D0903518

2/3/93 DP

WHO

KNOWS

WHAT

WHO
KNOWS
WHAT

The Essential Business
Resource Book

DANIEL STARER

A HENRY HOLT REFERENCE BOOK

HENRY HOLT AND COMPANY

NEW YORK

A Henry Holt Reference Book
Published by Henry Holt and Company, Inc.,
115 West 18th Street, New York, New York 10011.
Published in Canada by Fitzhenry & Whiteside Ltd.,
91 Granton Drive, Richmond Hill, Ontario L4B 2N5.

Library of Congress Cataloging-in-Publication Data
Starer, Daniel.
Who knows what : the essential business resource book / Daniel
Starer.—1st ed.
p.   cm.   — (A Henry Holt reference book)
Includes index.
1. Business information services—United States—Directories.
I. Title. II. Series.
HF54.52.U5S73   1992   92-17132
016.65—dc20   CIP

ISBN 0-8050-1853-0

Henry Holt Reference Books are available at special discounts
for bulk purchases for sales promotions, premiums,
fund-raising, or educational use. Special editions
or book excerpts can also be created to specification.

For details contact: Special Sales Director,
Henry Holt and Company, Inc., 115 West 18th Street,
New York, New York 10011.

First Edition—1992

Printed in the United States of America
Recognizing the importance of preserving the
written word, Henry Holt and Company, Inc.,
by policy, prints all of its first editions
on acid-free paper. ∞

1   3   5   7   9   10   8   6   4   2

For Nick Ellison

ACKNOWLEDGMENTS

My thanks to Ken Wright and Audrey Melkin at Henry Holt for their excellent ideas. I especially appreciate the insight and fine eye of my editor, Mary Kay Linge, whose help was invaluable. Thanks also to my assistant, Anne Smith.

CONTENTS

Introduction   xxiii

Abrasives Industry   1
Acids   3
Accounting   5
Actuarial Science   8
Additives and Flavorings   10
Adhesives and Sealants   12
Adult Education   15
Advertising   17
Aerosol Industry   21
Aerospace   24
AIDS   27
Affirmative Action and Equal Employment Opportunity   29
Agriculture   30
Air Conditioning, Refrigeration, and Heating Industry   37
Air Freight   41
Airline Industry   44
Air Pilots   46
Airplane and Helicopter Industry   47
Airports   50
Air Travel   52
Alabama   54
Alaska   56
Alcohol and Drug Abuse   59
Aluminum Industry   61
Antitrust   63
Appliances   65
Aquaculture   68
Arbitration and Mediation   70
Architecture   71
Arizona   72

Arkansas	75
Art and Antiques Market	78
Artificial Intelligence	80
Arts Management	82
Asbestos Industry	84
Asphalt Industry	86
Auctions	89
Audiovisual Industry	90
Automatic Identification Industry	93
Automobile Dealers	95
Automobile Equipment Industry	98
Automobile Lease/Rental Services	101
Automotive Industry	103
Avionics	106
Baking Industry	108
Bankruptcy	111
Banks and Banking	113
Barber and Beauty Shops	118
Barter and Countertrade	120
Battery Industry	121
Bearings and Ball Bearings	124
Beverage Industry	126
Bicycle Industry	129
Biotechnology	131
Boat Industry	133
Bookbinding	136
Book Publishing Industry	138
Bookselling Industry	141
Box Industry	143
Brewing Industry	145
Budgeting	148
Building Industry	149
Building Materials Industry	152
Business Ethics	155
Business History	156
Business Law	157
Cable Television Industry	158
California	160
Candy Industry	163
Canned Food Industry	165

Carpets and Rugs 168
Cash Management 170
Cattle Industry 171
Cement Industry 174
Census Data 176
Ceramics 177
Chain Stores 179
Chambers of Commerce 181
Cheese Industry 182
Chemical Engineering 184
Chemical Industry 186
Child Care 189
Civil Engineering 190
Civil Service 192
Clay Industry 193
Cleaning Products and Services 195
Clock and Watch Industry 198
Clothing Industry 200
Coal 204
Coffee and Tea Industry 206
Cogeneration 209
Collectibles 211
Collection Agencies 214
Colleges and Universities 216
Colorado 217
Commercial Art and Illustration 220
Commodity Futures 222
Compensation and Pay 224
Computer-aided Design/Manufacturing/Engineering (CAD/CAM/CAE) 226
Computer Graphics 229
Computers 231
Concession Industry 236
Concrete Industry 238
Connecticut 240
Consultants 243
Consumer Electronics Industry 244
Consumers 247
Container Industry 249
Copying and Duplicating Machine Industry 251
Cosmetics and Perfume Industry 254

Cotton Industry   257
Courts   259
Creativity   261
Credit   262
Credit Unions   265
Dairy Industry   267
Defense Industries   270
Delaware   273
Dental Industry   275
Desktop Publishing   278
Direct Mail and Marketing Industry   281
Distributors and Wholesalers   283
District of Columbia   285
Drug Stores   287
Economics   290
Education   292
Electrical Engineering   296
Electric Equipment Industry   297
Electric Power   300
Employee Benefits   302
Employee Stock Ownership Plans   305
Employment Services and Executive Search Firms   306
Energy   309
Engineering   315
Engines   316
Entrepreneurs   318
Environmental Conservation and Pollution Control   320
Fabrics and Textiles   324
Facsimile (Fax)   327
Fashion Industry   329
Federal Government   330
Feed Industry and Grain   333
Fertilizer Industry   336
Fiber Industry   338
Finance—Corporate   341
Finance—Public   343
Financial Analysts   344
Financial Planning   345
Firearm Industry   347
Fire Prevention and Protection   349

Fish and Seafood Industry 351
Floor Coverings and Flooring Industry 354
Florida 357
Florists and Flower Industry 360
Flour Industry 363
Food Industry 365
Food Machinery and Equipment Industry 368
Food Service Industry 371
Forest Products 375
Forms for Business 378
Foundations 380
Foundry Industry 381
Franchises 383
Freedom of Information and Access Laws 385
Freight Transportation 386
Fruit and Vegetable Industry 389
Fuel Oil Industry 394
Funeral and Mortuary Industry 396
Fur Industry 398
Furniture Industry 400
Gambling and Casino Industry 403
Garages and Service Stations 405
Garden Supply and Plant Nurseries 407
Gasoline Industry 410
Gem Industry 412
Georgia 414
Gift Industry 417
Glass and Glass Products 419
Graphic Arts Industry 422
Greeting Card Industry 425
Grocery Business 426
Hardware and Locksmith Industry 429
Hawaii 431
Health Care Industry 434
Health Food Industry 440
Hobby Industry 442
Home Improvement and Do-It-Yourself Industry 444
Honey Industry 446
Hospitals 448
Hotel and Motel Industry 451

Ice Cream Industry   453
Idaho   455
Illinois   457
Immigration and Emigration   460
Import-Export   461
Indiana   464
Industrial Coatings   467
Industrial Equipment Industry   470
Industrial Hygiene   473
Industrial Relations   475
Information Industry   477
Insulation Industry   479
Insurance—Automobile   481
Insurance—Casualty and Property   483
Insurance—Health and Accident   486
Insurance—Life   489
Insurance Agents   492
Intellectual Property   494
Interior Decoration   496
Internal Auditing   498
Inventions   499
Inventory Control   501
Investment Banking   502
Investments   504
Iowa   508
Jewelry Industry   511
Journalism   514
Kansas   515
Kentucky   518
Label Industry   521
Laboratories   523
Labor Unions   525
Laundry and Dry-Cleaning Industry   528
Lawyers   531
Leather Industry   533
Libraries   536
Lighting Industry   538
Liquor and Spirits Industry   540
Liquor Stores   543
Livestock Industry   544

Local Area Networks   547
Louisiana   549
Lubrication Industry   552
Luggage Industry   554
Macaroni and Pasta Industry   556
Machine Shops   557
Machine Tool Industry   559
Maine   562
Maintenance of Buildings   565
Management   567
Management Consultants   570
Management Information Systems (MIS)   572
Manufacturers' Representatives   574
Marketing   575
Market Research and Statistics   578
Maryland   580
Massachusetts   583
Materials   586
Materials Handling   588
Meat Industry   590
Medical and Hospital Equipment Industry   593
Mergers and Acquisitions   597
Metal Finishing Industry   599
Metallurgy   601
Metals Industry   603
Metal Working Industry   607
Michigan   610
Microforms   613
Mines and Mining Industry   615
Minnesota   617
Mississippi   620
Missouri   623
Mobile Home Industry   625
Mobile Telephone Industry   628
Montana   630
Mortgage Industry   633
Moving and Storage Industry   636
Motion Picture Industry   638
Motion Picture Theaters   641
Motivation (Psychology)   642

Motor Buses   644
Motorcycle Industry   646
Municipal Government   648
Musical Instruments Industry   650
Music Industry   654
Mutual Funds   657
Natural Gas Industry   659
Nebraska   663
Nevada   665
New Hampshire   668
New Jersey   671
New Mexico   674
Newsletters   677
Newspapers   678
New York   681
Noise Control   684
North Carolina   686
North Dakota   689
Novelty and Souvenir Industry   691
Nuclear Power   693
Nursing Homes   695
Nut Industry   698
Occupational Therapy   701
Office Automation   703
Office Buildings   706
Office Equipment and Supplies   707
Office Furniture   711
Office Management   713
Ohio   714
Oils, Fats, and Margarine Industry   717
Oklahoma   720
Onion and Garlic Industries   722
Operations Research   724
Ophthalmic Industry   725
Optics Industry   728
Oregon   731
Packaging   734
Packaging Machinery Industry   738
Paint and Painting Industry   740
Paper and Plastic Bag Industry   743

Paper and Pulp Industry 745
Paperboard Industry 748
Pennsylvania 751
Pensions and Profit-Sharing Plans 754
Periodicals, Magazines, and Trade Journals 756
Personnel Management 759
Pesticide Industry 762
Pet Industry 765
Petrochemical Industry 768
Petroleum Equipment Industry 771
Petroleum Industry 774
Pharmaceutical Industry 778
Photographic Industry 782
Pipe and Pipe Fittings Industry 786
Pipeline Industry 789
Plaster and Plastering Industry 791
Plastics Industry 793
Plumbing Industry 797
Point-of-Sale Industry 799
Population and Demographics 801
Postal Services and Equipment 803
Potato Industry 805
Poultry Industry 807
Power (Mechanical) 809
Precious Metals Industry 811
Premiums and Incentives 814
Printing and Printing Equipment Industries 815
Printing Ink Industry 820
Privatization 822
Production and Process Control 823
Productivity 825
Product Liability 829
Product Safety 831
Propane and Butane Gas Industry 832
Property and Facility Management 834
Prosthetics Industry 836
Public Administration 838
Public Opinion and Polls 840
Public Relations and Publicity 842
Public Transportation 844

Public Utilities   846
Pump and Compressor Industry   849
Purchasing   851
Quality Control   852
Quarry and Stone Industry   855
Radio Broadcasting Industry   857
Railroad Industry   859
Real Estate Business   862
Real Estate Investments   865
Recording Industry   868
Records Management   871
Recreational Vehicles Industry   872
Recreation Industry   874
Recycling   878
Regulation of Industry   880
Relocation of Employees   882
Rental and Leasing Services   884
Research and Development   886
Restaurant Industry   889
Retail Trade   892
Retirement   895
Rhode Island   897
Rice Industry   900
Risk Management   902
Roads and Highways   904
Robot Industry   907
Roofing Industry   910
Rubber and Rubber Goods Industry   913
Safety   916
Sales Management   920
Salespeople and Sales Techniques   921
Sales Promotion   923
Salt Industry   925
Sanitation Industry   926
Savings and Loan Associations   928
Schools   930
Scientific Instruments and Supply Industry   932
Secretaries and Office Workers   935
Securities   937
Security and Detective Services and Equipment   941

Seed Industry	945
Semiconductor Industry	947
Sheep Industry	950
Ships and Shipping Industry	952
Shoe Industry	955
Shopping Centers and Malls	957
Shorthand and Shorthand Reporting	959
Sign Industry	960
Small Business and Self-employment	962
Social Security	965
Solar Energy	966
South Carolina	968
South Dakota	971
Soybean Industry	974
Spice Industry	975
Sporting Goods Industry	977
Standards, Weights, and Measurements	980
Statistics	982
Steel and Iron Industry	983
Store Displays	987
Sugar Industry	988
Superconductors	991
Supermarkets and Convenience Stores	992
Surplus Products	994
Swimming Pool Industry	996
Swine Industry	998
Tableware Industry	1000
Taxation	1003
Taxicab and Limousine Industry	1006
Technology Transfer	1007
Telecommunications Industry	1009
Telemarketing	1013
Telephone Answering Service Industry	1015
Television Broadcasting Industry	1016
Temporary Employees	1019
Tennessee	1021
Testing	1024
Texas	1026
Tile Industry	1029
Tire Industry	1031

Tobacco Industry   1033
Toy Industry   1037
Trade Shows, Conventions, and Fairs   1039
Traffic Engineering and Management   1042
Traffic Safety   1044
Training of Personnel   1047
Translation and Translators   1049
Travel Agencies   1051
Travel Industry   1053
Truck and Trailer Manufacturing   1056
Trucking Industry   1059
Trusts and Estates   1062
Ultrasonics   1063
Underwear, Hosiery, and Intimate Apparel Industry   1065
Unemployment and Unemployment Insurance   1068
Upholstery Industry   1070
Utah   1072
Valuation and Appraisal   1074
Valve Industry   1077
Vending Machine Industry   1079
Venture Capital   1081
Vermont   1083
Veterinary Products Industry   1086
Video Recording Industry   1089
Videotex/Teletext   1091
Virginia   1092
Vitamin and Diet Industry   1095
Wallpaper Industry   1097
Warehouses   1099
Washington   1101
Waste Management   1104
Waterways and Ports   1107
Weather and Weather Forecasting   1110
Welding   1112
West Virginia   1114
Wheat Industry   1117
Wine Industry   1119
Wire Industry   1122
Wisconsin   1124
Women Professionals and Employees   1127

Woodworking Industries 1130
Wool and Worsted Industry 1133
Word Processing 1136
Workers' Compensation 1138
Writing and Editing 1140
Writing Instrument Industry 1143
Wyoming 1144
Yarn Industry 1147

Appendix 1151
Index of Associations, Periodicals, and Companies 1157
Index of Subjects 1225

INTRODUCTION

For most people, the best way to find business information is to go right to the source: an industry expert. *Who Knows What* is a comprehensive, one-stop directory that will help you find an appropriate expert on any business topic, whether you're a manager, executive, entrepreneur, business owner, administrator, journalist, or student.

I decided to write *Who Knows What* because I've always needed a book just like it at my fingertips. For the last fourteen years I've run a research service in New York City that finds information on business-related and other subjects. I access more than 1,500 databases and do research at some of the finest libraries in the world. Still, many times the fastest, most cost-effective way to find up-to-date information is to talk to an expert by telephone. Each year, I spend thousands of dollars buying separate directories that list the associations, trade magazines, specialized libraries, companies, government offices, and other sources employing experts on business topics. Not only are these directories expensive, it takes time to look through them and compile a list of information sources for a particular industry or on a particular business topic.

The book I wished I owned—and wrote—is a convenient directory listing on one or two pages the best information sources for a specific topic. *Who Knows What* lets people needing business information scan the one or two dozen choices in a particular industry or topic, quickly determine which ones seem most appropriate for their current research project, and call for help with a minimal waste of time and money.

SIX BEST SOURCES

In my experience, six kinds of organizations and/or experts yield the best results when researching business topics by telephone, fax, or letter. The first kind—state government offices—are listed alphabetically by state. The other five kinds of sources—associations, periodicals, libraries, companies, and agencies of the federal government—are listed in other sections throughout the book.

ASSOCIATIONS

The U.S. has more than 20,000 national associations that cover every topic imaginable. In the business world, you can find at least one association for virtually every industry, managerial and administrative function, profession, and even business-related concerns such as productivity.

Associations are comprised of industry professionals who organize to share information and further their common interests. In many industries, the main association is often the central information source and should be your first contact. Most associations are used to dealing with the public. Many consider themselves to be the public relations arm of their industry and employ researchers to help not only their dues-paying members but anyone who calls.

Under the Associations heading of each section throughout the book you'll find not only trade associations but professional societies, labor unions, information clearinghouses, think tanks, research institutes, and other organizations that can be loosely described as associations. Some are more helpful than others, but all will at least provide referrals to others in their industry or specialty.

Most of the associations listed in *Who Knows What* perform public relations activities that promote their special interests and members, supply speakers if requested, lobby before Congress or other governmental bodies from time to time, and publish at least one newsletter, fact sheet, or other publication. I generally do not mention these functions or publications in the brief description for each association. However, if an association has a special constituency or mission, or provides other special services to members or the public, I highlight this. Such services include educational programs, merchandising programs, research, and funding of other programs.

PERIODICALS

Editors of trade magazines and professional journals can be superb sources of information and referrals. Ideally, an editor has been with his or her periodical for several years, regularly surveys the entire industry, and speaks often to leading industry experts. If the information you need is fairly general, periodical editors are good contacts since they tend to be generalists in their field. If you need in-depth information about a narrow topic or about a specific industry sector, a periodical editor may be able to refer you to an appropriate expert. The editor's job is to write about and edit—not to create or consult about—the industry's news, ideas, and trends. As such, editors frequently can tell you who knows what in their field, but may not know certain information themselves.

Typically, for small publications the best editor to contact (sometimes the only editor on staff) is the editor-in-chief. However, if you know the publication to be quite large, a senior editor is your best choice. Unlike associations—which generally expect calls from the public and even employ researchers to field these calls—periodical editors are under no obligation to help you. Editors are hard-working people with tight deadlines to meet. But many will talk to callers who make intelligent use of their time. Your research project may interest them or even lead to an article in their magazine.

Beware of new or very junior editors at a trade journal. They have often not worked previously in the industry and are not yet good sources of information. However, there are many fine exceptions to this rule.

If you subscribe to the periodical by all means say so when you first talk to an editor. If you don't subscribe, say you are thinking about it. Since you may need ongoing information about the industry or topic, a subscription may be a good idea. When editors say they are working against a deadline, ask them to refer you to another industry expert or call at a later time.

Although many of the best business periodicals are included in *Who Knows What,* a few have been omitted intentionally to minimize duplication. In cases where the editor of an association's publication is that association's chief, I've omitted the periodical. In situations where the same publisher puts out two or more similar periodicals, only one of them is listed unless the editors are different. For example, the Watt Publishing Company dominates trade magazines in the poultry industry. They publish *Egg Industry, Poultry Digest,* and *Turkey World.* Since each magazine focuses on a different industry segment and since each has a different editorial staff with specialized expertise, all three sources are listed.

LIBRARIES

The U.S. has special-subject libraries that concentrate on virtually all topics covered in this book. Librarians who work at specialized libraries can be wonderful sources. They know the methods and materials for research and often have instant knowledge, or at least a smart intuition, of where to find data in their special field. If you contact a library, be sure to ask for a *reference* librarian, whose main job it is to help people find information. Unfortunately, it may not be the librarian's job to help *you.*

This book lists a wide variety of libraries. They must all be approached tactfully. Public, university, and association libraries are most accustomed to helping outside callers. If you call at a convenient time (usually first thing in the morning), and if your question is specific and limited, a librarian may spend a few minutes looking up information for you or at least refer you to another source. However, librarians are very busy people who may have a stack of requests in front of them from people in their own organization.

Librarians at companies and research institutes are the least obliged to help outside callers. But they may help under certain conditions. You should probably call the company's public relations office for permission to contact the library. If you are a customer, expect to become a customer, have any other affiliation with the firm, or can at least acknowledge the company's help in a way beneficial to it, say so immediately. The corporate librarian will be much more likely to help if the request comes from inside her or his own organization.

Never expect librarians to do substantial research for you. Unless you hire a librarian or researcher yourself, it is generally not their job to sift through a mass of material to find what is pertinent to your query, provide numerous photocopies, or make telephone calls on your behalf. Fortunately, a talented librarian may be able to find just what you need in the limited time he or she can devote to an outside caller.

COMPANIES

Corporations can be excellent sources of information. Of all the organizations listed in this book, companies may feel the least obligated to help outside callers. However, unlike associations, periodicals, and libraries, where only a handful of people are available to help an outside caller, large companies may employ dozens or even hundreds with the specialized knowledge you seek. Your problem is finding the right people and getting them to help you.

The obvious place to start when calling a company is the public relations or public affairs office. If your call is potentially welcome there is no reason to avoid the public relations office, though it can slow you down. As with any organization in this book, if you are the company's customer, potential customer, or can benefit the firm in any way, say so up front. If you pass muster, the public relations officer can find the right experts within the firm and get them to help you.

If you are a competitor, a journalist suspected of working on an unfavorable story, or someone who poses some other danger to the company, the public relations office should not be your first choice. But don't be surprised if a company's expert on your topic asks you to be cleared through the public relations office if you start asking sensitive questions. If company officials seem suspicious of you, try sending a letter on your organization's letterhead to prove your identity.

Often the company's telephone operator will be just as helpful in steering you to the right expert or at least the right department. Operators are trained to direct calls quickly. Don't start a long tale about who you are and what information you need. Simply ask for the administrative function (such as marketing, purchasing, or human resources) or the product group (such as light bulb manufacturing) that sounds most appropriate to your topic. With luck, you won't get transferred too many times before finding someone to help. Always write down the name and extension of each person with whom you talk. If you get cut off during a telephone transfer you can retrace your steps. More importantly, if an expert on your topic is too busy or unwilling to help, someone you had spoken to earlier may suggest another contact within the company.

Large companies often have many facilities and offices nationwide. Although only the national headquarters are listed in this book, don't limit yourself to headquarters if they prove unhelpful. In fact, an expert in a distant office, far from the watchful eyes of the main office, may talk much more freely. Ask the operator where, aside from headquarters, a specific product, process, or function is handled.

In an effort to provide a rich variety of sources, many sections of *Who Knows What* list midsized and even some fairly small companies along with the well-known behemoths. Large companies employ many experts who can potentially help you, though it may take time to find the right people. If you call one of the large companies, be sure to find out which division or subsidiary is most appropriate. Smaller firms have fewer experts, but they are easier to identify.

FEDERAL GOVERNMENT

The federal government employs several hundred thousand people at dozens of agencies who gather information on every subject imaginable. Most of the experts who can help with business research work for a handful of massive organizations (such as the Department of Commerce). The telephone operators (sometimes called "locators") at these large departments often use computerized directories that can make it surprisingly easy to help the public find an appropriate expert. Technically, all information and publications (with the exception of sensitive, private, or security-related materials) are publicly available at no charge or low cost, since our taxes pay to produce them.

So, theoretically, if the experts are easy to locate and they are supposed to help you, the government should be a fabulous source for research. That's true in many cases, if those you contact have the information you seek and it is not secret. Individual government experts receive well-defined missions to gather and analyze data in their specific industry or field. Their mission is often defined by whom they serve, such as their department's public policy makers, Congress, firms seeking to export American goods and services, firms and individuals seeking patents, or others. Government experts are generally not familiar with as wide a range of information as association executives, company experts, and trade journal editors. But for information which the government itself collects, analyzes, or publishes, they are often the best source.

Most of the federal offices listed in *Who Knows What* expect calls from the public. But sooner or later you will find officials who refuse to help because they are too busy or consider their information private. If a tactful yet firm request fails, and if a second and third call yields no results, call the agency's public affairs office. Be very specific about why you need the information. Remind them that as a tax-paying American citizen (or as a company trying to compete in world markets) you have a right to the information. If that doesn't break the logjam, mention contacting your senator and congressional representative. Your final ploy is to see the Freedom of Information and Access Laws section of this book for organizations that offer advice on using the Freedom of Information Act. The Act provides a mechanism for any American citizen to obtain many types of government information in a reasonable amount of time.

GETTING INFORMATION BY TELEPHONE

If you know whom to contact, the telephone is the fastest, least expensive way to find information. There's nothing like finding a real expert on your problem. That person can give you the most up-to-date answers customized to your needs. If you need detailed information that cannot be answered over the phone, an expert can tell you exactly which printed materials to see and where to find them. Many will even send the answers you need if you ask politely.

It is a common misconception that you can find the right expert within ten phone calls. In my experience it can usually be done in two or three calls, or even one, if you start with the right sources. How can you get the best information in the fewest calls?

PREPARING FOR THE CALL

Never waste an expert's time. You may not get another chance. Experts will generally help those callers who make quick and intelligent use of their time. Before you pick up the phone (or send a letter or fax) ask yourself these nine questions:

1. Why do I need the information and what will I do with it?

If others have asked you to do research for them it is particularly important to find out not only what they need to know but how they plan to use the information. Whenever clients ask me to do research, I interview them carefully to determine their true purpose. Are they starting a new company? Manufacturing or marketing a new product? Checking up on a competitor? Making an investment? Writing a speech? Obviously, each of these purposes requires a different kind of approach, resulting in different kinds of information.

If you are doing the research for yourself, consider interviewing yourself to better understand the project. In most circumstances the amount of information available on a subject is much greater than you realize. To avoid becoming bogged down in a morass of data, be sure you know why you need that data.

2. If there were one perfect book or article on my subject, what would be its title?

An excellent way to narrow down your topic, clarify your thinking, and focus on getting useful information is to jot down the imaginary title to an ultimate resource that would answer your questions. Be as specific as possible. Don't imagine an article called "Survey of the Desktop Publishing Industry" when what you really need is something called "How to Market IBM-Compatible Desktop Publishing Software to Independent Retailers in Southern California." Of course, it is extremely unlikely someone has written an article or report with that title. But by thinking about all the elements of your search, you are likely to reach your research goal much more quickly.

3. How can I separate my subject into its component questions?

As you define the title of an imaginary book or article, you may find that more than one research topic is needed to reach your goal. For example, you've determined that aside from finding the best distribution and marketing channels, sales will probably be higher if the software is packaged more attractively and you obtain some inexpensive publicity.

As you think through your goals, write them down, prioritize them, and ask the separate research questions that will bring you closer to your goals. Now you need to contact not only sources listed in the Desktop Publishing section of this book, but sources listed in the Packaging and the Public Relations and Publicity sections as well. You will also realize that creating new packaging takes the longest and probably requires your immediate attention.

4. What restrictions or limitations help define my questions?

To focus your search more effectively, consider excluding certain types of information. For example, do you want to limit your search by geography, data source, age of the information, or other factors?

5. How much time or money am I prepared to invest in my search?

Many people start looking for information without setting certain limits. If financial considerations are important (and they usually are), set a budget. In doing research, time and money generally have an inverse relation. That is, the more money you have the less time it will take to find your answers. By the same token, the more time you can devote to doing research, the less it will cost you. Luckily, the time and money involved may be minimal if an association, trade magazine, or other organization can provide the information for you.

6. If the data I want is not readily available, what is my second choice?

As the famous song says, "you can't always get what you want." Some information—most often statistical or financial data, or certain business lists—has not been created or compiled in the form you need. In other cases, the only source for certain information—usually a company or government office—considers the data proprietary or confidential.

If you are certain the data you need is not available, change the focus of your research. You may find that your second or third choice of research is almost as good for your purposes.

7. How much information do I really need?

Most people believe you can never have enough information. After all, a great deal of data on your exact topic plus data on related topics can only help you make the correct decisions, right? Not always. As the saying goes: "We are drowning in information but starved for knowledge."

It is very tempting to plunge into research, gathering information furiously while losing sight of your goals. Some people have a sensible idea about how much information they need for their project. Others become too absorbed with research because it is fun, because it offers an excuse to avoid making difficult business decisions, or because it delays the start of an arduous task, like writing a report based on the research.

Unless your topic is extremely arcane, you may be drowning in information before too long. Along with setting limits on the time and money you will devote to research, also decide *beforehand* how much information is enough. You can control your project in two ways. First, understand your goals and how the information will help you reach those goals. Second, read the information as you gather it, so you don't gather more than necessary.

8. From what source and in what form will the answers be most useful?

For some research projects it doesn't really matter what the information source is or in what form it arrives. For other projects it may matter a great deal if the information comes from interviews with experts over the telephone, computer database searches, primary sources such as government or company documents, secondary sources such as books or magazine articles, or other sources. Before starting research, ask yourself if the source is important. If the answer is yes, you can avoid inappropriate sources.

Aside from the source of information, the physical form in which information arrives may be important. Do you prefer a mailing list on a computer floppy disk rather than in printed form? Does an impressive-looking, original government report serve your needs better than a short magazine article that summarizes this report?

9. Which organization should I contact first?

A rule of thumb in information research is to *start* with the source that seems most targeted or specific to your subject. You generally save time by shooting for the bull's-eye right away. If you need information on store displays, see the Store Displays section before looking at the Retail Trade section. If you want data on printed fabrics, call the American Printed Fabrics Council before calling the American Textile Manufacturers Institute.

MAKING THE CALL

Once you prepare your questions and decide which organization to call, it is time for action.

1. How to present yourself

When talking to (or writing to) an expert, be clear and concise and get down to business right away. It is best to give the expert some basic information about yourself, the exact topic you are researching, and how you expect to use the information. For example: "Good morning. My name is Mary Smith. I'm with the legal department at the XYZ Corporation, a midsize manufacturer of pharmaceuticals. Could you please advise where I could find information about proposed legislation and regulations regarding genetically engineered plants?" Not only is it courteous to give experts all this information, it will help them tailor their answers more effectively.

2. Telephone manners that get the best results

Never take experts for granted. Unless they're your employees, they don't have to help you. While many experts are happy to share their knowledge, you should always treat them with respect, as if they are doing you a favor. If they sound harried, ask if you may call back at a different time.

Never ask a question in a negative way. For example: "You don't have any information on my topic, do you?" invites the response, "No, I don't."

If you are a complete novice in the field, say so. A generous, intelligent expert may—time permitting—ask appropriate questions for you, suggest types of information you don't yet realize you need, provide that information, and suggest additional sources for help. If you already know quite a bit about the subject, tell the expert right away to save time. If the expert seems genuinely interested in your topic, offer to share your research with that person. At the very least, offer free publicity and acknowledgment for the expert's help if possible. If you can establish a relationship from which you both benefit, the expert will obviously be more generous with his or her time and knowledge.

3. Getting past the secretary

In some cases you can find what you want by talking with knowledgeable assistants or junior executives at a company or organization. In other cases, you need to talk with a senior person who is zealously guarded by a secretary. Several methods will help you avoid this problem. Try calling before 9:00 A.M., when many executives are at their desks but secretaries have not yet arrived. Or try calling when you think the secretary might be at lunch. If you do get the secretary on the phone, try to make your need sound urgent. If you're calling long distance, by all means say so. If you are a customer, a member, or are affiliated in any way with the organization or are thinking of becoming affiliated, say so. If you have any interesting information to share with the executive, also say so. Treat the secretary with as much respect as you would his or her boss. Refer to the secretary as an assistant to—or even better, a colleague of—the executive. If possible, try to interest the secretary in what you are doing. Your enthusiasm may rub off and inspire the secretary to help rather than hinder you. If all else fails, call the public relations office or a superior of the person you are trying to reach. Even if these sources can't provide the information you seek, they may ask the executive with the protective secretary to help you.

4. Dealing with difficult, busy, or self-important experts

As mentioned earlier, most experts will help if you make intelligent use of their time. If an expert spends a career studying a specific industry or topic, he or she probably has a natural love for it and enjoys the role of helping others who value this knowledge.

Sooner or later you will come up against experts who are reluctant to help. Try to find out why they are reluctant. If it is because they are busy, ask for a time when it is convenient to call back. Polite persistence pays off. Call as many times as necessary during the times the expert suggests. Tell the expert that what you need will not take more than ten or fifteen minutes. If the expert is really pressed for time, he or she may tell you everything you need in that time frame.

Some experts act self-important. They feel it is beneath their dignity to help people who are not already quite familiar with their topic. Frankly, they are correct in that you should read about their area of expertise rather than ask them to explain the basics. A good strategy is to ask them what to read to familiarize yourself and call again after you have finished. Once you are in a position to ask very specific questions, having done the homework the expert assigned, it is reasonable to ask for his or her help.

Some experts remain difficult despite your best efforts. Try to build up a rapport with these people. Get them interested in your project. Offer them some kind of nonmonetary reward if that is appropriate: perhaps a copy of something you wrote, a sample of your company's products, a public acknowledgment of their contribution to your research. If you sense they'd rather be guaranteed anonymity, offer them your assurances, in writing if needed. Sometimes a consulting fee is needed to get results. But try offering something else first.

If they seem worried about giving away information they may consider secret, try to win over their trust. If they seem suspicious of who you are, tell them more about yourself and your intended use of the information. To prove you are who you claim to be, write a letter on your letterhead requesting the information. Offer as much evidence as possible that your use of the information is not competitive or derogatory. Offer to let them see the report (or whatever) you'll write up with your findings. Ask your less controversial or uncomfortable questions first so the expert gets used to giving you information. If the expert still resists giving the specific answers you need, rephrase your questions. Sometimes it is better to ask for a personal opinion about the subject rather than an organizational opinion. Also ask what others outside the organization have said about the subject. If you seek statistical or numerical information, ask for estimates or approximate figures if the expert is reluctant to give an exact figure. All these techniques will take the heat off the expert and should make him or her more cooperative.

5. Evaluating each expert's bias toward the subject

If you talk to a variety of experts from different types of organizations (such as companies, associations, and government offices) and they all give the same information, you can be fairly confident the information is correct. However, if conflicts or differences emerge, you need to discover why.

In some cases, experts simply have differences of opinion based on different sets of information or personal preferences. In other cases, experts may be strongly biased by their affiliations. For example, an opinion about the tobacco industry will obviously differ from a Phillip Morris employee than that of an American Medical Association representative. The biases of experts are often not so glaring. Keep in mind that experts will support whatever "party line" helps their specific organization or industry. Company and association experts generally present a pro-business, optimistic point of view. Public interest groups are generally more critical and negative. Government experts tend toward neutrality except where the information they give out reflects positively or negatively on their own government agency.

Whenever you find conflicting information or opinions, never hesitate to call the experts again and ask why. Let the experts justify what they told you in light of the other information you gathered. Beware that some experts will not openly contradict what another has said. Some feel it discourteous to publicly contradict a colleague. When asking one expert to comment on another's information or opinion, it is best not mention the other expert's name if possible. Ask instead about the information or opinion itself, saying the source wishes to remain anonymous.

6. Checking the expert's reputation

Not all experts are created equal. If you rely heavily on one source, make sure that source is reliable. First of all, be sure the expert is at the appropriate level within his or her organization. An inexperienced assistant may be eager to help you and save the boss's time, but an assistant may not really know the topic. A very senior person in the organization, while once an expert on your topic, may now be too involved with internal or administrative matters to be current on the topic.

Once you feel confident the expert you rely on is at the appropriate level, how do you evaluate his or her reputation? First of all, find out what that expert has written and where it is published. To publish widely the expert will need to constantly pass the scrutiny of editors and other experts. As a rule of thumb, the longer the paper trail an expert has left, the more reliable he or she is as an information source. If an expert has published in one or two periodicals, that should arouse your suspicions. However, keep in mind that in some fields one periodical is considered "the bible of the industry" and it may be the only prestigious place to publish.

If the expert on whom you rely has not published much, ask other experts "off the record" about his or her reputation in the industry. Don't ask point-blank about what they think of the expert. By asking in an impersonal way, you are more likely to get an honest answer from someone who might normally be reluctant to bad-mouth a colleague.

Just because an expert has not published does not mean this person is potentially unreliable. But it does take more work to check the reputation of an unpublished expert.

7. *Making the expert interested in talking to you again*

If an expert has been particularly helpful or has obviously spent some time on your behalf, send that person a thank-you note. Not only will it be appreciated, it will certainly make that expert open to future discussions. If you use the expert's information in writing a report or some other document, by all means send him or her a copy. The expert may correct any errors you made and send additional data you'll find useful.

8. *Ending the conversation*

No matter what kind of expert you talk to, make sure you ask these four questions:

- "Is there anything else I should have asked you?"
- "Is there any published material on the subject that you could send me?"
- "Are there any published materials that I should obtain from other sources?"
- "Who else should I speak with for additional help at other organizations or within your organization?"

Sometimes, despite calling appropriate organizations listed in *Who Knows What*, you may not find the information you need by talking with experts. In these cases, experts will often suggest where you can find information, whether in a library or on a computer database.

If you live near a major business library, call first and ask a reference librarian if it is likely to have the information you need. When visiting a library, go first thing in the morning; you may be the only person asking for the librarian's help. If you can't visit a library or need business information on a regular basis, you should become familiar with the vast world of business information available via computer. See the Appendix for an introduction to computerized databases.

No matter how you seek information, remember that persistence usually pays off. The data you need is probably out there. With a little planning, a little sweat, and a little luck, you will find it. Good hunting!

Daniel Starer
Research Network
59 West 85th Street
New York, NY 10024
(212) 877-5400

WHO

KNOWS

WHAT

ABRASIVES INDUSTRY

ASSOCIATIONS

Abrasive Engineering Society
108 Elliott Dr.
Butler, PA 16001-1118
412-282-6210
412-282-6210 Fax
Ted Giese, Business Manager
A technical society for those using abrasives in metalworking and other applications.

Coated Abrasives Manufacturers Institute
c/o Thomas Assocs., Inc.
1230 Keith Bldg.
Cleveland, OH 44115
216-241-7333
216-241-0105 Fax
Charles Stockinger, Managing Director
A small group of researchers and manufacturers.

Grinding Wheel Institute
30200 Detroit Rd.
Cleveland, OH 44145-1967
216-899-0010
216-892-1404 Fax
Allen Wherry, Manager
A group for manufacturers of abrasive products for grinding, polishing, and sharpening.

PERIODICALS

Abrasive Engineering Society Magazine
108 Elliot Dr.
Butler, PA 16001
412-282-6210
Theodore Giese, Editor
Follows trends and new technologies in the industry.

LIBRARIES

Norton Co.
Coated Abrasive Division
Technical Library
Box 808
Troy, NY 12181-0808
518-266-2741
518-266-2299 Fax
Abrasives, polymers, and organic chemistry.

Norton Co.
Library
One New Bond St.
Worcester, MA 01615-0008
508-795-2278
Abrasives, ceramics, metallurgy, and other subjects.

3M -251 Technical Library
3M Center, 251-2A-06
St. Paul, MN 55144
612-733-5236
Abrasives and other subjects.

COMPANIES

Abrasive Industries Inc.
Bay State Abrasives Div.
12 Union St.
Westborough, MA 01581
508-366-4431
Abrasive products.

Exolon-ESK Co.
1000 E. Niagara St.
Tonawanda, NY 14150
716-693-4550
Abrasive materials and products.

General Electric Co.
G.E. Superabrasives
6325 Huntley Rd.
Worthington, OH 43085
614-438-2000
Abrasive products.

Hermes Abrasives Ltd.
P.O. Box 2389
Virginia Beach, VA 23450
804-486-6623
Abrasive products.

Metallurg Inc.
25 E. 39th St.
New York, NY 10016
212-686-4010
Abrasives and other types of products.

Midwest Waltham Abrasive Co.
510 S. Washington St.
Owosso, MI 48867
517-725-7161
Abrasive products.

Norton Co. Coated Abrasives
P.O. Box 808
Troy, NY 21281
518-266-2200
Abrasives, coatings, and other products.

Radiac Abrasives, Inc.
1015 S. College Ave.
Salem, IL 62881
618-548-4200
Abrasive materials and products.

SinterMet Corp.
200 Egbert Rd.
Bedford, OH 44146
216-232-2400
Abrasive products.

Standard Abrasives Co.
9351 Deering Ave.
Chatsworth, CA 91311
818-718-7070
Abrasive products.

FEDERAL GOVERNMENT

U.S. International Trade Administration
Department of Commerce
14th St. and Constitution Ave., N.W.
Washington, DC 20230
202-377-2000
Ask for the Commodity Analyst who is an expert in abrasives.

U.S. International Trade Commission
500 E St., S.W.
Washington, DC 20436
202-205-2000 Office of the Secretary
202-205-3296 Industries locator
Ask for the Trade Analyst who is an expert in abrasives.

U.S. Patent and Trademark Office
Crystal Plaza 2
2011 Jefferson Davis Highway
Arlington, VA 22202
703-305-8000
Ask for the Examining Group Director who is a specialist in abrasives.

ACIDS

ASSOCIATIONS

Soap and Detergent Association
475 Park Ave. South
New York, NY 10016
212-725-1262
212-213-0685 Fax
Theodore Brenner, Manager
Members include manufacturers of fatty acids, glycerine, soaps, and detergents.

National Association of Corrosion Engineers
PO Box 218340
Houston, TX 77218
713-492-0535
713-492-8254 Fax
T. Lee, Executive Director
This group of scientists and engineers studies the prevention of corrosion and the corrosive properties of many substances, including acids.

PERIODICALS

C A Selects. Amino Acids, Peptides and Proteins
Chemical Abstracts Service
2540 Olentangy River Rd.
Box 3012
Columbus, OH 43210
614-447-3600
Technical information on amino acids, peptides, proteins, and their synthesis.

C A Selects. Omega-3 Fatty Acids & Fish Oil
Chemical Abstracts Service
2540 Olentangy River Rd.
Box 3012
Columbus, OH 43210
614-447-3600
Technical information on fatty acids and fish oils.

Chemistry and Biochemistry of Amino Acids, Peptides, and Proteins
Marcel Dekker, Inc.
270 Madison Ave.
New York, NY 10016
212-696-9000
B. Weinstein, Editor
Information for chemists on amino acids, peptides, and proteins.

LIBRARIES

American Chemical Society—Library
1155 16th St., N.W.
Washington, DC 20036
202-872-4509
Covers the full range of chemical subjects, including acids.

National Association of Corrosion Engineers Library
PO Box 218340
Houston, TX 77218
713-492-0535
713-492-8254 Fax
Corrosives, such as acids, and corrosive-inhibitors.

COMPANIES

Aceto Corp.
One Hollow Lane
Lake Success, NY 11042
516-627-6000
Specialty chemicals.

Acheson Industries, Inc.
511 Fort St.
Port Huron, MI 48060
313-984-5583
Specialty chemicals.

Ausimont N.V.
(Subsidiary of Montedison SpA)
128 Technology Dr.
Waltham, MA 02254
617-736-1400
Specialty chemicals

Biddle Sawyer Corp.
2 Pennsylvania Plaza
New York, NY 10121
212-736-1580
Enzymes, compounds, and other chemicals

Chevron Chemical Co.
(Subsidiary of Chevron Corp.)
6001 Bollinger Canyon Rd.
San Ramon, CA 94583
415-842-1000
Industrial detergents, olefins, acids, and many other chemicals.

Harcros Chemicals Inc.
(Subsidiary of Harrisons & Crosfield plc)
5200 Speaker Rd.
Kansas City, KS 66106
913-321-3131
Acids, emulsifiers, and other chemicals.

Henkel Corp.
(Subsidiary of Henkel of America, Inc.)
2200 Renaissance Blvd.
Gulph Mills, PA 19406
215-270-8100
Acids, resins, fatty nitrogen chemicals, gums, and other chemicals.

MacDermid Inc.
245 Freight St.
Waterbury, CT 06702
203-575-5700
Chemicals used for cleaning, polishing, and stripping.

Jacob Stern & Sons, Inc.
1464 E. Valley Rd., Box 50740
Santa Barbara, CA 93150
805-565-1411
Fats, fatty acids, grease, and vegetable oils.

FEDERAL GOVERNMENT

U.S. International Trade Administration
Department of Commerce
14th St. and Constitution Ave., N.W.
Washington, DC 20230
202-377-2000
Ask for the Commodity Analyst who is an expert in acids.

U.S. International Trade Commission
500 E St., S.W.
Washington, DC 20436
202-205-2000 Office of the Secretary
202-205-3296 Industries locator
Ask for the Trade Analyst who is an expert in acids.

U.S. Patent and Trademark Office
Crystal Plaza 2
2011 Jefferson Davis Highway
Arlington, VA 22202
703-305-8000
Ask for the Examining Group Director who is a specialist in acids.

ACCOUNTING

See also: ACTUARIAL SCIENCE; INTERNAL AUDITING; and individual state chapters

ASSOCIATIONS

American Institute of Certified Public
    Accountants
1211 Ave. of the Americas
New York, NY 10036
212-575-6200
212-575-3846 Fax
800-223-4155 Library services
800-522-5434 Library services in NY state
800-223-4158 Technical information
800-522-5430 Technical information in NY state
Philip Chenok, President
By far the largest organization of accountants in the U.S., this group sets accounting standards, offers training, and conducts research.

American Society of Women Accountants
35 E. Wacker Dr., Ste. 1068
Chicago, IL 60601
312-726-9030
312-726-4543 Fax
Shauna Babcock, Executive Director
Serves women CPAs and others working in accounting professions.

Associated Accounting Firms International
1612 K St. N.W., Ste. 900
Washington, DC 20006
202-463-7900
202-296-0741 Fax
Robert Taylor, President
Helps regional accounting firms improve business practices and marketing of their services. Offers training in computerization, taxes, and other subjects.

Controllers Council
10 Paragon Dr.
Montvale, NJ 07645-1760
201-573-6219
J. B. Schiff, Director
This group of controllers and chief financial officers provides career and professional information.

Foundation for Accounting Education
200 Park Ave., 10th Floor
New York, NY 10166
212-973-8300
212-972-5714 Fax
Robert Gray, Executive Director
Offers workshops and conferences for CPAs.

Institute of Certified Management Accoun-
    tants
10 Paragon Dr.
Montvale, NJ 07645
201-573-6300
800-638-4427
James Bulloch, Managing Director
Works to help people earn the Certified Management Accountant (CMA) designation.

Institute of Internal Auditors
249 Maitland Ave.
Altamonte Springs, FL 32701-4201
407-830-7600
800-CIA-DESK
407-831-5171 Fax
G. Peter Wilson, President
*Provides information to all accounting profes-
sionals who function as internal auditors in
companies, non-profits, and government
offices.*

National Association of Accountants
10 Paragon Dr.
Montvale, NJ 07645
201-573-9000
800-638-4427
201-573-8185 Fax
Gary Scopes, Executive Director
*A large organization of accountants that pro-
vides continuing education, conducts research,
and offers placement services.*

National Society of Public Accountants
1010 N. Fairfax St.
Alexandria, VA 22314
703-549-6400
703-549-2984 Fax
Stanley Stearman, Executive Vice President
*A society of independent tax practitioners and
accountants. Offers courses, seminars, and
accounting systems.*

PERIODICALS

Accounting News
Lebhar-Friedman, Inc.
425 Park Ave.
New York, NY 10022
212-371-9400
Bob Crane, Editor
*Covers news and developments in the account-
ing field.*

Accounting Today
Lebhar—Friedman, Inc.
425 Park Ave.
New York, NY 10022
212-371-9400
Thomas Kothman, Editor
*Primarily for accountants in public practice,
this newspaper provides news about issues,
strategies, and key industry people and organizations.*

CPA Client Bulletin
American Institute of Certified Public
    Accountants
1211 Ave. of the Americas
New York, NY 10036
212-575-6277
Arthur Lodge, Editor
*Offers information to CPAs on issues affecting
small businesses.*

Current Issues in the Financial Services
    Industries
Ernst & Young
787 Seventh Ave.
New York, NY 10019
212-830-6000
Richard Brezover, Editor
*Covers tax matters and other issues that con-
cern business.*

Government Accountants Journal
Association of Government Accountants
2200 Mount Vernon Ave.
Alexandria, VA 22301-1314
703-684-6931
Charles Hamilton, Editor
*Covers developments in accounting, data pro-
cessing, and budgeting.*

Journal of Accountancy
American Institute of Certified Public
    Accountants
1211 Ave. of Americas
New York, NY 10036-8775
212-575-3857
Collen Katz, Editor
Information on management of accounting firms, accounting issues, and other matters of concern to CPAs.

Practical Accountant
Warren, Gorham & Lamont, Inc.
One Penn Plaza
New York, NY 10119
800-950-1217
Information to help accountants run their practice.

LIBRARIES

American Institute of Certified Public
    Accountants
1211 Ave. of the Americas
New York, NY 10036
212-575-6200
212-575-3846 Fax
800-223-4155 Library services
800-522-5434 Library services in NY state
800-223-4158 Technical information
800-522-5430 Technical information in NY state
Philip Chenok, President
Covers the full range of accounting and taxation subjects.

Deloitte & Touche
Business Information Center
95 Wellington St., W., Ste. 1000
Toronto, ON, Canada M5J 2P4
416-861-9700
416-947-8247 Fax
Accounting, business, and auditing.

National Association of Accountants
10 Paragon Dr.
Montvale, NJ 07645
201-573-9000
800-638-4427
201-573-8185 Fax
Gary Scopes, Executive Director
Accounting, taxation, accounting practice management, and related topics.

COMPANIES

Arthur Andersen & Co.
69 West Washington St.
Chicago, IL 60602
312-346-6262
Accounting firm.

Coopers & Lybrand
1251 Avenue of the Americas
New York, NY 10020
212-536-2000
Accounting firm.

Deloitte & Touche
10 Westport Road
P.O. Box 820
Wilton, CT 06897-0820
203-761-3000
Accounting firm.

Ernst & Young
277 Park Avenue
New York, NY 10017
212-922-2000
Accounting firm.

Kenneth Leventhal & Co.
2049 Century Park East
Los Angeles, CA 90067
213-277-0880
Accounting firm.

Laventhol & Horwath
1845 Walnut St.
Philadelphia, PA 19103
215-299-1700
Accounting firm.

Moss, Adams & Co.
2830 Bank of California Center
Seattle, WA 98164
206-223-1820
Accounting firm.

Peat, Marwick, Main & Co.
345 Park Avenue
New York, NY 10022
212-758-9700
Accounting firm.

Price Waterhouse & Co.
1251 Avenue of the Americas
New York, NY 10020
212-489-8900
Accounting firm.

Seidman & Seidman/BDO
15 Columbus Circle
New York, NY 10023
212-765-7500
Accounting firm.

FEDERAL GOVERNMENT

U.S. International Trade Administration
Department of Commerce
14th St. and Constitution Ave., N.W.
Washington, DC 20230
202-377-2000
*Ask for the analyst who is an expert in
accounting services.*

ACTUARIAL SCIENCE

*Actuaries are professionals in the insurance and other industries who compute risks, pensions,
employee benefits, and insurance premiums based on statistical information.*

ASSOCIATIONS

American Society of Pension Actuaries
2029 K St. N.W., 4th Floor
Washington, DC 20006
202-659-3620
202-785-9594 Fax
Chester Salkind, Executive Director
*Offers information on various aspects of
employee benefits.*

American Academy of Actuaries
1720 I St. N.W., 7th Floor
Washington, DC 20006
202-223-8196
202-872-1948 Fax
J. Murphy, Executive Officer
*Promotes standards in actuarial science and
represents members in dealings with the government.*

Casualty Actuarial Society
One Penn Plaza
250 W. 34th St., 51st Floor
New York, NY 10119
212-560-1018
Robert Conger, Vice President
Promotes the use of actuarial science and statistics in researching casualty, fire, and other types of insurance.

Society of Actuaries
475 N. Martingale Rd., Ste. 800
Schaumburg, IL 60173-2226
708-706-3500
708-706-3599 Fax
John O'Connor, Executive Director
Members include actuaries who create programs in the fields of employee benefits, insurance, and pensions.

PERIODICALS

Actuarial Digest
Actuarial Digest Publishing Co.
5600 Rosewell Rd., NE, Ste. 276N
Atlanta, GA 30342-1103
404-256-5871
Gene Hubbard, Editor
News and industry trends for actuaries working in all fields.

Actuarial Update
American Academy of Actuaries
1720 I St., N.W., 7th Floor
Washington, DC 20006
202-223-8196
Jeanne Casey, Editor
Includes news for actuaries working in the fields of insurance, employee benefits, and pensions.

Society of Actuaries. Transactions: Reports of Mortality and Morbidity Experience
Society of Actuaries
475 N. Martingale, Ste. 800
Schaumburg, IL 60173-2226
708-706-3599
Statistics used by actuaries.

LIBRARIES

Davis Library
College of Insurance
Insurance Society of New York
101 Murray St.
New York, NY 10007
212-962-4111
Covers most insurance subjects, including actuarial science.

State Mutual Companies
Library
440 Lincoln St., G9
Worcester, MA 01605
508-855-2435
508-853-6332 Fax
Actuarial science, insurance, and business.

Society of Actuaries
475 N. Martingale Rd., Ste. 800
Schaumburg, IL 60173-2226
708-706-3500
708-706-3599 Fax
John O'Connor, Executive Director
Actuarial sciences, insurance, and employee benefits.

University of Michigan
Mathematics Library
3027 Angell Hall
Ann Arbor, MI 48109-1003
313-764-7266
Actuarial insurance, statistics, and mathematics.

ADDITIVES AND FLAVORINGS

ASSOCIATIONS

Chemical Sources Association
1620 I St. N.W., Ste. 925
Washington, DC 20006
202-293-5800
202-463-8998
Richard Heinze, President
This group of fragrance and flavor manufacturers helps find suppliers of unusual or rare oils and chemicals for use in creating products.

Flavor and Extract Manufacturers Association
     of the United States
1620 I St. N.W., Ste. 925
Washington, DC 20006
202-293-5800
202-463-8998 Fax
Daniel Thompson, Executive Secretary
Manufacturers and wholesalers of flavors, extracts, syrups, food color, and other food additives.

Society of Flavor Chemists
c/o Denise McCafferty
McCormick and Co.
204 Wight Ave.
Hunt Valley, MD 21031
301-771-7491
Denise McCafferty, Secretary
Chemists who create new flavors and new products that use flavors.

PERIODICALS

Bioresearch Today: Food Additives & Residues
BIOSIS
2100 Arch St.
Philadelphia, PA 19103-1399
215-587-4800
Technical information about food additives.

C A Selects. Flavors & Fragrances
Chemical Abstracts Service
2540 Olentangy River Rd.
Box 3012
Columbus, OH 43210
614-447-3600
Provides technical information about the full range of flavor and fragrances: essential oils, perfumes, flavoring materials, deodorants, artificial sweeteners, and other compounds that change taste and aroma.

Food Chemical News Guide
Food Chemical News, Inc.
1101 Pennsylvania Ave., S.E.
Washington, DC 20003
202-544-1980
Louis Rothschild, Editor
Covers food additives, particularly their current status regarding government approval and federal regulations.

Perfumer & Flavorist
Allured Publishing
Bldg. C, Ste. 1600
2100 Manchester Rd.
Box 318
Wheaton, IL 60189-0318
708-653-2155
Stanley Allured, Editor
Technical information for those working in the flavor and perfume fields.

LIBRARIES

Givaudan Corp—Library
125 Delawanna Ave.
Clifton, NY 07015-5034
201-365-8563
Food additives and other subjects.

COMPANIES

Coca-Cola Enterprises Inc.
(Subsidiary of Coca-Cola Co.)
One Coca-Cola Plaza, N.W.
Atlanta, GA 30313
404-676-2100
Flavoring extracts and flavoring syrups.

Crompton & Knowles Corp.
One Station Pl., Metro Center
Stamford, CT 06902
203-353-5400
Flavorings, fragrances, essential oils.

Florasynth, Inc.
410 East 62nd St.
New York, NY 10021
212-371-7700
Flavoring extracts, finished flavors, fragrances, perfumes, and essential oils.

Givaudan Corp.
(Subsidiary of L. Givaudan & Cie, S. A.)
100 Delawanna Ave.
Clifton, NJ 07015
201-365-8151
Fragrances and flavors.

International Flavors & Fragrances Inc.
521 W. 57th St.
New York, NY 10019
212-765-5500
Fragrances and flavors.

Mallinckrodt Inc.
(Subsidiary of Imcera Group Inc.)
675 McDonnell Blvd.
St. Louis, MO 63134
314-895-2000
Flavors, fragrances, and other types of chemicals.

McCormick Stange Flavor Division
(Division of McCormick & Co. Inc.)
230 Shilling Circle S.
Hunt Valley, MD 21031
301-771-7400
Flavorings and soluble seasonings.

A. E. Staley Mfg. Co.
(Subsidiary of Tate & Lyle PLC)
2200 E. Eldorado St.
Decatur, IL 62525
217-423-4411
Food flavorings, corn sweeteners, and other additives.

Universal Group Ltd.
(Subsidiary of Universal Foods Corp.)
5600 W. Raymond St.
Indianapolis, IN 46241
317-243-3521
Flavors and fragrances.

FEDERAL GOVERNMENT

U.S. International Trade Administration
Department of Commerce
14th St. and Constitution Ave., N.W.
Washington, DC 20230
202-377-2000
Ask for the Commodity Analyst who is an expert in additives or flavorings.

U.S. International Trade Commission
500 E St., S.W.
Washington, DC 20436
202-205-2000 Office of the Secretary
202-205-3296 Industries locator
Ask for the Trade Analyst who is an expert in additives or flavorings.

U.S. Patent and Trademark Office
Crystal Plaza 2
2011 Jefferson Davis Highway
Arlington, VA 22202
703-305-8000
Ask for the Examining Group Director who is a specialist in additives or flavorings.

ADHESIVES AND SEALANTS

ASSOCIATIONS

Adhesive and Sealant Council
1627 K St. N.W., Ste. 1000
Washington, DC 20006
202-452-1500
202-452-1501 Fax
Kerry Lake, Executive Vice President
Offers information on manufacturers and marketers of adhesives and sealants, raw materials, and suppliers of equipment.

Adhesives Manufacturers Association
111 E. Wacker Dr., Ste. 600
Chicago, IL 60601
312-644-6610
J. Dollard Carey, Executive Secretary
Represents manufacturers of formulated adhesives and coatings used in industry.

Gummed Industries Association
PO Box 92
Greenlawn, NY 11740
516-261-0114
Robert McKellar, Managing Director
Manufacturers and distributors of gummed paper, sealing tapes, and other tapes.

Pressure Sensitive Tape Council
104 Wilmot Rd., Ste. 201
Deerfield, IL 60015
708-940-8800
Glen Anderson, Executive Vice President
Offers information on virtually all types of pressure sensitive tapes, with the exception of surgical tape.

Sealant Waterproofing and Restoration Institute
3101 Broadway, Ste. 585
Kansas City, MO 64111
816-561-8230
816-561-7765 Fax
Kenneth Bowman, Executive Vice President
Members include sealant contractors, manufactures of sealants, and others in the waterproofing industry.

PERIODICALS

Adhesive Trends
Adhesive Manufacturers Association
111 E. Wacker Dr., Ste. 600
Chicago, IL 60611-4267
312-644-6610
Pamela Lubelfeld, Editor
Information on packaging adhesives, hot melts, pastes, gums, and glues.

Adhesives Age
Communication Channels, Inc.
6255 Barfield Rd.
Atlanta, GA 30328-4369
404-256-9800
Ann Barker, Editor
Covers all aspects of the manufacture, application, and marketing of adhesives and sealants.

Adhesives Age Directory
Communication Channels, Inc.
6255 Barfield Rd.
Atlanta, GA 30328-4369
404-256-9800
Barbara Katinsky, Editor
Lists supplies of adhesives and sealants.

Adhesives D.A.T.A. Digest
D.A.T.A. Business Publishing
15 Inverness Way E.
Box 6510
Englewood, CO 80155-6510
800-447-4666
Covers industry trends.

C A Selects. Adhesives
Chemical Abstracts Service
2540 Olentangy River Rd.
Box 3012
Columbus, OH 43210
614-447-3600
Technical information on adhesives, glues, sealants, grouts, and related products.

C A Selects. Hot-Melt Adhesives
Chemical Abstracts Service
2540 Olentangy River Rd.
Box 3012
Columbus, OH 43210
614-447-3600
Technical information on hot-melt adhesives and sealants.

Composites & Adhesives Newsletter
T C Press
Box 36006
Los Angeles, CA 90036
213-938-6923
George Epstein, Editor
Provides technical and industry information on adhesive and composite materials.

LIBRARIES

Avery Dennison
Research Center
Information Center
2900 Bradley St.
Pasadena, CA 91107-1599
818-398-2555
818-398-2553 Fax
Adhesives, polymer chemistry, and engineering.

Loctite Corp.—Research Library
705 N. Mountain Rd.
Newington, CT 06111
203-278-1280
Adhesives and other topics.

3M -209 Technical Library
3M Center, 209-BC-06
St. Paul, MN 55144-1000
612-733-6973
Adhesives, surface sciences, glass, and other subjects.

COMPANIES

Borden Packaging & Industrial Products Division
(Division of Borden Inc.)
180 E. Broad St.
Columbus, OH 43215
614-225-4000
Adhesives, resins, and other products.

Dennison Mfg. Co.
(Subsidiary of Avery Dennison Corp.)
300 Howard St.
Framingham, MA 01701
508-879-0511
Office supplies including adhesives.

H.B. Fuller Co.
2400 Energy Park Dr.
St. Paul, MN 55108
612-645-3401
Industrial adhesives, sealants, and coatings.

Grow Group Inc.
200 Park Ave.
New York, NY 10166
212-599-4400
Sealants, paints, and other coatings.

Minnesota Mining & Mfg. Co.
3M Center
St. Paul, MN 55144
612-733-1110
Adhesives among many other products.

Morgan Adhesives Co.
(Subsidiary of Bemis Co., Inc.)
4560 Darrow Rd.
Stow, OH 44224
216-688-1111
Adhesive print stock and adhesive films.

Reichhold Chemicals, Inc.
(Subsidiary of DIC Americas, Inc.)
525 N. Broadway
White Plains, NY 10603
914-682-5700
Adhesives and polymers.

Sherwin-Williams Co.
101 Prospect Ave., N. W.
Cleveland, OH 44115
216-566-2000
Paints, varnishes, lacquers, adhesives, and sealants.

Tremco Inc.
(Subsidiary of BF Goodrich Co.)
3735 Green Rd.
Beachwood, OH 44122
216-292-5000
Protective coatings, sealants, and adhesives.

FEDERAL GOVERNMENT

U.S. International Trade Administration
Department of Commerce
14th St. and Constitution Ave., N.W.
Washington, DC 20230
202-377-2000
Ask for the Commodity Analyst who is an expert in adhesives, sealants, or glues.

U.S. International Trade Commission
500 E St., S.W.
Washington, DC 20436
202-205-2000 Office of the Secretary
202-205-3296 Industries locator
Ask for the Trade Analyst who is an expert in adhesives, sealants, or glues.

ADULT EDUCATION

ASSOCIATIONS

American Association for Adult and Continuing Education
1112 16th St. N.W., Ste. 420
Washington, DC 20036
202-463-6333
Judith Koloski, Executive Director
Offers information and referrals on a wide range of adult-education subjects.

American Council on Education
1 Dupont Circle N.W., Ste. 800
Washington, DC 20036
202-939-9300
Robert Atwell, President
Among its many activities, the Council administers the GED high-school equivalency exam.

Coalition of Adult Education Organizations
c/o Elena Morris
Office of Adult Learning Services
The College Board
45 Columbus Ave.
New York, NY 10023
212-713-8000
Elena Morris, President
Offers information on a wide range of programs in adult and continuing education.

General Educational Development Institute
16211 6th Ave. N.E.
Seattle, WA 98155
206-362-2055
Chuck Herring, Director
Members include high-school dropouts, adults who need to develop skills, and employers, teachers, schools, and others who assist these individuals.

National Council of Administrators of Adult Education
c/o Morton S. Horowitz
Oceanside Public Schools
Community Activities Center
School No. 4, Oceanside Rd.
Oceanside, NY 11572
516-678-1200
516-678-1224 Fax
Morton Horowitz, President
Members run adult- and community-education programs nationwide.

PERIODICALS

Adult & Continuing Education Today
Learning Resources Network
1554 Hayes Dr.
Manhattan, KS 66502
913-539-5376
William Draves, Editor
A newsletter covering issues in continuing education.

Adult Education Quarterly
American Association for Adult and Continuing Education
1112 16th St. N.W., Ste. 420
Washington, DC 20036
202-463-6333
Roger Hiemstra, Editor
Offers information on research findings and theory in the field of adult education.

Adult Learning
American Association for Adult and Continu-
    ing Education
1112 16th St. N.W., Ste. 420
Washington, DC 20036
202-463-6333
Jeanette Smith, Editor
*Practical and how-to information for teaching
adults.*

Journal of Continuing Higher Education
Association for Continuing Higher Education
210 J. Orbis Keller Bldg.
Pennsylvania State University
University Park, PA 16802
814-863-7752
Donna Queeney, Editor
*A scholarly journal for those working in adult
education.*

LIBRARIES

Center on Education and Training for
    Employment
Research Library
Ohio State University
1900 Kenny Rd.
Columbus, OH 43210
614-292-4353
Training, employment, and related topics.

General Educational Development Institute
16211 6th Ave. N.E.
Seattle, WA 98155
206-362-2055
Adult-education materials.

Teachers College
Milbank Memorial Library
Columbia University
DB, Box 307
New York, NY 10027
212-678-3494
Education, technology, and related topics.

FEDERAL GOVERNMENT

U.S. Department of Education
400 Maryland Ave., S.W.
Washington, DC 20202
202-708-5366
*Ask for the Vocational and Adult Education
department.*

ADVERTISING

See also: MARKETING and SALES PROMOTION

ASSOCIATIONS

Advertising Club of New York
155 E. 55th St., Ste. 5-D
New York, NY 10022
212-935-8080
Denise Harbin, Executive Director
Members include prominent executives working in advertising and marketing. Provides classes in the advertising arts.

Advertising Research Foundation
3 E. 54th St.
New York, NY 10022
212-751-5656
212-319-5265 Fax
Michael Naples, President
This group of agencies, advertisers, and researchers use objective techniques to evaluate advertising and marketing campaigns. The Foundation develops new research methods, establishes research standards, and maintains an information center.

Affiliated Advertising Agencies International
2280 S. Xanadu Way, Ste. 300
Aurora, CO 80014
303-671-8551
303-337-9576 Fax
Patricia Parker, President
The agencies in this association help each other service accounts, find new business, and improve management practices.

American Association of Advertising Agencies
666 3rd Ave., 13th Floor
New York, NY 10017
212-682-2500
212-682-8391 Fax
John O'Toole, President
Promotes the advertising agency business and helps agencies operate more effectively.

American Council of Highway Advertisers
8803 Chesapeake Ave., Ste. 809
North Beach, MD 20714
301-855-8886
301-855-4452 Fax
Richard Roberts, President
Represents advertisers who use private property on public highways.

Association of National Advertisers
155 E. 44th St.
New York, NY 10017
212-697-5950
DeWitt Helm, President
Provides information on a wide variety of subjects to major advertising firms.

Institute of Outdoor Advertising
342 Madison Ave.
New York, NY 10173
212-986-5920
212-983-9808 Fax
Don Byer, President
Represents firms that advertise outdoors.

International Newspaper Advertising and
  Marketing Executives
PO Box 17210
Washington, DC 20041
703-648-1168
703-476-6015 Fax
Reggie Hall, Executive Director
*Offers information about advertising in daily
newspapers.*

National Advertising Division
c/o Council of Better Business Bureaus
845 Third Ave.
New York, NY 10022
212-754-1320
212-832-1296 Fax
Ronald Smithies, Director
*Investigates advertisers accused of product
misrepresentation and arbitrates cases where
the public interest is involved.*

Newspaper Advertising Bureau
1180 Ave. of the Americas
New York, NY 10036
212-704-4547
212-704-4616 Fax
Julie Nowhall, Communication Director
*Represents over 1,000 daily newspapers and
promotes newspaper advertising.*

Point-of-Purchase Advertising Institute
66 N. Van Brunt St.
Englewood, NJ 07631
201-894-8899
John Kawula, President
*Offers information on point-of-purchase
advertising signs and displays.*

Radio Advertising Bureau
304 Park Ave. South
New York, NY 10010
212-254-4800
800-232-3131
212-254-8713 Fax
Warren Potash, President
*Promotes advertising on radio. Maintains a
library and a database of information on radio
marketing.*

Retail Advertising Conference
500 N. Michigan Ave., Ste. 600
Chicago, IL 60611
312-245-9011
312-245-9015 Fax
Douglas Raymond, President
*Offers information on promotion of retail
sales.*

Specialty Advertising Association International
1404 Walnut Hill Ln.
Irving, TX 75038-3094
214-580-0404
214-550-8331 Fax
H. Ted Olson, President
*Represents firms selling such specialty adver-
tising products as calendars, imprinted items,
and executive gifts.*

Television Bureau of Advertising
477 Madison Ave.
New York, NY 10022
212-486-1111
James Joyella, President
Promotes advertising on television.

Yellow Pages Publishers Association
340 E. Big Beaver Rd., 5th Floor
Troy, MI 48083
313-680-8880
313-680-1251 Fax
J. Raymond Avedian, President
*Offers information on advertising in yellow
pages nationwide.*

PERIODICALS

Advertising Age, the International Newspaper
of Marketing
Crain Communications Inc.
220 E. 42nd St.
New York, NY 10017-5806
212-210-0171
Fred Danzig, Editor
*Covers the full range of developments in
advertising, sales promotion, and marketing.*

Adweek/East
B P I Communications, Inc.
49 E. 21st St.
New York, NY 10010
212-529-5500
Noreen O'Leary, Editor
*Advertising news with a focus on the East
coast. Call for information on other editions
with a focus on the Southeast, Midwest, New
England, Southwest, and West.*

Adweek's Marketer's Guide to Media
A S M Communications, Inc.
49 E. 21st St.
New York, NY 10010
212-529-5500
Gerri Lee, Editor
*A directory of various media used by adver-
tisers.*

Communication Arts
Coyne & Blanchard, Inc.
410 Sherman Ave.
Box 10300
Palo Alto, CA 94303
415-326-6040
Patrick Coyne, Editor
*Read by professionals involved with visual
communications, especially advertisers.*

Creative, the Magazine of Promotion and
Marketing
Magazines Creative, Inc.
37 W. 39th St.
New York, NY 10018
212-840-0160
David Flaserstein, Editor
*Information on sales promotion and adver-
tising.*

M P A Newsletter of Research
Magazine Publishers Association, Inc.
575 Lexington Ave.
New York, NY 10022
212-752-0055
Marian Confer, Editor
*Follows trends in magazine advertising among
other subjects.*

Madison Avenue Handbook
Peter Glenn Publications, Inc.
17 E. 48th St.
New York, NY 10017
212-688-7940
Chip Brill, Editor
*A yellow pages directory for the advertising
industry.*

Media Week
B P I Communications, Inc.
49 E. 21st St.
New York, NY 10010
212-529-5500
Craig Reiss, Editor
Covers news and trends in advertising media.

Nielsen Newscast
Nielsen Media Research
Nielsen Plaza
Northbrook, IL 60062
708-498-6300
L. Frerk, Editor
*Data on television audiences, media, trends,
and new products.*

Standard Directory of Advertisers
National Register Publishing Co.
Macmillan Directory Division
3004 Glenview Rd.
Wilmette, IL 60091
708-441-2210
*An alphabetical directory of advertisers with
listings also by industry, state, and city.*

LIBRARIES

Advertising Research Foundation
Library
3 E. 54th St.
New York, NY 10022
212-751-5656
212-319-5265 Fax
Advertising, research, and related subjects.

American Association of Advertising Agencies
Library
666 3rd Ave., 13th Floor
New York, NY 10017
212-682-2500
212-682-8391 Fax
John O'Toole, President
Advertising and the media.

COMPANIES

N.W. Ayer Inc.
825 Eighth Ave.
New York, NY 10019
212-474-5000
Advertising agency.

BBDO Worldwide Inc.
(Subsidiary of Omnicom Group Inc.)
1285 Avenue of the Americas
New York, NY 10019
212-459-5000
Advertising agency.

Backer Spielvogel Bates Worldwide Inc.
(Subsidiary of Saatchi & Saatchi Co. p.l.c.)
405 Lexington Ave.
New York, NY 10174
212-297-7000
Advertising agency.

D'Arcy Masius Benton & Bowles, Inc.
1675 Broadway
New York, NY 10019
212-468-3622
Advertising agency.

Interpublic Group of Companies, Inc.
1271 Ave. of the Americas
New York, NY 10020
212-399-8000
*Advertising agencies and other marketing ser-
vices.*

Ketchum Communications inc.
Six PPG Pl.
Pittsburgh, PA 15222
412-456-3500
Advertising and public relations.

McCann-Erickson USA, Inc.
(Subsidiary of Interpublic Group of Compa-
    nies, Inc.)
750 Third Ave.
New York, NY 10017
212-697-6000
Advertising agency.

Ogilvy Group Inc.
2 E. 48th St.
New York, NY 10017
212-907-3400
Advertising agency.

Ross Roy, Inc.
100 Bloomfield Hills Pkwy.
Bloomfield Hills, MI 48304
313-433-6000
Advertising agency.

Saatchi & Saatchi Compton Inc.
(Subsidiary of Saatchi & Saatchi Compton
    Worldwide)
375 Hudson St.
New York, NY 10014
212-463-2000
Advertising agency.

J. Walter Thompson Co.
(Subsidiary of WPP Group plc)
466 Lexington Ave.
New York, NY 10017
212-210-7000
Advertising agency.

Young & Rubicam Inc.
285 Madison Ave.
New York, NY 10017
212-210-3000
Advertising agency.

FEDERAL GOVERNMENT

Federal Trade Commission
Pennsylvania Ave. at 6th St., N.W.
Washington, DC 20580
202-326-2000
Ask for the Consumer Protection Bureau.

U.S. International Trade Administration
Department of Commerce
14th St. and Constitution Ave., N.W.
Washington, DC 20230
202-377-2000
*Ask for the Commodity Analyst who is an
expert in advertising.*

U.S. International Trade Commission
500 E St., S.W.
Washington, DC 20436
202-205-2000 Office of the Secretary
202-205-3296 Industries locator
*Ask for the Trade Analyst who is an expert in
advertising.*

AEROSOL INDUSTRY

ASSOCIATIONS

National Aerosol Association
584 Bellerive Dr., Ste. 3D
Annapolis, MD 21401
301-974-4472
301-757-3809 Fax
George Brown, Executive Director
*Represents aerosol packagers and manufactur-
ers of cans and valves.*

American Association for Aerosol Research
c/o Dr. John Seinfeld
5530 Wisconsin Ave., Ste. 1149
Washington, DC 20815
301-907-9873
301-656-0989 Fax
Dr. John Seinfeld, President
*Engineers and scientists engaged in aerosol
research.*

PERIODICALS

Advances in Aerosol Physics
John Wiley & Sons Ltd.
605 Third Ave.
New York, NY 10016
212-870-6000
V.A. Fedoseev, Editor
Technical information for manufacturers and engineers.

Aerosol Age, the Magazine of Pressure Packaging
Industry Publications, Inc.
389 Passaic Ave.
Fairfield, NJ 07006
201-227-5151
M. SanGiovanni, Editor
Trade magazine for manufacturers and marketers of aerosol products.

Aerosol Science and Technology
American Association for Aerosol Research
Elsevier Science Publishing Co., Inc.
655 Ave. of the Americas
New York, NY 10010
212-989-5800
Technical information with an emphasis on experimental new processes and products.

HAPPI: Household & Personal Products Industry
Rodman Publications, Inc.
17 S. Franklin Trnpk.
Ramsey, NJ 07446
201-825-2552
Hamilton Carson, Editor
Covers the detergent, soap, cosmetic and toiletry, wax, polish and aerosol industries.

Journal of Aerosol Medicine
Mary Ann Liebert, Inc.
1651 Third Ave.
New York, NY 10128
212-289-2300
Dr. Gerald Smaldone, Editor
Covers aerosols as they apply to the delivery of medication.

Journal of Aerosol Science
Pergamon Press, Inc., Journals Division
Maxwell House
Fairview Park
Elmsford, NY 10523
914-592-7700
G. Kaspert, Editors
Technical data on aerosols and their use in new products.

LIBRARIES

California Institute of Technology
Environmental Engineering Library
136 W.M. Keck Laboratory
Pasadena, CA 91125
818-356-4381
818-795-1547 Fax
Aerosol physics, atmospheric chemistry, air quality management, and air quality modeling.

Calvert Environmental, Inc./APT
Library
5985 Santa Fe
San Diego, CA 92109
619-272-0050
Aerosol science, chemistry, and fluids.

Lovelace Biomedical & Environmental
   Research Institute, Inc.
Inhalation Toxicology Research Institute
Library
Box 5890
Albuquerque, NM 87185
505-844-2600
505-847-1900 Fax
*Aerosol physics, inhalation toxicology, and
medicine.*

COMPANIES

APG, Inc.
2730 Middlebury St.
Elkhart, IN 46514
219-295-0000
Aerosol packaging.

Demert & Dougherty, Inc.
814 Commerce Dr.
Oak Brook, IL 60521
708-655-3450
Aerosol and liquid packaging.

Fuller Brush Co.
Westport Addition, Box 729
Great Bend, KS 67530
316-792-1711
*Cosmetics, aerosols, brushes, and other prod-
ucts.*

Novo Corp.
1075 Central Park Ave.
Scarsdale, NY 10583
914-472-2252
*Aerosol paints, anti-corrosive agents, and cork
products.*

Pittway Corp.
(Subsidiary of Standard Shares, Inc.)
333 Skokie Blvd.
Northbrook, IL 60065
708-498-1260
*Aerosol products, aerosol valves, and other
products.*

Plasti-Kote Co., Inc.
1000 Lake Rd.
Medina, OH 44256
216-725-4511
Aerosol paints.

Professional Packaging Corp.
208 E. Benton St.
Aurora, IL 60507
708-896-0574
Pharmaceutical aerosols.

Puritan-Bennett Corp.
9401 Indian Creek Pkwy., Box 25905
Overland Park, KS 66225
913-661-0444
*Propellant gases for aerosol packaging and
other gases.*

Risdon Corp.
(Subsidiary of CMB Packaging S.A.)
One Risdon St.
Naugatuck, CT 06770
203-729-8231
Aerosol valves and other products.

FEDERAL GOVERNMENT

U.S. International Trade Administration
Department of Commerce
14th St. and Constitution Ave., N.W.
Washington, DC 20230
202-377-2000
*Ask for the Commodity Analyst who is an
expert in aerosols.*

U.S. International Trade Commission
500 E St., S.W.
Washington, DC 20436
202-205-2000 Office of the Secretary
202-205-3296 Industries locator
Ask for the Trade Analyst who is an expert in aerosols.

U.S. Patent and Trademark Office
Crystal Plaza 2
2011 Jefferson Davis Highway
Arlington, VA 22202
703-305-8000
Ask for the Examining Group Director who is a specialist in aerosols.

AEROSPACE

See also: AIRPLANE AND HELICOPTER INDUSTRY and AIRPORTS

ASSOCIATIONS

Flight Safety Foundation
2200 Wilson Blvd., Ste. 500
Arlington, VA 22201
703-522-8300
703-525-6047 Fax
John Enders, President
Members include manufacturers, airlines, insurance companies, and others who promote safe flight.

American Astronautical Society
6352 Rolling Mill Pl., Ste. 102
Springfield, VA 22152
703-866-0020
703-866-3526 Fax
Carolyn Brown, Executive Director
Members include scientists, executives, and others who work in astronautics.

American Institute of Aeronautics and Astro-
    nautics
370 L'Enfant Promenade, S.W.
Washington, DC 20024
202-646-7400
202-646-7508 Fax
Cort Durocher, Executive Director
Engineers and scientists who exchange techni-cal data concerning aeronautics and astronau-tics.

National Space Society
922 Pennsylvania Ave., SE
Washington, DC 20003
202-543-1900
Lori Garver, Executive Director
Promotes the exploration of space.

Space Studies Institute
PO Box 82
Princeton, NJ 08540
609-921-0377
Dr. Gerard O'Neill, President
Companies and individuals promoting research into space exploration.

United States Space Foundation
PO Box 1838
Colorado Springs, CO 80901
719-550-1000
Richard MacLeod, President
Develops and promotes educational programs about space exploration.

PERIODICALS

Aerospace America
American Institute of Aeronautics and Astro-
    nautics, Inc.
370 L'Enfant Promenade, S.W.
Washington, DC 20024
202-646-7471
Robert daCosta, Editor
Information on all major aerospace issues, including space, electronics, design, defense, computers, and other technologies.

Aerospace Products
Gordon Publications, Inc.
301 Gibraltar Dr.
Morris Plains, NJ 07950
201-361-9060
Mary Franciscus, Editor, Editor
A trade magazine for executives and scientists in aerospace field.

Aviation Week & Space Technology
McGraw-Hill, Inc.
1221 Ave. of the Americas
New York, NY 10020
212-512-3288
Donald Fink, Editor
Covers news and trends in the aviation and aerospace industry.

LIBRARIES

American Institute of Aeronautics and Astro-
    nautics
Technical Information Service
555 W. 57th St., Ste. 1200
New York, NY 10019
212-247-6500
212-582-4861 Fax
Barbara Lawrence, Administrator
Aeronautics, air transportation, space explo-ration, air traffic control, and many related topics.

NASA
Ames Research Center
Library
Moffett Field, Mail Stop 604-3
Mountain View, CA 94035-1000
415-604-6325
Aeronautics, flight engineering, and related topics.

COMPANIES

Aerojet
(Subsidiary of GenCorp Inc.)
10300 N. Torrey Pines Rd.
La Jolla, CA 92037
619-455-8500
Aerospace and defense products.

Allied-Signal Inc.
Columbia Road & Park Ave.
Morristown, NJ 07962
201-455-2000
Aerospace and automobile products.

B.F. Goodrich Co.
3925 Embassy Pkwy.
Akron, OH 44333
216-374-2000
Aerospace components and other products.

Interlake Corp.
550 Warrenville Rd.
Lisle, IL 60532
708-852-8800
Engineered materials, including aerospace components.

LTV Aerospace and Defense Co.
(Subsidiary of LTV Corp.)
2001 Ross Ave., Box 655003
Dallas, TX 75265
214-979-7711
Space vehicles, military aircraft, and commercial aircraft components.

Martin Marietta Corp.
6801 Rockledge Dr.
Bethesda, MD 20817
301-897-6000
Aerospace, electronics, and defense products.

Parker Hannifin Corp.
17325 Euclid Ave.
Cleveland, OH 44112
216-531-3000
Motion-control components for aerospace applications.

Pneumo Abex Corp.
(Subsidiary of Whitman Corp.)
4800 Prudential Tower
Boston, MA 02199
617-375-1200
Aerospace products including flight controls and landing gear.

Textron Inc.
40 Westminster St.
Providence, RI 02903
401-421-2800
Aerospace systems and helicopters.

United Technologies Corp.
United Technologies Bldg.
Hartford, CT 06101
203-728-7000
Aircraft engines and many other aerospace products.

FEDERAL GOVERNMENT

National Aeronautics and Space Administration
600 Independence Ave., S.W.
Washington, DC 20546
202-453-1000
Ask for the Aeronautics department.

U.S. International Trade Administration
Department of Commerce
14th St. and Constitution Ave., N.W.
Washington, DC 20230
202-377-2000
Ask for the Commodity Analyst who is an expert in aerospace.

U.S. International Trade Commission
500 E St., S.W.
Washington, DC 20436
202-205-2000 Office of the Secretary
202-205-3296 Industries locator
Ask for the Trade Analyst who is an expert in aerospace.

AIDS

ASSOCIATIONS

Americans for a Sound AIDS Policy
PO Box 17433
Washington, DC 20041
703-471-7350
W. Shephard Smith, President
Helps create public policies towards AIDS.

Gay Men's Health Crisis
129 W. 20th St.
New York, NY 10011
212-807-6664
Helps AIDS victims through a variety of services and disseminates AIDS-prevention literature.

People With AIDS Coalition
31 W. 26th St.
New York, NY 10010
212-532-0290
800-828-3280
212-447-1508 Fax
William Case, Executive Director
Offers support and information for victims of AIDS.

National AIDS Information Clearinghouse
PO Box 6003
Rockville, MD 20850
301-217-0023
800-458-5231
301-738-6616 Fax
Ruthann Bates, Project Director
This service, operated by the Centers for Disease Control, offers free AIDS and AIDS-prevention information to health professionals, businesses, and individuals.

National Leadership Coalition on AIDS
1150 17th St., N.W., Ste. 202
Washington, DC 20036
202-429-0930
202-872-1977 Fax
B. J. Stiles, President
Members include a wide variety of corporations, labor unions, trade groups, and others. Helps businesses deal with AIDS in the workplace and promotes AIDS research.

PERIODICALS

AIDS & Public Policy Journal
University Publishing Group, Inc.
107 E. Church St.
Frederick, MD 21701
800-654-8188
Edward Brandt, M.D., Editor
Publishes information about the social, legal, and political issues regarding AIDS.

AIDS—HIV Treatment Directory
American Foundation for AIDS Research
1515 Broadway, Ste. 3601
New York, NY 10036-8901
212-719-0033
Dr. Donald Abrams, Editors
A listing of experimental and approved pharmaceuticals and methods used in treating AIDS.

AIDS Clinical Care
Massachusetts Medical Society
1440 Main St.
Waltham, MA 02154-1649
800-843-6356
Information about the latests AIDS treatments.

AIDS Education and Prevention
International Society of AIDS Education
Guilford Publications, Inc.
72 Spring St., 4th Floor
New York, NY 10012
212-431-9800
Dr. Francisco Sy, Editor
Covers AIDS-prevention trends for use by physicians, health educators, and others.

AIDS Litigation Reporter
Andrews Publications
1646 West Chester Pike
Box 1000
Westtown, PA 19395
215-399-6600
Ronald Baker, Editor
Reports on AIDS-related litigation nationwide.

AIDS Policy and Law
Buraff Publications
1350 Connecticut Ave. N.W., Ste. 1000
Washington, DC 20036
202-862-0990
Richard Hagan, Editor
Covers legislation, litigation, government regulations, policies, employment practices, and other issues regarding AIDS.

LIBRARIES

AIDS Library of Philadelphia
32 N. 3rd St.
Philadelphia, PA 19106
215-922-5120
AIDS.

U.S. National Institutes of Health
National Cancer Institute
Frederick Cancer Research & Development
    Center
Scientific Library
Box B-Bldg. 549
Frederick, MD 21702-1013
301-846-1093
AIDS, biomedical research, cancer, and related topics.

U.S. National Library of Medicine
8600 Rockville Pike
Bethesda, MD 20894
301-496-6308
301-496-4450 Fax
Biomedical research, AIDS, and related topics.

FEDERAL GOVERNMENT

National Institutes of Health
9000 Rockville Pike
Bethesda, MD 20892
301-496-4000
Ask for AIDS Treatment Research.

U.S. Centers for Disease Control
1600 Clifton Rd. N.E.
Atlanta, GA 30333
404-639-3311
Ask for the AIDS program.

AFFIRMATIVE ACTION AND EQUAL EMPLOYMENT OPPORTUNITY

Affirmative action and equal employment opportunity refer to laws designed to offer women, minorities, and the handicapped equal access and equal opportunities in the workplace.

ASSOCIATIONS

Employment Management Association
4101 Lake Boone Tr., Ste. 201
Raleigh, NC 27607
919-787-6010
919-787-4916 Fax
Susan Rexer, Executive Director
This group provides information on many issues concerning employment, including affirmative action.

American Association for Affirmative Action
11 E. Hubbard St., Ste. 200
Chicago, IL 60611
312-329-2512
312-329-9131 Fax
Judith Burnison, Executive Director
Members include executives, administrators, and educators in charge of equal opportunity and affirmative action matters.

Equal Employment Advisory Council
1015 15th St. N.W.
Washington, DC 20005
202-789-8650
Jeffrey Norris, President
Offers information and training to those concerned with equal employment.

Together, Inc.
3739A S. Peoria Ave.
Tulsa, OK 75152
918-587-2405
Bern Gentry, President
Helps businesses, governments, and other groups facilitate the employment of poor people who have been unemployed for a long time. Publishes a manual on affirmative action.

PERIODICALS

Affirmative Action Register
Affirmative Action, Inc.
8356 Olive Blvd.
St. Louis, MO 63132
314-991-1335
Warren Green, Editor
A publication with information for minority, female, and handicapped employees and candidates for employment.

EEO Report
Institute for Management
Panel Publishers, Inc.
14 Plaza Rd.
Greenvale, NY 11548
516-484-0006
Diane Rabin, Editor
Covers issues that concern company officials in charge of affirmative action and equal opportunity programs.

Fair Employment Practices Summary of Latest Developments
The Bureau of National Affairs, Inc.
1231 25th St., N.W.
Washington, DC 20037
202-452-4200
Bill Manville, Editor
Describes current trends, rules, guidelines, and other issues affecting equal employment and affirmative action practices.

From the State Capitals. Civil Rights
Wakeman-Walworth, Inc.
300 N. Washington St.
Alexandria, VA 22314
703-549-8606
Provides news of state and local rules and guidelines regarding discrimination, affirmative action, and civil rights.

Minorities in Business Insider
Community Development Services, Inc.
C D Publications
8204 Fenton St.
Silver Spring, MD 20910-2889
301-588-6380
News on the employment of minorities, affirmative action, government contracts, and related subjects.

FEDERAL GOVERNMENT

U.S. Department of Housing and Urban Development
451st St., S.W.
Washington, DC 20410
202-755-5111
Ask for the Affirmative Action program.

AGRICULTURE

GENERAL SUBJECTS

Associations

Agriculture Council of America
1250 I St. N.W., Ste. 601
Washington, DC 20005
202-682-9200
202-289-6648 Fax
Judith O'Hara, Executive Director
This group of agribusiness companies, farmers, and ranchers works to build confidence in the quality of the U.S. food supply. It provides information on a wide range of agricultural subjects.

Communicating for Agriculture
101 E. Lincoln Ave.
Fergus Falls, MN 56537
218-739-3241
800-432-FARM
M. E. Smedsrud, Chief Executive
Businesses and individuals who earn their living through agriculture. Offers information and referrals to the public and members.

American Farm Bureau Research Foundation
225 Touhy Ave.
Park Ridge, IL 60068
312-399-5700
Dean Kleckner, President
Sponsors agricultural research in such areas as production, marketing, quality control, conservation, safety, mechanization, and new technologies.

American Society of Agronomy
677 S. Segoe Rd.
Madison, WI 53711
608-273-8080
Robert Barnes, Executive Vice President
This scientific society offers information on breeding, soil, crop management, and many other subjects.

National Council of Farmer Cooperatives
50 F St. N.W., Ste. 900
Washington, DC 20001
202-626-8700
Wayne Boutwell, President
This group of cooperatives helps 2 million farmers with their purchasing, marketing, and credit needs.

American Agricultural Law Association
Univ. of Arkansas
Leflar Law Center
Fayetteville, AR 72701
501-575-7389
501-575-2053 Fax
William Babione, Executive Officer
This association of law professors and attorneys offers information and referrals on all issues relating to agricultural law.

Periodicals

Agweek
Knight-Ridder Inc.
113 N. Third St.
Box 6008
Grand Forks, ND 58206
701-780-1230
Juan Pedraza, Editor
Covers agricultural news, particularly stories relating to markets.

American Agriculturist
H B J Farm Publications, Inc.
6277 Sea Harbor Dr.
Orlando, FL 32887
407-345-2727
Farming news written for farmers.

Progressive Farmer
Southern Progress Corp.
2100 Lakeshore Dr.
Birmingham, AL 35209
205-877-6263
Jack Odle, Editor
Primarily for farmers in the South and Southwest.

Today's Farmer
Midcontinent Farmers Association Incorporated
M F A, Inc.
615 Locust St.
Columbia, MO 65201
314-876-5252
Chuck Lay, Editor
Management and marketing information for farmers.

Libraries

Farm Journal, Inc.
Marketing Library
230 W. Washington Sq.
Philadelphia, PA 19105
215-829-4734
Farm markets, agriculture, and marketing.

U. S. Department of Agriculture
National Agricultural Library
10301 Baltimore Blvd.
Beltsville, MD 20705
301-344-3212
301-344-5472 Fax
By far the largest agricultural library in the U.S.

University of Illinois
Agriculture Library
226 Mumford Hall
1301 W. Gregory Dr.
Urbana, IL 61801
217-333-2416
216-244-0398 Fax
Agricultural engineering, food science, agricultural history, animal science, and agricultural economics.

University of Minnesota, St. Paul
Central Library
1984 Buford Ave.
St. Paul, MN 55108
612-624-1212
612-624-9245 Fax
Agricultural economics, agricultural engineering, agronomy, animal science, and related topics.

Companies

American Cyanamid Co.
One Cyanamid Plaza
Wayne, NJ 07470
201-831-2000
Agricultural chemicals and other products.

Andersons
P.O. Box 119
Maumee, OH 43537
419-893-5050
Grain, fertilizer, mill products, seeds, and chemicals.

Butler Mfg. Co.
BMA Tower
Kansas City, MO 64108
816-968-3000
Non-field agricultural equipment.

J. I. Case Co.
(Subsidiary of Tenneco Inc.)
700 State St.
Racine, WI 53404
414-636-6011
Tractors, combines, and other agricultural vehicles.

Conagra, Inc.
One Central Park Plaza
Omaha, NE 68102
402-978-4000
Agricultural chemicals, poultry products, flour, grain, and other products.

Countrymark, Incorporated
4565 Columbus Pike
Delaware, OH 43015
614-548-8200
Grain, feed, and other farm supplies.

Dow Chemical Co.
2030 Willard H. Dow Ctr.
Midland, MI 48674
517-636-1000
Agricultural chemicals and other products.

FMC Corp.
200 E. Randolph Dr.
Chicago, IL 60601
312-861-6000
Agricultural chemicals and other products.

Farm Credit Bank of Baltimore
14114 York Rd.
Sparks, MD 21152
301-329-5500
Agricultural lending.

Farmers Union Central Exchange, Inc.
5500 Cenex Dr.
Inver Grove Heights, MN 55075
612-451-5151
*Wholesale distributor of farm equipment,
seed, fertilizer, and feed.*

Land O'Lakes, Inc.
4001 Lexington Ave., N.
Arden Hills, MN 55112
612-481-2222
Agricultural services.

Eli Lilly and Co.
Lilly Corporate Center
Indianapolis, IN 46285
317-276-2000
Agricultural and other products.

Monsanto Co.
800 N. Lindbergh Blvd.
St. Louis, MO 63167
314-694-1000
Agricultural and other products.

Sandoz Corp.
(Subsidiary of Sandoz Ltd.)
608 Fifth Ave.
New York, NY 10020
212-307-1122
Agricultural chemicals, seed, and farm supplies.

Southern States Cooperative, Incorporated
6606 West Broad St.
Richmond, VA 23230
804-281-1000
Fertilizer, seed, and other farm supplies.

Stauffer Chemical Co.
(Subsidiary of Rhone-Poulenc Inc.)
One Corporate Dr.
Shelton, CT 06484
203-925-3300
*Agricultural chemicals, seeds, and other
products.*

Terra Intl., Inc.
(Subsidiary of Inspiration Resources Corp.)
600 Fourth St.
Sioux City, IA 51101
712-277-1340
Feed, agricultural chemicals, and fertilizer.

Farms

Bell Farms, Inc.
Rte. 1
Pantego, NC 27860
919-935-5311

DM Camp and Sons
P.O. Box 80007
Bakersfield, CA 93303
805-399-5511

Gilkey Farms, Inc.
P.O. Box 426
Corcoran, CA 93212
209-992-2136

Huntsinger Farms, Inc.
P.O. Box 360
Eau Claire, WI 54702
715-832-9739

Oji Brothers Farms, Inc.
8547 Sawtelle
Yuba City, CA 95991
916-673-0845

Proprietary Holding, Inc.
Agrinorthwest
P.O. Box 2308
Tri Cities, WA 99302
509-735-6461

River Garden Farms Co.
41758 County Rd. 112
Knights Landing, CA 95645
916-735-6274

Sherrill Farms, Inc
5001 E. Washington St.
Phoenix, AZ 85034
602-275-5402

Vogel and Fey Farms, Inc.
1500 S. Zarzamora St.
San Antonio, TX 78207
512-223-6267

Woodland Farms, Inc.
P.O. Box 238
Story City, IA 50248
515-733-4582

ALTERNATIVE AND ORGANIC FARMING

Associations

Committee for Sustainable Agriculture
PO Box 1300
Colfax, CA 95713
916-346-2777
916-346-6884 Fax
Otis Wollen, Executive Director
These organic farmers and sellers of natural foods promote ecological farming practices.

Institute for Alternative Agriculture
9200 Edmonston Rd., Ste. 117
Greenbelt, MD 20770
301-441-8777
I. Garth Youngberg, Executive Director
Provides information on agricultural practices that are ecologically and economically sound.

International Alliance for Sustainable Agriculture
Newman Center
1701 University Ave. S.E.
Minneapolis, MN 55414
612-331-1099
612-379-1527 Fax
Terry Gips, Executive Director
Offers technical information and referrals on ecological, profitable systems for farming.

Organic Crop Improvement Association
3185 Township Rd. 179
Bellefontaine, OH 43311
513-592-4983
513-592-4983 Fax
Betty Kananen, Administrative Director
Works to regulate producers of organically-grown food.

Periodicals

Biological Farming News
701 Madison St., N.E.
Albuquerque, NM 87110
505-298-1748
Leland Taylor, Editor
Provides information on organic farming techniques.

CHEMICALS

Associations

National Agricultural Chemicals Association
1155 15th St., N.W., Ste. 900
Washington, DC 20005
202-296-1585
Jay Vroom, President
Manufacturers of a wide range of chemicals used in agriculture.

Weed Science Society of America
309 W. Clark St.
Champaign, IL 61820
217-356-3182
217-398-4119 Fax
Robert Schmidt, Executive
Offers information on weed control.

Periodicals

Agrichemical Age
H B J Farm Publications, Inc.
731 Market St.
San Francisco, CA 94103-2011
415-495-3340
Len Richardson, Editor
Written for dealers, applicators, and consultants involved with agricultural chemicals.

Farm Chemicals
Meister Publishing Co.
37733 Euclid Ave.
Willoughby, OH 44094
216-942-2000
Charlotte Sine, Editor
Information for manufacturers of fertilizers and pesticides.

ECONOMICS AND RESEARCH

Associations

Agricultural Research Institute
9650 Rockville Pike
Bethesda, MD 20814
301-530-7122
301-571-1858 Fax
William Cath, Executive Director
Exists to solve agricultural problems, particularly those involving technology.

American Agricultural Economics Association
80 Heady Hall
Iowa State Univ.
Ames, IA 50011-1070
515-294-8700
515-294-1234 Fax
Raymond Beneke, Secretary
Agricultural economists working for industry and government.

International Association of Agricultural
    Economists
1211 W. 22nd St., Ste. 216
Oak Brook, IL 60521
708-571-9393
708-571-9580 Fax
Dr. R. Hildreth, Secretary
Agricultural economists from around the world.

Periodicals

Agricultural Research
U.S. Agricultural Research Service
Bldg. 005, Rm. 318
BARC-West
Beltsville, MD 20705
202-655-4000
Lloyd McLaughlin, Editor
Reports on government agricultural research.

IRRIGATION

Associations

Irrigation Association
1911 N. Ft. Myer Dr., Ste. 1009
Arlington, VA 22209
703-524-1200
703-524-9544 Fax
R. Sears, Executive Vice President
Irrigation equipment manufacturers, wholesalers, and contractors.

American Society of Irrigation Consultants
425 Oak St.
Brentwood, CA 94513
415-516-1300
415-516-1301 Fax
Wanda Sarsfield, Executive Secretary
Members include manufacturers, consultants, and landscape architects involved with irrigation.

Periodicals

Landscape & Irrigation
Gold Trade Publications, Inc.
Box 8420
Van Nuys, CA 91409
818-781-8300
Anne Goldstein, Editor
Reports on the irrigation industry.

LABOR

Associations

Farm Labor Research Project
PO Box 550
Toledo, OH 43693
419-243-3456
Rick Velasquez, Legal Counsel
Represents the interests of farm workers.

National Council of Agricultural Employers
1735 I St., N.W., Ste. 704
Washington, DC 20006
202-728-0300
Sharon Hughes, Executive Vice President
Growers and food processors who employ hand laborors.

United Farm Workers of America
PO Box 62-LaPaz
Keene, CA 93531
805-822-5571
805- 822-653 Fax
Cesar Chavez, President
The largest union representing farm workers.

MACHINERY

Associations

Equipment Manufacturing Institute
10 S. Riverside Plaza
Chicago, IL 60606
312-321-1470
312-321-1480 Fax
Emmett Barker, President
Manufacturers of farming machinery and other equipment.

Farm Equipment Wholesalers Association
1927 Keokuk St.
Iowa City, IA 52240
319-354-5156
319-354-5157 Fax
Thomas Irwin, Executive Vice President
Wholesalers of light farm equipment and recreational equipment.

International Silo Association
8725 Rosehill, Ste. 210
Lenexa, KS 66215
913-599-1919
913-599-6500 Fax
James Knight, President
Firms that manufacture silos and other structures for storing agricultural products.

Periodicals

Farm & Power Equipment Dealer
North American Equipment Dealers Association
Admore Publishing Co., Inc.
9701 Gravois Ave.
St. Louis, MO 63123
314-638-4050
Rick Null, Editor
Information for dealers of farming equipment.

Farm Equipment Catalog
Johnson Hill Press, Inc.
1233 Janesville Ave.
Fort Atkinson, WI 53538
414-563-6388
A listing of equipment for farmers and ranchers.

Hot Line Farm Equipment Guide
Heartland Communications Group, Inc.
900 Central Ave.
Box 916
Fort Dodge, IA 50501
515-955-1600
Keeps readers abreast of the prices for farm equipment.

Implement & Tractor
Farm Press Publications
Box 1420
Clarksdale, MS 38614
601-624-8503
Edward Philips, Editor
Information on trends in farming equipment.

FEDERAL GOVERNMENT

U.S. Department of Agriculture
14th St. and Independence Ave., S.W.
Washington, DC 20250
202-720-8732
Ask for the Economic Research Service.

U.S. International Trade Administration
Department of Commerce
14th St. and Constitution Ave., N.W.
Washington, DC 20230
202-377-2000
Ask for the Commodity Analyst who is an expert in agricultural machinery or chemicals.

U.S. International Trade Commission
500 E St., S.W.
Washington, DC 20436
202-205-2000 Office of the Secretary
202-205-3296 Industries locator
Ask for the Trade Analyst who is an expert in agricultural machinery or chemicals.

AIR CONDITIONING, REFRIGERATION, AND HEATING INDUSTRY

ASSOCIATIONS

Automotive Refrigeration Products Institute
4600 E. West Hwy., Ste. 300
Bethesda, MD 20814
301-657-2774
Timothy Tierney, Executive Director
Offers information on products for car refrigeration.

Air Conditioning Contractors of America
1513 16th St. N.W.
Washington, DC 20036
202-483-9370
202-234-4721 Fax
James Norris, Executive Vice President
These contractors install and service air conditioning, refrigeration, and heating systems.

Air-Conditioning and Refrigeration Institute
1501 Wilson Blvd., 6th Fl.
Arlington, VA 22209
703-524-8800
Arnold Braswell, President
Members include manufacturers of air conditioning, refrigeration, and heating products. The institute provides information about and certification for these products.

Air-Conditioning and Refrigeration Wholesalers
6360 N.W. 5th Way, Ste. 202
Ft. Lauderdale, FL 33309
305-771-1000
305-491-8100 Fax
David Kellough, Executive Director
Distributors (but not installers) of air conditioning and refrigeration equipment and supplies.

American Society of Heating, Refrigerating and Air-Conditioning Engineers
1791 Tullie Circle N.E.
Atlanta, GA 30329
404-636-8400
404-321-5478 Fax
Frank Coda, Executive Director
Provides technical information about heating, ventilation, refrigeration, and air-conditioning.

International Association of Refrigerated Warehouses
7315 Wisconsin Ave., 1200N
Bethesda, MD 20814
301-652-5674
301-652-7269 Fax
J. William Hudson, President
Represents owners of refrigerated warehouses storing perishable products.

Mobile Air Conditioning Society
1709 N. Broad St.
PO Box 1307
Lansdale, PA 19446
215-362-5800
215-855-7257 Fax
Elvis Hoffpauir, Managing Director
Manufacturers and others that provide air conditioning equipment to cars and trucks.

National Commercial Refrigeration Sales Association
1900 Arch St.
Philadelphia, PA 19103
215-564-3484
215-564-2175 Fax
Kenneth Dickson, Executive Director
Manufacturers and distributors of commercial refrigeration equipment.

Refrigeration Service Engineers Society
1666 Rand Rd.
Des Plaines, IL 60016-3552
708-297-6464
Nari Sethna, Executive Vice President
Dealers, installers, and maintenance workers in the refrigeration, air-conditioning and heating indutry.

PERIODICALS

ACCA Quality Contractor's Catalog of Materials, Products and Services
Air Conditioning Contractors of America
1513 16th St., N.W.
Washington, DC 20036
202-483-9370
Elaine Smith, Editor
A listing of books, videos, and technical materials for air conditioning contractors.

ASHRAE Journal
American Society of Heating, Refrigerating
    and Air-Conditioning Engineers, Inc.
1791 Tullie Circle, N.E.
Atlanta, GA 30329
404-636-8400
William Coker, Editor
*Industry and technological news for engineers
in the air conditioning and related industries.*

Air Conditioning & Heating Service & Repair—
    Domestic Cars, Light Trucks & Vans
Mitchell International, Inc.
9889 Willow Creek Rd.
Box 26260
San Diego, CA 92196-0260
800-648-8010
For automobile technicians.

Air Conditioning, Heating & Refrigeration
    News
Business News Publishing Co.
Box 2600
Troy, MI 48007
313-362-3700
Thomas Mahoney, Editor
*News for contractors, manufacturers, and dis-
tributors.*

Consumer Selection Guide for Room Air
    Conditioners
Association of Home Appliance Manufac-
    turers
20 N. Wacker Dr.
Chicago, IL 60606
312-984-5800
Marian Stamos, Editor
*Advises consumers on how to evaluate and
purchase home air conditioners.*

Contracting Business
Penton Publishing
1100 Superior Ave.
Cleveland, OH 44114-2543
216-696-7000
James Wheeler, Editor
*Covers maintenance and marketing of air con-
ditioning, heating, and refrigeration systems.*

Contractor: The Newsmagazine of Mechanical
    Contracting
Cahners Publishing Co.
Division of Reed Publishing Inc.
1350 E. Touhy Ave.
Des Plaines, IL 60017-5080
John Schweizer, Editor
News and advice for contractors.

Engineered Systems
Business News Publishing Co.
Box 2600
Troy, MI 48007
313-362-3700
Robert Schwed, Editor
*Advises those working in commercial and
industrial buildings about the air conditioning
industry.*

H V A C Product News
Delta Communications Inc.
400 N. Michigan Ave., 13th Fl.
Chicago, IL 60611
312-222-2000
Roland Winkler, Editor
*Information on the latest products for the air
conditioning, heating, refrigeration, and ventilation industry.*

Heating—Piping—Air Conditioning
Penton Publishing
1100 Superior Ave.
Cleveland, OH 44114-2543
216-969-7000
Robert Korte, Editor
Informs those involved with construction and renovation about advances in the HVACR industry.

Koldfax
Air-Conditioning and Refrigeration Institute
1501 Wilson Blvd., 6th Fl.
Arlington, VA 22209-2403
703-524-8800
Maura Shannon, Editor
Industry news.

LIBRARIES

Carrier Corp.
Logan Lewis Library
Box 4808
Syracuse, NY 13221-4808
315-432-6306
315-432-6741 Fax
Air conditioning, ventilation, heating, refrigeration, and related topics.

Milwaukee Area Technical College
South Campus Library
6665 S. Howell Ave.
Oak Creek, WI 53154
414-768-5720
414-768-1054 Fax
Science and technology, including heating and air conditioning.

Thermo King Corp.
Library
314 W. 90th St.
Minneapolis, MN 55420
612-887-2336
612-887-2617 Fax
Air conditioning and refrigerated transportation.

COMPANIES

Amana Refrigeration, Inc.
(Subsidiary of Raytheon Co.)
Amana, IA 52204
319-622-5511
Air conditioners, freezers, refrigerators, and other products.

American Building Maintenance Industries
50 Fremont St.
San Francisco, CA 94105
415-597-4500
Sales and maintenance of air conditioning systems, and other products.

Bell Industries, Inc.
11812 San Vicente Blvd.
Los Angeles, CA 90049
213-826-6778
Distributors of heating, ventilating, and air conditioning products.

Commerical Products Division
(Subsidiary of SnyderGeneral Corp.)
13600 Industrial Park Blvd.
Minneapolis, MN 55441
612-553-5330
Air conditioning equipment and industrial fans.

Copeland Corp.
(Subsidiary of Emerson Electric Co.)
1675 Campbell Rd.
Sidney, OH 45365
513-498-3011
Compressors and condensing units for air conditioners and refrigerators.

Inter-City Products Corp.
(Subsidiary of CHL Holdings, Inc.)
1136 Heil-Quaker Blvd.
LaVergne, TN 37086
615-793-0450
Central heating and air conditioning equipment.

MLX Corp.
4781 Lewis Rd.
Stone Mountain, GA 30083
404-939-5910
Distributor of refrigeration and air condition-
ing products.

Noland Co.
2700 Warwick Blvd.
Newport News, VA 23607
804-928-9000
Wholesaler of air conditioning, heating, and
plumbing equipment.

SnyderGeneral Corp.
3232 McKinney Ave.
Dallas, TX 75204
214-740-1400
Air conditioning and heating products.

Welbilt Corp.
3333 New Hyde Park Rd.
New Hyde Park, NY 11042
516-365-5040
Air conditioners, furnaces, refrigerators, and
other products.

FEDERAL GOVERNMENT

U.S. International Trade Administration
Department of Commerce
14th St. and Constitution Ave., N.W.
Washington, DC 20230
202-377-2000
Ask for the Commodity Analyst who is an
expert in air conditioning, heating, refrigera-
tion, or ventilation.

U.S. International Trade Commission
500 E St., S.W.
Washington, DC 20436
202-205-2000 Office of the Secretary
202-205-3296 Industries locator
Ask for the Trade Analyst who is an expert in
air conditioning, heating, refrigeration, or
ventilation.

U.S. Patent and Trademark Office
Crystal Plaza 2
2011 Jefferson Davis Highway
Arlington, VA 22202
703-305-8000
Ask for the Examining Group Director who is
a specialist in air conditioning, heating, refrig-
eration, or ventilation.

AIR FREIGHT

See also: FREIGHT TRANSPORTATION

ASSOCIATIONS

Air Freight Association of America
1710 Rhode Island Ave., 2nd Fl.
Washington, DC 20036
202-293-1030
Stephen Alterman, Executive Vice President
Companies that offer air freight forwarding
and air cargo transportation.

Air Transport Association of America
1709 New York Ave., N.W.
Washington, DC 20006
202-626-4000
Robert Aaronson, President
Airlines that transport goods as well as people.

PERIODICALS

Air Cargo News
Air Cargo News, Inc.
Box 777
Jamaica, NY 11431
718-479-0176
Milton Caine, Editor
News about the air cargo industry.

Air Cargo World
Communication Channels, Inc.
6255 Barfield Rd.
Atlanta, GA 30328-4369
404-256-9800
David Premo, Editor
*Covers distribution, bulk freight, small pack-
ages, couriers, and other subjects of interest to
those using air cargo.*

OAG Air Cargo Guide
Official Airline Guides, Inc.
2000 Clearwater Dr.
Oak Brook, IL 60521
708-574-6000
*Schedules of air cargo services and connecting
flights worldwide.*

Jet Cargo News
Hagall Publishing Co.
Box 920952, Ste. 398
Houston, TX 77292-0952
713-681-4760
Pat Chandler, Editor
Information for those using air cargo services.

LIBRARIES

Air Transport Association of America
Library
1709 New York Ave., N.W.
Washington, DC 20006
202-626-4184
202-626-4181 Fax
*Air transportation, aeronautics, scheduled air
carrier financial statistics, and related topics.*

American Airlines, Inc.
Corporate Library
MD 5190 HDQ
P.O. Box 619616
DFW Airport, TX 75261
817-355-1464
817-967-9631
Air transportation.

Trans World Airlines, Inc.
Corporate Library
110 S. Bedford Rd.
Mount Kisco, NY 10549
914-242-3521
914-242-3109 Fax
Air transportation.

COMPANIES

Airborne Freight Corp.
P.O. Box 662
Seattle, WA 98111
206-285-4600
Air freight forwarding services.

Burlington Air Express Inc.
(Subsidiary of Pittston Co.)
18200 Von Karman Ave.
Irvine, CA 92715
714-752-4000
Air freight forwarding.

DHL Airways Inc.
333 Twin Dolphin Dr.
Redwood City, CA 94065
415-593-7474
International air courier service.

Emery Worldwide
(Subsidiary of Consolidated Freightways Inc.)
Wilton, CT 06897
203-762-8601
Domestic and international air freight delivery.

Empire Airlines Inc.
11101 Airport Dr.
Hayden Lake, ID 83835
208-772-4048
Air cargo transportation.

Federal Express Corp.
2005 Corporate Ave.
Memphis, TN 38132
901-369-3600
Domestic and international air courier service.

Pittston Co.
One Pickwick Plaza, Box 8900
Greenwich, CT 06836
203-622-0900
Air freight forwarding and other services.

Profit Freight Systems, Inc.
(Subsidiary of Profit Systems, Inc.)
1950 Spectrum Circle
Marietta, GA 30067
404-951-8100
Air freight forwarder.

SonicAir Couriers, Inc.
P.O. Box C-6010
Scottsdale, AZ 85261
602-991-1891
International air freight and courier.

TNT Ltd.
TNT Skypak
990 Stewart Ave.
Garden City, NY 11530
516-745-9000
International air freight and courier.

FEDERAL GOVERNMENT

U.S. International Trade Commission
500 E St., S.W.
Washington, DC 20436
202-205-2000 Office of the Secretary
202-205-3296 Industries locator
Ask for the Trade Analyst who is an expert in air freight or air transportation.

U.S. Department of Transportation
400 Seventh St., S.W.
Washington, DC 20590
202-366-4000
Ask for the Federal Aviation Administration's expert on air freight or air transportation.

U.S. International Trade Administration
Department of Commerce
14th St. and Constitution Ave., N.W.
Washington, DC 20230
202-377-2000
Ask for the Commodity Analyst who is an expert in air freight or air transportation.

AIRLINE INDUSTRY

ASSOCIATIONS

Air Transport Association of America
1709 New York Ave., N.W.
Washington, DC 20006
202-626-4000
Robert Aaronson, President
Scheduled airlines that carry passengers and cargo.

National Air Transportation Association
4226 King St.
Alexandria, VA 22302
703-845-9000
703-845-8116
Lawrence Burian, President
Represents companies that provide air taxi services and other aviation services.

Regional Airline Association
1101 Connecticut Ave. N.W., Ste. 700
Washington, DC 20036
202-857-1170
202-775-2625 Fax
Duane Ekedahl, President
Members are commuter airlines that transport passengers or cargo. Studies safety, airline regulations, and other topics.

PERIODICALS

Air Transport World
Penton Publishing
600 Summer St.
Box 1361
Stamford, CT 06904
203-348-7531
James Woolsey, Editor
Covers the equipment, management, and operation of support services for the airline industry.

Airline Executive International
Communication Channels, Inc.
6255 Barfield Rd.
Atlanta, GA 30328-4369
404-256-9800
David Premo, Editor
Follows news about aircraft, equipment, industry trends, support services, and other topics for executives of major airlines.

Airline Newsletter
Roadcap Aviation Publications
1030 S. Green Bay Rd.
Lake Forest, IL 60045
708-234-4730
Roy Roadcap, Editor
Surveys trends and news in commercial aviation.

Commuter Air International
Communication Channels, Inc.
6255 Barfield Rd.
Atlanta, GA 30328-4369
404-256-9800
David Premo, Editor
Management advice for executives of regional, commuter, and short haul airlines.

Commuter—Regional Airline News
Phillips Publishing, Inc.
1925 N. Lynn St., Ste. 304
Arlington, VA 22209
703-522-2332
Kelly Murphy, Editor
Follows news of interest to commuter and regional airlines.

44

OAG Pocket Flight Guide North American
     Edition
Official Airline Guides, Inc.
2000 Clearwater Dr.
Oak Brook, IL 60521
708-574-6000
A directory of all commercial flights in the U.S.

LIBRARIES

Air Transport Association of America
Library
1709 New York Ave., N.W.
Washington, DC 20006
202-626-4184
202-626-4181 Fax
*Air transportation, aeronautics, airline indus-
try, and related topics.*

American Airlines, Inc.
Corporate Library
MD 5190 HDQ
P.O. Box 619616
DFW Airport, TX 75261
817-355-1464
817-967-9631
Air transportation.

Trans World Airlines, Inc.
Corporate Library
110 S. Bedford Rd.
Mount Kisco, NY 10549
914-242-3521
914-242-3109 Fax
Air transportation.

COMPANIES

Aloha Airlines Inc.
P.O. Box 30028
Honolulu, HI 96820
808-836-4172
Domestic airline.

America West Airlines Inc.
4000 Sky Harbor Blvd.
Phoenix, AZ 85034
602-894-0800
Domestic airline.

American Airlines Inc.
P.O. Box 619616
Dallas-Ft. Worth Airpt., TX 75261
817-355-1234
Domestic and international airline.

Continental Airlines Inc.
P.O. Box 4607
Houston, TX 77210
713-834-5000
Domestic and international airline.

Delta Air Lines Inc.
Hartsfield Atlanta
Atlanta, GA 30320
404-765-2600
Domestic and international airline.

Northwest Airlines Inc.
5101 Northwest Dr.
St. Paul, MN 55111
612-726-2111
Domestic and international airline.

Southwest Airlines Co.
P.O. Box 36611
Dallas, TX 75235
214-904-4000
Domestic and international airline.

Trans World Airlines Inc.
100 S. Bedford Rd.
Mount Kisco, NY 10549
914-242-3000
Domestic and international airline.

United Airlines Inc.
P.O. Box 66100
Chicago, IL 60666
708-952-4000
Domestic and international airline.

USAir Inc.
2345 Crystal Dr.
Arlington, VA 22227
703-418-7000
Domestic and international airline.

FEDERAL GOVERNMENT

U.S. Department of Transportation
400 Seventh St., S.W.
Washington, DC 20590
202-366-4000
Ask for the Federal Aviation Administration.

U.S. International Trade Administration
Department of Commerce
14th St. and Constitution Ave., N.W.
Washington, DC 20230
202-377-2000
Ask for the Commodity Analyst who is an expert in the airline industry.

U.S. International Trade Commission
500 E St., S.W.
Washington, DC 20436
202-205-2000 Office of the Secretary
202-205-3296 Industries locator
Ask for the Trade Analyst who is an expert in the airline industry.

AIR PILOTS

ASSOCIATIONS

Air Line Pilots Association, International
1625 Massachusetts Ave., N.W.
Washington, DC 20036
703-689-2270
202-797-4052 Fax
Henry Duffy, President
Represents professional pilots in collective bargaining and other matters.

Aircraft Owners and Pilots Association
421 Aviation Way
Frederick, MD 21701
301-695-2000
800-USA-AOPA
301-695-2375 Fax
John Baker, President
Provides information for and about pilots and aircraft owners.

Society of Experimental Test Pilots
PO Box 986
Lancaster, CA 93534
805-942-9574
805-940-0398 Fax
Thomas Smith, Executive Director
Members are pilots who test and develop new aircraft and engines.

PERIODICALS

Air Line Pilot
Air Line Pilots Association
535 Herndon Parkway
Box 1169
Herndon, VA 22070
703-689-4176
Esperison Martinez, Editor
Information of interest to professional pilots.

Career Pilot
Future Aviation Professionals
4959 Massachusetts Blvd.
Atlanta, GA 30337
404-997-8097
Teresa Greer, Editor
Employee information for airline employees.

Private Pilot
Fancy Publications, Inc.
Box 6050
Mission Viejo, CA 92690
714-855-8822
Mary Silitch, Editor
Covers news and activities for owner-flyers.

FEDERAL GOVERNMENT

U.S. Department of Transportation
400 Seventh St., S.W.
Washington, DC 20590
202-366-4000
Ask for the Federal Aviation Administration.

AIRPLANE AND HELICOPTER INDUSTRY

See also: AEROSPACE

ASSOCIATIONS

Aerospace Industries Association of America
1250 I St. N.W.
Washington, DC 20005
202-371-8400
202-371-8470 Fax
Don Fuqua, President
Manufacturers of aircraft, spacecraft, and a wide variety of aviation equipment.

American Helicopter Society
217 N. Washington St.
Alexandria, VA 22314
703-684-6777
703-739-9279 Fax
John Zugschwert, Executive Director
Engineers, government officials, and executives who work with V/STOL (vertical/short takeoff and landing) aircraft.

Aviation Distributors and Manufacturers
Association
1900 Arch St.
Philadelphia, PA 19103
215-564-3484
215-564-2175 Fax
Patricia Lilly, Executive Director
*Firms that make and sell equipment, parts,
and supplies used in aircraft.*

Aviation Maintenance Foundation International
PO Box 2826
Redmond, WA 98073
206-828-3917
206-827-6895 Fax
Richard Kost, President
*Members include aircraft mechanics, companies that repair and maintain aircraft, and
others.*

PERIODICALS

Aircraft Technician
Johnson Hill Press, Inc.
1233 Janesville Ave.
Fort Atkinson, WI 53538
414-563-6388
Greg Napert, Editor
Information for aviation executives.

D M S Market Intelligence Reports: Civil Aircraft
Forecast International Inc.
22 Commerce Rd.
Newtown, CT 06470
203-426-0800
*Offers market information on civil aircraft,
including new technologies, production, costs,
and test results.*

Helicopter News
Phillips Publishing, Inc.
7811 Montrose Rd.
Potomac, MD 20854
301-340-2100
Frank McGuire, Editor
Follows the helicopter industry.

Journal of Aircraft
American Institute of Aeronautics and Astronautics, Inc.
370 L'Enfant Promenade, S.W.
Washington, DC 20024
202-646-7400
Thomas Weeks, Editor
*Covers advances in aeronautical science and
technology as applied to the production of airplane and helicopters.*

LIBRARIES

General Dynamics Corp.
Convair Division
Research Library
Box 85386
San Diego, CA 92186-5386
619-547-4876
619-547-4000 Fax
Aircraft technology and related topics.

McDonnell Douglas Helicopter Co.
Library
5000 E. McDowell Rd.
Mesa, AZ 85205
602-891-5675
*Aeronautical and helicopter engineering and
technology.*

Newport Aeronautical Sales
Library
23221 Peralta Dr., No. A
Laguna Hills, CA 92653
714-454-2588
714-454-8288 Fax
Aircraft technical manuals.

COMPANIES

Beech Aircraft Corp.
(Subsidiary of Raytheon Co.)
P. O. Box 85
Wichita, KS 67201
Commercial and military aircraft and systems.

Boeing Co.
7755 E. Marginal Way S.
Seattle, WA 98108
206-655-2121
Aircraft and helicopters.

Cessna Aircraft Co.
(Subsidiary of General Dynamics Corp.)
P. O. Box 1521
Wichita, KS 67201
316-685-9111
Aircraft and equipment.

General Electric Canada Inc.
(Subsidiary of General Electric Co.)
2300 Meadowvale Blvd.
Mississauga, Canada L5N 5P9
416-858-5100
Aircraft engines and other products.

Gulfstream Aerospace Corp.
P.O. Box 2206
Savannah, GA 31402
912-964-3000
Aircraft manufacturer.

Learjet Corp.
(Subsidiary of Integrated Resources, Inc.)
8220 W. Harry, Box 7707
Wichita, KS 67277
316-946-2000
*Business aircraft, used aircraft, and mainte-
nance of aircraft.*

LTV Aerospace and Defense Co.
(Subsidiary of LTV Corp.)
2001 Ross Ave., Box 655003
Dallas, TX 75265
214-979-7711
*Space vehicles, military aircraft, and commer-
cial aircraft components.*

McDonnell Douglas Corp.
P. O. Box 516
St. Louis, MO 63166
314-232-0232
Military and commercial aircraft.
Northrop Corp.
1840 Century Park, E.
Los Angeles, CA 90067
213-553-6262
*Military aircraft, commercial airframe assem-
blies, and electronics systems.*

United Technologies Corp.
United Technologies Bldg.
Hartford, CT 06101
203-728-7000
*Aircraft engines and many other aerospace
products.*

FEDERAL GOVERNMENT

U.S. Customs Service
Department of the Treasury
U.S. Customshouse
6 World Trade Center
New York, NY 10048
212-466-5550
*Ask for the Commodity Specialist in charge of
airplanes or helicopters.*

U.S. International Trade Administration
Department of Commerce
14th St. and Constitution Ave., N.W.
Washington, DC 20230
202-377-2000
Ask for the Commodity Analyst who is an expert in airplanes or helicopters.

U.S. International Trade Commission
500 E St., S.W.
Washington, DC 20436
202-205-2000 Office of the Secretary
202-205-3296 Industries locator
Ask for the Trade Analyst who is an expert in airplanes or helicopters.

AIRPORTS

See also: AEROSPACE

ASSOCIATIONS

Air Traffic Control Association
2020 N. 14th St., Ste. 410
Arlington, VA 22201
703-522-5717
703-527-7251 Fax
Gabriel Hartl, President
Provides information on all aspects of air traffic control, particularly the implementation of safe systems.

Airport Consultants Council
421 King St., Ste. 220
Alexandria, VA 22314
703-683-5908
703-549-4749 Fax
Paul Bollinger, Executive Director
Companies that offer security, design, engineering, environmental, and other services to airports.

Airport Operators Council International
1220 19th St. N.W., Ste. 200
Washington, DC 20036
202-293-8500
202-331-1362 Fax
George Howard, President
Represents commissions, boards, authorities, and municipalities that own or operate airports.

American Association of Airport Executives
4212 King St.
Alexandria, VA 22302
703-824-0500
703-820-1395 Fax
Charles Barclay, Executive Vice President
Managers, engineers, superintendents, and government officers who share information on airports.

International Association of Airport Duty Free
 Stores
1101 Connecticut Ave. N.W., Ste. 700
Washington, DC 20036
202-857-1184
202-429-5184 Fax
Robert Chancler, Executive Director
*Firms that own and operate duty-free shop
concessions at airports.*

PERIODICALS

Airport Pocket Guide
A M Data Services, Inc.
67 S. Bedford St., Ste. 400W
Burlington, MA 01803
617-229-5853
Andy Migliorini, Editor
*This aid for frequent flyers diagrams the gates
and services at 80 major airports in the U.S.*

Airport Services Management
Lakewood Publications, Inc.
50 S. Ninth
Minneapolis, MN 55402
612-333-0471
Gordon Gilbert, Editor
*Offers information on managing airports, new
products and services, and other topics to
interest airport executives.*

Airports
McGraw-Hill, Inc.
Aviation Week Group
1156 15th St., N.W.
Washington, DC 20005
202-822-4600
Avery Vise, Editor
*Prints articles on management, fees, FAA mat-
ters, noise problems, and other subjects.*

LIBRARIES

Airport Operators Council International
Library
1220 19th St., N.W., Ste. 200
Washington, DC 20036
202-293-8500
202-331-1362 Fax
*Airport security and other airport related
topics.*

KPMG Peat Marwick
Library
P.O. Box 8007
San Francisco Intl. Airport
San Francisco, CA 94128-8007
415-571-7722
415-571-5220 Fax
Airport planning and other topics.

TRA Architecture Engineering Planning Interiors
Library
215 Columbia
Seattle, WA 98104
206-682-1133
206-621-8782 Fax
Airport planning, design, and other topics.

COMPANIES

Butler Intl., Inc.
(Subsidiary of North American Ventures Inc.)
110 Summit Ave.
Montvale, NJ 07645
201-573-8000
Aviation services.

S. J. Groves & Sons Co.
P. O. Box 1267
Minneapolis, MN 55440
612-546-6943
*Building and contracting services for airports
and other major projects.*

Host International, Inc.
(Subsidiary of Marriott Corp.)
One Marriott Dr.
Washington, DC 20058
202-380-3677
*Restaurants, gift shops, and other airport
facilities.*

Hudson General Corp.
111 Great Neck Rd., Box 355
Great Neck, NY 11022
516-487-8610
Aviation services.

Lockheed Air Terminal, Inc.
(Subsidiary of Lockheed Corp.)
P. O. Box 7229
Burbank, CA 91510
818-503-1500
Management of airport terminal equipment.

Sky Chefs, Inc.
(Subsidiary of Onex Food Services, Inc.)
601 Ryan Plaza
Arlington, TX 76012
817-792-2123
Airport restaurants and inflight food services.

Temco Service Industries Inc.
One Park Ave.
New York, NY 10016
212-889-6353
*Cleaning, maintenance, and security services
for airports and other facilities.*

Wackenhut Corp.
1500 San Remo Ave.
Coral Gables, FL 33146
305-666-5656
*Security services and pre-departure screening
for airports.*

H. B. Zachry Co.
P. O. Box 21130
San Antonio, TX 78285
512-922-1213
Construction of airports and other facilities.

FEDERAL GOVERNMENT

U.S. Department of Transportation
400 Seventh St., S.W.
Washington, DC 20590
202-366-4000
Ask for the Federal Aviation Administration.

AIR TRAVEL

ASSOCIATIONS

Airline Passengers of America
4212 King St.
Alexandria, VA 22302
703-824-0505
Jack Corbett, General Counsel
*Promotes the rights of airline travelers and
offers insurance.*

Association of Corporate Travel Executives
PO Box 5394
Parsippany, NJ 07054
201-537-7630
800-228-3669
Robert Graze, Executive Director
*Members include a wide range of those who
plan and purchase travel for business purposes.*

Association of Travel Marketing Executives
PO Box 43563
Washington, DC 20010
202-232-7107
Marj Jensen, Executive Director
Executives who market travel products and services.

International Airline Passengers Association
4341 Lindburg Dr.
Dallas, TX 75244
214-404-9980
James Dunne, Chairman
Provides information to frequent flyers on safety, savings, convenience, and related subjects.

National Business Travel Association
516 Fifth Ave., Ste. 406
New York, NY 10036
212-221-6782
212-944-5513 Fax
Margie Crace, President
Executives who promote and purchase business travel.

PERIODICALS

Facts and Advice for Airline Passengers
Aviation Consumer Action Project
Box 19029
Washington, DC 20036
202-785-3704
Helps passengers avoid inconvenience and the service problems of airlines.

OAG Business Travel Planner. North American Edition
Official Airline Guides, Inc.
2000 Clearwater Dr.
Oak Brook, IL 60521
708-574-6000
Listings of hotels, maps, and ground and air transportation.

Travel News
Connie Gibson Wehrman Connor
1530 Key Blvd., Ste. 230
Arlington, VA 22209-1534
703-281-9323
Ed Wojtas, Editor
A newsletter of travel bargains.

FEDERAL GOVERNMENT

U.S. Department of Transportation
400 Seventh St., S.W.
Washington, DC 20590
202-366-4000
Ask for the Federal Aviation Administration.

ALABAMA

STATE OFFICE LOCATOR (*for referrals to all state government offices*)

205-261-2500

ARCHIVES AND RECORDS

Archives & History Department
624 Washington Avenue
Montgomery, AL 36130
205-242-4361

ATTORNEY GENERAL

Attorney General's Office
State House
11 S. Union Street
Montgomery, AL 36130
205-261-7305

BANKING

Banking Department
101 S. Union Street
Montgomery, AL 36130
205-242-3452

COMMERCE

Development Office
State Capitol
Montgomery, AL 36130
205-263-0048

CONSUMER AFFAIRS

Consumer Protection Division
State House
11 S. Union Street
Montgomery, AL 36130
205-242-7300

EDUCATION

Education Department
50 N. Ripley Street
Montgomery, AL 36130-3901
205-242-9700

ENERGY

Science, Technology & Energy Division
P.O. Box 2939
Montgomery, AL 36105-0939
205-284-8943

ENVIRONMENTAL AFFAIRS

Environmental Management Department
1751 Congressman William L. Dickerson Drive
Montgomery, AL 36130
205-271-7700

HEALTH

Public Health Department
381 State Office Building
Montgomery, AL 36130-1701
205-242-5052

HOUSING

Community Services Division
P.O. Box 2939
Montgomery, AL 36105-0939
205-284-8955

INSURANCE

Insurance Department
135 S. Union Street
Montgomery, AL 36130
205-269-3550

LABOR

Labor Department
64 N. Union Street
Room 651
Montgomery, AL 36130
205-242-3460

LEGISLATION

Legislative Reference Service
State House
11 S. Union Street
Room 613
Montgomery, AL 36130-6701
205-242-7560

LIBRARY SERVICES

Public Library Service
6030 Monticello Drive
Montgomery, AL 36130
205-277-7330

LICENSING—CORPORATE

Corporations Division
State Office Building
501 Dexter Avenue
Room 524
Montgomery, AL 36130
205-242-5324

MOTOR VEHICLES

Motor Vehicle Tax Division
Gordon Persons Building
50 N. Ripley Street
Montgomery, AL 36130
205-242-9000

OCCUPATIONAL HEALTH AND SAFETY

Division of Safety & Inspection
P.O. Box 10444
Birmingham, AL 35202
205-254-1275

PUBLIC UTILITIES

Public Service Commission
P.O. Box 991
Montgomery, AL 36101
205-242-5218

PURCHASING

Purchasing Division
State House
11 S. Union Street
Montgomery, AL 36130
205-242-7250

REAL ESTATE

Real Estate Commission
State Capitol
Montgomery, AL 36130
205-242-5544

SECURITIES

Securities Commission
166 Commerce Street
2nd Floor
Montgomery, AL 36130
205-242-2984

TAXATION AND REVENUE

Revenue Department
Gordon Persons Building
50 N. Ripley Street
Montgomery, AL 36130
205-242-1175

TOURISM

Department of Tourism & Travel
532 S. Perry Street
Montgomery, AL 36104
205-261-4169
800-252-2262
800-392-8096 (in Alabama)

TRANSPORTATION

Transportation Division
P.O. Box 991
Montgomery, AL 36101
205-242-5980

UNEMPLOYMENT

Unemployment Compensation Division
649 Monroe Street
Montgomery, AL 36130
205-242-8025

WORKER'S COMPENSATION

Industrial Relations Department
649 Monroe Street
Montgomery, AL 36130
205-242-8890

ALASKA

STATE OFFICE LOCATOR (*for referrals to all state government offices*)

907-465-2111

ARCHIVES AND RECORDS

Archives
141 Willoughby Avenue
Juneau, AK 99811
907-465-2275

ATTORNEY GENERAL

Law Department
P.O. Box K
Juneau, AK 99811
907-465-3600

BANKING

Banking, Securities & Corporations Division
P.O. Box D
Juneau, AK 99811
907-465-2506

COMMERCE

Commerce & Economic Development
   Department
P.O. Box D
Juneau, AK 99811
907-465-2500

EDUCATION

Education Department
P.O. Box F
Juneau, AK 99811
907-465-2800

ENERGY

Oil Spill Coordinating Office
P.O. Box AV
Juneau, AK 99811-0115
907-465-4125

ENVIRONMENTAL AFFAIRS

Environmental Conservation Department
P.O. Box O
Juneau, AK 99811-1800
907-465-2600

HEALTH

Health & Social Services Department
P.O. Box H
Juneau, AK 99811-0601
907-465-3030

HOUSING

State Housing Agency
P.O. Box 230329
Anchorage, AK 99523
907-562-2813

HUMAN RIGHTS

Human Rights Commission
800 A Street
Ste. 202
Anchorage, AK 99501-3628
907-276-7474

INSURANCE

Insurance Division
P.O. Box D
Juneau, AK 99811
907-465-2515

LABOR

Labor Department
P.O. Box 21149
Juneau, AK 99802-1149
907-465-2700

LEGISLATION

Legal Services Division
P.O. Box Y
Juneau, AK 99811
907-465-3867

LIBRARY SERVICES

State Libraries
P.O. Box G
Juneau, AK 99811-0500
907-465-2910

LICENSING—CORPORATE

Commerce & Economic Development
    Department
P.O. Box D
Juneau, AK 99811
907-465-2500

LICENSING—PROFESSIONAL AND OCCUPATIONAL

Occupational Licensing Division
P.O. Box D
Juneau, AK 99811
907-465-2534

MOTOR VEHICLES

Motor Vehicles Division
P.O. Box 6188
Anchorage, AK 99507
907-269-5551

OCCUPATIONAL HEALTH AND SAFETY

Occupational Safety & Health
P.O. Box 21149
Juneau, AK 99802
907-465-4855

OMBUDSMAN

Office of the Ombudsman
P.O. Box WO
Mail Stop 3000
Juneau, AK 99811
907-465-4970
800-478-4970

PUBLIC UTILITIES

Public Utilities Commission
420 L Street
Ste. 100
Anchorage, AK 99501
907-276-6222

PURCHASING

General Services & Supply Division
P.O. Box C
Juneau, AK 99811
907-465-2250

REAL ESTATE

Real Estate Commission
3601 C Street
Ste. 700
Anchorage, AK 99503
907-563-2169

SECURITIES

Banking, Securities & Corporations Division
P.O. Box D
Juneau, AK 99811

907-465-2521

TAXATION AND REVENUE

Revenue Department
P.O. Box S
Juneau, AK 99811
907-465-2300

TOURISM

Division of Tourism
P.O. Box E
Juneau, AK 99811
907-465-2010

TRANSPORTATION

Transportation & Public Facilities Department
P.O. Box Z
Juneau, AK 99811-2500
907-465-3900

UNEMPLOYMENT

Unemployment Insurance
P.O. Box 3-7000
Juneau, AK 99802-1218
907-465-2712

WORKER'S COMPENSATION

Workers Compensation Division
P.O. Box 25512
Juneau, AK 99802-5512
907-465-2790

ALCOHOL AND DRUG ABUSE

ASSOCIATIONS

Alcoholics Anonymous World Services
PO Box 459, Grand Central Station
New York, NY 10163
212-686-1100
212-576-8497 Fax
The largest self-help group of recovering alcoholics in the world. A chapter can be found in most communities.

American Council on Alcoholism
White Marsh Bus. Center
5024 Campbell Blvd., Ste. H
Baltimore, MD 21236
301-931-9393
Walter Pidgeon, President
Offers a wide variety of educational and information services regarding alcoholism, including help in developing employee assistance programs in the workplace.

American Council for Drug Education
204 Monroe St., Ste. 110
Rockville, MD 20850
301-294-0600
301-294-0603 Fax
Lee Dogoloff, Executive Director
Provides information and resource kits about the dangers of cocaine, marijuana, and other drugs.

Cocaine Anonymous World Services
3740 Overland Ave., Ste. G
Los Angeles, CA 90034
213-559-5833
Offers fellowship and help for those who wish to break their addiction to cocaine.

Drugs Anonymous
PO Box 473, Ansonia Station
New York, NY 10023
212-874-0700
James Kaplow, Executive Officer
Helps those addicted to all types of drugs.

Hazelden Foundation
15245 Pleasant Valley Rd.
PO Box 11
Center City, MN 55012
612-257-4010
800-257-7800
612-257-5101 Fax
Harold Swift, Director
Offers education and rehabilitation to those with chemical and alcohol dependencies.

Institute for a Drug-Free Workplace
PO Box 65708
Washington, DC 20035-5708
202-828-4590
202-828-4448 Fax
Mark Bernardo, Executive Director
Represents the rights of businesses and employees who take part in programs to prevent drug abuse.

Partnership for a Drug-Free America
666 3rd Ave.
New York, NY 10017
212-922-1560
212-922-1560 Fax
Thomas Hedrick, President
Members of the advertising and communications fields who create advertising campaigns to combat drug abuse.

Potsmokers Anonymous
208 W. 23rd St., Apt. 1414
New York, NY 10011-2139
212-254-1777
Francis Duffy, Director
Offers courses and advice for those addicted to marijuana.

PERIODICALS

Addictions Alert
American Health Consultants
Six Piedmont Center, Ste. 400
3525 Piedmont Rd., N.E.
Atlanta, GA 30305
404-262-7436
Dr. David Smith, Editor
Follows trends in the treatment of addictions.

Advances in Alcohol & Substance Abuse
Haworth Press, Inc.
10 Alice St.
Binghamton, NY 13904
800-342-9678
Dr. Barry Stimmel, Editor
Describes current issues in treating addictions.

Alcohol Health & Research World
U.S. National Institute on Alcohol Abuse and
    Alcoholism
1400 Eye St., N.W., Ste. 600
Washington, DC 20005
202-842-7600
Dianne Welsh, Editor
Follows government research in alcohol abuse.

Drugs in the Workplace
Business Research Publications, Inc.
817 Broadway, 3rd Fl.
New York, NY 10003
212-673-4700
Alison Knopf, Editor
Offers employers advice on how to lawfully detect, prevent, and treat alcoholism and drug addiction among employees.

Recovery Now
Box 280, Throgs Neck Station
New York, NY 10465
212-653-0321
Joyce DeRubba, Editor
Provides information and advice to the victims, friends, and family of alcoholics and drug abusers.

LIBRARIES

Addiction Research Foundation
Library
33 Russell St.
Toronto, ON, Canada M5S 2S1
416-595-6144
416-595-5017 Fax
Drug abuse and alcoholism.

Alcohol Research Group
Library
2000 Hearst
Berkley, CA 94709-2176
510-642-5208
510-642-7175 Fax
Alcohol and drug use and abuse.

U.S. Dept. of Justice
Bureau of Justice Statistics
Drugs and Crime Data Center and Clearing-
    house
1600 Research Blvd.
Rockville, MD 20850
800-666-3332
301-251l-5212 Fax
Illegal drug use, drug-related crimes, and laws.

FEDERAL GOVERNMENT

National Institutes of Health
9000 Rockville Pike
Bethesda, MD 20892
301-496-4000
*Ask for the National Institute on Alcohol
Abuse and Alcoholism.*

U.S. Department of Transportation
400 Seventh St., S.W.
Washington, DC 20590
202-366-4000
*Ask for the National Highway Traffic Safety
Administration for information on drunk
driving.*

ALUMINUM INDUSTRY

See also: METALS INDUSTRY

ASSOCIATIONS

Aluminum Association
900 19th St. N.W., Ste. 300
Washington, DC 20006
202-862-5100
202-862-5164 Fax
David Parker, President
*Members include manufacturers of aluminum
and aluminum products.*

Aluminum, Brick and Glass Workers International Union
3362 Hollenberg Dr.
Bridgeton, MO 63044
314-739-6142
314-739-1216 Fax
Ernest LaBaff, President
*The largest union representing workers in the
aluminum industry.*

Aluminum Extruders Council
1000 N. Rand Rd., Ste. 214
Wauconda, IL 60084
708-526-2010
708-526-3993 Fax
Donn Sanford, President
Members are extruders of aluminum shapes.

Aluminum Foil Container Manufacturers
Association
PO Box 1177
Lake Geneva, WI 53147
(414) 248-9208
Paul Uetzmann, Executive Secretary
Offers information on aluminum foil containers for food.

National Association of Aluminum Distributors
1900 Arch St.
Philadelphia, PA 19103
215-564-3484
215-564-2175 Fax
Kenneth Hutton, Executive Vice President
*Members sell aluminum rods, sheets, bars,
tubes, and other products.*

PERIODICALS

Bottle—Can Recycling Update
Resource Recycling, Inc.
Box 10540
Portland, OR 97210
800-227-1424
Jerry Powell, Editor
Information on various aspects of the recycling industry.

World Aluminium Databook
Metal Bulletin Inc.
220 Fifth Ave, 10th Fl.
New York, NY 10001
800-638-2525
*A directory of aluminum products and manu-
facturers.*

World Aluminum Abstracts
900 19th St., N.W., Ste. 300
Washington, DC 20006
202-862-5100
Reviews technical literature on aluminum.

LIBRARIES

Aluminum Association
Library
900 19th St. N.W., Ste. 300
Washington, DC 20006
202-862-5100
202-862-5164 Fax
David Parker, President
*Technical and industry information about alu-
minum.*

Aluminum Co. of America
Alcoa Laboratories
Information Center
Alcoa Center, PA 15069
412-337-2438
412-337-5436 Fax
Aluminum and other related materials.

Kaiser Aluminum & Chemical Corp.
Technical Information Center
Center for Technology
6177 Sunol Blvd.
Box 877
Pleasanton, CA 94566
510-847-4264
510-484-2472 Fax
*Aluminum, metallurgy, refractories, nonfer-
rous metals, and related areas.*

Reynolds Metals Co.
Alumina Division Technology
Technical Information Center
Box 9911
Corpus Christi, TX 78469
512-777-2676
512-777-2218 Fax
Aluminum industry and aluminum engineering.

COMPANIES

Alcan Aluminium Corp.
(Subsidiary of Alcan Aluminium Limited)
100 Erieview Plaza
Cleveland, OH 44114
216-523-6800
*Aluminum ingots, sheets, foil, and other prod-
ucts.*

Alcoa International Holdings Co.
(Subsidiary of Aluminum Co. of America)
1501 Alcoa Bldg.
Pittsburgh, PA 15219
412-553-4705
Aluminum products.

Amax Inc.
200 Park Ave.
New York, NY 10166
212-856-4200
*Aluminum, other metals, petroleum, and natu-
ral gas.*

Central Steel & Wire Co.
3000 W. 51st St.
Chicago, IL 60632
312-471-3800
*Sheets, coils, bars, and tubing made of alu-
minum and other metals.*

Edgcomb Metals Co.
(Subsidiary of Edgcomb Corp.)
Two W. Second St.
Tulsa, OK 74136
918-588-2623
Aluminum and steel.

Kaiser Aluminum & Chemical Corp.
(Subsidiary of KaiserTech Ltd.)
300 Lakeside Dr
Oakland, CA 94643
415-271-3300
Alumina and aluminum products.

Metallurg, Inc.
25 East 39th St.
New York, NY 10016
212-686-4010
Aluminum alloys and other metal products.

Reynolds Metals Co.
6601 W. Broad St., Box 27003
Richmond, VA 23261
804-281-2000
Primary and reclaimed aluminum, and other products.

Southwire Co.
One Southwire Dr.
Carrollton, GA 30119
404-832-4242
Aluminum and copper wire and cable.

FEDERAL GOVERNMENT

U.S. Bureau of Mines
810 7th St., N.W.
Washington, D.C. 20747
202-501-9770
Ask for the Commodity Specialist who is an
    expert in aluminum.

U.S. Customs Service
Department of the Treasury
U.S. Customshouse
6 World Trade Center
New York, NY 10048
212-466-5550
Ask for the Commodity Specialist in charge of aluminum.

U.S. International Trade Administration
Department of Commerce
14th St. and Constitution Ave., N.W.
Washington, DC 20230
202-377-2000
Ask for the Commodity Analyst who is an expert in aluminum.

ANTITRUST

ASSOCIATIONS

American Bar Association
750 N. Lake Shore Dr.
Chicago, IL 60611
312-988-5000
The Antitrust Law Section of the American Bar Association provides information and publishes two journals, Antitrust *and* Antitrust Law Journal.

Committee to Support the Antitrust Laws
c/o Jonathan W. Cuneo
1300 I St. N.W., E. Tower, Ste. 480
Washington, DC 20005
202-962-3862
Jonathan W. Cuneo, General Counsel
Supports federal and state antitrust laws.

National Association of Forensic Economists
PO Box 30067
Kansas City, MO 64112
816-276-1309
816-235-5263 Fax
Robert Thornton, President
Forensic economists compute damages during litigation arising from the economic harm caused by injury and death, negligence, antitrust, and other causes.

PERIODICALS

Antitrust
Antitrust Law Section
American Bar Association
750 N. Lake Shore Dr.
Chicago, IL 60611
US Telephone: 312-988-5555
Covers trends and news in antitrust law.

Antitrust Bulletin
Federal Legal Publications, Inc.
157 Chambers St.
New York, NY 10007
212-619-4949
William Curran, Editor
A newsletter for antitrust lawyers.

LIBRARIES

U.S. Dept. of Commerce
Law Library
14th & Penn St., N.W., Rm. 1894
Washington, DC 20230
202-377-5517
Numerous legal topics, including antitrust.

U.S. Dept. of Justice
Antitrust Branch Library
10th & Pennsylvania Ave., N.W.
Rm. 3310
Washington, DC 20530
202-514-2431
Antitrust, business, and other legal topics.

U.S. Federal Trade Commission
Library
6th St. & Pennsylvania Ave., N.W., Rm 630
Washington, DC 20580
202-326-2395
Antitrust and numerous business topics.

FEDERAL GOVERNMENT

U.S. Department of Justice
Constitution Ave. and 10th St., N.W.
Washington, DC
202-514-2000
Ask for the Antitrust department.

APPLIANCES

ASSOCIATIONS

Appliance Parts Distributors Association
228 E. Baltimore
Detroit, MI 48202
313-875-8455
Kenneth Adler, Executive Vice President
Wholesalers of appliance parts and accessories who promote independent distribution channels.

Association of Home Appliance Manufacturers
20 N. Wacker Dr.
Chicago, IL 60606
312-984-5800
Robert Holding, Pres.
Manufacturers of both major and portable appliances.

Gas Appliance Manufacturers Association
1901 N. Moore St., Ste. 1100
Arlington, VA 22209
703-525-9565
703-525-8159 Fax
C. Reuben Autery, President
Provides information on gas appliances used in residential, commercial, and industrial settings.

Independent Sewing Machine Dealers Association
PO Box 338
Hilliard, OH 43026
614-870-7211
J. Finney, Executive Director
Retailers and distributors of sewing machines.

National Housewares Manufacturers Association
1324 Merchandise Mart
Chicago, IL 60654
312-644-3333
312-644-3911 Fax
Kimberly Rawn, Communications Director
Provides information on housewares and small appliances.

Vacuum Cleaner Manufacturers Association
Box 2642
North Canton, OH 44720
216-499-5998
216-499-5292 Fax
Clifford Wood, Exeutive Secretary
Members manufacture vacuum cleaners and electric floor polishers.

Vacuum Dealers Trade Association
1200 Locust
Des Moines, IA 50309
515-282-9101
800-367-5651
Dick Beall, Executive Director
Independent dealers and distributors of vacuum cleaner and sewing machines.

PERIODICALS

Alternative Energy Retailer
Zackin Publications, Inc.
Box 2180
Waterbury, CT 06722
203-755-0158
John Florian, Editor
News and advice for retailers of gas-, wood-, and coal-burning appliances.

Appliance Manufacturer
Corcoran Communications, Inc.
29100 Aurora Rd., Ste. 200
Solon, OH 44139
216-349-3060
Norman Remich, Editor
Covers trends affecting manufacturers.

Appliance Service News
Gamit Enterprises, Inc.
110 W. St. Charles Rd.
Box 789
Lombard, IL 60148
708-932-9550
William Wingstedt, Editor
For servicers of major and portable appliances.

Consumer Reports
Consumers Union of U.S., Inc.
256 Washington St.
Mount Vernon, NY 10553
914-667-9400
Irwin Landau, Editor
Evaluates and rates all types of consumer appliances.

E E Product News
Intertec Publishing Corp.
707 Westchester Ave.
White Plains, NY 10604
914-949-8500
Edward Walter, Editor
Information on new appliances for those in the industry.

Global Appliance Report
Association of Home Appliance
    Manufacturers
20 N. Wacker Dr.
Chicago, IL 60606
312-984-5800
Craig Schulz, Editor
Concentrates on worldwide news of interest to manufacturers of home appliances.

Kitchen & Bath Business
Gralla Publications
1515 Broadway
New York, NY 10036
212-869-1300
Leslie Hart, Editor
Information on appliances among other subjects.

Television, Audio & Appliance Dealer
Target Publishing, Inc.
3821 W. 226th St.
Torrance, CA 90505
213-375-8786
C. Lee Thornton, Editor
Advice and product news for retailers of appliances.

LIBRARIES

General Electric Co.
Corporate Research & Development
Whitney Library
Box 8
KWF 116
Schenectady, NY 12301
518-387-6563
518-387-7593 Fax
Electronics, appliances, energy, physics, and chemistry.

COMPANIES

Allegheny International Inc.
Two Oliver Plaza, Box 456
Pittsburgh, PA 15230
412-562-4000
Manufactures small electric appliances and other products.

Circuit City Stores Inc.
9950 Maryland Dr.
Richmond, VA 23233
804-527-4000
Retailer of major and minor appliances.

Gillette Co.
Prudential Tower Bldg.
Boston, MA 02199
617-421-7000
Manufactures small appliances, such as electric shavers, and other products.

Gold Star Electronics Co. Inc.
1000 Sylvan Ave.
Englewood Cliffs, IL 60631
312-693-0450
Electrical appliances.

Masco Corp.
21001 Van Born Rd.
Taylor, MI 48180
313-274-7400
Maker of kitchen appliances, among other products.

Matsushita Electric Corp. of America
1 Panasonic Way
Secaucus, NJ 07094
201-348-7000
Electronic and other appliances.

Pioneer Electronics (USA), Inc.
2265 E. 220th St.
Long Beach CA 90810
310-835-6177
Electronic appliances.

Tatung Co. of America, Inc.
2850 El Presidio St.
Long Beach, CA 90810
213-979-7055
Electronic and other appliances.

Maytag Corp.
Newton, IA 50208
515-792-8000
Makes major and minor home appliances.

Toshiba America, Inc.
(Subsidiary of Toshiba Corp.)
375 Park Ave.
New York, NY 10152
212-308-2040
Manufactures home appliances and other types of equipment.

FEDERAL GOVERNMENT

U.S. Customs Service
Department of the Treasury
U.S. Customshouse
6 World Trade Center
New York, NY 10048
212-466-5550
Ask for the Commodity Specialist in charge of the specific type of appliance that interests you.

U.S. International Trade Administration
Department of Commerce
14th St. and Constitution Ave., N.W.
Washington, DC 20230
202-377-2000
Ask for the Commodity Analyst who is an expert in the specific type of appliance that interests you.

U.S. International Trade Commission
500 E St., S.W.
Washington, DC 20436
202-205-2000 Office of the Secretary
202-205-3296 Industries locator
Ask for the Trade Analyst who is an expert in the specific type of appliance that interests you.

AQUACULTURE

Aquaculture, sometimes called underwater agriculture, refers to the growing of plants, fish, and shellfish in a controlled aquatic environment.

See also: FISH AND SEAFOOD INDUSTRY

ASSOCIATIONS

Catfish Farmers of America
100 Hwy. 82, E.
Indianola, MS 38751
601-887-2699
Hugh Warren, Executive Vice President
Farmers who grow catfish.

Fish Culture Section
c/o American Fisheries Society
5410 Grosvenor Ln., Ste. 110
Bethesda, MD 20814
301-897-8616
301-897-8096 Fax
Carl Sullivan, Executive Director
Members include farmers of fish and shellfish, and manufacturers and dealers of equipment used in aquaculture.

Hydroponic Society of America
PO Box 6067
Concord, CA 94524
415-682-4193
Gene Brisbon, Executive Director
Hydroponic growers, scientists, and makers of hydroponic equipment.

World Aquaculture Society
Louisiana State Univ.
143 J. M. Parker Coliseum
Baton Rouge, LA 70803
504-388-3137
504-388-3493 Fax
Juiette Massey, Manager
Provides information to researchers, farmers, business people, and others.

PERIODICALS

Journal of Applied Aquaculture
Haworth Press, Inc.
10 Alice St.
Binghamton, NY 13904
607-722-1695
Douglas Tave, Editor
News about new technologies and methods that improve the farming of aquatic animals and plants.

Water Farming Journal
Carroll Trosclair and Associates, Inc.
3400 Neyrey Dr.
Metairie, LA 70002
504-885-9583
Carroll Trosclair, Editor
Includes news on the farming, selling, technology, and equipment of aquaculture.

LIBRARIES

Aquatic Research Institute
Aquatic Sciences & Technology Archive
2242 Davis Court
Hayward, CA 94545
510-784-0945
Aquaculture, aquatic sciences, and related areas.

Auburn University
International Center for Aquaculture
Library
Swingle Hall
Auburn University, AL 36849
205-844-4786
205-844-9208 Fax
Aquaculture management; aquaculture in fresh, brackish, and marine water; and related information.

U.S. National Marine Fisheries Service
Milford Laboratory Library
212 Rogers Ave.
Milford, CT 06460
203-783-4200
203-783-4217 Fax
Aquaculture, marine biology and pollution, fisheries, and related information.

COMPANIES

Atlantic Seafarms, Inc.
7994 White Point Rd.
Yonges Island, SC 29449
803-889-6086
Fish farming.

Aquatic Systems, Inc.
11125 Flintkote Ave.
San Diego, CA 92121
619-452-5765
Aquaculture farming.

Domsea Farms, Inc.
1656 Kraft Rd.
Pocatello, ID 82304
208-232-3080
Aquaculture farming.

Farm Fish, Inc.
P.O. Box 23109
Jackson, MS 39225
601-354-3801
Fish farming.

Fritz Chemical Co.
500 Sam Houston Rd.
Mesquite, TX 75149
214-285-5471
Makes aquaculture products among other items.

Sea Farms West, Inc.
P.O. Box 1540
Carlsbad, CA 92008
619-438-2444
Fish farming.

Triple H Fish Farms
Rte. 2
Indianola, MS 38751
601-887-1988
Fish farming.

Zeigler Brothers, Inc.
P.O. Box 95
Gardners, PA 17324
717-677-6181
Food for aquaculture and animals.

FEDERAL GOVERNMENT

U.S. Department of Agriculture
14th St. and Independence Ave., S.W.
Washington, DC 20250
202-720-8732
Ask for the Economic Research Service or the National Agricultural Statistic Service expert in aquaculture.

ARBITRATION AND MEDIATION

ASSOCIATIONS

American Arbitration Association
140 W. 51st St.
New York, NY 10020
212-484-4100
212-765-4874 Fax
Robert Coulson, President
Arbitrators, businesses, unions, and others working with arbitrators.

American Bar Association Standing Committee on Dispute Resolution
1800 M St. N.W., Ste. 200
Washington, DC 20036
202-331-2258
202-331-2220 Fax
Larry Ray, Staff Director
This committee offers referrals on dispute resolution and maintains a small library.

Center for Dispute Settlement
1666 Connecticut Ave. N.W., Ste. 501
Washington, DC 20009
202-265-9572
Linda Singer, Executive Director
Provides mediation for businesses, communities, and individuals.

National Academy of Arbitrators
Cornell University
School of Industrial and Labor Relations
20 Thornwood Dr., Ste. 107
Ithaca, NY 14850
607-257-9925
607-257-9942 Fax
Dana Eischen, Executive Secretary
Arbitrators who specialize in disputes between labor and management.

National Institute for Dispute Resolution
1901 L St. N.W., Ste. 600
Washington, DC 20036
202-466-4764
202-466-4769 Fax
Madeleine Crohn, Presdent
Offers information on alternatives to litigation.

PERIODICALS

B N A's Alternative Dispute Resolution Report
The Bureau of National Affairs, Inc.
1231 25th St., N.W.
Washington, DC 20037
202-452-4200
Sophie Eilperin, Editor
News of controversies that are settled without litigation.

Discipline and Grievances
Bureau of Business Practice
24 Rope Ferry Rd.
Waterford, CT 06386
203-442-4365
Emily Mitchell, Editor
Offers analyses of labor arbitration cases.

LIBRARIES

American Arbitration Association
Eastman Arbitration Library
140 W. 51st St.
New York, NY 10020
212-484-4127
212-765-4874 Fax
Arbitration and mediation.

Cornell University
New York State School of Industrial and
    Labor Relations
Sanford V. Lenz Library
15 E. 26th St.
New York, NY 10010-1565
212-340-2845
212-340-2822 Fax
*Arbitration, industrial and labor relations,
and collective bargaining.*

National Center for the Study of Collective
    Bargaining in Higher Education and the
    Professions
Elias Lieberman Higher Education Contract
    Library
17 Lexington Ave.
Box 322
New York, NY 10012
212-387-1510
*Arbitration, collective bargaining, and
grievance procedures.*

ARCHITECTURE

ASSOCIATIONS

International Institute of Site Planning
914 11th St. N.W.
Washington, DC 20001
202-737-2227
Beatriz Coffin, President
*Offers information on site selection and
design.*

American Institute of Architects
1735 New York Ave. N.W.
Washington, DC 20006
202-626-7300
James Cramer, Chief Executive
*The largest professional society of architects in
the U.S.*

American Institute of Building Design
1412 19th St.
Sacramento, CA 95814
916-447-2422
800-366-AIBD
Tammy Thomas, Executive Officer
*Members include designers, drafters, and
others.*

American Society of Landscape Architects
4401 Connecticut Ave. N.W.
Washington, DC 20008
202-466-7730
David Bohardt, Executive Vice President
*The largest professional group of landscape
architects in the U.S.*

PERIODICALS

Architectural Record
McGraw-Hill, Inc.
1221 Ave. of the Americas
New York, NY 10020
212-512-2000
Stephen Kliment, Editor
Covers architecture, design, and engineering.

Business Interiors
BusFac Publishing Co., Inc.
121 Monmouth St.
Box 2060
Red Bank, NJ 07701
201-842-7433
Heidi Schwartz, Editor
Information for planners of business facilities and offices.

Practicing Architect
Society of American Registered Architects
1245 S. Highland Ave.
Lombard, IL 60148
312-932-4622
Stanley Banash, Editor
Offers management advice for small architectural firms.

Progressive Architecture
Penton Publishing
600 Summer St.
Box 1361
Stamford, CT 06904
203-348-7531
John Dixon, Editor
Follows trends in design, governmental regulations, products for architects, and more.

LIBRARIES

American Institute of Architects
AIA Library
1735 New York Ave., N.W.
Washington, DC 20006
202-626-7492
Architecture and building technology.

Columbia University
Avery Architectural and Fine Arts Library
New York, NY 10027
212-854-3501
Architecture and city planning.

U.S. Department of Housing and Urban
  Development
Library
451 7th St., S.W., Rm. 8141
Washington, DC 20410
202-708-2376
Urban planning, housing, and architecture.

ARIZONA

STATE OFFICE LOCATOR (*for referrals to all state government offices*)

602-542-4900

ARCHIVES AND RECORDS

Library, Archives & Public Records Department
1700 W. Washington
Room 200
Phoenix, AZ 85007
602-542-4035

ATTORNEY GENERAL

Attorney General's Office
1275 W. Washington
Phoenix, AZ 85007
602-542-4266

BANKING

Banking Department
3225 N. Central Avenue
Ste. 815
Phoenix, AZ 85012
602-255-4421

COMMERCE

Commerce Department
3800 N. Central Avenue
Ste. 1400
Phoenix, AZ 85012
602-280-1300

CONSUMER AFFAIRS

Financial Fraud Protection
1275 W. Washington
Phoenix, AZ 85007
602-542-3702

EDUCATION

Education Services Department
1535 W. Jefferson
Phoenix, AZ 85007
602-542-4361

ENERGY

Energy Division
3800 N. Central Avenue
Ste. 1400
Phoenix, AZ 85012
602-280-1300

ENVIRONMENTAL AFFAIRS

Environmental Quality Department
2005 N. Central Avenue
Phoenix, AZ 85004
602-257-6917

HEALTH

Health Services Department
1740 W. Adams
Phoenix, AZ 85007
602-542-1024

HOUSING

Contractors Registrar
800 W. Washington
6th Floor
Phoenix, AZ 85007
602-542-1525

HUMAN RIGHTS

Civil Rights Division
1275 W. Washington
Phoenix, AZ 85007
602-542-5263

INSURANCE

Insurance Department
303 N. 3rd Street
Ste. 1100
Phoenix, AZ 85012
602-255-5400

LABOR

Labor Division
800 W. Washington
Phoenix, AZ 85007
602-542-4515

LEGISLATION

Legislative Council
1700 W. Washington
Room 100
Phoenix, AZ 85007
602-542-4617

LIBRARY SERVICES

Labor, Archives & Public Research Department
1700 W. Washington
Room 200
Phoenix, AZ 85007
602-542-4035

LICENSING—CORPORATE

Corporation Commission
1200 W. Washington
Phoenix, AZ 85007
602-542-4143

LICENSING—PROFESSIONAL AND OCCUPATIONAL

State Boards Office
1645 W. Jefferson
Room 410
Phoenix, AZ 85007
602-542-3095

MOTOR VEHICLES

Motor Vehicles Division
1801 W. Lewis
Phoenix, AZ 85009
602-255-8152

OCCUPATIONAL HEALTH AND SAFETY

Division of Occupational Safety Health
P.O. Box 19070
Phoenix, AZ 85005
602-255-5795

PUBLIC UTILITIES

Corporate Commission
1200 W. Washington
Phoenix, AZ 85007
602-542-4251

PURCHASING

Purchasing Department
1688 W. Adams
Room 220
Phoenix, AZ 85007
602-542-5511

REAL ESTATE

Real Estate Department
202 E. Earl Drive
4th Floor
Phoenix, AZ 85012
602-255-4670

SECURITIES

Securities Division
1200 W. Washington
Phoenix, AZ 85007
602-542-4242

TAXATION AND REVENUE

Revenue Department
1600 W. Monroe
Room 910
Phoenix, AZ 85007
602-542-3572

TOURISM

Office of Tourism
1100 W. Washington
Phoenix, AZ 85007
602-542-3618

TRANSPORTATION

Transportation Department
206 S. 17th Avenue
Phoenix, AZ 85007
602-255-7226

UNEMPLOYMENT

Unemployment Insurance Administration
P.O. Box 6123
Phoenix, AZ 85005
602-542-3667

WORKER'S COMPENSATION

State Compensation Fund
3031 N. 2nd Street
Phoenix, AZ 85012
602-631-2050

ARKANSAS

STATE OFFICE LOCATOR (*for referrals to all state government offices*)

501-371-3000

ARCHIVES AND RECORDS

Archives Secretary
1 Capitol Mall
Little Rock, AR 72201
501-682-6900

ATTORNEY GENERAL

Attorney General's Office
323 Center Street
Ste. 200
Little Rock, AR 72201
501-682-5437

BANKING

Bank Department
323 Center Street
Ste. 50
Little Rock, AR 72201
501-324-9019

COMMERCE

Industrial Development Commission
One Capitol Mall
Room 4C-300
Little Rock, AR 72201
501-682-1121

CONSUMER AFFAIRS

Attorney General
323 Center Street
Ste. 200
Little Rock, AR 72201
501-682-2007

EDUCATION

General Education Division
Arch-Ford Education Building
4 Capitol Mall
Room 304-A
Little Rock, AR 72201
501-682-4204

ENERGY

Arkansas Energy Office
1 Capitol Mall
Little Rock, AR 72201
501-682-1370

ENVIRONMENTAL AFFAIRS

Pollution Control & Ecology Department
P.O. Box 9583
Little Rock, AR 72219
501-562-7444

HEALTH

Health Department
4815 W. Markham
Little Rock, AR 72205-3867
501-661-2111

HOUSING

Development Finance Authority
P.O. Box 8023
Little Rock, AR 72203
501-682-5900

INSURANCE

Insurance Department
400 University
Little Rock, AR 72204
501-371-1325

LABOR

Labor Department
10421 W. Markham
Little Rock, AR 72205
501-682-4500

LEGISLATION

Legislative Research Bureau
State Capitol
5th & Woodlane
Room 315
Little Rock, AR 72201
501-682-1937

LIBRARY SERVICES

State Librarian
1 Capitol Mall
Little Rock, AR 72201
501-371-1526

LICENSING—CORPORATE

Industrial Development Commission
1 Capitol Mall
Little Rock, AR 72201
501-682-2052

MOTOR VEHICLES

Motor Vehicle Office
P.O. Box 3278
Little Rock, AR 72203
501-682-4630

OCCUPATIONAL HEALTH AND SAFETY

Safety Division
10421 W. Markham
Little Rock, AR 72205
501-682-4522

OMBUDSMAN

State Claims Commission
State Capitol
5th & Woodlane
Room 021
Little Rock, AR 72201
501-682-1619

PUBLIC UTILITIES

Public Service Commission
P.O. Box C-400
Little Rock, AR 72203
501-682-1453

PURCHASING

State Purchasing Office
P.O. Box 3278
Little Rock, AR 72032
501-324-9312

REAL ESTATE

Real Estate Commission
Twin City Bank Building
1 Riverfront Place
Ste. 660
N. Little Rock, AR 72114
501-371-1247

SECURITIES

Securities Department
201 E. Markham
Room 300
Little Rock, AR 72201
501-324-9260

TAXATION AND REVENUE

Revenue Division
P.O. Box 3278
Little Rock, AR 72203
501-682-7000

TOURISM

Department of Parks & Tourism
1 Capitol Mall
Little Rock, AR 72201
501-371-7777
800-828-8974
800-482-8999 (in Arkansas)

TRANSPORTATION

Highway & Transportation Department
P.O. Box 2261
Little Rock, AR 72203
501-569-2211

UNEMPLOYMENT

Unemployment Insurance
P.O. Box 2981
Little Rock, AR 72203
501-682-3201

WORKER'S COMPENSATION

Workers Compensation Commission
Justice Building
625 Marshall Street
Little Rock, AR 72201
501-372-3930

ART AND ANTIQUES MARKET

ASSOCIATIONS

Antique Appraisal Association of America
11361 Garden Grove Blvd.
Garden Grove, CA 92643
714-530-7090
Andrew Noland, Secretary
Membership is limited to antiques appraisers.

Antiques Dealers' Association of America
Box 335
Greens Farms, CT 06436
203-259-3844
203-255-3197 Fax
Satenig St. Marie, Executive Director
*Dealers of 17th-, 18th-, and 19th-century
antiques.*

Art Dealers Association of America
575 Madison Ave.
New York, NY 10022
212-940-8590
212-935-0679 Fax
Gilbert Edelson, Vice President
Art dealers who own or work for art galleries.

National Antique and Art Dealers Association
of America
15 E. 57th St.
New York, NY 10022
212-826-9707
212-308-2105 Fax
Christian Jussell, President
*Dealers of top quality and rare art and
antiques.*

PERIODICALS

Antique Market Report
Web Communications
Box 12830
Wichita, KS 67277
316-946-0600
Debra Roark, Editor
*Covers sales results from major antiques auc-
tions.*

Antique Monthly
Trans World Publishing Co.
2100 Powers Ferry Rd., Ste. 300
Atlanta, GA 30339
404-955-5656
Elizabeth McKenzie, Editor
Covers antiques shows and exhibits.

Antique Trader Price Guide to Antiques and
Collectors' Items
Babka Publishing Co.
Box 1050-PG
Dubuque, IA 52001
319-588-2073
Kyle Husfloen, Editor
Covers prices for antiques and collectibles.

Antiques and Auction News
Engle Publishing Co.
Rte. 230 W., Box 500
Mount Joy, PA 17552
717-653-9797
John Finsand, Editor
*Surveys the antiques scene on the eastern
seaboard.*

Art & Antiques
Art & Antiques Associates L.P.
Allison Publications, Inc.
89 Fifth Ave.
New York, NY 10003
212-206-7050
Jeffrey Schaire, Editor
*A consumer magazine for art and antiques
lovers and collectors.*

Magazine Antiques
Brant Publications
980 Madison Ave., 3rd Fl.
New York, NY 10021
212-941-2800
Wendell Garrett, Editor
Focuses on antique furniture.

LIBRARIES

New York Public Library
Miriam and Ira D. Wallach Division of Art,
    Prints & Photographs
Art and Architecture Collection
Fifth Ave. & 42nd St., Rm. 313
New York, NY 10018
212-930-0834
Painting, drawing, applied art, and antiques.

Sotheby's Library
1334 York Ave.
New York, NY 10021
212-606-7000
212-606-7011
Art and antiques.

FEDERAL GOVERNMENT

U.S. Customs Service
Department of the Treasury
U.S. Customshouse
6 World Trade Center
New York, NY 10048
212-466-5550
*Ask for the Commodity Specialist in charge of
art or antiques.*

U.S. International Trade Administration
Department of Commerce
14th St. and Constitution Ave., N.W.
Washington, DC 20230
202-377-2000
*Ask for the Commodity Analyst who is an
expert in art or antiques.*

U.S. International Trade Commission
500 E St., S.W.
Washington, DC 20436
202-205-2000 Office of the Secretary
202-205-3296 Industries locator
*Ask for the Trade Analyst who is an expert in
art or antiques.*

ARTIFICIAL INTELLIGENCE

See also: COMPUTERS

ASSOCIATIONS

American Association for Artificial Intelligence
445 Burgess Dr.
Menlo Park, CA 94025
415-328-3123
415-321-4457 Fax
Claudia Mazzetti, Executive Director
Scientists, executives, and others who share information on artifical intelligence and expert systems.

Association for Intelligent Systems Technology
6310 Fly Rd.
East Syracuse, NY 13057
315-433-1010
James Brule, President
Members explore the uses of artificial intelligence in science, business, medicine, and government.

Society for Machine Intelligence
100 Farnsworth
Detroit, MI 48202
313-832-5400
Dr. Thomas Kaczmarek, Chairman
Engineers and others who develop and use artificial intelligence software.

Special Interest Group on Artificial Intelligence
c/o Association for Computing Machinery
11 W. 42nd St., 3rd Fl.
New York, NY 10036
212-869-7440
Jon Doyle, Chairman
Members exchange information on the applications of artificial intelligence.

PERIODICALS

A I Expert
Miller Freeman Publications, Inc.
600 Harrison St.
San Francisco, CA 94107
415-905-2200
Alan Zeichick, Editor
Provides practical information for programmers and managers of artificial intelligence systems.

A I Today
Yellowstone Information Services
7 View Dr.
Elkview, WV 25071
304-965-5548
Roger Thibault, Editor
Subjects include expert systems, natural language, AI languages, and robotics.

Artificial Intelligence Abstracts
R.R. Bowker
Bowker A & I Publishing
121 Chanlon Rd.
New Providence, NJ 07974
908-771-7714
Judy Salk, Editor
Reviews developments and new literature in neural networks, expert systems, machine vision, natural language, and other AI subjects.

Artificial Intelligence Markets
AIM Publications, Inc.
Box 156
Natick, MA 01760
617-653-1622
Carol Weiszmann, Editor
Follows trends and business news in the AI field.

ISR: Intelligent Systems Report
A I Week, Inc.
2555 Cumberland Pkwy., Ste. 299
Atlanta, GA 30339
404-434-2187
David Blanchard, Editor
Covers expert systems, fuzzy logic, neural networks, and related subjects.

LIBRARIES

FMC Corp.
Corporate Technology Center
Information Services
1205 Coleman Ave.
Box 580
Santa Clara, CA 95052
408-289-2529
Artificial intelligence, robotics, and related topics.

Martin Marietta Laboratories
Library and Information Services
1450 S. Rolling Rd.
Baltimore, MD 21227-3898
301-247-0700
Artificial intelligence, materials science, microelectronics and other technologies.

Pennsylvania State University
Mathematics Library
109 McAllister Bldg.
University Park, PA 16802
814-865-6822
Mathematics, computer science, and artificial intelligence.

COMPANIES

Aicorp, Inc.
100 Fifth Ave.
Waltham, MA 02254
617-890-8400
Artificial intelligence software.

Analytics
2500 Maryland Rd.
Willow Grove, PA 19090
215-657-4100
Military systems, including those that employ artificial intelligence.

Artificial Intelligence Technologies, Inc.
40 Saw Mill River Rd.
Hawthorne, NY 10532
914-347-6860
Artificial intelligence software.

Expert Systems, Inc.
1010 Hunt Cliff
Atlanta, GA 30350
404-642-7575
Artificial intelligence software.

Titan Corp.
5910 Pacific Ctr. Blvd.
San Diego, CA 92122
619-453-9500
Artificial intelligence and expert systems cores and other products.

FEDERAL GOVERNMENT

U.S. International Trade Administration
Department of Commerce
14th St. and Constitution Ave., N.W.
Washington, DC 20230
202-377-2000
*Ask for the Commodity Analyst who is an
expert in artificial intelligence or computers.*

U.S. International Trade Commission
500 E St., S.W.
Washington, DC 20436
202-205-2000 Office of the Secretary
202-205-3296 Industries locator
*Ask for the Trade Analyst who is an expert in
artificial intelligence or computers.*

ARTS MANAGEMENT

ASSOCIATIONS

Association of Talent Agents
9255 Sunset Blvd., Ste. 318
Los Angeles, CA 90069
213-274-0628
Representatives of movie and stage actors.

International Society of Performing Arts
    Administrators
Box 200328
Austin, TX 78720
512-346-1328
*Members are administrators and managers of
performing arts companies and performing
artists.*

National Association of Performing Arts Man-
    agers and Agents
PO Box 1515
New York, NY 10023
212-799-5080
212-874-7652 Fax
John Gingrich, President
*Members include managers of performing
artists, publicists, and others.*

Professional Arts Management Institute
408 W. 57th St.
New York, NY 10019
212-245-3850
Alvin Reiss, Director
*Offers training to students and working man-
agers of performing arts programs and cultural institutions.*

FEDAPT
270 Lafayette St., Ste. 810
New York, NY 10012
212-966-9344
Nello McDaniel, Executive Director
*Offers management guidance to a variety of
performing arts groups.*

PERIODICALS

Arts Management
Radius Group Inc.
408 W. 57th St.
New York, NY 10019
212-245-3850
Alvin Reiss, Editor
News and issues for those managing the arts.

Backstage
B P I Communications, Inc.
330 W. 42nd St.
New York, NY 10036
212-947-0020
Steve Elish, Editor
Covers the theater scene and lists auditions, managers, coaches, and others.

Billboard's International Talent and Touring
   Directory
Billboard Publications, Inc.
1515 Broadway, 39th Fl.
New York, NY 10036
212-764-7300
Lists acts, shows, managers, booking agencies, services, and much more.

LIBRARIES

American Council for the Arts
Library
1285 Avenue of the Americas, 3rd Fl.
New York, NY 10019
212-245-4510
Arts management and policy.

National Endowment for the Arts
Arts Library
1100 Pennsylvania Ave., N.W.
Washington, DC 20506
202-682-5485
Arts management, law and the arts, visual arts, design, and related areas.

United Arts
Resources & Counseling Division
Library
75 W. 5th St., Rm. 429
St. Paul, MN 55102
612-292-4381
Arts management, nonprofit management, and business skills.

ASBESTOS INDUSTRY

See also: PRODUCT LIABILITY

ASSOCIATIONS

Asbestos Information Association/North
America
1745 Jefferson Davis Hwy., Ste. 509
Arlington, VA 22202
703-979-1150
B. J. Pigg, President
*Offers information on asbestos and asbestos
dust hazards, and also the benefits of asbestos
products. Maintains a library.*

Asbestos Litigation Group
c/o Ness, Motley, Loadholt, Richardson, and
Poole
PO Box 1137
Charleston, SC 29402
803-577-6747
Ronald Motley, President
*Attorneys involved with litigation concerning
asbestos-related disease cases.*

Asbestos Victims of America
PO Box 559
Capitola, CA 95010
408-476-3646
Heather Maurer, Chief Executive
*An information center and self-help group for
people suffering from asbestos-related diseases.*

Association of the Wall and Ceiling Industries—International
1600 Cameron St., Ste. 200
Alexandria, VA 22314
703-684-2924
703-684-2935 Fax
Joe Baker, Executive Vice President
*Firms which provide asbestos abatement and
other services.*

National Asbestos Council
1777 N.E. Expressway, Ste. 150
Atlanta, GA 30329
404-633-2622
404-633-5714 Fax
Paul Skoglund, Executive Director
*A clearinghouse for information on safe use
and removal of asbestos.*

National Insulation and Abatement Contractors Association
99 Canal Center Plaza, Ste. 222
Alexandria, VA 22314
703-683-6422
703-549-4838 Fax
William Pitkin, Executive Vice President
*Contractors and manufacturers who work
with insulation and asbestos abatement.*

PERIODICALS

Asbestos Abatement Report
Buraff Publications
1350 Connecticut Ave. N.W., Ste. 1000
Washington, DC 20036
202-862-0990
Corby Anderson, Editor
Follows technical and business developments in asbestos control.

Asbestos Case Law Quarterly
Butterworth Legal Publishers
90 Stiles Rd.
Salem, NH 03079
603-898-9664
Jerry Nates, Editor
A journal for lawyers.

Asbestos Control Report
Business Publishers, Inc.
951 Pershing Dr.
Silver Spring, MD 20910-4464
301-587-6300
Bryan Lee, Editor
Reports on removal, maintenance alternatives, federal standards, state regulations, insurance, and medical research.

Occupational Health & Safety Asbestos Control Buyer's Guide
Stevens Publishing Corp.
225 N. New Rd.
Waco, TX 76710
817-776-9000
Lists products, services, and equipment used in asbestos control.

LIBRARIES

Manville Coporation
HS & E/Technical Information Center
P.O. Box 5108
Denver, CO 80217
303-978-5200
Asbestos, occupational health, toxicology, and related topics.

Versar Inc.
Information Services
6850 Versar Center
Box 1549
Springfield, VA 22151
703-750-3000
703-642-6807 Fax
Asbestos, waste management, risk assessment, environmental research, and related topics.

White Lung Association
Library
1601 St. Paul St.
Baltimore, MD 21202-2816
301-727-6029
Asbestos hazards.

COMPANIES

Advatex Associates, Inc.
1501 Broadway
New York, NY 10036
212-921-0600
Asbestos removal services.

Chempower Inc.
807 E. Turkey Foot Lake Rd.
Akron, OH 44319
216-896-4202
Asbestos abatement.

Commodore Environmental Services Inc.
150 E. 58th St.
New York, NY 10155
212-308-5800
Hazardous materials and asbestos removal.

Critical Industries Inc.
5815 Gulf Freeway
Houston, TX 77023
713-923-1300
Manufactures equipment used for asbestos removal.

Environmental Control Group Inc.
115 Twinbridge Dr.
Pennsauken, NJ 08110
609-866-1616
Asbestos abatement.

LVI Group Inc.
345 Hudson St.
New York, NY 10014
212-337-6600
Asbestos abatement, construction, dredging, and energy-recovery equipment and services.

NSC Corp.
49 Danton Dr.
Methuen, MA 01844
508-686-6417
Asbestos abatement.

FEDERAL GOVERNMENT

U.S. International Trade Administration
Department of Commerce
14th St. and Constitution Ave., N.W.
Washington, DC 20230
202-377-2000
Ask for the Commodity Analyst who is an expert in asbestos.

U.S. International Trade Commission
500 E St., S.W.
Washington, DC 20436
202-205-2000 Office of the Secretary
202-205-3296 Industries locator
Ask for the Trade Analyst who is an expert in asbestos.

ASPHALT INDUSTRY

ASSOCIATIONS

Asphalt Emulsion Manufacturers Association
Three Church Circle, Ste. 250
Annapolis, MD 21401
301-267-0023
Michael Krissoff, Executive Director
Information about asphalt emulsion and its uses.

Asphalt Institute
Research Park Dr.
PO Box 14052
Lexington, KY 40512-4052
606-288-4960
606-288-4999 Fax
Members refine asphalt products out of petroleum.

Asphalt Recycling and Reclaiming Association
3 Church Circle, Ste. 250
Annapolis, MD 21401
301-267-0023
Michael Krissoff, Executive Director
*Offers information on the reworking and
reclaiming of asphalt.*

Asphalt Roofing Manufacturers Association
6288 Montrose Rd.
Rockville, MD 20852
301-231-9050
301-881-6572 Fax
Richard Snyder, Executive Vice President
*Manufacturers of asphalt shingles and other
materials.*

Asphalt Rubber Producers Group
3336 N. 32nd St., Ste. 106
Phoenix, AZ 85018
602-955-1141
602-956-3506 Fax
Timothy Baker, President
*Manufacturers and distributors of asphalt
rubber products, especially those that use the
rubber from ground-up scrap tires.*

National Asphalt Pavement Association
5100 Forbes Blvd.
Lanhan, MD 20706-4413
301-731-4748
301-779-8817 Fax
John Gray, President
*Members include hot mix asphalt contractors,
engineers, and equipment manufacturers.*

PERIODICALS

Association of Asphalt Paving Technologists.
    Proceedings
Association of Asphalt Paving Technologists
1404 Concordia Ave.
St. Paul, MN 55104
612-642-1350
E.L. Skok, Editor
Technical information about asphalt paving.

Lightweight Concrete Information Sheets
Expanded Shale, Clay and Slate Institute
2225 E. Murray Holladay Rd., Ste. 102
Salt Lake City, UT 84117
801-272-7070
John Ries, Editor
*Follows the use of ceramic lightweight aggre-
gate in concrete, asphalt, and other materials.*

LIBRARIES

Asphalt Institute
Research Library
P.O. Box 14052
Lexington, KY 40512-4052
606-288-4950
606-288-4999 Fax
Asphalt technology, history, and industry.

National Asphalt Pavement Association
Charles R. Foster Technical Library
5100 Forbes Ave.
Lanham, MD 20706-4413
301-731-4748
*Technology and applications of hot mix
asphalt.*

Witco Chemical Corp.
Golden Bear Division
QC/R & D Library
Ferguson & Manor Rds.
Box 5446
Oildale, CA 93388
805-393-7110
805-393-2083 Fax
*Asphalt, petroleum refining, rubber, and
related areas.*

COMPANIES

Astec Industries, Inc.
4101 Jerome Ave., Box 72787
Chattanooga, TN 37407
615-867-4210
*Asphalt plants, asphalt storage equipment,
paving equipment, and related products.*

Barber-Greene Co.
(Division of Astec Industries, Inc.)
3000 Barber-Greene Rd.
DeKalb, IL 60115
815-756-5600
Asphalt pavers and road wideners.

Chevron Corp.
225 Bush St.
San Francisco, CA 94104
415-894-7700
Asphalt and petroleum products.

Giles & Ransome, Inc.
2975 Galloway Rd.
Bensalem, PA 19020
215-639-4300
*Asphalt and concrete paving equipment and
other types of equipment.*

Huntway Partners
23822 W. Valencia Blvd.
Valencia, CA 91355
805-253-1799
*Liquid asphalt and other products for road
paving.*

Edward C. Levy Co.
8800 Dix Ave.
Detroit, MI 48209
313-843-7200
*Asphalt mixtures, concrete, and other prod-
ucts.*

Vecellio & Grogan, Inc.
P. O. Drawer V
Beckley, WV 25801
304-252-6575
Asphalt paving and contracting.

Vulcan Materials Co.
One Metroplex Dr.
Birmingham, AL 35209
205-877-3000
*Construction materials, including various
forms of asphalt.*

FEDERAL GOVERNMENT

U.S. Department of Transportation
400 Seventh St., S.W.
Washington, DC 20590
202-366-4000
*Ask for the Pavement Division, which is part
of the Federal Highway Administration.*

U.S. International Trade Administration
Department of Commerce
14th St. and Constitution Ave., N.W.
Washington, DC 20230
202-377-2000
*Ask for the Commodity Analyst who is an
expert in asphalt.*

U.S. International Trade Commission
500 E St., S.W.
Washington, DC 20436
202-205-2000 Office of the Secretary
202-205-3296 Industries locator
*Ask for the Trade Analyst who is an expert in
asphalt.*

AUCTIONS

ASSOCIATIONS

National Auctioneers Association
8880 Ballentine
Overland Park, KS 66214
913-541-8084
913-894-5281 Fax
Joseph Keefhaver, Executive Director
Provides certification and training to auction-eers.

National Auto Auction Association
Box 129
Monrovia, MD 21770
301-831-8077
Peter Lukasiak, Executive Director
Members operate wholesale auctions of cars and trucks.

PERIODICALS

Antiques and Auction News
Engle Publishing Co.
Rte. 230 W., Box 500
Mount Joy, PA 17552
717-653-9797
Doris Johnson, Editor
Information for antiques collectors and auc-tioneers with an emphasis on the East coast.

Appraisers Standard
New England Appraisers Association
5 Gill Terrace
Ludlow, VT 05149
802-228-7444
Linda Tucker, Editor
Advice and information for appraisers and auctioneers.

Art at Auction: the Year at Sotheby's and
    Parke-Bernet
Sotheby Publications
Philip Wilson Publishers Ltd.
c/o Harper & Row
10 E. 53 St.
New York, NY 10022
Sally Liddell, Editor
Covers the market for precious art and antiques.

Auction and Surplus
News Circle Publishing House
1250 W. Glenoaks Blvd., Unit E.
Box 3684
Glendale, CA 91201-0684
818-545-0333
Joseph Haiek, Editor
Reports on auctions and liquidations of close-outs and surplus from the government and companies.

Auction Prices of American Artists
Apollo Book
5 Schoolhouse Ln.
Poughkeepsie, NY 12603
914-462-0040
Lists auction prices of the works of over 5,000 American artists.

Auction Weekly
SouthAtlantic Communications
3020 Pickett Rd.
Durham, NC 27705
919-490-5472
Burton K. Fox, Editor
Advice on buying and selling at auctions.

Government Auctions Update
Publishing & Business Consultants
951 S. Oxford, No. 109
Los Angeles, CA 90006
213-732-3477
Atia Napoleon, Editor
A listing of government auctions nationwide.

COMPANIES

Cox Enterprises Inc.
1400 Lake Hearn Dr.
Atlanta, GA 30319
404-843-5000
Automobile auctions and other types of businesses.

Great Western Systems Inc.
5353 E. Washington St.
Phoenix, AZ 85034
602-244-0361
Used car auctions and other businesses.

Interstate Auto Auction, Inc.
(Subsidiary of Consumers Financial Corp.)
P. O. Box 550
Mercer, PA 16137
412-662-4500
Automobile auctions.

Lugbill Brothers, Inc.
Box 198
Archbold, OH 43502
419-445-2010
Livestock auctions and other farm businesses.

Sotheby's Inc.
(Subsidiary of Sotheby's Holdings, Inc.)
1334 York Ave.
New York, NY 10021
212-606-7000
Art, jewelry, and real estate auctions.

AUDIOVISUAL INDUSTRY

ASSOCIATIONS

American Video Association
2885 N. Nevada St., No. 140
Chandler, AZ 85225
602-892-8553
800-926-8358
800-528-7400
602-926-8358 Fax
John Power, President
Retailers of video products for consumers.

Association of Audio-Visual Technicians
2378 S. Broadway
Denver, CO 80210
303-698-1820
303-777-3261 Fax
Elsa Kaiser, Executive Director
Members include producers of audiovisual materials and repairers of equipment.

Audio-Visual Management Association
7907 N.W. 53rd St., Ste. 346
Miami, FL 33166
305-887-0446
Bob McEmber, Executive Director
Members run the audiovisual departments of businesses.

Independent Professional Representatives
   Organization
25820 Orchard Lake Rd.
Farmington, MI 48336
313-442-9661
Ray Wright, Executive Vice President
Manufacturers representatives of audiovisual products.

International Communications Industries
   Association
3150 Spring St.
Fairfax, VA 22031
703-273-7200
703-278-8082 Fax
Kenton Pattie, Executive Vice President
Manufacturers and dealers of video, audiovisual, and other products.

Professional Audiovideo Retailers Association
9140 Ward Pkwy.
Kansas City, MO 64114
816-444-3500
816-444-0330 Fax
John Carey, Executive Vice President
Dealers of expensive, specialized audiovisual equipment.

Video Software Dealers Association
3 Eves Dr., Ste. 307
Marlton, NJ 08053
609-596-8500
Pamela Cohen, Executive Vice President
Dealers and wholesalers of videocassettes.

PERIODICALS

A V Market Place
R.R. Bowker, Database Publishing Group
121 Chanlon Rd.
New Providence, NJ 07974
800-521-8110
A listing of firms that offer audiovisual equipment and services for all markets.

A V Video
Montage Publishing, Inc.
701 Westchester Ave.
White Plains, NY 10604
914-329-9157
Phillip Kurz, Editor
Follows news and technology, and offers how-to information on most fields within the audiovisual industry.

Audio-Visual Communications
P T N Publishing Corp.
445 Broad Hollow Rd., Ste. 25
Melville, NY 11646
516-845-2700
Mike Yuhas, Editor
Practical information for executives who use audiovisual tools for presentations.

Communications Industries Report
International Communications Industries
   Association, Inc.
3150 Spring St.
Fairfax, VA 22031-2399
703-273-7200
Dick Larsen, Editor
Covers audiovisuals, multimedia, video, and other communications technologies.

Educational Technology
Educational Technology Publications, Inc.
720 Palisade Ave.
Englewood Cliffs, NJ 07632
201-871-4007
Lawrence Lipsitz, Editor
Follows trends in computers, audiovisuals, and other technologies used in education.

NICEM Index to AV Producers and Distributors
National Information Center for Educational Media
Access Innovations, Inc
Box 40130
Albuquerque, NM 87196
505-265-3591
A directory of firms that offer audiovisual products.

LIBRARIES

Brooklyn Public Library
Audio Visual/Media Room Division
Grand Army Plaza
Brooklyn, NY 11238
718-780-7793
Audiovisual products.

Cleveland Public Library
Audio-Video Department
325 Superior Ave.
Cleveland, OH 44114-1271
216-623-2942
Audiovisual products.

COMPANIES

Apollo Space Systems, Inc.
60 Trade Zone Ct.
Ronkonkoma, NY 11779
516-467-8033
Audiovisual projectors.

Blumberg Communications, Inc.
525 N. Washington Ave.
Minneapolis, MN 55401
612-333-1271
Distributes audiovisual equipment and supplies.

Highsmith Co., Inc.
W 5527 Hwy. 106, Box 800
Fort Atkinson, WI 53538
414-563-9571
Mail order school supplies, including audiovisual equipment.

Minnesota Mining & Manufacturing Co.
3M Center
St. Paul, MN 55144
612-733-1110
Manufactures audiovisual equipment and supplies, among many other products.

Photo & Sound Co.
116 Natoma St.
San Francisco, CA 94105
415-822-7555
Sales and rental of audiovisual and related products.

School Specialty Supply, Inc.
3525 S. 9th At Berg Rd., Box 1547
Salina, KS 67402
913-827-0451
Audiovisual equipment and other school and office supplies.

FEDERAL GOVERNMENT

U.S. Customs Service
Department of the Treasury
U.S. Customshouse
6 World Trade Center
New York, NY 10048
212-466-5550
Ask for the Commodity Specialist in charge of audiovisual equipment.

U.S. International Trade Administration
Department of Commerce
14th St. and Constitution Ave., N.W.
Washington, DC 20230
202-377-2000
*Ask for the Commodity Analyst who is an
expert in audiovisual equipment.*

U.S. International Trade Commission
500 E St., S.W.
Washington, DC 20436
202-205-2000 Office of the Secretary
202-205-3296 Industries locator
*Ask for the Trade Analyst who is an expert in
audiovisual equipment.*

U.S. Patent and Trademark Office
Crystal Plaza 2
2011 Jefferson Davis Highway
Arlington, VA 22202
703-305-8000
*Ask for the Examining Group Director who is
a specialist in audiovisual equipment.*

AUTOMATIC IDENTIFICATION INDUSTRY

*Automatic identification technology uses bar-codes, scanners, optical character recognition, and other
types of equipment to help automate inventory control, pricing, accounting, and related functions.*

ASSOCIATIONS

Automatic Identification Manufacturers
1326 Freeport Rd.
Pittsburgh, PA 15238
412-963-8588
412-963-8753
William Hakanson, Secretary
*A clearinghouse for information about auto-
matic identification products.*

Uniform Code Council
8163 Old Yankee St.
Dayton, OH 45458
513-435-3870
Harold Juckett, Executive Vice President
*Provides information about universal product
codes (in which a unique number is assigned
to every product sold through check-out counters). These codes are used by automatic identification equipment to speed up sales,
improve inventory control, and for other purposes.*

PERIODICALS

G C A Bar Code Reporter
Graphic Communications Association
100 Daingerfield Rd.
Alexandria, VA 22314
703-519-8160
Alan Kotok, Editor
Focuses on how automatic identification products improve inventory control and automation for printers and publishers.

I D Systems
Helmers Publishing, Inc.
174 Concord St.
Box 874
Peterborough, NH 03458-0874
603-924-9631
Deb Navas, Editor
Surveys trends and products for users of automatic identification systems and bar-code equipment.

Modern Materials Handling
Cahners Publishing Company
275 Washington St.
Newton, MA 02158-1630
617-964-3030
Raymond Kulwiec, Editor
Reports on all types of equipment used for materials handling, including automatic identification systems.

SCAN Newsletter
Scanning, Coding & Automation Newsletter
   Ltd.
11 Middle Neck Rd.
Great Neck, NY 11021
516-487-6370
George Goldberg, Editor
Advice for managers who use automatic identification and bar-code scanning technologies.

COMPANIES

Accu-Sort Systems, Inc.
511 School House Rd.
Telford, PA 18969
215-723-0981
Bar-code readers and inventory control systems.

CheckRobot Inc.
692 S. Military Trail
Deerfield Beach, FL 33442
305-426-1600
Supermarket self-service check-out products that use bar-code scanners.

Graphic Technology, Incorporated
(Subsidiary of Nitto Denko America)
301 Gardner Dr.
Industrial Airport, KS 66031
913-764-5550
Labels used for bar-coding and other purposes.

Intermec Corp.
(Subsidiary of Litton Industries, Inc.)
6001-36th Ave. W., Box 4280
Everett, WA 98203
206-348-2600
Various types of bar-code systems and components.

Logan Co.
(Division of Figgie International Inc.)
200 Cabel St.
Louisville, KY 40206
502-587-1361
Conveyor, sorting, and bar-code equipment.

Metrologic Instruments, Inc.
Coles Rd. at Rte. 42
Blackwood, NJ 08012
609-228-8100
Bar-code equipment and portable data collection terminals.

Symbol Technologies, Inc.
116 Wilbur Pl.
Bohemia, NY 11716
516-563-2400
A wide variety of bar-code systems.

Zebra Technologies Corp.
333 Corporate Woods Pkwy.
Vernon Hills, IL 60061
708-634-6700
Printers and labels for the bar-code industry.

FEDERAL GOVERNMENT

U.S. International Trade Administration
Department of Commerce
14th St. and Constitution Ave., N.W.
Washington, DC 20230
202-377-2000
Ask for the Commodity Analyst who is an expert in bar-code equipment.

U.S. Patent and Trademark Office
Crystal Plaza 2
2011 Jefferson Davis Highway
Arlington, VA 22202
703-305-8000
Ask for the Examining Group Director who is a specialist in bar-code equipment.

AUTOMOBILE DEALERS

See also: AUTOMOTIVE INDUSTRY

ASSOCIATIONS

National Association of Fleet Resale Dealers
PO Box 34028
Los Angeles, CA 90034
213-838-3168
Bill Nerenberg, Executive Director
Offers public relations and management infor-mation to used-car wholesalers who handle large fleets of automobiles.

National Automobile Dealers Association
8400 Westpark Dr.
McLean, VA 22102
703-827-7407
703-821-7075 Fax
Frank McCarthy, Executive Vice President
New car and truck dealers who are franchised.

National Independent Automobile Dealers
   Association
2521 Brown Blvd.
Arlington, TX 76006-5203
817-640-3838
817-649-5866 Fax
Charles Tupper, Executive Vice President
*A clearinghouse for information about the
retail used-car industry.*

PERIODICALS

Automotive Executive
National Automobile Dealers Association
8400 Westpark Dr.
McLean, VA 22102
703-821-7150
Joe Phillips, Editor
Information and advice for new-car dealers.

Car Dealer Insider Newsletter
Atcom, Inc.
Atcom Bldg.
2315 Broadway
New York, NY 10024-4397
212-873-5900
Al Burns, Editor
*Covers industry news and trends for new-car
dealers.*

Chilton's Automotive Marketing
Chilton Co.
Chilton Way
Radnor, PA 19089
215-964-4395
*News for dealers of automotive accessories and
products.*

NADA Official Used Car Guide
National Automobile Dealers Association
Used Car Guide Co.
8400 Westpark Dr.
McLean, VA 22102
703-821-7000
A price guide for used cars.

Used Car Dealer
National Independent Automobile Dealers
   Association
2521 Brown Blvd., Ste. 100
Arlington, TX 76006-5203
817-640-3838
Don Harris, Editor
*Follows the practical and legal aspects of sell-
ing used cars.*

LIBRARIES

Automotive Information Council
Library
13505 Dulles Technology Dr.
Herndon, VA 22071-3415
703-904-0700
703-904-0727 Fax
*Wide-ranging information on the automotive
industry.*

Ford Motor Co.
Technical Information Section
20000 Rotunda Dr.
Box 1602
Dearborn, MI 48121
313-323-1059
313-323-7936 Fax
*Automotive engineering, automobile industry,
transportation, and other subjects.*

General Motors Corp.
Public Affairs Information Services
General Motors Bldg., Rm. 11-235
3044 W. Grand Blvd.
Detroit, MI 48202
313-556-2051
*Automotive business, economics, and related
nontechnical automotive industry information.*

COMPANIES

Allen County Motors, Inc.
2300 W. Jefferson Blvd.
Fort Wayne, IN 46802
219-432-9545
Automobile and truck retailer.

Autoland Chevrolet Inc.
Route 37 & Peter Ave.
Toms River, NJ 08754
908-244-8400
New and used cars.

Bland Cadillac Co.
P. O. Box 2147
Houston, TX 77252
713-527-6600
New and used Cadillacs.

Dart Group Corp.
3300 75th Ave.
Landover, MD 20785
301-731-1200
Very large retailer of cars.

Ferman Motor Car Co.
P.O. Box 1321
Tampa, FL 33601
813-623-2411
Large car dealership.

Parkway Ford, Inc.
2104 Peters Creek Pkwy.
Winston-Salem, NC 27107
919-724-5921
New and used cars and trucks.

Richmond Motor Co.
4600 W. Broad St.
Richmond, VA 23230
804-358-5521
New and used cars.

Jake Sweeney Automotive, Inc.
33 W. Kemper Rd.
Cincinnati, OH 45246
513-782-2800
New and used cars.

FEDERAL GOVERNMENT

U.S. International Trade Administration
Department of Commerce
14th St. and Constitution Ave., N.W.
Washington, DC 20230
202-377-2000
Ask for the Commodity Analyst who studies automobile dealerships.

AUTOMOBILE EQUIPMENT INDUSTRY

See also: TIRE INDUSTRY

ASSOCIATIONS

Association of Automotive Aftermarket Distributors
5050 Poplar Ave., Ste. 2020
Memphis, TN 38157-2001
901-682-9090
800-727-8112
901-682-9098 Fax
Marvin Almy, President
Distributors of automotive parts and accessories.

Automotive Body Parts Association
2500 Wilcrest Dr., Ste. 510
Houston, TX 77042-2752
713-977-5551
800-323-5832
713-531-9411 Fax
Stanley Rodman, Executive Director
Suppliers of recycled and recovered automotive parts from crashed and damaged cars.

Automotive Market Research Council
300 Sylvan Ave.
PO Box 1638
Englewood Cliffs, NJ 07632
607-257-6700
607-277-2953 Fax
Tod Morrow, President
Manufacturers of automotive parts and equipment.

Automotive Parts and Accessories Association
5100 Forbes Blvd.
Lanham, MD 20706
301-459-9110
301-459-8145 Fax
Julian Morris, President
Manufacturers, dealers, and distributors of car parts and accessories.

Automotive Parts Rebuilders Association
6849 Old Dominion Dr., Ste. 352
McLean, VA 22101
703-790-1050
703-790-1057 Fax
William Gager, Executive Vice President
Rebuilders of car and truck parts.

Automotive Service Industry Association
444 N. Michigan Ave.
Chicago, IL 60611-3975
312-836-1300
312-836-1009 Fax
John Nerlinger, President
Representatives of wholesalers and distributors of many automotive products, including parts and equipment.

Motor and Equipment Manufacturers Association
300 Sylvan Ave.
PO Box 1638
Englewood Cliffs, NJ 07632-0638
201-569-8500
201-569-0159 Fax
James Conner, Executive Vice President.
Members manufacture automotive and other heavy-duty equipment and replacement parts. Offers market research services.

PERIODICALS

Aftermarket Business
Edgell Communications
7500 Old Oak Blvd.
Cleveland, OH 44130
216-826-2839
Richard Weinberg, Editor
Offers retailers of automotive aftermarket products with industry news and product descriptions.

Auto Merchandising News
Mortimer Communications, Inc.
Box 1185
Fairfield, CT 06430
203-384-9323
Bill Mortimer, Editor
Advice for retailers of automobile parts and accessories.

Jobber—Retailer
Bill Communications, Inc.
633 Third Ave.
New York, NY 10017
212-986-4800
Mike Mavrigian, Editor
Covers the retail market for automotive equipment and parts.

LIBRARIES

Automotive Service Industry Association
444 N. Michigan Ave.
Chicago, IL 60611-3975
312-836-1300
312-836-1009 Fax
John Nerlinger, President
Automotive parts, equipment, servicing, and related topics.

General Motors Corp.
Delco Products Information Resource Center
2000 Forrer Blvd.
Dayton, OH 45420
513-455-9208
Motor vehicle and automotive equipment manufacturing, marketing, management, and related information.

United Automobile, Aerospace & Agricultural
  Implement Workers of America
Research Library
8000 E. Jefferson Ave.
Detroit, MI 48214
313-926-5386
313-823-6016 Fax
Automotive and motor vehicle equipment economics and collective bargaining and industrial relations.

COMPANIES

Alexander-Seewald Co., Inc.
1420 Seaboard Industrial Blvd., N.W.
Atlanta, GA 30318
404-355-3411
Replacement parts, supplies, and accessories for cars.

Allen Group Inc.
534 Broadhollow Rd.
Melville, NY 11747
516-293-5500
Diagnostic and other equipment used for cars.

BWD Automotive Corp.
(Division of Echlin Inc.)
11045 Gage Ave.
Franklin Park, IL 60131
708-455-3120
A wide variety of automotive replacement parts and testing equipment.

Douglas & Lomason Co.
24600 Hallwood Ct.
Farmington Hills, MI 48335
313-478-7800
Automotive hardware, bumpers, and other products.

Hickok Electrical Instrument Co.
10514 Dupont Ave.
Cleveland, OH 44108
216-541-8060
Automotive diagnostic instrumentation and other products.

Mr. Gasket Co.
8700 Brookpark Rd.
Cleveland, OH 44129
216-398-8300
Automotive accessories and parts.

Monroe Auto Equipment Co.
(Subsidiary of Tenneco Inc.)
International Dr.
Monroe, MI 48161
313-243-8000
Shock absorbers and other automotive ride control equipment.

Motorola, Inc.
1303 E. Algonquin Rd.
Schaumburg, IL 60196
708-397-5000
Electronic equipment for cars and many other products.

Parts, Inc.
(Subsidiary of GKN/Parts Industries Corp.)
601 S. Dudley, Box 429
Memphis, TN 38101
901-523-7711
Distributor of automotive parts, equipment, and supplies.

Sun Electric Corp.
One Sun Pkwy.
Crystal Lake, IL 60014
815-459-7700
Electronic and computerized test equipment for cars.

Underwriters Salvage Co.
1270 W. Northwest Hwy.
Palatine, IL 60067
708-705-9550
Distressed and reclaimed automobiles and parts.

Wickes Companies, Inc.
(Subsidiary of WCI Holdings Corp.)
3340 Ocean Park Blvd., Box 4056
Santa Monica, CA 90405
213-452-0161
Automotive aftermarket products and many other types of products.

FEDERAL GOVERNMENT

U.S. Customs Service
Department of the Treasury
U.S. Customshouse
6 World Trade Center
New York, NY 10048
212-466-5550
Ask for the Commodity Specialist in charge of automobile equipment.

U.S. International Trade Administration
Department of Commerce
14th St. and Constitution Ave., N.W.
Washington, DC 20230
202-377-2000
Ask for the Commodity Analyst who is an expert in automobile equipment.

U.S. International Trade Commission
500 E St., S.W.
Washington, DC 20436
202-205-2000 Office of the Secretary
202-205-3296 Industries locator
Ask for the Trade Analyst who is an expert in automobile equipment.

U.S. Patent and Trademark Office
Crystal Plaza 2
2011 Jefferson Davis Highway
Arlington, VA 22202
703-305-8000
Ask for the Examining Group Director who is a specialist in automobile equipment.

AUTOMOBILE LEASE/RENTAL SERVICES

ASSOCIATIONS

Alliance of State Car and Truck Renting and
    Leasing Associations
2011 I St., N.W., 5th Floor
Washington, DC 20006
202-775-4859
202-457-9121 Fax
Roger Murch, Executive Vice President
Represents renting and leasing associations in over 20 states.

American Automotive Leasing Association
1001 Connecticut Ave. N.W., Ste. 1201
Washington, DC 20036
202-223-2600
202-331-1899 Fax
John Fitch, Executive Director
Companies that offer long-term leases of cars, trucks, and vans for commercial use.

American Car Rental Association
2011 I. St, N.W., 5th Floor
Washington, DC 20006
202-223-2118
Jan Armstrong, Executive Director
Members include car rental companies, licensees, and independent rental agencies.

National Association of Fleet Administrators
120 Wood Ave. S., Ste. 615
Iselin, NJ 08830
201-494-8100
David Lefever, Executive Director
Members include administrators of mid- and large-sized fleets of vehicles.

National Vehicle Leasing Association
P.O. Box 34028
Los Angeles, CA 90034
213-838-3170
Bill Nerenberg, Executive Director
Members are car and truck leasing firms. Offers education and information services about the industry.

PERIODICALS

Auto Age
M H West, Inc.
6633 Odessa Ave.
Van Nuys, CA 91406
818-997-0644
C.D. Bohon, Editor
Information for new-car and truck dealers, manufacturers, finance and leasing firms.

Car Rental & Leasing Insider Newsletter
Atcom, Inc.
Atcom Bldg.
2315 Broadway
New York, NY 10024-4397
212-873-5900
Jim Koscs, Editor
Covers news and trends of interest to executives in the automobile rental and leasing industry.

Vehicle Leasing Today
National Vehicle Leasing Association
3710 S. Robertson Blvd., Ste. 225
Culver City, CA 90232-2349
213-838-3170
Lorraine Alkire, Editor
News about the car and truck leasing business.

LIBRARIES

American Car Rental Association
Library
2011 I. St, N.W., 5th Floor
Washington, DC 20006
202-223-2118
Automobile rental industry.

COMPANIES

Agency Rent-a-Car, Inc.
30000 Aurora Rd.
Solon, OH 44139
216-349-1000
Rents cars and other motor vehicles.

Alamo Rent A Car, Inc.
110 Twr-S.E. 6th St.
Fort Lauderdale, FL 33335
305-463-2604
Rents cars and other motor vehicles.

Avis, Inc.
900 Old Country Rd.
Garden City, NY 11530
516-222-3000
Rents cars and other motor vehicles.

Budget Rent a Car Corp.
200 N. Michigan Ave.
Chicago, IL 60601
312-580-5000
Rents cars and other motor vehicles.

Enterprise Leasing Co.
8850 Ladue Rd.
St. Louis, MO 63124
314-863-7000
Rents cars and other motor vehicles.

Hertz Corp.
225 Brae Blvd.
Park Ridge, NJ 07656
201-307-2000
Rents cars and other motor vehicles.

National Car Rental Systems, Inc.
7700 France Ave. S.
Minneapolis, MN 55435
612-830-2121
Rents cars and other motor vehicles.

Snappy Car Rental, Inc.
P.O. Box 21018
Tulsa, OK 74121
918-621-1100
Rents cars and other motor vehicles.

Thrifty Rent-A-Car System, Inc.
P.O. Box 35250
Tulsa, OK 74153
918-665-3930
Rents cars and other motor vehicles.

FEDERAL GOVERNMENT

Federal Trade Commission
Pennsylvania Ave. at 6th St., N.W.
Washington, DC 20580
202-326-2000
Ask for the Credit Practices Department which is part of the Consumer Protection Bureau.

U.S. International Trade Administration
Department of Commerce
14th St. and Constitution Ave., N.W.
Washington, DC 20230
202-377-2000
Ask for the Commodity Analyst who is an expert in automobile leasing and rental.

AUTOMOTIVE INDUSTRY

See also: AUTOMOBILE DEALERS; AUTOMOBILE EQUIPMENT INDUSTRY; and each of the 50 states under motor vehicles

ASSOCIATIONS

Association of International Automobile Manufacturers
1001 19th St. N., Ste. 1200
Arlington, VA 22209
703-525-7788
703-525-8817 Fax
George Nield, President
A clearinghouse for information about the automobile industry with a special interest in regulatory and legislative matters.

Automotive Industry Action Group
26200 Lahser Rd., Ste. 200
Southfield, MI 48034
313-358-3570
313-358-3253 Fax
Darlene Miller, Managing Director
Promotes engineering standards, competition, and productivity in the automotive industry.

Automotive Information Council
13505 Dulles Technology Dr.
Herndon, VA 22071-3415
703-904-0700
703-904-0727 Fax
Ronald Weiner, President
Represents the automotive industry by offering public relations and information services about numerous automotive topics.

Japan Automobile Manufacturers Association, Washington Office
1050 17th St. N.W., Ste. 410
Washington, DC 20036
202-296-8537
Akihiko Miyoshi, Manager
Provides information about the Japanese auto industry, trade policy, import/export, and related topics.

Motor Vehicle Manufacturers Association of
the United States
7430 2nd Ave., Ste. 300
Detroit, MI 48202
313-872-4311
313-872-5400 Fax
Thomas Hanna, Executive Officer
*Offers information on automotive safety,
energy efficiency, pollution control, legislation,
and other topics.*

PERIODICALS

Automotive Industries
Chilton Co.
Chilton Way
Radnor, PA 19089
215-964-4255
J. McElroy, Editor
*Covers such topics as automobile manufactur-
ing methods, industry sales figures, and man-
agement techniques.*

Automotive News
Crain Communications Inc. (Detroit),
Automotive News
1400 Woodbridge Ave.
Detroit, MI 48207
313-446-6000
Peter Brown, Editor
*Reports news in the fields of automotive engi-
neering, finance, manufacturing, sales, mar-
keting, and servicing.*

AutoWeek
Crain Communications Inc.
1400 Woodridge Ave.
Detroit, MI 48207-3187
313-446-6000
Matt DeLorenzo, Editor
Surveys the automotive industry.

Car and Driver
Hachette Magazines, Inc.
1633 Broadway
New York, NY 10009
212-767-6000
William Jean, Editor
A consumer magazine for car enthusiasts.

LIBRARIES

Automotive Information Council
Library
13505 Dulles Technology Dr.
Herndon, VA 22071-3415
703-904-0700
703-904-0727 Fax
Ronald Weiner, President
*Automotive business, regulations, and other
topics.*

Chrysler Motors
Chrysler Information Resources Center
12000 Chrysler Dr.
Highland Park, MI 48288
313-956-4881
313-353-7858 Fax
*Automotive engineering and the automotive
industry.*

General Motors Corp.
Research Laboratories Library
General Motors Technical Center
30500 Mound Rd.
Warren, MI 48090
313-986-3314
313-986-9378
*Automotive engineering, mechanical engineer-
ing, chemistry, and related sciences.*

University of Michigan
Transportation Research Institute
Research Information & Publications Center
2901 Baxter Rd.
Ann Arbor, MI 48109-2150
313-764-2171
313-936-1081
*Automotive industry, highway safety, accident
investigation, and related information.*

COMPANIES

BMW of North America, Inc.
P.O. Box 1227
Westwood, NJ 07675
201-307-4000

Chrysler Corp.
12000 Chrysler Dr.
Highland Park, MI 48288
313-956-5741

Ford Motor Co.
P.O. Box 1899
Dearborn, MI 48121
313-322-3000

General Motors Corp.
3044 W. Grand Blvd.
Detroit, MI 48202
313-566-5000

Honda of America Manufacturing, Inc.
Honda Pkwy.
Maysville, OH 43040
513-642-5000

Mazda Motor Manufacturing (USA) Corp.
1 Mazda Dr.
Flat Rock, MI 48134
313-782-7800

Mercedes-Benz of North America, Inc.
1 Mercedes Dr.
Montvale, NJ 07645
201-573-0600

Mitsubishi Motor Sales of America, Inc.
6400 Katella Ave.
Cypress, CA 90630
714-372-6000

Nissan Motor Manufacturing Corp. USA
Nissan Dr.
Smyrna, TN 37167
615-459-1400

Subaru of America, Inc.
2235 Rte. 70 W.
Cherry Hill, NJ 08002
609-488-8500

Toyota Motor Manufacturing USA, Inc.
1001 Cherry Blossom
Georgetown, KY 40324
502-868-2000

Volkswagen of America, Inc.
888 W. Big Beaver Rd.
Troy, MI 48007
313-361-6000

Volvo North America Corp.
535 Madison Ave.
New York, NY 10022
212-754-3300

FEDERAL GOVERNMENT

U.S. Customs Service
Department of the Treasury
U.S. Customshouse
6 World Trade Center
New York, NY 10048
212-466-5550
*Ask for the Commodity Specialist in charge of
automobiles.*

U.S. International Trade Administration
Department of Commerce
14th St. and Constitution Ave., N.W.
Washington, DC 20230
202-377-2000
*Ask for the Commodity Analyst who is an
expert in the automotive industry.*

U.S. International Trade Commission
500 E St., S.W.
Washington, DC 20436
202-205-2000 Office of the Secretary
202-205-3296 Industries locator
*Ask for the Trade Analyst who is an expert in
the automotive industry.*

AVIONICS

ASSOCIATIONS

Aircraft Electronics Association
PO Box 1981
Independence, MO 64055
816-373-6565
816-478-3100 Fax
Monte Mitchell, Executive Director
*Firms that design, sell, and service electronic
aviation equipment.*

General Aviation Manufacturers Association
1400 K St. N.W., Ste. 801
Washington, DC 20005
202-393-1500
202-842-4063 Fax
James Gormley, President
*Manufacturers of avionics, airframes, engines,
and components.*

National Avionics Society
PO Box 16322
St. Paul, MN 55116
612-690-1746
John Gera, Secretary
Engineers and others who work with avionics.

PERIODICALS

Aerospace Electronics Business
Phillips Publishing, Inc.
7811 Montrose Rd.
Potomac, MD 20854
301-340-2100
*Information of interest to avionics manufac-
turers.*

Avionics
Phillips Publishing, Inc.
7811 Montrose Rd.
Potomac, MD 20854
301-340-2100
Len Buckwalter, Editor
*Covers industry news and trends for all types
of aircraft avionics.*

Avionics News Magazine
Aircraft Electronics Association
Box 1981
Independence, MO 64055
816-373-6565
Monte Mitchell, Editor
Surveys the avionics industry.

Avionics Newsletter
National Avionics Society
401 W. Chester
Lafayette, CO 80026
Follows avionics technology.

Avionics Review
Belvoir Publications, Inc.
75 Holly Hill Lane
Box 2626
Greenwich, CT 06836-2626
203-661-6111
Perry Gray-Reneberg, Editor
News of technological and business developments.

World Military Avionics Inventory & Forecast
Forecast International Inc.—D M S
Forecast International Inc.
22 Commerce Rd.
Newtown, CT 06470
203-426-0800
Provides in-depth market information about military avionics.

LIBRARIES

U.S. Federal Aviation Administration
Technical Center Library (ACM-651)
Atlantic City International Airport
Atlantic City, NJ 08405
609-484-5772
Avionics, collision avoidance, radar, navigation, and other technical information.

University of Sourthern California
NASA Industrial Application Center (NIAC)
3716 S. Hope St., Rm. 200
Los Angeles, CA 90007-4344
213-743-6132
213-746-9043 Fax
Avionics, biosciences, chemistry, geophysics, and many other subjects regarding air and space travel.

COMPANIES

Base Ten Systems Inc.
One Electronics Dr., Box 3151
Trenton, NJ 08619
609-586-7010
Telemetry and avionics equipment.

Collins Commercial Avionics
(Division of Rockwell International Corp.)
400 Collins Rd. N. E.
Cedar Rapids, IA 52498
319-395-1000
Avionics and other types of equipment for aircraft.

Grumman Electronics Systems Division
(Division of Grumman Corp.)
Bethpage, NY 11714
516-575-0574
Avionics equipment.

Kaiser Aerospace & Electronics Corp.
(Subsidiary of K Systems, Inc.)
950 Tower Lane
Foster City, CA 94404
415-349-7400
Avionics displays and other aerospace products.

Lucas Epsco, Incorporated
(Subsidiary of Lucas Industries Inc.)
99 S. St.
Hopkinton, MA 01748
508-435-2400
Avionics systems and components and other products.

R E A International Corp.
1414 Randolph Ave.
Avenel, NJ 07001
908-382-7100
Avionics equipment.

Sundstrand Data Control, Inc.
(Subsidiary of Sundstrand Corp.)
15001 N.E. 36th St., Box 97001
Redmond, WA 98073
206-885-3711
Avionics and navigation equipment.

FEDERAL GOVERNMENT

U.S. Department of Transportation
400 Seventh St., S.W.
Washington, DC 20590
202-366-4000
Ask for the Federal Aviation Administration.

U.S. International Trade Administration
Department of Commerce
14th St. and Constitution Ave., N.W.
Washington, DC 20230
202-377-2000
*Ask for the Commodity Analyst who is an
expert in avionics.*

U.S. International Trade Commission
500 E St., S.W.
Washington, DC 20436
202-205-2000 Office of the Secretary
202-205-3296 Industries locator
*Ask for the Trade Analyst who is an expert in
avionics.*

U.S. Patent and Trademark Office
Crystal Plaza 2
2011 Jefferson Davis Highway
Arlington, VA 22202
703-305-8000
*Ask for the Examining Group Director who is
a specialist in avionics equipment.*

BAKING INDUSTRY

ASSOCIATIONS

American Bakers Association
1111 14th St. N.W., Ste. 300
Washington, DC 20005
202-296-5800
202-371-0017 Fax
Paul Abenante, President
*A sizable group of baking firms, distributors,
and suppliers to the baking industry.*

American Institute of Baking
1213 Bakers Way
Manhattan, KS 66502
913-537-4750
913-537-1493 Fax
William Hoover, President
*Actively researches new baking products,
techniques, sanitation methods, and more.*

American Society of Bakery Engineers
2 N. Riverside Plaza, Rm. 1733
Chicago, IL 60606
312-332-2246
Robert Fischer, President
Chemists, production managers, engineers, and others interested in the technical side of baking.

Bakery Equipment Manufacturers Association
401 N. Michigan Ave.
Chicago, IL 60611
312-644-6610
312-321-6869 Fax
J. Dollard Carey, Secretary
Members manufacture and service bakery equipment, ovens, and other machinery.

Biscuit and Cracker Manufacturers Association
1400 L St. N.W., Ste. 400
Washington, DC 20005
202-898-1636
Francis Rooney, President
Cookie and cracker bakers, and suppliers to the baking industry.

Independent Bakers Association
1223 Potomac St. N.W.
Washington, DC 20007
202-333-8190
202-337-3809 Fax
Robert Pyle, President
Small- and mid-sized bakers.

Retail Bakers of America
Presidential Bldg., Ste. 250
6525 Belcrest Rd.
Hyattsville, MD 20782
301-277-0990
800-638-0924
301-277-2090 Fax
Richard Gohla, Executive Vice President
Advises bakeries on such subjects as merchandising, production techniques, and store management.

PERIODICALS

B C & T News
Bakery, Confectionery and Tobacco Workers International Union
10401 Connecticut Ave.
Kensington, MD 20895
301-933-8600
News for unionized workers in the baking industry.

Bakery Production and Marketing
Gorman Publishing Co.
Triangle Plaza
8750 W. Bryn Mawr Ave.
Chicago, IL 60631
312-693-3200
Ray Lahvic, Editor
Offers management and marketing advice for retail and wholesale bakers.

Bakery Production and Marketing Red Book
Gorman Publishing Co.
Triangle Plaza
8750 W. Bryn Mawr Ave.
Chicago, IL 60631
312-693-3200
Ray Lahvic, Editor
A listing of products that wholesale bakers and confectioners sell.

Milling & Baking News
Sosland Publishing Co.
4800 Main St., Ste. 100
Kansas City, MO 64112
816-756-1000
Gordon Davidson, Editor
News and trends in the baking industry.

Proceedings of the Annual Meeting American Society of Bakery Engineers
2 N. Riverside Plaza, Ste. 1733
Chicago, IL 60606
312-332-2246
Jan Aaron, Editor
Technical information for bakers.

Retail Bakers of America. Government Bulletin
Retail Bakers of America
6525 Belcrest Rd., Ste. 250
Hyattsville, MD 20782-2096
301-277-0990
Gerard Panaro, Editor
Follows legislative news that affects bakers.

LIBRARIES

American Institute of Baking
Ruth Emerson Library
1213 Bakers Way
Manhattan, KS 66502
913-537-4750
913l-537-1493 Fax
Industry-related science and nutrition.

American Society of Baker Engineers
Information Service and Library
2 N. Riverside Plaza, Rm. 1733
Chicago, IL 60606
312-332-2246
Baking and related topics.

Kansas State University
Grain Science and Industry
Swanson Resource Room
Shellenberger Hall
Manhattan, KS 66506
913-532-6161
913-532-7010 Fax
Baking technology, nutrition, and grain.

COMPANIES

Allied-Lyons North America Corp.
(Subsidiary of Allied-Lyons PLC)
Two Trap Falls Rd.
Huntington, CT 06484
203-925-4400
Bakery goods and baking equipment.

Archer-Daniels-Midland Co.
4666 Faries Pkwy.
Decatur, IL 62525
217-424-5200
Bakery flours and other products used for baking.

CPC International Inc.
International Plaza
Englewood Cliffs, NJ 07632
201-894-4000
Specialty baked goods, baking aids, and many other food products.

DCA Food Industries Inc.
(Subsidiary of J. Lyons Inc.)
919 Third Ave.
New York, NY 10022
212-207-2000
Prepared mixes, including those used for doughnuts, cakes, and many other bakery items.

Dawn Food Products, Inc.
2021 Micor Dr.
Jackson, MI 49203
517-789-4400
A wide range of products and services for the baking industry.

Entenmann's, Inc.
(Subsidiary of General Foods Corp.)
1724 Fifth Ave.
Bay Shore, NY 11706
516-273-6000
Bakers and distributors of bakery products.

Flowers Industries, Inc.
U.S. Highway 19 S., P.O. Box 1338
Thomasville, GA 31799
912-226-9110
Wholesale bakery products and other foods.

Interstate Bakeries Corp.
(Subsidiary of IBC Holdings Corp.)
P.O. Box 1627
Kansas City, MO 64141
816-561-6600
Baker of bread, cakes, and doughnuts.

Merico Inc.
(Subsidiary of Campbell Taggart, Inc.)
1820 N. Josey Lane
Carrollton, TX 75006
214-416-4385
Producer of snack cakes, crackers, refrigerated dough, and other items.

Ralston Purina Co.
Checkerboard Sq.
St. Louis, MO 63164
314-982-1000
Bakery products and many other consumer goods.

FEDERAL GOVERNMENT

U.S. International Trade Administration
Department of Commerce
14th St. and Constitution Ave., N.W.
Washington, DC 20230
202-377-2000
Ask for the Commodity Analyst who is an expert in the baking industry.

U.S. International Trade Commission
500 E St., S.W.
Washington, DC 20436
202-205-2000 Office of the Secretary
202-205-3296 Industries locator
Ask for the Trade Analyst who is an expert in the baking industry.

BANKRUPTCY

ASSOCIATIONS

American Bankruptcy Institute
510 C St. N.E.
Washington, DC 20002
202-543-1234
202-543-2764 Fax
Caroline Rossanda, Administrator
Lawyers, accountants, lenders, government officials, and others who exchange information about bankruptcy.

American College of Bankruptcy
510 C St. N.E.
Washington, DC 20002
202-546-6725
202-543-2762 Fax
Richard Gitlin, Executive Officer
A small group that honors attorneys and others who distinguish themselves in the bankruptcy field.

National Association of Bankruptcy Trustees
3008 Millwood Ave.
Columbia, SC 29205
803-252-5646
Carol Davis, Executive Secretary
*Court-appointed trustees, bankers, and others
involved with companies in bankruptcy.*

Turnaround Management Association
1152 Executive Circle, Ste. 203
Carey, NC 27511
919-481-1888
919-969-0200 Fax
David Post, Executive Director
*Individuals and firms that help manage busi-
nesses facing bankruptcy and other serious
problems.*

PERIODICALS

Bankruptcy Strategist
Leader Publications, Inc.
111 8th Ave., Ste. 900
New York, NY 10011
800-888-8300
Herbert Schlagman, Editor
*Information and advice for attorneys practic-
ing bankruptcy law.*

Law & Business Directory of Bankruptcy
    Attorneys 1992
Prentice Hall Law & Business
270 Sylvan Ave.
Englewood Cliffs, NJ 07632-2513
201-894-8484
Lynn LoPucki, Editor
*Lists most of the bankruptcy attorneys prac-
ticing in the U.S.*

NCLC Reports: Bankruptcy & Foreclosures
National Consumer Law Center
11 Beacon St., Ste. 821
Boston, MA 02108
617-523-8010
Kathleen Keest, Editor
*Follows trends in consumer law, with a special
interest in foreclosures and bankruptcy.*

National Bankruptcy Reporter
Andrews Publications
1646 West Chester Pike
Box 1000
Westtown, PA 19395
215-399-6600
Aleka Agapitides, Editor
Reports on new business bankruptcies.

LIBRARIES

American Bankruptcy Institute
Library
510 C St. N.E.
Washington, DC 20002
202-543-1234
202-543-2764 Fax
Bankruptcy and related topics.

BANKS AND BANKING

See also: each of the 50 states under banking

ASSOCIATIONS

American Bankers Association
1120 Connecticut Ave. N.W.
Washington, DC 20036
202-663-5000
202-663-5430 Banker Education Network
800-872-7747 Financial Information
800-424-2871 News Service
202-637-8983 Fax
Don Ogilvie, Executive Vice President
*By far the largest banking association in the
U.S. Offers information services through its
huge library and training programs through
the American Institute of Banking, and
engages in many other activities.*

The American Safe Deposit Association
c/o Joyce A. McLin
330 W. Main St.
Greenwood, IN 46142
317-888-1118
Joyce McLin, Executive Manager
*Represents associations of banks and other
institutions who offer safe deposit services.*

Association of Bank Holding Companies
730 15th St. N.W.
Washington, DC 20005
202-393-1158
Thomas Ashley, President
*Members are bank holding companies regis-
tered with the Federal Reserve Board.*

Bank Administration Institute
2550 W. Golf Rd.
Rolling Meadows, IL 60008
708-228-6200
800-323-8552
708-228-2426 Fax
Ronald Burke, President
*A major information source for bankers
regarding administration, management, and
bank technology.*

Bank Capital Markets Association
Natl. Press Bldg., Ste. 200
Washington, DC 20045
202-347-5510
202-347-6211 Fax
Thomas Rideout, Executive Director
*Includes commercial banks that deal in certain
securities, money market instruments, and foreign exchange.*

Banking Law Institute
22 W. 21st St.
New York, NY 10010
212-645-7880
800-223-0787
James Slabe, Executive Vice President
*Acts as an clearinghouse for information on
regulations and laws governing banks and
other financial institutions.*

Bank Marketing Association
309 W. Washington St.
Chicago, IL 60606
312-782-1442
800-433-9013
J. Douglas Adamson, Executive Vice President
Marketing specialists and public relations executives who work for banks and the advertising agencies who serve banks.

Electronic Funds Transfer Association
1421 Prince St., Ste. 310
Alexandria, VA 22314
703-549-9800
703-683-7614 Fax
Sean Kennedy, President
Banks, retailers, telecommunications firms, and others who use or provide electronic funds transfer systems.

Independent Bankers Association of America
1 Thomas Circle N.W., Ste. 950
Washington, DC 20005
202-659-8111
800-422-8439 Library Research Services
800-422-7285 Seminar and Convention Information
Kenneth Guenther, Executive Vice President
Represents many of the small- and mid-sized community banks in the U.S.

Institute of Financial Education
111 E. Wacker Dr.
Chicago, IL 60601-4680
312-644-3100
312-856-0497 Fax
Dale Bottom, President
Offers courses for executives in banks and credit unions.

Mortgage Bankers Association of America
1125 15th St. N.W.
Washington, DC 20005
202-861-6500
Warren Lasko, Executive Vice President
Firms involved with the financing of mortgages, including banks, title companies, S & L assocations, and life insurance companies.

National Association of Bank Women
500 N. Michigan Ave., Ste. 1400
Chicago, IL 60611
312-661-1700
Susan Rex, President
A very large group representing women bankers nationwide.

National Second Mortgage Association
8300 Utica Ave., Ste. 173
Rancho Cucamonga, CA 91730
714-941-7080
714-941-8248 Fax
Jeffrey Zeltzer, Executive Director
Banks, finance companies, and others who offer second mortgages and support services.

PERIODICALS

A B A Banking Journal
American Bankers Association
Simmons-Boardman Publishing Corp.
345 Hudson St.
New York, NY 10014-4502
212-620-7200
William Streeter, Editor
Surveys news, products, and trends in the banking industry.

American Bank Directory
McFadden Business Publications
6195 Crooked Creek Rd.
Norcross, GA 30092
404-448-1011
A listing of banks in the U.S.

American Banker
Thomson Publishing Corp.
One State St. Plaza
New York, NY 10004
800-221-1809
Thomas Ferris, Editor
Covers issues that interest the financial community.

Bank Director
Private Business Inc.
Box 1603
Brentwood, TN 37024
615-371-9095
E. Thomas Wood, Editor
Offers advice on interstate banking, sales of credit card portfolios, and many other topics.

Bank Management
Bank Administration Institute
60 E. Gould Center
2550 Golf Rd.
Rolling Meadows, IL 60008
312-228-6200
J. Christopher Svave, Editor
Provides senior bank executives with management advice.

Bank New Product News
Faulkner & Gray, Inc.
118 S. Clinton St., Ste. 450
Chicago, IL 60606
312-648-0264
Reports on new technology and other products that improve banking practices.

Bankers Magazine
Warren, Gorham and Lamont Inc.
One Penn Plaza
New York, NY 10119
800-950-1217
Richard Miller, Editor
Provides the advice and how-to suggestions of important bankers on a wide range of issues.

Bankers Monthly
Hanover Publishers, Inc.
200 W. 57th St.
New York, NY 10019
212-399-1084
R.B. Slater, Editor
Follows industry trends and management practices.

Commercial Lending Newsletter
Robert Morris Associates
One Liberty Place, Ste. 2300
1650 Market St.
Philadelphia, PA 19103
215-851-9100
Luis Morales, Editor
Information for bank officers responsible for commerial lending.

Computers in Banking
Dealers Digest Inc.
2 World Trade Center, 18th Fl.
New York, NY 10048
212-227-1200
Brian Tracey, Editor
Covers all facets of bank automation.

Journal of Commercial Bank Lending
Robert Morris Associates
One Liberty Place, Ste. 2300
1650 Market St.
Philadelphia, PA 19107
215-851-9100
Charlotte Weisman, Editor
Covers the world of commercial and institutional lending.

Mortgage Banking
Mortgage Bankers Association of America
1125 15th St., N.W.
Washington, DC 20005
202-861-6555
Richard Helgerson, Editor
Reviews issues of concern to mortgage bankers.

Polk's Bank Directory. North American Edition
R. L. Polk & Co.,
Box 305100
Nashville, TN 37230-5100
615-889-3350
A complete listing of banks in North America.

LIBRARIES

American Banker, Inc.
Editorial Library
One State St. Plaza
New York, NY 10004
212-943-4844
Banks and banking.

American Bankers Association
Center for Banking Information
1120 Connecticut Ave., N.W.
Washington, DC 20036
202-663-5221
212-828-4535 Fax
Banking, finance, law, and related topics.

Citicorp/Citibank
Citiinformation
399 Park Ave., 4th Fl.
New York, NY 10022
212-559-1000
Banking, investment, economics, and related topics.

FEDERAL RESERVE BANKS

Board of Governors of the Federal Reserve
    System
Washington, DC 20551
202-452-3244

Federal Reserve Bank Atlanta
Public Information Dept.
104 Marietta Street, N.W.
Atlanta, GA 30303-2713
404-521-8788

Federal Reserve Bank Boston
Public Services Dept.
P.O. Box 2076
Boston, MA 02106-2076
617-973-3459

Federal Reserve Bank Chicago
Public Information Center
230 S. LaSalle Street
Chicago, IL 60690
312-322-5111

Federal Reserve Bank Cleveland
Public Affairs Dept.
P.O. Box 6387
Cleveland, OH 44101-1387
216-579-3079

Federal Reserve Bank Dallas
Public Affairs Dept.
Station K
Dallas, TX 75222
214-651-6289 or 6266

Federal Reserve Bank Kansas City
Public Affairs Dept.
925 Grand Avenue
Kansas City, MO 64198
816-881-2402

Federal Reserve Bank Minneapolis
Public Affairs Dept.
250 Marquette Avenue
Minneapolis, MN 55480
612-340-2446

Federal Reserve Bank New York
Public Information Dept.
33 Liberty Street
New York, NY 10045
212-720-6134

Federal Reserve Bank Philadelphia
Public Information Dept.
P.O. Box 66
Philadelphia, PA 19105
215-574-6115

Federal Reserve Bank Richmond
Public Services Dept.
P.O. Box 27622
Richmond, VA 23261
804-697-8109

Federal Reserve Bank St. Louis
Public Information Office
P.O. Box 442
St. Louis, MO 63166
314-444-8444

Federal Reserve Bank San Francisco
Public Information Dept.
P.O. Box 7702
San Francisco, CA 94120
415-974-2163

COMMERCIAL BANKS

BankAmerica Corp.
P.O. Box 37002
San Francisco, CA 94137
415-622-3456

Chase Manhattan Corp.
1 Chase Manhattan Plaza
New York, NY 10081
212-552-2222

Citicorp
399 Park Ave.
New York, NY 10043
212-559-1000

JP Morgan and Co., Inc.
60 Wall St.
New York, NY 10260
212-483-2323

NCNB Corp.
1 NCNB Plz.
Charlotte, NC 28255
704-374-5000

Security Pacific Corp.
333 S. Hope St.
Los Angeles, CA 90071
213-345-6211

FEDERAL GOVERNMENT

U.S. Department of the Treasury
1500 Pennsylvania Ave., N.W.
Washington, DC 20220
202-566-2111
*Ask for the Financial Institution Policy Office
or the Bank Organization & Structure department.*

BARBER AND BEAUTY SHOPS

ASSOCIATIONS

American Beauty Association
401 N. Michigan Ave.
Chicago, IL 60611
312-644-6610
312-565-4658 Fax
Paul Dykstra, Executive Director
*Members include manufacturers and others
who sell products used in beauty and barber
shops.*

Association of Cosmetologists and Hair-
    dressers
1811 Monroe
Dearborn, MI 48124
313-563-0360
Mary Ann Neuman, President
*Beauticians, cosmetics professionals, and man-
ufacturers.*

Beauty and Barber Supply Institute
271 Rt. 46 W., Ste. F-209
Fairfield, NJ 07004
201-808-7444
201-808-9099 Fax
Frederic Polk, Executive Director
*Serves manufacturers and distributors of
equipment and supplies used in beauty salons
and barber shops.*

National Beauty Culturists' League
25 Logan Circle N.W.
Washington, DC 20005
202-332-2695
Cleolif Richardson, President
*Offers information to beauticians, cosmetolo-
gists, and others.*

World International Nail and Beauty Associa-
    tion
1221 N. Lake View
Anaheim, CA 92807
714-779-9883
714-779-9971 Fax
Jim George, President
Represents the nail- and skin-care industries.

PERIODICALS

American Salon
National Cosmetology Association
Edgell Communications
270 Madison Ave.
New York, NY 10016
212-951-6600
Jayne Morehouse, Editor
*Offer technical and management information
to full-service salons.*

Beauty Age
113 W. 85th St.
New York, NY 10024
212-580-2756
Paul Cohen, Editor
*Reports on new cosmetics, accessories, and
fragrances.*

IFMT Magazine
Andres Aquino, Editor
Aquino Productions
One Bank St., Ste.201
Box 15760
Stamford, CT 06901
203-978-0562
Eileen McCarthy, Editor
*Follows news about fashion photographers,
models, designers, and make-up artists.*

Modern Salon
Vance Publishing Corp.
400 Knightsbridge Parkway
Lincolnshire, IL 60069
708-634-2600
Mary Atherton, Editor
Reports on business practices and new hair styles.

LIBRARIES

Association of Cosmetologists and Hairdressers
1811 Monroe
Dearborn, MI 48124
313-563-0360
Beauty culture, beauty products, and related topics.

COMPANIES

Aerial Co., Inc.
116 Hosmer St.
Marinette, WI 54143
715-735-9323
Beauty and barber supplies.

Burmax Co., Inc.
939 Motor Pkwy.
Hauppauge, NY 11788
516-582-9797
Wholesaler of beauty and barber suppliers.

Chicago Hair Goods Co.
428 S. Wabash Ave.
Chicago, IL 60605
312-427-8600
Beauty shop equipment and supplies.

Fromm Industries
8040 Ridgeway Ave.
Skokie, IL 60076
708-982-9292
Combs, brushes, and other tools used by beauticians and barbers.

Helene Curtis Industries, Inc.
325 N. Wells St.
Chicago, IL 60610
312-661-0222
Beauty shop supplies, beauty equipment, skincare products, shampoos, conditioners, and toiletries.

Koken Manufacturing Co., Inc.
(Subsidiary of Takara Co. New York Inc.)
1631 Dr. Martin Luther King Dr.
St. Louis, MO 63106
314-231-7383
Equipment used in barber and beauty shops.

Oster/Sunbeam Appliance Co.
(Subsidiary of Allegheny International Inc.)
5055 N. Lydell Ave.
Milwaukee, WI 53217
414-332-8300
Hair clippers and other tools used in beauty and barber shops.

Smith Investment Co.
P.O. Box 23976
Milwaukee, WI 53223
414-359-4030
Barber and beauty shop equipment.

BARTER AND COUNTERTRADE

ASSOCIATIONS

International Reciprocal Trade Association
5152 Woodmire Ln.
Alexandria, VA 22311
703-931-0105
703-931-4010 Fax
Paul Suplizio, Executive Director
Provides information on barter.

PERIODICALS

Barter Communique
Full Circle Marketing Corp.
Box 2527
Sarasota, FL 33578
813-349-3300
Robert Murley, Editor
Reports on barter opportunities and techniques.

Barter Update
Update Publicare Co.
c/o Prosperity & Profits Unlimited
Distribution Services
Box 570213
Houston, TX 77257-0213
Barter information for small businesses.

BarterNews
BarterNews Publications
Box 3024
Mission Viejo, CA 92690
714-831-0607
Bob Meyer, Editor
Includes barter listings and how-to advice for corporate marketers.

Countertrade Outlook
D P Publications Co.
Box 7188
Fairfax Sta., VA 22039
703-425-1322
Michael Morrison, Editor
Follows unconventional reciprocal trade deals around the world.

LIBRARIES

International Reciprocal Trade Association
5152 Woodmire Ln.
Alexandria, VA 22311
703-931-0105
703-931-4010 Fax
Barter and countertrade.

COMPANIES

Atwood Richards, Inc.
99 Park Ave.
New York, NY 10016
212-490-1414
Advertising barter.

Barter Advantage, Inc.
1751 2nd Ave.
New York, NY 10028
212-534-7500
Barter services.

Barter Exchange, Inc.
1106 Clayton Ln.
Austin, TX 78723
512-467-9989
Barter services.

Integrated Barter International, Inc.
210 E. 39th St.
New York, NY 10016
212-685-0066
Barter specialists.

Lino & Associates
5665 Central Ave.
St. Petersburg, FL 33710
813-384-3700
Reciprocal trading and barter.

Transmedia Network Inc.
509 Madison Ave.
New York, NY 10022
212-308-7676
Media bartering.

FEDERAL GOVERNMENT

U.S. Department of Agriculture
14th St. and Independence Ave., S.W.
Washington, DC 20250
202-720-8732
Ask for the Foreign Agriculture Service expert in barter or countertrade.

BATTERY INDUSTRY

See also: AUTOMOBILE EQUIPMENT INDUSTRY

ASSOCIATIONS

Association of Battery Recyclers
Sanders Lead Co. Corp.
Sanders Rd.
PO Drawer 707
Troy, AL 36081
205-566-1563
N. Kenneth Campbell, Executive Secretary
Firms that recycle the components of old batteries.

Battery Council International
111 E. Wacker Dr.
Chicago, IL 60601
312-644-6610
312-565-4658 Fax
Edward Craft, Executive Secretary
Manufacturers and distributors of lead-acid storage batteries.

Independent Battery Manufacturers Association
100 Larchwood Dr.
Largo, FL 34640
813-586-1408
813-586-1400 Fax
Celwyn Hopkins, Executive Secretary
Manufacturers of lead-acid storage batteries.

PERIODICALS

Advanced Battery Technology
Robert Morey Associates
Box 30
Cooperstown, NY 13326-0030
607-547-5314
Robert Morey, Editor
Reports on advances in battery research.

B C I News
Battery Council International
401 N. Michigan Ave.
Chicago, IL 60611
312-644-6610
Larry Fleischman, Editor
Covers industry news for manufacturers.

Battery Man
Independent Battery Manufacturers Association, Inc.
100 Larchwood Dr.
Largo, FL 34640
813-586-1408
Celwyn Hopkins, Editor
Focuses on the servicing of automobile electrical systems.

C A Selects. Batteries & Fuel Cells
Chemical Abstracts Service
2540 Olentangy River Rd.
Box 3012
Columbus, OH 43210
614-447-3600
Reports on technological advances in the design and manufacture of batteries and their components. Also covers battery recyling.

Industry Statistics
Battery Council International
401 N. Michigan Ave.
Chicago, IL 60611
312-644-6610
Provides annual statistics about batteries.

LIBRARIES

Duracell WTC
Technical Information Center
37 A St.
Needham Heights, MA 02194-2806
617-449-7600
617-449-7613 Fax
Batteries, electrochemistry, and related topics.

Eveready Battery Co., Inc.
Technical Information Center
25225 Detroit Rd.
Westlake, OH 44145
216-835-7641
216-835-7772 Fax
Batteries.

Rayovac Corp.
Technology Center Library
601 Rayovac Dr.
Madison, WI 53711-2497
608-275-4714
608-275-4992 Fax
Batteries, electrochemistry, and chemical engineering.

COMPANIES

C & D Power Systems, Inc.
3043 Walton Rd.
Plymouth Meeting, PA 19462
215-828-9000
Industrial batteries and chargers.

Charter Power Systems, Inc.
3043 Walton Rd.
Plymouth Meeting, PA 19462
215-828-9000
Batteries and chargers for consumers and industry.

Duracell Inc.
Berkshire Industrial Park
Bethel, CT 06801
203-796-4000
Consumer batteries.

East Penn Manufacturing Co.
Deka Rd.
Lyon Station, PA 19536
215-682-6361
Electric storage batteries and accessories.

Eveready Battery Co.
Checkerboard Sq.
St. Louis, MO 63164
314-982-1000
Various types of batteries.

Exide Corp.
P.O. Box 14205
Reading, PA 19612
215-378-0500
Industrial and automotive batteries.

Gates Corp.
900 S. Broadway
Denver, CO 80209
303-744-1911
Automotive batteries and other products.

GNB, Inc.
P.O. Box 64100
St. Paul, MN 55164
612-681-5000
Various types of batteries.

Ralston Purina Co.
Checkerboard Sq.
St. Louis, MO 63164
314-982-1000
Consumer batteries and many other products.

Rayovac Corp.
601 Rayovac Dr., Box 4960
Madison, WI 53711
608-275-3340
Dry cell batteries and lamps.

Western Auto Supply Co.
(Subsidiary of Sears, Roebuck and Co.)
2107 Grand Ave.
Kansas City, MO 64108
816-346-4000
Retailer of automobile accessories, including batteries.

FEDERAL GOVERNMENT

U.S. Customs Service
Department of the Treasury
U.S. Customshouse
6 World Trade Center
New York, NY 10048
212-466-5550
Ask for the Commodity Specialist in charge of batteries.

U.S. International Trade Administration
Department of Commerce
14th St. and Constitution Ave., N.W.
Washington, DC 20230
202-377-2000
Ask for the Commodity Analyst who is an expert in the battery industry.

U.S. International Trade Commission
500 E St., S.W.
Washington, DC 20436
202-205-2000 Office of the Secretary
202-205-3296 Industries locator
Ask for the Trade Analyst who is an expert in the battery industry.

U.S. Patent and Trademark Office
Crystal Plaza 2
2011 Jefferson Davis Highway
Arlington, VA 22202
703-305-8000
Ask for the Examining Group Director who is a specialist in batteries.

BEARINGS AND BALL BEARINGS

ASSOCIATIONS

Anti-Friction Bearing Manufacturers Association
1101 Connecticut Ave. N.W., Ste. 700
Washington, DC 20036
202-429-5155
202-223-4579 Fax
Michael Payne, President
Manufacturers of anti-friction bearings and the parts used in making bearings.

Ball Manufacturers Engineers Committee
1101 Connecticut Ave. N.W., Ste. 700
Washington, DC 20036-4303
202-429-5155
202-775-2625 Fax
Gary Satterfield, Technical Director
Engineers who construct balls for use in bearings.

Bearing Specialists Association
Bldg. C, Ste. 20
800 Roosevelt Rd.
Glen Ellyn, IL 60137
708-858-3838
708-790-3095 Fax
Richard Church, Executive Director
Wholesalers of anti-friction bearings.

PERIODICALS

Power Transmission Design
Penton Publishing
1100 Superior Ave.
Cleveland, OH 44114-2543
216-696-7000
Phil Kingsley, Editor
Offers practical and technical information on bearings, motors, transmissions, and related subjects.

LIBRARIES

MRC Bearings Inc.
Research & Development Technical Library
402 Chandler St.
Jamestown, NY 14701
716-661-2812
Ball bearings and related topics.

Timken Co.
Research Library
1835 Deuber Ave.
Canton, OH 44706
216-497-2049
216-497-2282 Fax
Bearing design, engineering research, and other topics.

COMPANIES

Bearings, Inc.
P.O. Box 6925
Cleveland, OH 44101
216-881-2838
Ball and linear motion bearings.

Detroit Ball Bearing Co. of Michigan
(Subsidiary of Invetech Co.)
1400 Howard St.
Detroit, MI 48216
313-963-6011
Ball, roller, thrust bearings, and other products.

Federal-Mogul
P. O. Box 1966
Detroit, MI 48235
313-354-7700
Bearings and many other types of products.

Ingersoll-Rand Co.
200 Chestnut Ridge Rd.
Woodcliff Lake, NJ 07675
201-573-0123
Antifriction bearings and many other products.

MPB Corp.
(Subsidiary of Timken Co.)
P. O. Box 547
Keene, NH 03431
603-352-0310
Ball and roller bearings and bearing assemblies.

New Hampshire Ball Bearings, Inc.
(Subsidiary of NMB USA)
Rte. 202
Peterborough, NH 03458
603-924-3311
Various types of bearings and sub-assemblies.

SKF USA, Inc.
(Subsidiary of AB SKF)
1100 First Ave.
King of Prussia, PA 19406
215-962-4300
Rolling bearings and accessories.

Timken Co.
1835 Dueber Ave, S. W.
Canton, OH 44706
216-438-3000
Tapered roller bearings and other products.

FEDERAL GOVERNMENT

U.S. Customs Service
Department of the Treasury
U.S. Customshouse
6 World Trade Center
New York, NY 10048
212-466-5550
Ask for the Commodity Specialist in charge of bearings or ball bearings.

U.S. Patent and Trademark Office
Crystal Plaza 2
2011 Jefferson Davis Highway
Arlington, VA 22202
703-305-8000
Ask for the Examining Group Director who is a specialist in bearings or ball bearings.

BEVERAGE INDUSTRY

See also: COFFEE AND TEA INDUSTRY

ASSOCIATIONS

Beverage Network
4437 Concord
Skokie, IL 60076
708-673-4614
Russell Hopkins, President
Represents distributors who offer non-alcoholic beverages, primarily from new and small manufacturers.

Carbonated Beverage Institute
1101 16th St. N.W.
Washington, DC 20036
202-463-6745
Donald Prescott, Administrator
Bottlers of carbonated beverages.

Cider Association of North America
North Branch Cider Mill
Main St.
PO Box 13
North Branch, NY 12766
717-224-6154
Robert Bernthal, President
Apple cider producers.

Coffee Development Group
1400 I St. N.W., Ste. 650
Washington, DC 20005
202-682-4034
Mike Levin, President
Represents coffee suppliers in the U.S.

International Bottled Water Association
113 N. Henry St.
Alexandria, VA 22314
703-683-5213
703-683-4074 Fax
William Deal, Executive Vice President
Members include water bottling plants and suppliers to the industry.

National Beverage Dispensing Equipment Association
2011 I St. N.W., 5th Fl.
Washington, DC 20006
202-775-4885
202-457-9121 Fax
Pamela Boyajian, Executive Director
Companies that sell and service equipment for dispensing all kinds of drinks.

National Coffee Association of U.S.A.
110 Wall St.
New York, NY 10005
212-344-5596
212-425-7059 Fax
Robert N. DeChillo, Secretary
Coffee importers, brokers, processors, and roasters who share information about the industry.

National Juice Products Association
PO Box 1531
215 Madison St.
Tampa, FL 33601
813-229-1089
813-224-9060 Fax
David Kerr, Secretary
Members include juice processors, brokers, and suppliers of containers.

National Soft Drink Association
1101 16th St. N.W.
Washington, DC 20036
202-463-6732
202-463-6731 Fax
William Ball, President
Soft drink bottlers and manufacturers of bottling equipment and supplies.

Tea Council of the United States of America
230 Park Ave.
New York, NY 10169
212-986-6998
Donald Wiederecht, Executive Director
Represents the world's leading tea boards and associations.

PERIODICALS

Beverage Beacon—Ledger
Evans Publishing
6601 S. Hoover St.
Los Angeles, CA 90044-3695
213-778-2522
Richard Evans, Editor
Covers most facets of the non-alcoholic beverage industry.

Beverage Industry
Edgell Communications
7500 Old Oak Blvd.
Cleveland, OH 44130
216-826-2839
Gary Hemphill, Editor
Provides information on marketing and distribution.

Beverage World
Keller International Publishing Corp.
150 Great Neck Rd.
Great Neck, NY 11021
516-829-9210
Larry Jabbonsky, Editor
Covers alcoholic and non-alcoholic beverages.

Beverage World's Databank
Keller International Publishing Corp.
150 Great Neck Rd.
Great Neck, NY 11021
516-829-9210
Sandy Beckerman, Editor
A directory of the beverage industry.

U S Non-Alcoholic Beverage Market: Impact
    Databank Review and Forecast
M. Shanken Communications, Inc.
387 Park Ave. So.
New York, NY 10016
212-684-4224
Lynn Rittenband
Market research for non-alcoholic beverages in the U.S.

LIBRARIES

Coca-Cola Co.
Technical Information Services
Drawer 1734
Atlanta, GA 30301
404-676-2008
404-676-5010 Fax
Beverages, food technology, and the beverage industry.

Pepsico
Information Access Center
100 Stevens Ave.
Valhalla, NY 10595
914-742-4882
914-742-4501 Fax
Beverages, food science, nutrition, and related topics.

COMPANIES

Arrowhead Mountain Spring Water Co.
601 E. Potrero Grande
Monterey Park, CA 91754
213-888-8000
Water and other beverages.

Brooks Beverage Management, Inc.
777 Brooks Ave.
Holland, MI 49423
616-396-1281
Soda and other beverages.

Cadbury Beverages, Inc.
P.O. Box 3800
Stamford, CT 06905
203-329-0911
Soda and other beverages.

Coca-Cola Enterprises, Inc.
1 Coca-Cola Plz. N.W.
Atlanta, GA 30313
404-676-2100
Soda and other beverages.

Delta Beverage Group
860 Ridge Lake Blvd.
Memphis, TN 38187
901-682-5660
Soda and other beverages.

LaCroix Water Co.
100 Harborview Plz.
LaCrosse, WI 54602
608-785-1000
Water and other beverages.

National Beverage Corp.
P.O. Box 16720
Fort Lauderdale, FL 33318
305-581-0922
Soda and other beverages.

Pepsi-Cola Co.
Rte. 100
Somers, NY 10589
914-767-6000
Soda and other beverages.

Royal Crown Cola Co.
6917 Collins Ave.
Miami Beach,FL 33141
305-876-3281
Soda and other beverages.

Shasta Beverages Inc.
26901 Industrial Blvd.
Hayward, CA 94545
510-783-3200
Soda and other beverages.

FEDERAL GOVERNMENT

U.S. Customs Service
Department of the Treasury
U.S. Customshouse
6 World Trade Center
New York, NY 10048
212-466-5550
Ask for the Commodity Specialist in charge of beverage products.

U.S. International Trade Administration
Department of Commerce
14th St. and Constitution Ave., N.W.
Washington, DC 20230
202-377-2000
Ask for the Commodity Analyst who is an expert in the beverage industry.

U.S. International Trade Commission
500 E St., S.W.
Washington, DC 20436
202-205-2000 Office of the Secretary
202-205-3296 Industries locator
Ask for the Trade Analyst who is an expert in the beverage industry.

BICYCLE INDUSTRY

See also: SPORTING GOODS INDUSTRY

ASSOCIATIONS

Bicycle Institute of America
1818 R St. N.W.
Washington, DC 20009
202-332-6986
212-332-6989 Fax
William Wilkinson, Executive Director.
Bicycle manufacturers, importers, dealers, and sponsors of races. Its Cycling News Service offers information on the industry.

Bicycle Manufacturers Association of America
3050 K St. N.W., Ste. 400
Washington, DC 20007
202-944-9297
202-338-5534 Fax
Thomas Shannon, Executive Director
A small group of domestic manufacturers.

Cycle Parts and Accessories Association
181 Salem Rd.
East Hills, NY 11577
516-484-7194
John Auerbach, Director
Represents suppliers of components for bicycles.

National Bicycle Dealers Association
129 Cabrillo St., Ste. 201
Costa Mesa, CA 92627
714-722-6909
714-722-6975 Fax
Steve Ready, Executive Director
Retailers who sell and service bikes.

PERIODICALS

American Bicyclist & Motorcyclist
Cycling Press, Inc.
80 Eighth Ave.
New York, NY 10011
212-206-7230
Konstantin Doren, Editor
Industry news for bicycle dealers, distributors, importers, and manufacturers.

Bicycle Dealer Showcase
Miramar Publishing Co.
Box 3640
Culver City, CA 90231-3640
213-337-9717
Walt Jarvis, Editor
Advice on how to sell bicycles and mopeds.

Bicycle Dealer Showcase Buyers Guide
Miramar Publishing Co.
Box 3640
Culver City, CA 90231-3640
213-337-9717
Walt Jarvis, Editor
Listing of products and manufacturers.

Bicycle Guide
Raben Publishing Co.
711 Boylston St.
Boston, MA 02116
617-236-1885
Theodore Constantino, Editor
A consumer magazine.

Bicycling
Rodale Press, Inc.
33 E. Minor St.
Emmaus, PA 18098
215-967-5171
Ed Pavelka, Editor
A consumer magazine.

Cycle World
Diamandis Communications, Inc.
1633 Broadway
New York, NY 10009
212-767-6000
Dave Edwards, Editor
A consumer magazine.

COMPANIES

American Cycle Systems, Inc.
P.O. Box 2597
City of Industry, CA 91746
818-961-3942
Bicycles and accessories.

Cycle Composites, Inc.
265 Westridge Dr.
Watsonville, CA 95076
408-724-9079
Bicycles and accessories.

Greendale Bicycle Co.
5610 S. Division St.
Grand Rapids, MI 49548
616-530-5556
Bicycles and accessories.

Huffy Corp.
Huffy Bicycle Div.
P.O. Box 318
Celina, OH 45822
419-586-5171
Bicycles and accessories.

Rand International, Inc.
Ross Bicycles U.S.A. Ltd.
51 Executive Blvd.
Farmingdale, NY 11735
516-249-6000
Bicycles and accessories.

Schwinn Bicycle Co.
217 N. Jefferson St.
Chicago, IL 60606
312-454-7400
Bicycles and accessories.

Trek Bicycle Corp.
P.O. Box 183
Waterloo, WI 53594
414-478-2191
Bicycles and accessories.

FEDERAL GOVERNMENT

U.S. Customs Service
Department of the Treasury
U.S. Customshouse
6 World Trade Center
New York, NY 10048
212-466-5550
*Ask for the Commodity Specialist in charge of
bicycles.*

U.S. International Trade Administration
Department of Commerce
14th St. and Constitution Ave., N.W.
Washington, DC 20230
202-377-2000
*Ask for the Commodity Analyst who is an
expert in the bicycle industry.*

U.S. International Trade Commission
500 E St., S.W.
Washington, DC 20436
202-205-2000 Office of the Secretary
202-205-3296 Industries locator
*Ask for the Trade Analyst who is an expert in
the bicycle industry.*

BIOTECHNOLOGY

ASSOCIATIONS

Association of Biotechnology Companies
1666 Connecticut Ave. N.W., Ste. 330
Washington, DC 20009-1039
202-234-3330
800-435-9222
202-234-3565 Fax
Dr. Pamela Bridgen, Executive Director
Firms researching biotechnology in the fields of health care, veterinary medicine, and industrial chemicals.

Industrial Biotechnology Association
1625 K St. N.W., Ste. 1100
Washington, DC 20006
202-857-0244
202-857-0237 Fax
Richard Godown, President
Pharmaceutical, chemical, food, and agricultural firms using biotechnology.

PERIODICALS

American Biotechnology Laboratory
International Scientific Communications, Inc.
30 Controls Dr.
Box 870
Shelton, CT 06484-0870
203-926-9300
Brian Howard, Editor
Follows new developments in biotechnology.

Applied Biochemistry and Biotechnology
Humana Press Inc.
Crescent Manor
Box 2148
Clifton, NJ 07015
201-773-4389
Howard Weetall, Editor
Reports on new techniques and products.

BioEngineering News
Deborah J. Mysiewicz Publishers, Inc.
Box 2009
Oak Harbor, WA 98277
800-359-6042
Thomas Mysiewicz, Editor
Provides news for the scientific and business communities.

Biotech Business
Worldwide Videotex
Box 138
Babson Park
Boston, MA 02157
617-449-1603
Mark Wright, Editor
Follows news of licensing agreements, patents, new products, and other developments in genetic engineering.

Biotechnology and Bioengineering
John Wiley & Sons, Inc., Journals
605 Third Ave.
New York, NY 10158-0012
212-850-6000
Daniel Wang, Editor
A scientific journal publishing new papers.

Biotechnology Directory
Stockton Press
15 E. 26th St.
New York, NY 10010
212-481-1334
Jim Coombs, Editor
A listing of research centers, corporations, and others using biotechnology.

Biotechnology Progress
American Chemical Society
1155 16th St., N.W.
Washington, DC 20036
202-872-4363
Jerome Schultz, Editor
Information on new technology.

Genetic Engineering News
Mary Ann Liebert Inc.
1651 Third Ave.
New York, NY 10128
212-289-2300
Reports on such business subjects as regulatory issues, company profiles, public offerings, patents, and other industry news.

LIBRARIES

Amgen, Inc.
Information Service Group
Amgen Center
Thousand Oaks, CA 91320-1789
805-499-5725
805-498-1425 Fax
Biotechnology, molecular biology, and related topics.

Biotechnology Research Institute
Library
1330-A Piccard Dr.
Rockville, MD 20850-4373
301-258-5200
301-840-2161 Fax
Biotechnology, immunology, and related topics.

DNAX Research Institute
Library
901 California Ave.
Palo Alto, CA 94304-1104
415-496-1285
415-496-1200 Fax
Biotechnology, molecular biology, immunology, genetic engineering and related topics.

COMPANIES

Biogen Research Corp.
14 Cambridge Ctr.
Cambridge, MA 02142
617-252-9200
Genetically engineered products.

BioTechnica International, Inc.
7300 W. 110th St.
Overland Park, KS 66210
913-661-0611
Genetically engineered products.

Calgene, Inc.
1920 5th St.
Davis, CA 95616
916-753-6313
Genetic engineering.

Cell Technology, Inc.
1668 Valtec Lane
Boulder, CO 80301
303-443-8155
Biotechnology research with a specialty in immunotherapy.

Cetus Corp.
1400 53rd St.
Emeryville, CA 94608
415-420-3300
Biotechnology research.

Immunex Research and Development Corp.
51 University St.
Seattle, WA 98101
206-587-0430
Genetically engineered products.

Lubrizol Corp.
29400 Lakeland Blvd.
Wickliffe, OH 44092
216-943-4200
A specialty chemicals firm that employs biotechnology.

Nova Pharmaceutical Corp.
6200 Freeport Ctr.
Baltimore, MD 21224
301-522-7000
Biotechnology pharmaceuticals.

Research Organics, Inc.
4353 E. 49th St.
Cuyahoga Heights, OH 44125
216-883-8025
Biochemicals created using genetic engineering.

Vega Biotechnologies, Inc.
1250 E. Aero Park Blvd.
Tuscon, AZ 85706
602-746-1401
Biotechnology equipment.

FEDERAL GOVERNMENT

National Institutes of Health
9000 Rockville Pike
Bethesda, MD 20892
301-496-4000
Ask for National Center for Biotechnology Information.

U.S. Department of Agriculture
14th St. and Independence Ave., S.W.
Washington, DC 20250
202-720-8732
Ask for the Agricultural Biotechnology Office.

U.S. Patent and Trademark Office
Crystal Plaza 2
2011 Jefferson Davis Highway
Arlington, VA 22202
703-305-8000
Ask for the Examining Group Director who is a specialist in biotechnology.

BOAT INDUSTRY

ASSOCIATIONS

American Boat and Yacht Council
405 Headquarters Dr., Ste. 3
PO Box 747
Millersville, MD 21108
301-923-3932
301-923-3988 Fax
Lysle Gray, Executive Director
Small craft manufacturers, architects, engineers, Navy personnel, and others who sponsor research on boats.

Marine Retailers Association of America
150 E. Huron St., No. 802
Chicago, IL 60611-2912
312-944-5080
312-938-9035 Fax
Paul Keeter, Executive Director
Retail dealers of marine products and services.

National Association of Marine Products and
    Services
401 N. Michigan Ave., Ste. 1150
Chicago, IL 60611
312-836-4747
312-329-9815 Fax
George Rounds, President
Members make equipment used for recreational boating.

National Marine Electronics Association
PO Box 50040
Mobile, AL 36605
205-473-1793
205-473-1669 Fax
Robert Sassaman, Executive Director
Firms that manufacture, sell, and service marine electronics.

National Marine Manufacturers Association
401 N. Michigan Ave., Ste. 1150
Chicago, IL 60611
312-836-4747
Jeff Napier, President
The nation's largest association of manufacturers of boats and supplies.

PERIODICALS

Boat & Motor Dealer
Van Zevern Publications, Inc.
3949 Oakton St.
Skokie, IL 60076
708-982-1810
George Van Zevern, Editor
Industry news and marketing advice for dealers.

Boat & Motor Dealer's Market Manual
Van Zevern Publications, Inc.
3949 Oakton St.
Skokie, IL 60076
708-982-1810
George Van Zevern, Editor
A listing of boats and boating products.

Boating
Diamandis Communications, Inc.
1633 Broadway, 45th Fl.
New York, NY 10009
212-767-6000
G. Douglas Schryver, Editor
A consumer publication.

Boating Industry
Communication Channels, Inc.
6255 Barfield Rd.
Atlanta, GA 30328-4369
404-256-9800
Richard Porter, Editor
Offers management and marketing advice to boat retailers.

Cruising World
Cruising World Publications, Inc.
5 John Clarke Rd.
Newport, RI 02840
401-847-1588
Bernadette Bernon, Editor
A consumer magazine.

Motor Boating & Sailing
Hearst Magazines
224 W. 57th St.
New York, NY 10019
212-649-3065
Peter Janssen, Editor
A consumer magazine.

Sailboat & Equipment Directory
Cahners Publishing Co.
275 Washington St.
Newton, MA 02158-1630
617-964-3030
Patience Wales, Editor
A listing of sail boats, equipment, and accessories.

Yachting
Times Mirror Magazines, Inc.
2 Park Ave.
New York, NY 10016
212-779-5000
Olive Moore, Editor
A consumer magazine.

COMPANIES

Carver Boat Corp.
(Subsidiary of Miramar Marine Corp.)
Industrial Dr.
Pulaski, WI 54162
414-822-3214
Pleasure boats.

E Z Loader Boat Trailers, Inc.
N. 717 Hamilton, Box 3263
Spokane, WA 99220
509-489-0181
Boat trailers.

Genmar Industries, Inc.
(Subsidiary of Minstar Inc.)
100 S. Fifth St.
Minneapolis, MN 55402
612-339-7600
Recreational power boats.

Marks-O'Donnell Industries, Inc.
Aloe & Leipzig Aves.
Cologne, NJ 08213
609-965-5188
Boat building and repairing.

Minstar Inc.
100 S. 5th St.
Minneapolis, MN 55402
612-339-7900
Boating products and sporting goods.

Outboard Marine Corp.
100 Sea Horse Dr.
Waukegan, IL 60085
708-689-6200
Outboard motors, boats, and boating accessories.

Peterson Builders, Inc.
101 Pennsylvania St., Box 650
Sturgeon Bay, WI 54235
414-743-5574
Boatbuilding and repair.

Thunderbird Products Corp.
(Subsidiary of Porter, Inc.)
P.O. Box 501
Decatur, IN 46733
219-724-9111
Fiberglass and pleasure boats.

FEDERAL GOVERNMENT

U.S. Department of Transportation
400 Seventh St., S.W.
Washington, DC 20590
202-366-4000
Ask for the Recreational Boating Product Assurance Department.

U.S. International Trade Administration
Department of Commerce
14th St. and Constitution Ave., N.W.
Washington, DC 20230
202-377-2000
Ask for the Commodity Analyst who is an expert in the boat industry.

U.S. International Trade Commission
500 E St., S.W.
Washington, DC 20436
202-205-2000 Office of the Secretary
202-205-3296 Industries locator
Ask for the Trade Analyst who is an expert in the boat industry.

BOOKBINDING

See also: PRINTING AND PRINTING EQUIPMENT INDUSTRIES

ASSOCIATIONS

Book Manufacturers Institute
111 Prospect
Stamford, CT 06901
203-324-9670
203-324-9674 Fax
Douglas Horner, Executive Vice President
Manufacturers of books and the materials used to make books.

Guild of Book Workers
521 5th Ave., 17th Fl.
New York, NY 10175
212-757-6454
John Mowery, President
Hand book binders, calligraphers, and fine press workers.

PERIODICALS

Abbey Newsletter
Abbey Publications, Inc.
320 E. Center St.
Provo, UT 84606
801-373-1598
Ellen R. McCrady, Editor
Reports on bookbinding and conservation of books and paper materials.

Abracadabra
Alliance for Contemporary Book Arts
USC Fine Arts Press
c/o USC—RAN
3716 S. Hope St.
Los Angeles, CA 90007
213-743-3939
Gerald Lange, Editor
Covers book arts, including printing, paper-making, calligraphy, and bookbinding.

LIBRARIES

Book Club of California
Library
312 Sutter St., Ste. 510
San Francisco, CA 94108
415 781-7532
415-391l-9603 Fax
Bookbinding, printing, and related topics.

Yale University
Arts of the Book Collectioin
Sterling Memorial Library
New Haven, CT 06520
203-432-1712
Bookbinding, book design, printing, and related topics.

COMPANIES

Book Binders, Inc.
251 Cornellson Ave.
Jersey City, NJ 07302
201-451-5400
Bookbinding services.

John H. Dekker & Sons, Inc.
2941 Clydon Ave., S. W.
Grand Rapids, MI 49509
616-538-5160
Bookbinding services.

Forest City Bookbindery
812 Huron Rd. E
Cleveland, OH 44115
216-621-5464
Bookbinding services.

Gane Bros. & Lane, Inc.
1400 Greenleaf St.
Elk Grove Village, IL 60007
708-593-3360
Bookbinding supplies, tools, and machinery.

Hartford Bindery, Inc.
2882 Main St.
Hartford, CT 06120
203-522-4174
Bookbinding services.

Hartman Bindery, Inc.
7115 Airport Hwy.
Pennsauken, NJ 08109
609-665-8700
Bookbinding services.

W. O. Hickok Mfg. Co.
9th & Cumberland Sts.
Harrisburg, PA 17103
717-234-8041
Bookbinding equipment and other products.

Printers' Bindery, Inc.
345 Hudson St.
New York, NY 10014
212-924-4200
Bookbinding services.

Smyth Manufacturing Co.
(Subsidiary of Beacon Group)
85 Granby St.
Bloomfield, CT 06002
203-242-2201
Bookbinding machinery.

FEDERAL GOVERNMENT

U.S. International Trade Administration
Department of Commerce
14th St. and Constitution Ave., N.W.
Washington, DC 20230
202-377-2000
Ask for the Commodity Analyst who is an expert in bookbinding.

U.S. International Trade Commission
500 E St., S.W.
Washington, DC 20436
202-205-2000 Office of the Secretary
202-205-3296 Industries locator
Ask for the Trade Analyst who is an expert in bookbinding.

U.S. Patent and Trademark Office
Crystal Plaza 2
2011 Jefferson Davis Highway
Arlington, VA 22202
703-305-8000
Ask for the Examining Group Director who is a specialist in bookbinding equipment.

BOOK PUBLISHING INDUSTRY

See also: BOOKSELLING INDUSTRY

ASSOCIATIONS

American Book Producers Association
41 Union Sq., W., Rm. 936
New York, NY 10003
212-645-2368
Stephen Ettlinger, President
*Firms that create concepts for books, sell the
idea to publishers, and usually provide a finished manuscript or even printed books.*

American Medical Publishers' Association
PO Box 944
Crystal Lake, IL 60014
815-459-3712
William Keller, Secretary
Firms publishing medical books.

Association of American Publishers
220 E. 23rd St.
New York, NY 10010
212-689-8920
Nicholas Veliotes, President
*Represents publishers of all kinds of hard-
bound and softbound books, including educational, trade, medical, religious, reference, and
technical books.*

Association of Jewish Book Publishers
838 Fifth Ave.
New York, NY 10021
212-249-0100
Charles Lieber, President
*Publishers of general books and textbooks on
Jewish subjects.*

Association of North American Directory
Publishers
7115 Suntide Pl.
Colorado Springs, CO 80919
719-528-1857
Carol Hill, Executive Director
*Firms that publish telephone, city, and spe-
cial-sbuject directories.*

Book Industry Study Group
160 5th Ave.
New York, NY 10010
212-929-1393
212-989-7542 Fax
Sandra Paul, Manager
*This collection of publishers, booksellers,
librarians, and others researches various
aspects of the book publishing industry.*

Catholic Book Publishers Association
Roth Advertising, Inc.
333 Glen Head Rd.
Old Brookville, NY 11545
516-671-9292
516-759-4227 Fax
Charles Roth, Secretary
*Book publishers with a specialty in Catholic
subjects.*

Children's Book Council
568 Broadway
New York, NY 10012
212-966-1990
John Donovan, President
Publishers of children's books.

National Association of Independent
Publishers
Riverside Dr. and Ave. M
PO Box 850
Moore Haven, FL 33471-0850
813-946-0293
813-946-0293 Fax
Betty Wright, Executive Director
Small, independent publishing companies.

Society for Scholarly Publishing
1918 18th St., N.W., Ste. 21
Washington, DC 20009
202-328-3555
*Publishers, booksellers, authors, and others
with an interest in scholarly publishing.*

PERIODICALS

Book Industry Trends
Book Industry Study Group, Inc.
160 5th Ave.
New York, NY 10010
212-929-1393
Reports on book sales and other news.

C B C Features
Children's Book Council, Inc.
568 Broadway
New York, NY 10012-3225
212-966-1990
John Donovan, Editor
*Features news of interest to publishers of chil-
dren's books, libraries, and others.*

Literary Market Place
R.R. Bowker, Inc.
121 Chanlon Rd.
New Providence, NJ 07974
800-521-8110
*A directory of publishers, literary agents, book
distributors, editorial and art services, and
others in the book publishing industry.*

Publishers Weekly
Cahners Publishing Co.
Bowker Magazine Group
249 W. 17th St.
New York, NY 10011
212-463-6758
Nora Rawlinson, Editor
*Wide-ranging news and trends that concern
booksellers, publishers, and librarians in all
fields of book publishing.*

LIBRARIES

American Booksellers Association
Information Center
560 White Plains Rd.
Tarrytown, NY 10591
914-631-7800
914-631-8391 Fax
Book publishing and selling.

R. R. Bowker Co.
Frederic G. Melcher Library
245 W. 17th St.
New York, NY 10011
212-463-6850
Book publishing industry and libraries.

COMPANIES

Bantam Doubleday Dell Publishing Group,
Inc.
666 5th Ave.
New York, NY 10103
212-765-6500
Book publisher.

Grolier, Inc.
Sherman Tpk.
Danbury, CT 06816
203-797-3500
Book publisher.

Harcourt Brace Jovanovich, Inc.
6277 Sea Harbor Dr.
Orlando, FL 32887
407-345-2000
Book publisher.

HarperCollins Publishers
10 E. 53rd St.
New York, NY 10022
212-207-7000
Book publisher.

Houghton Mifflin Co.
1 Beacon St.
Boston, MA 02108
617-725-5000
Book publisher.

Putnam Berkeley Group, Inc.
200 Madison Ave.
New York, NY 10016
212-951-8400
Book publisher.

Random House, Inc.
201 E. 50th St.
New York, NY 10022
212-572-2120
Book publisher.

Reed Publishing (USA), Inc.
275 Washington St.
Newton, MA 02158
617-964-3030
Book publisher.

Time-Life Books, Inc.
777 Duke St.
Alexandria, VA 22314
703-838-7000
Book publisher.

Western Publishing Group, Inc.
444 Madison Ave.
New York, NY 10022
212-688-4500
Book publisher.

FEDERAL GOVERNMENT

U.S. Customs Service
Department of the Treasury
U.S. Customshouse
6 World Trade Center
New York, NY 10048
212-466-5550
Ask for the Commodity Specialist in charge of books.

U.S. International Trade Administration
Department of Commerce
14th St. and Constitution Ave., N.W.
Washington, DC 20230
202-377-2000
Ask for the Commodity Analyst who is an expert in the book publishing industry.

U.S. International Trade Commission
500 E St., S.W.
Washington, DC 20436
202-205-2000 Office of the Secretary
202-205-3296 Industries locator
Ask for the Trade Analyst who is an expert in the book publishing industry.

BOOKSELLING INDUSTRY

See also: BOOK PUBLISHING INDUSTRY

ASSOCIATIONS

American Booksellers Association
560 White Plains Rd.
Tarrytown, NY 10591
914-631-7800
914-631-8391 Fax
Bernard Rath, Executive Director
*This association of book retailers is the by far
the largest group in the book publishing
industry.*

Christian Booksellers Association
PO Box 200
Colorado Springs, CO 80901
719-576-7880
719-576-0795 Fax
William Anderson, President
*Represents stores selling religious books and
church supplies.*

National Association of College Stores
528 E. Lorain St.
Oberlin, OH 44074
216-775-7777
800-622-7498
216-774-1335 Fax
Garis Distelhorst, Executive Director
*College stores that sell books and other materi-
als to students.*

PERIODICALS

Book Dealers World
North American Bookdealers Exchange
Box 606
Cottage Grove, OR 97424
503-942-7455
Al Galasso, Editor
*Information on books being marketed by mail
for mail order book dealers and self-publishers.*

Magazine & Bookseller
North American Publishing Co.
322 Eighth Ave., 18th Fl.
New York, NY 10001
212-620-7330
Mark Hinckley, Editor
*Offers how-to information for the effective
sales of magazines and paperback books
through retailers.*

Publishers Weekly
Cahners Publishing Co.
Bowker Magazine Group
249 W. 17th St.
New York, NY 10011
212-463-6758
Nora Rawlinson, Editor
*Surveys the book publishing industry for
booksellers, publishers, and librarians.*

COMPANIES

B. Dalton Bookseller, Inc.
1400 Old Country Rd.
Westbury, NY 11590
516-338-8000
Book retail chain.

Barnes and Noble, Inc.
122 5th Ave.
New York, NY 10003
212-633-3300
Book retail chain.

Crown Books Corp.
3300 75th Ave.
Landover, MD 20785
301-731-1200
Book retail chain.

Follet Corp. (Chicago Illinois)
1000 W. Washington
Chicago, IL 60607
312-666-4300
Booksellers.

Harvard Cooperative Society
1400 Massachusetts Ave.
Cambridge, MA 02138
617-492-1000
Booksellers.

Kroch's and Brentano's, Inc.
29 S. Wabash Ave.
Chicago, IL 60603
312-332-7500
Book retail chain.

Walden Book Co., Inc.
201 High Ridge Rd.
Stamford, CT 06904
203-352-2000
Book retail chain.

FEDERAL GOVERNMENT

U.S. Customs Service
Department of the Treasury
U.S. Customshouse
6 World Trade Center
New York, NY 10048
212-466-5550
Ask for the Commodity Specialist in charge of books.

U.S. International Trade Administration
Department of Commerce
14th St. and Constitution Ave., N.W.
Washington, DC 20230
202-377-2000
Ask for the Commodity Analyst who is an expert in the book retailing industry.

U.S. International Trade Commission
500 E St., S.W.
Washington, DC 20436
202-205-2000 Office of the Secretary
202-205-3296 Industries locator
Ask for the Trade Analyst who is an expert in book retailing.

BOX INDUSTRY

See also: CONTAINER INDUSTRY

ASSOCIATIONS

Fibre Box Association
2850 Golf Rd.
Rolling Meadows, IL 60008
708-364-9600
708-364-9639 Fax
Bruce Benson, President
Manufacturers of corrugated and fiber boxes.

National Paperbox and Packaging Association
1201 E. Abingdon Dr., Ste. 203
Alexandria, VA 22314
703-684-2212
703-683-6920 Fax
R. Mickey Gorman, President
Makers of rigid and folding paper boxes.

National Wooden Pallet and Container Association
1625 Massachusetts Ave. N.W., Ste. 200
Washington, DC 20036
202-667-3670
John Healy, Executive Vice President
Manufacturers of wooden containers of all types.

Western Wooden Box Association
Box 670
Turlock, CA 95381
209-667-1021
Reuben Carlson, Secretary
Firms that make and distribute wooden boxes used for shipping fresh fruit and vegetables.

PERIODICALS

Boxboard Containers
Maclean Hunter Publishing Co.
29 N. Wacker Dr.
Chicago, IL 60606
312-726-2802
Charles Huck, Editor
Industry news about shipping containers, setup paper boxes, folding cartons, and other products.

Journal of Packaging Technology
Technical Publications, Inc.
One Lethbridge Plaza
Mahwah, NJ 07430
201-529-3380
Tom Farley, Editor
Surveys many facets of the packaging industry, including boxes.

Packaging
Cahners Publishing Co.
1350 E. Touhy Ave.
Box 5080
Des Plaines, IL 60017-5080
708-635-8800
Robin Ashton, Editor
Reports on packaging innovations, designs, marketing, consumer protection, and other subjects.

Packaging Digest
Delta Communications, Inc.
400 N. Michigan Ave., 13th Fl.
Chicago, IL 60611
312-222-2000
Robert Heitzman, Editor
*Covers packaging design, manufacture, mar-
keting, equipment, and materials.*

Paperboard Packaging
Edgell Communications
7500 Old Oak Blvd.
Cleveland, OH 44130
216-826-2839
Mark Arzoumanian, Editor
*Information on the paperboard box industry
and related industries.*

COMPANIES

Central States Diversified Inc.
9322 Manchester Rd.
St. Louis, MO 63119
314-961-4300
Acetate boxes and other types of containers.

Entwistle Co.
Bigelow St.
Hudson, MA 01749
508-481-4000
*Machines for making corrugated boxes and
other products.*

Great Northern Corp.
P.O. Box 939
Appleton, WI 54912
414-739-3671
Corrugated boxes and displays.

Old Dominion Box Co.
Amherst County
Lynchburg, VA 24505
804-846-2791
*Folding cartons, paper boxes, and corrugated
boxes.*

Rock-Tenn Co.
504 Thrasher St.
Norcross, GA 30071
404-448-2193
*Folding cartons, corrugated boxes, and related
products.*

Westvaco Corp.
299 Park Ave.
New York, NY 10171
212-688-5000
*Corrugated boxes, folding boxes, and many
other paper and paperboard products.*

Willamette Industries, Inc.
3800 First Interstate Tower
Portland, OR 97201
503-227-5581
Corrugated boxes and other products.

FEDERAL GOVERNMENT

U.S. International Trade Administration
Department of Commerce
14th St. and Constitution Ave., N.W.
Washington, DC 20230
202-377-2000
*Ask for the Commodity Analyst who is an
expert in the box industry.*

U.S. International Trade Commission
500 E St., S.W.
Washington, DC 20436
202-205-2000 Office of the Secretary
202-205-3296 Industries locator
*Ask for the Trade Analyst who is an expert in
the box industry.*

BREWING INDUSTRY

See also: BEVERAGE INDUSTRY and LIQUOR AND SPIRITS INDUSTRY

ASSOCIATIONS

Beer Institute
1225 I St. N.W., Ste. 825
Washington, DC 20005
202-737-BEER
202-737-7004 Fax
James Sanders, President
Represents brewers and suppliers to the beer industry.

Brewers' Association of America
PO Box 727
Wilkes-Barre, PA 18703-0727
717-822-3442
Lee Holland, Executive Director
Members include regional and small brewers.

National Beer Wholesalers' Association
5205 Leesburg Pike, Ste. 1600
Falls Church, VA 22041
703-578-4300
703-931-3216 Fax
Ronald Sarasin, President
Independent distributors of beer.

PERIODICALS

American Brewer Magazine
American Brewer Inc.
Box 510
Hayward, CA 94541
415-538-9500
Bill Owens, Editor
Follows micro brewers, pub breweries, and other very small brewing operations.

Journal of the American Society of Brewing Chemists
American Society of Brewing Chemists
A P S Press
3340 Pilot Knob Rd.
St. Paul, MN 55121-2097
612-454-7250
W.M. Ingledew, Editor
Technical and practical data for brewers.

Beer Marketer's Insights
Beer Marketer's Insights, Inc.
51 Virginia Ave.
West Nyack, NY 10994
914-358-7751
Jerry Steinman, Editor
Offers beer industry statistics and news of legal, social, market, and other factors that impact on the industry.

Beer Statistics News
Beer Marketer's Insights, Inc.
51 Virginia Ave.
W. Nyack, NY 10994
914-358-7751
Eric Shepard, Editor
Reports on beer shipments by region, state, and brewer. Also provides industry forecasts and other information.

Beer Wholesaler
Beverage Management Associates, Inc.
11460 W. 44th Ave., Ste. 4
Wheat Ridge, CO 80033
303-425-4668
Daniel Morales Brink, Editor
*Reports on a wide range of news and issues
that interest wholesalers.*

Beverage Alcohol Business Scene
Northwest Beverage Journal, Inc.
Diamond Publications
4504 Excelsior Blvd.
Minneapolis, MN 55416
612-920-7711
Gary Diamond, Editor
*Written for beverage alcohol licensees buying
large amounts of beer, wine, and liquor.*

Brewers Digest
Siebel Publishing Co.
4049 W. Peterson Ave.
Chicago, IL 60646
312-463-3401
Dori Witney, Editor
*Practical information for brewers, including
advice on plant operation, packaging, purchasing, quality control, and sanitation.*

LIBRARIES

Anheuser-Busch Companies, Inc.
Corporate Library
One Busch Place
St. Louis, MO 63118
314-577-2669
314-577-2006
Brewing industry and technology.

Miller Brewing Co.
Scientific and Technical Information Facility
3939 W. Highland Blvd.
Milwaukee, WI 53201
414-931-3640
414-931-3986 Fax
Brewing industry and related topics.

Stroh Brewery Co.
Stroh Technical Library
100 River Place
Detroit, MI 48207
313-446-2033
313-446-2638 Fax
Brewing and related topics.

COMPANIES

Anheuser-Busch Companies, Inc.
One Busch Pl.
St. Louis, MO 63118
314-577-2000
Beer and other products.

Adolph Coors Co.
12th and Ford Sts.
Golden, CO 80401
303-279-6565
Beer and ale.

Genesee Brewing Co., Inc.
(Subsidiary of Genesee Corp.)
445 St. Paul St.
Rochester, NY 14605
716-546-1030
Beer and ale.

Ben E. Keith Co.
9th & Pecan
Fort Worth, TX 76102
817-332-9171
Wholesaler of food and beer.

Lewis Bear Co.
4150 W. Blount St.
Pensacola, FL 32505
904-438-9651
Beer and food distributor.

Miller Brewing Co.
(Subsidiary of Philip Morris Incorporated)
3939 W. Highland Blvd.
Milwaukee, WI 53201
414-931-2000
Beer and ale.

Pabst Brewing Co.
(Subsidiary of S & P Co.)
917 W. Juneau Ave., Box 766
Milwaukee, WI 53201
414-223-3500
Beer, ale, malt, and other products.

Stroh Brewery Co.
(Subsidiary of Stroh Companies, Inc.)
100 River Pl.
Detroit, MI 48207
313-446-2000
Beer, coolers, and soft drinks.

FEDERAL GOVERNMENT

U.S. Customs Service
Department of the Treasury
U.S. Customshouse
6 World Trade Center
New York, NY 10048
212-466-5550
*Ask for the Commodity Specialist in charge of
beer.*

U.S. Department of the Treasury
1500 Pennsylvania Ave., N.W.
Washington, DC 20220
202-566-2111
*Ask for the Wine & Beer Compliance Bureau
of the Bureau of Alcohol, Tobacco and
Firearms.*

U.S. International Trade Administration
Department of Commerce
14th St. and Constitution Ave., N.W.
Washington, DC 20230
202-377-2000
*Ask for the Commodity Analyst who is an
expert in the brewing industry.*

U.S. International Trade Commission
500 E St., S.W.
Washington, DC 20436
202-205-2000 Office of the Secretary
202-205-3296 Industries locator
*Ask for the Trade Analyst who is an expert in
the brewing industry.*

BUDGETING

ASSOCIATIONS

American Association for Budget and Program
   Analysis
PO Box 1157
Falls Church, VA 22041
703-941-4300
703-941-1535 Fax
Christine LaChance, Executive Secretary
*Executives in government and business who
are involved with budgeting and related topics.*

National Association of State Budget Officers
Hall of States
400 N. Capitol St. N.W., No. 295
Washington, DC 20001
202-624-5382
Gerald Miller, Executive Director
State budget directors and their assistants.

PERIODICALS

Planning Review
International Society for Strategic Manage-
   ment and Planning
Planning Forum
5500 College Corner Pike
Box 70
Oxford, OH 45056
513-523-4185
Liam Fahey, Editor
*Offers advice on a wide range of issues that
interest corporate planners, including
budgeting.*

Public Budgeting and Finance
American Association for Budget and Program
   Analysis
Transaction Publishers
Department 3091
Rutgers University
New Brunswick, NJ 08903
908-932-2280
Naomi Caiden, John Mikesell, Editors
*A theoretical journal that covers government
planning and budgeting.*

Public Budgeting and Financial Management
Marcel Dekker Journals
270 Madison Ave.
New York, NY 10016
212-696-9000
Jack Rabin, Editor
*A business journal that covers the applications
of budgeting and planning in the public and
private sectors.*

BUILDING INDUSTRY

See also: BUILDING MATERIALS INDUSTRY

ASSOCIATIONS

Associated Builders and Contractors
729 15th St. N.W.
Washington, DC 20005
202-637-8800
Daniel Bennet, Executive Vice President
A large group of contractors and subcontractors.

Log House Builder's Association of North
    America
22203 S.R. 203
Monroe, WA 98272
206-794-4469
Skip Ellsworth, President
Log cabin and house builders.

National Association of Home Builders of the
    U.S.
15th and M Streets N.W.
Washington, DC 20005
202-822-0200
800-221-NAHB
Kent Colton, Executive Vice President
*By far the largest association of builders in
the U.S.*

National Association of the Remodeling
    Industry
1901 N. Moore St., Ste. 808
Arlington, VA 22209
703-276-7600
703-243-3465 Fax
Alan Campbell, Executive Director
Remodeling contractors, manufacturers, distributers, lenders, and others.

National Council of the Housing Industry
15th and M Streets N.W.
Washington, DC 20005
202-822-0520
800-368-5242
Herb Ferlmann, Vice President
*Providers of a wide range of services and
goods to the constuction industry.*

National Frame Builders Association
8725 Rosehill Rd., Ste. 210
Lenexa, KS 66215
915-599-0606
915-599-6500 Fax
James Knight, President
Contractors who build commercial and agricultural structures.

Systems Builders Association
28 Lowry Dr.
PO Box 117
West Milton, OH 45383
513-698-4127
Christopher Long, Executive Vice President
Manufacturers of metal buildings.

PERIODICALS

Automated Builder
C M N Publications
4371 Carpinteria Ave.
Box 120
Carpinteria, CA 93013
805-684-7659
Don Carlson, Editor
Provides practical information for manufacturers of mobile homes and panelized homes who use automated hardware and components.

Builder-Dealer
16 First Ave.
Corry, PA 16407
814-664-8624
Charles Mancin, Editor
Advice and news for builders of single-family homes.

Building Design & Construction
Cahners Publishing Co.
1350 E. Touhy Ave.
Box 5080
Des Plaines, IL 60017-5080
708-635-8800
Philip Schreiner, Editor
Offers information on new designs and technology, financing, government regulations, and other industry news to owners and contractors of non-residential buildings.

Cockshaw's Construction Labor News &
    Opinion
Communications Counselors, Inc.
Box 427
Newtown Square, PA 19073
215-353-0123
Peter Cockshaw, Editor
Focuses on labor-management news and issues in the construction industry.

E N R
McGraw-Hill, Inc.
1221 Ave. of the Americas
New York, NY 10020
212-512-2000
Howard Stussman, Editor
Follows news and trends affecting large construction firms worldwide.

E N R Directory of Contractors
McGraw-Hill, Inc.
1221 Ave. of the Americas
New York, NY 10020
212-512-2000
Charles Pinyan, Editor
A listing of U.S. and foreign contractors.

Multi Housing News
Gralla Publications
1515 Broadway
New York, NY 10036
212-869-1300
Audrey Fields, Editor
Offers news of interest to builders of multi-unit dwellings.

Professional Builder & Remodeler
Cahners Publishing Co.
1350 E. Touhy Ave.
Box 5080
Des Plaines, IL 60017-5080
708-635-8800
Roy Diez, Editor
Provides news of market conditions, financing, new technologies, legislation, and other issues that affect the residential and remodeling industries.

LIBRARIES

Bechtel Corp.
Central Library
50 Beale St.
San Francisco, CA 94105
415-768-5306
415-768-6997 Fax
Construction and engineering.

Georgia Institute of Technology
Price Gilbert Memorial Library
Architecture Library
225 North Ave., N.W.
Atlanta, GA 30332-0900
404-894-4877
Building construction and urban planning.

National Association of Home Builders of the
    U.S.
15th and M Streets N.W.
Washington, DC 20005
202-822-0200
800-221-NAHB
Building and construction.

National Council of the Housing Industry
15th and M Streets N.W.
Washington, DC 20005
202-822-0520
800-368-5242
Housing and construction.

COMPANIES

Barton-Malow Co.
(Subsidiary of Barton-Malow Enterprises,
    Inc.)
P. O. Box 5200
Detroit, MI 48235
313-351-4500
General contractor.

George A. Fuller Co.
(Subsidiary of Fuller Group, Inc.)
919 Third Ave.
New York, NY 10022
212-355-2700
Construction management and contracting.

Jacobs Engineering Group Inc.
251 S. Lake Ave.
Pasadena, CA 91101
818-449-2171
Engineering and construction.

Perini Corp.
73 Mt. Wayte Ave.
Framingham, MA 01701
508-875-6171
Real estate development and construction.

Ryan Homes, Inc.
(Subsidiary of NVR L.P.)
100 Ryan Ct.
Pittsburgh, PA 15205
412-276-8000
Home building.

United Dominion Industries Ltd.
301 S. College St.
Charlotte, NC 28202
704-347-5454
Pre-engineered buildings and other products.

Walbridge Aldinger Co.
38099 Schoolcraft
Livonia, MI 48150
313-591-6000
*General contractors and construction man-
agers.*

Whiting-Turner Contracting Co.
300 E. Joppa Rd.
Baltimore, MD 21204
301-821-1100
Construction and construction management.

Bechtel Group, Inc.
Fifty Beale St., Box 3965
San Francisco, CA 94119
415-768-1234
Engineering, construction, and related businesses.

FEDERAL GOVERNMENT

Department of Housing and Urban Development
451 Seventh St., S.W.
Washington, DC 20410
202-755-5111
Ask for the public relations office for help finding an expert on the topic that interests you.

U.S. International Trade Administration
Department of Commerce
14th St. and Constitution Ave., N.W.
Washington, DC 20230
202-377-2000
Ask for the Commodity Analyst who is an expert in the building industry.

U.S. International Trade Commission
500 E St., S.W.
Washington, DC 20436
202-205-2000 Office of the Secretary
202-205-3296 Industries locator
Ask for the Trade Analyst who is an expert in the building industry.

BUILDING MATERIALS INDUSTRY

See also: BUILDING INDUSTRY

ASSOCIATIONS

American Architectural Manufacturers Association
2700 River Rd., Ste. 118
Des Plaines, IL 60018
708-699-7310
William Anton, Executive Director
Manufacturers of storm windows and doors, skylights, gutters, enclosures, and components used in mobile homes.

Architectural Woodwork Institute
2310 S. Walter Reed Dr.
Arlington, VA 22206
703-671-9100
703-820-7839 Fax
H. Keith Judkins, Executive Vice President
Firms that make wooden fixtures, paneling, and casework.

Associated Building Material Distributors of America
7100 E. Lincoln Dr., Ste. D-220
Scottsdale, AZ 85253
602-998-0696
602-948-2969 Fax
John Mackin, Executive Vice President
Small wholesalers of building materials.

Associated Construction Distributors International
1505 Johnson Ferry Rd., Ste. 150
Marietta, GA 30062
404-971-2342
404-971-4147 Fax
Daniel Guntin, Executive Vice President
Distributors who offer masonry, concrete, and related supplies.

Association of the Wall and Ceiling Industries—International 1600 Cameron St., Ste. 200
Alexandria, VA 22314
703-684-2924
703-684-2935 Fax
Joe Baker, Executive Vice President
Manufacturers and construction firms specializing in drywall, plastering, tiles, and other industries.

Brick Institute of America
11490 Commerce Park Dr.
Reston, VA 22091
703-620-0010
Nelson Cooney, President
Firms that make bricks made from clay.

National Building Material Distributors Association
1417 Lake Cook Rd., Ste. 130
Deerfield, IL 60015
708-945-7201
Al Leitschuh, Executive Vice President
Distributors throughout the U.S.

PERIODICALS

Better Homes and Gardens Home Products Guide
Meredith Corp.
1716 Locust St.
Des Moines, IA 50336
515-284-3000
A consumer magazine that illustrates materials used in home building and remodeling.

Building Products Digest
Cutler Publishing, Inc.
4500 Campus Dr., Ste. 480
Newport Beach, CA 92660
714-852-1990
Juanita Lovret, Editor
Offers news concerning building materials of all types.

Building Supply Home Centers
Cahners Publishing Co.
1350 E. Touhy Ave.
Box 5080
Des Plaines, IL 60017-5080
708-635-8800
Craig Shutt, Editor
Offers information on marketing, new products, and management to retailers of building materials.

Chilton's Hardware Age
Chilton Co.
Chilton Way
Radnor, PA 19089
215-964-4275
Follows news and trends in the do-it-yourself hardware market.

Fine Homebuilding
Taunton Press, Inc.
63 S. Main St.
Box 5506
Newtown, CT 06470-5506
203-426-8171
Mark Feirer, Editor
Offers news and advice about building materials.

LIBRARIES

Manville Sales Corp.
Technical Information Center
P.O. Box 5108
Denver, CO 80217
303-978-5374
303-978-5094 Fax
Building materials and engineering.

U.S. Army
Corps of Engineers
Construction Engineering Research Laboratory
H. B. Zachrison Memorial Library
Interstate Research Park
Box 4005
Champaign, IL 61824-4005
217-373-7217
217-373-7222 Fax
Construction materials, civil engineering, structural engineering, and related topics.

Jim Walter Research Corp.
Technical Information Center
10301 9th St., N.
P.O. Box 42010
St. Petersburg, FL 33716
813-576-4171
Building materials, material science, and related topics.

COMPANIES

American Standard Inc.
(Subsidiary of ASI Holding Corp.)
1114 Ave. of the Americas
New York, NY 10036
212-703-5100
Building products and other types of products.

Berke Co.
225 S. Fairbank St.
Addison, IL 60101
708-543-7710
Building materials and products.

Builders Specialties Co.
P.O. Box 969
Pawtucket, RI 02862
401-722-2988
Building materials and products.

Henry Bacon Building Materials
P.O. Box 6669
Bellevue, WA 98008
206-641-8000
Building materials and products.

Hardware Wholesalers, Inc.
P. O. Box 868
Fort Wayne, IN 46801
219-749-8531
Wholesaler of hardware and building materials.

Holston Builders Supply Co., Inc.
645 E. Main St.
Kingsport, TN 37660
615-247-8131
Building products.

Hughes Supply, Inc.
521 W. Central Blvd., Box 2273
Orlando, FL 32802
407-841-4755
Building supplies for electricians and plumbers, and construction tools.

L and W Supply Corp.
1 S. Wacker Dr.
Chicago, IL 60606
312-606-5400
Building products.

Riggs Supply Co.
320 Cedar St.
Kennett, MO 63857
314-888-4639
Building supplies.

Scotty's Inc.
P. O. Box 939
Winter Haven, FL 33882
813-299-1111
Retailer of building materials, supplies, house-hold fixtures, and tools.

FEDERAL GOVERNMENT

U.S. Department of Commerce
14th St. and Constitution Ave., N.W.
Washington, DC 20230
202-377-2000
Ask for the Center for Building Technology.

U.S. International Trade Administration
Department of Commerce
14th St. and Constitution Ave., N.W.
Washington, DC 20230
202-377-2000
Ask for the Commodity Analyst who is an expert in the building materials industry.

U.S. International Trade Commission
500 E St., S.W.
Washington, DC 20436
202-205-2000 Office of the Secretary
202-205-3296 Industries locator
Ask for the Trade Analyst who is an expert in the building materials industry.

BUSINESS ETHICS

ASSOCIATIONS

Society for Business Ethics
Loyola Univ. of Chicago
Dept. of Philosophy
6525 N. Sheridan Rd.
Chicago, IL 60626
312-508-2291
Patricia Werhane, Contact
Members include professors of business, philosophy, religion, and business executives.

PERIODICALS

Annual Editions: Business Ethics
Dushkin Publishing Group, Inc.
Sluice Dock
Guilford, CT 06437-9989
203-453-4351
John Richardson, Editor
Contains articles, mainly from the popular press, about business ethics.

Business & Professional Ethics Journal
Center for Applied Philosophy
University of Florida
240 Dauer Hall
Gainesville, FL 32611
904-392-2084
Robert Baum, Editor
Scholarly articles about business ethics.

Business Ethics Resource
Reheven Consultants
28 Marshal St., Ste. 3
Brookline, MA 02146
617-232-1820
Judith Ewing, Editor
Written for senior management, this periodical offers news and practical advice on how to handle ethics issues.

LIBRARIES

Center for the Study of Ethics in the Professions
Library
IIT Center
Illinois Institute of Technology
3300 S. Federal St.
Chicago, IL 60616
312-567-3017
Business ethics, education, codes of conduct, social responsibility, and related subjects.

Georgetown University
Kennedy Institute of Ethics
National Reference Center for Bioethics Literature
Washington, DC 20057
202-687-3885
202-687-6770 Fax
Ethics with an emphasis on medical and biological ethics.

BUSINESS HISTORY

ASSOCIATIONS

Academy of Accounting Historians
James Madison Univ.
School of Accounting
Harrisonburg, VA 22807
703-568-6607
703-568-6619 Fax
Ashton Bishop, Secretary
Accountants, accounting firms, professors, and students with an interest in business and accounting history.

Business History Conference
Coll. of William and Mary
Dept. of Economics
Williamsburg, VA 23185
804-221-2381
William Hausman, Secretary
Economic and business historians, mostly from colleges and universities.

PERIODICALS

Business History Review
Harvard Business School
Soldiers Field
Boston, MA 02163
617-495-6154
Steven Tolloday, Editor
Prints scholarly articles covering business history and its methodology.

LIBRARIES

Columbia University
Thomas J. Watson Library of Business and Economics
130 Uris Hall
New York, NY 10027
212-854-4000
Business, economics, business history, and related subjects.

Harvard University
Harvard Business School
Baker Library
Soldiers Field
Boston, MA 02163
617-495-6044
617-495-6001 Fax
Economics, business, business history, and many other topics.

University of Oklahoma
Harry W. Bass Collection in Business History
401 W. Brooks
Norman, OK 73019
405-324-3941
Business history.

BUSINESS LAW

See also: LAWYERS and each of the 50 states under attorney general

ASSOCIATIONS

American Bar Association
Business Law Section
750 N. Lake Shore Dr.
Chicago, IL 60611
312-988-5588
Corporate counsel and others who practice business law.

American Business Law Association
Western Carolina Univ.
School of Business
Cullowhee, NC 28723
704-586-1423
Daniel Herron, Executive Secretary
Professors who teach business law.

American Corporate Counsel Association
1225 Connecticut Ave. N.W., Ste. 302
Washington, DC 20036
202-296-4522
Nancy Nord, Executive Director
Members include attorneys who work for the legal departments of corporations.

PERIODICALS

Business Law Monographs
Matthew Bender & Co., Inc.
11 Penn Plaza
New York, NY 10001
212-967-7707
Provides indepth articles about common business law problems and their resolution.

Business Lawyer
American Bar Association
Business Law Section
750 N. Lake Shore Dr.
Chicago, IL 60611
312-988-5588
Linda Sypolt, Editor
Follows trends in financial and business law.

CABLE TELEVISION INDUSTRY

See also: TELEVISION BROADCASTING INDUSTRY

ASSOCIATIONS

Cable Television Administration and Marketing Society
635 Slaters Ln., Suite 250
Alexandria, VA 23314
703-549-4200
Margaret Combs, President
Offers training programs to marketers and administrators who work for cable television stations.

National Cable Television Association
1724 Massachusetts Ave. N.W.
Washington, DC 20036
202-775-3550
James Mooney, President
Offers research and educational programs to cable networks, station operators, equipment manufacturers, and others.

National Cable Television Institute
PO Box 27277
Denver, CO 80227
303-761-8554
303-761-8556 Fax
Byron Leech, President
Provides technical seminars and prepares technical materials for the cable television industry.

Women in Cable
c/o P.M. Haeger & Assocs.
500 N. Michigan Ave., Suite 1400
Chicago, IL 60611
312-661-1700
312-661-0769 Fax
Karen Wojdyla, Representative
Promotes the opportunities of women in the cable television industry.

PERIODICALS

Cable T V Advertising
Paul Kagan Associates, Inc.
126 Clock Tower Place
Carmel, CA 93923
408-624-1536
Larry Gerbrandt, Editor
Reports on the sale of commercial time by cable TV systems.

Cable T V and New Media Law and Finance
Leader Publications, Inc.
New York Law Publishing Co.
111 Eighth Ave., Ste. 900
New York, NY 10011
800-888-8300
Michael Botein, Editor
Focuses on the legal and financial aspects of the cable industry.

Cable T V Programming
Paul Kagan Associates, Inc.
126 Clock Tower Place
Carmel, CA 93923
408-624-1536
Paul Kagan, Editor
Offers studies of cable TV economics and valuations.

Cable T V Technology
Paul Kagan Associates, Inc.
126 Clock Tower Place
Carmel, CA 93923
408-624-1536
John Mansell, Editor
Reports news about cable systems and the technologies they employ.

Cable World
Cable World Associates
1905 Sherman St.
Denver, CO 80203
303-837-0900
Stewart Schley, Editor
Covers business news and trends concerning the cable industry.

CableVision
Cable Publishing Group
600 S. Cherry St., Ste. 400
Denver, CO 80222
303-393-7449
Kathy Haley, Editor
Analysis and feature articles regarding the cable television industry.

Lewis Letter on Cable Marketing
Lewis Associates, Inc.
292 Main St.
Great Barrington, MA 01230
413-528-9445
Eiken Willner, Editor
Offers how-to information to cable executives about public relations, marketing, and advertising.

LIBRARIES

Library of Congress
John F. Kennedy Center for the Performing Arts
The Performing Arts Library
John F. Kennedy Ctr.
Washington, DC 20566
202-707-5507
Broadcasting, theater, film, music, and related topics.

U.S. Federal Communications Commission Library
1919 M St., N.W.
Washington, DC 20554
202-632-7100
Telecommunications, broadcasting, and other topics.

COMPANIES

American Television & Communications Corp.
(Subsidiary of Time Warner Inc.)
300 First Stamford Pl.
Stamford, CT 06902
203-328-0600
Cable television broadcasting.

Cablevision Systems Corp.
One Media Crossways
Woodbury, NY 11797
516-364-8450
Cable television broadcasting.

Comcast Corp.
1414 S. Penn Sq.
Philadelphia, PA 19102
215-665-1700
Cable television broadcasting.

Continental Cablevision Inc.
The Pilot House, Lewis Wharf
Boston, MA 02110
617-742-9500
Cable television broadcasting.

Home Shopping Network, Inc.
12000 25th Ct. N.
St. Petersburgh, FL 33716
813-572-8585
Cable television broadcasting.

MTV Networks
(Division of Viacom International Inc.)
1515 Broadway
New York, NY 10036
212-258-8000
Cable television broadcasting.

Scripps Howard Broadcasting Co.
(Subsidiary of E. W. Scripps Co.)
1100 Central Trust Tower
Cincinnati, OH 45202
513-977-3000
Cable television broadcasting and other businesses.

Storer Communications, Inc.
(Subsidiary of SCI Holdings, Inc.)
12000 Biscayne Blvd.
Miami, FL 33181
305-899-1000
Cable television broadcasting.

CALIFORNIA

STATE OFFICE LOCATOR (*for referrals to all state government offices*)

916-322-9900

ARCHIVES AND RECORDS

State Archives Division
Public Market Building
1230 J Street
Sacramento, CA 95814
916-445-4293

ATTORNEY GENERAL

Justice Department
P.O. Box 944255
Sacramento, CA 94244
916-324-5437

BANKING

Banking Department
111 Pine Street
11th Floor
San Francisco, CA 94111
415-557-3535

COMMERCE

Commerce Department
801 K Street
Ste. 1700
Sacramento, CA 95814
916-322-3962

CONSUMER AFFAIRS

Consumer Affairs Department
1020 N Street
Room 510
Sacramento, CA 95814
916-445-4465

EDUCATION

Education Department
P.O. Box 944272
Sacramento, CA 94244-2720
916-445-4338

ENERGY

Energy Commission
1516 9th Street
Sacramento, CA 95814
916-324-3326

ENVIRONMENTAL AFFAIRS

Environmental Affairs Agency
P.O. Box 2815
Sacramento, CA 95812
916-445-3846

HEALTH

Health Services Department
714 P Street
Sacramento, CA 95814
916-445-1351

HOUSING

Housing & Community Development Department
P.O. Box 952050
Sacramento, CA 94252-2050
916-445-4775

INSURANCE

Insurance Department
100 Van Ness Avenue
17th Floor
San Francisco, CA 94102
415-557-3848

LABOR

Industrial Relations Department
P.O. Box 603
San Francisco, CA 94101
415-737-2600

LEGISLATION

Assembly Office of Research
1100 J Street
Room 535
Sacramento, CA 95814
916-445-1638

LIBRARY SERVICES

Libraries Division
P.O. Box 2037
Sacramento, CA 95809
916-445-4027

LICENSING—CORPORATE

Corporate Filing Division
Public Market Building
1230 J Street
Sacramento, CA 95814
916-445-0620

LICENSING—PROFESSIONAL AND OCCUPATIONAL

Consumer Affairs Department
1020 N Street
Room 510
Sacramento, CA 95814
916-445-4465

MOTOR VEHICLES

Motor Vehicles Department
P.O. Box 932328
Sacramento, CA 94232-3280
916-732-7281

OCCUPATIONAL HEALTH AND SAFETY

Occupational Safety & Health Division
P.O. Box 603
San Franciso, CA 94101
415-737-2959

PUBLIC UTILITIES

Energy Commission
1516 8th Street
Sacramento, CA 95814
916-324-3326

PURCHASING

Office of Procurement
1823 14th Street
Room 100
Sacramento, CA 95814
916-445-6942

REAL ESTATE

Real Estate & Building Division
915 Capitol Mall
Ste. 590
Sacramento, CA 95814
916-445-7213

SECURITIES

Corporation Department
3700 Wilshire Boulevard
Ste. 600
Los Angeles, CA 90010-2901
213-736-2741

TAXATION AND REVENUE

Equalization Board
1020 N Street
Sacramento, CA 95814
916-445-3956

TOURISM

Office of Tourism
1121 L Street
Ste. 600
Sacramento, CA 95814
916-332-1396 or 1397
800-862-2543

TRANSPORTATION

Transportation Department
1120 N Street
Sacramento, CA 95814
916-445-2201

UNEMPLOYMENT

Employment Development Department
P.O. Box 826880
Sacramento, CA 94280-0001
916-445-9212

Worker's Compensation
Industrial Accidents Division
P.O. Box 603
San Francisco, CA 94101
415-557-1946

CANDY INDUSTRY

ASSOCIATIONS

National Candy Brokers Association
PO Box 486
North Andover, MA 01845
508-685-3893
Edward Bjornson, Executive Vice President
Members include independent candy salespeople and brokers.

National Candy Wholesalers Association
1120 Vermont Ave. N.W., Ste. 1120
Washington, DC 20005
202-463-2124
202-467-0559 Fax
David Strachan, Executive Vice President
Candy and confectionery wholesalers, salespeople, brokers, manufacturers, and others.

National Confectioners Association of the U.S.
7900 Westpark Dr., Ste. A-320
McLean, VA 22102
703-790-5750
Richard O'Connell, President
Confectionery manufacturers and suppliers to the candy industry.

Retail Confectioners International
1807 Glenview Rd., Ste. 204
Glenview, IL 60025
708-724-6120
Evans Billington, Executive Director
Candy manufacturers who sell their products in stores they own.

PERIODICALS

Candy Buyers Directory
Manufacturing Confectioner Publishing Co.
Directory Division
175 Rock Rd.
Glen Rock, NJ 07452
201-652-2655
Allen Allured, Editor
A listing of confectionery manufacturers for buyers of candy.

Edgell Communications
7500 Old Oak Blvd.
Cleveland, OH 44130
216-826-2839
Susan Tiffany, Editor
Provides executives in the confectionery industry with management advice and news of technological improvements.

Candy Wholesaler
National Candy Wholesalers Association, Inc.
1120 Vermont Ave., N.W., Ste. 1120
Washington, DC 20005
202-463-2124
Advice for distributors of candy, tobacco, and other consumer products.

Fancy Food
Talcott Communications Corp.
1414 Merchandise Mart
Chicago, IL 60654
312-670-0800
Follows industry trends for buyers of candy and other specialty foods.

Manufacturing Confectioner
Manufacturing Confectioner Publishing Co.
175 Rock Rd.
Glen Rock, NJ 07452
201-652-2655
Allen Allured, Editor
Advises on plant operations, financial matters, and advances in the candy making process.

United States Distribution Journal
BMT Publications, Inc.
7 Penn Plaza
New York, NY 10001-3900
212-594-4120
Kevin Francella, Editor
Information for distributors of tobacco, candy, and groceries.

LIBRARIES

Hershey Foods Corp.
Information Analysis Center
1025 Reese Ave.
Hershey, PA 17033
717-534-5106
717-523-5069 Fax
Chocolate, confectionery, nutrition, chemistry, and business.

M&M/Mars Library Research Services
800 High St.
Hackettstown, NJ 07840
201-850-2244
201-850-0918 Fax

Confectionery and business.
Westreco, Inc.
Food Research and Development
Library
577 S. Fourth St.
Fulton, NY 13069
315-593-8402
315-593-6793 Fax
Confectionery industry, chocolate, chemistry, and other topics.

COMPANIES

Farley Candy Co.
2945 W. 31st St.
Chicago, IL 60623
312-254-0900
Confectionery products.

HB Reese Candy Co., Inc.
Rte. 422 W.
Hershey, PA 17033
717-534-4100
Confectionery products.

Hershey Foods Corp.
Y and S Candies
400 Running Pump Rd.
Lancaster, PA 17603
717-299-1261
Confectionery products.

Lance, Inc.
8600 South Blvd., Box 32368
Charlotte, NC 28232
704-554-1421
Bakery and candy products.

MEI Diversified Inc.
90 S. Sixth St.
Minneapolis, MN 55402
612-339-8853
Candy, health foods, and snacks.

Mars, Inc.
6885 Elm St.
McLean, VA 22101
703-821-4900
Confectionery products.

Midial USA Fanny Farmer Candy Shops, Inc.
5885 Grant Ave.
Cleveland, OH 44105
216-883-9700
Chain of candy stores.

Nestle Foods Corp.
(Subsidiary of Nestle S.A.)
100 Manhattanville Rd.
Purchase, NY 10577
914-251-3000
Chocolate bars, confections, and other products.

Sathers, Inc.
Sather Plaza
Round Lake, MN 56167
507-945-8181
Distributor of confectionery products.

See's Candy Shops, Inc.
(Subsidiary of Berkshire Hathaway Inc.)
210 El Camino Real
South San Francisco, CA 94080
415-583-7307
Retailer of candy.

Tootsie Roll Industries, Inc.
7401 S. Cicero Ave.
Chicago, IL 60629
312-838-3400
Candy and confectionery products.

FEDERAL GOVERNMENT

U.S. Customs Service
Department of the Treasury
U.S. Customshouse
6 World Trade Center
New York, NY 10048
212-466-5550
Ask for the Commodity Specialist in charge of candy or confectionery products.

U.S. International Trade Administration
Department of Commerce
14th St. and Constitution Ave., N.W.
Washington, DC 20230
202-377-2000
Ask for the Commodity Analyst who is an expert in candy or confectionery products.

U.S. International Trade Commission
500 E St., S.W.
Washington, DC 20436
202-205-2000 Office of the Secretary
202-205-3296 Industries locator
Ask for the Trade Analyst who is an expert in candy or confectionery products.

CANNED FOOD INDUSTRY

See also: FOOD MACHINERY AND EQUIPMENT INDUSTRY and FOOD INDUSTRY

ASSOCIATIONS

Canned Food Information Council
500 N. Michigan Ave., Ste. 300
Chicago, IL 60611
312-836-7279
312-836-7170 Fax
Julie Well, Supervisor
Manufacturers of canned food.

Food Processing Machinery and Supplies
  Association
200 Daingerfield Rd.
Alexandria, VA 22314
703-684-1080
800-331-8816
703-548-6563 Fax
George Melnykovich, President
Companies that supply the freezing, canning, and food processing industries with machinery and supplies.

Food Processors Institute
1401 New York Ave., N.W., Ste. 400
Washington, DC 20005
202-393-0890
202-639-5932 Fax
Ken Stevenson, Executive Director
Offers education and training to people who work in food precessing.

National Food Processors Association
1401 New York Ave. N.W., 4th Fl.
Washington, DC 20005
202-639-5900
202-639-5932 Fax
John Cady, President
A large group of food packers, canners, and preservers.

PERIODICALS

Directory of the Canning, Freezing, Preserv-
  ing Industries
Edward E. Judge & Sons, Inc.
Box 866
Westminster, MD 21157
301-876-2052
Daniel Judge, Editor
Lists businesses that can, freeze, and preserve food in North America.

Prepared Foods
Gorman Publishing Co.
8750 Bryn Mawr Ave.
Chicago, IL 60631
312-693-3200
Mike Pehanich, Editor
Follows trends in food preserving, canning, and related topics.

LIBRARIES

Beatrice/Hunt-Wesson
Technical Library
1645 W. Valencia Dr., M.S. 506
Fullerton, CA 92633-3899
724-680-2158
724-449-5166 Fax
Food packaging, science, and technology.

H.J. Heinz Co.
Technical Information Center
1062 Progress St.
Pittsburgh, PA 15212
412-237-5948
412-237-5725 Fax
Food packaging and processing, bacteriology, nutrition, and agriculture.

National Food Processors Association
National Food Laboratory
Library
6363 Clark Ave.
Box 2277
Dublin, CA 94568
425-828-1440
415-833-8795 Fax
Food processing and engineering, product development, and related topics.

COMPANIES

Atalanta Corp.
Atalanta Plaza
Elizabeth, NJ 07206
201-351-8000
Canned meats, frozen foods.

Beatrice/Hunt-Wesson Foods
(Subsidiary of Beatrice Co.)
1645 W. Valencia Dr.
Fullerton, CA 92634
714-680-1000
Canned tomato products and other foods.

CPC International Inc.
International Plaza
Englewood Cliffs, NJ 07632
201-894-4000
*Canned vegetables and fruits, and many other
kinds of foods.*

Curtice-Burns Foods Inc.
One Lincoln First Sq.
Rochester, NY 14603
716-383-1850
*Canned fruits, vegetables, desserts, and many
other kinds of foods.*

H. J. Heinz Co.
600 Grant St.
Pittsburgh, PA 15219
412-456-5700
Canned and processed foods of all kinds.

Seneca Foods Corp.
1162 Pittsford-Victor Rd.
Pittsford, NY 14534
716-385-9500
*Canned vegetables and many other types of
foods.*

Star-Kist Foods, Inc.
(Subsidiary of H. J. Heinz Co.)
180 E. Ocean Blvd.
Long Beach, CA 90802
213-590-7900
Canned tuna.

Tri/Valley Growers Inc.
1255 Battery St.
San Francisco, CA 94111
415-445-1600
Vegetable and fruit production and canning.

FEDERAL GOVERNMENT

U.S. International Trade Administration
Department of Commerce
14th St. and Constitution Ave., N.W.
Washington, DC 20230
202-377-2000
*Ask for the Commodity Analyst who is an
expert in canned fruits and vegetables and also
in packaging machinery.*

U.S. International Trade Commission
500 E St., S.W.
Washington, DC 20436
202-205-2000 Office of the Secretary
202-205-3296 Industries locator
*Ask for the Trade Analyst who is an expert in
canned fruits and vegetables and also in packaging machinery.*

CARPETS AND RUGS

ASSOCIATIONS

Carpet Manufacturers Marketing Association
300 Emery Sq.
Dalton, GA 30720
404-278-4101
Jane Osborne, Executive Director
*Carpet manufacturers and suppliers to the
carpeting industry.*

Carpet and Rug Institute
P.O. Box 2048
Dalton, GA 30722
Ronald VanGelderen, President
404-278-3176
404-278-8835
*Offers research and technical services to manu-
facturers of carpets, rugs, and similar products.*

Oriental Rug Importers Association
100 Park Plaza Dr.
Secaucus, NJ 07094
201-866-5054
Lucille Laufer, Executive Director
Members import and wholesale oriental rugs.

PERIODICALS

Carpet & Rug Industry
Rodman Publications, Inc.
17 S. Franklin Tpk.
Box 555
Ramsey, NJ 07446
201-825-2552
Frank O'Neill, Editor
Follows news and trends in the carpet industry.

Carpet and Rug Industry Review
Carpet and Rug Institute
310 Holiday Ave., S.
Box 2048
Dalton, GA 30720-2048
404-278-3176
*Reports on new products and issues in the car-
pet and rug business.*

Oriental Rug Review
Oriental Rug Auction Review, Inc.
Box 709
Meredith, NH 03253
603-744-9191
Ron O'Callaghan, Editor
*News and in-depth articles for collectors and
dealers of orientals rugs and textiles.*

LIBRARIES

Textile Museum
Arthur D. Jenkins Library
2320 S. St., N.W.
Washington, DC 20008
202-667-0441
Rare and ancient oriental rugs and textiles.

COMPANIES

Burlington Industries, Inc.
Lees Commercial Carpet Div.
3330 W. Friendly Ave.
Greensboro, NC 27420
919-379-2000
Carpeting and related products.

Columbus Mills, Inc.
4600 River Rd.
Columbus, GA 31904
404-324-0111
Carpeting and related products.

Diamond Rug and Carpet Mills, Inc.
P.O. Box 46
Eton, GA 30724
404-695-9446
Carpeting and related products.

Galaxy Carpet Mills, Inc.
P.O. Box 800
Chatsworth, GA 30705
404-695-9611
Carpeting and related products.

HMK Enterprises, Inc.
800 South St.
Waltham, MA 02154
627-891-6660
Carpeting and related products.

Image Carpets, Inc.
P.O. Box 5555
Armuchee, GA 30105
404-235-8444
Carpeting and related products.

Mohawk Carpet Corp.
1755 The Exchange
Atlanta, GA 30339
404-951-6000
Carpeting and related products.

Salem Carpet Mills, Inc.
P.O. Box 2818
Winston-Salem, NC 27102
919-727-1200
Carpeting and related products.

Shaw Industries, Inc.
P.O. Drawer 2128
Dalton, GA 30722
404-278-3812
Carpeting and related products.

World Carpets, Inc.
P.O. Box 1448
Dalton, GA 30722
404-278-8000
Carpeting and related products.

FEDERAL GOVERNMENT

U.S. Customs Service
Department of the Treasury
U.S. Customshouse
6 World Trade Center
New York, NY 10048
212-466-5550
Ask for the Commodity Specialist in charge of rugs or carpeting.

U.S. International Trade Administration
Department of Commerce
14th St. and Constitution Ave., N.W.
Washington, DC 20230
202-377-2000
Ask for the Commodity Analyst who is an expert in the carpet industry.

U.S. International Trade Commission
500 E St., S.W.
Washington, DC 20436
202-205-2000 Office of the Secretary
202-205-3296 Industries locator
Ask for the Trade Analyst who is an expert in the carpet industry.

CASH MANAGEMENT

ASSOCIATIONS

National Association of Corporate Treasurers
1101 Connecticut Ave. N.W., Ste. 700
Washington, DC 20036
202-857-1115
202-429-5154 Fax
Robert Chancler, Executive Director
Offer seminars on cash management and many other topics.

National Corporate Cash Management Association
52 Church Hill Rd.
Newtown, CT 06470
203-426-3007
Donald Manger, Executive Director
Offers executives information on how to improve the management of corporate cash.

PERIODICALS

Cash Flow Enhancement Report
Institute of Management and Adminstration
29 W. 35th St., 5th fl.
New York, NY 10001-2200
212-244-0360
Reports on new techniques that make cash flow more efficient.

Cash Management Performance Report
Warren, Gorham and Lamont Inc.
One Penn Plaza
New York, NY 10119
800-950-1217
Offers information on strategies and innovations to executives responsible for corporate cash management.

Corporate Cashflow
Communication Channels, Inc.
6255 Barfield Rd.
Atlanta, GA 30328-4369
404-256-9800
Richard H. Gamble, Editor
Advises treasurers and others how to control cash, risk, credit, investments, and accounts receivable.

Journal of Cash Management
National Corporate Cash Management Association
145 Route 46 W.
Wayne, NJ 07470
201-812-1922
Kenneth Parkinson, Editor
Prints lengthy articles on investments, banking, and other issues of concern to treasurers.

Treasury Manager
I B C—U S A Inc.
360 Woodland St.
Box 6640
Holliston, MA 01746
508-429-5930
Bruce Fraser, Editor
Surveys such issues as improving cash flow, bank services, investment strategies, and management techniques.

CATTLE INDUSTRY

See also: LIVESTOCK INDUSTRY

ASSOCIATIONS

American Angus Association
3201 Frederick Blvd.
St. Joseph, MO 64506
816-233-3101
Richard Spader, Executive Vice President
Owners and breeders of Angus cattle.

American Hereford Association
PO Box 014059
1501 Wyandotte
Kansas City, MO 64101
816-842-3757
816-842-6931 Fax
H. H. Dickenson, Executive Vice President
Owner and breeders of Hereford cattle.

American National Cattle Women
5420 S. Quebec
PO Box 3881
Englewood, CO 80155
303-694-0313
303-694-0305 Fax
Laurie Stotts, Executive Vice President
A large group of women who work in the cattle industry.

American Polled Hereford Association
4700 E. 63rd St.
Kansas City, MO 64130
816-333-7731
816-333-7365 Fax
Larry Heidebrecht, President
Owners and breeders of Polled Hereford cattle.

Holstein-Friesian Association of America
1 Holstein Pl.
Brattleboro, VT 05301-0808
802-254-4551
James Yanizyn, Executive Officer
Breeders and owners of Holstein cattle.

National Cattlemen's Association
PO Box 3469
Englewood, CO 80155
303-694-0305
John Meetz, Executive Vice President
This huge organization of farmers and ranchers coordinates industrywide efforts in the areas of public relations, legislation, and other matters.

North American Limousin Foundation
PO Box 4467
Englewood, CO 80155
303-220-1693
Wayne Vanderwert, Executive Vice President
Owners and breeders of Limousin cattle.

PERIODICALS

Beef Business Bulletin
National Cattlemen's Association
5420 S. Quebec St.
Englewood, CO 80111
303-694-0305
Scott Cooper, Editor
Follows trends in the cattle breeding industry.

Beef Today
Farm Journal, Inc.
230 W. Washington Sq.
Philadelphia, PA 19105
215-829-4700
John Byrne, Editor
Reports on business and technological matters of interest to cattle breeders.

Beefweek
Livestock Breeder Journal, Inc.
567 Arlington Place
Box 4264
Macon, GA 31208
912-746-4815
A news weekly for ranchers and breeders.

Hornsmatch
Rt. 198
Woodstock Valley, CT 06282
203-974-2223
Focuses on horned cattle, bison, and related breeds.

LIBRARIES

Michigan State University
Animal Industries Reference Room
208 Anthony Hall
East Lansing, MI 48824
517-355-8483
517-353-9806 Fax
Animal breeding and production.

National Association of Animal Breeders
Library
401 Bernadette Dr.
Box 1033
Columbia, MO 65205
314-445-4406
314-446-2279 Fax
Cattle breeding and related topics.

University of Illinois
Agriculture Library
226 Mumford Hall
1301 W. Gregory Dr.
Urbana, IL 61801
217-333-2416
217-244-0398 Fax
Animal science and food science.

COMPANIES

Bartlett Cattle Co.
4800 Main St.
Kansas City, MO 64112
816-753-6300
Beef cattle feedlot.

Brookover Feed Yards
P.O. Box 917
Garden City, KS 67846
316-276-6662
Beef cattle feedlot.

Cactus Feeders, Inc.
P.O. Box 3050
Amarilla, TX 79116
806-373-2333
Beef cattle feedlot.

Granada Foods Corp.
10900 Richmond Ave.
Houston, TX 77042
713-229-8000
Beef cattle feedlot.

Hollandia Dairy
662 E. Mission Ave.
San Marcos, CA 92069
619-744-3222
Cattle ranch.

Honda Co.
720 E. College Blvd.
Roswell, NM 88201
505-625-8670
Cattle ranch.

King Ranch, Inc.
16825 Northchase Ave.
Houston, TX 77060
713-872-5566
Cattle ranch.

Orita Land and Cattle
P.O. Box 1420
Brawley, CA 92227
619-344-4040
Cattle ranch.

Pioneer Feed Yards, Inc.
P.O. Box 547
Oakley, KS 67748
913-672-3257
Beef cattle feedlot.

Tejon Ranch Co.
P.O. Box 1000
Lebec, CA 93243
805-327-8481
Cattle ranch.

FEDERAL GOVERNMENT

U.S. Department of Agriculture
14th St. and Independence Ave., S.W.
Washington, DC 20250
202-720-8732
*Ask for the Economic Research Service or the
National Agricultural Statistics Service.*

U.S. International Trade Administration
Department of Commerce
14th St. and Constitution Ave., N.W.
Washington, DC 20230
202-377-2000
*Ask for the Commodity Analyst who is an
expert in the cattle industry.*

U.S. International Trade Commission
500 E St., S.W.
Washington, DC 20436
202-205-2000 Office of the Secretary
202-205-3296 Industries locator
*Ask for the Trade Analyst who is an expert in
the cattle industry.*

CEMENT INDUSTRY

ASSOCIATIONS

American Cement Alliance
1212 New York Ave. N.W., Ste. 528
Washington, DC 20005
202-408-9494
202-408-9392 Fax
Richard Creighton, President
Firms that make Portland cement.

Portland Cement Association
5420 Old Orchard Rd.
Skokie, IL 60077
708-966-6200
708-966-9781 Fax
John Gleason, President
Firms that manufacture and sell Portland cement.

PERIODICALS

American Cement Directory
Bradley Pulverizer Co.
Box 1318
123 S. Third St.
Allentown, PA 18105
215-434-5191
Veronica M. Saylor, Editor
A listing of companies and individuals in the cement industry.

Cement and Concrete Research
Pergamon Press, Inc., Journals Division
Maxwell House
Fairview Park
Elmsford, NY 10523
914-592-7700
Della Roy, Editor
A technical journal for engineers and technicians.

Mineral Industry Surveys. Cement
U.S. Bureau of Mines
Production and Distribution
Cochrans Mill Rd.
Box 18070
Pittsburgh, PA 15236
412-892-4411
Offers statistical data on cement production in the U.S.

Pit & Quarry
Edgell Communications
7500 Old Oak Blvd.
Cleveland, OH 44130
216-243-8100
Robert Drake, Editor
Reports industry news about sand, gravel, crushed stone, cement, and other products.

Rock Products
Maclean Hunter Publishing Co.
29 N. Wacker Dr.
Chicago, IL 60606
312-726-2802
Richard Hunta, Editor
Follows trends for manufacturers and distributors of sand, gravel, crushed stone, cement, lime, and other products.

LIBRARIES

Holnam Inc.
Library
Box 1468
LaPorte, CO 80535
303-482-5600
303-482-5608 Fax
Concrete, mineralogy, and related topics.

Portland Cement Association
Library Services
5420 Old Orchard Rd.
Skokie, IL 60077
708-966-6200
708-966-9781 Fax
*Cement chemistry, concrete technology, and
related topics.*

COMPANIES

Ash Grove Cement Co.
P. O. Box 25900
Overland Park, KS 66225
913-451-8900
Portland cement and lime.

California Portland Cement Co.
(Division of CalMat Co.)
3200 San Fernando Rd.
Los Angeles, CA 90065
213-258-2777
Portland cement and other types of cement.

Coplay Cement Co.
(Subsidiary of Societe Des Ciments Francais)
P.O. Box 32
Nazareth, PA 18064
215-837-6725
Cement.

Dundee Cement Co.
(Subsidiary of Holnam Inc.)
Dundee, MI 48131
313-529-2411
Portland cement.

Fuller Co.
2040 Ave. C
Bethlehem, PA 18001
215-264-6011
*Design and construction of cement plants and
other types of heavy equipment.*

Gifford-Hill Cement Co.
(Subsidiary of Gifford-Hill & Co., Inc.)
2515 McKinney Ave., LB30
Dallas, TX 75201
214-754-5500
Portland cement.

Glen-Gery Corp.
(Subsidiary of Ibstock Johnsen PLC)
1166 Spring St., Box 7001
Wyomissing, PA 19610
215-374-4011
Bricks and cement blocks.

Lafarge Corp.
(Subsidiary of LaFarge Coppee)
11130 Sunrise Valley Dr., Box 4600
Reston, VA 22090
703-264-3600
Cement, concrete, and related products.

Southdown, Inc.
1200 Smith St.
Houston, TX 77002
713-650-6200
Cement and concrete.

Tilcon Inc.
Blackrock Ave.
New Britain, CT 06050
203-223-3651
Concrete, cement, and other building materials.

FEDERAL GOVERNMENT

U.S. Customs Service
Department of the Treasury
U.S. Customshouse
6 World Trade Center
New York, NY 10048
212-466-5550
*Ask for the Commodity Specialist in charge of
cement products.*

U.S. International Trade Administration
Department of Commerce
14th St. and Constitution Ave., N.W.
Washington, DC 20230
202-377-2000
*Ask for the Commodity Analyst who is an
expert in the cement industry.*

U.S. International Trade Commission
500 E St., S.W.
Washington, DC 20436
202-205-2000 Office of the Secretary
202-205-3296 Industries locator
*Ask for the Trade Analyst who is an expert in
the cement industry.*

U.S. Patent and Trademark Office
Crystal Plaza 2
2011 Jefferson Davis Highway
Arlington, VA 22202
703-305-8000
*Ask for the Examining Group Director who is
a specialist in cement.*

CENSUS DATA

LIBRARIES

U.S. Bureau of the Census
Information Services Program
Los Angeles Regional Office
Library
15350 Sherman Way
Van Nuys, CA 91406
818-904-6339
818-892-6339 Fax
U.S. census and survey reports.

U.S. Bureau of the Census
Library & Information Service Branch
Federal Bldg. No. 3, Rm. 2455
Washington, DC 20233
301-763-5042
301-763-7322 Fax
*Population, survey and statistical methodol-
ogy, urban studies, and related topics.*

U.S. Dept. of Commerce
Library
14th & Constitution Ave., N.W., Rm. 8060
Washington, DC 20230
202-377-3611
*U.S. Census publications, statistics, economics,
marketing, legislation, and related subjects.*

FEDERAL GOVERNMENT

U.S. Bureau of the Census
Public Information Office
Washington, DC 20233
301-763-4040

CERAMICS

ASSOCIATIONS

Technical Ceramics Manufacturers Association
25 N. Broadway
Tarrytown, NY 10591
914-332-0040
Richard Byrne, Executive Director
Members include manufacturers of the ceramics used to make components for electronic products.

United States Advanced Ceramics Association
1440 New York Ave. N.W., Ste. 300
Washington, DC 20005
202-638-1200
202-639-8685 Fax
Steven Hellem, Executive Director
A clearinghouse for information about advanced ceramics used in electronics and other industrial applications.

PERIODICALS

C A Selects. Ceramic Materials
Chemical Abstracts Service
2540 Olentangy River Rd.
Box 3012
Columbus, OH 43210
614-447-3600
Surveys the manufacture and use of ceramics as building materials, insulators, cutting tools, and other uses.

Ceramic Engineering and Science Proceedings
American Ceramic Society, Inc.
757 Brooksedge Plaza Dr.
Box 6136
Westerville, OH 43081-6136
614-890-4700
John Wachtman, Editor
Technical data on the manufacture and use of ceramics.

Ceramic Industry
Business News Publishing Co.
Box 2600
Troy, MI 48007
313-362-3700
Patricia Janeway, Editor
Business information about the ceramics industry.

LIBRARIES

Harbison-Walker Refractories Co.
Garber Research Center Library
1001 Pittsburgh-McKeesport Blvd.
West Mifflin, PA 15122
412-469-3880
Ceramics, refractories, and related topics.

Norton Co.
Advanced Ceramics
Loring Coes, Jr. Library
Goddard Rd.
Northborough, MA 01532
508-393-5810
508-393-2270 Fax
Advanced ceramics.

Ohio State University
Materials Engineering Library
197 Watts Hall
2041 N. College Rd.
Columbus, OH 43210
614-292-9614
Ceramic engineering and materials science.

COMPANIES

AVX Corp.
(Subsidiary of Kyocera Corp.)
750 Lexington Ave.
New York, NY 10022
212-935-6363
Multilayer ceramic components and other products.

JE Baker Co.
P.O. Box 1189
York, PA 17405
717-848-1504
Refractories, ceramics, and other products.

Brush Wellman Inc.
1200 Hanna Bldg
Cleveland, OH 44115
216-443-1000
Beryllia ceramics and other products.

Carborundum Co.
(Subsidiary of British Petroleum Co. p.l.c.)
345 Third St., Carborundum Ctr.
Niagara Falls, NY 14302
716-278-2000
Ceramic fiber, refractories, structural and electronic ceramics.

Coors Porcelain Co.
(Subsidiary of Adolph Coors Co.)
600 9th St.
Golden, CO 80401
303-278-4000
Structural ceramic products and other types of products.

Ferro Corp.
1000 Lakeside Ave.
Cleveland, OH 44114
216-641-8580
Chemicals, ceramics, theromoplastics, and other products.

Resco Products, Inc.
1302 Conshohocken Rd.
Norristown, PA 19401
215-279-5010
Refractories, ceramics, and other products.

Unitrode Corp.
Five Forbes Rd.
Lexington, MA 02173
617-861-6540
Ceramic capacitors and other types of electronic parts and components.

FEDERAL GOVERNMENT

U.S. Customs Service
Department of the Treasury
U.S. Customshouse
6 World Trade Center
New York, NY 10048
212-466-5550
Ask for the Commodity Specialist in charge of ceramics products.

U.S. International Trade Administration
Department of Commerce
14th St. and Constitution Ave., N.W.
Washington, DC 20230
202-377-2000
Ask for the Commodity Analyst who is an expert in the ceramics industry.

U.S. International Trade Commission
500 E St., S.W.
Washington, DC 20436
202-205-2000 Office of the Secretary
202-205-3296 Industries locator
Ask for the Trade Analyst who is an expert in the ceramics industry.

CHAIN STORES

See also: RETAIL TRADE and SHOPPING CENTERS AND MALLS

ASSOCIATIONS

International Center for Companies of the
   Food Trade and Industry
3800 Moore Pl.
Alexandria, VA 22305
703-549-4525
703-549-0406 Fax
Sally Adamy-McMullen, Representative
*Members include large chain stores that sell
food and firms that supply the chain food store
industry.*

National Association of Convenience Stores
1605 King St.
Alexandria, VA 22314-2792
703-684-3600
703-836-4564 Fax
Kerley LeBoeuf, President
*Stores that sell food, gasoline, grocery items,
and other items. Many of these stores belong
to a chain.*

National Retail Federation
100 W. 31st St.
New York, NY 10001
212-244-8780
212-594-0487 Fax
John Schultz, President
*A variety of stores, including chain stores, that
sell home furnishings and apparel.*

PERIODICALS

Chain Store Age General Merchandise Trends
Lebhar-Friedman, Inc.
425 Park Ave.
New York, NY 10022
212-371-9400
Murray Forseter, Editor
*Offers chain store executives an overview of
industry news.*

Directory of Leading Chain Stores
Chain Store Guide Information Services
425 Park Ave.
New York, NY 10022
212-371-9400
An annual listing of major chain stores.

Shopping Center World
Communication Channels, Inc.
6255 Barfield Rd.
Atlanta, GA 30328-4369
404-256-9800
Teresa DeFranks, Editor
*Provides information to executives who build
and manage shopping centers and chain stores.*

LIBRARIES

Lebhar-Friedman, Inc.
Chain Store Age
Reader Service Research Library
425 Park Ave.
New York, NY 10022
212-371-9400
212-838-9487 Fax
*Chain stores, retailing, merchandising, shop-
ping centers, and related subjects.*

National Association of Convenience Stores
1605 King St.
Alexandria, VA 22314-2792
703-684-3600
703-836-4564 Fax
Convenience stores and other retailing topics.

COMPANIES

Arnold Constable Corp.
240 West 40th St.
New York, NY 10018
212-997-0080
Chain stores.

D & C Stores
N. Clinton St.
Stockbridge, MI 49285
517-851-7925
Chain stores.

E-II Holdings
(Subsidiary of Riklis Family Corp.)
725 Fifth Ave.
New York, NY 10022
212-735-9500
Retail chain stores.

Fisher Foods, Inc.
(Subsidiary of Riser Foods Inc.)
5300 Richmond Rd.
Bedford Heights, OH 44146
216-292-7000
Retail food chain stores.

Lerner Stores Corp.
(Subsidiary of Limited, Inc.)
460 W. 33 St.
New York, NY 10001
212-736-1222
Chain stores that sell women's and children's clothing.

McCrory Corp.
(Subsidiary of E-II Holdings)
888 Seventh Ave.
New York, NY 10106
212-621-4500
Variety chain stores.

Morse Shoe, Inc.
555 Turnpike St.
Canton, MA 02021
617-828-9300
Chain stores selling footwear.

Pep Boys
32nd & Allegheny
Philadelphia, PA 19132
215-229-9000
Automobile parts and accessories chain stores.

Western Auto Supply Co.
(Subsidiary of Sears, Roebuck and Co.)
2107 Grand Ave.
Kansas City, MO 64108
816-346-4000
Automotive chain stores.

CHAMBERS OF COMMERCE

ASSOCIATIONS

American Chamber of Commerce Executives
4232 King St.
Alexandria, VA 22302
703-998-0072
703-931-5624 Fax
Paul Greeley, President
Staff members who work for chambers of commerce nationwide.

American Chamber of Commerce
   Researchers Association
c/o Amer. Chamber of Commerce Executives
4232 King St.
Alexandria, VA 22302
703-998-4172
703-931-5624 Fax
Deborah Mason, Staff Liaison
Researchers who work for chambers of commerce.

Chamber of Commerce of the United States
1615 H St. N.W.
Washington, DC 20062
202-659-6000
202-463-5836 Fax
Richard Lesher, President
The national representative of chambers of commerce nationwide. Maintains a large library.

CHEESE INDUSTRY

See also: DAIRY INDUSTRY

ASSOCIATIONS

American Cheese Society
c/o Food Work
34 Downing St.
New York, NY 10014
212-727-7939
212-316-6664 Fax
Ari Weinzweig, President
Manufacturers, distributors, and retailers of cheese.

Cheese Importers Association of America
460 Park Ave.
New York, NY 10022
212-753-7500
212-688-2870 Fax
Virginia Sheahan, Executive Secretary
Importers and brokers of cheese.

National Cheese Institute
888 16th St. N.W.
Washington, DC 20006
202-659-1454
202-659-1496 Fax
Floyd Gaibler, Executive Director
Cheese makers and distributors.

United States Cheese Makers Association
Three S. Pinckney St., Ste. 215
Madison, WI 53703
608-255-2027
Linda Leger, Executive Director
Represents cheese manufacturers.

PERIODICALS

Cheese Market News
Gorman Publishing Co.
8750 W. Bryn Mawr Ave.
Chicago, IL 60631
312-693-3200
Alan Lenitt, Editor
Covers the cheese industry for producers and distributors.

Cheese Reporter
Cheese Reporter Publishing Co., Inc.
6401 Odana Rd.
Madison, WI 53719-1157
608-273-1300
Richard Groves, Editor
Reports on the technological and business aspects of manufacturing and marketing of cheese and cultured milk products.

LIBRARIES

Kraft USA
Technical Information Research
801 Waukegan Rd.
Glenview, IL 60025
708-998-3707
708-998-5150 Fax
Dairy science, food technology, and related topics.

Ohio State University
Agriculture Library
45 Agriculture Bldg.
2120 Fyffe Rd.
Columbus, OH 43210
614-292-6125
614-292-7859 Fax
Dairy science, food science, and nutrition.

U.S.D.A.
National Agricultural Library
10301 Baltimore Blvd.
Beltsville, MD 20705
301-344-3755
301-344-5472 Fax
*Animal industry, veterinary medicine, food
industry, dairy products, and nutrition.*

COMPANIES

Amfac Foods Inc.
(Subsidiary of Amfac, Inc.)
7000 S. W. Hampton St.
Portland, OR 97223
503-620-3600
*Natural and processed cheese, and other
foods.*

Borden, Inc.
277 Park Ave.
New York, NY 10172
212-573-4000
*Cheeses, other dairy products, and other types
of food.*

Crowley Foods, Inc.
(Subsidiary of Wessanen U.S.A. Inc.)
Metrocenter
Binghamton, NY 13902
607-722-6441
Dairy products, including cheeses.

Dairymen, Inc.
10140 Linn Station Rd.
Louisville, KY 40223
502-426-6455
*An agriculture cooperative that produces
cheese and other dairy products.*

H. P. Hood Inc.
(Subsidiary of Agway Inc.)
500 Rutherford Ave.
Boston, MA 02129
617-242-0600
*Food processor that makes cheese and other
products.*

Mid-America Dairymen, Inc.
3253 E. Chestnut Expressway
Springfield, MO 65802
417-865-7100
Cheese and other dairy products.

Morning Glory Farms Region
(Division of Associated Milk Producers, Inc.)
116 N. Main St.
Shawano, WI 54166
715-526-2131
Dairy products, including cheese.

Wisconsin Dairies Co-Op
Rte. 3 Hwy. 12 N.
Baraboo, WI 53913
608-356-8316
Dairy products, including cheese.

FEDERAL GOVERNMENT

U.S. Customs Service
Department of the Treasury
U.S. Customshouse
6 World Trade Center
New York, NY 10048
212-466-5550
*Ask for the Commodity Specialist in charge of
cheeses.*

U.S. Department of Agriculture
14th St. and Independence Ave., S.W.
Washington, DC 20250
202-720-8732
Ask for dairy products in Economic Research Service or the Agricultural Marketing Service.

U.S. International Trade Administration
Department of Commerce
14th St. and Constitution Ave., N.W.
Washington, DC 20230
202-377-2000
Ask for the Commodity Analyst who is an expert in the cheese industry.

U.S. International Trade Commission
500 E St., S.W.
Washington, DC 20436
202-205-2000 Office of the Secretary
202-205-3296 Industries locator
Ask for the Trade Analyst who is an expert in the cheese industry.

CHEMICAL ENGINEERING

See also: CHEMICAL INDUSTRY

ASSOCIATIONS

American Institute of Chemical Engineers
345 E. 47th St.
New York, NY 10017
212-705-7338
212-752-3294 Fax
Richard Emmert, Executive Director
A very large society of chemical engineers. Publishes numerous technical journals.

Association of Consulting Chemists and
    Chemical Engineers
310 Madison Ave., Ste. 1423
New York, NY 10017
212-983-3160
212-983-3161 Fax
Elizabeth Jones, Executive Secretary
Offers a referral service to help industrial firms and others find chemical engineers who provide consulting services.

PERIODICALS

Chemical and Engineering News
American Chemical Society
1155 16th St., N.W.
Washington, DC 20036
202-872-4363
Michael Heylin, Editor
Reports on technological and business matters relating to the chemical industry.

Chemical Engineering
McGraw-Hill, Inc.
1221 Ave. of the Americas
New York, NY 10020
212-512-2000
Nicholas Chopey, Editor
Offers information for chemical engineers and others working in the chemical process industries.

Chemical Engineering Progress
American Institute of Chemical Engineers
345 E. 47th St.
New York, NY 10017
212-705-7663
Attilio Bisio, Editor
Follows news of technological advances, new products, regulatory issues, and related subjects.

Chemical Week
Chemical Week Associates
810 Seventh Ave.
New York, NY 10019
212-586-3430
Peter Coombes, Editor
Covers the technology and business sides of the chemical process industries.

LIBRARIES

Babcock and Wilcox Co.
Corporate Information Center
Box 835
Alliance, OH 44601
216-821-9110
216-823-0639 Fax
Chemical engineering, chemistry, electronics, nuclear science, and related topics.

Chemists' Club Library
Chemical International Information Center
295 Madison Ave., 27th Fl.
New York, NY 10017
212l-679-6383
212-779-0349 Fax
Chemical engineering, pure chemistry, and applied chemistry.

University of Texas, Austin
Chemistry Library
General Libraries, WEL 2.132
Austin, TX 78713-7330
512-471-1303
512-471-6983 Fax
Chemical engineering, chemistry, and biochemistry.

FEDERAL GOVERNMENT

U.S. Patent and Trademark Office
Crystal Plaza 2
2011 Jefferson Davis Highway
Arlington, VA 22202
703-305-8000
Ask for the Examining Group Director who is a specialist in chemical engineering.

U.S. Department of Commerce
14th St. & Constitution Ave., N.W.
Washington, DC 20230
202-377-2000
Ask for the Center for Chemical Engineering or the Center for Chemical Technology.

CHEMICAL INDUSTRY

See also: CHEMICAL ENGINEERING

ASSOCIATIONS

Chemical Manufacturers Association
2501 M St., N.W.
Washington, DC 20037
202-887-1100
800-CMA-8200
202-887-1237 Fax
Charles Van Vlack, Secretary
This group of chemical manufacturers oper-
ates the Chemical Referral Center, which
answers questions on health, safety, pollution,
and many other subjects.

Chemical Specialties Manufacturers Association
1913 I St., N.W.
Washington, DC 20006
202-872-8110
202-872-8114 Fax
Ralph Engel, President
Manufacturers and sellers of such products as
household cleaners, polishes, and pesticides.

Industrial Chemical Research Association
1811 Monroe St.
Dearborn, MI 48124
313-563-0360
Harold Castor, President
Researchers, manufacturers, marketers, and
others who share information on research,
safety, and selling techniques.

National Association of Chemical Distributors
1200 17th St. N.W., Ste. 400
Washington, DC 20036
202-296-9200
202-296-0023 Fax
Joseph Cook, Executive Vice President
Distributors and transporters of chemicals.

PERIODICALS

Chemical and Engineering News
American Chemical Society
1155 16th St., N.W.
Washington, DC 20036
202-872-4363
Michael Heylin, Editor
Reports on technological and business matters
relating to the chemical industry.

Chemical Engineering
McGraw-Hill, Inc.
1221 Ave. of the Americas
New York, NY 10020
212-512-2000
Nicholas Chopey, Editor
Offers information for chemical engineers and
others working in the chemical process indus-
tries.

Chemical Week
Chemical Week Associates
810 Seventh Ave.
New York, NY 10019
212-586-3430
Peter Coombes, Editor
Covers the technology and business sides of
the chemical process industries.

Chemical Worker
International Chemical Workers Union
International Chemical Workers Bldg.
1655 W. Market St.
Akron, OH 44313
216-867-2444
Frank Martino, Editor
News of interest to unionized workers in the chemical industry.

Industrial Chemical News
McGraw-Hill, Inc.
1221 Ave. of the Americas
New York, NY 10020
212-512-2000
Irvin Schwartz, Editor
News for executives of chemical firms.

LIBRARIES

American Chemical Society
Library
1155 16th St., N.W.
Washington, DC 20036
202-872-4509
202-872-6257 Fax
Chemical industry and chemical engineering.

Chemists' Club Library
Chemical International Information Center
295 Madison Ave., 27th Fl.
New York, NY 10016
212-679-6383
212-779-0349 Fax
Chemical engineering, chemistry, and the chemical industry.

COMPANIES

Air Products And Chemicals, Inc.
Box 538
Allentown, PA 18105
215-481-4911
Industrial gases and chemicals.

American Cyanamid Co.
One Cyanamid Plaza
Wayne, NJ 07470
201-831-2000
Specialty chemicals and other products.

Arco Chemical Co.
3801 W. Chester Pike
Newtown Square, PA 19073
215-359-2000
Intermediate chemicals and specialty chemicals.

Bayer USA Inc.
(Subsidiary of Bayer AG)
500 Grant St., One Mellon Ctr.
Pittsburgh, PA 15219
412-394-5500
Industrial and agricultural chemicals, and other products.

Degussa Corp.
(Subsidiary of Degussa AG)
65 Challenger Rd.
Ridgefield Park, NJ 07660
201-641-6100
Organic and inorganic chemicals.

Dow Plastics & Hydro-Carbons
(Division of Dow Chemical USA)
2040 Willard H. Dow Center
Midland, MI 48674
517-636-3050
Chemicals and other products.

W. R. Grace & Co.
1114 Ave. of the Americas
New York, NY 10036
212-819-5500
Specialty chemicals and other businesses.

Great Lakes Chemical Corp.
P.O. Box 2200, Hwy. 52, N.W.
West Lafayette, IN 47906
317-497-6100
Specialty chemicals, agricultural chemicals, water treatment and oil field chemicals.

Lubrizol Corp.
29400 Lakeland Blvd.
Wickliffe, OH 44092
216-943-4200
Specialty chemicals and chemical additives.

Morton International Inc.
110 N. Wacker Dr.
Chicago, IL 60606
312-807-2000
Specialty chemicals.

Occidental Chemical Corp.
(Subsidiary of Occidental Petroleum Corp.)
5005 LBJ Frwy.
Dallas, TX 75244
214-404-3800
Chemicals and plastics.

Olin Corp.
120 Long Ridge Rd.
Stamford, CT 06904
203-356-2000
Specialty and industrial chemicals.

Rohm & Haas Co.
Independence Mall W.
Philadelphia, PA 19105
215-592-3000
Industrial and agricultural chemicals.

Union Carbide Corp.
39 Old Ridgebury Rd.
Danbury, CT 06817
203-794-2000
Chemicals, plastics, and other products.

FEDERAL GOVERNMENT

U.S. Customs Service
Department of the Treasury
U.S. Customshouse
6 World Trade Center
New York, NY 10048
212-466-5550
Ask for the Commodity Specialist in charge of chemicals.

U.S. International Trade Administration
Department of Commerce
14th St. and Constitution Ave., N.W.
Washington, DC 20230
202-377-2000
Ask for the Commodity Analyst who is an expert in the specific type of chemical that interests you.

U.S. International Trade Commission
500 E St., S.W.
Washington, DC 20436
202-205-2000 Office of the Secretary
202-205-3296 Industries locator
Ask for the Trade Analyst who is an expert in the specific type of chemical that interests you.

CHILD CARE

ASSOCIATIONS

American Council of Nanny Schools
Delta College
University Center, MI 48710
517-686-9417
*The Council represents 25 schools nationwide
that train nannies. Offers referrals.*

Child Care Action Campaign
99 Hudson Street
Room 1233
New York, NY 10013
212-334-9595
*Although primarily a lobbying group, this
organization publishes a newsletter, Childcare
ActioNews, that follows trends in child care
for working parents.*

National Association of Child Care Resource
 & Referral Agencies
2116 Campus Drive, S.E.
Rochester, MN 55904
507-287-2220
*Directs parents to local child care referral
agencies nationwide.*

National Association for Family Day Care
725 Fifteenth Street, N.W.
Ste. 505
Washington, DC 20005
202-347-3356
800-359-3817
Makes referrals to local child care providers.

PERIODICALS

Center Management
Engel Communications, Inc.
820 Bear Tavern Rd.
W. Trenton, NJ 08628
609-530-0044
Bob Smite, Editor
*Offers business and management advice to
owners and operators of day care centers.*

ChildCare
Cara Communications Ltd.
100 Court Ave.
Des Moines, IA 50309
515-282-2888
Debra Steilen, Editor
*Provides information on how to improve the
management of day care centers.*

Nanny Times
Jack & Jill Enterprises, Inc.
Box 31
Rutherford, NJ 07070
201-935-5575
Gillian Gordon, Editor
*Written for in-home child care providers and
the parents who employ them.*

LIBRARIES

Child Welfare League of America
Information Service
Dorothy L. Bernhard Library
440 First St., N.W.
Washington, DC 20001
202-638-2952
202-638-4004 Fax
*Child development, child welfare, and social
work.*

International Child Resource Institute
Information Clearinghouse
1810 Hopkins
Berkeley, CA 94707
510-644-1000
510-845-1115 Fax
Child care, health, and related subjects.

CIVIL ENGINEERING

ASSOCIATIONS

American Society of Civil Engineers
345 E. 47th St.
New York, NY 10017
212-705-7496
Edward Pfrang, Executive Director
This very large group of civil engineers offers research services through the Engineering Societies Library.

PERIODICALS

A P W A Reporter
American Public Works Association
1313 E. 60th St.
Chicago, IL 60637
312-667-2200
Kenneth Bauder, Editor
Follows news of building trends that interest civil engineers.

E N R
McGraw-Hill, Inc.
1221 Ave. of the Americas
New York, NY 10020
212-512-2000
Howard Stussman, Editor
National and international news of construction projects.

Highway and Heavy Construction
Cahners Publishing Co.
1350 E. Touhy Ave.
Box 5080
Des Plaines, IL 60017-5080
708-635-8800
Daniel Brown, Editor
Reports on new products, methods, and other information for heavy construction managers and civil engineers.

National Utility Contractor
National Utility Contractors Association
1235 Jefferson Davis Hwy., Ste. 606
Arlington, VA 22202
703-486-2100
James Gardner, Editor
Follows news in the water and sewer construction industry.

Professional Surveyor
American Surveyors Publishing Co.
901 S. Highland, Ste. 105
Arlington, VA 22204
703-892-0733
Nick Harrison, Editor
Provides technical information to surveyors, mappers, and civil engineers.

Roads & Bridges
Scranton Gillette Communications, Inc.
380 E. Northwest Hwy.
Des Plaines, IL 60016
708-298-6622
Tom Kuennen, Editor
Informs contruction executives and civil engineers about trends in road and bridge construction and repair.

LIBRARIES

Engineering Societies Library
United Engineering Center
345 E. 47th St.
New York, NY 10017
212-705-7611
212-486-1086 Fax
Civil engineering and other engineering topics.

COMPANIES

Bechtel Group, Inc.
P.O. Box 193965
San Francisco, CA 94119
415-768-1234
Civil engineering and many other services.

CRS Sirrine Engineers, Inc.
P.O. Box 5456
Greenville, SC 29606
803-676-6000
Civil engineering and many other services.

Foster Wheeler Corp.
Perryville Corporate
Clinton, NJ 08809
908-730-4000
Civil engineering and many other services.

Foster Wheeler International Corp.
Perryville Corporate
Clinton, NJ 08809
908-730-4030
Civil engineering and many other services.

Henkels and McCoy, Inc.
985 Jolly Rd.
Blue Bell, PA 19422
215-283-7600
Civil engineering and many other services.

ICF Kaiser Engineers, Inc.
1800 Harrison St.
Oakland, CA 94612
510-268-6000
Civil engineering and many other services.

Jacobs Engineering Group, Inc.
251 S. Lake Ave.
Pasadena, CA 91101
818-449-2171
Civil engineering and many other services.

United Engineers and Constructors International, Inc.
P.O. Box 8223
Philadelphia, PA 19101
215-422-3000
Civil engineering and many other services.

FEDERAL GOVERNMENT

U.S. Department of Transportation
400 Seventh St., S.W.
Washington, DC 20590
202-366-4000
Ask for Civil Engineering in the Office of Engineering.

CIVIL SERVICE

See also: FEDERAL GOVERNMENT and MUNICIPAL GOVERNMENT

ASSOCIATIONS

Blacks in Government
1820 11th St. N.W.
Washington, DC 20001
202-667-3280
Marion Bowden, President
Afro-American civil service employees who work for local, state, or federal offices.

Civil Service Employees Association
PO Box 125, Capitol Station
143 Washington Ave.
Albany, NY 12210
518-434-0191
Joseph McDermott, President
A very large group of state and local government employees that provides legal assistance and other services.

National Association of Civil Service Employees
7185 Navajo Rd., Ste. C
San Diego, CA 92119
619-464-1014
S. K. Gossman, Secretary
Promotes the interests of city, county, state, and federal civil service employees.

National Federation of Federal Employees
1016 16th St., N.W.
Washington, DC 20036
202-862-4400
Represents the interests of federal civil service employees.

PERIODICALS

Federal Times
Army Times Publishing Co.
6883 Commercial Dr.
Springfield, VA 22159
703-750-2000
Marianne Lester, Editor
Covers news of interest to civil service workers.

Management
U.S. Office of Personnel Management
Office of Public Affairs
Washington, DC 20415
202-655-4000
David Turner, Editor
A government periodical that offers management advice to supervisors.

LIBRARIES

Institute of Public Administration
Library
55 W. 44th St.
New York NY 10036
212-730-5631
212-398-9305 Fax
Civil service, public administration, local government, and related topics.

FEDERAL GOVERNMENT

Office of Personnel Management
1900 E St. N.W.
Washington, DC 20415
202-606-2424
Ask for Employee & Labor Relations.

CLAY INDUSTRY

ASSOCIATIONS

Clay Minerals Society
PO Box 880
Evergreen, CO 80439
303-674-8095
Jo Eberl, Manager
A professional society of scientists, engineers, and executives interested in clay mineralogy.

Expanded Shale Clay and Slate Institute
2225 E. Murray Holladay Rd., Ste. 102
Salt Lake City, UT 84117
801-272-7070
801-272-3377 Fax
John Ries, Executive Director
Members include firms that produce shales, clays, and lightweight aggregate (which is used in concrete).

LIBRARIES

Engelhard Corp.
Technical Information Center
Menlo Park
Edison, NJ 08818
201-205-5271
201-205-5300 Fax
Clays, pigments, catalysts, and related topics.

Thiele Kaolin Co.
Research & Development Library
Box 1056
Sandersville, GA 31082
912-552-3951
912-552-4105 Fax
Clays, mineralogy, and related topics.

United Catalysts, Inc.
Technical Library
Box 32370
Louisville, KY 40232
502-634-7200
Clays.

COMPANIES

J. H. France Refractories Co.
(Subsidiary of Adience Inc.)
1944 France Road
Snow Shoe, PA 16874
814-387-6811
Brick and clay products.

Freeport Area Inc.
(Subsidiary of Freeport Area Enterprises Inc.)
Mill St., Drawer F
Freeport, PA 16229
412-295-2111
Clay refractories, bricks, clay mortar.

Holmes Limestone Co.
SR 39
Berlin, OH 44610
216-893-2721
Coal, clay, and limestone.

Inland Enterprises, Inc.
38600 Chester Rd., Box 239
Avon, OH 44011
216-934-6600
Clay refractories.

Justin Industries, Inc.
2821 W. 7th St.
Fort Worth, TX 76101
817-336-5125
Brick and clay products.

Kentucky-Tennessee Clay Co.
(Subsidiary of Hecla Mining Co.)
P.O. Box 449
Mayfield, KY 42066
502-247-3061
Mining and processing of ball clay.

Pacific Clay Products, Inc.
(Subsidiary of Pacific Holding Co.)
Temescal Canyon Rd.
Corona, CA 91719
714-735-6020
Clay sewer pipes.

Richards Brick Co.
234 Springer Ave
Edwardsville, IL 62025
618-656-0230
Face brick and other structural clay products.

Southern Clay Products Inc.
(Subsidiary of ECC America, Inc.)
1212 Church St.
Gonzales, TX 78629
512-672-2891
Clay and clay products.

J. C. Steele & Sons, Inc.
710 S. Mulberry St.
Statesville, NC 28677
704-872-3681
Machines for manufacturing clay products.

FEDERAL GOVERNMENT

Bureau of Mines
810 7th St., N.W.
Washington, DC 20747
202-501-9770
Ask for the Commodity Specialist who is an expert in clay products.

U.S. Customs Service
Department of the Treasury
U.S. Customshouse
6 World Trade Center
New York, NY 10048
212-466-5550
Ask for the Commodity Specialist in charge of the clay industry.

U.S. International Trade Administration
Department of Commerce
14th St. and Constitution Ave., N.W.
Washington, DC 20230
202-377-2000
Ask for the Commodity Analyst in charge of the clay industry.

U.S. International Trade Commission
500 E St., S.W.
Washington, DC 20436
202-205-2000 Office of the Secretary
202-205-3296 Industries locator
Ask for the Trade Analyst who is an expert in the clay industry.

CLEANING PRODUCTS AND SERVICES

See also: SANITATION INDUSTRY

ASSOCIATIONS

Association of Specialists in Cleaning and
    Restoration
10830 Annapolis Junction Rd., Ste. 312
Annapolis Junction, MD 20701
301-604-4411
Martin Berry, Executive Vice President
*Provides technical and business information
about the cleaning of carpets, draperies, and
upholstery.*

Cleaning Equipment Trade Association
111 E. Wacker Dr., No. 600
Chicago, IL 60601
312-644-6610
800-634-6119
312-565-4658 Fax
Maxine Couture, Executive Vice President
*Manufacturers of powered cleaning systems
including floor polishers and self-service car
washes.*

Cleaning Management Institute
13 Century Hill Dr.
Latham, NY 12110-2197
518-783-1281
518-783-1386 Fax
Ellen Evans, Executive Officer
*Provides training and educational materials to
cleaning and maintenence organizations.*

International Window Cleaning Association
27 Oak Creek Rd.
El Sobrante, CA 94803
415-222-7080
Represents the window cleaning industry.

Society of Cleaning Technicians
PO Box 981
Americus, GA 31709
912-928-3534
John Bass, Executive Director
*Members share technical information on
cleaning.*

PERIODICALS

C A Selects. Detergents, Soaps, & Surfactants
Chemical Abstracts Service
2540 Olentangy River Rd.
Box 3012
Columbus, OH 43210
614-447-3600
*Technical data regarding the manufacture and
use of soaps and synthetic detergents.*

Cleaning Business
1512 Western Ave.
Box 1273
Seattle, WA 98111
206-622-4241
W. R. Coriffin, Editor
*Provides self-employed cleaning and mainte-
nance firms advice regarding cleaning techniques and business management.*

Professional Cleaning Journal
Target Trade
2626 Valley View Ln., No. 11
Dallas, TX 75234
214-484-4474
Keven Todd, Editor
*Offers technical and business information to
those who clean drapery, carpet, and upholstery.*

LIBRARIES

Dixo Engineering
Library
158 Central Ave.
Box 7038
Rochelle Park, NJ 07662
201-845-6000
201-845-6004 Fax
Dry cleaning.

Ecolab, Inc.
Corporate Information Center
840 Sibley Memorial Hwy.
St. Paul, MN 55118
612-451-5651
612-451-2574 Fax
Cleaning technologies, environmental affairs and related topics.

International Fabricare Insitute
Library
12251 Tech Rd.
Silver Spring, MD 20904
301-622-1900
301-236-9320 Fax
Dry cleaning, textiles, and laundering.

COMPANIES

Clorox Co.
1221 Broadway
Oakland, CA 94612
415-271-7000
Household cleaning products.

Dial Corp.
(Subsidiary of Armour And Co.)
Greyhound Tower
Phoenix, AZ 85077
602-248-2800
Household cleaning, floor care, and personal hygiene products.

Dubois Chemicals, Inc.
(Subsidiary of Diversey Corp.)
1100 DuBois Tower
Cincinnati, OH 45202
513-762-6000
Chemical cleaning compounds and equipment.

Hoover Co.
(Subsidiary of Maytag Corp.)
101 E. Maple St.
North Canton, OH 44720
216-499-9200
Vacuum cleaning and floor washing equipment.

ISS International Service System, Inc.
1430 Broadway
New York, NY 10018
212-382-9800
Building cleaning and maintenance.

NCH Corp.
2727 Chemsearch Blvd.
Irving, TX 75062
214-438-0211
Cleaning and sanitation chemicals.

National Service Industries, Inc.
1420 Peachtree St., N.E.
Atlanta, GA 30309
404-853-1000
Cleaning and sanitation chemicals, and other products.

National Union Electric Corp.
(Subsidiary of Electrolux (AB)
1201 E. Bell St.
Bloomington, IL 61701
309-828-2367
Household vacuum cleaners and industrial cleaning equipment.

Ogden Allied Services Corp.
(Subsidiary of Ogden Corp.)
2 Pennsylvania Plaza
New York, NY 10121
212-868-6000
Maintenance and cleaning services.

Procter & Gamble Co.
One Procter & Gamble Plaza
Cincinnati, OH 45202
513-983-1100
Soaps, detergents, and other cleaning products.

Stanhome Inc.
333 Western Ave.
Westfield, MA 01085
413-562-3631
Direct sale of household cleaning supplies and other products.

FEDERAL GOVERNMENT

U.S. International Trade Administration
Department of Commerce
14th St. and Constitution Ave., N.W.
Washington, DC 20230
202-377-2000
Ask for the Commodity Analyst who is an expert in cleaning products, soaps, and equipment.

U.S. International Trade Administration
Department of Commerce
14th St. and Constitution Ave., N.W.
Washington, DC 20230
202-377-2000
Ask for the Commodity Analyst who is an expert in cleaning products, soaps, and equipment.

U.S. Patent and Trademark Office
Crystal Plaza 2
2011 Jefferson Davis Highway
Arlington, VA 22202
703-305-8000
Ask for the Examining Group Director who is a specialist in cleaning products, soaps, and equipment.

CLOCK AND WATCH INDUSTRY

ASSOCIATIONS

American Watch Association
PO Box 464
1201 Pennsylvania Ave. N.W.
Washington, DC 20044
703-759-3377
Emilio Collado, Executive Officer
Manufacturers, importers, assemblers, and servicers of watches and clocks.

American Watchmakers Institute
3700 Harrison Ave.
Cincinnati, OH 45211
513-661-3838
513-661-3131 Fax
Michael Danner, Administrative Director
Provides technical and vocational information to watchmakers, clockmakers, jewelers, and others.

Clock Manufacturers and Marketing Association
710 E. Ogden Ave., Ste. 113
Naperville, IL 60563
708-369-2406
Arthur Seeds, Executive Vice President
Provides industry information about the manufacturing and marketing of clocks.

PERIODICALS

Chilton's Jewelers' Circular-Keystone
Chilton Co.
Chilton Way
Radnor, PA 19089
215-964-4474
George Holmes, Editor
Reports on the retail jewelry and watch industry.

Jewelry Workers' Bulletin
Amalgamated Jewelry, Diamond and Watchcase Worker's Union
Local No. 1-J
AFL-CIO
133 W. 44th St.
New York, NY 10036
212-246-2335
Joseph Tarantola, Editor
News for unionized watchmakers, repairers, and others.

Watch and Clock Review
Bell Publications
2403 Champa St.
Denver, CO 80205
303-296-1600
Jayne Barrick, Editor
Covers business news for manufacturers, importers, and retailers of watches and clocks.

LIBRARIES

American Watchmakers Institute
3700 Harrison Ave.
Cincinnati, OH 45211
513-661-3838
513-661-3131 Fax
Technical information about watch and clock making and repair.

Joseph Bulova School
Library
40-24 62nd St.
Box 465
Woodside, NY 11377
718-424-2929
718-335-0545 Fax
Clock and watchmaking, computer repair, and related topics.

National Association of Watch and Clock Collectors, Inc.
Watch & Clock Museum of the NAWCC
Library
514 Poplar St.
Columbia, PA 17512
717-684-8261
717-684-0878 Fax
Horology.

COMPANIES

W. Bell & Co.
12401 Twinbrook Pkwy.
Rockville, MD 20852
301-881-2000
Watches, clocks, jewelry, housewares, and other products.

Elgin Watch Co.
(Subsidiary of M. Z. Berger & Co., Inc.)
33-00 Northern Blvd.
Long Island City, NY 11101
718-361-7720
Watches and jewelry.

Frequency Electronics, Inc.
55 Charles Lindbergh Blvd.
Mitchel Field, NY 11553
516-794-4500
Time and frequency control equipment, digital clocks.

Gruen Marketing Corp.
(Subsidiary of Jewelcor Incorporated)
117 Seaview Dr.
Secaucus, NJ 07094
201-865-8787
Watches.

Michael Anthony Jewelers Inc.
70 S. MacQursted Pkwy.
Mount Vernon, NY 10550
914-699-9840
Jewelry and watches.

North American Watch Corp.
650 Fifth Ave.
New York, NY 10019
212-397-7800
Manufactures and distributes watches.

Pulaski Furniture Corp.
P.O. Box 1371
Pulaski, VA 24301
703-980-7330
Furniture and clocks, including mantel, wall, and grandfather clocks.

Simplex Time Recorder Co.
Simplex Plaza
Gardner, MA 01441
508-632-2500
Master clocks and other time equipment.

FEDERAL GOVERNMENT

U.S. International Trade Administration
Department of Commerce
14th St. and Constitution Ave., N.W.
Washington, DC 20230
202-377-2000
Ask for the Commodity Analyst who is an expert in the clock and watch industry.

U.S. International Trade Commission
500 E St., S.W.
Washington, DC 20436
202-205-2000 Office of the Secretary
202-205-3296 Industries locator
Ask for the Trade Analyst who is an expert in the clock and watch industry.

CLOTHING INDUSTRY

See also: UNDERWEAR, HOSIERY, AND INTIMATE APPAREL INDUSTRY

ASSOCIATIONS

American Apparel Contractors Association
140 Maryeanna Dr.
Atlanta, GA 30342
404-843-3171
Sue Strickland, Director
Members include apparel contractors, suppliers, and manufacturers.

American Apparel Manufacturers Association
2500 Wilson Blvd., Ste. 301
Arlington, VA 22201
703-524-1864
703-522-6741 Fax
G. Stewart Boswell, President
A large group of apparel manufacturers and suppliers of equipment, fabrics, and services to the industry.

Bureau of Salesmen's National Associations
1819 Peachtree Rd. N.E., Ste. 210
Atlanta, GA 30309
404-351-7355
404-728-1520 Fax
Sherwyn Syna, Managing Director
Salespeople of wholesale apparel and accessories.

Childrenswear Manufacturers Association
2 Greentree Centre, Ste. 225
PO Box 955
Marlton, NJ 08053
609-985-2878
William MacMillan, Executive Director
Firms that make children's apparel.

Federation of Apparel Manufacturers
225 W. 34th St., Ste. 1416
New York, NY 10122
212-594-0810
212-268-7152 Fax
Cory Greenspan, Executive Director
Represents over 1,000 apparel manufacturers.

International Formalwear Association
401 N. Michigan Ave.
Chicago, IL 60611
312-644-6610
312-321-6869 Fax
Jack Springer, Executive Director
Promotes sales of formalwear.

Ladies Apparel Contractors Association
450 7th Ave.
New York, NY 10123
212-564-6161
Sidney Reiff, Executive Director
Provides a variety of services, including labor negotiations, for members.

Menswear Retailers of America
2011 I St. N.W., Ste. 600
Washington, DC 20006
202-347-1932
Douglas Wiegand, Executive Director
Firms that retail men's and boy's clothing.

National Knitwear and Sportswear Association
386 Park Ave. South
New York, NY 10016
212-683-7520
Seth Bodner, Executive Director
Offers information and maintains a library of swatches for manufacturers.

National Outerwear and Sportswear Association
240 Madison Ave.
New York, NY 10016
212-686-3440
Jack Carver, Executive Officer
Firms that make men's and boys' outerwear and sportswear.

PERIODICALS

Activewear Business Magazine
Virgo Publishing, Inc.
Box C-5400
Scottsdale, AZ 85261
602-483-0014
Brent Diamond, Editor
Written for sportswear retailers and manufacturers.

Apparel Industry Magazine
Shore Communications, Inc.
180 Allen Rd., N.E., Ste. 300 N.
Atlanta, GA 30328
404-252-8831
Meg Thornton, Editor
Focuses on apparel manufacturing, new technology, and quality control.

Apparel Merchandising
Lebhar-Friedman, Inc.
425 Park Ave.
New York, NY 10022
212-371-9400
Paula Lashinsky, Editor
Offers marketing advice to retailers.

Earnshaw's Infants, Girls and Boys Wear Review
Earnshaw Publications Inc.
225 W. 34th St.
New York, NY 10001
212-563-2742
Thomas Hudson, Editor
Follows trends and new products for retailers of children's clothing.

Earnshaw's Plus Sizes
Earnshaw Publications, Inc.
225 W. 34th St.,
New York, NY 10001
212-563-2742
Christina Gruber, Editor
For retailers of large-sized clothing.

Made to Measure
Halper Publishing Co.
600 Central Ave., Ste. 226
Highland Park, IL 60035
708-831-6678
News for retailers and manufacturers of uniforms, career apparel, and tailers.

Sportswear International
Opal Publishing
29 W. 38th St., 15th fl.
New York, NY 10018
212-768-8450
Michael Belluomo, Editor
A fashion magazine for those in the sportswear industry.

Women's Wear Daily
Fairchild Publications, Inc.
Women's Wear Daily
7 E. 12th St.
New York, NY 10003
212-741-4000
Michael Coady, Editor
A daily newspaper that reports on all aspects of the fashion industry.

LIBRARIES

Amalgamated Clothing & Textile Workers
    Union, AFL-CIO
Research Department Library
15 Union Square
New York, NY 10003
212-242-0700
212-255-7230 Fax
Industry data on men's clothing, textiles, labor economics, and related topics.

Fashion Institute of Design & Merchandising
Cyril Magnin Resource and Research Center
55 Stockton St., 5th Fl.
San Francisco, CA 94108-5804
415-433-6691
Fashion merchandising and design, and apparel manufacturing.

Fashion Institute of Technology
Library
7th Ave. at 27th St.
New York, NY 10001-5992
212-760-7884
212-594-9206 Fax
Fashion, textiles, fashion buying, and related topics.

International Ladies' Garment Workers Union
Research Department Library
1710 Broadway
New York, NY 10019
212-265-7000
Women's clothing industry.

COMPANIES

Blue Bell, Inc.
(Division of VF Corp.)
335 Church St.
Greensboro, NC 27401
919-373-3400
Work clothes, western wear, sportswear, and children's clothes.

Edison Brothers Stores, Inc.
501 N. Broadway
St. Louis, MO 63102
314-331-6000
Retail stores that carry ready-to-wear apparel.

Hartmarx Corp.
101 N. Wacker Dr.
Chicago, IL 60606
312-372-6300
Manufactures a wide variety of men's and women's suits, outerwear, and other clothes.

K Mart Apparel Corp.
(Subsidiary of K Mart Corp.)
7373 Westside Ave. N.
North Bergen, NJ 07047
201-861-9100
Men's and women's clothing.

Levi Strauss Associates, Inc.
1155 Battery St.
San Francisco, CA 94111
415-544-6000
Blue jeans and other casual clothing.

Liz Claiborne, Inc.
1441 Broadway
New York, NY 10018
212-354-4900
Designs and sells women's clothing.

Marshalls Inc.
(Subsidiary of Melville Corp.)
30 Harvard Mill Sq., Box 1000-34
Wakefield, MA 01880
617-721-3001
Apparel for the whole family.

Nordstrom, Inc.
1501 5th Ave.
Seattle, WA 98101
206-628-2111
Men's, women's and children's apparel.

Petrie Stores Corp.
70 Enterprise Ave.
Secaucus, NJ 07094
201-866-3600
*Stores that sell women's, juniors', and misses'
apparel.*

Talon Inc.
626 Arch St.
Meadville, PA 16335
814-337-1281
Zippers and other fasteners.

TJX Companies, Inc.
Framingham, MA 01701
508-390-1000
Self-service apparel stores.

VF Corp.
1047 N. Park Rd.
Wyomissing, PA 19610
215-378-1151
*Jeans, sportswear, intimate apparel, and other
types of clothes.*

FEDERAL GOVERNMENT

U.S. Customs Service
Department of the Treasury
U.S. Customshouse
6 World Trade Center
New York, NY 10048
212-466-5550
*Ask for the Commodity Specialist in charge of
clothing.*

U.S. International Trade Administration
Department of Commerce
14th St. and Constitution Ave., N.W.
Washington, DC 20230
202-377-2000
*Ask for the Commodity Analyst who is an
expert in the clothing industry.*

U.S. International Trade Administration
Department of Commerce
14th St. and Constitution Ave., N.W.
Washington, DC 20230
202-377-2000
*Ask for the Commodity Analyst who is an
expert in the clothing industry.*

COAL

See also: ENERGY

ASSOCIATIONS

American Coal Foundation
1130 17th St. N.W., Ste. 220
Washington, DC 20036
202-466-8630
202-466-8632 Fax
Beatrice Burns, Executive Director
This group of coal mining firms, coal suppliers, utilities, and others promotes the use of coal.

Association of Bituminous Contractors
2020 K St., Ste. 800
Washington, DC 20006
202-785-4440
William Howe, Secretary
Firms that build coal mines and other coal facilities.

Bituminous Coal Operators' Association
303 World Center Bldg.
918 16th St. N.W.
Washington, DC 20006
202-783-3195
202-783-4862 Fax
Robert Vines, Secretary
Companies that mine bituminous coal. Promotes safe operations and help firms negotiate with the International Union United Mine Workers of America.

Coal and Slurry Technology Association
1156 15th St. N.W., Ste. 525
Washington, DC 20005
202-296-1133
202-223-3504 Fax
Stuart Serkin, Executive Director
Members include companies that assist in the production, transportation, and efficient use of coal and coal-related products.

National Coal Association
1130 17th St. N.W.
Washington, DC 20036
202-463-2625
202-463-6152 Fax
Richard Lawson, President
This large association of coal manufacturers, equipment suppliers, utilities, consultants, and others informs the public and governement about a wide range of issues affecting the coal industry.

PERIODICALS

Clean Coal Technologies
Department of Energy
U.S. National Technical Information Service
5825 Port Royal Rd.
Springfield, VA 22161
703-487-4630
Surveys technologies for coal cleaning, gasification, liquefaction, desulfurization, and related subjects.

Coal
Maclean Hunter Publishing Co.
29 N. Wacker Dr.
Chicago, IL 60606
312-726-2802
Mark Sprouls, Editor
Reports news of coal exploration, mining, and distribution nationwide.

Coal Mine Directory
Mining Information Services
Maclean Hunter Publishing Inc.
4 Stamford Forum
Stamford, CT 06901
203-977-2812
Charles Richardson, Editor
A listing of coal mines nationwide.

Coal Mining Newsletter
National Safety Council
444 N. Michigan Ave.
Chicago, IL 60611
800-621-7619
Discusses coal mining safety issues.

Coal Week
McGraw-Hill, Inc.
1221 Ave. of the Americas, 36th Fl.
New York, NY 10020
212-512-6410
John Higgins, Editor
Covers the technology and business of coal mining.

LIBRARIES

U.S. Bureau of Mines
SSI
Library
Cochrans Mill Rd.
Box 18070
Pittsburgh, PA 15236
412-892-4431
412-892-4292 Fax
Coal research, mining, and geology.

U.S. Department of Energy
Morgantown Energy Technology Center
Library
Box 880
Morgantown, WV 26507-0880
304-291-4184
305-291-4403 Fax
Coal, petroleum, chemistry, chemical engineering, and geology.

University of Kentucky
Center for Applied Energy Research
3572 Iron Works Pike
Lexington, KY 40511-8433
606-257-0309
606-257-0220 Fax
Coal, energy, and oil shale.

COMPANIES

Amax Inc.
200 Park Ave.
New York, NY 10166
212-856-4200
Aluminum, gold, coal, and other mined products.

Atlantic Richfield Co.
515 S. Flower St.
Los Angeles, CA 90071
213-486-3511
Coal, petroleum, chemicals, and other products

Consolidation Coal Co.
(Subsidiary of E. I. du Pont de Nemours & Co.)
Consol Plaza
Pittsburgh, PA 15241
412-831-4000
Coal mining.

Mapco Inc.
1800 S. Baltimore Ave.
Tulsa, OK 74119
918-581-1800
Coal, natural gas, and other products.

Nacco Industries, Inc.
12800 Shaker Blvd.
Cleveland, OH 44120
216-752-1000
Coal and other products.

Peabody Coal Co.
(Subsidiary of Peabody Holding Co., Inc.)
1951 Barrett Ct., Box 1990
Henderson, KY 42420
502-827-0800
Coal mining.

Pittston Co.
One Pickwick Plaza, Box 8900
Greenwich, CT 06836
203-622-0900
Coal and other products.

USX Corp.
600 Grant St.
Pittsburgh, PA 15219
412-433-1121
Coal, oil, steel, and other products.

FEDERAL GOVERNMENT

Bureau of Mines
810 7th St., N.W.
Washington, DC 20747
202-501-9770
Ask for the Commodity Specialist who is an expert in coal.

U.S. International Trade Administration
Department of Commerce
14th St. and Constitution Ave., N.W.
Washington, DC 20230
202-377-2000
Ask for the Commodity Analyst in charge of the coal industry.

U.S. International Trade Commission
500 E St., S.W.
Washington, DC 20436
202-205-2000 Office of the Secretary
202-205-3296 Industries Locator
Ask for the Trade Analyst who is an expert in the coal industry.

COFFEE AND TEA INDUSTRY

See also: BEVERAGE INDUSTRY

ASSOCIATIONS

Coffee Development Group
1400 Eye St., N.W., Ste. 650
Washington, DC 20005
202-682-4034
Michael Levin, President
Promotes coffee drinking and provides information about technical and business subjects.

National Coffee Association of U.S.A.
110 Wall St.
New York, NY 10005
212-344-5596
George Boecklin, President
Coffee importers, brokers, roasters, processors, and others in the industry.

Tea Board of India
445 Park Ave.
New York, NY 10022
212-838-4150
Rahul Bedi, Director
Represents producers and importers of India tea.

Tea Council of the United States of America
230 Park Ave.
New York, NY 10169
212-986-6998
Donald Wiederecht, Executive Director
Represents importers of tea from all over the world.

PERIODICALS

Tea and Coffee Trade Journal
Lockwood Trade Journal Co., Inc.
130 W. 42nd St.
New York, NY 10036-7802
212-391-2060
News about tea and coffee products and markets.

Tea Talk
R & R Publications
419 N. Larchmont
Los Angeles, CA 90004-3000
213-871-6901
Diana Rosen, Editor
A magazine for tea lovers.

World Coffee & Tea
McKeand Publications, Inc.
636 First Ave.
West Haven, CT 06516
203-934-5288
Richard Hanley, Editor
Follows news and trends in the coffee and tea business.

LIBRARIES

Hurty-Peck Library of Beverage Literature
5600 W. Raymond St.
Indianapolis, IN 46241
317-243-3521
317-240-1524 Fax
Tea, coffee, soft drinks, and related subjects.

Thomas J. Lipton, Inc.
Library/Information Services
800 Sylvan Ave.
Englewood Cliffs, NJ 07632
201-894-7568
201-871-8149 Fax
Tea and food technology.

COMPANIES

American Tea & Coffee Co., Inc.
2500 Heiman St.
Nashville, TN 37202
615-329-0077
Coffee and tea.

Chock Full o'Nuts Corp.
370 Lexington Ave.
New York, NY 10017
212-532-0300
Coffee and tea.

Wilbur Curtis Co., Inc.
1781 N. Indiana St.
Los Angeles, CA 90063
213-269-8121
Coffee and tea dispensing and brewing equipment.

Imperial Commodities Corp.
(Subsidiary of Deli Universal, Inc.)
17 Battery Pl.
New York, NY 10004
212-837-9400
Rubber, coffee, tea, and other foods.

Ireland Coffee-Tea, Inc.
350 Canale Dr., Box 1103
Pleasantville, NJ 08232
609-646-7200
Coffee and tea.

Thomas J. Lipton, Inc.
(Subsidiary of Unilever United States, Inc.)
800 Sylvan Ave.
Englewood Cliffs, NJ 07632
201-567-8000
Tea, soups, and other foods.

Wm. B. Reily & Co.
P. O. Box 60296
New Orleans, LA 70160
504-524-6131
Coffee, tea, and other foods.

Tone Bros. Inc
(Subsidiary of Rykoff-Sexton Inc.)
4141 McDonald Ave.
Des Moines, IA 50301
515-262-9721
Spices, tea, and food processing.

FEDERAL GOVERNMENT

U.S. International Trade Administration
Department of Commerce
14th St. and Constitution Ave., N.W.
Washington, DC 20230
202-377-2000
Ask for the Commodity Analyst who is an expert in tea or coffee.

U.S. International Trade Commission
500 E St., S.W.
Washington, DC 20436
202-205-2000 Office of the Secretary
202-205-3296 Industries locator
Ask for the Trade Analyst who is an expert in tea or coffee.

COGENERATION

Cogeneration is the conversion of wasted heat produced by industrial or power plants into usable electricity.

See also: ELECTRICAL ENGINEERING and ENERGY

ASSOCIATIONS

Association of Energy Engineers
4025 Pleasantdale Rd., Ste. 420
Atlanta, GA 30340
404-447-5083
Albert Thumann, Executive Director
Many engineers in this association are experts on energy management and cogeneration.

Cogeneration and Independent Power Coalition of America
Two Lafayette Center
1133 21st St. N.W., Ste. 420
Washington, DC 20036
202-785-8776
202-785-8897 Fax
Christine Nolin, Executive Director
Supports the creation of incentives to develop cogeneration and independent power projects.

PERIODICALS

Cogeneration
Pequot Publishing
Box 44
Southport, CT 06490
203-259-1812
Earl Dunckel, Editor
News and advice for managers of cogeneration systems.

Cogeneration Journal
Fairmont Press, Inc.
700 Indian Trail
Lilburn, GA 30247
404-925-9388
F. William Payne, Editor
Technical information about cogeneration.

Directory of Selected U S Cogeneration, Small Power and Industrial Power Plants
Utility Data Institute, Inc.
1700 K St., N.W., Ste. 400
Washington, DC 20006
202-466-3660
A listing of nearly 5,000 power projects, which include cogeneration systems.

Independent Energy
Alternative Sources of Energy, Inc.
107 S. Central Ave.
Milaca, MN 56353
612-983-6892
Donald Marier, Editor
Information for operators of independent electric power plants, including cogeneration systems.

Purpa Lines
Hydro Consultants, Inc.
H C I Publications
410 Archibald St.
Kansas City, MO 64111-3046
816-931-1311
John Braden, Editor
*Follows business, legislative, and financial
news regarding cogeneration.*

World Cogeneration
Edgell Communications
7500 Old Oak Blvd.
Cleveland, OH 44130
216-243-8100
Jim Watts, Editor
*Follows technological and business news about
cogeneration.*

LIBRARIES

National Center for Appropriate Technology
Research Library
3040 Continental Dr.
Box 3838
Butte, MT 59702
406-494-4572
406-494-2905 Fax
*Community energy planning, agriculture,
biomass, appropriate technology, solar and
wind energy, superinsulation, community
development, and economic development.*

COMPANIES

Bonneville Pacific Corp.
257 E. 200 S.
Salt Lake City, UT 84111
801-363-2520
*Designs, builds, and operates cogeneration
electric facilities.*

C N F Constructors, Inc.
(Subsidiary of C N F Industries, Inc.)
One Research Pkwy.
Meriden, CT 06450
203-237-5580
*Contractor for cogeneration and other energy
facilities.*

Energy Factors, Inc.
(Subsidiary of Sithe-Energies L. P.)
401 B St.
San Diego, CA 92101
619-239-9900
Cogeneration systems.

Fermont Co.
(Division of Dynamics Corp. of America)
141 North Ave.
Bridgeport, CT 06606
203-366-5211
*Power generators, cogeneration equipment,
and related supplies.*

Harbert Corp.
P. O. Box 1297
Birmingham, AL 35201
205-987-5500
*Construction and engineering of cogeneration
and other resource recovery systems.*

Long Lake Energy Corp.
420 Lexington Ave.
New York, NY 10170
212-986-0440
Cogeneration and hydroelectric systems.

O'Brien Environmental Energy Inc.
225 S. 8th St.
Philadelphia, PA 19106
215-627-5500
Designs and operates cogeneration projects.

PSE Inc.
(Subsidiary of Dow Chemical Co.)
9432 Old Katy Rd.
Houston, TX 77055
713-464-9451
Designs, builds, and operates cogeneration and other energy recovery systems.

Public Service Enterprise Group Inc.
80 Park Plaza
Newark, NJ 07101
201-430-7000
Cogeneration and other energy businesses.

Thermo Electron Corp.
101 First Ave.
Waltham, MA 02254
617-622-1000
Cogeneration systems and other products.

FEDERAL GOVERNMENT

U.S. Department of Energy
1000 Independence Ave., S.W.
Washington, DC 20585
202-586-5000
Ask for the public affairs office to find an appropriate expert.

COLLECTIBLES

See also: ART AND ANTIQUES MARKET

COINS

Associations

American Numismatic Association
818 N. Cascade Ave.
Colorado Springs, CO 80903-3279
719-632-2646
800-367-9723
719-634-4085 Fax
Robert Leuver, Executive Director
Collectors and dealers of coins and paper money. Operates a library and provides various services to collectors.

American Numismatic Society
Broadway and 155th & 156th St.
New York, NY 10032
212-234-3130
Leslie Elam, Director
This association of collectors maintains a very large numismatic museum.

Professional Numismatists Guild
PO Box 430
Van Nuys, CA 91408
818-781-1764
Paul Koppenhaver, Executive Director
A group of full-time coin dealers.

Periodicals

Certified Coin Dealer Newsletter
Coin Dealer Newsletter
Box 11099
Torrance, CA 90510-1099
213-515-7369
Dennis Baker, Editor
Management advice for coin dealers.

Coin Prices
Krause Publications, Inc.
700 E. State St.
Iola, WI 54990
715-445-2214
Bob Wilhite, Editor
A listing of market values for U.S. coins.

Coin World
Amos Press Inc.
Box 4315
Sidney, OH 45365
513-498-0800
Beth Deisher, Editor
Reports on news that interests dealers and collectors.

Coins
Krause Publications, Inc.
700 E. State St.
Iola, WI 54990
715-445-2214
Arlyn Sieber, Editor
A magazine for collectors that offers news and pricing information.

Libraries

American Numismatic Society
Library
Broadway at 155th St.
New York, NY 10032
212-234-3130
212-234-3381 Fax
Numismatics.

Stack's Rare Coin Co. of New York
Technical Information Center
123 W. 57th St.
New York, NY 10019
212-582-2580
212-245-5018 Fax
Rare coins, medals, and related subjects.

Companies

American Coin Portfolios Inc.
600 B St.
San Diego, CA 92101
619-231-1400
Sells rare U.S. coins.

Calstar, Inc.
7401 Cahill Rd.
Minneapolis, MN 55435
612-941-0110
Stamps, coins & jewelry.

John Dannreuther Rare Coins, Inc.
868 Mt. Moriah
Memphis, TN 38117
901-683-2492
Dealer of rare American coins.

First Coinvestors, Inc.
One Old Country Rd.
Carle Place, NY 11514
516-294-0040
Rare coins, stamps, and baseball cards.

J. J. Teaparty
51 Bromfield St.
Boston, MA 02108
617-482-2398
Rare coins and baseball cards.

Renrob Coins Incorporated
4 Cornwall Dr.
East Brunswick, NJ 08816
908-238-3080
Rare U. S. coins.

Rex, Inc.
3444 Crest Rd.
Cincinnati, OH 45251
513-874-3700
Coin dealers.

Stack's
123 W. 57th St.
New York, NY 10019
212-582-2580
Rare coin dealers.

Federal Government

U.S. Mint Bureau
633 3rd St., N.W.
Washington, DC 20220
202-622-2000
Ask for Numismatic Marketing.

STAMPS

Associations

American Stamp Dealers Association
3 School St., Ste. 205
Glen Cove, NY 11542
516-759-7000
Joseph Savarese, Executive Officer
Dealers of stamps and collectors' supplies.

American Philatelic Society
100 Oakwood Ave.
PO Box 8000
State College, PA 16803
814-237-3803
814-237-6128 Fax
Keith Wagner, Executive Director
Collectors of stamps and other philatelic materials.

Periodicals

Linn's Stamp News
Amos Press Inc.
Box 29
Sidney, OH 45365
513-498-0801
Michael Laurence, Editor
Weekly news for stamp dealers and hobbyists.

Scott Stamp Monthly
Scott Publishing Co.
911 Vandemark Rd.
Box 828
Sidney, OH 45365
513-498-0802
Mark Goldberg, Editor
Emphasizes the fun side of stamp collecting.

Stamp Collector
Van Dahl Publications
Box 10
Albany, OR 97321
503-928-3569
Dane Claussen, Editor
Surveys new issues and many other subjects.

Libraries

American Philatelic Society
100 Oakwood Ave.
PO Box 8000
State College, PA 16803
814-237-3803
814-237-6128 Fax
Philatelic materials.

Collectors Club
Library
22 E. 35th St.
New York, NY 10016
212-683-0559
Postal history and philately.

International Stamp Collectors Society
Library
Box 854
Van Nuys, CA 91408
818-997-6496
818-988-4337 Fax
Philately.

Companies

Calstar, Inc.
7401 Cahill Rd.
Minneapolis, MN 55435
612-941-0110
Stamps, coins & jewelry.

First Coinvestors, Inc.
One Old Country Rd.
Carle Place, NY 11514
516-294-0040
Rare coins, stamps, and baseball cards.

Gerson's International
520 S.W. Yamhill St.
Portland, OR 97204
503-228-5233
Stamps.

Federal Government

U.S. Postal Service
475 L'Enfant Plaza, S.W.
Washington, DC 20260
202-268-2020
Ask for Philatelic Sales.

COLLECTION AGENCIES

ASSOCIATIONS

American Collectors Association
4040 W. 70th St.
PO Box 39106
Minneapolis, MN 55439-0106
612-926-6547
John Johnson, Executive Vice President
This group of collection services pursue over-due accounts of all types.

American Commercial Collectors Association
4040 W. 70th St.
Minneapolis, MN 55435
612-925-0760
David Peterson, Executive Vice President
Collection services that mainly handle commercial accounts.

AMR Recovery Association Inc.
PO Box 6788
New Orleans, LA 70174
504-367-0711
504-392-2612 Fax
Huey Mayronne, Executive Director
Offers information on the repossession industry.

PERIODICALS

Collector
American Collectors Association Inc.
4040 W. 70th St.
Box 39106
Minneapolis, MN 55435
612-926-6547
Jeffrey Benson, Editors
Reports on collection techniques, management tips, and regulations that impact on the customer debt collection industry.

N C L C Reports: Debt Collection & Repossessions
National Consumer Law Center
11 Beacon St., Ste. 821
Boston, MA 02108
617-523-8010
Kathleen Keest, Editor
Offers news of the consumer law field, with a focus on debt collection.

LIBRARIES

American Collectors Association, Inc.
Ralph Smith Memorial Library
4040 W. 70th St.
Minneapolis, MN 55435
612-926-6547
612-926-1624 Fax
Debt collection.

COMPANIES

Capital Credit Corp.
(Subsidiary of Union Corp.)
1320 Fenwick Lane
Silver Springs, MD 20910
301-588-9222
Collection agency for past due receivables.

Credit Bureau Reports, Inc.
(Subsidiary of Transcon Services, Inc.)
7204 Harwin Dr.
Houston, TX 77036
713-781-0262
Consumer collection agencies and credit bureaus.

Dun & Bradstreet Receivable Management Services
(Subsidiary of Dun & Bradstreet Corp.)
One Diamond Hill Rd.
Murray Hill, NJ 07974
908-665-5000
Collection of past due commercial accounts.

G C Services Corp.
6330 Gulfton
Houston, TX 77081
713-777-4441
Collection of delinquent accounts.

House of Adjustments Inc.
715 Mamaroneck Ave., Box 780
Mamaroneck, NY 10543
914-381-6000
Collection agency for commercial past due accounts.

National Corporate Investigations Bureau, Inc.
1001 Howard Ave.
New Orleans, LA 70113
504-568-9211
Collection of commercial accounts and other services.

Vengroff Williams & Assoc. Inc./Western Division
(Division of Vengroff Williams & Assoc., Inc./Eastern)
18090 Beach Blvd.
Huntington Beach, CA 92648
714-842-1534
Collection agency.

FEDERAL GOVERNMENT

Federal Trade Commission
Pennsylvania Ave. at 6th St., N.W.
Washington, DC 20580
202-326-2000
Ask for Credit Practices in the Bureau of Consumer Protection.

COLLEGES AND UNIVERSITIES

See also: ADULT EDUCATION and EDUCATION

ASSOCIATIONS

American Association for Higher Education
1 Dupont Circle, Ste. 600
Washington, DC 20036
202-293-6440
202-293-0073 Fax
Russell Edgerton, President
Serves as a forum to discuss a wide range of issues affecting colleges and universities.

American Association of State Colleges and
    Universities
1 Dupont Circle, Ste. 700
Washington, DC 20036
202-293-7070
202-296-5819 Fax
Allan Ostar, President
Represents colleges and universities that receive support from state governments.

Association of American Colleges
1818 R St. N.W.
Washington, DC 20009
202-387-3760
202-265-9532 Fax
Paula Brownlee, President
Helps colleges and universities develop academic curricula.

Council of Graduate Schools
1 Dupont Circle N.W., Ste. 430
Washington, DC 20036
202-223-3791
Jules LaPidus, President
Provides a wide range of information about graduate schools.

PERIODICALS

Academe
American Association of University Professors
1012 14th St., Ste. 500
Washington, DC 20005
202-737-5900
Paul Strohm, Editor
Reports on issues affecting higher education.

Chronicle of Higher Education
Chronicle of Higher Education, Inc.
1255 23rd St., N.W., Ste. 700
Washington, DC 20037
202-466-1000
Corbin Gwaltney, Editor
Covers the gamut of news and issues that interest college administrators and faculty.

Higher Education and National Affairs
American Council on Education
One Dupont Circle, N.W.
Washington, DC 20036
202-939-9300
Follows trends in higher education.

U: The National College Newspaper
American Collegiate Network
3110 Main St., 3rd fl.
Santa Monica, CA 90405
213-450-2921
Rebecca Robbins, Editor
News that interests college students.

LIBRARIES

Teachers College
Milbank Memorial Library
Columbia University
DB, Box 307
New York, NY 10027
212-678-3494
Education, psychology, technology, and other subjects.

FEDERAL GOVERNMENT

U.S. Department of the Interior
1800 C St., N.W.
Washington, DC 20240
202-208-7220
Ask for the Historically Black College & University Program.

U.S. International Trade Administration
Department of Commerce
14th St. and Constitution Ave., N.W.
Washington, DC 20230
202-377-2000
Ask for the Commodity Analyst who is an expert in college facilities.

COLORADO

STATE OFFICE LOCATOR (*for referrals to all state government offices*)

303-866-5000

ARCHIVES AND RECORDS

Archives & Public Records Division
1525 Sherman Street
7th Floor
Denver, CO 80203
303-866-2055

ATTORNEY GENERAL

Law Department
1525 Sherman Street
3rd Floor
Denver, CO 80203
303-620-4500

BANKING

Banking Division
303 W. Colfax
Denver, CO 80204
303-866-6440

CONSUMER AFFAIRS

Law Department
1525 Sherman Street
3rd Floor
Denver, CO 80203
303-620-4500

EDUCATION

Education Department
201 E. Colfax
Denver, CO 80203
303-866-6806

ENERGY

Energy Conservation Division
112 E. 14th Street
Denver, CO 80203
303-894-2144

ENVIRONMENTAL AFFAIRS

Natural Resources Department
1313 Sherman Street
Room 718
Denver, CO 80203
303-866-3311

HEALTH

Health Department
4210 E. 11th Avenue
Denver, CO 80220
303-331-4600

HOUSING

Local Affairs Department
1313 Sherman Street
Room 518
Denver, CO 80203
303-866-2771

HUMAN RIGHTS

Civil Rights Division
1560 Broadway
Ste. 1050
Denver, CO 80202
303-894-2997

INSURANCE

Insurance Division
303 W. Colfax
Denver, CO 80204
303-866-6400

LABOR

Labor Division
1120 Lincoln Street
Denver, CO 80203
303-837-3800

LEGISLATION

Legislative Council
State Capitol Building
200 E. Colfax
Room 029
Denver, CO 80203
303-866-3521

LICENSING—CORPORATE

Uniform Commercial Recordings Division
1560 Broadway
Ste. 200
Denver, CO 80202
303-894-2249

LICENSING—PROFESSIONAL AND OCCUPATIONAL

Regulatory Agencies Department
1560 Broadway
Ste. 1550
Denver, CO 80202
303-894-7855

MOTOR VEHICLES

Motor Vehicle Division
140 W. 6th Avenue
Denver, CO 80204
303-572-5653

OMBUDSMAN

Citizen's Advocate Office
State Capitol Building
Room 136
Denver, CO 80203
303-866-2885

PUBLIC UTILITIES

Public Utilities Commission
1525 Sherman Street
Room 110
Denver, CO 80203
303-894-2001

PURCHASING

Purchasing Division
1525 Sherman Street
7th Floor
Denver, CO 80203
303-866-6100

REAL ESTATE

Real Estate Commission
1776 Logan Street
4th Floor
Denver, CO 80204
303-894-2166

SECURITIES

Securities Division
1560 Broadway
Ste. 1450
Denver, CO 80203
303-894-2320

TAXATION AND REVENUE

Revenue Department
1375 Sherman Street
Denver, CO 80261
303-866-3091

TOURISM

Department of Tourism
1625 Broadway
Ste. 1700
Denver, CO 80202
303-592-5410
800-255-5550

TRANSPORTATION

Highways Department
4201 E. Arkansas Avenue
Room 262
Denver, CO 80222
303-757-9201

UNEMPLOYMENT

Unemployment Insurance Office
600 Trant Street
Ste. 900
Denver, CO 80203-3528
303-866-6032

WORKER'S COMPENSATION

Workers Compensation Section
1120 Lincoln Street
Denver, CO 80203
303-764-2906

COMMERCIAL ART AND ILLUSTRATION

See also: GRAPHIC ARTS INDUSTRY

ASSOCIATIONS

American Institute of Graphic Arts
1059 Third Ave.
New York, NY 10021
212-752-0813
800-548-1634
212-755-6749 Fax
Caroline Hightower, Executive Director
Members include graphic designers, illustrators, art directors, and others.

American Institute of Technical Illustrators
    Association
2424 Sylvan Ave., Ste. 908
Alton, IL 62002-5502
618-462-3720
John White, Executive Vice President
A forum for technical illustrators.

Graphic Artists Guild
11 W. 20th St., 8th Fl.
New York, NY 10011
212-463-7730
Paul Basista, Executive Director
Members include graphic, computer, textile, and other commercial artists. Cartoonists and illustrators are also members.

Society of Illustrators
128 E. 63rd St.
New York, NY 10021
212-838-2560
212-838-2561 Fax
Terrence Brown, Director
Members include illustrators and art directors.

PERIODICALS

Illustrator
Art Instruction Schools
500 S. Fourth St.
Minneapolis, MN 55415
612-339-8721
Don Jardine, Editor
A how-to magazine for illustrators.

RSVP: The Directory of Illustration and
    Design
253 Washington Ave.
Box 314
Brooklyn, NY 11205
718-857-9267
Richard Lebenson, Editor
*An illustrated directory of work by illustrators
and designers.*

LIBRARIES

Pratt Institute
Pratt Manhattan Library
295 Lafayette St.
New York, NY 10012
212-925-8481
212-941-6397 Fax
*Advertising design and illustration, art tech-
niques, fashion illustration and related subjects.*

Rhode Island School of Design
Library
2 College St.
Providence, RI 02903
401-331-3511
Applied and fine arts, and architecture.

University of Oregon
Architecture and Allied Arts Library
200 Lawrence Hall
Eugene, OR 97403-1206
503-346-3637
*Fine and applied arts, interior architecture,
computer graphics, and related subjects.*

COMMODITY FUTURES

Commodity futures are speculative contracts to buy or sell grains, vegetables, precious metals, and other unprocessed or partially processed commodities to be delivered on a future date.

ASSOCIATIONS

Futures Industry Association
2001 Pennsylvania Ave. N.W., Ste. 600
Washington, DC 20006-1807
202-466-5460
202-296-3184 Fax
John Damgard, President
Brokerage companies that deal in commodity futures and options.

Managed Futures Trade Association
1 Glendinning Pl.
Westport, CT 06880
203-221-1260
Kenneth Tropin, Chairman
Brokers, advisors, investors, and others with an interest in commodity futures.

National Association of Futures Trading Advisors
1919 Pennsylvania Ave. N.W., Ste. 300
Washington, DC 20006
202-872-9186
202-872-9189 Fax
William Seale, President
Members include commodity trading advisors and firms that offer services to them.

National Futures Association
200 W. Madison St. Ste. 1600
Chicago, IL 60606
312-781-1300
800-621-3570
Robert Wilmouth, President
Operates an information center about commodities futures and related subjects.

PERIODICALS

C R B Futures Chart Service
Commodity Research Bureau
75 Wall St., 22nd Fl.
New York, NY 10005
212-504-7754
Stuart Shinbein, Editor
Provides charts for 67 futures markets around the world.

Comex Weekly Market Report
Commodity Exchange, Inc.
c/o Fabian Joseph, Statistics Dept.
Room 9108
4 World Trade Center
New York, NY 10048
212-938-2937
A variety of statistics generated by the Comex market.

Commodity Closeup
Oster Communications, Inc.
219 Main St.
Cedar Falls, IA 50613
319-277-1271
Glen Ring, Editor
Follows 27 major futures markets.

Commodity Perspective
30 S. Wacker Dr., Ste. 1820
Chicago, IL 60606
312-454-1801
Gerald Becker, Editor
Provides prices for 51 major futures markets.

Futures Magazine Reference Guide to
Futures Markets
Oster Communications, Inc.
219 Main St.
Cedar Falls, IA 50613
319-277-1271
Darrell Jobman, Editor
A directory of brokerage firms, computer analysis services, exchanges, and other firms involved with futures.

Journal of Futures Markets
John Wiley & Sons, Inc.
605 Third Ave.
New York, NY 10158-0012
212-850-6000
Mark Powers, Editor
A technical journal that covers forecasting, hedging, trading systems, tax consequences, and related matters.

LIBRARIES

Chicago Board of Trade
Education Department
Library
141 W. Jackson Blvd.
Chicago, IL 60604
312-435-3552
Commodity exchanges, options, business, agriculture economics, and related topics.

Chicago Mercantile Exchange
Library/Resource Center
30 S. Wacker Dr.
Chicago, IL 60606
312-930-8239
Options on futures and futures.

Commodity Futures Trading Commission
Library
2033 K St., N.W., Rm. 540
Washington, DC 20581
202-254-5901
202-254-6265 Fax
Futures and options trading, economics, and related subjects.

COMPANIES

Jack Carl/312 Futures, Inc.
222 W. Adams St.
Chicago, IL 60603
312-207-5700
Futures broker.

Coffee, Sugar & Cocoa Exchange, Inc.
Four World Trade Center
New York, NY 10048
212-938-2800
Commodity futures.

Dean Witter
2 World Trade Center
New York, NY 10048
212-392-2222
Commodities futures and many other financial businesses.

First Options of Chicago, Inc.
(Subsidiary of Continental Bank, N.A.)
One Financial Pl., 440 LaSalle St.
Chicago, IL 60605
312-362-3000
Futures and options clearing brokers.

Holco Commodities Inc.
(Subsidiary of Holco Trading Co., Inc.)
Two World Trade Ctr.
New York, NY 10048
212-912-8900
Futures brokerage.

International Trading Group Ltd.
60 E. Third Ave.
San Mateo, CA 94401
415-340-8000
Commodity/futures brokerage.

Interstate/Johnson Lane, Inc.
2700 NCNB Plaza
Charlotte, NC 28280
704-379-9000
Securities and futures brokerage.

Stotler Group, Inc.
200 West Adams
Chicago, IL 60606
312-704-9000
Futures broker.

Wolcott & Lincoln, Inc.
4800 Main St.
Kansas City, MO 64112
816-753-6750
Wholesale grain and commodity futures.

FEDERAL GOVERNMENT

U.S. Department of Agriculture
14th St. and Independence Ave., S.W.
Washington, DC 20250
202-720-8732
*Ask for the commodity futures expert in the
Economic Research Service.*

COMPENSATION AND PAY

See also: EMPLOYEE BENEFITS

ASSOCIATIONS

American Compensation Association
14040 Northsight Blvd.
Scottsdale, AZ 85260
602-951-9191
Jesse Smith, Executive Director
*Compensation managers and advisors who
exchange information about wages, pensions,
salaries, and other forms of payment.*

Classification and Compensation Society
1730 K St. N.W., Ste. 713
Washington, DC 20006
202-296-1900
Ann Finlay, Executive Vice President
*Government officials who make compensation
decisions and create compensation systems.*

Employers Council on Flexible Compensation
927 15th St. N.W., Ste. 1000
Washington, DC 20005
202-659-4300
K. E. Feltman, Executive Director
*Offers information and training manuals to
firms that already use or plan to use a flexible
compensation plan.*

PERIODICALS

Compensation & Benefits Management
Panel Publishers, Inc.
36 W. 44th St., Bar Bldg.
New York, NY 10036
516-484-0006
Madelyn Roesch, Editor
Offers advice on how to design and manage compensation programs.

Compensation and Benefits Review
American Management Association
135 W. 50th St.
New York, NY 10020
212-903-8069
Hermine Levine, Editor
Surveys the compensation and benefits field.

Compensation Strategy and Management
Professional and Business Reference
    Publishing
Maxwell Macmillan
910 Sylvan Ave.
Englewood Cliffs, NJ 07632-3310
800-562-0245
Reports on the business and legal aspects of compensation, benefits, and employee evaluation.

Employee Benefits Report
Warren, Gorham & Lamont Inc.
One Penn Plaza
New York, NY 10119
800-950-1217
John Reynolds, Editor
Follows trends and news about employee benefits and compensation, including IRS matters, new laws and regulations, social security changes, and more.

Executive Compensation Reports
D P Publications Co.
Box 7188
Fairfax Station, VA 22039
703-425-1322
Carol Bowie, Editor
Recommends procedures and policies for companies to use in their compensation programs.

LIBRARIES

Detroit Public Library
Labor Collection
5201 Woodward Ave.
Detroit, MI 48202
313-833-1440
Statistics on wages, U.S. and foreign labor laws and legislation, labor relations, and related subjects.

The Hay Group
Corporate Library
229 S. 18th St.
Philadelphia, PA 19103
215-875-2300
Compensation, pensions, and benefits.

Hewitt Associates
Library
100 Half Day
Lincolnshire, IL 60069
708-295-5000
Compensation, wage and salary administration, employee benefits, and related topics.

FEDERAL GOVERNMENT

U.S. Department of Labor
200 Constitution Ave., N.W.
Washington, DC 20210
202-523-6666
Ask for the Workers Compensation Programs.

COMPUTER-AIDED DESIGN/ MANUFACTURING/ENGINEERING (CAD/CAM/CAE)

ASSOCIATIONS

Computer Aided Manufacturing International
1250 E. Copeland Rd., No. 500
Arlington, TX 76011
817-860-1654
817-275-6450 Fax
Ben Kaminski, President
Conducts research and offers seminars and software in the field of computer-aided manufacturing.

National Society for Computer Applications in Engineering, Planning, and Architecture
Robert Marshall
Edwards and Kelcey, Inc.
705 S. Orange Ave.
Livingston, NJ 07039
201-994-4520
201-994-7174 Fax
Robert Marshall, Representative
Conducts research into the use of computers in engineering, architecture, and design.

Society for Computer-Aided Engineering
5411 E. State St.
Rockford, IL 61108
815-399-8700
800-338-5646
815-399-7279 Fax
John Nandzik, Executive Director
A clearinghouse for information about computer-aided engineering. Offers educational programs.

PERIODICALS

A-E-C Automation Newsletter
Automation Newsletter Companies Inc.
Box 18418
Fountain Hills, AZ 85269-8418
602-837-7050
E. Forrest, Editor
Reports on the use of computers in engineering, architecture, and construction.

C A D—C A M Abstracts
Bowker A & I Publishing
121 Chanlon Rd.
New Providence, NJ 07974
908-771-7714
Judy Salk, Editor
Summarizes and indexes technical articles printed in other periodicals concerning CAD/CAM and related topics.

Design for Manufacturability Alert
Management Roundtable, Inc.
1050 Commonwealth Ave., No. 301
Boston, MA 02215-1109
617-232-8080
Alex Cooper, Editor
Technical and how-to information for CAD/CAM professionals.

Computer Aided Design Report
C A D—C A M Publishing, Inc.
841 Turquoise St.
San Diego, CA 92109-1159
619-488-0533
Jeannette Dewyze, Editor
Follows news and trends for CAD/CAM engineers.

Computer-Aided Engineering
Penton Publishing
1100 Superior Ave.
Cleveland, OH 44114-2543
216-696-7000
John Krouse, Editor
Surveys the CAE field.

LIBRARIES

Computer Aided Manufacturing-International, Inc.
Library
1250 E. Copeland Rd., Ste. 500
Arlington, TX 76011
817-860-1654
817-275-6450 Fax
Computer-aided manufacturing and design, factory management.

IIT Research Institute
Manufacturing Technology Information Analysis Center
10 W. 35th St.
Chicago, IL 60616
312-567-47830
312-567-4736 Fax
CAD/CAM, metals, electronics, and related topics.

Industrial Technology Institute
Information Resources Center
2901 Hubbard
Box 1485
Ann Arbor, MI 48106
313-769-4290
313-769-4064 Fax
Computerized integrated manufacturing, software development, manufacturing engineering, and related topics.

COMPANIES

Autodesk, Inc.
2320 Marinship Way
Sausalito, CA 94965
415-332-2344
Computer-aided design software.

Cadnetix Corp.
5775 Flatiron Pkwy.
Boulder, CO 80301
303-444-8075
Computer-aided products which automate electronic systems.

Daisy/Cadnetix Inc.
(Subsidiary of Daisy Systems Corp.)
5775 Flat Iron Pkwy.
Boulder, CO 80301
303-444-8075
CAD/CAM software and hardware.

Index Technology Corp.
(Subsidiary of Sage Software, Inc.)
One Main St.
Cambridge, MA 02142
617-494-8200
Computer-aided engineering software products.

Prime Computer, Inc.
(Subsidiary of DR Holdings Inc. of Delaware)
Prime Park
Natick, MA 01760
508-655-8000
Integrated CAD/CAM systems.

Silvar-Lisco
1080 Marsh Rd.
Menlo Park, CA 94025
408-991-6000
Computer-aided engineering software.

Structural Dynamics Research Corp.
2000 Eastman Dr.
Milford, OH 45150
513-576-2400
Computer-aided engineering systems.

Valid Logic Systems Inc.
2820 Orchard Pkwy.
San Jose, CA 95134
408-432-9400
Computer-aided engineering systems.

FEDERAL GOVERNMENT

U.S. International Trade Administration
Department of Commerce
14th St. and Constitution Ave., N.W.
Washington, DC 20230
202-377-2000
Ask for the Commodity Analyst who is an expert in computer-aided design, computer-aided manufacturing, or computer-aided engineering.

U.S. International Trade Commission
500 E St., S.W.
Washington, DC 20436
202-205-2000 Office of the Secretary
202-205-3296 Industries locator
Ask for the Trade Analyst who is an expert in computer-aided design, computer-aided manufacturing, or computer-aided engineering.

U.S. Patent and Trademark Office
Crystal Plaza 2
2011 Jefferson Davis Highway
Arlington, VA 22202
703-305-8000
Ask for the Examining Group Director who is a specialist in computer-aided design, computer-aided manufacturing, or computer-aided engineering.

COMPUTER GRAPHICS

See also: COMPUTERS and DESKTOP PUBLISHING

ASSOCIATIONS

National Computer Graphics Association
2722 Merrilee Dr., Ste. 200
Fairfax, VA 22031
703-698-9600
800-225-NCGA
705-560-2752 Fax
Victor Parra, Executive Vice President
Members include manufacturers, dealers, and users of computer graphics hardware and software.

Special Interest Group on Computer Graphics
Association for Computing Machinery
11 W. 42nd St.
New York, NY 10036
212-869-7440
212-764-5537 Fax
Lois Blankstein, Executive Officer
Offers technical information about computer graphics.

PERIODICALS

ACM Transactions on Graphics
Association for Computing Machinery
11 W. 42nd St.
New York, NY 10036
212-869-7440
John Beatty, Editor
A technical journal that covers such topics as algorithms, geometric modelling, and computer graphics hardware.

Anderson Report on Computer Graphics
Anderson Publishing Co.
4525 E. Industrial St., Ste. 4L
Simi Valley, CA 93063
805-581-1184
Ken Anderson, Editor
Reports on industry news, products, and new technologies.

CG Professional
Graphic Channels Inc.
1714 Stockton St.
San Francisco, CA 94133
415-956-5350
Scott Lowe, Editor
Helps readers buy and use computer graphics hardware and software.

Computer Graphics World
PennWell Publishing Co.
Advanced Technology Group
One Technology Park Dr.
Box 987
Westford, MA 01886
Phil LoPiccolo, Editor
617-443-4671
Reports on a wide range of computer graphics topics for manufacturers, retailers, and users.

IEEE Computer Graphics and Applications
IEEE Computer Society
10662 Los Vaqueros Circle
Los Alamitos, CA 90720-1264
714-821-8380
True Seaborn, Editor
A technical journal for professional users of computer graphics.

LIBRARIES

IBM Corp.
Data Systems Division
MVH Kingston Technical Library Learning
   Center
Dept. 65P/687
Neighborhood Rd.
Kingston, NY 21401
914-385-3698
914-385-1963 Fax
Computer graphics, physics, software/hardware development, and related topics.

National Computer Graphics Association
2722 Merrilee Dr., Ste. 200
Fairfax, VA 22031
703-698-9600
800-225-NCGA
705-560-2752 Fax
Computer graphics hardware and software.

Tektronix, Inc.
Wilsonville Library
Box 1000, M/S 63-531
Wilsonville, OR 97070
503-685-3986
503-682-3408 Fax
Computer graphics, computer programming, and electronics.

University of Oregon
Architecture and Allied Arts Library
200 Lawrence Hall
Eugene, OR 97403-1206
503-346-3637
Computer graphics and art and architecture.

COMPANIES

Adobe Systems, Inc.
P.O. Box 7900
Mountain View, CA 94039
415-961-4400
Computer graphics software.

Aldus Corp.
411 First Ave. S.
Seattle, WA 98104
206-622-5500
Computer graphics software.

Adage, Inc.
615 Willbrook Lane
West Chester, PA 19382
215-430-3900
Computer graphics terminals.

Bitstream, Inc.
215 1st St.
Cambridge, MA 02142
617-497-6222
Computer graphics software.

Evans & Sutherland Computer Corp.
580 Arapeen Dr.
Salt Lake City, UT 84108
801-582-5847
Computer graphics systems.

Intergraph Corp.
One Madison Industrial Park
Huntsville, AL 35807
205-730-2000
Interactive computer graphics systems.

Raster Technologies, Inc.
(Subsidiary of Alliant Computer Systems
   Corp.)
One Monarch Dr.
Littleton, MA 01460
508-692-7900
Computer graphics systems.

Sanders Associates, Inc.
(Subsidiary of Lockheed Corp.)
Daniel Webster Highway, S.
Nashua, NH 03061
603-885-4321
Products for defense and computer graphics markets.

Silicon Graphics Inc.
2011 N. Shoreline Blvd.
Mountain View, CA 94039
415-960-1980
Computer graphics systems.

Summagraphics
60 Silvermine Rd.
Seymour, CT 06483
203-881-2000
Computer graphics and related systems.

FEDERAL GOVERNMENT

U.S. Customs Service
Department of the Treasury
U.S. Customshouse
6 World Trade Center
New York, NY 10048
212-466-5550
Ask for the Commodity Specialist in charge of computer graphics products.

U.S. International Trade Administration
Department of Commerce
14th St. and Constitution Ave., N.W.
Washington, DC 20230
202-377-2000
Ask for the Commodity Analyst who is an expert in computer graphics.

U.S. International Trade Commission
500 E St., S.W.
Washington, DC 20436
202-205-2000 Office of the Secretary
202-205-3296 Industries locator
Ask for the Trade Analyst who is an expert in computer graphics.

U.S. Patent and Trademark Office
Crystal Plaza 2
2011 Jefferson Davis Highway
Arlington, VA 22202
703-305-8000
Ask for the Examining Group Director who is a specialist in computer graphics.

COMPUTERS

ASSOCIATIONS

Association of Computer Users
P.O. Box 2189
Berkeley, CA 94702-0189
415-549-4336
415-549-4331 Fax
Margaret Buckley, Manager
Helps computer users choose hardware and software.

Association for Computing Machinery
11 W. 42nd St., 3rd Fl.
New York, NY 10036
212-869-7440
212-944-1318 Fax
Joseph DeBlasi, Executive Director
A forum for computer scientists, systems analysts, engineers, and others to share technical information on a wide range of subjects.

Boston Computer Society
One Center Plaza
Boston, MA 02108
617-367-8080
Mary McCann, Exec. Dir.
A large organization offering information, instruction, software, and advice.

Data Processing Management Association
505 Busse Hwy.
Park Ridge, IL 60068
708-825-8124
Brian Kennedy, Exec. Director
Offers self-study courses and seminars covering management principles and the electronic data processing business.

IEEE Computer Society
1730 Massachusetts Ave. N.W.
Washington, DC 20036
202-371-0101
202-728-9614 Fax
This professional society of engineers and computer professionals offers educational programs.

Independent Computer Consultants Association
933 Gardenview Office Pkwy.
St. Louis, MO 63141
314-997-4633
800-GET-ICCA
314-567-5133 Fax
Carolyn Karelitz, Executive Director
Offers financial and business advisory services, standard contracts, and educational programs to computer consultants.

International Association for Computer Systems Security
6 Swarthmore Ln.
Dix Hills, NY 11746
516-499-1616
516-462-9178 Fax
Robert Wilk, President
Provides advice and seminars on computer system security and protection against computer viruses.

National Association of Computer Consultant Businesses
1250 Connecticut Ave. N.W., Ste. 700
Washington, DC 20036
202-637-6483
202-637-9195 Fax
Randy Evans, President
Offers technical support and information on a wide range of computer topics to computer consultants.

North American Computer Service Association
100 Silver Beach, No. 918
Daytona Beach, FL 32118
904-255-9040
904-258-1502 Fax
David Glascock, Director
Offers advice to computer repair and service firms on such subjects as purchasing and contract negotiation.

PERIODICALS

Adweek's Marketing Computers
ASM Communications, Inc.
49 E. 21st St.
New York, NY 10010
212-995-7306
Donna Tapellini, Editor
Reports on marketing and advertising of computers, electronics, and business systems.

Byte
McGraw-Hill, Inc., Byte Publications
One Phoenix Mill Lane
Peterborough, NH 03458
603-924-9281
Frederic Langa, Editor
Offers information on microcomputer products, applications, and technology.

Compute
Compute Publications, Inc.
324 W. Wendover Ave., Ste. 200
Greensboro, NC 27408
212-496-6100
Peter Scisco, Editor
Covers news about IBM, Tandy, and compatible machines.

Computer Shopper
Coastal Associates Publishing, L.P.
Computer Publications Division
One Park Ave.
New York, NY 10016
800-999-7467
Bob Lindstrom, Editor
Targeted towards consumers who buy computers and software by mail order.

Computerworld
Computerworld, Inc.
375 Cochituate Rd.
Box 9171
Framingham, MA 01701-9171
508-879-0700
Bill Laberis, Editor
News about networking, systems, and software.

Home Office Computing
Scholastic Inc.
730 Broadway
New York, NY 10003-9538
212-505-3580
Claudia Cohl, Editor
Targeted towards computer users who work at home or have a home-based business.

InCider—A Plus
I D G Communications
80 Elm St.
Peterborough, NH 03458
603-924-0100
Dan Muse, Editor
Reports on Apple computer software, hardware, programming, and trends.

InfoWorld
InfoWorld Publishing
1060 Marsh Rd.
Menlo Park, CA 94025
415-328-4602
Michael Miller, Editor
Reports on PC peripherals, software, and hardware.

MacWorld
MacWorld Communications
501 Second St.
San Francisco, CA 94107
415-243-0505
Jerry Borrell, Editor
Covers Macintosh computers.

P C Magazine
Ziff-Davis Publishing Co.
One Park Ave.
New York, NY 10016
212-503-5100
Bill Machrone, Editor
Surveys the news, trends, software, and hardware for IBM and compatible microcomputers.

P C Sources
Coastal Associates Publishing
One Park Ave.
New York, NY 10016
800-999-7467
Peter McKie, Editor
Reports on microcomputer products for consumers who buy via mail order.

LIBRARIES

Apple Computer Inc.
Library and Information Resources
10381 Bandley Dr., 8C
Cupertino, CA 95014
408-974-2400
408-725-8502 Fax
Microcomputers, computer programming, and software.

Lotus Development Corp.
Information Resources Group
Resource Center
55 Cambridge Pkwy.
Cambridge, MA 02142
617-693-5300
Microcomputer hardware and software.

University of Oregon
Computing Center
Library
Eugene, OR 97403
503-346-1722
Microcomputers, educational computing, and computer science.

University of Pittsburgh
Computer Science Library
200 Alumni Hall
Pittsburgh, PA 15260
412-624-8294
412-624-8296 Fax
Covers the full range of computer science subjects.

University of Washington
Computing Information Center
University Computing Services, HG-45
Seattle, WA 98195
206-543-5818
206-543-3090 Fax
Computing, hardware, software, data communications, and related topics.

COMPUTER HARDWARE COMPANIES

Apple Computer, Inc.
20525 Mariani Ave.
Cupertino, CA 95014
408-996-1010

Compaq Computer Corp.
P.O. Box 692000
Houston, TX 77269
713-370-0670

Control Data Corp.
8100 34th Ave. S.
Minneapolis, MN 55420
612-853-8100

Data General Corp.
4400 Computer Dr.
Westborough, MA 01580
508-366-8911

Dell Computer Corp.
9505 Arboretum Blvd.
Austin, TX 78759
512-338-4400

Digital Equipment Corp.
146 Main St.
Maynard, MA 01754
508-493-5111

International Business Machines Corp.
Old Orchard Rd.
Armonk, NY 10504
914-765-1900

NCR Corp.
1700 S. Patterson Blvd.
Dayton, OH 45479
513-445-5000

COMPUTER SOFTWARE COMPANIES

Borland International, Inc.
1800 Green Hills Rd.
Scotts Valley, CA 95066
408-438-8400

Central Point Software, Inc.
15220 N.W. Greenbrier
Beaverton, OR 97006
503-690-8090

Computer Associates International, Inc.
711 Stewart Ave.
Garden City, NY 11530
516-227-3300

Lotus Development Corp.
55 Cambridge Pkwy.
Cambridge, MA 02142
617-577-8500

Mentor Graphics Corp.
8005 S.W. Boeckman Rd.
Wilsonville, OR 97070
503-685-7000

Microsoft Corp.
1 Microsoft Way
Redmond, WA 98052
206-882-8080

Oracle Corp.
500 Oracle Pkwy.
Redwood City, CA 94065
415-506-7000

WordPerfect Corp.
1555 N. Technology Way
Orem, UT 84057
801-222-7900

COMPUTER REPAIR AND MAINTENANCE COMPANIES

Bell Atlantic Business Systems Services, Inc.
50 E. Swedesford Rd.
Frazer, PA 19355
215-296-6000

National Repair Center, Inc.
823 E. Holmes Rd.
Memphis, TN 38116
901-348-1422

TRW, Inc.
Customer Service Div.
15 Law Dr.
Fairfield, NJ 07006
201-575-7110

Volt Delta Resources, Inc.
Maintech Div.
1133 Ave. of the Americas
New York, NY 10036
212-827-2603

Westinghouse Electric Corp.
Integrated Logistics Support Div.
111 Schilling Rd.
Hunt Valley, MD 21030
301-584-1000

FEDERAL GOVERNMENT

National Science Foundation
1800 G. St., N.W.
Washington, DC 20550
202-357-9859
Ask for the Advanced Scientific Computing department or the Computer & Computational Research department.

U.S. Customs Service
Department of the Treasury
U.S. Customshouse
6 World Trade Center
New York, NY 10048
212-466-5550
Ask for the Commodity Specialist in charge of computers.

U.S. International Trade Administration
Department of Commerce
14th St. and Constitution Ave., N.W.
Washington, DC 20230
202-377-2000
*Ask for the Commodity Analyst who is an
expert in the computer industry.*

U.S. International Trade Commission
500 E St., S.W.
Washington, DC 20436
202-205-2000 Office of the Secretary
202-205-3296 Industries locator
*Ask for the Trade Analyst who is an expert in
the computer industry.*

U.S. Patent and Trademark Office
Crystal Plaza 2
2011 Jefferson Davis Highway
Arlington, VA 22202
703-305-8000
*Ask for the Examining Group Director who is
a specialist in computer products.*

CONCESSION INDUSTRY

ASSOCIATIONS

Conference of National Park Concessioners
PO Box 29041
Phoenix, AZ 85038
602-967-6006
Rex Maughan, Chairman
*Members operate concessions within U.S.
national parks.*

International Association of Airport Duty Free
   Stores
1101 Connecticut Ave. N.W., Ste. 700
Washington, DC 20036
202-857-1184
202-429-5184 Fax
Robert Chancler, Executive Director
*Operators and owners of duty-free concessions
at airports.*

Outdoor Amusement Business Association
4600 W. 77th St.
Minneapolis, MN 55435
612-831-4643
Roland Larson, Executive Director
*Includes concessionaires and other types of
firms that are found in carnivals and arcades.*

National Association of Concessionaires
35 E. Wacker Dr., Ste. 1545
Chicago, IL 60601
312-236-3858
312-236-7809 Fax
Charles Winans, Executive Director
*The largest group of concessionaires in the
U.S.*

PERIODICALS

Concessionaire
National Association of Concessionaires
35 E. Wacker Dr., Ste. 1545
Chicago, IL 60601
312-236-3858
Mandy Pava, Editor
Reports on legislative and market news that impacts on the industry.

COMPANIES

Carson International Inc.
(Subsidiary of Greyhound Dial Corp.)
O'Hare Field, Box 66048
Chicago, IL 60666
312-686-6180
Operates concessions at airports.

Dobbs Houses, Inc.
(Subsidiary of Greyhound Dial Corp.)
5100 Poplar Ave.
Memphis, TN 38137
901-766-3600
Operate airport concession restaurants, bars, gift shops, and newsstands.

Glazier Park, Inc.
(Subsidiary of Greyhound Dial Corp.)
Greyhound Tower
Phoenix, AZ 85077
602-248-2600
Operates concessions at national parks.

Harry M. Stevens, Inc.
(Subsidiary of Harry M. Stevens Holding
    Corp.)
Two Commerce Dr., Box 8700
Cranbury, NJ 08512
609-395-0400
Operates concessions at athletic stadiums and elsewhere.

Yosemite Park & Curry Co.
(Subsidiary of MCA, Inc.)
Yosemite Natl. Park, CA 95389
209-372-1000
Operates concessions at national parks.

FEDERAL GOVERNMENT

U.S. Department of the Interior
1800 C St., N.W.
Washington, DC 20240
202-208-7220
Ask for the concessions department in the Operations Division of the National Park Service.

CONCRETE INDUSTRY

ASSOCIATIONS

American Concrete Pavement Association
3800 N. Wilke Rd., Ste. 490
Arlington Heights, IL 60004
708-394-5577
M. J. Knutson, President
Members include concrete paving contractors, equipment manufacturers, and those offering services to the industry.

American Society for Concrete Construction
3330 Dundee Rd., Ste. N-4B
Northbrook, IL 60062
312-291-0270
W. Burr Bennett, Executive Vice President
Contractors and others who build using concrete.

International Association of Concrete Repair
   Specialists
PO Box 17402
Dulles Intl. Airport
Washington, DC 20041
703-260-0009
703-661-8013 Fax
Milton Collins, Executive Director
Offers technical information about the repair of concrete.

National Concrete Masonry Association
PO Box 781
Herndon, VA 22070-0781
703-435-4900
John Heslip, President
Concrete block manufacturers.

National Precast Concrete Association
825 E. 64th St.
Indianapolis, IN 46220
317-253-0486
800-428-5732
317-259-7230 Fax
James Tilford, Executive Vice President
Manufacturers of all kinds of precast concrete products.

National Ready Mixed Concrete Association
900 Spring St.
Silver Spring, MD 20910
301-587-1400
Vincent Ahearn, President
Firms that make ready mixed concrete.

Prestressed Concrete Institute
175 W. Jackson Blvd.
Chicago, IL 60604
312-786-0300
312-786-0353 Fax
Thomas Battles, President
The manufacturers, engineers, and technicians in this group share information about prestressed concrete design and construction methods.

PERIODICALS

Cement and Concrete Research
Pergamon Press, Inc.
Maxwell House
Fairview Park
Elmsford, NY 10523
914-592-7700
Della Roy, Editor
Technical data about concrete and cement.

Concrete Construction
Aberdeen Group
426 S. Westgate
Addison, IL 60101
708-543-0870
Ward Malisch, Editor
*How-to advice for contractors and others
using concrete.*

Concrete Products
Maclean Hunter Publishing Co.
29 N. Wacker Dr.
Chicago, IL 60606
312-726-2802
William Blaha, Editor
*Surveys the industry for users and manufac-
turers of concrete and concrete products.*

LIBRARIES

Cresset Chemical Co.
Library
P.O. Box 367
Weston, OH 43569
419-669-2041
419-669-2200 Fax
Concrete and other topics.

Holnam Inc.
Library
Box 1468
LaPorte, CO 80535
303-482-5600
303-482-5608 Fax
*Concrete, cement, mineralogy, and inorganic
chemistry.*

Portland Cement Association
Library Services
5420 Old Orchard Rd.
Skokie, IL 60077
708-966-6200
708-966-9781 Fax
*Cement chemistry, concrete technology, struc-
tural engineering, and related subjects.*

COMPANIES

Florida Rock Industries, Inc.
155 E. 21st St.
Jacksonville, FL 32206
904-355-1781
*Concrete blocks, ready mix concrete, and
related products.*

Gifford-Hill Cement Co.
(Subsidiary of Gifford-Hill & Co., Inc.)
2515 McKinney Ave., LB30
Dallas, TX 75201
214-754-5500
Concrete and portland cement.

Lafarge Corp.
(Subsidiary of LaFarge Coppee)
11130 Sunrise Valley Dr., Box 4600
Reston, VA 22090
703-264-3600
Cement, concrete, and related products.

Justin Industries, Inc.
2821 W. 7th St.
Fort Worth, TX 76101
817-336-5125
Concrete blocks, brick, and other products.

Kiewit Construction Group Inc.
(Subsidiary of Peter Kiewit Sons', Inc.)
One Thousand Kiewit Plaza
Omaha, NE 68131
402-342-2052
Construction and concrete.

Lone Star Industries, Inc.
300 First Stamford Pl., Box 120014
Stamford, CT 06912
203-969-8546
Concrete and cement.

Rinker Materials Corp.
(Subsidiary of RMC Holdings (USA , Ltd.)
1501 Belvedere Rd.
West Palm Beach, FL 33406
407-833-5555
Concrete blocks, ready mix concrete, and related products.

Southdown, Inc.
1200 Smith St.
Houston, TX 77002
713-650-6200
Cement and concrete.

Tilcon Inc.
Blackrock Ave.
New Britain, CT 06050
203-223-3651
Concrete, cement, and other building materials.

FEDERAL GOVERNMENT

U.S. Department of Transportation
400 Seventh St., S.W.
Washington, DC 20590
202-366-4000
Ask for the Pavement Division, which is part of the Federal Highway Administration.

U.S. International Trade Administration
Department of Commerce
14th St. and Constitution Ave., N.W.
Washington, DC 20230
202-377-2000
Ask for the Commodity Analyst who is an expert in the concrete industry.

U.S. International Trade Commission
500 E St., S.W.
Washington, DC 20436
202-205-2000 Office of the Secretary
202-205-3296 Industries locator
Ask for the Trade Analyst who is an expert in the concrete industry.

CONNECTICUT

STATE OFFICE LOCATOR (*for referrals to all state government offices*)

203-566-2211

ARCHIVES AND RECORDS

State Library
231 Capitol Avenue
Hartford, CT 06106
203-566-5650

ATTORNEY GENERAL

Attorney General's Office
55 Elm Street
Hartford, CT 06106
203-566-2026

BANKING

Banking Department
44 Capitol Avenue
Hartford, CT 06106
203-566-4560

COMMERCE

Economic Development Department
865 Brook Street
Rocky Hill, CT 06067-3405
203-258-4201

CONSUMER AFFAIRS

Consumer Protection Department
165 Capitol Avenue
Hartford, CT 06106
203-566-4999

EDUCATION

Department of Education
165 Capitol Avenue
Hartford, CT 06145
203-566-5061

ENERGY

Powerfeed Development & Planning
80 Washington Street
Hartford, CT 06106
203-566-2800

ENVIRONMENTAL AFFAIRS

Environmental Protection Department
165 Capitol Avenue
Hartford, CT 06106
203-566-2110

HEALTH

Health Services Department
150 Washington Street
Hartford, CT 06106
203-566-2038

HUMAN RIGHTS

Human Rights & Opportunities Commission
90 Washington Street
Hartford, CT 06106
203-566-3350

INSURANCE

Insurance Department
165 Capitol Avenue
Hartford, CT 06106
203-297-3800

LABOR

Labor Department
200 Folly Brook Boulevard
Wethersfield, CT 06109
203-566-4384

LEGISLATION

Legislative Research Office
Legislative Office Building
Room 5300
Hartford, CT 06106
203-240-8400

LIBRARY SERVICES

State Library
231 Capitol Avenue
Hartford, CT 06106
203-566-4301

LICENSING—CORPORATE

Commercial Recording Division
30 Trinity Street
Hartford, CT 06106
203-566-2448

LICENSING—PROFESSIONAL AND OCCUPATIONAL

Licensing & Administration Division
165 Capitol Avenue
Hartford, CT 06106
203-566-7177

MOTOR VEHICLES

Motor Vehicles Department
60 State Street
Wethersfield, CT 06109
203-566-2240

OCCUPATIONAL HEALTH AND SAFETY

Occupational Safety & Health Division
200 Folly Brook Boulevard
Wethersfield, CT 06109
203-566-4550

PUBLIC UTILITIES

Department of Public Utility Control
1 Central Park Plaza
New Britain, CT 06051
203-827-1553

PURCHASING

Purchasing Bureau
460 Silver Street
Middleton, CT 06457
203-638-6237

REAL ESTATE

Real Estate Division
165 Capitol Avenue
Hartford, CT 06106
203-566-5130

SECURITIES

Securities Division
44 Capitol Avenue
Hartford, CT 06106
203-566-4560

TAXATION AND REVENUE

Revenue Services Department
92 Farmington Avenue
Hartford, CT 06105
203-297-5650

TOURISM

Department of Economic Development/Vacations
210 Washington Street
Hartford, CT 06106
203-566-3948
800-243-1685
800-842-7492 (in Connecticut)

TRANSPORTATION

Transportation Department
P.O. Drawer A
Wethersfield, CT 06109
203-566-3477

UNEMPLOYMENT

Unemployment Compensation Division
401 Trumbull Street
Hartford, CT 06103
203-566-5790

WORKER'S COMPENSATION

Workers Compensation Commission
1890 Dixwell Avenue
Hamden, CT 06514
203-789-7783

CONSULTANTS

ASSOCIATIONS

American Association of Professional Consultants
9140 Ward Pkwy.
Kansas City, MO 64114
816-444-3500
Bill Steinhardt, Executive Vice President
A small group that helps consultants manage their businesses.

American Consultants League
1290 Palm Ave.
Sarasota, FL 34236
813-952-9290
Hubert Bermont, Executive Officer
Offers educational and advisory services to consultants in all fields.

Professional and Technical Consultants Association
1330 S. Bascom Ave., Ste. D
San Jose, CA 95128
408-287-8703
408-286-8988 Fax
Jan Shepherd, Executive Director
Helps consultants market their services.

PERIODICALS

Consultants and Consulting Organizations Directory
Gale Research Inc.
835 Penobscot Bldg.
Detroit, MI 48226
313-961-2242
Janice McLean, Editor
Lists individuals, companies, and other organizations that are consultants for business, industry and government.

Consultation
Human Sciences Press, Inc.
233 Spring St.
New York, NY 10013-1578
212-620-8000
Alan Glassman, Editor
Offers detailed advice on how to improve a consulting practice.

Consulting Rates and Business Practices.
    Annual Survey
Professional and Technical Consultants Asso-
    ciation
1330 S. Bascom Ave., Ste. D
San Jose, CA 95158
Gary Cunningham, Editor
408-287-8703
*Reports on fees paid to consultants and their
operating methods.*

LIBRARIES

Council of Consulting Organizations, Inc.
Library
230 Park Ave.
New York, NY 10169
212-697-9693
212-949-6571 Fax
Management and management consulting.

Fry Consultants Inc.
MacFarlane & Co., Inc.
Management Centre, Inc.
One Park Place, Ste. 450
1900 Emery St., N.W.
Atlanta, GA 30318
404-352-2293
404-352-2299 Fax
*Management consulting, executive search,
marketing, and related topics.*

FEDERAL GOVERNMENT

U.S. International Trade Administration
Department of Commerce
14th St. and Constitution Ave., N.W.
Washington, DC 20230
202-377-2000
*Ask for the Commodity Analyst who is an
expert in consulting services.*

CONSUMER ELECTRONICS INDUSTRY

See also: APPLIANCES

ASSOCIATIONS

Electronic Industries Association
2001 Pennsylvania Ave. N.W., Ste. 1100
Washington, DC 20006-1813
202-457-4900
202-457-4985 Fax
Peter McCloskey, President
*A large group of manufacturers that make
radios, televisions, and many other types of
electronic products and parts.*

IEEE Consumer Electronics Society
c/o Institute of Electrical and Electronics
    Engineers
345 E. 47th St.
New York, NY 10017
212-705-7867
*A clearinghouse for technical information
about consumer electronics design and manufacture.*

National Electronic Sales and Service Dealers
　　Association
2708 W. Berry St., Ste. 3
Ft. Worth, TX 76109
817-921-9061
817-921-3741 Fax
Clyde Nabors, Executive Officer
*Offers technical and education programs to
servicers of electronic equipment, and management training to electronic service dealers.*

PERIODICALS

Audiovideo International
Dempa Publications Inc.
400 Madison Ave.
New York, NY 10017
212-752-3003
Takao Tsukahara, Editor
*Covers the consumer electronics industry for
retailers and distributors.*

Dealerscope Merchandising
North American Publishing Co.
401 N. Broad St.
Philadelphia, PA 19108
215-238-5300
Murray Slovik, Editor
*Advice about marketing, advertising, and
management for retailers of consumer electronics and major appliances.*

Directory of Consumer Electronics 1992
Chain Store Guide Information Services
3922 Coconut Palm Dr.
Tampa, FL 33619
813-664-6800
Carl Skeps, Editor
*A listing of retailers and distributors who sell
consumer electronics and appliances.*

Electronic Market Trends
Electronic Industries Association
2001 Pennsylvania Ave. N.W.
Washington, DC 20006
202-457-4955
Carol Benda, Editor
*Surveys trends and statistics for all electronics
products, including consumer electronics.*

Electronic Servicing & Technology
C Q Communications, Inc.
76 N. Broadway
Hicksville, NY 11801
516-681-2922
Conrad Persson, Editor
*Practical information for technicians who
repair electronic goods.*

On!
I D G Communications
80 Elm St.
Peterborough, NH 03458
603-924-0100
Martin Levine, Editor
*A consumer magazine for lovers of gadgets
and consumer electronics.*

Radio-Electronics
Gernsback Publications, Inc.
500-B Bi-county Blvd.
Farmingdale, NY 11735
516-293-3000
Brian Fenton, Editor
*A consumer magazine for electronics hobby-
ists.*

LIBRARIES

Electronic Industries Association
2001 Pennsylvania Ave. N.W., Ste. 1100
Washington, DC 20006-1813
202-457-4900
202-457-4985 Fax
Consumer electronics and related topics.

COMPANIES

Amkor Electronics Inc.
1345 Enterprise Dr.
West Chester, PA 19380
215-431-9600
Consumer electronics and semiconductor assembly.

Emerson Radio Corp.
1 Emerson Lane
N. Bergen, NJ 07047
201-854-6600
Consumer electronics.

Highland Superstores, Inc.
909 N. Sheldon Ave.
Plymouth, MI 48170
313-451-3200
Chain of consumer electronics stores.

Matsushita Industrial
9401 W. Grand Ave.
Franklin Park, IL 60131
312-451-1200
Consumer electronics.

Philips Consumer Electronics Co.
(Subsidiary of North American Philips Corp.)
One Philips Dr.
Knoxville, TN 37914
615-521-4316
Consumer electronics.

Sanyo Manufacturing
3333 Sanyo Rd.
Forrest City, AR 72335
501-633-5030
Consumer electronics.

Tandy Corp.
1800 One Tandy Center
Fort Worth, TX 76102
817-390-3700
Chain of consumer electronics stores.

Toshiba America, Inc.
(Subsidiary of Toshiba Corporation)
375 Park Ave.
New York, NY 10152
212-308-2040
Consumer electronics.

FEDERAL GOVERNMENT

U.S. Customs Service
Department of the Treasury
U.S. Customshouse
6 World Trade Center
New York, NY 10048
212-466-5550
Ask for the Commodity Specialist in charge of consumer electronics.

U.S. International Trade Administration
Department of Commerce
14th St. and Constitution Ave., N.W.
Washington, DC 20230
202-377-2000
Ask for the Commodity Analyst who is an expert in consumer electronics.

U.S. International Trade Commission
500 E St., S.W.
Washington, DC 20436
202-205-2000 Office of the Secretary
202-205-3296 Industries locator
Ask for the Trade Analyst who is an expert in consumer electronics.

U.S. Patent and Trademark Office
Crystal Plaza 2
2011 Jefferson Davis Highway
Arlington, VA 22202
703-305-8000
Ask for the Examining Group Director who is a specialist in consumer electronics.

CONSUMERS

See also: MARKET RESEARCH AND STATISTICS and each of the 50 states under consumer affairs

ASSOCIATIONS

Association for Consumer Research
Graduate School of Mgmt.
632 TNRB
Brigham Young Univ.
Provo, UT 84602
801-378-2080
Keith Hunt, Executive Secretary
Professors and executives who share information on consumer research.

Consumer Federation of America
1424 16th St. N.W., Ste. 604
Washington, DC 20036
202-387-6121
Stephen Brobeck, Executive Director
Represents consumer protection groups nationwide.

Consumers' Research
800 Maryland Ave., N.E.
Washington, DC 20002
202-546-1713
John Merline, Editor
This service analyzes and rates consumer products and services. It also collects information on consumer issues.

Consumers Union of United States
256 Washington St.
Mt. Vernon, NY 10553
914-667-9400
Rhoda Karpatkin, Executive Director
This well-known publisher of Consumer Reports tests and rates a wide range of consumer products and services.

PERIODICALS

Affluent Markets Alert
Alert Publishing, Inc.
37-06 30th Ave.
Long Island City, NY 11103-3808
718-626-3356
Ann Longhlin, Editor
Helps marketers sell all kinds of products and services to the wealthy.

American Demographics
American Demographics, Inc.
Box 68
Ithaca, NY 14851-0068
607-273-6343
Brad Edmondson, Editor
Reports on all aspects of the American population and their buying habits. Sells a wide range of books and reports about consumers.

American Marketplace
Business Publishers, Inc.
951 Pershing Dr.
Silver Spring, MD 20910-4464
301-587-6300
Dede Ryan, Editor
Offer marketers information on population and consumer trends.

Consumer Confidence Survey
Conference Board, Inc.
845 Third Ave.
New York, NY 10022
212-759-0900
Fabian Linden, Editor
Surveys consumer confidence and business conditions.

Consumer Trends
International Credit Association
Box 27357
St. Louis, MO 63141-1757
314-991-3030
Robert Johnson, Editor
Follows news that relates to consumer credit and other consumer financial affairs.

LIBRARIES

Purdue University
Consumer and Family Sciences Library
Stone Hall
West Lafayette, IN 47907
317-494-2914
317-494-9007 Fax
Consumer affairs, financial counseling and planning, home economics, and related topics.

J. Walter Thompson Co.
Information Center
900 N. Michigan Ave.
Chicago, IL 60611
312-951-4000
312-951-4571 Fax
Consumer products, services, and behaviors.

University of Illinois
Survey Research Laboratory
SRL Library
1005 W. Nevada St.
Urbana, IL 61801-3883
217-333-7109
217-244-4408 Fax
Consumer behavior and survey research.

FEDERAL GOVERNMENT

U.S. Department of Labor
200 Constitution Ave., N.W.
Washington, DC 20210
202-523-6666
Ask for Consumer Prices & Consumption Studies.

U.S. Department of Commerce
14th St. & Constitution Ave., N.W.
Washington, DC 20230
202-377-2000
Ask for the Demographic Surveys division.

U.S. International Trade Administration
Department of Commerce
14th St. and Constitution Ave., N.W.
Washington, DC 20230
202-377-2000
Ask for the Commodity Analyst who is an expert in consumer goods consumption.

CONTAINER INDUSTRY

See also: BOX INDUSTRY; PACKAGING; PAPER AND PLASTIC BAG INDUSTRY

ASSOCIATIONS

Container Marketing Committee
c/o Amer. Iron and Steel Inst.
1133 15th St. N.W.
Washington, DC 20005-2701
202-452-7100
202-463-6573 Fax
Helps promote all types of containers made of iron and steel.

Containerization and Intermodal Institute
PO Box 1593
North Caldwell, NJ 07007
201-226-0160
Barbara Yeninas, Executive Director
Members include manufacturers and users of shipping containers and shipping equipment.

Fibre Box Association
2850 Golf Rd.
Rolling Meadows, IL 60008
708-364-9600
708-364-9639 Fax
Bruce Benson, President
Firms that make fiber shipping containers of all types.

National Association of Container Distributors
c/o William L. Robinson
1900 Arch St.
Philadelphia, PA 19103
215-564-3484
William Robinson, Executive Director
Wholesaler distributors of metal, glass, and plastic containers.

Plastic Shipping Container Institute
4913 Main St.
PO Box 578
Downers Grove, IL 60515
708-969-2300
708-969-2529 Fax
Robert Hultquist, Secretary
Manufacturers of plastic shipping containers.

Steel Shipping Container Institute
2204 Morris Ave.
Union, NJ 07083
201-688-8750
201-688-9468 Fax
Malcolm Anderson, Executive Director
Manufacturers of steel barrels, drums, barrels, and other containers.

PERIODICALS

Container News
Communication Channels, Inc.
6255 Barfield Rd.
Atlanta, GA 30328-4369
404-256-9800
Herb Schild, Editor
Reports on intermodal and container shipping around the world.

Packaging Strategies
122 S. Church St.
West Chester, PA 19382
215-436-4220
William LeMaire, Editor
Covers packaging materials, containers, and the equipment used to make them.

COMPANIES

Anchor Glass Container Corp.
4343 Anchor Plaza Pkwy.
Tampa, FL 33634
813-884-0000
Glass containers of all sizes.

Constar International Inc.
P.O. Box 6339
Chattanooga, TN 37401
615-267-2973
Plastic containers.

Gaylord Container Corp.
500 Lake Cook Rd.
Deerfield, IL 60015
708-405-5500
Corrugated containers and other products.

Inland Container Corp.
(Subsidiary of Temple-Inland Inc.)
4030 Vincennes Rd.
Indianapolis, IN 46268
317-262-0222
Corrugated shipping containers.

Itel Corp.
Two N. Riverside Plaza
Chicago, IL 60606
312-902-1515
*Leases intermodal cargo containers and other
equipment.*

Jefferson Smurfit Corp.
(Subsidiary of Jefferson Smurfit Group p.l.c.)
8182 Maryland
St. Louis, MO 63105
314-746-1100
Corrugated containers and other products.

Owens-Illinois, Inc.
(Subsidiary of Kohlberg Kravis Roberts &
    Co.)
One Seagate
Toledo, OH 43666
419-247-5000
Glass containers and other products.

Packaging Corp. of America
(Subsidiary of Tenneco Inc.)
1603 Orrington Ave.
Evanston, IL 60204
708-492-5713
*Cartons, corrugated containers, plastic and
aluminum containers.*

Stone Container Corp.
150 N. Michigan Ave.
Chicago, IL 60601
312-346-6600
*Corrugated containers, multiwall shipping
sacks, and other types of containers.*

Trinity Industries, Inc.
2525 Stemmons Freeway, Box 10587
Dallas, TX 75207
214-631-4420
*Pressure and non-pressure containers, and
other products.*

FEDERAL GOVERNMENT

U.S. Customs Service
Department of the Treasury
U.S. Customshouse
6 World Trade Center
New York, NY 10048
212-466-5550
*Ask for the Commodity Specialist in charge of
containers.*

U.S. International Trade Administration
Department of Commerce
14th St. and Constitution Ave., N.W.
Washington, DC 20230
202-377-2000
Ask for the Commodity Analyst who is an
expert in the container industry.

U.S. International Trade Commission
500 E St., S.W.
Washington, DC 20436
202-205-2000 Office of the Secretary
202-205-3296 Industries locator
Ask for the Trade Analyst who is an expert in
the container industry.

COPYING AND DUPLICATING MACHINE INDUSTRY

See also: OFFICE EQUIPMENT AND SUPPLIES

ASSOCIATIONS

Copier Dealers Association
12200 W. Adler Ln.
West Allis, WI 53214
414-778-0210
James Fuchs, Secretary
Dealers of photocopiers who share marketing
and management information.

National Office Machine Dealers Association
12411 Wornall
Kansas City, MO 64145
816-941-3100
816-941-3100 Fax
Frank Fonteyn, Executive Director
A large group of retailers who sell photocopies
and other office machines.

National Office Machine Service Association
Total Copy System
15544 Minnesota Ave.
Paramount, CA 90723
213-633-4724
Paul Sprangel, Executive Director
Companies and technicians who repair photo-
copiers and other types of office machines.

PERIODICALS

Copier Duplicator News
Datapro Research Corp.
1805 Underwood Blvd.
Delran, NJ 08075
609-764-0100
Follows technical developments and reports on
new models.

Datapro Reports on Copiers & Duplicators
Datapro Research Corp.
1805 Underwood Blvd.
Delran, NJ 08075
609-764-0100
A listing of machines and their capabilities.

Office Dealer
Office Systems
941 Danbury Rd.
Box 150
Georgetown, CT 06829
203-544-9526
William Hogan, Editor
Reports on news of interest to dealers of new office machines, including copiers.

Office Products Analyst
Industry Analysts, Inc.
50 Chestnut St.
Rochester, NY 14604
716-232-5320
Louis Slawetsky, Editor
Details the features and prices of copying, duplicating, word processing, and FAX equipment.

Office Products Dealer Buying Guide and
    Directory
Hitchcock Publishing
191 S. Gary Ave.
Carol Stream, IL 60188
708-462-2275
Wayne Siatt, Editor
Describes numerous office machines, reports industry news, and advises retailers of office supplies on business matters.

LIBRARIES

3M
235 Technical Library
3M Center, 235-1A-25
St. Paul, MN 55144
612-733-2592
Reprographics, printing, imaging technology, optics, and related subjects.

Xerox Corp.
Technical Information Center
800 Philips
Mail Stop 01205-C
Webster, NY 14580
716-422-3505
Reprography, xerography, photography, and related topics.

COMPANIES

A. B. Dick Co.
(Subsidiary of General Electric Co. p.l.c.)
5700 W. Touhy Ave.
Chicago, IL 60648
312-763-1900
Copying, duplicating, and printing equipment and supplies.

Brother International Corp.
(Subsidiary of Brother Industries, Ltd.)
Eight Corporate Pl.
Piscataway, NJ 08854
908-981-0300
Color copiers and other types of office equipment.

Canon Business Machines, Inc.
3191 Red Hill Ave.
Costa Mesa, CA 92626
714-556-4700
Copiers and other types of equipment.

Gestetner Corp.
(Subsidiary of Gestetner Holdings (U.S.A.
    Ltd.)
599 West Putnam Ave., Box 2656
Greenwich, CT 06836
203-625-7600
Copying equipment and other office machines.

Gradco Systems, Inc.
7 Morgan St.
Irvine, CA 92718
714-770-1223
Sorters and feeders for copiers.

Modern Business Systems, Inc.
(Division of Alco Standard Corp.)
2211 St. Mary's Blvd.
Jefferson City, MO 65109
314-634-1800
*Sales and service of copiers and other office
supplies.*

Monroe Systems For Business, Inc.
The American Rd.
Morris Plains, NJ 07950
201-993-2000
Copiers and other equipment.

Savin Corp.
9 W. Broad St., Box 10270
Stamford, CT 06904
203-967-5000
Color and black-and-white copiers.

Toshiba America Information Systems, Inc.
9740 Irvine Blvd.
Irvine, CA 92718
714-583-3000
Copiers and other types of equipment.

Xerox Corp.
Long Ridge Rd., Box 1600
Stamford, CT 06904
203-968-3000
*Copiers, duplicators, and other office
machines.*

FEDERAL GOVERNMENT

U.S. International Trade Administration
Department of Commerce
14th St. and Constitution Ave., N.W.
Washington, DC 20230
202-377-2000
*Ask for the Commodity Analyst who is an
expert in the copying and duplicating machine
industry.*

U.S. International Trade Commission
500 E St., S.W.
Washington, DC 20436
202-205-2000 Office of the Secretary
202-205-3296 Industries locator
*Ask for the Trade Analyst who is an expert in
the copying and duplicating machine industry.*

COSMETICS AND PERFUME INDUSTRY

See also: ADDITIVES AND FLAVORINGS

ASSOCIATIONS

American Society of Perfumers
P.O. Box 1551
West Caldwell, NJ 07006
No phone listed.
A small group of perfumers that share infor-mation on technological subjects.

Cosmetic Industry Buyers and Suppliers
J. Palazzolo Son, Inc.
36 Lakeville Rd.
New Hyde Park, NY 11040
Joseph Palazzolo, Executive Director
516-775-0220
Offers information to suppliers and buyers of essential oils, packaging, finished cosmetics, and related materials.

Cosmetic, Toiletry and Fragrance Association
1110 Vermont Ave., N.W., Ste. 800
Washington, DC 20005
202-331-1770
202-331-1969
Members include manufacturers and distribu-tors of essential oils, finished cosmetics, fra-grances, and other beauty and personal care items. Offers information on business, legal, and regulatory subjects.

Independent Cosmetic Manufacturers and
  Distributors
1230 W. Northwest Hwy.
Palatine, IL 60067
312-991-4499
800-33-ICMAD
312-934-3697 Fax
Represents small manufacturers and distribu-tors of cosmetics.

Society of Cosmetic Chemists
1995 Broadway, Ste. 1701
New York, NY 10023
212-874-0600
Theresa Cesario, Administrator
Professional group of scientists and techni-cians that produce cosmetics.

PERIODICALS

C A Selects. Food, Drugs, & Cosmetics—
  Legislative & Regulatory Aspects
Chemical Abstracts Service
2540 Olentangy River River
Box 3012
Columbus, OH 43210
614-447-3600
News of U.S. and foreign government findings and regulations regarding food, drugs, and cosmetics.

Cosmetic Insider's Report
Edgell Communications
270 Madison Ave.
New York, NY 10017
212-951-6600
Don Davis, Editor
Covers news of interest to executives in the cosmetics industry.

Cosmetic Science and Technology Series
Marcel Dekker, Inc.
270 Madison Ave.
New York, NY 10016
212-696-9000
Eric Jungerman, Editor
Technical information about the formulation of cosmetics.

Cosmetic World
Cosmetic World, Inc.
48 E. 43rd St.
New York, NY 10017
212-687-6190
John Ledes, Editor
News for cosmetics marketers and other industry executives.

Perfumer & Flavorist
Allured Publishing
Bldg. C, Ste. 1600
2100 Manchester Rd.
Wheaton, IL 60189-0318
708-653-2155
Stanley Allured, Editor
Reports on industry developments for scientists and executives in the perfume trade.

LIBRARIES

Colgate Palmolive Co.
Technical Information Cetner
909 River Rd.
Piscataway, NJ 08854
908-878-7573
908-878-7128 Fax
Perfumes, comestics, fats and oils, essential oils, chemistry, and related topics.

International Flavors and Fragrances, Inc.
Technical Information Center
1515 Hwy. 35
Union Beach, NJ 07735
201-888-2435
Perfume, flavors, organic chemistry, and related subjects.

Estee Lauder Inc.
Information Center
125 Pine Lawn Rd.
Melville, NY 11747
516-531-1174
Cosmetics, dermatology, chemistry, and biochemistry.

Mary Kay Cosmetics, Inc.
Technical Information Center
1330 Regal Row
Dallas, TX 75247
214-905-6299
214-631-5938 Fax
Cosmetics, chemistry, and dermatology.

COMPANIES

Avon Products, Inc.
9 W. 57th St.
New York, NY 10019
212-546-6015
Cosmetics and toiletries.

Cardinal Distribution Inc.
655 Metro Pl. S.
Dublin, OH 43017
614-761-8700
Wholesaler of cosmetics, pharmaceuticals, and other products.

Chesebrough-Pond's USA Co.
(Subsidiary of Unilever N.V.)
33 Benedict Pl., Box 6000
Greenwich, CT 06836
203-661-2000
Creams and beauty aids, colognes, and related products.

Coty Division
(Division of Pfizer Inc.)
235 E. 42nd St.
New York, NY 10017
212-573-3500
Cosmetics and fragrances.

Estee Lauder, Inc.
767 Fifth Ave.
New York, NY 10153
212-572-4200
Cosmetics.

Florasynth, Inc.
410 East 62 St.
New York, NY 10021
212-371-7700
Essential oils, flavoring extracts, perfume materials, and finished fragrances.

Glemby Co.
120 East 16th St.
New York, NY 10003
212-477-8300
Hair, skin, nail products, and cosmetics.

Mary Kay Cosmetics, Inc.
(Subsidiary of Mary Kay Corp.)
8787 Stemmons Freeway
Dallas, TX 75247
214-630-8787
Cosmetics and toiletries.

Max Factor & Co.
(Subsidiary of Revlon Group Inc.)
12100 Wilshire Blvd.
Los Angeles, CA 90025
213-442-2000
Cosmetics, nail care, and hair care products.

Quintessence Incorporated
980 N. Michigan Ave.
Chicago, IL 60611
312-951-7000
Cosmetics, fragrances, and toiletries.

St. Ives Laboratories, Inc.
8944 Mason Ave.
Chatsworth, CA 91311
818-709-5500
Perfumes and cosmetics.

FEDERAL GOVERNMENT

U.S. Customs Service
Department of the Treasury
U.S. Customshouse
6 World Trade Center
New York, NY 10048
212-466-5550
Ask for the Commodity Specialist in charge of cosmetics or perfumes.

U.S. Department of Agriculture
14th St. and Independence Ave., S.W.
Washington, DC 20250
202-720-8732
Ask for the Topical Information Center for information on cosmetics testing using animals.

U.S. International Trade Administration
Department of Commerce
14th St. and Constitution Ave., N.W.
Washington, DC 20230
202-377-2000
Ask for the Commodity Analyst who is an expert in cosmetics or perfumes.

U.S. International Trade Commission
500 E St., S.W.
Washington, DC 20436
202-205-2000 Office of the Secretary
202-205-3296 Industries locator
Ask for the Trade Analyst who is an expert in cosmetics or perfumes.

U.S. Patent and Trademark Office
Crystal Plaza 2
2011 Jefferson Davis Highway
Arlington, VA 22202
703-305-8000
Ask for the Examining Group Director who is a specialist in cosmetics or perfumes.

COTTON INDUSTRY

ASSOCIATIONS

Cotton Council International
1110 Vermont Ave. N.W., No. 430
Washington, DC 20005
202-833-2943
202-331-0622 Fax
K. Adrian Hunnings, Executive Director
Growers, marketers, and all others involved in the cotton industry are represented in this group.

Cotton Foundation
PO Box 12284
Memphis, TN 38182
901-274-9030
George Slater, Executive Director
Companies that sponsor research and educational programs to promote cotton.

Cotton Incorporated
1370 Ave. of the Americas
New York, NY 10019
212-586-1070
William Daddi, Public Relations Director
Promotes the interests of cotton producers.

International Cotton Advisory Committee
1901 Pennsylvania Ave. N.W., Ste. 201
Washington, DC 20006
202-463-6660
L. H. Shaw, Executive Director
Provides information on the cotton industry.

National Cotton Council of America
1918 N. Parkway
Memphis, TN 38112
901-274-9030
Phillip Burnett, Executive Vice President
Offers technical and industry information on behalf of cotton producers nationwide.

PERIODICALS

Cotton Digest International
Cotton Digest Co., Inc.
Box 820768
Houston, TX 77282-0768
713-977-1644
Elizabeth Edwards Abbey, Editor
Surveys trends in the cotton industry.

Cotton Farming
Little Publications, Inc.
6263 Poplar Ave., Ste. 540
Memphis, TN 38119
901-767-4020
Patrick Shepard, Editor
News and advice for cotton producers.

Cotton Gin and Oil Mill Press
Haughton Publishing Co. of Texas
Box 180218
Dallas, TX 75218
214-288-7511
Don Swanson, Editor
Follows the cotton ginning and oilseed processing industries.

Cotton Grower
Meister Publishing Co.
37733 Euclid Ave.
Willoughby, OH 44094
216-942-2000
William Spencer, Editor
Report news of interest to cotton producers.

Weekly Cotton Trade Report
New York Cotton Exchange
4 World Trade Center
New York, NY 10048
212-938-7909
Tom Bertolini, Editor
Analyzes the cotton futures and cash for cotton markets.

LIBRARIES

National Cotton Council of America
Library
1918 N. Parkway
Memphis, TN 38112
901-274-9030
901-725-0510 Fax
Cotton and related topics.

COMPANIES

Calcot, Ltd.
P. O. Box 259
Bakersfield, CA 93302
805-327-5961
Marketing and storage of raw cotton.

Plains Cotton Cooperative Association
3301 E. 50th St.
Lubbock, TX 79408
806-763-8011
Merchandisers of raw cotton.

Staplcotn
214 W. Market St., Box 547
Greenwood, MS 38930
601-453-6231
Marketing and warehousing of cotton.

FEDERAL GOVERNMENT

U.S. Department of Agriculture
14th St. and Independence Ave., S.W.
Washington, DC 20250
202-720-8732
Ask for the Economic Research Service, the Agricultural Marketing Service, the Cotton & Seed Division, or the Cotton Division.

U.S. International Trade Administration
Department of Commerce
14th St. and Constitution Ave., N.W.
Washington, DC 20230
202-377-2000
Ask for the Commodity Analyst who is an expert in cotton.

U.S. International Trade Commission
500 E St., S.W.
Washington, DC 20436
202-205-2000 Office of the Secretary
202-205-3296 Industries locator
Ask for the Trade Analyst who is an expert in cotton.

COURTS

ASSOCIATIONS

American Judges Association
300 Newport Ave.
Williamsburg, VA 23187
804-253-2000
Shelley Rockwell, Representative
Offers information on managing courts.

Conference of State Court Administrators
Natl. Center for State Courts
300 Newport Ave.
Williamsburg, VA 23187
804-253-2000
Robert Baldwin, Exeutive Officer
Administrators who work for state courts.

Federal Court Clerks Association
c/o Candice Quinn
120 Oriole Ln.
La Plata, MD 20646
Candice Quinn, Executive Secretary
Members are clerks to the U.S. Courts of Appeal, U.S. District Courts, and other courts.

National Association for Court Management
Natl. Center for State Courts
300 Newport Ave.
Williamsburg, VA 23187
804-253-2000
804-220-0449 Fax
Karen Wick, President
Court administrators and clerks.

National Center for State Courts
300 Newport Ave.
Williamsburg, VA 23187
804-253-2000
804-220-0449 Fax
Larry Sipes, President
Serves as a clearinghouse for information about state courts.

PERIODICALS

Modern Courts
Fund for Modern Courts, Inc.
36 W. 44th St., Ste. 310
New York, NY 10036-8181
212-575-1577
D. Bernadette Parker, Editor
Follows a wide variety of judicial issues that concern judges and other court officers.

Third Branch
United States Courts
Administrative Office
811 Vermont Ave., N.W.
Washington, DC 20544
202-633-6040
David Sellers, Editor
News about the federal courts.

LIBRARIES

National Center for State Courts
Library
300 Newport Ave.
Williamsburg, VA 23187
804-253-2000
804-220-0449 Fax
Information about state courts.

U.S. Court of Appeals, 2nd Circuit
Library
U.S. Court House, Rm. 2801, Foley Square
40 Centre St.
New York, NY 10007
212-791-1052
Law, courts, and other subjects.

U.S. Department of Justice
Civil Branch Library
10th & Pennsylvania Ave., N.W., Rm. 3344
Washington, DC 20530
202-514-3523
Law, government contracts, copyright, courts, and related topics.

U.S. Supreme Court
Library
One First St., N.E.
Washington, DC 20543
202-479-3000
202-479-3477 Fax
Law and legislative histories.

CREATIVITY

ASSOCIATIONS

Creative Education Foundation
1050 Union Rd.
Buffalo, NY 14224
716-675-3181
John Meyerhoff, Executive Vice President
Offers training programs, research, and publications about creativity.

National Association for Creative Children
    and Adults
8080 Springvalley Dr.
Cincinnati, OH 45236
513-631-1777
Ann Isaacs, Chief Executive
Provides information on how to foster creativity.

PERIODICALS

Creativity in Action
Creative Education Foundation, Inc.
1050 Union Rd.
Buffalo, NY 14224
716-675-3181
Arthur Van Gundy, Editor
Reports on new developments in the study of creativity.

Creativity Research Journal
Ablex Publishing Corp.
355 Chestnut St.
Norwood, NJ 07648
201-767-8450
Mark Runco, Editor
A scholarly journal about creativity.

Northern Lights Studies in Creativity
University of Maine at Presque Isle
181 Main St.
Presque Isle, ME 04769
207-762-7761
Stanley Scott, Editor
A scholarly journal about creativity.

LIBRARIES

Center for Creative Leadership
Library
5000 Laurinda Dr.
P.O. Box 26300
Greensboro, NC 27438-6300
919-288-7210
919-288-2999 Fax
Creative management, innovation, social psychology, leadership, and related subjects.

National Association for Creative Children
    and Adults
Library
8080 Springvalley Dr.
Cincinnati, OH 45236
513-631-1777
Creativity, talent, art, and writing.

Creative Studies Library
SUNY
College at Buffalo
Edward H. Butler Library
1300 Elmwood Ave.
Buffalo, NY 14222
716-878-6314
716-878-3134 Fax
Creativity, education, humanities, fine arts, applied arts, and related subjects.

CREDIT

ASSOCIATIONS

Associated Credit Bureaus
16211 Park Ten Pl.
PO Box 218300
Houston, TX 77218
713-492-8155
713-492-8372 Fax
Walter Kurth, President
Represents credit reporting and collection services.

Bankcard Holders of America
560 Herndon Pkwy., Ste. 120
Herndon, VA 22070
703-481-1110
Elgie Holstein, President
Informs consumers who have credit and bank cards about their rights.

Credit Professionals International
50 Crestwood Exec. Center, Ste. 204
St. Louis, MO 63126
314-842-6280
314-842-6310 Fax
Esther Worthington, Executive Vice President
Members work in the credit or collection offices of businesses and organizations.

Credit Research Foundation
8815 Center Park Dr.
Columbia, MD 21045
301-740-5499
301-740-4620 Fax
R. F. Thompson, President
Members include bankers and executives responsible for credit and related financial decisions. The Foundation researches the effect of credit on the economy, credit trends, and management practices regarding credit.

International Credit Association
243 N. Lindbergh Blvd.
St. Louis, MO 63141
314-991-3030
314-991-3029 Fax
William Henderson, President
A professional society of credit executives.

PERIODICALS

Comments on Money and Credit
D R I—McGraw-Hill
24 Hartwell Ave.
Lexington, MA 02173
617-863-5100
Reports on credit and money conditions in the U.S.

Credit
American Financial Services Association
1101 14th St., N.W.
Washington, DC 20005
202-289-0400
Barbara Van Gorder, Editor
Covers governmental and marketplace developments that impact on the financial services industry.

Credit & Finance
Publishing & Business Consulting
951 S. Oxford, No. 109
Los Angeles, CA 90006
213-732-3477
Atia Napoleon, Editor
Follows news and trends in personal credit.

LIBRARIES

Beneficial Management Corp.
Information Services-Corporate Community
    Affairs
200 Beneficial Center
Peapack, NJ 07977
201-781-3744
Consumer finance and credit.

Credit Research Foundation
Library
8815 Center Park Dr.
Columbia, MD 21045
301-740-5499
301-740-4620 Fax
Credit, economics, management of credit in banks and corporations.

Farm Credit Administration
Library
1501 Farm Credit Dr.
McLean, VA 22102-5090
703-883-4296
703-734-5784 Fax
Banking, finance, and agricultural credit.

Federal Reserve System
Board of Governors
Research Library
20th & Constitution Ave., N.W.
Washington, DC 20551
202-452-3332
202-452-3819 Fax
Credit, money, finance, banking, and related topics.

COMPANIES

Avco Financial Services, Inc.
(Subsidiary of Textron Inc.)
3349 Michelson Dr.
Irvine, CA 92715
714-553-1200
Consumer credit services.

Beneficial Corp.
400 Bellevue Pkwy.
Wilmington, DE 19809
302-798-0800
Consumer loans, credit insurance, and related financial services.

Comdata Holdings Corp.
5301 Maryland Way
Brentwood, TN 37027
615-370-7000
Funds transfer, cash advances on credit cards, and related services.

Diners Club International
(Subsidiary of Citibank N.A.)
8430 Bryn Mawr
Chicago, IL 60631
312-380-5237
Credit card system.

Discover Credit Corp.
(Subsidiary of Sears, Roebuck and Co.)
3711 Kennett Pike
Greenville, DE 19807
Credit card system.

Dun and Bradstreet Information Services NA
1 Diamond Hill Rd.
Murray Hill, NJ 07974
908-665-5000
Credit reporting service.

Equifax, Inc.
P.O. Box 4081
Atlanta, GA 30302
404-885-8000
Credit reporting service.

First Data Resources Inc.
(Subsidiary of American Express Co.)
10825 Farnum Dr.
Omaha, NE 68154
402-399-7050
Bank credit card processing and related services.

IBM Credit Corp.
(Subsidiary of International Business
    Machines Corp.)
290 Harbor Dr.
Stamford, CT 06904
203-352-7100
Commercial credit.

Telecredit, Inc.
(Subsidiary of Equifax Inc.)
6171 W. Century Blvd.
Los Angeles, CA 90045
213-410-4600
Credit card authorization and transaction services.

TRW, Inc.
Credit Data Div.
500 City Pkwy. W.
Orange, CA 92668
714-385-7012
Credit reporting service.

FEDERAL GOVERNMENT

Federal Deposit Insurance Corp.
550 17th St., N.W.
Washington, DC 20429
202-393-8400
Ask for Consumer Affairs.

Federal Reserve System
20th St. and Constitution Ave., N.W.
Washington, DC 20551
202-452-3000
Ask for Consumer Credit, Housing Credit, or Current Estimates and Analysis.

Federal Trade Commission
Pennsylvania Ave. at 6th St.,N.W.
Washington, DC 20580
202-326-2000
Ask for Credit Practices in the Bureau of Consumer Protection.

U.S. Department of Agriculture
14th St. and Independence Ave., S.W.
Washington, DC 20250
202-720-8732
Ask for the Loan Division in the Farmers Home Administration.

CREDIT UNIONS

Credit unions are cooperatives of consumers, usually employees of the same organization, that make loans to their members at low interest rates.

ASSOCIATIONS

Association of Credit Union League Executives
PO Box 431
Madison, WI 53701
608-231-4000
These chief executives and other senior executives of credit union leagues share information about management and policy.

Community Service Credit Union Council
1001 Connecticut Ave. N.W., Ste. 728
Washington, DC 20036
202-223-3920
800-446-7453
202-223-1311 Fax
Melanie Durkin, Executive Officer
Does research and offers educational programs to credit unions who work for more than one employer.

Credit Union Executives Society
2801 Coho St., Ste. 300
PO Box 14167
Madison, WI 53714-0167
608-271-2664
Fred Johnson, President
A professional society for credit union executives that offers management conferences and seminars.

Credit Union National Association
PO Box 431
Madison, WI 53701
608-231-4000
Ralph Swoboda, President
This association represents most of the local credit unions in the U.S. Offers information on laws, innovations in credit union services, and training of executives.

National Credit Union Management Association
c/o J.K. Anchors
4989 Rebel Trail, N.W.
Atlanta, GA 30327
404-255-6828
404-851-1752 Fax
J. K. Anchors, Treasurer
Helps credit union managers run and market their service.

PERIODICALS

Credit Union News
B K B Publications Inc.
150 Nassau St.
New York, NY 10038
212-267-7707
Charlene Storey, Editor
Offers news of government regulations for credit union executives.

Credit Union Week
Credit Union Week, Inc.
Box 088888
N. Palm Beach, FL 33408-8888
407-627-7330
Robert Heady, Editor
Reports news of interest rates, regulatory matters, administrative techniques, and trends in the industry.

LIBRARIES

Credit Union National Association
Information Resource Center
5710 W. Mineral Point Rd.
Box 431
Madison, WI 53701
608-231-4170
608-231-1869 Fax
Credit unions, business, and finance.

CUNA Mutual Insurance Group
Library & Research Center
Box 33430
Detroit, MI 48232-5430
313-357-8100
Credit unions and banking.

CREDIT UNIONS

American Airlines Employees Federal Credit
    Union
2100 P.O. Box 619001
DFW Airport, TX 75261-9001
817-963-6590

Boeing Employees Credit Union
Box 97050
Seattle, WA 98124-9750
206-439-5700

Golden 1 Credit Union
401 N. Middleton Rd.
Pearl River, NY 10965
916-732-2804

Hughes Aircraft Employees Federal Credit
    Union
P.O. Box 10003
Mahattan Beach, CA 90266
213-643-5400

LMSC Federal Credit Union
Box 3643
Sunnyvale, CA 94088-3643
408-742-2801

Navy Federal Credit Union
Box 3000
Maryfield, VA 22119-3000
703-255-8904

Pentagon Federal Credit Union
Box 1432
Alexandria, VA 22313
703-838-1000

State Employees Credit Union
310 Pittsboro
Chapel Hill, NC 27514
919-962-9191

United Airlines Employees Credit Union
125 E. Algonquin
Arlington Heights, IL 60005
708-952-6630

DAIRY INDUSTRY

See also: CHEESE INDUSTRY

ASSOCIATIONS

American Butter Institute
888 16th St., N.W.
Washington, DC 20006
202-659-1454
202-659-1496 Fax
Floyd Gaibler, Executive Director
Manufacturers and distributors of butter.

American Cultured Dairy Products Institute
888 16th St. N.W., 2nd Fl.
Washington, DC 20006
202-223-1931
202-331-7820 Fax
Thomas Balmer, Executive Director
Firms that make yogurt, buttermilk, cottage cheese, and sour cream.

American Dairy Association
6300 N. River Rd.
Rosemont, IL 60018
708-696-1880
708-696-1033 Fax
Grover Simpson, Vice President
A very large federation of state and regional dairy associations.

American Dairy Products Institute
130 N Franklin St.
Chicago, IL 60606
312-782-4888
312-782-5299 Fax
Warren Clark, Executive Director
Members produce evaporated, condensed, and powdered milk.

Dairy and Food Industries Supply Association
6245 Executive Blvd.
Rockville, MD 20852
301-984-1444
301-881-7832 Fax
John Martin, Executive Vice President
Firms that sell machinery and supplies used in making dairy and other food products.

PERIODICALS

Dairy Foods
Gorman Publishing Co.
8750 W. Bryn Mawr Ave.
Chicago, IL 60631
312-693-3200
Mike Pehanich, Editor
Reports news of interest to all executives in the dairy industry, including information on management, plant operation, and marketing.

Dairy Herd Management
Miller Publishing Co.
12400 Whitewater Dr., Ste. 160
Box 2400
Minnetonka, MN 55343
612-931-0211
Ed Clark, Editor
News and advice for large dairy farmers.

Dairy Today
Farm Journal, Inc.
230 W. Washington Sq.
Philadelphia, PA 19105
215-829-4700
Follows government regulations, news about market conditions, and other industry information.

Dairyman
Holstein-Friesian World, Inc.
8036 Lake Rd.
Box 299
Sandy Creek, NY 13145
315-387-3441
Dennis J. Halladay, Editor
Offers news and advice about business and technical matters for farmers of large dairy herds.

LIBRARIES

American Dairy Products Institute
Library
130 N. Franklin St.
Chicago, IL 60606
312-782-5455
312-782-5299 Fax
Dairy products of all kinds.

Ohio State University
Agriculture Library
45 Agriculture Bldg.
2120 Fyffe Rd.
Columbus, OH 43210
614-292-6125
614-292-7859 Fax
Dairy science, animal science, food science, and nutrition.

U.S.D.A.
National Agricultural Library
10301 Baltimore Blvd.
Beltsville, MD 20705
301-344-3755
301-344-5472 Fax
Milk sanitation, animal industry, veterinary medicine, and related topics.

COMPANIES

Agway Inc.
Box 4933
Syracuse, NY 13221
315-449-6127
Various products used on dairy farms.

Atlantic Dairy Cooperative
1225 Industrial Hwy.
Southhampton, PA 18966
215-322-0200
Cooperative that sells a wide variety of dairy products.

CPC International Inc.
International Plaza
Englewood Cliffs, NJ 07632
201-894-4000
Dairy products and many other types of food.

Finevest Foods, Inc.
191 Mason St.
Greenwich, CT 06830
203-629-8750
Wholesaler of dairy products and frozen foods.

H. P. Hood Inc.
(Subsidiary of Agway Inc.)
500 Rutherford Ave.
Boston, MA 02129
617-242-0600
Processes and distributes dairy and other food products.

Land O'Lakes, Inc.
4001 Lexington Ave., N.
Arden Hills, MN 55112
612-481-2222
Dairy and other food products.

Morning Glory Farms Region
(Division of Associated Milk Producers, Inc.)
116 N. Main St.
Shawano, WI 54166
715-526-2131
Dairy products.

Morningstar Foods Inc.
5956 Sherry Lane
Dallas, TX 75225
214-360-4700
Dairy products.

Prairie Farms Dairy, Inc.
P. O. Box 499
Carlinville, IL 62626
217-854-2547
Dairy products.

FEDERAL GOVERNMENT

U.S. Customs Service
Department of the Treasury
U.S. Customshouse
6 World Trade Center
New York, NY 10048
212-466-5550
*Ask for the Commodity Specialist in charge of
dairy products.*

U.S. Department of Agriculture
14th St. and Independence Ave., S.W.
Washington, DC 20250
202-720-8732
*Ask for dairy products in Economic Research
Service or the Agricultural Marketing Service.*

U.S. International Trade Administration
Department of Commerce
14th St. and Constitution Ave., N.W.
Washington, DC 20230
202-377-2000
*Ask for the Commodity Analyst who is an
expert in dairy products.*

U.S. International Trade Commission
500 E St., S.W.
Washington, DC 20436
202-205-2000 Office of the Secretary
202-205-3296 Industries locator
*Ask for the Trade Analyst who is an expert in
dairy products.*

DEFENSE INDUSTRIES

ASSOCIATIONS

Aerospace Industries Association of America
1250 I St. N.W.
Washington, DC 20005
202-371-8400
202-371-8470 Fax
Don Fuqua, President
Firms that manufacture guided missiles, aircraft, and other products.

Council of Defense and Space Industry Associations
1225 I St. N.W., Ste. 950
Washington, DC 20005
202-682-4435
202-682-9111 Fax
Jon Englund, Executive Secretary
Serves all parts of the defense industry by offering information about procurement policies, government regulations, and other broad issues.

International Defense Equipment Exhibitors Association
25 S. Quaker Ln., Ste. 20
Alexandria, VA 22314
703-461-3808
David Whiteree, Chairman
Promotes defense trade shows worldwide.

National Security Industrial Association
1025 Connecticut Ave. N.W., Ste. 300
Washington, DC 20036
202-775-1440
202-775-1309 Fax
Wallace Robinson, President
Studies defense trends and offers educational programs to officers in the defense industry and the U.S. government.

PERIODICALS

Armed Forces Journal International
Armed Forces Journal International, Inc.
2000 L St., N.W., Ste. 520
Washington, DC 20036
202-296-0450
B.F. Schemmer, Editor
Covers defense news for military officers and federal government officials.

Defense—Aerospace Business Digest
Phillips Publishing, Inc.
7811 Montrose Rd.
Potomac, MD 20854
301-340-2100
Ed Hazelwood, Editor
Reports news from the Pentagon and Congress on such topics as new arms programs and contracts.

Defense and Aerospace Markets
Forecast International Inc.—D M S
Forecast International Inc.
22 Commerce Rd.
Newtown, CT 06470
203-426-0800
Analyses of business opportunities for arms sales outside of the U.S.

Defense Organization Service—Industry
Carroll Publishing Co.
1058 Thomas Jefferson St., N.W.
Washington, DC 20007
202-333-8620
Provides organizational charts of companies that produce military goods.

Journal of Electronic Defense
Horizon—House—Microwave, Inc.
685 Canton St.
Norwood, MA 02062
617-769-9750
Hal Gershanoff, Editor
Business and technical information about electronic defense equipment.

Military Market
Army Times Publishing Co.
6883 Commercial Dr.
Springfield, VA 22159
703-750-8676
Nancy Tucker, Editor
Written for buyers who work for military base stores.

LIBRARIES

Center for Defense Information
Library
1500 Massachusetts Ave., N.W.
Washington, DC 20005
202-862-0700
202-862-0708 Fax
Defense information, foreign affairs, Defense Department budgets, and related subjects.

FMC Corp.
Ground Systems Division Library
2890 De La Cruz Blvd.
Box 58123, PO5
Santa Clara, CA 95052
408-289-3490
408-289-3323 Fax
Defense business, weapons systems, mechanical engineering, human factors, and related subjects.

U.S. National Defense University
Library
Fort Lesley J. McNair
4th & P Sts., S.W.
Washington, DC 20319-6000
202-475-1905
202-475-1745 Fax
Miltary science, national security affairs, political affairs, wargaming, and related subjects.

University of Pennsylvania
John Penman Wood Library of National
    Defense
504 Hollenback Center
3000 South St.
Philadelphia, PA 19104-6325
215-898-7757
Principles of war, officer education, tactics, organization, and related topics.

COMPANIES

AM General Division
(Division of LTV Missiles & Electronics
    Group)
105 N. Niles Ave.
South Bend, IN 46480
219-237-6222
Military vehicles.

ITT Corp.
320 Park Ave.
New York, NY 10022
212-752-6000
Defense and many other types of products.

Loral Corp.
600 Third Ave.
New York, NY 10016
212-697-1105
Military computers, telecommunications, other types of equipment.

LTV Aerospace and Defense Co.
(Subsidiary of LTV Corp.)
2001 Ross Ave., Box 655003
Dallas, TX 75265
214-979-7711
Military aircraft, missles, vehicles, and other products.

Martin Marietta Corp.
6801 Rockledge Dr.
Bethesda, MD 20817
301-897-6000
Aerospace, defense, electronics, and related products.

Northrop Corp.
1840 Century Park, E.
Los Angeles, CA 90067
213-553-6262
Military aircraft, electronic systems, and other products.

Paccar Inc
777 106th Ave., N. E.
Bellevue, WA 98004
206-455-7400
Military vehicles and other products.

TRW Space & Defense Sector
One Space Park
Redondo Beach, CA 90278
213-535-4321
Computers, software, comunications equipment, and other military products.

Textron Inc.
40 Westminster St.
Providence, RI 02903
401-421-2800
Aerospace, computers, and other defense products.

Thiokol Corp.
2475 Washington Blvd.
Ogden, UT 84401
801-629-2200
Ordnance and other defense products.

Tracor, Inc.
(Subsidiary of Westmark Systems Inc.)
6500 Tracor Lane
Austin, TX 78725
512-322-2360
Defense electronics.

United Technologies Corp.
United Technologies Bldg.
Hartford, CT 06101
203-728-7000
A wide range of military products.

FEDERAL GOVERNMENT

U.S. Department of Defense
The Pentagon
Washington, DC 20301
202-545-66700
Ask for the public affairs office to find the appropriate expert.

DELAWARE

STATE OFFICE LOCATOR (*for referrals to all state government offices*)

302-736-4000

ARCHIVES AND RECORDS

Historical & Cultural Affairs Division
Hall of Records
P.O. Box 1401
Dover, DE 19903
302-739-5318

ATTORNEY GENERAL

Justice Department
820 N. French Street
Wilmington, DE 19801
302-577-3838

BANKING

State Bank Commission
540 S. DuPont Highway
Dover, DE 19903
302-739-4235

COMMERCE

Development Office
99 Kings Highway
Dover, DE 19903
302-739-4271

CONSUMER AFFAIRS

Consumer Affairs Division
820 N. French Street
Dover, DE 19903
302-577-3250

EDUCATION

Public Instruction Department
P.O. Box 1402
Dover, DE 19903
302-739-4601

ENERGY

Energy Office
P.O. Box 1401
Dover, DE 19903
302-739-5644

ENVIRONMENTAL AFFAIRS

Natural Resources & Environmental Control
    Department
89 Kings Highway
Dover, DE 19903
302-739-4764

HEALTH

Community Health Bureau
Jesse Cooper Building
P.O. Box 637
Dover, DE 19903
302-736-4700

HOUSING

Housing Authority
18 The Green
Dover, DE 19901
302-739-4263

HUMAN RIGHTS

Human Relations Department
820 N. French Street
Wilmington, DE 19801
302-577-3485

INSURANCE

Insurance Department
841 Silver Lake Boulevard
Dover, DE 19901
302-739-4251

LABOR

Labor Department
820 N. French Street
Wilmington, DE 19801
302-577-2710

LEGISLATION

Legislative Council
Legislative Hall
Dover, DE 19901
302-739-4114

LIBRARY SERVICES

Library Services
Edgehill Shopping Center
Dover, DE 19901
302-739-4748

LICENSING—CORPORATE

Corporations Administration
State Department
Townsend Building
Dover, DE 19901
302-739-3073

LICENSING—PROFESSIONAL AND OCCUPATIONAL

Professional Regulation Division
P.O. Box 1401
Dover, DE 19903
302-739-4522

MOTOR VEHICLES

Motor Vehicles Division
P.O. Box 698
Dover, DE 19903
302-739-4421

OCCUPATIONAL HEALTH AND SAFETY

Occupational Safety & Health
820 N. French Street
Wilmington, DE 19801
302-577-3908

PUBLIC UTILITIES

Public Services Commission
P.O. Box 457
Dover, DE 19903
302-739-4247

PURCHASING

Purchasing
Purchasing Building
P.O. Box 299
Delaware City, DE 19706
302-577-3070

REAL ESTATE

Real Estate Commission
P.O. Box 1401
Dover, DE 19903
302-739-4522

SECURITIES

Securities Office
820 N. French Street
Wilmington, DE 19801
302-577-3847

TAXATION AND REVENUE

Revenue Division
820 N. French Street
Wilmington, DE 19801
302-577-3315

TOURISM

Tourism Office
P.O. Box 1401
Dover, DE 19903
302-739-4271
800-441-8846
800-282-8667 (in Delaware)

TRANSPORTATION

Transportation Department
P.O. Box 778
Dover, DE 19903
302-739-4303

UNEMPLOYMENT

Unemployment Insurance Division
P.O. Box 9029
Newark, DE 19714-9029
302-368-6730

WORKER'S COMPENSATION

Industrial Accident Board
820 N. French Street
Wilmington, DE 190801
302-571-3594

DENTAL INDUSTRY

ASSOCIATIONS

American Dental Trade Association
4222 King St. W.
Alexandria, VA 22302-1597
703-379-7755
703-931-9429 Fax
Nik Petrovic, President
Most of the firms that manufacture and distribute dental equipment, tools, and supplies are members of this association. It offers training programs and a variety of services to members.

Dental Dealers of America
1118 Land Title Bldg.
Philadelphia, PA 19110
215-563-2588
215-561-3267 Fax
Edward Shils, Executive Secretary
A small group of dealers that wholesale dental instruments and supplies.

Dental Laboratory Conference
Warwick Hotel, Ste. 411
17th and Locust Sts.
Philadelphia, PA 19103
215-546-2313
215-546-9595 Fax
Robert Gitman, Executive Director
Dental laboratories that make prosthetic restorations at the request of dentists.

Dental Manufacturers of America
1118 Land Title Bldg.
Philadelphia, PA 19110
215-563-2588
215-561-3267 Fax
Edward Shils, Executive Director
Members manufacture dental equipment and supplies.

PERIODICALS

Dental Economics
PennWell Publishing Co.
Box 3408
Tulsa, OK 74101
918-835-3161
Dick Hale, Editor
Helps dentists run the business aspects of their practice and manage their personal financial affairs.

Dental Lab Products
Medical Economics Co. Inc.
680 Kinderkamack Rd.
Oradell, NJ 07649
201-262-3030
Jeanne Matson, Editor
Reports on new dental products and their uses.

Dental Laboratory Review Buyer's Guide
Dental Survey Publications
7500 Old Oak Blvd.
Cleveland, OH 44130
216-243-8100
A listing of dental products.

Dental Management
Edgell Communications
7500 Old Oak Blvd.
Cleveland, OH 44130
216-826-2839
Alice Luddington, Editor
Offers dentists help in managing their offices and delivering their services.

General Dentistry
Academy of General Dentistry
211 E. Chicago Ave., Ste. 1200
Chicago, IL 60611
312-440-4300
William Howard, Editor
Provides dentists advice on management and new products.

LIBRARIES

National Institute of Dental Research
Research Data and Management Information
5333 Westbard Ave.
Bethesda, MD 20016
301-496-7220
301-496-9241 Fax
Dental research.

Northwestern University
Dental School Library
311 E. Chicago Ave.
Chicago, IL 60611-3008
312-503-6896
312-503-3831 Fax
Dental office practice, oral surgery, oral hygiene, forensic dentistry, and related topics.

University of Rochester
School of Medicine & Dentistry
Edward G. Miner Library
601 Elmwood Ave.
Rochester, NY 14642
716-275-3364
716-275-4799 Fax
Dental research, medicine, and nursing.

COMPANIES

Dentsply International Inc.
(Subsidiary Of Dentsply Holdings Inc.)
570 W. College Ave.
York, PA 17405
717-845-7511
Dental equipment and supplies.

Healthco International Inc.
25 Stuart St.
Boston, MA 02116
617-423-6045
Sales and service of dental equipment and dental supplies.

North American Philips Corp.
(Subsidiary of Philips Industries, N. V.)
100 E. 42nd St.
New York, NY 10017
212-697-3600
Dental X-ray machines and many other types of products.

Patterson Dental Co.
1100 E. 80 St.
Minneapolis, MN 55420
612-854-2881
Dental equipment and supplies.

Henry Schein, Inc.
5 Harbor Park Dr.
Port Washington, NY 11050
516-621-4300
Dental, medical, and pharmaceutical supplies.

Sherwood Medical Co.
(Subsidiary of American Home Products
    Corp.)
1831 Olive St.
St. Louis, MO 63103
314-621-7788
Medical, dental, surgical, and related products.

Sterling Optical Corp.
1025 Westchester Ave.
White Plains, NY 10604
914-682-4500
Dental, optical, and medical supplies.

Sybron Acquisition Co.
411 E. Wisconsin Ave.
Milwaukee, WI 53202
414-274-6600
Supplies for dental laboratories.

FEDERAL GOVERNMENT

National Institutes of Health
9000 Rockville Pike
Bethesda, MD 20892
301-496-4000
Ask for Surgical-Dental Drugs at the Center for Drug Evaluation and Research or for the Laboratory of Oral Medicine.

U.S. Customs Service
Department of the Treasury
U.S. Customshouse
6 World Trade Center
New York, NY 10048
212-466-5550
Ask for the Commodity Specialist in charge of dental products and equipment.

U.S. International Trade Administration
Department of Commerce
14th St. and Constitution Ave., N.W.
Washington, DC 20230
202-377-2000
Ask for the Commodity Analyst who is an expert in the dental industry.

U.S. International Trade Commission
500 E St., S.W.
Washington, DC 20436
202-205-2000 Office of the Secretary
202-205-3296 Industries locator
Ask for the Trade Analyst who is an expert in the dental industry.

U.S. Patent and Trademark Office
Crystal Plaza 2
2011 Jefferson Davis Highway
Arlington, VA 22202
703-305-8000
Ask for the Examining Group Director who is a specialist in dental products and equipment.

DESKTOP PUBLISHING

See also: COMPUTER GRAPHICS and COMPUTERS

ASSOCIATIONS

Desktop Publishing Applications Association
c/o Herbert Communication
3 Post Office Rd., No. 104
Waldorf, ND 20602-2710
No telephone listed.
Herbert Boeckenhaupt, Executive Director
Offers training, certification, and information to those interested in desktop publishing.

National Association of Desktop Publishers
1260 Boylston St.
Boston, MA 02205
617-426-2885
800-874-4113
617-437-0014 Fax
Barry Harrington, Chairman
A large group of hardware and software manufacturers, and others who use microcomputers and mainframes to create documents on desktop publishing systems. Offers information services, discount prices on software, and much more.

PERIODICALS

Desktop Communications
International Desktop Communications, Ltd.
48 E. 43rd. St.
New York, NY 10017
212-867-9650
Pauline Ores, Editor
Offers design and technical information for those who create newsletters, presentations, and other documents on desktop publishing systems.

Desktop Publishing: Office Automation
    Buyer's Guide & Handbook
Computer Information Publishing
150 Fifth Ave.
New York, NY 10011
212-807-8220
A listing of desktop publishing products.

MicroPublishing Report
Micro Publishing Press
21150 Hawthorne Blvd., Ste. 104
Torrance, CA 90503
213-371-5787
James Cavuoto, Editor
*Reports on industry trends, vendors, trade
shows, and other matters of interest to executives in the desktop publishing industry.*

Personal Publishing
Hitchcock Publishing
191 S. Gary Ave.
Carol Stream, IL 60188
708-462-2286
Terry Ulick, Editor
*A how-to magazine for users of desktop sys-
tems.*

Publish!
P C W Communications, Inc.
501 Second St.
San Francisco, CA 94107
415-546-7722
Susan Gubernat, Editor
*A how-to magazine for users of desktop sys-
tems.*

Seybold Report on Desktop Publishing
Seybold Publications, Inc.
Box 644
Media, PA 19063
215-565-2480
Peter Dyson, Editor
*Covers the software, hardware, and tech-
niques used by desktop publishers.*

LIBRARIES

Apple Computer Inc.
Library and Information Resources
10381 Bandley Dr., 8C
Cupertino, CA 95014
408-974-2400
408-725-8502 Fax
*Microcomputers, computer programming, and
software.*

National Computer Graphics Association
2722 Merrilee Dr., Ste. 200
Fairfax, VA 22031
703-698-9600
800-225-NCGA
705-560-2752 Fax
Computer graphics hardware and software.

University of Oregon
Computing Center
Library
Eugene, OR 97403
503-346-1722
*Microcomputers, educational computing, and
computer science.*

University of Washington
Computing Information Center
University Computing Services, HG-45
Seattle, WA 98195
206-543-5818
206-543-3090 Fax
*Computing, hardware, software, data commu-
nications, and related topics.*

COMPANIES

Adobe Systems, Inc.
P.O. Box 7900
Mountain View, CA 94039
415-961-4400
Desktop publishing software.

Aldus Corp.
411 1st Ave. S.
Seattle, WA 98104
206-622-5500
Desktop publishing software.

Apple Computer, Inc.
20525 Mariani Ave.
Cupertino, CA 95014
408-996-1010
Desktop publishing and many other types of software.

International Business Machines Corp.
Old Orchard Rd.
Armonk, NY 10504
914-765-1900
Desktop publishing and many other types of software.

Microsoft Corp.
1 Microsoft Way
Redmond, WA 98052
206-882-8080
Desktop publishing and many other types of software.

Ventura Software, Inc.
15175 Innovation Drive
San Diego, CA 92128
619-673-0172
Desktop publishing software.

WordPerfect Corp.
1555 N. Technology Way
Orem, UT 84057
801-222-7900
Desktop publishing and other types of software.

FEDERAL GOVERNMENT

U.S. Customs Service
Department of the Treasury
U.S. Customshouse
6 World Trade Center
New York, NY 10048
212-466-5550
Ask for the Commodity Specialist in charge of computer products.

U.S. International Trade Administration
Department of Commerce
14th St. and Constitution Ave., N.W.
Washington, DC 20230
202-377-2000
Ask for the Commodity Analyst who is an expert in the computer industry.

U.S. International Trade Commission
500 E St., S.W.
Washington, DC 20436
202-205-2000 Office of the Secretary
202-205-3296 Industries locator
Ask for the Trade Analyst who is an expert in the computer industry.

U.S. Patent and Trademark Office
Crystal Plaza 2
2011 Jefferson Davis Highway
Arlington, VA 22202
703-305-8000
Ask for the Examining Group Director who is a specialist in the computer industry.

DIRECT MAIL AND MARKETING INDUSTRY

See also: MARKETING

ASSOCIATIONS

Direct Marketing Association
11 W. 42nd St.
New York, NY 10036-8096
212-768-7277
212-768-4546 Fax
Jonah Gitlitz, President
By far the largest association of firms in the direct marketing industry. Members include retailers, publishers, mail order firms, list brokers, lettershops, research firms, and advertisers. Offers a wide range of educational and information services to members and the public.

Direct Marketing Educational Foundation
6 E. 43rd St.
New York, NY 10017-4646
212-768-7277
212-599-1268 Fax
Richard Montesi, President
Furthers the education of direct marketing executives at the college level through granting fellowships, internships, and creating course outlines.

Mail Advertising Service Association International
1421 Prince St., Ste. 200
Alexandria, VA 22314-2814
703-836-9200
703-548-8204 Fax
David Weaver, President
Members offer a variety of direct mail services, including mailing list rental, fulfillment, and related services. The Association provides training and research.

National Mail Order Association
3875 Wilshire Blvd., Ste. 604
Los Angeles, CA 90010
213-380-3686
Paul Muchnick, Chairman
Offers direct mail marketers information on new products, techniques, mailing lists, and other data that improves mail order sales.

PERIODICALS

Direct
Cowles Business Media
Six River Bend Center
911 Hope St.
Stamford, CT 06907
203-358-9900
Mercedes Erickson, Editor
Follows the latest trends in direct marketing.

Direct Mail List Rates and Data
Standard Rate & Data Service, Inc.
3004 Glenview Rd.
Wilmette, IL 60091
800-323-4588
A directory of mailing lists available for rental and firms that service the direct mail industry.

Direct Marketing Magazine
Lighthouse Communications Group
224 Seventh St.
Garden City
Long Island, NY 11530
516-746-6700
Raymond Roel, Editor
Reports on the companies and strategies that are making news in the industry.

Direct Marketing Market Place
Hilary House Publishers, Inc.
980 N. Federal Hwy., Ste. 206
Boca Raton, FL 33432-2704
*A directory of individuals and companies who
work in direct marketing.*

Direct Response Specialist
Stilson & Stilson
Box 1075
Tarpon Springs, FL 34688-1075
813-786-1411
Galen Stilson, Editor
Offers tips for improving response rates.

Journal of Direct Marketing
John Wiley & Sons, Inc., Journals
605 Third Ave.
New York, NY 10158-0012
212-850-6000
Don Schultz, Editor
*Serves both academics and practitioners of
direct marketing.*

Target Marketing
North American Publishing Co.
401 N. Broad St.
Philadelphia, PA 19100
215-238-5300
Jo Anne Parke, Editor
*Reports on various direct mail and other mar-
keting media. Includes articles on new techniques, lists, equipment, and strategies.*

LIBRARIES

Direct Marketing Association, Inc.
Information Central
11 W. 42nd St.
New York NY 10036-8096
212-768-7277
212-768-4546 Fax
*Direct mail advertising and marketing,
research studies, and related subjects.*

Harris Catalog Library
Catalog World: America's Mail Order Theater
4555 Auburn Blvd., Ste. 11
Sacramento, CA 95841
916-487-6964
A full range of mail order catalogs.

COMPANIES

Advo-System Inc.
One Univac Lane
Windsor, CT 06095
203-285-6100
Direct mail advertising.

American Transtech
(Subsidiary of American Telephone & Telegraph Co.)
8000 Baymeadows Way
Jacksonville, FL 32256
904-636-1000
*Direct marketing programs, especially tele-
marketing.*

Ed Burnett Consultants, Inc.
2 Park Ave
New York, NY 10016
800-223-7777
Consumer and business mailing list rental.

Barry Blau & Partners Inc.
1960 Bronson Rd.
Fairfield, CT 06430
203-254-3700
Direct mail advertising.

Columbian Advertising, Inc.
201 E. Ohio St.
Chicago, IL 60611
312-943-7600
Direct marketing sales promotion.

Direct Mail Corp. of America
1533 Washington Ave.
St. Louis, MO 63103
314-436-1122
Direct mail advertising agency.

Johnson & Quin, Inc.
7460 N. Lehigh Ave.
Niles, IL 60648
708-647-6900
Personalized direct mail packages.

Mars Graphic Services Inc.
1 Deadline Dr.
Westville, NJ 08093
609-456-8666
Direct mail brochures and letters.

R. L. Polk & Co.
431 Howard St.
Detroit, MI 48231
313-961-9470
Direct mail lists.

Roy Thomas, Inc.
701 E. Prospect
Mount Prospect, IL 60056
708-577-9890
Direct mail marketing.

Wiland Services Inc.
6707 Winchester Ct.
Boulder, CO 80301
303-530-0606
*Data processing and related services to the
direct mail industry.*

FEDERAL GOVERNMENT

U.S. International Trade Commission
500 E St., S.W.
Washington, DC 20436
202-205-2000 Office of the Secretary
202-205-3296 Industries locator
*Ask for the Trade Analyst who is an expert in
the direct mail industry.*

DISTRIBUTORS AND WHOLESALERS

ASSOCIATIONS

Council of Logistics Management
2803 Butterfield Rd., Ste. 380
Oak Brook, IL 60521
708-574-0985
708-574-0989 Fax
George Gecowets, Executive Vice President
*Members include executives, educators, and
consultants involved with the physical distribution of goods. Offers information on management and coordination of transportation,
warehousing, and handling.*

General Merchandise Distributors Council
1275 Lake Plaza Dr.
Colorado Springs, CO 80906
719-576-4260
Richard Tilton, President
*Works to increase the efficiency of distribu-
tion, management, marketing, and merchandising of its members.*

National Association of Wholesaler-Distributors
1725 K St. N.W., Ste. 710
Washington, DC 20006
202-872-0885
202-785-0586 Fax
Dirk Van Dongen, President
By far the largest association of wholesalers and distributors in the U.S. Acts as a lobbying group and offers management courses.

PERIODICALS

Chilton's Distribution Magazine
Chilton Co.
Chilton Way
Radnor, PA 19089
215-964-4379
Thomas Foster, Editor
How-to information on inventory control, traffic management, transportation, and business logistics.

Distribution Center Management
Customer Service Institute
1010 Wayne Ave., Ste. 440
Silver Spring, MD 20910
301-585-0730
Offers advice about operational and personnel issues to supervisors of warehouses and distribution centers.

Distributors & Wholesalers' Advisory
Alexander Research & Communications, Inc.
1133 Broadway, Ste. 1407
New York, NY 10010
212-206-7979
News and advice for executives in charge of distribution.

LIBRARIES

Bergen Brunswig Corp.
Library
4000 Metropolitan Dr.
Orange, CA 92668
714-385-4454
Pharmaceuticals distribution, consumer electronics distribution, and prerecorded video cassettes distribution.

Validata Computer and Research Corp.
Library
428 S. Perry St.
Box 4719
Montgomery, AL 36104
205-834-2324
Physical distribution management.

FEDERAL GOVERNMENT

U.S. International Trade Administration
Department of Commerce
14th St. and Constitution Ave., N.W.
Washington, DC 20230
202-377-2000
Ask for the Commodity Analyst who is an expert in wholesale trade.

DISTRICT OF COLUMBIA

DISTRICT OFFICE LOCATOR (*for referrals to all district government offices*)

202-727-1000

ARCHIVES AND RECORDS

Public Records Office
1350 Pennsylvania Avenue, N.W.
Room 504
Washington, DC 20004
202-727-2052

ATTORNEY GENERAL

Corporation Counsel Office
1350 Pennsylvania Avenue, N.W.
Washington, DC 20004
202-727-6248

COMMERCE

Business & Economic Development
717 14th Street, N.W.
10th Floor
Washington, DC 20005
202-727-6600

CONSUMER AFFAIRS

Consumer & Regulatory Affairs Department
614 H Street, N.W.
Room 1120
Washington, DC 20001
202-727-7170

EDUCATION

Board of Education
415 12th Street, N.W.
Washington, DC 20004
202-724-4223

ENERGY

Energy Office
613 G Street, N.W.
Washington, DC 20001
202-727-1800

ENVIRONMENTAL AFFAIRS

Environmental Control Division
614 H Street, N.W.
Room 1120
Washington, DC 20001
202-404-1120

HEALTH

Public Health Commission
801 N. Capitol Street, N.E.
Washington, DC 20002
202-673-7700

HOUSING

Housing & Community Development Department
51 N Street, N.E.
Washington, DC 20002
202-535-1970

HUMAN RIGHTS

Human Rights & Minority Business Opportunity
2000 14th Street, N.W.
Washington, DC 20009
202-939-8740

INSURANCE

Insurance Adminstration
614 H Street, N.W.
Room 1120
Washington, DC 20001
202-727-8000

LEGISLATION

Intergovernmental Relations Office
1350 Pennsylavnia Avenue, N.W.
Washington, DC 20004
202-727-6265

LICENSING—CORPORATE

Corporations Division
614 H Street, N.W.
Room 1120
Washington, DC 20001
202-727-7278

LICENSING—PROFESSIONAL AND OCCUPATIONAL

Occupational & Professional Licensure
    Administration
614 H Street, N.W.
Room 1120
Washington, DC 20001
202-727-7480

MOTOR VEHICLES

Transportation Systems Administration
2000 14th Street, N.W.
6th Floor
Washington, DC 20009
202-727-1737

OCCUPATIONAL HEALTH AND SAFETY

Occupational Safety & Health Division
950 Upshur Street, N.W.
Washington, DC 20011
202-576-6339

OMBUDSMAN

Corporation Counsel Office
1350 Pennsylvania Avenue, N.W.
Washington, DC 20004
202-727-6248

PUBLIC UTILITIES

Public Service Commission
450 5th Street, N.W.
Ste. 309
Washington, DC 20001
202-727-1822

PURCHASING

Office of Policy & Management
613 G Street, N.W.
Ste. 900
Washington, DC 20001
202-727-1179

REAL ESTATE

Real Estate Commission
P.O. Box 37200
Washington, DC 20013-7200
202-727-7468

SECURITIES

Securities Division
450 5th Street, N.W.
Washington, DC 20001
202-626-5100

TAXATION AND REVENUE

Finance & Revenue Department
300 Indiana Avenue, N.W.
Room 4136
Washington, DC 20001
202-727-6020

TOURISM

Convention & Visitor's Center
1212 New York Avenue, N.W.
Washington, DC 20005
202-789-7000

TRANSPORTATION

Transportation Systems
200 14th Street, N.W.
6th Floor
Washington, DC 20009
202-727-1737

UNEMPLOYMENT

Office of Unemployment Compensation
500 C Street, N.W.
Room 515
Washington, DC 20001
202-639-1163

WORKER'S COMPENSATION

Office of Workers Compensation
1100 L Street, N.W.
Room 9101
Washington, DC 20211
202-724-0702

DRUG STORES

ASSOCIATIONS

Affiliated/Associated Drug Stores
c/o Ira Shain
330 Seventh Ave.
New York, NY 10001
212-967-9890
212-967-9896 Fax
Ira Shain, President
A small group that represents drug store chains.

American Pharmaceutical Association
2215 Constitution Ave. N.W.
Washington, DC 20037
202-628-4410
800-237-APHA
202-783-2351 Fax
John Gans, Executive Vice President
This large professional society of pharmacists, researchers, educators and others offers educational services, lobbying, and information about the industry.

Drug Information Association
PO Box 3113
Maple Glen, PA 19002
215-628-2288
Thomas Teal, Director
This association is for people who collect, analyze, and report drug information in industry, government, and other fields.

National Association of Chain Drug Stores
c/o Ronald Ziegler
PO Box 1417
Alexandria, VA 22313-1480
703-549-3001
703-836-4869 Fax
Ronald Ziegler, President
The main purpose of this large group of chain drug retailers is to keep members informed about new and existing government regulations, taxes, and related matters.

National Association of Retail Druggists
205 Dangerfield Rd.
Alexandria, VA 22314
703-683-8200
800-547-7447
703-683-3619 Fax
Charles West, Executive Vice President
A very large association of independent drugstores and pharmacists. Provides education and management assistance.

PERIODICALS

Chain Drug Review
Racher Press Inc.
220 Fifth Ave.
New York, NY 10001
212-213-6000
David Pinto, Editor
News for chain drug store executives.

Drug Store Market Guide
Melnor Publishing, Inc.
1739 Horton Ave.
Mohegan Lake, NY 10547
914-528-7147
Melanie Buse, Editor
A analysis of distribution within the chain and wholesale drug store industry.

Drug Store News
Lebhar-Friedman, Inc.
425 Park Ave.
New York, NY 10022
212-371-9400
Bruce Buckley, Editor
Follows trends, regulations, and other matters that interest drug store executives and managers.

Drug Topics Red Book
Medical Economics Co. Inc.
680 Kinderkamack Rd.
Oradell, NJ 07649
201-262-3030
Valentine Cardinale, Editor
A huge listing of drug store products. Also prints articles about merchandising techniques.

LIBRARIES

American Pharmaceutical Association
Library
2215 Constitution Ave. N.W.
Washington, DC 20037
202-628-4410
800-237-APHA
202-783-2351 Fax
Covers pharmaceutical subjects including drug stores.

COMPANIES

Arbor Drugs, Inc.
3331 W. Big Beaver
Troy, MI 48084
313-643-9420
Retail drug stores.

Drug Emporium, Inc.
7760 Olentangy River Rd.
Worthington, OH 43085
614-888-6876
Discount drug stores.

Jack Eckerd Corp.
8333 Bryan Dairy Rd.
Clearwater, FL 33518
813-397-7461
Drug store chain.

Genovese Drug Stores, Inc.
80 Marcus Dr.
Melville, NY 11747
516-420-1900
Drug store chain.

Osco Drug, Inc.
(Subsidiary of American Stores Co.)
1818 Swift Dr
Oak Brook, IL 60521
708-887-5000
Retail drug stores.

Peoples Drug Stores, Inc.
(Subsidiary of Melville Corp.)
6315 Bren Mar Drive
Alexandria, VA 22312
703-750-6100
Chain of drug stores.

Perry Drug Stores Inc.
5400 Perry Dr., P.O. Box 1957
Pontiac, MI 48340
313-334-1300
Retail drug stores.

Revco D.S.
1925 Enterprise Pkwy.
Twinsburg, OH 44087
216-425-9811
Chain of discount drug stores.

Rite Aid Corp.
Railroad Ave. & Trindle Rd.
Shiremanstown, PA 17011
717-761-2633
Chain of retail drug stores.

Thrift Drug Co.
(Division of J. C. Penney Co., Inc.)
615 Alpha Dr.
Pittsburgh, PA 15238
412-963-6600
Retail drug stores.

Walgreen Co.
200 Wilmot Rd.
Deerfield, IL 60015
708-940-2500
Chain drug stores.

FEDERAL GOVERNMENT

U.S. International Trade Administration
Department of Commerce
14th St. and Constitution Ave., N.W.
Washington, DC 20230
202-377-2000
Ask for the Commodity Analyst who is an expert in drug stores.

ECONOMICS

ASSOCIATIONS

American Economic Association
2014 Broadway, Ste. 305
Nashville, TN 37203-2418
615-322-2595
615-343-7590 Fax
Elton Hinshaw, Secretary
This large group of economists, executives, educators, and government officials provides a forum to exchange information on economic problems and solutions.

American Institute for Economic Research
Great Barrington, MA 01230
413-528-1216
Rollo Handy, President
Provides publications and research on a wide variety of financial and economic topics.

The Conference Board
845 3rd Ave.
New York, NY 10022
212-759-0900
Preston Townley, President
The Board publishes reports and conducts research into many economics and management subjects. The Board operates a Work and Family Information Center, which studies the effect of work on family relationships, and a Consumer Research Center, which studies demographic trends, consumer attitudes, and related subjects.

International Association of Business Forecasting
1587 Town Hill Rd.
York Springs, PA 17372
309-827-0350
Charles Chase, President
Offers information on forecasting techniques and systems.

Joint Council on Economic Education
432 Park Ave. South
New York, NY 10016
212-685-5499
Stephen Buckles, President
These economists, educators, and executives work to increase and improve the level of economics education at the school and college levels.

National Association of Business Economists
28790 Chagrin Blvd., Ste. 300
Cleveland, OH 44122
216-464-7986
216-464-6352 Fax
David Williams, Executive Director
Business economists who work in industry, government, and academia.

PERIODICALS

Advances in Econometrics
J A I Press Inc.
55 Old Post Rd., No. 2
Box 1678
Greenwich, CT 06836-1678
203-661-7602
George Rhodes, Editor
A scholarly journal about the mathematical study of economics.

American Economic Review
American Economic Association
2014 Broadway, Ste. 305
Nashville, TN 37203
615-322-2595
Short and long articles about a wide range of subjects that concern economists.

Business Economics
National Association of Business Economists
28790 Chagrin Blvd., Ste. 300
Cleveland, OH 44122
216-464-7986
Edmund Mennis, Editor
Offers working economists information on such subjects as monetary policy, forecasting, deregulation, interest rates, and many other subjects.

Journal of Business and Economic Perspectives
University of Tennessee at Martin
School of Business Administration
102 Business Administration Building
Martin, TN 38238-5015
901-587-7225
Saul Barr, Editor
Provides scholarly articles on economic issues that relate to business.

Journal of Economic Theory
Academic Press, Inc.
1250 Sixth Ave.
San Diego, CA 92101
619-230-1840
Karl Shell, Editor
Prints papers in economics.

Quarterly Journal of Economics
Harvard University. Department of Economics
M I T Press
55 Hayward St.
Cambridge, MA 02142
617-253-2889
For economists in business and academia.

LIBRARIES

American Institute for Economic Research
E. C. Harwood Library
Division St.
Great Barrington, MA 01230
413-528-1216
413-528-0103 Fax
Business cycles, money and banking, and a full range of economics topics.

Federal Reserve Bank of New York
Research Library
33 Liberty St.
New York, NY 10045
212l-720-5670
212-720-1372 Fax
Business conditions, economics, finance, international finance, and related topics.

New York Public Library
Economic and Public Affairs Division
Fifth Ave, & 42nd St., Rm. 228
New York, NY 10018
212-930-0750
Covers the full range of business and economics subjects.

University of Pennsylvania
Lippincott Library
Van Pelt-Dietrich Library Center
3420 Walnut St.
Philadelphia, PA 19104-6207
215-898-2261
215-898-2261 Fax
Applied economics, finance, econometrics, statistics, and related topics.

University of Pittsburgh
Joseph M. Katz Graduate School of Business
Library
130 Mervis Hall
Pittsburgh, PA 15260
412-648-1669
412-648-1586 Fax
Economics, econometrics, accounting, marketing, finance, and related topics.

Yale University
Cowles Foundation for Research in Economics
Library
30 Hillhouse Ave.
New Haven, CT 06520
203-432-3697
Economic theory, econometrics, macroeconomic theory, and related subjects.

FEDERAL GOVERNMENT

National Science Foundation
1800 G. St., N.W.
Washington, DC 20550
202-357-9859
Ask for the Social & Economic Sciences Division.

U.S. Department of Commerce
14th St. and Constitution Ave., N.W.
Washington, DC 20230
202-377-2000
Ask for the Economic and Agriculture Census.

U.S. Department of Labor
200 Constitution Ave., N.W.
Washington, DC 202210
202-523-6666
Ask for the Bureau of Labor Statistics.

EDUCATION

See also: ADULT EDUCATION; COLLEGES AND UNIVERSITIES; SCHOOLS; and each of the 50 states under education

BUSINESS EDUCATION

Associations

American Assembly of Collegiate Schools of
Business
605 Old Ballas Rd., Ste. 220
St. Louis, MO 63141-7077
314-872-8481
William Laidlaw, Executive Vice President
Members offer accredited college programs in business administration and accounting. Conducts seminars and research about business education.

American Society for Training and Development
Box 1443
1640 King St.
Alexandria, VA 22313
703-683-8100
703-683-8103 Fax
Curtis Plott, Executive Vice President
This large association serves as an information clearinghouse for questions about training and human resource development.

Decision Sciences Institute
University Plaza
Atlanta, GA 30303
404-651-4000
404-651-2804 Fax
Carol Latta, Executive Director
*Members include professors at business
schools and business executives.*

National Business Education Association
1914 Association Dr.
Reston, VA 22091
703-860-8300
Janet Treichel, Executive Director
*A large organization of business teachers
working in high schools, colleges, and other
postsecondary schools.*

Periodicals

Business Education Forum
National Business Education Association
1914 Association Dr.
Reston, VA 22091
703-860-8300
Diana Stein, Editor
*Prints articles for business education teachers
and administrators.*

Business Education Index
Delta Pi Epsilon, Inc.
National Office
Box 4340
Little Rock, AR 72214
501-562-1233
Carol Lundgren, Editor
*This index lists articles about business educa-
tion that were published in selected business
and education periodicals.*

Business Education World
Glencoe—McGraw-Hill
1221 Ave. of the Americas
New York, NY 10020
212-512-4736
Wendy Spiegel, Editor
*Reports on innovative teaching methods,
materials, and curricula in the field of business
and office education.*

Business Horizons
Indiana University
School of Business
Bloomington, IN 47405
812-855-6342
Harvey Bunke, Editor
*Scholarly articles on a wide range of business
subjects, including business education.*

Companies

Careercom Corp.
1801 Oberlin Rd.
Middletown, PA 17057
717-939-1981
*Private schools that teach business subjects as
well as tractor/trailer driving and mechanic
skills.*

Commercial Programming Unlimited, Inc.
25 W. 17th St.
New York, NY 10011
212-243-7800
Business education products.

Grumman Data Systems Institute
(Division of Grumman Corp.)
250 Crossways Park Dr.
Woodbury, NY 11797
516-346-2055
Computer business education.

TECHNICAL AND VOCATIONAL EDUCATION

Associations

American Association for Vocational Instructional Materials
745 Gaines School Rd.
Athens, GA 30605
404-543-7557
800-228-4689
404-542-0806 Fax
Richard Hylton, Executive Director
Offers information on teaching aids and instructional materials used for vocational education.

American Technical Education Association
North Dakota State College of Science
Wahpeton, ND 58076
701-671-2240
701-471-2145 Fax
Betty Krump, Executive Director
Teachers of technical subjects, mainly at the college level.

American Vocational Association
1410 King St.
Alexandria, VA 22314
703-683-3111
800-826-9972
703-739-9098 Fax
Charles Buzzell, Executive Director
A large group of teachers and others involved with vocational and technical education.

International Technology Education Association
1914 Association Dr.
Reston, VA 22091
703-860-2100
Kendall Starkweather, Executive Director
Technology teachers at all levels of education.

National Association of Trade and Technical Schools
2251 Wisconsin Ave. N.W.
Washington, DC 20007
202-333-1021
Stephen Blair, President
Acts as a clearinghouse for private schools that train students for technical careers.

Periodicals

Career Success
Target Marketing, Inc.
115 Blue Jay Dr.
Liberty, MO 64068
816-781-7557
Targeted to vocational students or prospective students. Reports on the employment outlook, success stories, and career opportunities.

Journal of Studies in Technical Careers
Southern Illinois University at Carbondale
College of Technical Careers
Carbondale, IL 62901
618-453-7288
Susan Rehwaldt, Editor
Advice and descriptions of existing programs for teachers of technical subjects.

Technical Education News
Glencoe—McGraw-Hill
1221 Ave. of the Americas
New York, NY 10020
212-512-4736
Wendy Spiegel, Editor
Reports on trends and innovations in the field.

Vocational Training News
Capitol Publications, Inc.
1101 King St., Ste. 444
Alexandria, VA 22314
703-683-4100
David Harrison, Editor
Covers federal and state government training acts and initiatives.

Companies

Brodhead-Garrett Co.
(Subsidiary of FSC Educational Inc.)
223 S. Illinois Ave.
Mansfield, OH 44905
419-589-8222
*Equipment and supplies for industrial arts
and vocational schools.*

Concord Career Colleges Inc.
12 & Baltimore, Box 26610
Kansas City, MO 64196
816-474-4750
Vocational training schools.

Graves-Humphreys Co.
(Subsidiary of Frank Paxton Co.)
1948 Franklin Rd. S.W.
Roanoke, VA 24014
703-343-8011
*Supplies and equipment for vocational and
industrial arts schools.*

Herzing Institutes, Inc.
161 W. Wisconsin Ave.
Milwaukee, WI 53203
414-271-8103
Operates vocational training schools.

L. J. Technical Systems, Inc.
(Subsidiary of L. J. Technical Systems Ltd.)
19 Power Dr.
Hauppauge, NY 11788
516-234-2100
*Training equipment for technical and voca-
tional schools.*

National Institute Of Careers Inc.
6151 Miramar Pkwy.
Miramar, FL 33023
305-981-0112
Vocational school.

R. Tolerton Co.
265 N. Freedom Ave.
Alliance, OH 44601
216-821-1220
Vocational school equipment.

LIBRARIES

Columbus Technical Institute
Educational Resources Center
550 E. Spring St.
Box 1609
Columbus, OH 43216
614-227-2400
614-227-2467 Fax
Vocational and technical education subjects.

Teachers College
Milbank Memorial Library
Columbia University
DB, Box 307
New York, NY 10027
212-678-3494
212-678-4048 Fax
*Education, speech, psychology, communica-
tions, and related topics.*

FEDERAL GOVERNMENT

U.S. Department of Education
400 Maryland Ave., S.W.
Washington, DC 20202
202-708-5366
Ask for Vocational and Adult Education.

U.S. Department of Veterans Affairs
810 Vermont Ave., N.W.
Washington, DC 20420
202-233-4000
Ask for Vocational Rehabilitation.

U.S. Patent and Trademark Office
Crystal Plaza 2
2011 Jefferson Davis Highway
Arlington, VA 22202
703-305-8000
Ask for the Examining Group Director who is a specialist in educational equipment.

ELECTRICAL ENGINEERING

See also: ENGINEERING

ASSOCIATIONS

Institute of Electrical and Electronics Engineers
345 E. 47th St.
New York, NY 10017
212-705-7900
Eric Herz, General Manager
The main professional society for electrical engineers.

Eta Kappa Nu
c/o Dr. J. Robert Betten
Box HKN
Univ. of Missouri-Rolla
Rolla, MO 65401
314-341-6400
Dr. J. Robert Betten, Executive Secretary
An honorary fraternity of electrical engineers.

PERIODICALS

IEEE Engineering Management Review
Engineering Management Society
Institute of Electrical and Electronics Engineers, Inc.
345 E. 47th St.
New York, NY 10017-2394
212-705-7366
David Scott Lewis, Editor
Advice on management for electronic and other engineers.

IEEE Spectrum
Institute of Electrical and Electronics Engineers, Inc.
345 E. 47th St.
New York, NY 10017-2394
212-705-7900
Donald Christiansen, Editor
Detailed technical information for electrical and electronic engineers.

LIBRARIES

Battell Memorial Institute
Library
505 King Ave.
Columbus, OH 43201-2693
614-424-6302
614-424-3607 Fax
Engineering and other sciences.

University of California, Berkeley
Kresge Engineering Library
110 Bechtel Engineering Center
Berkeley, CA 94720
510-642-3339
Engineering.

Unversity of Illinois
Engineering Library
221 Engineering Hall
1308 W. Green St.
Urbana, IL 61801
217-333-3576
Engineering.

FEDERAL GOVERNMENT

U.S. Department of Commerce
14th St. & Constitution Ave., N. W.
Washington, DC 20230
202-377-2000
Ask for the National Engineering Laboratory at the National Institute for Standards and Technology.

ELECTRIC EQUIPMENT INDUSTRY

ASSOCIATIONS

Electrical Apparatus Service Association
1331 Baur Blvd.
St. Louis, MO 63132
314-993-2220
August Baechle, Executive Vice President
Firms that service and sell electrical apparatus. Offers information on repair and rebuilding of generators, electric motors, and transformers.

Electrical Generating Systems Association
PO Box 9257
Coral Springs, FL 33065-9257
305-755-2677
305-755-2679 Fax
A. Tony Raucci, Executive Director
Members include manufacturers of machines that produce electrical power.

International Coil Winding Association
PO Box 278
Imperial Beach, CA 92032
619-575-4191
Charles Thurman, President
Manufacturers of electric transformers, motors, and coils. Offers technical education programs.

National Association of Electrical Distributors
45 Danberry Rd.
Wilson, CT 06897
203-834-1908
Marvin Schylling, President
Wholesalers of electrical apparatus and supplies.

National Electrical Manufacturers Association
2101 L St. N.W.
Washington, DC 20037
202-457-8400
202-457-8411 Fax
Bernard Falk, President
A large group of firms that make equipment used for electric power generation, distribution, and control. Offers information on safety, conservation, product liability, and business subjects.

PERIODICALS

Electronic and Electrical Equipment
  Newsletter
National Safety Council
444 N. Michigan Ave.
Chicago, IL 60611
800-621-7619
Issues safety recommendations for electronic and electrical equipment.

Electronics Purchasing
Cahners Publishing Co.
275 Washington St.
Newton, MA 02158-1630
617-964-3030
John Kerr, Editor
Reports on products, prices, information about suppliers, and industry trends.

LIBRARIES

General Electric Co.
Corporate Research & Development
Whitney Library
Box 8
KWF 116
Schenectady, NY 12301
518-387-6563
518-387-7593 Fax
Electronics, energy, mathematics, physics, chemistry, and related topics.

COMPANIES

All-Phase Electric Supply Co. Inc.
875 Riverview Dr.
Benton Harbor, MI 49022
616-926-6194
Wholesaler of electric supplies.

CAL Electric Supply Inc.
1585 Folsom St.
San Francisco, CA 94103
415-863-2020
Electric supplies.

Economy Electric Supply, Inc.
428 Tolland Tpke.
Manchester, CT 06040
203-647-5000
Electric materials and supplies used in construction and industry.

Electric Specialty & Supply Corp.
817 Albany St.
Boston, MA 02119
617-442-6400
Electric supplies.

General Electric Co.
3135 Easton Tpke.
Fairfield, CT 06431
203-373-2211
Electrical equipment and many other types of products.

W.W. Grainger, Inc.
5500 W. Howard St.
Skokie, IL 60077
708-982-9000
Wholesaler of electric motors, fans, pumps, and other electrical supplies.

Koontz-Wagner Electric Co., Inc.
3801 Voorde Dr.
South Bend, IN 46628
219-232-2051
Electrical supplies and equipment.

W. A. Kraft Corp.
45 Sixth Rd.
Woburn, MA 01888
617-938-9100
Electric generators and engines.

Reliance Electric Co.
29325 Chagrin Blvd.
Cleveland, OH 44122
216-266-7000
Electric equipment for industrial automation.

FEDERAL GOVERNMENT

U.S. Customs Service
Department of the Treasury
U.S. Customshouse
6 World Trade Center
New York, NY 10048
212-466-5550
Ask for the Commodity Specialist in charge of electric equipment.

U.S. International Trade Administration
Department of Commerce
14th St. and Constitution Ave., N.W.
Washington, DC 20230
202-377-2000
Ask for the Commodity Analyst who is an expert in the electric equipment industry.

U.S. International Trade Commission
500 E St., S.W.
Washington, DC 20436
202-205-2000 Office of the Secretary
202-205-3296 Industries locator
Ask for the Trade Analyst who is an expert in the electric equipment industry.

U.S. Patent and Trademark Office
Crystal Plaza 2
2011 Jefferson Davis Highway
Arlington, VA 22202
703-305-8000
Ask for the Examining Group Director who is a specialist in electric equipment.

ELECTRIC POWER

See also: ELECTRIC EQUIPMENT INDUSTRY and ENERGY

ASSOCIATIONS

American Public Power Association
2301 M St., N.W.
Washington, DC 20037
202-467-2900
202-467-2910
*Represents electric utilities owned by munici-
palities and other publicly owned electric systems and cooperatives.*

Edison Electric Institute
1111 19th St., N.W.
Washington, DC 20036
202-778-6400
202-778-6542
William McCollam, President
*Represents many electric utility companies
that are owned by investors.*

Electric Power Research Institute
3412 Hillview Ave.
Palo Alto, CA 94303
415-855-2000
Richard Balzhiser, Executive Director
*Conducts a wide range of research programs
in the technological aspects of electric power
generation, transmission, and use.*

National Rural Electric Cooperative Association
1800 Massachusetts Ave. N.W.
Washington, DC 20036
202-857-9500
Bob Bergland, Executive Vice President
*Members include public utility districts, rural
electric systems, and other public power districts.*

North American Electric Reliability Council
101 College Rd. E.
Princeton, NJ 08540
609-452-8060
Michael Gent, President
*Composed of electric utility systems. Research
how to maintain and plan for reliable electric
power.*

PERIODICALS

Electric Light and Power
PennWell Publishing Co.
1421 S. Sheridan Rd.
Tulsa, OK 74112
918-835-3161
Robert Lincicome, Editor
*Reports on news and trends that interest pub-
licly- and investor-owned electric utilities and
electric cooperatives.*

Electrical World
McGraw-Hill, Inc.
1221 Ave. of the Americas
New York, NY 10020
212-512-3288
Herbert Cavanaugh, Editor
*Practical information for engineers and man-
agers in the electrical power industry.*

Public Power
American Public Power Association
2301 M St., N.W.
Washington, DC 20037
202-467-2948
Jeanne LaBella, Editor
*Monitors regulatory and legislative matters,
and technological innovations.*

LIBRARIES

Centerior Energy Corp.
Library
Public Square, Rm. 504
Box 5000
Cleveland, OH 44101
216-479-4764
216-479-1665 Fax
Electric power engineering, public utilities, energy, and public utilities.

Consolidated Edison Co. of New York, Inc.
Library
4 Irving Pl., Rm. 1650-S
New York, NY 10003
212-460-4228
Electricity, public utility economics, atomic power, and gas.

Electric Power Research Institute
Technical Library
3412 Hillview Ave.
Palo Alto, CA 94304
415-855-2354
415-855-1080 Fax
Electric power, energy, engineering, and related topics.

Florida Power Corp.
Corporate Library
Library A3
3201 34th St., S.
St. Petersburg, FL 33711-3828
813-866-5304
813-866-4390 Fax
Electric power, electric utilities, electrical engineering, ecology, manpower, and related topics.

COMPANIES

American Electric Power Co., Inc.
One Riverside Plaza
Columbus, OH 43215
614-223-1000
Electric light and power ulitity.

Central Maine Power Co.
Edison Dr.
Augusta, ME 04336
207-623-3521
Electric utility.

Illinois Power Co.
500 S. 27th St.
Decatur, IL 62525
217-424-6600
Electric and gas utility.

Memphis Light Gas and Water Division
220 S. Main St.
Memphis, TN 38101
901-528-4011
Electric and gas utility.

Potomac Electric Power Co.
1900 Pennsylvania Ave., N. W.
Washington, DC 20068
202-872-2000
Electric utility.

San Diego Gas & Electric Co.
P.O. Box 1831
San Diego, CA 92112
619-696-2000
Electric and gas utility.

Scana Corp.
1426 Main St., Box 764
Columbia, SC 29202
803-748-3000
Electric and gas utility.

Texas Utilities Electric Co.
(Subsidiary of Texas Utilities Co.)
2001 Bryan Tower
Dallas, TX 75201
214-812-4600
Electric utility.

FEDERAL GOVERNMENT

U.S. Department of Agriculture
14th St. and Independence Ave., S.W.
Washington, DC 20250
202-720-8732
Ask for the Rural Electrification Administration department.

U.S. Department of Energy
1000 Independence Ave., S.W.
Washington, DC 20585
202-586-5000
Ask for the Electric Power Analysis & Forecasting department or the Electric Power Division.

U.S. International Trade Administration
Department of Commerce
14th St. and Constitution Ave., N.W.
Washington, DC 20230
202-377-2000
Ask for the analyst who is an expert in power transmission and distribution equipment, or in electric power plants.

U.S. International Trade Commission
500 E St., S.W.
Washington, DC 20436
202-205-2000 Office of the Secretary
202-205-3296 Industries locator
Ask for the Trade Analyst who is an expert in electric power plants.

EMPLOYEE BENEFITS

See also: COMPENSATION AND PAY; EMPLOYEE STOCK OWNERSHIP PLANS; and PENSIONS AND PROFIT-SHARING PLANS

ASSOCIATIONS

American Society of Pension Actuaries
2029 K St. N.W., 4th Fl.
Washington, DC 20006
202-659-3620
202-785-9594 Fax
Chester Salkind, Executive Director
Members are actuaries who design and administer employee benefit plans.

Employee Benefit Research Institute
2121 K St. N.W., Ste. 600
Washington, DC 20037
202-659-0670
202-775-6312 Fax
Dallas Salisbury, President
Studies disability, retirement, health, and other employee benefit programs.

ERISA Industry Committee
1726 M St. N.W., Ste. 1101
Washington, DC 20036
202-833-2800
202-833-1026 Fax
Mark Ugoretz, Executive Director
*ERISA stands for the Employee Retirement
Income Security Act of 1974. The companies
that belong to the Committee study how to
create and administer employee pension and
benefit programs.*

International Foundation of Employee Bene-
    fit Plans
18700 W. Bluemound Rd.
PO Box 69
Brookfield, WI 53008
414-786-6700
414-786-6647 Fax
John Altobelli, Chief Executive
*This large foundation consists of executives in
charge of employee benefit plans, benefit consultants, and others. Offers college-level
courses on employee benefit management.*

International Society of Certified Employee
    Benefit Specialists
18700 W. Bluemound Rd.
PO Box 209
Brookfield, WI 53008-0209
414-786-8771
414-786-6647 Fax
Daniel Graham, Director
*This society offers a certification program for
employee benefits professionals.*

National Employee Benefits Institute
2445 M St., N.W., Ste. 400
Washington, DC 20037
800-558-7258
Steven Huff, Associate Director
*Members are Fortune 1000 corporations that
study the government regulation of employee
benefits.*

PERIODICALS

Benefits
Applied Benefits Research, Inc.
3255 U.S. Hwy. 19N
Clearwater, FL 34621
813-785-2819
G.E. Lackey, Editor
*Offers news and advice on managing employee
benefit plans.*

Benefits News Analysis
Benefits News Analysis, Inc.
Box 4033
New Haven, CT 06525
203-393-2272
Faisal Saleh, Editor
*Analyses of employee benefit programs at
major corporations.*

Compensation Strategy and Management
Maxwell Macmillan
Professional and Business Reference
    Publishing
910 Sylvan Ave.
Englewood Cliffs, NJ 07632-3310
800-562-0245
*Covers employee benefits and related compen-
sation topics.*

Employee Benefit Cases
The Bureau of National Affairs, Inc.
1231 25th St., N.W.
Washington, DC 20037
202-452-4200
David Sayre, Editor
*Prints the full text of federal and state court
decisions and arbitrators' decisions relating to
employee benefits.*

Employee Benefit News
Enterprise Communications Inc.
1483 Chain Bridge Rd., Ste. 202
McLean, VA 22101
703-448-0336
Robert Hicbox, Editor
Reports on trends in insurance, health care, day care, and other topics that concern employee benefits managers.

LIBRARIES

Employee Benefit Research Institute
Library
2121 K St., N.W., Ste. 600
Washington, DC 20037-1896
202-775-6349
202-775-6312 Fax
Employee benefits, pension plans, health care benefits, disability, and retirement incomes.

Hewitt Associates
Library
100 Half Day
Lincolnshire, IL 60069
708-295-5000
Employee benefits, compensation, personnel, finance, and related topics.

Kwasha Lipton
Library
2100 N. Central Rd.
Box 1400
Fort Lee, NJ 07024
201-592-1300
201-592-9012 Fax
Employee benefits and taxation.

William M. Mercer-Meidinger-Hansen Inc.
Information Research Center
10 S. Wacker Dr.
Chicago, IL 60606
312-902-7760
Employee benefits, pension plans, health plans, executive compensation, wages, and related topics.

COMPANIES

Alexander & Alexander Services Inc.
1211 Ave. of the Americas
New York, NY 10036
212-840-8500
Employee benefit planning and other services.

Hewitt Associates
100 Half Day
Lincolnshire, IL 60069
708-295-5000
Employee benefits consulting and other services.

Johnson & Higgins
125 Broad St.
New York, NY 10004
212-574-7000
Employee benefits consulting and other services.

Kwasha Lipton
2100 N. Central Rd.
Fort Lee, NJ 07024
201-592-1300
Employee benefits consulting.

Marsh & McClennan Companies, Inc.
1211 Ave. of the Americas
New York, NY 10036
212-997-2000
Management consultants in employee benefits and other topics.

William M. Mercer-Meidinger-Hansen Inc.
10 S. Wacker Dr.
Chicago, IL 60606
312-902-7760
Employee benefits consulting.

Trust Services of America, Inc.
(Subsidiary of CalFed Inc.)
700 Wilshire Blvd.
Los Angeles, CA 90017
213-614-7000
Employee benefit plan management and other services.

FEDERAL GOVERNMENT

U.S. Department of Labor
200 Constitution Ave., N.W.
Washington, DC 20210
202-523-6666
Ask for the Bureau of Labor Statistics or for the Pension Welfare Benefits Administration.

EMPLOYEE STOCK OWNERSHIP PLANS

See also: EMPLOYEE BENEFITS

ASSOCIATIONS

ESOP Association
1100 17th St. N.W., Ste. 1207
Washington, DC 20036
202-293-2971
David Binns, Executive Director
The major clearinghouse for information about employee stock ownership plans.

PERIODICALS

Benefits Today
The Bureau of National Affairs, Inc.
1231 25th St., N.W.
Washington, DC 20037
202-452-4200
David Sayre, Editor
Covers news concerning many employee benefits, one of which is the Employee Stock Ownership Plan.

LIBRARIES

ESOP Association
Library
1100 17th St. N.W., Ste. 1207
Washington, DC 20036
202-293-2971
David Binns, Executive Director
Employee stock ownership plans and related topics.

Benefit Capital Co. Inc.
Library
721 Bonhill Rd.
Los Angeles, CA 90049
213-820-8768
213-417-5478 Fax
Employee stock ownership plans.

International Foundation of Employee Benefit Plans
Information Center
18700 W. Bluemound Rd.
Borrkfield, WI 53005
414-786-6700
414-786-2990 Fax
Employee benefits and investments.

EMPLOYMENT SERVICES AND EXECUTIVE SEARCH FIRMS

ASSOCIATIONS

Association of Executive Search Consultants
17 Sherwood Pl.
Greenwich, CT 06830
203-661-6606
Glenn Van Doren, President
Members include over 100 executive search firms that recruit executives who earn in excess of $75,000.

Association of Outplacement Consulting Firms
364 Parsippany Rd.
Parsippany, NJ 07054
201-887-6667
201-887-8145 Fax
Jeanne O'Donnell, Executive Director
Comprised of outplacement firms (which are hired by companies whose fired employees need help finding a new employer or deciding what career to pursue).

National Association of Corporate and Professional Recruiters
4000 Woodstone Way
Louisville, KY 40241
502-228-4500
Linda Meagher, Executive Director
Helps executive search consultants run their services more effectively and profitably.

National Association of Executive Recruiters
222 S. Westmonte Dr., Ste. 101
Altamonte Springs, FL 32714
407-774-7880
407-774-6440 Fax
Willard Kautter, Executive Vice President
This association of recruiters offers seminars and helps recruiters market their services and manage their businesses more effectively.

National Association of Personnel Consultants
3133 Mt. Vernon Ave.
Alexandria, VA 22305
703-684-0180
703-684-0071 Fax
John Lisack, Executive Vice President
The private employment agencies that comprise this group offer a certification program and other services.

PERIODICALS

Current Employment
Publishing & Business Consultants
951 S. Oxford, No. 109
Los Angeles, CA 90006
213-732-3477
Atia Napoleon, Editor
Surveys the government employment field.

Directory of Executive Recruiters
Consultants News
Templeton Rd.
Fitzwilliam, NH 03447
603-585-2200
James Kennedy, Editor
A listing of nearly 3,000 executive recruiting offices.

Dun's Employment Opportunities
    Directory—The Career Guide
Dun's Marketing Services
3 Sylvan Way
Parsippany, NJ 07054-3896
201-455-0900
A listing of job opportunities and major companies that wish to receive resumes.

Journal of Career Development
Human Sciences Press, Inc.
233 Spring St.
New York, NY 10013-1578
212-620-8000
Norman Gysbers, Editor
News and advice for career development executives and counselors.

Journal of Employment Counseling
National Employment Counselors Association
American Association for Counseling and
    Development
5999 Stevenson Ave.
Alexandria, VA 22304
703-823-9800
Robert Drummond, Editor
Reports of personnel practices and employment counseling.

Recruiting and Search Report
Box 9433
Panama City Beach, FL 32407
904-235-3733
Kenneth Cole, Editor
News of the executive search industry.

Recruiting Trends
Remy Publishing Co.
350 W. Hubbard St., No. 440
Chicago, IL 60610-4011
312-464-0300
Elizabeth Hintch, Editor
Advice for recruiting executives.

LIBRARIES

Korn/Ferry International
Research Library
120 S. Riverside Plaza, Ste. 918
Chicago, IL 60606
312-726-1841
312-726-2836 Fax
Executive search and other topics.

LaMalie Associates, Inc.
Research Department
13920 N. Dale Mabry
Tampa, FL 33618
813-961-7494
813-962-2138 Fax
Management consulting, executive search, and business.

COMPANIES

CDI Corp.
10 Penn Center Plz.
Philadelphia, PA 19103
215-569-2200
Employment services.

Diversified Human Resources Group, Inc.
5001 Spring Valley Rd.
Dallas, TX 75244
214-458-8500
Employment services.

Fairfax Opportunities Unlimited, Inc.
5510 Port Royal Rd.
Springfield, VA 22151
703-321-8890
Employment services.

General Employment Enterprises, Inc.
1 Tower Ln.
Oak Brook Terrace, IL 60181
708-954-0400
Employment services.

HealthStaffers, Inc.
5636 N. Broadway
Chicago, IL 60660
312-561-5400
Employment services.

Korn-Ferry International
1800 Century Park E.
Los Angeles, CA 90067
213-879-1834
Employment services.

Management Recruiters International, Inc.
1127 Euclid Ave.
Cleveland, OH 44115
216-696-1122
Employment services.

North American Ventures, Inc.
110 Summit Ave.
Montvale, NJ 07645
201-573-8000
Employment services.

Russell Reynolds Associates, Inc.
200 Park Ave., 23rd Fl.
New York, NY 10166
212-351-2000
Employment services.

FEDERAL GOVERNMENT

U.S. Department of Labor
200 Constitution Ave., N.W.
Washington, DC 20210
202-523-6666
Ask for the Information Service Department in the Bureau of Labor Statistics.

U.S. International Trade Administration
Department of Commerce
14th St. and Constitution Ave., N.W.
Washington, DC 20230
202-377-2000
Ask for the analyst who is an expert in employment services and agencies.

U.S. International Trade Commission
500 E St., S.W.
Washington, DC 20436
202-205-2000 Office of the Secretary
202-205-3296 Industries locator
*Ask for the Trade Analyst who is an expert in
employment services and agencies.*

ENERGY

See also: COAL; ELECTRIC POWER; FUEL OIL INDUSTRY; GASOLINE
INDUSTRY; NUCLEAR POWER; PETROLEUM INDUSTRY; SOLAR
ENERGY; and each of the 50 states under energy

CONVENTIONAL ENERGY

Associations

Alliance to Save Energy
1725 K St. N.W., No. 914
Washington, DC 20006-1401
202-857-0666
James Wolf, Executive Director
*Executives, government officials, and others
who conduct and sponsor research into efficient use of oil, coal, natural gas, and other
forms of conventional energy.*

American Council for an Energy Efficient
    Economy
1001 Connecticut Ave. N.W., Ste. 535
Washington, DC 20036
202-429-8873
Howard Geller, Associate Director
*Researches energy conservation and cost-effec-
tive energy alternatives.*

Association of Professional Energy Managers
3104 O St., Ste. 301
Sacramento, CA 95816
916-454-4338
916-736-3581 Fax
Tim Speller, President
*This professional society offers energy man-
agers and others practical information on the
use and control of energy.*

International Association for Energy Eco-
    nomics
1101 14th St. N.W., Ste. 1100
Washington, DC 20005
202-371-1191
202-775-9631 Fax
Joan Cassedy, Executive Director
*Offers energy economists and others a forum
to exchange information.*

National Energy Specialist Association
NESA Bldg.
518 Gordon St. N.W.
Topeka, KS 66608
913-232-1702
Frank Newbraugh, Executive Director
*Helps marketers, sellers, and managers of
energy and energy products to increase sales.*

Energy Conservation Coalition
1525 New Hampshire Ave. N.W.
Washington, DC 20036
202-745-4874
Nancy Hirsh, Director
*Helps individuals, businesses, factories, and
organizations to increase their efficient use of
energy.*

PERIODICALS

Energy
Pergamon Press, Inc.
Maxwell House
Fairview Park
Elmsford, NY 10523
914-592-7700
S.S. Penner, Editor
*International news and technical information
about energy technologies.*

Energy Daily
King Publishing Group, Inc.
627 National Press Bldg.
Washington, DC 20045
202-638-4260
John McCaughey, Editor
Surveys the energy industry.

Energy Report
Pasha Publications Inc.
1401 Wilson Blvd., Ste. 900
Arlington, VA 22209-9970
703-528-1244
Beth McConnell, Editor
*Focusses on policy, regulatory, and legislative
issues that concern all energy industries.*

Energy Review
International Academy at Santa Barbara
800 Garden St.
Santa Barbara, CA 93101
805-965-5010
Mary Ann Short, Editor
*Reviews books and technical reports involving
all energy fields.*

Energy Sources
Taylor & Francis
1900 Frost Rd., Ste. 101
Bristol, PA 19007-1598
215-785-5800
G. Ali. Mansoori, Editor
*Technical information about harnessing all
types of energy.*

Energy Today
Trends Publishing Inc.
National Press Bldg.
Washington, DC 20045
202-393-0031
A. Kranish, Editor
*Reports on issues, policy matters, and regula-
tions that involve energy industries.*

LIBRARIES

Babcock and Wilcox Co.
Corporate Information Center
Box 835
Alliance, OH 44601
216-821-9110
216-823-0639 Fax
Energy and other subjects.

Engineering Societies Library
United Engineering Center
345 E. 47th St.
New York, NY 10017
212-705-7611
212-486-1086 Fax
Engineering topics of all kinds including those involving the energy industry.

U.S. Department of Energy
Energy Information Administration
National Energy Information Center
Forrestal Bldg., Rm. 1F-048
Washington, DC 20585
202-586-8800
Energy information of all kinds.

U.S. Department of the Interior
Natural Resources Library
18th & C Sts., N.W.
Washington, DC 20240
202-208-5815
Energy, power, conservation, and related topics.

COMPANIES

Diversified Energies, Inc.
(Subsidiary of Arkla, Inc.)
201 S. 7th St.
Minneapolis, MN 55402
612-342-5101
Owns a wide range of energy businesses.

Dresser Industries, Inc.
1600 Pacific Bldg., Box 718
Dallas, TX 75221
214-740-6000
Provides services and products to the energy and natural resource industries.

Enron Corp.
1400 Smith St.
Houston, TX 77002
713-853-6161
Owns a wide range of energy businesses.

Enserch Corp.
300 S. St. Paul St.
Dallas, TX 75201
214-651-8700
Owns a wide range of energy businesses.

W. R. Grace & Co.
1114 Ave. of the Americas
New York, NY 10036
212-819-5500
A diversified company with strong holdings in energy.

Midcon Corp.
(Subsidiary of Occidental Petroleum Corp.)
701 E. 22nd St.
Lombard, IL 60148
708-691-2500
Owns a wide range of energy businesses.

Phibro Energy, Inc.
(Subsidiary of Salomon Inc.)
600 Steamboat Rd.
Greenwich, CT 06830
203-661-4770
Owns a wide range of energy businesses.

Sun Co., Inc.
100 Matsonford Rd.
Radnor, PA 19087
215-293-6000
Owns a wide range of energy businesses.

Wheelabrator Technologies Inc.
(Subsidiary of Waste Management, Inc.)
Liberty Lane
Hampton, NH 03842
603-929-3000
Products and services for the energy industry and other industries.

ALTERNATIVE ENERGY

Associations

American Wind Energy Association
777 N. Capitol St. N.E., Ste. 805
Washington, DC 20002
202-408-8988
202-408-8536 Fax
Randall Swisher, Executive Director
*Manufacturers, dealers, scientists and others
who work with wind energy and exchange
technological and business information about
the subject.*

Biomass Energy Research Association
1825 K St. N.W., Ste. 503
Washington, DC 20006
202-785-2856
312-567-5209 Fax
Donald Klass, President
*Companies and researchers who work with
biomass and related waste-to-energy fuels.*

Conservation and Renewable Energy Inquiry
    and Referral Service
PO Box 8900
Silver Spring, MD 20907
800-523-2929
Grace Gilden, Manager
*This branch of the U.S. Department of Energy
offers information and referrals regarding
solar, biomass, ocean, wind, and other alternative energy sources.*

Council on Alternate Fuels
1225 I St. N.W., Ste. 320
Washington, DC 20005
202-898-0711
Michael Koleda, President
*Firms and researchers that work with syn-
thetic fuels.*

Research Institute
6850 Rattlesnake Hammock Rd.
Hwy. 951
Naples, FL 33962
813-793-1922
J. C. Caruthers, President
*Provides information on wide range of alter-
native energy technologies with an emphasis
on alcohol-based fuels.*

National Wood Energy Association
777 N. Capitol St. N.E., Ste. 805
Washington, DC 20002
202-408-0664
202-408-8536 Fax
Scott Sklar, Executive Director
*Researches and promotes the use of wood as
an energy source.*

Renew America
1400 16th St. N.W., Ste. 710
Washington, DC 20036
202-232-2252
202-232-2617 Fax
Tina Hobson, Executive Director
*Helps communities find renewable energy and
conservation technologies.*

Periodicals

Alternate Energy Transportation Newsletter
Campbell Publishing
327 Central Park W.
New York, NY 10025
212-222-0160
E.A. Campbell, Editor
*Follows news of alternative fuels used to
power vehicles.*

Alternative Energy Digests
International Academy at Santa Barbara
Environmental Studies Institute
800 Garden St., Ste. D
Santa Barbara, CA 93101
805-965-5010
Mary Ann Short, Editor
Lists books, articles, and other publications about alternative energy.

Alternative Energy Retailer
Zackin Publications, Inc.
Box 2180
Waterbury, CT 06722
203-755-0158
John Florian, Editor
Information for dealers of home heating appliances that use wood, gas, coal, and other alternative fuel sources.

Alternative Energy Sourcebook
Real Goods
966-A Mazzoni St.
Ukiah, CA 95482
800-762-7325
Covers alternative sources for generating electical power for the home.

Independent Energy
Alternative Sources of Energy, Inc.
107 S. Central Ave.
Milaca, MN 56353
612-983-6892
Donald Marier, Editor
Offers information for managers of solar, wind, geothermal, water-powered, and other alternative energy systems.

Synerjy
Box 1854
Cathedral Sta., NY 10025
212-865-9595
Jeffrey Twine, Editor
Listing of publications and organizations concerned with wind, biomass, solar, and other alternative energy sources.

Wind Energy News
Wind Books, Inc.
Box 4008
St. Johnsbury, VT 05819
802-748-2425
Farrell Seiler, Editor
Covers the business and technology of the windmill industry.

Libraries

Atlantic-Richfield Co.
ARCO Oil & Gas Co.
Research & Technical Services
Technical Information Center
PRC-F1100
2300 W. Plano Pkwy.
Plano, TX 75075
214-754-6965
214-754-6502 Fax
Synthetic fuels, chemistry, petroleum production, and petroleum exploration.

Conservation and Renewable Energy Inquiry
    and Referral Service
Library
PO Box 8900
Silver Spring, MD 20907
800-523-2929
Grace Gilden, Manager
Solar, biomass, ocean, wind, and other alternative energy sources.

Fluor Daniel
Technical Information Center-CNQ
3333 Michelson Dr.
Irvine, CA 92730
712-975-5532
*Synthetic fuels, environmental engineering,
chemical engineering, and human resources.*

Companies

Conversion Industries Inc.
101 E. Green St.
Pasadena, CA 91105
818-793-7526
Develops alternative energy systems.

O'Brien Environmental Energy Inc.
225 S. 8th St.
Philadelphia, PA 19106
215-627-5500
*Develops and operates a variety of alternative
fuel projects.*

Surrette America
(Subsidiary of Atlantic Battery Co.)
P.O. Box 429
Tilton, NH 03276
508-745-4444
*Batteries for wind and solar energy, and many
other products.*

Vawtpower Inc.
134 Rio Rancho Dr.
Rio Rancho, NM 87124
505-892-9463
Wind turbines for electric power generation.

FEDERAL GOVERNMENT

U.S. Department of Energy
1000 Independence Ave., S.W.
Washington, DC 20585
202-586-5000
*Ask for public affairs office to find an expert
on your specific topic.*

U.S. International Trade Administration
Department of Commerce
14th St. and Constitution Ave., N.W.
Washington, DC 20230
202-377-2000
*Ask for the Commodity Analyst who is an
expert in energy equipment.*

U.S. International Trade Commission
500 E St., S.W.
Washington, DC 20436
202-205-2000 Office of the Secretary
202-205-3296 Industries locator
*Ask for the Trade Analyst who is an expert in
energy.*

ENGINEERING

See also: CHEMICAL ENGINEERING; CIVIL ENGINEERING; and ELECTRICAL ENGINEERING

ASSOCIATIONS

National Society of Professional Engineers
1420 King St.
Alexandria, VA 22314
703-684-2800
703-836-4875 Fax
Donald Weinert, Executive Director
This very large professional society includes engineers and engineering students in all fields. Helps engineers in their professional life.

Society of Women Engineers
345 E. 47th St., Rm. 305
New York, NY 10017
212-705-7855
212-319-0947 Fax
B. J. Harrod, Executive Director
Helps women engineers advance their careers.

United Engineering Trustees
345 E. 47th St.
New York, NY 10017
212-705-7828
212-705-7441 Fax
Alexander Korwek, Secretary
This group of major engineering societies offers referrals to engineering information of all kinds.

LIBRARIES

Engineering Societies Library
United Engineering Center
345 E. 47th St.
New York, NY 10017
212-705-7611
212-486-1086 Fax
All engineering subjects.

FEDERAL GOVERNMENT

National Science Foundation
1800 G. St., N.W.
Washington, DC 20550
202-357-9859
Ask for Studies & Programs in the Science & Engineering Education Division.

U.S. International Trade Administration
Department of Commerce
14th St. and Constitution Ave., N.W.
Washington, DC 20230
202-377-2000
Ask for the analyst who is an expert in engineering services.

ENGINES

ASSOCIATIONS

Association of Diesel Specialists
9140 Ward Pkwy.
Kansas City, MO 64114
816-444-3500
816-444-0330 Fax
Barbara St. Aubin, Executive Director
Offers information about supercharger, turbocharger, fuel injection, and related engine systems.

Engine Manufacturers Association
111 E. Wacker Dr.
Chicago, IL 60601
312-644-6610
Glenn Keller, Executive Director
Members manufacture engines except those primarily used for aircraft and automobiles.

Engine Service Association
1900 Arch St.
Philadelphia, PA 19103
215-564-3484
215-564-2175 Fax
William Robinson, Executive Director
Distributors and servicers of internal combustion engines.

National Engine Parts Manufacturers Association
One Grand Lake Dr.
Port Clinton, OH 43452
419-734-2501
419-732-3780 Fax
Bill Herring, Executive Vice President
Firms that make pistons, piston rings, and other parts for internal combustion engines.

PERIODICALS

Diesel & Gas Turbine Worldwide
Diesel & Gas Turbine Publications
13555 Bishop's Ct.
Brookfield, WI 53005-6286
414-784-9177
Joseph Kane, Editor
Covers news about the design and use of large diesel and gas engines.

Engineers and Engines Magazine
1118 N. Raynor Ave.
Joliet, IL 60435
815-727-1830
Donald Knowles, Editor
A magazine for hobbyists working with small engines.

Ward's Engine Update and Vehicle
Technology
Ward's Communications, Inc.
28 W. Adams St.
Detroit, MI 48226
313-962-4532
Joel Pietrangelo, Editor
Summarizes technological information concerning automotive engines, drive trains, and related subjects.

LIBRARIES

Caterpillar Inc.
Technical Information Center
100 N.E. Adams St.
Peoria, IL 61629
309-675-1000
Enginology, mechanical engineering, and metallurgy.

John Deere Tractor Works
Library
Product Engineering Ctr.
6725 Cedar Hts. Dr.
Cedar Falls, IA 50613
319-292-8000
Engines, fuels, lubricants, and applied mechanics.

General Motors Corp.
Electro-Motive Division
Engineering Library
9301 55th St.
La Grange, IL 60525
708-387-6706
312-387-3530 Fax
Engines, gas turbines, locomotives, and power plants.

COMPANIES

Briggs & Stratton Corp.
12301 W. Wirth St.
Wauwatosa, WI 53222
414-259-5333
Gasoline engines.

Deere & Co.
John Deere Rd.
Moline, IL 61265
309-765-8000
Engines used for farm equipment and other products.

Echlin Inc.
100 Double Beach Rd.
Branford, CT 06405
203-481-5751
Automotive and truck parts, including engine parts.

General Electric Co.
3135 Easton Tpke.
Fairfield, CT 06431
203-373-2211
Aircraft engines and many other products.

General Motors Corp.
3044 W. Grand Blvd.
Detroit, MI 48202
313-556-5000
Aircraft engines, automotive engines, and many other products.

Outboard Marine Corp.
100 Sea Horse Dr.
Waukegan, IL 60085
708-689-6200
Outboard motors, boats, and other marine products.

Sequa Corp.
200 Park Ave.
New York, NY 10166
212-986-5500
Gas turbine and jet engine components, and other products.

Stewart & Stevenson Services, Inc.
2707 N. Loop W., Box 1637
Houston, TX 77251
713-868-7700
Diesel and turbine engines.

Tecumseh Products Co.
100 E. Patterson St.
Tecumseh, MI 49286
517-423-8411
Small gasoline engines and other products.

FEDERAL GOVERNMENT

U.S. Department of Energy
1000 Independence Ave., S.W.
Washington, DC 20585
202-586-5000
*Ask for the Transportation Technologies
department.*

U.S. International Trade Administration
Department of Commerce
14th St. and Constitution Ave., N.W.
Washington, DC 20230
202-377-2000
*Ask for the Commodity Analyst who is an
expert in motor vehicle, aircraft, or other types
of engines.*

U.S. International Trade Commission
500 E St., S.W.
Washington, DC 20436
202-205-2000 Office of the Secretary
202-205-3296 Industries locator
*Ask for the Trade Analyst who is an expert in
motor vehicle, aircraft, or other types of
engines.*

ENTREPRENEURS

See also: SMALL BUSINESS AND SELF-EMPLOYMENT

ASSOCIATIONS

Association of Collegiate Entrepreneurs
1845 N. Fairmount
Box 147
Wichita, KS 67208
316-689-3000
316-689-3687 Fax
Donald Herman, Director
*Helps student entrepreneurs by introducing
them to venture capitalists and successful
entrepreneurs.*

Center for Entrepreneurial Management
180 Varick St., Penthouse Ste.
New York, NY 10014
212-633-0060
212-627-9247 Fax
Joseph Mancuso, President
*Offers publications, courses, and information
on how to start, grow, and manage an
entrepreneurial venture.*

The Entrepreneurship Institute
3592 Corporate Dr., Ste. 101
Columbus, OH 43231
614-895-1153
Jan Zupnick, Executive Officer
Offers consulting help on financial, legal, and marketing issues to new companies and individual entrepreneurs.

Young Entrepreneurs Organization
1221 Pennsylvania Ave. S.E.
Washington, DC 20003
202-544-7100
202-543-2720 Fax
Verne Harnish, Executive Officer
Exclusively for entrepreneurs whose firms' revenues exceed $1 million per year and who are less than 35 years old.

PERIODICALS

Entrepreneur
Entrepreneur Inc.
2392 Morse Ave.
Irvine, CA 92714
714-261-2325
Rieva Lesonsky, Editor
Offers help choosing and running a small business.

Entrepreneurial Economy Review
Corporation for Enterprise Development
777 N. Capitol St., N.E., Ste. 801
Washington, DC 20002
202-408-9788
Reports of private and government programs designed to encourage new enterprises that create jobs and economic growth.

Entrepreneurial Woman
Entrepreneur Inc.
2392 Morse Ave.
Irvine, CA 92714
714-261-2325
Rieva Lesonsky, Editor
Articles help women start and manage a business.

Entrepreneurship: Theory and Practice
Baylor University. Hankamer School of Business
John F. Baugh Center for Entrepreneurship
BU Box 8011
Waco, TX 76798-8011
817-755-2265
Ray Bagby, Editor
Scholarly articles about small businesses.

Journal of Business Venturing
Elsevier Science Publishing Co., Inc.
655 Ave. of the Americas
New York, NY 10010
212-989-5800
Ian MacMillan, Editor
Reports of new research about entrepreneurial ventures.

LIBRARIES

Alameda County Library
Business Library
2201 Broadway
Oakland, CA 94612-3044
510-271-4292
Starting a business, managing a business, investments, international business personnel, and related topics.

Center for Entrepreneurial Management
180 Varick St., Penthouse Ste.
New York, NY 10014
212-633-0060
212-627-9247 Fax
Joseph Mancuso, President
Entrepreneurship, small businesses management, and venture capital.

University of Southern Maine
Small Business Development Center
Business Information Service
96 Falmouth St.
Portland, ME 04103
207-780-4949
207-780-4810 Fax
Small business management.

ENVIRONMENTAL CONSERVATION AND POLLUTION CONTROL

See also: RECYCLING; WASTE MANAGEMENT; and each of the 50 states under environmental affairs

ASSOCIATIONS

American Forestry Association
1516 P St. N.W.
Washington, DC 20005
202-667-3300
800-368-5748
202-667-7751 Fax
R. Neil Sampson, Executive Vice President
A citizens' group that works to protect forests and other natural resources.

Citizens for Sensible Control of Acid Rain
1301 Connecticut Ave. N.W., Ste. 700
Washington, DC 20036
202-659-0330
A pro-business group concerned with air pollution.

National Audubon Society
950 Third Ave.
New York, NY 10022
212-832-3200
212-727-1773 Fax
Peter Berle, President
Members are individuals concerned with conservation, with a special interest in wildlife and forests.

Natural Resources Defense Council
40 W. 20th St.
New York, NY 10011
212-727-4412
John Adams, Executive Director
A group of scientists, economists, and planners involved with pollution and conservation issues.

National Wildlife Federation
1400 16th St. N.W.
Washington, DC 20036-2266
202-797-6800
Jay Hair, President
A huge federation of state and local conserva-
tion organizations.

Water Pollution Control Federation
601 Wythe St.
Alexandria, VA 22314-1994
703-684-2400
800-556-8700
703-684-2492 Fax
Quincalee Brown, Executive Director
Represents engineers and others who work
with municipal water works, industrial
wastewater, and others who seek to control
water pollution.

PERIODICALS

Environment Today
Enterprise Communications Inc.
1483 Chain Bridge Rd., Ste. 202
McLean, VA 22101
703-448-0336
News for executives, environmental engineers,
and others directly responsible for controlling
pollution and hazardous waste.

Environment Week
King Communications Group, Inc.
627 National Press Bldg.
Washington, DC 20045
202-638-4260
Dennis Wamsted, Editor
Keeps abreast of policy discussions in and out
of government.

Environmental Business Journal
Environmental Business Publishing, Inc.
827 Washington St.
San Diego, CA 92103
619-295-7685
Grant Ferrier, Editor
Follows news in the pollution control industry.

Environmental Compliance Update
High Tech Publishing Co.
Box 1923
Brattleboro, VT 03501
802-254-3539
Helps executives comply with environmental
law and find cost-effective ways to do so.

Environmental Protection
Stevens Publishing Corporation
225 N. New Rd.
Waco, TX 76710
817-776-9000
Carol Mouche, Editor
How-to information for business people and
scientists involved with pollution control.

Pollution Engineering Locator
Cahners Publishing Co.
1350 E. Touhy Ave.
Box 5080
Des Plaines, IL 60017-5080
708-635-8800
A directory and advisor for products and ser-
vices used to control pollution and hazardous
waste.

Pollution Equipment News
Rimbach Publishing, Inc.
8650 Babcock Blvd.
Pittsburgh, PA 15237
412-364-5366
David Lavender, Editor
News of equipment and supplies used to con-
trol pollution.

Environmental Manager
Executive Enterprises Publications Co., Inc.
22 W. 21st St.
New York, NY 10010-6904
212-645-7880
Uses case studies to inform executives about avoiding and dealing with environmental problems.

LIBRARIES

U.S. Environmental Protection Agency
Andrew W. Breidenbach Environmental
   Research Library
26 W. Martin Luther King Dr.
Cincinnati, OH 45268
513-569-7707
Environmental studies, biotechnology, water pollution, and related subjects.

U.S. Environmental Protection Agency
Headquarters Library
Rm. 2904 PM-211-A
401 M St., S.W.
Washington, DC 20460-0001
202-382-5921
202-382-7883 Fax
Water pollution, air pollution, hazardous wastes, solid waste management, resource recovery, pesticides, management aspects of environmental policy, and other subjects.

World Resources Institute
Library
1709 New York Ave., N.W., 7th Fl.
Washington, DC 20006
202-622-2504
202-638-0036 Fax
Environmental conservation, natural resources, climate, forestry, agriculture, and related topics.

COMPANIES

Air & Water Technologies Corp.
U.S. Hwy. 22 W. & Station Rd.
Branchburg, NJ 08876
201-685-4600
Services and products used for water protection, air pollution control, and disposal of waste products.

Allwaste Inc.
3040 Post Oak Blvd.
Houston, TX 77056
713-623-8777
A variety of environmental services.

Camp Dresser & McKee Inc.
One Cambridge Center
Cambridge, MA 02142
617-621-8181
Control of wastewater, air pollution, and solid waste.

Clean Harbors Inc.
325 Wood Rd.
Braintree, MA 02184
617-849-1800
Environmental services.

Donaldson Industrial Group
(Division of Donaldson Co. Inc.)
1400 W. 94th St.
Minneapolis, MN 55431
612-887-3900
Control of industrial air pollution and dust.

Envirosource, Inc.
Five High Ridge Park, Box 10309
Stamford, CT 06904
203-322-8333
Handling, recycling, and landfilling of wastes.

International Recovery Corp.
700 S. Royal Poinciana Blvd.
Miami Springs, FL 33166
305-884-2001
Environmental services and waste management.

International Technology Corp.
23456 Hawthorne Blvd.
Torrance, CA 90505
213-378-9933
Environmental services and hazardous waste disposal.

NUS Corp.
(Subsidiary of Halliburton Co.)
910 Clopper Rd., Box 6032
Gaithersburg, MD 20877
301-258-6000
A variety of environmental protection services.

Ohm Corp.
P.O. Box 551
Findlay, OH 45839
419-423-3526
Environmental services and waste disposal.

Venture Dyne Ltd.
10201 W. Lincoln Ave.
Milwaukee, WI 53227
414-327-2211
Air pollution instruments and other products.

Roy F. Weston, Inc.
Weston Way
West Chester, PA 19380
215-692-3030
Environmental consulting and laboratory services.

FEDERAL GOVERNMENT

National Institutes of Health
9000 Rockville Pike
Bethesda, MD 20892
301-496-4000
Ask for the National Institute of Environmental Health Sciences.

U.S. Department of the Interior
1800 C St., N.W.
Washington, DC 20240
202-208-7220
Ask the public relations office for an appropriate expert in environmental conservation and pollution.

U.S. Department of Justice
Constitution Ave. and 10th St., N.W.
Washington, DC
202-514-2000
Ask for the Environmental Crimes office in the Land & Natural Resources Division.

U.S. Department of Transportation
400 Seventh St., S.W.
Washington, DC 20590
202-366-4000
Ask for the Environmental Division in the Transportation Regulatory Affairs office.

U.S. Environmental Protection Agency
401 M St., S.W.
Washington, DC 20460
202-260-2090
Ask for the Center for Environmental Research Information.

U.S. Patent and Trademark Office
Crystal Plaza 2
2011 Jefferson Davis Highway
Arlington, VA 22202
703-305-8000
Ask for the Examining Group Director who is a specialist in environmental control equipment.

FABRICS AND TEXTILES

See also: COTTON INDUSTRY and WOOL AND WORSTED INDUSTRY

ASSOCIATIONS

American Printed Fabrics Council
45 W. 36th St., 3rd Fl.
New York, NY 10018
212-695-2254
Frank Strauss, President
Promotes the sale of printed textiles.

American Textile Manufacturers Institute
1801 K St. N.W., Ste. 900
Washington, DC 20006
202-862-0500
Carlos Moore, Executive Vice President
Members include companies that make wool, cotton, synthetic, and other textiles.

INDA, Association of the Nonwoven Fabrics Industry
1001 Winstead Dr., Ste. 460
Cary, NC 27513
919-677-0060
919-677-0211 Fax
John Mead, President
Firms that make and sell nonwoven fabrics.

Knitted Textile Association
386 Park Ave. S.
New York, NY 10016
212-689-3807
212-889-6160 Fax
David Herrick, Executive Director
Manufacturers of knitted fabrics and providers of materials to the textile industry.

National Association of Decorative Fabric Distributors
3008 Milwood Ave.
Columbia, SC 29205
803-252-5646
800-445-8629
803-765-0860 Fax
Mary Eubanks, Executive Director
Wholesalers of upholstery and drapery fabrics.

Textile Distributors Association
45 W. 36th St., 3rd Fl.
New York, NY 10018
212-563-0400
Bruce Roberts, Executive Director
Distributors of natural and synthetic fabrics.

PERIODICALS

Clothing & Textiles Research Journal
Association of College Professors of Textiles and Clothing, Inc.
Box 1360
Monument, CO 80132
719-488-3716
Nancy Owens, Editor
Reports on new research in the fields of clothing and textiles.

Home Textiles Today
Cahners Business Newspapers
200 S. Main St.
High Point, NC 27261
212-679-9755
Warren Shoulberg, Editor
Offers business advice on selling to the home textile market.

Textile Business Outlook
Statistikon Corp.
Box 246
E. Norwich, NY 11732
516-922-0882
Jordan Yale, Editor
Statistics and forecasts about textile sales.

Textile Chemist and Colorist
American Association of Textile Chemists and
    Colorists
Box 12215
Research Triangle Park, NC 27709
919-549-8141
Jack Kissiah, Editor
Technical information about textile manufacture and treatment.

Textile Manufacturing
Merit Publications, Inc.
18 Perimeter Park Dr., Ste. 108
Atlanta, GA 30341
404-451-4990
Earl Whited, Editor
News and how-to information for managers and engineers at textile plants.

Textile Research Journal
Textile Research Institute
601 Prospect Ave.
Box 625
Princeton, NJ 08542
609-924-3150
Richard Toner, Editor
Technological reports about the manufacture of textiles.

LIBRARIES

American Textile Manufacturers Institute
Library
1801 K St. N.W., Ste. 900
Washington, DC 20006
202-862-0500
Carlos Moore, Executive Vice President
Cotton, wool, synthetic, and other textiles.

Cone Mills Corp.
Library
1106 Maple St.
Greensboro, NC 27405
919-379-6215
919-379-6423 Fax
Textile technology, industrial relations, marketing, and management.

E.I. Du Pont de Nemours & Co., Inc.
Dacron Research
Laboratory
Box 800
Kinston, NC 28501
919-522-6111
Textile industry, fabrics, textile fibers, and related topics.

Institute of Textile Technology
Textile Information Services
Roger Milliken Textile Library
P.O. Box 391
Charlottesville, VA 22902
804-296-5511
804-977-5400 Fax
Textile technology, polymers, and dyeing.

COMPANIES

Bibb Co.
237 Coliseum Dr.
Macon, GA 31208
912-752-6700
A wide variety of fabrics.

Collins & Aikman Corp.
(Subsidiary of Wickes Companies, Inc.)
210 Madison Ave.
New York, NY 10016
212-578-1200
Textiles for upholstery and clothing.

Cone Mills Corp.
1201 Maple St.
Greensboro, NC 27405
919-379-6220
A wide range of fabrics.

Delta Woodside Industries
233 N. Main St., Hammond Sq.
Greenville, SC 29601
803-232-8301
Woven and knitted fabrics.

Dominion Textile (USA) Inc.
(Subsidiary of Dominion Textile Inc.)
120 W. 45th St.
New York, NY 10036
212-704-7600
A wide variety of apparel fabrics.

Guilford Mills, Inc.
4925 W. Market St.
Greensboro, NC 27407
919-292-7550
Knitted fabrics.

Springs Industries, Inc.
205 N. White St., Box 70
Fort Mill, SC 29715
803-547-3650
A wide range of fabrics.

J. P. Stevens & Co., Inc.
(Subsidiary of West Point-Pepperell, Inc.)
1185 Avenue of the Americas
New York, NY 10036
212-930-2000
Fabrics for apparel, home furnishings, and industry.

West Point-Pepperell, Inc.
P.O. Box 71
West Point, GA 31833
404-645-4000
A wide range of fabrics.

FEDERAL GOVERNMENT

U.S. Customs Service
Department of the Treasury
U.S. Customshouse
6 World Trade Center
New York, NY 10048
212-466-5550
Ask for the Commodity Specialist in charge of fabrics and textiles.

U.S. International Trade Administration
Department of Commerce
14th St. and Constitution Ave., N.W.
Washington, DC 20230
202-377-2000
Ask for the Commodity Analyst who is an expert in the fabrics industry.

U.S. International Trade Commission
500 E St., S.W.
Washington, DC 20436
202-205-2000 Office of the Secretary
202-205-3296 Industries locator
Ask for the Trade Analyst who is an expert in the fabrics industry.

FACSIMILE (FAX)

See also: OFFICE EQUIPMENT AND SUPPLIES

ASSOCIATIONS

American Facsimile Association
1528 Walnut St.
Philadelphia, PA 19102
215-875-0975
215-875-0987 Fax
G. L. Brodsky, Executive Director
*Acts as a clearinghouse for information about
the fax industry.*

International Facsimile Association
4023 Lakeview Dr.
Lake Havasu City, AZ 86403
602-453-3850
Jonathan Bart, Executive Director
*Members include manufacturers, retailers,
and users of facsimile equipment and supplies.*

PERIODICALS

Fax Magazine
Technical Data Publishing Corp.
91 N. Bertrand Rd.
Box 458
Mt. Arlington, NJ 07856
201-770-2633
William Rowe, Editor
Covers new fax products and fax trends.

Office Products Analyst
Industry Analysts, Inc.
50 Chestnut St.
Rochester, NY 14604
716-232-5320
Louis Slawetsky, Editor
*Compares a variety of office equipment,
including fax machines. Also covers technological trends.*

COMPANIES

Brother International Corp.
(Subsidiary of Brother Industries, Ltd.)
Eight Corporate Pl.
Piscataway, NJ 08854
908-981-0300
*Typewriters, printers, fax machines, and other
products.*

Canon Business Machines, Inc.
3191 Red Hill Ave.
Costa Mesa, CA 92626
714-556-4700
Fax machines and other products.

Fujitsu Imaging Systems of America, Inc.
3 Corporate Dr.
Danbury, CT 06810
203-796-5400
Fax machines and other products.

Sanyo Business Systems Corp.
51 Joseph St.
Moonachie, NJ 07074
201-440-9300
Fax machines and other products.

Savin Corp.
9 W. Broad St., Box 10270
Stamford, CT 06904
203-967-5000
Copiers and facsimile machines.

Toshiba America Information Systems, Inc.
9740 Irvine Blvd.
Irvine, CA 92718
714-583-3000
Fax machines and other products.

Xerox Corp.
Long Ridge Rd., Box 1600
Stamford, CT 06904
203-968-3000
*Manufactures copiers, fax machines, and other
products.*

FEDERAL GOVERNMENT

U.S. Customs Service
Department of the Treasury
U.S. Customshouse
6 World Trade Center
New York, NY 10048
212-466-5550
*Ask for the Commodity Specialist in charge of
facsimile equipment and products.*

U.S. International Trade Administration
Department of Commerce
14th St. and Constitution Ave., N.W.
Washington, DC 20230
202-377-2000
*Ask for the Commodity Analyst who is an
expert in facsimile equipment.*

U.S. International Trade Commission
500 E St., S.W.
Washington, DC 20436
202-205-2000 Office of the Secretary
202-205-3296 Industries locator
*Ask for the Trade Analyst who is an expert in
facsimile equipment.*

U.S. Patent and Trademark Office
Crystal Plaza 2
2011 Jefferson Davis Highway
Arlington, VA 22202
703-305-8000
*Ask for the Examining Group Director who is
a specialist in facsimile equipment.*

FASHION INDUSTRY

See also: CLOTHING INDUSTRY

ASSOCIATIONS

Council of Fashion Designers of America
1412 Broadway, Ste. 1006
New York, NY 10018
212-302-1821
Robert Raymond, Executive Director
Fashion designers who have achieved a certain level of recognition.

National Association of Fashion and Accessory
  Designers
2180 E. 93rd St.
Cleveland, OH 44106
216-231-0375
Beatrice Spencer, President
An association of Afro-American fashion designers.

World Modeling Association
PO Box 100
Croton-on-Hudson, NY 10520
914-736-3046
914-658-8367 Fax
Ruth Tolman, President
Members include teachers of fashion merchandising and modeling.

PERIODICALS

Fashion Newsletter
Fashion Newsletter Inc.
Newsletter Services, Inc.
c/o Peter S. Nagan, Pub.
1545 New York Ave., N.E.
Washington, DC 20002
202-529-5700
Alice Meyers, Editor
Reports new fashion trends from around the world for designers, manufacturers, and store buyers.

Women's Wear Daily
Fairchild Publications, Inc.
7 E. 12th St.
New York, NY 10003
212-741-4000
Michael Coady, Editor
Covers all aspects of the fashion industry.

LIBRARIES

Academy of Art College
Library
2300 Stockton St.
San Francisco, CA 94133
415-765-4202
Fashion, commercial arts, and related topics.

Fashion Institute of Design & Merchandising
Cyril Magnin Resource and Research Center
55 Stockton St., 5th Fl.
San Francisco, CA 94108-5805
415-433-6691
Fashion design and merchandising, apparel manufacturing, and related subjects.

Fashion Institute of Technology
Library
7th Ave. at 27th St.
New York, NY 10001-5992
212-760-7884
212-594-9206 Fax
Fashion, fashion buying, fashion merchandising, textiles, and other topics.

FEDERAL GOVERNMENT

To find the national headquarters of a federal government department check the appropriate subject heading in the index. Alternatively, call 202-555-1212 and ask directory assistance for help.

If you need to identify which local or state branch office of the federal government can answer a particular question, the referral services below will help. Note that not every state has a federal office referral number. If your state is not listed below, call the number of the state nearest you.

Alabama

Birmingham 205-322-8591
Mobile 205-438-1421

Alaska

Anchorage 907-271-3650

Arizona

Phoenix 602-261-3313

Arkansas

Little Rock 501-378-6177

California

Los Angeles 213-894-3800
Sacramento 916-551-2380
San Diego 619-557-6030
San Francisco 415-556-6600
Santa Ana 714-836-2386

Colorado

Colorado Springs 719-471-9491
Denver 303-844-6575
Pueblo 303-544-9523

Connecticut

Hartford 203-527-2617
New Haven 203-624-4720

Florida

Ft. Lauderdale 305-522-8531
Jacksonville 904-354-4756
Miami 305-536-4155
Orlando 305-422-1800
St. Petersburgh 813-893-3495
Tampa 813-229-7911
West Palm Beach 407-833-7566

Georgia

Atlanta 404-331-6891

Hawaii

Honolulu 808-551-1365

Illinois

Chicago 312-353-4242

Indiana

Gary 219-883-4110
Indianapolis 317-269-7373

Iowa

All points 800-532-1556

Kansas

All points 800-432-2934

Kentucky

Louisville 502-582-6261

Louisiana

New Orleans 504-589-6696

Maryland

Baltimore 301-962-4980

Massachusetts

Boston 617-565-8121

Michigan

Detroit 313-226-7016
Grand Rapids 616-451-2628

Minnesota

Minneapolis 612-370-3333

Missouri

St. Louis 314-425-4106
All other points 800-392-7711

Nebraska

Omaha 402-221-3353
All other points 800-642-8383

New Jersey

Newark 201-645-3600
Trenton 609-396-4400

New Mexico

Albuquerque 505-766-3091

New York

Albany 518-463-4421
Buffalo 716-846-4010
New York 212-264-4464
Rochester 716-546-5075
Syracuse 315-476-8545

North Carolina

Charlotte 704-376-3600

Ohio

Akron 216-375-5638
Cincinnati 513-684-2801
Cleveland 216-522-4040
Columbus 614-221-1014
Dayton 513-223-7377
Toledo 419-241-3223

Oklahoma

Oklahoma City 405-231-4868
Tulsa 918-584-4193

Oregon

Portland 503-221-2222

Pennsylvania

Philadelphia 215-597-7042
Pittsburgh 412-644-3456

Rhode Island

Providence 401-331-5565

Tennessee

Chattanooga 615-265-8231
Memphis 901-521-3285
Nashville 615-242-5056

Texas

Austin 512-472-5494
Dallas 214-767-8585
Fort Worth 817-334-3624
Houston 713-229-2552
San Antonio 512-224-4471

Utah

Salt Lake City 801-524-5353

Virginia

Norfolk 804-441-3101
Richmond 804-643-4928
Roanoke 703-982-8591

Washington

Seattle 206-442-0570
Tacoma 206-383-5230

Wisconsin

Milwaukee 414-271-2273

LIBRARIES

U.S. Executive Office of the President
Library
725 17th St., N.W., Rm. G-102
Washington, DC 20503
202-395-3654
Federal legislation, public administration, political science, the Presidency, and related topics.

U.S. House of Representatives
Library
B-18 Cannon Bldg.
Washington, DC 20515
202-225-0462
Law and legislation.

U.S. Senate
Library
Capitol Bldg., Ste. S-332
Washington, DC 20510
202-224-7106
202-224-0879 Fax
Government, political science, legislation, and economics.

FEED INDUSTRY AND GRAIN

ASSOCIATIONS

American Feed Industry Association
1501 Wilson Blvd.
Arlington, VA 22209
703-524-0810
703-524-1921 Fax
Oakley Ray, President
Members manufacture formula feed.

National Feed Ingredients Association
One Corporate Pl., Ste. 375
West Des Moines, IA 50265
515-225-9611
515-225-6130 Fax
Marvin Vinsand, President
Members manufacture additives used in making feed.

National Grain and Feed Association
1201 New York Ave., N.W., Ste. 830
Washington, DC 20005
202-289-0873
Kendell Keith, Executive Vice President
Firms that distribute and retail feed and grain.

National Hay Association
5445 Mariner St., No. 102
Tampa, FL 33609
813-286-3655
813-286-1924 Fax
Donald Kieffer, Executive Officer
Hay producers, dealers and others.

U.S. Feed Grains Council
1400 K St. N.W., Ste. 1200
Washington, DC 20005
202-789-0789
202-898-0522 Fax
Kenneth Hobbie, Executive Officer
A group of organizations that represent feed grain producers.

PERIODICALS

Feed and Grain Times
Johnson Hill Press, Inc.
1233 Janesville Ave.
Ft. Atkinson, WI 53538
414-563-6388
Mary Modaff, Editor
Offers advice to firms that handle and process feed and grain.

Feed Control Comment
American Feed Industry Association
1501 Wilson Blvd., Ste. 1100
Arlington, VA 22209
703-524-0180
Follows regulatory issues that interest the feed industry.

Feed Industry Red Book
Communications Marketing, Inc.
7535 Office Ridge Circle
Eden Prairie, MN 55344
612-941-5820
Bruce Smith, Editor
Information for buyers of feed.

Feed Management
Watt Publishing Co.
Sandstone Bldg.
Mount Morris, IL 61054
815-734-4171
Clayton Gill, Editor
How-to advice and industry information for manufacturers and mixers of animal feed.

Grain & Feed Marketing
K.R. Publishing
Box 1036
Mercer Island, WA 98040
206-236-2353
Donald Kinnan, Editor
News and market information relating to grain.

Grain Age
Communications Marketing, Inc.
7535 Office Ridge Circle.
Eden Prairie, MN 55344
612-941-5820
Bruce Smith, Editor
Information on how to condition, store, process, and transport grains and related products.

LIBRARIES

Cargill, Inc.
Information Center
Box 5670
Minneapolis, MN 55440
612-475-6498
612-475-7899 Fax
Grain storage, hybrid corn breeding, commodities, and related topics.

Kansas State University
Food and Feed Grain Institute
Post-Harvest Documentation Service
Farrell Library
Manhattan, KS 66502
913-532-7452
913-532-6144 Fax
Grain harvesting, storage facilities, stored-product pests, and related topics.

U.S.D.A.
Agricultural Research Service
Western Regional Research Center Library
800 Buchanan St.
Albany, CA 94710
415-559-5603
415-559-5777 Fax
Cereals, field crops, grain, food technology, chemistry, and nutrition.

COMPANIES

Bunge Corp.
1 Chase Manhattan Plaza
New York, NY 10005
212-943-6600
Grain, feedstuffs, and other products.

Central Soya Co., Inc.
(Subsidiary of SMRK Equity Holdings, Inc.)
1300 Ft. Wayne National Bank Bldg.
Ft. Wayne, IN 46802
219-425-5100
Livestock and poultry feeds, and related products.

Conagra, Inc.
One Central Park Plaza
Omaha, NE 68102
402-978-4000
Manufactures feed and many other products.

Farmers Union Central Exchange, Inc.
5500 Cenex Dr.
Inver Grove Heights, MN 55075
612-451-5151
Distributor of agricultural supplies, including feed.

Farmland Industries, Inc.
3315 N. Oak Trafficway
Kansas City, MO 64116
816-459-6000
Distributor of many farm supplies, including feed and grain.

Gold Kist Inc.
244 Perimeter Center Pkwy., N.E.
Atlanta, GA 30346
404-393-5000
Grain mill products, feed, seed, and other farm products.

Harvest States Cooperatives
P. O. Box 64594
St. Paul, MN 55164
612-646-9433
Cooperative that produces and markets grain, feed, and other products.

Holly Farms Corp.
(Subsidiary of Tyson Foods, Inc.)
P. O. Box 17236
Memphis, TN 38187
901-761-3610
Animal feeds, mill feed, and many other products.

International Multifoods Corp.
Multifoods Tower, Box 2942
Minneapolis, MN 55402
612-340-3300
Animal feed and many other products.

FEDERAL GOVERNMENT

U.S. Customs Service
Department of the Treasury
U.S. Customshouse
6 World Trade Center
New York, NY 10048
212-466-5550
Ask for the Commodity Specialist in charge of feed and grain.

U.S. Department of Agriculture
14th St. and Independence Ave., S.W.
Washington, DC 20250
202-720-8732
Ask for Economic Research Service or the Grain and Feed Division.

U.S. International Trade Administration
Department of Commerce
14th St. and Constitution Ave., N.W.
Washington, DC 20230
202-377-2000
Ask for the Commodity Analyst who is an expert in feed and grain.

U.S. International Trade Commission
500 E St., S.W.
Washington, DC 20436
202-205-2000 Office of the Secretary
202-205-3296 Industries locator
Ask for the Trade Analyst who is an expert in feed and grain.

FERTILIZER INDUSTRY

See also: AGRICULTURE

ASSOCIATIONS

The Fertilizer Institute
501 Second Ave., N.E.
Washington, DC 20002
202-675-8250
202-544-8123 Fax
Gary Myers, President
Members include manufacturers and dealers of fertilizer and fertilizer materials.

National Fertilizer Solutions Association
339 Consort Dr.
Manchester, MO 63011
314-256-4900
314-256-4901 Fax
James Boillot, Executive Vice President
Firms that make and sell nitrogen solutions and other liquid fertilizers.

PERIODICALS

Custom Applicator
Little Publications, Inc.
6263 Poplar Ave., Ste. 540
Memphis, TN 38119
901-767-4020
Rob Wiley, Editor
How-to information on the application of fertilizers and insecticides.

Dealer Progress
Fertilizer Institute
501 Second St., N.E.
Washington, DC 20002
202-675-8250
K. Elliott Nowels, Editor
Industry news for retailers of fertilizer and other agricultural chemicals.

Farm Chemicals
Meister Publishing Co.
37733 Euclid Ave.
Willoughby, OH 44094
216-942-2000
Charlotte Sine, Editor
Follows trends in the manufacturing of fertilizers and pesticides.

Fertilizer and Agricultural Chemical
    Newsletter
National Safety Council. Industrial Section
444 N. Michigan Ave.
Chicago, IL 60611
800-621-7619
Makes safety suggestions for handlers of fertilizers and other agricultural chemicals.

Fertilizer Science and Technology Series
Marcel Dekker, Inc.
270 Madison Ave.
New York, NY 10016
212-696-9000
T.P. Hignett, Editor
Technical data for manufacturers of fertilizers.

LIBRARIES

Tennessee Valley Authority
National Fertilizer and Environmental
    Research Center Library
Muscle Shoals, AL 35660
205-386-3071
205-386-2453 Fax
*Fertilizer, chemical engineering, agriculture,
waste management, and environmental sciences.*

U.S.D.A.
Agricultural Research Service
Northern Regional Research Center Library
1815 N. University St.
Peoria, IL 61604
309-685-4011
309-671-7065 Fax
Agricultural subjects including fertilizers.

COMPANIES

Cargill Fertilizer, Inc.
8813 Hwy. 41 S.
Riverview, FL 33569
813-677-9111
Fertilizer and other products.

CF Industries, Inc.
Salem Lake Dr.
Long Grove, IL 60047
708-438-9500
Fertilizers.

Farmland Industries, Inc.
3315 N. Oak Trafficway
Kansas City, MO 64116
816-459-6000
Fertilizer and many other farm supplies.

Freeport-McMoRan Resource Partners LP
1615 Poydras St.
New Orleans, LA 70112
504-582-4000
Fertilizer and other products.

Gold Kist Inc.
244 Perimeter Center Pkwy., N.E.
Atlanta, GA 30346
404-393-5000
Fertilizers and other products.

Growmark, Inc.
1701 Towanda Ave.
Bloomington, IL 61701
309-557-6000
Fertilizers and other products.

IMC Fertilizer Group, Inc.
2100 Sanders Rd.
Northbrook, IL 60062
708-272-9200
Phosphate chemical fertilizers and mixed fertilizers.

Nu-West Industries, Inc.
8400 E. Prentice Ave.
Englewood, CO 80111
303-721-1396
Fertilizer and other products.

Royster Co.
Royster Fertilizer
P.O. Box 797
Mulberry, FL 33860
813-425-1176
Fertilizer and other products.

Vigoro Industries, Inc.
P.O. Box 4139
Fairview Heights, IL 62208
618-624-5522
Fertilizer and other products.

FEDERAL GOVERNMENT

U.S. Customs Service
Department of the Treasury
U.S. Customshouse
6 World Trade Center
New York, NY 10048
212-466-5550
Ask for the Commodity Specialist in charge of fertilizer equipment and products.

U.S. Department of Agriculture
14th St. and Independence Ave., S.W.
Washington, DC 20250
202-720-8732
Ask for Economic Research Service.

U.S. International Trade Administration
Department of Commerce
14th St. and Constitution Ave., N.W.
Washington, DC 20230
202-377-2000
Ask for the Commodity Analyst who is an expert in the fertilizer industry.

U.S. International Trade Commission
500 E St., S.W.
Washington, DC 20436
202-205-2000 Office of the Secretary
202-205-3296 Industries locator
Ask for the Trade Analyst who is an expert in the fertilizer industry.

FIBER INDUSTRY

ASSOCIATIONS

American Fiber Manufacturers Association
1150 17th St. N.W.
Washington, DC 20036
202-296-6508
202-296-3052 Fax
Paul O'Day, President
Manufacturers of fibers used in household items, apparel, and other products.

American Fiber, Textile, Apparel Coalition
1801 K St. N.W., Ste. 900
Washington, DC 20006
202-862-0500
Carlos Moore, Associate
Coalition of trade groups and labor unions in the fiber, textile, and apparel industries.

Fiber Society
Box 625
Princeton, NJ 08542
609-924-3150
George Lamb, Secretary
Scientists and engineers that research fibers and products made with fibers.

Textile Fibers and By-Products Association
PO Box 11065
Charlotte, NC 28220
704-527-5593
John Coleman, Executive Secretary
Companies the buy and sell textile fiber by-products.

PERIODICALS

Fabric & Fiber Sourcebook
Taunton Press
63 S. Main St.
Box 5506
Newtown, CT 06470
800-283-7252
Bobbi McRae, Editor
A directory of manufacturers of fibers and textiles.

International Fiber Journal
McMickle Publications, Inc.
2919 Spalding Dr.
Atlanta, GA 30350-4628
404-394-6098
Wilbur Newcomb, Editor
Information for senior and mid-level executives in the fiber industry.

International Fiber Science and Technology
  Series
Marcel Dekker, Inc.
270 Madison Ave.
New York, NY 10016
212-696-9000
Technical data for fiber manufacturers and users.

LIBRARIES

Hoechst Celanese Corp.
R.L. Mitchell Technical Center
Technical Information Center
86 Morris Ave.
Summit, NJ 07901
908-522-7939
908-522-3902 Fax
Fibers, polymers, plastics, chemistry, and coatings.

Textile Research Institute
Library
601 Prospect Ave.
Box 625
Princeton, NJ 08540
609-924-3150
609-683-7836 Fax
Fibers, polymers, chemistry, engineering, and related topics.

University of Texas, Austin
Natural Fibers Research and Information
  Center
P.O. Box 7459, University Sta.
Austin, TX 78713-7459
512-471-1616
512-471-1063 Fax
Natural fibers, agricultural statistics, economic statistics, production, and related topics.

COMPANIES

Basf Corp.
(Subsidiary of Basfin Corp.)
8 Campus Dr.
Parsippany, NJ 07054
201-397-2700
A wide range of chemicals, fibers, plastics, and other products.

Burlington Industries, Inc.
(Subsidiary of Burlington Holdings Inc.)
3330 W. Friendly Ave.
Greensboro, NC 27410
919-379-2000
Textiles and synthetic fibers.

Dixie Yarns, Inc.
1100 S. Watkins St.
Chattanooga, TN 37404
615-698-2501
Synthetic fiber yarns and other products.

E. I. Du Pont de Nemours & Co.
1007 Market St.
Wilmington, DE 19898
302-774-1000
Diversified chemicals, plastics, fibers, and other products.

Hercules Incorporated
1313 N. Market St.
Wilmington, DE 19894
302-594-5000
Polypropylene and graphite fibers, cellulose, and other products.

Hoechst Celanese Corp.
(Subsidiary of Hoechst AG)
Rte. 202-206
Somerville, NJ 08876
201-231-2000
A wide range of synthetic fibers, chemicals, and other products.

Manville Sales Corp.
(Subsidiary of Manville Corp.)
P.O. Box 5108
Denver, CO 80217
303-978-2000
Fibers made from glass, and many other products.

Temple-Inland Forest Products Corp.
(Subsidiary of Temple-Inland Inc.)
P. O. Drawer N
Diboll, TX 75941
409-829-5511
Fiber products made from wood, and many other wood products.

Wellman, Inc.
1040 Broad St.
Shrewsbury, NJ 07702
908-542-7300
Synthetic fibers.

FEDERAL GOVERNMENT

U.S. Customs Service
Department of the Treasury
U.S. Customshouse
6 World Trade Center
New York, NY 10048
212-466-5550
Ask for the Commodity Specialist in charge of fibers.

U.S. Department of Agriculture
14th St. and Independence Ave., S.W.
Washington, DC 20250
202-720-8732
Ask for the Agricultural Research Service.

U.S. International Trade Administration
Department of Commerce
14th St. and Constitution Ave., N.W.
Washington, DC 20230
202-377-2000
Ask for the Commodity Analyst who is an expert in the fiber industry.

FINANCE—CORPORATE

See also: CASH MANAGEMENT; FINANCE—PUBLIC; FINANCIAL
ANALYSTS; and FINANCIAL PLANNING

ASSOCIATIONS

American Finance Association
New York University
Graduate School of Business Administration
100 Trinity Pl.
New York, NY 10006
212-285-8915
Michael Keenan, Executive Secretary
*Academics, analysts, bankers, financiers, and
other concerned with corporate and public
finance.*

Financial Executives Research Foundation
10 Madison Ave.
PO Box 1938
Morristown, NJ 07962-1938
201-898-4600
201-898-4649 Fax
P. Norman Roy, President
*Members include treasurers, controllers, and
other corporate financial officers. The Foundation conducts research in business and
financial management.*

Financial Managers Society
111 E. Wacker Dr.
Chicago, IL 60601
312-938-2576
Richard Yingst, President
*A clearinghouse for technical information
needed by financial managers.*

International Association for Financial Planning
2 Concourse Pkwy., Ste. 800
Atlanta, GA 30328
404-395-1605
Charles M. Finn, President
*Offers seminars and information services for
financial planners.*

PERIODICALS

Corporate Finance
C F—V H Associates, Inc.
415 Madison Ave.
New York, NY 10017
212-754-0850
Al Ehrbar, Editor
*Information on investment, legislation, and
other topics to interest managers responsible
for financial strategy.*

Corporate Finance Sourcebook
National Register Publishing Co.
3004 Glenview Rd.
Wilmette, IL 60091
708-256-6067
*Provides information about lenders, venture
capital firms, banks, leasing firms, and wide
range of other financial services.*

Financial Manager
Financial Management Center
American Bankers Association
1120 Connecticut Ave., N.W.
Washington, DC 20036
202-663-5087
News for financial officers regarding regulatory and legislative matters.

Journal of Applied Corporate Finance
Stern Stewart Management Services, Inc.
450 Park Ave.
New York, NY 10022
212-751-3900
How-to information for executives working in corporate finances.

Treasury Manager
I B C—U S A, Inc.
360 Woodland St.
Box 6640
Holliston, MA 01746
508-429-5930
Bruce Fraser, Editor
Follows trends and technologies that help treasurers with cash management, investments, and other financial issues.

LIBRARIES

Financial Executives Research Foundation
10 Madison Ave.
PO Box 1938
Morristown, NJ 07962-1938
201-898-4600
201-898-4649 Fax
Financial and business management.

U.S. Securities and Exchange Commission
Library
450 5th St., N.W.
Washington, DC 20549
202-272-2618
Finance, corporations, investments, securities, accounting, government, and other subjects.

University of Illinois
Commerce Library
Rm. 101, Main Library
1408 W. Gregory Dr.
Urbana, IL 61801
217-333-3619
Finance, business administration, accounting, and economics.

FINANCE—PUBLIC

See also: CASH MANAGEMENT; FINANCE—CORPORATE;
FINANCIAL ANALYSTS; and FINANCIAL PLANNING

ASSOCIATIONS

American Finance Association
New York University
Graduate School of Business Administration
100 Trinity Pl.
New York, NY 10006
212-285-8915
Michael Keenan, Executive Secretary
*Academics, analysts, bankers, financiers, and
others concerned with corporate and public
finance.*

Government Finance Officers Association of
United States and Canada 180 N.
Michigan Ave., Ste. 800
Chicago, IL 60601
312-977-9700
312-977-4806 Fax
Jeffrey Esser, Executive Director
*Members serve as finance officers for a wide
range of local, state, and federal government
entities.*

Municipal Treasurers Association of the U.S.
and Canada
1420 16th St. N.W.
Washington, DC 20036
202-797-7347
Stacey Crane, Executive Director
*Treasurers, finance directors, controllers, and
others who work with municipal finance.*

National Association of County Treasurers and
Finance Officers
c/o National Association of Counties
440 1st St. N.W., 8th Fl.
Washington, DC 20001
202-393-6226
John Thomas, Executive Director
*Offers management and accounting advice to
treasurers working for counties.*

National Association of State Auditors,
Comptrollers, and Treasurers
2401 Regency Rd.
Lexington, KY 40503
606-276-1147
Relmond Van Daniker, Executive Director
*Offers training and services to officials respon-
sible for state financial matters.*

National Association of State Treasurers
c/o Council of State Governments
Iron Works Pike
PO Box 11910
Lexington, KY 40578
606-252-2291
Jimmie Fisher, President
*Teaches state treasurers techniques for cash
management and investment strategies.*

PERIODICALS

Government Finance Review
Government Finance Officers Association
180 N. Michigan Ave., Ste. 800
Chicago, IL 60601
312-977-9700
Karen Utterback, Editor
*Follows trends and news of interest to govern-
ment finance officers.*

LIBRARIES

U.S. Dept. of the Treasury
Information & Library Services
Treasury Department Library
Main Treasury Bldg., Rm. 5030
Washington, DC 20220
202-566-2777
202-566-8066 Fax
*Public finance, economic conditions, law, taxa-
tion, and economics.*

National League of Cities
Municipal Reference Service
1301 Pennsylvania Ave., N.W.
Washington, DC 20004
202-626-3130
202-626-3043 Fax
*Public finance, community development,
municipal government, and related topics.*

Urban Institute
Library
2100 M St., N.W.
Washington, DC 20037
202-857-8688
202-223-3043 Fax
*Public finance, public policy, housing and
urban development, human resources
research, economic development, and related
topics.*

FINANCIAL ANALYSTS

See also: FINANCE—CORPORATE; FINANCIAL PLANNING;
INVESTMENTS; and SECURITIES

ASSOCIATIONS

Association for Investment Management and
    Research
5 Boar's Head Ln.
PO Box 3668
Charlottesville, VA 22903
804-977-6600
800-247-8132
804-977-1103 Fax
Darwin Bayston, President
*A nationwide group of societies of investment
analysts.*

Financial Analysts Federation
Boar's Head Lane, Ste. 5
Charlottesville, VA 22903
804-977-8977
804-977-1103 Fax
Alfred Morley, President
*A large group of financial, security, and
investment analysts. Offers education programs.*

New York Society of Security Analysts
71 Broadway, 2nd Fl.
New York, NY 10006
212-344-8450
212-809-6439 Fax
T. Wayne Whipple, Executive Director
*Members are financial and securities analysts
who work for banks, brokerage firms, and
other institutions.*

PERIODICALS

Financial Analysts Journal
Association for Investment Management and
    Research
5 Boar's Head Ln.
PO Box 3668
Charlottesville, VA 22903
804-977-6600
800-247-8132
Charles D'Ambrosio, Editor
Technical information for financial analysts.

Financial Management
Financial Management Association
University of South Florida
College of Business
Tampa, FL 33620
813-974-2084
James Awg, Editor
Covers a wide range of financial topics.

Journal of Financial and Quantitative Analysis
Graduate School of Business Administration
University of Washington
DJ-10, Lewis Hall
Seattle, WA 98195
Publishes original papers in financial analysis.

FINANCIAL PLANNING

See also: FINANCE—CORPORATE; FINANCE—PUBLIC; and
FINANCIAL ANALYSTS

ASSOCIATIONS

National Resource Network
3631 Fairmount
Dallas, TX 75219
214-528-9080
Beverly Redfearn, President
*Members include banks and other institutions
that offer financial planning services to individuals.*

International Association for Financial
    Planning
2 Concourse Pkwy., Ste. 800
Atlanta, GA 30328
404-395-1605
Charles Finn, President
*Offers training and information to profes-
sional financial planners.*

Institute of Certified Financial Planners
2 Denver Highlands, Ste. 320
10065 E. Harvard Ave.
303-751-7600
303-751-1037 Fax
Denver, CO 80231
Robert Goss, Executive Director
A large group that offers educational programs which culminate in designating students as Certified Financial Planners.

International Association of Registered Financial Planners
305 E. Franklin Ave.
El Paso, TX 79901
915-544-7947
800-749-7947
Ronald Combs, President
A small group of financial planners who have passed certain tests.

National Association of Personal Financial Advisors
1130 Lake Cook Rd., Ste. 105
Buffalo Grove, IL 60089
708-537-7722
800-366-2732
708-520-5475 Fax
Mike Kabarec, Executive Officer
Financial planners who work on a fee-only basis. Promotes the practice of fee-only planning.

PERIODICALS

Advances in Financial Planning and Forecasting
J A I Press Inc.
55 Old Post Rd., No. 2
Box 1678
Greenwich, CT 06836-1678
203-661-7602
Cheng Lee, Editor
Strategies and techniques for finanacial planners.

Estate and Financial Planners Alert
Research Institute of America, Inc.
90 Fifth Ave.
New York, NY 10011
212-645-4800
News and advice for financial planners with an emphasis on tax matters.

Financial Planners and Planning Organizations Directory
Gale Research Inc.
835 Penobscot Bldg.
Detroit, MI 48226
313-961-2242
A listing of financial planners.

Financial Planning
Macmillan Information Co. Inc.
910 Sylvan Ave.
Englewood Cliffs, NJ 07632
800-562-0245
Technical information for financial planners.

Personal Financial Planning
Warren, Gorham and Lamont Inc.
One Penn Plaza
New York, NY 10119
800-950-1217
Case studies and advice for financial planners, certified public accountants, and investment managers.

Practical Financial Planning
Matthew Bender & Co., Inc.
11 Penn Plaza
New York, NY 10001
212-867-7707
Technical information about investments, taxes, insurance, and management advice on running a financial planning service.

FIREARM INDUSTRY

ASSOCIATIONS

American Custom Gunmakers Guild
PO Box 812
Burlington, IA 52601-0812
319-752-6114
Jan Billeb, Executive Director
*Stockmakers, metalsmiths and others involved
with making custom guns.*

National Association of Federally Licensed
    Firearms Dealers
2801 E. Oakland Park Blvd.
Ft. Lauderdale, FL 33306
305-561-3505
Andrew Molchan, President
*Offers gun dealers merchandising informa-
tion, industry information, product information, and literature with a pro-firearm stance.*

National Reloading Manufacturers Association
1 Centerpointe Dr., Ste. 300
Lake Oswego, OR 97035
503-639-9190
William Chevalier, Executive Secretary
*Promotes the handloading of ammunition for
all small arms.*

National Rifle Association of America
1600 Rhode Island Ave., N.W.
Washington, DC 20036
202-828-6000
J. Warren Cassidy, Executive Vice President
*Represents hunters, gunsmiths, police officers,
and gun collectors.*

PERIODICALS

American Firearms Industry
National Association of Federally Licensed
    Firearms Dealers
c/o Andrew Molchan
2801 E. Oakland Park Blvd.
Ft. Lauderdale, FL 33306
305-561-3505
R.A. Lesmeister, Editor
*Industry and product information for licensed
firearms dealers.*

LIBRARIES

Keystone State Consultants
Library
Box 5071
Philadelphia, PA 19111
215-742-5107
Firearms, ammunition, and forensics.

National Rifle Association of America
NRA-ILA Library
1600 Rhode Island Ave., N.W., 7th Fl.
Washington, DC 20036
202-828-6332
Firearms and criminal justice.

U.S. Bureau of Alcohol, Tobacco and
    Firearms
National Laboratory Library
1401 Research Blvd.
Rockville, MD 20850
301-294-0410
Firearms, forensic sciences, and other topics.

COMPANIES

Browning
(Subsidiary of Browning America)
Rte. 1
Morgan, UT 84050
801-876-2711
Firearms for hunting and other hunting and fishing equipment.

Charter Arms Corp.
430 Sniffens Lane
Stratford, CT 06497
203-377-8080
Revolvers and rifles.

Firearms Import & Export Corp.
(Subsidiary of Southern General Diversified)
4530 N.W. 135th St.
Opa-Locka, FL 33054
305-685-5966
Firearms importer.

Lyman Products Corp.
Rte. 147
Middlefield, CT 06455
203-349-3421
Accessories for firearm users.

O. F. Mossberg & Sons, Inc.
7 Grasso Ave.
North Haven, CT 06473
203-288-6491
Sporting firearms, including shotguns and rifles.

Riley's Inc.
121 N. Main St.
Avilla, IN 46710
219-897-2351
Firearm and accessory distributor.

Savage Industries, Inc.
Springdale Rd.
Westfield, MA 01085
413-562-2361
Firearms and accessories for hunting.

Smith & Wesson Corp.
(Subsidiary of Tomkins Corp.)
2100 Roosevelt Ave.
Springfield, MA 01102
413-781-8300
Handguns.

Sturm Ruger & Co., Inc.
Lacey Pl.
Southport, CT 06490
203-259-7843
Revolvers, pistols, and other firearms.

K. W. Thompson Co., Inc.
Farmington Rd.
Rochester, NH 03867
603-332-2333
Firearms.

FEDERAL GOVERNMENT

U.S. Customs Service
Department of the Treasury
U.S. Customshouse
6 World Trade Center
New York, NY 10048
212-466-5550
Ask for the Commodity Specialist in charge of firearms.

U.S. Department of the Treasury
1500 Pennsylvania Ave., N.W.
Washington, DC 20220
202-566-2111
Ask for the Bureau of Alcohol, Tobacco, and Firearms.

U.S. International Trade Administration
Department of Commerce
14th St. and Constitution Ave., N.W.
Washington, DC 20230
202-377-2000
Ask for the Commodity Analyst who is an expert in the firearm industry.

U.S. International Trade Commission
500 E St., S.W.
Washington, DC 20436
202-205-2000 Office of the Secretary
202-205-3296 Industries locator
Ask for the Trade Analyst who is an expert in the firearm industry.

U.S. Patent and Trademark Office
Crystal Plaza 2
2011 Jefferson Davis Highway
Arlington, VA 22202
703-305-8000
Ask for the Examining Group Director who is a specialist in firearms.

FIRE PREVENTION AND PROTECTION

ASSOCIATIONS

National Fire Protection Association
One Batterymarch Park
P.O. Box 9101
Quincy, MA 02269-9101
617-770-3000
617-770-0700 Fax
Provides information on fire safety, fire suppression, fire prevention, and related topics.

Society of Fire Protection Engineers
60 Batterymarch St.
Boston, MA 02110
617-482-0686
Offers fire protection education.

Society of Fire Protection Technicians
c/o John Fannin
2106 Silver Side Rd.
Wilmington, DE 19810
302-479-9200
Provides information about fire protection and enforcement regulations and trains fire professionals in fire protection technologies.

PERIODICALS

American Fire Journal
Fire Publications, Inc.
c/o J.A. Ackerman, Pub.
9072 E. Artesia Blvd.
Bellflower, CA 90706
213-866-1664
Carol Brooks , Editor
Covers techniques and equipment used in fire prevention and fire suppression.

Fire News
National Fire Protection Association
1 Batterymarch Park
Quincy, MA 02269
617-770-3500
Catherine Cronin , Editor
*Follows news in the areas of fire prevention
and suppression.*

Fire Protection Contractor
H.B. Brumbeloe & Associates
1115 High St., Ste. 11
Auburn, CA 95603
916-823-0706
Brant Brumbeloe , Editor
*News about sprinkler systems and other piped
fire protection systems.*

Fire Technology
National Fire Protection Association
1 Batterymarch Park
Quincy, MA 02269
617-770-3000
*Technical information about fire protection
and suppression.*

LIBRARIES

Industrial Risk Insurers
Library
85 Woodland St.
Hartford, CT 06102
203-520-7412
203-527-3160 Fax
Fire protection and engineering.

Rolf Jensen & Associates
Library
1751 Lake Cook Rd., Ste. 400
Deerfield, IL 60015
708-948-0700
312-948-0866 Fax
*Fire protection, building research, and fire
safety.*

U.S. National Institute of Standards and Technology
Fire Research Information Services
Bldg. 224, Rm. A252
Gaithersburg, MD 20899
301-975-6862
301-975-4052 Fax
Fire safety, combustion, arson, extinguishment, and related topics.

COMPANIES

Baker Industries, Inc.
(Subsidiary of Borg-Warner Corp.)
1633 Littleton Rd.
Parsippany, NJ 07054
201-267-5300
Fire detection and alarm systems, fire extinguishing products, and related products.

Central Sprinkler Corp.
451 N. Cannon Ave.
Lansdale, PA 19446
215-362-0700
Sprinkler systems.

Encomp Corp.
4120 Scottsdale
Dallas, TX 75227
214-388-2171
Sprinkler systems.

Figgie International Inc.
4420 Sherwin Rd.
Willoughby, OH 44094
216-953-2700
*Fire protection equipment and many other
types of products.*

Holmes Protection, Inc.
(Subsidiary of Holmes Protection Group Inc.)
440 9th Ave.
New York, NY 10001
212-760-0530
Fire and burglar alarms.

Reliable Automatic Sprinkler Co., Inc.
525 N. MacQuesten Pkwy.
Mount Vernon, NY 10552
914-668-3470
Sprinkler systems and other fire protection equipment.

Smith Industries, Inc.
2781 Gunter Park Dr., E., Box 3237
Montgomery, AL 36109
205-277-8520
Fire protection equipment and other products.

Sunbelt Marketing Investment Corp.
610 Water Front Dr.
Atlanta, GA 30336
404-696-1690
Fire protection equipment and other types of products.

Tyco Laboratories, Inc.
Tyco Park
Exeter, NH 03833
603-778-9700
Fire protection and other types of industrial equipment.

FEDERAL GOVERNMENT

Federal Emergency Management Agency
500 C St., S.W.
Washington, DC 20472
202-646-2500
Ask for the U.S. Fire Administration or the National Fire Academy.

U.S. Patent and Trademark Office
Crystal Plaza 2
2011 Jefferson Davis Highway
Arlington, VA 22202
703-305-8000
Ask for the Examining Group Director who is a specialist in fire prevention and protection equipment.

FISH AND SEAFOOD INDUSTRY

See also: AQUACULTURE

ASSOCIATIONS

American Seafood Retailers Association
PO Box 1500
Cos Cob, CT 06807
203-661-2959
R. Woodman Harris, President
A small group working to boost sales of seafood.

American Tunaboat Association
1 Tuna Ln.
San Diego, CA 92101
619-233-6405
619-233-7913 Fax
August Felando, President
Members include tuna boat owners and others in the industry. Conducts research into conservation, law, and technology.

International Institute of Fisheries Economics
  and Trade
Oregon State University
Office of International Research and Development
Snell Hall 400
Corvallis, OR 97331
503-737-2228
503-737-3447 Fax
Ann Shriver, Executive Director
*University, government, and fisheries industry
officials who share information about fisheries
economics, market conditions, and trade practices.*

Maine Lobstermen's Association
PO Box 147
Damariscotta, ME 04543
207-563-5254
Edward Blackmore, President
*Offers information about new equipment and
conservation methods.*

National Fisheries Institute
1525 Wilson Blvd., Ste. 500
Arlington, VA 22209
703-524-8880
Lee Weddig, Executive Vice President
*Offers technical and industry information to
boat owners, processors, wholesalers, canners,
and others in the fisheries and shellfish business.*

Pacific Coast Oyster Growers Association
1023 S. Adams St., No. 129
Olympia, WA 98501
206-459-2828
206-459-2829 Fax
Tim Smith, Executive Director
*Growers and packers of oysters and clams
along the Pacific Coast.*

PERIODICALS

Fisheries Product News
Compass Publications Inc.
Box 37
Stonington, ME 04681
207-367-2396
Robin Alden, Editor
*Reports on equipment used in commercial
fishing, seafood processing, and related topics.*

Pacific Fishing
Salmon Bay Communications
1515 N.W. 51st St.
Seattle, WA 98107
206-789-5333
Steve Shapiro, Editor
*Provides news for fishermen, seafood proces-
sors, and sellers on the West Coast of the U.S.
and Canada.*

Seafood Business
Journal Publications
Box 908
Rockland, ME 04841-0908
207-594-6222
Nancy Hasselback, Editor
*Covers the technology of fishing and the mar-
keting of seafood.*

Seafood Leader
Waterfront Press Co.
1115 N.W. 46th St.
Seattle, WA 98107
206-789-6506
Peter Redmayne, Editor
*Follows the technology and marketing of
seafood.*

Seafood Price-Current
Urner Barry Publications, Inc.
Box 389
Toms River, NJ 08754
908-240-5330
Paul Brown, Editor
News of market prices for seafood.

LIBRARIES

U.S. Fish & Wildlife Service
National Fisheries Research Center (Lee-
    town)
Technical Information Services
Box 700
Kearneysville, WV 25430
304-725-8461
*Aquaculture, fish diseases, fish pathology,
freshwater biology, and related topics.*

University of Washington
Fisheries-Oceanography Library
151 Oceanography Teaching Bldg., WB-30
Seattle, WA 98195
206-543-4279
206-685-8049 Fax
*Fisheries science, food science, marine biology,
marine policy, and oceanography.*

COMPANIES

Arctic Alaska Fisheries
4250 24th Ave. W.
Seattle, WA 98199
206-282-3445
Commercial fishing and seafood processing.

California Shellfish Co., Inc.
655 Beach St.
San Francisco, CA 94109
415-923-7400
Seafood.

Coast Oyster Co.
2375 130th Ave. N.E.
Bellevue, WA 98005
206-885-7734
Seafood.

Fishery Products International USA
18 Electronics Ave.
Danvers, MA 01923
508-777-2660
Seafood.

Iceland Seafood Corp.
(Subsidiary of Samband of Iceland)
1250 State Hill Rd.
Camp Hill, PA 17011
717-761-2600
Packaged frozen fish.

Ocean Beauty Seafoods, Inc.
(Subsidiary of Sealaska Corp.)
P. O. Box C-70739
Seattle, WA 98107
206-285-6800
Seafood products.

Pan Pacific Fisheries
(Subsidiary of GR Foods Inc.)
338 Cannery St.
Terminal Island, CA 90731
213-833-3564
Canned tuna fish.

Sea View Fillet Co., Inc.
16 Hassey St.
New Bedford MA 02740
508-994-1233
Seafood.

Singleton Seafood Co.
(Division of ConAgra, Inc.)
P. O. Box 2819
Tampa, FL 33601
813-247-1171
Processed and breaded seafood of all types.

Zapata Haynie Corp.
(Subsidiary of Zapata Corp.)
P. O. Box 2868
Hammond, LA 70404
504-345-2035
Commercial fishing and processing.

FEDERAL GOVERNMENT

U.S. Department of Commerce
14th St. & Constitution Ave., N.W.
Washington, DC 20230
202-377-2000
*Ask for the National Marine Fisheries Service
in the National Oceanic and Atmospheric
Administration.*

U.S. Department of the Interior
1800 C St., N.W.
Washington, DC 20240
202-208-7220
Ask for the Fish & Wildlife Service.

U.S. International Trade Administration
Department of Commerce
14th St. and Constitution Ave., N.W.
Washington, DC 20230
202-377-2000
*Ask for the Commodity Analyst who is an
expert in the fish and seafood industry.*

U.S. International Trade Commission
500 E St., S.W.
Washington, DC 20436
202-205-2000 Office of the Secretary
202-205-3296 Industries locator
*Ask for the Trade Analyst who is an expert in
the fish and seafood industry.*

FLOOR COVERINGS AND FLOORING INDUSTRY

See also: CARPETS AND RUGS

ASSOCIATIONS

American Floorcovering Association
13-154 Merchandise Mart
Chicago, IL 60654
312-644-1243
800-621-8020
312-644-2787 Fax
Edward Korczak, Executive Director
*Members include floor covering manufactur-
ers, wholesalers, and owners of retail stores.
Offers information on all segments of the
industry.*

Floor Covering Installation Contractors Association
PO Box 948
Dalton, GA 30722-0948
404-226-5488
404-278-8835 Fax
Ronald Van Gelderen, President
*Carpet installation contractors and carpet
manufacturers.*

National Association of Floor Covering Distributors
85 W. Algonquin Rd.
Arlington, IL 60005
708-364-9040
708-364-9083 Fax
Wade Newman, Exec.Dir.
Collects data of interest to wholesalers of floor covering and others.

National Congress of Floor Covering Associations
470 Merchandise Mart
Chicago, IL 60654
312-527-4141
James Bidwill, Vice President
Offers educational programs designed to promote the floor covering industry.

National Wood Flooring Association
11046 Manchester Rd.
St. Louis, MO 63122
314-821-8654
800-422-4556
314-821-7242 Fax
Bonnie Holmes, Executive Director
Members include manufacturers, distributors, and installers of wood flooring. Offers training seminars and information on all aspects of the industry.

Resilient Floor Covering Institute
966 Hungerford Dr., Ste. 12-B
Rockville, MD 20805
301-340-8580
301-340-7283 Fax
Walter Anderson, Director
Manufacturers of vinyl tiles of all kinds.

PERIODICALS

Eastern Floors
Specialist Publications, Inc.
17835 Ventura Blvd., Ste. 312
Encino, CA 91316
818-345-3550
Howard Olansky, Editor
Offers industry and convention news to floor covering retailers and manufacturers in the eastern U.S.

Floor Covering News
Altron Communications, Inc.
29-10 Thomson Ave.
Long Island City, NY 11101
718-706-7830
Albert Wahnon, Editor
News for manufacturers, distributors, and retailers.

Flooring
Edgell Communications
7500 Old Oak Blvd.
Cleveland, OH 44130
216-826-2839
Mark Kuhar, Editor
Information for sellers and installers of flooring.

Western Floors
Specialist Publications, Inc.
17835 Ventura Blvd., Ste. 312
Encino, CA 91316
213-873-1411
Howard Olansky, Editor
Offers industry and convention news to floor covering retailers and manufacturers in the western U.S.

LIBRARIES

Congoleum Corp.
Technical Research Library
Box 3127
Trenton, NJ 08619
609-584-3329
609-584-3305 Fax
Floor coverings, coatings, and plastics.

National Wood Flooring Association
11046 Manchester Rd.
St. Louis, MO 63122
314-821-8654
800-422-4556
314-821-7242 Fax
Manufacture, sales, and installation of wood flooring.

COMPANIES

Armstrong World Industries Inc.
Liberty & Charlotte Sts.
Lancaster, PA 17604
717-397-0611
Floor coverings and other interior furnishings.

Centimark Corp.
3000 Industrial Blvd.
Bethel Park, PA 15102
800-558-4100
Flooring and roofing materials.

Cohen Furniture Co.
336 Adams St., S.W.
Peoria, IL 61602
309-673-0711
Furniture, floor covering, and other products.

Congoleum Corp.
989 Lenox Dr.
Lawrenceville, NJ 08648
609-584-3000
Floor coverings.

Hoboken Wood Flooring Corp.
Seven Demerest Dr.
Wayne, NJ 07470
201-694-2888
Wholesaler and installer of hardwood and other flooring.

Hamburg Brothers Co.
40 24th St.
Pittsburgh, PA 15222
412-227-6200
Floor coverings and other products.

J. E. Higgins Lumber Co.
1485 Enea Ct., Box 4124
Concord, CA 94524
415-674-9300
Wholesaler of wood flooring and other products.

Lasalle-Deitch Co., Inc.
640 Industrial Pkwy., Box 2347
Elkhart, IN 46515
219-294-2661
Vinyl flooring and other products.

Potlatch Corp.
P. O. Box 3591
San Francisco, CA 94119
415-947-5500
Hardwood flooring and other products.

Standard Brands Paint Co.
4300 W. 190th St.
Torrance, CA 90509
213-214-2411
Paint, floor coverings, and other home decorating products.

Triangle Pacific Corp.
(Subsidiary Of Tripac Holding Corp.)
16803 Dallas Pkwy., Box 660100
Dallas, TX 75266
214-931-3000
Hardwood flooring and kitchen/bathroom cabinets.

FEDERAL GOVERNMENT

U.S. Customs Service
Department of the Treasury
U.S. Customshouse
6 World Trade Center
New York, NY 10048
212-466-5550
Ask for the Commodity Specialist in charge of floor coverings.

U.S. International Trade Administration
Department of Commerce
14th St. and Constitution Ave., N.W.
Washington, DC 20230
202-377-2000
Ask for the Commodity Analyst who is an expert in floor coverings and the flooring industry.

U.S. International Trade Commission
500 E St., S.W.
Washington, DC 20436
202-205-2000 Office of the Secretary
202-205-3296 Industries locator
Ask for the Trade Analyst who is an expert in floor coverings and the flooring industry.

FLORIDA

STATE OFFICE LOCATOR (*for referrals to all state government offices*)

904-488-1234

ARCHIVES AND RECORDS

Library Development Bureau
R. A. Gray Building
Tallahassee, FL 32301
904-487-2651

ATTORNEY GENERAL

Legal Affairs Department
Capitol Building
Tallahassee, FL 32399
904-487-1963

BANKING

Banking & Finance Department
Capitol Building
Plaza Level, PL-09
Tallahassee, FL 32399-0350
904-488-0370

COMMERCE

Commerce Department
Collins Building
Ste. 510 C
Tallahassee, FL 32399-1024
904-488-3104

CONSUMER AFFAIRS

Consumer Services Division
Mayo Building
Tallahassee, FL 32399-0800
904-488-2226

EDUCATION

Education Department
Capitol Building
Plaza Level, PL-08
Tallahassee, FL 32399
904-487-1785

ENERGY

Energy Office
Capitol Building
Tallahassee, FL 32399-0001
904-488-6764

ENVIRONMENTAL AFFAIRS

Environmental Regulation Department
2600 Blairstone Road
Tallahassee, FL 32399-2400
904-488-4805

HEALTH

Health
1317 Winewood Boulevard
Tallahassee, FL 32399-0700
904-487-2705

HOUSING

Housing & Community Assistance Bureau
2740 Centerview Drive
Tallahassee, FL 32399-2100
904-488-7541

HUMAN RIGHTS

Human Relations Commission
325 John Knox Road
Tallahassee, FL 32301
904-488-7082

INSURANCE

Insurance & Treasurer Department
Capitol Building
Plaza Level, PL-11
Tallahassee, FL 32399-0300
904-488-3440

LABOR

Labor Employment & Training Division
Atkins Building
Ste. 300
Tallahassee, FL 32399-0667
904-488-7228

LEGISLATION

Legislative Library Services Division
Capitol Building
Room 701
Tallahassee, FL 32399-1400
904-488-2812

LIBRARY SERVICES

Library Servies Division
R. A. Gray Building
Tallahassee, FL 32301
904-487-2651

LICENSING—CORPORATE

Corporate Information Systems Bureau
P.O. Box 6327
Tallahassee, FL 32314
904-487-6802

LICENSING—PROFESSIONAL AND OCCUPATIONAL

Professional Regulation Department
1940 N. Monroe Street
Tallahassee, FL 32399-0750
904-487-2252

MOTOR VEHICLES

Motor Vehicles Division
Neil Kirkman Building
Tallahassee, FL 32399-0500
904-488-4597

OCCUPATIONAL HEALTH AND SAFETY

Consultation & Enforcement Division
349 Forrest Building
2728 Centerview Drive
Tallahassee, FL 32399-0663
904-488-7421

OMBUDSMAN

Citizens' Assistance Program
Capitol Building
Room 207-S
Tallahassee, FL 32399-0001
904-488-7146

PUBLIC UTILITIES

Public Service Commission
Fletcher Building
101 E. Gaines Street
Tallahassee, FL 32399-0850
904-488-7001

PURCHASING

Purchasing Division
Knight Building
2737 Centerview Drive
Room 110
Tallahassee, FL 32399-0950
904-488-7307

REAL ESTATE

Real Estate Commission
400 W. Robinson Street
Orlando, FL 32801
407-423-6053

SECURITIES

Securities Division
Capitol Building
Plaza Level, PL-09
Tallahassee, FL 32399-0350
904-488-9805

TAXATION AND REVENUE

Revenue Department
104 Carlton Building
Tallahassee, FL 32399-0100
904-488-5050

TOURISM

Department of Commerce
Division of Tourism
107 W. Gaines Street
Tallahassee, FL 32399-2000
904-487-1462

TRANSPORTATION

Transportation Department
605 Suwannee Street
Tallahassee, FL 32399-0450
904-488-6721

UNEMPLOYMENT

Unemployment Compensation Division
Caldwell Building
Ste. 201
Tallahassee, FL 32399-0206
904-488-6093

WORKER'S COMPENSATION

Workers Compensation Division
Hartman Building
2012 Capitol Circle, S.E.
Tallahassee, FL 32399-2152
904-488-2514

FLORISTS AND FLOWER INDUSTRY

See also: GARDEN SUPPLY AND PLANT NURSERIES

ASSOCIATIONS

American Institute of Floral Designers
720 Light St.
Baltimore, MD 21230
301-752-3318
301-752-8295 Fax
Thomas Shaner, Executive Director
Floral designers interested in promoting their industry.

Florists' Transworld Delivery Association
29200 Northwestern Hwy.
Southfield, MI 48037
313-355-9300
John Borden, Executive Vice President
Serves retail florists who accept orders by wire for flower, candy, and other gifts. Maintains a computerized clearinghouse which transmits these orders.

Society of American Florists
1601 Duke St.
Alexandria, VA 22314
703-836-8700
800-336-4743
703-836-8705 Fax
Betty Sapp, Executive Vice President
A large group of flower growers, distributors, and store owners.

Teleflora
12233 W. Olympic Blvd.
Los Angeles, CA 90064
213-826-5253
Cynthia Cleveland, President
Provides a network for florists to send and receive orders around the world.

Wholesale Florists and Florist Suppliers of
    America
5313 Lee Hwy.
Arlington, VA 22207
703-241-1100
703-237-6438 Fax
Archie Clapp, Executive Vice President
Represents wholesalers of flowers, plants, and related products.

PERIODICALS

Floral and Nursery Times
XXX Publishing Enterprises Ltd.
629 Green Bay Rd.
Wilmette, IL 60091
708-256-8777
Barbara Gilbert, Editor
Industry news for growers and sellers of flowers and plants.

Florists' Review
3641 S.W. Plass
Topeka, KS 66611
913-266-0888
John Saxtan, Editor
News for growers and retailers of flowers.

Flower News
Cenflo, Inc.
549 W. Randolph St.
Chicago, IL 60661
312-236-8648
Rosemary Martin, Editor
Business for retail florists.

LIBRARIES

American Floral Art School
Floral Library
539 S. Wabash Ave.
Chicago, IL 60605
312-922-9328
Floral design, flower arrangement, and flower symbolism.

Horticultural Society of New York
Library
128 W. 58th St.
New York, NY 10019
212-757-0915
212-246-1207 Fax
Flower arrangement, horticulture, landscape gardening, supply catalogs, and related topics.

International Bulb Society
Research Library
Box 985
National City, CA 92151
619-477-5333
Flowers, taxonomy, and botany.

COMPANIES

Amlings Flowerland
540 W. Ogden Ave.
Hinsdale, IL 60521
708-654-8820
Gardening supplies and flowers.

Bachman's Inc.
6010 Lyndale Ave. S.
Minneapolis, MN 55419
612-861-7600
Flowers.

Fruit Basket Gardens, Inc.
(Subsidiary of Fruit Basket Flowerland)
765 W. 28th St.
Grand Rapids, MI 49509
616-532-2934
Garden supplies and flowers.

Greenleaf Wholesale Florists
P.O. Box 537
Brighton, CO 80601
303-659-8000
Flower wholesaler.

Leider Horticultural
855 E. Aptakisic Rd.
Buffalo Grove, IL 60089
708-634-4060
Flowers and plants.

Pennock Co.
Stukley St.
Philadelphia, PA 19129
215-844-6600
Wholesaler of flowers and floral supplies.

National Potteries Corp.
7800 Bayberry Rd.
Jacksonville, FL 32256
904-737-8500
Ceramic containers for flowers.

Melridge, Inc.
14075 N. E. Arndt Rd.
Aurora, OR 97002
503-678-1235
Distributor of cut flowers.

Rancho Flowers, Inc.
8605 S.W. Beaverton
Portland, OR 97225
503-292-0154
Flowers and plants.

Shemin Nurseries, Inc.
641 Danbury Rd.
Ridgefield, CT 06877
203-531-0540
Flowers and plants.

FEDERAL GOVERNMENT

U.S. Customs Service
Department of the Treasury
U.S. Customshouse
6 World Trade Center
New York, NY 10048
212-466-5550
*Ask for the Commodity Specialist in charge of
artificial or cut flowers.*

U.S. Department of Agriculture
14th St. and Independence Ave., S.W.
Washington, DC 20250
202-720-8732
Ask for the Economic Research Service.

U.S. International Trade Administration
Department of Commerce
14th St. and Constitution Ave., N.W.
Washington, DC 20230
202-377-2000
*Ask for the Commodity Analyst who is an
expert in the flower industry.*

U.S. International Trade Commission
500 E St., S.W.
Washington, DC 20436
202-205-2000 Office of the Secretary
202-205-3296 Industries locator
*Ask for the Trade Analyst who is an expert in
the flower industry.*

FLOUR INDUSTRY

See also: BAKING INDUSTRY

ASSOCIATIONS

Home Baking Association
2150 W. 29th Ave., Ste. 500
Denver, CO 80211
303-455-5100
R. J. Yurkus, Secretary
Flour millers and sellers who promote home baking, especially in the Southeast.

National Association of Flour Distributors
c/o Harold Gardner
2096 E. Imperial Dr.
Naples, FL 33942
813-591-1043
813-591-1043 Fax
Harold Gardner, Executive Secretary
Distributors, mill sales representatives, and brokers who deal in flour for baking.

Millers' National Federation
600 Maryland Ave. S.W., Ste. 305-W
Washington, DC 20024
202-484-2200
Roy Henwood, President
Members mill all types of flour, including most of the flour made in the U.S.

PERIODICALS

Cereal Foods World
American Association of Cereal Chemists, Inc.
3340 Pilot Knob Rd.
St. Paul, MN 55121-2097
800-328-7560
Elwood Caldwell, Editor
Covers technical aspects of cereals, including the use of flour in cereals.

Durum Kernels
U S Durum Growers Association
824 Thompson St.
Bottinenu, ND 58318
701-228-3057
News for growers of wheat and millers of wheat flour.

Milling & Baking News
Sosland Publishing Co.
4800 Main St., Ste. 100
Kansas City, MO 64112
816-756-1000
Gordon Davidson, Editor
Reports news for the milling and baking industry.

LIBRARIES

National Agricultural Library
10301 Baltimore Blvd.
Beltsville, MD 20705
301-344-3755
301-344-5472 Fax
Agricultural and food topics.

Pillsbury Co.
Technical Information Center
330 University Ave., S.E.
Minneapolis, MN 55414
612-330-4750
612-330-4099
Food sciences, cereal chemistry, flour, and other topics.

COMPANIES

ADM Milling Co.
P.O. Box 7007
Shawnee Mission, KS 66207
913-491-9400
Flour and other products.

Bartlett and Co.
4800 Main St.
Kansas City, MO 64112
816-753-6300
Flour milling and other products.

Cargill, Inc.
Cargill Flour Milling
P.O. Box 2696
Wichita, KS 67201
316-292-2200
Flour and other products.

ConAgra Flour Milling Co.
1 Central Park Plz.
Omaha, NE 68102
402-595-4002
Flour and other products.

Hubbard Milling Co.
424 N. Riverfront Dr.
Mankato, MN 56001
507-388-9400
Flour and other milled products.

International Multifoods Corp.
Multifoods Tower, Box 2942
Minneapolis, MN 55402
612-340-3300
Flour and other types of foods.

Lauhoff Grain Co.
P.O. Box 571
Danville, IL 61834
217-442-1800
Flour and other products.

National Oats Co., Inc.
(Division of Curtice-Burns Foods Inc.)
1515 H Ave., N.E.
Cedar Rapids, IA 52402
319-364-9161
Oat flour and other foods.

Pillsbury Co.
200 S. 6th St.
Minneapolis, MN 55402
612-330-4966
Flour and other products.

Seaboard Corp.
(Subsidiary of Seaboard Flour Corp.)
200 Boylston St.
Newton, MA 02167
617-332-8492
Milling and marketing of flour.

FEDERAL GOVERNMENT

U.S. International Trade Administration
Department of Commerce
14th St. and Constitution Ave., N.W.
Washington, DC 20230
202-377-2000
Ask for the Commodity Analyst who is an expert in the flour industry.

U.S. International Trade Commission
500 E St., S.W.
Washington, DC 20436
202-205-2000 Office of the Secretary
202-205-3296 Industries locator
Ask for the Trade Analyst who is an expert in the flour industry.

FOOD INDUSTRY

See also: CANNED FOOD INDUSTRY; FOOD MACHINERY AND
EQUIPMENT INDUSTRY; and HEALTH FOOD INDUSTRY

ASSOCIATIONS

American Institute of Food Distribution
28-12 Broadway
Fair Lawn, NJ 07410
201-791-5570
201-791-5222 Fax
Roy Harrison, President
*Offers information about all facets of the food
industry. Members include food manufacturers, packers, freezers, canners, distributors,
retailers, and those who provide services to the
food industry.*

Association of Food Industries
Sravine Dr.
PO Box 776
Matawan, NJ 07747
201-583-8188
201-583-0798 Fax
Richard Sullivan, Executive Vice President
*Members include food importers, exporters,
and processors.*

Chilled Foods Association
5775 Peachtree-Dunwoody Rd.
Atlanta, GA 30342
404-252-3663
404-252-0774 Fax
Richard Cristol, Executive Director
Promotes sales of chilled foods.

Food Processors Institute
1401 New York Ave., N.W., Ste. 400
Washington, DC 20005
202-393-0890
202-639-5932 Fax
Ken Stevenson, Executive Director
*Offers education and training to people who
work in food precessing.*

International Frozen Food Association
1764 Old Meadow Ln.
McLean, VA 22102
703-821-0770
703-821-1350 Fax
Thomas House, Director
*Producers, packers, distributors, and mar-
keters of frozen foods.*

National Association for the Specialty Food
    Trade
215 Park Ave. S., Ste. 1606
New York, NY 10003
212-505-1770
800-255-2502
212-353-2356 Fax
John Roberts, Executive Director
*Offers information on specialty and gourmet
foods to members of the industry and others.*

National Food Processors Association
1401 New York Ave. N.W., 4th Fl.
Washington, DC 20005
202-639-5900
202-639-5932 Fax
John Cady, President
A large group of food packers, canners, and preservers.

National Frozen Food Association
4755 Linglestown Rd., Ste. 300
PO Box 6069
Harrisburg, PA 17112
717-657-8601
717-657-9862 Fax
Nevin Montgomery, President
Members include processors, marketers, and others involved with the frozen food industry.

National Kosher Food Trade Association
21 W. 38th St.
New York, NY 10018
212-302-6677
212-302-3731 Fax
Aharon Ungar, Executive Director
Manufacturers and suppliers of kosher foods.

PERIODICALS

Chilton's Food Engineering
Chilton Co.
Chilton Way
Box 2035
Radnor, PA 19089
215-964-4440
Charles Haberstroh, Editor
Practical information for food technicians and executives.

Fancy Food
Talcott Communications Corp.
1414 Merchandise Mart
Chicago, IL 60654
312-670-0800
Advice for buyers of specialty foods.

Food & Beverage Marketing
Charleson Publishing
505 Eighth Ave., Ste. 1403
New York, NY 10018
212-695-0704
Alan Urbanski, Editor
Follows trends in the marketing of food and beverages.

Food Production—Management
C T I Publications Inc.
2619 Maryland Ave.
Baltimore, MD 21218
301-467-3338
Arthur Judge, Editor
Covers the business and technical aspects of canning, glass-packing, preserving, and freezing foods.

Food Technology
Institute of Food Technologists
221 N. LaSalle St.
Chicago, IL 60601
312-782-8424
John Klis, Editor
Technical information for food technologists.

Food Processing
Putman Publishing Co.
301 E. Erie St.
Chicago, IL 60611
312-644-2020
Roy Hlavacek, Editor
News and advice for commercial food processors.

Food Production—Management
C T I Publications Inc.
2619 Maryland Ave.
Baltimore, MD 21218
301-467-3338
Arthur I. Judge, II, Editor
Technical information for the canning, glass-packing and frozen food industry.

Journal of Food Process Engineering
Food & Nutrition Press, Inc.
2 Corporate Dr.
Box 374
Trumbull, CT 06611
203-261-8587
D.R. Heldman, Editor
Technical information for food processors.

LIBRARIES

Archer Daniels Midland Co.
Library
4666 Faries Pkwy.
Decatur, IL 62526
217-424-5397
Agribusiness, foods, agricultural economics, finance, and nutrition.

H.J. Heinz Co.
Technical Information Center
1062 Progress St.
Pittsburgh, PA 15212
412-237-5948
412-237-5725 Fax
Food processing, food engineering, nutrition, agriculture, and related subjects.

Westreco, Inc.
Technical Library
140 Boardman Rd.
New Milford, CT 06776
203-355-0911
203-355-3446 Fax
Food science, nutrition, analytical chemistry, and related topics.

COMPANIES

Beatrice/Hunt-Wesson Foods
(Subsidiary of Beatrice Co.)
1645 W. Valencia Dr.
Fullerton, CA 92634
714-680-1000 .
A wide range of foods.

Chiquita Brands International, Inc.
(Subsidiary of American Financial Corp.)
250 E. Fifth St.
Cincinnati, OH 45202
513-784-8000
Foods and food processing.

H. J. Heinz Co.
600 Grant St.
Pittsburgh, PA 15219
412-456-5700
Processed and canned foods.

Hershey Foods Corp.
P. O. Box 814
Hershey, PA 17033
717-534-4000
Candy and food.

International Multifoods Corp.
Multifoods Tower, Box 2942
Minneapolis, MN 55402
612-340-3300
A wide range of foods.

Kellogg Co.
One Kellogg Sq., Box 3599
Battle Creek, MI 49016
616-961-2000
Cereals and other types of foods.

Kraft General Foods, Inc.
(Subsidiary of Philip Morris Companies Inc.)
Kraft Court
Glenview, IL 60025
708-998-2000
A wide range of foods.

Nash-Finch Co.
3381 Gorham Ave.
Minneapolis, MN 55426
612-929-0371
A wide range of foods.

Quaker Oats Co.
321 N. Clark St., Quaker Tower
Chicago, IL 60610
312-222-7111
A wide range of foods.

RJR Nabisco, Inc.
(Subsidiary of Kohlberg Kravis Roberts &
    Co.)
1301 Ave. of the Americas
New York, NY 10019
212-258-5600
Tobacco and foods.

Scrivner, Inc.
(Subsidiary of Haniel Corp.)
5701 N. Shartel, Box 26030
Oklahoma City, OK 73126
405-841-5500
Wholesaler and retailer of food.

Sysco Corp.
1390 Enclave Pkwy.
Houston, TX 77077
713-584-1390
Distributor of food and other products.

FEDERAL GOVERNMENT

U.S. Department of Agriculture
14th St. and Independence Ave., S.W.
Washington, DC 20250
202-720-8732
*Ask the public information office to find an
appropriate expert.*

U.S. Patent and Trademark Office
Crystal Plaza 2
2011 Jefferson Davis Highway
Arlington, VA 22202
703-305-8000
*Ask for the Examining Group Director who is
a specialist in food products and processes.*

FOOD MACHINERY AND EQUIPMENT
INDUSTRY

See also: CANNED FOOD INDUSTRY and FOOD INDUSTRY

ASSOCIATIONS

Commercial Food Equipment Service Associ-
    ation
9240 N. Meridian St., Ste. 355
Indianapolis, IN 46260
317-844-4700
317-844-4745 Fax
Carla M. Helm, Exec.Dir.
*Repairers of food preparation equipment used
by restaurants.*

Food Industries Suppliers Association
P.O. Box 2084
Fairfield Glade, TN 38557
615-456-2205
615-456-2279 Fax
Thomas Watkin, Executive Vice President
*Members distribute dairy and food processing
equipment.*

Food Machinery Service Institute
7297 Lee Hwy., Ste. N
Falls Church, VA 22042
703-533-1159
Clay Tyeryar, Secretary
Companies that service cutting equipment used in the meat and food industries.

Food Processing Machinery and Supplies
Association
200 Dangerfield Rd.
Alexandria, VA 22314
703-684-1080
800-331-8816
703-548-6563 Fax
George Melnykovich, President
Members manufacture equipment or offer services used by food processing, freezing, and canning plants.

Foodservice Equipment Distributors Association
332 S. Michigan Ave.
Chicago, IL 60604
312-427-9605
Raymond Herrick, Executive Director
Wholesalers of ranges, ovens, china, and many other products used by restaurants and institutions.

National Association of Food Equipment
Manufacturers
401 N. Michigan Ave.
Chicago, IL 60611-4390
312-644-6610
312-321-6869 Fax
William Carpenter, Executive Vice President
Firms that make equipment used by commercial food preparers such as restaurants and hotels.

PERIODICALS

Food Processing
Putman Publishing Co.
301 E. Erie St.
Chicago, IL 60611
312-644-2020
Roy Hlavacek, Editor
News and advice for commercial food processors.

Food Production—Management
C T I Publications Inc.
2619 Maryland Ave.
Baltimore, MD 21218
301-467-3338
Arthur Judge, Editor
Technical information for the canning, glass-packing and frozen food industry.

Foodservice Equipment & Supplies Specialist
Cahners Publishing Co.
1350 E. Touhy Ave.
Box 5080
Des Plaines, IL 60017-5080
708-635-8800
Gregory Richards, Editor
Reports on new products and other subjects for buyers and sellers of commercial food equipment.

Foodservice Product News
Young-Conway Publications, Inc.
104 Fifth Ave.
New York, NY 10011
212-206-7440
Judy Young, Editor
News of products and services for the foodservice market.

Journal of Food Process Engineering
Food & Nutrition Press, Inc.
2 Corporate Dr.
Box 374
Trumbull, CT 06611
203-261-8587
D.R. Heldman, Editor
Technical information for food processors.

LIBRARIES

H.J. Heinz Co.
Technical Information Center
1062 Progress St.
Pittsburgh, PA 15212
412-237-5948
412-237-5725 Fax
Food engineering, equipment, packaging, processing, and chemistry.

COMPANIES

APV Crepaco, Inc.
(Subsidiary of APV plc)
8303 W. Higgins Rd.
Chicago, IL 60631
312-693-4000
Food processing, refrigeration, and freezing equipment.

Alfa-Laval, Inc.
(Subsidiary of Alfa-Laval AB)
One Maynard Dr.
Park Ridge, NJ 07656
201-307-9100
Food processing and other types of equipment.

Blaw Knox Corp.
One Oliver Plaza
Pittsburgh, PA 15222
412-263-2300
Equipment for food processing and other purposes.

DEC International, Inc.
P.O. Box 8050
Madison, WI 53708
608-222-4778
Food processing, milking, and other types of equipment.

Dorr-Oliver Inc.
612 Wheelers Farm Rd.
Milford, CT 06460
203-876-5400
Heavy equipment for processing food, chemicals, and many other products.

Illinois Range Co.
708 W. Central Rd.
Mount Prospect, IL 60056
312-775-2500
Commercial food service equipment.

Middleby Corp.
8300 Austin Ave.
Morton Grove, IL 60053
708-966-8300
Commercial ovens, mixers, and other types of food service equipment.

Specialty Equipment Companies Inc.
750 Blackhawk Blvd.
Rockton, IL 61072
815-624-4100
Food service equipment.

Vulcan-Hart Corp.
(Division of Premark International Inc.)
P. O. Box 696
Louisville, KY 40201
502-778-2791
Commercial food service and refrigeration equipment.

Welbilt Corp.
3333 New Hyde Park Rd.
New Hyde Park, NY 11042
516-365-5040
*Home and commercial food service equipment,
and other products.*

FEDERAL GOVERNMENT

U.S. Customs Service
Department of the Treasury
U.S. Customshouse
6 World Trade Center
New York, NY 10048
212-466-5550
*Ask for the Commodity Specialist in charge of
food machinery and equipment.*

U.S. Department of Agriculture
14th St. and Independence Ave., S.W.
Washington, DC 20250
202-720-8732
Ask for the Food Technology department.

U.S. International Trade Administration
Department of Commerce
14th St. and Constitution Ave., N.W.
Washington, DC 20230
202-377-2000
*Ask for the Commodity Analyst who is an
expert in food preparing machines.*

U.S. International Trade Commission
500 E St., S.W.
Washington, DC 20436
202-205-2000 Office of the Secretary
202-205-3296 Industries locator
*Ask for the Trade Analyst who is an expert in
food preparing machines.*

FOOD SERVICE INDUSTRY

See also: FOOD MACHINERY AND EQUIPMENT INDUSTRY and
RESTAURANT INDUSTRY

ASSOCIATIONS

Foodservice Consultants Society International
12345 30th Ave., N.E., Ste. A
Seattle, WA 98125-5405
206-367-3274
206-367-1121 Fax
C. Russell Nickel, Executive Vice President
*Members design and manage food service
operations.*

Foodservice Equipment Distributors Association
332 S. Michigan Ave.
Chicago, IL 60604
312-427-9605
Raymond Herrick, Executive Director
*Wholesalers of ranges, ovens, china, and many
other products used by restaurants and institutions.*

Inflight Food Service Association
304 W. Liberty St., Ste. 201
Louisville, KY 40202
502-583-3783
502-589-3602 Fax
Phillip Cooke, Administrator
*A forum for airlines and the catering compa-
nies that serve airlines to share information.*

International Food Service Executive's Association
1100 S. State Rd. 7, Ste. 103
Margate, FL 33068
305-977-0767
305-977-0874 Fax
Edward Manley, Executive Director
*Members include owners, operators, and man-
agers of hotels, restaurants, food service operations, and cafeterias.*

International Foodservice Distributors Association
201 Park Washington Ct.
Falls Church, VA 22046
703-532-9400
703-538-4673 Fax
Gilbert Kretzer, Executive Director
*Members wholesale grocery products to the
foodservice industry.*

Society for Foodservice Management
304 W. Liberty St., Ste. 201
Louisville, KY 40202
502-583-3783
502-589-3602 Fax
Claudia O'Mahoney, Executive Vice President
*Companies that provide food services in
industrial plants, office buildings, and other
work sites.*

PERIODICALS

Cameron's Foodservice Promotions Reporter
5325 Sheridan Dr.
Box 1160
Williamsville, NY 14231-1160
716-833-4369
Nina Cameron, Editor
*Covers promotions and advertising for the
food service industry.*

Catering Today
ProTech Publishing and Communications
Box 222
Santa Claus, IN 47579
812-937-4464
Paula Werne, Editor
*Follows news, trends, and products for cater-
ing services.*

FoodService Director
Bill Communications, Inc.
633 Third Ave.
New York, NY 10017
212-986-4800
Walter Schruntek, Editor
*Offers advice to directors of food services at
hospitals, schools, and many other types of
institutions.*

Foodservice Distributor
Penton Publishing
1100 Superior Ave.
Cleveland, OH 44114-2543
216-696-7000
John Lawn, Editor
*Helps managers and sales people of food ser-
vices to improve their marketing, sales, and
promotional programs.*

Foodservice Product News
Young-Conway Publications, Inc.
104 Fifth Ave.
New York, NY 10011
212-206-7440
Judy Young, Editor
Reports on new products and services for the food service industry.

Journal of Foodservice Systems
Society of Foodservice Systems
Food & Nutrition Press, Inc.
2 Corporate Dr.
Box 374
Trumbull, CT 06611
203-261-8587
Oscar Snyder, Editor
Reports on issues of concern to executives in the food service industry.

School Food Service Journal
American School Food Service Association
1600 Duke St., 7th Fl.
Alexandria, VA 22314
800-877-8822
Follows trends in school food services.

LIBRARIES

City College of San Francisco
Hotel and Restaurant Department
Alice Statler Library
50 Phelan Ave.
San Francisco, CA 94112
415-239-3460
Public hospitality industries, nutrition, tourism, wines, and beverages.

Pennsylvania State University, Berks Campus
Memorial Library
Tulpehocken Rd.
Box 7009
Reading, PA 19610-6009
215-320-4822
215-320-4914 Fax
Food service amd other subjects.

U.S.D.A.
National Agricultural Library
Food and Nutrition Information Center
10301 Baltimore Blvd., Rm. 304
Beltsville, MD 20705
301-344-3719
301-344-5472 Fax
Food service management, food technology, and nutrition.

COMPANIES

ARA Services, Inc.
Campus Dining Div.
1101 Market St.
Philadelphia, PA 19107
215-238-3000
Food services at universities.

Dalgety, Inc.
(Subsidiary of Dalgety plc London)
901 Mariners Island Blvd.
San Mateo, CA 94404
415-572-8000
Food processing and foodservice distribution.

Horn & Hardart Co.
101 Convention Center Dr.
Las Vegas, NV 89109
702-369-9500
Food service and restaurants.

International Catering Corp.
153 2nd Ave.
Waltham, MA 02254
617-890-6200
Food services.

International Multifoods Corp.
Multifoods Tower, Box 2942
Minneapolis, MN 55402
612-340-3300
Food production and service.

Piccadilly Cafeterias, Inc.
3232 Sherwood Forest Blvd.
Baton Rouge, LA 70821
504-293-9440
Restaurant food services.

Sky Chefs, Inc.
(Subsidiary of Onex Food Services, Inc.)
601 Ryan Plaza
Arlington, TX 76012
817-792-2123
Institutional food services and catering in airports and inflight.

Harry M. Stevens, Inc.
2 Commerce Dr.
Cranbury, NJ 08512
609-395-0400
Food services at stadiums and elsewhere.

TW Services, Inc.
(Subsidiary of TW Holdings Inc.)
203 E. Main St.
Spartanburg, SC 29302
803-596-8000
Owns food service businesses and restaurants.

FEDERAL GOVERNMENT

U.S. Department of Agriculture
14th St. and Independence Ave., S.W.
Washington, DC 20250
202-720-8732
Ask for the public information office to find an appropriate expert.

U.S. International Trade Administration
Department of Commerce
14th St. and Constitution Ave., N.W.
Washington, DC 20230
202-377-2000
Ask for the Commodity Analyst who is an expert in food service.

U.S. International Trade Commission
500 E St., S.W.
Washington, DC 20436
202-205-2000 Office of the Secretary
202-205-3296 Industries locator
Ask for the Trade Analyst who is an expert in food service.

FOREST PRODUCTS

See also: PAPER AND PULP INDUSTRY
and PAPERBOARD INDUSTRY

ASSOCIATIONS

American Plywood Association
PO Box 11700
Tacoma, WA 98411
206-565-6600
206-565-7265 Fax
William T. Robison, Pres.
This group of plywood and composite manu-
facturers conducts technological research.

American Wood-Preservers' Association
PO Box 849
Stevensville, MD 21666
301-643-4163
301-643-2708 Fax
John Ferry, Secretary
Firms that process and use chemically treated
wood.

Forest Products Research Society
2801 Marshall Ct.
Madison, WI 53705
608-231-1361
608-231-2152 Fax
Arthur Brauner, Executive Vice President
Executives and researchers who study the pro-
duction, distribution, and uses of forest prod-
ucts at all stages.

Hardwood Manufacturers Association
2831 Airways Blvd., Ste. 205, Bldg. B
Memphis, TN 38132
901-346-2222
901-346-2233 Fax
Susan Regan, Executive Vice President
Firms that make hardwood products and
lumber.

National Forest Products Association
1250 Connecticut Ave. N.W., Ste. 200
Washington, DC 20036
202-463-2700
202-463-2785 Fax
Barry Cullen, Pres.
Provides lobbying and public relations ser-
vices to the forest products industry.

National Hardwood Lumber Association
P.O. Box 34518
Memphis, TN 38184-0518
901-377-1818
901-382-6419 Fax
Ernest Stebbins, Executive Manager
This group of manufacturers and distributors
of hardwood products offers training and
research.

PERIODICALS

Northern Logger and Timber Processer
N L Publishing, Inc.
Box 69
Old Forge, NY 13420
315-369-3078
Eric Johnson, Editor
Industry news for forest products executives in the northern U.S.

Paper Tree Letter
Miller Freeman Publications, Inc.
600 Harrison St.
San Francisco, CA 94107
415-905-2200
Will Mies, Editor
Analyses market conditions for the paper and forest products industries.

Timber Harvesting
Hatton-Brown Publishers, Inc.
225 Hanrick St.
Montgomery, AL 36104
205-834-1170
David Knight, Editor
Reports on the lumbering industry.

Timber Processing
Hatton-Brown Publishers, Inc.
225 Hanrick St.
Montgomery, AL 36104
205-834-1170
David Knight, Editor
Reports on the wood processing industry.

Timber Producer
Box 39
Tomahawk, WI 54487
715-453-5159
Carl Theiler, Editor
Covers equipment, techniques, and business information for the forest products industry.

LIBRARIES

Forest Products Research Society
FOREST Information Retrieval System
2801 Marshall Ct.
Madison, WI 53705
608-231-1361
608-231-2152 Fax
Timber resources, wood, plywood, and particleboard.

U.S. Forest Service
Forest Products Laboratory Library
One Gifford Pinchot Dr.
Madison, WI 53705-2398
608-231-9313
Wood processing, paper, wood engineering, timber, wood products economics, and related topics.

Weyerhaeuser Co.
Technical Information Center
WTC-TIC
Tacoma, WA 98477
206-924-6267
Forestry, wood products, paper chemistry, and related subjects.

COMPANIES

Boise Cascade Corp.
One Jefferson Sq.
Boise, ID 83728
208-384-6161
Lumber, plywood, and other forest products.

Great Northern Nekoosa Corp.
(Subsidiary of Georgia-Pacific Corp.)
401 Merritt, Box 5120
Norwalk, CT 06856
203-845-9000
Paper, lumber, and other wood-based products.

Hechinger Co.
1616 McCormick Dr.
Landover, MD 20785
301-925-3185
Retailer of lumber and building supplies.

ITT Rayonier, Inc.
(Subsidiary of ITT Corp.)
1177 Summer St.
Stamford, CT 06904
203-348-7000
Lumber, logs, paper pulps, and chemicals.

Louisiana-Pacific Corp.
111 S. W. Fifth Ave.
Portland, OR 97204
503-221-0800
A wide variety of lumber and wood, particle-board, and other wood-based products.

Manville Corp.
P.O. Box 5108
Denver, CO 80217
303-978-2000
A wide variety of products including forest products.

Mead Corp.
Courthouse Plaza, N. E.
Dayton, OH 45463
513-495-6323
Paper, pulp, lumber and other forest products.

Potlatch Corp.
P. O. Box 3591
San Francisco, CA 94119
415-947-5500
Paper, lumber, flooring, and related products.

Scott Paper Co.
Scott Plaza
Philadelphia, PA 19113
215-522-5000
Paper, logs, lumber, and other products.

Servistar Corp.
P.O. Box 1510
Butler, PA 16003
412-283-4567
Wholesaler of lumber and building materials.

Weyerhaeuser Co.
Tacoma, WA 98477
206-924-2345
A wide variety of wood products.

Willamette Industries, Inc.
3800 First Interstate Tower
Portland, OR 97201
503-227-5581
Lumber, plywood, and other wood-based products.

FEDERAL GOVERNMENT

U.S. Department of Agriculture
14th St. and Independence Ave., S.W.
Washington, DC 20250
202-720-8732
Ask for the Forest Service Information Network.

U.S. International Trade Administration
Department of Commerce
14th St. and Constitution Ave., N.W.
Washington, DC 20230
202-377-2000
Ask for the Commodity Analyst who is an expert in forest products.

U.S. International Trade Commission
500 E St., S.W.
Washington, DC 20436
202-205-2000 Office of the Secretary
202-205-3296 Industries locator
Ask for the Trade Analyst who is an expert in forest products.

FORMS FOR BUSINESS

See also: OFFICE EQUIPMENT AND SUPPLIES

ASSOCIATIONS

Business Forms Management Association
519 SW 3rd St., No. 712
Portland, OR 97204
503-227-3393
Andrew Palatka, Executive Director
Members include manufacturers, designers, and others who work with forms and information management.

International Business Forms Industries
2111 Wilson Blvd., Ste. 350
Arlington, VA 22201
703-841-9191
703-522-5750 Fax
Christopher Bevevino, President
This group of business forms manufacturers conducts market research.

National Business Forms Association
433 E. Monroe Ave.
Alexandria, VA 22301
703-836-6232
703-836-2241 Fax
Meredith Smith, Executive Vice President
Members design, manufacture, and sell business forms.

PERIODICALS

Business Forms, Labels and Systems
North American Publishing Co.
401 N. Broad St.
Philadelphia, PA 19108
215-238-5300
William Drennan, Editor
Covers new products, designs, manufacturing techniques, and marketing data.

Forms Tech Reference Series
International Business Forms Industries
2111 Wilson Blvd., Ste. 350
Arlington, VA 22201-3008
703-841-9191
Mary Coffman, Editor
Technical data for forms manufacturers.

LIBRARIES

International Business Forms Industries
Library
2111 Wilson Blvd., Ste. 350
Arlington, VA 22201
703-841-9191
703-522-5750 Fax
Business forms and related subjects.

LIBRARIES

Standard Register Co.
Corporate Library
Box 1167
Dayton, OH 45401
513-443-1130
Printing, paper, forms, and related topics.

COMPANIES

Allied Paper, Inc.
P. O. Box 125, W. C. Br.
Dayton, OH 45449
513-866-7421
Continuous and standard business forms.

Dennison Mfg. Co.
(Subsidiary of Avery Dennison Corp.)
300 Howard St.
Framingham, MA 01701
508-879-0511
A wide range of office supplies including accounting forms.

Duplex Products Inc.
1947 Bethany Rd.
Sycamore, IL 60178
815-895-2101
Business forms.

New England Business Service, Inc.
500 Main St.
Groton, MA 01471
508-448-6111
A printer of business forms.

Reynolds and Reynolds Co.
115 S. Ludlow St.
Dayton, OH 45402
513-449-4216
Business forms and other products.

Standard Register Co.
600 Albany St.
Dayton, OH 45408
513-443-1000
Continuous business forms and form-handling equipment.

Uarco Inc.
(Subsidiary of Settsu Corp.)
West County Line Rd.
Barrington, IL 60010
708-381-7000
Business forms and related equipment.

Vanier Graphics Corp.
(Subsidiary of American Business Products, Inc.)
8787 Olive Lane
Santee, CA 92071
619-448-3000
Snap-out and continuous business forms.

Wallace Computer Services Inc.
4600 Roosevelt Rd.
Hillside, IL 60162
312-626-2000
Business forms and printing.

Wilson Jones Co.
(Subsidiary of American Brands, Inc.)
6150 Touhy Ave.
Chicago, IL 60648
312-774-7700
A wide variety of business forms.

FEDERAL GOVERNMENT

U.S. International Trade Administration
Department of Commerce
14th St. and Constitution Ave., N.W.
Washington, DC 20230
202-377-2000
Ask for the Commodity Analyst who is an expert in forms and blanks.

U.S. International Trade Commission
500 E St., S.W.
Washington, DC 20436
202-205-2000 Office of the Secretary
202-205-3296 Industries locator
Ask for the Trade Analyst who is an expert in forms and blanks.

FOUNDATIONS

ASSOCIATIONS

Foundation Center
79 5th Ave.
New York, NY 10003
212-620-4230
800-424-9836
212-691-1828 Fax
Thomas Buckman, President
*Offers a wide range of information about
foundations and the grants they award.*

PERIODICALS

Foundation Directory
Foundation Center
79 Fifth Ave.
New York, NY 10003
212-620-4230
Stan Olson, Editor
*Detailed information on the largest founda-
tions offering grants in the U.S.*

Foundation Giving Watch
Taft Group
12300 Twinbrook Pkwy., Ste. 450
Rockville, MD 20852
301-816-0210
Louis LaBreque, Editor
*Provides information to non-profit organiza-
tions that seek the support of foundations.*

Foundation Grants Index
Foundation Center
79 Fifth Ave.
New York, NY 10003
212-620-4230
*Data on all foundation grants in the U.S. of
$10,000 or more.*

Foundation News
Council on Foundations
1828 L St., N.W., Ste. 1200
Washington, DC 20036
202-466-6512
Jody Curtis, Editor
*Reports news and trends for those who offer
and those who seek grants.*

National Data Book of Foundations
Foundation Center
79 Fifth Ave.
New York, NY 10003
212-620-4230
*Contains data on more than 32,000 founda-
tions that make grants.*

LIBRARIES

Ford Foundation
Library
320 E. 43rd St.
New York, NY 10017
212-573-5155
212-599-4584 Fax
*Economic assistance, technical assistance, edu-
cation, urban affairs, philanthropy, and
related topics.*

Foundation Center
Washington Library
1001 Connecticut Ave., N.W., Ste. 938
Washington, DC 20036
202-331-1400
202-331-1739 Fax
Foundations and corporations.

Funding Information Center
507 Brooklyn
San Antonio, TX 78215
512-227-4333
Foundations, nonprofit organizations, proposal writing, and funding.

FOUNDRY INDUSTRY

See also: METALS INDUSTRY and STEEL AND IRON INDUSTRY

ASSOCIATIONS

American Cast Metals Association
455 State St.
Des Plaines, IL 60016
312-299-9160
Peter Dudchenko, President
Offers research, training, and lobbying services to all segments of the foundry industry.

American Foundrymen's Society
505 State St.
Des Plaines, IL 60016-8399
708-824-0181
202-833-3636 Fax
Charles Jones, President
This technical society offers training. Its Technical Information Center provides published information of interest to foundry workers.

Casting Industry Suppliers Association
6990 Rieber St.
Worthington, OH 43085
614-848-8199
614-848-5717 Fax
William Bergdahl, Executive Secretary
Makers of equipment used in foundries including molding machines, tumblers, and dust controllers.

Non-Ferrous Founders Society
455 State St., Ste. 100
Des Plaines, IL 60016
708-299-0950
708-299-3598 Fax
James Mallory, Executive Director
Firms that manufacture nonferrous castings such as those made from bronze and brass.

Steel Founders' Society of America
Cast Metals Fed. Bldg.
455 State St.
Des Plaines, IL 60016
708-299-9160
708-299-3105 Fax
Raymond Monroe, Executive Vice President
Manufacturers of steel castings.

PERIODICALS

Directory of Steel Foundries in the United
    States, Canada and Mexico
Steel Founders' Society of America
455 State St.
Des Plaines, IL 60016
708-299-9160
Kathleen Reese, Editor
A listing of foundries in North America.

Foundry Focus
Metal Bulletin Inc.
220 Fifth Ave., 10 Fl.
New York, NY 10001
800-638-2525
Milton Murse, Editor
Reports on technological and business news about the foundry industry.

Foundry Management & Technology
Penton Publishing
1100 Superior Ave.
Cleveland, OH 44114-2543
216-696-7000
Robert Rodgers, Editor
Advises on management, operational, and technical issues of interest to foundry workers and supervisors.

LIBRARIES

Ajax Magnethermic Corp.
Research & Development Library
1745 Overland, N.E.
Warren, OH 44482
216-372-8781
216-372-8644 Fax
Foundries, steelmaking, induction melting, and related topics.

American Cast Iron Pipe Co.
Technical Library
2930 N. 16th St.
Birmingham, AL 35207-4806
205-325-8978
205-325-8095 Fax
Foundry practices, corrosion, metallurgy, and engineering.

American Foundrymen's Society, Inc.
Technical Information Center
505 State St.
Des Plaines, IL 60016
708-824-0181
708-824-7848 Fax
Foundry practice, cast metals, and air pollution control.

COMPANIES

Alamo Iron Works
P. O. Box 231
San Antonio, TX 78291
512-223-6161
A foundry.

Brenlin Corp.
670 W. Market St.
Akron, OH 44303
216-762-2420
Iron and steel forgings.

BMI Refractories
(Division of Adience Inc.)
27 Noblestown Rd.
Carnegie, PA 15106
412-276-1750
Refractory mixtures and other materials used by foundries.

George Fischer Corp.
(Subsidiary of George Fischer Limited)
555 Business Center Dr.
Mt. Prospect, IL 60056
708-635-7990
Foundry equipment and other products.

Intermet Corp.
2859 Paces Ferry Rd.
Atlanta, GA 30339
404-431-6000
Iron casting foundries.

Earle M. Jorgensen Holdings Co., Inc.
3050 E. Birch St.
Brea, CA 92621
213-567-1122
Iron and steel forgings.

Lake Shore, Inc.
900 W. Brietung
Kingsford, MI 49801
906-774-1500
Foundry products.

Laldish Co., Inc.
5481 S. Packard Ave.
Cudahy, WI 53110
414-747-2611
Iron and steel forgings.

National Forge Co.
100 Front St.
Irvine, PA 16329
814-563-7522
Iron and steel forgings.

Pettibone Corp.
4225 Naperville Rd.
Wildes, IL 60018
708-955-0220
Foundry machinery and other equipment.

FEDERAL GOVERNMENT

U.S. International Trade Administration
Department of Commerce
14th St. and Constitution Ave., N.W.
Washington, DC 20230
202-377-2000
Ask for the Commodity Analyst who is an expert in foundry equipment and products.

U.S. International Trade Commission
500 E St., S.W.
Washington, DC 20436
202-205-2000 Office of the Secretary
202-205-3296 Industries locator
Ask for the Trade Analyst who is an expert in foundry equipment and products.

FRANCHISES

See also: SMALL BUSINESS AND SELF-EMPLOYMENT

ASSOCIATIONS

American Franchise Association
2730 Wilshire Blvd., Ste. 400
Santa Monica, CA 90403
213-829-0841
Russell Berney, Executive Director
Members include franchise owners and the many services which assist them, including attorneys, bankers, accountants, and others.

Franchise Consultants International Association
5147 S. Angela Rd.
Memphis, TN 38117
901-761-3085
William Richey, President
Aside from consultants, the Association includes lawyers, brokers, bankers, and others who offer or seek information about franchising.

PERIODICALS

Business Organizations: Franchising
Matthew Bender & Co., Inc.
11 Penn Plaza
New York, NY 10011
212-967-7707
Gladys Glickman, Editor
Legal, tax, and other information about franchising.

Entrepreneur's Guide to Franchise & Business Opportunities
Entrepreneur Inc.
2392 Morse Ave.
Irvine, CA 92714
Rieva Lesonsky, Editor
714-261-2325
Lists franchises and advises on how to find the suitable opportunity.

Franchise Annual
International Franchise Opportunities
Info Press, Inc.
728 Center St.
Box 550
Lewiston, NY 14092
716-754-4669
E.L. Dixon, Editor
A directory of franchises.

Franchise Law Journal
American Bar Association. Forum Commission on Franchising
A B A Press
750 N. Lake Shore Dr.
Chicago, IL 60611
312-988-6068
Follows all legal matters that relate to franchising.

Franchising Adviser
Shepard's—McGraw-Hill, Inc.
Box 35300
Colorado Springs, CO 80935-3530
800-525-2474
W. Michael Garner, Editor
Offers advice on trademarks, legal matters, regulations, and related subjects concerning franchises.

Franchising World
International Franchise Association
1350 New York Ave., N.W., Ste. 900
Washington, DC 20005
202-628-8000
Polly Larson, Editor
Follows trends and news in franchising.

Opportunity Magazine
Opportunity Associates
6 N. Michigan Ave., Ste. 1405
Chicago, IL 60602
312-346-4790
Jack Weissman, Editor
Information about small, inexpensive businesses and franchises for the opportunity seeker.

Source Book of Franchise Opportunities
Business One Irwin
1818 Ridge Rd.
Homewood, IL 60430
708-206-2700
Robert Bond, Editor
A directory of companies that sell franchises.

LIBRARIES

Arnold, White & Durkee
Library
Box 4433
Houston, TX 77210
713-787-1400
713-789-2679 Fax
Franchising, copyright, patent, and related subjects.

Brownstein, Zeidman & Schomer
Law Library
1401 New York Ave., N.W., Ste. 900
Washington, DC 20005
202-879-5854
202-879-5773 Fax
*Franchising, trademarks, real estate, and
related topics.*

International Franchise Association
IFA World Resource Center
1350 New York Ave., N.W., Ste. 900
Washington, DC 20005
202-628-8000
202-628-0812 Fax
Franchising.

FREEDOM OF INFORMATION AND ACCESS LAWS

The Freedom of Information Act (1966) and subsequent information access laws are designed to help American citizens gain access to many types of records kept by the federal government. Most federal agencies maintain a Freedom of Information office that fields written requests for information. You should call the appropriate federal agency, or the sources listed below, for help using these laws.

ASSOCIATIONS

American Society of Access Professionals
7910 Woodmont Ave., Ste. 1208
Bethesda, MD 20814-3015
301-913-0030
Claire Shanley, Manager
Journalists, lawyers, and others with an interest in effectively using the Freedom of Information Act, the Fair Credit Reporting Act, and other laws that provide access to or privacy on information.

Freedom of Information Center
Univ. of Missouri
20 Walter Williams Hall
Columbia, MO 65211
314-882-4856
Kathleen Edwards, Manager
A clearinghouse for data on how to use the Freedom of Information laws.

Freedom of Information Clearinghouse
PO Box 19367
Washington, DC 20036
202-785-3704
Eleanor Smith, Director
Offers anyone information and advice on how best to use the Freedom of Information Act and other laws to access government information.

National Center for Freedom of Information Studies
Loyola Univ. of Chicago
820 N. Michigan Ave.
Chicago, IL 60611
312-670-3116
Edmund Rooney, Director
A resource center for those interested in using the Freedom of Information Act.

PERIODICALS

FOIA Update
U.S. Department of Justice. Office of Information and Privacy
Constitution Ave. & 10th Sts., N.W.
Washington, DC 20530
202-514-3642
Pamela Maida, Editor
Offers information about the Freedom of Information Act to officers and managers in federal agencies.

Federal Information Disclosure, 2-E
Shepard's—McGraw-Hill, Inc.
Box 35300
Colorado Springs, CO 80935-3530
800-525-2474
Advises attorneys and others on how to use the Freedom of Information Act, including how to litigate.

Litigation Under the Federal Open Government Laws
American Civil Liberties Union Foundation
122 Maryland Ave., N.E.
Washington, DC 20002
202-544-1681
Allan Adler, Editor
Information on suing the U.S. government to enforce the Freedom of Information Act and related access laws.

LIBRARIES

University of Missouri, Columbia
Freedom of Information Center
20 Walter Williams Hall
Columbia, MO 65211
314-882-4856
314-882-8044 Fax
Economic, governmental, and societal controls on information.

FREIGHT TRANSPORTATION

See also: AIR FREIGHT; SHIPS AND SHIPPING INDUSTRY; and TRUCKING INDUSTRY

ASSOCIATIONS

Air and Expedited Motor Carriers Conference
2200 Mill Rd.
Alexandria, VA 22314
703-838-1887
George Mundell, Executive Vice President
Member firms are motor carriers that transport freight which airlines have already taken part of the journey.

National Association of Freight Transportation Consultants
PO Box 21418
Albuquerque, NM 87154
D. F. Behme, Executive Director
Provides educational programs to companies and individuals who offer consulting services to carrier and freight shippers.

National Freight Transportation Association
PO Box 21856
Roanoke, VA 24018
703-774-7725
W. C. Mayo, Executive Secretary
A resource for freight transporters of all kinds.

PERIODICALS

Freight Management Report
Transportation Research Associates
Box 4150
Toms River, NJ 08756-4150
908-787-5814
Thomas F. Dillon, Editor
Reports on transportation cost reduction.

Highway Common Carrier Newsletter
Regular Common Carrier Conference
2200 Mill Rd., Ste. 350
Alexandria, VA 22314-4677
703-898-1970
Shawn Fields, Editor
*Follows regulatory and legislative matters for
the freight industry.*

Inbound Logistics
Thomas Publishing Co.
Five Penn Plaza, 8th Fl.
250 W. 34th St.
New York, NY 10001
212-290-7336
Richard Sexton, Editor
*Covers the equipment and services used for
inbound freight.*

Transportation in America
Eno Foundation for Transportation, Inc.
270 Saugatuck Ave.
Box 2055
Westport, CT 06880-0055
203-227-4852
Frank A. Smith, Editor
*A statistical analysis of freight and passenger
transportation in the United States.*

LIBRARIES

American Trucking Associations, Inc.
Information Center
2200 Mill Rd.
Alexandria, VA 22314
703-838-1880
703-634-4324 Fax
Trucking and freight transportation.

Transportation Institute
Research Documentation Center
301-303 Merrick Bldg.
North Carolina Agricultural & Tech. State
    Univ.
Greensboro, NC 27411
919-334-7093 Fax
Freight transportation.

Western Highway Institute
Research Library
1200 Bayhill Dr., Ste. 112
San Bruno, CA 94066
415-952-4900
415-588-0424 Fax
Trucking and transportation.

COMPANIES

ABF Freight System, Inc.
(Subsidiary of Arkansas Best Corp.)
P.O. Box 48
Fort Smith, AR 72902
501-785-8700
Common carrier of freight.

Burlington Air Express Inc.
(Subsidiary of Pittston Co.)
18200 Von Karman Ave.
Irvine, CA 92715
714-752-4000
Air freight forwarding.

Carolina Freight Carriers Corp.
(Subsidiary of Carolina Freight Corp.)
P. O. Box 697
Cherryville, NC 28021
704-435-6811
Motor freight carrier.

Consolidated Rail Corp.
6 Penn Center Plaza
Philadelphia, PA 19103
215-977-4699
Rail freight transportation.

Emery Worldwide
(Subsidiary of Consolidated Freightways Inc.)
Wilton, CT 06897
203-762-8601
*Domestic and international air freight
delivery.*

Harper Group Inc.
260 Townsend
San Francisco, CA 94107
415-978-0600
Ocean and air freight forwarding.

Lykes Bros. Steamship Co., Inc.
Lykes Center, 300 Poydras St.
New Orleans, LA 70130
504-523-6611
Ocean freight.

Overnite Transportation Co.
(Subsidiary of Union Pacific Corp.)
1000 Semmes Ave.
Richmond, VA 23224
804-231-8000
Motor freight carrier.

Roadway Package System, Inc.
410 Rouser Rd.
Coraopolis, PA 15108
412-236-1000
Motor freight carrier.

United Parcel Service of America, Inc.
Greenwich Office Pk.
Greenwich, CT 06831
203-862-6000
Courier and motor freight carrier.

FEDERAL GOVERNMENT

Federal Maritime Commission
1100 L St., N.W.
Washington, DC 20573
202-523-5773
*Ask for the public affairs office to find an
appropriate expert.*

U.S. Department of Transportation
400 Seventh St., S.W.
Washington, DC 20590
202-366-4000
*Ask for the public affairs office to find an
appropriate expert.*

FRUIT AND VEGETABLE INDUSTRY

See also: GROCERY BUSINESS; ONION AND GARLIC INDUSTRIES; and POTATO INDUSTRY

ASSOCIATIONS

American Greenhouse Vegetable Growers
Association
31 N. Market St.
Elysburg, PA 17824
Carol Laymon, Executive Secretary
*A clearinghouse for information about the
greenhouse vegetable growing industry.*

American Mushroom Institute
907 E. Baltimore Pike
Kennett Square, PA 19348
215-388-7806
215-388-0243 Fax
Alma Rigler, Representative
*Provides information to mushroom growers
and processors.*

American Produce Association
1146 19th St. N.W.
Washington, DC 20036
George Carstens, President
Importers of fruits and vegetables.

Apricot Producers of California
1064 Woodland Ave., Ste. E
Modesto, CA 95351
209-524-0801
209-524-3840 Fax
Les Rose, Operations Vice President
Offers information on the apricot industry.

Blue Anchor, Inc.
PO Box 15498
Sacramento, CA 95851
916-929-3050
916-921-9362 Fax
Patrick Sanguinetti, President
*A cooperative that helps growers market their
table grapes and other fruits from deciduous
trees.*

California Fig Institute
PO Box 709
Fresno, CA 93712
209-445-5626
209-224-3447 Fax
Ron Klamm, Managing Director
*Conducts research for fig growers in Califor-
nia.*

California Iceberg Lettuce Commission
PO Box 3354
Monterey, CA 93942
408-375-8277
Wade Whitfield, President
*Members are commissioners who offer a vari-
ety of marketing and promotional services on
behalf of California's iceburg lettuce industry.*

California Melon Research Board
531-D N. Alta Ave.
Dinuba, CA 93618
209-591-0435
Represents melon growers in California.

California Raisin Advisory Board
PO Box 5335
Fresno, CA 93755
209-224-7010
Clyde Nef, Manager
Studies the growing, processing, and marketing of raisins.

California Table Grape Commission
PO Box 5498
Fresno, CA 93755
209-224-4997
209-224-4756 Fax
Bruce Obbink, President
Promotes the sale of table grapes.

Florida Citrus Mutual
Citrus Mutual Bldg.
302 S. Massachusetts Ave.
Lakeland, FL 33801
813-682-1111
Bobby McKown, Executive Vice President
Supplies information about the prices and the fruit market to Florida citrus growers.

Florida Citrus Packers
PO Box 1113
Lakeland, FL 33802
813-682-0151
Richard Kinney, Executive Vice President
Firms that pack and ship citrus fruits from Florida.

Florida Fruit and Vegetable Association
PO Box 140155
Orlando, FL 32814-0155
407-894-1351
407-894-7840 Fax
George Sorn, Executive Vice President
Represents firms in Florida that grow and ship fruits and vegetables of all kinds.

Florida Tomato Exchange
P.O. Box 140635
Orlando, FL 32814
407-894-3071
407-898-4296 Fax
Wayne Hawkins, Executive Vice President
Sponsors research in the growing, packaging, and shipping of tomatoes.

Frozen Vegetable Council
c/o American Frozen Food Institute
1838 El Camino Real, Rm. 202
Burlingame, CA 94010
415-697-6835
M. J. Bohannan, Secretary
Provides public relations and advertising services to the frozen vegetable industry.

International Apple Institute
6707 Old Dominion Dr., Ste. 320
PO Box 1137
McLean, VA 22101
703-442-8850
703-790-0845 Fax
Derl Derr, President
Represents apple growers around the world.

International Banana Association
1101 Vermont Ave., N.W., Ste. 306
Washington, DC 20005
202-371-1620
Robert Moore, President
Studies the growing, harvesting, transport, and selling of bananas.

National Cherry Growers and Industries
    Foundation
1105 N.W. 31st St.
Corvallis, OR 97330
503-753-8508
Norm Gutzwiler, President
Offers information on the cherry industry.

National Peach Council
PO Box 11280
Columbia, SC 29211
803-492-7724
Offers research into the peach industry.

National Red Cherry Institute
2220 University Park Dr., Ste. 200
Okemos, MI 48864
517-321-1231
C. Richard Johnston, Execurive Director
Studies the cherry industry.

North American Blueberry Council
c/o Myrtle L. Ruch
PO Box 166
Marmora, NJ 08223
609-399-1559
Myrtle Ruch, Secretary
*A clearinghouse for information about the
blueberry industry.*

Rare Fruit Council International
PO Box 561914
Miami, FL 33256
305-378-4457
800-262-6688
Efrain Santiago, President
Promotes the study and sale of tropical fruits.

Sunkist Growers
PO Box 7888
Van Nuys, CA 91409-7888
818-986-4800
Russell Hanlin, President
A cooperative of citrus fruit growers.

United Fresh Fruit and Vegetable Association
727 N. Washington St.
Alexandria, VA 22314
703-836-7745
George Dunlop, President
*Offers research, marketing, and educational
services to growers, distributors, retailers, and
others in fresh fruit and vegetable industry.*

Washington State Apple Commission
PO Box 18
Wenatchee, WA 98807-0018
509-663-9600
509-662-5824 Fax
Thomas Hale, President
*Helps Washington state apple growers to
advertise and promote their fruit.*

PERIODICALS

American Fruit Grower
Meister Publishing Co.
37733 Euclid Ave.
Willoughby, OH 44094
216-942-2000
Gary Acuff, Editor
*Covers technical and business news for the
fruit growing industry.*

American Vegetable Grower
Meister Publishing Co.
37733 Euclid Ave.
Willoughby, OH 44094
216-942-2000
Stella Nacgely, Editor
Covers vegetable growing and marketing.

California Tomato Grower
California Tomato Growers Association, Inc.
9036 Thornton Rd.
Box 7398
Stockton, CA 95207
209-478-1761
David Zollinger, Editor
Surveys the tomato industry.

Citrus and Vegetable Magazine
Box 7595
Tampa, FL 33673-7595
813-223-7628
E. Shaunn Alderman, Editor
*Helps farmers, processors, and packers keep
abreast of the citrus and vegetable industry.*

Citrus Industry Magazine
Associated Publications Corp.
495 E. Summerlin St.
Box 89
Bartow, FL 33830
813-533-4114
Richard Frisbie, Editor
Advice on citrus fruit growing.

Florida Grower and Rancher
F.G.R., Incorporated
1331 N. Mills Ave., 2nd fl.
Orlando, FL 32803-2598
407-894-6522
Sondra Abrahamson, Editor
Reports on farming, processing, and marketing of vegetables and citrus fruits.

Fruit Country
Columbia Publishing and Design
2809-A Fruitvale Blvd.
Box 1467
Yakima, WA 98907-1467
509-248-2452
Ken Hodge, Editor
Covers fruit growing in Washington and Northern Oregon.

Fruit Varieties Journal
American Pomological Society
c/o Dr. Robert M. Crassweller, Business Manager
103 Tyson Bldg.
University Park, PA 16802
814-863-6163
David Ferree, Editor
Technical information for horticulturists and fruit breeders and growers.

Mushroom
Box 3156, University Sta.
Moscow, ID 83843
208-882-8720
H. Coombs, Editor
Reports on wild mushroom hunting and mushroom cultivation.

Mushroom News
American Mushroom Institute
907 E. Baltimore Pike
Kennett Sq., PA 19348
215-388-7806
Analyzes the mushroom industry and provides growing tips.

Vegetable and Specialty Crop Situation and Outlook
U.S. Department of Agriculture
Information Division
1301 New York Ave., N.W.
Washington, DC 20005
202-783-3238
Surveys current and expected market conditions for fresh and processed vegetables.

LIBRARIES

U.S.D.A.
Agricultural Research Service
Horticultural Research Laboratory
Library
2120 Camden Rd.
Orlando, FL 32803
407-897-7301
407-897-7309 Fax
Citrus fruit, vegetables, plant pathology, transportation, and the marketing of fruits and vegetables.

U.S.D.A.
Agricultural Research Service
Western Regional Research Center Library
800 Buchanan St.
Albany, CA 94710
415-559-5603
415-559-5777 Fax
Fruits, vegetables, food technology, chemistry, and nutrition.

University of Florida
Agricultural Research & Education Center
Library
Box 728
Hastings, FL 32145-0728
904-692-1792
Agriculture, including fruits and vegetables.

COMPANIES

Auster Co. Inc.
51 S. Water Market
Chicago, IL 60608
312-829-6550
Wholesalers of fresh produce.

Calavo Growers of California
15661 Red Hill Ave.
Tustin, CA 92680
714-259-1166
Fresh and frozen fruits.

Curtice-Burns Foods Inc.
90 Linden Pl., Box 681
Rochester, NY 14603
716-383-1850
Frozen and canned fruits and vegetables.

De Bruyn Produce Co.
101 Washington St.
Zeeland, MI 49464
616-772-2101
Vegetable growing and packing.

Fadler Co., Inc.
(Subsidiary of Hale Halsell Co.)
6511 E. 44th St.
Tulsa, OK 74145
918-627-0770
Wholesaler of fresh fruits and other foods.

Naturipe Berry Growers
P. O. Box A
Watsonville, CA 95077
408-722-2439
Fresh fruits and vegetables.

Prevor Marketing International, Inc.
(Subsidiary of Polly Peck International PLC)
Hunts Point Market
Bronx, NY 10474
212-589-5200
Fresh fruits and vegetables.

Pro-Fac Cooperative, Inc.
P.O. Box 682
Rochester, NY 14603
716-325-1020
Cooperative of firms selling fruits and vegetables.

Red's Market, Inc.
(Subsidiary of Albert Fisher Group PLC)
8801 Exchange Dr.
Orlando, FL 32809
407-857-3930
Wholesaler of fruits and vegetables.

Snokist Growers
P. O. Box 1587
Yakima, WA 98907
509-453-5631
Fresh and processed fruits.

Sun-Land Products of California
(Subsidiary of Sun-Diamond Growers of Cali-
    fornia)
16500 W. 103rd St.
Lemont, IL 60439
708-739-3000
*Wholesaler of fresh fruits, vegetables, and
nuts.*

Tri/Valley Growers Inc.
1255 Battery St.
San Francisco, CA 94111
415-445-1600
Fruit and vegetable growing and canning.

Valley Packing Service
310 Walker St.
Watsonville, CA 95076
408-724-7551
Fruit and vegetable brokers.

FEDERAL GOVERNMENT

U.S. Customs Service
Department of the Treasury
U.S. Customshouse
6 World Trade Center
New York, NY 10048
212-466-5550
*Ask for the Commodity Specialist in charge of
fruits or vegetables.*

U.S. Department of Agriculture
14th St. and Independence Ave., S.W.
Washington, DC 20250
202-720-8732
*Ask for the Agricultural Marketing Service,
the Economic Research Service, or the Agricultural Statistics Service.*

U.S. International Trade Administration
Department of Commerce
14th St. and Constitution Ave., N.W.
Washington, DC 20230
202-377-2000
*Ask for the Commodity Analyst who is an
expert in the fruit and vegetable industry.*

FUEL OIL INDUSTRY

See also: PETROLEUM INDUSTRY

ASSOCIATIONS

Petroleum Marketers Association of America
1120 Vermont Ave. N.W., Ste. 1130
Washington, DC 20005
202-331-1198
202-467-6330 Fax
Phillip Chisholm, Executive Vice President
*A federation of regional associations that rep-
resent marketers of petroleum products,
including fuel oil and heating oil.*

PERIODICALS

Fuel Oil News
Hunter Publishing Limited Partnership
950 Lee St.
Des Plaines, IL 60016
708-296-0770
Howard Shingle, Editor
*Information for fuel oil dealers and suppiers of
oil burning equipment.*

LIBRARIES

Diamond Petroleum Co.
(Subsidiary of Diamond Industries Inc.)
S. Heald & A St.
Wilmington, DE 19801
302-658-3591
Wholesaler of fuel oil.

Fletcher Oil & Refining Co.
(Subsidiary of Hondo Oil & Gas Co.)
24721 S. Main
Carson, CA 90744
213-518-4270
Refiner of gasoline, fuel oil, and other petroleum products.

G & M Oil Co., Inc.
1549 N. Warwick Ave.
Baltimore, MD 21216
301-728-0333
Fuel oil distributor.

Griffith-Consumers Co.
2510 Schuster Dr.
Cheverly, MD 20781
301-322-5114
Fuel oil and fuel-oil burning equipment.

Petroleum Heat & Power Co.
Davenport St.
Stamford, CT 06904
203-323-2121
Retailer of fuel oil.

Steuart Petroleum Co.
6531 Evergreen Ave.
Jacksonville, FL 32206
904-355-9675
Wholesaler of fuel oil.

Stuart Petroleum Co.
4646 40th St., N.W.
Washington, DC 20016
202-537-8900
Retail and wholesale fuel oil, kerosene, and other petroleum products.

Watkins Oil Co., Inc.
120 W. Fayette
Hillsdale, MI 49242
517-437-3140
Distributor of fuel oil and gasoline.

FEDERAL GOVERNMENT

U.S. Department of Energy
1000 Independence Ave., S.W.
Washington, DC 20585
202-586-5000
Ask for the public relations office.

U.S. International Trade Administration
Department of Commerce
14th St. and Constitution Ave., N.W.
Washington, DC 20230
202-377-2000
Ask for the Commodity Analyst who is an expert in the fuel oil industry.

U.S. International Trade Commission
500 E St., S.W.
Washington, DC 20436
202-205-2000 Office of the Secretary
202-205-3296 Industries locator
Ask for the Trade Analyst who is an expert in the fuel oil industry.

FUNERAL AND MORTUARY INDUSTRY

ASSOCIATIONS

American Cemetery Association
3 Skyline Pl., Ste. 1111
5201 Leesburg Pike
Falls Church, VA 22041
703-379-5838
703-998-0162 Fax
Stephen Morgan, Executive Vice President
Represents owners of cemeteries and funeral homes.

Associated Funeral Directors Service International
PO Box 23023
St. Petersburg, FL 33742
813-579-1113
800-346-7151
813-522-3237 Fax
Richard Santore, Executive Officer
Offers funeral homes and mortuaries help with public relations, advertising, and cooperative buying of supplies.

Casket Manufacturers Association of America
708 Church St.
Evanston, IL 60201
708-866-8383
George Lemke, Executive Director
Members make and distribute burial caskets and related funeral supplies.

Embalming Chemical Manufacturers Association
1370 Honeyspot Rd.
Stratford, CT 06497
800-243-6104
Firms that make embalming chemicals.

Monument Builders of North America
1612 Central St.
Evanston, IL 60201
708-869-2031
708-869-2056 Fax
John Dianis, Executive Vice President
Manufacturers and dealers of monuments.

National Funeral Directors Association
11121 W. Oklahoma Ave.
Milwaukee, WI 53227
414-541-2500
Robert Harden, Executive Director
Represents state associations of funeral directors.

PERIODICALS

American Funeral Director
Kates-Boylston Publications, Inc.
1501 Broadway
New York, NY 10036
212-398-9266
Charles Kates, Editor
Technical and business advice for directors of funeral homes.

Mortuary Management
Berg Publications Inc.
315 Silverlake Blvd.
Los Angeles, CA 90026
213-665-0101
Ronald Hast, Editor
Provides industry news and management advice to funeral directors, cemetery directors, and others.

Yellow Book News
Nomis Publications, Inc.
Box 5122
Youngstown, OH 44514
800-321-7479
Chester Simon, Editor
Reports on funeral industry news.

LIBRARIES

Cincinnati College of Mortuary Science
Library
Cohen Center
3860 Pacific Ave.
Cincinnati, OH 45207-1033
513-745-3631
*Funeral service, mortuary science, and
embalming.*

National Foundation of Funeral Service
Beryl L. Boyer Library
1614 Central St.
Evanston, IL 60201
708-328-6545
312-328-6778 Fax
*Funeral service, mortuary science, embalming,
death customs, and burial.*

National Funeral Directors Association
Library
11121 W. Oklahoma Ave.
Milwaukee, WI 53227
414-541-2500
*Technical and business information about
funerals and mortuary science.*

San Francisco College of Mortuary Science
Library
1363 Divisadero St.
San Francisco, CA 94115-3912
415-567-0674
*Funeral directing, embalming, and funeral
management.*

COMPANIES

Arlington Corp.
950 E. Paces Ferry Rd.
Atlanta, GA 30326
404-266-8877
Funeral homes.

Aurora Casket Co., Inc.
P.O. Box 29
Aurora, IN 47001
812-926-1111
Burial caskets and other mortuary supplies.

Batesville Casket Co., Inc.
Hwy. 46 E.
Batesville, IN 47006
812-934-7500
Burial caskets and other mortuary supplies.

Champion Co.
400 Harrison St., Box 967
Springfield, OH 45501
513-324-5681
Embalming and funeral products.

Paragon Family Services, Inc.
16825 Northchase Dr.
Houston, TX 77060
713-872-0996
Funeral homes.

Rose Hills Co.
P.O. Box 110
Whittier, CA 90608
310-699-0921
Funeral homes.

Service Corporation International
1929 Allen Pkwy.
Houston, TX 77019
713-522-5141
*Owns and operates funeral homes and ceme-
teries, offers financial services for other
funeral homes and cemeteries.*

Toccoa Casket Co.
726 W. Currahee St.
Toccoa, GA 30577
404-886-3153
Burial caskets and other mortuary supplies.

Uniservice Corp.
415 N. Killingsworth
Portland, OR 97217
503-283-1980
Owns funeral parlors and operates cemeteries.

York Group, Inc.
York Casket Co.
2880 Blackbridge Rd.
York, PA 17402
717-854-9566
Burial caskets and other mortuary supplies.

FUR INDUSTRY

ASSOCIATIONS

American Fur Industry
363 7th Ave., 7th Fl.
New York, NY 10001
212-564-5133
Sandra Blye, Executive Vice President
This group of fur manufacturers promotes the acceptance and sales of furs.

Fur Takers of America
Rt. 3, Box 211A1
Aurora, IN 47001
812-926-1049
Marcia Walston, Treasurer
Members include fur trappers, equipment suppliers, fur buyers, and others in the industry. Promotes trapping as humane.

PERIODICALS

Business of Fur
Fur Publishing Plus Inc.
19 W. 21st St., Ste. 403
New York, NY 10010
212-727-1210
Richard Harrow, Editor
News and advice for fur retailers.

Fur Rancher
Communications Marketing, Inc.
7535 Office Ridge Circle
Eden Prairie, MN 55344
612-941-5820
Bruce Smith, Editor
Covers news of interest to ranchers and trappers of mink and other fur animals.

COMPANIES

Banyan Corp.
360 W. 31st St.
New York, NY 10001
212-736-8620
Retail and wholesale fur apparel.

Dubrowsky & Perlbinder, Inc.
512 Seventh Ave.
New York, NY 10018
212-221-1450
Fur coats and other coats.

Michael Forrest Inc.
333 Seventh Ave.
New York, NY 10001
212-564-4726
Fur coats.

Fur Vault Inc.
360 W. 31st St.
New York, NY 10001
212-563-7070
Retail and wholesale fur coats.

Goldin-Karabeles International, Inc.
345 Seventh Ave.
New York, NY 10001
212-594-4415
Fur coats.

Hudson's Bay New York Inc.
(Subsidiary of Hudson's Bay Co.)
410 Commerce Blvd.
Carlstadt, NJ 07072
201-438-0414
Fur auctioneers.

Pacific Hide & Fur Depot
1401 3rd St. N.W.
Great Falls, MT 59403
406-727-6222
Wholesaler of furs.

Silberman Fur Corp.
332 S. Michigan Ave.
Chicago, IL 60604
312-922-2468
Raw and dressed furs.

FEDERAL GOVERNMENT

U.S. International Trade Administration
Department of Commerce
14th St. and Constitution Ave., N.W.
Washington, DC 20230
202-377-2000
*Ask for the Commodity Analyst who is an
expert in the fur industry.*

FURNITURE INDUSTRY

ASSOCIATIONS

American Furniture Manufacturers Association
PO Box HP-7
High Point, NC 27261
919-884-5000
Douglas Brackett, Executive Vice President
*Provides a wide range of market research
information to furniture manufacturers and
others.*

American Society of Furniture Designers
PO Box 2688
High Point, NC 27261
919-884-4074
919-882-2555 Fax
Judith Reagan, Administrator
*Furniture designers who share design and
industry information.*

Business and Institutional Furniture Manufacturers Association
2335 Burton S.E.
Grand Rapids, MI 49506
616-243-1681
616-243-1011 Fax
Stephen Channer, Executive Director
*Manufacturers of furniture used in offices and
institutions.*

Furniture Rental Association of America
Blendonview Office Park
5008 Pine Creek Dr.
Westerville, OH 43081-4899
614-895-1273
800-FOR-RENT.
James Bannister, Executive Director
*Firms that rent or lease furniture and acces-
sories used in homes.*

National Association of Casual Furniture
Retailers
1190 Merchandise Mart
Chicago, IL 60654
312-321-0563
M. B. Gregory, Executive Director
*A forum for manufacturers and retailers of
casual furniture.*

National Home Furnishings Association
PO Box 2396
High Point, NC 27261
919-883-1650
800-888-9590
919-883-1195 Fax
David Schmitt, Executive Vice President
*This group of furniture and furnishings retail-
ers conducts research and offers marketing
and management training.*

National Unfinished Furniture Institute
1850 Oak St.
Northfield, IL 60093
708-446-8434
800-323-5462
708-446-3523 Fax
Ray Passis, Director
*Represents manufacturers and retailers of
unfinished furniture.*

National Waterbed Retailers Association
36 S. State St., No. 1806
Chicago, IL 60603
312-236-6662
800-832-3553
312-236-1140 Fax
Ralph Bloch, Executive Director
Conducts research for the waterbed industry.

PERIODICALS

F D M—Furniture Design & Manufacturing
Delta Communications, Inc.
400 N. Michigan Ave., 13th Fl.
Chicago, IL 60611
312-222-2000
Michael Chazin, Editor
News about furniture, upholstery, and bed manufacturing.

Furniture—Today
Cahners Business Newspapers
200 S. Main St.
High Point, NC 27261
919-889-0113
Bill Peterson, Editor
Reports business news of interest to furniture manufacturers and retailers.

Furniture Retailer
Pace Communications Inc.
1301 Carolina St.
Greensboro, NC 27401
919-378-6065
Patricia Bowling, Editor
Advice and information about new products for furniture retailers.

Furniture Transporter
Bohman Industrial Traffic Consultants, Inc.
335 E. Broadway
Gardner, MA 01440
617-632-1913
Raynard Bohman, Editor
News for executives of firms that transport furniture.

H F D—Retailing Home Furnishings
Fairchild Publications, Inc.
7 E. 12th St.
New York, NY 10003
212-741-4000
Geri Brin, Editor
Advice for retailers and suppliers of furniture, housewares, and bedding.

Home Furnishings Review
Southwest Homefurnishings Association
110 World Trade Center
Box 581207
Dallas, TX 75258
214-741-7632
Darrell Hofheinz, Editor
Summaries of how-to articles printed elsewhere which help furnishings retailers run their businesses more effectively.

LIBRARIES

Bernice Bienenstock Furniture Library
1009 N. Main St.
High Point, NC 27262
919-883-4011
Furniture design and furniture styles, dating from the 1600 to the present.

Harrington Institute of Interior Design
Design Library
410 S. Michigan Ave.
Chicago, IL 60605
312-939-4975
312-939-8005 Fax
Furniture, interior design, and building materials.

COMPANIES

Brodhead-Garrett Co.
223 S. Illinois Ave.
Mansfield, OH 44905
419-589-8222
Furniture.

Chaselle, Inc.
9645 Gerwig Ln.
Columbia, MD 21046
301-381-9611
Furniture.

Harvard Industries, Inc.
Central Ave.
Farmingdale, NJ 07727
201-938-3000
Furniture and other products.

Interco Incorporated
101 S. Hanley Rd.
St. Louis, MO 63105
314-863-1100
Furniture and home furnishings.

Joyce International, Inc.
114 5th Ave.
New York, NY 10011
212-463-9044
Furniture.

La-Z-Boy Chair Co.
1284 N. Telegraph Rd.
Monroe, MI 48161
313-242-1444
Upholstered furniture.

Levitz Furniture Corp.
(Subsidiary of LFC Holding Corp.)
6111 Broken Sound Pkwy., N.W.
Boca Raton, FL 33487
407-994-6006
Retailer of furniture.

Ohio Mattress Co.
1228 Euclid Ave.
Cleveland, OH 44115
216-522-1310
Mattresses, box springs, sofabeds, and other furniture.

Schottenstein Stores Corp.
1800 Moler Rd.
Columbus, OH 43207
614-221-9200
Furniture retailers.

Steelcase Inc.
901 44th St., S.E.
Grand Rapids, MI 49508
616-247-2710
Office furniture.

FEDERAL GOVERNMENT

General Services Administration
18th & F St., N.W.
Washington, DC 20405
202-708-5082
Ask for the Furniture Commodity Center division of the Federal Supply Service.

U.S. Customs Service
Department of the Treasury
U.S. Customshouse
6 World Trade Center
New York, NY 10048
212-466-5550
Ask for the Commodity Specialist in charge of furniture.

U.S. International Trade Administration
Department of Commerce
14th St. and Constitution Ave., N.W.
Washington, DC 20230
202-377-2000
Ask for the Commodity Analyst who is an expert in the furniture industry.

U.S. International Trade Commission
500 E St., S.W.
Washington, DC 20436
202-205-2000 Office of the Secretary
202-205-3296 Industries locator
Ask for the Trade Analyst who is an expert in furniture industry.

GAMBLING AND CASINO INDUSTRY

ASSOCIATIONS

National Association of Gambling Regulatory
    Agencies
PO Box 66614
Baton Rouge, LA 70896
504-925-1835
Frank Brown, President
*Officers in governments that regulate all types
of gambling activity.*

National Association of Off-Track Betting
700 Ellicott St.
Batavia, NY 14020
716-343-1423
Martin Basinait, President
Represents legal off-track betting operations.

Nevada Association Race and Sports Book
    Operators
37-65 Central Park Circle, #8
Las Vegas, NV 89109
702-731-0749
Andrew Jerry, Executive Director
*Legal bookmakers for off-track betting and
betting on other sports.*

PERIODICALS

Card Player
1455 E. Tropicana Ave., No. 450
Las Vegas, NV 89119
702-798-5170
June Field, Editor
*Reports on casino gambling news for gam-
blers.*

Casino World
Gramercy Information Services, Inc.
Box 2003, Madison Sq. Sta.
New York, NY 10159
212-228-4769
Nancy Dunnan, Editor
*Industry news for executives connected with
casinos in the U.S. and around the world.*

Journal of Gambling Studies
National Council on Compulsive Gambling
Human Sciences Press, Inc.
233 Spring St.
New York, NY 10013-1578
212-620-8000
Henry Lesieur, Editor
*A scholarly magazine covering the nature of
and treatment for compulsive gambling.*

Player
Casino Journal Publishing Group
2524 Arctic Ave.
Atlantic City, NJ 08401
609-344-9000
Glenn Fine, Editor
*News and statistics designed to help gamblers
who bet in casinos, on sporting events, horses,
and lotteries.*

Win
Gambling Times, Inc.
16760 Stagg St., Ste. 213
Van Nuys, CA 91406
818-781-9355
Advice and news for gamblers.

LIBRARIES

Princeton Antiques Bookfinders
Art Marketing Reference Library
2915-17-31 Atlantic Ave.
Atlantic City, NJ 08401
609-344-1943
Gambling and other topics.

University of Nevada, Las Vegas
Gambling Research Center
4505 Maryland Pkwy.
Las Vegas, NV 89154
702-739-3252
Gambling, lotteries, and related topics.

COMPANIES

Aztar Corp.
2390 E. Camelback Rd.
Phoenix, AZ 85016
602-381-4100
Casinos and hotels.

Bally Manufacturing Corp.
8700 W. Bryn Mawr
Chicago, IL 60631
312-399-1300
Gaming equipment, lottery products, fitness centers, and other products.

Bally's Grand, Inc.
3645 Las Vegas Blvd. S.
Las Vegas, NV 89109
702-739-4855
Casinos and hotels.

Mirage Resorts Inc.
3400 Las Vegas Blvd. S.
Las Vegas, NV 89109
702-791-7111
Casinos and hotels.

Resorts International/Casino Hotel Inc.
(Subsidiary of Resorts International, Inc.)
Atlantic City, NJ 08404
609-344-6000
Casinos and hotels.

Sands Hotel & Casino Corp.
(Subsidiary of Pratt Hotel Corp.)
Indiana Ave. at Brighton Park
Atlantic City, NJ 08401
609-441-4000
Casino and hotel.

Showboat Inc.
2800 E. Fremont St.
Las Vegas, NV 89104
702-385-9141
Casino and hotel.

GARAGES AND SERVICE STATIONS

See also: AUTOMOBILE EQUIPMENT INDUSTRY and GASOLINE INDUSTRY

ASSOCIATIONS

Automotive Service Association
1901 Airport Fwy., Ste. 100
PO Box 929
Bedford, TX 76095-0929
817-283-6205
817-685-0225 Fax
George Merwin, President
Provides techical, management, and industry information to automotive service companies, such as body shops, transmission shops, paint shops, and others.

Car Wash Owners and Suppliers Association
PO Box 4067
Racine, WI 53404
414-639-4393
Don Morgan, President
1983
Promotes the car washing industry.

Convenient Automotive Services Institute
PO Box 34595
Bethesda, MD 20817
301-897-3191
Glenn Northup, Executive Director
Members offer quick oil change and lubrication services.

Gasoline and Automotive Service Dealers Association
6338 Ave. N
Brooklyn, NY 11234
718-241-1111
718-763-6589 Fax
Stanley Schuer, Executive Director
Owners and operators of gas stations and car repair shops. Offers training programs.

Interstate Towing Association
PO Box 916430
Longwood, FL 32791-6430
407-260-0088
800-327-8542
Kevin Fritz, President
Represents firms that transport disabled and wrecked cars and trucks. Offers technical, safety, legislative, and management information.

National Association of Independent Lubes
12800 Hillcrest, Ste. 214
Dallas, TX 75230
214-458-9468
800-331-0329
214-458-9539 Fax
Thomas Whennen, Executive Director
Oil change shops that are independently owned and operated.

Service Station Dealers of America
499 S. Capital St. S.W.
Washington, DC 20003-4013
202-479-0196
Joseph Koach, Executive Director
*Members are owners and operators of service
stations.*

Society of Collision Repair Specialists
1201 Landmark, Ste. 3
Liberty, MO 64068
816-781-5225
816-781-5615 Fax
John Loftus, Executive Director
*Members include auto collision repair shops,
insurance firms, auto supply firms, and others.
Offers technical information.*

PERIODICALS

Service Station Management
Hunter Publishing Limited Partnership
950 Lee St.
Des Plaines, IL 60016
708-296-0770
Peggy Smedley, Editor
*Industry news and management advice for
gasoline stations that offer car repair.*

Super Automotive Service
Irving-Cloud Publishing Co.
7300 N. Cicero Ave.
Lincolnwood, IL 60646
708-647-7300
Bob Weber, Editor
*Covers industry trends and new products for
service stations and repair shops.*

LIBRARIES

Automotive Information Council
Library
13505 Dulles Technology Dr.
Herndon, VA 22071-3415
703-904-0700
708-904-0727 Fax
Motor vehicle maintenance, repair, and safety.

COMPANIES

ABC-Treadco, Inc.
P.O. Box 48
Fort Smith, AR 72901
501-785-6000
Tire retreading shops.

American Oil Change Corp.
31 Moody Rd.
Enfield, CT 06082
203-763-2881
Automotive services.

Auto Glass Specialists, Inc.
P.O. Box 9500
Madison, WI 53715
608-271-5484
Automotive glass replacement shops.

Bandag, Inc.
Bandag Ctr.
Muscatine, IA 52761
319-262-1400
Tire retreading shops.

Haygood, Inc.
185 W. McLemore St.
Memphis, TN 38106
901-775-8300
General automotive repair shops.

Jiffy Lube International, Inc.
P.O. Box 2967
Houston, TX 77252
713-546-4100
General automotive repair shops.

Monro Muffler and Brake, Inc.
P.O. Box 22720
Rochester, NY 14692
716-427-2280
Muffler and brake repair.

Northwest Motor Welding, Inc.
519 E. La Palma Ave.
Anaheim, CA 92801
714-776-1500
General automotive repair shops.

Parts Industries Corp.
601 Dudley St.
Memphis, TN 38104
901-523-7711
General automotive repair shops.

SpeeDee Oil Change and Tune-up
6660 Riverside Dr.
Metairie, LA 70003
504-454-3783
General automotive repair shops.

U.S. Auto Glass Centers, Inc.
1880 W. Fullerton Ave.
Chicago, IL 60614
312-278-6900
Automotive glass replacement shops.

GARDEN SUPPLY AND PLANT NURSERIES

See also: FLORISTS AND FLOWER INDUSTRY

ASSOCIATIONS

American Association of Nurserymen
1250 I St. N.W., Ste. 500
Washington, DC 20005
202-789-2900
Growers, wholesalers, and garden centers that provide all types of plants and trees. Provides a wide range of management and business information.

American Horticultural Society
7931 E. Boulevard Dr.
Alexandria, VA 22308
703-768-5700
800-777-7931
703-765-6032 Fax
Frank Robinson, Executive Director
The amateur and professional gardeners that belong to the Society share technical information and seeds.

Garden Club of America
598 Madison Ave.
New York, NY 10022
212-753-8287
212-753-0134 Fax
Mary Walsh, Executive Secretary
A group for amateur gardeners.

Professional Plant Growers Association
PO Box 27517
Lansing, MI 48909
517-694-7700
517-694-8560 Fax
Terry Humfeld, Executive Director
Members include plant growers, distributors, and retailers. Offers technical and marketing information.

PERIODICALS

American Nurseryman
American Nurseryman Publishing Co.
111 N. Canal St., Ste. 545
Chicago, IL 60606-7276
312-782-5505
Cynthia Champney Urbano, Editor
News and how-to information for nurseries.

Floral and Nursery Times
XXX Publishing Enterprises Ltd.
629 Green Bay Rd.
Wilmette, IL 60091
708-256-8777
Barbara Gilbert, Editor
News and market information for nurseries.

Florida Nurseryman
Florida Nurserymen & Growers Association
5401 Kirkman Rd., Ste. 650
Orlando, FL 32819
407-345-8137
Janice Herbster, Editor
Follows industry trends, marketing opportunities, and new research findings.

Garden Supply Retailer
Chilton Co.
201 King of Prussia Rd.
Radnor, PA 19089
215-964-4275
Terrence Gallagher, Editor
Offers management and merchandising advice to garden centers and firms that sell outdoor power equipment.

Nursery Business
Brantwood Publications, Inc.
Northwood Plaza Sta.
Clearwater, FL 33519-0360
813-796-3877
Richard Morey, Editor
Industry news and management advice for nurseries.

LIBRARIES

American Horticultural Society
Library
7931 E. Boulevard Dr.
Alexandria, VA 22308
703-768-5700
800-777-7931
Technical information about horticultural subjects.

Ohio State University
Agricultural Technical Institute
Library
1328 Dover Rd.
Wooster, OH 44691
216-264-3911
216-262-0859 Fax
Nurseries, greenhouse production, agricultural engineering, and related topics.

U.S. National Arboretum
Library
3501 New York Ave., N.E.
Washington, DC 20002
202-475-4828
202-475-5252 Fax
Gardening, horticulture, botany, and plant breeding.

COMPANIES

Ames Co.
(Subsidiary of HM Acquisition Corp.)
P.O. Box 1774
Parkersburg, WV 26101
304-424-3000
Lawn and garden tools.

Bachman's, Inc.
6010 Lyndale Ave., S.
Minneapolis, MN 55419
612-861-7600
Merchandise sold in flower shops, nurseries, and garden centers.

Channel Home Centers Inc.
945 Rte. 10
Whippany, NJ 07981
201-887-7000
Retailer of paint, hardware, and lawn and garden products.

Frank's Nursery & Crafts Inc.
(Subsidiary of General Host Corp.)
6501 E. Nevada
Detroit, MI 48234
313-366-8400
Retail garden centers.

Fuqua Industries, Inc.
4900 Georgia-Pacific Center
Atlanta, GA 30303
404-658-9000
Lawn care and garden products, and other products.

General Host Corp.
22 Gate House Rd., Box 10045
Stamford, CT 06904
203-357-9900
Retailer of nursery products and crafts.

Hunter-Melnor Inc.
(Subsidiary of L M Acquisition, Inc.)
2500 Frisco Ave
Memphis, TN 38114
901-743-1360
Lawn and garden accessories, and other products.

Scotts Co.
1411 Scottslawn Rd.
Marysville, OH 43041
513-644-0011
Garden and lawn products.

Sunbelt Nursery Group Inc.
(Subsidiary of Pier 1 Imports, Inc.)
6500 W. Frwy.
Fort Worth, TX 76116
817-738-8111
Nurseries and retail garden supply stores.

FEDERAL GOVERNMENT

U.S. International Trade Administration
Department of Commerce
14th St. and Constitution Ave., N.W.
Washington, DC 20230
202-377-2000
Ask for the Commodity Analyst who is an expert in garden and lawn equipment.

U.S. International Trade Commission
500 E St., S.W.
Washington, DC 20436
202-205-2000 Office of the Secretary
202-205-3296 Industries locator
Ask for the Trade Analyst who is an expert in garden and lawn equipment.

GASOLINE INDUSTRY

See also: GARAGES AND SERVICE STATIONS and PETROLEUM INDUSTRY

ASSOCIATIONS

American Petroleum Institute
1220 L St. N.W.
Washington, DC 20005
202-682-8000
202-682-8030 Fax
Charles DiBona, President
Members refine and market the full range of petroleum products, including gasoline. Provides information on technical and industry subjects.

Mid-Continent Oil and Gas Association
1919 Pennsylvania Ave. N.W., Ste. 503
Washington, DC 20006
202-785-3515
Stephen Ward, Vice President
Members include oil and gas producers, refiners, gasoline manufacturers, and others in the industry.

Society of Independent Gasoline Marketers of America
Reston Town Center
11911 Freedom Dr., 1 Fountain Square
Reston, VA 22090-5603
703-709-7000
Kenneth Doyle, Executive Vice President
Represents marketers of private brand gasoline.

PERIODICALS

Independent Gasoline Marketing
Society of Independent Gasoline Marketers of America
11911 Freedom Dr., No. 590
Reston, VA 22090-5602
703-709-7000
Angela Angerosa, Editor
Reports about legislation and other topics that affect the gasoline industry.

COMPANIES

Amerada Hess Corp.
1185 Ave. of the Americas
New York, NY 10036
212-997-8500
Refines and markets numerous petroleum products, including gasoline.

Ashland Oil, Inc.
P.O. Box 391
Ashland, KY 41114
606-329-3333
Refines and markets numerous petroleum products, including gasoline.

Chevron Corp.
225 Bush St.
San Francisco, CA 94104
415-894-7700
Refines and markets numerous petroleum products, including gasoline.

Cumberland Farms, Inc.
777 Dedham St.
Canton, MA 02021
617-828-4900
Retailer of milk, other dairy products, and gasoline.

Diamond Shamrock Inc.
P.O. Box 696000
San Antonio, TX 78269
512-641-6800
Refiner and retailer of gasoline and other products.

Getty Petroleum Corp.
125 Jericho Tpke.
Jericho, NY 11753
516-338-6000
Gasoline and other petroleum products.

Rip Griffin Truck/Travel Center, Inc.
P.O. Box 10128
Lubbock, TX 79408
806-795-8785
Gasoline service stations.

Phillips Petroleum Co.
6A1 Phillips Bldg.
Bartlesville, OK 74004
918-661-8710
Refines and markets numerous petroleum products, including gasoline.

Racetrac Petroleum, Inc.
300 Technology Ct.
Smyrna, GA 30082
404-431-7600
Retailer of gasoline.

Roadway Motor Plazas, Inc.
760 Brooks Ave.
Rochester, NY 14619
716-235-3615
Gasoline service stations.

Tenneco Oil Co.
(Subsidiary of Tenneco Corp.)
P. O. Box 2511
Houston, TX 77001
713-757-2131
Refines and markets numerous petroleum products, including gasoline.

Truckstops of America
200 Public Sq.
Cleveland, OH 44114
216-586-4141
Gasoline service stations.

FEDERAL GOVERNMENT

U.S. International Trade Administration
Department of Commerce
14th St. and Constitution Ave., N.W.
Washington, DC 20230
202-377-2000
Ask for the Commodity Analyst who is an expert in the gasoline industry.

U.S. International Trade Commission
500 E St., S.W.
Washington, DC 20436
202-205-2000 Office of the Secretary
202-205-3296 Industries locator
Ask for the Trade Analyst who is an expert in the gasoline industry.

GEM INDUSTRY

See also: JEWELRY INDUSTRY

ASSOCIATIONS

Accredited Gemologists Association
915 Lootens
San Rafael, CA 94901
415-454-8553
Dance Richardson, Executive Officer
Offers training to gemologists.

American Gem and Mineral Suppliers Association
PO Box 741
Patton, CA 92369
714-885-3918
Renata Williams, Executive Secretary
Members include manufacturers, distributors, and retailers of gems, minerals, and related supplies.

American Gem Society
5901 W. Third St.
Los Angeles, CA 90036
213-936-4367
213-936-9629 Fax
Thomas Dorman, Executive Director
Helps retail jewelry firms though its educational and promotional programs.

American Gem Trade Association
181 World Trade Center
PO Box 581043
Dallas, TX 75258
214-742-GEMS
800-972-1162
214-742-7334 Fax
Peggy Willett, Executive Director
Manufacturers and retail jewelers who supply colored gemstones.

Gemological Institute of America
1660 Stewart St.
Santa Monica, CA 90404
213-829-2991
800-421-7250
213-828-0247 Fax
Bill Boyajian, President
Offers a wide range of educational and gem testing services.

PERIODICALS

Diamond Insight
Tryon Mercantile Inc.
790 Madison Ave., Ste. 602
New York, NY 10021
212-772-1286
Guido Giovannini-Torelli, Editor
Profiles major diamonds, their prices, and diamond industry news.

Gems & Gemology
Gemological Institute of America
1660 Stewart St.
Santa Monica, CA 90404
213-829-2991
Alice Keller, Editor
Offers business and technological news about gems.

Jewelry Appraiser
National Association of Jewelry Appraisers
4210 N. Brown Ave., No. A
Scottsdale, AZ 85251
602-941-8088
Richard Baron, Editor
Advises on how to value jewels and gems.

National Jeweler
Gralla Publications
1515 Broadway
New York, NY 10036
212-869-1300
Lynn Diamond, Editor
Follows news and trends in the gem and jewelry industry.

Rock & Gem
Miller Magazines, Inc.
2660 E. Main St.
Ventura, CA 93003-2888
805-643-3664
W.R.C. Shedenhelm, Editor
Written for amateur rockhounds and mineral hobbiests.

LIBRARIES

Gemological Institute of America
Library
1660 Stewart St.
Santa Monica, CA 90404
213-829-2991
800-421-7250
213-828-0247 Fax
Bill Boyajian, President
The full range of gemological topics.

Lizzadro Museum of Lapidary Art
Library
220 Cottage Hill Ave.
Elmhurst, IL 60126
708-833-1616
Gemology, lapidary, mineralogy, jewelry, and geology.

U.S. Geological Survey
Library System
12201 Sunrise Valley Dr.
National Center, Mail Stop 950
Reston, VA 22092
703-648-4302
Minerology, geology, gems, and other topics.

COMPANIES

Empire Diamond Corp.
350 5th Ave.
New York, NY 10001
212-564-4777
Diamonds and gems.

Gem East Corp.
2124 2nd Ave.
Seattle, WA 98121
206-441-1700
Diamonds and gems.

Grieger's Inc.
900 S. Arroyo Pkwy.
Pasadena, CA 91109
818-795-9775
Gems and tools for hobbiests.

Lazare Kaplan International Inc.
529 Fifth Ave.
New York, NY 10017
212-972-9700
Cutting and polishing of diamonds.

Michael Anthony Jewelers Inc.
70 S. MacQursted Pkwy.
Mount Vernon, NY 10550
914-699-9840
Jewelry, diamonds, and precious gems.

Pan American Diamond Corp.
71 Fifth Ave.
New York, NY 10003
212-929-3100
Cut diamonds and diamond jewelry.

Zale Corp.
(Subsidiary of Peoples Jewellers Ltd.)
901 W. Walnut Hill Lane
Irving, TX 75038
214-580-4000
Retail jewelry stores and wholesaler of diamonds.

FEDERAL GOVERNMENT

Bureau of Mines
810 7th St., N.W.
Washington, DC 20747
202-501-9770
Ask for Commodity Specialist who is an expert in the gem industry.

U.S. International Trade Administration
Department of Commerce
14th St. and Constitution Ave., N.W.
Washington, DC 20230
202-377-2000
Ask for the Commodity Analyst who is an expert in the gem industry.

U.S. International Trade Commission
500 E St., S.W.
Washington, DC 20436
202-205-2000 Office of the Secretary
202-205-3296 Industries locator
Ask for the Trade Analyst who is an expert in the gem industry.

GEORGIA

STATE OFFICE LOCATOR (*for referrals to all state government offices*)

404-656-2000

ARCHIVES AND RECORDS

Archives & History Department
330 Capitol Avenue, S.E.
Atlanta, GA 30334
404-656-2358

ATTORNEY GENERAL

Law Department
132 State Judicial Building
Atlanta, GA 30334
404-656-4585

BANKING

Banking & Finance Department
2990 Brandywine Road
Ste. 200
Atlanta, GA 30341
404-986-1633

COMMERCE

Industry, Trade & Tourism Department
P.O. Box 1776
Atlanta, GA 30301
404-656-3556

CONSUMER AFFAIRS

Consumer Affairs
State Capitol
Room 203
Atlanta, GA 30334
404-656-1760

EDUCATION

Education Department
Twin Towers East
205 Butler Street, S.E.
Room 2066
Atlanta, GA 30334
404-656-2800

ENERGY

Energy Resources Division
270 Washington Street, S.W.
Room 611
Atlanta, GA 30334
404-656-5176

ENVIRONMENTAL AFFAIRS

Natural Resources Department
205 Butler Street, S.E.
Ste. 1252
Atlanta, GA 30334
404-656-3500

HEALTH

Public Health Division
47 Trinity Avenue, S.W.
Atlanta, GA 30334-1202
404-894-7505

HOUSING

Residential Finance Authority
60 Executive Parkway, S.
Ste. 250
Atlanta, GA 30334
404-679-4840

INSURANCE

Insurance Department
716 West Tower
2 Martin Luther King, Jr. Drive
Atlanta, GA 30334
404-656-2056

LABOR

Labor Department
148 International Boulevard
Atlanta, GA 30303
404-656-3011

LEGISLATION

State Legislature
State Capitol
Room 316
Atlanta, GA 30334
404-656-5000

LIBRARY SERVICES

Public Library Services Division
Twin Towers East
205 Butler Street, S.E.
Room 2066
Atlanta, GA 30334
404-656-2461

LICENSING—CORPORATE

Secretary of State
State Capitol
Room 214
Atlanta, GA 30334
404-656-2881

LICENSING—PROFESSIONAL AND OCCUPATIONAL

Professional Examining Boards
166 Pryor Street, S.W.
Atlanta, GA 30303
404-656-3900

MOTOR VEHICLES

Motor Vehicle Division
270 Washington Street, S.W.
Atlanta, GA 30334
404-656-4156

OCCUPATIONAL HEALTH AND SAFETY

Division of Public Health
878 Peachtree Street, N.E.
Ste. 100
Atlanta, GA 30309
404-894-6644

OMBUDSMAN

Consumer Affairs
State Capitol
Room 203
Atlanta, GA 30334
404-656-1760

PUBLIC UTILITIES

Public Service Commission
244 Washington Street, S.W.
Atlanta, GA 30334
404-656-4512

PURCHASING

Purchasing Division
Piedmont Avenue
Atlanta, GA 30334
404-656-3240

REAL ESTATE

Real Estate Commission
40 Pryor Street, S.W.
Atlanta, GA 30303-3184
404-656-3916

SECURITIES

Secretary of State
State Capitol
Room 214
Atlanta, GA 30334
404-656-2881

TAXATION AND REVENUE

Revenue Department
270 Washington Street, S.W.
Atlanta, GA 30334
404-656-4015

TOURISM

Tourist Division
Box 1776
Atlanta, GA 30301
404-656-3590
800-847-4842

TRANSPORTATION

Transportation & Certification
Enforcement & Safety Division
1007 Virginia Avenue
Hapeville, GA 30354
404-559-6600

UNEMPLOYMENT

Unemployment Insurance Division
148 International Boulevard
Atlanta, GA 30303
404-656-3050

WORKER'S COMPENSATION

Workers Compensation Board
1000 South Tower
1 CNN Center
Atlanta, GA 30303-2788
404-656-2034

GIFT INDUSTRY

See also: TABLEWARE INDUSTRY

ASSOCIATIONS

China, Glass and Giftware Association
1115 Clifton Ave.
Clifton, NJ 07013
201-779-1600
201-779-3242 Fax
Donald Doctorow, Executive Secretary
*Manufacturers and wholesalers of tableware
and other gift items.*

Gift Association of America
PO Box 147
Royersford, PA 19468
215-948-3832
215-948-4277 Fax
Jennifer DeCock, Managing Director
*Represents manufacturers, distributors, and
retailers of gifts such as china and decorative
items.*

PERIODICALS

Gift & Stationery Business
Gralla Publications
1515 Broadway
New York, NY 10036
212-869-1300
Joyce Washnick, Editor
*Reports on new products and industry trends
for retailers of gifts and stationery.*

Gift Basket Review
Festivities Publications, Inc.
1205 W. Forsyth St.
Jacksonville, FL 32204
904-634-1902
Recommends new designs for gift baskets.

Gift Digest
Market Place Publications
170 World Trade Mart
Dallas, TX 75258
214-747-4274
Misty Smailer, Editor
*Industry news and new-product evaluations
for retailers of gifts.*

Gifts & Decorative Accessories
Geyer-McAllister Publications, Inc.
51 Madison Ave.
New York, NY 10010
212-689-4411
Phyllis Sweed, Editor
News for manufacturers and retailers of gifts, gourmet products, home accessories, greeting cards, and social stationery.

Giftware News
Talcott Communications Corp.
1414 Merchandise Mart
Chicago, IL 60654
312-670-0800
Anthony Demasi, Editor
For store buyers who purchase gifts, china and glass, fine stationery, and home accessories.

Souvenirs and Novelties
Kane Communications, Inc.
7000 Terminal Square, Ste. 210
Upper Darby, PA 19082
215-734-2420
Sandy Meskow, Editor
For manufacturers and retailers of souvenirs, novelties, and gifts.

COMPANIES

American Greetings Corp.
10500 American Rd.
Cleveland, OH 44144
216-252-7300
Greeting cards, gift wrappings, and gifts.

Claire's Stores Inc.
6095 N.W. 167th St.
Miami, FL 33014
305-558-2577
Retailer of gifts.

Cracker Barrel Old Country Store, Inc.
Hartman Dr., Box 787
Lebanon, TN 37088
615-444-5533
Retailer of gifts, gasoline, and also restaurant food.

Duty Free International Inc.
19 Catoonah St.
Ridgefield, CT 06877
203-431-6057
Retail gift and duty free shops.

Host International, Inc.
(Subsidiary of Marriott Corp.)
One Marriott Dr.
Washington, DC 20058
202-380-3677
Restaurants, airport facilities, gift shops, and other businesses.

Lancaster Colony Corp.
37 W. Broad St.
Columbus, OH 43215
614-224-7141
Gift glassware and other products.

Munford, Inc.
497 Semoran Blvd.
Casselberry, FL 32707
407-331-4300
Gift shops, arts and crafts stores, and other businesses.

Papercraft Corp.
(Subsidiary of Amalgamated Investment
    Corp.)
Papercraft Park
Pittsburgh, PA 15238
412-362-8000
Gift wrappings and other products.

Russ Berrie & Co., Inc.
111 Bauer Dr.
Oakland, NJ 07436
201-337-9000
Gifts such as stuffed animals, mugs, and figurines.

Spencer Gifts, Inc.
(Subsidiary of MCA Inc.)
1050 Black Horse Pike
Pleasantville, NJ 08232
609-645-3300
Retail gift stores.

Swank, Inc.
6 Hazel St.
Attleboro, MA 02703
508-222-3400
Retailers of jewelry, leather items, and gifts.

FEDERAL GOVERNMENT

U.S. International Trade Administration
Department of Commerce
14th St. and Constitution Ave., N.W.
Washington, DC 20230
202-377-2000
Ask for the Commodity Analyst who is an expert in giftware.

U.S. International Trade Commission
500 E St., S.W.
Washington, DC 20436
202-205-2000 Office of the Secretary
202-205-3296 Industries locator
Ask for the Trade Analyst who is an expert in giftware.

GLASS AND GLASS PRODUCTS

See also: TABLEWARE INDUSTRY

ASSOCIATIONS

Flat Glass Marketing Association
White Lakes Professional Bldg.
3310 Harrison
Topeka, KS 66611
913-266-7013
William Birch, Executive Vice President
Distributors and retailers of plate and window glass. Provides technical and industry information. Affiliated with the Glass Tempering Association at the same address.

National Glass Association
8200 Greensboro Dr., Ste. 302
McLean, VA 22102
703-442-4890
703-442-0603 Fax
Philip James, Chief Executive
Members manufacture, distribute, and install glass of all kinds, including flat, automotive, architectural, and other types of glass. Offers market and technical information.

Society for Glass Science and Practices
PO Box 166
Clarksburg, WV 26301
412-225-4400
Paul Pakula, Secretary
Members share information on making glass by hand rather than machine.

PERIODICALS

Auto and Flat Glass Journal
Grawin Publications, Inc.
303 Harvard E., No. 101
Seattle, WA 98102
206-322-5120
Burton Winters, Editor
Provides retailers of flat and automobile glass with product and business news, and technical advice for glass installation.

Glass Digest
Ashlee Publishing Co., Inc.
310 Madison Ave.
New York, NY 10017
212-682-7681
Charles Cumpston, Editor
For executives in the flat glass and architectural glass industry.

US Glass, Metal & Glazing
US Glass Publications, Inc.
560 Oakwood Ave., Ste. 202
Lake Forest, IL 60045-1906
708-295-2900
John Lawo, Editor
News for manufacturers, distributors, and retailers of flat glass and other products.

LIBRARIES

Corning Inc.
Technical Information Center
Sullivan Park
Corning, NY 14831
607-974-3359
607-962-6067 Fax
Glass technology, physics, ceramics, and related topics.

Pittsburgh Corning Corp.
Technical Library
800 Presque Isle Dr.
Pittsburgh, PA 15239
412-327-6100
412-733-4815 Fax
Glass, physics, ceramics, and materials engineering.

PPG Industries, Inc.
Glass Research Center
Information Services
Box 11472
Pittsburgh, PA 15238
412-665-8566
412-665-8512 Fax
Glass technology and engineering.

COMPANIES

AFG Industries, Inc.
301 Commerce St.
Fort Worth, TX 76102
817-332-5006
Flat glass.

Anchor Glass Container Corp.
4343 Anchor Plaza Pkwy.
Tampa, FL 33634
813-884-0000
Many kinds of glass products.

Apogee Enterprises, Inc.
7900 Xerxes Ave., S.
Minneapolis, MN 55431
612-835-1874
Automobile and flat glass, and other specialty glass products.

Beals Royal Glass and Mirror
5353 S. Valley View
Las Vegas, NV 89118
702-735-8788
Many kinds of glass.

Binswanger Glass Co.
(Subsidiary of ACI International Limited)
965 Ridge Lake Blvd.
Memphis, TN 38119
901-767-7111
Mirrors, auto glass, and other types of glass.

Corning Glass Works/Corning Engineering
Houghton Park
Corning, NY 14831
607-974-9000
Glass of all kinds.

Kerr Glass Mfg. Corp.
1840 Century Park E.
Los Angeles, CA 90067
213-556-2200
Glass containers.

Lancaster Colony Corp.
37 W. Broad St.
Columbus, OH 43215
614-224-7141
Glass tubes, table glassware, and other glass products.

SDI Operating Partners L. P.
One Logan Sq.
Philadelphia, PA 19103
215-665-3650
Glass products and other businesses.

Tempglass, Inc.
291 M St.
Perrysburg, OH 43551
419-666-2000
Glass products.

FEDERAL GOVERNMENT

U.S. Customs Service
Department of the Treasury
U.S. Customshouse
6 World Trade Center
New York, NY 10048
212-466-5550
Ask for the Commodity Specialist in charge of glass and glass products.

U.S. International Trade Administration
Department of Commerce
14th St. and Constitution Ave., N.W.
Washington, DC 20230
202-377-2000
Ask for the Commodity Analyst who is an expert in glass and the glass products industry.

U.S. International Trade Commission
500 E St., S.W.
Washington, DC 20436
202-205-2000 Office of the Secretary
202-205-3296 Industries locator
Ask for the Trade Analyst who is an expert in glass and the glass products industry.

U.S. Patent and Trademark Office
Crystal Plaza 2
2011 Jefferson Davis Highway
Arlington, VA 22202
703-305-8000
Ask for the Examining Group Director who is a specialist in glass and glass products.

GRAPHIC ARTS INDUSTRY

See also: COMPUTER GRAPHICS and PRINTING
AND PRINTING EQUIPMENT INDUSTRIES

ASSOCIATIONS

American Institute of Graphic Arts
1059 Third Ave.
New York, NY 10021
212-752-0813
800-548-1634
212-755-6749 Fax
Caroline Hightower, Executive Director
A professional society for designers, illustrators, art directors, and others in the graphic arts field.

Graphic Artists Guild
11 W. 20th St., 8th Fl.
New York, NY 10011
212-463-7730
Paul Basista, Executive Director
Designers, illustrators, cartoonists, and other graphic artists. Offers a variety of services to members.

Graphic Arts Marketing Information Service
1730 N. Lynn St.
Arlington, VA 22209
703-841-8179
703-841-8178 Fax
Jacqueline Bland, Managing Director
Printing firms, printing equipment manufacturers, and suppliers to the printing trade that share marketing information.

Graphic Arts Suppliers Association
c/o Jennifer S. Cochran
1900 Arch St.
Philadelphia, PA 19103
215-564-3484
215-564-2175 Fax
Jennifer Cochran, Executive Director
Helps manufacturers and dealers of graphic arts supplies to manage and market their businesses more effectively.

Graphic Arts Technical Foundation
4615 Forbes Ave.
Pittsburgh, PA 15213
412-621-6941
412-621-3049 Fax
John Burgess, Executive Director
Offers technical and educational information regarding graphic processes. Performs research and quality control tests.

Research and Engineering Council of the
Graphic Arts Industry
PO Box 639
Chadds Ford, PA 19317
215-388-7394
215-388-2708 Fax
Fred Rogers, Managing Director
Sets standards and coordinates research for printing companies, manufacturers, and others in the graphic arts.

National Graphic Arts Dealers Association
116 W. Ottawa St., Ste. 600
Lansing, MI 48933-1602
517-372-4440
517-487-3830 Fax
Maureen Miller, Executive Director
Independent retailers of graphic arts supplies and printing equipment.

PERIODICALS

Advertising & Graphic Arts Techniques
Advertising Trade Publications, Inc.
10 E. 39th St., 6th Fl.
New York, NY 10016
212-889-6500
Dan Barron, Editor
Technical and how-to information for graphic artists, mainly those working in advertising.

Art Direction
Advertising Trade Publications, Inc.
10 E. 39th St., 6th Fl.
New York, NY 10016
212-889-6500
Don Barron, Editor
Provides business and practical information to advertising art directors, photograpers, and others in the industry.

Dealer Communicator
Fichera Publications
777 S. State Rd. 7
Margate, FL 33068
800-327-8999
Reports on new products for graphic arts suppliers and dealers.

Graphic Arts Monthly
Cahners Publishing Co.
249 W. 17th St.
New York, NY 10011
212-463-6834
Rodger Ynostroza, Editor
Management and production advice for those in the printing industries.

Graphic Arts Product News
Maclean Hunter Publishing Co.
29 N. Wacker Dr.
Chicago, IL 60606
312-726-2802
Jill Roth, Editor
Reports on new trends and products for printers and others in the graphic arts field.

LIBRARIES

ANPA
Technical Research Department
Library
The Newspaper Center
Box 17407
Dulles International Airport
Washington, DC 20041
703-648-1000
703-620-4557 Fax
Printing, ink, and paper.

Graphic Arts Technical Foundation
E.H. Wadewitz Memorial Library
4615 Forbes Ave.
Pittsburgh, PA 15213
412-621-6941
412-621-3049 Fax
Graphic design, desktop publishing, printing processes, paper, and photography.

Graphic Communications World
Library
P.O. Box 727
Hartsdale, NY 10530-0727
914-472-3051
904-656-7506 Fax
Graphic communication and printing technology.

COMPANIES

Appleton Papers Inc.
(Subsidiary of Wiggins Teape Appleton p.l.c.)
825 E. Wisconsin Ave.
Appleton, WI 54912
414-734-9841
Paper and graphic arts supplies.

H. S. Crocker Co., Inc.
321 Allenton Ave.
San Francisco, CA 94080
415-872-8300
Graphic arts and lithography services.

Esselte Business Systems Inc.
(Subsidiary of Esselte AB)
71 Clinton Rd.
Garden City, NY 11530
516-741-3200
Office supplies and graphic arts supplies.

Phillips & Jacobs, Inc.
(Subsidiary of Tasty Baking Co.)
Fox St. & Roberts Ave.
Philadelphia, PA 19129
215-221-8800
Graphic arts equipment and supplies.

Polychrome Corp.
(Subsidiary of DIC Americas, Inc.)
137 Alexander St., Box 817
Yonkers, NY 10702
914-965-8800
Graphic arts and printing equipment and supplies.

Royal Zenith Corp.
(Subsidiary of Dyson-Kissner-Moran Corp.)
222 Community Dr.
Great Neck, NY 11021
516-466-3900
Importer of graphic arts machinery.

Stendig Industries Inc.
Five Daniel Road E.
Fairfield, NJ 07006
201-227-6500
Graphic arts supplies and other businesses.

Techtron
Two N. Riverside Plaza
Chicago, IL 60606
312-876-0533
Graphic arts servives.

Young-Phillips Sales Co.
3250 Healy Dr.
Winston-Salem, NC 27108
919-768-0110
Wholesaler of photographic and graphic arts supplies.

FEDERAL GOVERNMENT

U.S. International Trade Administration
Department of Commerce
14th St. and Constitution Ave., N.W.
Washington, DC 20230
202-377-2000
Ask for the Commodity Analyst who is an expert in graphic arts products and services.

U.S. International Trade Commission
500 E St., S.W.
Washington, DC 20436
202-205-2000 Office of the Secretary
202-205-3296 Industries locator
Ask for the Trade Analyst who is an expert in graphic arts products and services.

GREETING CARD INDUSTRY

See also: GIFT INDUSTRY

ASSOCIATIONS

Greeting Card Association
1350 New York Ave. N.W., Ste. 615
Washington, DC 20005
202-393-1778
202-393-0336 Fax
Marianne McDermott, Executive Vice President
Members publish greeting cards and supply materials to publishers.

PERIODICALS

Gifts & Decorative Accessories
Geyer-McAllister Publications, Inc.
51 Madison Ave.
New York, NY 10010
212-689-4411
Phyllis Sweed, Editor
News for retailers and others who sell gifts, home accessories, greeting cards, and fine stationery.

Party and Paper Retailer
4Ward Corp.
500 Summer St., Ste. 300
Stamford, CT 06901
203-964-0900
Nancy Paoli, Editor
News for retailers of party supplies, gift wrap, and greeting cards.

LIBRARIES

Hallmark Cards, Inc.
Creative Research Library
25th & McGee
Kansas City, MO 64108
816-274-5525
Graphic art, design, illustration, and lettering.

COMPANIES

American Greetings Corp.
10500 American Rd.
Cleveland, OH 44144
216-252-7300
Greeting cards, gift wrap, and other products.

Artistic Greetings Inc.
409 William St.
Elmira, NY 14901
607-733-5541
Greeting cards and stationery sold by mail order.

Burgoyne, Inc.
2030 E. Byberry Rd.
Philadelphia, PA 19116
215-677-8000
Greeting cards and stationery.

Current, Inc.
(Subsidiary of Deluxe Corp.)
P.O. Box 2559
Colorado Springs, CO 80901
719-594-4100
Greeting and note cards, stationery, gift wrap, and other products.

Gibson Greetings Inc.
2100 Section Rd.
Cincinnati, OH 45237
513-841-6600
Greeting cards and gift wrap.

Hallmark Cards Inc.
2501 McGee Trafficway, Box 419580
Kansas City, MO 64141
816-274-5111
Greeting cards and related products.

Leanin Tree Inc.
P. O. Box 9500
Boulder, CO 80301
303-530-1442
Greeting cards and stationery.

P V A—EPVA, Inc.
Stoney Brook Dr.
Wilton, NH 03086
603-654-6141
Greeting cards.

FEDERAL GOVERNMENT

U.S. International Trade Administration
Department of Commerce
14th St. and Constitution Ave., N.W.
Washington, DC 20230
202-377-2000
Ask for the Commodity Analyst who is an expert in the greeting card industry.

U.S. International Trade Commission
500 E St., S.W.
Washington, DC 20436
202-205-2000 Office of the Secretary
202-205-3296 Industries locator
Ask for the Trade Analyst who is an expert in the greeting card industry.

GROCERY BUSINESS

See also: FOOD INDUSTRY; FRUIT AND VEGETABLE INDUSTRY; and SUPERMARKETS AND CONVENIENCE STORES

ASSOCIATIONS

Grocery Manufacturers of America
1010 Wisconsin Ave., N.W., Ste. 800
Washington, DC 20007
202-337-9400
202-337-4508 Fax
C. Manly Molpus, President
Manufacturers of food and other products sold by grocers.

National-American Wholesale Grocers' Association
201 Park Washington Ct.
Falls Church, VA 22046
703-532-9400
703-538-4673 Fax
John Block, President
Provides wholesale grocers with information and education on management techniques, warehouse operations, food transport, and related topics.

National Grocers Association
1825 Samuel Morse Dr.
Reston, VA 22090
703-437-5300
703-437-7768 Fax
Thomas Zaucha, President
A large group of food distributors and retailers. Offers educational programs designed to improve efficiency within the industry.

PERIODICALS

Food People
Associated Grocers Inc.
Box 3763
Seattle, WA 98124
206-764-7585
Robb Zerr, Editor
Follows industry trends, new products, and technology.

Grocery Marketing
Ryan Mathews, Editor
Gorman Publishing Co.
8750 W. Bryn Mawr Ave.
Chicago, IL 60631
312-693-3200
Richard Mulville, Editor
Industry news for grocers and food distributors.

Marketing Grocery Products
American Institute of Food Distribution, Inc.
28-12 Broadway
Fair Lawn, NJ 07410
201-791-5570
Frank Panyko, Editor
Covers the business of food brokering, distribution, and sales.

Modern Grocer
Grocers Publishing Co., Inc.
15 Emerald St.
Hackensack, NJ 07601
201-488-1800
Howard Ackerman, Editor
News and advice for grocers.

Progressive Grocer
Progressive Grocer Co.
4 Stamford Forum
Stamford, CT 06901
203-325-3500
Michael Sansolo, Editor
Written for executives and managers of supermarkets.

LIBRARIES

National Association of Convenience Stores
NACS Information Center
1605 King St.
Alexandria, VA 22314-2792
703-684-3600
703-836-4564 Fax
Convenience stores, food service and marketing, and retail trade.

Safeway, Inc.
Library
201 4th St.
Oakland, CA 94660
510-891-3236
Retail food chains, food, and the grocery business.

COMPANIES

Associated Wholesale Grocers, Inc.
5000 Kansas Ave
Kansas City, KS 66106
913-321-1313
Wholesale grocers.

Giant Food Inc.
P.O. Box 1804
Washington, DC 20013
301-341-4100
Retail grocery chain.

Great Atlantic & Pacific Tea Co., Inc.
(Subsidiary of Tengelmann Warenhandels-
   gellschaft)
2 Paragon Dr., Box 418
Montvale, NJ 07645
201-573-9700
Retail grocery chain.

McLane Co., Inc.
P.O. Box 6115
Temple, TX 76503
817-778-7500
Grocery distribution.

National Convenience Stores Inc.
100 Waugh Dr.
Houston, TX 77007
713-863-2200
Retail grocery chain.

P&C Food Markets, Inc.
(Subsidiary of Penn Traffic Co.)
P.O. Box 4965
Syracuse, NY 13221
315-457-9460
Retail and wholesale groceries.

Riser Foods Inc.
5300 Richmond Rd.
Bedford Heights, OH 44146
216-292-7000
Grocery distributor.

Super Food Services, Inc.
3233 Newmark Dr.
Miamisburg, OH 45342
513-439-7500
Wholesale grocery.

Winn-Dixie Stores, Inc.
5050 Edgewood Ct.
Jacksonville, FL 32203
904-783-5000
Retail grocery chain.

West Coast Grocery Co.
(Subsidiary of Super Valu Stores, Inc.)
1525 E. D St.
Tacoma, WA 98401
206-593-3200
Wholesaler of groceries.

HARDWARE AND LOCKSMITH INDUSTRY

See also: HOME IMPROVEMENT AND DO-IT-YOURSELF INDUSTRY

ASSOCIATIONS

American Hardware Manufacturers Association
931 N. Plum Grove Rd.
Schaumburg, IL 60173
708-605-1025
708-605-1093 Fax
William Farrell, President
Members make all kinds of products sold through hardware wholesalers.

American Ladder Institute
401 N. Michigan Ave.
Chicago, IL 60611
312-644-6610
Dan Brady, Executivve Director
Firms that make ladders of all kinds.

Associated Locksmiths of America
3003 Live Oak St.
Dallas, TX 75204
214-827-1701
William Mathisen
Offers training programs and research services to retail locksmiths.

Builders' Hardware Manufacturers Association
355 Lexington Ave., 17th Fl.
New York, NY 10017
212-661-4261
212-370-9047 Fax
Mark Holland, Executive Director
Members manufacture builders' hardware such as latches, cabinet hardware, door hinges, and locks.

Door and Hardware Institute
7711 Old Springhouse Rd.
McLean, VA 22102
703-556-3990
703-356-3533 Fax
Richard Hornaday, Executive Vice President
Wholesalers of builders' hardware such as latches, cabinat hardware, door hinges, and locks.

National Locksmith Suppliers Association
1900 Arch St.
Philadelphia, PA 19103
215-564-3484
Patricia Lilly, Executive Director
Firms that distribute supplies for locksmiths.

National Retail Hardware Association
5822 W. 74th St.
Indianapolis, IN 46278
317-290-0338
317-290-0378 Fax
Hal Marsotais, Managing Director
A large group of hardware retailers that conducts market research and offers educational programs.

National Wholesale Hardware Association
1900 Arch St.
Philadelphia, PA 19103
Wholesalers of hardware supplies.

PERIODICALS

Chilton's Hardware Age
Chilton Co.
Chilton Way
Radnor, PA 19089
215-964-4275
News and product information for hardware and do-it-yourself retailers.

Hardware Trade
Master Publications, Inc.
2965 Broadmoor Valley Rd., Ste. B
Colorado Springs, CO 80906
719-576-5277
Edward Gonzales, Editor
Marketing and merchandising advice for hardware distributors and retailers.

Keynotes
Associated Locksmiths of America, Inc.
3003 Live Oak St.
Dallas, TX 75204
214-827-1701
Margaret Hons, Editor
News of the locksmithing industry.

Locksmith Ledger International
Locksmith Publishing Corp.
850 Busse Hwy.
Park Ridge, IL 60068-5980
708-692-5940
William Reed, Editor
Follows new products and technologies for locksmiths who sell physical and electronic security devices.

COMPANIES

Cotter & Co.
2740 N. Clybourn Ave.
Chicago, IL 60614
312-975-2700
Manufactures and distributes hardware and variety items.

Hardware Wholesalers, Inc.
P. O. Box 868
Fort Wayne, IN 46801
219-749-8531
Wholesaler of hardware and building materials.

Lowe's Companies, Inc.
P.O. Box 1111
North Wilkesboro, NC 28656
919-651-4000
Wholesaler and retailer of hardware and building materials.

Masco Corp.
21001 Van Born Rd.
Taylor, MI 48180
313-274-7400
Locks, hardware, and home improvement products.

Payless Cashways, Inc.
2300 Main St., Box 419466
Kansas City, MO 64141
816-234-6000
Retail chain of hardware, lumber, and building materials.

Price Co.
P.O. Box 85466
San Diego, CA 92138
619-581-4600
Retailer of numerous products, including hardware.

Servistar Corp.
P.O. Box 1510
Butler, PA 16003
412-283-4567
Wholesaler of hardware and building materials.

Stanley Works
1000 Stanley Dr.
New Britain, CT 06053
203-225-5111
Hardware and tools.

FEDERAL GOVERNMENT

U.S. International Trade Administration
Department of Commerce
14th St. and Constitution Ave., N.W.
Washington, DC 20230
202-377-2000
*Ask for the Commodity Analyst who is an
expert in the hardware industry.*

U.S. International Trade Commission
500 E St., S.W.
Washington, DC 20436
202-205-2000 Office of the Secretary
202-205-3296 Industries locator
*Ask for the Trade Analyst who is an expert in
the hardware industry.*

U.S. Patent and Trademark Office
Crystal Plaza 2
2011 Jefferson Davis Highway
Arlington, VA 22202
703-305-8000
*Ask for the Examining Group Director who is
a specialist in hardware.*

HAWAII

STATE OFFICE LOCATOR (*for referrals to all state government offices*)

808-548-2211

ARCHIVES AND RECORDS

Archives Division
Iolani Palace Grounds
Honolulu, HI 96813
808-548-2355

ATTORNEY GENERAL

Attorney General's Office
425 S. Beretania Street
Room 405
Honolulu, HI 96813
808-548-4740

BANKING

Financial Institutions Division
P.O. Box 2054
Honolulu, HI 96805
808-586-2820

COMMERCE

Commerce & Consumer Affairs Department
P.O. Box 541
Honolulu, HI 96809
808-586-2850

CONSUMER AFFAIRS

Consumer Protection Division
250 S. King Street
Room 520
Honolulu, HI 96813
808-586-2630

EDUCATION

Education Department
P.O. Box 2360
Honolulu, HI 96804
808-586-3310

ENERGY

Energy Division
335 Merchant Street
Room 110
Honolulu, HI 96813
808-548-4150

ENVIRONMENTAL AFFAIRS

Environmental Quality Control Office
550 Halekauwila Street
Room 301
Honolulu, HI 96813
808-548-6915

HEALTH

Health Department
P.O. Box 3378
Honolulu, HI 96801
808-548-6505

HOUSING

Human Services Department
P.O. Box 339
Honolulu, HI 96809
808-548-6260

INSURANCE

Insurance Division
P.O. Box 3614
Honolulu, HI 96811
808-546-2799

LABOR

Labor & Industrial Relations Department
830 Punchbowl Street
Honolulu, HI 96813
808-548-3150

LEGISLATION

Legislative Reference Bureau
State Capitol
415 S. Beretania Street
Honolulu, HI 96813
808-548-6237

LIBRARY SERVICES

Library Services Division
P.O. Box 2360
Honolulu, HI 96804
808-548-5596

LICENSING—CORPORATE

Business Registration Division
P.O. Box 40
Honolulu, HI 96810
808-586-2744

LICENSING—PROFESSIONAL AND OCCUPATIONAL

Professional & Vocational Licensing Division
P.O. Box 3469
Honolulu, HI 96801
808-586-2690

OCCUPATIONAL HEALTH AND SAFETY

Occupational Safety & Health Division
677 Ala Moana Boulevard
Ste. 910
Honolulu, HI 96813
808-548-4155

OMBUDSMAN

Ombudsman's Office
465 S. King Street
4th Floor
Honolulu, HI 96813
808-548-7811

PUBLIC UTILITIES

Public Utilities Commission
455 S. King Street
1st Floor
Honolulu, HI 96813
808-548-3990

PURCHASING

Purchasing & Supply
Kalanimoku Building
Box 119
Honolulu, HI 96810
808-548-4057

REAL ESTATE

Real Estate Commission
1010 Richards Street
Honolulu, HI 96813
808-548-7464

SECURITIES

Business Registration Division
P.O. Box 40
Honolulu, HI 96810
808-586-2744

TAXATION AND REVENUE

Taxation Department
P.O. Box 259
Honolulu, HI 96809
808-548-7650

TOURISM

Visitors Bureau
Waikiki Business Plaza
Ste. 801
2270 Kalakaua Avenue
Honolulu, HI 96815
808-923-1811

TRANSPORTATION

Transportation Department
869 Punchbowl Street
Honolulu, HI 96813
808-548-3205

UNEMPLOYMENT

Unemployment Insurance Research Bureau
830 Punchbowl Street
Honolulu, HI 96813
808-548-4064

WORKER'S COMPENSATION

Labor & Industrial Relations Department
830 Punchbowl Street
Honolulu, HI 96813
808-548-5414

HEALTH CARE INDUSTRY

See also: HOSPITALS; MEDICAL AND HOSPITAL EQUIPMENT INDUSTRY; NURSING HOMES; and each of the 50 states under health and occupational health and safety

GENERAL

Associations

Academy for Health Services Marketing
c/o American Marketing Association
250 S. Wacker Dr., Ste. 200
Chicago, IL 60606
312-648-0536
Carla Windhorst, Executive Director
*Executives from hospitals and health mainte-
nance organizations who share information on
the marketing of health care.*

American Medical Association
See under Physicians (below)

Distributors Association
225 Reinekers Ln., No. 650
Alexandria, VA 22314
703-549-4432
703-549-6495 Fax
James Stover, President
*Firms that distribute medical, surgical, home
health care, and related products. Offers education in management, sales, and other topics.*

Health Industry Manufacturers Association
1030 15th St. N.W., Ste. 1100
Washington, DC 20005
202-452-8240
Alan Magazine, President
*Companies that make medical equipment and
supplies of all types.*

National Association of Medical Equipment
    Suppliers
625 Slaters Ln., Ste. 200
Alexandria, VA 22314
703-836-6263
703-836-6730 Fax
Thomas Antone, President
*Firms that supply medical equipment and
oxygen.*

National Mental Health Association
1021 Prince St.
Alexandria, VA 22314
703-684-7722
Preston Garrison, Executive Director
*A large consumer group that promotes mental
health treatment and research.*

Periodicals

Healthcare Information Management
Healthcare Information and Management
   Systems Society
840 N. Lake Shore Dr.
Chicago, IL 60657
312-280-6148
Bonnie Million, Editor
Covers computers and other tools that auto-mate the handling of health-related informa-tion.

Health Care Marketer
United Communications Group
4550 Montgomery Ave., Ste. 700-N
Bethesda, MD 20814
301-961-8777
Lorraine Coffey, Editor
Outlines marketing plans for health care providers.

Health Care Strategic Management
Business Word
770 N. La Salle St., Ste. 701
Chicago, IL 60610-3541
800-521-7210
Donald Johnson, Editor
Offers advice on planning, marketing, and allocation of resources.

Health Marketing Quarterly
Haworth Press, Inc.
10 Alice St.
Binghamton, NY 13904
800-342-9678
William Winston, Editor
Provides detailed analysis of marketing for group practices, nursing homes, and other health care organizations.

Healthcare Community Relations & Market-ing Letter
Health Resources Publishing
Brinley Professional Plaza, 3100 Hwy. 138
Wall Township, NJ 07719
908-681-1133
Robert Jenkins, Editor
Contains news and advice for public relations and marketing executives at health care orga-nizations.

Medical Products Sales
Health Industry Distributors Association
McKnight Medical Communications Co.
1419 Lake Cook Rd.
Deerfield, IL 60015
708-949-0345
Bill Briggs, Editor
Written for manufacturers and marketers of medical products.

Libraries

New York Academy of Medicine
Library
2 E. 103rd St.
New York, NY 10029
212-876-8200
212-722-7650 Fax
Health sciences and medicine.

Quorum Health Resources
Corporate Information Center
1 Park Plaza
Box 24347
Nashville, TN 37203
615-340-5852
615-340-5895 Fax
Health care industry, hospital management, and health care marketing.

U.S. National Library of Medicine
8600 Rockville Pike
Bethesda, MD 20894
301-496-6308
301-496-4450 Fax
Public health, medicine, health sciences, and nursing.

HOME HEALTH CARE

Associations

American Rental Association
1900 19th St.
Moline, IL 61265
309-764-2475
800-334-2177
James Irish, Executive Vice President
Renters of medical equipment and many other types of products.

National Association for Home Care
519 C St. N.E.
Washington, DC 20002
202-547-7424
202-547-3540 Fax
Val Halamandaris, President
Members provide home health care and related services. Conducts industry research offers educational programs.

Periodicals

Home Health Care Dealer
Curant Communications, Inc.
1849 Sawtelle Blvd., Ste. 770
Los Angeles, CA 90025
213-479-1769
Follows trends and offers marketing advice for dealers of home health care products.

Home Health Care Services Quarterly
Haworth Press, Inc.
10 Alice St.
Binghamton, NY 13904
800-342-9678
Brahna Trager, Editor
Detailed articles concerning policy and organizational issues concerning the home health care industry.

Companies

Baxter International Inc.
One Baxter Pkwy.
Deerfield, IL 60015
708-948-2000
A wide range of medical products including home dialysis units.

Clinical Homecare Ltd.
45 Kulick Rd.
Fairfield, NJ 07004
201-227-0222
Home health care services.

Diversicare Corp. of America
105 Reynolds Dr., Box 1675
Franklin, TN 37065
615-794-3313
Nursing and home health care services.

Geer Drug Co.
(Division of Alco Health Services Corp.)
P.O. Box V
Charleston, SC 29402
803-723-2541
Wholesaler of pharmaceuticals, medical supplies, and home health care products.

Healthdyne Inc.
1850 Parkway Pl.
Marietta, GA 30067
404-423-4500
Home care products and services.

Lifetime Corp.
75 State St.
Boston, MA 02109
617-330-5080
Home health care services.

National Healthcorp L.P.
100 Vine St.
Murfreesboro, TN 37130
615-890-2020
Nursing homes and home health care services.

Sci-O-Tech, Co.
(Subsidiary of McKesson Corp.)
501 Richardson Dr.
Lancaster, PA 17603
717-397-0308
Home health care products.

Syracuse Supply Co.
5921 Court St. Rd.
Syracuse, NY 13221
315-463-9511
Home health care products and other businesses.

HEALTH MAINTENANCE ORGANIZATIONS AND PREFERRED PROVIDER ORGANIZATIONS

Associations

American Association of Preferred Provider
    Organizations
111 E. Wacker Dr., Ste. 600
Chicago, IL 60601
312-644-6610
312-565-4658 Fax
Jacqueline Berkelhamer, Executive Officer
Preferred provider organizations and individuals associated with the PPO industry. A PPO is a health provider that negotiates health care with a client organization in advance.

American Managed Care and Review Association
1227 25th St. N.W., No. 610
Washington, DC 20037
202-728-0506
202-728-0609 Fax
Charles Stellar, Executive Vice President
Members include health maintenance organizations, preferred provider organizations, and other groups offering managed health care.

Group Health Association of America
1129 20th St. N.W., Ste. 600
Washington, DC 20036
202-778-3200
202-331-7487 Fax
James Doherty, President
Members include health maintenance organizations and other group medical practices that take prepayment.

Periodicals

Employer's Guide Purchasing Managed
    Health Care Services
National Association of Employers on Health
    Care Action
Blue Book, Inc.
Box 220
Key Biscayne, FL 33149
305-361-2810
Advice for employers who purchase group health care.

Executive Report on Managed Care
American Business Publishing
3100 Hwy. 138
Box 1442
Wall Township, NJ 07719-1442
908-681-1133
Ruth Stack, Editor
Describes the experiences large firms are having with a variety of managed care programs. Offers advice on how to choose and control health care.

Managed Care Outlook
Capitol Publications, Inc.
1101 King St., Ste. 444
Alexandria, VA 22314
703-683-4100
Russ Jackson, Editor
*Follows business, legal, and government news
that affects the managed care industry.*

P P O Letter
Business Information Services, Inc.
12811 N. Point Lane
Laurel, MD 20708
301-792-0927
James Gutman, Editor
*News of interest to preferred provider organi-
zations and their clients.*

H M O Practice
J.B. Lippincott Co.
E. Washington Sq.
Philadelphia, PA 19105
215-238-4200
Leonard Katz, Editor
*Covers innovations and issues that interest the
executives and physicians who work for health
maintenance organizations.*

Libraries

Group Health Association of America, Inc.
Gertrude Sturges Memorial Library
1129 20th St., N.W.
Washington, DC 20036
202-778-3200
202-331-7487 Fax
*Health maintenance organizations, health
administration, and medical economics.*

Kaiser Foundation Hospitals
Center for Health Research Library
4610 S.E. Belmont St.
Portland, OR 97215
503-233-5631
503-233-4328 Fax
*Health maintenance organizations, health care
utilization, and group practice.*

PHYSICIANS

Associations

American Medical Association
515 N. State St.
Chicago, IL 60610
312-464-5000
312-645-4184 Fax
James Todd, Executive Vice President
*A huge organization representing a vast
majority of the physicians in the U.S. Offers
many enducational services, and publishes
many journals.*

National Association of VA Physicians
3400 International Dr. N.W.,
Washington, DC 20008
202-363-3838
Paul Schafer, Executive Director
*Physicians who work at Veterans Administra-
tion hospitals.*

Periodicals

Medical Economics
Medical Economics Co. Inc.
680 Kinderkamack Rd.
Oradell, NJ 07649
201-262-3030
Don Berg, Editor
*Advises physicians on how to manage their
medical practices and personal finances.*

Physician's Management
Edgell Communications
7500 Old Oak Blvd.
Cleveland, OH 44130
216-826-2839
Bob Feigenbaum, Editor
Suggests ways to improve the management of medical practices.

U S Medicine
U S Medicine, Inc.
2033 M St., N.W., Ste. 505
Washington, DC 20036
202-463-6000
Nancy Tomich, Editor
Follows news and reports on management techniques that help physicians.

Libraries

American Medical Association
515 N. State St.
Chicago, IL 60610
312-464-5000
312-645-4184 Fax
James Todd, Executive Vice President
Medical and health industry topics.

FEDERAL GOVERNMENT

National Institutes of Health
9000 Rockville Pike
Bethesda, MD 20892
301-496-4000
Ask for the public affairs office to find an appropriate expert.

U.S. Centers for Disease Control
1600 Disease Control
1600 Clifton Rd., N.E.
Atlanta, GA 30333
404-639-3311
Ask for the National Institute for Occupational Safety and Health.

U.S. Department of Health and Human Services
200 Independence Ave., S.W.
Washington, DC 20201
202-619-0257
Ask for the Health Care Financing Administration.

U.S. Department of Labor
200 Constitution Ave., N.W.
Washington, DC 20210
202-523-6666
Ask for the Occupational Safety and Health Administration.

HEALTH FOOD INDUSTRY

See also: FOOD INDUSTRY and VITAMIN AND DIET INDUSTRY

ASSOCIATIONS

Committee for Sustainable Agriculture
PO Box 1300
Colfax, CA 95713
916-346-2777
916-346-6884 Fax
Otis Wollen, Executive Director
Members include natural food farmers, distributors, and retailers, and also researchers who study organic foods.

Natural Product Broker Association
4720 Lincoln Blvd., Ste. 331
Marina Del Rey, CA 90292
213-827-8771
Karen Kahan, Secretary
Works to convince natural food manufacturers and distributors to use food brokers.

Organic Crop Improvement Association
3185 Township Rd. 179
Bellefontaine, OH 43311
513-592-4983
513-592-4983 Fax
Betty Kananen, Director
Organic farmers and retailers who share information on quality control and other topics.

Organic Foods Production Association of
  North America
PO Box 1078
Greenfield, MA 01301
507-452-6332
Frederick Kircashmann, President
Growers, wholesalers, and retailers of organic foods who work to increase productivity and standards.

PERIODICALS

Health Foods Business
Howmark Publishing Corp.
567 Morris Ave.
Elizabeth, NJ 07208
908-353-7373
Ging Geslewitz, Editor
Offers news and product descriptions to retailers of health and natural foods.

Specialty Food Merchandising
Tarter Communications, Inc.
29 Park Ave.
Manhasset, NY 11030
516-365-9088
Saul Tarter, Editor
Helps distributors and retailers of ethnic, natural, and other specialty foods run their businesses more effectively.

Whole Foods
W F C, Inc.
3000 Hadley Rd.
S. Plainfield, NJ 07080
908-769-1160
Daniel McSweenney, Editor
*Follows industry trends for producers, distrib-
utors, and retailers of health foods.*

COMPANIES

Atlantic Group Inc.
10 W. Adams St.
Jacksonville, FL 32202
904-359-3075
Retailer of health foods and natural foods.

Ener-G Foods Inc.
5960-1st Ave. S., Box 84487
Seattle, WA 98124
206-767-6660
Health foods and baking mixes.

IVCI Corp.
P.O. Box 810004
Boca Raton, FL 33481
407-750-9691
Health foods.

MEI Diversified Inc.
90 S. Sixth St.
Minneapolis, MN 55402
612-339-8853
Snacks, candy, and health foods.

Nutritional Enterprises, Inc.
1019 Grand Blvd.
Deer Park, NY 11729
516-242-6222
Health foods and dietary supplements.

Tree of Life, Inc.
(Subsidiary of Wessanen)
1750 Tree Blvd., Box 410
St. Augustine, FL 32086
904-824-8181
Manufacturer and wholesaler of natural foods.

Vestro Foods Inc.
13 Corporate Plaza
Newport Beach, CA 92660
714-760-0354
Natural foods and desserts.

FEDERAL GOVERNMENT

U.S. Department of Agriculture
14th St. and Independence Ave., S.W.
Washington, DC 20250
202-720-8732
*Ask for the public affairs office to find an
appropriate expert in the health food industry.*

U.S. International Trade Administration
Department of Commerce
14th St. and Constitution Ave., N.W.
Washington, DC 20230
202-377-2000
*Ask for the Commodity Analyst who is an
expert in the health food industry.*

U.S. International Trade Commission
500 E St., S.W.
Washington, DC 20436
202-205-2000 Office of the Secretary
202-205-3296 Industries locator
*Ask for the Trade Analyst who is an expert in
the health food industry.*

HOBBY INDUSTRY

See also: COLLECTIBLES and TOY INDUSTRY

ASSOCIATIONS

American Craft Council
72 Spring St.
New York, NY 10012
212-274-0630
212-274-0650 Fax
Lois Moran, Executive Director
Professional crafts people, designers, architects and others concerned with ceramic, wood, glass, and other crafts.

Association of Crafts and Creative Industries
1100-H Brandywine Blvd.
PO Box 2188
Zanesville, OH 43702
614-452-4541
614-452-2552 Fax
Walter Offinger, President
Manufacturers, distributors, and retailers of hobby and crafts supplies.

Hobby Industry Association of America
319 E. 54th St.
Elmwood Park, NJ 07407
201-794-1133
201-797-0657 Fax
Patricia Koziol, Executive Director
Manufacturers, distributors, and retailers of hobby and crafts supplies. Sponsors a national trade show and educational seminars.

PERIODICALS

Hobby Merchandiser
Hobby Publications, Inc.
225 Gordons Corner Plaza
Box 420
Manalapan, NJ 07726
201-446-4900
Andrew Hecht, Editor
Management and merchandising advice for hobby distributors and retailers.

Playthings
Geyer-McAllister Publications, Inc.
51 Madison Ave.
New York, NY 10010
212-689-4411
Frank Reysen, Editor
Reports on new hobby products, toys, and industry trends.

Toy & Hobby World
463 Seventh Ave., Ste. 202
New York, NY 10018
212-594-4237
Larry Carlat, Editor
Informs those who buy toys and hobby products for stores about new products and promotions by manufacturers.

COMPANIES

America's Hobby Center, Inc.
146-148 West 22nd St.
New York, NY 10011
212-675-8922
Retailer of models and hobby items.

Felix V. Bass & Co., Inc.
611 Delsea Dr.
Westville, NJ 08093
609-848-8800
Wholesaler of hobby and crafts supplies.

M.W. Kasch Co.
5401 W. Donges Bay Rd.
Mequon, WI 53092
414-242-5000
*Wholesaler of toys, hobby needs, and school
supplies.*

Michaels Stores, Inc.
5931 Campus Circle Dr.
Irving, TX 75063
214-580-8242
Retailer of hobby, arts, and crafts supplies.

Model Rectifier Corp.
200 Carter Dr.
Edison, NJ 08818
908-248-0730
Importer of hobby kits and supplies.

Monogram Models Inc.
8601 Waukegan Rd.
Morton Grove, IL 60053
312-966-3500
Hobby kits.

Testor Corp.
(Subsidiary of RPM Inc.)
620 Buckbee St.
Rockford, IL 61104
815-962-6654
Hobby products and kits.

Tiny Tots
199 U.S. Rt. 22
Green Brook, NJ 08812
908-752-7200
*Retailer of toys, hobby supplies, and other
juvenile products.*

Tri-Chem, Inc.
One Cape May St.
Harrison, NJ 07029
201-482-5500
Hobby products, decorative paints.

FEDERAL GOVERNMENT

Federal Trade Commission
Pennsylvania Ave. at 6th St., N.W.
Washington, DC 20580
202-326-2000
Ask for the Bureau of Consumer Protection.

U.S. International Trade Administration
Department of Commerce
14th St. and Constitution Ave., N.W.
Washington, DC 20230
202-377-2000
*Ask for the Commodity Analyst who is an
expert in a specific hobby product.*

U.S. International Trade Commission
500 E St., S.W.
Washington, DC 20436
202-205-2000 Office of the Secretary
202-205-3296 Industries locator
*Ask for the Trade Analyst who is an expert in a
specific hobby product.*

HOME IMPROVEMENT AND DO-IT-YOURSELF INDUSTRY

See also: HARDWARE AND LOCKSMITH INDUSTRY

ASSOCIATIONS

Home Improvement Research Institute
400 Knightsbridge Pkwy.
Lincolnshire, IL 60069
708-634-4368
708-634-4379 Fax
Judith Riggs, Executive Director
Firms that make, distribute, and sell products used by consumers who improve their homes themselves.

National Retail Hardware Association
5822 W. 74th St.
Indianapolis, IN 46278
317-290-0338
Hal Marsotais, Managing Director
A large association of hardware retailers.

National Supply Distributors Association
PO Box 31248
5134 Bower Ave.
Dayton, OH 45431
513-258-2424
800-922-8645
513-258-3112 Fax
Glenn Valentine, President
Firms that distribute hardware, building, and other supplies to do-it-yourself stores. Offers information and consulting services.

PERIODICALS

Building Supply Home Centers
Cahners Publishing Co.
1350 E. Touhy Ave.
Des Plaines, IL 60017
708-635-8800
Craig Shutt, Editor
Advises how building materials dealers can sell effectively to do-it-yourselfers as well as to professional builders.

Do-it-Yourself Retailing
National Retail Hardware Association
5822 W. 74th St.
Indianapolis, IN 46278
317-297-1190
Mark Parrott, Editor
Helps retailers of hardware, lumber, and home repair products market their stores more effectively.

Family Handyman
Home Service Publications, Inc.
7900 International Dr., Ste. 950
Minneapolis, MN 55425
612-854-3000
Gary Havens, Editor
How-to information for the do-it-yourself consumer.

Home Improvement Center
Vance Publishing Corp.
400 Knightsbridge Parkway
Lincolnshire, IL 60669
312-634-2600
Cori Dunn, Editor
Covers industry trends and new products for home improvement centers.

LIBRARIES

National Retail Hardware Association
Library
5822 W. 74th St.
Indianapolis, IN 46278
317-290-0338
Hardware and business topics.

COMPANIES

Automotive & Consumer Group
(Division of Loctite Corp.)
4450 Cranwood Ct.
Cleveland, OH 44128
216-475-3600
Do-it-yourself supplies for cars, homes, and boats.

Busy Beaver Building Centers, Inc.
701 Alpha Dr.
Pittsburgh, PA 15238
412-963-1980
Retailer of home improvement products.

Home Depot, Inc.
2727 Paces Ferry Rd.
Atlanta, GA 30339
404-433-8211
Retailer of home improvement products.

Leichtung Inc.
4944 Commerce Pkwy.
Cleveland, OH 44128
216-831-6191
Tools, do-it-yourself products, and housewares.

Masco Corp.
21001 Van Born Rd.
Taylor, MI 48180
313-274-7400
Home improvement products and hardware.

PNP Prime Corp.
(Subsidiary of PNP Holdings Corp.)
1209 S. Central Ave.
Kent, WA 98032
206-854-5450
Retailer of home improvement products.

Tapjac Home Centers
(Subsidiary of TAPJAC Co., Inc.)
221 W. 4th St.
Carthage, MO 64836
417-358-6081
Building materials and home improvement products.

Wickes Companies, Inc.
(Subsidiary of WCI Holdings Corp.)
3340 Ocean Park Blvd., Box 4056
Santa Monica, CA 90405
213-452-0161
Home improvement products, furnishings, and other businesses.

FEDERAL GOVERNMENT

Federal Trade Commission
Pennsylvania Ave. at 6th St., N.W.
Washington, DC 20580
202-326-2000
Ask for Marketing Practices in the Bureau of Consumer Protection.

U.S. International Trade Administration
Department of Commerce
14th St. and Constitution Ave., N.W.
Washington, DC 20230
202-377-2000
Ask for the Commodity Analyst who is an expert in the hardware industry.

U.S. International Trade Commission
500 E St., S.W.
Washington, DC 20436
202-205-2000 Office of the Secretary
202-205-3296 Industries locator
Ask for the Trade Analyst who is an expert in the hardware industry.

U.S. Patent and Trademark Office
Crystal Plaza 2
2011 Jefferson Davis Highway
Arlington, VA 22202
703-305-8000
Ask for the Examining Group Director who is a specialist in hardware.

HONEY INDUSTRY

ASSOCIATIONS

National Honey Packers and Dealers Association
5 Ravine Dr.
Matawan, NJ 07747
201-583-8188
201-583-0798 Fax
Richard Sullivan, Executive Vice President
Packers and dealers of honey.

American Honey Producers Association
Box 368
Bruce, SD 57220
405-352-4944
Richard Adey, President
Members are beekeepers, both hobbyists and commercial producers.

PERIODICALS

American Beekeeping Federation. Newsletter
American Beekeeping Federation, Inc.
Box 1038
Jesup, GA 31545
912-427-8447
Troy Fore, Editor
Reports on organizational activities and news of interest to commercial beekeepers.

Honey Market News
U.S. Agricultural Marketing Service
2015 South First St., Rm. 4
Yakima, WA 98903
509-575-2494
Technical and industry news.

COMPANIES

Dutch Gold Honey, Inc.
2220 Dutch Gold Dr.
Lancaster, PA 17601
717-393-1716
Honey producer.

Walter T. Kelley Co.
3107 Elizabeth Town Road
Clarkson, KY 42726
502-242-2012
Equipment used by the honey industry.

A. I. Root Co.
623 W. Liberty St.
Medina, OH 44256
216-725-6677
Beekeeping equipment.

Sioux Honey Association Co-op
509 Lewis Blvd.
Sioux City, IA 51106
712-258-0638
Packing and wholesaling of honey.

W. F. Straub & Co.
5520 Northwest Hwy.
Chicago, IL 60630
312-763-5520
Honey and molasses producer.

FEDERAL GOVERNMENT

U.S. Department of Agriculture
14th St. and Independence Ave., S.W.
Washington, DC 20250
202-720-8732
Ask for the Commodity Economics Division or the National Agricultural Statistics Service.

HOSPITALS

See also: HEALTH CARE INDUSTRY and NURSING HOMES

ASSOCIATIONS

American Hospital Association
840 N. Lake Shore Dr.
Chicago, IL 60611
312-280-6000
800-621-6712
312-280-5979 Fax
Carol McCarthy, President
A large association of executives, doctors, and others who work for hospitals and other health care institutions. It conducts research on many topics and sponsors educational programs.

American Society for Healthcare Human
    Resources Administration
c/o American Hospital Association
840 N. Lake Shore Dr.
Chicago, IL 60611
312-280-6434
800-621-6712
Beverly Rogers, Director
Offers health care administrators a forum to exchange information.

American Society for Hospital Materials Man-
    agement
c/o American Hospital Association
840 N. Lake Shore Dr.
Chicago, IL 60611
312-280-6137
312-280-4152 Fax
Terry Montgomery, Director
Members handle purchasing and distribution of materials for hospitals and other health care institutions.

Federation of American Health Systems
1405 N. Pierce, No. 311
Little Rock, AR 72207
501-661-9555
501-663-4903 Fax
Michael Bromberg, Executive Director
Members are for-profit hospitals. Provides information about investor-owned hospitals.

PERIODICALS

Hospital
5790 Eaglesridge Lane
Cincinnati, OH 45230
513-232-0511
Gregory Loomis, Editor
Covers new medical equipment and technologies.

Hospital & Health Services Administration
Foundation of the American College of
    Healthcare Executives
Health Administration Press
1021 E. Huron
Ann Arbor, MI 48104-9990
312-943-0544
Samuel Levey, Editor
Reports on news and innovations that concern executives at hospitals and other health care organizations.

Hospital News
H. Robert Jacobs Publishing Co., Inc.
2022 E. Allegheny Ave.
Philadelphia, PA 19134
215-739-2033
Marybeth Caracci, Editor
Discusses a wide range of issues that interest hospital administrators and physicians.

Hospital Practice
H P Publishing Co.
10 Astor Pl., 7th Fl.
New York, NY 10003-6903
212-477-2727
David Fisher, Editor
Offers medical and technological information to physicians practicing in a hospital setting.

Hospital Purchasing News
McKnight Medical Communications Co.
1419 Lake Cook
Deerfield, IL 60015
708-945-0345
Mark Thill, Editor
Product news and industry trends for buyers and managers of hospital supplies.

Hospitals
American Hospital Publishing, Inc.
211 E. Chicago Ave., Ste. 700
Chicago, IL 60611
312-440-6800
Maria Grayson, Editor
News for hospital and other health care executives.

LIBRARIES

American Hospital Association
Resource Center
840 N. Lake Shore Dr.
Chicago, IL 60611
312-280-6263
312-280-3061 Fax
Health care administration, financing, planning, medical administration, and related topics.

Hospital Association of New York (State)
Hospital Educational and Research Fund
Lillian R. Hayt Memorial Library
74 N. Pearl St.
Albany, NY 12207
518-434-7600
518-434-7812 Fax
Hospital administration, health economics, and management.

University of California, Berkeley
Public Health Library
42 Earl Warren Hall
Berkeley, CA 94720
510-642-2511
510-642-7623 Fax
Hospital administration, public health, environmental issues, and related subjects.

COMPANIES

American Medical International, Inc.
(Subsidiary of American Medical Holdings
    Inc.)
8201 Preston Rd.
Dallas, TX 75225
214-360-6300
Owns and operates hospitals.

Epic Healthcare Group Inc.
433 E. Las Colinas Blvd.
Irving, TX 75039
214-869-0707
Owns and operates hospitals.

Healthtrust Inc.
4525 Harding Rd.
Nashville, TN 37205
615-383-4444
Owns and operates hospitals.

Hospital Corp. of America
One Park Plaza
Nashville, TN 37202
615-327-9551
Owns and operates hospitals.

Humana Inc
500 W. Main St., Box 1438
Louisville, KY 40201
502-580-1000
Owns and operates hospitals.

Manor Healthcare Corp.
(Subsidiary of Manor Care, Inc.)
10770 Columbia Pike
Silver Spring, MD 20901
301-593-9600
Owns and operates nursing centers and hospitals.

National Medical Enterprises, Inc.
2700 Colorado Ave.
Santa Monica, CA 90404
213-315-8000
Owns and operates hospitals.

Paracelsus Healthcare Corp.
155 N. Lake Ave.
Pasadena, CA 91101
818-792-8600
Owns and operates hospitals.

Republic Health Corp.
15303 Dallas Pkwy.
Dallas, TX 75248
214-851-3100
Owns and operates hospitals, nursing homes, and substance abuse and psychiatric facilities.

Universal Health Services, Inc.
367 S. Gulph Rd.
King of Prussia, PA 19406
215-768-3300
Owns and operates hospitals.

FEDERAL GOVERNMENT

U.S. Department of Health and Human Services
200 Independence Ave., S.W.
Washington, DC 20201
202-619-0257
Ask for Facilities Compliance in the Health Resources and Services Administration.

U.S. International Trade Administration
Department of Commerce
14th St. and Constitution Ave., N.W.
Washington, DC 20230
202-377-2000
Ask for the Commodity Analyst who is an expert in hospitals.

U.S. International Trade Commission
500 E St., S.W.
Washington, DC 20436
202-205-2000 Office of the Secretary
202-205-3296 Industries locator
Ask for the Trade Analyst who is an expert in hospitals.

HOTEL AND MOTEL INDUSTRY

ASSOCIATIONS

American Hotel & Motel Association
1201 New York Ave. N.W., Ste. 600
Washington, DC 20005
202-289-3100
202-289-3199 Fax
Kenneth Hine, Executive Vice President
A large group of hotels and motels that provide public relations and promotional programs, management training, and research services.

Hotel Sales and Marketing Association International
1300 L St. N.W., Ste. 800
Washington, DC 20005
202-789-0089
202-789-1725 Fax
Leonard Hoyle, Executive Vice President
Owners, sales managers, and others concerned with the marketing of hotel services.

Preferred Hotels Association
1901 S. Meyers Rd., Ste. 220
Oakbrook Terrace, IL 60181
708-953-0404
800-323-7500
708-953-0176 Fax
Ronald Beaumont, President
Luxury hotels not affiliated with hotel chains. Offers marketing assistance and a reservations service to members.

Small Luxury Hotels Association
c/o Jayne Levant
337 S. Robertson Blvd., Ste. 202
Beverly Hills, CA 90211
213-659-5050
800-345-3457
817-685-9443 Fax
Jayne Levant, Executive Vice President
Helps promote independent luxury hotels with fewer than 200 rooms.

PERIODICALS

Hospitality Management
Delmont Communications, Inc.
1700 Livingston Ave.
St. Paul, MN 55118
612-457-2289
Joe Delmont, Editor
Ideas and advice for managers of hotels.

Hospitality Manager
Kassis Communications
120 Hayward
Ames, IA 50010
515-296-2400
Terry Lowman, Editor
Practical management advice for hotel managers and supervisors.

Hotel and Motel Management
Edgell Communications
7500 Old Oak Blvd.
Cleveland, OH 44130
216-826-2839
Robert Nozar, Editor
Covers new products, security techniques, and management strategies for executives of hotels, motels, and meeting facilities.

U S Lodging Industry
Laventhol & Horwath
1845 Walnut St.
Philadelphia, PA 19103
215-299-1600
An annual report on hotel and motel opera-
tions.

LIBRARIES

City College of San Francisco
Hotel and Restaurant Department
Alice Statler Library
50 Phelan Ave.
San Francisco, CA 94112
415-239-3460
Hotels, motels, tourism, and related topics.

Cornell University
School of Hotel Administration Library
Statler Hall
Ithaca, NY 14853-6901
607-255-3673
607-255-4179 Fax
Hotel and motel administration, public rela-
tions, tourist industry, and related subjects.

Hotel Sales and Marketing Association International
Sales Research Library
1300 L St., N.W., Ste. 800
Washington, DC 20005
202-789-0089
Sales promotion, merchandising, direct mail,
marketing, advertising, and public relations of
hotels.

COMPANIES

Caesars World, Inc.
1801 Century Park East
Los Angeles, CA 90067
213-552-2711
Resort hotels and casinos.

Carlson Hospitality Group Inc.
(Subsidiary of Carlson Companies, Inc.)
Carlson Pkwy., Box 59159
Minneapolis, MN 55459
612-540-5526
Owns and operates hotels and resorts.

Hilton Hotels Corp.
9336 Civic Center Dr.
Beverly Hills, CA 90209
213-278-4321
Owns and operates hotels.

Holiday Corp.
(Subsidiary of Bass PLC)
1023 Cherry Rd.
Memphis, TN 38117
901-762-8600
Owns and operates hotels, casinos, and restau-
rants.

Host International, Inc.
(Subsidiary of Marriott Corp.)
One Marriott Dr.
Washington, DC 20058
202-380-3677
Owns and operates restaurants, shops, and
hotels, primarily at airports.

ITT Sheraton Corp.
(Subsidiary of ITT Corp.)
60 State St.
Boston, MA 02109
617-367-3600
Owns and operates hotels, inns, and resorts.

Loews Corp.
667 Madison Ave.
New York, NY 10021
212-545-2000
Owns and operates hotels, movie theaters, and
other businesses.

Marriott Corp.
10400 Fernwood Rd.
Bethesda, MD 20817
301-380-9000
Owns and operates hotels and food service businesses.

Stouffer Hotel Co.
(Division of Nestle Enterprises, Inc.)
29800 Bainbridge
Solon, OH 44139
216-248-3600
Owns and operates hotels.

FEDERAL GOVERNMENT

U.S. International Trade Administration
Department of Commerce
14th St. and Constitution Ave., N.W.
Washington, DC 20230
202-377-2000
Ask for the Commodity Analyst who is an expert in hotels and hotel equipment.

U.S. International Trade Commission
500 E St., S.W.
Washington, DC 20436
202-205-2000 Office of the Secretary
202-205-3296 Industries locator
Ask for the Trade Analyst who is an expert in hotels and hotel equipment.

ICE CREAM INDUSTRY

ASSOCIATIONS

International Ice Cream Association
888 16th St. N.W.
Washington, DC 20006
202-296-4250
202-331-7820 Fax
E. Linwood Tipton, President
Offers market research, training, and public relations for ice cream manufacturers.

National Ice Cream Mix Association
5610 Crawfordsville Rd., Ste. 1104
Indianapolis, IN 46224
317-243-9342
Peter Holm, Exec.Dir.
Soft-serve ice cream and dessert mix manufacturers.

National Ice Cream and Yogurt Retailers
    Association
1429 King Ave., Ste. 210
Columbus, OH 43212
614-486-1444
614-486-0694 Fax
Don Buckley, Executive Director
Owners of ice cream stores and the manufacturers who supply them.

PERIODICALS

National Dipper
U S Exposition Corp.
1850 Oak St.
Northfield, IL 60093
708-446-8434
Lynda Utterback, Editor
Reports on new products and trends for ice cream store owners.

LIBRARIES

Borden Inc.
Gail Borden Research Centre
Library
1 Gail Borden Dr.
Syracuse, NY 13204
315-477-0218
315-477-0203 Fax
Ice cream and many other foods.

COMPANIES

Ambrit Inc.
(Subsidiary of Clabir Corp.)
10101 9th St. N.
St. Petersburg, FL 33716
813-576-8424
Ice cream bars and frozen novelties.

Baskin-Robbins USA Co.
P.O. Box 1200
Glendale, CA 91209
818-956-0031
Ice cream.

Ben & Jerry's Homemade Inc.
Rte. 100, Box 240
Waterbury, VT 05676
802-244-5641
Ice cream producer and ice cream parlor franchises.

Borden, Inc.
277 Park Ave.
New York, NY 10172
212-573-4000
Ice cream and other products.

Carvel Corp.
201 Saw Mill River Rd.
Yonkers, NY 10701
914-476-6200
Retail ice cream stores.

Clabir Corp
5400 118th Ave., N.
Clearwater, FL 34620
813-572-7088
Ice cream and popsicles.

Dreyer's Grand Ice Cream, Inc.
5929 College Ave.
Oakland, CA 94618
415-652-8187
Ice cream products.

Friendly Ice Cream Corp.
1855 Boston Rd.
Wilbraham, MA 01095
413-534-2400
Ice cream manufacturing and chain of ice cream restaurants.

Gold Bond Ice Cream Inc.
(Subsidiary of Thomas J. Lipton, Inc.)
909 Packerland St.
Green Bay, WI 54307
414-499-5151
Ice cream bars, sandwiches, and popsicles.

Häagen-Dazs Co., Inc.
Glen Pointe
Teaneck, NJ 07666
201-692-0900
World's best ice cream.

Stewart's Ice Cream Co., Inc.
P.O. Box 435
Saratoga Springs, NY 12866
518-584-8700
Ice cream producer and retailer.

FEDERAL GOVERNMENT

U.S. Department of Agriculture
14th St. and Independence Ave., S.W.
Washington, DC 20250
202-720-8732
Ask for the National Agricultural Statistics Service.

IDAHO

STATE OFFICE LOCATOR (*for referrals to all state government offices*)

208-334-2411

ARCHIVES AND RECORDS

Archives Office
325 W. State Street
Boise, ID 83702
208-334-3356

ATTORNEY GENERAL

Attorney General's Office
State House
Room 210
Boise, ID 83720
208-334-2400

BANKING

Finance Department
700 W. State Street
Boise, ID 83720
208-334-5159

COMMERCE

Commerce Department
700 W. State Street
Boise, ID 83720
208-334-2470

CONSUMER AFFAIRS

Attorney General
State House
Room 210
Boise, ID 83720
208-334-2400

EDUCATION

Education Department
Len B. Jordan Building
650 W. State Street
Boise, ID 83720
208-334-3300

ENERGY

Energy Resources Division
State House
Boise, ID 83720
208-327-7900

ENVIRONMENTAL AFFAIRS

Environment Division
450 W. State Street
Boise, ID 83720
208-334-5840

HEALTH

Preventive Medicine Bureau
450 W. State Street
Boise, ID 83720
208-334-5930

HOUSING

Building Division
State House
Boise, ID 83720
208-334-3896

HUMAN RIGHTS

Human Rights Commission
450 W. State Street
Boise, ID 83720
208-334-2873

INSURANCE

Insurance Department
500 S. 10th Street
Boise, ID 83720
208-334-2250

LABOR

Labor & Industrial Services Department
State House
Boise, ID 83720
208-334-3950

LEGISLATION

Legislative Unit
State Capitol Building
700 W. Jefferson Street
Boise, ID 83720
208-334-2475

LIBRARY SERVICES

State Library
325 W. State Street
Boise, ID 83702
208-334-5124

LICENSING—CORPORATE

Corporation Division
State House
Room 203
Boise, ID 83720
208-334-2300

LICENSING—PROFESSIONAL AND OCCUPATIONAL

Occupational Licenses Bureau
24417 Bank Drive
Room 312
Boise, ID 83705-2598
208-334-3233

MOTOR VEHICLES

Motor Vehicle Bureau
P.O. Box 7129
Boise, ID 83707
208-334-8606

OCCUPATIONAL HEALTH AND SAFETY

Labor & Industrial Services Department
State House Mall
Boise, ID 83720
208-334-3950

PUBLIC UTILITIES

Public Utilities Commission
State House
Boise, ID 83720
208-334-3427

PURCHASING

Purchasing Division
650 W. State Street
Room 100
Boise, ID 83720
208-327-7465

REAL ESTATE

Real Estate Commission
633 N. 4th Street
Boise, ID 83720
208-334-3285

SECURITIES

Securities Bureau
700 W. State Street
Boise, ID 83720
208-334-3684

TAXATION AND REVENUE

Revenue & Taxation Department
700 W. State Street
Boise, ID 83720
208-334-7500

TOURISM

Department of Commerce
Capitol Building
Room 108
Boise, ID 83720
208-334-2470
800-635-7820

TRANSPORTATION

Transportation Department
3311 W. State Street
Boise, ID 83707
208-334-8800

UNEMPLOYMENT

Unemployment Insurance Division
317 Main Street
Boise, ID 83735
208-334-6466

WORKER'S COMPENSATION

Industrial Commission
State House
Boise, ID 83720
208-334-6000

ILLINOIS

STATE OFFICE LOCATOR (*for referrals to all state government offices*)

217-782-2000

ARCHIVES AND RECORDS

Archives & Records Division
213 Capitol Building
Springfield, IL 62756
217-782-4682

ATTORNEY GENERAL

Attorney General's Office
500 S. 2nd Street
Springfield, IL 62706
217-782-1090

BANKING

Banks & Trust Companies
Reisch Building
117 S. 5th Street
Room 100
Springfield, IL 62701
217-782-7966

COMMERCE

Department of Commerce & Community
Affairs
620 E. Adams
Springfield, IL 62701
217-782-7500

CONSUMER AFFAIRS

Attorney General
500 S. 2nd Street
Springfield, IL 62706
217-782-1090

EDUCATION

Board of Education
100 N. 1st Street
Springfield, IL 62777
217-782-2221

ENERGY

Energy & Natural Resources Department
325 W. Adams Street
Room 300
Springfield, IL 62704
217-785-2800

ENVIRONMENTAL AFFAIRS

Environmental Protection Agency
P.O. Box 19276
Springfield, IL 62794
217-782-3397

HEALTH

Public Health Department
535 W. Jefferson Street
Springfield, IL 62761
217-782-4977

HOUSING

Housing & Community Development
620 E. Adams
Springfield, IL 62701
217-785-6154

HUMAN RIGHTS

Human Rights Department
100 W. Randolph Street
Ste. 10-100
Chicago, IL 60601
312-814-6245

INSURANCE

Insurance Department
320 W. Washington Street
4th Floor
Springfield, IL 62767
217-782-4515

LABOR

Labor Department
310 S. Michigan
10th Floor
Chicago, IL 60604
312-793-2800

LEGISLATION

Legislative Research Unit
222 S. College Street
3rd Floor, Ste. A
Springfield, IL 62704
217-782-6851

LIBRARY SERVICES

State Library Division
213 Capitol Building
Springfield, IL 62756
217-782-7845

LICENSING—CORPORATE

Business Services Division
213 Capitol Building
Springfield, IL 62756
217-785-3285

LICENSING—PROFESSIONAL AND OCCUPATIONAL

Professional Regulation Department
320 W. Washington Street
Springfield, IL 62786
217-785-0800

MOTOR VEHICLES

Motor Vehicle Service Division
213 Capitol Building
Springfield, IL 62756
217-785-3000

OMBUDSMAN

Consumer Service Office
100 W. Randolph Street
10th Floor
Chicago, IL 60601
312-814-4794

PUBLIC UTILITIES

Public Utilities Division
Commerce Commission
P.O. Box 19280
Springfield, IL 62794-9280
217-782-7295

PURCHASING

Support Services Bureau
715 William Stratton Building
Springfield, IL 62706
217-782-9349

REAL ESTATE

Real Estate Division
715 William Stratton Building
Springfield, IL 62706
217-782-5410

SECURITIES

Securities Division
213 Capitol Building
Springfield, IL 62756
217-782-2256

TAXATION AND REVENUE

Revenue Department
101 W. Jefferson
Springfield, IL 62708
217-785-2602

TOURISM

Office of Tourism
310 S. Michigan Avenue
Chicago, IL 60604
312-793-2094
800-545-7300
800-359-9299 (in Illinois)

TRANSPORTATION

Transportation Department
2300 S. Dirksen Parkway
Springfield, IL 62764
217-782-5597

UNEMPLOYMENT

Unemployment Insurance
401 S. State Street
Chicago, IL 60605
312-793-4240

WORKER'S COMPENSATION

Industrial Commission
100 W. Randolph Street
Ste. 8-272
Chicago, IL 60601
312-814-6555

IMMIGRATION AND EMIGRATION

ASSOCIATIONS

American Council on International Personnel
510 Madison Ave.
New York, NY 10022
212-688-2437
212-593-4697 Fax
Lucia A. Trovato, Exec.Dir.
Member firms supply immigration information to international corporations and others.

American Immigration Lawyers Association
1000 16th St. N.W., Ste. 604
Washington, DC 20036
202-331-0046
202-463-6325 Fax
Warren Leiden, Executive Director
Attorneys with a specialty in immigration law.

Association of Immigration Attorneys
401 Broadway, Ste. 1602
New York, NY 10013
212-226-3913
Peter Hirsch, Legal Counsel
Attorneys with a specialty in immigration law.

National Immigration Law Center
1636 W. Eighth St., Ste. 215
Los Angeles, CA 90017
213-487-2531
213-380-4319 Fax
Charles Wheeler, Executive Officer
An information center supporting immigrants' rights.

PERIODICALS

I and N Reporter
U.S. Immigration and Naturalization Service
425 I St. N.W.
Washington, DC 20536
202-724-7796
Janet Graham, Editor
Official news from the federal government about immigration.

Immigration and Nationality Law Review
Clark Boardman Co., Ltd.
435 Hudson St.
New York, NY 10014
212-929-7500
Maurice Roberts, Editor
News and legal analysis for immigration attorneys.

Immigration Briefings
Federal Publications, Inc.
1120 20th St., N.W., Ste. 500 S.
Washington, DC 20036
202-337-7000
Bruce Hake, Editor
An analysis of U.S. immigration and national-
ity law aimed at employers and others.

Immigration Policy & Law
Buraff Publications
1350 Connecticut Ave. N.W., Ste. 1000
Washington, DC 20036
202-862-0990
Corby Anderson, Editor
Covers the activities and regulations of the
U.S. government regarding immigration.

U S Immigration
Publishing & Business Consulting
951 S. Oxford, No. 109
Los Angeles, CA 90006
213-732-3477
Atia Napoleon, Editor
News and advice for those seeking green cards
and citizenship in the U.S.

FEDERAL GOVERNMENT

U.S. Department of Justice
Constitution Ave. and 10th St., N.W.
Washington, DC
202-514-2000
Ask for the Office of Immigration Review or
the Immigration and Naturalization Service.

IMPORT-EXPORT

ASSOCIATIONS

American Association of Exporters and
Importers
11 W. 42nd St.
New York, NY 10036
212-944-2230
212-382-2606 Fax
Eugene Milosh, President
Members include exporters, importers, for-
warders, customs brokers, and others who
serve the industry.

Association of Foreign Trade Representatives
PO Box 300
New York, NY 10024
212-877-8900
John McCabe, Executive Director
Members are foreign trade representatives in
the United States.

Committee for Small Business Exports
PO Box 6
Aspen, CO 81612
303-925-7567
Richard Fenton, President
Promotes the exports of small businesses.

Council for Export Trading Companies
1200 19 St. N.W., Ste. 605
Washington, DC 20036
202-861-4705
Ronald Wakeford, Executive Director
Helps companies export more competitively by
forming export trading companies, which are
exempt from certain antitrust laws and are
allowed to sell abroad.

International Trade Council
3144 Circle Hill Rd.
PO Box 2478
Alexandria, VA 22305
703-548-1234
703-548-6126 Fax
Peter Nelsen, President
A large group of import and export firms that conducts research, offers educational programs, and information on such topics as market conditions abroad, trade regulations, and transportation costs.

International Traders Association
c/o The Mellinger Co.
6100 Variel Ave.
Woodland Hills, CA 91367
818-884-4400
818-594-5804 Fax
Brainerd Mellinger, President
Members are international traders who promote their role in world commerce.

National Association of Export Companies
17 Battery Pl., Ste. 1425
New York, NY 10004
516-487-0700
Luke Ambrose, Director
Members are export companies that represent and distribute for U.S. corporations.

National Customs Brokers and Forwarders
    Association of America
1 World Trade Center, Ste. 1153
New York, NY 10048
212-432-0050
212-432-5709 Fax
John Hammon, Executive Vice President
Customs brokers, ocean freight forwarders, and air cargo agents who share industry information.

NCITD—The International Trade Facilitation
    Council
350 Broadway, Ste. 205
New York, NY 10013
212-925-1400
212-941-0371 Fax
Eugene Hemley, Executive Director
Helps importers, exporters, and the firms that service them to simplify the paperwork and procedures that accompany world trade.

World Export Processing Zones Association
PO Box 986
Flagstaff, AZ 86002
602-779-0052
602-774-8589 Fax
Richard Bolin, Director
Members are export processing zones (in which the local customs service allows inexpensive assembly and manufacture of goods made with imported parts).

PERIODICALS

Export
Hunter Publishing Limited Partnership
950 Lee St.
Des Plaines, IL 60016
708-296-0770
Jack Dobson, Editor
Written for distributors and dealers of consumer durables outside the U.S. and Canada.

Export Today
Trade Communications Inc.
733 15th St. N.W., Ste. 1100
Washington, DC 20005
202-737-1060
John Chewning, Editor
Practical information for executives at midsized U.S. firms that wish to increase their export sales.

Exporter
Trade Data Reports, Inc.
6 W. 37th St.
New York, NY 10018
212-563-2772
L. Stroh, Editor
*Practical information about the business of
exporting.*

Global Trade
North American Publishing Co.
401 N. Broad St.
Philadelphia, PA 19108
215-238-5300
Karen Theurman, Editor
*Written for executives responsible for import
and export transportation, finance, marketing,
and commercial services.*

U S Industrial Export Directory
Cahners Publishing Co.
8 Stamford Forum
Box 10277
Stamford, CT 06904-2277
203-328-2500
Anne Brickley, Editor
*A buyer's guide for foreigners who are inter-
ested in U.S. industrial products.*

LIBRARIES

American Association of Exporters and
 Importers
11 W. 42nd St.
New York, NY 10036
212-944-2230
212-382-2606 Fax
Eugene Milosh, President
Import/export, shipping, and related topics.

Business International
Information Center
215 Park Ave. S.
New York, NY 10003
212-460-0600
212-995-8837 Fax
*International trade, foreign investment,
finance, economics, and related topics.*

U.S. Court of International Trade
Law Library
One Federal Plaza
New York, NY 10007
212-264-2816
212-264-1085 Fax
International trade, customs, tariffs, and law.

U.S. Department of Commerce
Library
14th & Constitution Ave., N.W., Rm. 8060
Washington, DC 20230
202-377-3611
*Export-import, foreign trade, economics, busi-
ness, and related topics.*

U.S. International Trade Commission
National Library of International Trade
500 E St., S.W.
Washington, DC 20436
202-252-1630
*International trade, U.S. trade policy, tariffs,
and foreign trade statistics.*

FEDERAL GOVERNMENT

U.S. Customs Service
Department of the Treasury
U.S. Customshouse
6 World Trade Center
New York, NY 10048
212-466-5550
Ask for the public affairs office to find an appropriate expert.

U.S. International Trade Administration
Department of Commerce
14th St. and Constitution Ave., N.W.
Washington, DC 20230
202-377-2000
Ask for the analyst who is an expert in import programs.

INDIANA

STATE OFFICE LOCATOR (*for referrals to all state government offices*)

317-232-3140

ARCHIVES AND RECORDS

Public Records Commission
501 State Office Building
Indianapolis, IN 46204
317-232-3373

ATTORNEY GENERAL

Attorney General's Office
State House
Room 219
Indianapolis, IN 46204
317-232-6201

BANKING

Financial Institutions Department
1024 State Office Building
Indianapolis, IN 46204-2294
317-232-3955

COMMERCE

Commerce Department
1 N. Capitol Street
Ste. 700
Indianapolis, IN 46204-2248
317-232-8800

CONSUMER AFFAIRS

Consumer Protection Division
State House Building
Room 219
Indianapolis, IN 46204
317-232-6205

EDUCATION

Education Department
State House Building
Room 229
Indianapolis, IN 46204
317-232-6667

ENERGY

Energy Policy Division
1 N. Capitol Street
Ste. 700
Indianapolis, IN 46204-2248
317-232-8942

ENVIRONMENTAL AFFAIRS

Solid & Hazardous Waste Management
    Bureau
P.O. Box 6015
Indianapolis, IN 46206-6015
317-232-3210

HEALTH

Health Board
P.O. Box 1964
Indianapolis, IN 46206
317-633-8400

HOUSING

Housing Unit
P.O. Box 7802
Indianapolis, IN 46207
317-232-7045

HUMAN RIGHTS

Civil Rights Commission
32 E. Washington Street
Ste. 900
Indianapolis, IN 46204
317-232-2612

INSURANCE

Insurance Department
311 W. Washington Street
Ste. 300
Indianapolis, IN 46204
317-232-2385

LABOR

Labor Department
100 N. Senate Avenue
Room 1013
Indianapolis, IN 46204
317-232-2655

LEGISLATION

Legislative Services Agency
State House Building
Room 302
Indianapolis, IN 46204
317-232-9550

LIBRARY SERVICES

State Library
140 N. Senate Avenue
Indianapolis, IN 46204
317-232-3692

LICENSING—PROFESSIONAL AND OCCUPATIONAL

Professional Licensing Agency
1021 State Office Building
Indianapolis, IN 46204
317-232-3997

MOTOR VEHICLES

Motor Vehicles Bureau
401 State Office Building
Indianapolis, IN 46204
317-232-2800

OCCUPATIONAL HEALTH AND SAFETY

Industrial Hygiene & Radiological Health
    Division
1330 W. Michigan Street
Indianapolis, IN 46206
317-633-0692

OMBUDSMAN

Community Development Division
1 N. Capitol Street
Ste. 600
Indianapolis, IN 46204-2248
317-232-8926

PUBLIC UTILITIES

Utilities Division
913 State Office Building
Indianapolis, IN 46205
317-232-2737

PURCHASING

Procurement Division
508 State Office Building
Indianapolis, IN 46204
317-232-3032

REAL ESTATE

Professional Licensing Agency
1021 State Office Building
Indianapolis, IN 46204
317-232-3997

SECURITIES

Securities Division
State House Building
Room 201
Indianapolis, IN 46204
317-232-6690

TAXATION AND REVENUE

Revenue Department
202 State Office Building
Indianapolis, IN 46204
317-232-2101

TOURISM

Tourism Development Office
1 N. Capitol Street
Ste. 700
Indianapolis, IN 46225-2288
317-232-8860
800-W-WANDER

TRANSPORTATION

Transportation Department
100 N. Senate Avenue
Indianapolis, IN 46204
317-232-5526

UNEMPLOYMENT

Unemployment Insurance
10 N. Senate Avenue
Room 109
Indianapolis, IN 46204
317-232-7670

WORKER'S COMPENSATION

Workers Compensation Board
601 State Office Building
Indianapolis, IN 46204
317-232-3809

INDUSTRIAL COATINGS

See also: PAINT AND PAINTING INDUSTRY

ASSOCIATIONS

American Electroplaters and Surface Finishers Society
12644 Research Pkwy.
Orlando, FL 32826
407-281-6441
407-281-6446 Fax
J. Howard Schumacher, Executive Director
*Offers education and information services to
scientists and manufacturers who use electroplating and surface finishing.*

American Galvanizers Association
PO Box 80
Clarendon Hills, IL 60514
708-352-6884
800-535-0344
708-352-9335 Fax
Keith Windross, Vice President
*Firms apply coats of zinc to steel and iron
using a hot dip process.*

Association for Finishing Processes of Society
of Manufacturing Engineers
PO Box 930
1 SME Dr.
Dearborn, MI 48121
313-271-1500
313-271-2861 Fax
Eileen McGuire, Manager
*Engineers and others who share information
about all types of industrial finishes and coatings.*

Association of Industrial Metallizers, Coaters
and Laminators
2604 Pennington Dr.
Wilmington, DE 19810
302-475-7079
Robert Marsh, Executive Director
*Supplies technical and industry information to
metallizers, coaters, laminators, and suppliers
to the industry.*

Federation of Societies for Coatings Technology
1315 Walnut, Ste. 830
Philadelphia, PA 19107
215-545-1506
Robert Ziegler, Executive Vice President
*Engineers, technicians, and others who work
with coatings. Offers technical data.*

National Paint and Coatings Association
1500 Rhode Island Ave. N.W.
Washington, DC 20005
202-462-6272
James Doyle, Executive Director
*Firms that make paint, chemical coatings, and
associated equipment.*

Powder Coating Institute
1800 Diagonal Rd., Ste. 370
Alexandria, VA 22314
703-684-1770
Gregory Bocchi, Executive Director
*Members provide powder coating materials
and equipment used to coat and finish industrial goods.*

Society of Vacuum Coaters
440 Live Oak Loop
Albuquerque, NM 87122
505-298-7624
505-298-7942 Fax
Robert Gelber, Secretary
Individuals and companies that study and promote the vacuum coating process.

PERIODICALS

Advanced Coatings & Surface Technology
Technical Insights, Inc.
32 N. Dean St.
Englewood, NJ 07631
201-568-4744
Irv Schwartz, Editor
Reports on technological innovations in coatings used throughout industry.

C A Selects. Corrosion-Inhibiting Coatings
Chemical Abstracts Service
2540 Olentangy River Rd.
Box 3012
Columbus, OH 43210
614-447-3600
Technical information about the manufacture and use of corrosion-preventing coatings for metal surfaces.

Journal of Protective Coatings and Linings
Technology Publishing Co.
24 S. 18th St.
Pittsburgh, PA 15203
412-431-8300
Information about the use of protective coatings specifically on steel structures.

Modern Paint and Coatings
Communication Channels, Inc.
6255 Barfield Rd.
Atlanta, GA 30328-4369
404-256-9800
Larry Anderson, Editor
Reports on technological improvements in paints, coatings, and equipment used to make and apply them.

Paint & Coatings Industry
Business News Publishing, Co.
Box 2600
Troy, MI 48007
313-362-3700
Larry Dill, Editor
Business and technological news for manufacturers and distributors of paint and coatings.

LIBRARIES

The Glidden Co.
Technical Information Services
Glidden Research Center
16651 Sprague Rd.
Strongsville, OH 44136
216-826-5260
216-826-5555 Fax
Coatings, resins, polymer chemistry, and related topics.

Powder Coating Institute
1800 Diagonal Rd., Ste. 370
Alexandria, VA 22314
703-684-1770
Gregory Bocchi, Executive Director
Powder coating industry.

Rust-Oleum Corp.
R & D Library
8105 Fergusson Dr.
P.O. Box 70
Pleasant Prairie, WI 53158
414-947-7220
Coatings, resins, and corrosion.

COMPANIES

Akzo Coatings Inc.
(Subsidiary of Akzo America Inc.)
1930 Bishop Lane
Louisville, KY 40218
502-459-9110
Coatings of all kinds.

Ferro Corp.
1000 Lakeside Ave.
Cleveland, OH 44114
216-641-8580
Coatings and other chemicals.

H.B. Fuller Co.
2400 Energy Park Dr.
St. Paul, MN 55108
612-645-3401
Adhesives, sealants, coatings, and other chemicals.

Grow Group Inc.
200 Park Ave.
New York, NY 10166
212-599-4400
Solvents, sealants, paints, and coatings.

Loctite Corp.
Ten Columbus Blvd.
Hartford, CT 06106
203-520-5000
Adhesives, sealants, and coatings.

RPM Inc.
2628 Pearl Rd.
Medina, OH 44256
216-273-5090
Specialty coatings and other businesses.

Tremco Inc.
(Subsidiary of BF Goodrich Co.)
3735 Green Rd.
Beachwood, OH 44122
216-292-5000
Coatings and sealants.

FEDERAL GOVERNMENT

U.S. International Trade Administration
Department of Commerce
14th St. and Constitution Ave., N.W.
Washington, DC 20230
202-377-2000
Ask for the Commodity Analyst who is an expert in industrial coatings.

U.S. International Trade Commission
500 E St., S.W.
Washington, DC 20436
202-205-2000 Office of the Secretary
202-205-3296 Industries locator
Ask for the Trade Analyst who is an expert in industrial coatings.

U.S. Patent and Trademark Office
Crystal Plaza 2
2011 Jefferson Davis Highway
Arlington, VA 22202
703-305-8000
Ask for the Examining Group Director who is a specialist in coating apparatus and compositions.

INDUSTRIAL EQUIPMENT INDUSTRY

See also: MACHINE TOOL INDUSTRY

ASSOCIATIONS

American Supply and Machinery Manufacturers Association
Thomas Assocs., Inc.
1230 Keith Bldg.
Cleveland, OH 44115
216-241-7333
216-241-0105 Fax
Charles Stockinger, Executive Officer
Firms that make industrial machinery and supplies.

Associated Equipment Distributors
615 W. 22nd St.
Oak Brook, IL 60521
708-574-0650
708-574-0132 Fax
Toby Mack, Executive Vice President
Manufacturers of construction, forestry, and related types of equipment.

Industrial Distribution Association
3 Corporate Sq., Ste. 201
Atlanta, GA 30329
404-325-2776
404-325-2784 Fax
Gary Buffington, Executive Vice President
Firms that distribute industrial equipment and supplies. Offers management and marketing training.

Machinery Dealers National Association
1110 Spring St.
Silver Spring, MD 20910
301-585-9494
301-588-7830 Fax
Darryl McEwen, Executive Vice President
Dealers of used and reconditioned industrial machinery.

Manufacturers Alliance for Productivity and Innovation
1200 18th St. N.W., Ste. 400
Washington, DC 20036
202-331-8430
202-331-7160 Fax
Kenneth McLennan, President
Manufacturers of machinery and industrial equipment. Sponsors research on the capital goods industry.

PERIODICALS

Control Engineering
Cahners Publishing Co.
1350 E. Touhy Ave.
Box 5080
Des Plaines, IL 60017-5080
708-635-8800
Michael Babb, Editor
Advice and news for designers and users of control and instrumentation equipment.

IEN: Industrial Equipment News
Thomas Publishing Co.
Five Penn Plaza
250 W. 34th St.
New York, NY 10001
212-695-0500
Mark Devlin, Editor
Surveys new industrial equipment, parts, and materials.

Industrial Machinery News
Hearst Business Media Corp.
5700 Crooks Rd., Ste. 219
Troy, MI 48098-2809
313-828-7000
Gregory Jones, Editor
Follows new equipment for manufacturers, distributors, and buyers.

Industrial Market Place
Wineberg Publications
7842 N. Lincoln Ave.
Skokie, IL 60077
708-676-1900
Joel Wineberg, Editor
Prints advertisements for industrial equipment and machinery.

New Equipment Digest
Penton Publishing
1100 Superior Ave.
Cleveland, OH 44114-2543
216-696-7000
Robert King, Editor
Reports on new industrial products.

New Equipment Reporter
De Roche Publications
777 W. 19th St., Ste. W
Costa Mesa, CA 92627
714-642-9978
David De Roche, Editor
Reports on new products.

Used Equipment Directory
Penton Publishing
601 Pavonia Ave.
Jersey City, NJ 07306
800-526-6052
James Mack, Editor
A listing of used industrial equipment available for sale.

LIBRARIES

FMC Corp.
Corporate Technology Center
1205 Coleman Ave.
Santa Clara, CA 95052
408-289-2529
Engineering, materials, robotics, industrial machinery, and related topics.

Industrial Distribution Association
Library
3 Corporate Sq., Ste. 201
Atlanta, GA 30329
404-325-2776
404-325-2784 Fax
Industrial equipment and supplies.

COMPANIES

Axel Johnson Inc.
(Subsidiary of Lexa International Corp.)
110 E. 59th St.
New York, NY 10022
212-758-3200
Industrial machinery and capital equipment.

Darr Equipment Co., Inc.
P.O. Box 540788
Dallas, TX 75354
214-721-2000
Industrial machinery and equipment.

EAC USA, Inc.
73-45 Woodhaven Blvd.
Glendale, NY 11385
718-830-7800
Industrial machinery and equipment.

FMC Corp.
200 E. Randolph Dr.
Chicago, IL 60601
312-861-6000
Machinery, equipment, and other products.

General Signal Corp.
High Ridge Park, P.O. Box 10010
Stamford, CT 06904
203-357-8800
Equipment for the process control industry and other industries.

Motorola, Inc.
1303 E. Algonquin Rd.
Schaumburg, IL 60196
708-397-5000
Industrial electronic equipment and many other types of products.

Ringhaver Equipment Co.
P.O. Box 30169
Tampa, FL 33630
813-671-3700
Industrial machinery and equipment.

Sammons Enterprises, Inc.
403 S. Akard St.
Dallas, TX 75202
214-670-9790
A diversified company that makes industrial machinery.

White Consolidated Industries, Inc.
(Subsidiary of Electrolux AB)
11770 Berea Rd.
Cleveland, OH 44111
216-252-3700
Equipment for industry and consumers.

Wilson Industries, Inc.
P.O. Box 1492
Houston, TX 77251
713-237-3700
Industrial machinery and equipment.

FEDERAL GOVERNMENT

U.S. Customs Service
Department of the Treasury
U.S. Customshouse
6 World Trade Center
New York, NY 10048
212-466-5550
Ask for the Commodity Specialist in charge of industrial equipment.

U.S. International Trade Administration
Department of Commerce
14th St. and Constitution Ave., N.W.
Washington, DC 20230
202-377-2000
Ask for the Commodity Analyst who is an expert in the industrial equipment industry.

U.S. International Trade Commission
500 E St., S.W.
Washington, DC 20436
202-205-2000 Office of the Secretary
202-205-3296 Industries locator
Ask for the Trade Analyst who is an expert in the industrial equipment industry.

U.S. Patent and Trademark Office
Crystal Plaza 2
2011 Jefferson Davis Highway
Arlington, VA 22202
703-305-8000
Ask for the Examining Group Director who is a specialist in industrial equipment.

INDUSTRIAL HYGIENE

Industrial hygiene refers to the preservation of workers' health in industrial settings.

ASSOCIATIONS

American Board of Industrial Hygiene
4600 W. Saginaw, Ste. 101
Lansing, MI 48917-2737
517-321-2638
James Barrett, Executive Secretary
A board that certifies industrial hygienists.

American Industrial Hygiene Association
345 White Pond Dr.
Akron, OH 44320
216-873-2442
216-873-1642 Fax
O. Gordon Banks, Executive Director
The main professional society for industrial hygienists.

Industrial Health Foundation
34 Penn Circle, W.
Pittsburgh, PA 15206
412-363-6600
Industrial companies that share information about maintaining health in industrial plants.

PERIODICALS

American Journal of Industrial Medicine
Wiley-Liss, Inc.
41 E. 11th St.
New York, NY 10003
212-475-7700
Irving Selikoff, Editor
A professional journal for physicians and health care workers concerned with industrial medicine.

Applied Occupational & Environmental Hygiene
Applied Industrial Hygiene, Inc.
6500 Glenway Ave., Bldg. D-7
Cincinnati, OH 45211
513-661-7881
Sharon Ziggler, Editor
News and advice of interest to professionals in fields of occupational and environmental health and safety.

Chilton's Industrial Safety & Hygiene News
Chilton Co.
One Chilton Way
Radnor, PA 19089
215-964-4028
Dave Johnson, Editor
Covers equipment used in industrial settings to control safety, hygiene, fire, security, and the environment.

Industrial Hygiene News
Rimbach Publishing, Inc.
8650 Babcock Blvd.
Pittsburgh, PA 15237
412-364-5366
David Lavender, Editor
Reports news about occupational health and safety in industrial settings.

LIBRARIES

Clayton Environmental Consultants, Inc.
Library and Information Center
22345 Roethel Dr.
Novi, MI 48050
313-344-1770
313-344-2654 Fax
Industrial hygiene, environmental pollution, waste management, toxicology, and other subjects.

Industrial Health Foundation
Library
34 Penn Circle, W.
Pittsburgh, PA 15206
412-363-6600
Industrial hygiene.

U.S. Department of Labor
OSHA
Technical Data Center
200 Constitution Ave., N.W.
Rm. N-2625
Washington, DC 20210
202-523-9700
202-523-5046 Fax
Industrial hygiene, carcinogens, process safety, occupational safety, electrical safety, and related topics.

University of California, Berkeley
Public Health Library
42 Earl Warren Hall
Berkeley, CA 94720
510-642-2511
510-642-7623 Fax
Public health, environmental health, epidemiology, industrial hygiene, and other topics.

FEDERAL GOVERNMENT

U.S. Department of Labor
200 Constitution Ave., N.W.
Washington, DC 20210
202-523-6666
Ask for the Occupational Safety and Health Administration.

U.S. Centers for Disease Control
1600 Clifton Rd., N.E.
Atlanta, GA 30333
404-639-3311
Ask for the National Institute for Occupational Safety and Health.

INDUSTRIAL RELATIONS

See also: LABOR UNIONS and each
of the 50 states under labor

ASSOCIATIONS

Industrial Relations Counselors
PO Box 1530
New York, NY 10101
212-764-4198
Charles Tasso, President
*Offers information about relations between
employers and employees.*

Industrial Relations Research Association
7226 Social Science Bldg.
Univ. of Wisconsin
Madison, WI 53706
608-262-2762
David Zimmerman, Secretary.
*Professors, executives, union officials, and oth-
ers who study employee-employer relations.*

Institute of Labor and Industrial Relations
Victor Vaughan Bldg.
Univ. of Michigan
1111 E. Catherine St.
Ann Arbor, MI 48109-2054
313-763-3116
313-763-0913 Fax
Malcolm Cohen, Director
*Offers research assistance to businesses and
labor unions who study labor and employee-
employer relations.*

PERIODICALS

Cornell International Industrial and Labor
    Relations Reports
New York State School of Industrial and
    Labor Relations
I L R Press
Cornell University
Ithaca, NY 14851-0952
607-255-3061
*Reports on trends in industrial and labor rela-
tions.*

Discipline and Grievances
Bureau of Business Practice
24 Rope Ferry Rd.
Waterford, CT 06386
203-442-4365
Emily Mitchell, Editor
*Helps executives analyze labor arbitration
cases.*

Employee Relations in Action
Business Research Publications, Inc.
817 Broadway
New York, NY 10003
212-673-4700
Elmer Ellentuck, Editor
*Uses the case study method to explore the
many issues that confront managers and
employees.*

Employee Relations Report
Business Communication Services
Box 671
Richmond, VA 23206
804-355-0214
Ann Black, Editor
Offers advice to employee relations managers
on how to improve communications.

Industrial and Labor Relations Review
Cornell University
New York State School of Industrial and
    Labor Relations
Ithaca, NY 14853-3901
607-255-2763
Donald Cullen, Editor
Articles cover a wide range of employment
issues and problems.

Industrial Relations Law Journal
University of California Press
Journals Division
2120 Berkeley Way
Berkeley, CA 94720
415-642-4191
Follows trends in labor and employment law.

Journal of Labor Research
Department of Economics
George Mason University
4400 University Dr.
Fairfax, VA 22030
703-323-2744
James Bennett, Editor
Covers issues that concern unions and
employers.

Labor Relations Today
United States Department of Labor
Bureau of Labor Management Relations
200 Constitution Ave., No. N5419
Washington, DC 20210
202-523-6098
Barbara Schrader, Editor
Follows trends in labor and industrial rela-
tions.

LIBRARIES

Cornell University
New York State School of Industrial and
    Labor Relatioins
Martin P. Catherwood Library
Ives Hall
Ithaca, NY 14851-0952
607-255-2184
607-255-9641 Fax
Labor-management relations, industrial psy-
chology, organizational behavior, and other
subjects.

University of Massachusetts, Amherst
Labor Relations & Research Center Library
Draper Hall
Amherst, MA 01003
413-545-3870
Industrial relations.

University of Minnesota
Industrial Relations Center
Reference Room
Management & Economics, West Campus
271 19th Ave., S.
Minneapolis, MN 55455
612-624-7011
612-724-6374 Fax
Industrial psychology, labor relations, indus-
trial sociology, personnel administration, and
management.

FEDERAL GOVERNMENT

Office of Personnel Management
1900 E St., N.W.
Washington, DC 20415
202-606-2424
Ask for Employee & Labor Relations.

INFORMATION INDUSTRY

The information industry provides data, news, and other forms of information on all topics. Information is delivered in printed or electronic form, which includes computerized databases.

See also: APPENDIX

ASSOCIATIONS

Information Industry Association
555 New Jersey Ave. N.W., Ste. 800
Washington, DC 20001
202-639-8262
202-638-4403 Fax
David Fullerton, President
Members create, report, package, and sell information. Offers information on how new technologies improve the information industry.

PERIODICALS

Information Broker
Burwell Enterprises
3724 F.M. 1960 W., Ste. 214
Houston, TX 77068
713-537-9051
Helen Burwell, Editor
News of interest to professional information researchers.

Information Industry Alert
Industry News Service Inc.
Box 457
Wilton, CT 06897-0457
203-762-3206
Reports on how companies use new technologies to deliver information effectively.

Information Industry Bulletin
Digital Information Group
51 Bank St.
Stamford, CT 06901
203-348-2751
Chris Elwell, Editor
Covers news and trends of interest to publishers of information products, including electronic and print products.

Information Today
Learned Information, Inc.
143 Old Marlton Pike
Medford, NJ 08055
609-654-6266
Patricia Lane, Editor
*News about online and CD-ROM products
and services for users and producers of electronic information.*

Information Week
C M P Publications, Inc.
600 Community Dr.
Manhasset, NY 11030
516-562-5000
Laton McCartney, Editor
*Advice and news for managers of information
systems.*

LIBRARIES

Decision Information Services, Ltd.
Library
2130 Hanover St.
Palo Alto, CA 94306
415-856-3666
*Information technology, microcomputers, and
related topics.*

COMPANIES

CompuServe, Inc.
5000 Arlington Center
Columbus, OH 43220
614-457-8600
*Online database service that covers numerous
subjects.*

Dialog Information Services, Inc.
3460 Hillview Ave.
Palo Alto, CA 94304
800-3-DIALOG
*Online database service that covers numerous
subjects.*

Disclosure, Inc.
5161 River Rd.
Bethesda, MD 20816
301-951-1300
*Online database producer that focusses on
business information.*

Find/SVP
625 Ave. of the Americas
New York, NY 10011
212-645-4500
Information services.

Information on Demand
8000 Westpark Dr.
McLean, VA 22102
703-442-0303
*Photocopies of published articles and other
documents.*

Institute for Scientific Information
3501 Market St.
Philadelphia, PA 19104
215-386-0100
*Online database producer that focusses on sci-
entific and technical information.*

Mead Data Central, Inc.
P.O. Box 933
Dayton, OH 45401
513-865-6800
*Online database service that focusses on legal,
news, and business information.*

Predicasts, Inc.
11001 Cedar Ave.
Cleveland, OH 44106
216-795-3000
*Online database producer that focusses on
business information.*

Research Network
59 West 85th St.
New York, NY 10024
212-877-5400
Customized research service that finds information on any topic.

Quotron Systems, Inc.
12731 W. Jefferson
Los Angeles, CA 90066
310-827-4600
Online database service that focusses on stock quotes.

SilverPlatter Information
100 River Ridge Dr.
Norwood, MA 02062
800-343-0064
CD-ROM information products.

INSULATION INDUSTRY

ASSOCIATIONS

Exterior Insulation Manufacturers Association
30 Holley St.
Wakefield, RI 02879-3309
401-782-3687
401-782-4796 Fax
J. Dick Hopkins, Executive Director
Manufacturers of exterior insulation.

Insulation Contractors Association of America
15819 Crabbs Branch Way
Rockville, MD 20855
301-590-0030
301-590-0713 Fax
R. Hartley Edes, Executive Director
Contractors who install insulation in homes and businesses. Offers education and research.

National Insulation and Abatement Contractors Association
99 Canal Center Plaza, Ste. 222
Alexandria, VA 22314
703-683-6422
703-549-4838 Fax
William Pitkin, Executive Vice President
Insulation and asbestos abatement contractors.

Thermal Insulation Manufacturers Association
29 Bank St.
Stamford, CT 06901
203-324-7533
203-324-5132 Fax
Frank Rauscher, Executive Director
Firms that make thermal insulation products. Conducts research and testing.

PERIODICALS

Contractor's Guide
Century Communications, Inc.
6201 W. Howard St.
Niles, IL 60648
312-647-1200
Russ Gager, Editor
How-to information for contractors working with insulation, roofing materials, and window installations.

Journal of Thermal Insulation
Technomic Publishing Co., Inc.
851 New Holland Ave.
Lancaster, PA 17604
717-291-5609
Charles Gilbo, Editor
Technical information for the thermal insulation industry.

LIBRARIES

Certainteed Corp.
Corporate Library/Information Center
1400 Union Meeting Rd.
Blue Bell, PA 19422
215-341-6283
215-341-6429 Fax
Insulation, roofing, science, and technology.

Drexel University
Center for Insulation Technology
Library
Mechanical Engr. & Mechanics Dept.
Philadelphia, PA 19104
215-895-2000
Insulation.

Owens-Corning Fiberglass Corp.
Technical Data Center
2790 Columbus Rd., Rte. 16
Granville, OH 43023-0415
614-587-7265
Glass, fiberglass, chemistry, insulation, and other topics.

COMPANIES

Allied Building Products Corp.
15 E. Union Ave.
East Rutherford, NJ 07073
201-935-0800
Insulation materials and other building products.

Fibreboard Corp.
1000 Burnett Ave.
Concord, CA 94520
415-686-0700
Insulation and wood products.

General Refractories Co.
(Subsidiary of Belmont Industries Inc.)
2661 Audubon Rd.
Audubon, PA 19407
215-666-0104
Insulating, building, and other products.

Georgia-Pacific Corp.
133 Peachtree St., N. E.
Atlanta, GA 30303
404-521-4000
A wide variety of wood and building products, including insulation.

Insulation Materials Corp. of America
4325 Murray Ave.
Haltom City, TX 76117
817-485-5290
Insulation materials.

Irex Corp.
P.O. Box 1268
Lancaster, PA 17603
717-397-3633
Insulation contracting and distribution of insulation materials.

Manville Sales Corp.
(Subsidiary of Manville Corp.)
P.O. Box 5108
Denver, CO 80217
Fiberglass insulation and other products.

Owens-Corning Fiberglas Corp.
Fiberglas Tower
Toledo, OH 43659
419-248-8000
Insulation and other fiberglass products.

FEDERAL GOVERNMENT

U.S. Customs Service
Department of the Treasury
U.S. Customshouse
6 World Trade Center
New York, NY 10048
212-466-5550
Ask for the Commodity Specialist in charge of insulation.

Federal Trade Commission
Pennsylvania Ave. at 6th St., N.W.
Washington, DC 20580
202-326-2000
Ask for the Consumer Protection Bureau.

INSURANCE—AUTOMOBILE

See also: INSURANCE AGENTS

ASSOCIATIONS

American Insurers Highway Safety Alliance
1501 Woodfield Rd., Ste. 400 W.
Schaumburg, IL 60173
708-330-8500
708-330-8602 Fax
Franklin Nutter, President
This group of automobile insurance companies promotes traffic safety.

Independent Automotive Damage Appraisers Association
707 N. York Rd., 2nd Fl.
Elmhurst, IL 60126
708-834-0010
708-834-0052
Richard Devermann, Executive Vice President
Members are independent appraisers hired by insurance companies and other firms to estimate automobile damages.

National Automobile Theft Bureau
10330 S. Roberts Rd., Executive Office 3A
Palos Hills, IL 60465
708-430-2430
Paul Gilliland, President
Members are insurers that write policies covering physical damage to motor vehicles. Offers information about theft prevention and related topics.

PERIODICALS

Automobile Insurance Losses, Collision Coverages, Variations by Make and Series
Highway Loss Data Institute
c/o Stephen Oesch, General Counsel
1005 N. Glebe Rd., Ste. 800
Arlington, VA 22201
703-247-1600
Insurance statistics concerning cars.

Automobile Law Reports—Insurance Cases
Commerce Clearing House, Inc.
4025 W. Peterson Ave.
Chicago, IL 60646
312-583-8500
A.E. Schechter, Editor
Follows insurance law as it relates to automotive cases.

LIBRARIES

College of Insurance
Insurance Society of New York
Kathryn and Shelby Cullom Davis Library
101 Murray St.
New York, NY 10007
212-962-4111
212-964-3381 Fax
All types of insurance including automotive, casualty, health, life, fire, and worker's compensation.

COMPANIES

Aetna Casualty and Surety Co.
151 Farmington
Hartford, CT 06156
203-273-0123
Automobile and other types of insurance.

Allstate Insurance Co.
Allstate Plz.
Northbrook, IL 60062
708-402-5000
Automobile and other types of insurance.

Crum and Forster, Inc.
211 Mount Airy Rd.
Basking Ridge, NJ 07920
908-204-3500
Automobile and other types of insurance.

Chubb Corp.
15 Mountain View Rd.
Warren, NJ 07061
908-580-2000
Automobile and other types of insurance.

ITT Hartford Insurance Group
Hartford Plz.
Hartford, CT 06115
203-547-5000
Automobile and other types of insurance.

State Farm Mutual Automobile Insurance Co.
1 State Farm Plz
Bloomington, IL 61710
309-766-2311
Automobile and other types of insurance.

FEDERAL GOVERNMENT

U.S. International Trade Administration
Department of Commerce
14th St. and Constitution Ave., N.W.
Washington, DC 20230
202-377-2000
*Ask for the Commodity Analyst who is an
expert in insurance.*

U.S. International Trade Commission
500 E St., S.W.
Washington, DC 20436
202-205-2000 Office of the Secretary
202-205-3296 Industries locator
*Ask for the Trade Analyst who is an expert in
insurance.*

INSURANCE—CASUALTY AND PROPERTY

See also: ACTUARIAL SCIENCE; INSURANCE AGENTS; and each of
the 50 states under insurance

ASSOCIATIONS

Alliance of American Insurers
1501 Woodfield Rd., Ste. 400 W
Schaumburg, IL 60173
708-330-8500
708-330-8602 Fax
Franklin Nutter, President
Property and casualty insurers.

American Association of Insurance Services
1035 S. York Rd.
Bensenville, IL 60106
708-595-3225
708-595-4647 Fax
P. A. Baiocchi, President
*This association of property and casualty
insurers creates rates and forms, and offers
various services to the industry.*

American Insurance Association
1130 Connecticut Ave., N.W. Ste. 1000
Washington, DC 20036
202-828-7100
202-293-1219 Fax
Robert Vagley, President
*Acts as an information clearinghouse to prop-
erty and casualty insurers.*

American Insurance Services Group
85 John St.
New York, NY 10038
212-669-0400
Lawrence Zippin, President
*Offers information on safety promotion, insur-
ance claims, and other subjects that concern
property and casualty insurers.*

Conference of Casualty Insurance Companies
3707 Woodview Trace
Indianapolis, IN 46268
317-872-4061
Larry Forrester, Executive Vice President
*Casualty insurance companies that collectively
sponsor management training programs.*

Insurance Crime Prevention Institute
15 Franklin St.
Westport, CT 06880
203-226-6347
800-221-5715
203-227-4663 Fax
Wendall Harness, Director
*Works to prevent and investigate casualty and
property insurance claim fraud.*

National Association of Casualty and Surety
   Executives
1130 Connecticut Ave., N.W., Ste. 1000
Washington, DC 20036
202-828-7104
202-293-1219 Fax
Lawrence Zippin, Executive Director
*Professional society of executives who work for
casualty and surety insurers.*

PERIODICALS

Best's Insurance Report: Property—Casualty
A.M. Best Co.
Ambest Rd.
Oldwick, NJ 08858
908-439-2200
C. Burton Kellogg, Editor
*Surveys all aspects of the property and casu-
alty insurance industry.*

Fire, Casualty & Surety Bulletin
National Underwriter Co.
505 Gest St.
Cincinnati, OH 45203
513-721-2140
*Surveys news in the property and casualty
insurance field.*

Insurance Law Reports: Fire & Casualty
Commerce Clearing House, Inc.
4025 W. Peterson Ave.
Chicago, IL 60646
312-583-8500
*Follows the legal issues involving property,
casualty, and fire insurance.*

InsuranceWeek
1001 Fourth Ave. Plaza, Ste. 3029
Seattle, WA 98154
206-624-6965
Richard Rambeck, Editor
*News for agents and insurance executives in
the property and casualty field who live in the
Western U.S.*

National Underwriter. Property & Casualty
   Insurance Edition
National Underwriter Co.
505 Gest St.
Cincinnati, OH 45203
513-721-2410
*Reports on insurance products, the insurance
market, government regulations, and other
issues.*

LIBRARIES

College of Insurance
Insurance Society of New York
Kathryn and Shelby Cullom Davis Library
101 Murray St.
New York, NY 10007
212-962-4111
212-964-3381 Fax
All types of insurance including automotive, casualty, health, life, fire, and worker's compensation.

Insurance Information Institute
Library
110 William St.
New York, NY 10038
212-669-9200
212-732-1916 Fax
Property and casualty insurance.

Insurance Library Association of Boston
156 State St.
Boston, MA 02109
617-227-2087
617-723-8524 Fax
Fire insurance, health insurance, casualty insurance, life insurance, and property insurance.

Travelers Insurance Companies
The Information Exchange 2G5
One Tower Square
Hartford, CT 06183
203-954-4636
203-277-9167 Fax
Insurance.

COMPANIES

Aetna Casualty and Surety Co.
151 Farmington
Hartford, CT 06156
203-273-0123
Property/casualty and other types of insurance.

Allstate Insurance Co.
Allstate Plz.
Northbrook, IL 60062
708-402-5000
Property/casualty and other types of insurance.

Crum and Forster, Inc.
211 Mount Airy Rd.
Basking Ridge, NJ 07920
908-204-3500
Property/casualty and other types of insurance.

Chubb Corp.
15 Mountain View Rd.
Warren, NJ 07061
908-580-2000
Property/casualty and other types of insurance.

ITT Hartford Insurance Group
Hartford Plz.
Hartford, CT 06115
203-547-5000
Property/casualty and other types of insurance.

Liberty Mutual Insurance Co.
175 Berkeley St.
Boston, MA 02117
617-357-9500
Property/casualty and other types of insurance.

Nationwide Mutual Insurance Group
1 Nationwide Plz.
Columbus, OH 43216
614-249-7111
Property/casualty and other types of insurance.

St. Paul Fire and Marine Insurance Co.
385 Washington St.
St. Paul, MN 55102
612-221-7911
Property/casualty and other types of insurance.

State Farm Fire and Casualty Co.
1 State Farm Plz.
Bloomington, IL 61710
309-766-2311
Property/casualty and other types of insurance.

Travelers Insurance Co.
1 Tower Sq.
Harford, CT 06183
203-277-0111
Property/casualty and other types of insurance.

FEDERAL GOVERNMENT

U.S. International Trade Administration
Department of Commerce
14th St. and Constitution Ave., N.W.
Washington, DC 20230
202-377-2000
Ask for the Commodity Analyst who is an expert in insurance.

U.S. International Trade Commission
500 E St., S.W.
Washington, DC 20436
202-205-2000 Office of the Secretary
202-205-3296 Industries locator
Ask for the Trade Analyst who is an expert in insurance.

U.S. Securities and Exchange Commission
450 5th St., N.W.
Washington, DC 20549
202-272-3100
Ask for the Insurance Products Compliance department in the Investment Management Office.

INSURANCE—HEALTH AND ACCIDENT

See also: INSURANCE AGENTS

ASSOCIATIONS

Health Insurance Association of America
1025 Connecticut Ave. N.W., Ste. 1200
Washington, DC 20036
202-223-7780
Carl Schramm, President
Insurance firms that write accident and health policies.

National Association of Health Underwriters
1000 Connecticut Ave. N.W., Ste. 1111
Washington, DC 20036
202-223-5533
William Flood, Executive Vice President
Insurance agencies and others who sell health insurance and pay disability claims. Sponsors research seminars.

National Health Care Anti-Fraud Association
1255 23rd St. N.W., Ste. 850
Washington, DC 20037
202-659-5955
202-833-3636 Fax
Richard Ekfelt, Executive Director
Insurance companies and agencies that work to prevent health insurance fraud by sharing information.

PERIODICALS

Best's Insurance Report: Life—Health
A.M. Best Co.
Ambest Rd.
Oldwick, NJ 08858
908-439-2200
Robert King, Editor
Surveys the life and health insurance field.

Broker World
Insurance Publications, Inc.
10709 Barkley, Ste. 3
Overland Park, KS 66211
800-762-3387
Sharon Chace, Editor
Follows insurance news and trends for independent agents and brokers who specialize in health and life insurance.

Business and Health
Medical Economics Co. Inc.
680 Kinderkamack Rd.
Oradell, NJ 07649
201-262-3030
Karen Hunt, Editor
Covers a wide range of health issues of concern to corporations, including health insurance issues.

Health Insurance Medical Records Risk Management Report
Cox Publications
Box 20316
Billings, MT 59104-0316
406-256-8822
Meridith Cox, Editor
Helps health insurers and others create policies regarding the dissemination of patients' medical records.

Insurance Law Reports: Life, Health & Accident
Commerce Clearing House, Inc.
4025 W. Peterson Ave.
Chicago, IL 60646
312-583-8500
Covers legal issues relating to health, accident, and life insurance.

Journal of Insurance Medicine
Association of Life Insurance Medical Directors of America
Transamerica Life Companies
Box 2101, Tower 60
Los Angeles, CA 90051
213-742-2751
W. John Elder, Editor
Reports on actuarial, claims, underwriting, and other medical medicine issues.

Risk & Insurance
Axon Group
747 Dresher Rd., Ste. 500
Horsham, PA 19044
215-784-0860
Richard Jaccoma, Editor
Reports on all types of liability and insurance benefits for executives in the insurance industry and for corporate insurance managers.

LIBRARIES

Blue Cross and Blue Shield Association
Library
676 N. St. Clair
Chicago, IL 60611
312-440-5510
Health insurance and related topics.

College of Insurance
Insurance Society of New York
Kathryn and Shelby Cullom Davis Library
101 Murray St.
New York, NY 10007
212-962-4111
212-964-3381 Fax
*All types of insurance including automotive,
casualty, health, life, fire, and workmen's compensation.*

Insurance Library Association of Boston
156 State St.
Boston, MA 02109
617-227-2087
617-723-8524 Fax
*Fire insurance, health insurance, casualty
insurance, life insurance, and property insurance.*

COMPANIES

American Family Corp.
1932 Wynnton Rd.
Columbus, GA 31999
404-323-3431
Health and accident insurance.

American Republic Insurance Co.
P.O. Box 1
Des Moine, IA 50309
515-245-2000
Health and accident insurance.

Blue Cross and Blue Shield of the National
Capital Area
550 12th St. S.W.
Washington, DC 20065
202-479-8000
Health and accident insurance.

Blue Cross and Blue Shield of Michigan
600 E. Lafayette
Detroit, MI 48226
313-225-9000
Health and accident insurance.

Blue Cross of Western Pennsylvania
Fifth Ave. Pl.
Pittsburgh, PA 15222
412-255-7000
Health and accident insurance.

Hartford Accident and Indemnity Co.
Hartford Plz.
Hartford, CT 06115
203-547-5000
Health and accident insurance.

Medical Services Association
P.O. 890089
Camp Hill, PA 17098
717-763-6526
Health and accident insurance.

Michigan Mutual Insurance Co.
28 W. Adams Ave.
Detroit, MI 48226
313-965-8600
Health and accident insurance.

Pioneer Financial Services, Inc.
304 N. Main St.
Rockford, IL 61101
815-987-5000
Health and accident insurance.

Washington National Insurance Co.
1630 Chicago Ave.
Evanston, IL 60201
708-570-5500
Health and accident insurance.

FEDERAL GOVERNMENT

U.S. International Trade Administration
Department of Commerce
14th St. and Constitution Ave., N.W.
Washington, DC 20230
202-377-2000
Ask for the Commodity Analyst who is an expert in insurance.

U.S. International Trade Commission
500 E St., S.W.
Washington, DC 20436
202-205-2000 Office of the Secretary
202-205-3296 Industries locator
Ask for the Trade Analyst who is an expert in insurance.

INSURANCE—LIFE

See also: INSURANCE AGENTS

ASSOCIATIONS

American Council of Life Insurance
1001 Pennsylvania Ave. N.W.
Washington, DC 20004-2599
202-624-2000
202-624-2319 Fax
L. Charles FitzGerald, Secretary
Promotes the life insurance industry through educational and research programs.

Life Insurance Marketing and Research Association
Box 208
Hartford, CT 06141
203-677-0033
203-678-0187 Fax
Ernest Cragg, President.
Members are life insurance companies. The Association studies a wide range of issues that effect the life insurance industry.

National Association of Life Companies
1455 Pennsylvania Ave. N.W., Ste. 1250
Washington, DC 20004
202-783-6252
S. Roy Woodall, President
Studies life insurance with an emphasis on legislative matters.

National Association of Life Underwriters
1922 F St. N.W.
Washington, DC 20006
202-331-6001
Jack Bobo, Executive Vice President
A very large association representing life insurance agents and executives at insurance firms. Works to standardize industry practices and to promote sales of life insurance.

PERIODICALS

Best's Agents Guide to Life Insurance Companies
A.M. Best Co.
Ambest Rd.
Oldwick, NJ 08858
908-439-2200
Robert King, Editor
Helps independent life insurance agents choose among the competing life insurance policies.

Best's Insurance Management Reports: Life—Health Edition
A.M. Best Co.
Ambest Rd.
Oldwick, NJ 08858
908-439-2200
D. Hall, Editor
Surveys the life and health insurance field.

Broker World
Insurance Publications, Inc.
10709 Barkley, Ste. 3
Overland Park, KS 66211
800-762-3387
Sharon Chace, Editor
Follows insurance news and trends for independent agents and brokers who specialize in health and life insurance.

Insurance Law Reports: Life, Health & Accident
Commerce Clearing House, Inc.
4025 W. Peterson Ave.
Chicago, IL 60646
312-583-8500
News of the legal issues relating to life and health insurance.

Life Insurance Selling
Commerce Publishing Co.
408 Olive St.
St. Louis, MO 63102
314-421-5445
Larry Albright, Editor
How-to information to help life insurance agents increase their sales.

LIBRARIES

College of Insurance
Insurance Society of New York
Kathryn and Shelby Cullom Davis Library
101 Murray St.
New York, NY 10007
212-962-4111
212-964-3381 Fax
All types of insurance including automotive, casualty, health, life, fire, and worker's compensation.

Insurance Library Association of Boston
156 State St.
Boston, MA 02109
617-227-2087
617-723-8524 Fax
Fire insurance, health insurance, casualty insurance, life insurance, and property insurance.

Life Insurance Marketing and Research Association
William J. Mortimer Library
Box 208
Hartford, CT 06141
203-677-0033
203-678-0187 Fax
Life insurance, life insurance company history, statistics, and related topics.

COMPANIES

Aetna Life and Casualty Co.
151 Farmington Ave.
Hartford, CT 06156
203-273-0123
Life insurance.

Connecticut General Life Insurance Co.
900 Cottage Grove Rd.
Bloomfield, CT 06002
203-726-6000
Life insurance.

Equitable Life Assurance Society of the
    United States
787 7th Ave.
New York, NY 10019
212-554-1234
Life insurance.

John Hancock Mutual Life Insurance Co.
P.O. Box 111
Boston, MA 02117
617-572-6000
Life insurance.

Massachusetts Mutual Life Insurance Co.
1295 State St.
Springfield, MA 01111
413-788-8411
Life insurance.

Metropolitan Life Insurance Co.
1 Madison Ave.
New York, NY 10010
212-578-2211
Life insurance.

New York Life Insurance Co.
51 Madison Ave.
New York, NY 10010
212-576-7000
Life insurance.

Northwestern Mutual Life Insurance Co.
720 E. Wisconsin Ave.
Milwaukee, WI 53202
414-271-1444
Life insurance.

Prudential Insurance Co. of America
751 Broad St.
Newark, NJ 07102
201-877-6000
Life insurance.

Travelers Corp.
1 Tower Sq.
Hartford, CT 06183
203-277-0111
Life insurance.

FEDERAL GOVERNMENT

U.S. International Trade Administration
Department of Commerce
14th St. and Constitution Ave., N.W.
Washington, DC 20230
202-377-2000
Ask for the Commodity Analyst who is an expert in insurance.

U.S. International Trade Commission
500 E St., S.W.
Washington, DC 20436
202-205-2000 Office of the Secretary
202-205-3296 Industries locator
Ask for the Trade Analyst who is an expert in insurance.

INSURANCE AGENTS

See also: ALL ENTRIES OF INSURANCE

ASSOCIATIONS

American Society of CLU and ChFC
270 Bryn Mawr Ave.
Bryn Mawr, PA 19010
215-526-2500
215-527-4010 Fax
John Driskill, Executive Vice President
Members are insurance agents designated Chartered Life Underwriter (CLU) and also professionals in financial services who are designated Chartered Financial Consultant (ChFC). Offers education programs.

Independent Insurance Agents of America
127 Peyton St.
Alexandria, VA 22314
703-683-4422
Offers selling and management advice to independent agencies that sell all types of insurance.

Million Dollar Round Table
325 W. Touhy
Park Ridge, IL 60068
708-692-6378
Roderick Geer, Executive Vice President
Life insurance agents who sell over $2.3 million of life insurance annually.

Society of Certified Insurance Counselors
PO Box 27027
Austin, TX 78755-1027
512-345-7932
512-343-2167 Fax
William Hold, President
This professional society offers educational programs that lead to the Certified Insurance Counselor designation.

PERIODICALS

American Agent and Broker
Commerce Publishing Co.
408 Olive St.
St. Louis, MO 63102
314-421-5445
D.A. Baetz, Editor
Offers how-to information regarding sales and agency management. Written for agents who handle more than one line of insurance.

Broker World
Insurance Publications, Inc.
10709 Barkley, Ste. 3
Overland Park, KS 66211
800-762-3387
Sharon Chace, Editor
Follows insurance trends and offers advice to independent agents.

Rough Notes
Rough Notes Co., Inc.
1200 N. Meridian
Box 564
Indianapolis, IN 46206
800-428-4384
Thomas McCoy, Editor
Sales and marketing advice for property and casualty insurance agents.

COMPANIES

Alexander and Alexander Services, Inc.
1211 Ave. of the Americas
New York, NY 10036
212-840-8500
Insurance agencies.

Crawford and Co.
P.O. Box 5047
Atlanta, GA 30342
404-256-0830
Insurance agencies.

Frank B. Hall and Co., Inc.
261 Madison Ave.
New York, NY 10016
212-922-1300
Insurance agencies.

Jardine Insurance Brokers, Inc.
333 Bush St.
San Francisco, CA 94104
415-391-2600
Insurance agencies.

Johnson and Higgins
125 Broad St.
New York, NY 10004
212-574-7000
Insurance agencies.

Lawrence Agency Corp.
108 Union St.
Schenectady, NY 12305
518-3710-1720
Insurance agencies.

Lawrence Insurance Group, Inc.
500 5th Ave.
New York, NY 10110
212-944-8242
Insurance agencies.

Marsh and McLennan Companies, Inc.
1166 Ave. of the Americas
New York, NY 10036
212-345-5000
Insurance agencies.

Willis Corroon Corp.
Wall Street Plz.
New York, NY 10005
212-363-4100
Insurance agencies.

INTELLECTUAL PROPERTY

Intellectual property includes patents, copyrights, and trademarks.

See also: INVENTIONS (for information sources on patenting, trademarking, and copyrighting property)

ASSOCIATIONS

American Copyright Society
345 W. 58th St.
New York, NY 10019
212-582-5705
Gerard Delachapelle, Managing Director
This group of composers, authors, and publishers of music works to protect the property of its members.

American Intellectual Property Law Association
2001 Jefferson Davis Hwy., Ste. 203
Arlington, VA 22202
703-521-1680
703-892-2752 Fax
Michael Blommer, Executive Director
Attorneys who practice copyright, patent, and trademark law.

Brand Names Education Foundation
6 E. 45th St.
New York, NY 10017
212-986-5880
212-687-8267 Fax
Robin Rolfe, President
Promotes the use of brand names and trademarks.

Copyright Clearance Center
27 Congress St.
Salem, MA 01970
508-744-3350
508-741-2318 Fax
Eamon Fennessy, President
Collect fees from companies and others who use and distribute photocopies of copyrighted materials.

Copyright Society of the U.S.A.
Columbia University School of Law
435 W. 116th St.
New York, NY 10017
212-854-7696
212- 854-794 Fax
Deborah Sommer, Contact
Lawyers and others who share information about copyright and other types of intellectual property.

Intellectual Property Owners
1255 23rd St. N.W., Ste. 850
Washington, DC 20037
202-466-2396
Herbert Wamsley, Executive Director
Companies, attorneys, and others who work towards strengthening the laws that protect copyrights, patents, trademarks, and trade secrets.

International Intellectual Property Association
Box 476
New Vernon, NJ 07976
201-538-6473
201-538-7062 Fax
Jeremiah McAuliffe, President
Attorneys and others concerned with protecting all kinds of American-owned intellectual property abroad.

PERIODICALS

Attorneys and Agents Registered to Practice Before the U.S. Patent and Trademark Office
U.S. Patent and Trademark Office
Washington, DC 20231
703-557-1728
An official directory of persons who can legally practice before the U.S. Patent and Trademark Office.

B. N. A.'s Patent, Trademark & Copyright Journal
The Bureau of National Affairs, Inc.
1231 25th St., N.W.
Washington, DC 20037
202-452-4200
Jeffrey Samuels, Editor
Reports on the activities and decisions of the courts, Congress, the Patent and Trademark Office, and the Copyright Office.

Copyright Law Reports
Commerce Clearing House, Inc.
4025 W. Peterson Ave.
Chicago, IL 60646
312-583-8500
Follows trends in copyright law.

Index of Patents Issued from the United States
Patent and Trademark Office
U.S. Patent and Trademark Office
Washington, DC 20231
703-557-3341
A listing of new patents.

Intellectual Property Law
Harwood Academic Publishers
270 Eighth Ave.
New York, NY 10011
212-206-8900
A scholarly journal on patent, trademark, and copyright law.

Intellectual Property Law Review
Clark Boardman Co., Ltd.
435 Hudson St.
New York, NY 10014
212-929-7500
Thomas Costner, Editor
A journal for patent, trademark, and copyright attorneys.

LIBRARIES

U.S. Patent & Trademark Office
Scientific and Technical Information Center
Crystal Plaza Bldg. 3
2021 Jefferson Davis Hwy.
Arlington, VA 22202
703-308-0810
Patents, trademarks, technology, and related topics.

FEDERAL GOVERNMENT

Department of State
2201 C St., N.W.
Washington, DC 20520
202-647-3686
Ask for the International Intellectual Property Advisory Committee.

U.S. International Trade Administration
Department of Commerce
14th St. and Constitution Ave., N.W.
Washington, DC 20230
202-377-2000
Ask for the Commodity Analyst who is an expert in patent, trademark, copyright, and related services.

U.S. Patent and Trademark Office
Crystal Plaza 2
2011 Jefferson Davis Highway
Arlington, VA 22202
703-305-8000
Ask for the Examining Group Director who is a specialist in the technology or product that interests you.

INTERIOR DECORATION

ASSOCIATION

American Society of Interior Designers
608 Massachusetts Ave. N.E.
Washington, DC 20002
202-546-3480
Robert Angle, Executive Director
A professional society of working interior designers that offers educational programs.

Association of Professional Design Firms
118 N. Clinton St., No. U5
Chicago, IL 60606
614-888-3301
614-888-3373 Fax
David Smith, President
Helps design companies and individual designers improve their marketing and management practices.

Institute of Business Designers
341 Merchandise Mart
Chicago, IL 60654
312-467-1950
Designers who work primarily on offices, businesses, and institutional facilities.

Interior Design Society
PO Box 2396
High Point, NC 27261
800-888-9590
Faye Laverty, Executive Director
Designers that specialize in working for retailers, particularly home furnishing stores.

International Society of Interior Designers
433 S. Spring St., 10th Fl.
Los Angeles, CA 90013
213-680-4240
213-680-7704 Fax
Carole Shanis, President
A large group of designers and educators that helps members find employment.

PERIODICALS

Architectural Digest
Knapp Communications Corp.
5900 Wilshire Blvd.
Los Angeles, CA 90036
213-965-3700
Paige Rense, Editor
A glossy magazine that highlights buildings, homes, and other interiors.

Business Interiors
BusFac Publishing Co., Inc.
121 Monmouth St.
Red Bank, NJ 07701
201-842-7433
Heidi Schwartz, Editor
Follows trends and offers advice to interior designers of offices and facilities planners.

Designers Illustrated
Select Communications, Inc.
4410 El Camino Real, Ste. 111
Los Altos, CA 94022
415-941-6200
Paul Nyberg, Editor
Portrays interior design ideas and home furnishings for consumers.

Interior Design
Cahners Publishing Co.
Interior Design Group
249 W. 17th St.
New York, NY 10011
212-645-0067
Stanley Abercrombie, Editor
Follows design trends and new products for professional designers.

LIBRARIES

Academy of Art College
Library
2300 Stockton St.
San Francisco, CA 94133
415-765-4202
Interior design, commercial arts, related subjects.

Bauder Fashion College
Library
508 S. Center St.
Arlington, TX 76010
817-277-6666
Interior design, fashion, and related subjects.

Fashion Institute of Technology
Library
7th Ave. at 27th St.
New York, NY 10001-5992
212-760-7884
212-594-9206 Fax
Interior design, fashion, commercial arts, technology, and management.

INTERNAL AUDITING

During an internal audit, a company's own accountants check financial accounts or other company records.

ASSOCIATIONS

Financial Managers Society
111 E. Wacker Dr.
Chicago, IL 60601
312-938-2576
Richard Yingst, President
Offers educational programs on internal auditing and other subjects for financial managers.

Institute of Internal Auditors
249 Maitland Ave.
Altamonte Springs, FL 32701-4201
407-830-7600
800-CIA-DESK
407-831-5171 Fax
G. Peter Wilson, President
A large group of internal auditors and comptrollers that sponsors educational seminars.

PERIODICALS

Handbook for Internal Auditors
Matthew Bender & Co., Inc.
11 Penn Plaza
New York, NY 10001
212-967-7707
Keagle Davis, Editor
Advice on all aspects of setting up and managing a corporate internal audit department.

Internal Auditing
Warren, Gorham and Lamont Inc.
One Penn Plaza
New York, NY 10119
800-950-1217
Offers practical advice to the managers of internal audit programs.

LIBRARIES

Institute of Internal Auditors
249 Maitland Ave.
Altamonte Springs, FL 32701-4201
407-830-7600
800-CIA-DESK
407-831-5171 Fax
G. Peter Wilson, President
Technical information for internal auditors.

INVENTIONS

See also: INTELLECTUAL PROPERTY

ASSOCIATIONS

American Association of Inventors
2853 State
Saginaw, MI 48602
517-791-3444
John McRae, President
Helps inventors develop, protect, and sell their ideas.

Affiliated Inventors Foundation
2132 E. Bijou St.
Colorado Springs, CO 80909-5950
719-635-1234
800-525-5885
John Farady, President
Offers information to inventors who wish to patent or sell their ideas.

Invention Marketing Institute
345 W. Cypress St.
Glendale, CA 91204
818-246-6540
Ted DeBoer, Executive Director
Members include both inventors and manufacturers who are looking for new products.

Inventors Clubs of America
PO Box 450261
Atlanta, GA 30345
404-938-5089
800-336-0169
Alexander Marinaccio, President
Represents clubs nationwide that assist inventors to protect and sell their inventions.

Inventors Workshop International Education Foundation
3201 Corte Malpaso, Ste. 304-A
Camarillo, CA 93012
805-484-9786
Alan Tratner, President
Helps inventors gain patent protection and market their products.

National Inventors Foundation
345 W. Cypress St.
Glendale, CA 91204
818-246-6540
Ted DeBoer, Executive Director
Helps inventors protect and market their ideas.

PERIODICALS

Abstract Newsletter: Government Inventions for Licensing
U.S. National Technical Information Service
5285 Port Royal Rd.
Springfield, VA 22161
703-487-4630
Linda LaGarde, Editor
Lists inventions and patents that are owned by the U.S. government and may be licensed.

Inventing and Patenting Sourcebook
Gale Research Inc.
835 Penobscot Bldg.
Detroit, MI 48226
800-877-4253
Robert Hoffman, Editor
Offers inventors advice on how to protect and sell their ideas.

Inventor's Gazette
Inventors Association of America
7780 Klusman Ave.
Box 1531
Rancho Cucamonga, CA 91730
714-980-6446
L. Troy Hall, Editor
Highlights inventors and their inventions.

LIBRARIES

Inventors Clubs of America
Library
Box 450261
Atlanta, GA 30345
404-938-5089
Inventions, patents, manufacturing, and marketing.

Inventors Workshop
Library
3201 Corte Malpaso, Ste. 304-A
Camarillo, CA 93012
805-484-9786
Inventions, technology, and related topics.

FEDERAL GOVERNMENT

U.S. Department of Commerce
14th St. & Constitution Ave., N.W.
Washington, DC 20230
202-377-2000
Ask for the National Engineering Laboratory in the National Institute for Standards and Technology.

U.S. Patent and Trademark Office
Crystal Plaza 2
2011 Jefferson Davis Highway
Arlington, VA 22202
703-305-8000
Ask for the Examining Group Director who is a specialist in the technology or product that interests you.

INVENTORY CONTROL

See also: MATERIALS HANDLING and OPERATIONS RESEARCH

ASSOCIATIONS

American Production and Inventory Control
  Society
500 W. Annandale Rd.
Falls Church, VA 22046
703-237-8344
800-444-2742
703-237-1071 Fax
Michael Stack, Executive Director
*Offers technical information about production
and inventory control.*

North American Association of Inventory Services
1609 Holbrook St.
Greensboro, NC 27403
919-294-2216
Lois Rasnake, Executive Director
*Helps inventory services promote their
industry.*

PERIODICALS

Chilton's Distribution Magazine
Chilton Co.
Chilton Way
Radnor, PA 19089
215-964-4379
Thomas Foster, Editor
*Provides advice on transportation, traffic
management, business logistics, and inventory
control.*

Directions
Health Care Material Management Society
99 E. Weber Rd.
Columbus, OH 43202
614-263-5927
S. Anne Sostrom, Editor
*Advises material management executives in
the health care field about a variety of subjects, including inventory control.*

Production and Inventory Management
American Production & Inventory Control
  Society
500 W. Annandale Rd.
Falls Church, VA 22046-4274
703-237-8344
800-444-2742
R. Woolsey, Editor
*Evaluates production and inventory manage-
ment systems.*

COMPANIES

Accu-Sort Systems, Inc.
511 School House Rd.
Telford, PA 18969
215-723-0981
*Optical systems and scanners for inventory
control and other purposes.*

Amherst Systems, Inc.
30 Wilson Rd.
Williamsville, NY 14221
716-631-0610
*Computerized inventory control systems for
retailers.*

Diebold, Inc.
P.O. Box 8230
Canton, OH 44711
216-489-4000
Inventory control and other products.

Huffy Corp.
7701 Byers Rd.
Miamisburg, OH 45401
513-866-6251
Provides inventory services to retailers, and manufactures a variety of other products.

International Identification, Inc.
721 York St., Box 430
Newport, KY 41071
606-261-2035
Identification tags used for inventory control and other purposes.

National Computer Systems, Inc.
11000 Prairie Lakes Dr.
Eden Prairie, MN 55344
612-829-3000
Inventory control and other products.

Symbol Technologies, Inc.
116 Wilbur Pl.
Bohemia, NY 11716
516-563-2400
Bar-code products used for inventory control and other purposes.

INVESTMENT BANKING

See also: BANKS AND BANKING; INVESTMENTS; MERGERS AND ACQUISITIONS; and SECURITIES

ASSOCIATIONS

Securities Industry Association
120 Broadway
New York, NY 10271
212-608-1500
212-608-1604 Fax
Edward O'Brien, President
Members include investment bankers, underwriters of securities, and stock dealers. Conducts research and offers educational programs.

PERIODICALS

Corporate Financing Week
Institutional Investor, Inc.
488 Madison Ave.
New York, NY 10022
212-303-3591
Tom Lamont, Editor
Reports news and trends about corporate finance, mergers and acquisitions, investment banking, tax issues, and other subjects of concern to corporate finance executives.

M & A Dealmaker
New York Law Publishing Co.
Marketing Department
111 Eighth Ave.
New York, NY 10011
212-741-8300
Offers news and statistics to lawyers, investment bankers, and others who assist in mergers and acquisitions.

COMPANIES

Alex Brown & Sons, Incorporated
(Subsidiary of Alex. Brown Incorporated)
135 E. Baltimore St.
Baltimore, MD 21202
301-727-1700
Investment bankers and security dealers.

Donaldson, Lufkin & Jenrette, Inc.
140 Broadway
New York, NY 10005
212-504-3000
Investment bankers.

A. G. Edwards, Inc.
One N. Jefferson Ave.
St. Louis, MO 63103
314-289-3000
Securities dealers and investment bankers.

Kidder, Peabody and Co.
10 Hanover Sq.
New York, NY 10005
212-510-3000
Securities dealers and investment bankers.

Legg Mason, Inc.
111 S. Calvert St.
Baltimore, MD 21203
301-539-3400
Investment brokers and investment bankers.

Merrill Lynch and Co.
North Tower
World Financial Center
New York, NY 10281-1332
212-449-1000
Investment brokers and investment bankers.

Morgan Stanley and Co.
1251 Ave. of the Americas
New York, NY 10020
212-703-4000
Securities dealers and investment bankers.

Nikko Securities Co. International, Inc.
(Subsidiary of Nikko Securities Co., Ltd.)
200 Liberty St.
New York, NY 10201
212-416-5400
Investment bankers and securities dealers.

Nomura Securities Co.
180 Maiden Lane
New York, NY 10038
212-208-9300
Securities dealers and investment bankers.

Oppenheimer and Co.
Oppenheimer Tower
World Financial Center
New York, NY 10281
212-667-7000
Securities dealers and investment bankers.

S.G. Warburg & Co. Inc.
(Subsidiary of S.G. Warburg Group)
787 Seventh Ave., Equitable Tower
New York, NY 10019
212-459-7000
Securities dealers and investment bankers.

FEDERAL GOVERNMENT

U.S. Securities and Exchange Commission
450 5th St., N.W.
Washington, DC 20549
202-272-3100
*Ask for the Office of Advisor Regulation or the
Investment Company Regulation Office.*

INVESTMENTS

See also: FINANCIAL ANALYSTS; MUTUAL FUNDS; REAL ESTATE
INVESTMENTS; and SECURITIES

ASSOCIATIONS

American Association of Individual Investors
625 N. Michigan Ave., Ste. 1900
Chicago, IL 60611
312-280-0170
James Cloonan, President
*Offers educational programs to individual
investors who research and choose their own
investments.*

Association for Investment Management and
    Research
5 Boar's Head Ln.
PO Box 3668
Charlottesville, VA 22903
804-977-6600
800-247-8132
804-977-1103 Fax
Darwin Bayston, President
*Provides research and educational programs
to investment analysts.*

Coalition of Publicly Traded Partnerships
1625 K St. N.W., Ste. 200
Washington, DC 20006
202-857-0670
Letitia Chambers, Executive Officer
*Studies and represents publicly traded part-
nerships and master limited partnerships.*

Council of Institutional Investors
1420 16th St. N.W., Ste. 405
Washington, DC 20036
202-745-0800
Sarah Teslik, Executive Director
*Helps pension funds, endowment funds, and
nonprofit foundations increase their return on
investment while protecting the interests of
shareholders.*

Independent Investor Protective League
PO Box 5031
Ft. Lauderdale, FL 33310
305-749-1551
Merrill Sands, Executive Vice President
Acts as an advisory and referral service for individual investors who may need protection from unscrupulous investment firms or services.

Investment Company Institute
1600 M St. N.W., Ste. 600
Washington, DC 20036
202-293-7700
202-293-7016 Fax
David Silver, President
A clearinghouse for information about mutual funds.

Investment Counsel Association of America
20 Exchange Pl.
New York, NY 10005
212-344-0999
Gail Edwards, Executive Director
Firms that offer investment advice on a continuing basis for steady clients.

Investment Management Consultants Association
10200 E. Girard Ave., Ste. 340
Denver, CO 80231
303-337-2424
303-337-0873 Fax
Evelyn Brust, Executive Director
Members include money managers, stock brokers, and investment advisors.

Investment Partnership Association
1100 Connecticut Ave. N.W., Ste. 500
Washington, DC 20036
202-775-9750
202-331-8446 Fax
Christopher Davis, President
Promotes investment partnerships.

Investor Responsibility Research Center
1755 Massachusetts Ave., N.W., Ste. 600
Washington, DC 20036
202-234-7500
202-332-8570 Fax
Margaret Carroll, Executive Director
Informs corporate and individual investors about the societal impact of certain investments in South Africa and elsewhere.

MicroComputer Investors Association
902 Anderson Dr.
Fredericksburg, VA 22405
703-371-5474
Jack Williams, Administrator
Provides advice, seminars, and software to investors who use microcomputers for stock analysis and portfolio management.

National Association of Investors Corp.
1515 E. 11 Mile Rd.
Royal Oak, MI 48067
313-543-0612
Thomas O'Hara, Executive Director
A large group of investor clubs whose individual members pool money to buy securities.

National Investor Relations Institute
2000 L St. N.W., Ste. 701
Washington, DC 20036
202-861-0630
202-861-0633 Fax
Louis Thompson, President
Conducts research and offers educational programs for corporate executives responsible for investor relations.

PERIODICALS

Barron's National Business and Financial
    Weekly
Dow Jones & Co., Inc.
200 Liberty St.
New York, NY 10281
212-416-2000
Alan Abelson, Editor
*Covers news, trends, financial indexes, and
specific investments for individual and institutional investors.*

DollarSense
E.F. Baumer & Co.
401 Shatto Pl., Ste. 105
Los Angeles, CA 90020
213-386-2111
Richard Baumer, Editor
*A consumer magazine offering advice on per-
sonal finances, retirement, and estate planning.*

Financial Product News
Enterprise Communications Inc.
1483 Chain Bridge Rd., Ste. 202
McLean, VA 22101
703-448-0322
Richard Stolz, Editor
*Describes new investment products for stock-
brokers and other investment professionals.*

Individual Investor
Financial Data Systems, Inc.
38 E. 29th St., 4th Fl.
New York, NY 10016
212-689-2777
*A consumer magazine that focuses on invest-
ing in small companies.*

Investment Reporter
Olympia Capital Corp.
325 N. Newport Blvd., No. 100
Newport Beach, CA 92663
714-548-8035
Peggy Powel, Editor
*News and advice for institutional investors,
stockbrokers, securities analysts, and corporate managers who make investment decisions.*

Pensions & Investments
Crain Communications, Inc.
220 E. 42nd St.
New York, NY 10017-5806
212-210-0100
Jamie Gilmore, Editor
*Surveys investment trends and issues that con-
cern corporate and institutional investors.*

Professional Investor
Lynatrace, Inc.
Box 2144
Pompano Beach, FL 33061-2144
800-826-2122
Robert Gross, Editor
*Financial data, indexes, and news for stock
market investors.*

Wall Street Journal
200 Liberty St.
New York, NY 10005
212-416-2000
Financial and investment news of all kinds.

LIBRARIES

Bear, Stearns & Co. Inc.
Library
245 Park Ave.
New York, NY 10167
212-272-2607
212-272-3083 Fax
*Investments, securities, business conditions,
and finance.*

Moody's Investors Service
Information Center
99 Church St.
New York, NY 10007-2787
212-553-0300
Investment information about publicly held municipalities, corporations, and governments.

Paine Webber Inc.
Library
1285 Ave. of the Americas
New York, NY 10019
212-713-3669
Investments, economic conditions, finance, money, and banking.

Standard & Poor's Corp.
Business Information Center
25 Broadway
New York, NY 10004
212-208-8514
Investments, securities, finance, corporations, and public utilities.

U.S. Securities and Exchange Commission
Library
450 5th St., N.W.
Washington, DC 20549
202-272-2618
Investments, finance, economics, accounting, securities, and related topics.

COMPANIES

Bear, Stearns & Co. Inc.
(Subsidiary of Bear Stearns Companies Inc.)
245 Park Ave.
New York, NY 10167
212-272-2000
Securities and other investments.

Charles Schwab Corp.
101 Montgomery St.
San Francisco, CA 94104
415-627-7000
Discount securities brokerage.

A. G. Edwards, Inc.
One N. Jefferson Ave.
St. Louis, MO 63103
314-289-3000
Securities and other investments.

Merrill Lynch and Co.
North Tower
World Financial Center
New York, NY 10281-1332
212-449-1000
Securities and other investments.

Morgan Stanley Group Inc.
1251 Ave. of the Americas
New York, NY 10020
212-703-4000
Securities and other investments.

Oppenheimer & Co., Inc.
(Subsidiary of Oppenheimer & Co., L.P.)
Oppenheimer Tower, World Fin. Ctr.
New York, NY 10281
212-667-7000
Securities and other investments.

Salomon Brothers Inc
(Subsidiary of Salomon Inc)
One New York Plaza
New York, NY 10004
212-747-7000
Securities and other investments.

Shearson Lehman Brothers Inc.
(Subsidiary of American Express Co.)
World Financial Center
New York, NY 10285
212-298-2000
Securities and other investments.

S.G. Warburg & Co. Inc.
(Subsidiary of S.G. Warburg Group)
787 Seventh Ave., Equitable Tower
New York, NY 10019
212-459-7000
Securities and other investments.

FEDERAL GOVERNMENT

Federal Trade Commission
Pennsylvania Ave. at 6th St., N.W.
Washington, DC 20580
202-326-2000
Ask for the Service Industry Practices office in the Consumer Protection Bureau.

U.S. Bureau of the Census
Washington, DC 20233
301-763-4040
Ask for the Business Investment Bureau.

U.S. Department of Commerce
14th St. & Constitution Ave., N.W.
Washington, DC 20230
202-377-2000
Ask for the International Investment Division in the Bureau of Economic Affairs.

U.S. International Trade Administration
Department of Commerce
14th St. and Constitution Ave., N.W.
Washington, DC 20230
202-377-2000
Ask for the Commodity Analyst who is an expert in investment management.

U.S. Securities and Exchange Commission
450 5th St., N.W.
Washington, DC 20549
202-272-3100
Ask for the Office of Advisor Regulation or the Investment Company Regulation Office.

IOWA

STATE OFFICE LOCATOR (*for referrals to all state government offices*)

515-281-5011

ARCHIVES AND RECORDS

Cultural Affairs Department
Historical Building
Des Moines, IA 50319
319-335-3916

ATTORNEY GENERAL

Attorney General's Office
Hoover State Office Building
2nd Floor
Des Moines, IA 50319
515-281-8373

BANKING

Banking Division
200 E. Grand Avenue
Des Moines, IA 50309
515-281-6514

COMMERCE

Commerce Department
1918 S. E. Hulsizer Avenue
Ankeny, IA 50021
515-281-7401

CONSUMER AFFAIRS

Consumer Protection Division
Hoover State Office Building
2nd Floor
Des Moines, IA 50319
515-281-5926

EDUCATION

Education Department
Grimes State Office Building
Des Moines, IA 50319-0146
515-281-5924

ENERGY

Energy & Geological Resources Division
Wallace State Office Building
Des Moines, IA 50319
515-281-4308

ENVIRONMENTAL AFFAIRS

Environmental Protection Division
Wallace State Office Building
Des Moines, IA 50319
515-281-6284

HEALTH

Public Health Deapartment
Lucas State Office Building
Des Moines, IA 50319
515-281-5605

HOUSING

Iowa Finance Authority
Grimes State Office Buildig
Ste. 222
Des Moines, IA 50309
515-281-4058

HUMAN RIGHTS

Civil Rights Commission
211 E. Maple Street
2nd Floor
Des Moines, IA 50319
515-281-4121

INSURANCE

Insurance Division
Lucas State Office Building
Des Moines, IA 50319
515-281-5523

LABOR

Labor Services Commission
1000 E. Grand Avenue
Des Moines, IA 50319
515-281-8067

LEGISLATION

Legislative Service Bureau
State Capitol Building
3rd Floor
Des Moines, IA 50319
515-281-3566

LIBRARY SERVICES

State Library Division
E. 12th & Grand Street
Des Moines, IA 50319
515-281-4105

LICENSING—CORPORATE

Uniform Commercial Code Division
State House
Des Moines, IA 50319
515-281-6560

LICENSING—PROFESSIONAL AND OCCUPATIONAL

Professional Licensing & Regulation Division
1918 S.E. Hulsizer Avenue
Ankeny, IA 50021
515-281-5596

MOTOR VEHICLES

Motor Vehicle Division
5268 2nd Avenue, N.W.
Des Moines, IA 50313
515-237-3265

OCCUPATIONAL HEALTH AND SAFETY

Employment Appeal Board
Lucas State Office Building
Des Moines, IA 50319
515-281-8113

OMBUDSMAN

Citizen's Aide & Ombudsman's Office
215 E. 6th Street
Des Moines, IA 50319
515-281-3592

PUBLIC UTILITIES

Utilities Division
Lucas State Office Building
Des Moines, IA 50319
515-281-5167

PURCHASING

Purchasing & Material Management
Hoover State Office Building
Level A
Des Moines, IA 50319
515-281-3089

REAL ESTATE

Real Estate Commission
1918 S.E. Hulsizer Avenue
Ankeny, IA 50021
515-281-7361

SECURITIES

Securities Bureau
Lucas State Office Building
Des Moines, IA 50319
515-281-4441

TAXATION AND REVENUE

Revenue & Finance Department
Hoover State Office Building
Des Moines, IA 50310
515-281-3204

TOURISM

Tourism Office
200 E. Grand Avenue
Des Moines, IA 50309-2882
515-281-3679
800-345-4692

TRANSPORTATION

Transportation Department
800 Lincoln Way
Ames, IA 50010
515-239-1111

UNEMPLOYMENT

Job Insurance Bureau
100 E. Grand Avenue
Des Moines, IA 50319
515-281-4986

WORKER'S COMPENSATION

Industrial Services Commission
100 E. Grand Avenue
Des Moines, IA 50319
515-281-5934

JEWELRY INDUSTRY

See also: GEM INDUSTRY

ASSOCIATIONS

American Gem Society
5901 W. Third St.
Los Angeles, CA 90036
213-936-4367
213-936-9629 Fax
Thomas Dorman, Executive Director
Members are jewelry retailers.

Independent Jewelers Organization
2 Railroad Pl.
Westport, CT 06880
203-226-6941
800-624-9252
203-454-4371 Fax
Jack Gredinger, President
*Helps independent jewelers by providing
advertising and promotion programs.*

Jewelers of America
Time-Life Bldg.
1271 Ave. of the Americas
New York, NY 10020
212-489-0023
800-223-0673
212-586-9396 Fax
Michael Roman, Chairman
*Helps retail jewelers improve their manage-
ment and marketing practices.*

Jewelry Industry Council
8 W. 19th St., 4th Fl.
New York, NY 10011
212-727-0130
Steffan Aletti, President
*Members are manufacturers, distributors, and
retailers of jewelry products. Sponsors educational, marketing, and promotional activities.*

Jewelry Manufacturers Association
475 5th Ave., Ste. 1908
New York, NY 10017
212-725-5599
Alex Glauberman, Representatives
Members manufacture jewelry products.

Jewelry Manufacturers Guild
PO Box 46099
Los Angeles, CA 90046
714-769-1820
Moshe Pereg, President
Represents the manufacturers of fine jewelry at trade shows and through a lobbying program.

PERODICALS

Chilton's Jewelers' Circular-Keystone
Chilton Co.
Chilton Way
Radnor, PA 19089
215-964-4474
George Holmes, Editor
Covers industry news and products for retail jewelers.

Costume Jewelry Review
Retail Reporting Bureau
101 Fifth Ave.
New York, NY 10003
212-255-9595
Reports on fashions in and merchandising of costume jewelry.

Lapidary Journal
Lapidary Journal, Inc.
Box 80937
San Diego, CA 92138
619-275-3505
Merle Berk, Editor
Advises jewelers and others about gemology and jewelry making.

Modern Jeweler National
Vance Publishing Corporaiton
7950 College Blvd.
Shawnee Mission, KS 66201
913-451-2200
Joseph Thompson, Editor
Follows jewelry trends and offers retailing advice.

LIBRARIES

Joseph Bulova School
Library
40-24 62nd St.
Box 465
Woodside, NY 11377
718-424-2929
718-335-0545 Fax
Jewelry repair, watches, mineralogy, gems, and other topics.

COMPANIES

Barry's Jewelers, Inc.
111 W. Lemon Ave.
Monrovia, CA 91016
818-303-4741
Jewelry retailer.

Cartier, Inc.
(Subsidiary of Cartier International Inc.)
653 Fifth Ave.
New York, NY 10022
212-753-0111
Jewelry and silverware retailer.

Finlay Fine Jewelry Corp.
(Subsidiary of Finlay Enterprises, Inc.)
521 5th Ave.
New York, NY 10175
212-382-7400
Operates fine jewelry concessions in department stores.

Kay Jewelers Inc.
(Subsidiary of Ratners Group plc)
320 King St.
Alexandria, VA 22314
703-683-3800
Operates jewelry stores.

Leach & Garner Co.
57 John L. Dietsch Sq.
North Attleborough, MA 02760
508-695-7800
*Manufactures precious metal chains, bracelets,
and other jewelry items.*

Lori Corp.
(Subsidiary of Artra Group Incorporated)
500 Central Ave.
Northfield, IL 60093
708-441-7300
Manufacturer and distributor of fashion jewelry.

Sotheby's Inc.
(Subsidiary of Sotheby's Holdings, Inc.)
1334 York Ave.
New York, NY 10021
212-606-7000
Auctioneer of fine art, jewelry, and other precious items.

Sterling Inc.
(Subsidiary of Ratners Group PLC)
375 Ghent Rd.
Akron, OH 44313
216-867-1230
Operates jewelry stores.

Zale Corp.
(Subsidiary of Peoples Jewellers Ltd.)
901 W. Walnut Hill Lane
Irving, TX 75038
214-580-4000
Operates jewelry stores.

FEDERAL GOVERNMENT

U.S. International Trade Administration
Department of Commerce
14th St. and Constitution Ave., N.W.
Washington, DC 20230
202-377-2000
*Ask for the Commodity Analyst who is an
expert in the jewelry industry.*

U.S. International Trade Commission
500 E St., S.W.
Washington, DC 20436
202-205-2000 Office of the Secretary
202-205-3296 Industries locator
*Ask for the Trade Analyst who is an expert in
the jewelry industry.*

JOURNALISM

See also: CABLE TELEVISION INDUSTRY; NEWSLETTERS; NEWS-
PAPERS; PERIODICALS, MAGAZINES, AND TRADE JOURNALS;
RADIO BROADCASTING INDUSTRY; TELEVISION BROADCASTING
INDUSTRY; and WRITING AND EDITING

ASSOCIATIONS

National Center for Business and Economic
   Communication
The American Univiversity
Cassell Bldg., No. 107
4400 Massachusetts Ave.
Washington, DC 20016
202-885-6167
Louis Kohlmeier, Director
*Offers seminars to executives and journalists
on business and economic communications.*

Society of Professional Journalists
16 S. Jackson
Greencastle, IN 46135
317-653-3333
317-653-4631 Fax
Ira Perry, Executive Director
*Offers a variety of seminars and services to
journalists.*

PERIODICALS

Columbia Journalism Review
Graduate School of Journalism
Columbia University
700 Journalism Bldg.
New York, NY 10027
212-854-1881
Suzanne Braun Levine, Editor
*Provides in-depth analysis of trends in jour-
nalism.*

Presstime
American Newspaper Publishers Association
Box 17407 Dulles Airport
Washington, DC 20041
703-648-1000
Maurice Fliess, Editor
Reports on the newspaper business.

St. Louis Journalism Review
8380 Olive Blvd.
St. Louis, MO 63132
314-991-1699
Charles Klotzer, Editor
*Covers a wide variety of issues of concern to
journalists.*

LIBRARIES

Columbia University
Sulzberger Journalism Library
304 Journalism Bldg.
Broadway & 116th St.
New York, NY 10027
212-854-3860
Journalism and current events.

National Press Club
Eric Friedheim Library
529 14th St., N.W.
Washington, DC 20045
202-662-7523
202-879-6725 Fax
Journalism, history, current events, broadcast media, and print media.

University of Illinois
Communications Library
122 Gregory Hall
Urbana, IL 61801
217-333-2216
Journalism, newspapers, communication theory, magazines, publishing, broadcasting, and related topics.

KANSAS

STATE OFFICE LOCATOR (*for referrals to all state government offices*)

913-296-0111

ARCHIVES AND RECORDS

State Historical Society
120 W. 10th Street
Topeka, KS 66612
913-296-4792

ATTORNEY GENERAL

Attorney General's Office
Kansas Judicial Center
2nd Floor
Topeka, KS 66603
913-296-2215

BANKING

Banking Department
700 Jackson Street
Ste. 300
Topeka, KS 66603
913-296-2266

COMMERCE

Commerce Department
400 S.W. 8th Street
5th Floor
Topeka, KS 66603
913-296-3480

CONSUMER AFFAIRS

Consumer Protection Divison
Kansas Judicial Center
2nd Floor
Topeka, KS 66612
913-296-3751

EDUCATION

Education Department
120 E. 10th Street
Topeka, KS 66612
913-296-3202

ENERGY

Energy Division
1500 Arrowhead
Topeka, KS 66604
913-271-3100

ENVIRONMENTAL AFFAIRS

Environment Division
Landon State Office Building
901 S.W. Jackson Street
Topeka, KS 66612
913-296-1535

HEALTH

Health Division
Landon State Office Building
901 S.W. Jackson Street
Topeka, KS 66612
913-296-1343

HOUSING

Housing Programs Section
915 Harrison Street
Topeka, KS 66612
913-296-4100

HUMAN RIGHTS

Civil Rights Commission
Landon State Office Building
901 S.W. Jackson Street
Ste. 851-S
Topeka, KS 66612-1258
913-296-3206

INSURANCE

Insurance Department
420 S.W. 9th Street
Topeka, KS 66612
913-296-3071

LABOR

Public Employee Relations Board
501 Topeka Avenue
Topeka, KS 66603
913-296-3094

LEGISLATION

Legislative Research Department
State House
Room 545-N
Topeka, KS 66612
913-296-3181

LIBRARY SERVICES

State Library
State House
3rd Floor
Topeka, KS 66612
913-296-3296

LICENSING—CORPORATE

Corporation Commission
1500 S.W. Arrowhead Road
Topeka, KS 66604-4027
913-271-3100

MOTOR VEHICLES

Vehicles Division
915 Harrison Street
Topeka, KS 66612-1588
913-296-3601

OCCUPATIONAL HEALTH AND SAFETY

Industrial Safety & Health Division
401 Topeka Avenue
Topeka, KS 66603
913-296-4386

OMBUDSMAN

Constituent Services Division
State Capitol
2nd Floor
Topeka, KS 66612-1504
913-296-3232

PUBLIC UTILITIES

Utilities Division
Corporation Commission
1500 S.W. Arrowhead Road
Topeka, KS 66604-4027
913-271-3100

PURCHASING

Purchasing Division
State Capitol
Room 263-E
Topeka, KS 66612
913-296-2376

REAL ESTATE

Real Estate Commission
109 W. 9th Street
Room 501
Topeka, KS 66612
913-296-3411

SECURITIES

Securities Division
420 S.W. 9th Street
Topeka, KS 66612
913-296-7846

TAXATION AND REVENUE

Revenue Department
915 Harrison Street
Topeka, KS 66612-1588
913-296-3041

TOURISM

Travel & Tourism Division
400 W. 8th Street
Ste. 500
Topeka, KS 66603
913-296-2009 or 7091
800-252-6727 (in Kansas)

TRANSPORTATION

Transportation Department
Docking State Office Building
Topeka, KS 66612
913-296-3461

UNEMPLOYMENT

Unemployment Insurance Program
401 Topeka Avenue
Topeka, KS 66603
913-296-3534

WORKER'S COMPENSATION

Workers Compensation Division
401 Topeka Avenue
Topeka, KS 66603
913-296-3441

KENTUCKY

STATE OFFICE LOCATOR (*for referrals to all state government offices*)

502-564-2500

ARCHIVES AND RECORDS

Libraries & Archives Department
P.O. Box 537
Frankfort, KY 40602
502-875-7000

ATTORNEY GENERAL

Attorney General's Office
116 Capitol Building
Frankfort, KY 40601
502-564-7600

BANKING

Financial Institutions Department
911 Leawood Drive
Frankfort, KY 40601
502-564-3390

COMMERCE

Economic Development Cabinet
Capitol Plaza Tower
24th Floor
Frankfort, KY 40601
502-564-7670

CONSUMER AFFAIRS

Consumer Protection Division
116 Capitol Building
Frankfort, KY 40601
502-564-2200

EDUCATION

Public Instruction Department
Capitol Plaza Tower
Frankfort, KY 40601
502-564-4770

ENERGY

Governor's Office for Coal & Energy Policy
P.O. Box 11888
Lexington, KY 40578-1916
606-252-5535

ENVIRONMENTAL AFFAIRS

Environmental Protection Department
Fort Boone Plaza
18 Reilly Road
Frankfort, KY 40601
502-564-2150

HEALTH

Health Services Department
275 E. Main Street
Frankfort, KY 40621
502-564-3970

HOUSING

Housing Corp.
1231 Louisville Road
Frankfort, KY 40601
502-564-7630

HUMAN RIGHTS

Human Rights Commission
Capital Plaza Tower
Room 832
Frankfort, KY 40601
502-564-3550

INSURANCE

Insurance Department
229 W. Maine
Frankfort, KY 40601
502-564-3630

LABOR

Labor Cabinet
127 Building
U.S. Highway 127 S.
Frankfort, KY 40601
502-564-3070

LEGISLATION

Legislative Research Commission
State Capitol Building
Room 300
Frankfort, KY 40601
502-564-8100

LIBRARY SERVICES

Public Records Division
P.O. Box 537
Frankfort, KY 40602
502-875-7000

LICENSING—CORPORATE

Corporation Division
Capitol Building
Room 150
Frankfort, KY 40601
502-564-2848

LICENSING—PROFESSIONAL AND OCCUPATIONAL

Occupations & Professions Division
301 Capitol Annex
Frankfort, KY 40601
502-564-3296

MOTOR VEHICLES

Vehicle Regulation Department
State Office Building
Frankfort, KY 40601
502-564-7000

OCCUPATIONAL HEALTH AND SAFETY

Occupational Safety & Health Review Commission
Airport Building
Louisville Road
Frankfort, KY 40601
502-564-6892

PUBLIC UTILITIES

Public Protection & Regulation Cabinet
P.O. Box 615
Frankfort, KY 40602
502-564-3940

PURCHASING

Purchasing Division
301 Capitol Annex
Frankfort, KY 40601
502-564-3633

REAL ESTATE

Real Estate Commission
10200 Linn Station Road
Ste. 201
Louisville, KY 40223
502-425-4273

SECURITIES

Securities Division
911 Leawood Drive
Frankfort, KY 40601
502-564-2180

TAXATION AND REVENUE

Revenue Cabinet
Capitol Annex
Frankfort, KY 40601
502-564-3226

TOURISM

Department of Travel Development
Capital Plaza Tower
22nd Floor
Frankfort, KY 40601
502-564-4270 or 4930
800-225-8747

TRANSPORTATION

Transportation Cabinet
State Office Building
Frankfort, KY 40622
502-564-4890

UNEMPLOYMENT

Unemployment Insurance Services Division
275 E. Main Street
Frankfort, KY 40621
502-564-2900

WORKER'S COMPENSATION

Workers Compensation Board
127 Building
U.S. Highway 127 S.
Frankfort, KY 40601
502-564-5550

LABEL INDUSTRY

See also: PACKAGING

ASSOCIATIONS

Label Printing Industries of America
100 Dangerfield Rd.
Alexandria, VA 22314
703-519-8122
Lois Eck, Executive Director
Printers of labels for household items, food, and many other products.

Tag and Label Manufacturers Institute
104 Wilmot Rd., Ste. 201
Deerfield, IL 60015-5195
708-940-8800
708-940-7218 Fax
Carol Godiksen, Executive Director
Members include label and tag producers, and manufacturers of equipment and supplies.

PERIODICALS

Forms & Label Purchasing
North American Publishing Co.
401 N. Broad St.
Philadelphia, PA 19108
215-238-5300
William Drennan, Editor
Offers advice and reports on new products for buyers of business forms and labels.

LIBRARIES

Avery Dennison
Research Center
Information Center
2900 Bradley St.
Pasadena, CA 91107-1599
818-398-2555
818-398-2553 Fax
Labels and other subjects.

COMPANIES

Avery Dennison Corp.
150 N. Orange Grove Blvd.
Pasadena, CA 91103
818-304-2000
Pressure-sensitive labels and other products.

Double Envelope Corp.
7702 Plantation Rd., N.W.
Roanoke, VA 24019
703-362-3311
Envelopes and labels.

Fort Dearborn Lithograph Co.
6035 Gross Pt. Rd.
Chicago, IL 60648
312-774-4321
Labels and greeting cards.

Graphic Technology, Incorporated
(Subsidiary of Nitto Denko America)
301 Gardner Dr.
Industrial Airport, KS 66031
913-764-5550
Pressure sensitive labels and bar-coded products.

Intermec Corp.
(Subsidiary of Litton Industries, Inc.)
6001-36th Ave. W., Box 4280
Everett, WA 98203
206-348-2600
Bar-code products including label printers.

Manco, Inc.
830 Canterbury Rd.
Westlake, OH 44145
216-228-3100
Pressure-sensitive labels and other products.

Monarch Marking Systems, Inc.
(Subsidiary of Pitney Bowes Inc.)
P. O. Box 608
Dayton, OH 45401
513-865-2123
Price marking devices and labels.

Paper Manufacturers Co.
9800 Bustleton Ave.
Philadelphia, PA 19115
215-673-4500
Various types of labels.

Paxar Corp.
275 N. Middletown Rd.
Pearl River, NY 10965
914-735-9200
Labels and tags.

Symbol Technologies, Inc.
116 Wilbur Pl.
Bohemia, NY 11716
516-563-2400
Bar-code products including labels and label-reading equipment.

Weber Marking Systems, Inc.
711 W. Algonquin Rd.
Arlington Heights, IL 60005
708-364-8500
Label printing machines and other types of machines.

Wurzburg, Inc.
710 S. Fourth St.
Memphis, TN 38102
901-525-1441
Label printing machines and other types of products.

FEDERAL GOVERNMENT

Federal Trade Commission
Pennsylvania Ave. at 6th St., N.W.
Washington, DC 20580
202-326-2000
Ask for the Bureau of Consumer Protection.

U.S. International Trade Administration
Department of Commerce
14th St. and Constitution Ave., N.W.
Washington, DC 20230
202-377-2000
Ask for the Commodity Analyst who is an expert in labels and labeling.

U.S. International Trade Commission
500 E St., S.W.
Washington, DC 20436
202-205-2000 Office of the Secretary
202-205-3296 Industries locator
Ask for the Trade Analyst who is an expert in labels and labeling.

LABORATORIES

See also: MEDICAL AND HOSPITAL EQUIPMENT INDUSTRY and RESEARCH AND DEVELOPMENT

ASSOCIATIONS

American Council of Independent Laboratories
1725 K St. N.W.
Washington, DC 20006
202-887-5872
202-887-0021 Fax
Joseph O'Neil, Executive Director
Members are laboratories that test, research, and analyze products for a wide range of clients.

National Conference of Standards Laboratories
1800 30th St., Ste. 305B
Boulder, CO 80301
303-440-3339
Wilbur Anson, Manager
Members work for laboratories that standardize measurements and calibrations.

Underwriters Laboratories
333 Pfingsten Rd.
Northbrook, IL 60062
708-272-8800
Tom Castino, President
This well-known product safety laboratory certifies a wide range of consumer products.

PERIODICALS

American Laboratory News
International Scientific Communications, Inc.
Box 870
Shelton, CT 06484-0870
203-926-9300
Brian Howard, Editor
Follows trends in laboratories and the products they use.

Clinical Laboratory Science
American Society of Medical Technology, Inc.
2021 L St., N.W., Ste. 400
Washington, DC 20036
202-785-3311
L. Michael Posey, Editor
Reports on issues and developments that concern medical technologists at all levels.

Labmedica
Globetech Publishing
30 Cannon Rd.
Wilton, CT 06897
203-762-3432
Jill Roberge, Editor
Follows the latest news involving medical technology in laboratories.

Laboratory Equipment
Gordon Publications, Inc.
301 Gibraltar Dr.
Morris Plains, NJ 07950
201-361-9060
Helen Robinson, Editor
Covers new products for laboratories.

Medical Laboratory Products
Medical Economics Co., Inc.
680 Kinderkamack Rd.
Oradell, NJ 07649
201-262-3030
Deborah Kaplan, Editor
Offers practical advice and reports on new products for medical laboratories.

COMPANIES

Baxter International Inc.
One Baxter Pkwy.
Deerfield, IL 60015
708-948-2000
Products and services for hospitals, clinical laboratories, and other markets.

Becton, Dickinson & Co.
One Becton Dr.
Franklin Lakes, NJ 07417
201-848-6800
Products for hospitals, laboratories, and other markets.

Damon Corp.
(Subsidiary of Nomad Partners L.P.)
115 Fourth Ave.
Needham Heights, MA 02194
617-449-0800
Clinical laboratory testing services.

Fisher Scientific
(Subsidiary of Henley Group, Inc.)
711 Forbes Ave.
Pittsburgh, PA 15219
412-562-8300
Instruments, chemicals, and apparatus for laboratories.

Groundwater Technology Inc.
100 River Ridge Dr.
Norwood, MA 02062
617-769-7600
Environmental laboratory services and related services.

Metpath Inc.
(Subsidiary of Corning Incorporated)
One Malcolm Ave.
Teterboro, NJ 07608
201-288-0900
Clinical laboratory testing services.

National Health Laboratories Inc.
(Subsidiary of National Health Care Group, Inc.)
7590 Fay Ave.
La Jolla, CA 92037
619-454-3314
Clinical laboratory testing services.

SmithKline Beecham Corp.
(Subsidiary of SmithKline Beecham p.l.c.)
One Franklin Plaza
Philadelphia, PA 19101
215-751-4000
Pharmaceutical products and clinical laboratory services.

VWR Corp.
1400 N. Providence Rd.
Media, PA 19063
215-891-2770
Distributors of products to educational and government laboratories.

Roy F. Weston, Inc.
Weston Way
West Chester, PA 19380
215-692-3030
Environmental laboratory services and related services.

FEDERAL GOVERNMENT

National Institutes of Health
9000 Rockville Pike
Bethesda, MD 20892
301-366-4000
Ask for Animal Care and Use.

U.S. Department of Commerce
14th St. & Constitution Ave., N.W.
Washington, DC 20230
202-377-2000
Ask for the Laboratory Accreditation office in the National Institute of Standards and Technology.

U.S. International Trade Administration
Department of Commerce
14th St. and Constitution Ave., N.W.
Washington, DC 20230
202-377-2000
Ask for the Commodity Analyst who is an expert in lab instruments.

U.S. International Trade Commission
500 E St., S.W.
Washington, DC 20436
202-205-2000 Office of the Secretary
202-205-3296 Industries locator
Ask for the Trade Analyst who is an expert in lab instruments.

LABOR UNIONS

ASSOCIATIONS

Coalition of Labor Union Women
15 Union Sq., W.
New York, NY 10003
212-242-0700
212-255-7230 Fax
Sandy Pope, Executive Director
Provides educational, research, and organizing activities.

Congress of Independent Unions
303 Ridge St.
Alton, IL 62002
618-462-2447
R. Richard Davis, President
Helps independent labor unions to organize employees and to bargain with management.

National Federation of Independent Unions
1166 S. 11th St.
Philadelphia, PA 19147
215-336-3300
F. J. Chiappardi, President
Helps promote the 300 independent labor unions that are members.

PERIODICALS

AFL—CIO News
American Federation of Labor—Congress of
    Industrial Organizations
815 16th St., N.W.
Washington, DC 20006
202-637-5032
Rex Hardesty, Editor
Reports news of interest to AFL-CIO members and leaders.

Allied Industrial Worker
Allied Industrial Workers of America, AFL—
    CIO
3520 W. Oklahoma Ave.
Milwaukee, WI 53215
414-645-9500
Dominick D'Ambrosio, Editor
*Covers a wide range of issues that concern
industrial workers.*

International Teamster
International Brotherhood of Teamsters,
    Chauffeurs, Warehousemen and Helpers
    of America
25 Louisiana Ave., N.W.
Washington, DC 20001
202-624-6800
Linda Fisher, Editor
Written for teamsters.

Labor Today
Labor Today Associates
7917 S. Exchange no.211
Chicago, IL 60617
312-933-4900
James Cavanaugh, Editor
*Provides how-to information for rank-and-file
labor activitists.*

LIBRARIES

American Federation of Labor and Congress
    of Industrial Organizations (AFL-CIO)
Library
815 16 St., N.W.
Washington, DC 20006
202-637-5297
202-637-5058 Fax
Labor, trade unions, and industrial relations.

Cornell University
New York State School of Industrial and
    Labor Relations
Martin P. Catherwood Library
Ives Hall
Ithaca, NY 14851-0952
607-255-2184
608-255-9641 Fax
*Labor organization, labor-management rela-
tions, industrial psychology, and related
topics.*

U.S. Department of Labor
Library
200 Constitution Ave., N.W., Rm. N-2439
Washington, DC 20210
202-523-6992
Labor, trade unions, and economics.

LABOR UNIONS

American Federation of State, County and
    Municipal Employees
1625 L St., N.W.
Washington, DC 20036
202-452-4800
Gerald McEntee, President

Communications Workers of America
1925 K St., N.W.
Washington, DC 20006
202-728-2300
James Booe, Secretary-Treasurer

International Association of Machinists and
    Aerospace Workers
1300 Connecticut Ave.
Washington, DC 20036
202-857-5200
George Kourpias, President

International Brotherhood of Electrical
    Workers
1125 15th St., N.W.
Washington, DC 20005
202-833-7000
J.J. Barry, President

International Brotherhood of Teamsters,
    Chauffeurs, Warehousemen and Helpers
    of America
25 Louisiana Ave., N.W.
Washington, DC 20001
202-624-6800
William McCarthy, Executive Officer

International Union, United Automobile,
    Aerospace and Agricultural Implement
    Workers of America
3000 E. Jefferson
Detroit, MI 48214
313-926-5000
Owen Bieber, President

National Education Association
1201 16th St., N.W.
Washington, DC 20036
202-833-4000
Don Cameron, Executive Director

Service Employees International Union
1313 L St., N.W.
Washington, DC 20005
202-898-3200
John Sweeney, President

United Brotherhood of Carpenters and Join-
    ers of America
101 Constitution Ave., N.W.
Washington, DC 20001
202-546-6206
Sigurd Lucassen, General President

United Food and Commercial Workers Inter-
    national Union
Suffridge Bldg.
1775 K St., N.W.
Washington, DC 20006
202-223-3111
William Wynn, President

LAUNDRY AND DRY-CLEANING INDUSTRY

See also: CLEANING PRODUCTS AND SERVICES

ASSOCIATIONS

Coin Laundry Association
1315 Butterfield Rd., Ste. 212
Downers Grove, IL 60515
708-963-5547
Frank Vitek, President
*Members include operators of dry-cleaning
and laundry stores, manufacturers of equipment and supplies used in coin-operated laundries, and wholesalers of these supplies.*

Institute of Industrial Launderers
1730 M St., N.W., Ste. 610
Washington, DC 20036
202-296-6744
202-296-2309 Fax
Lawrence Graham, President
*Offers information about cleaning technologies
and marketing to industrial launderers who
rent uniforms, towels, and other items.*

International Drycleaners Congress
PO Box I
Cupertino, CA 95015-3009
408-252-1746
George Laumann, Executive Director
*Acts as an information clearinghouse for tech-
nical and business information that concern
dry cleaners and laundry services.*

International Fabricare Institute
12251 Tech Rd.
Silver Spring, MD 20904
301-622-1900
301-236-9320 Fax
Charles Riggott, Executive Vice President
*A large group of dry cleaners, industrial and
hospital laundries, equipment supplies, and
others. Tests fabrics to determine their suit-
ability for washing and dry cleaning.*

Multi-Housing Laundry Association
4101 Lake Boone Tr., Ste. 201
Raleigh, NC 27607
919-787-5181
919-787-4916 Fax
Michael Olson, Executive Director
*Members own and operate laundry routes and
coin laundry equipment. Provides business
and tax information.*

Textile Laundry Council
316 Chestnut St.
Moorestown, NJ 08057
609-722-1182
Susan Heath, Executive Vice President
*Members are companies that offer diaper ser-
vice.*

PERIODICALS

American Coin-Op
Crain Associated Enterprises
500 N. Dearborn St.
Chicago, IL 60610
312-337-7700
Ben Russell, Editor
Follows news, trends, and new products for owners of coin-operated laundries.

American Drycleaner
Crain Associated Enterprises
500 N. Dearborn St.
Chicago, IL 60610
312-337-7700
Earl Fischer, Editor
Practical advice and new-product information for owners of dry-cleaning establishments.

Drycleaners News
Zackin Publications, Inc.
Box 2180
Waterbury, CT 06722
203-755-0158
Dave Johnston, Editor
Written for dry cleaners, primarily in the northeastern part of the U.S.

Laundry News
Mill Hollow Publications
19 W. 21st St.
New York, NY 10010
212-741-2095
Sylvia Levine, Editor
Covers news, issues, and products for the laundry industry.

LIBRARIES

Dixo Engineering
Library
158 Central Ave.
Box 7038
Rochelle Park, NJ 07662
201-845-6000
201-845-6004 Fax
Dry-cleaning procedures, standards, technologies, applications, and policy.

International Fabricare Institute
Library
12251 Tech Rd.
Silver Spring, MD 20904
301-622-1900
301-236-9320 Fax
Dry cleaning, textiles, and chemistry.

COMPANIES

Angelica Corp.
10176 Corporate Sq. Dr.
St. Louis, MO 63132
314-854-3800
Rental and laundry services of garments, and other products and services.

American Laundry Machinery Inc.
5050 Section Ave.
Cincinnati, OH 45212
513-731-5500
Commercial laundry and dry-cleaning machinery.

Cissell Mfg. Co.
(Subsidiary of Dyson-Kissner-Moran Corp.)
831 S. First St.
Louisville, KY 40203
502-587-1292
Dry-cleaning, laundry, and steam pressing equipment.

Concord Custom Cleaners
(Subsidiary of Rite Aid Corp.)
370 Boggs
Richmond, KY 40475
606-623-2550
Dry-cleaning services.

Dryclean U.S.A., Inc.
(Subsidiary of Johnson Group)
9100 S. Dadeland Blvd.
Miami, FL 33156
305-270-0000
Dry-cleaning stores.

Healthcare Services Group, Inc.
2643 Huntingdon Pike
Huntingdon Valley, PA 19006
215-938-1661
Housekeeping, linen, and laundry services.

Jensen Corp.
2775 N.W. 63rd Ct.
Fort Lauderdale, FL 33309
305-974-6300
Commercial laundry, dry-cleaning, and laundry-marking equipment.

Kahler Corp.
20 2nd Ave. S. W.
Rochester, MN 55902
507-285-2710
Operates hotels, motels, and laundries.

Solon Automated Services, Inc.
1101 Market St.
Philadelphia, PA 19107
215-238-3300
Operates coin-operated laundry machines in apartment buildings, motels, and university dormitories.

Spic and Span, Inc.
4301 N. Richards St.
Milwaukee, WI 53212
414-964-5050
Laundry and drycleaning services.

Sterling Supply Corp.
5697 Rising Sun Ave.
Philadelphia, PA 19120
215-342-7700
Dry-cleaning and laundry supplies and chemicals.

FEDERAL GOVERNMENT

U.S. Customs Service
Department of the Treasury
U.S. Customshouse
6 World Trade Center
New York, NY 10048
212-466-5550
Ask for the Commodity Specialist in charge of laundry and dry-cleaning equipment.

U.S. International Trade Administration
Department of Commerce
14th St. and Constitution Ave., N.W.
Washington, DC 20230
202-377-2000
Ask for the Commodity Analyst who is an expert in laundry and dry-cleaning machinery or services.

U.S. International Trade Commission
500 E St., S.W.
Washington, DC 20436
202-205-2000 Office of the Secretary
202-205-3296 Industries locator
Ask for the Trade Analyst who is an expert in laundry and dry-cleaning machinery or services.

LAWYERS

See also: BUSINESS LAW

ASSOCIATIONS

American Bar Association
750 N. Lake Shore Dr.
Chicago, IL 60611
312-988-5000
312-988-6281 Fax
By far the largest group of lawyers in the U.S. Conducts a very large range of research and educational activities. Offers numerous publications.

American Academy of Matrimonial Lawyers
20 N. Michigan Ave., Ste. 540
Chicago, IL 60602
312-263-6477
Lorraine West, Executive Director
Provides educational programs to lawyers practicing matrimonial and family law.

American Corporate Counsel Association
1225 Connecticut Ave. N.W., Ste. 302
Washington, DC 20036
202-296-4522
Nancy Nord, Executive DIrector
Offers research, management advice, and educational programs to attorneys who work in law departments of corporations.

Association of Trial Lawyers of America
1050 31st St. N.W.
Washington, DC 20007
202-965-3500
202-337-0977 Fax
Thomas Henderson, Executive Director
Members are attorneys, law professors, judges, and others involved in trial work, primarily lawyers representing plaintiffs. Offers a substantial research and education program.

National Association of Criminal Defense
    Lawyers
1110 Vermont Ave., Ste. 1150
Washington, DC 20005
202-872-8688
202-331-8269 Fax
Keith Stroup, Executive Director
Represents the interest of attorneys who handle criminal defense cases.

National Bar Association
1225 11th St. N.W.
Washington, DC 20001
202-842-3900
John Crump, Executive Director
Provides a variety of educational programs to black and other minority attorneys.

PERIODICALS

A B A Journal
American Bar Association
750 N. Lake Shore Dr.
Chicago, IL 60611
312-988-5000
Gary Hengstler, Editor
*Advice, news, trends, and how-to information
for practicing attorneys.*

American Lawyer
American Lawyer Newspapers Group, Inc.
Am-Law Media L.P.
600 Third Ave.
New York, NY 10016
212-973-2800
*Follows major issues and news that concern
the legal profession.*

Barrister
American Bar Association. Young Lawyers
    Division
750 N. Lake Shore Dr.
Chicago, IL 60611
312-988-6047
Anthony Monahan, Editor
*Covers issues and trends regarding the legal
profession and the law.*

Litigation
American Bar Association. Litigation Section
750 N. Lake Shore Dr.
Chicago, IL 60611
312-988-5555
Miriam Kass, Editor
*In-depth coverage of topics of concern to trial
lawyers and judges.*

Trial
Association of Trial Lawyers of America
1050 31st St., N.W.
Washington, DC 20007
202-965-3500
Elizabeth Yeary, Editor
*Advises trial lawyers on litigation techniques
and follows news that interests litigators.*

LIBRARIES

American Bar Association
750 N. Lake Shore Dr.
Chicago, IL 60611
312-988-5000
312-988-6281 Fax
*Legal issues and professional information for
attorneys.*

LAW FIRMS

Davis Polk and Wardwell
1 Chase Manhattan Plz.
New York, NY 10005
212-530-4000

Gibson Dunn and Crutcher
333 S. Grand Ave.
Los Angeles, CA 90071
213-229-7000

Jones Day Reavis and Pogue
901 Lakeside Ave.
Cleveland, OH 44114
216-586-3939

Latham and Watkins
520 S. Grand Ave.
Los Angeles, CA 90071
213-891-1200

Shearman and Sterling
599 Lexington Ave.
New York, NY 10022
212-848-4000

Sidley and Austin
1 1st National Plz.
Chicago, IL 60603
312-853-7000

Skadden Arps Slate Meagher and Flom
919 3rd Ave.
New York, NY 10022
212-371-6000

Sullivan and Cromwell
125 Broad St.
New York, NY 10004
212-558-4000

Vinson and Elkins
3300 1st City Tower
Houston, TX 77002
713-651-2222

Well Gotshal and Manges
767 5th Ave.
New York, NY 10153
212-310-8000

FEDERAL GOVERNMENT

U.S. International Trade Administration
Department of Commerce
14th St. and Constitution Ave., N.W.
Washington, DC 20230
202-377-2000
Ask for the Commodity Analyst who is an expert in attorney's services.

U.S. International Trade Commission
500 E St., S.W.
Washington, DC 20436
202-205-2000 Office of the Secretary
202-205-3296 Industries locator
Ask for the Trade Analyst who is an expert in attorney's services.

LEATHER INDUSTRY

ASSOCIATIONS

International Leather Goods, Plastic and Novelty Workers' Union
265 W. 14th St., 14th Fl.
New York, NY 10011
212-675-9240
Dominick DiPaola, President
The main union that serves workers in the leather industry.

Leather Industries of America
1000 Thomas Jefferson St. N.W., Ste. 515
Washington, DC 20007
202-342-8086
202-342-9063 Fax
Charles Myers, President
This group of leather tanning firms shares technical and business information.

Luggage and Leather Goods Manufacturers of
America
350 5th Ave., Ste. 2624
New York, NY 10118
212-695-2340
212-643-8021 Fax
Robert Ermatinger, Executive Vice President
*Manufacturers and distributors of luggage,
briefcases, and other items made from leather.*

National Luggage Dealers Association
245 5th Ave.
New York, NY 10016
212-684-1610
212-684-1736 Fax
M. Howard Kaplan, Executive Director
*These luggage, handbag, and leather goods
retailers share information and promotional
materials.*

U.S. Hide, Skin and Leather Association
1700 N. Moore St., Ste. 1600
Arlington, VA 22209
703-841-5485
703-841-9656 Fax
Jerome Breiter, President
*Firms that produce and sell hides and skins.
Offers educational and marketing programs.*

PERIODICALS

Hide and Leather Bulletin
Jacobsen Publishing Co.
300 W. Adams St.
Chicago, IL 60606
312-726-6600
*Covers news for the leather tanning and shoe
manufacturing industry.*

Leather Crafters Journal
Leather Crafters Journal Inc.
4307 Oak Dr.
Rhinelander, WI 54501
715-362-5393
William Reis, Editor
*How-to information for those who work with
hand-crafted leather.*

World Leather
61 Massachusetts
Arlington, MA 02174
617-648-8160
Iain Howie, Editor
*Reports news about tanning around the U.S.
and around the world.*

LIBRARIES

Henkel Corp.
Technical Library
Bldg. 23
300 Brookside Ave.
Ambler, PA 19002
215-628-1526
*Chemicals used for leather treatment and
other purposes.*

U.S.D.A.
Agricultural Research Service
Eastern Regional Research Center Library
600 E. Mermaid Lane
Philadelphia, PA 19118
215-233-6602
215-233-6606 Fax
Leather and many other topics.

COMPANIES

Bond Leather Co., Inc.
2 Summit St. Rear, Ind Park
Peabody, MA 01960
508-531-3227
Leather coloring services.

Amdur Braude Riley, Inc.
P.O. Box 3636
Peabody, MA 01961
508-531-0400
Leather uppers for shoes, belts, and handbags.

American Leather Mfg. Co.
(Subsidiary of Elmo US Holding Co.)
2195 Elizabeth Ave.
Rahway, NJ 07065
908-382-1700
Leather for upholstery and automobiles.

Feuer Leather Corp.
3 Park Ave.
New York, NY 10016
212-686-7666
Leather tanning and finishing.

A. F. Gallun & Sons Co., L.P.
1818 N. Water St.
Milwaukee, WI 53202
414-271-4400
Calfskin, kidskin, and pigskin tanning.

Howes Leather Co. Inc.
439 W. Main St.
Ridgway, PA 15853
814-772-3015
Leather shoe soles and leather cut stock.

Irving Tanning Co.
(Subsidiary of Vista Resources, Inc.)
Main St.
Hartland, ME 04943
207-938-4491
Leather splits and leather uppers.

Prime Tanning Co., Inc.
Sullivan St.
Berwick, ME 03901
207-698-1100
Leather tanning and finishing.

Albert Trostel and Sons Co.
P.O. Box 743
Milwaukee, WI 53201
414-327-4870
Leather tanning and finishing.

United States Leather Holdings, Inc.
777 E. Wisconsin Ave.
Milwaukee, WI 53202
414-765-1040
Leather tanning and finishing.

FEDERAL GOVERNMENT

U.S. Customs Service
Department of the Treasury
U.S. Customshouse
6 World Trade Center
New York, NY 10048
212-466-5550
Ask for the Commodity Specialist in charge of leather.

U.S. International Trade Administration
Department of Commerce
14th St. and Constitution Ave., N.W.
Washington, DC 20230
202-377-2000
Ask for the Commodity Analyst who is an expert in the leather industry.

U.S. International Trade Commission
500 E St., S.W.
Washington, DC 20436
202-205-2000 Office of the Secretary
202-205-3296 Industries locator
Ask for the Trade Analyst who is an expert in the leather industry.

LIBRARIES

See also: Each of the 50 states under library services

ASSOCIATIONS

American Library Association
50 E. Huron St.
Chicago, IL 60611
312-944-6780
800-545-2433
312-440-9374 Fax
Linda Crismond, Executive Director
This large group of librarians and libraries offers educational and research services about subjects concerning libraries.

Medical Library Association
6 N. Michigan Ave., Ste. 300
Chicago, IL 60602
312-419-9094
Raymond Palmer, Executive Director
Offers education programs to librarians working in medical libraries.

Special Libraries Association
1700 18th St. N.W.
Washington, DC 20009
202-234-4700
202-265-9317 Fax
David Bender, Executive Director
Members include librarians and others who work in business, government, universities, and other libraries that specialize in certain subjects.

PERIODICALS

American Libraries
American Library Association
50 E. Huron St.
Chicago, IL 60611-2795
800-545-2433
Thomas Gaughan, Editor
Reports on news and trends affecting libraries in the U.S.

Library Journal
Cahners Publishing Co.
249 W. 17th St.
New York, NY 10011
800-669-1002
John Berry, Editor
Covers news of interest to libraries and reviews books and audiovisual materials.

School Library Journal
Cahners Publishing Co.
249 W. 17th St.
New York, NY 10011
800-669-1002
Lillian Gerhardt, Editor
Written for librarians who work with children, young adults, and adults in schools and public libraries.

LIBRARIES

Special Libraries Association
Information Resources Center
1700 18th St., N.W.
Washington, DC 20009
202-234-4700
202-265-9317 Fax
*Library management, special libraries, and
librarianship.*

University of Michigan
Information and Library Studies Library
300 Hatcher Graduate Library
Ann Arbor, MI 48109-1205
313-764-9375
*Library science, online information, informa-
tion storage, history of libraries, and related
topics.*

COMPANIES

Brodart Co.
500 Arch St.
Williamsport, PA 17705
717-326-2461
Library automation and cataloging systems.

Checkpoint Systems, Inc.
550 Grove Rd.
Thorofare, NJ 08086
609-848-1800
*Equipment to prevent library book theft and
other types of security equipment.*

CLSI, Inc.
320 Nevada St.
Newtonville, MA 02160
617-965-6310
Library automation systems.

Dynix, Inc.
151 E. 1700 S.
Provo, UT 84606
801-375-2770
Library automation systems.

Faxon Co., Inc.
15 Southwest Park
Westwood, MA 02090
617-329-3350
Library magazine subscription services.

Gaylord Bros.
(Division of Croydon Co. Inc.)
7272 Morgan Rd.
Liverpool, NY 13088
315-457-5070
Library furniture, shelving, and supplies.

Ingram Library Services, Inc.
1125 Heil Quaker Blvd.
Lavergne, TN 37086
800-937-5300
Book ordering service.

Kapco Library Products
P.O. Box 626
Kent, OH 44240
800-843-5368
Book repair products.

Library Bureau, Inc.
801 Park Ave.
Herkimer, NY 13350
315-866-1330
Library furniture and shelving.

OCLC
6565 Frantz Rd.
Dublin, OH 43017
800-848-5878
Online database and cataloging systems.

LIGHTING INDUSTRY

ASSOCIATIONS

American Lighting Association
435 N. Michigan Ave., Ste. 1717
Chicago, IL 60611
312-644-0828
312-644-8557 Fax
James Nicol, Managing Director
Represents firms that make, distribute, and retail lighting fixtures, lamps, bulbs, and accessories. Offers educational, marketing, and merchandising services.

Illuminating Engineering Society of North America
345 E. 47th St.
New York, NY 10017
212-705-7926
William Hanley, Executive Vice President
Offers technical information to designers, manufacturers, engineers, architects, and others interested in illumination.

International Association of Lighting Management Companies
14 Washington Rd., Bldg. 5
Princeton Junction, NJ 08550-1028
609-799-5501
Jeffry Barnhart, Executive Officer
Members are contractors that repair and maintain lighting systems for commercial and industrial clients.

National Association of Independent Lighting Distributors
320 Grote St.
Buffalo, NY 14207
716-875-3670
716-875-9764 Fax
C. W. Cooley, President
Helps distributors of lighting products through management and marketing education.

National Ornament and Electric Lights Christmas Association
230 5th Ave., Ste. 1611
New York, NY 10001
212-889-8343
212-683-3701 Fax
Phyllis Southad, Executive Secretary
Offers public relations, credit, and other services to manufacturers of Christmas lights and ornaments.

PERIODICALS

Architectural Lighting
Gralla Publications
1515 Broadway
New York, NY 10036
212-869-1300
Michael MacRae, Editor
Product information and how-to advice for professionals in architectural lighting.

Home Lighting & Accessories
Doctorow Communications, Inc.
1115 Clifton Ave.
Clifton, NJ 07013
201-779-1600
Peter Wulff, Editor
A consumer magazine that covers lamps and lighting fixtures.

Lighting Dimensions
Lighting Dimensions Associates
135 Fifth Ave.
New York, NY 10010-7193
212-677-5997
Laura Scholes, Editor
Design advice for lighting professionals in the fields of architecture, stage, and interior design.

LIBRARIES

GTE Sylvania
Engineering Library
100 Endicott St.
Danvers, MA 01923
508-750-2349
Engineering, chemistry, lighting products, and other subjects.

Lighting Technologies Inc.
Library
10 Downing Pkwy.
Pittsfield, MA 01201
413-499-2135
Lighting for aircraft, buildings, and related subjects.

COMPANIES

Day-brite Lighting Inc.
(Subsidiary of Thomas Industries Inc.)
1015 S. Green St.
Tupelo, MS 38802
601-842-7212
Industrial and consumer lighting fixtures.

GTE Products Corp.
(Subsidiary of GTE Products of Connecticut Corp.)
100 Endicott St.
Danvers, MA 01923
508-777-1900
Lamps, lighting fixtures, automotive lighting products.

Genlyte Group, Inc.
100 Lighting Way
Secaucus, NJ 07094
201-864-3000
Fluorescent, incandescent, track, and outdoor lighting.

Lights of America, Inc.
611 Reyes Dr.
Walnut, CA 91789
213-968-0414
Fluorescent lighting products.

Lithonia Lighting
(Division of National Service Industries, Inc.)
P. O. Box A
Conyers, GA 30207
404-922-9000
Fluorescent, incandescent, emergency, and high intensity lighting equipment.

Philips Lighting Co.
(Subsidiary of North American Philips Corp.)
P.O. Box 6800
Somerset, NJ 08875
908-563-3000
Light bulbs and lamps.

Prescolite Inc.
(Subsidiary of Hanson Industries North America)
1251 Doolittle Dr.
San Leandro, CA 94577
415-562-3500
Lighting fixtures.

Thomas Industries Inc.
4360 Brownsboro Rd.
Louisville, KY 40207
502-893-4600
Lighting fixtures and other products.

Valmont Industries, Inc.
Valley, NE 68064
402-359-2201
Street lighting poles and other products.

FEDERAL GOVERNMENT

U.S. Department of Transportation
400 Seventh St., S.W.
Washington, DC 20590
202-366-4000
*Ask for the Safety & Operations Division in
the Federal Highway Administration department.*

U.S. International Trade Administration
Department of Commerce
14th St. and Constitution Ave., N.W.
Washington, DC 20230
202-377-2000
*Ask for the Commodity Analyst who is an
expert in lighting equipment.*

U.S. International Trade Commission
500 E St., S.W.
Washington, DC 20436
202-205-2000 Office of the Secretary
202-205-3296 Industries locator
*Ask for the Trade Analyst who is an expert in
lighting equipment.*

U.S. Patent and Trademark Office
Crystal Plaza 2
2011 Jefferson Davis Highway
Arlington, VA 22202
703-305-8000
*Ask for the Examining Group Director who is
a specialist in lighting fixtures.*

LIQUOR AND SPIRITS INDUSTRY

See also: LIQUOR STORES; BREWING INDUSTRY; and WINE INDUSTRY

ASSOCIATIONS

Distilled Spirits Council of the United States
1250 I St. N.W., Ste. 900
Washington, DC 20005
202-628-3544
202-682-8888 Fax
F. A. Meister, President
*Acts as an information clearinghouse to manu-
facturers and distributors of distilled spirits
and to the public.*

National United Affiliated Beverage Association
PO Box 9308
Philadelphia, PA 19139
215-748-5670
Joseph Finn, President
*A large organization of Afro-American and
minority distributors of beverages, including
alcoholic beverages.*

Wine and Spirits Shippers Association
11800 Sunrise Valley Dr., Ste. 332
Reston, VA 22091
703-860-2300
800-368-3167
703-860-2422 Fax
Howard Rappin, President
Offers money-saving shipping options to importers and distributors of alcoholic beverages.

Wine and Spirits Wholesalers of America
1023 15th St. N.W., 4th Fl.
Washington, DC 20005
202-371-9792
Douglas Metz, Executive Vice President
Members distribute wine and distilled spirits.

PERIODICALS

Food & Beverage Marketing
Charleson Publishing
505 Eighth Ave., Ste. 1403
New York, NY 10018
212-695-0704
Alan Urbanski, Editor
Covers news for marketers of food, beverages, beer, wine, liquor, and tobacco.

Impact
M. Shanken Communications, Inc.
387 Park Ave. So.
New York, NY 10016
212-684-4224
Marvin Shanken, Editor
Reports news and research for the the wine, spirits, and beer industries.

Jobson's Liquor Handbook
Jobson Publishing Corp.
352 Park Ave. So.
New York, NY 10010
212-685-4848
Nicolas Furlotte, Editor
Covers statistics, trends, and analysis for the distilled spirits industry.

Mixin'
American Bartenders' Association
Box 15527
Sarasota, FL 34277
813-922-3316
Douglas Ferguson, Editor
Covers news about spirits, wines, and new products of interest to bartenders.

LIBRARIES

Joseph E. Seagram & Sons, Inc.
Corporate Library
800 Third Ave.
New York, NY 10022
212-572-7873
Distilled spirits, wine, and related topics.

COMPANIES

Bacardi Imports, Inc.
2100 Biscayne Blvd.
Miami, FL 33137
305-573-8511
Liquor importer and distributor.

Block Distributing Co., Inc.
Box 8157
San Antonio, TX 78208
512-224-7531
Liquor and wine distributors.

Continental Distributing Co. Inc.
9800 W. Balmoral Ave.
Rosemont, IL 60018
708-671-7700
Liquor and wine wholesalers.

DEC International, Inc.
P.O. Box 8050
Madison, WI 53708
608-222-4778
Liquor dispensing equipment and other types of equipment.

Kronheim Co.
99 Ray Rd.
Baltimore, MD 21227
301-242-8000
Liquor, beer, and wine wholesalers.

National Winex Spirits
700 W. Morris St.
Indianapolis, IN 46206
317-636-4880
Liquor and wine wholesalers.

Julius Schepps Wholesale Liquors, Inc.
2535 Manana St.
Dallas, TX 75220
214-357-8300
Liquor, beer, and wine wholesalers.

Joseph E. Seagram and Sons, Inc.
House of Seagram
375 Park Ave.
New York, NY 10152
212-572-7000
Liquor producer and distributor.

Stimson Lane Wine and Spirits Ltd.
P.O. Box 1976
Woodinville, WA 98072
206-488-1133
Liquor producer and distributor.

United Liquors Ltd.
1 United Dr.
West Bridgewater, MA 02379
508-588-2300
Liquor producer and distributor.

FEDERAL GOVERNMENT

U.S. International Trade Administration
Department of Commerce
14th St. and Constitution Ave., N.W.
Washington, DC 20230
202-377-2000
Ask for the Commodity Analyst who is an expert in the liquor and spirits industry.

U.S. International Trade Commission
500 E St., S.W.
Washington, DC 20436
202-205-2000 Office of the Secretary
202-205-3296 Industries locator
Ask for the Trade Analyst who is an expert in the liquor and spirits industry.

LIQUOR STORES

See also: LIQUOR AND SPIRITS INDUSTRY; BREWING INDUSTRY; and WINE INDUSTRY

ASSOCIATIONS

National Licensed Beverage Association
4214 King St., W.
Alexandria, VA 22302
703-671-7575
Gerald Murphy, Executive Director
Offers educational programs to owners and operators of bars, taverns, and other establishments that serve alcoholic beverages.

National Liquor Stores Association
5101 River Rd., Ste. 108
Bethesda, MD 20816
301-656-1494
John Burcham, Executive Director
Represents state associations of liquor stores.

PERIODICALS

Beverage Alcohol Business Scene
Diamond Publications
4504 Excelsior Blvd.
Minneapolis, MN 55416
612-920-7711
Gary Diamond, Editor
Covers the business scene for licensees who purchase more than $1 million of liquor, beer, or wine annually.

Beverage Dynamics
Jobson Publishing Corp.
352 Park Ave. So.
New York, NY 10010
212-685-4848
Nicolas Furlotte, Editor
Reports on the beverage alcohol industry.

COMPANIES

ABC Liquors, Inc
P.O. Box 593688
Orlando, FL 32859
407-851-0000
Liquor stores.

Armanetti, Inc.
7324 N. Western Ave.
Chicago, IL 60645
312-465-5300
Liquor stores.

Berbiglia, Inc.
1101 E. Bannister Rd.
Kansas City, MO 64131
816-942-0070
Liquor stores.

Flanigan's Enterprises, Inc.
2841 Cypress Creek Rd.
Fort Lauderdale, FL 33309
305-974-9003
Liquor stores.

Gold Standard Enterprises, Inc.
5100 W. Dempster St.
Skokie, IL 60077
708-674-4200
Liquor stores.

Kash-n-Karry Food Stores Inc.
6422 Harney Rd.
Tampa, FL 33610
813-621-0200
Food and liquor stores.

Price Co.
P.O. Box 85466
San Diego, CA 92138
619-581-4600
Retailer and wholesaler of many products,
including liquor.

Sigel Liquor Stores, Inc.
2960 Anode Ln.
Dallas, TX 75220
214-350-1271
Liquor stores.

FEDERAL GOVERNMENT

U.S. International Trade Administration
Department of Commerce
14th St. and Constitution Ave., N.W.
Washington, DC 20230
202-377-2000
Ask for the Commodity Analyst who is an
expert in liquor stores.

LIVESTOCK INDUSTRY

See also: CATTLE INDUSTRY; MEAT INDUSTRY; SHEEP INDUSTRY; and SWINE INDUSTRY

ASSOCIATIONS

Livestock Conservation Institute
6414 Copps Ave., Ste. 204
Madison, WI 53716
608-221-4848
John Lang, President
Members are livestock producers, meat indus-
try executives, transportation experts, and oth-
ers who share information about preventing
diseases and accidents that harm the value of
livestock.

Livestock Industry Institute
1 E. 9th Ave.
Hutchinson, KS 64501
316-669-8885
Robert Campbell, Executive Director
Offers information on increasing profitability
in the red meat and livestock industry.

Livestock Marketing Association
7509 Tiffany Springs Pkwy.
Kansas City, MO 64190
816-891-0502
800-821-2048
James Frost, General Manager
Provides marketing, public relations, and pro-
motional services to livestock companies.

National Association of Animal Breeders
401 Bernadette Dr.
Columbia, MO 65205
314-445-4406
314-446-2279 Fax
Gordon Doak, President
Sponsors research into new techniques for ani-
mal breeding.

PERIODICALS

Breeders Journal
American Breeders Service
Box 459
DeForest, WI 53532-0459
608-846-3721
Kathleen Bee, Editor
Technical information for livestock breeders.

Livestock Market Digest
Livestock Market Digest, Inc
Box 7458
Albuquerque, NM 87194
Emil Reutzel, Editor
505-243-9515
Advises on livestock production and marketing.

Livestock Weekly
Southwest Publishers, Inc.
Box 3306
San Angelo, TX 76902
915-949-4611
Stanley Frank, Editor
Covers news and trends in the livestock industry.

Weekly Livestock Reporter
Livestock Service, Inc.
120 N. Rayner St.
Box 7655
Fort Worth, TX 76111
817-831-3147
Ted Gouldy, Editor
Provides information for all segments of the livestock industry, including ranchers, breeders, operators of feedlots, and others.

Western Livestock Reporter
Western Livestock Reporter, Inc.
Box 30758
Billings, MT 59107
406-259-4589
Marcia Krings, Editor
Covers the livestock industry for the western part of the U.S.

LIBRARIES

Delaware Valley College of Science and Agriculture
Joseph Krauskopf Memorial Library
Doylestown, PA 18901
215-345-1500
215-345-1711 Fax
Animal science, dairy science, poultry husbandry, agribusiness, and related topics.

Michigan State University
Animal Industries Reference Room
208 Anthony Hall
East Lansing, MI 48824
517-355-8483
517-353-9806 Fax
Animal breeding and animal production.

University of Illinois
Agriculture Library
226 Mumford Hall
1301 W. Gregory Dr.
Urbana, IL 61801
217-333-2416
217-244-0398 Fax
Animal science and agricultural economics.

COMPANIES

E. Barber and Sons Livestock
P.O. Box 1327
Lexington, KY 40590
606-255-8751
Livestock.

Equity Cooperative Livestock Sales Association
E. 10890 Penny Ln.
Baraboo, WI 53913
608-356-8311
Livestock.

Finger Lakes Livestock Exchange, Inc.
Rte. 5 & Rte. 20
Canandaigua, NY 14424
716-394-1515
Livestock.

Garrard County Stockyard
P.O. Box 654
Lancaster, KY 40444
606-792-2118
Livestock.

Heinold Hog Market, Inc.
P.O. Box 375
Kouts, IN 46347
219-766-2211
Livestock.

Pontiac Livestock Sales
Rte. 116 E.
Pontiac, IL 61764
815-844-6951
Livestock.

Michigan Livestock Exchange
806 Coolidge Rd.
East Lansing, MI 48823
517-337-2856
Livestock.

Prairie Livestock, Inc.
P.O. Drawer 636
West Point, MS 39773
601-494-5651
Livestock.

Vintage Sales Stables, Inc.
3451 Lincoln Hwy. E.
Prardise, PA 17562
717-442-4181
Livestock.

FEDERAL GOVERNMENT

U.S. Department of Agriculture
14th St. and Independence Ave., S.W.
Washington, DC 20250
202-720-8732
Ask for the Livestock & Poultry Sciences Institute.

U.S. International Trade Administration
Department of Commerce
14th St. and Constitution Ave., N.W.
Washington, DC 20230
202-377-2000
Ask for the Commodity Analyst who is an expert in livestock.

U.S. International Trade Commission
500 E St., S.W.
Washington, DC 20436
202-205-2000 Office of the Secretary
202-205-3296 Industries locator
Ask for the Trade Analyst who is an expert in livestock.

LOCAL AREA NETWORKS

See also: COMPUTERS and TELECOMMUNICATIONS INDUSTRY

ASSOCIATIONS

Special Interest Group on Data Communication
c/o Won Kim
UniSQL, Inc.
9390 Research Blvd.
Kaledo I, Ste. 214
Western, TX 78759
512-343-7297
512-258-0487 Fax
Won Kim, President
This chapter of the Association for Computing Machinery studies computer communications equipment, including computer networks.

PERIODICALS

Applied Networks Report
International Data Corp.
Five Speen St.
Box 9015
Framingham, MA 01701
508-872-8200
Caroline Michel, Editor
Detailed information about local area network technology and its application in business.

IEEE Network
Institute of Electrical and Electronics Engineers, Inc.
345 E. 47th St.
New York, NY 10017-2394
212-705-7900
Warren Gifford, Editor
Highly technical information about local area network design, architecture, and management.

L A N
Miller Freeman Publications, Inc.
600 Harrison St.
San Francisco, CA 94107
415-905-2200
Patricia Schnaidt, Editor
Covers new products and their applications.

L A N Computing
Professional Press, Inc.
101 Witmer Rd.
Horsham, PA 19044
215-957-1500
News, product tests, and advice for managers of LAN systems.

L A N Reporter
National Software Testing Laboratories, Inc.
Plymouth Corporate Center
Box 1000
Plymouth Meeting, PA 19462
215-941-9600
Michael Stern, Editor
Evaluates LAN products.

L A N Technology
M & T Publishing, Inc.
501 Galveston Dr.
Redwood City, CA 94063
415-366-3600
Eric Maloney, Editor
Practical information for network technicians and managers.

L A N Times
McGraw-Hill, Inc.
1221 Ave. of the Americas
New York, NY 19929
212-512-2000
Edward Liebine, Editor
Follows industry trends and product innovations for network users.

LIBRARIES

University of Pittsburgh
Computer Science Library
200 Alumni Hall
Pittsburgh, PA 15260
412-624-8294
412-624-8296 Fax
Covers the full range of computer science subjects.

University of Washington
Computing Information Center
University Computing Services, HG-45
Seattle, WA 98195
206-543-5818
206-543-3090 Fax
Computing, LAN's, hardware, software, data communications, and related topics.

University of Oregon
Computing Center
Library
Eugene, OR 97403
503-346-1722
Microcomputers, LAN's, educational computing, and computer science.

COMPANIES

3Com Corp.
3165 Kifer Rd.
Santa Clara, CA 95052
800-NET-3COM
LAN products.

American Systems Corp.
14200 Park Meadow Dr.
Chantilly, VA 22021
703-968-6300
Installs and maintains various communications systems, including local area networks.

Artsoft Inc.
575 East River Rd.
Tucson, AZ 85704
602-293-6363
LAN products.

Banyan Systems, Inc.
115 Flanders Rd.
Westboro, MA 01581
508-898-1000
LAN products.

Cheyenne Software, Inc.
55 Bryant Ave.
Roslyn, NY 11576
516-484-5110
Software for LAN's.

Interphase Corp.
13800 Senlac Dr.
Dallas, TX 75234
214-919-9000
Local area network controllers and other microcomputer peripherals.

NetFrame Systems Inc.
894 Ross Dr.
Sunnyvale, CA 94186
408-745-0633
Network hardware.

Network General Corp.
4200 Bohannon Dr.
Menlo Park, CA 94025
415-688-2700
Tools for analyzing LAN's.

Novell Inc.
122 E. 1700 S.
Provo, UT 84601
801-379-5900
LAN software and systems.

Standard Microsystems Corp.
35 Marcus Blvd.
Hauppauge, NY 11788
516-273-3100
Hardware and software used in LAN's.

FEDERAL GOVERNMENT

U.S. International Trade Administration
Department of Commerce
14th St. and Constitution Ave., N.W.
Washington, DC 20230
202-377-2000
Ask for the Commodity Analyst who is an expert in computers.

U.S. International Trade Commission
500 E St., S.W.
Washington, DC 20436
202-205-2000 Office of the Secretary
202-205-3296 Industries locator
Ask for the Trade Analyst who is an expert in computers.

LOUISIANA

STATE OFFICE LOCATOR (*for referrals to all state government offices*)

504-342-6600

ARCHIVES AND RECORDS

Archives & Records Division
P.O. Box 94125
Baton Rouge, LA 70804
504-922-1200

ATTORNEY GENERAL

Justice Department
P.O. Box 94005
Baton Rouge, LA 70804
504-342-7013

BANKING

Economic Development Department
P.O. Box 94185
Baton Rouge, LA 70804-9185
504-342-5388

COMMERCE

Economic Development Department
P.O. Box 94185
Baton Rouge, LA 70804-9185
504-342-5388

CONSUMER AFFAIRS

Consumer Protection Section
P.O. Box 94005
Baton Rouge, LA 70804
504-342-7013

EDUCATION

Education Department
P.O. Box 94064
Baton Rouge, LA 70804-9064
504-342-3602

ENERGY

Energy Division
P.O. Box 44156
Baton Rouge, LA 70804
504-342-1399

ENVIRONMENTAL AFFAIRS

Environmental Quality Department
P.O. Box 44066
Baton Rouge, LA 70804
504-342-1266

HEALTH

Public Health Services Office
P.O. Box 60630
New Orleans, LA 70160
504-568-5052

HOUSING

Housing Finance Agency
5815 Corporate Boulevard
Ste. 6A
Baton Rouge, LA 70808
504-925-3675

HUMAN RIGHTS

Civil Rights
P.O. Box 3776
Baton Rouge, LA 70821
504-342-6729

INSURANCE

Insurance Department
P.O. Box 94214
Baton Rouge, LA 70804-9214
504-342-5900

LABOR

Labor Department
P.O. Box 94094
Baton Rouge, LA 70804-9094
504-342-3011

LEGISLATION

Legislative Services
P.O. Box 44486
Baton Rouge, LA 70804
504-342-7393

LIBRARY SERVICES

State Library Office
P.O. Box 131
Baton Rouge, LA 70821
504-342-4923

LICENSING—CORPORATE

Corporations Division
P.O. Box 94125
Baton Rouge, LA 70804-9125
504-925-4716

LICENSING—PROFESSIONAL AND OCCUPATIONAL

Licensing & Certification Division
P.O. Box 3767
Baton Rouge, LA 70821
504-342-5774

MOTOR VEHICLES

Motor Vehicles & Drivers License
P.O. Box 64886
Baton Rouge, LA 70896
504-925-6335

OCCUPATIONAL HEALTH AND SAFETY

Occupational Safety & Health Survey
P.O. Box 94094
Baton Rouge, LA 70804
504-342-3126

OMBUDSMAN

Citizen's Affairs
P.O. Box 94004
Baton Rouge, LA 60804-9004
504-342-0910

PURCHASING

Purchasing Office
P.O. Box 94095
Baton Rouge, LA 70804-9095
504-342-7000

REAL ESTATE

Real Estate Division
P.O. Box 94245
Baton Rouge, LA 70804-9245
504-379-1096

SECURITIES

Security Commission
325 Loyola Avenue
Room 315
New Orleans, LA 70112
504-568-5515

TAXATION AND REVENUE

Revenue & Taxation Department
P.O. 201
Baton Rouge, LA 70821
504-925-7680

TOURISM

Office of Tourism
P.O. Box 94291
Baton Rouge, LA 70804-9291
504-342-8119
800-334-8626

TRANSPORTATION

Transportation & Development Department
P.O. Box 94245
Baton Rouge, LA 70804-9245
504-379-1200

UNEMPLOYMENT

Unemployment Insurance Division
P.O. Box 94094
Baton Rouge, LA 70804-9094
504-342-3017

WORKER'S COMPENSATION

Workers Compensation & Administration
P.O. Box 94094
Baton Rouge, LA 70804-9094
504-342-7836

LUBRICATION INDUSTRY

See also: GARAGES AND SERVICE STATIONS (for information about the lubrication of motor vehicles)

ASSOCIATIONS

National Lubricating Grease Institute
4635 Wyandotte St.
Kansas City, MO 64112
816-931-9480
816-753-5026 Fax
Duane Fike, General Manager
Offers technical information and sponsors research into new and better lubricating greases.

Society of Tribologists and Lubrication Engineers
840 Busse Hwy.
Park Ridge, IL 60068
708-825-5536
708-825-1456 Fax
Maxine Hensley, Executive Director
Offers a forum to exchange technical information about lubrication methods and materials.

PERIODICALS

C A Selects. Lubricants, Greases, & Lubrication
Chemical Abstracts Service
2540 Olentangy River Rd.
Columbus, OH 43210
614-447-3600
Technical information on lubricants, greases, oils, and related topics.

Journal of Tribology
American Society of Mechanical Engineers
345 E. 47th St.
New York, NY 10017
212-705-7722
W.O. Winer, Editor
Technical data on lubricants and lubrication techniques.

LIBRARIES

Dylon Industries, Inc.
Library
7700 Clinton Rd.
Cleveland, OH 44144
216-234-1600
Lubricants, release agents, and related topics.

E.F. Houghton Technical Center
Library
Madison & Van Buren Aves.
Valley Forge, PA 19482
215-666-4146
215-666-7354 Fax
Lubricants, industrial oils, organic chemistry, and industrial chemicals.

Lubrizol Corp.
Chemical Library
29400 Lakeland Blvd.
Wickliffe, OH 44092
216-943-4200
Chemistry, lubrication, and petroleum.

COMPANIES

Aro Corp.
(Subsidiary of Ingersoll-Rand Co.)
One Aro Center
Bryan, OH 43506
419-636-4242
Industrial, farm, and automotive lubricating equipment, and other types of equipment.

Chevron Chemical Co.
(Subsidiary of Chevron Corp.)
6001 Bollinger Canyon Rd.
San Ramon, CA 94583
415-842-1000
Lubricating oil and many other types of chemicals.

Cit-Con Oil Corp.
(Subsidiary of Citgo Petroleum Corp.)
P.O. Box 1578
Lake Charles, LA 70602
318-491-8581
Lubricating oils.

Industrial Lubricants Co.
P.O. Box 10290
San Antonio, TX 78210
512-533-1264
Lubricating oils and greases.

Lincoln
(Subsidiary of Pentair Inc.)
One Lincoln Way
St. Louis, MO 63120
314-679-4200
Lubricating equipment and other types of equipment.

Lubricating Specialties Co.
8015 Paramount Blvd.
Pico Rivera, CA 90660
310-928-3311
Lubricating oils and greases.

Lubrizol Corp.
Lubrizol Petroleum Chemicals Co.
P.O. Box 158
Deer Park, TX 77536
713-479-2851
Lubricating oils and greases.

Pentair Inc.
1700 W. Hwy. 36
St. Paul, MN 55113
612-636-7920
Lubricating equipment and systems, and other types of products.

Penzoil Products Co.
P.O. Box 2967
Houston, TX 77252
713-546-4000
Lubricating oils and greases.

Stewart-Warner Corp.
(Subsidiary of BTR Inc.)
799 Bierman Ct.
Mt. Prospect, IL 60056
708-391-1300
Lubricating equipment and other types of equipment.

D. A. Stuart Ltd.
7575 Plaza Ct.
Willowbrook, IL 60521
708-655-4595
Lubricating oils.

FEDERAL GOVERNMENT

U.S. International Trade Administration
Department of Commerce
14th St. and Constitution Ave., N.W.
Washington, DC 20230
202-377-2000
Ask for the Commodity Analyst who is an expert in lubricating grease and oil.

U.S. International Trade Commission
500 E St., S.W.
Washington, DC 20436
202-205-2000 Office of the Secretary
202-205-3296 Industries locator
Ask for the Trade Analyst who is an expert in lubricating grease and oil.

LUGGAGE INDUSTRY

ASSOCIATIONS

American Luggage Dealers Cooperative
610 Anacapa St.
Santa Barbara, CA 93101
805-966-6909
805-966-3517 Fax
Marion Jones, Executive Director
Offers merchandising programs to luggage retailers.

Luggage and Leather Goods Manufacturers of
America
350 5th Ave., Ste. 2624
New York, NY 10118
212-695-2340
212-643-8021 Fax
Robert Ermatinger, Executive Vice President.
Members manufacture and distribute luggage of all kinds.

National Luggage Dealers Association
245 5th Ave.
New York, NY 10016
212-684-1610
212-684-1736 Fax
M. Howard Kaplan, Executive Director
Offers promotional assistance for retailers of luggage, handbags, and related goods.

PERIODICALS

Travelware
Business Journals, Inc.
50 Day St.
Box 5550
Norwalk, CT 06856
203-853-6015
Dana Carpenter, Editor
Reports on news and trends in the luggage industry.

COMPANIES

American Tourister, Inc.
91 Main St.
Warren, RI 02885
401-245-2100
Luggage.

Hartmann Luggage Co.
P.O. Box 550
Lebanon, TN 37087
615-444-5000
Luggage.

Koret, Inc.
136 Madison Ave.
New York, NY 10016
212-683-8544
Luggage, handbags, and leather goods.

Monarch Luggage Co.,Inc.
5 Delavan St.
Brooklyn, NY 11231
718-858-6900
Luggage.

Samsonite Corp.
11200 E. 45th Ave.
Denver, CO 80239
303-373-2000
Luggage.

Seward Luggage Co.
434 High St.
Petersburg, VA 23803
804-733-5111
Luggage.

Sirco International Corp.
700 S. Fulton Ave.
Mount Vernon, NY 10550
914-664-4400
Importers of handbags, soft luggage, and tote bags.

Skyway Luggage Co.
10 Wall St.
Seattle, WA 98121
206-441-5300
Luggage.

United States Luggage Corp.
(Affiliate of London Leather, Inc.)
366 Fifth Ave.
New York, NY 10001
212-594-3313
Leather luggage and attache cases.

Universal Luggage Co., Inc.
32-33 47 Ave.
Long Island City, NY 11101
718-392-6200
Luggage and attache cases.

FEDERAL GOVERNMENT

U.S. Customs Service
Department of the Treasury
U.S. Customshouse
6 World Trade Center
New York, NY 10048
212-466-5550
Ask for the Commodity Specialist in charge of luggage.

U.S. International Trade Administration
Department of Commerce
14th St. and Constitution Ave., N.W.
Washington, DC 20230
202-377-2000
Ask for the Commodity Analyst who is an expert in the luggage industry.

U.S. International Trade Commission
500 E St., S.W.
Washington, DC 20436
202-205-2000 Office of the Secretary
202-205-3296 Industries locator
Ask for the Trade Analyst who is an expert in the luggage industry.

MACARONI AND PASTA INDUSTRY

See also: FOOD INDUSTRY

ASSOCIATIONS

National Pasta Association
2101 Wilson Blvd., No. 920
Arlington, VA 22201
703-841-0818
703-528-6507 Fax
Joseph Lichtenberg, President
Offers education in agricultural subjects, plant operations, and other technical subjects to pasta manufacturers.

PERIODICALS

Pizza & Pasta
Talcott Communications, Inc.
222 Merchandise Mart Plaza, Ste. 1529
Chicago, IL 60654-1301
312-664-4040
Eileen Mullin, Editor
Offers news for pizza and restaurant owners, and equipment dealers.

COMPANIES

Borden, Inc.
Borden Pasta Div.
428 1st St. N.
Minneapolis, MN 55401
612-333-4281
Macaroni and spaghetti.

De Francisci Machine Corp.
46-45 Metropolitan Ave.
Ridgewood, NY 11385
718-456-6600
Macaroni making machines.

Gioia Pasta Co., Inc.
(Subsidiary of Borden, Inc.)
1700 Elmwood Ave.
Buffalo, NY 14207
716-873-8600
Macaroni, spaghetti, and egg noodles.

Golden Grain Co.
1111 139th Ave.
San Leandro, CA 94578
510-357-8400
Macaroni and spaghetti.

Hershey Pasta Group
San Giorgio Macaroni Div.
749 Gilford St.
Lebanon, PA 17042
717-273-7641
Macaroni and spaghetti.

Philadelphia Macaroni Co., Inc.
Catherine & 11th Sts.
Philadelphia, PA 19147
215-923-3614
Macaroni and spaghetti.

Prince Co., Inc.
(Subsidiary of Borden, Inc.)
Prince Ave.
Lowell, MA 01852
508-458-4111
Macaroni products, sauces, and other Italian-style foods.

Provena Foods Inc.
420 W. Central Ave.
Santa Ana, CA 92707
714-557-9833
Produces specialty foods, including macaroni and spaghetti.

Ravarino & Freschi, Inc.
(Subsidiary of Borden, Inc.)
4651 Shaw Blvd.
St. Louis, MO 63110
314-773-2700
Macaroni and spaghetti.

Ronzoni Macaroni Co., Inc.
(Subsidiary of General Foods Corp.)
50-02 Northern Blvd.
Long Island City, NY 11101
718-278-3500
Macaroni, spaghetti, egg noodles, and sauces.

FEDERAL GOVERNMENT

U.S. Department of Agriculture
14th St. and Independence Ave., S.W.
Washington, DC 20250
202-720-8732
Ask for the Economic Research Service.

U.S. International Trade Administration
Department of Commerce
14th St. and Constitution Ave., N.W.
Washington, DC 20230
202-377-2000
Ask for the Commodity Analyst who is an expert in pasta.

MACHINE SHOPS

See also: METAL WORKING INDUSTRY

ASSOCIATIONS

Automotive Engine Rebuilders Association
330 Lexington Dr.
Buffalo Grove, IL 60089-6998
708-541-6550
312-541-5808 Fax
Barry Soltz, President
Members are machine shops that specialize in rebuilding automotive products.

National Blacksmiths and Weldors Association
Box 327
Arnold, NE 69120
308-848-2913
James Holman, Information Director
Members include blacksmiths, welders, and machine shops that share technical data.

PERIODICALS

Automotive, Tooling, Metalworking, and Associated Industries Newsletter
National Safety Council
444 N. Michigan Ave.
Chicago, IL 60611
800-621-7619
Offers safety advice for machine shops.

Modern Machine Shop
Gardner Publications, Inc.
6600 Clough Pike
Cincinnati, OH 45244-4090
513-231-8020
Kenneth Gettelman, Editor
Covers a wide range of technical, business, and safety information for those working in the machining industry.

LIBRARIES

Joseph Bulova School
Library
40-24 62nd St.
Box 465
Woodside, NY 11377
718-424-2929
718-335-0545 Fax
Watch repair and watchmaking, computer repair, machine-shop procedures, and other topics.

Woodward Governor Co.
Woodward Library
5001 N. Second St.
Rockford, IL 61101
815-877-7441
815-877-0001 Fax
Machine-shop practices and other topics.

COMPANIES

Advance Mfg. Co., Inc.
Tpke. Industrial Park
Westfield, MA 01085
508-568-2411
Machine shop.

B & C Corp.
366 Fairview Ave.
Barberton, OH 44203
216-848-3714
Machine shop.

Babco Textron, Inc.
(Subsidiary of Textron Inc.)
28 Water St.
Danvers, MA 01923
508-777-1980
Job machine shop, components and assemblies for aircraft.

General Ship Corp.
400 Border St.
East Boston, MA 02128
617-569-4200
Shipbuilding, repairing, and machine-shop work.

Hydro-Mill Co.
9301 Mason Ave.
Chatsworth, CA 91311
213-873-4161
Job machine shop making aircraft parts.

Landis Manufacturing Systems, Inc.
456 Milford Sq. Pike
Quakertown, PA 18951
215-536-6944
Machine shop.

McSwain Manufacturing Corp.
(Subsidiary of Heroux Inc.)
189 Container Pl.
Cincinnati, OH 45246
513-671-6130
Machine shop.

Metalex Manufacturing, Inc.
5750 Cornell Rd.
Cincinnati, OH 45242
513-489-0507
Machine shop.

Seaberg Precision Corp.
165 Field St.
West Babylon, NY 11704
516-694-3871
Machine shop.

West Homestead Engineering & Machine Co.
(Division of Park Corp.)
W. Seventh Ave.
Homestead, PA 15120
412-464-4400
Machine shop and steel foundry.

MACHINE TOOL INDUSTRY

See also: INDUSTRIAL EQUIPMENT INDUSTRY

ASSOCIATIONS

American Machine Tool Distributors' Association
1335 Rockville Pike
Rockville, MD 20852
301-738-1200
301-738-9499 Fax
Robert Gale, President
Provides help with sales and technical training to distributors of machine tools that shape metal.

National Machine Tool Builders' Association—Association for Manufacturing Technology
7901 Westpark Dr.
McLean, VA 22102
703-893-2900
800-544-3597
703-893-1151 Fax
Albert Moore, President
Manufacturers of machine tools, molding machines, assemblers, and other machines that make durable goods. Sponsors educational programs in technological, safety, and business subjects.

Numerical Control Society/AIM Tech
5411 E. State St.
Rockford, IL 61108
800-399-8700
815-399-7279 Fax
Mike Mastroianni, Executive Director
This professional society of engineers and executives offers information on how numerical control can improve manufacturing processes.

PERIODICALS

Industrial Machine Trader
Heartland Communications, Inc.
1003 Central Ave.
Fort Dodge, IA 50501
515-955-1600
Reports on the availability of industrial machinery and machine tools for buyers and sellers.

International Journal of Machine Tools & Manufacture
Pergamon Press, Inc., Journals Division
Maxwell House
Fairview Park
Elmsford, NY 10523
914-592-7700
R. Davies, Editor
Technical information about the design, manufacture, and use of machine tools.

Surplus Record
Surplus Record, Inc.
20 N. Wacker Dr.
Chicago, IL 60606
312-372-9077
Thomas Scanlan, Editor
An extensive directory of used industrial equipment, machine tools, and parts available from dealers in the U.S. and Canada.

LIBRARIES

Cincinnati Milacron Inc.
Information Resource Center
4701 Marburg Ave.
Cincinnati, OH 45209-1025
513-841-8589
513-841-8059 Fax
Machine tools, automated manufacturing, metalworking, and other topics.

Doall Co.
Library
245 N. Laurel Ave.
Des Plaines, IL 60016
708-824-1122
Machine tools, equipment, metallurgy, and related topics.

Wayne State University
College of Engineering
Machine Tool Research Laboratory
Library
Department of Mechnical Engineering
5050 Anthony Wayne Dr.
Detroit, MI 48202
313-577-3898
313-577-3881 Fax
Machine tools, mechanical design, robotics, and related topics.

COMPANIES

Acme-Cleveland Corp.
30195 Chagrin Blvd.
Cleveland, OH 44124
216-292-2100
Machine tools and other machinery.

Cincinnati Milacron Inc.
4701 Marburg Ave.
Cincinnati, OH 45209
513-841-8100
Machine tools and other machinery.

Doall Co.
254 N. Laurel Ave.
Des Plaines, IL 60016
708-824-1122
Machine tools, cutting tools, and other machinery.

Fadal Engineering Co., Inc.
7260 Atoll Ave.
North Hollywood, CA 91605
818-765-9838
Machine tools.

Famtec International, Inc.
509 N. Third Ave.
Des Plaines, IL 60016
708-803-3200
Machine tools.

Giddings & Lewis, Inc.
142 Doty St.
Fond du Lac, WI 54935
414-921-4100
Automated machine tools.

Gosiger Inc.
108 McDonough St.
Dayton, OH 45402
513-228-5174
Dealer of machine tools and machinery.

Hurco Companies Inc.
6460 Saguaro Ct., Box 68180
Indianapolis, IN 46268
317-293-5309
Automated machine tools.

Oerlikon Motch Corp.
(Subsidiary of Oerlikon-Buhrle)
1250 E. 222nd St.
Cleveland, OH 44117
216-486-3600
Metal working machine tools and other machinery.

FEDERAL GOVERNMENT

U.S. Customs Service
Department of the Treasury
U.S. Customshouse
6 World Trade Center
New York, NY 10048
212-466-5550
Ask for the Commodity Specialist in charge of machine tools and equipment.

U.S. International Trade Administration
Department of Commerce
14th St. and Constitution Ave., N.W.
Washington, DC 20230
202-377-2000
Ask for the Commodity Analyst who is an expert in the machine tool industry.

U.S. International Trade Commission
500 E St., S.W.
Washington, DC 20436
202-205-2000 Office of the Secretary
202-205-3296 Industries locator
Ask for the Trade Analyst who is an expert in the machine tool industry.

MAINE

STATE OFFICE LOCATOR (*for referrals to all state government offices*)

207-289-1110

ARCHIVES AND RECORDS

State Archives Division
State House
Station 148
Augusta, ME 04333
207-289-5790

ATTORNEY GENERAL

Attorney General's Office
State House
Station 6
Augusta, ME 04333
207-289-3661

BANKING

Banking Bureau
State House
Station 35
Augusta, ME 04333
207-582-8713

COMMERCE

Economic & Community Development Office
State House
Station 59
Augusta, ME 04333
207-289-2656

CONSUMER AFFAIRS

Consumer Credit Protection Bureau
State House
Station 35
Augusta, ME 04333
207-582-8718

EDUCATION

Educational & Cultural Services Department
State House
Station 23
Augusta, ME 04333
207-289-5800

ENERGY

Energy Resources Office
State House
Station 53
Augusta, ME 04333
207-289-3811

ENVIRONMENTAL AFFAIRS

Environmental Protection Department
State House
Station 17
Augusta, ME 04333
207-289-2811

HEALTH

Health Planning
State House
Station 11
Augusta, ME 04333
207-289-2716

HOUSING

Housing Authority
P.O. Box 2669
Augusta,, ME 04338-2669
207-626-4600

HUMAN RIGHTS

Human Rights Commission
State House
Station 51
Augusta, ME 04333
207-289-2326

INSURANCE

Insurance Bureau
State House
Station 35
Augusta, ME 04333
207-582-8707

LABOR

Labor Department
P.O Box 309
Augusta, ME 04332-0309
207-289-3788

LEGISLATION

Policy & Legal Anaylsis Office
State House
Station 13
Augusta, ME 04333
207-289-1670

LIBRARY SERVICES

Library Services Bureau
State House
Station 23
Augusta, ME 04333
207-289-5600

LICENSING—CORPORATE

Uniform Commercial Code Bureau
State House
Station 148
Augusta, ME 04333
207-289-4177

LICENSING—PROFESSIONAL AND OCCUPATIONAL

Licensing & Enforcement Division
State House
Station 35
Augusta, ME 04333
207-582-8723

MOTOR VEHICLES

Motor Vehicles Division
State House
Station 148
Augusta, ME 04333
207-289-2761

OCCUPATIONAL HEALTH AND SAFETY

Labor Statistics Bureau
P.O. Box 309
Augusta, ME 04332-0309
207-289-6400

OMBUDSMAN

Community Services Division
State House
Station 1
Augusta, ME 04333
207-289-3771

PUBLIC UTILITIES

Public Utilities Commission
State House
Station 18
Augusta, ME 04333
207-289-3831

PURCHASING

Purchasing Bureau
State House
Station 74
Augusta, ME 04333
207-289-3521

REAL ESTATE

Real Estate Commission
State House
Station 35
Augusta, ME 04333
207-582-8727

SECURITIES

Securities Division
State House
Station 35
Augusta, ME 04333
207-582-8700

TAXATION AND REVENUE

Taxation Bureau
State House
Station 78
Augusta, ME 04333
207-289-2076

TOURISM

Publicity Bureau
P.O. Box 23000
Hallowell, ME 04347
207-289-2423 or 5710
800-533-9595

TRANSPORTATION

Transportation Department
State House
Station 16
Augusta, ME 04333-0016
207-289-2551

UNEMPLOYMENT

Unemployment Compensation Division
P.O. Box 309
Augusta, ME 04332-0309
207-289-2316

WORKER'S COMPENSATION

Workers Compensation
State House
Station 27
Augusta, ME 04333
207-289-3751

MAINTENANCE OF BUILDINGS

See also: CLEANING PRODUCTS AND SERVICES

ASSOCIATIONS

Association of Physical Plant Administrators of
   Universities and Colleges
1446 Duke St.
Alexandria, VA 22314
703-684-1446
703-549-2772 Fax
Walter Shaw, Executive Director
*Provides research and education to adminis-
trators of the buildings, grounds, and power
plants at colleges and universities.*

Building Service Contractors Association
   International
10201 Lee Hwy., Ste. 225
Fairfax, VA 22030
703-359-7090
800-368-3414
703-352-0493 Fax
Carol Dean, Executive Vice President
*Offers certification, public relations, manage-
ment training and other services to building
maintenance and cleaning services.*

Cleaning Management Institute
13 Century Hill Dr.
Latham, NY 12110-2197
518-783-1281
518-783-1386 Fax
Ellen Evans, Executive Officer
*Provides home study courses and computer
software to cleaning and building maintenance
firms.*

Environmental Management Association
255 Detroit St., Ste. 200
Denver, CO 80206
303-320-7855
303-393-0770 Fax
Dianna Rampy, Contact
*Offers educational programs to people respon-
sible for environmental sanitation and maintenance programs in buildings and industrial
plants.*

PERIODICALS

Cleaning Business
1512 Western Ave.
Box 1273
Seattle, WA 98111
206-622-4241
W. R. Coriffin, Editor
*Provides self-employed cleaning and mainte-
nance firms advice regarding cleaning techniques and business management.*

LIBRARIES

American Public Works Association
Information Services
1313 E. 60th St.
Chicago, IL 60637
312-667-2200
*Building management, grounds management,
and related subjects.*

Building Service Contractors Association
    International
Information Central
10201 Lee Hwy., Ste. 225
Fairfax, VA 22030-2202
703-359-7090
703-352-0493 Fax
Floor care, janitorial service, cleaning technologies, and related subjects.

Cleaning Management Institute
13 Century Hill Dr.
Latham, NY 12110-2197
518-783-1281
518-783-1386 Fax
Cleaning technologies and products.

COMPANIES

American Building Maintenance Industries
50 Fremont St.
San Francisco, CA 94105
415-597-4500
Building maintenance and janitorial services.

ARA Environmental Services, Inc.
1101 Market St.
Philadelphia, PA 19107
215-238-3000
Building maintenance services.

Arcade Building Maintenance, Inc.
1290 Ave. of the Americas
New York, NY 10104
212-246-3200
Building maintenance services.

Commercial Building Maintenance Co., Inc.
220 Spruce Ave.
South San Francisco, CA 94080
415-871-6740
Building maintenance services.

Diversco Inc.
105 Diversco Dr., Box 5527
Spartanburg, SC 29304
803-579-3420
Building maintenance services and other types of services.

ISS International Service System Inc.
(Subsidiary of ISS International Service System A/S)
1430 Broadway
New York, NY 10018
212-382-9800
Building maintenance and other types of services.

Jani-King International, Inc.
4950 Keller Springs Rd.
Dallas, TX 75248
214-991-0900
Building maintenance services.

Ogden Services Corp.
2 Penn Plz.
New York, NY 10121
212-868-6000
Building maintenance services.

ServiceMaster Co. LP
2300 Warrensville Rd.
Downers Grove, IL 60515
708-964-1300
Building maintenance services.

Temco Service Industries, Inc.
1 Park Ave.
New York, NY 10016
212-889-6353
Building maintenance services.

FEDERAL GOVERNMENT

U.S. International Trade Administration
Department of Commerce
14th St. and Constitution Ave., N.W.
Washington, DC 20230
202-377-2000
Ask for the Commodity Analyst who is an expert in building maintenance and operations.

U.S. International Trade Commission
500 E St., S.W.
Washington, DC 20436
202-205-2000 Office of the Secretary
202-205-3296 Industries locator
Ask for the Trade Analyst who is an expert in building maintenance.

U.S. Department of Housing and Urban
  Development
451 7th St., S.W.
Washington, DC 20410
202-755-5111
Ask for a specialist in the maintenance of buildings.

MANAGEMENT

See also: MANAGEMENT CONSULTANTS and MANAGEMENT INFORMATION SYSTEMS (MIS)

ASSOCIATIONS

American Institute of Management
PO Box 7039
Quincy, MA 02269
617-472-0277
Barbara Doll, President
Conducts research and offers educational programs to improve the efficiency and measurement of management.

American Management Association
135 W. 50th St.
New York, NY 10020
212-586-8100
212-903-8168 Fax
Thomas Horton, Chief Executive
By far the largest professional group of managers in the U.S. Offers a wide range of educational programs and materials.

Center for Management Effectiveness
427 Beirut Ave.
Pacific Palisades, CA 90272
213-459-6052
213-459-9307 Fax
Herbert Kindler, Director
Teaches the trainers of managers such subjects as stress control, resolving differences, decision-making, and risk-taking.

The Institute of Management Sciences
290 Westminster St.
Providence, RI 02903
401-274-2525
M. R. DeMelim, Executive Director
This professional society sponsors research on the science of management.

International Management Council
430 S. 20th St., Ste. 3
Omaha, NE 68102
402-345-1904
402-345-4480 Fax
John Shepherd, Executive Director
Offers leadership training programs to managers and supervisors.

Issues Management Association
1785 Massachusetts Ave. N.W., Ste. 501
Washington, DC 20036
202-232-3405
Provides research and training to help executives who deal with public policy, financial planning, governmental matters, and other large issues that are important to corporations.

National Management Association
2210 Arbor Blvd.
Dayton, OH 45439
513-294-0421
Ronald Leigh, President
Offers training and seminars in a variety of management, communications, and human resources subjects.

Society for Advancement of Management
126 Lee Ave., Ste. 11
Vinton, VA 24179
703-342-5563
703-342-6413 Fax
Joseph Bush, Executive Director
Gives seminars and conferences on such subjects as management, materials handling, industrial relations, quality control, and distribution.

PERIODICALS

Across the Board
Conference Board, Inc.
845 Third Ave.
New York, NY 10022
212-759-0900
A.J. Vogl, Editor
Reports on trends and issues that concern senior executives.

Administrative Management
Dalton Communications, Inc.
1123 Broadway, Ste. 1100
New York, NY 10010
212-924-8989
Don Johnson, Editor
Advises on business management techniques and new uses of technology.

Association Management
American Society of Association Executives
1575 Eye St., N.W.
Washington, DC 20005
202-626-2735
Ann Mahoney, Editor
Advice for managers of associations.

Chief Executive Magazine
Chief Executive Publishing
233 Park Ave. S.
New York, NY 10003
212-979-4810
J.P. Donlon, Editor
Information on policy, strategy, and management of interest to CEO's.

D & B Reports
Dun & Bradstreet
299 Park Ave.
New York, NY 10171
212-593-6800
Patricia Hamilton, Editor
Management news and advice for small businesses.

Harvard Business Review
Harvard University
Graduate School of Business Administration
Soldiers Field Rd.
Boston, MA 02163-1099
617-495-6182
Rosebeth Kanter, Editor
Detailed articles on business trends and issues.

Management Review
American Management Association
135 W. 50th St.
New York, NY 10020-1201
212-586-8100
Martha Peak, Editor
Reports news and advises executives on management techniques.

Sloan Management Review
Sloan Management Review Association
Massachusetts Institute of Technology
Sloan School of Management
1 Amherst St.
Cambridge, MA 02139
617-253-7170
Detailed articles on major issues and new technologies of concern to senior management.

LIBRARIES

American Management Association
135 W. 50th St.
New York, NY 10020
212-586-8100
212-903-8168 Fax
Management topics of all kinds.

University of Michigan
Kresge Business Administration Library
School of Business Administration
Tappan & Monroe Sts.
Ann Arbor, MI 48109-1234
313-764-7356
313-763-5688 Fax
Human resource management, general business, organizational behavior, marketing, and finance.

University of Pennsylvania
Lippincott Library
Van Pelt-Dietrich Library Center
3420 Walnut St.
Philadelphia, PA 19104-6207
215-898-2261
215-898-2261 Fax
Management, finance, labor, industrial relations, and business.

University of Washington
Business Administration Library
100 Balmer Hall, DJ-10
Seattle, WA 98195
206-543-4360
206-545-8049 Fax
Management, personnel, labor, and marketing.

MANAGEMENT CONSULTANTS

See also: CONSULTANTS and MANAGEMENT

ASSOCIATIONS

ACME—The Association of Management
  Consulting Firms
230 Park Ave.
New York, NY 10169
212-697-9693
Edward Hendricks, President
*Offers general information about management
consulting organizations and referrals to specific firms.*

Association of Internal Management Consultants
PO Box 304
East Bloomfield, NY 14443
716-657-7878
Margaret Custer, Executive Secretary
*Promotes the use of internal management con-
sultants and acts as a clearinghouse for the
exchange of techniques and methods.*

Council of Consulting Organizations
230 Park Ave.
New York, NY 10169
212-697-9693
Edward Hendricks, President
*Members are management consultants who
are independent or work for a consulting firm.*

PERIODICALS

Consultants News
Kennedy & Kennedy, Inc.
Templeton Rd.
Fitzwilliam, NH 03447
603-585-2200
James Kennedy, Editor
*Reports on news and trends of interest to man-
agement consultants.*

Directory of Management Consultants
Consultants News
Templeton Rd.
Fitzwilliam, NH 03447
603-585-2200
James Kennedy, Editor
*A descriptive listing of over 1200 firms provid-
ing management consulting services.*

Professional Consultant and Information
Marketing Report
20750 Ventura Blvd., No. 206
Woodland Hills, CA 91364
818-703-1415
Howard Shenson, Editor
*Advises on how to market consulting services
and describes seminars and information products for consultants.*

LIBRARIES

Boston Consulting Group
Research Library
200 S. Wacker Dr.
Chicago, IL 60606
312-993-3300
312-715-2250 Fax
Finance, industry, management consulting, and statistics.

Ernst & Young
Library
277 Park Ave.
New York, NY 10172
212-733-1975
212-773-3441 Fax
Management consulting, accounting, and taxation.

Fry Consultants Inc.
MacFarlane & Co., Inc.
Management Centre, Inc.
One Park Place, Ste. 450
1900 Emery St., N.W.
Atlanta, GA 30318
404-352-2293
404-352-2299 Fax
Management consulting, general business reference, marketing, and related topics.

COMPANIES

Philip Crosby Associates, Inc.
(Subsidiary of Alexander Proudfoot plc)
807 W. Morse Blvd., Box 2369
Winter Park, FL 32790
407-645-1733
Management consultants.

Harbridge House, Inc.
11 Arlington St.
Boston, MA 02116
617-267-6410
Management consultants.

Heidrick and Struggles International, Inc.
(Subsidiary of Heidrick and Struggles, Inc.)
125 S. Wacker
Chicago, IL 60606
312-372-8811
Management consultants with a specialty in executive recruiting.

Arthur D. Little, Inc.
25 Acorn Park
Cambridge, MA 02140
617-864-5770
Management consulting services.

McKinsey and Co., Inc.
55 E. 52nd St.
New York, NY 10022
212-446-7000
Management consulting services.

William M. Mercer, Inc.
1166 Ave. of the Americas
New York, NY 10036
212-345-7000
Management consulting services.

Kurt Salmon Associates, Inc.
12 E. 49th St.
New York, NY 10017
212-319-9450
Management consultants.

Science Management Corp.
P.O. Box 0600
Basking Ridge, NJ 07920
201-647-7000
Management and technology consultants.

Strategic Planning Associates, Inc.
(Subsidiary of Marsh & McLennan Companies Inc.)
2300 N Street, N.W.
Washington, DC 20037
202-778-7000
Management consultants.

Towers, Perrin, Forster & Crosby, Inc.
245 Park Ave.
New York, NY 10016
212-309-3400
Management consultants.

FEDERAL GOVERNMENT

U.S. International Trade Administration
Department of Commerce
14th St. and Constitution Ave., N.W.
Washington, DC 20230
202-377-2000
*Ask for the Commodity Analyst who is an
expert in management consulting.*

U.S. International Trade Commission
500 E St., S.W.
Washington, DC 20436
202-205-2000 Office of the Secretary
202-205-3296 Industries locator
*Ask for the Trade Analyst who is an expert in
management consulting.*

MANAGEMENT INFORMATION SYSTEMS (MIS)

See also: RECORDS MANAGEMENT

ASSOCIATIONS

Association for Systems Management
1433 W. Bagley Rd.
Cleveland, OH 44138
216-243-6900
Steve Adamson, Executive Director
*Helps MIS professionals and others responsi-
ble for administrative and organizational
information systems to be more efficient.*

Society for Information Management
401 N. Michigan Ave.
Chicago, IL 60611-4267
312-644-6610
312-321-6869 Fax
Henry Givray, Executive Director
*Offers technical information to directors of
management information systems and others
who manage the flow of information within
corporations.*

PERIODICALS

Computerworld
Computerworld, Inc.
375 Cochituate Rd.
Box 9171
Framingham, MA 01701-9171
508-879-0700
Bill Laberis, Editor
Reports on many aspects of computers and the use of automation in MIS systems.

Computing & Management
Management Science Associates
11016 Malaguena Lane, N.E.
Albuquerque, NM 87111
505-296-3017
John Hoover, Editor
Written for executives who use computers to help make management decisions.

Information Management: Strategies, Systems, and Technologies
Auerbach Publishers
One Penn Plaza
New York, NY 10119
212-971-5000
Reports on a wide range of technologies and practices used by data processing and MIS managers.

Information Processing & Management
Pergamon Press, Inc.
Maxwell House
Fairview Park
Elmsford, NY 10523
914-592-7700
Tefko Saracevic, Editor
Covers innovative techniques and technologies used for managing information, library systems, electronic publishing, and related topics.

Information Week
C M P Publications, Inc.
600 Community Dr.
Manhasset, NY 11030
516-562-5000
Laton McCartney, Editor
Reports news and trends for executives who run information systems.

Journal of Information Systems Management
Auerbach Publishers
One Penn Plaza
New York, NY 10119
212-971-5000
Robert Umbaugh, Editor
Offers advice on data communications, management, information center operations, and related topics of concern to MIS and data processing executives.

Journal of Management Information Systems
M. E. Sharpe, Inc.
80 Business Park Dr.
Armonk, NY 10504
914-273-1800
Vladimir Zwass, Editor
Prints detailed articles about how to improve MIS operations.

LIBRARIES

Association for Systems Management
Library
1433 W. Bagley Rd.
Cleveland, OH 44138
216-243-6900
Systems management technologies and related topics.

Howard University
School of Business and Public Administration
Library
2600 6th St., N.W., Rm. 120
Washington, DC 20059
202-806-1561
MIS, management, business administration, public administration, computer-based management, and related subjects.

Pennsylvania State University
College of Business Administration
Center for Research
Research Support Center
104 Beam Business Adm. Bldg.
University Park, PA 16802
814-863-0598
814-863-2753 Fax
MIS, organizational behavior, operations management, marketing, and other business topics.

University of New Mexico
William J. Parish Memorial Library
Albuquerque, NM 87131-1496
505-277-5912
MIS, management, personnel, marketing, and related topics.

MANUFACTURERS' REPRESENTATIVES

See also: SALESPEOPLE AND SALES TECHNIQUES

ASSOCIATIONS

Agricultural and Industrial Manufacturers'
Representatives Association
5818 Reeds Rd.
Mission, KS 66202-2740
913-262-4511
913-262-0174 Fax
Frank Bistrom, Executive Director
Offers education and research to independent manufacturers' representatives of light industrial, agricultural, and garden equipment.

Independent Manufacturers Representatives
Forum
c/o National Office Products Association
301 N. Fairfax St.
Alexandria, VA 22314
703-549-9040
800-542-6672
703-683-7552 Fax
James Herman, Coordinator
Offers training programs to independent manufacturers' representatives who sell office products.

Manufacturers' Agents National Association
23016 Mill Creek Rd.
Laguna Hills, CA 92654
714-859-4040
Kathleen Mahan, Director
A large association of agents who represent at least two manufacturers and are paid by commission. Offers referrals and assists with legal paperwork.

PERIODICALS

Agency Sales
Manufacturers' Agents National Association
23016 Mill Creek Rd.
Laguna Hills, CA 92654
714-859-4040
Bert Holtje, Editor
Covers marketing news and trends for manufacturers' agents.

Sales Rep's Advisor
Alexander Research & Communications, Inc.
1133 Broadway, Ste. 1407
New York, NY 10010
212-228-0246
Laurence Alexander, Editor
Offers news, advice, and case studies for independent manufacturer's representatives who wish to improve their productivity.

MARKETING

See also: ADVERTISING; CONSUMERS; DIRECT MAIL AND MARKETING INDUSTRY; MARKET RESEARCH AND STATISTICS; PREMIUMS AND INCENTIVES; and TELEMARKETING

ASSOCIATIONS

Academy of Marketing Science
University of Miami
School of Business Administration
PO Box 248012
Coral Gables, FL 33124
305-284-6673
Harold Berkman, Executive Vice President
Professors of marketing and executives who share information on the theoretical and practical aspects of marketing.

American Marketing Association
250 S. Wacker Dr., Ste. 200
Chicago, IL 60606
312-648-0536
312-993-7542 Fax
Jeffrey Heilbrunn, President
Offers research and seminars to marketers, sales managers, market researchers, and others.

Association for Innovative Marketing
c/o Alan Rosenspan
34 Summit Ave.
Sharon, MA 02067
800-729-1747
Alan Rosenspan, President
*Members share innovations in marketing
high-tech products.*

Marketing Science Institute
1000 Massachusetts Ave.
Cambridge, MA 02138
617-491-2060
617-491-2065 Fax
H. Paul Root, President
*Helps develop more effective marketing tech-
niques, sponsors research, and offers information about research results.*

Multi-Level Marketing International Associa-
    tion
119 Stanford
Irvine, CA 92715
714-854-5488
Doris Wood, Executive Director
*Multi-level marketers sell their products
directly, often from their homes. This association offers educational programs to members.*

National Account Marketing Association
310 Madison Ave., Ste. 724
New York, NY 10017
212-983-5140
Ernest Biglow, Executive Director
*Corporate sales and marketing representatives
who sell directly to national accounts.*

National Association of Market Developers
1422 W. Peachtree N.W., Ste. 500
Atlanta, GA 30309
404-892-0244
404-874-7100 Fax
Bunnie Ransom, Executive Director
*Marketers, advertisers, and others who sell to
minority markets. Conducts research.*

PERIODICALS

Advertising Age
Crain Communications, Inc.
220 E. 42nd St.
New York, NY 10017-5806
212-210-0171
Fred Danzig, Editor
*Reports on news and trends that concern
advertisers and marketers worldwide.*

Marketing Insights
Focused Communications, Ltd.
295 Madison Ave., Ste. 4400
New York, NY 10017
212-599-4600
*Advice for corporate executives who make
marketing and advertising decisions.*

Sales & Marketing Management
Bill Communications, Inc.
633 Third Ave.
New York, NY 10017
212-986-4800
Richard Kern, Editor
*Aimed at sales and marketing executives who
sell and promote with their own company.*

LIBRARIES

American Marketing Association
Library
250 S. Wacker Dr., Ste. 200
Chicago, IL 60606
312-648-0536
312-993-7542 Fax
The full range of marketing subjects.

Booz, Allen & Hamilton, Inc.
Research Service
101 Park Ave.
New York, NY 10178
212-697-1900
212-880-9732 Fax
*Industrial marketing, consumer marketing,
production, and other topics.*

Chicago Public Library Central Library
Business/Science/Technology Division
Harold Washington Library Center
400 S. State St.
Chicago, IL 60605
312-269-2814
*Marketing, technology, management, small
business, investments, and corporate reports.*

Marketing Science Institute
1000 Massachusetts Ave.
Cambridge, MA 02138
617-491-2060
617-491-2065 Fax
Marketing and related topics.

University of California, Los Angeles
John E. Anderson Graduate School of Man-
    agement
Library
Los Angeles, CA 90024-1460
213-825-3138
*Marketing, operations research, full range of
management areas, business economics,
investments, and related topics.*

FEDERAL GOVERNMENT

Federal Trade Commission
Pennsylvania Ave. at 6th St., N.W.
Washington, DC 20580
202-326-2000
Ask for the Consumer Protection Bureau.

U.S. International Trade Administration
Department of Commerce
14th St. and Constitution Ave., N.W.
Washington, DC 20230
202-377-2000
*Ask for the Commodity Analyst who is an
expert in marketing.*

MARKET RESEARCH AND STATISTICS

See also: ADVERTISING; CONSUMERS; MARKETING; and PUBLIC
OPINION AND POLLS

ASSOCIATIONS

American Marketing Association
250 S. Wacker Dr., Ste. 200
Chicago, IL 60606
312-648-0536
312-993-7542 Fax
Jeffrey Heilbrunn, President
*Members are marketers, market research executives, and others concerned with marketing.
The association sponsors research, conferences, and offers other services.*

Marketing Research Association
111 E. Wacker Dr., Ste. 600
Chicago, IL 60601
312-644-6610
312-565-4658 Fax
Shelley Ball, Chief of Operations
*Members are market researchers or users of
market research. Offers information on data
collection and analysis.*

Technical Marketing Society of America
PO Box 7275
Long Beach, CA 90807
714-821-8672
James Pearson, Executive Director
*Marketers, engineers, and others concerned
with the marketing of high-tech products and
services.*

PERIODICALS

Advances in Consumer Research
Association for Consumer Research
Brigham Young University
Graduate School of Management
632 TNRB
Provo, UT 84602
801-378-2080
*A scholarly journal of new market research
techniques and findings.*

Findex
Cambridge Information Group Directories,
   Inc.
7200 Wisconsin Ave.
Bethesda, MD 20814
301-961-6750
Stuart Stern, Editor
*A directory and description of thousands of
published market research studies and reports
about companies and industries.*

Journal of Marketing Research
American Marketing Association
250 S. Wacker Dr., Ste. 200
Chicago, IL 60606
312-648-0536
Michael Houston, Editor
*Detailed information about the methods and
analyses used in market research.*

Marketing Research Review
High Tech Publishing Co.
Box 1923
Brattleboro, VT 05301
802-254-3539
Philip Diperi, Editor
Reviews market research reports that are commercially available.

Research Alert
Alert Publishing, Inc.
37-06 30th Ave.
Long Island City, NY 11103-3808
718-626-3356
Eric Miller, Editor
Reports on the results of consumer marketing studies.

Research in Marketing
J A I Press Inc.
55 Old Post Rd., No. 2
Greenwich, CT 06836
203-661-7602
Jagdish Sheth, Editor
An annual compilation of market research.

LIBRARIES

Advertising Research Foundation
Library
3 E. 54th St.
New York, NY 10022
212-751-5656
212-319-5265 Fax
Market research, research methods, and media research.

Business Trend Analysis
Library
2171 Jericho Tpke.
Commack, NY 11725
516-462-5454
516-462-1842 Fax
Business, marketing, and economics.

Frankel & Co.
Information Center
111 E. Wacker Dr.
Chicago, IL 60601
312-938-3434
312-938-1901 Fax
Marketing research.

Marketemps
Marketing Intelligence Center
3435 Ocean Pacific Blvd., Ste. 202-B
Santa Monica, CA 90405
213-452-9610
213-450-1130 Fax
Marketing intelligence, growth industries, market trends, and related topics.

COMPANIES

Admar Research Co.
304 Park Ave. S.
New York, NY 10010
212-677-1700
Market research.

Burke Marketing Research, Inc.
800 Broadway
Cincinnati, OH 45202
513-852-8585
Market research.

CACI Marketing Systems
1100 N. Glebe Rd.
Arlington, VA 22201
800-292-2240
Demographic information and market research.

Claritas/NPDC
11 W. 42 St.
New York, NY 10036
212-789-3580
Demographic information and market research.

Data Probe Inc.
770 Broadway
New York, NY 10003
212-255-3355
Data processing for market research.

I.M.S. International, Inc.
(Subsidiary of Dun & Bradstreet Corp.)
1209 Orange St.
Wilmington, DE 19801
302-834-5000
Market research and publishing.

MRCA Information Services
4 Landmark Sq.
Stamford, CT 06901
203-324-9600
Market research.

Market Facts, Inc.
676 N. St. Clair St.
Chicago, IL 60611
312-280-9100
Market research.

Nielsen Marketing Research
70 Seaview Ave.
Stamford, CT 06902
203-353-7000
Market research.

Starch/Inra/Hooper, Inc.
E. Boston Post Rd.
Mamaroneck, NY 10543
914-698-0800
Market research and public opinion polls.

Survey Sampling, Inc.
1 Post Rd.
Fairfield, CT 06430
203-255-4200
Surveys and market research.

MARYLAND

STATE OFFICE LOCATOR (*for referrals to all state government offices*)

301-974-2000

ARCHIVES AND RECORDS

Archives Department
350 Rawe Boulevard
Annapolis, MD 21401
301-974-3915

ATTORNEY GENERAL

Attorney General's Office
200 St. Paul Place
Baltimore, MD 21202
301-576-6300

BANKING

Financial Regulation Division
34 Market Place
Baltimore, MD 21202
301-333-6262

COMMERCE

Economic & Employment Development
    Department
217 E. Redwood Street
Baltimore, MD 21202
301-333-6901

CONSUMER AFFAIRS

Consumer Protection
200 St. Paul Place
Baltimore, MD 21202
301-576-6550

EDUCATION

Education Department
200 W. Baltimore Street
Baltimore, MD 21201
301-333-2100

ENERGY

Energy Office
45 Calvert Street
Annapolis, MD 21401
301-974-3755

ENVIRONMENTAL AFFAIRS

Environmental Service
2020 Industrial Drive
Annapolis, MD 21401
301-974-7281

HEALTH

Health & Mental Hygiene Department
201 W. Preston Street
5th Floor
Baltimore, MD 21201
301-225-6500

HOUSING

Community Development Administrative
    Division
45 Calvert Street
Annapolis, MD 21401
301-974-3161

HUMAN RIGHTS

Human Relations Commission
20 E. Franklin Street
Baltimore, MD 21202
301-333-1715

INSURANCE

Insurance Division
501 St. Paul Place
Baltimore, MD 21202
301-333-6300

LABOR

Labor & Industry Divison
501 St. Paul Place
Baltimore, MD 21202
301-333-4179

LEGISLATION

Legislative Reference Department
Legislative Services Building
90 State Circle
Annapolis, MD 21401-1991
301-841-3865

LIBRARY SERVICES

Library Development & Services
200 W. Baltimore Street
Baltimore, MD 21201
301-333-2113

LICENSING—CORPORATE

Labor & Industry Division
501 St. Paul Place
Baltimore, MD 21202
301-333-4179

LICENSING—PROFESSIONAL AND OCCUPATIONAL

Licensing & Regulation Department
501 St. Paul Place
Baltimore, MD 21202
301-333-6200

MOTOR VEHICLES

Motor Vehicle Administration
6601 Ritchie Highway
Glen Burnie, MD 21062
301-768-7275

OCCUPATIONAL HEALTH AND SAFETY

Occupational Safety & Health Section
501 St. Paul Place
Baltimore, MD 21202
301-333-4195

OMBUDSMAN

Office of the State Prosecutor
Investment Building
1 Investment Place
Room 100
Towson, MD 21204
301-321-4067

PUBLIC UTILITIES

Public Service Commission
231 E. Baltimore Street
Baltimore, MD 21202
301-333-6071

PURCHASING

Purchasing Bureau
301 W. Preston Street
Room 1401
Baltimore, MD 21201
301-225-4620

REAL ESTATE

Real Estate Office
301 W. Preston Street
Room 1401
Baltimore, MD 21201
301-225-4322

SECURITIES

Securities Division
200 St. Paul Place
Baltimore, MD 21202
301-576-6360

TAXATION AND REVENUE

State Treasurer Office
Box 666
Annapolis, MD 21404
301-974-3533

TOURISM

Office of Tourist Development
217 E. Redwood Avenue
Baltimore, MD 21202
301-974-3517
301-333-6611
800-331-1750

TRANSPORTATION

Transportation Department
P.O. Box 8755
BWI Airport
Baltimore, MD 21240
301-859-7397

UNEMPLOYMENT

Unemployment Insurance Office
1100 N. Eutaw Street
Room 501
Baltimore, MD 21201
301-333-5306

WORKER'S COMPENSATION

Workers Compensation Commission
6 N. Liberty Street
Baltimore, MD 21201
301-333-4700

MASSACHUSETTS

STATE OFFICE LOCATOR (*for referrals to all state government offices*)

617-727-2121

ARCHIVES AND RECORDS

Archivist
State House
Room 337
Boston, MA 02133
617-727-2816

ATTORNEY GENERAL

Attorney General's Office
1 Ashburton Place
Room 2010
Boston, MA 02108
617-727-2200

BANKING

Banks Division
100 Cambridge Street
Room 2004
Boston, MA 02202
617-727-3145

COMMERCE

Economic Affairs Executive Office
1 Ashburton Place
Room 2101
Boston, MA 02108
617-727-8380

CONSUMER AFFAIRS

Consumer Affairs & Business
1 Ashburton Place
Room 1411
Boston, MA 02108
617-727-7755

EDUCATION

Education Department
1385 Hancock Street
Quincy, MA 02169
617-770-7300

ENERGY

Energy Facilities Siting Council
100 Cambridge Street
Room 2109
Boston, MA 02202
617-727-1136

ENVIRONMENTAL AFFAIRS

Environmental Affairs Executive Office
100 Cambridge Street
20th Floor
Boston, MA 02202
617-727-9800

HEALTH

Public Health Department
150 Tremont Street
Boston, MA 02111
617-727-0201

HOUSING

Communities & Development Executive
    Office
100 Cambridge Street
Room 1404
Boston, MA 02202
617-727-7765

HUMAN RIGHTS

Commission Against Discrimination
1 Ashburton Place
Room 601
Boston, MA 02108
617-727-3990

INSURANCE

Insurance Division
1 Ashburton Place
Room 2010
Boston, MA 02108
617-727-2200

LABOR

Labor & Industries Department
100 Cambridge Street
Room 1100
Boston, MA 02202
617-727-3454

LIBRARY SERVICES

State Library
State House
Room 341
Boston, MA 02133
617-727-2592

LICENSING—CORPORATE

Corporations Division
State House
Room 337
Boston, MA 02133
617-727-2853

LICENSING—PROFESSIONAL AND OCCUPATIONAL

Registration Division
100 Cambridge Street
Room 1115
Boston, MA 02202
617-727-3074

MOTOR VEHICLES

Motor Vehicles Registry
100 Nashua Street
2nd Floor
Boston, MA 02114
617-727-7912

OCCUPATIONAL HEALTH AND SAFETY

Industrial Safety Division
100 Cambridge Street
Room 1100
Boston, MA 02202
617-727-3567

OMBUDSMAN

Consumer Affairs & Business Regulation
    Executive Office
1 Ashburton Place
Room 1411
Boston, MA 02108
617-727-7755

PUBLIC UTILITIES

Public Utilities Commission
100 Cambridge Street
12th Floor
Boston, MA 02202
617-727-3500

PURCHASING

Procurement Department
1 Ashburton Place
Boston, MA 02108
617-727-2882

REAL ESTATE

Real Estate Management Division
10 Park Plaza
Room 3910
Boston, MA 02116
617-722-3258

SECURITIES

Securities Division
State House
Room 337
Boston, MA 02133
617-727-3548

TAXATION AND REVENUE

Revenue Department
100 Cambridge Street
Room 806
Boston, MA 02202
617-727-4201

TOURISM

Division of Tourism
100 Cambridge Street
13th Floor
Boston, MA 02202
617-727-3201 or 3205
800-533-6277

TRANSPORTATION

Transportation & Construction Executive
    Office
10 Park Plaza
Room 3510
Boston, MA 02116-3969
617-973-7000

UNEMPLOYMENT

Unemployment Insurance
Charles F. Hurley Building
Government Center
19 Staniford Street
Boston, MA 02114
617-727-6638

WORKER'S COMPENSATION

Industrial Accident Department
600 Washington Street
7th Floor
Boston, MA 02111
617-727-4900

MATERIALS

Materials—sometimes called engineered materials or advanced materials—are synthetic substances made from metals, plastics, or other components.

See also: METALLURGY

ASSOCIATIONS

Federation of Materials Societies
1707 L St. N.W., Ste. 333
Washington, DC 20036
202-296-9282
202-833-3014 Fax
Betsy Houston, Executive Director
Offers scientists, engineers, and business people a wide range of research, educational, and referral services.

Materials Research Society
9800 McKnight Rd.
Pittsburgh, PA 15237
412-367-3003
412-367-4373 Fax
John Ballance, Executive Director
This professional society promotes the exchange of information between scientists, engineers, and executives who work with inorganic and organic materials.

Society for the Advancement of Material and
    Process Engineering
PO Box 2459
Covina, CA 91722
818-331-0616
818-332-8929 Fax
Marge Smith, Business Director
A professional society of material and process engineers and scientists.

Suppliers of Advanced Composite Materials
    Association
1600 Wilson Blvd., Ste. 1008
Arlington, VA 22209
703-841-1556
703-841-1559 Fax
Joseph Jackson, Executive Director
Firms that manufacture products made from fiber-reinforced, advanced materials.

PERIODICALS

Advanced Materials & Processes
A S M International
Materials Park, OH 44073
216-338-5151
William Scott, Editor
Reports on breakthroughs in the field of engineered materials and manufacturing processes.

Chemical Engineering Progress
American Institute of Chemical Engineers
345 E. 47th St.
New York, NY 10017
212-705-7663
Attilio Bisio, Editor
Covers chemical processes, new materials, and related topics.

Materials Edge
Metal Bulletin Inc.
220 Fifth Ave., 10th Fl.
New York, NY 10001
800-638-2525
John Mack, Editor
Reports on new materials and their uses in various industries.

Materials Engineering
Penton Publishing
1100 Superior Ave.
Cleveland, OH 44114-2543
216-696-7000
Clifford Lewis, Editor
Technical information about new materials and their properties.

LIBRARIES

MRA Laboratories, Inc.
Materials Research and Analysis
Information Services
96 Marshall St.
North Adams, MA 01247-2411
413-664-4524
413-663-5535 Fax
Materials sciences, engineering, and electronic ceramics.

University of California, Berkeley
Kresge Engineering Library
110 Bechtel Engineering Center
Berkeley, CA 94720
510-642-3339
Materials science and the full range of engineering subjects.

COMPANIES

Allied-Signal Inc.
101 Columbia Rd.
Morristown, NJ 07962
201-455-2000
Engineered materials and other products.

Battelle Memorial Institute
5050 King Ave.
Columbus, OH 43201
614-424-6424
Research into advanced materials and many other areas.

Engelhard Corp.
Menlo Park, CN 40
Edison, NJ 08818
908-205-6000
Specialty chemicals and engineered materials.

Interlake Corp.
550 Warrenville Rd.
Lisle, IL 60532
708-852-8800
Engineered materials and other products.

Materials Research, Inc.
790 E. 700 S.
Centerville, UT 84014-2514
801-298-4000
Analyses of materials.

Witco Corp.
520 Madison Ave.
New York, NY 10022
212-605-3800
Specialty chemicals and engineered materials.

FEDERAL GOVERNMENT

U.S. Department of Commerce
14th St. & Constitution Ave., N.W.
Washington, DC 20230
202-377-2000
*Ask for Institute for Materials, Science &
Engineering in the National Institute of Science and Technology.*

U.S. International Trade Administration
Department of Commerce
14th St. and Constitution Ave., N.W.
Washington, DC 20230
202-377-2000
*Ask for the Commodity Analyst who is an
expert in advanced materials.*

National Science Foundation
1800 G St., N.W.
Washington, DC 20550
202-357-9859
*Ask for Ceramics & Electronic Materials,
Mathematics & Physical Sciences or Materials
Research, Mathematical, and Physical Sciences.*

MATERIALS HANDLING

See also: DISTRIBUTORS AND WHOLESALERS; INVENTORY CONTROL; OPERATIONS RESEARCH; and WAREHOUSES

ASSOCIATIONS

International Material Management Society
8720 Red Oak Blvd., Ste. 224
Charlotte, NC 28217
704-525-4667
William Clayburg, Executive Director
*A professional group of engineers, scientists,
and managers who share information about
the theory and practice of managing and handling materials in manufacturing, transportation, and warehousing.*

PERIODICALS

Material Handling Engineering
Penton Publishing
1100 Superior Ave.
Cleveland, OH 44114-2543
216-696-7000
Bernard Knill, Editor
*Reports on successful operations and new
products for specialists in materials handling,
packaging, and shipping.*

Material Handling Product News
Gordon Publications, Inc.
301 Gibraltar Dr.
Morris Plains, NJ 07950
201-292-5100
Dolly Grobstein, Editor
Describes products and systems that can be used for materials handling and warehousing.

Modern Materials Handling
Cahners Publishing Co.
275 Washington St.
Newton, MA 02158-1630
617-964-3030
Raymond Kulwiec, Editor
Reports on products and techniques for materials handling in manufacturing plants and warehouses.

Progress in Materials Handling and Logistics
Springer-Verlag
175 Fifth Ave.
New York, NY 10010
212-460-1500
Ira Pence, Editor
Follows the state-of-the-art in materials handling and logistics.

LIBRARIES

Hyster Co.
Engineering Library
2701 N.W. Vaughn, Ste. 900
Portland, OR 97210
503-721-6238
503-721-6001 Fax
Materials handling, safety, design standards, metallurgy, and other subjects.

Timken Co.
Research Library
1835 Deuber Ave.
Canton, OH 44706
216-497-2049
216-497-2282 Fax
Materials handling, steel process research, engineering research, and management.

COMPANIES

Baldwin Technology Co., Inc.
65 Rowayton Ave.
Rowayton, CT 06853
203-348-4400
Materials handling equipment, primarily for the printing industry.

Blaw Knox Corp.
One Oliver Plaza
Pittsburgh, PA 15222
412-263-2300
Materials handling equipment and other types of equipment.

Briggs-Weaver, Inc.
(Subsidiary of Sammons Enterprises, Inc.)
5000 Harry Hines Blvd.
Dallas, TX 75235
214-631-3600
Materials handling equipment, industrial tools, and other products.

Columbus McKinnon Corp.
140 Audubon Pkwy.
Amherst, NY 14228
716-689-5400
Materials handling equipment, including chains and hoists.

Harnischfeger Industries, Inc.
13400 Bishops Lane
Brookfield, WI 53005
414-671-4400
Materials handling systems, including hoists and cranes.

JLG Industries, Inc.
JLG Dr.
McConnellsburg, PA 17233
717-485-5161
Trolleys and other materials handling products.

Pettibone Corp.
4225 Naperville Rd.
Wildes, IL 60018
708-955-0220
Materials handling equipment and other equipment.

Rapistan Corp.
(Division of Lear Siegler Diversified Holdings Corp.)
507 Plymouth Ave., N. E.
Grand Rapids, MI 49505
616-451-6200
Conveyors and other types of materials handling equipment.

Raymond Corp.
S. Canal St.
Greene, NY 13778
607-656-2466
Materials handling systems.

MEAT INDUSTRY

See also: CATTLE INDUSTRY and LIVESTOCK INDUSTRY

ASSOCIATIONS

American Association of Meat Processors
PO Box 269
Elizabethtown, PA 17022
717-367-1168
717-367-9096 Fax
Stephen Krut, Executive Director
Members operate meat processing plants and storage facilities.

American Meat Institute
PO Box 3556
Washington, DC 20007
703-841-2400
703-527-0938 Fax
C. Manly Molpus, President
Offers information about meat processing, packing, storage, marketing, and other subjects to all facets of the meat industry.

Meat Importers' Council of America
1901 N. Ft. Myer Dr.
Arlington, VA 22209
703-522-1910
William Morrison, Executive Director
A small group of meat importers.

Meat Industry Suppliers Association
7297 Lee Hwy., Ste. N
Falls Church, VA 22042
703-533-1159
Harry Buzzerd, Secretary
Suppliers of machinery, packaging supplies, seasonings, other products, and services to the meat industry.

National Association of Meat Purveyors
1920 Association Dr., Ste. 400
Reston, VA 22091-1547
703-758-1900
703-758-8001 Fax
Stanley Emerling, Executive Vice President
Members distribute meat to hotels, restaurants, and institutions of all types.

National Live Stock and Meat Board
444 N. Michigan Ave.
Chicago, IL 60611
312-467-5520
John Huston, President
Represents almost 150 organizations concerned with livestock and meat. Offers a wide range of educational, scientific research, and promotional services to increase meat sales.

United States Meat Export Federation
600 S. Cherry St., Ste. 1000
Denver, CO 80222
303-399-7151
303-321-7075 Fax
Philip Seng, President
Offers seminars, research services, and other services to promote the sales of U.S. meats abroad.

PERIODICALS

Advances in Meat Research Series
Van Nostrand Reinhold—A V I
115 Fifth Ave.
New York, NY 10003-1004
800-926-2665
A.M. Pearson, Editor
Technical information about meat production.

Livestock, Meat and Wool Market News
Livestock and Grain Market News Branch
Livestock and Seed Division
U.S. Agricultural Marketing Service
Rm. 2623-S, Box 96456
Washington, DC 20090-6456
202-447-6231
Reports government statistics and news for the meat industry.

Meat and Poultry
Oman Publishing, Inc.
90 Throckmorton Ave.
Box 1059
Mill Valley, CA 94942
415-388-7575
Steve Bjerklie, Editor
Business and technical information of interest to the meat and poultry industry.

Meat Business Magazine
Admore Publishing Co., Inc.
9701 Gravois Ave.
St. Louis, MO 63123
314-638-4050
Louise King, Editor
Technical and financial information for meat industry executives.

Meat Price Report
National Provisioner, Inc.
15 W. Huron St.
Chicago, IL 60610
312-944-3380
Lists prices currently being paid to wholesalers and purveyors of meat by restaurants, hotels, and institutions.

Meat Processing
Edgell Communications
7500 Old Oak Blvd.
Cleveland, OH 44130
216-826-2839
Dan Murphy, Editor
Technical and business information about meat processing, rendering, and the corporate customers who buy meat.

Meat Sheet
Box 124
Westmont, IL 60559-0124
708-963-2252
William Albanos, Editor
Lists wholesale beef, poultry, and pork prices.

LIBRARIES

Iowa Beef Processors, Inc.
Corporate Library
Box 515
Dakota City, NE 68731
402-494-2061
Meat science and industry, and management topics.

National Livestock and Meat Board
Meat Industry Information Center
444 N. Michigan Ave.
Chicago, IL 60611
312-467-5520
312-467-9729 Fax
Meat, food economics, and nutrition.

Swift-Eckrich, Inc.
Research Library
3131 Woodcreek Dr.
Downers Grove, IL 60515
708-512-1084
708-512-1125 Fax
Meat science, fats, chemistry, and microbiology.

COMPANIES

Farmland Foods Inc.
(Subsidiary of Farmland Industries, Inc.)
P.O. Box 7527
Kansas City, MO 64116
816-891-1200
Meat packing plants.

Hudson Foods, Inc.
1225 Hudson Rd., Box 777
Rogers, AR 72757
501-636-1100
Meat products.

IBP, Inc.
(Subsidiary of Occidental Petroleum Corp.)
Dakota City, NE 68731
402-494-2061
Meat products.

Monfort, Inc.
(Subsidiary of ConAgra Inc.)
1930 AA St., Box G
Greeley, CO 80632
303-353-2311
Meat processing and distributing.

John Morrell & Co.
(Subsidiary of Chiquita Brands International, Inc.)
250 E. 5th St.
Cincinnati, OH 45202
513-852-3500
Slaughterers and processors of meats.

Packerland Packing Co., Inc.
(Subsidiary of Gillett Group, Inc.)
P.O. Box 1184
Green Bay, WI 54305
414-468-4000
Meat products and hides.

Smithfield Foods, Inc.
501 N. Church St.
Smithfield, VA 23430
804-357-4321
Meat processing.

Swift-Eckrich, Inc.
(Subsidiary of Beatrice Co.)
2001 Butterfield Rd.
Downers Grove, IL 60515
708-512-1000
Meat products.

FEDERAL GOVERNMENT

U.S. Department of Agriculture
14th St. and Independence Ave., S.W.
Washington, DC 20250
202-720-8732
*Ask for the Food Safety & Inspection Service
or the Meat and Poultry Inquiry Hotline.*

U.S. International Trade Administration
Department of Commerce
14th St. and Constitution Ave., N.W.
Washington, DC 20230
202-377-2000
*Ask for the Commodity Analyst who is an
expert in the meat industry.*

U.S. International Trade Commission
500 E St., S.W.
Washington, DC 20436
202-205-2000 Office of the Secretary
202-205-3296 Industries locator
*Ask for the Trade Analyst who is an expert in
meat industry.*

MEDICAL AND HOSPITAL EQUIPMENT INDUSTRY

See also: HEALTH CARE INDUSTRY and LABORATORIES

ASSOCIATIONS

American Orthotic and Prosthetic Association
717 Pendleton St.
Alexandria, VA 22314
703-836-7116
Ian Horen, Executive Director
*Manufacturers of artificial limbs and other
replacement parts of the human body.*

American Rental Association
1900 19th St.
Moline, IL 61265
309-764-2475
800-334-2177
James Irish, Executive Vice President
*Firms that rent medical equipment and many
other types of products.*

Association for the Advancement of Medical
Instrumentation
3330 Washington Blvd., Ste. 400
Arlington, VA 22201-4598
703-525-4890
800-332-2264
703-276-0793 Fax
Michael Miller, Executive Director
*Scientists and engineers working to improve
the quality of medical instrumentation.*

Health Industry Distributors Association
225 Reinekers Ln., No. 650
Alexandria, VA 22314
703-549-4432
703-549-6495 Fax
James Stover, President
*Distributors of medical, surgical, and other
health care supplies and equipment.*

Health Industry Manufacturers Association
1030 15th St. N.W., Ste. 1100
Washington, DC 20005
202-452-8240
Alan Magazine, President
*Manufacturers of medical devices of all kinds,
including information systems used by hospitals.*

Independent Medical Distributors Association
5818 Reeds Rd.
Shawnee Mission, KS 66202
913-262-4510
913-262-0174 Fax
Frank Bistrom, Executive Director
*Firms that distribute medical products, espe-
cially those products that employ high technology.*

National Association of Medical Equipment
Suppliers
625 Slaters Ln., Ste. 200
Alexandria, VA 22314
703-836-6263
703-836-6730 Fax
Thomas Antone, President
*Members supply medical and oxygen equip-
ment.*

PERIODICALS

C L R
Medical Laboratory Observer
Medical Economics Co. Inc.
680 Kinderkamack Rd.
Oradell, NJ 07649
201-262-3030
Robert Fitzgibbon, Editor
*Describes new equipment and instruments
used in medical laboratories.*

Health Devices Sourcebook
Emergency Care Research Institute
5200 Butler Pike
Plymouth Meeting, PA 19462
215-825-6000
Dorothy Wood, Editor
*This directory lists manufacturers of medical
devices, their products, and firms that service
and deal in used devices.*

Hospital
5790 Eaglesridge Lane
Cincinnati, OH 45230
513-232-0511
Gregory Loomis, Editor
*Describes new equipment and technology used
in hospitals.*

Medical Electronics and Equipment News
Reilly Publishing Co.
532 Busse Hwy.
Park Ridge, IL 60068
312-693-3773
Marianne Schmidt, Editor
Reports on new medical electronics.

Medical Product Manufacturing News
Canon Communications, Inc.
3340 Ocean Park Blvd., Ste. 1000
Santa Monica, CA 90405-3207
213-392-5509
John Bethune, Editor
Reports on the products, services, and components that are used by manufacturers of medical devices.

Orthopedic Products News
Lippincott Healthcare Publications
130 Madison Ave.
New York, NY 10016
212-679-9710
Britta Herlitz, Editor
Covers new equipment used by orthopedic surgeons.

LIBRARIES

CIBA Corning Diagnostics Corp.
Steinberg Information Center
63 North St.
Medfield, MA 02052
508-359-3606
508-359-4426 Fax
Clinical medicine and medical engineering.

ECRI
Library
5200 Butler Pike
Plymouth Meeting, PA 19462
215-825-6000
215-834-7366 Fax
Medical equipment and biomedical engineering.

Imed Corp.
Library
9775 Businesspark Ave.
San Diego, CA 92131
619-566-9000
619-695-8796 Fax
Medical instrumentation, medicine, and engineering.

U.S. Food & Drug Administration
Center for Devices & Radiological Health
Library HFZ-46
1390 Piccard Dr.
Rockville, MD 20850
301-427-1235
301-427-1997 Fax
Medical equipment, biomedical engineering, artificial organs, and related topics.

COMPANIES

Abbott Laboratories
Abbott Park, IL 60064
708-937-6100
Equipment and pharmaceuticals for hospitals and laboratories.

Becton, Dickinson & Co.
One Becton Dr.
Franklin Lakes, NJ 07417
201-848-6800
Medical equipment for hospitals and laboratories.

Boehringer Mannheim Corp.
(Subsidiary of Boehringer Mannheim U.S.
Holdings Inc.)
9115 Hague Rd.
Indianapolis, IN 46250
317-845-2000
Orthopedic and diagnostic equipment, and pharmaceuticals.

Cobe Laboratories, Inc.
(Subsidiary of Gambro A.B.)
1185 Oak St.
Lakewood, CO 80215
303-232-6800
*Equipment used in surgery, blood therapy,
and nephrology.*

Kendall-Futuro Co.
(Division of Kendall Co.)
One Riverfront Pl.
Newport, KY 41071
606-655-3400
*Equipment used for surgery, convalescence,
and other medical products.*

Spacelabs Inc.
(Subsidiary of Westmark International Inc.)
4200 150th St., N.E.
Redmond, WA 98052
206-882-3700
*Monitoring equipment used for patients in
hospitals.*

Stryker Corp.
P.O. Box 4085
Kalamazoo, MI 49003
616-385-2600
*Hospital beds, surgical instruments, orthope-
dic equipment, and other medical equipment.*

Valleylab, Inc.
5920 Longbow Dr.
Boulder, CO 80301
303-530-2300
A variety of equipment used in hospitals.

Zinetics Medical, Inc.
(Subsidiary of Zinetics Medical Technology
   Corp.)
2212 S.W. Temple
Salt Lake City, UT 84115
801-466-7809
*A variety of medical devices and electronic
equipment.*

FEDERAL GOVERNMENT

U.S. Customs Service
Department of the Treasury
U.S. Customshouse
6 World Trade Center
New York, NY 10048
212-466-5550
*Ask for the Commodity Specialist in charge of
medical instruments.*

U.S. International Trade Administration
Department of Commerce
14th St. and Constitution Ave., N.W.
Washington, DC 20230
202-377-2000
*Ask for the Commodity Analyst who is an
expert in medical and hospital instruments.*

U.S. International Trade Commission
500 E St., S.W.
Washington, DC 20436
202-205-2000 Office of the Secretary
202-205-3296 Industries locator
*Ask for the Trade Analyst who is an expert in
medical and hospital instruments.*

U.S. Patent and Trademark Office
Crystal Plaza 2
2011 Jefferson Davis Highway
Arlington, VA 22202
703-305-8000
*Ask for the Examining Group Director who is
a specialist in medical and hospital apparatus.*

MERGERS AND ACQUISITIONS

See also: INVESTMENT BANKING and SECURITIES

ASSOCIATIONS

International Association of Merger and
   Acquisition Consultants
200 S. Frontage Rd., Ste. 103
Burr Ridge, IL 60521
708-323-0233
708-323-0237 Fax
Cheryl Cade, Administrator
*Offers information about the buying, selling,
and merging of small and medium-sized businesses.*

PERIODICALS

Acquisition Mart
Business Publications, Inc.
9605 Scranton Rd., Ste. 840
San Diego, CA 92121-1774
619-457-7577
Lynn Mason, Editor
*Describes mid-sized companies that are for
sale.*

Directory of Merger and Acquisition Firms
   and Professionals
I B C—U S A Inc.
360 Woodland St.
Box 6640
Holliston, MA 01746
508-429-5930
Kathryn Wolden, Editor
*A listing of merger and acquisition
professionals.*

M & A Dealmaker
New York Law Publishing Co.
Marketing Department
111 Eighth Ave.
New York, NY 10011
212-741-8300
*Reports on the law firms, bankers, and other
services who are assisting current mergers and
acquisitions.*

Merger Management Report
Securities Data Co., Inc.
S D C Publishing
40 W. 57th St., 8th Fl.
New York, NY 10019
212-765-5311
Ted Weissberg, Editor
*Profiles and interviews of key personnel in the
mergers industry.*

Merger Yearbook: Domestic Edition
Securities Data Co., Inc.
S D C Publishing
40 W. 57th St., 8th Fl.
New York, NY 10019
212-765-5311
Evan Simonoff, Editor
*Lists all the mergers and acquisitions of the
prior year.*

Mergers & Acquisitions
M L R Publishing Co.
229 S. 18th St.
Philadelphia, PA 19103
215-790-7000
Martin Sikora, Editor
News of merger trends and how-to advice for professionals in the industry.

Mergers and Acquisitions Law Reporter
Computer Law Reporter, Inc.
1519 Connecticut Ave., N.W., Ste. 200
Washington, DC 20036
202-462-5755
Neil Cohen, Editor
Advises attorneys on the legal aspects of mergers and acquisitions.

COMPANIES

Bushkin Associates, Inc.
117 E. 57th St.
New York, NY 10022
212-371-9102
Investment bankers that help negotiate mergers and acquisitions.

Kutzen Co., Inc.
Purchase St.
Purchase, NY 10577
914-253-9120
Merger and acquisition consultants.

Lepercq de Neuflize & Co. Inc.
(Subsidiary of Lepercq Inc.)
1675 Broadway
New York, NY 10019
212-698-0700
Advisors on investments and mergers and acquisitions.

MacDonald & Co., Inc.
630 Fifth Ave.
New York, NY 10111
212-246-0515
Mergers and acquisitions consultants.

Morgan Stanley Group Inc.
1251 Ave. of the Americas
New York, NY 10020
212-703-4000
Security brokerage, mergers and acquisitions consultants, and other financial services.

A. R. Wolfson Associates
409 Salisbury Rd.
Wyncote, PA 19095
215-884-1500
Mergers and acquisitions consultants.

FEDERAL GOVERNMENT

Federal Deposit Insurance Corp.
550 17th St., N.W.
Washington, DC 20429
202-393-8400
Ask for the Research Statistics department.

Securities and Exchange Commission
450 5th St., N.W.
Washington, DC 20549
202-272-3100
Ask for the Tender Offers division in the Corporate Finance Office.

METAL FINISHING INDUSTRY

See also: METALLURGY; METALS INDUSTRY; and METAL WORKING INDUSTRY

ASSOCIATIONS

American Electroplaters and Surface Finishers Society
12644 Research Pkwy.
Orlando, FL 32826-3298
305-281-6441
J. Howard Schumacher, Editor
Offers educational programs to job shop tech-
nicians, scientists, and engineers.

Metal Finishing Suppliers' Association
801 N. Cass Ave., Ste. 300
Westmount, IL 60555
708-887-0797
King Ruhly, Executive Director
Firms that make metal finishing and plating
equipment and the materials and chemicals
used in the process. Offers educational pro-
grams to both industry members and firms
that buy finished metal products.

National Association of Metal Finishers
111 E. Wacker Dr., Ste. 600
Chicago, IL 60601
312-644-6610
Brad Parcells, Executive Director
Firms that plate, galvanize, polish, chrome,
anodize, and otherwise finish metal surfaces.

PERIODICALS

Cleaning-Finishing-Coating Digest
A S M International, Materials Information
Materials Park, OH 44073
216-338-5151
Technical advice for metal finishers.

Finishers' Management
Publications Management, Inc.
4350 DiPaolo Center
Deerlove Rd.
Glenview, IL 60025
708-699-1700
Hugh Morgan, Editor
Management advice and industry trends for
metal finishers.

Metal Finishing
Metals and Plastics Publications, Inc.
Three University Plaza
Hackensack, NJ 07601
201-487-3700
Palmer Langdon, Editor
Technical and business information about the
treatment of metallic surfaces.

LIBRARIES

AMP, Inc.
Tchnical Library
Mail Stop 21-02
Box 3608
Harrisburg, PA 17105-3608
717-541-3050
717-541l-3028 Fax
All types of engineering and electroplating.

Atochem North America
Technical & Business Information Center
P.O. Box 1295
620 Old York Rd.
Somerville, NJ 08876
201-704-2437
201-707-4928 Fax
Electroplating, chemicals, reagents, and other subjects.

McGean-Rohco, Inc.
2910 Harvard Ave.
Cleveland, OH 44105
216-441-4900
Electroplating, metallurgy, and chemistry.

COMPANIES

API Industries
1250 Morse Ave.
Elk Grove Village, IL 60007
708-437-7474
Metal finishing.

Auric Corp.
470 Frelinghuysen Ave.
Newark, NJ 07114
201-242-4110
Chemicals used for metal finishing.

Commercial Steel Treating Corp.
31440 Stephenson Hwy.
Madison Heights, MI 48071
313-588-3300
Metal finishing and heat treating.

EC Industries, Inc.
1401 Park Ave.
Emeryville, CA 94608
415-653-5303
Metal finishing products and services.

Enthone, Inc.
(Subsidiary of Asarco Incorporated)
P.O. Box 1900
New Haven, CT 06508
203-934-8611
Chemicals and equipment used in metal finishing.

Hubbard Hall Inc.
P.O. Box 780
Waterbury, CT 06720
203-756-5521
Metal finishing chemicals.

MacDermid Inc.
245 Freight St.
Waterbury, CT 06702
203-575-5700
Chemicals used for polishing, electroplating, and galvanizing metal surfaces.

OMI International Corp.
(Subsidiary of Asarco Incorporated)
21441 Hoover Rd.
Warren, MI 48089
313-497-9100
Chemicals and equipment used in metal finishing and electroplating.

Whyco Chromium Co.
Thomaston, CT 06787
203-283-5826
Electroplating and metal finishing.

FEDERAL GOVERNMENT

U.S. International Trade Administration
Department of Commerce
14th St. and Constitution Ave., N.W.
Washington, DC 20230
202-377-2000
Ask for the Commodity Analyst who is an expert in metal finishing machinery.

U.S. International Trade Commission
500 E St., S.W.
Washington, DC 20436
202-205-2000 Office of the Secretary
202-205-3296 Industries locator
Ask for the Trade Analyst who is an expert in metal finishing machinery.

U.S. Patent and Trademark Office
Crystal Plaza 2
2011 Jefferson Davis Highway
Arlington, VA 22202
703-305-8000
Ask for the Examining Group Director who is a specialist in metal finishing equipment.

METALLURGY

See also: FOUNDRY INDUSTRY; MATERIALS; METALS INDUSTRY; METAL WORKING INDUSTRY; and STEEL AND IRON INDUSTRY

ASSOCIATIONS

ASM International
9639 Kinsman
Materials Park, OH 44073
216-338-5151
216-338-4634 Fax
Edward Langer, Managing Director
Offers technical information to metallurgists, engineers, and executives in the metals and materials industries.

Metal Powder Industries Federation
105 College Rd. E.
Princeton, NJ 08540
609-452-7700
609-987-8523 Fax
Donald White, Executive Director
Offers information and does research on metal powders and powder metallurgy products.

Minerals, Metals, and Materials Society
420 Commonwealth Dr.
Warrendale, PA 15086
412-776-9000
412-776-3770 Fax
Alexander Scott, Executive Director
A professional society of engineers and scientists who work with metals and materials.

PERIODICALS

Acta Metallurgica et Materialia
Pergamon Press, Inc., Journals Division
Maxwell House
Fairview Park
Elmsford, NY 10523
914-592-7700
M. Ashby, Editor
Technical information for scientists, engineers, and metallurgists.

Materials Edge
Metal Bulletin Inc.
220 Fifth Ave., 10th Fl.
New York, NY 10001
800-638-2525
John Mack, Editor
Reports on new materials and metallurgical processes.

LIBRARIES

Engineering Societies Library
United Engineering Center
345 E. 47th St.
New York, NY 10017
212-705-7611
212-486-1086 Fax
All types of engineering, including metallurgy.

U.S. Bureau of Mines
Twin Cities Research Center
Library
5629 Minnehaha Ave., S.
Minneapolis, MN 55417-3099
612-725-4503
Metallurgy, mining engineering, mineral industries, and related topics.

University of Missouri, Rolla
Curtis Laws Wilson Library
Rolla, MO 65401
314-341-4227
314-341-4233 Fax
Metallurgy, mining, geology, and related topics.

COMPANIES

American Powdered Metals
(Affiliate of Worldmark Group)
407 Thornburg Dr., Box 915
Conover, NC 28613
704-464-0642
Powdered metallurgy products.

Davy McKee Corp.
(Subsidiary of Davy Inc.)
One Oliver Plaza
Pittsburgh, PA 15222
412-566-4500
Metallurgical plants and metal forming equipment.

Dorr-Oliver Inc.
612 Wheelers Farm Rd.
Milford, CT 06460
203-876-5400
Equipment for the metallurgical industry and many other industries.

ICM/Krebsoge
(Division of Pullman Co.)
38701 Seven Mile Rd.
Livonia, MI 48152
313-462-3840
Powder metallurgy parts.

Kennametal Inc.
P.O. Box 346
Latrobe, PA 15650
412-539-5000
Powder metallurgy products and tools used for metalcutting and other purposes.

Leco Corp.
3000 Lakeview Ave.
St. Joseph, MI 49085
616-983-5533
Instruments and equipment used in the metallurgical and energy industries.

New York Testing Laboratories, Inc.
81 Urban Ave.
Westbury, NY 11590
516-334-7770
Metallurgical and other types of testing.

Reactive Metal & Alloys Corp.
Rte. 168
West Pittsburg, PA 16160
412-535-4357
Metallurgical additives.

FEDERAL GOVERNMENT

National Science Foundation
1800 G. St., N.W.
Washington, DC 20550
202-357-9859
Ask for the Metallurgy Program in the Mathematics & Physical Sciences department.

U.S. Department of Commerce
14th St. & Constitution Ave., N.W.
Washington, DC 20230
202-377-2000
Ask for the Institute for Materials Science & Engineering department in the National Institute of Standards and Technology.

U.S. Department of Energy
1000 Independence Ave., S.W.
Washington, DC 20585
202-586-5000
Ask for the Metallurgy & Ceramics Bureau in the Energy Research Administration.

U.S. Patent and Trademark Office
Crystal Plaza 2
2011 Jefferson Davis Highway
Arlington, VA 22202
703-305-8000
Ask for the Examining Group Director who is a specialist in metallurgy.

METALS INDUSTRY

See also: ALUMINUM INDUSTRY; STEEL AND IRON INDUSTRY; and PRECIOUS METALS INDUSTRY

ASSOCIATIONS

American Bureau of Metal Statistics
PO Box 1405
400 Plaza Dr.
Secaucus, NJ 07094
201-863-6900
201-863-6050 Fax
W. J. Lambert, President
Provides statistics on all nonferrous metals, including copper, zinc, aluminum, silver, and many others.

American Copper Council
333 Rector Place, Ste. 10P
New York, NY 10280
212-945-4990
Mary Boland, Director
An information clearinghouse for firms involved in all facets of the copper industry.

American Institute for Hollow Structural Sections
929 McLaughlin Run Rd., Ste. 8
Pittsburgh, PA 15017
412-221-8880
412-221-9119 Fax
Frederick Palmer, Director
Manufacturers of steel hollow structural sections used in the construction of bridges and buildings.

American Tin Trade Association
PO Box 1347
New York, NY 10150
201-364-2280
Karen Salberg, Secretary
Members import and trade tin.

Brass and Bronze Ingot Manufacturers
300 W. Washington, Rm. 1500
Chicago, IL 60606
312-236-2715
Julie Sculthorpe, Administrator
Firms that make ingots from brass and bronze.

Cadmium Council, Inc.
Greenwich Office Park, Bldg. 2
Greenwich, CT 06830
203-625-0911
203-625-0918 Fax
Hugh Morrow, Executive Director
Offers technical and market information regarding cadmium.

Copper and Brass Servicenter Association
Adams Bldg., Ste. 109
251 W. DeKalb Pike
King of Prussia, PA 19406
215-265-6658
215-265-3419 Fax
R. Franklin Brown, Executive Vice President
Firms that distribute copper and brass pipe, sheet, and similar products.

Independent Zinc Alloyers Association
1000 16th St. N.W., Ste. 603
Washington, DC 20036
202-785-0558
Richard Cooperman, Executive Director
Manufacturers of zinc alloys.

International Magnesium Association
2010 Corporate Ridge, Ste. 700
McLean, VA 22102
703-442-8888
703-821-1824 Fax
Byron Clow, Executive Vice President
Firms that mine, process, and use magnesium.

Lead Industries Association
295 Madison Ave.
New York, NY 10017
212-578-4750
212-684-7714 Fax
Jerome Smith, Executive Director
Firms that mine and refine lead, and firms that manufacture products out of lead.

Non-Ferrous Metals Producers Committee
c/o Kenneth Button
Economic Consulting Service
1225 19th St. N.W., Ste. 210
Washington, DC 20036
202-466-7720
Kenneth Button, Exec.Sec.
Producers of lead, copper, and zinc.

Sheet Metal and Air Conditioning Contractors' National Association
PO Box 70
Merrifield, VA 22116
703-790-9890
703-893-5710 Fax
John Sroka, Executive Vice President
Members are contractors who use sheet metal ducts in the construction of heating, air conditioning, and other systems.

Tin Research Institute
1353 Perry St.
Columbus, OH 43201
614-424-6200
William Hampshire, Manager
Provides technical information about the use of tin.

Titanium Development Association
11 W. Monument Ave., Ste. 510
Dayton, OH 45401
513-223-TIDA
513-223-6307 Fax
Francine Rickenbach, Executive Director
Firms that produce and use titanium.

PERIODICALS

33 Metal Producing
Penton Publishing
1100 Superior Ave.
Cleveland, OH 44114
216-696-7000
Wally Huskonen, Editor
Technical information on all stages of metal production, from smelting through distribution.

American Metal Market
Capital Cities—A B C, Inc.
825 Seventh Ave.
New York, NY 10019
212-887-8532
Michael Botta, Editor
Surveys news and trends throughout the metals industry. Covered are metal production, commodities, scrap metal, precious metals, and related subjects.

Engineering & Mining Journal
Maclean Hunter Publishing Co.
29 N. Wacker Dr.
Chicago, IL 60606
312-726-2802
Robert Wyllie, Editor
Offers technical information on how to mine, mill, refine, and smelt metals and nonmetallic substances.

Metals Week
Commodity Services Group
McGraw-Hill, Inc.
1221 Avenue of the Americas, 42nd Fl.
New York, NY 10020
212-512-2000
Ken Jacobson, Editor
Pricing and other business information about the metals markets.

Modern Metals
Delta Communications, Inc.
400 N. Michigan Ave., 13th Fl.
Chicago, IL 60611
F.L. Church, Editor
Information for executives at industrial plants about metals engineering, design, production, use, and purchasing.

LIBRARIES

ASM International
Materials Information
Materials Park, OH 44073
216-338-5151
216-338-4634 Fax
Metals engineering and industry information.

Bethlehem Steel Corp.
Corporate Information Center
701 E. Third St., Rm. 320A
Bethlehem, PA 18016
215-694-3325
215-794-3290 Fax
Metallurgy, steelmaking technology, and engineering.

USX Corp.
USS Division
Information Resource Center
4000 Tech Center Dr.
MS 88
Monroeville, PA 15146
412-825-2344
412-825-2050 Fax
Metallurgy, steel manufacture, materials science, and related topics.

COMPANIES

Bethlehem Steel Corp.
1170 Eighth Ave.
Bethlehem, PA 18016
215-694-2424
Steel products.

Degussa Corp.
(Subsidiary of Degussa AG)
65 Challenger Rd.
Ridgefield Park, NJ 07660
201-641-6100
Refined and precious metals, products from metals, and chemicals.

Dow U.S.A.
(Division of Dow Chemical USA)
2020 Dow Ctr.
Midland, MI 48674
517-636-3989
Chemicals, metals, and many other types of products.

Mitsubishi International Corp.
(Subsidiary of Mitsubishi Corp.)
520 Madison Ave.
New York, NY 10022
212-605-2000
Importer of metals and many other types of products.

Philipp Brothers, Inc.
(Subsidiary of Salomon Inc)
1221 Ave. of the Americas
New York, NY 10020
212-575-5900
Non-ferrous and precious metals, minerals, and other products.

Royal Dutch/Shell Group
30 Rockefeller Plaza
New York, NY 10112
212-632-4800
Oil, gas, chemicals, metals, and other products.

Timken Co.
1835 Dueber Ave, S. W.
Canton, OH 44706
216-438-3000
Steel, steel alloys, and other metals.

Union Pacific Corp.
Eighth & Eaton Aves.
Bethlehem, PA 18018
215-861-3200
Many types of products including metals.

FEDERAL GOVERNMENT

Bureau of Mines
810 7th St., N.W.
Washington, DC 20747
202-501-9770
Ask for the public affairs office to find the expert on the topic that interests you.

U.S. International Trade Administration
Department of Commerce
14th St. and Constitution Ave., N.W.
Washington, DC 20230
202-377-2000
Ask for the Commodity Analyst who is an expert in the metal industry.

U.S. International Trade Commission
500 E St., S.W.
Washington, DC 20436
202-205-2000 Office of the Secretary
202-205-3296 Industries locator
Ask for the Trade Analyst who is an expert in the metal industry.

METAL WORKING INDUSTRY

See also: MACHINE SHOPS; METAL FINISHING INDUSTRY; METALS INDUSTRY; and STEEL AND IRON INDUSTRY

ASSOCIATIONS

Copper and Brass Fabricators Council
1050 17th St. N.W., Ste. 440
Washington, DC 20036
202-833-8575
Joseph Mayer, President
Represents fabricators of copper and brass.

Custom Roll Forming Institute
522 Westgate Tower
Cleveland, OH 44116
216-333-8848
216-333-4554 Fax
Robert Boeddener, President
Offers engineering and manufacturing information regarding the forming of metal custom roll sections.

Industrial Perforators Association
710 N. Plankinton Ave., Ste. 622
Milwaukee, WI 53203
414-271-2263
414-271-5154 Fax
Jean McKey, Secretary
Provides technical and market information to firms that make perforated metal products.

Metal Treating Institute
302 Third St., Ste. 1
Neptune Beach, FL 32233
904-249-0448
904-249-0459 Fax
M. Lance Miller, Executive Director
Studies the technology and business of treating metals and metal products with heat.

National Metal Spinners Association
Box 358
Farmingdale, NY 11735
516-249-2468
Richard Goldhaber, Secretary
Firms that spin and stamp metal.

National Ornamental and Miscellaneous Metals Association
804-10 Main St., Ste. E
Forest Park, GA 30050
404-363-4009
404-366-1852 Fax
Barbara Cook, Executive Director
Members produce ornamental and miscellaneous metal products, and supply equipment and services to the industry.

Precision Metalforming Association
27027 Chardon Rd.
Richmond Heights, OH 44143
216-585-8800
216-585-3126 Fax
Jon Jenson, President
Firms that stamp, spin, and otherwise fabricate metal into many types of products.

Metal Fabricating Institute
PO Box 1178
Rockford, IL 61105
815-965-4031
Ronald Fowler, President
Offers technical education to the metal fabricating industry.

PERIODICALS

Dun's Industrial Guide—The Metalworking Directory
Dun's Marketing Services
3 Sylvan Way
Parsippany, NJ 07054-3896
201-455-0900
An exhaustive listing of maufacturers of metalworking equipment.

Stamping Quarterly
Croydon Group, Ltd.
5411 E. State St.
Rockford, IL 61108-2378
815-399-8700
Kathy Velasco, Editor
Advises the metal stamping industry about new techniques and products.

LIBRARIES

Cincinnati Milacron Inc.
Information Resource Center
4701 Marburg Ave.
Cincinnati, OH 45209-1025
513-841-8589
513-841-8059 Fax
Metalworking, machinery, and other topics.

Fabricators & Manufacturers Association, International
Technical Information Center
5411 State St.
Rockford, IL 61108
815-399-8700
815-399-7279 Fax
Metal fabricating.

Ladish Co.
Technical Information Center
5481 S. Packard Ave.
Cudahy, WI 53110
414-747-2611
Metalworking technology, metal cleaning, metal testing, corrosion, and other subjects.

COMPANIES

Avondale Industries, Inc.
P. O. Box 50280
New Orleans, LA 70150
504-436-2121
Heavy metal fabrications and shipbuilding.

Cambridge Street Metal Co. Inc.
500 Lincoln St.
Boston, MA 02134
617-254-7580
Fabricated metal products.

Creative Industries Group, Inc.
275 Rex Blvd.
Auburn Hills, MI 48326
313-852-5700
Sheet metal fabrication and related products.

Idex Corp.
630 Dundee Rd.
Northbrook, IL 60062
708-498-7070
Metal fabrication equipment and other types of machinery.

JSJ Corp.
700 Robbins Rd., Box 687
Grand Haven, MI 49417
616-842-6350
Metal stampings and other products.

Metalink, Inc.
(Subsidiary of TBG Inc.)
302 Ashfield St.
Belding, MI 48809
312-763-1200
Cold rolled steel and metal fabrication.

Parish Div.
(Division of Dana Corp.)
Robeson & Weiser Sts.
Reading, PA 19612
215-371-70
Metal stampings and assemblies.

Stern Metals, Inc.
(Subsidiary of Cookson America Inc.)
320 Washington St.
Mount Vernon, NY 10553
914-668-4300
Precious metals fabrication.

FEDERAL GOVERNMENT

U.S. Customs Service
Department of the Treasury
U.S. Customshouse
6 World Trade Center
New York, NY 10048
212-466-5550
Ask for the Commodity Specialist in charge of metal working equipment.

U.S. International Trade Administration
Department of Commerce
14th St. and Constitution Ave., N.W.
Washington, DC 20230
202-377-2000
Ask for the Commodity Analyst who is an expert in the metal working industry.

U.S. International Trade Commission
500 E St., S.W.
Washington, DC 20436
202-205-2000 Office of the Secretary
202-205-3296 Industries locator
Ask for the Trade Analyst who is an expert in the metal working industry.

U.S. Patent and Trademark Office
Crystal Plaza 2
2011 Jefferson Davis Highway
Arlington, VA 22202
703-305-8000
Ask for the Examining Group Director who is a specialist in metal working equipment.

MICHIGAN

STATE OFFICE LOCATOR (*for referrals to all state government offices*)

517-373-1837

ARCHIVES AND RECORDS

State Historic Preservation Officer
Treasury Building
1st Floor
Lansing, MI 48918
517-373-1666

ATTORNEY GENERAL

Attorney General's Office
P.O. Box 30212
Lansing, MI 48909
517-373-1110

BANKING

Financial Institutions Bureau
P.O. Box 30224
Lansing, MI 48909
517-373-3460

COMMERCE

Commerce Department
P.O. Box 30004
Lansing, MI 48909
517-373-7230

CONSUMER AFFAIRS

Consumer Protection & Charitable Trusts
    Division
P.O. Box 30212
Lansing, MI 48909
517-373-1140

EDUCATION

Education Department
P.O. Box 30008
Lansing, MI 48909
517-373-3354

ENERGY

Energy Program Office
P.O. Box 30221
Lansing, MI 48909
517-334-6272

ENVIRONMENTAL AFFAIRS

Environmental Protection Division
P.O. Box 30028
Lansing, MI 48909
517-373-7917

HEALTH

Public Health Department
P.O. Box 30195
Lansing, MI 48909
517-335-8022

HOUSING

State Housing Development Authority
P.O. Box 30044
Lansing, MI 48909
517-373-6022

HUMAN RIGHTS

Civil Rights Department
303 W. Kalamazoo
4th Floor
Lansing, MI 48913
517-335-3165

INSURANCE

Insurance Bureau
P.O. Box 30220
Lansing, MI 48909
517-373-9273

LABOR

Labor Department
Victor Office Building
201 N. Washington Square
Lansing, MI 48909
517-373-9600

LEGISLATION

Legislative Service Bureau
P.O. Box 30036
Lansing, MI 48909
517-373-0170

LIBRARY SERVICES

State Library
P.O. Box 30007
Lansing, MI 48909
517-373-1580

LICENSING—CORPORATE

Corporation & Securities Bureau
P.O. Box 30222
Lansing, MI 48909
517-334-6212

LICENSING—PROFESSIONAL AND OCCUPATIONAL

Licensing & Regulations Department
P.O. Box 30018
Lansing, MI 48909
517-373-1870

MOTOR VEHICLES

Automotive Regulation Bureau
Treasury Building
1st Floor
Lansing, MI 48918
517-373-7245

OCCUPATIONAL HEALTH AND SAFETY

Environmental & Occupational Health
  Bureau
P.O. Box 30195
Lansing, MI 48909
517-335-9218

OMBUDSMAN

Civil Service Department
P.O. Box 30002
Lansing, MI 48909
517-373-6497

PUBLIC UTILITIES

Public Service Commission
P.O. Box 30221
Lansing, MI 48909
517-334-6368

PURCHASING

Purchasing Division
P.O. Box 30026
Lansing, MI 48909
517-373-0300

REAL ESTATE

Commercial Services Bureau
P.O. Box 30018
Lansing, MI 48909
517-373-0490

SECURITIES

Corporation & Securities Bureau
P.O. Box 30222
Lansing, MI 48909
517-334-6212

TAXATION AND REVENUE

Revenue Division
P.O. Box 30212
Lansing, MI 48909
517-373-3203

TOURISM

Travel Bureau
P.O. Box 30226
Lansing, MI 48909
517-373-1195
800-543-2-YES

TRANSPORTATION

Transportation Department
P.O. Box 30050
Lansing, MI 48909
517-373-2114

UNEMPLOYMENT

Bureau of Unemployment Insurance
7310 Woodward Avenue
Room 506
Detroit, MI 48202
313-876-5467

WORKER'S COMPENSATION

Workers Disability Compensation Office
Victor Office Building
201 N. Washington Square
Lansing, MI 48909
517-322-1296

MICROFORMS

See also: RECORDS MANAGEMENT

ASSOCIATIONS

Association for Information and Image Management
1100 Wayne Ave., Ste. 1100
Silver Spring, MD 20910
301-587-8202
301-587-2711 Fax
Sue Wolk, Executive Director
Offers information to firms that manufacture, sell, and use information and image management equipment and services.

Library and Information Technology Association
50 E. Huron St.
Chicago, IL 60611-2729
312-280-4270
312-440-9374 Fax
Linda Knutson, Executive Director
This division of the American Library Association provides information about library automation, information storage, microforms, and related subjects.

PERIODICALS

I M C Journal
International Information Management Congress
345 Woodcliff Dr.
Fairport, NY 14450-4201
716-383-8330
William McArthur, Editor
Covers various aspects of electronic and non-electronic records management, including microfilms and micrographics.

International Journal of Micrographics & Optical Technology Pergamon Press, Inc., Journals Division
Maxwell House
Fairview Park
Elmsford, NY 10523
914-592-7700
Don Avedon, Editor
Surveys the electronic information transfer and storage field.

Micrographics and Optical Storage Equipment Review
Meckler Publishing Corp.
11 Ferry Lane W.
Westport, CT 06880-5808
203-226-6967
William Saffady, Editor
Detailed product information and advice for buyers and users of information storage systems, including microforms.

Micrographics Newsletter
Microfilm Publishing, Inc.
Box 950
Larchmont, NY 10538-0950
914-834-3044
Mitchell Badler, Editor
Covers news, trends, and products for executives who use or market microfilm services and equipment.

LIBRARIES

Association for Information and Image Management
Resource Center
1100 Wayne Ave.
Silver Spring, MD 20910
301-587-8202
301-587-2711 Fax
Micrographics, electronic imaging, imaging industry, records management, and related topics.

General Microfilm Co.
Microform Library
30 Coolidge Hill Rd.
Watertown, MA 02172
617-927-5557
Microform technology and related subjects.

COMPANIES

Bell & Howell Publication Systems Co.
(Subsidiary of Bell & Howell Co.)
Old Mansfield Rd.
Wooster, OH 44691
216-264-6666
Microfilm publishing and related products.

Computer Microfilm Corp.
(Subsidiary of Microfilm Reprographics, Inc.)
1706 N.E. Expressway
Atlanta, GA 30329
404-321-0886
Microfilm publishing services and microfilm equipment.

Dukane Corp.
2900 Dukane Dr.
St. Charles, IL 60174
708-584-2300
Microfilm and audiovisual equipment.

Endata, Inc.
(Division of First Financial Management Corp.)
501 Great Circle Rd.
Nashville, TN 37228
615-244-0244
Microfilming and other services.

Microfilm Holding Co., Inc.
1105 Fairchild Dr.
Winston-Salem, NC 27105
919-767-7886
Microfilming of goverment, hospital, and other types of records.

Micrographic Technology Corp.
520 Logue Ave.
Mountain View, CA 94043
415-965-3700
Microfilm information systems.

Southern Microfilm Corp.
1820 L & A Rd.
Metairie, LA 70001
504-834-0701
Microfilming services.

Spaulding Co., Inc.
(Subsidiary of Semco Industries, Inc.)
90 Hawes Way
Stoughton, MA 02072
800-441-4500
Microfilming services and equipment.

University Microfilms Inc.
(Division of Bell & Howell Co.)
300 N. Zeeb Rd.
Ann Arbor, MI 48106
313-761-4700
Microfilm copies of periodicals, books, and educational materials.

FEDERAL GOVERNMENT

U.S. International Trade Administration
Department of Commerce
14th St. and Constitution Ave., N.W.
Washington, DC 20230
202-377-2000
Ask for the Commodity Analyst who is an expert in microforms.

U.S. International Trade Commission
500 E St., S.W.
Washington, DC 20436
202-205-2000 Office of the Secretary
202-205-3296 Industries locator
Ask for the Trade Analyst who is an expert in microforms.

MINES AND MINING INDUSTRY

See also: COAL

ASSOCIATIONS

American Mining Congress
1920 N St. N.W., Ste. 300
Washington, DC 20036
202-861-2800
202-861-7535 Fax
John Knebel, President
Members include mining firms, suppliers of mining equipment, and firms that provide services to the industry.

International Union United Mine Workers of
America
900 15th St. N.W.
Washington, DC 20005
202-842-7200
Richard Trumka, President
By far the largest union of mine workers in the U.S.

Interstate Mining Compact Commission
459B Carlisle Dr.
Herndon, VA 22070
703-709-8654
703-709-8655 Fax
Gregory Conrad, Executive Director
Represents states that seek to control damage to the environment caused by surface mining.

Mining and Metallurgical Society of America
210 Post St., Ste. 1102
San Francisco, CA 94108
415-398-6925
Robert Crum, Executive Officer
Provides information on mineral conservation, mining, and related topics.

PERIODICALS

American Mining Congress Journal
American Mining Congress
1920 N St., N.W., Ste. 300
Washington, DC 20036
202-861-2800
Joyce Morgan, Editor
Surveys the mining field.

California Mining Journal
California Mining Journal, Inc.
Box 2260
Aptos, CA 95001
408-662-2899
Kenneth Harn, Editor
Reports on news, trends, technologies, and legal and business matters for the mining industry around the U.S.

Mine & Quarry Trader
Allied Publications
7355 N. Woodland
Box 603
Indianapolis, IN 46206-0603
317-297-5500
Business, equipment, and merchandising information for the mining and quarry industries.

Mining Engineering
Society for Mining, Metallurgy and Exploration
Box 625002
Littleton, CO 80162-5002
303-973-9550
Technical information for mining engineers.

LIBRARIES

Colorado School of Mines
Arthur Lakes Library
Golden, CO 80401
303-273-3690
303-278-4931 Fax
Mining, geology, mineral economics, metallurgy, and related topics.

Mine Safety Appliances Co.
Business Library
Box 426
Pittsburgh, PA 15230
412-967-3131
412-967-3460 Fax
Coal mining, industrial hygiene, and occupational safety.

Newmont Mining Corp.
Engineering Library
200 Park Ave., 36th Fl.
New York, NY 10166-0105
212-953-1935
212-351-2875 Fax
Mining, geology, and exploration.

COMPANIES

BHP-Utah International Inc.
(Subsidiary of Broken Hill Proprietary Co., Ltd.)
550 California St.
San Francisco, CA 94104
415-981-1515
Mining of coal and other minerals.

Freeport-McMoran Resource Partners, L.P.
(Subsidiary of Freeport-McMoRan Inc.)
1615 Poydras St.
New Orleans, LA 70112
504-582-4000
Mining and other businesses.

Ingersoll-Rand Co.
200 Chestnut Ridge Rd.
Woodcliff Lake, NJ 07675
201-573-0123
Equipment used for mining and industry.

Kennecott Corp.
(Subsidiary of RTZ Corp. Plc)
10 E. South Temple, Box 11248
Salt Lake City, UT 84147
801-322-7000
Mining of copper, silver, and gold.

Magma Copper Co.
P.O. Box M, Hwy. 76
San Manuel, AZ 85631
602-575-5670
Copper mining.

Manville Corp.
P.O. Box 5108
Denver, CO 80217
303-978-2000
Mining and other businesses.

Newmont Mining Corp.
1700 Lincoln St.
Denver, CO 80203
303-863-7414
Gold mining.

Peabody Coal Co.
(Subsidiary of Peabody Holding Co., Inc.)
1951 Barrett Ct., Box 1990
Henderson, KY 42420
502-827-0800
Coal mining.

Terex Corp.
201 W. Walnut St.
Green Bay, WI 54305
414-435-5322
Equipment used in mining and construction.

FEDERAL GOVERNMENT

Bureau of Mines
810 7th St., N.W.
Washington, DC 20747
202-501-9770
Ask for the Mining & Quarrying Trends or the Statistical Summary department.

U.S. Department of Labor
200 Constitution Ave., N.W.
Washington, DC 20210
202-523-6666
Ask for the Mine Safety and Health Adminis-tration.

U.S. International Trade Administration
Department of Commerce
14th St. and Constitution Ave., N.W.
Washington, DC 20230
202-377-2000
Ask for the Commodity Analyst who is an expert in mines and the mining industry.

U.S. International Trade Commission
500 E St., S.W.
Washington, DC 20436
202-205-2000 Office of the Secretary
202-205-3296 Industries locator
Ask for the Trade Analyst who is an expert in mines and the mining industry.

MINNESOTA

STATE OFFICE LOCATOR (*for referrals to all state government offices*)

612-296-6013

ARCHIVES AND RECORDS

Historical Society
Historical Building
690 Cedar Street
St. Paul, MN 55101
612-296-6980

ATTORNEY GENERAL

Attorney General's Office
State Capitol
St. Paul, MN 55155
612-297-4272

BANKING

Financial Examinations Division
133 E. 7th Street
St. Paul, MN 55101
612-296-2135

COMMERCE

Commerce Department
133 E. 7th Street
St. Paul, MN 55101
612-296-6848

CONSUMER AFFAIRS

Consumer Enforcement
State Capitol
St. Paul, MN 55155
612-296-2306

EDUCATION

Education Department
Capitol Square Building
550 Cedar Street
St. Paul, MN 55101
612-296-2358

ENERGY

Energy Regulation & Resources Management
150 E. Kellogg Boulevard
Room 790
St. Paul, MN 55101
612-296-6026

ENVIRONMENTAL AFFAIRS

Environmental Quality Board
Centennial Office Building
658 Cedar Street
Room 300
St. Paul, MN 55155
612-296-2603

HEALTH

Health Department
P.O. Box 9441
Minneapolis, MN 55440
612-623-5460

HOUSING

Housing Finance Agency
400 Sibley Street
Room 300
St. Paul, MN 55101
612-296-5738

HUMAN RIGHTS

Human Rights Department
500 Bremer Tower
7th Place & Minnesota Street
St. Paul, MN 55101
612-296-5665

INSURANCE

Commerce Department
133 E. 7th Street
St. Paul, MN 55101
612-296-6848

LABOR

Labor & Industry Department
443 Lafayette Road
St. Paul, MN 55155
612-296-2342

LEGISLATION

Legislative Reference Library
State Office Building
100 Constitution Avenue
Room 645
St. Paul, MN 55155
612-296-3398

LIBRARY SERVICES

Library Development & Services Section
Capitol Square Building
550 Cedar Street
St. Paul, MN 55101
612-296-2821

LICENSING—CORPORATE

Corporation Division
180 State Office Building
St. Paul, MN 55155
612-296-9215

LICENSING—PROFESSIONAL AND OCCUPATIONAL

Commerce Department
133 E. 7th Street
St. Paul, MN 55101
612-296-6848

MOTOR VEHICLES

Driver & Vehicle Services Bureau
Transportation Building
Room 211
St. Paul, MN 55155
612-296-9525

OCCUPATIONAL HEALTH AND SAFETY

Occupational Safety & Compliance Unit
443 Lafayette Road
St. Paul, MN 55155
612-296-4532

OMBUDSMAN

Lieutenant Governor's Office
130 State Capitol
St. Paul, MN 55155
612-296-2374

PUBLIC UTILITIES

Public Utilities Commission
American Center Building
150 E. Kellogg Boulevard
Room 780
St. Paul, MN 55101
612-296-2354

PURCHASING

Material Management Divison
50 Sherburne Avenue
St. Paul, MN 55155
612-296-1442

REAL ESTATE

Enforcement & Licensing Division
133 E. 7th Street
St. Paul, MN 55101
612-296-3528

SECURITIES

Securities Registration Unit
500 Metro Square Building
7th & Roberts Streets
St. Paul, MN 55106
612-296-2284

TAXATION AND REVENUE

Revenue Department
10 River Park Plaza
St. Paul, MN 55146
612-297-4160

TOURISM

Tourist Information Center
Farm Credit Service Building
375 Jackson Street
St. Paul, MN 55101
612-296-5029
800-328-1461
800-652-9747 (in Minnesota)

TRANSPORTATION

Transportation Department
John Ireland Boulevard
St. Paul, MN 55155
612-296-3000

UNEMPLOYMENT

Jobs & Training Department
390 N. Robert Street
St. Paul, MN 55101
612-296-3711

WORKER'S COMPENSATION

Workers' Compensation Unit
443 Lafayette Road
St. Paul, MN 55155
612-296-6490

MISSISSIPPI

STATE OFFICE LOCATOR (*for referrals to all state government offices*)

601-354-7011

ARCHIVES AND RECORDS

Archives & History Department
P.O. Box 571
Jackson, MS 39205
601-359-6850

ATTORNEY GENERAL

Attorney General's Office
P.O. Box 220
Jackson, MS 39205
601-359-3680

BANKING

Banking & Consumer Finance Department
P.O. Drawer 23729
Jackson, MS 39225-3729
601-359-1031

COMMERCE

Agriculture & Commerce Department
P.O. Box 1609
Jackson, MS 39215-1609
601-354-7050

CONSUMER AFFAIRS

Consumer Protection Division
P.O. Box 1609
Jackson, MS 39215-1609
601-354-7063

EDUCATION

Education Department
P.O. Box 771
Jackson, MS 39205
601-359-3513

ENERGY

Energy & Transportation Division
P.O. Box 849
Jackson, MS 39205
601-359-6600

ENVIRONMENTAL AFFAIRS

Office of Pollution Control
P.O. Box 10385
Jackson, MS 39289-0385
601-961-5100

HEALTH

Health Department
P.O. Box 1700
Jackson, MS 39215-1700
601-960-7634

HOUSING

Housing Finance Corp.
Dickson Building
510 George Street
Room 204
Jackson, MS 39201
601-359-6700

HUMAN RIGHTS

Appeals Board
301 N. Lamar Street
Room 100
Jackson, MS 39201
601-359-1406

INSURANCE

Insurance Department
P.O. Box 79
Jackson, MS 39205
601-359-3569

LABOR

Employment Security Commission
P.O. Box 1699
Jackson, MS 39215
601-354-8711

LEGISLATION

Legislative Reference Bureau
P.O. Box 1018
Jackson, MS 39215-1018
601-359-3135

LIBRARY SERVICES

Library Commission
P.O. Box 10700
Jackson, MS 39289-0700
601-359-1036

LICENSING—CORPORATE

Corporations Division
P.O. Box 136
Jackson, MS 39205
601-359-1350

LICENSING—PROFESSIONAL AND OCCUPATIONAL

Medical Licensure Board
2688D Insurance Center Drive
Jackson, MS 39216
601-354-6645

MOTOR VEHICLES

Motor Vehicle Commission
P.O. Box 16873
Jackson, MS 39236-7459
601-987-3995

OCCUPATIONAL HEALTH AND SAFETY

Occupational Safety & Health
P.O. Box 1700
Jackson, MS 39215-1700
601-987-3981

PUBLIC UTILITIES

Public Service Commission
P.O. Box 1174
Jackson, MS 39215-1174
601-961-5450

PURCHASING

Purchasing & Travel Division
P.O. Box 267
Jackson, MS 39205
601-354-7107

REAL ESTATE

Real Estate Commission
1920 Dunbarton
Jackson, MS 39216-5087
601-987-3969

SECURITIES

Securities Division
P.O. Box 136
Jackson, MS 39205
601-359-1350

TAXATION AND REVENUE

Tax Commission
P.O. Box 22828
Jackson, MS 39225
601-359-1098

TOURISM

Division of Tourism
P.O. Box 22825
Jackson, MS 39205
601-359-3297 or 3414
800-647-2290

TRANSPORTATION

Department of Energy & Transportation
Dickson Building
510 George Street
Jackson, MS 39202
601-961-4733

UNEMPLOYMENT

Unemployment Insurance Division
P.O. Box 1699
Jackson, MS 39215-1699
601-961-7700

WORKER'S COMPENSATION

Workers Compensation Commission
P.O. Box 5300
Jackson, MS 39296-5300
601-987-4200

MISSOURI

STATE OFFICE LOCATOR (*for referrals to all state government offices*)

314-751-2000

ARCHIVES AND RECORDS

Archives Division
P.O. Box 778
Jefferson City, MO 65102
314-751-4717

ATTORNEY GENERAL

Attorney General's Office
P.O. Box 899
Jefferson City, MO 65102
314-751-3321

BANKING

Finance Division
P.O. Box 716
Jefferson City, MO 65102
314-751-3397

COMMERCE

Economic Development Department
P.O. Box 1157
Jefferson City, MO 65102
314-751-3946

CONSUMER AFFAIRS

Public Protection Division
P.O. Box 899
Jefferson City, MO 65102
314-751-3321

EDUCATION

Elementary & Secondary Education Department
P.O. Box 480
Jefferson City, MO 65102
314-751-4446

ENERGY

Energy Division
P.O. Box 176
Jefferson City, MO 65102
314-751-2254

ENVIRONMENTAL AFFAIRS

Environmental Quality Division
P.O. Box 176
Jefferson City, MO 65102
314-751-4810

HEALTH

Health Department
P.O. Box 570
Jefferson City, MO 65102
314-751-6001

HOUSING

Housing Development Commission
3770 Broadway
Kansas City, MO 64111
816-756-3790

HUMAN RIGHTS

Human Rights Commission
3315 W. Truman Boulevard
Jefferson City, MO 65109
314-751-3325

INSURANCE

Insurance Division
P.O. Box 690
Jefferson City, MO 65102
314-751-4126

LABOR

Labor & Industrial Relations Department
3315 W. Truman Boulevard
Jefferson City, MO 65109
314-751-4091

LIBRARY SERVICES

State Library
P.O. Box 387
Jefferson City, MO 65102
314-751-3615

LICENSING—CORPORATE

Corporation Division
P.O. Box 778
Jefferson City, MO 65102
314-751-4194

LICENSING—PROFESSIONAL AND OCCUPATIONAL

Professional Registration Division
P.O. Box 1335
Jefferson City, MO 65102
314-751-1081

MOTOR VEHICLES

Motor Vehicles & Driver Licensing Division
P.O. Box 311
Jefferson City, MO 65105
314-751-4429

OCCUPATIONAL HEALTH AND SAFETY

Safety & Health Consultation Services
P.O. Box 449
Jefferson City, MO 65102
314-751-3403

OMBUDSMAN

Lieutenant Governor's Office
P.O. Box 563
Jefferson City, MO 65102
314-751-3000

PUBLIC UTILITIES

Public Service Commission
P.O. Box 360
Jefferson City, MO 65102
314-751-4132

PURCHASING

Purchasing Division
P.O. Box 809
Jefferson City, MO 65102
314-751-4169

REAL ESTATE

Real Estate Commission
P.O. Box 1339
Jefferson City, MO 65102
314-751-2628

SECURITIES

Securities Division
P.O. Box 778
Jefferson City, MO 65102
314-751-4704

TAXATION AND REVENUE

Revenue Department
P.O. Box 311
Jefferson City, MO 65105
314-751-4450

TOURISM

Division of Tourism
P.O. Box 1055
Jefferson City, MO 65101
314-751-4133

TRANSPORTATION

Highway & Transportation Department
P.O. Box 270
Jefferson City, MO 65102
314-751-4622

UNEMPLOYMENT

Unemployment Insurance Section
421 E. Dunklin Street
Jefferson City, MO 65101
314-751-3641

WORKER'S COMPENSATION

Workers Compensation Division
3315 W. Truman Boulevard
Jefferson City, MO 65109
314-751-4231

MOBILE HOME INDUSTRY

See also: BUILDING INDUSTRY

ASSOCIATIONS

American Mobilehome Association
12929 W. 26th Ave.
Golden, CO 80401
303-232-6336
R. Earnest White, President
An association of mobile home owners.

Manufactured Housing Institute
1745 Jefferson Davis Hwy., Ste. 511
Arlington, VA 22202
703-979-6620
Jerry Connors, President
Firms that make manufactured homes and supply components and services to the industry.

National Foundation Manufactured Home
     Owners
PO Box 33
Redmond, WA 98073
206-885-4650
John Jensen, Treasurer
*Represents the interests of people who own
mobile and manufactured homes.*

National Manufactured Housing Federation
1701 K St. N.W., No. 400
Washington, DC 20006
202-822-6470
Daniel Gilligan, President
*Represents firms that make manufactured
housing, operators of mobile home parks, and
developers of these parks.*

PERIODICALS

Automated Builder
C M N Publications
4371 Carpinteria Ave.
Carpinteria, CA 93014
805-684-7659
Don Carlson, Editor
*How-to information and case studies for
builders of mobile homes and other manufactured housing.*

MH—RV Builders News
Dan Kamrow & Associates, Inc.
Box 72367
Roselle, IL 60172
708-893-8872
Pat Finn, Editor
*Reports on trends and offers advice to builders
of mobile and manufactured homes and recre-
ational vehicles.*

Mobile Homes and Mobile Home Parks
Shepard's—McGraw-Hill, Inc.
Box 35300
Colorado Springs, CO 80935-3530
800-525-2474
*Covers developments in the laws that affect
mobile home owners and mobile home parks.*

Western Mobile News
Modern Housing Inc.
Coast Media, Inc.
4043 Irving Place
Culver City, CA 90230
213-839-5271
Edward Ely, Editor
*Reports on the mobile home industry in the
western part of the U.S.*

COMPANIES

Clayton Homes, Inc.
7131 Clinton Hwy., Box 15169
Knoxville, TN 37901
615-970-7200
Manufactured homes.

Elixir Industries
17925 S. Broadway
Gardena, CA 90248
213-321-1191
*Components for mobile homes and other prod-
ucts.*

Fleetwood Enterprises, Inc.
3125 Myers St., Box 7638
Riverside, CA 92523
714-351-3500
*Manufactured homes, motor homes and trail-
ers, and financing services for these products.*

Manufactured Homes, Inc.
3410 Healy Dr., Box 24549
Winston-Salem, NC 27114
919-768-9890
Retailer of mobile homes.

National Enterprises Inc.
Earl & Wallace, Box 7680
Lafayette, IN 47902
317-448-2000
Manufactured homes.

Oakwood Homes Corp.
2225 South Holden Rd.
Greensboro, NC 27407
919-855-2400
Wholesaler and retailer of mobile homes, and financing of mobile homes.

Schult Homes Corp.
P. O. Box 151
Middlebury, IN 46540
219-825-5881
Mobile homes.

Silvercrest Corp.
303 N. Placentia Ave.
Fullerton, CA 92631
714-572-1878
Manufactured and mobile homes.

Wick Building Systems, Inc.
404 Walter Rd., Box 490
Mazomanie, WI 53560
608-795-4281
Mobile and panelized homes.

FEDERAL GOVERNMENT

Federal Emergency Management Agency
500 C St., S.W.
Washington, DC 20472
202-646-2500
Ask for the Temporary Housing Bureau in the State & Local Programs & Support department.

U.S. Department of Housing and Urban
    Development
451 7th St., S.W.
Washington, DC 20410
202-755-5111
Ask for the Manufactured Housing & Construction Standards department.

U.S. International Trade Administration
Department of Commerce
14th St. and Constitution Ave., N.W.
Washington, DC 20230
202-377-2000
Ask for the Commodity Analyst who is an expert in mobile homes.

MOBILE TELEPHONE INDUSTRY

See also: TELECOMMUNICATIONS INDUSTRY

ASSOCIATIONS

National Association of Cellular Agents
1716 Woodhead St.
Houston, TX 77019
713-522-0528
Bob Hutchinson, President
Members include sales people, manufacturers and others working in the cellular mobile telephone industry. Offers promotional and training services.

National Cellular Resellers Association
c/o Thomas Assocs., Inc.
1230 Keith Bldg.
Cleveland, OH 44115
216-241-7333
216-241-0105 Fax
John Addington, Executive Director
Helps cellular resellers promote their industry.

Telocator, The Mobile Communications
    Industry Association
2000 M St., N.W., Ste. 230
Washington, DC 20036
202-467-4770
800-922-7626
202-467-6987 Fax
Thomas Stroup, President
An information clearinghouse for those interested in mobile telephone and radio paging communications.

PERIODICALS

Advanced Wireless Communication
Telecom Publishing Group
Capitol Publications Inc.
1101 King St., Ste. 444
Alexandria, VA 22313-2055
800-327-7205
Ed Warner, Editor
Reports business information on all the newest forms of wireless communications, including digital cellular, in-flight phones, paging systems, and other technologies.

Cellular Business
Intertec Publishing Corp.
9221 Quivira Rd.
Box 12901
Overland Park, KS 66212
913-888-4664
Rhonda Wickham, Editor
Covers business and technological news for the cellular telecommunications industry.

Cellular Marketing
Cardiff Publishing Co.
6300 S. Syracuse Way, Ste. 650
Englewood, CO 80111
303-220-0600
Information and advice for sales and marketing executives in the cellular industry.

Cellular Sales & Marketing
Creative Communications Inc.
Box 1519-BKC
Herndon, VA 22070-1519
703-742-9696
Stuart Crump, Editor
Highlights new products and sales techniques.

Communications
Cardiff Publishing Co.
6300 S. Syracuse Way, Ste. 650
Englewood, CO 80111
303-220-0600
George Dennis, Editor
*Covers governmental, business, and techno-
logical subjects for industry professionals.*

Mobile Product News
Phillips Publishing, Inc.
7811 Montrose Rd.
Potomac, MD 20854
301-340-2100
Lisa Portner, Editor
*Features new mobile communications prod-
ucts and systems.*

COMPANIES

Centel Corp.
8725 Higgins Rd.
Chicago, IL 60631
312-399-2500
Telephone and cellular telephone services.

Cellcom Corp.
15 Gardner Rd.
Fairfield, NJ 07004
201-808-1121
Mobile telephone services.

Metro Mobile CTS, Inc.
110 E. 59th St.
New York, NY 10022
212-605-0800
Operates a cellular telephone system.

Nationwide Cellular Service Inc.
20 E. Sunrise Hwy.
Valley Stream, NY 11582
516-568-2000
*Cellular telephone services and sales of cellu-
lar telephones.*

U.S. Cellular Corp.
(Subsidiary of Telephone & Data Systems,
   Inc.)
9410 W. Bryn Mawr
Chicago, IL 60631
312-399-8900
Cellular telephone services.

U S West NewVector Group, Inc.
(Subsidiary of U S West, Inc.)
3350 161st Ave. S.E.
Bellevue, WA 98008
206-747-4900
Cellular telephone services.

Vanguard Cellular Systems, Inc.
2002 Pisgah Church Rd.
Greensboro, NC 27408
919-282-3690
Cellular telephone services.

FEDERAL GOVERNMENT

Federal Communications Commission
1919 M St., N.W.
Washington, DC 20554
202-632-7106
*Ask for the Cellular Branch in the Common
Carrier Bureau.*

U.S. International Trade Administration
Department of Commerce
14th St. and Constitution Ave., N.W.
Washington, DC 20230
202-377-2000
*Ask for the Commodity Analyst who is an
expert in mobile telephone equipment.*

U.S. International Trade Administration
Department of Commerce
14th St. and Constitution Ave., N.W.
Washington, DC 20230
202-377-2000
Ask for the Commodity Analyst who is an expert in mobile telephone equipment.

U.S. Patent and Trademark Office
Crystal Plaza 2
2011 Jefferson Davis Highway
Arlington, VA 22202
703-305-8000
Ask for the Examining Group Director who is a specialist in mobile telephone equipment.

MONTANA

STATE OFFICE LOCATOR (*for referrals to all state government offices*)

406-444-2511

ARCHIVES AND RECORDS

State Archivist
225 N. Roberts Street
Helena, MT 59620
406-444-4775

ATTORNEY GENERAL

Justice Department
Justice Building
215 N. Sanders
Helena, MT 59620
406-444-2026

BANKING

Financial Institutions Division
1424 9th Avenue
Helena, MT 59620
406-444-2091

COMMERCE

Commerce Department
1424 9th Avenue
Helena, MT 49620
406-444-3494

CONSUMER AFFAIRS

Consumer Affairs Unit
1424 9th Avenue
Helena, MT 59620
406-444-4312

EDUCATION

Public Instruction Office
State Capitol
Room 106
Helena, MT 59620
406-444-3680

ENERGY

Energy Division
1520 E. 6th Avenue
Helena, MT 59620
406-444-6697

ENVIRONMENTAL AFFAIRS

Health & Environmental Sciences Department
Cogswell Building
Helena, MT 59620
406-444-3948

HEALTH

Department of Health & Environmental Sciences
Cogswell Building
Helena, MT 59620
406-444-2544

HOUSING

Board of Housing Division
1424 9th Avenue
Helena, MT 59620
406-444-3040

HUMAN RIGHTS

Human Rights Division
P.O. Box 1728
Helena, MT 59624
406-444-2884

INSURANCE

Auditor
P.O. Box 4009
Helena, MT 59604-4009
406-444-2040

LABOR

Labor & Industry Department
P.O. Box 1728
Helena, MT 59624
406-444-3555

LEGISLATION

Legislative Council
Capitol Building
Room 138
Helena, MT 59620
406-444-3064

LIBRARY SERVICES

State Library
1515 E. 6th Avenue
Helena, MT 59620
406-444-3115

LICENSING—CORPORATE

Corporation Bureau
State Capitol
Room 225
Helena, MT 59620
406-444-3665

LICENSING—PROFESSIONAL AND OCCUPATIONAL

Professional & Occupational Licensing Bureau
1424 9th Avenue
Helena, MT 59620
406-444-3737

MOTOR VEHICLES

Motor Vehicle Division
Scott Hart Building
Helena, MT 59620
406-444-4536

OCCUPATIONAL HEALTH AND SAFETY

Occupational Health Bureau
Cogswell Building
Helena, MT 59620
406-444-3671

OMBUDSMAN

Citizen's Advocate's Office
Capitol Station
Helena, MT 59620
406-444-3468

PUBLIC UTILITIES

Utility Division
2701 Prospect Avenue
Helena, MT 59620-2701
406-444-6187

PURCHASING

Purchasing Bureau
Sam W. Mitchell Building
Room 155
Helena, MT 59620
406-444-2575

REAL ESTATE

Board of Realty Regulation
1424 9th Avenue
Helena, MT 59620-0407
406-444-2961

SECURITIES

Securities Division
P.O. Box 4009
Helena, MT 59604-4009
406-444-2040

TAXATION AND REVENUE

Revenue Department
Sam W. Mitchell Building
Room 455
Helena, MT 59620
406-444-2460

TOURISM

Promotion Division
1424 9th Avenue
Helena, MT 59620
406-444-2654
800-541-1447

TRANSPORTATION

Transportation Division
2701 Prospect Avenue
Helena, MT 59620-2601
406-444-6195

UNEMPLOYMENT

Unemployment Insurance Division
P.O. Box 1728
Helena, MT 59624
406-444-2723

WORKER'S COMPENSATION

Workers Compensation Court
P.O. Box 537
Helena, MT 59624
406-444-7794

MORTGAGE INDUSTRY

See also: BANKS AND BANKING and REAL ESTATE BUSINESS

ASSOCIATIONS

National Association of Mortgage Brokers
706 E. Bell Rd., Ste. 101
Phoenix, AZ 85022
602-992-6181
602-493-8711 Fax
Michael Hoogendyk, Executive Vice President
Offers educational programs to mortgage brokers.

National Second Mortgage Association
8300 Utica Ave., Ste. 173
Rancho Cucamonga, CA 91730
714-941-7080
800-342-1121
714-941-8248 Fax
Jeffrey Zeltzer, Executive Director
Members include banks, finance firms, companies that offer second mortgages, and firms offering services to the mortgage industry. Compiles statistics and offers educational programs.

Mortgage Bankers Association of America
1125 15th St. N.W.
Washington, DC 20005
202-861-6500
Warren Lasko, Executive Vice President
Members include mortgage and commercial banks, savings and loan firms, title companies, and others involved with mortgage lending. Offers research and educational services on technical and business-related subjects.

Mortgage Insurance Companies of America
805 15th St. N.W., Ste. 1110
Washington, DC 20005
202-371-2899
Suzan Hutchinson, President
Mortgage insurance companies that share information and compile statistics.

United Mortgage Bankers of America
800 Ivy Hill Rd.
Philadelphia, PA 19150
215-242-6060
215-247-1580 Fax
Gene Hatton, President
Afro-American and other minority mortgage bankers and mortgage brokers.

PERIODICALS

Mortgage and Real Estate Executives Report
Warren, Gorham and Lamont Inc.
One Penn Plaza
New York, NY 10119
800-950-1217
Alvin Arnold, Editor
Offers information about market conditions and advice for increasing profitability to professionals in the mortgage industry.

Mortgage Commentary
Mortgage Commentary Publications
Box 30240
Bethesda, MD 20814
301-654-5580
Andrew Mandala, Editor
News and trends that interest corporate executives in charge of mortgage investing.

Mortgage Market Insight
Community Development Services, Inc.
C D Publications
8204 Fenton St.
Silver Spring, MD 20910-2889
301-588-6380
John Bancroft, Editor
Reports on the residential and commercial mortgage market.

Secondary Marketing Executive
L D J Corp.
70 Edwin Ave.
Box 2330
Waterbury, CT 06722-2330
203-755-0158
John Florian, Editor
Advice and industry analysis for marketers of secondary mortgages.

LIBRARIES

MGIC Investment Corp.
Corporate Library
MGIC Plaza
Milwaukee, WI 53202
414-347-6409
414-347-6959 Fax
Mortgage insurance, real estate statistics, housing, banking, and related topics.

United Mortgage Bankers of America
Library
800 Ivy Hill Rd.
Philadelphia, PA 19150
215-242-6060
215-247-1580 Fax
Minority mortgage banking and minority mortgage brokering.

U.S. Department of Housing and Urban Development
Library
451 7th St., S.W., Rm. 8141
Washington, DC 20410
202-708-2376
Mortgage finance, community development, law, construction finance, and related topics.

U.S. League of Savings Institutions
Library
111 E. Wacker Dr.
Chicago, IL 60601
312-644-3100
312-938-2541 Fax
Mortgages, banking services, housing finance, and related topics.

COMPANIES

American Southwest Mortgage Investments Corp.
335 N. Wilmot St.
Tucson, AZ 85711
602-748-2111
Mortgage-based investments.

Federal National Mortgage Association
3900 Wisconsin Ave., N.W.
Washington, DC 20016
202-752-7000
This quasi-governmental body, known popularly as Fannie Mae, facilitates loans for residential mortgages.

FirstFed Financial Corp.
401 Wilshire Blvd.
Santa Monica, CA 90401
213-319-6001
Residential mortgages and consumer loans.

Inland Mortgage Co.
(Subsidiary of Irwin Financial Corp.)
9265 Counselor's Row
Indianapolis, IN 46240
317-844-7788
Involved in residential and commercial loans.

M.D.C. Holdings, Inc.
3600 S. Yosemite St.
Denver, CO 80237
303-773-1100
Mortgage banking and real estate development.

PHM Corp.
33 Bloomfield Hills Pky.
Bloomfield Hills, MI 48304
313-647-2750
Residential house builders and mortgage financing.

FEDERAL GOVERNMENT

Federal Home Loan Mortgage Coporation
8200 Jones Branch Dr.
McLean, VA 22102
703-903-2000
Ask for the Risk Management department.

Federal Reserve System
20th St. and Constitution Ave., N.W.
Washington, DC 20551
202-452-3000
Ask for the Market Data & Analysis department, the Consumer & Community Affairs department, or the Housing Credit department.

Federal Trade Commission
Pennsylvania Ave. at 6th St., N.W.
Washington, DC 20580
202-326-2000
Ask for the Marketing Practices department in the Bureau of Consumer Protection.

U.S. Department of Housing and Urban
    Development
451 7th St., S.W.
Washington, DC 20410
202-755-5111
Ask for the Government National Mortgage Association.

U.S. Department of the Treasury
1500 Pennsylvania Ave., N.W.
Washington, DC 20220
202-566-2111
Ask for the Thrift Supervision Office.

MOVING AND STORAGE INDUSTRY

See also: WAREHOUSES

ASSOCIATIONS

American Movers Conference
2200 Mill Rd.
Alexandria, VA 22314
703-838-1930
703-838-1925 Fax
Charles Irions, President
Represents movers of office, household, and other types of goods. Offers a variety of publications to moving companies.

National Council of Moving Associations
1500 N. Beauregard St.
Alexandria, VA 22311-1715
703-671-8813
703-671-6712 Fax
Gary Petty, President
Conducts research and training programs for moving and storage companies. Associated with the National Moving and Storage Association at the same address.

National Mini-Storage Institute
1331 P St. N.W.
Washington, DC 20005
202-943-9162
Frank Mason, President
Offers educational seminars for owners and operators of self-storage facilities.

Self Storage Association
60 Revere Dr., Ste. 500
Northbrook, IL 60062
708-480-9627
708-480-9282 Fax
Provides public relations, marketing, and educational services to self-storage facility owners.

Storage Council
8720 Red Oak Blvd., Ste. 201
Charlotte, NC 28217
704-522-8644
704-522-7826 Fax
John Nofsinger, Managing Director
A federation of trade associations representing storage firms.

PERIODICALS

Direction
National Moving & Storage Association
1500 Beauregard St.
Alexandria, VA 22311-1715
703-671-8813
Joyce McDowell, Editor
Covers equipment, management, regulations, labor matters, and other concerns of the moving and storage industry.

Mayflower Warehouseman
9247 N. Meridian St., Ste. 120
Indianapolis, IN 46260
317-844-6226
Katherine Armington, Editor
Reports news and trends in the moving and storage industry.

Mini-Storage Messenger
Mini Co., Inc.
2531 W. Dunlap Ave., Ste. 201
Phoenix, AZ 85021
800-824-6864
Business information for owners and operators of self-storage firms.

COMPANIES

Alexander & Baldwin, Inc.
822 Bishop St., Box 3440
Honolulu, HI 96801
808-525-6611
Trucking and storage and other businesses.

Allied Van Lines, Inc.
(Subsidiary of NFC plc)
P.O. Box 4403
Chicago, IL 60680
708-717-3000
Long distance and local moving.

Bekins Moving & Storage Co.
777 Flower St.
Glendale, CA 91201
818-507-1200
Local and long distance moving and storage.

CSX Corp.
1 James Ctr.
Richmond, VA 23219
804-782-1400
Moving and shipping services.

Mayflower Group, Inc.
9998 N. Michigan Rd.
Carmel, IN 46032
317-875-1000
Moving and transportation of household items and other products.

Norfolk Southern Corp.
3 Commercial Pl.
Norfolk, VA 23510
804-629-2600
Moving and shipping services.

North American Van Lines of Texas
2307 Springlake, #516
Dallas, TX 75234
214-241-0522
Moving and storage services.

U-Haul International, Inc.
(Subsidiary of Amerco)
2727 N. Central Ave.
Phoenix, AZ 85004
602-263-6011
Rentals of trailers, trucks, and other products for moving.

MOTION PICTURE INDUSTRY

ASSOCIATIONS

Academy of Motion Picture Arts and Sciences
8949 Wilshire Blvd.
Beverly Hills, CA 90211
213-859-9619
Bruce Davis, Executive Director
This group of actors, producers, and others in the motion picture industry is best known for presenting the Oscars. Its National Film Information Service maintains a library which answers questions about films and the film industry.

Alliance of Motion Picture and Television Producers
14144 Ventura Blvd., 3rd Fl.
Sherman Oaks, CA 91423
818-995-3600
818-789-7431 Fax
J. Nicholas Counter, President
A professional society of producers.

American Cinema Editors
1041 N. Formosa Ave.
West Hollywood, CA 90046
213-850-2900
George Grenville, President
A professional society of editors.

American Film Marketing Association
12424 Wilshire Blvd., Ste. 600
Los Angeles, CA 90025-1040
213-558-1170
Tim Kittleson, Executive Director
Members are responsible for selling film rights in the U.S. and abroad.

American Society of Cinematographers
1782 N. Orange Dr.
Hollywood, CA 90028
213-876-5080
213-876-4973 Fax
Richard Rawlings, Secretary
A professional society of cinematographers.

International Documentary Association
1551 S. Robertson Blvd., Ste. 201
Los Angeles, CA 90035
213-284-8422
213-785-9334 Fax
Lora Fox, Executive Director
A professional society of documentary makers.

PERIODICALS

Boxoffice
R L D Communications
1800 N. Highland Ave., Ste. 710
Hollywood, CA 90028
213-465-1186
Harley Lond, Editor
Covers all business subjects of concern to the motion picture industry.

Entertainment Law Reporter
Entertainment Law Reporter Publishing Co.
2210 Wilshire Blvd., No. 311
Santa Monica, CA 90403
213-892-9335
Lionel Sobel, Editor
Covers legal and regulatory matter for the motion picture, television, radio, music, theater, and publishing industries.

Hollywood Reporter
H.R. Industries, Inc.
6715 Sunset Blvd.
Hollywood, CA 90028
213-464-7411
Teri Ritzer, Editor
Surveys the movie industry.

Variety
Variety, Inc.
Cahners Publishing Co.
475 Park Ave. S.
New York, NY 10016-6901
212-779-1999
Peter Bart, Editor
*Extensive coverage of all entertainment busi-
nesses, including motion pictures, television,
theater, and music.*

LIBRARIES

American Film Institute
Louis B. Mayer Library
2021 N. Western Ave.
Box 27999
Los Angeles, CA 90027
213-856-7660
Motion pictures and video.

New York Public Library
Performing Arts Research Center
Billy Rose Theatre Collection
111 Amsterdam Ave.
New York, NY 10023
212-870-1639
212-787-3852 Fax
Cinema, television, theater, and related topics.

University of California, Los Angeles
Theater Arts Library
22478 University Research Library
Los Angeles, CA 90024-1575
213-825-4880
Film, television, motion pictures, and theater.

University of California, Los Angeles
UCLA Film and Television Archive
Research and Study Center
46 Powell Library
405 Hilgard Ave.
Los Angeles, CA 90024-1517
213-206-5388
213-206-3592 Fax
*Films, broadcast television programs, and
related topics.*

COMPANIES

Carolco Pictures Inc.
8800 Sunset Blvd.
Los Angeles, CA 90069
213-850-8800
Finances and produces motion pictures.

Walt Disney Co.
500 S. Buena Vista St.
Burbank, CA 91521
818-560-1000
*Produces and distributes motion pictures and
TV programs.*

De Laurentiis Entertainment Group Inc.
8670 Wilshire Blvd.
Beverly Hills, CA 90211
213-854-7000
Produces and distributes motion pictures.

MGM/UA Communications Co.
(Subsidiary of Pathe Communications Corp.)
10000 W. Washington Blvd.
Culver City, CA 90230
213-280-6000
Produces and distributes motion pictures.

New Line Cinema Corp.
575 Eighth Ave.
New York, NY 10018
212-239-8880
Produces and distributes motion pictures.

Orion Pictures Corp.
1325 Ave. of the Americas
New York, NY 10019
212-956-3800
Finances, produces, and distributes motion pictures.

Reeves Communications Corp.
(Subsidiary of Thames Televison PLC)
708 Third Ave.
New York, NY 10017
212-573-8600
Produces and distributes motion pictures.

Paramount Pictures Corp.
5555 Melrose Ave.
Los Angeles, CA 90038
213-956-5000
Produces and distributes motion pictures.

Twentieth Century-Fox Film Corp.
P.O. Box 900
Beverly Hills, CA 90213
213-277-2211
Produces and distributes motion pictures and TV programs.

Warner Bros. Inc.
(Subsidiary of Time Warner Inc.)
4000 Warner Blvd.
Burbank, CA 91522
818-954-6000
Produces and distributes motion pictures and TV programs.

FEDERAL GOVERNMENT

U.S. International Trade Administration
Department of Commerce
14th St. and Constitution Ave., N.W.
Washington, DC 20230
202-377-2000
Ask for the Commodity Analyst who is an expert in the motion picture industry.

U.S. International Trade Commission
500 E St., S.W.
Washington, DC 20436
202-205-2000 Office of the Secretary
202-205-3296 Industries locator
Ask for the Trade Analyst who is an expert in the motion picture industry.

MOTION PICTURE THEATERS

ASSOCIATIONS

National Association of Theatre Owners
4605 Lankershim Blvd., Ste. 340
North Hollywood, CA 91602
818-506-1778
818-506-0269 Fax
Mary Grasso, Executive Director
Members are owners and operators of motion picture theaters.

Theatre Equipment Association
244 W. 49th St.
New York, NY 10019
212-246-6460
212-265-6428 Fax
Robert Sunshine, Executive Director
Manufacturers and distributors of supplies and equipment used by motion picture theatres.

PERIODICALS

See the periodicals listed in MOTION PICTURE INDUSTRY

COMPANIES

AMC Entertainment Inc.
106 W. 14th St.
Kansas City, MO 64105
816-221-4000
Exhibitor of motion pictures in theaters.

General Cinema Corp.
27 Boylston St.
Chestnut Hill, MA 02167
617-232-8200
Owns motion picture theaters.

Loews Corp.
667 Madison Ave.
New York, NY 10021
212-545-2000
Owns and operates motion picture theaters and hotels.

Neumade Products Corp.
200 Connecticut Ave., Box 5001
Norwalk, CT 06856
203-866-7600
Theater projection equipment and other types of equipment.

TPI Enterprises, Inc.
885 Third Ave.
New York, NY 10022
212-230-2233
Owns restaurants and motion picture theaters.

United Artists Entertainment Co.
(Subsidiary of Tele-Communications, Inc.)
2930 E. Third Ave.
Denver, CO 80206
303-321-4242
Owns and operates motion picture theaters and cable television systems.

FEDERAL GOVERNMENT

U.S. International Trade Administration
Department of Commerce
14th St. and Constitution Ave., N.W.
Washington, DC 20230
202-377-2000
*Ask for the Commodity Analyst who is an
expert in motion picture theaters.*

U.S. International Trade Commission
500 E St., S.W.
Washington, DC 20436
202-205-2000 Office of the Secretary
202-205-3296 Industries locator
*Ask for the Trade Analyst who is an expert in
motion picture theaters.*

MOTIVATION (PSYCHOLOGY)

*Motivation is the psychological study of how to inspire employees to work more effectively or to
increase sales.*

ASSOCIATIONS

Association for Quality and Participation
801-B W. 8th St., Ste. 501
Cincinnati, OH 45203
513-381-1959
Cathy Kramer, Executive Vice President
*This group of executives, trainers, and others
share information about how quality circles
can improve productivity, quality, and motivation.*

Human Resources Research Organization
1100 S. Washington St.
Alexandria, VA 22314
703-549-3611
William Osborn, President
*Members are researchers, educators, and exec-
utives that share information on improving
performance, motivation, and other subjects.*

PERIODICALS

Advances in Motivation and Achievement
J A I Press Inc.
55 Old Post Rd., No. 2
Box 1678
Greenwich, CT 06836-1678
203-661-7602
Martin Maehr, Editor
*A scholarly journal for those interested in
motivation.*

Human Performance
Lawrence Erlbaum Associates, Inc.
365 Broadway
Hillsdale, NJ 07642
201-666-4110
Frank Landy, Editor
*A scholarly journal reporting on factors that
improve human performance and increase
motivation.*

Industry Week
Penton Publishing
1100 Superior Ave.
Cleveland, OH 44114-2543
216-696-7000
Charles Day, Editor
Reports news from various industries and also advises on management approaches that increase motivation and productivity.

Psychology of Learning and Motivation
Academic Press, Inc.
1250 Sixth Ave.
San Diego, CA 92101
619-231-0926
K.W. Spence, Editor
A scholarly journal that reports new research in learning and motivation.

LIBRARIES

Harvard University
Psychology Research Library
33 Kirkland St.
Cambridge, MA 02138
617-495-3858
A wide variety of psychology subjects including the psychology of motivation.

Ohio Poetry Therapy Center and Library
Pudding House
60 N. Main St.
Johnstown, OH 43031
614-967-6060
Psychology, self-help, and motivation.

COMPANIES

L. G. Balfour Co., Inc.
(Subsidiary of Town & Country Corp.)
25 County St.
Attleboro, MA 02703
508-222-3600
Motivation and incentive products for industry and schools.

Carlson Marketing Group Inc.
(Subsidiary of Carlson Companies, Inc.)
Carlson Parkway, Box 59159
Minneapolis, MN 55459
612-449-1000
Motivation and training programs, and other services.

Maritz Inc.
1375 N. Highway Dr.
Fenton, MO 63026
314-827-4000
Motivation and training programs.

MOTOR BUSES

See also: AUTOMOTIVE INDUSTRY
and PUBLIC TRANSPORTATION

ASSOCIATIONS

American Bus Association
1015 15th St. N.W., Ste. 250
Washington, DC 20005
202-842-1645
800-422-1400
202-842-0850 Fax
George Snyder, Executive Vice President
*Members are bus manufacturers and privately
owned bus companies.*

American Public Transit Association
1201 New York Ave. N.W., Ste. 400
Washington, DC 20005
202-898-4000
202-898-4070 Fax
Jack Gilstrap, Executive Vice President
*Publicly owned bus and rail systems in North
America.*

Motor Vehicle Manufacturers Association of
the United States
7430 2nd Ave., Ste. 300
Detroit, MI 48202
313-872-4311
313-872-5400 Fax
Thomas Hanna, Executive Officer
*Manufacturers of cars, trucks, and buses. Pro-
vides research services.*

National Bus Traffic Association
506 S. Wabash Ave., Rm. 518
Chicago, IL 60605
312-922-3700
L. W. Harlow, Chairman
Members are intercity bus carriers.

National School Transportation Association
PO Box 2639
Springfield, VA 22152
703-644-0700
Karen Finkel, Executive Director
*Members manufacture and operate school
buses.*

United Bus Owners of America
1300 L St. N.W., Ste. 1050
Washington, DC 20005
202-484-5623
202-898-0484 Fax
Wayne Smith, Executive Director
*Bus companies that share information about
safety, regulations, and related subjects.*

PERIODICALS

Bus Operator
Tom Jackson & Associates, Inc.
1210 Eighth Ave. S.
Nashville, TN 37203
615-242-7747
*News and management advice for those
involved with intercity bus operations.*

Bus World
Stauss Publications
Box 39
Woodland Hills, CA 91365
818-710-0208
Julian Wolinsky, Editor
*Covers news of interest to bus owners and bus
systems operators.*

Chilton's Commercial Carrier Journal
Chilton Co.
1 Chilton Way
Radnor, PA 19089
215-964-4000
Gerald Standley, Editor
Advice and news for managers of bus and truck fleets.

Moody's Transportation News Reports
Moody's Investors Service
99 Church St.
New York, NY 10007-0300
212-553-0300
Robert Hanson, Editor
Follows news and trends of interest to railroads, airlines, and shipping, bus, and truck firms.

National Bus Trader
National Bus Trader, Inc.
9698 Judson Rd.
Polo, IL 60614
815-946-2341
Larry Plachno, Editor
Reports on developments in bus design and bus equipment.

National School Bus Report
National School Transportation
Box 2639
Springfield, VA 22152
703-644-0700
Karen Finkel, Editor
News for owners and operaters of school buses.

LIBRARIES

Motor Bus Society, Inc.
Library
P.O. Box 10503
New Brunswick, NJ 08906
Motor bus transportation history.

COMPANIES

Collins Industries, Inc.
421 E. 30th Ave., Box 2064
Hutchinson, KS 67504
316-663-5551
Small buses and transportation equipment.

Flexible Corp.
970 Pittsburgh
Delaware, OH 43015
614-362-2600
Motor buses and other vehicles.

General Motors Truck and Bus Div.
31 Judson St.
Pontiac, MI 48058
313-857-5000
Trucks and buses.

Greyhound Lines Inc.
901 Main St.
Dallas, TX 75202
214-744-6500
Bus transportation services.

Grumman Allied Div.
4170 Veterans Memorial Hwy.
Bohemia, NY 11716
516-737-5400
Buses and other vehicles.

New Jersey Transit Bus Operation Inc.
(Subsidiary of New Jersey Transit Corp.)
180 Boyden Ave.
Maplewood, NJ 07040
201-378-6300
Interstate and intrastate bus services.

Southern California Rapid Transit District
425 S. Main St.
Los Angeles, CA 90013
213-972-6000
Buses and other forms of public transportation.

FEDERAL GOVERNMENT

Interstate Commerce Commission
12th St. and Constitution Ave., N.W.
Washington, DC 20423
202-275-0885
Ask for the Motor Carrier Leasing Board.

U.S. Department of Transportation
400 7th St., S.W.
Washington, DC 20590
202-366-4000
Ask for the Motor Carrier Standards Review department in the Federal Highway Administration department; or for the Urban Mass Transportation Administration.

U.S. International Trade Administration
Department of Commerce
14th St. and Constitution Ave., N.W.
Washington, DC 20230
202-377-2000
Ask for the Commodity Analyst who is an expert in motor buses.

U.S. International Trade Commission
500 E St., S.W.
Washington, DC 20436
202-205-2000 Office of the Secretary
202-205-3296 Industries locator
Ask for the Trade Analyst who is an expert in motor buses.

MOTORCYCLE INDUSTRY

See also: AUTOMOTIVE INDUSTRY

ASSOCIATIONS

Motorcycle Industry Council
2 Jenner St., Ste. 150
Irvine, CA 92718
714-727-4211
714-727-4217 Fax
Carol Kington, Vice President
This group of motorcycle manufacturers and distributors compiles statistics and conducts research.

Independent Motorcycle Retailers of America
3345 W. Montrose
Chicago, IL 60618
James Rashid, President
A small group of independent distributors and retailers of motorcycles.

PERIODICALS

Cycle News
C N Publishing Group
2201 Cherry Ave.
Box 498
Long Beach, CA 90801
310-427-7433
Jack Mangus, Editor
A weekly newspaper for motorcycle enthusiasts.

Motorcycle Dealernews Buyers Guide
Edgell Communications
7500 Old Oak Blvd.
Cleveland, OH 44130
216-826-2839
Leslie Frohoff, Editor
Product descriptions for motorcycle dealers.

Motorcycle Industry Magazine
Industry Shopper Publishing, Inc.
31194 La Baya Dr., Ste. 200
Westlake Village, CA 91362
818-991-2070
Rick Campbell, Editor
Surveys news and trends of interest to the motorcycle industry.

Motorcycle Product News
M H West, Inc.
6633 Odessa Ave.
Van Nuys, CA 91406
818-997-0664
Bob Jackson, Editor
Covers new products for dealers, distributors, and servicers of mopeds, and other small powered vehicles.

LIBRARIES

Harley-Davidson, Inc.
Engineering Libraqry
3700 W. Juneau Ave.
Box 653
Milwaukee, WI 53208
414-341-4680
Motorcycles and engineering.

Motorcycle Safety Foundation
Information Resource Center
2 Jenner St., Ste. 150
Irvine, CA 92718
714-727-3227
714-727-4217 Fax
Motorcycle awareness, motorcycle rider education, and related topics.

COMPANIES

Cambridge Holdings Ltd.
370 17th St.
Boulder, CO 80202
303-573-8866
Motorcycle and ski glasses and goggles.

Douglas Battery Mfg. Co.
500 Battery Dr.
Winston-Salem, NC 27117
919-650-7000
Batteries for cars, motorcycles, and other types of batteries.

Harley-Davidson Motor Co., Inc.
3700 W. Juneau Ave.
Milwaukee, WI 53201
414-935-4680
Motorcycles and parts.

Honda of America Manufacturing
Honda Pkwy.
Marysville, OH 43040
513-866-6251
Motorcycles and cars.

Kawasaki Motor Manufacturing Corp. USA
6600 N.W. 27th St.
Lincoln, NE 68524
402-476-6600
Motorcycles and parts.

KK Motorcycle Supply
431 E. 3rd St.
Dayton, OH 45401
513-222-1303
Motorcycle tires, parts, and supplies.

Midwest Mutual Insurance Co.
1111 Ashworth Rd.
West Des Moines, IA 50265
515-223-2000
Insurance for motorcycle, recreational and other non-standard vehicles.

Shoreline Products Inc.
P.O. Box 848
Arlington, TX 76010
817-465-1351
Trailers for boats, snowmobiles, and motorcycles.

Vetter Products, Inc.
Rte. 136 East
Rantoul, IL 61866
217-893-9300
Accessories for motorcycles.

Yuasa Exide Battery Corp.
(Subsidiary of Yuasa Battery & Exide Battery)
Montrose & Angeline Sts.
Laureldale, PA 19605
215-929-5781
Batteries for motorcycles and other types of batteries.

FEDERAL GOVERNMENT

U.S. Customs Service
Department of the Treasury
U.S. Customshouse
6 World Trade Center
New York, NY 10048
212-466-5550
Ask for the Commodity Specialist in charge of motorcycles.

U.S. International Trade Administration
Department of Commerce
14th St. and Constitution Ave., N.W.
Washington, DC 20230
202-377-2000
Ask for the Commodity Analyst who is an expert in motorcycles.

U.S. International Trade Commission
500 E St., S.W.
Washington, DC 20436
202-205-2000 Office of the Secretary
202-205-3296 Industries locator
Ask for the Trade Analyst who is an expert in motorcycles.

MUNICIPAL GOVERNMENT

See also: CIVIL SERVICE and each of the 50 states

ASSOCIATIONS

American Association of Small Cities
Rte. 2, PO Box 128
De Leon, TX 76444
817-893-5818
Roy Dugger, Executive Director
Members are towns, villages, boroughs, and small cities whose population is under 50,000. Provides information on issues of concern to small cities.

ICMA—The Professional Local Government
  Management Association
777 N. Capitol St., N.E., Ste. 500
Washington, DC 20002-4201
202-289-ICMA
202-962-3500 Fax
William Hansell, Executive Director
Offers management education to municipal administrators.

Local Government Center
2716 Ocean Park Blvd., Ste. 1062
Santa Monica, CA 90405
213-392-0443
213-392-0942 Fax
Philip Fixler, Director
*Studies how local governments can reduce
costs, especially in the delivery of services.*

National Association of Towns and Townships
1522 K St. N.W., Ste. 730
Washington, DC 20005
202-737-5200
Jeffrey Schiff, Executive Director
*Offers information and educational programs
to teach small communities how to improve
the quality of life.*

National League of Cities
1301 Pennsylvania Ave., N.W.
Washington, DC 20004
202-626-3000
202-626-3043 Fax
Donald Borut, Executive Director
*Teaches officials of municipalities how to
improve the services and functioning of local
governments.*

United States Conference of Mayors
1620 I St., N.W.
Washington, DC 20006
202-293-7330
J. Thomas Cochran, Executive Director
*Offers technical assistance and educational
programs to mayors and municipal employees
of cities with more than 30,000 citizens.*

PERIODICALS

American City & County
Communication Channels, Inc.
6255 Barfield Rd.
Atlanta, GA 30328-4369
404-256-9800
Janet Ward, Editor
*Reports on the trends and issues that concern
those in charge of local government administration, engineering, and operations.*

City Hall Digest
City Hall Communications
Box 309
Seabrook, MD 20703-0309
301-557-3681
Raymond Bancroft, Editor
*Suggests management techniques and innova-
tions that can help municipal officials in all
fields.*

Governing
Congressional Quarterly Inc.
1414 22nd St., N.W.
Washington, DC 20037
800-432-2250
Peter Harkness, Editor
*Covers the policy issues, trends, and politics
that concern municipal officials at all levels.*

Municipal Litigation Reporter
Strafford Publications, Inc.
1201 Peachtree St., N.E., Ste. 1150
Atlanta, GA 30361
404-881-1141
*Reports on litigation against local govern-
ments all over the U.S.*

State and Local Government Review
University of Georgia. Carl Vinson Institute
of Government
Terrell Hall
Athens, GA 30602
404-542-2736
Richard Campbell, Editor
A scholarly journal that reports on state and local government issues.

LIBRARIES

National League of Cities
Municipal Reference Service
1301 Pennsylvania Ave., N.W.
Washington, DC 20004
202-626-3130
202-626-3043 Fax
Municipal government, finance, community development, urban affairs, and related topics.

Program Planners, Inc.
Library/Information Center
230 W. 41st St., 19th Fl.
New York, NY 10036
212-840-2600
Local government, urban affairs, insurance, collective bargaining, and related subjects.

MUSICAL INSTRUMENTS INDUSTRY

See also: MUSIC INDUSTRY

ASSOCIATIONS

American Federation of Violin and Bow
    Makers
288 Richmond Terrace
Staten Island, NY 10301
718-816-7818
800-99-AMATI
William Monical, President
Offers educational programs for makers and repairers of violins and bows.

Associated Pipe Organ Builders of America
475 Riverside Dr., Ste. 1260
New York, NY 10115
212-870-2310
Jack Bethards, President
Offers industry and technical information to manufacturers of pipe organs and to the public.

Guitar and Accessories Music Marketing
    Association
136 W. 21st St., 3rd Fl.
New York, NY 10011-3212
212-924-9175
212-675-3577 Fax
Jerome Hershman, Executive Vice President
*Members manufacture and sell guitars and
other stringed instruments.*

International Association of Electronic Key-
    board Manufacturer
c/o Korg USA
89 Frost St.
Westbury, NY 11590
516-333-9100
800-482-1616
Mike Kovins, President
*Members are U.S. manufacturers of electronic
keyboards.*

International MIDI Association
5316 W. 57th St.
Los Angeles, CA 90056
213-649-6434
213-215-3380 Fax
S. D. Westfall, Executive Officer
*Members manufacture and sell musical instru-
ments, computers, software, and other products used to make music electronically.*

Music Distributors Association
136 W. 21st St., 3rd Fl.
New York, NY 10011-3212
212-924-9175
212-675-3577 Fax
Jerome Hershman, Executive Vice President
*Offers information about the wholesaling and
distribution of musical instruments, accessories, and sheet music.*

Music Industry Conference
c/o Music Educators National Conference
1902 Association Dr.
Reston, VA 22091
703-860-4000
703-860-1531 Fax
Michael Bennett, President
*An information clearinghouse for music edu-
cators and instrument manufacturers, publishers, and others in the music industry.*

National Association of Band Instrument
    Manufacturers
136 W. 21st St., 3rd Fl.
New York, NY 10011-3212
212-924-9175
212-675-3577 Fax
Jerome Hershman, Executive Vice President
*Members make and import musical instru-
ments used in bands.*

National Association of Music Merchants
5140 Avenida Encinas
Carlsbad, CA 92008
619-438-8001
Larry Linkin, Executive Vice President
*Offers marketing and industry information to
manufacturers, distributors, and retailers of
music products.*

Piano Manufacturers Association Interna-
    tional
c/o Donald W. Dillon Assocs.
4020 McEwen St., Ste. 105
Dallas, TX 75244
214-233-9107
Donald Dillon, Executive Director
*Provides industry information for piano man-
ufacturers.*

PERIODICALS

Instrumentalist
Instrumentalist Co.
200 Northfield Rd.
Northfield, IL 60093-3390
708-446-5000
Judy Nelson, Editor
*Written for school band leaders, and musical
instrument teachers.*

Music and Sound Retailer
Testa Communications, Inc.
25 Willowdale Ave.
Port Washington, NY 11050
516-767-2500
Jon Mayer, Editor
*Industry trends, new products, and merchan-
dising advice for retailers of musical instruments.*

Strings
String Letter Press, Inc.
Box 767
San Anselmo, CA 94979-0767
415-485-6946
David Brin, Editor
*Written for the manufacturer and performer
of stringed instuments.*

Music Retailing
W G E Publishing, Inc.
Forest Rd.
Hancock, NH 03449
603-525-4201
Mark Lo, Editor
*Business management techniques for retailers
of musical instruments and other music prod-
ucts.*

LIBRARIES

New York Public Library
Performing Arts Research Center
Music Division
111 Amsterdam Ave.
New York, NY 10023
212-870-1650
Music and musical instruments.

COMPANIES

Allen Organ Co.
150 W. Locust St.
Macungie, PA 18062
215-966-2200
Electronic keyboard instruments.

Gibson Guitar Corp.
641 Massam Dr.
Nashville, TN 37210
615-871-4500
Guitars and other fretted instruments.

Kimball Piano & Organ Co.
(Division of Kimball International, Inc.)
1549 Royal St.
Jasper, IN 47546
812-482-1600
Pianos and organs.

Kurzweil Music Systems, Inc.
411 Waverly Oaks Rd.
Waltham, MA 02154
617-893-5900
*Electronic keyboards and instruments based
on computers.*

C. F. Martin & Co.
510 Sycamore St.
Nazareth, PA 18064
215-759-2837
*Guitars, banjos, and other fretted and stringed
instruments.*

Mission Bay Investments, Inc.
3132 Jefferson St.
San Diego, CA 92110
619-296-0292
Retailer and wholesalers of pianos and organs.

Musicland Group Inc.
(Subsidiary of Musicland Stores Corp.)
7500 Excelsior Blvd.
Minneapolis, MN 55426
612-932-7700
Chain of musical instrument and accessories stores.

Ohio Art Co.
P.O. Box 111
Bryan, OH 43506
419-636-3141
Musical instruments, games, and toys.

Peaches Entertainment Corp.
(Subsidiary of URT Industries Inc.)
3451 Executive Hwy.
Limiramar, FL 33025
305-432-4200
Retail music stores.

Sam Ash Music Corp.
278 Duffy Ave.
Hicksville, NY 11801
516-932-6400
Retailer of instruments of all kinds and recording equipment.

Yamaha Music Manufacturing Inc. USA
(Subsidiary of Yamaha Corp. of America)
100 Yamaha Park
Thomaston, GA 30286
404-647-9601
Pianos and other instruments.

FEDERAL GOVERNMENT

U.S. Customs Service
Department of the Treasury
U.S. Customshouse
6 World Trade Center
New York, NY 10048
212-466-5550
Ask for the Commodity Specialist in charge of musical instruments.

U.S. International Trade Administration
Department of Commerce
14th St. and Constitution Ave., N.W.
Washington, DC 20230
202-377-2000
Ask for the Commodity Analyst who is an expert in musical instruments.

U.S. International Trade Commission
500 E St., S.W.
Washington, DC 20436
202-205-2000 Office of the Secretary
202-205-3296 Industries locator
Ask for the Trade Analyst who is an expert in musical instruments.

MUSIC INDUSTRY

See also: MUSICAL INSTRUMENTS INDUSTRY

ASSOCIATIONS

American Music Center
30 W. 26th St., Ste. 1001
New York, NY 10010
212-366-5260
Nancy Clarke, Executive Director
Promotes contemporary American music.

American Music Conference
303 E. Wacker Dr., Ste. 1214
Chicago, IL 60601
312-856-8820
Paul Bjorneberg, Director of Services
Conducts research into many aspects of the music business and music education.

American Society of Composers, Authors and
    Publishers
One Lincoln Plaza
New York, NY 10023
212-595-3050
This group, usually known as ASCAP, represents composers and music publishers, collects fees for composers, and performs other services.

Country Music Association
7 Music Circle, N.
Nashville, TN 37202
615-244-2840
Jo Walker-Meador, Executive Director
Promotes country music.

International Planned Music Association
735 E. Montecito St.
Santa Barbara, CA 93103
805-965-5268
David Payne, President
Members contract to supply Muzak (background music that is played in elevators, offices, and other places).

Jazz World Society
P.O. Box 777
Times Square Station
New York, NY 10108
Jan Byrczek, Executive Director
Promotes jazz music in the U.S.

Music Publishers' Association of the United
    States
130 W. 57th St.
New York, NY 10019
212-582-1122
212-974-0271 Fax
Howard Wattenberg, General Counsel
Members publish music that is heard in concerts and studied in schools. Offers information on copyright protection.

National Music Publishers' Association
205 E. 42nd St., 18th Fl.
New York, NY 10017
212-370-5330
Edward Murphy, President
Helps music publishers and songwriters increase sales and protect their copyrights.

PERIODICALS

American Music Teacher
Music Teachers National Association, Inc.
617 Vine St., Ste. 1432
Cincinnati, OH 45202-2434
513-421-1420
Robert Elias, Editor
Covers musical subjects for professional teachers.

Arts Management
Radius Group Inc.
408 W. 57th St.
New York, NY 10019
212-245-3850
Alvin Reiss, Editor
Reports news and offers advice for all facets of the arts management industry.

Billboard
Billboard Publications, Inc.
1515 Broadway, 39th Fl.
New York, NY 10036
212-764-7300
Ken Schlager, Editor
Covers news for the home entertainment and music business.

Cash Box
Cash Box Publishing Co., Inc.
157 W. 57th St., Ste. 1402
New York, NY 10019
212-586-2640
Fred Goodman, Editor
Reports news to the music record industry.

Down Beat
Maher Publications, Inc.
180 W. Park Ave.
Elmhurst, IL 60126
708-941-2030
Frank Alkyer, Editor
Written for musicians and audiences of jazz, blues, and other forms of contemporary music.

Music and Sound Retailer
Testa Communications, Inc.
25 Willowdale Ave.
Port Washington, NY 11050
516-767-2500
Jon Mayer, Editor
News of interest to retailers of musical instruments and related sound products.

Music City News
Music City News Publishing Co., Inc.
Box 22975
50 Music Sq. W.
Nashville, TN 37202
615-329-2200
Lydia Dixon-Harden, Editor
Surveys the country music industry.

Musical America
Capital Cities—A B C Publishing Companies,
    Inc.
825 Seventh Ave.
New York, NY 10019
212-887-8386
Shirley Fleming, Editor
Surveys the classical music field.

Rolling Stone
Straight Arrow Publishers, Inc.
1290 Ave. of Americas
New York, NY 10104
800-876-8138
Jann Wenner, Editor
Covers the fields of rock and pop music.

Variety
Variety, Inc.
Cahners Publishing Co.
475 Park Ave. S.
New York, NY 10016-6901
212-779-1999
Peter Bart, Editor
News of many entertainment industries, including music.

LIBRARIES

Bowling Green State University
Music Library
Jerome Library
Bowling Green, OH 43403-0179
419-372-2307
419-372-7996 Fax
Classical music, popular music, and the recording industry.

Chicago Public Library Cultural Center
Visual & Performing Arts
Music Information Center
Harold Washington Library Center
400 S. State St.
Chicago, IL 60605
312-269-2886
312-368-0918 Fax
Popular music, folk music, music history, music education, arranging, composing, and related topics.

New York Public Library
Performing Arts Research Center
Music Division
111 Amsterdam Ave.
New York, NY 10023
212-870-1650
All kinds of classical and popular music.

COMPANIES

Boosey & Hawkes, Inc.
(Subsidiary of Boosey & Hawkes PLC)
24 E. 21st St.
New York, NY 10003
212-228-3300
Publisher, wholesaler, and retailer of music.

Music Sales Corp.
225 Park Ave. S.
New York, NY 10003
212-254-2100
Publisher of music books.

National Music Services Inc.
(Subsidiary of Namsco Corp.)
122 Montgomery St. E.
Spokane, WA 99205
509-327-7784
Background music and equipment rental.

Theodore Presser Co.
Presser Pl.
Bryn Mawr, PA 19010
215-525-3636
Music publisher and retailer of sheet music.

Rowe International, Inc.
75 Troy Hills Rd.
Whippany, NJ 07981
201-887-0400
Background music systems and other products.

Twentieth Century-Fox Film Corp.
P.O. Box 900
Beverly Hills, CA 90213
213-277-2211
Motion pictures, music publishing, and other businesses.

Wenger Corp.
555 Park Dr.
Owatonna, MN 55060
507-455-4100
Music chairs, stands, stages, and related products.

FEDERAL GOVERNMENT

Copyright Royalty Tribunal
1825 Connecticut Ave., N.W.
Ste. 918
Washington, DC 20009
202-606-4400
Ask for information on music royalties.

U.S. International Trade Administration
Department of Commerce
14th St. and Constitution Ave., N.W.
Washington, DC 20230
202-377-2000
*Ask for the Commodity Analyst who is an
expert in the music industry.*

U.S. International Trade Commission
500 E St., S.W.
Washington, DC 20436
202-205-2000 Office of the Secretary
202-205-3296 Industries locator
*Ask for the Trade Analyst who is an expert in
the music industry.*

MUTUAL FUNDS

See also: INVESTMENTS and SECURITIES

ASSOCIATIONS

American Association of Individual Investors
625 N. Michigan Ave., Ste. 1900
Chicago, IL 60611
312-280-0170
James Cloonan, President
*A large group of investors who research
investments and make their own decisions.
Offers educational programs and materials
about mutual funds and other investments.*

Investment Co. Institute
1600 M St. N.W., Ste. 600
Washington, DC 20036
202-293-7700
202-293-7016 Fax
David Silver, President
*Operates an information clearinghouse on
mutual funds. Offers research services.*

Mutual Fund Education Alliance
Association of No-Load Funds
1900 Erie St., Ste. 120
Kansas City, MO 64116
816-471-1454
816-471-7646 Fax
Michelle Smith, Managing Director
*Members offer mutual funds that are marketed
directly to the public. Conducts research and
offers training to executives in the industry.*

PERIODICALS

Mutual Fund Charts
C D A Investment Technologies, Inc.
1355 Piccard Dr.
Rockville, MD 20850
301-975-9600
*Graphic statistical information about more
than 1,500 mutual funds.*

Mutual Fund Fact Book
Investment Co. Institute
1600 M St., N.W., Ste. 600
Washington, DC 20036
202-293-7700
Arlene Zuckerberg, Editor
Follows trends and statistical data for the mutual fund industry.

Mutual Fund Forecaster
Institute for Econometric Research
Coral Ridge Building
3471 N. Federal Highway
Ft. Lauderdale, FL 33306
305-563-9000
Norman Fosback, Editor
Statistics on profits and risks for mutual fund investors and traders.

Mutual Fund Performance Report
Morningstar, Inc.
53 W. Jackson Blvd.
Chicago, IL 60604
312-427-1985
Joe Mansueto, Editor
Rates the performance of mutual funds.

Mutual Fund Trends
Growth Fund Research, Inc.
Box 6600
Rapid City, SD 57709
607-341-1971
William Rouleau, Editor
A charting service for the most successful mutual funds.

United Mutual Fund Selector
Babson-United Investment Advisors, Inc.
101 Prescott St.
Wellesley Hills, MA 02181-3319
617-235-0900
Patricia Ganley, Editor
Statistical data for mutual fund investors.

LIBRARIES

Mutual Fund Education Alliance
Association of No-Load Funds
1900 Erie St., Ste. 120
Kansas City, MO 64116
816-471-1454
816-471-7646 Fax
Mutual fund prospectuses.

COMPANIES

Boston Co. Family of Funds
One Boston Place
Boston, MA 02108
800-225-5267
Mutual funds.

Dreyfus Corp.
200 Park Ave.
New York, NY 10166
212-922-6000
Mutual funds.

Franklin Custodian Funds, Inc.
777 Mariners Island Blvd.
San Mateo, CA 94404
415-570-3000
Mutual funds.

Money Market Trust
Federated Investors Tower
Pittsburgh, PA 15222
412-288-1900
Mutual funds.

Oppenheimer Fund Management, Inc.
2 World Trade Center
New York, NY 10048
212-323-0200
Mutual funds.

Rowe Price New Income Fund, Inc.
(Subsidiary of T. Rowe Price Associates, Inc.)
100 E. Pratt St.
Baltimore, MD 21202
301-547-2000
Mutual funds.

Twentieth Century Investors, Inc.
4500 Main St.
Kansas City, MO 64111
800-345-2021
Mutual fund dealer.

Wellington Fund, Inc.
P. O. Box 1100
Valley Forge, PA 19482
215-669-6000
Mutual funds.

Windsor Funds, Inc.
P. O. Box 1100
Valley Forge, PA 19482
215-669-6000
Mutual funds.

FEDERAL GOVERNMENT

U.S. International Trade Administration
Department of Commerce
14th St. and Constitution Ave., N.W.
Washington, DC 20230
202-377-2000
Ask for the Commodity Analyst who is an expert in mutual funds.

U.S. Securities and Exchange Commission
450 5th St., N.W.
Washington, DC 20549
202-272-3100
Ask for the Investment Company Regulation Office.

NATURAL GAS INDUSTRY

See also: PETROLEUM INDUSTRY and PIPELINE INDUSTRY

ASSOCIATIONS

American Gas Association
1515 Wilson Blvd.
Arlington, VA 22209
703-841-8400
Michael Baly, Contact
Provides information on all phases of gas transmission, distribution, management, safety, finance and related subjects.

Gas Processors Suppliers Association
6526 E. 60th St.
Tulsa, OK 74145
918-493-3872
R. E. Cannon, Secretary
Offers technical information about the equipment and supplies used in the natural gas industry.

Gas Research Institute
8600 W. Bryn Mawr Ave.
Chicago, IL 60631
312-399-8100
312-399-8170 Fax
Stephen Ban, President
Conducts research and seminars on the technical, safety, environmental, and business aspects of natural gas.

Institute of Gas Technology
3424 S. State St.
Chicago, IL 60616
312-567-3650
312-567-5209 Fax
Bernard Lee, President
Sponsors technical research and offers educational programs for executives in the natural gas industry.

Interstate Natural Gas Association of America
555 13th St. N.W., Ste. 300 W.
Washington, DC 20004
202-626-3200
Jerald Halvorsen, President
Member firms transport natural gas.

Natural Gas Supply Association
1129 20th St. N.W., Ste. 300
Washington, DC 20036
202-331-8900
Nicholas Bush, President
Member firms produce natural gas.

PERIODICALS

Advanced Oil and Gas Recovery Technologies
Department of Energy
U.S. National Technical Information Service
5285 Port Royal Rd.
Springfield, VA 22161
703-487-4630
Technical data on the recovery of petroleum, gas, oil shales, and related resources.

D R I—McGraw-Hill Energy Review: Natural
   Gas Review
D R I—McGraw-Hill
24 Hartwell Ave.
Lexington, MA 02173
617-863-5100
Surveys the natural gas business.

Foster Natural Gas Report
Foster Associates
1015 15th St., N.W.
Washington, DC 20005-2605
202-408-7710
M.W. Rockefeller, Editor
Covers technology and business aspects of natural gas.

Gas Price Index
Intelligence Press Inc.
425B Carlisle St.
Herndon, VA 22070
703-318-8848
Covers trading levels and prices for the natural gas spot market.

Gas Storage Report
Pasha Publications Inc.
1401 Wilson Blvd., Ste. 900
Arlington, VA 22209-9970
703-528-1244
Daniel Macey, Editor
Reports on natural gas inventories, new ventures, technological developments, government regulations, and industry trends.

King's North American Gas
King Publishing Co.
Box 52210
Knoxville, TN 37950
615-584-6294
Market report for the natural gas industry. Reports on the market for natural gas.

Natural Gas
Executive Enterprises Publications Co., Inc.
22 W. 21st St.
New York, NY 10010-6904
212-645-7880
Jane Bensahel, Editor
Covers finance, regulatory, pricing, and other business matters of interest to the natural gas industry.

LIBRARIES

Transco Energy Co.
Corporate Library
Box 1396
Houston, TX 77251
713-439-2321
713-439-2440 Fax
Petroleum industry and natural gas industry.

U.S. Department of Energy
Energy Information Administration
National Energy Information Center
Forrestal Bldg., Rm. 1F-048
Washington, DC 20585
202-586-8800
All types of energy including natural gas.

U.S. Geological Survey
Earth Science Information Center (ESIC)
4320 University Dr., Rm. 101
Anchorage, AK 99508-4664
907-786-7011
907-786-7050 Fax
Gas, oil, and minerals.

Wisconsin Gas Co.
Corporate and Law Library
626 E. Wisconsin Ave.
Milwaukee, WI 53202
414-291-6666
414-291-7025 Fax
Natural gas, public utility regulation, and related topics.

COMPANIES

Coastal Corp.
Nine Greenway Plaza E.
Houston, TX 77046
713-877-1400
Natural gas and petroleum products.

Panhandle Eastern Corp.
5400 Westheimer Court, Box 1642
Houston, TX 77251
713-627-5400
Transportation and sales of natural gas.

Phillips Petroleum Co.
6A1 Phillips Bldg.
Bartlesville, OK 74004
918-661-4710
Natural gas, crude oil, and refined products.

Shell Oil Co.
(Subsidiary of Shell Petroleum Inc.)
One Shell Plaza
Houston, TX 77001
713-241-6161
Natural gas, crude oil, and refined products.

Southern California Gas Co.
(Subsidiary of Pacific Enterprises)
555 W. Fifth St.
Los Angeles, CA 90013
213-689-2633
Natural gas.

Tennessee Gas Pipeline Co.
(Subsidiary of Tenneco Inc.)
Tenneco Bldg.
Houston, TX 77002
713-757-2131
Operates natural gas pipelines and other businesses.

Texas Gas Transmission Corp.
(Subsidiary of Transco Energy Co.)
3800 Frederica St.
Owensboro, KY 42301
502-926-8686
*Transports natural gas through a huge inter-
state pipeline system.*

United Gas Pipe Line Co.
(Subsidiary of United Gas Holding Corp.)
600 Travis
Houston, TX 77002
713-229-4123
Transmission of natural gas.

Valero Natural Gas Partners, L.P.
530 McCullough Ave.
San Antonio, TX 78215
512-246-2000
Distribution and marketing of natural gas.

Williams Companies
P.O. Box 2400
Tulsa, OK 74102
918-588-2000
Interstate natural gas pipelines.

FEDERAL GOVERNMENT

U.S. Department of Energy
1000 Independence Ave., S.W.
Washington, DC 20585
202-586-5000
*Ask for the Reserves & Natural Gas Division
in the Economic Regulatory Administration.*

U.S. Department of Transportation
400 7th St., S.W.
Washington, DC 20590
202-355-4000
*Ask for the Alaska Natural Gas Pipeline Pro-
ject in the Research and Special Programs
Administration.*

U.S. International Trade Administration
Department of Commerce
14th St. and Constitution Ave., N.W.
Washington, DC 20230
202-377-2000
*Ask for the Commodity Analyst who is an
expert in the natural gas industry.*

U.S. International Trade Commission
500 E St., S.W.
Washington, DC 20436
202-205-2000 Office of the Secretary
202-205-3296 Industries locator
*Ask for the Trade Analyst who is an expert in
the natural gas industry.*

NEBRASKA

STATE OFFICE LOCATOR (*for referrals to all state government offices*)

402-471-2311

ARCHIVES AND RECORDS

Historical Society
P.O. Box 82505
Lincoln, NE 68501
402-471-4750

ATTORNEY GENERAL

Attorney General's Office
State Capitol Building
Room 2115
Lincoln, NE 68509
402-471-2682

BANKING

Banking & Finance Department
P.O. Box 95006
Lincoln, NE 68509
402-471-2171

COMMERCE

Economic Development Department
P.O. Box 94666
Lincoln, NE 68509
402-471-3747

CONSUMER AFFAIRS

Consumer Protection Division
State Capitol Building
Room 2115
Lincoln, NE 68509
402-471-2682

EDUCATION

Education Department
P.O. Box 94987
Lincoln, NE 68509
402-471-2465

ENERGY

Policy Research & Energy Office
P.O. Box 94601
Lincoln, NE 68509
402-471-2414

ENVIRONMENTAL AFFAIRS

Environmental Control Department
P.O. Box 98922
Lincoln, NE 68509-8922
402-471-2186

HEALTH

Health Department
P.O. Box 95007
Lincoln, NE 68509
402-471-2133

HOUSING

Investment Finance Authority
1033 O Street
Ste. 218
Lincoln, NE 68508
402-434-3900

INSURANCE

Insurance Department
941 O Street
Ste. 400
Lincoln, NE 68508
402-471-2201

LABOR

Labor Department
P.O. Box 94600
Lincoln, NE 68509
402-471-9000

LEGISLATION

Legislative Council
State Capitol
1445 K Street
7th Floor
Lincoln, NE 68509
402-471-2221

LIBRARY SERVICES

Library Commission
1420 P Street
Lincoln, NE 68508
402-471-2045

LICENSING—CORPORATE

Corporation Division
P.O. Box 94608
Lincoln, NE 68509-4608
402-471-4079

LICENSING—PROFESSIONAL AND OCCUPATIONAL

Examining Boards Bureau
P.O. Box 95007
Lincoln, NE 68509
402-471-2115

MOTOR VEHICLES

Motor Vehicles Department
P.O. Box 94789
Lincoln, NE 68509
402-471-3900

OCCUPATIONAL HEALTH AND SAFETY

Safety Division
P.O. Box 94600
Lincoln, NE 68509
402-471-2239

OMBUDSMAN

Ombudsman's Office
State Capitol
Room 807
Lincoln, NE 68509
402-471-2035

PUBLIC UTILITIES

Public Service Commission
P.O. Box 94927
Lincoln, NE 68509-4927
402-471-3101

PURCHASING

Material Division
301 Centennial Mall S.
Lincoln, NE 68509
402-471-2401

REAL ESTATE

Real Estate Commission
P.O. Box 94667
Lincoln, NE 68509
402-471-2004

SECURITIES

Securities Division
P.O. Box 95006
Lincoln, NE 68509
402-471-2171

TAXATION AND REVENUE

Revenue Department
P.O. Box 94818
Lincoln, NE 68509
402-471-5607

TOURISM

Division of Travel & Tourism
P.O. Box 94666
Lincoln, NE 68509
402-471-3794 or 3796
800-228-4307
800-742-7595 (in Nebraska)

TRANSPORTATION

Roads Department
P.O. Box 94759
Lincoln, NE 68509
402-479-4615

UNEMPLOYMENT

Unemployment Insurance Division
P.O. Box 94600
Lincoln, NE 68509
402-471-9000

WORKER'S COMPENSATION

Workers Compensation Court
P.O. Box 98908
Lincoln, NE 68509-9808
402-471-2568

NEVADA

STATE OFFICE LOCATOR (*for referrals to all state government offices*)

702-885-5000

ARCHIVES AND RECORDS

State Library & Archives
Capitol Complex
Carson City, NV 89710
702-687-5210

ATTORNEY GENERAL

Attorney General's Office
Heroes Memorial Building
Carson City, NV 89710
702-687-4170

BANKING

Financial Institutions Division
4067 E. 2nd Street
Carson City, NV 89710
702-687-4259

COMMERCE

Commerce Department
1665 Hot Springs Road
Carson City, NV 89710
702-687-4250

EDUCATION

Education Department
400 W. King Street
Carson City, NV 89710
702-687-3100

ENERGY

Community Services Office
Capitol Complex
Carson City, NV 89710
702-687-4990

ENVIRONMENTAL AFFAIRS

Environmental Protection Division
123 W. Nye Lane
Carson City, NV 89710
702-687-4670

HEALTH

Health Division
505 E. King Street
Room 600
Carson City, NV 89701
702-687-4740

HOUSING

Housing Division
1050 E. William Street
Ste. 435
Carson City, NV 89710
702-687-4258

HUMAN RIGHTS

Equal Rights Commission
1515 E. Tropicana Avenue
Ste. 590
Las Vegas, NV 89109
702-486-7161

INSURANCE

Insurance Division
1665 Hot Springs Road
Carson City, NV 89710
702-687-4270

LABOR

Labor Commission
505 E. King Street
Room 602
Carson City, NV 89710
702-687-4850

LEGISLATION

Legislative Counsel Bureau
Legislative Building
401 S. Carson Street
Room 215
Carson City, NV 89710
702-687-6825

LIBRARY SERVICES

State Library & Archives
Capitol Complex
Carson City, NV 89710
702-687-5160

LICENSING—CORPORATE

Corporations Filing Division
Capitol Complex
Carson City, NV 89710
702-687-5203

MOTOR VEHICLES

Motor Vehicle & Public Safety Department
555 Wright Way
Carson City, NV 89711-0900
702-687-5375

OCCUPATIONAL HEALTH AND SAFETY

Occupational Safety & Health Division
1390 S. Curry Street
Carson City, NV 89710
702-687-5240

OMBUDSMAN

Consumer Affairs Division
2601 E. Sahara Avenue
Las Vegas, NV 89158
702-486-7355

PUBLIC UTILITIES

Public Service Commission
Capitol Complex
Carson City, NV 89703
702-687-6007

PURCHASING

Purchasing Division
505 E. King Street
Room 400
Carson City, NV 89701
702-687-4070

REAL ESTATE

Real Estate Division
Capitol Complex
Carson City, NV 89710
702-687-4280

SECURITIES

Securities Division
Capitol Complex
Carson City, NV 89710
702-687-5203

TAXATION AND REVENUE

Taxation Department
Capitol Complex
Carson City, NV 89710
702-687-4892

TOURISM

Commission on Tourism
Capitol Complex
Ste. 207
Carson City, NV 89710
702-687-4322
800-237-0774

TRANSPORTATION

Transportation Department
1263 S. Stewart Street
Carson City, NV 89712
702-687-5440

UNEMPLOYMENT

Unemployment Insurance Division
500 E. 3rd Street
Carson City, NV 89713
702-687-4510

WORKER'S COMPENSATION

Industrial Insurance System
515 E. Musser Street
Carson City, NV 89714
702-687-5284

NEW HAMPSHIRE

STATE OFFICE LOCATOR (*for referrals to all state government offices*)

603-271-1110

ARCHIVES AND RECORDS

State Archivist
State House
107 N. Main Street
Room 204
Concord, NH 03301
603-271-2236

ATTORNEY GENERAL

Attorney General's Office
208 State House Annex
Concord, NH 03301
603-271-3655

BANKING

Banking Department
45 S. Main Street
Concord, NH 03301
603-271-3561

COMMERCE

Resources & Economic Development Department
105 Loudon Road
Box 856
Concord, NH 03301
603-271-2411

CONSUMER AFFAIRS

Consumer Protection Division
208 State House Annex
Concord, NH 03301-6526
603-271-3641

EDUCATION

Education Department
101 Pleasant Street
Concord, NH 03301
603-271-3144

ENERGY

Energy Office
2 1/2 Beacon Street
Concord, NH 03301
603-271-2711

ENVIRONMENTAL AFFAIRS

Environmental Protection Division
208 State House Annex
Concord, NH 03301-6526
603-271-3679

HEALTH

Public Health Services Department
Hazen Drive
Concord, NH 03301
603-271-4501

HOUSING

Housing Finance Authority
P.O. Box 5087
Manchester, NH 03102
603-472-8623

HUMAN RIGHTS

Human Rights Commission
163 Loudon Road
Concord, NH 03301
603-271-2767

INSURANCE

Insurance Department
169 Manchester Street
Concord, NH 03301
603-271-2261

LABOR

Labor Department
19 Pillsbury Street
Concord, NH 03301
603-271-3171

LEGISLATION

Legislative Services Office
State House
107 N. Main Street
Room 109
Concord, NH 03301
603-271-3435

LIBRARY SERVICES

State Library
20 Park Street
Concord, NH 03301
603-271-2393

LICENSING—CORPORATE

Corporations Division
State House
107 N. Main Street
Room 204
Concord, NH 03301
603-271-3244

MOTOR VEHICLES

Motor Vehicles Division
Hazen Drive
Concord, NH 03301
603-271-2484

OCCUPATIONAL HEALTH AND SAFETY

Occupational Safety & Health
19 Pillsbury Street
Concord, NH 03301
603-271-2024

OMBUDSMAN

Executive Office of the Governor
State House
107 N. Main Street
Concord, NH 03301
603-271-3130

PUBLIC UTILITIES

Public Utilities Commission
8 Old Suncook Road
Concord, NH 03301
603-271-2431

PURCHASING

Plant & Property Management Division
State House Annex
Concord, NH 03301
603-271-2700

REAL ESTATE

Real Estate Commission
107 Pleasant Street
3rd Floor
Concord, NH 03301
603-271-2701

SECURITIES

Securities Regulation Office
157 Manchester Street
Concord, NH 03301
603-271-1463

TAXATION AND REVENUE

Revenue Administration Department
61 S. Spring Street
Concord, NH 03301
603-271-2191

TOURISM

Office of Vacation Travel
P.O. Box 856
Concord, NH 03301
603-271-2343 or 2666
800-258-3608 (in Northeast region, but not
      New Hampshire)

TRANSPORTATION

Transportation Department
P.O. Box 483
Concord, NH 03301
603-271-3734

UNEMPLOYMENT

Unemployment Compensation Bureau
32 S. Main Street
Concord, NH 03301-4857
603-224-3311

WORKER'S COMPENSATION

Workers Compensation Division
19 Pillsbury Street
Concord, NH 03301
603-271-3172

NEW JERSEY

STATE OFFICE LOCATOR (*for referrals to all state government offices*)

609-292-2121

ARCHIVES AND RECORDS

Archives & Record Management
2300 Stuyvesant Avenue
Trenton, NJ 08625
609-530-3200

ATTORNEY GENERAL

Attorney General's Office
Justice Complex
CN 081
Trenton, NJ 08625
609-292-9660

BANKING

Banking Department
20 W. State Street
CN 040
Trenton, NJ 08625
609-292-3420

COMMERCE

Commerce & Economic Development
  Department
20 W. State Street
CN 820
Trenton, NJ 08625
609-292-2444

CONSUMER AFFAIRS

Consumer Affairs Division
1100 Raymond Boulevard
Room 400
Newark, NJ 07102
201-648-4010

EDUCATION

Education Department
224 W. State Street
CN 500
Trenton, NJ 08625
609-292-4450

ENERGY

Energy Division
2 Gateway Center
Newark, NJ 07102
201-648-3078

ENVIRONMENTAL AFFAIRS

Environmental Protection Department
401 E. State Street
CN 402
Trenton, NJ 08625
609-292-2885

HEALTH

Health Department
John Fitch Plaza
CN 360
Trenton, NJ 08625
609-292-7837

HOUSING

Housing Division
101 S. Broad Street
CN 800
Trenton, NJ 08625
609-292-7899

HUMAN RIGHTS

Civil Rights Division
1100 Raymond Boulevard
Room 400
Newark, NJ 07102
201-648-2700

INSURANCE

Insurance Department
20 W. State Street
CN 325
Trenton, NJ 08625
609-292-5360

LABOR

Labor Department
John Fitch Plaza
CN 110
Trenton, NJ 08625
609-292-2323

LEGISLATION

Legislative Services Office
State House Annex
CN 068
Trenton, NJ 08625
609-292-4661

LIBRARY SERVICES

New Jersey State Library
225 W. State Street
CN 500
Trenton, NJ 08625
609-292-6200

LICENSING—CORPORATE

Corporation Division
State Capitol Building
CN 300
Trenton, NJ 08625
609-984-1900

LICENSING—PROFESSIONAL AND OCCUPATIONAL

Consumer Affairs Division
1100 Raymond Boulevard
Newark, NJ 07102
201-648-4010

MOTOR VEHICLES

Motor Vehicles Division
25 S. Montgomery Street
Trenton, NJ 08625
609-292-4570

OCCUPATIONAL HEALTH AND SAFETY

Workplace Standards
John Fitch Plaza
CN 110
Trenton, NJ 08625
609-292-2313

OMBUDSMAN

Citizens Complaints & Dispute Settlement
    Division
25 Market Street
CN 850
Trenton, NJ 08625
609-292-1770

PUBLIC UTILITIES

Public Utilities Board
Gateway Center
Newark, NJ 07102
201-648-2027

PURCHASING

Treasury Department
State House
CN 002
Trenton, NJ 08625
609-292-4330

REAL ESTATE

Real Estate Division
20 W. State Street
CN 325
Trenton, NJ 08625
609-292-8280

SECURITIES

Securities Bureau
2 Gateway Center
Newark, NJ 07102
201-648-2040

TAXATION AND REVENUE

Taxation Division
State House
CN 002
Trenton, NJ 08625
609-292-5185

TOURISM

Division of Travel & Tourism
CN 826
Trenton, NJ 08625
609-292-2470

TRANSPORTATION

Transportation Department
1035 Parkway Avenue
CN 600
Trenton, NJ 08625
609-530-3535

UNEMPLOYMENT

Unemployment & Disability Insurance Divi-
    sion
John Fitch Plaza
CN 110
Trenton, NJ 08625
609-292-2460

WORKER'S COMPENSATION

Workers Compensation Division
John Fitch Plaza
CN 110
Trenton, NJ 08625
609-232-2414

NEW MEXICO

STATE OFFICE LOCATOR (*for referrals to all state government offices*)

505-827-4011

ARCHIVES AND RECORDS

State Records Center & Archives
P.O. Box 25101
Santa Fe; NM 87503
505-827-7332

ATTORNEY GENERAL

Attorney General's Office
P.O. Box 1508
Santa Fe, NM 87504
505-827-6000

BANKING

Financial Institutions Division
P.O. Box 25101
Santa Fe, NM 87504
505-827-7100

COMMERCE

Economic Development & Tourism Department
Joseph Montoya Building
1100 St. Francis Drive
Santa Fe, NM 87503
505-827-0305

CONSUMER AFFAIRS

Consumer Protection Division
P.O. Box 1508
Santa Fe, NM 87504-1508
505-827-6060

EDUCATION

Education Department
Education Building
300 Don Gaspar Avenue
Santa Fe, NM 87501-2786
505-827-6635

ENERGY

Energy Conservation Management Division
2040 S. Pacheco Street
Santa Fe, NM 87505
505-827-5900

ENVIRONMENTAL AFFAIRS

Community Services Bureau
1190 St. Francis Drive
Santa Fe, NM 87503
505-827-2771

HEALTH

Public Health Division
1190 St. Francis Drive
Santa Fe, NM 87503
505-827-2389

HOUSING

State Housing Divison
Joseph Montoya Building
1100 St. Francis Drive
Santa Fe, NM 87503
505-827-0256

HUMAN RIGHTS

Human Rights Division
1596 S. Pacheco Street
Santa Fe, NM 87501
505-827-6838

INSURANCE

Insurance Division
P.O. Box 1269
Santa Fe, NM 87504-1269
505-827-4297

LABOR

Labor & Industrial Division
1596 S. Pacheco Street
Santa Fe, NM 87501
505-827-6808

LEGISLATION

Legislative Council Service
State Capitol
Room 334
Santa Fe, NM 87503
505-984-9600

LIBRARY SERVICES

Cultural Affairs Office
State Library Building
325 Don Gaspar Avenue
Sante Fe, NM 87503
505-827-3800

LICENSING—CORPORATE

Corporation Division
P.O. Box 1269
Santa Fe, NM 87504-1269
505-827-4508

LICENSING—PROFESSIONAL AND OCCUPATIONAL

Regulation & Licensing Department
P.O. Box 25101
Santa Fe, NM 87504
505-827-7004

MOTOR VEHICLES

Motor Vehicles Division
P.O. Box 630
Santa Fe, NM 87509-0630
505-827-2294

OCCUPATIONAL HEALTH AND SAFETY

Occupational Health & Safety Bureau
1990 St. Francis Drive
Santa Fe, NM 87503
505-827-2888

OMBUDSMAN

Consitutent Services Agency
PERA Building
5th Floor
Santa Fe, NM 87503
505-827-3000

PUBLIC UTILITIES

Public Service Commission
224 E. Palace Avenue
Santa Fe, NM 87503
505-827-6940

PURCHASING

Purchasing Division
715 Alta Vista
Santa Fe, NM 87503
505-827-0472

REAL ESTATE

Real Estate Commission
4125 Carlisle, N.E.
Albuquerque, NM 87107
505-841-6524

SECURITIES

Securities Division
P.O. Box 25101
Santa Fe, NM 87504
505-827-7140

TAXATION AND REVENUE

Taxation & Revenue Department
P.O. Box 630
Santa Fe, NM 87509-0630
505-827-0341

TOURISM

Travel Division
Joseph Montoya Building
1100 St. Francis Drive
Santa Fe, NM 87503
505-827-0291 or 0295
800-545-2020

TRANSPORTATION

Highway & Transportation Department
P.O. Box 1149
Santa Fe, NM 87504
505-827-5110

UNEMPLOYMENT

Unemployment Insurance Bureau
P.O. Box 1928
Albuquerque, NM 87103
505-841-8431

WORKER'S COMPENSATION

Workmans Compensation Division
P.O. Box 27198
Albuquerque, NM 87102
505-841-8787

NEWSLETTERS

ASSOCIATIONS

Newsletter Association
1401 Wilson Blvd., Ste. 403
Arlington, VA 22209
703-527-2333
800-356-9302
Frederick Goss, Executive Director
Offers research and educational seminars to for-profit newsletter publishers, and those who wish to start newsletters.

PERIODICALS

Newsletter on Newsletters
Newsletter Clearinghouse
44 W. Market St.
Rhinebeck, NY 12572
914-876-2081
Howard Penn Hudson, Editor
Covers all aspects of publishing newsletters, including the design, writing, marketing, and other subjects. Also sells a variety of how-to books for newsletter publishers.

COMPANIES

Bureau of Business Practice
(Division of Simon & Schuster Inc)
24 Rope Ferry Rd.
Waterford, CT 06386
203-442-4365
Publisher of various business newsletters and periodicals.

Alan Feinstein & Associates
37 Alhambra Circle
Providence, RI 02905
401-467-5155
Publisher of financial newsletters and publications.

Hearst Business Communications, Inc.
(Division of Hearst Corp.)
645 Stewart Ave.
Garden City, NY 11530
516-227-1300
Publisher of various industrial newsletters, periodicals, and other materials.

Kiplinger Washington Editors, Inc.
1729 H St., N.W.
Washington, DC 20006
202-887-6400
Publisher of current events and business newsletters.

Miller Freeman, Inc.
(Division of United Newspapers plc)
600 Harrison St.
San Francisco, CA 94107
415-905-2200
Various business publications, including newsletters.

New York Law Publishing Co.
(Subsidiary of Price Communications Corp.)
111 Eighth Ave.
New York, NY 10011
212-741-8300
Legal publications, including newsletters.

North American Publishing Co.
401 N. Broad St.
Philadelphia, PA 19108
215-238-5300
Professional and trade newsletters, and other publications.

Oil Daily Co.
1401 New York Ave., N.W.
Washington, DC 20005
201-662-0700
Oil industry newsletters.

Rodale Press, Inc.
33 E. Minor St.
Emmaus, PA 18098
215-967-5171
Health publications, including newsletters.

NEWSPAPERS

See also: JOURNALISM and WRITING AND EDITING

ASSOCIATIONS

American Society of Newspaper Editors
PO Box 17004
Washington, DC 20041
703-648-1144
703-620-4557 Fax
Lee Stinnett, Executive Director
Professional society of mid-level and senior editors at daily newspapers.

International Newspaper Advertising and
     Marketing Executives
PO Box 17210
Washington, DC 20041
703-648-1168
703-476-6015 Fax
Reggie Hall, Executive Director
Professional group of advertising and marketing executives who work for daily newspapers.

Newspaper Advertising Bureau
1180 Ave. of the Americas
New York, NY 10036
212-704-4547
212-704-4616 Fax
Julie Nowhall, Communication Director
Conducts research surveys about newspaper readership, content, advertising, and related topics.

National Newspaper Association
1627 K St. N.W., Ste. 400
Washington, DC 20006
202-466-7200
202-331-1403 Fax
David Simonson, Executive Vice President
Represents daily, semiweekly, weekly newspapers.

Newspaper Research Council
1000 2 Ruan Center
601 Locust St.
Des Moines, IA 50309
515-245-3828
Glenn Roberts, Executive Director
Professional group of research and marketing directors who work for newspapers.

Suburban Newspapers of America
401 N. Michgan Ave.
Chicago, IL 60611
312-644-6610
312-321-6869 Fax
James Elsener, Executive Director
Offers research and marketing services, educational programs, and sales training to publishers of suburban and urban newspapers with a local community focus.

PERIODICALS

American Newspaper Markets Circulation
American Newspaper Markets, Inc.
Box 994
Malibu, CA 90265
213-456-1863
Peter Sinding, Editor
Reports newspaper circulation figures.

Editor & Publisher—the Fourth Estate
Editor & Publisher Co., Inc.
11 W. 19th St.
New York, NY 10011
212-675-4380
Robert Brown, Editor
*Reports on the newspaper business and news-
paper advertising.*

Newspaper Financial Executives Journal
International Newspaper Financial Executives
Box 17573
Dulles International Airport
Washington, DC 20041
Jeanie Geib, Editor
*Advice on the financial aspects of running a
newspaper.*

Newspaper Research Journal
1621 College St.
Newspaper Division
University of South Carolina
Columbia, SC 29208-0251
803-777-2005
Gerald Stone, Editor
A scholarly journal about newspaper journalism.

Presstime
American Newspaper Publishers Association
Box 17407 Dulles Airport
Washington, DC 20041
703-648-1000
Maurice Fliess, Editor
*Reports news and trends of concern to news-
paper executives.*

Working Press of the Nation
National Research Bureau, Inc.
424 N. Third St.
Burlington, IA 52601
312-752-5415
Nancy Veatch, Editor
*A directory of editors and other personnel at
newspapers and other media sources nationwide.*

LIBRARIES

Columbia University
Sulzberger Journalism Library
304 Journalism Bldg.
Broadway & 116th St.
New York, NY 10027
212-854-3860
Current events and journalism.

Newspaper Advertising Bureau, Inc.
Information Center
1180 Avenue of the Americas
New York, NY 10036
212-704-4549
212-704-4616 Fax
Newspapers.

Washington Post
News Research Center
1150 15th St., N.W.
Washington, DC 20071
202-334-7341
202-334-5575 Fax
*Newspapers, politics, government, sports, for-
eign affairs, and related topics.*

COMPANIES

Chicago Tribune Co.
(Subsidiary of Tribune Co.)
435 N. Michigan Ave.
Chicago, IL 60611
312-222-3232
Newspaper publishing.

Gannett Co., Inc.
P.O. Box 7858
Washington, DC 20044
703-284-6000
Newspaper, broadcasting, and outdoor advertising businesses.

Harte-Hanks Communications, Inc.
(Subsidiary of HHC Holding Inc.)
P. O. Box 269
San Antonio, TX 78291
512-829-9000
Newspapers, television, and direct marketing businesses.

Knight-Ridder, Inc.
1 Herald Plaza
Miami, FL 33132
305-376-3800
Newspaper publishing.

Los Angeles Times
(Division of Times Mirror Co.)
Times Mirror Sq.
Los Angeles, CA 90053
213-237-5000
Newspaper publishing.

McClatchy Newspapers, Inc.
2100 Q St.
Sacramento, CA 95816
916-321-1000
Newspaper publishing.

New York Times Co.
229 W. 43rd St.
New York, NY 10036
212-556-1234
Newspaper, television, and radio businesses.

Pulitzer Publishing Co.
900 N. Tucker Blvd.
St. Louis, MO 63101
314-622-7000
Newspaper, television, and radio businesses.

E. W. Scripps Co.
1100 Central Trust Tower
Cincinnati, OH 45202
516-977-3000
Newspaper, television, and radio businesses.

Tribune Co.
435 N. Michigan Ave.
Chicago, IL 60611
312-222-9100
Newspapers and other media businesses.

Washington Post Co.
1150 15th St., N.W.
Washington, DC 20071
202-334-6600
Newspaper, magazine, and other media businesses.

FEDERAL GOVERNMENT

U.S. Customs Service
Department of the Treasury
U.S. Customshouse
6 World Trade Center
New York, NY 10048
212-466-5550
Ask for the Commodity Specialist in charge of newspapers.

U.S. International Trade Administration
Department of Commerce
14th St. and Constitution Ave., N.W.
Washington, DC 20230
202-377-2000
Ask for the Commodity Analyst who is an expert in newspapers.

U.S. International Trade Commission
500 E St., S.W.
Washington, DC 20436
202-205-2000 Office of the Secretary
202-205-3296 Industries locator
Ask for the Trade Analyst who is an expert in newspapers.

NEW YORK

STATE OFFICE LOCATOR (*for referrals to all state government offices*)

518-474-2121

ARCHIVES AND RECORDS

State Archives & Records Division
33 Cultural Education Center
Room 10A
Albany, NY 12230
518-474-1195

ATTORNEY GENERAL

Law Department
120 Broadway
New York, NY 10271
518-474-7330

BANKING

Banking Department
2 Rector Street
New York, NY 10006
212-618-6557

COMMERCE

Economic Development Office
1515 Broadway
New York, NY 10036
212-827-6100

CONSUMER AFFAIRS

Consumer Protection Board
99 Washington Avenue
Albany, NY 12210
518-474-3514

EDUCATION

Elementary & Secondary Education Office
Education Building Annex
Hawk & Elk Streets
Room 875
Albany, NY 12234
518-474-4688

ENERGY

Energy Office
2 Rockefeller Plaza
Albany, NY 12223
518-473-4376

ENVIRONMENTAL AFFAIRS

Environmental Conservation Department
50 Wolff Road
Albany, NY 12233
518-457-3446

HEALTH

Health Department
Corning Tower
Empire State Plaza
Albany, NY 12237-0001
518-474-2011

HOUSING

Housing & Community Renewal Division
Hampton Plaza
40 State Street
Albany, NY 12207
518-486-3370

HUMAN RIGHTS

Human Rights Division
55 W. 125th Street
New York, NY 10027
212-870-8790

INSURANCE

Insurance Department
Agency Building
1 Empire State Plaza
Albany, NY 12257
518-474-4550

LABOR

Labor Department
State Campus
Building 12
Albany, NY 12240
518-457-2741

LEGISLATION

Legislative Library
State Capitol
Room 337
Albany, NY 12224
518-455-4000

LIBRARY SERVICES

Cultural Education Office
33 Cultural Education Center
Room 10A
Albany, NY 12230
518-474-5930

LICENSING—CORPORATE

Corporations & State Records Division
162 Washington Avenue
Albany, NY 12231
518-474-6200

LICENSING—PROFESSIONAL AND OCCUPATIONAL

Professional Licensing Services Division
Cultural Education Center
Room 3029
Albany, NY 12230
518-474-0046

MOTOR VEHICLES

Motor Vehicles Department
Empire State Plaza
Albany, NY 12228
518-474-0841

OCCUPATIONAL HEALTH AND SAFETY

Occupational Safety & Health Division
State Campus
Building 12
Albany, NY 12240
518-457-3518

OMBUDSMAN

State Department
162 Washington Avenue
Albany, NY 12231
518-474-4750

PUBLIC UTILITIES

Public Service Department
3 Empire State Plaza
Albany, NY 12223
518-474-2530

PURCHASING

Standards & Purchasing Group
Corning Tower
Empire State Plaza
Albany, NY 12242
518-474-6710

REAL ESTATE

Licensing Services Division
162 Washington Avenue
Albany, NY 12231
518-474-4664

SECURITIES

Investor Protection & Securities Bureau
120 Broadway
New York, NY 10271
212-341-2200

TAXATION AND REVENUE

Taxation & Finance Department
State Campus
Building 9
Albany, NY 12227
518-457-2244

TOURISM

Division of Tourism
1 Commerce Plaza
Albany, NY 12245
518-474-4116
518-473-0715
800-225-5697 (in Northeast region, but not
    Maine)

TRANSPORTATION

Transportation Department
State Campus
Building 5
Albany, NY 12232
518-457-4422

UNEMPLOYMENT

Unemployment Insurance Division
State Campus
Building 12
Albany, NY 12240
518-457-2177

WORKER'S COMPENSATION

Workers Compensation Board
180 Livingston Street
Brooklyn, NY 11248
718-802-6700

NOISE CONTROL

ASSOCIATIONS

Institute of Noise Control Engineering
PO Box 3206, Arlington Br.
Poughkeepsie, NY 12603
914-462-4006
George Maling, Administrator
Professional society of noise control engineers.

National Association of Noise Control Officials
c/o Edward J. DiPolvere
53 Cubberly Rd.
Trenton, NJ 08690
609-984-4161
Edward DiPolvere, Administrator
Government officials at the state and local level concerned with controlling noise.

Noise Control Association
104 Cresta Verde Dr.
Rolling Hills, CA 90274
213-377-9958
213-377-9958 Fax
David Harris, Executive Director
Members are manufacturers of noise control products.

PERIODICALS

Noise—News
Noise Control Foundation
Institute of Noise Control Engineering
2469 Arlington Branch
Poughkeepsie, NY 12603
914-462-4006
G.C. Maling, Editor
Surveys the noise control field.

Noise Control Engineering Journal
Department of Mechanical Engineering
Auburn University
Auburn, AL 36849-3501
205-844-3306
Malcolm Crocker, Editor
Technical information about all aspects of noise control in buildings, industrial plants, transportation, and elsewhere.

Noise Regulation Reporter
Business Publishers, Inc.
951 Pershing Dr.
Silver Spring, MD 20910-4464
301-587-6300
Mary Worobec, Editor
Reports on state and federal regulations and legislation involving the control of noise.

Sound and Vibration
Acoustical Publications, Inc.
Box 40416
Bay Village, OH 44140
216-835-0101
Jack Mowry, Editor
Technical information about the testing, analysis, and control of noise and vibration in machinery and other situations.

LIBRARIES

U.S. Department of Labor
OSHA
Technical Data Center
200 Constitution Ave., N.S.
Rm. N-2625
Washington, DC 20210
202-523-9700
202-523-5046 Fax
Noise, occupational safety, and related topics.

U.S. Environmental Protection Agency
Headquarters Library
Rm. 2904 PM-211-A
401 M St., S.W.
Washington, DC 20460-0001
202-382-5921
202-382-7883 Fax
*Noise abatement, air pollution, and many
other environmental topics.*

Wyle Labortories
Wyle Research Library
128 Maryland St.
El Segundo, CA 90245
213-322-1763
213-322-9799 Fax
Noise control.

COMPANIES

A C G, Inc.
232 Front Ave.
West Haven, CT 06516
203-776-6990
Noise and vibration isolation systems.

Farr Co.
2221 Park Pl.
El Segundo, CA 90245
213-772-5221
Noise abatement equipment and other products.

Industrial Acoustics Co., Inc.
1160 Commerce Ave
Bronx, NY 10462
212-931-8000
Noise control products and contracting.

Isolatek Corp.
P.O. Box 56
Netcong, NJ 07857
201-347-1264
*Insulation products for fire, heat, cold, and
noise.*

Kinetics Noise Control, Inc.
6300 Irelan Pl.
Dublin, OH 43017
614-889-0480
Noise and vibration control products.

Lord Corp.
2000 W. Grandview Blvd.
Erie, PA 16514
814-868-0924
*Noise and vibration control products, and
other types of products.*

Dan T. Moore Co.
820 W. Superior Ave.
Cleveland, OH 44113
216-771-8444
*Noise and vibration damping products for
motor vehicles.*

Neiss Corp.
P.O. Box 478
Rockville, CT 06066
203-872-8528
Noise control products and enclosure systems.

United Process, Inc.
279 Silver St.
Agawam, MA 01001
413-789-1770
Curtains, foam, and other noise control products.

Vibration Mountings & Controls Inc.
(Subsidiary of ARX, Inc.)
113 Main St.
Bloomingdale, NJ 07403
201-838-1780
Products for the control of noise, vibration, and shock.

FEDERAL GOVERNMENT

Environmental Protection Agency
401 M St., S.W.
Washington, DC 20460
202-260-2090
Ask for the public affairs office to find an appropriate expert on noise control.

U.S. Department of Transportation
400 Seventh St., S.W.
Washington, DC 20590
202-366-4000
Ask for the Environmental Division in the Transportation Regulatory Affairs department; the Technology Division of the Federal Aviation Administration; or the Noise & Air Analysis department in the Federal Highway Administration.

NORTH CAROLINA

STATE OFFICE LOCATOR (*for referrals to all state government offices*)

919-733-1110

ARCHIVES AND RECORDS

Cultural Resources Department
109 E. Jones Street
Raleigh, NC 27601
919-733-7305

ATTORNEY GENERAL

Justice Department
P.O. Box 629
Raleigh, NC 27602
919-733-3377

BANKING

Banking Commission
430 N. Salisbury Street
Raleigh, NC 27611
919-733-3016

COMMERCE

Economic & Community Development
    Department
P.O. Box 629
Raleigh, NC 27602
919-733-4962

CONSUMER AFFAIRS

Consumer Protection Section
P.O. Box 629
Raleigh, NC 27602
919-733-7741

EDUCATION

Public Instruction Department
116 W. Edenton Street
Raleigh, NC 27603-1712
919-733-3813

ENERGY

Energy Division
430 N. Salisbury Street
Raleigh, NC 27611
919-733-2230

ENVIRONMENTAL AFFAIRS

Environmental Management Division
P.O. Box 27687
Raleigh, NC 27611
919-733-7015

HEALTH

Health Director's Office
P.O. Box 2091
Raleigh, NC 27602-2091
919-733-4984

HOUSING

Housing Finance Agency
3300 Drake Circle
Ste. 200
Raleigh, NC 27607
919-781-6115

HUMAN RIGHTS

Human Relations Council
121 W. Jones Street
Raleigh, NC 27603
919-733-7996

INSURANCE

Insurance Department
P.O. Box 26387
Raleigh, NC 27611
919-733-7343

LABOR

Labor Department
4 W. Edenton Street
Raleigh, NC 27601
919-733-7166

LEGISLATION

General Assembly of North Carolina
Legislative Building
16 W. Jones Street
Room 2129
Raleigh, NC 27611
919-733-7044

LIBRARY SERVICES

State Library Division
109 E. Jones Street
Raleigh, NC 27601-2807
919-733-2570

LICENSING—CORPORATE

Corporation Division
300 N. Salisbury Street
Raleigh, NC 27611
919-733-4161

MOTOR VEHICLES

Division of Motor Vehicles
1100 New Bern Avenue
Room 220
Raleigh, NC 27697
919-733-2403

OCCUPATIONAL HEALTH AND SAFETY

Safety & Health Review Board
121 W. Jones Street
Raleigh, NC 27603
919-733-3589

OMBUDSMAN

Citizen Affairs Office
116 W. Jones Street
Raleigh, NC 27603-8001
919-733-5017

PUBLIC UTILITIES

Utilities Commission
430 N. Salisbury Street
Raleigh, NC 27611
919-733-4249

PURCHASING

Purchasing & Contracts Division
116 W. Jones Street
Raleigh, NC 27603
919-733-3581

REAL ESTATE

Real Estate Commission
P.O. Box 17100
Raleigh, NC 27619
919-733-9580

SECURITIES

Securities Division
300 N. Salisbury Street
Raleigh, NC 27611
919-733-4161

TAXATION AND REVENUE

Revenue Department
P.O. Box 25000
Raleigh, NC 27640
919-733-7211

TOURISM

Travel & Tourism Division
430 N. Salisbury Street
Raleigh, NC 27611
919-733-4171
800-VISIT-NC

TRANSPORTATION

Transportation Department
P.O. Box 25201
Raleigh, NC 27611
919-733-2520

UNEMPLOYMENT

Benefit Claims Administration
P.O. Box 25903
Raleigh, NC 27611
919-733-7883

WORKER'S COMPENSATION

Industrial Commission
430 N. Salisbury Street
Raleigh, NC 27611
919-733-4820

NORTH DAKOTA

STATE OFFICE LOCATOR (*for referrals to all state government offices*)

701-224-2000

ARCHIVES AND RECORDS

State Archives & Historical Research Library
612 E. Boulevard
Bismarck, ND 58505
701-224-2668

ATTORNEY GENERAL

Attorney General Office
600 E. Boulevard
Bismarck, ND 58505
701-224-2210

BANKING

Banking & Financial Institutions Department
600 E. Boulevard
Bismarck, ND 58505
701-224-2253

COMMERCE

Economic Development Commission
604 E. Boulevard
Bismarck, ND 58505
701-224-2810

CONSUMER AFFAIRS

Consumer Fraud & Antitrust Division
600 E. Boulevard
Bismarck, ND 58505
701-224-3404

EDUCATION

Public Instruction Department
600 E. Boulevard
Bismarck, ND 58505
701-224-2261

ENERGY

Intergovernmental Assistance Division
600 E. Boulevard
Bismarck, ND 58505
701-224-2094

ENVIRONMENTAL AFFAIRS

Environmental Health Section
1200 Missouri Avenue
Bismarck, ND 58505
701-221-5150

HEALTH

Health & Consolidated Laboratories Department
600 E. Boulevard
Bismarck, ND 58505
701-224-2372

HOUSING

Housing Finance Agency
P.O. Box 1535
Bismarck, ND 58502-1535
701-224-3434

HUMAN RIGHTS

Labor Department
600 E. Boulevard
Bismarck, ND 58505
701-224-2661

INSURANCE

Insurance Department
600 E. Boulevard
Bismarck, ND 58505
701-224-2440

LABOR

Labor Department
600 E. Boulevard
Bismarck, ND 58505
701-224-2661

LEGISLATION

Legislative Council
600 E. Boulevard
Bismarck, ND 58505
701-224-2916

LIBRARY SERVICES

State Library
604 E. Boulevard
Bismarck, ND 58505
701-224-2492

LICENSING—CORPORATE

Corporation Division
600 E. Boulevard
Bismarck, ND 58505
701-224-2900

LICENSING—PROFESSIONAL AND OCCUPATIONAL

Licensing Department
State Capitol
17th Floor
Bismarck, ND 58505
701-224-2219

MOTOR VEHICLES

Driver & Vehicle Services Division
Capitol Grounds
Bismarck, ND 58505
701-224-2725

OCCUPATIONAL HEALTH AND SAFETY

Occupational Safety & Health Program
P.O. Box 5520
Bismarck, ND 58502-5520
701-221-5188

PUBLIC UTILITIES

Public Service Commission
State Capitol
12th Floor
Bismarck, ND 58505
701-224-2400

PURCHASING

Accounting Operations
600 E. Boulevard
Bismarck, ND 58505
701-224-2680

REAL ESTATE

Land Department
P.O. Box 5523
Bismarck, ND 58505
701-224-2800

SECURITIES

Securities Department
600 E. Boulevard
Bismarck, ND 58505
701-224-2910

TAXATION AND REVENUE

Tax Department
600 E. Boulevard
Bismarck, ND 58505
701-224-2770

TOURISM

Tourism Promotion
Liberty Memorial Building
State Capitol
Bismarck, ND 58505
701-224-2525 or 2527
800-437-2077
800-472-2100 (in North Dakota)

TRANSPORTATION

Transportation Department
608 E. Boulevard
Bismarck, ND 58505-0700
701-224-2581

UNEMPLOYMENT

Job Insurance Department
P.O. Box 1537
Bismarck, ND 58502
701-224-2833

WORKER'S COMPENSATION

Workers Compensation Bureau
Russell Building
4007 N. State Street
Bismarck, ND 58501
701-224-2700

NOVELTY AND SOUVENIR INDUSTRY

See also: GIFT INDUSTRY

ASSOCIATIONS

International Leather Goods, Plastic and Novelty Workers' Union
265 W. 14th St., 14th Fl.
New York, NY 10011
212-675-9240
Dominick DiPaola, President
*The main union that represents workers in the
souvenir and novelty industry.*

Souvenir and Novelty Trade Association
7000 Terminal Sq., Ste. 210
Upper Darby, PA 19082
215-734-2420
215-734-2426 Fax
Scott Borowsky, President
*Offers information and promotional services
to the manufacturers, distributors, and retailers of souvenirs and novelties.*

PERIODICALS

Souvenir
Talcott Communications Corp.
1414 Merchandise Mart
Chicago, IL 60654
312-670-0800
Offers news and product information for corporate buyers of tourist and souvenir items.

Souvenirs and Novelties
Kane Communications, Inc.
7000 Terminal Square, Ste. 210
Upper Darby, PA 19082
215-734-2420
Sandy Meskow, Editor
Follows trends and new products for the souvenir, gift, novelty, and post card industry.

COMPANIES

Frankford Candy & Chocolate Co., Inc.
2101 Washington Ave.
Philadelphia, PA 19146
215-735-5200
Chocolate and candy novelties.

Noveltex Miami Inc.
151 E. 10 Ave.
Hialeah, FL 33010
305-887-8191
Souvenirs and gifts made from shells and other materials.

Rennoc Corp.
3600 Southeast Blvd.
Vineland, NJ 08360
609-327-5400
Christmas novelties.

Russ Berrie & Co., Inc.
111 Bauer Dr.
Oakland, NJ 07436
201-337-9000
Wholesaler of novelty figures, stuffed animals, keyrings, and related products.

Shalom International Corp.
700 Milik St.
Carteret, NJ 07008
908-969-3200
Novelty items, hair accessories, and costume jewelry.

Takashimaya, Inc.
(Subsidiary of Takashimaya Co. Ltd., Tokyo, Japan)
509 Fifth Ave.
New York, NY 10017
212-682-1900
Novelty and gift items.

Telecom Corp.
1545 W. Mockingbird Lane
Dallas, TX 75235
214-638-0638
Distributor of novelty, souvenir, and gift items, and other types of products.

FEDERAL GOVERNMENT

U.S. International Trade Administration
Department of Commerce
14th St. and Constitution Ave., N.W.
Washington, DC 20230
202-377-2000
Ask for the Commodity Analyst who is an expert in the novelty and souvenir industry.

U.S. International Trade Commission
500 E St., S.W.
Washington, DC 20436
202-205-2000 Office of the Secretary
202-205-3296 Industries locator
Ask for the Trade Analyst who is an expert in the novelty and souvenir industry.

NUCLEAR POWER

See also: ENERGY

ASSOCIATIONS

American Nuclear Energy Council
410 1st St., S.E.
Washington, DC 20003
202-484-2670
Edward Davis, President
Members include nuclear engineering firms,
utilities, uranium suppliers, and equipment
suppliers. Promotes the use of nuclear power.

Institute of Nuclear Power Operations
1100 Circle 75 Pkwy., Ste. 1500
Atlanta, GA 30339
404-953-3600
Z. T. Pate, President
Represents most of the nuclear powered elec-
tric utilities in the U.S. Offers training and
information services.

Nuclear Information and Resource Service
1424 16th St. N.W., No. 601
Washington, DC 20036
202-328-0002
Michael Mariotte, Executive Director
An antinuclear group working to end the con-
struction of nuclear power plants.

Nuclear Management and Resources Council
1776 I St. N.W., Ste. 300
Washington, DC 20006
202-872-1280
202-785-1898 Fax
Byron Lee, President
Members include nuclear utilities, engineering
firms, and suppliers to the industry.

PERIODICALS

Annals of Nuclear Energy
Pergamon Press, Inc., Journals Division
Maxwell House
Fairview Park
Elmsford, NY 10523
M. Williams, Editor
914-592-7700
Technical data about harnessing nuclear energy.

Atomic Energy Clearinghouse
Congressional Information Bureau, Inc.
1325 G St., N.W., Ste. 1005
Washington, DC 20005
202-347-2257
Elyse Sternberg, Editor
Reports on business, Congressional, and legal
news affecting the nuclear energy industry.

International Directory of Nuclear Utilities
Nuexco
1515 Arapahoe St., Ste. 900
Denver, CO 80202
303-899-4500
Carolyn McCants, Editor
Lists nuclear utilities around the world.

Nuclear Plant Journal
EQES, Inc.
Bldg. 6, Ste. 208
799 Roosevelt Rd.
Glen Ellyn, IL 60137
708-858-6161
Newal Agnihotri, Editor
Reports on a variety of issues that concern the
designers, builders, and operators of nuclear
power plants.

Nuclear Reactors and Technology
Department of Energy
U.S. National Technical Information Service
5825 Port Royal Rd.
Springfield, VA 22161
703-487-4630
Reports innovations in nuclear reactor technology.

LIBRARIES

EG&G Idaho, Inc.
Idaho National Engineering Laboratory
INEL Technical Library
Box 1625, MS 2300
Idaho Falls, ID 83415-2300
208-526-1185
Nuclear energy, reactor engineering, material science, radioactive waste management, and related topics.

Virginia Power
Research/Records Services
Box 26666
Richmond, VA 23261
804-771-3657
804-771-3168 Fax
Nuclear power, electric power, and the environment.

Westinghouse Savannah River Co.
Technical Library
SRS-Bldg. 773A
Aiken, SC 29808
803-725-2940
Nuclear science, chemistry, engineering, and physics.

COMPANIES

Connecticut Yankee Atomic Power
Selden St.
Berlin, CT 06037
203-665-5000
Nuclear power plant.

CVI Incorporated
(Subsidiary of Pitt-DesMoines, Inc.)
P. O. 2138
Columbus, OH 43216
614-876-7381
Cleanup systems for nuclear power plants and other products.

E G & G Idaho, Inc.
(Subsidiary of EG & G, Inc.)
1955 Fremont St., Box 1625
Idaho Falls, ID 83415
208-526-0111
Support services for nuclear programs, including research and development in reactor safety.

Industrial Engineering Works
P.O. Box 8008
Trenton, NJ 08650
609-586-5005
Steel and iron work for radiation shielding and other purposes.

Maine Yankee Atomic Power Co.
Edison Dr.
Augusta, ME 04336
207-622-4868
Nuclear power plant.

Metropolitan Circuits Inc.
1330 E. Golf Rd.
Schaumburg, IL 60196
708-884-3600
Electronic equipment used in nuclear power plants and other businesses.

Moorco International Inc.
2700 Post Oak Blvd.
Houston, TX 77056
713-993-7450
Control systems for nuclear power plants and other industries.

Multi-Amp Institute
(Division of Multi-Amp Services Corp.)
4271 Bronze Way
Dallas, TX 75237
214-333-3201
Training for nuclear power plant employees.

Nutech, Inc.
(Subsidiary of Pacific Nuclear Systems, Inc.)
145 Martindale Ave.
San Jose, CA 95119
408-629-9800
Engineering services to nuclear power and other plants.

Vacco Industries
(Subsidiary of Emerson Electric Co.)
10350 Vacco St.
South El Monte, CA 91733
818-443-7121
Valves and filters for nuclear power plants and other systems.

FEDERAL GOVERNMENT

U.S. International Trade Administration
Department of Commerce
14th St. and Constitution Ave., N.W.
Washington, DC 20230
202-377-2000
Ask for the Commodity Analyst who is an expert in nuclear energy.

U.S. Department of Energy
1000 Independence Ave., S.W.
Washington, DC 20585
202-586-5000
Ask for the Nuclear, Electric, & Alternate Fuels Analysis department.

NURSING HOMES

See also: HEALTH CARE INDUSTRY and HOSPITALS

ASSOCIATIONS

American College of Health Care Administrators
325 S. Patrick St.
Alexandria, VA 22314
703-549-5822
703-739-7901 Fax
Richard Thorpe, Executive Officer
This professional group of nursing home and long-term-care administrators offers certification and educational programs.

American Medical Directors Association
10480 Little Patuxent Pkwy., Ste. 760
Columbia, MD 21044
800-321-AMDA
Lorraine Tarnove, Executive Director
A professional group of physicians who run or work in nursing homes and other long-term-care facilities.

National Institute on Community-Based
    Long-Term Care
c/o National Council on the Aging
600 Maryland Ave., S.W., Ste. 100
Washington, DC 20024
202-479-1200
Linda Redford, Chairperson
Helps develop programs that allow senior citi-
zens to stay in their own homes rather than be
sent to nursing homes.

Nursing Home Information Service
c/o National Council of Senior Citizens
925 15th St. N.W.
Washington, DC 20005
202-347-8800
202-624-9595 Fax
Annabel Seidman, Coordinator
Offer consumers information on the stan-
dards, regulations, and insurance procedures
relating to nursing homes.

PERIODICALS

Contemporary Long-Term Care
Bill Communications, Inc.
341 White Pond Dr.
Box 3599
Akron, OH 44309-3599
216-867-4401
James Bowe, Editor
Covers the nursing home and long-term-care
industry.

Health Marketing Quarterly
Haworth Press, Inc.
10 Alice St.
Binghamton, NY 13904
800-342-9678
William Winston, Editor
Advises on the marketing of various health
care services, including long-term care.

Journal of Long-Term Care Administration
American College of Health Care Administra-
    tors
325 S. Patrick St.
Alexandria, VA 22314
703-549-5822
Jan Lamoglia, Editor
Detailed articles about trends and advances in
the management of long-term-care facilities.

Later Years
Dunn & Hargitt
22 N. Second St.
Box 620
Lafayette, IN 47902
317-423-2624
Nancy Kleckner, Editor
A newsletter written for residents of retire-
ment and nursing homes.

Long Term Care Management
Faulkner & Gray, Healthcare Information
    Center
1133 15th St., N.W., Ste. 450
Washington, DC 20005
202-828-4150
Karen Migadale, Editor
Advises administrators in charge of long-term-
care facilities about health, legal, business, and
moral issues.

McKnight's Long Term Care News
McKnight Medical Communications Co.
1419 Lake Cook Rd.
Deerfield, IL 60015
708-945-0345
Suzanne Powills, Editor
News and practical information for those in
charge of long-term-care facilities.

Nursing Homes and Senior Citizen Care
International Publishing Group
4959 Commerce Pkwy.
Cleveland, OH 44128
216-464-1210
Richard Peck, Editor
Written for directors of nursing homes.

Senior Law Report
Community Development Services, Inc.
C D Publications
5204 Fenton St.
Silver Spring, MD 20910-2889
301-588-6380
Herb Weiss, Editor
Reports news, rulings, and legislation that affects senior citizens.

LIBRARIES

American College of Health Care Administrators
Information Central
325 S. Patrick St.
Alexandria, VA 22314
703-739-7932
Long-term care.

The National Council on the Aging, Inc.
Ollie A. Randall Library
600 Maryland Ave., S.W., West Wing 100
Washington, DC 20024
202-479-1665
202-479-0735 Fax
Nursing homes, aging, senior centers, and health care.

Philadelphia Geriatric Center
Library
5301 Old York Rd.
Philadelphia, PA 19141
215-456-2971
215-456-2017 Fax
Long-term-care administration, geriatrics, dying, and other subjects.

COMPANIES

American Medical Services, Inc.
(Subsidiary of AMS Holding Co.)
1051 E. Ogden St.
Milwaukee, WI 53202
414-271-1300
Owns and operates nursing homes.

Forum Group, Inc.
8900 Keystone Crossing, Box 40498
Indianapolis, IN 46240
317-846-0700
Develops, owns, and operates retirement communities, including those offering long-term health care.

Geriatric & Medical Centers, Inc.
5601 Chestnut St.
Philadelphia, PA 19139
215-476-2250
Operates retirement and nursing homes.

Health Care & Retirement Corp.
(Subsidiary of Owens-Illinois, Inc.)
One Seagate
Toledo, OII 43666
419-247-5000
Develops and operates long-term-care facilities that are owned by investors.

Horizon Healthcare Corp.
6001 Indian School Rd., N. E.
Albuquerque, NM 87110
505-881-4961
Operates long-term-care facilities.

National Healthcorp L.P.
100 Vine St.
Murfreesboro, TN 37130
615-890-2020
Operates retirement homes and long-term health care facilities.

National Heritage Inc.
15770 N. Dallas Pkwy.
Dallas, TX 75248
214-233-3900
Operates nursing homes.

Vari-Care Inc.
277 Alexander St.
Rochester, NY 14607
716-325-6940
Operates nursing homes.

FEDERAL GOVERNMENT

U.S. Department of Veterans Affairs
810 Vermont Ave., N.W.
Washington, DC 20420
202-233-4000
*Ask for the Geriatrics & Extended Care
Research & Evaluation department; or the
Nursing Home Care department in the Veter-
ans Health Service.*

NUT INDUSTRY

ASSOCIATIONS

Almond Board of California
PO Box 15920
Sacramento, CA 95852
916-338-2225
916-338-1019 Fax
Peggy Leong, Manager
*Provides research, quality control, and mar-
keting assistance to almond growers and
packers.*

Blue Diamond Growers
PO Box 1768
Sacramento, CA 95812
916-442-0771
916-446-8620 Fax
Roger Baccigaluppi, President
*California growers and processors of almonds,
hazelnuts, and other nuts using the cooperative Blue Diamond label.*

Diamond Walnut Growers
1050 S. Diamond St.
Stockton, CA 95201
209-467-6000
Gerald Barton, President
*A collective of walnut growers, processors, and
marketers.*

Federated Pecan Growers' Associations of the
    United States
c/o Dr. Earl Puls
Louisiana State Univ.
157 Miller
Baton Rouge, LA 70803
504-388-2222
Earl Puls, Secretary
Groups of pecan growers' associations.

Georgia Peanut Commission
110 E. 4th St.
Tifton, GA 31793
912-386-3470
912-386-3501 Fax
Don Koehler, Exec.Dir.
Offers research and promotion services and educational programs to peanut farmers.

National Peanut Council
1500 King St., Ste. 301
Alexandria, VA 22314
703-838-9500
703-838-9508 Fax
C. Edward Ashdown, President
Members include growers, processors, and marketers of peanuts.

National Pecan Marketing Council
4348 Carter Creek Pkwy., Ste. 101
Bryan, TX 77802
409-846-1681
409-846-1752 Fax
Norman Winter, Executive Director
Provides market research and marketing services to pecan growers.

Peanut Butter and Nut Processors Association
9005 Congressional Ct.
Potomac, MD 20854
301-365-4080
301-365-7705 Fax
James Mack, Managing Director
Members make peanut butter, packaged peanuts, and products containing peanut butter.

PERIODICALS

Chocolate and Nut World
Lott Publishing Co.
Box 710
Santa Monica, CA 90406
213-397-4217
Dave Lott, Editor
News for retailers of candy and nut shops and manufacturers of these products.

Nut Grower
Western Agricultural Publishing Co. Inc.
4974 E. Clinton Way, Ste. 123
Fresno, CA 93727
209-252-7000
Harry Cline, Editor
Technical and business information for nut growers.

Peanut Farmer
Specialized Agricultural Publications, Inc.
3000 Highwoods Blvd., Ste. 300
Box 95075
Raleigh, NC 27625
919-872-5040
Dayton Matlick, Editor
Technical and business information for peanut farmers.

Peanut Grower
Agri-Publications, Inc.
Box 83
Tifton, GA 31793
912-386-8591
J. Tyron Spearman, Editor
Reports on peanut growing techniques, legal matters, marketing and other business subjects of concern to growers.

Peanut Research
American Peanut Research and Education
    Society
c/o Dr. James R. Sholar
376 Ag Hall
Oklahoma State University
Stillwater, OK 74078
405-624-6423
Corley Holbrook, Editor
Technical information for growers.

COMPANIES

Birdsong Corp.
311 Factory St.
Suffolk, VA 23434
804-539-3456
Peanuts and peanut oil.

California Almond Growers Exchange
1802 C St.
Sacramento, CA 95814
916-442-0771
Wholesaler of almonds.

Diamond Walnut Growers, Inc.
1050 S. Diamond St.
Stockton, CA 95205
209-467-6000
Whole and shelled walnuts.

Dole Nut Co.
P.O. Box 845
Orland, CA 95963
916-865-5511
*Processors and packers of almonds and pista-
chios.*

Golden Peanuts Co.
1100 Johnson Ferry Rd.
Atlanta, GA 30342
404-843-7850
Peanuts and peanut oil.

Los Angeles Nut House
(Subsidiary of MEI Diversified Inc.)
1388 E. 7th St.
Los Angeles, CA 90021
213-623-2541
Distributor of candy, nuts, and dried fruit.

MEI Diversified Inc.
90 S. Sixth St.
Minneapolis, MN 55402
612-339-8853
*Nut and other snack foods, and other busi-
nesses.*

Sessions Co. Inc.
P. O. Box 1336
Enterprise, AL 36331
205-347-9551
Various peanut products.

J. M. Smucker Co.
Strawberry Lane
Orrville, OH 44667
216-682-3000
Peanut butter, jams, and other foods.

Sun-Diamond Growers of California
5568 Gibralter Dr.
Pleasanton, CA 94588
415-463-8200
*Processors of almonds, pecans, walnuts, fil-
berts, and dried fruits.*

FEDERAL GOVERNMENT

U.S. Department of Agriculture
14th St. and Independence Ave., S.W.
Washington, DC 20250
202-720-8732
*Ask for the State & County Operations
department in the Agricultural Stabilization
and Conservation Service; or for the Economic
Research Service.*

U.S. International Trade Administration
Department of Commerce
14th St. and Constitution Ave., N.W.
Washington, DC 20230
202-377-2000
Ask for the Commodity Analyst who is an expert in nuts.

U.S. International Trade Commission
500 E St., S.W.
Washington, DC 20436
202-205-2000 Office of the Secretary
202-205-3296 Industries locator
Ask for the Trade Analyst who is an expert in nuts.

OCCUPATIONAL THERAPY

ASSOCIATIONS

American Occupational Therapy Association
1383 Piccard Dr., Ste. 301
Rockville, MD 20850-4375
301-948-9626
301-948-5512 Fax
Jeanette Bair, Executive Director
Professional society of occupational therapists who help victims of accidents and illnesses adjust to their new lives.

PERIODICALS

American Journal of Occupational Therapy
American Occupational Therapy Association, Inc.
1383 Piccard Dr.
Rockville, MD 20850-0882
301-948-9626
Elaine Viseltear, Editor
Reports new research and offers how-to information to occupational therapists.

Occupational Therapy Forum
Forum Publishing, Inc.
251 W. Dekalb Pike, Ste. A-115
King of Prussia, PA 19406
215-337-0381
Focuses on new research, techniques, and equipment used by occupational therapists.

Occupational Therapy in Mental Health
Haworth Press, Inc.
10 Alice St.
Binghamton, NY 13904
800-342-9678
Diane Gibson, Editor
Covers methods used by occupational therapists working in the mental health field.

Rehab Management
Curant Communications, Inc.
4676 Admiralty Way, Ste. 202
Marina Del Rey, CA 90292-6603
213-479-1769
Tony Ramos, Editor
Covers the business side of rehabilitation programs and occupational therapy.

LIBRARIES

American Occupational Therapy Association
Wilma L. West Library
1383 Piccard Dr.
Box 1725
Rockville, MD 20850-4375
301-948-9626
301-948-5512 Fax
All types of occupational therapy.

Massachusetts Mental Health Center
Charles MacFie Campbell Memorial Library
74 Fenwood Rd.
Boston, MA 02115-6196
617-734-1300
Occupational therapy, neurology, psychology, and other subjects.

Texas (State) Rehabilitation Commission
Library
4900 N. Lamar
Austin, TX 78751
512-483-4240
512-483-4245 Fax
Occupational therapy, rehabilitation theory, caseload management, and management skills.

COMPANIES

Medgroup Inc.
4676 Admiralty Way
Marina del Rey, CA 90292
213-822-7015
Physical and occupational therapy services.

Novacare Inc.
2570 Boulevard of the Generals
Norristown, PA 19403
215-631-9300
Physical, speech, rehabilitative, and occupational therapy services.

FEDERAL GOVERNMENT

U.S. Department of Labor
200 Constitution Ave., N.W.
Washington, DC 20210
202-523-6666
Ask for the Workers' Medical & Rehabilitation Service.

OFFICE AUTOMATION

See also: COMPUTERS; LOCAL AREA NETWORKS;
MANAGEMENT INFORMATION SYSTEMS (MIS);
and OFFICE EQUIPMENT AND SUPPLIES

ASSOCIATIONS

International Information Management
  Congress
345 Woodcliff Dr.
Fairport, NY 14450
716-383-8330
716-383-8442 Fax
George Hoffman, Executive Director
U.S. and foreign associations that share information about office automation.

Office Automation Society International
6348 Munhall Ct.
McLean, VA 22101
703-821-6650
David Kahn, Executive Director
Serves as a forum for office managers and manufacturers who share information about office automation problems and their solution.

Special Interest Group on Office Information
  Systems
c/o Dr. Clarence Ellis
3500 Balcones Center Dr.
Austin, TX 78759
512-338-3384
Clarence Ellis, Chairman
This group of the Association for Computing Machinery serves as a clearinghouse on office information systems.

PERIODICALS

Administrative Management
Dalton Communications, Inc.
1123 Broadway, Ste. 1100
New York, NY 10010
212-924-8989
Don Johnson, Editor
Focuses on general management techniques, the successful incorporation of automation in offices, and the implementation of new systems.

Business Computer Digest
Association of Computer Users
4800 Riverbend Rd.
Boulder, CO 80301
303-241-0125
Lawrence Oakley, Editor
Reports on local area networks and their use in office automation.

Computerworld
Computerworld, Inc.
375 Cochituate Rd.
Box 9171
Framingham, MA 01701-9171
508-879-0700
Bill Laberis, Editor
Reports on all aspects of computers and the management of information systems, including office automation.

Datapro Management of Office Automation
Datapro Research Corp.
1805 Underwood Blvd.
Delran, NJ 08075
609-764-0100
*Offers advice on how to choose and use the
equipment, systems, and personnel needed
when automating an office.*

Modern Office Technology
Penton Publishing
1100 Superior Ave.
Cleveland, OH 44114-2543
216-696-7000
Lura Romei, Editor
*Covers new equipment and automation prod-
ucts for office managers and executives.*

Office Technology Management
F M Business Publications, Inc.
1225 Franklin Ave., Ste. 210
Garden City, NY 11530
516-739-0336
Eileen Feretic, Editor
*Reports on office automation equipment and
management strategies that increase office
productivity.*

LIBRARIES

InterConsult Inc.
Library
366 Massachusetts Ave.
Arlington, MA 02174
617-646-9600
617-646-9615 Fax
*Office automation, electronic publishing,
graphic arts automation, and other subjects.*

University of Oregon
Computing Center
Library
Eugene, OR 97403
503-346-1722
*Microcomputers, educational computing,
office automation, and computer science.*

University of Washington
Computing Information Center
University Computing Services, HG-45
Seattle, WA 98195
206-543-5818
206-543-3090 Fax
*Computing, hardware, software, data commu-
nications, office automation, and related
topics.*

COMPANIES

Datapoint Corp.
8400 Datapoint Dr.
San Antonio, TX 78229
512-593-7000
*Office automation equipment including com-
puters and local area networks.*

Digital Equipment Corp.
146 Main St.
Maynard, MA 01754
508-493-5111
*Computer hardware, software, and office
automation products.*

Informix Corp.
4100 Bohannon Dr.
Menlo Park, CA 94025
415-926-6300
*Office automation and database management
software.*

International Business Machines Corp.
Old Orchard Rd.
Armonk, NY 10504
914-765-1900
Computer hardware, software, and office automation products.

Internet Communications Corp.
7100 E. Belleview Ave.
Englewood, CO 80111
303-770-7600
Office automation consulting.

NCR Corp.
(Subsidiary of AT&T & Telegraph Co.)
1700 S. Patterson Blvd.
Dayton, OH 45479
513-445-5000
Personal computers, workstations, and other office automation products.

Network Equipment Technologies, Inc.
800 Saginaw Dr.
Redwood City, CA 94063
415-366-4400
Office automation systems.

Syntrex Inc.
246 Industrial Way W.
Eatontown, NJ 07724
908-542-1500
Office automation systems.

Systems Management American Corp.
254 Monticello Ave.
Norfolk, VA 23510
804-627-9331
Installation of office automation and local area network systems.

FEDERAL GOVERNMENT

General Services Administration
18th and F St., N.S.
Washington, DC 20405
202-708-5082
Ask for the Federal Office Automation Center.

U.S. Customs Service
Department of the Treasury
U.S. Customshouse
6 World Trade Center
New York, NY 10048
212-466-5550
Ask for the Commodity Specialist in charge of office automation.

U.S. Postal Service
475 L'Enfant Plaza, S.W.
Washington, DC 20260
202-268-2020
Ask for the Communications and Technology Office.

OFFICE BUILDINGS

See also: REAL ESTATE INVESTMENTS

ASSOCIATIONS

Building Owners and Managers Association
International
1201 New York Ave. N.W., Ste. 300
Washington, DC 20005
202-289-7000
202-371-0181 Fax
Mark Hurwitz, Executive Vice President
*Offers research and educational programs to
the investors, developers, managers, and owners of office buildings.*

PERIODICALS

Income-Expense Analysis: Office Buildings,
Downtown and Suburban
Institute of Real Estate Management
Box 109025
Chicago, IL 60610-9025
312-661-1930
Renato Pangan, Editor
*Provides an analysis of the expenses and rev-
enues of office buildings.*

Journal of Property Management
Institute of Real Estate Management
430 N. Michigan Ave.
Box 109025
Chicago, IL 60610-9025
312-661-1930
Mariwyn Evans, Editor
*Reports on trends and offers management
advice to those in charge of office buildings
and other forms of investment real estate.*

LIBRARIES

Building Owners and Managers Association
International
Library
1201 New York Ave., N.W., Ste. 300
Washington, DC 20005
202-408-2662
202-371-0181 Fax
Commercial office building management.

COMPANIES

Helmsley-Spear, Inc.
60 E. 42 St.
New York, NY 10017
212-687-6400
Owns and manages office buildings.

JMB Properties Urban Co.
(Subsidiary of JMB Realty Trust)
900 N. Michigan Ave.
Chicago, IL 60611
312-440-4800
*Develops and owns office buildings, hotels,
shopping centers, and other properties.*

Lennar Corp.
700 N. W. 107th Ave.
Miami, FL 33172
305-559-4000
*Builds homes, shopping centers, and office
buildings.*

May, Stern & Co., L.P.
914 Penn Ave.
Pittsburgh, PA 15222
412-281-5200
Owns and manages office buildings.

Rouse Co.
10275 Little Patuxent Pkwy.
Columbia, MD 21044
301-992-6000
*Buys, builds, owns, and manages retail malls,
office buildings, and other properties.*

Tishman Construction Corp.
666 5th Ave.
New York, NY 10103
212-399-3600
*Builds, owns, and manages office buildings
and other properties.*

Trump Organization
725 5th Ave.
New York, NY 10022
212-832-2000
*Builds, owns, and manages office buildings
and other properties.*

OFFICE EQUIPMENT AND SUPPLIES

See also: COMPUTERS; COPYING AND DUPLICATING MACHINE
INDUSTRY; FACSIMILE (FAX); FORMS FOR BUSINESS; LOCAL AREA
NETWORKS; and OFFICE AUTOMATION

ASSOCIATIONS

Center for Office Technology
575 Eighth Ave., 14th Fl.
New York, NY 10018-3011
212-560-1298
212-465-2488 Fax
O. Bruce Dickerson, Executive Officer
*Members are concerned with the use and
safety of office equipment, particularly video
display terminals.*

Computer and Business Equipment Manufacturers Association
311 1st St. N.W., Ste. 500
Washington, DC 20001
202-737-8888
202-638-4922 Fax
John Pickitt, President
*Offers research and helps to create standards
for manufacturers of computers and other
business and office equipment.*

INCODA
789 Main St.
Hackensack, NJ 07601
201-489-7722
201-489-7997 Fax
Robert Woletz, Chairman
Members are trade associations that represent distributors and retailers of business equipment.

ISDA—The Office Systems Cooperative
37 W. Yokuts, Ste. A-4
Stockton, CA 95207
209-474-0919
William Highfil, Executive Vice President
Members are dealers of office filing and microfilm equipment.

National Office Machine Dealers Association
12411 Wornall
Kansas City, MO 64145
816-941-3100
Frank Fonteyn, Executive Director
Offers research and educational programs for office machine and copier retailers.

National Office Machine Service Association
Total Copy System
15544 Minnesota Ave.
Paramount, CA 90723
213-633-4724
Paul Sprangel, Executive Director
Helps office machine repair and service firms find parts and information. Also conducts educational programs.

National Office Products Association
301 N. Fairfax St.
Alexandria, VA 22314
703-549-9040
800-542-NOPA
703-683-7552 Fax
Donald Haspel, Executive Vice President
Provides research, management training, and other services to firms that manufacture office machines, computers, office furniture, and supplies.

PERIODICALS

Geyer's Office Dealer
Geyer-McAllister Publications, Inc.
51 Madison Ave.
New York, NY 10010
212-689-4411
R. Rauch, Editor
Follows news and trends of interest to dealers of office equipment and supplies.

Office
Office Publications, Inc.
1600 Summer St.
Box 120031
Stamford, CT 06912-0031
203-327-9670
William Schulhof, Editor
Offers the office manager or executive a look at new technology and equipment. Reviews computers and other office products.

Office Dealer
Office Systems
941 Danbury Rd.
Box 150
Georgetown, CT 06829
203-544-9526
William Hogan, Editor
Product and merchandising information for office equipment dealers.

Office Products Analyst
Industry Analysts, Inc.
50 Chestnut St.
Rochester, NY 14604
716-232-5320
Louis Slawetsky, Editor
*Reviews trends in copiers, duplicators, fax
machines, and word processing equipment.*

Office Products Dealer Buying Guide and
    Directory
Hitchcock Publishing
191 S. Gary Ave.
Carol Stream, IL 60188
708-462-2275
Wayne Siatt, Editor
*Provides product, management, and market-
ing information for retailers of office supplies,
office machines, computers, and word processing systems.*

Officemation Product Reports
Management Information Corp.
401 E. Route 70, Ste. 104
Cherry Hill, NJ 08034
609-428-1020
Pam Benham, Editor
*Evaluates office automation equipment, word
processors, work stations, and other hardware
and software.*

Patricia Seybold's Office Computing Report
Patricia Seybold's Office Computing Group
148 State St., Ste. 612
Boston, MA 02109
617-742-5200
Patricia Seybold, Editor
*Evaluates office equipment and word process-
ing products.*

COMPANIES

Acco World Corp.
(Subsidiary of American Brands, Inc.)
500 Lake Cook Rd.
Deerfield, IL 60015
708-405-9000
Computer and offices supplies.

Atapco Office Products Group
(Subsidiary of American Trading and Produc-
    tion Corp.)
12312 Olive Blvd., Ste. 400
St. Louis, MO 63141
314-542-5400
Office supplies.

Dennison Mfg. Co.
(Subsidiary of Avery Dennison Corp.)
300 Howard St.
Framingham, MA 01701
508-879-0511
*Labels, binders, markers, notebooks, and
many other types of office supplies.*

Eldon Industries, Inc.
(Subsidiary of Rubbermaid Incorporated)
9920 La Clenega Blvd.
Inglewood, CA 90301
213-642-7716
*Office supplies, furniture for conference
rooms, cabinets, and related products.*

Esselte Business Systems Inc.
(Subsidiary of Esselte AB)
71 Clinton Rd.
Garden City, NY 11530
516-741-3200
Office and graphics arts supplies.

Fellowes Manufacturing Co.
1789 Norwood Ave.
Itasca, IL 60143
708-893-1600
Office and records storage supplies.

Mead Corp.
Courthouse Plaza, N. E.
Dayton, OH 45463
513-495-6323
Paper and office supplies.

Office Club Inc.
1631 Challenge Dr.
Concord, CA 94520
415-682-2582
Wholesaler of office supplies.

Office Depot Inc.
851 Broken Sound Pkwy., N.W.
Boca Raton, FL 33487
407-994-2131
Chain of office supply retailers.

United Stationers Inc.
2200 E. Golf Rd.
Des Plaines, IL 60016
708-699-5000
Wholesaler of office supplies.

FEDERAL GOVERNMENT

General Services Administration
18th and F St., N.S.
Washington, DC 20405
202-708-5082
*Ask for the Office & Scientific Equipment
department in the Federal Supply Service.*

U.S. Customs Service
Department of the Treasury
U.S. Customshouse
6 World Trade Center
New York, NY 10048
212-466-5550
*Ask for the Commodity Specialist in charge of
office equipment and supplies.*

U.S. International Trade Administration
Department of Commerce
14th St. and Constitution Ave., N.W.
Washington, DC 20230
202-377-2000
*Ask for the Commodity Analyst who is an
expert in office equipment and supplies.*

U.S. International Trade Commission
500 E St., S.W.
Washington, DC 20436
202-205-2000 Office of the Secretary
202-205-3296 Industries locator
*Ask for the Trade Analyst who is an expert in
office equipment and supplies.*

OFFICE FURNITURE

See also: FURNITURE INDUSTRY and OFFICE EQUIPMENT
AND SUPPLIES

ASSOCIATIONS

Mobile Modular Office Association
PO Box 986
Irmo, SC 29063
803-781-1638
Toni Sylvester, Executive Director
Offers research for manufacturers and retailers of modular and mobile office products.

Retail Office Furniture Forum
c/o National Office Products Association
301 N. Fairfax St.
Alexandria, VA 22314
703-549-9040
800-542-6672
703-683-7552 Fax
Dan Scott, Staff Coordinator
Offers information about lower-cost office furniture.

PERIODICALS

Office Products Dealer Buying Guide and
    Directory
Hitchcock Publishing
191 S. Gary Ave.
Carol Stream, IL 60188
708-462-2286
Al Lehto, Editor
Surveys products for manufacturers and dealers of all office supplies, including office furniture. Also offers management and marketing advice to retailers.

COMPANIES

Eastman, Inc.
(Subsidiary of AAM, Inc.)
3366 E. Willow
Signal Hill, CA 90806
213-490-1000
Retailer of office furniture and supplies.

Kimball Office Furniture Co.
(Division of Kimball International, Inc.)
Route 60
Borden, IN 47106
812-967-2041
Office furniture.

Knoll International Inc.
(Subsidiary of Westinghouse Electric Corp.)
Water St.
East Greenville, PA 18041
215-679-7991
Furniture for offices, institutions, and homes.

Lane Co., Inc.
(Subsidiary of Interco Incorporated)
Altavista, VA 24517
804-369-5641
Residential and office furniture.

Herman Miller, Inc.
8500 Byron Rd.
Zeeland, MI 49464
616-772-3300
Office furniture systems.

Steelcase Inc.
901 44th St., S.E.
Grand Rapids, MI 49508
616-247-2710
Office furniture systems.

Sunarhauserman, Inc.
(Subsidiary of Hauserman, Inc.)
5711 Grant Ave.
Cleveland, OH 44105
216-883-1400
Office furniture systems.

Tab Products Co.
1400 Page Mill Rd.
Palo Alto, CA 94304
415-852-2400
Office furniture and filing systems.

21 International Holdings
153 E. 53rd St.
New York, NY 10022
212-230-0400
Open office systems, office furniture, and other types of products.

Virco Mfg. Corp.
15134 S. Vermont Ave.
Los Angeles, CA 90247
213-532-3570
Furniture for offices, institutions, and schools.

FEDERAL GOVERNMENT

U.S. Customs Service
Department of the Treasury
U.S. Customshouse
6 World Trade Center
New York, NY 10048
212-466-5550
Ask for the Commodity Specialist in charge of office furniture.

U.S. International Trade Administration
Department of Commerce
14th St. and Constitution Ave., N.W.
Washington, DC 20230
202-377-2000
Ask for the Commodity Analyst who is an expert in office furniture.

U.S. International Trade Commission
500 E St., S.W.
Washington, DC 20436
202-205-2000 Office of the Secretary
202-205-3296 Industries locator
Ask for the Trade Analyst who is an expert in office furniture.

OFFICE MANAGEMENT

See also: MANAGEMENT and SECRETARIES AND OFFICE WORKERS

ASSOCIATIONS

Administrative Management Society
1101 14th St. N.W., No. 1100
Washington, DC 20005-5601
202-371-8299
202-371-1090 Fax
M. Sutherland, Executive Director
Provides office managers, administrators, and other office personnel with information and seminars designed to increase productivity and quality of office work.

PERIODICALS

Administrative Management
Dalton Communications, Inc.
1123 Broadway, Ste. 1100
New York, NY 10010
212-924-8989
Don Johnson, Editor
Advises administrative personnel on management techniques. Also covers office automation.

Dynamic Supervision
Bureau of Business Practice
24 Rope Ferry Rd.
Waterford, CT 06386
203-442-4365
Shelley Wolf, Editor
Practical advice about people-handling for office managers and other supervisors.

Management
Office of Public Affairs
U.S. Office of Personnel Management
Washington, DC 20415
202-655-4000
David Turner, Editor
News and advice for government supervisors, managers, and private contractors.

Personal Report for the Professional Secretary
National Institute of Business Management
1328 Broadway
New York, NY 10001-0208
212-971-3300
Barry Lenson, Editor
Administrative and productivity advice for secretaries.

OHIO

STATE OFFICE LOCATOR (*for referrals to all state government offices*)

614-466-2000

ARCHIVES AND RECORDS

Historical Society
1982 Velma Avenue
Columbus, OH 43211
614-297-2300

ATTORNEY GENERAL

Attorney General's Office
30 E. Broad Street
Columbus, OH 43215
614-466-4320

BANKING

Banks Division
77 S. High Street
23rd Floor
Columbus, OH 43277-0544
614-466-2932

COMMERCE

Banks Division
77 S. High Street
23rd Floor
Columbus, OH 43277-0544
614-466-2932

CONSUMER AFFAIRS

Consumer Protection Section
30 E. Broad Street
Columbus, OH 43215
614-466-8831

EDUCATION

Education Department
65 S. Front Street
Columbus, OH 43266-0308
614-466-3304

ENERGY

Coal Development Office
P.O. Box 1001
Columbus, OH 43266-0101
614-466-3465

ENVIRONMENTAL AFFAIRS

Environmental Protection Agency
P.O. Box 1049
Columbus, OH 43266-0149
614-644-2782

HEALTH

Health Department
246 N. High Street
Columbus, OH 43266-0588
614-466-2253

HOUSING

Housing Finance Agency
77 S. High Street
26th Floor
Columbus, OH 43266-0319
614-466-7970

HUMAN RIGHTS

Civil Rights Commission
220 Parsons Avenue
Columbus, OH 43266-0543
614-466-2785

INSURANCE

Insurance Department
2100 Stella Court
Columbus, OH 43266
614-644-2651

LABOR

Industrial Relations Department
P.O. Box 825
Columbus, OH 43266-0567
614-644-2223

LEGISLATION

Legislative Service Commission
State House
Broad & High Streets
Columbus, OH 43215
614-466-3615

LIBRARY SERVICES

Library Board
65 S. Front Street
Columbus, OH 43266-0334
614-644-7061

LICENSING—CORPORATE

Corporations Division
30 E. Broad Street
14th Floor
Columbus, OH 43266-0418
614-466-1145

LICENSING—PROFESSIONAL AND OCCUPATIONAL

Licensing Division
77 S. High Street
23rd Floor
Columbus, OH 43266-0544
614-466-4130

MOTOR VEHICLES

Motor Vehicles Bureau
P.O. Box 16520
Columbus, OH 43266-0020
614-752-7621

OCCUPATIONAL HEALTH AND SAFETY

Industrial Hygiene & Engineering Section
William Green Building
30 W. Spring Street
20th Floor
Columbus, OH 43266-0581
614-466-3564

OMBUDSMAN

Office of the Governor
77 S. High Street
Columbus, OH 43215
614-466-3555

PUBLIC UTILITIES

Public Utilities Commission
180 E. Broad Street
Columbus, OH 43266-0573
614-466-3204

PURCHASING

Purchasing Section
30 E. Broad Street
Room 4040
Columbus, OH 43266-0401
614-644-6359

REAL ESTATE

Real Estate Division
77 S. High Street
23rd Floor
Columbus, OH 43266-0544
614-466-4100

SECURITIES

Securities Division
77 S. High Street
23rd Floor
Columbus, OH 43266-0544
614-644-7381

TAXATION AND REVENUE

Taxation Department
P.O. Box 530
Columbus, OH 43216
614-466-2166

TOURISM

Office of Tourism
P.O. Box 1001
Columbus, OH 43266-0101
614-466-8444
800-BUCKEYE

TRANSPORTATION

Transportation Department
25 S. Front Street
Columbus, OH 43215
614-466-2335

UNEMPLOYMENT

Unemployment Compensation Division
145 S. Front Street
Columbus, OH 43266
614-466-9755

WORKER'S COMPENSATION

Workers Compensation Bureau
246 N. High Street
Columbus, OH 43215
614-466-1935

OILS, FATS, AND MARGARINE INDUSTRY

ASSOCIATIONS

Institute of Shortening and Edible Oils
1750 New York Ave. N.W.
Washington, DC 20006
202-783-7960
202-393-1367 Fax
Robert Reeves, President
Members refine and manufacture edible oils, cooking oils, and shortening.

National Association of Margarine Manufacturers
1101 15th St., N.W., Ste. 202
Washington, DC 20005
202-785-3232
202-253-9741 Fax
Joseph Morris, Director
Manufacturers and distributors of margarine and suppliers to the margarine industry.

National Cottonseed Products Association
1255 Lynnfield, No. 143
Memphis, TN 38187
901-682-0800
901-682-2856 Fax
Allen Ater, Executive Vice President
Maintains a research program to increase the quality and productivity of oil mills and refiners.

National Institute of Oilseed Products
c/o Meyers & Associates
412 First St. S.E., Ste. 100
Washington, DC 20003
202-484-2773
202-484-0770 Fax
Larry Meyers, Executive Director
Members import and trade coconut and palm oils, and products made from these oils.

National Oilseed Processors Association
1255 23rd St. N.W., Ste. 850
Washington, DC 20037
202-452-8040
202-835-0400 Fax
Sheldon Hauck, President
Processors of oilseeds.

Olive Oil Association
5 Ravine Dr.
PO Box 776
Matawan, NJ 07747
201-583-8188
201-583-0798 Fax
Richard Sullivan, Executive Vice President.
Members import, process, and sell olive oil.

PERIODICALS

C A Selects. Fats & Oils
Chemical Abstracts Service
2540 Olentangy River Rd.
Box 3012
Columbus, OH 43210
614-447-3600
Technical information on the analysis, manufacture, and use of fats and oils.

Current Industrial Reports: Fats and Oils.
Customer Services Dept.
U.S. Bureau of the Census
Washington, DC 20233
301-763-4100
Reports on the production, consumption, and stocks of fats and oils in the U.S.

INFORM: International News on Fats, Oils &
    Related Materials
American Oil Chemists' Society
1608 Broadmoor Dr.
Box 3489
Champaign, IL 61821-0489
217-359-2344
*Covers worldwide technological news for the
fats and oils industry.*

Jacobsen's Fats & Oils Bulletin
Jacobsen Publishing Co.
300 W. Adams St.
Chicago, IL 60606
312-726-6600
R. Everett Hodgson, Editor
*Reports on business and technological news
and trends that concern the industry.*

LIBRARIES

A.E. Staley Manufacturing Co.
Technical Information Center
2200 E. Eldorado St.
Decatur, IL 62525
217-421-2543
217-421-2519 Fax
Fats, oils, polymers, and corn products.

Unilever Research U.S.
Research Library
45 River Rd.
Edgewater, NJ 07020
201-943-7100
Fats and oils.

U.S.D.A.
Agricultural Research Service
Southern Regional Research Center
1100 Robert E. Lee Blvd.
Box 19687
New Orleans, LA 70179
504-286-4287
504-286-4396 Fax
*Vegetable fats, vegetable oils, food processing,
and chemical engineering.*

COMPANIES

AG Processing Inc.
11717 Burt St.
Omaha, NE 68154
402-496-7809
*Soybean, salad, and other types of oils, and
other food products.*

Baker Commodities Inc.
4020 Bandini Blvd.
Los Angeles, CA 90023
213-268-2801
Animal fats and oils, tallow, and bone meal.

Conopco, Inc.
(Subsidiary of Unilever United States, Inc.)
390 Park Ave.
New York, NY 10022
212-688-6000
Margarines and other food products.

Karlshamns USA Inc.
(Subsidiary of Karlshamns AB)
525 W. First Ave.
Columbus, OH 43215
614-299-3131
*Oleomargarine, vegetable and cooking oils,
powdered fats, and related products.*

Level Valley Dairy Co.
807 Pleasant Valley Rd.
West Bend, WI 53095
414-377-3073
*Butter, anhydrous fat, butteroil, and other
dairy products.*

Madison Dairy Produce Co.
1018 E. Washington Ave.
Madison, WI 53701
608-256-5561
Butter and margarine.

Miami Margarine Co.
5226 Vine St.
Cincinnati, OH 45217
513-242-2310
Margarine, shortening, and related products.

National By-Products, Inc.
1020 Locust St., Box 615
Des Moines, IA 50303
515-288-2166
Animal fats and other animal by-products.

RJR Nabisco, Inc.
(Subsidiary of Kohlberg Kravis Roberts &
    Co.)
1301 Ave. of the Americas
New York, NY 10019
212-258-5600
Margarines and many other types of foods.

Jacob Stern & Sons, Inc.
1464 E. Valley Rd., Box 50740
Santa Barbara, CA 93150
805-565-1411
*Vegetable oils, fats, tallow, grease, and related
products.*

FEDERAL GOVERNMENT

U.S. Customs Service
Department of the Treasury
U.S. Customshouse
6 World Trade Center
New York, NY 10048
212-466-5550
*Ask for the Commodity Specialist in charge of
oils and fats.*

U.S. Department of Agriculture
14th St. and Independence Ave., S.W.
Washington, DC 20250
202-720-8732
Ask for the Economic Research Service.

U.S. International Trade Administration
Department of Commerce
14th St. and Constitution Ave., N.W.
Washington, DC 20230
202-377-2000
*Ask for the Commodity Analyst who is an
expert in the oils and fats industry.*

U.S. International Trade Commission
500 E St., S.W.
Washington, DC 20436
202-205-2000 Office of the Secretary
202-205-3296 Industries locator
*Ask for the Trade Analyst who is an expert in
the oils and fats industry.*

OKLAHOMA

STATE OFFICE LOCATOR (*for referrals to all state government offices*)

405-521-2011

ARCHIVES AND RECORDS

Archives & Records Branch
Libraries Department
200 N.E. 18th Street
Oklahoma City, OK 73105
405-521-2502

ATTORNEY GENERAL

Attorney General's Office
112 State Capitol Building
Oklahoma City, OK 73105
405-521-3921

BANKING

Banking Department
100 Stae Capitol Building
Oklahoma City, OK 73105
405-521-2783

COMMERCE

Commerce Department
6601 Broadway Extension
Oklahoma City, OK 73116-8214
405-843-9770

CONSUMER AFFAIRS

Consumer Protection Unit
4545 Lincoln Boulevard
Ste. 104
Oklahoma City, OK 73105
405-521-4274

EDUCATION

Education Department
2500 N. Lincoln Boulevard
Oklahoma City, OK 73105
405-521-3301

ENERGY

Community Affairs & Development Division
6601 Broadway Extension
Oklahoma City, OK 73116-8214
405-843-9770

ENVIRONMENTAL AFFAIRS

Pollution Control Department
P.O. Box 53504
Oklahoma City, OK 73152
405-271-4677

HEALTH

Health Department
P.O. Box 53551
Oklahoma City, OK 73152
405-271-4200

HUMAN RIGHTS

Human Rights Commission
2101 N. Lincoln Boulevard
Room 480
Oklahoma City, OK 73105
405-521-3441

INSURANCE

Insurance Department
P.O. Box 53408
Oklahoma City, OK 73152-3408
405-521-2828

LABOR

Labor Department
4001 Lincoln Boulevard
Oklahoma City, OK 73105
405-528-1500

LIBRARY SERVICES

Libraries Department
200 N.E. 18th Street
Oklahoma City, OK 73105
405-521-2502

LICENSING—CORPORATE

Secretary of State
101 State Capitol Building
Oklahoma City, OK 73105
405-521-3911

MOTOR VEHICLES

Motor Vehicles Division
4400 Will Rogers Parkway
Ste. 215
Oklahoma City, OK 73108
405-521-2375

OCCUPATIONAL HEALTH AND SAFETY

Safety Standards Division
4001 Lincoln Boulevard
Oklahoma City, OK 73105
405-528-1500

OMBUDSMAN

Office of the Governor
212 State Capitol
Oklahoma City, OK 73105
405-521-2342

PUBLIC UTILITIES

Public Utility Division
Jim Thorpe Building
Oklahoma City, OK 73116
405-521-3908

PURCHASING

Purchasing Division
104 State Capitol Building
Oklahoma City, OK 73105
405-521-2115

REAL ESTATE

Real Estate Commission
4040 N. Lincoln Boulevard
Ste. 100
Oklahoma City, OK 73105
405-521-3387

SECURITIES

Securities Department
P.O. Box 53595
Oklahoma City, OK 73105
405-521-2451

TAXATION AND REVENUE

Tax Commission
2501 Lincoln Boulevard
Oklahoma City, OK 73194
405-521-3115

TOURISM

Division of Tourism
500 William Rogers Building
Oklahoma City, OK 73105
405-521-2409 or 2413
800-652-6552 (in bordering states)
800-522-8565 (in Oklahoma)

TRANSPORTATION

Transportation Department
200 N.E. 21st Street
Oklahoma City, OK 73105
405-521-2631

UNEMPLOYMENT

Unemployment Insurance Division
2401 N. Lincoln Boulevard
Oklahoma City, OK 73105
405-557-7218

WORKER'S COMPENSATION

Workers Compensation Court
Denver N. Davidson Building
1915 N. Stiles
Oklahoma City, OK 73105
405-557-7600

ONION AND GARLIC INDUSTRIES

See also: FRUIT AND VEGETABLE INDUSTRY

ASSOCIATIONS

American Dehydrated Onion and Garlic Association
1 Maritime Plaza, Ste. 2300
San Francisco, CA 94111
415-392-7077
415-392-3969 Fax
J. Dennis McQuaid, Secretary
Firms that dehydrate onions and garlic products.

Fresh Garlic Association
c/o Caryl Saunders Assoc.
PO Box 2410
Sausalito, CA 94966-2410
415-383-5057
415-381-8185 Fax
Caryl Saunders, Executive Officer
Firms that grow, transport, and market fresh garlic.

National Onion Association
1 Greeley Natl. Plaza, Ste. 510
Greeley, CO 80631
303-353-5895
303-353-5897 Fax
Wayne Mininger, Executive Vice President
Members grow, ship, and wholesale onions.

PERIODICALS

Garlic Times
Lovers of the Stinking Rose
Harris Publishing
1621 Fifth St.
Berkeley, CA 94710
A newsletter for garlic eaters.

Onion World
Columbia Publishing and Design
2809-A Fruitvale Blvd.
Box 1467
Yakima, WA 98907-1467
509-248-2452
D. Brent Clement, Editor
Agricultural and business information for commercial onion growers.

LIBRARIES

American Dehydrated Onion and Garlic Association
1 Maritime Plaza, Ste. 2300
San Francisco, CA 94111
415-392-7077
415-392-3969 Fax
Business and technical information about onions and garlic.

COMPANIES

Big Gus Onion Rings
4500 Turney Rd.
Cleveland, OH 44105
216-883-9045
Breaded onion rings.

Wm. Bolthouse Farms, Inc.
13475 Spruce Ave.
Grant, MI 49327
616-834-5601
Growing, packaging, and selling of onions and carrots.

Fry Foods, Inc.
99 Maule Rd.
Tiffin, OH 44883
419-448-0831
Onion rings and other breaded foods.

Gilroy Foods, Inc.
(Subsidiary of McCormick & Co., Inc.)
1350 Pacheco Pass Hwy.
Gilroy, CA 95020
408-847-1414
Dehydrated garlic, onion, and other products.

Ore-Ida Foods Co., Inc.
(Subsidiary of H. J. Heinz Co.)
P. O. Box 10
Boise, ID 83707
208-383-6100
Frozen onion rings, chopped onions, and potatoes.

M. Polaner, Inc.
426 Eagle Rock Ave.
Roseland, NJ 07068
201-228-2500
Jams, syrups, pickles, and garlic.

Westin, Inc.
4727 Center
Omaha, NE 68106
402-553-3363
Onion rings, chopped onions, and other foods.

FEDERAL GOVERNMENT

U.S. Department of Agriculture
14th St. and Independence Ave., S.W.
Washington, DC 20250
202-720-8732
Ask for the Economic Research Service.

U.S. International Trade Administration
Department of Commerce
14th St. and Constitution Ave., N.W.
Washington, DC 20230
202-377-2000
*Ask for the Commodity Analyst who is an
expert in the onion industry or the garlic
industry.*

U.S. International Trade Commission
500 E St., S.W.
Washington, DC 20436
202-205-2000 Office of the Secretary
202-205-3296 Industries locator
*Ask for the Trade Analyst who is an expert in
the onion industry or the garlic industry.*

OPERATIONS RESEARCH

*Operations research is the mathematical or statistical study of a problem, process, or operation in
order to increase efficiency or effectiveness.*

ASSOCIATIONS

Operations Research Society of America
Mt. Royal and Guilford Aves.
Baltimore, MD 21202
301-528-4146
301-528-8556 Fax
Patricia Morris, Executive Director
*A professional society for educators, scientists
and others who practice operations research,
decision analysis, probability studies, and
related subjects in all types of industries and
non-business settings.*

PERIODICALS

Computers & Operations Research
Pergamon Press, Inc., Journals Division
Maxwell House
Fairview Park
Elmsford, NY 10523
914-592-7700
Samuel Raff, Editor
*Papers on the use of computers and operations
research to solve major world problems.*

Mathematics of Operations Research
Institute of Management Sciences
290 Westminister St.
Providence, RI 02903
401-274-2525
Erhan Cinlar, Editor
*Technical information for experts in opera-
tions research working primarily in business.*

Operations Research
Operations Research Society of America
Mount Royal and Guilford Aves.
Baltimore, MD 21202
301-528-4146
H. Donald Ratliff, Editor
*Technical information for operations research
professionals.*

Studies in Operations Research
Gordon & Breach Science Publishers
270 Eighth Ave.
New York, NY 10011
212-206-8900
A. Ghosal, Editor
Detailed papers for practitioners.

LIBRARIES

Computer Sciences Corp.
M/C 222 Library Services
3160 Fairview Park Dr.
Falls Church, VA 22042
703-641-2009
703-849-1001 Fax
*Operations research, communications, and
management science.*

University of California, Berkeley
Kresge Engineering Library
110 Bechtel Engineering Center
Berkeley, CA 94720
510-742-3339
Operations research and the full range of engineering subjects.

University of Pennsylvania
Lippincott Library
Van Pelt-Dietrich Library Center
3420 Walnut St.
Philadelphia, PA 19104-6207
215-989-2261
215-898-2261 Fax
*Operations research, management, business,
marketing, and other subjects.*

OPHTHALMIC INDUSTRY

The ophthalmic industry covers all services and products involving eye care, including optometrists.

See also: OPTICS INDUSTRY

ASSOCIATIONS

Optical Laboratories Association
PO Box 2000
Merrifield, VA 22116
703-849-8550
703-849-8554 Fax
Irby Hollans, Executive Director
*Represents ophthalmic laboratories and firms
that supply the industry.*

Optical Manufacturers Association
6055A Arlington Blvd.
Falls Church, VA 22044
703-237-8433
703-237-0643 Fax
Eugene Keeney, Executive Vice President
*Manufacturers of ophthalmic lenses, frames,
lenses, machinery used to make lenses, and
supplies.*

Vision Council of America
1800 Kent St., Ste. 1210
Rosslyn, VA 22209
703-243-1508
703-243-1537 Fax
Susan Allen, Executive Director
*A collection of firms that produce ophthalmic
trade shows.*

PERIODICALS

American Journal of Ophthalmology
Ophthalmic Publishing Co.
435 N. Michigan Ave., Ste. 1415
Chicago, IL 60611
312-787-3853
Frank Newell, Editor
A clinical journal for ophthalmologists.

Chilton's Review of Optometry
Chilton Co.
Chilton Way
Radnor, PA 19089
215-964-4370
Stan Herrin, Editor
*Follows news and trends for the optometry
industry.*

Eyecare Business
Viscom Publications, Inc.
50 Washington St.
Norwalk, CT 06854
203-838-9100
Leo Robert, Editor
Reports on news, trends, and new products.

Ophthalmology Times
Edgell Communications
7500 Old Oak Blvd.
Cleveland, OH 44130
216-243-8100
Dean Celia, Editor
*Covers industry news and announcements of
professional meetings.*

Optometric Economics
American Optometric Association
243 N. Lindbergh Blvd.
St. Louis, MO 63141
314-991-4100
Jack Runninger, Editor
*Advises on how to manage the business mat-
ters in an optometric practice.*

Optometric Management
Viscom Enterprises
656 E. Swedesford Rd., Ste. 218
Wayne, PA 19087
215-964-8801
Stan Herrin, Editor
*Marketing and business advice for optometry
practices.*

LIBRARIES

Allergan, Inc.
Corporate Information Center
2525 Dupont Dr.
Irvine, CA 92715-1599
714-752-4314
714-955-6756 Fax
*Ophthalmology, contact lenses, and general
medicine.*

American Academy of Ophthalmology
Library
P.O. Box 7424
San Francisco, CA 94966
415-561-8500
415-561-8533 Fax
Ophthalmology.

Iolab Corp.
Research Information Services
500 Iiolab Dr.
Claremont, CA 91711
714-399-1571
714-399-1425 Fax
Ophthalmology.

University of California, Berkeley
Optometry Library
490 Minor Hall
Berkeley, CA 94720
510-642-1020
Ophthalmology, optometry, and physiological optics.

COMPANIES

Alcon Laboratories, Inc.
(Subsidiary of Nestle S.A.)
P. O. Box 6600
Fort Worth, TX 76115
817-293-0450
Pharmaceuticals, surgical instruments, and ophthalmic products.

Allergan, Inc.
2525 DuPont Dr.
Irvine, CA 92715
714-752-4500
Contacts lenses, ophthalmic products, and pharmaceuticals.

Welch Allyn, Inc.
4341 State St.
Skaneateles Falls, NY 13153
315-685-8351
Ophthalmoscopes, and other medical examination equipment.

American Optical Corp.
14 Mechanic St.
Southbridge, MA 01550
508-765-9711
Ophthalmic lenses, eyeglass frames and cases, and related products.

Duffens Optical Inc.
400 Quincy St.
Topeka, KS 66601
913-234-3481
Wholesaler of prescription ophthalmic lenses, contact lenses, and ophthalmic equipment.

Optical Micro Systems
83 Pine St.
Peabody, MA 01960
508-535-2112
Ophthalmic surgical systems and other medical equipment.

Optical Radiation Corp.
1300 Optical Dr.
Azusa, CA 91702
818-969-3344
Ophthalmic lenses and other optical products.

Pearle, Inc.
(Subsidiary of Grandmet USA Inc.)
2534 Royal Lane, Box 226139
Dallas, TX 75266
214-241-3381
Operates and franchises retail eyecare stores.

Schott Glass Technologies Inc.
(Subsidiary of Schott Corp.)
400 York Ave.
Duryea, PA 18642
717-457-7485
Optical and ophthalmic glass.

Shuron Inc.
P.O. Box 331
Rochester, NY 14601
716-288-4130
Ophthalmic lenses and frames.

Western Optical Corp.
1200 Mercer St.
Seattle, WA 98109
206-622-7627
Optical goods including ophthalmic instruments.

FEDERAL GOVERNMENT

National Institutes of Health
9000 Rockville Pike
Bethesda, MD 20892
301-496-4000
Ask for the National Eye Institute.

U.S. International Trade Administration
Department of Commerce
14th St. and Constitution Ave., N.W.
Washington, DC 20230
202-377-2000
*Ask for the Commodity Analyst who is an
expert in the ophthalmic industry.*

U.S. International Trade Commission
500 E St., S.W.
Washington, DC 20436
202-205-2000 Office of the Secretary
202-205-3296 Industries locator
*Ask for the Trade Analyst who is an expert in
the ophthalmic industry.*

OPTICS INDUSTRY

See also: OPHTHALMIC INDUSTRY

ASSOCIATIONS

Optical Society of America
2010 Massachusetts Ave. N.W.
Washington, DC 20036
202-223-8130
202-223-1096 Fax
Jarus Quinn, Execurive Director
*Members are individuals involved in optics
research, manufacturing, and related fields.*

SPIE—The International Society for Optical
  Engineering
1000 20th St.
Bellingham, WA 98227
206-676-3290
206-647-1445 Fax
Joseph Yaver, Executive Director
*Scientists and engineers who share informa-
tion on optical engineering and related subjects.*

PERIODICALS

L D & A
Illuminating Engineering Society
345 E. 47th St.
New York, NY 10017
212-705-7926
Technical information for optics engineers.

O E Reports
International Society for Optical Engineering.
Society of Photo-Optical Instrumentation
    Engineers
1000 20th St.
Box 10
Bellingham, WA 98227-0010
206-676-3290
Rich Donnelly, Editor
Technical and industry information for professionals in the fields of optics and optoelectronics.

Optical Engineering
International Society for Optical Engineering
Society of Photo-Optical Instrumentation
    Engineers
Box 10
1000 20th St.
Bellingham, WA 98227-0010
206-676-3290
Brian Thompson, Editor
Technical information about the design, engineering, and manufacture of optical, laser, fiber optic, and electro-optical equipment.

Optical Materials and Engineering News
Business Communications Co.
25 Van Zant St.
Norwalk, CT 06855
203-853-4266
Richard Bryant, Editor
A business survey of new products, technologies, and trends within the optics industry.

Optical Physics and Engineering
Plenum Publishing Corp.
233 Spring St.
New York, NY 10013
212-620-8000
William Wolfe, Editor
Technical papers about optical theories and their applications.

LIBRARIES

American Optical Corp.
Research Center Library
14 Mechanic St.
Southbridge, MA 01550
508-765-9711
Ophthalmology, optometry, glass technology, and related subjects.

Illinois College of Optometry
Carl F. Shepard Memorial Library
3241 S. Michigan Ave.
Chicago, IL 60616
312-255-1700
312-791-1970 Fax
Optometry, optics, eye diseases, vision, and related topics.

Optikon Research Laboratories
Library
P.O. Box 259
West Cornwall, CT 06796
203-672-6614
Optics.

COMPANIES

Gerber Scientific Products, Inc.
(Subsidiary of Gerber Scientific Inc.)
151 Batson Dr.
Manchester, CT 06040
203-643-1515
Optical manufacturing equipment and other products.

IMO Industries Inc.
3450 Princeton Pike
Lawrenceville, NJ 08648
609-896-7600
Optical instruments and other businesses.

Kollmorgen Corp.
10 Mill Pond Lane
Simsbury, CT 06070
203-651-3757
Electro-optical products and other businesses.

Nikon Inc.
(Subsidiary of Nikon Corp.)
623 Stewart Ave.
Garden City, NY 11530
516-222-0200
Wholesaler of photographic and optical equipment.

Optical Coating Laboratory, Inc.
2789 Northpoint Pkwy.
Santa Rosa, CA 95407
707-545-6440
Optical thin film coated products.

Optical Radiation Corp.
1300 Optical Dr.
Azusa, CA 91702
818-969-3344
Intraocular and ophthalmic lenses, electro-optical products, and other products.

Recon/Optical, Inc.
(Subsidiary of Bourns Inc.)
550 W. Northwest Hwy.
Barrington, IL 60010
708-381-2400
Optics, coatings, electro-optical systems, and related products.

FEDERAL GOVERNMENT

U.S. Customs Service
Department of the Treasury
U.S. Customshouse
6 World Trade Center
New York, NY 10048
212-466-5550
Ask for the Commodity Specialist in charge of optical equipment and products.

U.S. International Trade Administration
Department of Commerce
14th St. and Constitution Ave., N.W.
Washington, DC 20230
202-377-2000
Ask for the Commodity Analyst who is an expert in the optics industry.

U.S. International Trade Commission
500 E St., S.W.
Washington, DC 20436
202-205-2000 Office of the Secretary
202-205-3296 Industries locator
Ask for the Trade Analyst who is an expert in the optics industry.

U.S. Patent and Trademark Office
Crystal Plaza 2
2011 Jefferson Davis Highway
Arlington, VA 22202
703-305-8000
Ask for the Examining Group Director who is a specialist in optical equipment and products.

OREGON

STATE OFFICE LOCATOR (*for referrals to all state government offices*)

503-378-3131

ARCHIVES AND RECORDS

Archives Division
1005 Broadway, N.E.
Salem, OR 97310
503-378-4241

ATTORNEY GENERAL

Justice Department
100 Justice Building
Salem, OR 97310
503-378-6002

BANKING

Finance & Corporate Securities Division
Busick Building
280 Court Street, N.E.
Salem, OR 97310
503-378-4140

COMMERCE

Insurance & Finance Department
Labor & Industries Building
Room 21
Salem, OR 97310
503-378-4100

CONSUMER AFFAIRS

Civil Enforcement Division
100 Justice Building
Salem, OR 97310
503-378-4732

EDUCATION

Education Department
700 Pringle Parkway, S.E.
Salem, OR 97310-0290
503-378-3573

ENERGY

Energy Department
625 Marion Street, N.E.
Salem, OR 97310
503-378-4131

ENVIRONMENTAL AFFAIRS

Environmental Quality Department
811 S.W. 6th Avenue
Portland, OR 97204
503-229-5395

HEALTH

Health Division
P.O. Box 231
Portland, OR 97207
503-229-5032

HOUSING

Housing Agency
1600 State Street
Ste. 100
Salem, OR 97310-0161
503-373-1614

HUMAN RIGHTS

Civil Rights Division
1400 S.W. 5th Avenue
Ste. 409
Portland, OR 97201
503-229-6600

INSURANCE

Insurance Division
21 Labor & Industries Building
Salem, OR 97310
503-378-4271

LABOR

Labor & Industries Bureau
1400 S.W. 5th Avenue
Ste. 409
Portland, OR 97201
503-229-5737

LEGISLATION

Legislative Administration Committee
State Capitol
Room S407
Salem, OR 97310
503-378-8179

LIBRARY SERVICES

State Library
State Library Building
Salem, OR 97310-0640
503-378-4367

LICENSING—CORPORATE

Corporate Securities Division
Busick Building
280 Court Street, N.E.
Salem, OR 97310
503-378-4140

LICENSING—PROFESSIONAL AND OCCUPATIONAL

Insurance & Finance Department
Labor & Industries Building
Room 21
Salem, OR 97310
503-378-4100

MOTOR VEHICLES

Motor Vehicles Division
1905 Lana Avenue, N.E.
Salem, OR 97314
503-371-2200

OCCUPATIONAL HEALTH AND SAFETY

OSHA
Labor & Industries Building
Salem, OR 97310
503-378-3272

OMBUDSMAN

Office of the Governor
State Capitol Building
Room 254
Salem, OR 97310
503-378-4582

PUBLIC UTILITIES

Public Utility Commission
Labor & Industries Building
Room 300
Salem, OR 97310
503-378-6611

PURCHASING

Purchasing Division
1225 Ferry Street, S.E.
Salem, OR 97310
503-378-4643

REAL ESTATE

Real Estate Agency
158 12th Street, N.E.
Salem, OR 97310
503-378-4170

SECURITIES

Finance & Corporate Securities Division
Busick Building
280 Court Street, N.E.
Salem, OR 97310
503-378-4140

TAXATION AND REVENUE

Revenue Department
955 Center Street, N.E.
Salem, OR 97310
503-378-3363

TOURISM

Tourism Division
539 Cottage Street, N.E.
Salem, OR 97310
503-378-1270 or 3451
800-547-7842
800-233-3306 (in Oregon)

TRANSPORTATION

Transportation Department
135 Transportation Building
Salem, OR 97310
503-378-6388

UNEMPLOYMENT

Programs & Methods Section
875 Union Street, N.E.
Salem, OR 97311
503-378-3214

WORKER'S COMPENSATION

Workers Compensation Board
480 Church Street, S.E.
Salem, OR 97310
503-378-3308

PACKAGING

See also: AEROSOL INDUSTRY; BOX INDUSTRY; and PACKAGING MACHINERY INDUSTRY

ASSOCIATIONS

Center for Packaging Education
PO Box 020240
Brooklyn Heights, NY 11202-0005
718-624-6157
Robert Goldberg, Executive Director
Offers educational programs on the design and manufacture of packaging.

Flexible Packaging Association
1090 Vermont Ave. N.W., Ste. 500
Washington, DC 20005
202-842-3880
202-842-3841 Fax
Glenn Braswell, President
Offers research and educational programs to firms that create flexible packaging out of paper, plastics, and other materials.

Institute of Packaging Professionals
Reston Intl. Center, Ste. 212
11800 Sunrise Valley Dr.
Reston, VA 22091
703-620-9380
703-391-6897 Fax
William Pflaum, Executive Director
Professional society of designers and others working in the packaging field.

Package Design Council
PO Box 3753, Grand Central Sta.
New York, NY 10017
212-682-1980
Jane Maslinoff, Executive Director
Professional group of packaging designers.

Paperboard Packaging Council
1101 Vermont Ave. N.W., Ste. 411
Washington, DC 20005
202-289-4100
202-289-4243 Fax
S. Edward Iciek, President
Offers public relations and educational services to firms that make paperboard packaging.

Polystyrene Packaging Council
1025 Connecticut Ave. N.W., Ste. 508
Washington, DC 20036
202-822-6424
202-331-0538 Fax
R. Jerry Johnson, Executive Director
Members make and recycle polystyrene packaging products.

Tube Council of North America
740 Broadway
New York, NY 10003
212-477-9007
212-460-9028 Fax
Ted Klein, Executive Secretary
Manufacturers of toothpaste tubes and other forms of squeeze tubes.

PERIODICALS

Folding Carton
E. Gilbert Mathews, Inc.
274 Tanner Marsh Rd.
Guilford, CT 06437
203-453-3963
E. Gilbert Mathews, Editor
Covers all aspects of manufacturing, printing, and using carton packaging.

Food and Drug Packaging
Edgell Communications
7500 Old Oak Blvd.
Cleveland, OH 44130
216-826-2839
Sophia Dilberakis, Editor
Reports industry trends, marketing innovations, and regulatory matters in the packaging of food and drugs.

Good Packaging Magazine
Pacific Trade Journals
1315 E. Julian St.
San Jose, CA 95116-1094
408-286-1661
J.E. Erich, Editor
Surveys the equipment, techniques, and new products used in the packaging of all consumer goods.

Packaging
Cahners Publishing Co.
1350 E. Touhy Ave.
Box 5080
Des Plaines, IL 60017-5080
708-635-8800
Robin Ashton, Editor
Offers information on design, equipment, legal matters and other subjects to the managers, engineers, and marketers of packaging.

Packaging Digest
Delta Communications, Inc.
400 N. Michigan Ave., 13th Fl.
Chicago, IL 60611
312-222-2000
Robert Heitzman, Editor
Surveys the design, marketing, equipment, and materials of packaging for manufacturers and users of packaging.

Packaging Marketplace
Gale Research Inc.
835 Penobscot Bldg.
Detroit, MI 48226
313-961-2242
Joseph Hanlon, Editor
An extensive listing of packaging manufacturers.

Packaging Strategies
122 S. Church St.
West Chester, PA 19382
215-436-4220
William LeMaire, Editor
Reports on the materials and equipment used in packaging.

Produce Packaging Handling Digest
Vance Publishing Corp.
7950 College Blvd.
Shawnee Mission, KS 66210
913-451-2200
Bill O'Neill, Editor
Advice on the handling and packaging of produce.

LIBRARIES

W.R. Grace & Co.-Conn.
Cryovac Division
Technical Library
Box 464
Duncan, SC 29334-464
803-433-2584
803-433-2689 Fax
Packaging, plastic film, and chemistry.

Rutgers University, the State University of
  New Jersey
Gottscho Packaging Information Center
Busch Campus, Bldg. 3529
Piscataway, NJ 08855
201-932-3044
Packaging.

TAPPI Information Resources Center
Box 105113
Atlanta, GA 30348
404-446-1400
404-446-6947 Fax
Packaging, paper, and other subjects.

COMPANIES

Aluminum & Plastic Packaging Group
(Division of Packaging Corp. of America)
2100 Sanders Rd.
Northbrook, IL 60065
708-205-2300
*Aluminum and plastic packaging materials
and packaging machinery.*

Bell Packaging Corp.
3102 S. Boots St.
Marion, IN 46953
317-664-1261
Corrugated containers and flexible packaging.

Bemis Co., Inc.
625 Marquette Ave.
Minneapolis, MN 55402
612-340-6000
Packaging.

Engraph, Inc.
2635 Century Pkwy., N. E.
Atlanta, GA 30345
404-329-0332
*Flexible packaging materials, blister packaging
cards, and related products.*

Kiewit Continental Inc.
(Subsidiary of Kiewit Holding Corp.)
800 Connecticut Ave.
Norwalk, CT 06856
203-855-5900
Packaging and wood products.

Manville Forest Products Corp.
(Subsidiary of Manville Corp.)
P.O. Box 35800
West Monroe, LA 71291
318-362-2000
Paperboard, wood, and packaging products.

Rexham Inc.
(Subsidiary of Bowater plc)
7315 Pineville/Matthews Rd,
Charlotte, NC 28247
704-541-2800
Plastic and other types of packaging materials.

Sealed Air Corp.
Park 80 Plaza E.
Saddle Brook, NJ 07662
201-791-7600
*Cushioning and protective packaging materi-
als such as bubble wrap.*

Tri-Pack Corp.
(Division of Jefferson Smurfit Corp.)
2828 S. Lock St.
Chicago, IL 60608
312-247-5500
Corrugated containers and packaging supplies.

Webster Industries, Inc.
(Division of Chelsea Industries, Inc.)
58 Pulaski St.
Peabody, MA 01960
508-532-2000
Polyethylene and poly film packaging products.

FEDERAL GOVERNMENT

U.S. Customs Service
Department of the Treasury
U.S. Customshouse
6 World Trade Center
New York, NY 10048
212-466-5550
Ask for the Commodity Specialist in charge of packaging.

U.S. International Trade Administration
Department of Commerce
14th St. and Constitution Ave., N.W.
Washington, DC 20230
202-377-2000
Ask for the Commodity Analyst who is an expert in packaging.

U.S. International Trade Commission
500 E St., S.W.
Washington, DC 20436
202-205-2000 Office of the Secretary
202-205-3296 Industries locator
Ask for the Trade Analyst who is an expert in packaging.

U.S. Patent and Trademark Office
Crystal Plaza 2
2011 Jefferson Davis Highway
Arlington, VA 22202
703-305-8000
Ask for the Examining Group Director who is a specialist in packaging.

PACKAGING MACHINERY INDUSTRY

See also: PACKAGING

ASSOCIATIONS

Packaging Machinery Manufacturers Institute
1343 L St., N.W.
Washington, DC 20005
202-347-3838
202-628-2471 Fax
Charles Yuska, Executive Director
Members make the equipment used for filling, labeling, wrapping, bagging, and other types of packaging.

PERIODICALS

Good Packaging Magazine
Pacific Trade Journals
1315 E. Julian St.
San Jose, CA 95116-1094
408-286-1661
J.E. Erich, Editor
Reports on packaging equipment, materials, and techniques.

Material Handling Engineering
Penton Publishing
1100 Superior Ave.
Cleveland, OH 44114-2543
216-696-7000
Bernard Knill, Editor
Covers the methods, equipment, and technology used for materials handling, shipping, packaging, and related industries.

Packaging Digest
Delta Communications, Inc.
400 N. Michigan Ave., 13th Fl.
Chicago, IL 60611
312-222-2000
Robert Heitzman, Editor
Information on packaging materials, equipment, and related subjects.

LIBRARIES

TAPPI Information Resources Center
Box 105113
Atlanta, GA 30348
404-446-1400
404-446-6947 Fax
Packaging, paper, and other subjects.

COMPANIES

Aluminum & Plastic Packaging Group
(Division of Packaging Corp. of America)
2100 Sanders Rd.
Northbrook, IL 60065
708-205-2300
Aluminum and plastic packaging materials and packaging machinery.

Charles Beseler Co.
1600 Lower Rd.
Linden, NJ 07036
908-862-7999
Shrink packaging machinery and photographic equipment.

Crown Cork & Seal Co., Inc.
9300 Ashton Rd.
Philadelphia, PA 19136
215-698-5100
*Packaging, handling, and filling machinery,
and closures used in packaging.*

Cryovac Division
(Division of W. R. Grace & Co.)
Box 464
Duncan, SC 29334
803-433-2000
Packaging equipment and materials.

Kliklok Corp.
5224 Snapfinger Woods Dr.
Decatur, GA 30035
404-981-5200
Packaging machinery.

Paxall Group, Inc.
(Subsidiary of Sasib S.P.A.)
7515 N. Linder Ave.
Skokie, IL 60077
708-677-7800
Package handling and packaging equipment.

Pneumatic Scale Corp.
(Subsidiary of Barry-Wehmiller Co.)
65 Newport Ave.
Quincy, MA 02171
617-328-6100
Bottling and packaging machinery.

Rodico, Inc.
18 Park Way
Upper Saddle River, NJ 07458
201-327-6303
Packaging equipment.

Simplimatic Engineering Co.
(Division of CMB Packaging)
1320 Wards Ferry Rd., Box 11709
Lynchburg, VA 24506
804-582-1200
Packaging and conveyor machinery.

Stevens Graphics Corp.
5500 Airport Freeway
Fort Worth, TX 76117
817-831-3911
Printing presses and packaging presses.

FEDERAL GOVERNMENT

U.S. Customs Service
Department of the Treasury
U.S. Customshouse
6 World Trade Center
New York, NY 10048
212-466-5550
*Ask for the Commodity Specialist in charge of
packaging machines.*

U.S. International Trade Administration
Department of Commerce
14th St. and Constitution Ave., N.W.
Washington, DC 20230
202-377-2000
*Ask for the Commodity Analyst who is an
expert in packaging machines.*

U.S. International Trade Commission
500 E St., S.W.
Washington, DC 20436
202-205-2000 Office of the Secretary
202-205-3296 Industries locator
*Ask for the Trade Analyst who is an expert in
packaging machines.*

U.S. Patent and Trademark Office
Crystal Plaza 2
2011 Jefferson Davis Highway
Arlington, VA 22202
703-305-8000
*Ask for the Examining Group Director who is
a specialist in packaging machines.*

PAINT AND PAINTING INDUSTRY

See also: WALLPAPER INDUSTRY

ASSOCIATIONS

Guild CPO
4730 Oakland, Ste. 300
Denver, CO 80239
303-371-4333
303-371-8945 Fax
Jerry Alderson, Executive Director
*Offers a cooperative for paint manufacturers
to buy raw materials.*

National Paint and Coatings Association
1500 Rhode Island Ave. N.W.
Washington, DC 20005
202-462-6272
James Doyle, Executive Director
*Provides research, public relations, and other
services to manufacturers of paint and coatings.*

National Paint Distributors
701 Lee St., Ste. 1020
Des Plaines, IL 60016
708-297-6400
Charles Schwarz, Executive Director
*Paint distributors who share information
about marketing and other subjects.*

National Spray Equipment Manufacturers
   Association
550 Randall Rd.
Elyria, OH 44035
216-366-6808
Don Scarbrough, Executive Secretary
Firms that make spray-painting equipment.

PERIODICALS

American Painting Contractor
American Paint Journal Co.
2911 Washington Ave.
St. Louis, MO 63103
314-530-0301
Paul Stoecklein, Editor
*News and how-to information for painters
whose worksites include factories, offices, and
homes.*

Modern Paint & Coatings Paint Red Book
Communication Channels, Inc.
6255 Barfield Rd.
Atlanta, GA 30328-4369
404-256-9800
Barbara Katinsky, Editor
A directory of the paint and coatings industry.

Modern Paint and Coatings
Communication Channels, Inc.
6255 Barfield Rd.
Atlanta, GA 30328-4369
404-256-9800
Larry Anderson, Editor
Surveys the raw materials, manufacture, and use of paints and coatings.

Paint & Coatings Industry
Business News Publishing, Co.
Box 2600
Troy, MI 48007
313-362-3700
Larry Dill, Editor
Covers industry news, products, and technological innovations for paint manufacturers, distributors, and suppliers of raw materials.

Painting and Wallcovering Contractor
Finan Publishing Co., Inc.
8730 Big Bend Blvd.
St. Louis, MO 63119
314-961-6644
Jeffery Beckner, Editor
Practical advice for contractors of painting and wallpapering services.

LIBRARIES

BASF Corp.
Colorants Library
491 Columbia Ave.
Holland, MI 49423-4899
616-392-2391
616-392-1340 Fax
Paint, resins, lacquers, pigments, and related topics.

The Glidden Co.
Technical Information Services
Glidden Research Center
16651 Sprague Rd.
Strongsville, OH 44136
216-826-5260
216-826-5555 Fax
Resins, coatings, polymer chemistry, paint, and other subjects.

PPG Industries, Inc.
C & R Group
Technical Information Center
Rosanna Dr.
Box 1009
Allison Park, PA 15101
412-492-5268
Paint, resins, polymer chemistry and related topics.

COMPANIES

Duron, Inc.
10406 Tucker St.
Beltsville, MD 20705
301-937-4600
Paints and wallcoverings.

Kelly-Moore Paint Co., Inc.
987 Commercial St.
San Carlos, CA 94070
415-592-8337
Paints and accessories.

George Koch Sons, Inc.
10 S. 11th Ave.
Evansville, IN 47744
812-426-9600
Paint finishing systems used in industry and other types of equipment.

Pratt & Lambert, Inc.
75 Tonawanda St.
Buffalo, NY 14207
716-873-6000
Paints, coatings, and adhesives.

Ransburg Corp.
(Subsidiary of Illinois Tool Works Inc.)
3939 W. 56th St.
Indianapolis, IN 46254
317-298-5000
Spray painting and other types of equipment.

Sherwin-Williams Co.
101 Prospect Ave., N. W.
Cleveland, OH 44115
216-566-2000
Paints, coatings, and painting accessories and equipment.

Standard Brands Paint Co.
4300 W. 190th St.
Torrance, CA 90509
213-214-2411
Paints, wall and floor coverings.

Stewart-Warner Corp.
(Subsidiary of BTR Inc.)
799 Bierman Ct.
Mt. Prospect, IL 60056
708-391-1300
Paint handling and other types of equipment.

Valspar Corp.
1101 Third St., S.
Minneapolis, MN 55415
612-332-7371
Paints and coatings.

FEDERAL GOVERNMENT

U.S. Customs Service
Department of the Treasury
U.S. Customshouse
6 World Trade Center
New York, NY 10048
212-466-5550
Ask for the Commodity Specialist in charge of paint or painting equipment.

U.S. International Trade Administration
Department of Commerce
14th St. and Constitution Ave., N.W.
Washington, DC 20230
202-377-2000
Ask for the Commodity Analyst who is an expert in paint or painting equipment.

U.S. International Trade Commission
500 E St., S.W.
Washington, DC 20436
202-205-2000 Office of the Secretary
202-205-3296 Industries locator
Ask for the Trade Analyst who is an expert in paint or painting equipment.

U.S. Patent and Trademark Office
Crystal Plaza 2
2011 Jefferson Davis Highway
Arlington, VA 22202
703-305-8000
Ask for the Examining Group Director who is a specialist in paint and painting equipment.

PAPER AND PLASTIC BAG INDUSTRY

ASSOCIATIONS

Paper Bag Institute
Plastic Bag Association
505 White Plains Rd., No. 206
Tarrytown, NY 10591
914-631-0909
Brent Dixon, Executive Vice President
Manufacturers of grocery bags and sacks made from paper and plastic.

PERIODICALS

Package Printing & Converting
North American Publishing Co.
401 N. Broad St.
Philadelphia, PA 19108
215-238-5300
David Wittenberger, Editor
Covers the techniques and equipment used in printing and converting (cutting, shaping, folding) bags, boxes, cartons, and other packaging materials.

LIBRARIES

TAPPI Information Resources Center
Box 105113
Atlanta, GA 30348
404-446-1400
404-446-6947 Fax
Packaging, paper, and related topics.

COMPANIES

Baumann Paper Co. Inc.
Baumann Dr.
Lexington, KY 40511
606-252-8891
Paper and plastic disposable bags, cups, napkins, and related items.

Cadillac Products, Inc.
530 Stephenson Hwy.
Troy, MI 48083
313-583-1525
Paper bags, containers, and other products.

Central States Diversified Inc.
9322 Manchester Rd.
St. Louis, MO 63119
314-961-4300
Plain and printed bags and other items made from paper and plastic.

Cupples Co. Manufacturers
9430 Page St., Box 8430
St. Louis, MO 63132
314-426-7750
Paper and plastic bags.

Gaylord Container Corp.
500 Lake Cook Rd.
Deerfield, IL 60015
708-405-5500
Paper multiwall bags, containers, and other products.

General Foods Manufacturing Corp.
(Division of Philip Morris Companies, Inc.)
49 Geyser Rd.
Saratoga Springs, NY 12866
518-584-7000
Paper cartons and multiwall bags.

Gift Box Corp. of America
305 Veterans Blvd.
Carlstadt, NJ 07072
201-933-9777
Gift boxes and bags.

Langston Co. Inc.
3294 Poplar
Memphis, TN 38111
901-454-1100
Bags made from paper, polypropylene, burlap, and other textiles.

Stone Container Corp.
150 N. Michigan Ave.
Chicago, IL 60601
312-346-6600
Containers, paper sacks and bags, and other products.

Studley Products Co., Inc.
(Division of Ply-Gem Industries Inc.)
95 Inip Dr.
Inwood, NY 11696
516-239-4000
Paper and vacuum cleaner bags.

Willamette Industries, Inc.
3800 First Interstate Tower
Portland, OR 97201
503-227-5581
Paper bags and other paper products.

FEDERAL GOVERNMENT

U.S. Customs Service
Department of the Treasury
U.S. Customshouse
6 World Trade Center
New York, NY 10048
212-466-5550
Ask for the Commodity Specialist in charge of bags and sacks.

U.S. International Trade Administration
Department of Commerce
14th St. and Constitution Ave., N.W.
Washington, DC 20230
202-377-2000
Ask for the Commodity Analyst who is an expert in the paper and plastic bag industry.

U.S. International Trade Commission
500 E St., S.W.
Washington, DC 20436
202-205-2000 Office of the Secretary
202-205-3296 Industries locator
Ask for the Trade Analyst who is an expert in the paper and plastic bag industry.

PAPER AND PULP INDUSTRY

See also: FOREST PRODUCTS and PAPERBOARD INDUSTRY

ASSOCIATIONS

American Paper Institute
260 Madison Ave.
New York, NY 10016
212-340-0600
Red Cavaney, President
Offers technical and industry information to manufacturers of paper, pulp, and paperboard.

National Paper Trade Association
c/o John J. Buckley
111 Great Neck Rd.
Great Neck, NY 11021
516-829-3070
John Buckley, President
Distributors of papers to printing plants and industrial firms.

Paper Industry Management Association
2400 E. Oakton St.
Arlington Heights, IL 60005
708-956-0250
708-956-0520 Fax
George Calimafde, Executive Director
Offers technical information to the managers and operations personnel of paper mills and pulp plants.

Pulp, Paper and Paperboard Export Association of the United States
528 N. New St.
Bethlehem, PA 18018
Robert Kerridge, Executive Director
Offers information to exporters of paper and paper products.

TAPPI
Technology Park/Atlanta
PO Box 105113
Atlanta, GA 30348
404-446-1400
800-332-8686
404-446-6947 Fax
William Cullison, Executive Director
Provides educational programs on a large range of subjects to professionals in the paper, pulp, and paperboard industries.

PERIODICALS

Converting Magazine
Delta Communications, Inc.
400 N. Michigan Ave., 13th Fl.
Chicago, IL 60611
312-222-2000
Yolanda Simonsis, Editor
Industry and technical news of firms that form, coat, extrude, and otherwise convert paper, paperboard, and other materials.

Hand Papermaking
Box 10571
Minneapolis, MN 55458
612-788-9440
Amanda Degener, Editor
Information for crafts people and artisans who make paper by hand.

Instrumentation in the Pulp and Paper
    Industry
Instrument Society of America
67 Alexander Dr.
Box 12277
Research Triangle Park, NC 27709
919-549-8411
*Technical information for the operations and
executive staff at paper mills.*

PIMA Magazine
Paper Industry Management Association
2400 E. Oakton St.
Arlington Heights, IL 60005
708-956-0250
Alan Rooks, Editor
*Covers industry trends, new products and
technologies, management issues, and related
topics.*

Paper Age
Global Publications
400 Old Hook Rd., Apt. G5
Westwood, NJ 07675
201-666-2262
Mark McCready, Editor
*Highlights major paper manufacturers and
mill operations.*

Paper Distribution Data Source
National Paper Trade Association, Inc.
111 Great Neck Rd., Ste. 603
Great Neck, NY 11021
516-829-3070
George Cain, Editor
Reports a variety of paper sales statistics.

Paper Recycler
Miller Freeman Publications, Inc.
600 Harrison St.
San Francisco, CA 94107
415-905-2200
Debra Garcia, Editor
Covers the paper recycling field.

Paper Sales
Edgell Communications
7500 Old Oak Blvd.
Cleveland, OH 44130
216-826-2839
Jane Seybolt, Editor
*Advises on selling techniques for sales people
working for paper, paperboard, and pulp
firms.*

Paper Stock Report
McEntee Media Corp.
1327 Holland Rd.
Cleveland, OH 44142-3290
216-362-7979
Ken McEntee, Editor
Covers the paper recycling industry.

Pulp & Paper International
Miller Freeman Publications, Inc.
600 Harrison St.
San Francisco, CA 94107
415-905-2200
Peter Sutton, Editor
*Operations advice for managers of paper and
pulp mills.*

LIBRARIES

International Paper Co.
Erling Riis Research Laboratory
ERRL Library
Box 2787
Mobile, AL 36652
205-470-3245
205-470-3280 Fax
*Paper, wood pulp, wood chemistry, forest
products, and related subjects.*

University of Minnesota, St. Paul
Forestry Library
B50 NRAB
2003 Upper Bufford Circle
St. Paul, MN 55108
612-624-3222
Paper, pulp, forest products, and natural resource conservation.

Weyerhaeuser Co.
Technical Information Center
WTC-TIC
Tacoma, WA 98477
206-924-6267
Paper, wood products, paper chemistry, and adhesives.

COMPANIES

Boise Cascade Corp.
One Jefferson Sq.
Boise, ID 83728
208-384-6161
Pulp, newsprint, many types of paper, and related products.

International Paper Co.
Two Manhallanville Rd.
Purchase, NY 10577
914-397-1500
Pulp, many types of paper, and related products.

Mead Corp.
Courthouse Plaza, N. E.
Dayton, OH 45463
513-495-6323
Pulp, many types of paper, paperboard, and related products.

Paper Corp. of America
(Subsidiary of Alco Standard Corp.)
P.O. Box 951
Valley Forge, PA 19487
215-296-8000
Paper and paper products.

Pentair Inc.
1700 W. Hwy. 36
St. Paul, MN 55113
612-636-7920
Many types of paper and other businesses.

Potlatch Corp.
P. O. Box 3591
San Francisco, CA 94119
415-947-5500
Various papers and wood-based products.

Scott Paper Co.
Scott Plaza
Philadelphia, PA 19113
215-522-5000
Numerous types of paper, pulp, and other wood-based products.

Union Camp Corp.
1600 Valley Rd
Wayne, NJ 07470
201-628-2000
Various types of paper, pulp, and related products.

Westvaco Corp.
299 Park Ave.
New York, NY 10171
212-688-5000
Paper, pulp, paperboard, and related products.

Weyerhaeuser Co.
Tacoma, WA 98477
206-924-2345
Various wood-based products, including paper.

FEDERAL GOVERNMENT

U.S. Customs Service
Department of the Treasury
U.S. Customshouse
6 World Trade Center
New York, NY 10048
212-466-5550
Ask for the Commodity Specialist in charge of paper and pulp.

U.S. International Trade Administration
Department of Commerce
14th St. and Constitution Ave., N.W.
Washington, DC 20230
202-377-2000
Ask for the Commodity Analyst who is an expert in the paper and pulp industry.

U.S. International Trade Commission
500 E St., S.W.
Washington, DC 20436
202-205-2000 Office of the Secretary
202-205-3296 Industries locator
Ask for the Trade Analyst who is an expert in the paper and pulp industry.

U.S. Patent and Trademark Office
Crystal Plaza 2
2011 Jefferson Davis Highway
Arlington, VA 22202
703-305-8000
Ask for the Examining Group Director who is a specialist in paper and pulp.

PAPERBOARD INDUSTRY

See also: BOX INDUSTRY; CONTAINER INDUSTRY; PACKAGING;
and PAPER AND PULP INDUSTRY

ASSOCIATIONS

Containerboard and Kraft Paper Group
260 Madison Ave.
New York, NY 10016
212-340-0760
William Driscoll, Vice President
Represents manufacturers of containerboard and containerboard products.

Paperboard Packaging Council
1101 Vermont Ave. N.W., Ste. 411
Washington, DC 20005
202-289-4100
202-289-4243 Fax
S. Edward Iciek, President
Provides research, public relations, labor bargaining, and other services to manufacturers of paperboard packaging.

PERIODICALS

Board Converting News
N V Business Publishers Corp.
602 Main St.
Belmar, NJ 07719-2702
908-280-1900
Ted Vilardi, Editor
*Reports on general news and new products for
the paperboard industry.*

Boxboard Containers
Maclean Hunter Publishing Co.
29 N. Wacker Dr.
Chicago, IL 60606
312-726-2802
Charles Huck, Editor
*Covers news about paperboard mills and the
cartons, boxes, and other products they produce.*

Converting Magazine
Delta Communications, Inc.
400 N. Michigan Ave., 13th Fl.
Chicago, IL 60611
312-222-2000
Yolanda Simonsis, Editor
*Follows trends for firms that extrude, coat,
print, form, slit, and other wise convert plastic, paper, and paperboard.*

Paper Age
Global Publications
400 Old Hook Rd., Apt. G5
Westwood, NJ 07675
201-666-2262
Mark McCready, Editor
*Covers news and company profiles for manu-
facturers and users of pulp, paper, and paperboard products.*

Paperboard Packaging
Edgell Communications
7500 Old Oak Blvd.
Cleveland, OH 44130
216-826-2839
Mark Arzoumanian, Editor
*Follows the production, management, engi-
neering, and marketing of packaging made
from paperboard.*

LIBRARIES

International Paper Co.
Erling Riis Research Laboratory
ERRL Library
Box 2787
Mobile, AL 36652
205-470-3245
205-470-3280 Fax
*Paper, wood pulp, paperboard, forest prod-
ucts, and related subjects.*

University of Minnesota, St. Paul
Forestry Library
B50 NRAB
2003 Upper Bufford Circle
St. Paul, MN 55108
612-624-3222
*Paper, pulp, forest products, paperboard, and
natural resource conservation.*

Weyerhaeuser Co.
Technical Information Center
WTC-TIC
Tacoma, WA 98477
206-924-6267
*Paper, wood products including paperboard,
paper chemistry, and adhesives.*

COMPANIES

Bleached Paperboard Group
(Division of Temple-Inland Forest Products
    Corp.)
P. O. Box 816
Silsbee, TX 77656
409-276-1411
Bleached paperboard and pulp.

Federal Paper Board Co., Inc.
75 Chestnut Ridge Rd.
Montvale, NJ 07645
201-391-1776
*Bleached pulps and paperboard, recycled
paperboard, and related products.*

Jefferson Smurfit Corp.
(Subsidiary of Jefferson Smurfit Group p.l.c.)
8182 Maryland
St. Louis, MO 63105
314-746-1100
Paperboard, containers, and related products.

Manville Forest Products Corp.
(Subsidiary of Manville Corp.)
P.O. Box 35800
West Monroe, LA 71291
318-362-2000
*Paperboard products, packaging, and other
wood-based products.*

Rock-Tenn Co.
504 Thrasher St.
Norcross, GA 30071
404-448-2193
*Recycled paperboard, cartons, paperboard
specialties, and other products.*

Shorewood Packaging Corp.
55 Engineers Lane
Farmingdale, NY 11735
516-694-2900
Cartons and other paperboard products.

Specialty Paperboard, Inc.
Brudies Rd.
Brattleboro, VT 05302
802-257-0365
Paperboard and related products.

Wisconsin Paperboard Corp.
(Subsidiary of Newark Group Inc.)
1514 E. Thomas Ave.
Milwaukee, WI 53211
414-271-9000
Paperboard.

FEDERAL GOVERNMENT

U.S. Customs Service
Department of the Treasury
U.S. Customshouse
6 World Trade Center
New York, NY 10048
212-466-5550
*Ask for the Commodity Specialist in charge of
paperboard.*

U.S. International Trade Administration
Department of Commerce
14th St. and Constitution Ave., N.W.
Washington, DC 20230
202-377-2000
*Ask for the Commodity Analyst who is an
expert in the paperboard industry.*

U.S. International Trade Commission
500 E St., S.W.
Washington, DC 20436
202-205-2000 Office of the Secretary
202-205-3296 Industries locator
*Ask for the Trade Analyst who is an expert in
the paperboard industry.*

PENNSYLVANIA

STATE OFFICE LOCATOR (*for referrals to all state government offices*)

717-787-2121

ARCHIVES AND RECORDS

Historical & Museum Commission
Box 1026
Harrisburg, PA 17108
717-783-9872

ATTORNEY GENERAL

Attorney General's Office
Strawberry Square
16th Floor
Harrisburg, PA 17120
717-787-3391

BANKING

Banking Department
333 Market Street
16th Floor
Harrisburg, PA 17101-2290
717-787-6991

COMMERCE

Commerce Department
433 Forum Building
Harrisburg, PA 17120
717-787-3003

CONSUMER AFFAIRS

Consumer Protection Division
Strawberry Square
16th Floor
Harrisburg, PA 17120
717-783-5048

EDUCATION

Education Department
333 Market Street
Harrisburg, PA 17126-0333
717-787-5820

ENERGY

Energy Office
116 Pine Street
Harrisburg, PA 17101-1227
717-783-9981

ENVIRONMENTAL AFFAIRS

Environmental Resources Department
P.O. Box 2063
Harrisburg, PA 17120
717-787-2814

HEALTH

Health Department
P.O. Box 90
Harrisburg, PA 17108
717-787-6436

HOUSING

Housing Finance Agency
P.O. Box 8029
Harrisburg, PA 17105
717-780-3800

HUMAN RIGHTS

Human Relations Commission
P.O. Box 3145
Harrisburg, PA 17105
717-787-4410

INSURANCE

Insurance Department
1326 Strawberry Street
Harrisburg, PA 17120
717-787-5173

LABOR

Labor & Industry Department
Labor & Industry Building
Harrisburg, PA 17120
717-787-3756

LEGISLATION

Legislative Reference Bureau
P.O. Box 1127
Harrisburg, PA 17013
717-787-4223

LIBRARY SERVICES

State Library Bureau
333 Market Street
Harrisburg, PA 17126-0333
717-787-2646

LICENSING—CORPORATE

Corporation Bureau
North Office Building
Harrisburg, PA 17120
717-787-1978

LICENSING—PROFESSIONAL AND OCCUPATIONAL

Professional & Occupational Affairs Bureau
618 Transport & Safety Building
Harrisburg, PA 17120
717-787-8503

MOTOR VEHICLES

Motor Vehicles Bureau
P.O. Box 1583
Harrisbury, PA 17105-1533
717-787-2304

OCCUPATIONAL HEALTH AND SAFETY

Occupational & Industrial Safety Bureau
Labor & Industry Building
Harrisburg, PA 17109
717-787-3323

OMBUDSMAN

Action Center
402 Finance Building
Harrisburg, PA 17120
717-783-1198

PUBLIC UTILITIES

Public Utility Commission
P.O. Box 3265
Harrisburg, PA 17120
717-787-4507

PURCHASING

Purchases Bureau
North Office Building
Room 515
Harrisburg, PA 17125
717-787-4718

REAL ESTATE

Real Estate Bureau
North Office Building
Room 515
Harrisburg, PA 17125
717-787-4394

SECURITIES

Securities Commission
1010 N. 7th Street
2nd Floor
Harrisburg, PA 17102
717-787-6828

TAXATION AND REVENUE

Revenue Department
Strawberry Square
11th Floor
Harrisburg, PA 17128-1100
717-783-3860

TOURISM

Bureau of Travel
439 Forum Building
Harrisburg, PA 17120
717-787-5453
800-847-4872

TRANSPORTATION

Transportation Department
1200 Transportation & Safety Building
Harrisburg, PA 17120
717-787-5574

UNEMPLOYMENT

Unemployment Compensation Review Board
Labor & Industry Building
Harrisburg, PA 17120
717-787-5122

WORKER'S COMPENSATION

Workers Compensation Appeal Board
Labor & Industry Building
Harrisburg, PA 17120
717-783-5421
800-482-2383

PENSIONS AND PROFIT-SHARING PLANS

See also: ACTUARIAL SCIENCE and EMPLOYEE BENEFITS

ASSOCIATIONS

Association of Private Pension and Welfare
   Plans
1212 New York Ave. N.W., Ste. 1250
Washington, DC 20005
202-289-6700
202-289-4582 Fax
Howard Weizmann, Executive Director
*Promotes the interests of corporate pension
and other employee benefit plans.*

National Council of Real Estate Investment
   Fiduciaries
PO Box 970
Tacoma, WA 92401-0970
206-596-5400
Joseph Diehl, Executive Officer
*Provides information promoting real estate as
an investment for pension funds.*

National Institute of Pension Administrators
145 W. First St., Ste. A
Tustin, CA 92680
714-731-3524
714-731-1284 Fax
Dean Davisson, Executive Director
*Provides educational programs to pension
administrators.*

Pension Real Estate Association
95 Glastonbury Blvd.
Glastonbury, CT 06033
203-657-2612
Robert Stavey, President
*Offers information for those who currently
invest or plan to invest pension funds in real
estate.*

Pension Research Council
3641 Locust Walk
Philadelphia, PA 19104
215-898-7762
Dan McGill, Director
*Conducts a broad research program on pri-
vate pensions.*

Pension Rights Center
918 16th St. N.W., Ste. 704
Washington, DC 20006
202-296-3776
Karen Ferguson, Director
*Works to insure the rights and benefits of
retirees and workers who recieve or should
receive pension and other retirement income.*

Profit-Sharing Council of America
20 N. Wacker Dr., No. 1722
Chicago, IL 60606
312-372-3411
800-255-2710
312-704-4020 Fax
David Wray, President
*Helps companies design, promote, and admin-
ister their profit-sharing and 401(K) plans.*

LIBRARIES

Teachers Insurance and Annuity Association
   of America
Business Library
730 Third Ave.
New York, NY 10017
212-490-9000
Pensions, annuities, and insurance.

Towers Perrin
Corporate Information Center
100 Summit Lake Dr.
Valhalla, NY 10595
914-745-4500
914-745-4100 Fax
Pensions, profit sharing, employee benefits, and insurance.

U.S. Social Security Administration
Information Resources Branch
Library Services Section
Altmeyer Bldg., Rm. 570
P.O. Box 17330
Baltimore, MD 21235
301-965-6107
Health insurance, social insurance, and related topics.

PERIODICALS

Fiduciary Standards in Pension and Trust
    Fund Management
Butterworth Legal Publishers
90 Stiles Rd.
Salem, NH 03079
800-548-4001
Betty Krikorian, Editor
Analyzes the legal and business aspects of pension and trust funds for the fiduciaries who set up and manage these funds.

Nelson's Directory of Pension Fund Consul-
    tants
Nelson Publications
1 Gateway Plaza
Box 591
Port Chester, NY 10573
914-937-8400
Lists over 200 consultants and consulting firms who work with pension funds.

Pension and Profit-Sharing Plans Compliance
    Guide
Matthew Bender & Co., Inc.
11 Penn Plaza
New York, NY 10001
212-967-7707
Carmine Scudere, Editor
Helps managers of pension and profit-sharing plans comply with the law.

Pension and Profit-Sharing Plans: Forms and
    Practice with Tax Analysis
Matthew Bender & Co., Inc.
11 Penn Plaza
New York, NY 10001
212-967-7707
Harvey Frutkin, Editor
Analyzes the tax ramifications of pension and profit-sharing plans.

Pension Fund Litigation Reporter
Andrews Publications
1646 West Chester Pike
Box 1000
Westtown, PA 19395
215-399-6600
Barbara Pizzirani, Editor
Reports on litigation against benefit plan fiduciaries.

Pension Fund News
Enterprise Communications Inc.
1483 Chain Bridge Rd., Ste. 202
McLean, VA 22101
203-448-0322
Richard Stolz, Editor
Covers news and trends for those who design, administer, and invest for pension funds.

Pension World
Communication Channels, Inc.
6255 Barfield Rd.
Atlanta, GA 30328-4369
404-256-9800
Ed LaBorwit, Editor
Follows the design, administration, and performance of employee benefit plans.

Pensions & Investments
Crain Communications, Inc.
220 E. 42nd St.
New York, NY 10017-5806
212-210-0100
Jamie Gilmore, Editor
News for pension fund investors and other institutional investors.

PERIODICALS, MAGAZINES, AND TRADE JOURNALS

See also: JOURNALISM; NEWSLETTERS; and WRITING AND EDITING

ASSOCIATIONS

Council for Periodical Distributors Associations
60 E. 42nd St., No. 2134
New York, NY 10165
212-818-0234
John Harrington, President
Offers educational programs to distributors of magazines and paperback books to newsstands.

Magazine and Paperback Marketing Institute
1621 Cole St.
Baltimore, MD 21223
301-525-3355
Don Devito, Executive Vice President
Distributors, jobbers, and other marketers of magazines and paperback books.

Magazine Publishers of America
575 Lexington Ave.
New York, NY 10022
212-752-0055
212-888-4217 Fax
Donald Kummerfeld, Executive Officer
Represents over 200 major and minor magazines.

Periodicals Institute
PO Box 899
West Caldwell, NJ 07007
201-882-1130
201-227-7475 Fax
John Fitzmaurice, President
Provides research, public relations, advertsing, and promotional services to publishers of periodicals.

PERIODICALS

Circulation Management
Ganesa Corp.
611 Broadway, Ste. 401
New York, NY 10012-2608
212-989-2133
James Fischer, Editor
Offers advice to magazine and newsletter executives in charge of circulation, postal matters, fulfillment of subscriptions, and related topics.

Editorial Eye
Editorial Experts, Inc.
66 Canal Center Plaza, Ste. 200
Alexandria, VA 22314
703-683-0683
Ann Moldus, Editor
Advice on editing, language, publishing practices, and management of publications.

Editors' Notes
Council of Editors of Learned Journals
Modern Language Association
c/o Prof. John N. Serio
Department of Liberal Studies
Clarkson University
Potsdam, NY 13699-5750
Edna Steeves, Editor
Editorial information for publishers and editors of scholarly journals.

Publishing Trends and Trendsetters
Oxbridge Communications, Inc.
150 Fifth Ave.
New York, NY 10011
212-741-0231
Jim Mann, Editor
Prints interviews with magazine executives who offer advice and discuss industry trends.

Strategic Planning for Magazine Executives
Cowles Business Media
6 River Bend Center
911 Hope St.
Stamford, CT 06907
203-358-9900
Richard Koff, Editor
Planning suggestions for senior magazine publishing executives.

LIBRARIES

Magazine Publishers Association
Magazine Information Center
575 Lexington Ave.
New York, NY 10022
212-752-0055
212-888-4217 Fax
Magazine publishing.

University of Illinois
Communications Library
122 Gregory Hall
Urbana, IL 61801
217-333-2216
Magazines, journalism, publishing, mass communication, and related topics.

COMPANIES

Chilton Co.
(Division of Capital Cities/ABC Inc.)
201 King of Prussia Rd.
Radnor, PA 19089
215-964-4000
Publishes numerous trade and industry journals.

Edgell Communications, Inc.
(Subsidiary of New Century Communications, Inc.)
7500 Old Oak Blvd.
Cleveland, OH 44130
216-243-8100
Publisher of business magazines.

Family Circle, Inc.
(Subsidiary of New York Times Co.)
110 5th Ave.
New York, NY 10011
212-463-1000
Magazines for consumers.

Institute for Scientific Information
3501 Market St.
Philadelphia, PA 19104
215-386-0100
Publishes scientific periodicals.

International Data Group, Inc.
Five Speen St.
Framingham, MA 01701
508-875-5000
Publishes and prints business periodicals.

McGraw-Hill, Inc.
1221 Ave. of the Americas
New York, NY 10020
212-512-2000
Business magazines, books, and information services.

Springhouse Corp.
(Subsidiary of Elsevier Business Press Inc.)
1111 Bethlehem Pike
Spring House, PA 19477
215-646-8700
Business periodicals and books.

Time, Inc.
Time & Life Bldg., Rockefeller Ctr.
New York, NY 10020
212-522-1212
Magazines for consumers.

Year Book Medical Publishers, Inc.
(Subsidiary of Times Mirror Co.)
200 N. LaSalle
Chicago, IL 60601
312-726-9733
Publisher of medical books and periodicals.

Ziff-Davis Publishing Co.
(Division of Ziff Communications Co.)
One Park Ave.
New York, NY 10016
212-503-3500
Magazines for consumers.

FEDERAL GOVERNMENT

U.S. Customs Service
Department of the Treasury
U.S. Customshouse
6 World Trade Center
New York, NY 10048
212-466-5550
Ask for the Commodity Specialist in charge of magazines.

U.S. International Trade Administration
Department of Commerce
14th St. and Constitution Ave., N.W.
Washington, DC 20230
202-377-2000
Ask for the Commodity Analyst who is an expert in periodicals and trade journals.

U.S. International Trade Commission
500 E St., S.W.
Washington, DC 20436
202-205-2000 Office of the Secretary
202-205-3296 Industries locator
Ask for the Trade Analyst who is an expert in periodicals and trade journals.

PERSONNEL MANAGEMENT

See also: INDUSTRIAL RELATIONS and MANAGEMENT

ASSOCIATIONS

Administrative Management Society
1101 14th St. N.W., No. 1100
Washington, DC 20005-5601
202-371-8299
202-371-1090 Fax
M. Sutherland, Executive Director
Members are administrators who share information about management methods to lower costs, increase productivity, improve human relations, and related topics.

American Management Association
135 W. 50th St.
New York, NY 10020
212-586-8100
212-903-8168 Fax
Thomas Horton, Chairman
Offers numerous educational programs for human resources and personnel managers, and executives of all kinds.

International Personnel Management Association
1617 Duke St.
Alexandria, VA 22314
703-549-7100
703-684-0948 Fax
Donald Tichenor, Executive Director
Offers research and educational programs to personnel officials and departments in government.

Human Resources Research Organization
1100 S. Washington St.
Alexandria, VA 22314
703-549-3611
William Osborn, President
Members are researchers into human behavior who share information on the motivation, evaluation, and training of employees.

PERIODICALS

Conference Board's Human Resources Briefing
Conference Board, Inc.
845 Third Ave.
New York, NY 10022
212-759-0900
Theresa Brothers, Editor
Offers senior executives news of such human resources issues as labor relations, compensation, and training.

Employee Communication
Management Resources, Inc.
379 W. Broadway
New York, NY 10012
212-966-8966
Advises managers on how to improve their communications with employees.

H R Reporter
Buraff Publications
1350 Connecticut Ave. N.W., Ste. 1000
Washington, DC 20036
202-862-0990
Tessa Jolls, Editor
Follows news and trends for human resources professionals.

Human Capital
Learning Ventures International
21 Elm St., 4th Fl.
Box 1328
Camden, ME 04843
207-236-6267
Bruce Taylor, Editor
Advice for human resource and other executives at large corporations on how to increase productivity among employees.

Human Resource Management Review
J A I Press Inc.
55 Old Post Rd., No. 2
Box 1678
Greenwich, CT 06836-1678
203-661-7602
H. John Bernardin, Editor
Scholarly papers on human resources.

Human Resource Professional
Faulkner & Gray, Inc.
106 Fulton St.
New York, NY 10038
212-766-7800
Christine Varholy, Editor
Showcases innovative and effective human resource programs.

Personnel
American Management Association
135 W. 50th St.
New York, NY 10020
212-586-8100
Authur Durity, Editor
Reports news and trends in the human resources field.

Personnel Management
The Bureau of National Affairs, Inc.
1231 25th St., N.W.
Washington, DC 20037
202-452-4200
Bill Manville, Editor
Advice on managing employee relations problems in such areas as hiring, firing, and grievances.

Personnel News
Human Resources Advertising, Inc.
4701 Patrick Henry Dr., Ste. 1301
Santa Clara, CA 95054
408-727-2118
George Tansill, Editor
Covers news and trends for human resources and labor relations managers.

Personnel Psychology
Personnel Psychology, Inc.
9660 Hillcroft, Ste. 337
Houston, TX 77096
713-728-3078
Michael Campion, Editor
Covers industrial psychology and the management of employee relations.

Public Personnel Management
International Personnel Management Association
1617 Duke St.
Alexandria, VA 22314
703-549-7100
Sarah Shiffert, Editor
Covers news and issues of concern to personnel managers in the public sector.

LIBRARIES

Human Resources Research Organization
Van Evera Library
1100 S. Washington St.
Alexandria, VA 22314
703-549-3611
*Human engineering, psychology, and educa-
tion.*

University of Minnesota
Industrial Relations Center
Reference Room
Management & Economics, West Campus
271 19th Ave., S.
Minneapolis, MN 55455
612-624-7011
612-624-6374 Fax
*Personnel administration, labor economics,
human resource management, labor relations,
and related topics.*

University of Washington
Business Administration Library
100 Balmer Hall, DJ-10
Seattle, WA 98195
206-543-4360
206-545-8049 Fax
*Personnel, management, labor, and other busi-
ness topics.*

COMPANIES

Caliper Management, Inc.
741 Mt. Lucas Rd.
Princeton, NJ 08540
609-924-3800
*Consultants who specialize in strategic human
resources.*

Digital Solutions, Inc.
One Rossmoor Dr.
Jamesburg, NJ 08831
609-655-4300
Personnel management services.

Drake Beam Morin, Inc.
(Subsidiary of Harcourt Brace Jovanovich,
    Inc.)
100 Park Ave.
New York, NY 10017
212-692-7700
*Human resource and outplacement
counseling.*

Dun & Bradstreet Software Services, Inc.
(Subsidiary of Dun & Bradstreet Corp.)
3445 Peachtree Rd., N.E.
Atlanta, GA 30326
404-239-2000
*Computer software for various business func-
tions, including human resources.*

Genesys Software Systems, Inc.
Five Branch St.
Methuen, MA 01844
508-685-5400
*Computer software for benefits, payroll, and
human resources.*

Intersearch Group, Inc.
115 E. 87St.
New York, NY 10128
212-831-5156
Human resources consulting.

National Education Training Group, Inc.
(Subsidiary of National Education Corp.)
1751 W.Diehl Rd.
Naperville, IL 60563
708-369-3000
*Training courses for many purposes, including
human resource development.*

Right Management Consultants, Inc.
1234 Market St.
Philadelphia, PA 19107
215-988-1588
*Outplacement and human resources
consulting.*

PESTICIDE INDUSTRY

See also: AGRICULTURE

ASSOCIATIONS

Association of American Pesticide Control
    Officials
RR 1, Box 1260
Greensboro, VT 05841
802-533-7704
Phil Gray, Secretary
*Local, state, and federal officials who control
the sale and use of pesticides.*

Chemical Specialties Manufacturers Associa-
    tion
1913 Eye St., N.W.
Washington, DC 20006
202-872-8110
202-872-8114 Fax
Ralph Engel, President
*Firms that manufacture and market a wide
range of chemicals, including pesticides.*

Interstate Professional Applicators Association
PO Box 1377
Milton, WA 98354
206-848-3407
Cindy Deffe, President
*Members are firms that apply pesticides and
share information about safety.*

National Pesticide Telecommunication Net-
    work
Texas Tech University
Dept. of Preventive Medicine and Commu-
    nity Hygiene
Thompson Hall, Rm. S-129
Lubbock, TX 79430
806-743-3091
800-858-7378
806-743-3094 Fax
Anthony Way, Executive Officer
*A clearinghouse for information about pesti-
cides, their correct use, dangers, and disposal.*

PERIODICALS

Agricultural Chemical Newsletter
Thomson Publications
Box 9335
Fresno, CA 93791
209-435-2163
W.T. Thomson, Editor
*Covers industry news regarding herbicides,
insecticides, and other pesticides.*

C A Selects. Pesticide Analysis
Chemical Abstracts Service
2540 Olentangy River Rd.
Box 3012
Columbus, OH 43210
614-447-3600
*Technical information about pesticide raw
materials and finished products.*

E P A Pesticide Label File
Environmental Protection Agency
U.S. National Technical Information Service
5825 Port Royal Rd.
Springfield, VA 22161
703-487-4630
*Provides a listing of registered pesticide labels,
their ingredients, usage, and related topics.*

Farm Chemicals International
Meister Publishing Co.
37733 Euclid Ave.
Willoughby, OH 44094
216-942-2000
Parry Klassen, Editor
*Reports news and trends about pesticides and
fertilizers for the manufacturers, mixers,
retailers, and others in the industry.*

Pesticide & Toxic Chemical News
Food Chemical News, Inc.
1101 Pennsylvania Ave., S.E.
Washington, DC 20003
202-544-1980
Ron Grandon, Editor
*Reports on legislation, regulations, and other
legal matters that involve toxic and hazardous
materials such as pesticides.*

LIBRARIES

Chevron Chemical Co.
Ortho Research & Development
Library
15049 San Pablo Ave.
Box 4010
Richmond, CA 94804
510-231-6372
510-231-6425 Fax
*Pesticide science, organic chemistry, plant sci-
ences, and agricultural chemicals.*

National Pesticide Telecommunication Network
Texas Tech University
Dept. of Preventive Medicine and Community Hygiene
Thompson Hall, Rm. S-129
Lubbock, TX 79430
806-743-3091
800-858-7378
806-743-3094 Fax
*Technical information about pesticide use, dis-
posal, and decontamination.*

Pesticide Action Network North America
Regional Center
Information Services
965 Mission St., No. 514
San Francisco, CA 94103
415-541-9141
415-541-9253 Fax
*Pesticides, environmental issues, and pesticide
alternatives.*

U.S. Environmental Protection Agency
Headquarters Library
Rm. 2904 PM-211-A
401 M St., S.W.
Washington, DC 20460-0001
202-382-5921
202-382-7883 Fax
*Pesticides, hazardous wastes, chemistry, toxi-
cology, social aspects of environmental policy,
water pollution, air pollution, and related
topics.*

University of California, Davis
Environmental Toxicology Department
Toxicology Documentation Center
Davis, CA 95616-8588
916-752-2587
*Pesticides, environmental pollutants, and haz-
ardous waste management.*

COMPANIES

Chevron Chemical Co.
6001 Bollinger Canyon Rd.
San Ramon, CA 94583
415-842-5500
Pesticides and other chemicals.

DuPont E. I. DeNemours and Co.
1007 Market St.
Wilmington, DE 19898
302-775-1000
Pesticides and other chemicals.

Gustafson Inc.
(Subsidiary of Uniroyal Chemical Co.)
1400 Preston
Plano, TX 75075
214-985-8877
Insecticides and fungicides.

Mid-Ohio Chemical Co., Inc.
717 Robinson Rd.
Wash. Court House, OH 43160
614-335-3810
Pesticides and fertilizers.

Miller Chemical & Fertilizer Corp.
(Subsidiary of Alco Industries, Inc.)
P. O. Box 333
Hanover, PA 17331
717-632-8921
*Pesticides, fertilizers, and other agricultural
chemicals.*

Monsanto Co.
800 N. Lindbergh Blvd.
St. Louis, MO 63141
314-694-1000
Pesticides and other chemicals.

Moyer Products, Inc.
1540 E. Shaw
Fresno, CA 93710
209-226-4664
Pesticides and fertilizers.

Orkin Exterminating Co.
2170 Piedmont Rd., N.E.
Atlanta, GA 30324
404-888-2000
*Residential and industrial insect exterminating
services.*

Oxford Chemicals Inc.
(Subsidiary of Diversey World Holdings, Inc.)
5001 Peachtree Ind. Blvd.
Chamblee, GA 30341
404-452-1100
Insecticides, herbicides, and other products.

Reckitt & Colman Inc.
(Subsidiary of Reckitt & Colman plc)
1655 Valley Rd., Box 943
Wayne, NJ 07474
201-633-3600
*Household insecticides and many other con-
sumer products.*

Willert Home Products, Inc.
4044 Park Ave.
St. Louis, MO 63110
314-772-2822
*Household insecticides and other consumer
products.*

FEDERAL GOVERNMENT

U.S. Department of Agriculture
14th St. and Independence Ave., S.W.
Washington, DC 20250
202-720-8732
Ask for the Economic Research Service.

U.S. Environmental Protection Agency
401 M St., S.W.
Washington, DC 20460
202-260-2090
*Ask for the Occupational & Residential Expo-
sure department or the Pesticides & Toxic
Substances department.*

U.S. International Trade Administration
Department of Commerce
14th St. and Constitution Ave., N.W.
Washington, DC 20230
202-377-2000
*Ask for the Commodity Analyst who is an
expert in the pesticide industry.*

U.S. International Trade Commission
500 E St., S.W.
Washington, DC 20436
202-205-2000 Office of the Secretary
202-205-3296 Industries locator
*Ask for the Trade Analyst who is an expert in
the pesticide industry.*

PET INDUSTRY

ASSOCIATIONS

American Boarding Kennels Association
4575 Galley Rd., #400A
Colorado Springs, CO 80915
719-591-1113
719-597-0006 Fax
James Krack, Executive Director
*Members operate kennels and supply the
industry.*

American Pet Products Manufacturers Association
60 E. 42nd St.
New York, NY 10165
212-867-2290
212-986-4497 Fax
Jules Schwimmer, Executive Director
*Provides public relations and other services to
firms that manufacture and import pet supplies.*

American Professional Pet Distributors, Inc.
c/o Doug Hughes
Dobo Tri-Kennel
Route 1
Purdy, MO 66734
404-498-2627
Doug Hughes, President
*Offers educational programs to those who
breed, distribute, and retail pets.*

National Dog Groomers Association of
America
Box 101
Clark, PA 16113
412-962-2711
412-962-1919 Fax
Jeffrey Reynolds, Executive Director
*Members are professional dog groomers and
supply grooming products.*

Pet Food Institute
1101 Connecticut Ave. N.W., Ste. 700
Washington, DC 20036
202-857-1120
Duane Ekedahl, Executive Director
Firms that make all kinds of pet food.

Pet Industry Distributors Association
5024-R Campbell Blvd.
Baltimore, MD 21236
301-931-8100
301-931-8111 Fax
Steven King, Executive Vice Presdent
Promotes the pet industry through a variety of
public relations and educational programs.

Pet Industry Joint Advisory Council
1710 Rhode Island Ave. N.W., 2nd Fl.
Washington, DC 20036
202-452-1525
800-553-7387
202-293-4377 Fax
N. Marshall Meyers, General Counsel
Monitors legislation and offers educational
programs for pet supply manufacturers and
retailers.

PERIODICALS

Bird Talk
Fancy Publications, Inc.
Box 6050
Mission Viejo, CA 92690
714-855-8822
Karyn New, Editor
A consumer magazine containing advice for
people who keep birds.

Cat Fancy
Fancy Publications, Inc.
Box 6050
Mission Viejo, CA 92690
714-855-8822
Kathryn Segnar, Editor
A consumer magazine containing advice for
people who take care of cats.

Dog Fancy
Fancy Publications, Inc.
Box 6050
Mission Viejo, CA 92690
714-855-8822
Kim Thornton, Editor
A consumer magazine containing advice for
people who take care of dogs.

Groom & Board
H.H. Backer Associates, Inc.
207 S. Wabash Ave., Ste. 504
Chicago, IL 60604
312-663-4040
Karen Long MacLeod, Editor
News and how-to information for professional
dog groomers and kennel operators.

Pet Dealer
Howmark Publishing Corp.
567 Morris Ave.
Elizabeth, NJ 07208
201-353-7373
Donna Eastman, Editor
Offers industry news and announcements of
new products to retail pet shops.

Petfood Industry
Watt Publishing Co.
Sandstone Bldg.
Mt. Morris, IL 61054
815-734-4171
Clay Gill, Editor
Written for manufacturers of pet foods.

Pets, Supplies, Marketing
Edgell Communications
7500 Old Oak Blvd.
Cleveland, OH 44130
216-826-2839
Hugh Bishop, Editor
Covers the entire pet industry for manufactur-
ers, distributors, and retailers.

LIBRARIES

American Kennel Club
Library
51 Madison Ave.
New York, NY 10010
212-696-8245
212-646-8299 Fax
Full range of topics about dogs.

Morris Animal Foundation
Library
45 Inverness Dr., E.
Englewood, CO 80112
303-790-2345
303-790-4066 Fax
Zoo medicine and veterinary medicine.

COMPANIES

Alpo Petfoods, Inc.
(Subsidiary of Grandmet Consumer Products
Inc.)
Box 2187
Allentown, PA 18001
215-398-4500
Pet food.

Carter-Wallace, Inc.
1345 Ave. of the Americas
New York, NY 10105
212-339-5007
Pharmaceuticals, pet products, and other businesses.

Hartz Mountain Corp.
700 Frank E. Rodgers Blvd., S.
Harrison, NJ 07029
201-481-4800
Pet products of all kinds.

Iams Co.
7520 Poe Ave.
Dayton, OH 45414
513-898-7387
Pet food.

Kal Kan Foods, Inc.
3250 E. 44th St.
Vernon, CA 90058
213-587-2727
Pet food and pet care accessories.

Oil-Dri Corp. of America
520 N. Michigan Ave.
Chicago, IL 60611
312-321-1515
Cat box absorbent and other types of products.

Quaker Oats Co.
321 N. Clark St., Quaker Tower
Chicago, IL 60610
312-222-7111
Pet food and food for people.

Ralston Purina Co.
Checkerboard Sq.
St. Louis, MO 63164
314-982-1000
Pet food and other types of products.

Star-Kist Foods, Inc.
(Subsidiary of H. J. Heinz Co.)
180 E. Ocean Blvd.
Long Beach, CA 90802
213-590-7900
Canned tuna and pet food.

Superior Brands, Inc.
(Subsidiary of Carnation Co.)
122 Quincy Shore Dr.
Quincy, MA 02171
617-770-0880
Various pet products, including cat litter and dog biscuits.

Warner-Lambert Co.
201 Tabor Rd.
Morris Plains, NJ 07950
201-540-2000
Pharmaceuticals, pet care products, and other businesses.

FEDERAL GOVERNMENT

U.S. International Trade Administration
Department of Commerce
14th St. and Constitution Ave., N.W.
Washington, DC 20230
202-377-2000
*Ask for the Commodity Analyst who is an
expert in pets, pet food, or pet products.*

U.S. International Trade Commission
500 E St., S.W.
Washington, DC 20436
202-205-2000 Office of the Secretary
202-205-3296 Industries locator
*Ask for the Trade Analyst who is an expert in
pets, pet food, or pet products.*

PETROCHEMICAL INDUSTRY

*Petrochemicals are chemical substances, such as gasoline and kerosene, manufactured from
petroleum or natural gas.*

See also: CHEMICAL ENGINEERING; CHEMICAL INDUSTRY; GASOLINE INDUSTRY; and PETROLEUM INDUSTRY

ASSOCIATIONS

National Petroleum Refiners Association
1899 L St. N.W., Ste. 1000
Washington, DC 20036
202-457-0480
Urvan Sternfels, President
Petroleum, refining, and petrochemical firms.

Petrochemical Energy Group
1100 15th St. N.W., Ste. 1200
Washington, DC 20005
202-452-1880
Dena Wiggins, Counsel
*Keeps petrochemical companies abreast of
government and business matters of concern
to the industry.*

PERIODICALS

Oil, Gas & Petrochem Equipment
PennWell Publishing Co.
Box 1260
Tulsa, OK 74101
918-835-3161
J.B. Avants, Editor
*Covers the equipment used in all phases of
petroleum, gas, and petrochemical production.*

PetroChemical News
William F. Bland, Co.
Box 16666
Chapel Hill, NC 27516-6666
909-490-0700
Susan Zaro, Editor
*Reports on worldwide news of petrochemical
plants, products, markets, new ventures,
mergers, and related subjects.*

Platt's Petrochemicalscan
McGraw-Hill, Inc.
1221 Ave. of the Americas
New York, NY 10020
Jorge Montepque, Editor
212-512-2563
Surveys the petrochemical industry.

LIBRARIES

Chevron Research & Technology Co.
Technical Information
576 Standard Ave.
Box 1627
Richmond, CA 94802-0627
510-620-4755
510-620-5621 Fax
Petroleum refining, chemistry, petrochemicals, fuels, and lubricants.

Shell Development Co.
Westhollow Research Center Library
3333 Hwy. 6, S.
Box 1378
Houston, TX 77001
713-493-7530
Petroleum refining, petrochemicals, and toxicology.

UOP Research Center
Technical Information Center
50 E. Algonquin Rd.
Des Plaines, IL 60017-5016
708-391-3109
708-391-3330 Fax
Petroleum refining processes, petrochemical processes, patents, catalysis, petroleum refining technology, and related subjects.

COMPANIES

Amerada Hess Corp.
1185 Ave. of the Americas
New York, NY 10036
212-997-8500
Oil, gas, refined petroleum products, and petrochemicals.

H-R International Inc.
(Subsidiary of HRI Holdings, Inc.)
2045 Lincoln Hwy.
Edison, NJ 08817
908-287-2111
Constructs plants for the petrochemical and other industries.

Litwin Engineers & Constructors Inc.
(Subsidiary of United Dominion Industries, Inc.)
1250 W. Sam Houston Pkwy. S.
Houston, TX 77042
713-268-8200
Designs and builds chemical, refinery, and petrochemical facilities.

Lyondell Petrochemical Co.
1221 McKinney St.
Houston, TX 77010
713-652-7200
Petroleum refining and petrochemicals.

Oxy Petrochemical Inc.
(Division of Occidental Chemical Corp.)
Five Greenway Plaza
Houston, TX 77046
713-623-6550
Petrochemicals.

Pro-Quip Corp.
8522 E. 61 St.
Tulsa, OK 74133
918-250-8522
Facilities for processing petrochemicals and natural gas.

Rosemount Varec Division
(Division of Emerson Electric Co.)
10800 Valley View
Cypress, CA 90630
714-761-1300
Petrochemical equipment.

Tenneco Oil Co.
(Subsidiary of Tenneco Corp.)
P. O. Box 2511
Houston, TX 77001
713-757-2131
*Oil, gas, refined petroleum products, and
petrochemicals.*

Texaco Chemical Co.
(Subsidiary of Texaco Inc.)
Box 430
Bellaire, TX 77401
713-666-8000
Petrochemicals.

UOP
(Subsidiary of Allied-Signal Inc. & Union Carbide, Inc.)
25 E. Algonquin Rd.
Des Plaines, IL 60017
708-391-2000
*Processes, catalysts, and chemicals used in
petroleum refining and petrochemicals.*

FEDERAL GOVERNMENT

U.S. International Trade Administration
Department of Commerce
14th St. and Constitution Ave., N.W.
Washington, DC 20230
202-377-2000
*Ask for the Commodity Analyst who is an
expert in the petrochemical industry.*

U.S. International Trade Commission
500 E St., S.W.
Washington, DC 20436
202-205-2000 Office of the Secretary
202-205-3296 Industries locator
*Ask for the Trade Analyst who is an expert in
petrochemical industry.*

PETROLEUM EQUIPMENT INDUSTRY

See also: PETROCHEMICAL INDUSTRY and PETROLEUM INDUSTRY

ASSOCIATIONS

Fiberglass Petroleum Tank and Pipe Institute
1 SeaGate, Ste. 1001
Toledo, OH 43604-1560
419-247-5412
419-247-5421 Fax
Edward Nieshoff, Executive Director
Manufacturers of fiberglass underground tanks and pipes used for petroleum.

Petroleum Equipment Suppliers Associatiom
9225 Katy Fwy., Ste. 310
Houston, TX 77024
713-932-0168
713-932-0497 Fax
J. Stephen Larkin, Executive Vice President
Offers research services and educational programs to firms that make, distribute, and service petroleum equipment.

Pipe Line Contractors Association
1700 Pacific Ave., Ste. 4100
Dallas, TX 75201
214-969-2700
Hailey Roberts, Managing Director
Contractors who lay cross-country pipes and firms that supply the industry.

PERIODICALS

Annual Directory of Pipelines and Equipment
Oildom Publishing Co. of Texas, Inc.
3314 Mercer St.
Houston, TX 77027
713-622-0676
Oliver Klinger, Editor
A listing of oil field equipment sources.

Composite Catalog of Oil Field Equipment & Services
Gulf Publishing Co.
Box 2608
Houston, TX 77252-2608
713-529-4301
Robert Rust, Editor
A directory of services and equipment used in oil exploration and recovery.

Directory of Oil Well Supply Companies
Midwest Register, Inc.
15 W. Sixth St., Ste. 1308
Tulsa, OK 74119-1505
918-582-2000
Lists supplies of petroleum equipment and pipeline.

Oil, Gas & Petrochem Equipment
PennWell Publishing Co.
Box 1260
Tulsa, OK 74101
918-835-3161
J.B. Avants, Editor
Reports on equipment used in all phases of oil and gas exploration, recovery, and refining.

LIBRARIES

Halliburton Services
Research Center Library
Box 1431
Duncan, OK 73536-0400
405-251-3516
405-251-3218 Fax
*Petroleum industry, equipment, engineering,
and chemistry.*

National Institute for Petroleum & Energy
    Research (NIPER)
Library
Box 2128
Bartlesville, OK 74005
918-337-4371
918-337-4365 Fax
*Petroleum technology, natural gas technology,
automotive fuels, and related topics.*

Sperry-Sun Drilling Services
Technical Information Center
3000 N. Sam Houston Pkwy. E.
Box 60070
Houston, TX 77205
713-987-4544
713-987-4015 Fax
*Petroleum, oil drilling, oil field equipment,
engineering, and materials science.*

COMPANIES

Daniel Industries, Inc.
9753 Pine Lake Dr., Box 19097
Houston, TX 77055
713-467-6000
*Equipment for oil and gas fields, and other
types of equipment.*

Glitsch, Inc.
(Subsidiary of Foster Wheeler Corp.)
4900 Singleton Blvd.
Dallas, TX 75212
214-631-3841
*Equipment for petroleum refining and chemi-
cal processing.*

Grace Energy Corp.
(Subsidiary of W. R. Grace & Co.)
13455 Noel Rd.
Dallas, TX 75240
214-770-0200
*Equipment and services for the oil and
petroleum industry and other industries.*

Halliburton Co.
500 N. Akard St.
Dallas, TX 75201
214-978-2600
*Drilling, oil field, and offshore equipment and
supplies.*

Hydril Co.
714 W. Olympic Blvd
Los Angeles, CA 90015
213-749-4180
Oil field equipment.

Baroid Drilling Fluids, Inc.
(Subsidiary of Baroid Corp.)
P. O. Box 1675
Houston, TX 77251
713-987-5900
*Drilling fluids and equipment used in oil and
gas exploration.*

Schlumberger Ltd.
277 Park Ave.
New York, NY 10017
212-350-9400
*Equipment and services for oil drillers and
producers.*

Varlen Corp.
305 E. Schuman Blvd.
Naperville, IL 60566
708-420-0400
Petroleum analysis equipment and other types of products.

Vinson Supply Co.
(Subsidiary of Sammons Enterprises, Inc.)
P.O. Box 1860
Tulsa, OK 74101
918-587-6681
Pipes, valves, and control equipment used in oil fields.

Wilson Industries, Inc.
1301 Conti St.
Houston, TX 77251
713-237-3700
Oil field equipment.

FEDERAL GOVERNMENT

U.S. Customs Service
Department of the Treasury
U.S. Customshouse
6 World Trade Center
New York, NY 10048
212-466-5550
Ask for the Commodity Specialist in charge of petroleum equipment.

U.S. International Trade Administration
Department of Commerce
14th St. and Constitution Ave., N.W.
Washington, DC 20230
202-377-2000
Ask for the Commodity Analyst who is an expert in the petroleum equipment industry.

U.S. International Trade Commission
500 E St., S.W.
Washington, DC 20436
202-205-2000 Office of the Secretary
202-205-3296 Industries locator
Ask for the Trade Analyst who is an expert in the petroleum equipment industry.

U.S. Patent and Trademark Office
Crystal Plaza 2
2011 Jefferson Davis Highway
Arlington, VA 22202
703-305-8000
Ask for the Examining Group Director who is a specialist in petroleum equipment.

PETROLEUM INDUSTRY

See also: FUEL OIL INDUSTRY; GASOLINE INDUSTRY; NATURAL GAS
INDUSTRY; and PETROLEUM EQUIPMENT INDUSTRY

ASSOCIATIONS

American Independent Refiners Association
649 S. Olive St., Ste. 500
Los Angeles, CA 90014
213-624-8407
W. Scott Lovejoy, Executive Director
Represents independent refiners of petroleum.

American Petroleum Institute
1220 L St. N.W.
Washington, DC 20005
202-682-8000
202-682-8030 Fax
Charles DiBona, President
*A large group that represents petroleum pro-
ducers, transporters, refiners, and marketers.
Operates substantial research program for the
public, industry, and government.*

Association of Oil Pipe Lines
1725 K St. N.W., Ste. 1205
Washington, DC 20006
202-331-8228
Patrick Corcoran, Executive Director
Common carriers who own oil pipelines.

Association of Oilwell Servicing Contractors
6060 N. Central Expy., Ste. 428
Dallas, TX 75206
214-692-0771
John Copeland, Executive Vice President
*An educational and safety organization of
firms that service oil wells and supply equipment to the industry.*

Independent Petroleum Association of
America
1101 16th St., N.W.
Washington, DC 20036
202-857-4722
800-433-2812
H. B. Scoggins, President
*Represents small and independent oil opera-
tors, suppliers, and royalty owners.*

International Association of Drilling Contractors
PO Box 4287
Houston, TX 77210
713-578-7171
713-578-0589 Fax
Edwin McGhee, Executive Vice President
*Offers educational and safety programs to oil
well drilling contractors.*

International Association of Geophysical Contractors
PO Box 460209
Houston, TX 77056
713-871-6444
713-871-6447 Fax
Charles Darden, President
*Firms that provide petroleum exploration ser-
vices and others connected with the exploration industry.*

National Petroleum Refiners Association
1899 L St. N.W., Ste. 1000
Washington, DC 20036
202-457-0480
202-467-6330 Fax
Urvan Sternfels, President
Firms that refine petroleum.

Petroleum Marketers Association of America
1120 Vermont Ave. N.W., Ste. 1130
Washington, DC 20005
202-331-1198
Phillip Chisholm, Executive Vice President
*Represents jobbers and wholesalers of
petroleum products.*

PERIODICALS

Hydrocarbon Processing
Gulf Publishing Co.
Box 2608
Houston, TX 77252-2608
713-529-4301
Harold Hoffman, Editor
*Technical and industry news for processors of
petroleum and gas products.*

J P T: Journal of Petroleum Technology
Society of Petroleum Engineers, Inc.
Box 833836
Richardson, TX 75083-3836
214-669-3377
Jim McInnis, Editor
Technical advice for petroleum engineers.

Journal of Petroleum Marketing
B M T Publications, Inc.
7 Penn Plaza
New York, NY 10001-3900
212-594-4120
Greg Pitkoff, Editor
*News and trends for managers of petroleum
marketing.*

Oil & Gas Journal
PennWell Publishing Co.
Box 1260
Tulsa, OK 74101
918-835-3161
Gene Kinney, Editor
*Reports on the exploration, recovery, refining,
and transportation of oil and gas.*

Oil and Gas Investor
Hart Publications, Inc.
1900 Grant St., Ste. 400
Box 1917
Denver, CO 80201
303-837-1917
News and advice for petroleum investors.

Petroleum Management
Management Publishing Services
7887 San Felipe, Ste. 100
Houston, TX 77063
713-789-7887
Thelma Marlowe, Editor
*Covers news, trends, and management tech-
niques to mid- and upper-level executives in
the oil and gas industry.*

Petroleum Taxation & Legislation Report
Barrows Co., Inc.
116 E. 66th St.
New York, NY 10021
212-772-1199
Gordon Barrows, Editor
*Reviews changes in laws and regulations
affecting the oil and gas business worldwide.*

Platt's Oilgram Marketscan. U S Edition
McGraw-Hill, Inc.
1221 Ave. of the Americas
New York, NY 10020
212-512-2563
Joseph Link, Editor
Surveys the U.S. petroleum industry.

World Oil
Gulf Publishing Co.
Box 2608
Houston, TX 77252-2608
713-529-4301
T.R. Wright, Editor
Covers news of the petroleum industry worldwide.

LIBRARIES

Atlantic-Richfield Co.
Information Resource Center
515 S. Flower St.
Box 2679, Terminal Annex
Los Angeles, CA 90051
312-486-2400
213-486-1472 Fax
Petroleum, petroleum refining, and management.

Sun Refining & Marketing Co.
Library and Information Center
Box 1135
Marcus Hook, PA 19061
215-447-1723
215-447-1645 Fax
Petroleum refining, engineering, and chemistry.

U.S. Department of Energy
Energy Information Administration
National Energy Information Center
Forrestal Bldg., Rm. 1F-048
Washington, DC 20585
202-586-8800
Petroleum, synthetic fuels, natural gas, energy statistics, and related topics.

COMPANIES

Ashland Oil, Inc.
P.O. Box 391
Ashland, KY 41114
606-329-3333
Oil and gas exploring, refining, and marketing, and other businesses.

Exxon Corp.
225 E. John W. Carpenter Freeway
Irving, TX 75062
214-444-1000
Oil and gas exploring, refining, and marketing, and other businesses.

Mobil Oil Corp.
(Subsidiary of Mobil Corp.)
3225 Gallows Rd.
Fairfax, VA 22037
703-846-3000
Oil and gas exploring, refining, and marketing, and other businesses.

Occidental Petroleum Corp.
10889 Wilshire Blvd.
Los Angeles, CA 90024
213-879-1700
Oil and gas exploring, refining, and marketing, and other businesses.

Phibro Energy, Inc.
(Subsidiary of Salomon Inc.)
600 Steamboat Rd.
Greenwich, CT 06830
203-661-4770
Refining and marketing of crude oil and other products.

Phillips Petroleum Co.
6A1 Phillips Bldg.
Bartlesville, OK 74004
918-661-4710
Oil and gas exploring, refining, and marketing, and other businesses.

Royal Dutch/Shell Group
30 Rockefeller Plaza
New York, NY 10112
212-632-4800
*Oil and gas exploring, refining, and market-
ing, and other businesses.*

Shell Oil Co.
(Subsidiary of Shell Petroleum Inc.)
One Shell Plaza
Houston, TX 77001
713-241-6161
*Oil and gas exploring, refining, and market-
ing, and other businesses.*

Tenneco Oil Co.
(Subsidiary of Tenneco Corp.)
P. O. Box 2511
Houston, TX 77001
713-757-2131
*Oil and gas exploring, refining, and market-
ing, and other businesses.*

Texaco Inc.
2000 Westchester Ave.
White Plains, NY 10650
914-253-4000
*Oil and gas exploring, refining, and market-
ing, and other businesses.*

FEDERAL GOVERNMENT

U.S. Department of Energy
1000 Independence Ave., S.W.
Washington, DC 20585
202-586-5000
*Ask for the petroleum industry analyst in the
Economic Regulatory Administration; or for
the Strategic Petroleum Reserve.*

U.S. International Trade Administration
Department of Commerce
14th St. and Constitution Ave., N.W.
Washington, DC 20230
202-377-2000
*Ask for the Commodity Analyst who is an
expert in the petroleum industry.*

U.S. International Trade Commission
500 E St., S.W.
Washington, DC 20436
202-205-2000 Office of the Secretary
202-205-3296 Industries locator
*Ask for the Trade Analyst who is an expert in
the petroleum industry.*

U.S. Patent and Trademark Office
Crystal Plaza 2
2011 Jefferson Davis Highway
Arlington, VA 22202
703-305-8000
*Ask for the Examining Group Director who is
a specialist in petroleum chemistry.*

PHARMACEUTICAL INDUSTRY

See also: DRUG STORES

ASSOCIATIONS

Council on Family Health
225 Park Ave. S., 17th Fl.
New York, NY 10003
212-598-3617
William Bergman, President
Sponsored by drug manufacturers, this group offers consumer education on the proper use of pharmaceuticals.

Generic Pharmaceutical Industry Association
200 Madison Ave., Ste. 2404
New York, NY 10016
212-683-1881
212-213-2105 Fax
Dee Fensterer, President
Promotes the use of generic prescription drugs.

National Association of Pharmaceutical Manufacturers
747 3rd Ave.
New York, NY 10017
212-838-3720
212-753-6832 Fax
Robert Milanese, President
Studies laws and regulations for the pharmaceutical industry.

Nonprescription Drug Manufacturers Association
1150 Connecticut Ave., N.W.
Washington, DC 20036
202-429-9260
202-223-6835 Fax
James Cope, President
Provides business and regulatory information to manufacturers of nonprescription drugs and their supplies.

Pharmaceutical Manufacturers Association
1100 15th St. N.W.
Washington, DC 20005
202-835-3400
Gerald Mossinghoff, President
Members include most of the pharmaceutical manufacturers in the U.S. who sell drugs under their own label. Keeps members informed about regulatory and other subjects.

PERIODICALS

Biopharm
Aster Publishing Corp.
859 Willamette St.
Box 10955
Eugene, OR 97440
503-343-1200
M. Jane Ganter, Editor
Information for scientists and executives reponsible for large-scale manufacturing of recently developed pharmaceuticals.

The Blue Sheet
F-D-C Reports, Inc.
5550 Friendship Blvd.
Chevy Chase, MD 20815-7278
Cole Werble, Editor
301-657-9830
Covers government policies regarding biomedical research and pharmaceuticals.

Clinical Pharmacology & Therapeutics
11830 Westline Industrial Dr.
St. Louis, MO 63146
800-325-4117
Marcus Reidenberg, Editor
A technical journal for pharmaceutical researchers.

Food and Drug Packaging
Edgell Communications
7500 Old Oak Blvd.
Cleveland, OH 44130
216-826-2839
Sophia Dilberakis, Editor
Covers packaging trends, products, and legislation for the pharmaceutical, food, and cosmetics industries.

Journal of Pharmaceutical Marketing and
    Management
Haworth Press, Inc.
10 Alice St.
Binghamton, NY 13904
800-342-9678
Mickey Smith, Editor
Advice for managers and marketers in the drug industry.

Medical Advertising News
Engel Communications, Inc.
820 Bear Tavern Rd.
Mountainview Corp. Park
W. Trenton, NJ 08628
609-530-0044
Styli Engel, Editor
Focuses on the advertising and marketing of medical products and drugs.

Medical Letter on Drugs and Therapeutics
Medical Letter, Inc.
1000 Main St.
New Rochelle, NY 10801
914-235-0500
Mark Abramowicz, Editor
Evaluations of pharmaceuticals for physicians.

Pharmaceutical Engineering
International Society of Pharmaceutical Engineers, Inc.
3816 W. Linebaugh Ave., Ste. 412
Tampa, FL 33624-4702
813-960-2105
Pamela Jones, Editor
Technical information and advice for researchers and manufacturers of pharmaceuticals.

Pharmaceutical Executive
Aster Publishing Corp.
859 Willamette St.
Eugene, OR 97440
503-343-1200
Wayne Koberstein, Editor
Covers marketing, management, sales, and regulatory issues for executives at pharmaceutical firms.

Pharmaceutical Representative
McKnight Medical Communications Co.
1419 Lake Cook Rd.
Deerfield, IL 60015
708-945-0345
Suzanne Powills, Editor
Sales and marketing advice for representatives of pharmaceutical companies.

Pharmaceutical Technology
Aster Publishing Corp.
859 Willamette St.
Box 10955
Eugene, OR 97440
503-343-1200
Stefan Schuber, Editor
How-to information about the manufacture of pharmaceuticals.

The Pink Sheet
F-D-C Reports, Inc.
5550 Friendship Blvd.
Chevy Chase, MD 20815-7278
Cole Werble, Editor
301-657-9830
Survey news about pharmaceutical research, tests, manufacturing, marketing, and regulatory matters.

LIBRARIES

Merck & Co., Inc.
Merck Sharp & Dohme Research Laboratories
Literature Resources, Rahway
R86-240
Box 2000
Rahway, NJ 07065
908-594-6754
908-594-6059 Fax
Pharmacology, biomedical sciences, biochemistry, science, and chemistry.

Pfizer, Inc.
Central Research
Research Library
Eastern Point Rd.
Groton, CT 06340
203-441-3687
203-441-4998 Fax
Pharmaceutical chemistry, pharmacology, organic chemistry, and antibiotics.

Schering-Plough Corp.
Library Information Center
60 Orange St.
Bloomfield, NJ 07003
201-429-3737
201-429-3706 Fax
Pharmacy, organic chemistry, biomedicine, and microbiology.

COMPANIES

Bristol-Myers Squibb Co.
345 Park Ave.
New York, NY 10154
212-546-4000
Pharmaceuticals, household and personal care products, and other businesses.

Marion Merrell Dow Inc.
(Subsidiary of Dow Chemical Co.)
P.O. Box 8480
Kansas City, MO 64114
816-966-4000
Pharmaceuticals and consumer health products.

Merck & Co., Inc.
P.O. Box 2000
Rahway, NJ 07065
908-594-4000
Pharmaceuticals, biologicals, and animal health products.

Miles Inc.
(Subsidiary of Bayer USA Inc.)
1127 Myrtle St.
Elkhart, IN 46515
219-264-8111
Pharmaceuticals, dermatologicals, and related products.

Pfizer Inc.
235 E. 42nd St.
New York, NY 10017
212-573-2323
Pharmaceuticals, toiletries, and other consumer products.

Schering-Plough Corp.
One Giralda Farms
Madison, NJ 07940
201-822-7000
Pharmaceuticals and other health care products.

SmithKline Beecham Corp.
(Subsidiary of SmithKline Beecham p.l.c.)
One Franklin Plaza
Philadelphia, PA 19101
215-751-4000
Pharmaceutical and animal health care products.

Sterling Drug Co.
(Subsidiary of Eastman Kodak Co.)
90 Park Ave.
New York, NY 10016
212-907-2000
Pharmaceuticals and consumer health products.

Upjohn Co.
7000 Portage Rd.
Kalamazoo, MI 49001
616-323-4000
Pharmaceuticals, chemicals, and agricultural products.

Warner-Lambert Co.
201 Tabor Rd.
Morris Plains, NJ 07950
201-540-2000
Pharmaceuticals and other types of products.

FEDERAL GOVERNMENT

U.S. Department of Health and Human Services
200 Independence Ave., S.W.
Washington, DC 20201
202-619-0257
Ask for the Pharmacological Sciences division in the National Institute of General Medical Sciences.

U.S. Food and Drug Administration
5600 Fishers Lane
Rockville, MD 20857
301-295-8012
Ask for the Center for Drug Evaluation & Research or the Over-the-Counter Compliance Branch.

U.S. International Trade Administration
Department of Commerce
14th St. and Constitution Ave., N.W.
Washington, DC 20230
202-377-2000
Ask for the Commodity Analyst who is an expert in the pharmaceutical industry.

U.S. International Trade Commission
500 E St., S.W.
Washington, DC 20436
202-205-2000 Office of the Secretary
202-205-3296 Industries locator
Ask for the Trade Analyst who is an expert in the pharmaceutical industry.

U.S. Patent and Trademark Office
Crystal Plaza 2
2011 Jefferson Davis Highway
Arlington, VA 22202
703-305-8000
Ask for the Examining Group Director who is a specialist in pharmaceuticals.

PHOTOGRAPHIC INDUSTRY

ASSOCIATIONS

Advertising Photographers of America
27 W. 20th St.
New York, NY 10011
212-807-0399
212-727-8120 Fax
J. Barry O'Rourke, President
A small group of advertising photographers who share information.

American Society of Magazine Photographers
419 Park Ave. S., No. 1407
New York, NY 10016
212-889-9144
212-779-9446 Fax
Richard Weisgrau, Executive Director
A professional group of freelance photographers who offer their services to magazines and other media.

Association of Professional Color Laboratories
3000 Picture Pl.
Jackson, MI 49201
517-788-8146
Roy Pung, Executive Director
Laboratories that develop and print color film for professional use.

International Minilab Association
2627 Grimsley St.
Greensboro, NC 27403
919-854-8088
919-854-8566 Fax
Roger McManus, Executive Director
Offers educational, marketing, and technical services to owners and operators of photographic minilabs and to industry suppliers.

National Association of Photographic Manufacturers
550 Mamaroneck Ave.
Harrison, NY 10528
914-698-7603
914-698-7609 Fax
Thomas Dufficy, Executive Vice President
Firms that make photographic equipment and supplies.

National Free Lance Photographers Association
Box 406
Solebury, PA 18963
H. Jeffrey Valentine, President
A large group of professional and amateur photographers.

National Press Photographers Association
3200 Croasdaile Dr., Ste. 306
Durham, NC 27705
919-383-7246
919-383-7261 Fax
Charles Cooper, Executive Director
Offers educational programs to professional photographers who work for newspapers and other segments of the press.

Photo Marketing Association International
3000 Picture Pl.
Jackson, MI 49201
517-788-8100
517-788-8371 Fax
Roy Pung, Executive Director
Offers research to retailers of photographic and video equipment and supplies.

Photographic Manufacturers and Distributors
  Association
866 United Nations Plaza
New York, NY 10017
212-688-3520
Norman Lipton, Executive Manager
*A small group of firms that manufacture and
distribute photographic equipment.*

Professional Photographers of America
1090 Executive Way
Des Plaines, IL 60018
708-299-8161
708-299-2685 Fax
Philip Kummerer, Executive Director
*A large group of professional photographers
who do wedding, industrial, portrait, and
other types of photography.*

PERIODICALS

Darkroom & Creative Camera Techniques
Preston Publications, Inc.
7800 N. Merrimac Ave.
Niles, IL 60648
708-965-0566
David Jay, Editor
*Focuses on darkroom techniques and equip-
ment for knowledgeable amateur and professional photographers.*

Mini Lab Focus
Photo Marketing Association International
3000 Picture Pl.
Jackson, MI 49201
517-788-8100
Gary Pageau, Editor
*Covers trends and new products for owners
and operators of photographic minilabs.*

Photo Business
Billboard Publications, Inc.
1515 Broadway, 39th Fl.
New York, NY 10036
212-764-7300
Willard Clark, Editor
*Surveys the photographic industry and new
products for professional photographers.*

Photo Lab Management
P L M Publishing
1312 Lincoln Blvd.
Box 1700
Santa Monica, CA 90406
213-451-1344
Carolyn Ryan, Editor
*Management advice for those in charge of
photographic labs.*

Popular Photography
Hachette Magazines, Inc.
1633 Broadway
New York, NY 10009
212-767-6000
Jason Schneider, Editor
*A widely read comsumer magazine for ama-
teur and professional photographers.*

Wedding Photographer
Wedding Photographers International
Rangefinder Publishing
1312 Lincoln Blvd.
Santa Monica, CA 90406
213-451-0090
Sandi Messana, Editor
*Management and how-to information for pro-
fessional wedding photographers.*

LIBRARIES

Eastman Kodak Co.
Building 69 Library
B69, Fl. 1, Kodak
Rochester, NY 14650-1917
716-722-2356
716-477-8161 Fax
Photography, electronic imagery, and chemical engineering.

Eastman Kodak Co.
Business Information Center
343 State St.
Rochester, NY 14650
716-724-3041
716-724-0663 Fax
Photography.

COMPANIES

CPI Corp.
1706 Washington
St. Louis, MO 63103
314-231-1575
Operator of one-hour photo finishing minilabs and also photographic studios located in department stores.

Eastman Kodak Co.
343 State St.
Rochester, NY 14650
716-724-4000
A wide range of photographic equipment and supplies.

General Chemical Corp.
(Subsidiary of New Hampshire Oak Inc.)
90 E. Halsey Rd.
Parsippany, NJ 07054
908-515-0900
Photographic chemicals and other types of chemicals.

C. R. Gibson Co.
32 Knight St.
Norwalk, CT 06856
203-847-4543
Photograph albums and other products.

Hasco International, Inc.
3613 Mueller Rd.
St. Charles, MO 63301
314-946-5115
Portrait and infant photography.

Image Bank Inc.
111 Fifth Ave.
New York, NY 10003
212-529-3080
Represents photographers whose pictures are available for reproduction in magazines and for many other purposes.

Nikon Inc.
(Subsidiary of Nikon Corp.)
623 Stewart Ave.
Garden City, NY 11530
516-222-0200
Photographic and optical equipment.

PCA International, Inc.
815 Matthews-Mint Hill Rd.
Matthews, NC 28105
704-847-8011
Photographic portrait services.

Polaroid Corp.
549 Technology Sq.
Cambridge, MA 02139
617-577-2000
Cameras, film, and accessories.

Traditional Industries, Inc.
5155 N. Clareton Dr.
Agoura Hills, CA 91301
818-991-2773
Distributor of photography equipment and supplies.

Vivitar Corp.
(Subsidiary of Hanimex Corp.)
9350 DeSoto Ave.
Chatsworth, CA 91313
818-700-2890
Cameras, lenses, and other types of photographic equipment.

FEDERAL GOVERNMENT

U.S. Customs Service
Department of the Treasury
U.S. Customshouse
6 World Trade Center
New York, NY 10048
212-466-5550
Ask for the Commodity Specialist in charge of photographic equipment and products.

U.S. International Trade Administration
Department of Commerce
14th St. and Constitution Ave., N.W.
Washington, DC 20230
202-377-2000
Ask for the Commodity Analyst who is an expert in photographic chemicals, film, equipment, or supplies.

U.S. International Trade Commission
500 E St., S.W.
Washington, DC 20436
202-205-2000 Office of the Secretary
202-205-3296 Industries locator
Ask for the Trade Analyst who is an expert in photographic chemicals, film, equipment, or supplies.

U.S. Patent and Trademark Office
Crystal Plaza 2
2011 Jefferson Davis Highway
Arlington, VA 22202
703-305-8000
Ask for the Examining Group Director who is a specialist in photographic equipment and products.

PIPE AND PIPE FITTINGS INDUSTRY

See also: PLUMBING INDUSTRY and VALVE INDUSTRY

ASSOCIATIONS

American Concrete Pipe Association
8300 Boone Blvd., Ste. 400
Vienna, VA 22182
703-821-1990
703-821-3054 Fax
Richard Barnes, President
Supplies engineering and business information to manufacturers of concrete pipe.

American Pipe Fittings Association
6203 Old Keene Mill Ct.
Springfield, VA 22152
703-644-0001
Paul Engle, Executive Director
Firms that make a variety of iron, brass, steel, and plastic pipe fittings, flanges, and other products.

Ductile Iron Pipe Research Association
245 Riverchase Pkwy. E.
Birmingham, AL 35244
205-988-9870
Troy Stroud, President
Manufacturers of ductile iron pipe and fittings for use in sewage, water utilities, and other settings.

National Association of Steel Pipe Distributors
1726 Augusta, Ste. 102
Houston, TX 77057
713-781-6405
713-781-1802 Fax
Ann Muffeny, Executive Director
Firms that distribute steel tubing and pipe.

National Clay Pipe Institute
PO Box 759
Lake Geneva, WI 53147
414-248-9094
E. J. Sikora, Vice President
Manufacturers of clay pipe and related products for use in sewer systems.

National Corrugated Steel Pipe Association
2011 I St. N.W.
Washington, DC 20006
202-223-2217
202-457-9121 Fax
Venlo Wolfsohn, Executive Director
Manufacturers of corrugated steel pipes used primarily for drainage.

Pipe Fabrication Institute
PO Box 173
Springdale, PA 15144
412-274-4722
Lois Moore, Executive Director
Manufacturers of pipes that can withstand high pressures and temperatures and are generally used in refineries and chemical plants.

Plastic Pipe and Fittings Association
Bldg. C, Ste. 20
800 Roosevelt Rd.
Glen Ellyn, IL 60137
708-858-6540
708- 858-654 Fax
Richard Church, Executive Director
Offers technical and industry information to manufacturers of plastic pipes, fittings, and suppliers of raw materials.

Plastics Pipe Institute
Wayne Interchange Plaza II
155 Rt. 46 W.
Wayne, NJ 07470
201-812-9076
Stanley Mruk, Executive Director
Provides technical information to plastic pipe manufacturers.

Tube and Pipe Fabricators Association, International
5411 E. State St.
Rockford, IL 61108
815-399-8700
800-338-5646
815-399-7279 Fax
John Nandzik, Executive Director
Offers a forum for individuals and firms in the pipe industry to exchange information.

PERIODICALS

Concrete Producers News
Edgell Communications
7500 Old Oak Blvd.
Cleveland, OH 44130
216-826-2839
Patrick Hernan, Editor
News for producers of various concrete products, including concrete pipe.

T P Q: The Tube & Pipe Quarterly
Croydon Group, Ltd.
5411 E. State St.
Rockford, IL 61108-2378
815-399-8700
Kathy Velasco, Editor
A wide range of industry and technical information for managers and engineers responsible for the manufacture of tubing and piping.

LIBRARIES

National Corrugated Steel Pipe Association
Library
2011 Eye St., N.W., 5th Fl.
Washington, DC 20006
202-223-2217
202-457-9121 Fax
Corrugated steel drainage pipes and pipe materials.

Uni-Bell PVC Pipe Association
Library
2655 Villa Creek, Ste. 155
Dallas, TX 75234
214-243-3902
214-243-3907 Fax
Pipe and design.

COMPANIES

Amcast Industrial Corp.
3931 S. Dixie Avenue
Kettering, OH 45439
513-298-5251
Brass, bronze, and iron pipe fittings, and other metal products.

Ameron, Inc.
4700 Ramona Blvd.
Monterey Park, CA 91754
213-268-4111
Concrete and steel pipe, reinforced pipe, and other products.

Duriron Co. Inc.
425 N. Findlay St.
Dayton, OH 45404
513-226-4000
Pipes, fittings, valves, and related products.

Geneva Steel
10 S. Geneva Rd.
Vineyard, UT 84058
801-227-9000
Steel pipe and other steel products.

Harsco Corp.
P.O. Box 8888
Camp Hill, PA 17011
717-763-7064
Plastic pipe, pipe fittings, and other products.

Maremont Exhaust Products, Inc.
250 E. Kehoe Blvd.
Carol Stream, IL 60188
708-462-8500
Exhaust and tail pipes, mufflers, and related products.

McJunkin Corp.
835 Hillcrest Dr.
Charleston, WV 25311
304-348-5211
Stainless steel pipes, fittings, valves, and other products.

McWane Inc.
23 Inverness City Pkwy.
Birmingham, AL 35243
305-991-9888
Cast and ductile iron pressure pipe and fittings.

U. S. Pipe & Foundry Co.
(Subsidiary of Walter Industries, Inc.)
3300 First Ave., N.
Birmingham, AL 35202
205-254-7000
Cast and ductile iron pressure pipes, fittings, valves, and other products.

Vinson Supply Co.
(Subsidiary of Sammons Enterprises, Inc.)
P.O. Box 1860
Tulsa, OK 74101
918-587-6681
Pipes, fittings, and valves designed for oil fields and refineries.

FEDERAL GOVERNMENT

U.S. International Trade Administration
Department of Commerce
14th St. and Constitution Ave., N.W.
Washington, DC 20230
202-377-2000
Ask for the Commodity Analyst who is an expert in fittings or pipes: specify rubber, plastic, or steel.

U.S. International Trade Commission
500 E St., S.W.
Washington, DC 20436
202-205-2000 Office of the Secretary
202-205-3296 Industries locator
Ask for the Trade Analyst who is an expert in fittings or pipes.

U.S. Patent and Trademark Office
Crystal Plaza 2
2011 Jefferson Davis Highway
Arlington, VA 22202
703-305-8000
Ask for the Examining Group Director who is a specialist in fittings or pipes.

PIPELINE INDUSTRY

See also: NATURAL GAS INDUSTRY and PETROLEUM INDUSTRY

ASSOCIATIONS

Association of Oil Pipe Lines
1725 K St. N.W., Ste. 1205
Washington, DC 20006
202-331-8228
Patrick Corcoran, Executive Director
Members are oil pipeline firms, primarily common carriers.

Pipe Line Contractors Association
1700 Pacific Ave., Ste. 4100
Dallas, TX 75201
214-969-2700
Hailey Roberts, Managing Director
Firms that contract to lay cross-country pipelines.

PERIODICALS

Huttlinger's Pipeline Report
Huttlinger's Energy News
Box 409
Poolesville, MD 20837
301-972-8100
Stan Janet, Editor
Follows the pipline industry.

Oil & Gas Journal
PennWell Publishing Co.
Box 1260
Tulsa, OK 74101
918-835-3161
Gene Kinney, Editor
Surveys the petroleum industry and includes news about the transportation of oil and gas through pipelines.

Pipe Line Industry
Gulf Publishing Co.
Box 2608
Houston, TX 77252-2608
713-529-4301
William Quarles, Editor
Covers the transportation of oil and gas through pipelines.

Pipeline & Gas Journal
Edgell Communications
7500 Old Oak Blvd.
Cleveland, OH 44130
216-243-8100
Jim Watts, Editor
Reports on the construction and operation of oil and gas pipelines.

LIBRARIES

Federal Energy Regulatory Commission
Library
825 N. Capitol St., N.E., Rm. 8502
Washington, DC 20426
202-208-0200
Oil pipelines, utility regulation, and electric power.

Mobil Pipe Line Co.
Engineering Library
Box 900
Dallas, TX 75221
214-658-2039
214-658-2241 Fax
Pipeline construction, transportation, and related topics.

U.S. Bureau of Land Management
Alaska State Office
Alaska Resources Library
222 W. 7th
No. 36
Anchorage, AK 99513
907-271-5025
Alaska pipeline, pollution, engineering, and land management.

Williams Brothers Engineering Co.
Technical Information Center
P.O. Box 21310
Tulsa, OK 74121-1310
918-561-9575
918-561-9510 Fax
Pipeline engineering, environmental engineering, petroleum industry, and related topics.

COMPANIES

Arco Pipe Line Co.
(Subsidiary of Atlantic Richfield Co.)
Arco Bldg.
Independence, KS 67301
316-331-1300
Oil transportation by pipeline.

Algonquin Gas Transmission Co.
(Subsidiary of Panhandle Eastern Corp.)
1284 Soldiers Field Rd.
Boston, MA 02135
617-254-4050
Operates piplines for gas transmission.

Exxon Pipeline Co.
(Subsidiary of Exxon Corp.)
Exxon Bldg., Box 2220
Houston, TX 77252
713-656-3636
Common carrier pipeline.

Henkels & McCoy, Inc.
985 Jolly Rd.
Blue Bell, PA 19422
215-283-7600
Engineering and construction of oil pipelines and other major projects.

Lakehead Pipe Line Co., Inc.
(Subsidiary of Interprovincial Pipe Line Inc.)
119 N. 25th St.
Superior, WI 54880
715-394-1400
Oil transportation by pipeline.

McDermott Inc.
(Subsidiary of McDermott International Inc.)
1010 Common St.
New Orleans, LA 70112
504-587-4411
Engineering and construction of pipelines and other major projects.

Sohio Pipe Line Co.
(Subsidiary of BP America Inc.)
P.O. Box 6098
Cleveland, OH 44101
216-586-4141
Oil transportation by pipeline.

Texas Gas Transmission Corp.
(Subsidiary of Transco Energy Co.)
3800 Frederica St.
Owensboro, KY 42301
502-926-8686
Operates an interstate pipeline system for the transmission of natural gas.

Williams Companies
P.O. Box 2400
Tulsa, OK 74102
918-588-2000
Common carrier pipeline systems.

H.B. Zachry Co.
P. O. Box 21130
San Antonio, TX 78285
512-922-1213
Construction of pipelines and other major projects.

FEDERAL GOVERNMENT

U.S. Department of Energy
1000 Independence Ave., S.W.
Washington, DC 20585
202-586-5000
Ask for the Pipeline Certificates department; or for the Gas Pipeline Rates department in the Federal Energy Regulatory Commission.

U.S. Department of Transportation
400 Seventh St., S.W.
Washington, DC 20590
202-366-4000
Ask for the Pipeline Safety Office in the Research and Special Programs Administration.

PLASTER AND PLASTERING INDUSTRY

See also: BUILDING MATERIALS INDUSTRY

ASSOCIATIONS

Association of the Wall and Ceiling Industries
1600 Cameron St., Ste. 200
Alexandria, VA 22314
703-684-2924
Joe Baker, Executive Vice President
Firms in the plastering, lathing, drywall, insulation, and related industries.

International Institute for Lath and Plaster
795 Raymond Ave.
St. Paul, MN 55114
612-645-0208
612-645-0208 Fax
Clint Fladland, Executive Director
Members include lathing and plastering contractors, and manufacturers of supplies.

PERIODICALS

Walls & Ceilings
I S I Publications
8602 N. 40th St.
Tampa, FL 33604
Lee Rector, Editor
Written for suppliers and contractors involved with plaster, drywall, and other products for walls and ceilings.

COMPANIES

Allied Construction Services, Inc.
2122 Fleur Dr.
Des Moines, IA 50304
515-288-4855
Interior construction services.

Cleveland Builders Supply Inc.
(Subsidiary of LaFarge Corp.)
2100 W. Third St.
Cleveland, OH 44113
216-621-4300
Brick, cement, plaster, and other building supplies.

Duncan Enterprises
5673 Shields Ave., E.
Fresno, CA 93727
209-291-4444
Plaster molds and other products.

John H. Hampshire, Inc.
(Subsidiary of Hampshire Industries, Inc.)
320 W. 24th St.
Baltimore, MD 21211
301-366-8900
Plastering and other construction work.

Hoge-Warren-Zimmerman Co.
1701 Mills Ave.
Cincinnati, OH 45212
513-631-8900
Plaster mixing equipment and other products.

Industrial Welding, Inc.
2200 Olds Ave., Box 20067
Lansing, MI 48901
517-372-0950
Heavy machinery for making molded plaster products and other purposes.

National Gypsum Co.
(Subsidiary of Aancor Holdings, Inc.)
4500 Lincoln Plaza
Dallas, TX 75201
214-740-4500
Gypsum wallboards, plasters, and many other building materials.

Stone Construction Equipment, Inc.
32 E. Main St.
Honeoye, NY 14471
716-229-5141
Equipment used to mix concrete, mortar, and plaster.

FEDERAL GOVERNMENT

U.S. International Trade Administration
Department of Commerce
14th St. and Constitution Ave., N.W.
Washington, DC 20230
202-377-2000
Ask for the Commodity Analyst who is an expert in plaster and plastering.

U.S. International Trade Commission
500 E St., S.W.
Washington, DC 20436
202-205-2000 Office of the Secretary
202-205-3296 Industries locator
Ask for the Trade Analyst who is an expert in plaster and plastering.

PLASTICS INDUSTRY

ASSOCIATIONS

Association of Rotational Molders
435 N. Michigan Ave., Ste. 1717
Chicago, IL 60611-4067
312-644-0828
Charles Fredrick, Executive Director
Firms that make plastics using the rotational molding process.

Decorative Laminate Products Association
600 S. Federal St., Ste. 400
Chicago, IL 60605
312-922-6222
Barbara Boden, Executive Director
Firms that make all types of products with plastic laminates.

National Association of Plastics Distributors
6333 Long St., Ste. 340
Shawnee, KS 66216
913-268-6273
913-268-6388 Fax
Carol Wagner, Executive Director
Distributors of plastic resins, materials, and other plastic products.

Plastics Institute of America
Stevens Institute of Technology
Castle Point Sta.
Hoboken, NJ 07030
201-420-5553
201-420-1606 Fax
William Sacks, Executive Director
Conducts scientific research for plastics manufacturers.

Society of Plastics Engineers
14 Fairfield Dr.
Brookfield, CT 06804-0403
203-775-0471
203-775-8490 Fax
Robert Forger, Executive Director
A professional group of engineers and scientists working in the plastics field.

Society of the Plastics Industry
1275 K St., N.W., Ste. 400
Washington, DC 20005
202-371-5200
202-371-1022 Fax
Larry Thomas, President
An information clearinghouse for firms that fabricate, mold, and otherwise manufacture plastics.

PERIODICALS

Advances in Polymer Technology
John Wiley & Sons, Inc.
605 Third Ave.
New York, NY 10158-0012
212-850-6000
James Throne, Editor
Covers new technologies, products, processes, and materials in the plastics industry.

Journal of Elastomers and Plastics
Technomic Publishing Co. Inc.
851 New Holland Ave.
Lancaster, PA 17604
717-291-5609
Melvyn Kohudic, Editor
Technical information about the use of elastomers in plastics.

Journal of Reinforced Plastics & Composites
Technomic Publishing Co., Inc.
851 New Holland Ave.
Lancaster, PA 17604
717-291-5609
George Springer, Editor
Technical information about advances in reinforced plastics and composites.

Journal of Thermoplastic Composite Materials
Technomic Publishing Co., Inc.
851 New Holland Ave.
Lancaster, PA 17604
717-291-5609
Selcuk Guceri, Editor
Technical information about thermoplastic composites.

Modern Plastics
McGraw-Hill, Inc.
1221 Ave. of the Americas
New York, NY 10020
212-512-6267
Robert Martino, Editor
Covers the entire plastics industry, including techological and manufacturing advances, new designs, and new markets.

Plastics Business News
Washington Business Information, Inc.
1117 N. 19th St., Ste. 200
Arlington, VA 22209
703-247-3422
Elaine Zablocki, Editor
Covers news of companies, products, production techniques, markets, and distribution of plastics.

Plastics Compounding
Edgell Communications
7500 Old Oak Blvd.
Cleveland, OH 44130
216-243-8100
Mary McMurrer, Editor
How-to information for plastics compounders, formulators, and resin producers.

Plastics Design Forum
Edgell Communications
7500 Old Oak Blvd.
Cleveland, OH 44130
216-243-8100
Mel Friedman, Editor
News for designers of plastic products and plastic components.

Plastics Machinery and Equipment
machinery and equipment
Edgell Communications
7500 Old Oak Blvd.
Cleveland, OH 44130
216-243-8100
Merle Snyder, Editor
Covers new products for executives who choose and purchase plastics machinery.

Plastics News
Crain Communications Inc.
1725 Merriman Rd.
Akron, OH 44313-3185
216-836-9180
Robert Grace, Editor
Surveys company news, advances in technology, and new products.

Plastics Technology
Bill Communications, Inc.
633 Third Ave.
New York, NY 10017
212-986-4800
Matthew Naitove, Editor
Covers the machinery and materials that improve productivity in the plastics industry.

Plastics World
Cahners Publishing Co.
275 Washington St.
Newton, MA 02158-1630
617-964-3030
Douglas Smock, Editor
Written for buyers of plastics-making equipment and raw materials.

LIBRARIES

Dow Chemical U.S.A.
Business Information Center
2020 Willard H. Dow Center
Midland, MI 48674
517-636-3779
517-636-8135 Fax
Plastics business intelligence and marketing research.

E.I. Du Pont de Nemours & Co., Inc.
Technical Library Network
P.O. Box 80014
Wilmington, DE 19880-0014
302-992-2666
302-992-6758 Fax
Plastics, polymers, fibers, and chemistry.

General Electric Co.
G.E. Plastics
Information Resource Center
One Plastics Ave.
Pittsfield, MA 01201
413-448-7345
413-448-7625 Fax
Plastics technology, plastics marketing, and organic chemistry.

COMPANIES

Atlantis Group, Inc.
2665 S. Bayshore Dr.
Miami, FL 33133
305-858-2200
Plastic films and molded products.

Chelsea Industries, Inc.
1360 Soldiers Field Rd.
Boston, MA 02135
617-787-9010
Plastic films and extruded products.

Dow Chemical Co.
2030 Willard H. Dow Ctr.
Midland, MI 48674
517-636-1000
Plastics, chemicals, and other products.

E. I. Du Pont de Nemours & Co.
1007 Market St.
Wilmington, DE 19898
302-774-1000
Diversified petroleum, chemical, and plastics products.

B.F. Goodrich Co.
3925 Embassy Pkwy.
Akron, OH 44333
216-374-2000
Plastics, chemicals, and other products.

Hoechst Celanese Corp.
(Subsidiary of Hoechst AG)
Rte. 202-206
Somerville, NJ 08876
908-231-2000
Chemicals, fibers, plastics, polyvinyl chloride, and other products.

Lacks Industries
5460 Cascade S.E.
Grand Rapids, MI 49506
616-949-6570
Plastic injection molding.

Occidental Chemical Corp.
(Subsidiary of Occidental Petroleum Corp.)
5005 LBJ Frwy.
Dallas, TX 75244
214-404-3800
Chemicals and plastics.

Rohm and Haas Co.
Independence Mall W.
Philadelphia, PA 19105
215-592-3000
Chemicals and plastics.

A. Schulman, Inc.
3550 W. Market St.
Akron, OH 44313
216-666-3751
Plastic compounds and resins.

Tuscarora Plastics, Inc.
737 Fifth Ave.
New Brighton, PA 15066
412-843-8200
Molded foam plastic products.

Union Carbide Corp.
39 Old Ridgebury Rd.
Danbury, CT 06817
203-794-2000
Chemicals, plastics, and carbon products.

FEDERAL GOVERNMENT

U.S. Customs Service
Department of the Treasury
U.S. Customshouse
6 World Trade Center
New York, NY 10048
212-466-5550
Ask for the Commodity Specialist in charge of plastics.

U.S. International Trade Administration
Department of Commerce
14th St. and Constitution Ave., N.W.
Washington, DC 20230
202-377-2000
Ask for the Commodity Analyst who is an expert in the plastics industry.

U.S. International Trade Commission
500 E St., S.W.
Washington, DC 20436
202-205-2000 Office of the Secretary
202-205-3296 Industries locator
Ask for the Trade Analyst who is an expert in the plastics industry.

U.S. Patent and Trademark Office
Crystal Plaza 2
2011 Jefferson Davis Highway
Arlington, VA 22202
703-305-8000
Ask for the Examining Group Director who is a specialist in plastics.

PLUMBING INDUSTRY

See also: HARDWARE AND LOCKSMITH INDUSTRY; PIPE AND PIPE FITTINGS INDUSTRY; and VALVE INDUSTRY

ASSOCIATIONS

American Supply Association
222 Merchandise Mart, Ste. 1360
Chicago, IL 60654
312-464-0090
312-464-0091 Fax
Peter Schwartz, Executive Vice President
*Offers research and educational programs to
firms that distribute heating and plumbing
supplies of all kinds.*

Central Wholesalers Association
PO Box 310
Caledonia, OH 43314-0310
419-845-2023
Dan Schlosser, Executive Vice President
*Members distribute plumbing and heating
supplies.*

Plumbing and Drainage Institute
c/o Sol Baker
1106 W. 77th St., South Dr.
Indianapolis, IN 46260
317-251-6970
Sol Baker, Executive Secretary
*Manufacturers of plumbing supplies and
fittings.*

Plumbing Manufacturers Institute
Bldg. C, Ste. 20
800 Roosevelt Rd.
Glen Ellyn, IL 60137
708-858-9172
Richard Church, President
Firms that make plumbing products.

United Association of Journeymen and
Apprentices of the Plumbing and Pipe Fit-
ting Industry of the U.S. and Canada
PO Box 37800
Washington, DC 20013
202-628-5823
202-628-5024 Fax
Marvin Boede, General President
The largest union that represents plumbers.

PERIODICALS

Contractor
Cahners Publishing Co.
1350 E. Touhy Ave.
Des Plaines, IL 60017
708-635-8800
John Schweizer, Editor
*News and products for heating, air condition-
ing, and plumbing contractors.*

Plumbing & Mechanical
Business News Publishing Co.
Box 2600
Troy, MI 48007
313-362-3700
Jim Olsztynski, Editor
*Covers products and trends for the plumbing
industry.*

Plumbing Business
Merit Publications, Inc.
18 Perimeter Park Dr., Ste. 108
Atlanta, GA 30341
404-451-4990
Earl Whited, Editor
Advises plumbing contractors how to improve their management and marketing.

Plumbing Engineer
American Society of Plumbing Engineers
Delta Communications Inc.
400 N. Michigan Ave., 13th Fl.
Chicago, IL 60611
312-222-2000
Technical information for engineers in the piping and plumbing fields.

Supply House Times
Cahners Publishing Co.
1350 E. Touhy Ave.
Box 5080
Des Plaines, IL 60017-5080
708-635-8800
John O'Reilly, Editor
News and how-to advice for wholesalers of plumbing, heating, and piping supplies.

LIBRARIES

New England Wholesalers Association
Lending Library
262 Main St.
Box 638
Milford, MA 01757-0638
508-478-8621
508-473-0302 Fax
Plumbing, industrial pipe, and heating.

COMPANIES

Briggs Industries, Inc.
4350 W. Cyprus St.
Tampa, FL 33607
813-878-0178
Vitreous china, procelain, and steel plumbing fixtures.

Bristol Corp.
(Subsidiary of Bristol Holding Corp.)
211 W. Washington St.
South Bend, IN 46601
219-232-0497
Plumbing supplies, plastic pipe and fittings, and related products.

Eljer Industries Inc.
901 Tenth St.
Plano, TX 75074
214-881-7177
Heating and plumbing fixtures.

Familian Pipe & Supply Co.
(Division of Familian Corp.)
7651 Woodman Ave.
Van Nuys, CA 91402
213-873-5050
Distributor of plumbing and heating supplies.

Lowe's Companies, Inc.
P.O. Box 1111
North Wilkesboro, NC 28656
919-651-4000
Wholesaler and retailer of building materials, including plumbing fixtures.

Mueller Brass Co.
(Subsidiary of Sharon Steel Corp.)
1925 Lapeer Ave.
Port Huron, MI 48060
313-987-4000
Tubes, fittings, plumbing and heating assemblies, and related products.

Nibco Inc.
P. O. Box 1167
Elkhart, IN 46515
219-295-3000
Faucets, valves, fittings, and other plumbing supplies.

Noland Co.
2700 Warwick Blvd.
Newport News, VA 23607
804-928-9000
Wholesaler of heating, plumbing, refrigeration, and air-conditioning supplies.

Universal-Rundle Corp.
(Subsidiary of Nortek Inc.)
P. O. Box 960
New Castle, PA 16103
412-658-6631
Plumbing fittings and fixtures.

FEDERAL GOVERNMENT

U.S. International Trade Administration
Department of Commerce
14th St. and Constitution Ave., N.W.
Washington, DC 20230
202-377-2000
Ask for the Commodity Analyst who is an expert in the plumbing industry.

U.S. International Trade Commission
500 E St., S.W.
Washington, DC 20436
202-205-2000 Office of the Secretary
202-205-3296 Industries locator
Ask for the Trade Analyst who is an expert in the plumbing industry.

POINT-OF-SALE INDUSTRY

Point-of-sale equipment is used by retailers at their customer-checkout counters to automate accounting and inventory control.

See also: AUTOMATIC IDENTIFICATION INDUSTRY and RETAIL TRADE

ASSOCIATIONS

Independent Cash Register Dealers Association
711 E. Morehead St.
Charlotte, NC 28202
704-376-8516
704-376-8301 Fax
Curt Kennington, Executive Secretary
Dealers of cash registers and retail point-of-sale systems.

PERIODICALS

P O S News
Faulkner & Gray, Inc.
118 S. Clinton St., Ste. 450
Chicago, IL 60606
312-648-0264
Lori Giesen, Editor
Reports on issues and developments in the retail point-of-sale industry.

LIBRARIES

Point of Purchase Advertising Institute
Information Center
66 N. Van Brunt St.
Englewood, NJ 07631-2707
201-984-8899
201-894-0529 Fax
Point-of-sale information.

COMPANIES

AW Computer Systems, Inc.
9000 A Commerce Pkwy.
Mount Laurel, NJ 08054
609-234-3939
Point-of-sale computer systems for retailers.

American Business Computers Corp.
451 Kennedy Rd.
Akron, OH 44305
216-733-2841
Point-of-sale systems for restaurants, and other products.

Chesapeake Corp.
1021 E. Cary St., Box 2350
Richmond, VA 23218
804-697-1000
Paper and paperboard point-of-sale displays and other products.

Control Transaction Corp.
14 Industrial Rd.
Fairfield, NJ 07006
201-575-9100
Computerized point-of-sale systems.

Fisher Business Systems, Inc.
3939 Roswell Rd.
Marietta, GA 30062
404-578-1771
Point-of-sale systems for retailers.

Massillon-Cleveland-Akron Sign Co.
681 1st St., S. W.
Massillon, OH 44646
216-833-3165
Signs and point-of-sale materials.

Micros Systems Inc.
(Subsidiary of Westinghouse Electric Corp.)
12000 Baltimore Ave.
Beltsville, MD 20705
301-490-2000
Point-of-sale and other specialized computer systems.

Packaging Concepts Ltd.
One Industrial Dr.
Smithfield, RI 02917
401-231-2300
Point-of-sale fixtures and displays.

POPULATION AND DEMOGRAPHICS

See also: CONSUMERS and MARKET RESEARCH AND STATISTICS

ASSOCIATIONS

Center for Migration Studies of New York
209 Flagg Pl.
Staten Island, NY 10304
718-351-8800
718-667-4598 Fax
Lydio Tomasi, Executive Director
Offers information on all aspects of migration, population shifts, and refugees. Does not provide demographic data for marketers.

Population Association of America
1722 N St. N.W.
Washington, DC 20036
202-429-0891
Jen Suter, Administrator
Professional group of people with an interest in population studies and demographics.

Population Reference Bureau
1875 Connecticut Ave. N.W., Ste. 520
Washington, DC 20009
202-483-1100
202-328-3937 Fax
Thomas Merrick, President
A clearinghouse for information on demographics and populations in the U.S. and abroad.

PERIODICALS

American Demographics
American Demographics, Inc.
Box 68
Ithaca, NY 14851-0068
607-273-6343
Brad Edmondson, Editor
Reports on demographic and other consumer trends that impact on marketers. Offers a substantial mail-order catalog of demographic materials for business executives.

Lifestyle Market Analyst
Standard Rate and Data Service, Inc.
3004 Glenview Rd.
Wilmette, IL 60091
800-323-4588
June Levy, Editor
Reports demographic data for local, regional, and national markets.

Population Trends and Public Policy
Population Reference Bureau, Inc.
1875 Connecticut Ave., N.W., Ste. 520
Washington, DC 20009
202-483-1100
Focuses on how demographic and population trends affect public policy.

LIBRARIES

U.S. Bureau of the Census
Library & Information Services Branch
Federal Bldg. No. #, Rm 2455
Washington, DC 20233
301-763-5042
301-763-7322 Fax
Population, urban studies, survey and statistical methodology, and related topics.

University of California, Berkeley
Program in Population Research
Library
2234 Piedmont Ave.
Berkeley, CA 94720
510-642-9800
Demography and population studies.

University of Pennsylvania
Population Studies Center
Demography Library
3718 Locust Walk
Philadelphia, PA 19104-6298
215-898-5375
215-898-2124 Fax
Population and demographic surveys, statistics, and census data.

University of Southern California
Population Research Laboratory
Library
University Park, Research Annex 385
Los Aneles, CA 90007
213-743-2950
213-743-7408 Fax
Demography, population, and urban sociology.

University of Wisconsin, Madison
Center for Demography
Library
4457 Social Science Bldg.
1180 Observatory Dr.
Madison WI 53706
608-262-2182
608-262-8400 Fax
Demography and population studies.

FEDERAL GOVERNMENT

U.S. Bureau of the Census
Washington, DC 20233
301-763-4040
Ask for the Population Projections Branch in the Population Division; the Center for Demographic Studies; or the Demographic Surveys Division.

U.S. Department of Housing and Urban
   Development
451 7th St., S.W.
Washington, DC 20410
202-755-5111
Ask for the Demographic Analysis division in the Office of Economic Affairs.

POSTAL SERVICES AND EQUIPMENT

ASSOCIATIONS

American Postal Workers Union
1300 L St. N.W.
Washington, DC 20005
202-842-4200
Moe Biller, President
A very large union of postal workers.

National Association of Letter Carriers of the
    U.S.A.
100 Indiana Ave. N.W., Ste. 713
Washington, DC 20001
202-393-4695
Vincent Sombrotto, President
A very large union of postal workers.

National Association of Postmasters of the
    United States
8 Herbert St.
Alexandria, VA 22305-2600
703-683-9027
703-683-6820 Fax
Jeffrey Thompson, Executive Director
*A forum for postmasters to exchange informa-
tion.*

PERIODICALS

Memo to Mailers
U.S. Postal Service. Communications Depart-
    ment
475 L'Enfant Plaza, Rm. 5300
Washington, DC 20260-3122
*Reports news of importance to the U.S. Postal
Service and mailers.*

Postal Watch
Intertec Publishing Corp.
Box 12988
Overland Park, KS 66212-0988
913-888-4664
Lori Billington, Editor
*Follows postal regulations and advises how to
save money and speed delivery of letters.*

Postal World
United Communications Group
11300 Rockville Pike, Ste. 1100
Rockville, MD 20852-3030
301-816-8950
Marcus Smith, Editor
*Advises mailers how to cuts costs, increase
productivity in the mailroom, speed delivery
of letters, and related subjects.*

LIBRARIES

National Association of Letter Carriers
Information Center
100 Indiana Ave., N.W.
Washington, DC 20001
202-393-4695
*The postal system, letter carriers, and labor
issues.*

COMPANIES

Friden-Alcatel Corp.
30955 Huntwood Ave.
Hayward, CA 94544
415-489-6800
*Postage meters, scales, mailing machines,
mailroom furniture, and related products.*

General Technologies Group Ltd.
11 Lincoln St.
Copiague, NY 11726
516-842-7676
Postage stamp vending machines and other equipment.

Mail Boxes Coast to Coast Inc.
701 N. Brand Blvd.
Glendale, CA 91203
818-956-5400
Franchises postal service and communications centers.

Mail Boxes Etc.
5555 Oberlin Dr.
San Diego, CA 92121
619-455-8800
Franchises postal service and communications centers.

Micro General Corp.
1740 E. Wilshire
Santa Ana, CA 92705
714-667-0557
Postal scales and parcel shipping systems.

Pitney Bowes Inc.
World Headquarters
Stamford, CT 06926
203-356-5000
A huge variety of mailing and shipping products and supplies.

Rockaway Corp.
(Subsidiary of Ascom Holding AG)
41 Pine St.
Rockaway, NJ 07866
201-627-4400
Postal scales and meters, and other types of products.

United States Banknote Corp.
345 Hudson St.
New York, NY 10014
212-697-6600
Designs and prints stamps, certificates, currency, securities, and other products.

FEDERAL GOVERNMENT

U.S. Customs Service
Department of the Treasury
U.S. Customshouse
6 World Trade Center
New York, NY 10048
212-466-5550
Ask for the Commodity Specialist in charge of postage meters.

U.S. International Trade Administration
Department of Commerce
14th St. and Constitution Ave., N.W.
Washington, DC 20230
202-377-2000
Ask for the Commodity Analyst who is an expert in postage franking equipment.

U.S. Postal Service
475 L'Enfant Plaza, S.W.
Washington, DC 20260
202-268-2020
Ask for the Regular Mail Services Market Research division or the National Accounts Market Research department.

POTATO INDUSTRY

See also: FRUIT AND VEGETABLE INDUSTRY

ASSOCIATIONS

Frozen Potato Products Institute
1764 Old Meadow Ln., Ste. 350
McLean, VA 22102
703-821-0770
Leslie Sarasin, Executive Director
Firms that process frozen potato products.

Idaho Potato Commission
PO Box 1068
Boise, ID 83701
208-334-2350
M. B. Anderson, Director
Promotes and advertises potatoes grown in Idaho.

National Potato Council
9085 E. Mineral Circle, Ste. 155
Englewood, CO 80112
303-790-1141
303-790-1142 Fax
Ron Walker, Executive Director
A large group of commercial potato growers.

National Potato Promotion Board
1385 S. Colorado Blvd., Ste. 512
Denver, CO 80222
303-758-7783
303-756-9256 Fax
Robert Mercer, President
Conducts research, educational, advertising, public relations, and marketing programs for commercial potato growers.

PERIODICALS

Maine Potato News
Maine Potato Board
Northeast Publishing Co.
Box 510
Presque Isle, ME 04769
207-764-7033
Covers the potato industry in Maine.

Potato Grower of Idaho
Potato Growers of Idaho, Inc.
Harris Publishing, Inc.
520 Park Ave.
Idaho Falls, ID 83402
208-524-7000
Covers the potato industry in Idaho.

Spudman
Box 1752
Monterey, CA 93942
408-373-7991
Donald Miller, Editor
News and advice for potato growers, packers, shippers, and processors.

COMPANIES

Idaho Supreme Potatoes, Inc.
Box 246
Firth, ID 83236
208-346-6841
Fresh potatoes and potato flakes.

Interstate Food Processing Corp.
P. O. Box 172
Fort Fairfield, ME 04742
207-472-3041
French fried potatoes and frozen vegetables.

Maine Potato Growers, Inc.
56 Parsons St.
Presque Isle, ME 04769
207-764-3131
Potatoes and many other products.

Ore-Ida Foods Co., Inc.
(Subsidiary of H. J. Heinz Co.)
P. O. Box 10
Boise, ID 83707
208-383-6100
Frozen potato products and other frozen foods.

Oregon Potato Co.
P. O. Box 169
Boardman, OR 97818
503-481-2715
Potato flakes.

Penford Products Co.
(Subsidiary of Penwest, Ltd.)
1001 First St., S.W.
Cedar Rapids, IA 52404
319-398-3700
Potato starch and flakes, and other products.

Penobscot Frozen Foods, Inc.
One Pierce St.
Belfast, ME 04915
207-338-4360
Frozen potato products.

J. C. Watson Co.
P.O. Box 278
Parma, ID 83660
208-722-5141
Fresh fruits and vegetables, including potatoes.

FEDERAL GOVERNMENT

U.S. Department of Agriculture
14th St. and Independence Ave., S.W.
Washington, DC 20250
202-720-8732
Ask for the Economic Research Service.

U.S. International Trade Administration
Department of Commerce
14th St. and Constitution Ave., N.W.
Washington, DC 20230
202-377-2000
Ask for the Commodity Analyst who is an expert in the potato industry.

U.S. International Trade Commission
500 E St., S.W.
Washington, DC 20436
202-205-2000 Office of the Secretary
202-205-3296 Industries locator
Ask for the Trade Analyst who is an expert in the potato industry.

POULTRY INDUSTRY

ASSOCIATIONS

National Broiler Council
Madison Bldg., No. 614
1155 15th St. N.W.
Washington, DC 20005
202-293-4005
George Watts, President
Firms that process and distribute broiler chickens.

National Turkey Federation
11319 Sunset Hills Rd.
Reston, VA 22090
703-435-7206
703-481-0837 Fax
Stuart Proctor, Executive Vice President
A clearinghouse for industry and technical information on turkeys.

Poultry Science Association
309 W. Clark St.
Champaign, IL 61820
217-356-3182
217-398-4119 Fax
C. D. Johnson, Business Manager
A professional society for researchers, educators, and others in the field of poultry science.

PERIODICALS

Egg Industry
Watt Publishing Co.
Mount Morris, IL 61054
815-734-4171
Gary Thornton, Editor
Covers commercial egg production, processing, and marketing.

Meat and Poultry
Oman Publishing, Inc.
90 Throckmorton Ave.
Box 1059
Mill Valley, CA 94942
415-388-7575
Steve Bjerklie, Editor
Reports on technical and business news for the meat and poultry industry.

Poultry and Egg Marketing
Poultry and Egg News
345 Green St., N.W.
Box 1338
Gainesville, GA 30503
404-536-2476
Jim Mathis, Editor
Advises how to market poultry products.

Poultry Digest
Watt Publishing Co.
Sandstone Bldg.
Mt. Morris, IL 61054
815-734-4171
Charles Perry, Editor
Covers such topics as husbandry, production, and sales of broilers, eggs, and turkeys.

Poultry Processing
Edgell Communications
7500 Old Oak Blvd.
Cleveland, OH 44130
216-243-8100
Dan Murphy, Editor
Technical information for those who slaughter and process poultry.

Turkey World
Watt Publishing Co.
Mount Morris, IL 61054
815-734-4171
Bernard Heffernan, Editor
Follows news of interest to growers, processors, and marketers of turkeys.

Who's Who in the Egg and Poultry Industries
Watt Publishing Co.
Mount Morris, IL 61054
815-734-4171
A directory of suppliers to the industry, processors, buyers, and sellers of eggs, broilers, and turkeys.

LIBRARIES

U.S.D.A.
National Agricultural Library
10301 Baltimore Blvd.
Beltsville, MD 20705
301-344-3755
301-344-5472 Fax
Covers most agricultural topics including poultry.

University of Wisconsin, Madison
Poultry Science Department
Halpin Memorial Library
Animal Science Bldg., Rm. 214
1675 Observatory Dr.
Madison, WI 53706
608-262-1243
Poultry science.

COMPANIES

Cagle's Inc.
2000 Hills Ave.
Atlanta, GA 30318
404-355-2820
Chicken growers and poultry products.

Golden Poultry Co., Inc.
(Subsidiary of Gold Kist, Inc.)
244 Perimeter Ctr. Pkwy., N.E.
Atlanta, GA 30346
404-393-5000
Poultry processing and distributing.

Holly Farms Foods, Inc.
(Subsidiary of Tyson Foods, Inc.)
P. O. Box 88
Wilkesboro, NC 28697
919-838-2171
Poultry and egg products.

Perdue Farms Inc.
P. O. Box 1537
Salisbury, MD 21801
301-543-3000
Poultry products, hatching eggs, and other food products.

Peterson Industries Inc.
Main St.
Decatur, AR 72722
501-752-3211
Poultry stock and dressed poultry.

Rocco Enterprises, Inc.
P.O. Box 549
Harrisonburg, VA 22801
703-568-1400
Poultry farming and processing.

Sanderson Farms, Inc.
225 N. Thirteenth Ave.
Laurel, MS 39440
601-649-4030
Frozen poultry and other foods.

Showell Farms, Inc.
P.O. Box 158
Showell, MD 21862
301-352-5411
Poultry products of all kinds.

FEDERAL GOVERNMENT

U.S. Department of Agriculture
14th St. and Independence Ave., S.W.
Washington, DC 20250
202-720-8732
*Ask for the Poultry Grading division in the
Agricultural Marketing Service department;
the Economic Research Service; or the Meat
and Poultry Inquiry Hotline.*

U.S. International Trade Administration
Department of Commerce
14th St. and Constitution Ave., N.W.
Washington, DC 20230
202-377-2000
*Ask for the Commodity Analyst who is an
expert in the poultry industry.*

U.S. International Trade Commission
500 E St., S.W.
Washington, DC 20436
202-205-2000 Office of the Secretary
202-205-3296 Industries locator
*Ask for the Trade Analyst who is an expert in
poultry industry.*

POWER (MECHANICAL)

See also: ENGINES and ENGINEERING

ASSOCIATIONS

National Association of Power Engineers
2350 E. Devon Ave., Ste. 115
Des Plaines, IL 60018
718-298-0600
718-298-1545 Fax
C. Dalgard, Executive Officer
*This professional group of stationary and
power engineers shares information on the
generating and transmitting of power.*

PERIODICALS

Diesel & Gas Turbine Worldwide
Diesel & Gas Turbine Publications
13555 Bishop's Ct.
Brookfield, WI 53005-6286
414-784-9177
Joseph Kane, Editor
Covers all aspects of engine power systems.

Power
McGraw-Hill, Inc.
1221 Ave. of the Americas
New York, NY 10020
212-512-2000
Robert Schwieger, Editor
News and and how-to information for engineers employed by utilities and industries that require a great deal of power.

Power Transmission Design
Penton Publishing
1100 Superior Ave.
Cleveland, OH 44114-2543
216-696-7000
Phil Kingsley, Editor
Advises on how to choose, use, and maintain engines and parts that transmit power.

LIBRARIES

United Technologies Corp.
Library & Information Services
United Technologies Research Center
East Hartford, CT 06108
203-727-7478
203-727-7316 Fax
Power plants, energy conversion, physics, and related topics.

Washington Public Power Supply System
Library
3000 George Washington Way
Box 968
Richland, WA 99352
509-372-5120
509-372-5328 Fax
Nuclear power, power transmission, and engineering standards.

Wisconsin Electric Power Co.
Library
231 W. Michigan St., Rm. P219
Milwaukee, WI 53203
414-221-2580
414-221-2139 Fax
The electric utility industry, including power plants and nuclear power.

FEDERAL GOVERNMENT

U.S. International Trade Administration
Department of Commerce
14th St. and Constitution Ave., N.W.
Washington, DC 20230
202-377-2000
Ask for the Commodity Analyst who is an expert in mechanical power.

U.S. International Trade Commission
500 E St., S.W.
Washington, DC 20436
202-205-2000 Office of the Secretary
202-205-3296 Industries locator
Ask for the Trade Analyst who is an expert in mechanical power.

U.S. Patent and Trademark Office
Crystal Plaza 2
2011 Jefferson Davis Highway
Arlington, VA 22202
703-305-8000
Ask for the Examining Group Director who is a specialist in power transmission equipment.

PRECIOUS METALS INDUSTRY

See also: METALS INDUSTRY and METALLURGY

ASSOCIATIONS

American Bureau of Metal Statistics
PO Box 1405
400 Plaza Dr.
Secaucus, NJ 07094
201-863-6900
201-863-6050 Fax
W. J. Lambert, President
Producers of nonferrous metals, including gold, silver, and platinum. Offers statistical and other types of data.

Dental Gold Institute
140 The Fenway
Boston, MA 02115
617-423-1645
Louis Calisti, Director
Members supply gold to the dental profession.

Gold Institute
1112 16th St. N.W., Ste. 240
Washington, DC 20036
202-835-0185
202-835-0155 Fax
John Lutley, Managing Director
Offers research services to firms that mine, refine, and sell gold, make products using gold, dealers of gold bullion, and others in the industry.

Silver Institute
1112 16th St. N.W.
Washington, DC 20036
202-835-0185
202-783-2127 Fax
John Lutley, Executive Director
Offers research and educational programs to silver mining and refining firms, manufacturers of products that use silver, suppliers of bullion, and others in the industry.

Silver Users Association
1730 M St. N.W., No. 911
Washington, DC 20036
202-785-3050
202-659-5760 Fax
Walter Frankland, Executive Vice President
Provides research to all users of silver including firms that make photographic, medical, jewelry, and mirror products.

International Precious Metals Institute
4905 Tilghman St., Ste. 160
Allentown, PA 18104
215-395-9700
215-395-5855 Fax
David Lundy, Executive Director
Provides technical information of all kinds to precious metal miners, refiners, users, scientists, and others.

PERIODICALS

American Metal Market
Capital Cities—A B C, Inc.
825 Seventh Ave.
New York, NY 10019
212-887-8532
Michael Botta, Editor
Reports on the mining, refining, trading, and markets for all metals, including precious metals.

Bullion Advisory
Moneypower
4247 46th Ave. N.
Minneapolis, MN 55422
612-537-8096
James Moore, Editor
Advice for investors about gold, silver and platinum.

Gold Mining Stock Report
Justim Publishing Co.
Box 1217
Lafayette, CA 94549
415-283-4848
Robert Bishop, Editor
Advice for investors about the stock of companies that mine precious metals.

Gold Standard News
Gold Standard Corp.
1805 Grand Ave.
Kansas City, MO 64108
816-842-4653
Conrad Brann, Editor
Reports on the gold, silver and platinum industry.

Mineral Industry Surveys. Gold and Silver
U.S. Bureau of Mines
Cochrans Mill Rd.
Box 18070
Pittsburgh, PA 15236
412-892-4411
Reports gold and silver production data. An additional publication, Platinum—Group Metals, covers production data for platinum.

North American Gold Mining Stocks
Taylor Hard Money Advisors, Inc.
33-42 61st St.
Woodside, NY 11377
718-457-1426
Jay Taylor, Editor
Advice for investors about gold mining stocks.

LIBRARIES

Engelhard Corp.
Technical Information Center
Menlo Park
Edison, NJ 08818
201-205-5271
201-205-5300 Fax
Fabrication of gold, silver, and platinum products, and other subjects.

Technic Inc.
Library
1 Spectacle St.
Cranston, RI 02910
401-781-6100
Metallurgy, jewelry, surface finishing, precious metals, and related topics.

U.S. Bureau of Mines
Twin Cities Research Center
Library
5629 Minnehaha Ave., S.
Minneapolis, MN 55417-3099
612-725-4503
Mining, mineral industries, metallurgy, and related topics.

COMPANIES

Degussa Corp.
(Subsidiary of Degussa AG)
65 Challenger Rd.
Ridgefield Park, NJ 07660
201-641-6100
Chemicals and precious metal products.

Handy & Harman
850 Third Ave.
New York, NY 10022
212-752-3400
Precious metals, alloys, and metal products.

Homestake Mining Co.
650 California St.
San Francisco, CA 94108
415-981-8150
Mining for gold, silver, and other minerals.

Johnson Matthey Investments, Inc.
(Subsidiary of Johnson, Matthey Public Limited Co.)
460 E. Swedesford Rd.
Wayne, PA 19087
215-971-3000
Refining of precious metals and precious metals products.

Kennecott Corp.
(Subsidiary of RTZ Corp. Plc)
10 E. South Temple, Box 11248
Salt Lake City, UT 84147
801-322-7000
Mining of copper, gold, silver, and other products.

Kiewit Mining Group Inc.
(Subsidiary of Peter Kiewit Sons', Inc.)
One Thousand Kiewit Plaza
Omaha, NE 68131
402-342-2052
Mining of gold, coal, and other products.

Newmont Gold Co.
(Subsidiary of Newmont Mining Corp.)
1700 Lincoln St.
Denver, CO 80203
303-863-7414
Gold mining and processing.

Phelps Dodge Corp.
2600 N. Central Ave.
Phoenix, AZ 85004
602-234-8100
Copper, gold, silver, and other products.

Reynolds Metals Co.
6601 W. Broad St., Box 27003
Richmond, VA 23261
804-281-2000
Precious and non-precious metals, and other types of products.

FEDERAL GOVERNMENT

Bureau of Mines
810 7th St., N.W.
Washington, DC 20747
202-501-9770
Ask for the commodity specialist who is an expert in the specific metal that interest you.

U.S. International Trade Administration
Department of Commerce
14th St. and Constitution Ave., N.W.
Washington, DC 20230
202-377-2000
Ask for the Commodity Analyst who is an expert in the specific metal that interests you.

U.S. International Trade Commission
500 E St., S.W.
Washington, DC 20436
202-205-2000 Office of the Secretary
202-205-3296 Industries locator
Ask for the Trade Analyst who is an expert in the specific metal that interests you.

PREMIUMS AND INCENTIVES

See also: MARKETING and SALES PROMOTION

ASSOCIATIONS

Incentive Manufacturers Representatives
  Association
710 E. Ogden Ave., Ste. 113
Naperville, IL 60563
708-369-2425
Ann Spehar, Administrator
Offers public relations and education programs designed to help representatives of manufacturers who sell products to the premium and incentive market.

National Premium Sales Executives
1600 Rt. 22
Union, NJ 07083
201-687-3090
201-687-0977 Fax
Howard Henry, Executive Director
Members include marketing and sales personnel that buy and sell premiums and incentives for their companies. Offers information about incentive merchandising.

PERIODICALS

Incentive
Bill Communications, Inc.
633 Third Ave.
New York, NY 10017
212-986-4800
Bruce Bolger, Editor
Advice for executives in charge of buying incentives.

Premium—Incentive Business
Gralla Publications
1515 Broadway
New York, NY 10036
212-869-1300
Reports on all aspects of the incentive and premium business.

COMPANIES

L. G. Balfour Co., Inc.
(Subsidiary of Town & Country Corp.)
25 County St.
Attleboro, MA 02703
508-222-3600
Motivation and incentive products for industry and schools.

Freeman Products Inc.
(Subsidiary of Avnet, Inc.)
86 Rte. 4
Englewood, NJ 07631
201-871-0750
Trophies, incentive awards, and related products.

Houze Glass Corp.
(Subsidiary of DWG Corp.)
Point Marion, PA 15474
412-725-5231
Glasses and other premium and advertising specialties.

Marden-Kane, Inc.
410 Lakeville Rd.
Lake Success, NY 11042
516-326-3666
Incentive programs, sales promotions, contests, and related services.

R. S. Owens & Co.
5535 N. Lynch Ave.
Chicago, IL 60630
312-282-6000
Trophies, plaques, and other recognition and incentive items.

Vernon Co.
604 W. Fourth St, N.
Newton, IA 50208
515-792-9000
Premium, incentive, and specialty advertising products and programs.

PRINTING AND PRINTING EQUIPMENT INDUSTRIES

See also: GRAPHICS ARTS INDUSTRY and PRINTING INK INDUSTRY

ASSOCIATIONS

Advertising Typographers Association
RD 3, Box 345
Stockton, NJ 08559
201-782-4055
Walter Dew, Executive Secretary
Companies that offer typesetting services.

International Association of Printing House Craftsmen
7599 Kenwood Rd.
Cincinnati, OH 45236
513-891-0611
513-891-3848 Fax
Milford Robertson, President
Provides educational and research services to owners, operators, supervisors, and others involved in the day-to-day operations of printing plants.

International Financial Printers Association
100 Daingerfield Rd
Alexandria, VA 22319
703-519-8122
Lois Eck, Executive Director
This section of the Printing Industries of America promotes firms that print company prospectuses, bonds, and other financial documents.

Magazine Printers Section
100 Daingerfield Rd.
Alexandria, VA 22314
703-519-8100
Mary Fuller, Executive Director
Serves as a forum for magazine printers to share information.

National Association of Printers and Lithographers
780 Palisade Ave.
Teaneck, NJ 07666
201-342-0700
Charles Alessandrini, President
Offers management and production consulations and seminars to printing firms.

National Association of Professional Print Buyers
15050 NE 20th Ave., Ste. A
North Miami, FL 33181
305-947-5100
Vincent Mallardi, Representative
Helps buyers of printing products and services to improve their procurement and negotiating skills.

National Association of Quick Printers
404 N. Michigan
Chicago, IL 60611
312-644-6610
Tracy Poyser, Executive Director
Provides business and technical information to firms that offer while-you-wait printing services.

National Printing Equipment and Supply Association
1899 Preston White Dr.
Reston, VA 22091-4326
703-264-7200
703-620-0994 Fax
Regis Delmontagne, President
Offers research and cosponsors trade exhibits for firms that manufacture and distribute printing equipment and supplies.

Printing Brokerage Association
1700 N. Moore St., No. 714
Arlington, VA 22209
703-243-3666
Vincent Mallardi, Executive Director
Offers promotional and educational programs to printing brokers and others in the printing industry.

Printing Industries of America
100 Daingerfield Rd.
Alexandria, VA 22314
703-519-8100
703-548-3227 Fax
Ray Roper, Executive Officer
A large association that provides many research and management education services to printing firms.

PERIODICALS

American Printer
Maclean Hunter Publishing Co.
29 N. Wacker Dr.
Chicago, IL 60606
312-726-2802
Jill Roth, Editor
Reports news and trends to professionals in the printing, lithographic, and printing equipment industries.

Graphic Arts Blue Book
A.F. Lewis Co., Inc.
79 Madison Ave.
New York, NY 10016
212-679-0770
*A series of regional directories that list print-
ing and other grahic arts firms and their suppliers.*

Graphic Communications World
Green Sheet Communications, Inc.
Box 727
Hartsdale, NY 10530-0727
914-472-3051
John Werner, Editor
*Management information for senior executives
at printing and publishing firms.*

High Volume Printing
Innes Publishing Co.
425 Huehl Rd.
Box 368
Northbrook, IL 60062
708-564-5940
Catherine Stanulis, Editor
*Covers technological and business develop-
ments for large printing firms.*

In-Plant Reproductions
North American Publishing Co.
401 N. Broad St.
Philadelphia, PA 19108
215-238-5300
Jody Bocklage, Editor
*Technical and operations advice for printers
and production personnel.*

Instant & Small Commercial Printer
Innes Publishing Co.
425 Huehl Rd.
Box 368
Northbrook, IL 60062
708-564-5940
Cathy Bazzon, Editor
*Business and product information for while-
you-wait and small printing firms.*

Pre-South Wind Publishing Co.
8340 Mission Rd., Ste. 106
Prairie Village, KS 66206
913-642-6611
Michael Scheibach, Editor
*Reports on the trends, techniques, and prod-
ucts of interest to the pre-press and electronic
design industry.*

Print Buyers Review
Successful Media
Box 36
S. Weymouth, MA 02190
617-340-2066
Robert Dixon, Editor
*Advises on how to effectively buy materials
and services for the printing and book pub-
lishing industry.*

Printers Hot Line
Heartland Communications Group, Inc.
900 Central Ave.
Box 916
Fort Dodge, IA 50501
515-955-1600
*Written for buyers and sellers of new and used
equipment.*

Printing News—East
Cahners Publishing Co.
249 W. 17th St.
New York, NY 10011
212-463-6727
Joann Strashun, Editor
One of several regional editions that covers industry news, technical data, and economic forecasts for the printing trade.

Quick Printing
Coast Publishing, Inc.
1680 S.W. Bayshore Blvd.
Port St. Lucie, FL 34984
407-879-6660
Bob Hall, Editor
Written for quick print and copy shops.

LIBRARIES

R.R. Donnelley & Sons, Co.
Corporate Library
2223 S. King Dr.
Chicago, IL 60616
312-326-7149
312-326-8543 Fax
Printing, publishing, and business.

Graphic Arts Technical Foundation
E.H. Wadewitz Memorial Library
4615 Forbes Ave.
Pittsburgh, PA 15213
412-621-6941
412-621-3049 Fax
Graphic design, printing processes, paper, and photography.

Graphic Communications World
Library
P.O. Box 727
Hartsdale, NY 10530-0727
914-472-3051
904-656-7506 Fax
Graphic communication and printing technology.

COMPANIES

Arcata Corp.
601 California St.
San Francisco, CA 94108
415-781-4200
Printing of books and other materials.

Banta Corp.
P.O. Box 8003
Mehasha, WI 54952
414-722-7777
Printing of books and other materials.

A. B. Dick Co.
(Subsidiary of General Electric Co. p.l.c.)
5700 W. Touhy Ave.
Chicago, IL 60648
312-763-1900
Copying, printing, and duplicating equipment and supplies.

Graphic Industries, Inc.
2155 Monroe Dr., N.E.
Atlanta, GA 30324
404-874-3327
Commercial printing.

John H. Harland Co.
2939 Miller Rd.
Decatur, GA 30035
404-981-9460
Printing of checks and other bank items.

Heidelberg Harris, Inc.
(Subsidiary of Heidelberger Druckmaschiner)
121 Broadway
Dover, NH 03820
603-749-6600
Printing presses and other printing equipment.

Polychrome Corp.
(Subsidiary of DIC Americas, Inc.)
137 Alexander St., Box 817
Yonkers, NY 10702
914-965-8800
Printing plates, prepress equipment, and supplies.

Quebecor Printing
1999 Sheppard Rd.
St. Paul, MN 55116
612-690-7200
Commercial printing.

Ringier America, Inc.
One Pierce Pl.
Itasca, IL 60143
708-285-6000
Printing of books, magazines, catalogs, inserts, and other items.

Sullivan Graphics, Inc.
100 Winners Circle
Brentwood, TN 37027
615-377-0377
Printing of books and other materials.

Western Paper Co.
(Division of International Paper Co.)
P.O. Box 2967
Shawnee Mission, KS 66201
913-451-1213
Paper and printing equipment.

World Color Press, Inc.
(Division of Printing Holdings, L.P.)
401 Industrial Ave., Box 1248
Effingham, IL 62401
217-342-9241
Printing of magazines, directories, catalogs, and other items.

FEDERAL GOVERNMENT

U.S. Customs Service
Department of the Treasury
U.S. Customshouse
6 World Trade Center
New York, NY 10048
212-466-5550
Ask for the Commodity Specialist in charge of printing equipment.

U.S. International Trade Administration
Department of Commerce
14th St. and Constitution Ave., N.W.
Washington, DC 20230
202-377-2000
Ask for the Commodity Analyst who is an expert in printing or the printing equipment industry.

U.S. International Trade Commission
500 E St., S.W.
Washington, DC 20436
202-205-2000 Office of the Secretary
202-205-3296 Industries locator
Ask for the Trade Analyst who is an expert in printing or the printing equipment industry.

U.S. Patent and Trademark Office
Crystal Plaza 2
2011 Jefferson Davis Highway
Arlington, VA 22202
703-305-8000
Ask for the Examining Group Director who is a specialist in printing equipment.

PRINTING INK INDUSTRY

See also: PRINTING AND PRINTING EQUIPMENT INDUSTRIES

ASSOCIATIONS

National Association of Printing Ink Manufacturers
47 Halstead Ave.
Harrison, NY 10528
914-835-5650
914-835-5988 Fax
James Renson, Executive Director
*Members manufacture printing inks of all
kinds.*

PERIODICALS

American Inkmaker
PTN Publishing Co.
445 Broad Hollow Rd.
Melville, NY 11747
516-845-2700
*Written for manufacturers of printing inks
and related graphic arts specialty colors.*

C A Selects. Coatings, Inks, & Related
Products
Chemical Abstracts Service
2540 Olentangy River Rd.
Box 3012
Columbus, OH 43210
614-447-3600
Francine Del Vescoro, Editor
*Technical data about the chemistry and manu-
facture of inks and other coatings.*

LIBRARIES

BASF Corp.
Coatings and Inks Division
Corporate Library
1255 Broad St.
Clifton, NJ 07015
201-365-3400
201-365-3561 Fax
*Printing inks, polymer chemistry, and automo-
tive paints.*

BASF Corp.
Colorants Library
491 Columbia Ave.
Holland, MI 49423-4899
616-392-2391
616-392-1340 Fax
*Paint, inks, resins, pigments, chemistry, and
related subjects.*

COMPANIES

Braden-Sutphin Ink Co.
3650 East 93rd St.
Cleveland, OH 44105
216-271-2300
Printing inks.

Daicolor-Pope, Inc.
(Subsidiary of Dainichiseika Color & Chemicals Manufacturing Co., Ltd.)
40 Wero Rd.
Clifton, NJ 07012
201-777-0200
Pigments used in printing inks.

A. J. Daw Printing Ink Co.
3559 S. Greenwood Ave.
Los Angeles, CA 90040
213-723-3253
Printing inks and related coatings.

Gans Ink & Supply Co., Inc.
1441 Boyd St.
Los Angeles, CA 90033
213-264-2200
Printing inks.

Heucotech Ltd.
99 Newbold Rd.
Fairless Hills, PA 19030
215-736-0712
*Pigments used in printing inks, paints, and
other products.*

J. M. Huber Corp.
333 Thornall St.
Edison, NJ 08818
908-549-8600
Printing inks, pigments, and other products.

Markem Corp.
150 Congress St.
Keene, NH 03431
603-352-1130
Printing inks and other printing supplies.

Millmaster Onyx Group, Inc.
500 Post Rd. E.
Westport, CT 06880
203-454-1800
*Printing inks for newspapers and other chemi-
cals.*

FEDERAL GOVERNMENT

U.S. Customs Service
Department of the Treasury
U.S. Customshouse
6 World Trade Center
New York, NY 10048
212-466-5550
*Ask for the Commodity Specialist in charge of
printing ink.*

U.S. International Trade Administration
Department of Commerce
14th St. and Constitution Ave., N.W.
Washington, DC 20230
202-377-2000
*Ask for the Commodity Analyst who is an
expert in the printing ink industry.*

U.S. International Trade Commission
500 E St., S.W.
Washington, DC 20436
202-205-2000 Office of the Secretary
202-205-3296 Industries locator
*Ask for the Trade Analyst who is an expert in
the printing ink industry.*

PRIVATIZATION

Privatization refers to the transfer or sale to a private enterprise of a service or organization owned by a government.

ASSOCIATIONS

Privatization Council, Inc.
1101 Connecticut Ave., N.W., Ste. 700
Washington, DC 20036
202-859-1142
Jenny Hefferon, Executive Director
Promotes the benefits of privatization and works to privatize public projects.

PERIODICALS

Annual Report on Privatization
Reason Foundation
2716 Ocean Park Blvd., Ste. 1062
Santa Monica, CA 90405
213-392-0443
A survey of privatization in the U.S.

Privatization
Government Information Services
1611 N. Kent St., Ste. 508
Arlington, VA 22209
703-528-1000
Laurence Alexander, Editor
Reports on the contracting out and privatization of a wide range of services. Includes practical information for those who set up and manage these arrangements.

Privatization Watch
Local Government Center
2716 Ocean Park Blvd., Ste. 1062
Santa Monica, CA 90405
213-392-0443
Philip Fixler, Editor
Follows privatization trends.

PRODUCTION AND PROCESS CONTROL

See also: COMPUTER-AIDED DESIGN/MANUFACTURING/ENGINEERING (CAD/CAM/CAE)

ASSOCIATIONS

American Production and Inventory Control
  Society
500 W. Annandale Rd.
Falls Church, VA 22046-4274
703-237-8344
Michael Stack, Executive Director
*An information clearinghouse for engineers,
production managers, and technical personnel
who select and operate production and inventory control systems and equipment.*

IEEE Industry Applications Society
c/o Institute of Electrical and Electonic Engineers
345 E. 47th St.
New York, NY 10017
212-705-7867
*Engineers who work to improve manufactur-
ing processes.*

Society of Logistics Engineers
125 W. Park Loop, Ste. 201
Huntsville, AL 35806
205-837-1092
*Offers educational programs to engineers
responsible for logistics in manufacturing and
other areas.*

Statistical Process Control Society
PO Box 1203
Avon, CT 06001
203-676-8890
Hab Weaver, President
*Provides information about statistical process
control methods that increase product quality
and manufacturing efficiency.*

PERIODICALS

American Machinist
Penton Publishing
1100 Superior Ave.
Cleveland, OH 44114-2543
216-696-7000
Joseph Jablonowski, Editor
*Reports on a wide range of manufacturing
topics including computer-assisted manufacturing and production control.*

Journal of Manufacturing and Operations
  Management
Elsevier Science Publishing Co., Inc.
655 Ave. of the Americas
New York, NY 10010
212-989-5800
Uday Karmarkar, Editor
*Detailed advice about how to manage and
automate manufacturing systems.*

P & I M Review
American Production and Inventory Control
   Society
T D A Publications, Inc.
2021 Coolidge St.
Hollywood, FL 33020-2012
305-925-5900
Raymond Feldman, Editor
*Reports developments in inventory and pro-
duction control for managers of manufactur-
ing operations.*

LIBRARIES

Avery Dennison
Research Center
Information Center
2900 Bradley St.
Pasadena, CA 91107-1599
818-398-2555
818-398-2553 Fax
*Control engineering and process engineering,
and other subjects.*

California Institute of Technology
Chemical Engineering Library
202 Spalding Laboratory
Pasadena, CA 91125
818-356-6423
818-795-1547 Fax
*Surface science, process control, and chemical
engineering.*

Fischer & Porter Co.
Corporate Engineering Library
125 E. County Line Rd.
Warminster, PA 18974
215-674-6000
Process control and engineering.

Monsanto Co.
Fisher Controls Co.
Information Center
R.A. Engel Technical Center
Box 11
Marshalltown, IA 50158
515-754-2161
515-754-3159 Fax
*Process control, mechanical engineering, auto-
matic control, and computer science.*

COMPANIES

ABB Process Automation Inc.
(Subsidiary of Asea Brown Boveri Inc.)
650 Ackerman Rd.
Columbus, OH 43202
614-261-2000
Computerized process automation systems.

Allen-Bradley Co.
(Subsidiary of Rockwell International Corp.)
1201 S. Second St.
Milwaukee, WI 53204
414-382-2000
Automated industrial control equipment.

Bra-Con/X-Mation, Inc.
(Subsidiary of CDI Transportation Group,
   Inc.)
43850 W. 10 Mile Rd.
Novi, MI 48376
313-348-0200
*Automated industrial control, robotics, and
material handling equipment.*

Fisher Controls Intl.
8000 Maryland Ave.
St. Louis, MO 63105
314-694-9900
Process control equipment.

Honeywell Inc.
Honeywell Plaza
Minneapolis, MN 55408
612-870-5200
Industrial control and automation systems, and other businesses.

Litton Industries, Inc.
360 N. Crescent Dr.
Beverly Hills, CA 90210
213-859-5000
Industrial automation systems, and other businesses.

Mark Controls Corp.
5202 Old Orchid Rd.
Skokie, IL 60077
708-470-8585
Process control equipment.

Micron Instrument Corp.
50 Alexander Ct.
Ronkonkoma, NY 11779
516-467-8000
Numerical control and other industrial production equipment.

Reichel & Drews Inc.
1025 W. Thorndale Ave.
Itasca, IL 60143
708-773-2500
Production, process, and automation equipment.

Robertshaw Controls Co.
(Subsidiary of Siebe plc)
P. O. Box 26544
Richmond, VA 23261
804-281-0700
Automatic control systems for industry and buildings.

FEDERAL GOVERNMENT

U.S. International Trade Administration
Department of Commerce
14th St. and Constitution Ave., N.W.
Washington, DC 20230
202-377-2000
Ask for the Commodity Analyst who is an expert in process control instruments.

PRODUCTIVITY

See also: QUALITY CONTROL

ASSOCIATIONS

American Productivity and Quality Center
123 N. Post Oak Ln., Ste. 300
Houston, TX 77024
713-681-4020
C. Jackson, Chairman
A clearinghouse for information on productivity.

Association of Productivity Specialists
Pan Am Bldg.
200 Park Ave., Ste. 303E
New York, NY 10017
212-286-0943
Robert Jacobson, Chairman
*Members are designated Productivity Special-
ists: management consultants who advise on
how to improve quality, reduce costs, speed
production, and related subjects.*

Manufacturers Alliance for Productivity and
  Innovation
1200 18th St. N.W., Ste. 400
Washington, DC 20036
202-331-8430
202-331-7160 Fax
Kenneth McLennan, President
*Offers a wide range of educational programs
on subjects designed to improve the productivity and competitiveness of U.S. manufacturing
firms.*

Productivity Communication Center
102 Braswell Rd.
Chapel Hill, NC 27516
919-968-0047
Daniel Dickinson, President
*Provides seminars to managers on productiv-
ity and quality.*

Quality and Productivity Management Association
300 N. Martingale Rd., Ste. 230
Schaumburg, IL 60173
708-619-2909
708-619-3383 Fax
Bill Ginnodo, Executive Director
*Provides information for companies concerned
with productivity and quality control.*

PERIODICALS

A Q P Report
Association for Quality and Participation
801-B W. 8th St., Ste. 501
Cincinnati, OH 45203
513-381-1959
Ned Hamson, Editor
*Advice on how to improve quality and produc-
tivity by using a team approach to solving
problems.*

Creative Management
Business Research Publications, Inc.
817 Broadway
New York, NY 10003
212-673-4700
Gail Hayden, Editor
*Information on a wide range of management
issues, including employee productivity.*

Industrial Management
Institute of Industrial Engineers
25 Technology Park-Atlanta
Norcross, GA 30092
404-449-0460
*Reports on such industrial management topics
as automation and productivity.*

Journal of Productivity Analysis
Kluwer Academic Publishers
101 Philip Dr.
Norwell, MA 02061
617-871-6600
Ali Dogramaci, Editor
*Technical analyses of how to improve produc-
tivity.*

National Productivity Review
Executive Enterprises Publications Co., Inc.
22 W. 21st St.
New York, NY 10010-6904
212-645-7880
Jane Bensahel, Editor
*Covers a wide range of issues about managing
productivity.*

Public Productivity and Management Review
Jossey-Bass Inc., Publishers
350 Sansome St., 5th Fl.
San Francisco, CA 94104
415-433-1767
Marc Holzer, Editor
*Provides examples of productivity programs
that work in both the public and private sectors.*

Productivity Measures for Selected Industries
U.S. Bureau of Labor Statistics
441 G Street, N.W.
Washington, DC 20212
202-523-9244
Productivity statistics in certain industries.

LIBRARIES

American Productivity & Quality Center
Information Services
123 N. Post Oak Ln.
Houston, TX 77024
713-681-4020
713-681-8578 Fax
*Productivity, industrial economics, and qual-
ity control.*

California Institute of Technology
Industrial Relations Center
Management Library
383 S. Hill (3-90)
Pasadena, CA 91125
818-356-4048
818-795-7174 Fax
*Productivity management, new product devel-
opment, advanced manufacturing systems,
and related topics.*

University of Maryland, College Park
Maryland Center for Quality and Productivity
Library
College of Business and Management
College Park, MD 20742
301-405-2189
301-454-0179 Fax
*Productivity, labor-management cooperation,
and related topics.*

Work in America Institute, Inc.
700 White Plains Rd.
Scarsdale, NY 10583
914-472-9600
914-472-9606 Fax
*Productivity, work innovations, and industrial
relations.*

COMPANIES

Forum Corp. of North America
One Exchange Pl.
Boston, MA 02109
617-523-7300
*Consulting and training services designed to
increase innovation, productivity and leadership qualities.*

HGH Associates, Inc.
9951 Atlantic Blvd.
Jacksonville, FL 32225
904-727-3417
*Management consultants that work to improve
productivity.*

Arthur D. Little, Inc.
25 Acorn Park
Cambridge, MA 02140
617-864-5770
Management consulting services.

McKinsey and Co., Inc.
55 E. 52nd St.
New York, NY 10022
212-446-7000
Management consulting services.

William M. Mercer, Inc.
1166 Ave. of the Americas
New York, NY 10036
212-345-7000
Management consulting services.

Science Management Corp.
P.O. Box 0600
Basking Ridge, NJ 07920
201-647-7000
Consulting and other services to increase productivity.

Strategic Planning Associates, Inc.
(Subsidiary of Marsh & McLennan Companies Inc.)
2300 N Street, N.W.
Washington, DC 20037
202-778-7000
Management consultants.

Towers, Perrin, Forster & Crosby, Inc.
245 Park Ave.
New York, NY 10016
212-309-3400
Management consultants.

FEDERAL GOVERNMENT

U.S. Department of Labor
200 Constitution Ave., N.W.
Washington, DC 20210
202-523-6666
Ask for the Industry Productivity & Technology Studies division; or for the Productivity Research division in the Bureau of Labor Statistics.

PRODUCT LIABILITY

See also: PRODUCT SAFETY

ASSOCIATIONS

Association of Trial Lawyers of America
1050 31st St. N.W.
Washington, DC 20007
202-965-3500
800-424-2725
202-337-0977 Fax
Thomas Henderson, Executive Director
Offers research and educational seminars to attorneys who represent plaintiffs in product liability and other cases involving damages to property or persons.

The Product Liability Alliance
c/o National Association of Wholesaler-Distributors
1725 K St. N.W., Ste. 710
Washington, DC 20006
202-872-0885
Dirk Van Dongen, Executive Secretary
A group of trade associations and manufacturers working to limit product liability through legislation.

Product Liability Prevention and Defense
7297 Lee Hwy., Ste. N
Falls Church, VA 22042
703-533-0251
703-241-5603 Fax
Clay Tyeryar, Executive Officer
Helps manufacturers of machinery improve their defense against litigation.

PERIODICALS

Consumer Product Litigation Reporter
Andrews Publications
1646 West Chester Pike
Box 1000
Westtown, PA 19395
215-399-6600
Kathy Knaub, Editor
Reports on a variety of issues in the liability of consumer products, including warning labels and merchantability.

Journal of Products Liability
Pergamon Press, Inc.
Maxwell House
Fairview Park
Elmsford, NY 10523
914-592-7700
Verne Roberts, Editor
Technical and legal information about issues that affect product liability and safety.

Law of Products Liability
Butterworth Legal Publishers
90 Stiles Rd.
Salem, NH 03079
400-548-4001
Marshall Shapo, Editor
Covers the legal issues that arise during product liability litigation.

Medico-Legal Advisor
Health Law Research Group
9041 Executive Park Dr.
Box 90220
Knoxville, TN 37990
615-482-6600
Laurence Dry, Editor
Analyzes trends in medical product liability.

Product Liability Law and Strategy
New York Law Publishing Co.
Marketing Dept.
111 Eighth Ave., Ste. 900
New York, NY 10011
212-741-8300
Stuart Wise, Editor
Court news and how-to information for attorneys in the product liability field.

Product Liability Trends
National Legal Research Group, Inc.
2421 Ivy Rd.
Box 7187
Charlottesville, VA 22906-7187
800-446-1870
Jeremy Taylor, Editor
Covers recent court cases and legislative trends.

Product Liability: Design and Manufacturing
Defects
Shepard's—McGraw-Hill, Inc.
Box 35300
Colorado Springs, CO 80935-3530
800-525-2474
Advice for manufactures on how to avoid product liability through improved attention to warning labels, packaging, advertising, and related topics.

LIBRARIES

Aetna Life & Casualty
Engineering Library
151 Farmington Ave.
Hartford, CT 06156
203-683-3648
203-683-3746 Fax
Product liability, industrial hygiene, and engineering topics.

Center for Auto Safety
Product Liability Research Service
Library
2001 S St., N.W., Ste. 410
Washington, DC 20009
202-328-7700
Automotive product liability.

PRODUCT SAFETY

See also: PRODUCT LIABILITY and SAFETY

ASSOCIATIONS

Board of Certified Product Safety Management
8009 Carita Ct.
Bethesda, MD 20817
301-984-8969
Harold Gordon, Executive Director
*Offers courses and certifies executives and
engineers responsible for product safety and
product liability.*

Underwriters Laboratories
333 Pfingsten Rd.
Northbrook, IL 60062
708-272-8800
Tom Castino, President
*A well-known certification laboratory con-
cerned with product safety.*

PERIODICALS

Hazard Prevention
System Safety Society, Inc.
Technology Trading Park
5 Export Drive., Ste. A
Sterling, VA 22170-4421
703-444-6520
Sonya Kaiser, Editor
*How-to and technical information for product
safety specialists.*

Product Safety & Liability Reporter
The Bureau of National Affairs, Inc.
1231 25th St., N.W.
Washington, DC 20037
202-452-4200
Stanley Gilbert, Editor
*News and analysis relating to product safety
and liability.*

Product Safety Letter
Washington Business Information, Inc.
c/o Karen Harrington
1117 N. 19th St., Ste. 200
Arlington, VA 22209
703-247-3434
Alice Rogers, Editor
*Follows legislative and regulatory news that
involves consumer products.*

Product Safety News
Institute for Product Safety
Box 1931
Durham, NC 27702
919-489-2356
Verne Roberts, Editor
*Summaries of technical articles about product
and transportation safety that have appeared
in other publications.*

Product Safety Up To Date
National Safety Council
444 N. Michigan Ave.
Chicago, IL 60611
800-621-7619
Kathleen Knowles, Editor
*One of several safety publications of the
National Safety Council concerned with the
manufacture of consumer products.*

LIBRARIES

Consumer Product Safety Commission
Library
5401 Westbard Ave., 4th Fl.
Washington, DC 20207
301-492-6544
*Consumer product safety and standards, and
product testing.*

Eastman Kodak Co.
Eastman Chemical Co.
Technical Information Center
Product Safety Library
P.O. Box 511
Bldg. 54B
Kingsport, TN 37662-0511
615-229-6109
615-229-6099
*Product safety and product toxicology, and
many other topics.*

FEDERAL GOVERNMENT

Consumer Product Safety Commission
Washington, DC 20207
800-638-2772
*Call this telephone number to report an injury
due to a product you feel is unsafe, or for
information about other products that have
been recalled or are considered hazardous.*

PROPANE AND BUTANE GAS INDUSTRY

See also: NATURAL GAS INDUSTRY

ASSOCIATIONS

National Propane Gas Association
1600 Eisenhower Ln.
Lisle, IL 60532
708-515-0600
D. N. Myers, Executive Vice President
*Offers promotional services, and safety and
management education to producers and distributors of propane and butane gas.*

PERIODICALS

Butane—Propane News
Butane—Propane News, Inc.
338 E. Foothill Blvd.
Box 419
Arcadia, CA 91006
818-357-2168
Steve Prowler, Editor
Follows butane and propane news and trends.

Weekly Propane Newsletter
Butane-Propane News, Inc.
338 E. Foothill Blvd.
Box 419
Arcadia, CA 91066
818-357-2168
Hal McWilliams, Editor
Surveys the butane and propane industry.

LIBRARIES

Gas Research Institute
Library Services
8600 W. Bryn Mawr Ave.
Chicago, IL 60631
312-399-8354
312-399-8170 Fax
Natural gas and engineering.

COMPANIES

Chesapeake Utilities Corp.
861 Silver Lake Blvd.
Dover, DE 19901
302-734-6713
Distributor of natural gas, propane, and other products.

Gas Incorporated
4205 Jonesboro Rd.
Union City, GA 30291
404-969-9500
Retailer of propane gas.

Pacific Resources Inc.
(Subsidiary of Broken Hill Proprietary Co.,
    Ltd.)
P.O. Box 3379
Honolulu, HI 96842
808-547-3111
Fuels, gasoline, propane, and other energy products.

Pennsylvania & Southern Gas Co.
102 Desmond St.
Sayre, PA 18840
717-888-6600
Natural gas, propane, and other products.

Silgas, Inc.
(Subsidiary of Star Gas Corp.)
P.O. Box 2487
Clarksville, IN 47131
812-246-6336
Propane gas and other types of fuel.

Suburban Propane
(Division of Quantum Chemical Corp.)
P. O. Box 206
Whippany, NJ 07981
201-540-0300
Propane gas, gas equipment and appliances.

United Cities Gas Co.
5300 Maryland Way
Brentwood, TN 37027
615-373-0104
Distributor of natural gas and propane.

FEDERAL GOVERNMENT

U.S. International Trade Administration
Department of Commerce
14th St. and Constitution Ave., N.W.
Washington, DC 20230
202-377-2000
Ask for the Commodity Analyst who is an expert in the propane and butane gas industry.

U.S. International Trade Commission
500 E St., S.W.
Washington, DC 20436
202-205-2000 Office of the Secretary
202-205-3296 Industries locator
Ask for the Trade Analyst who is an expert in the propane and butane gas industry.

PROPERTY AND FACILITY MANAGEMENT

See also: MAINTENANCE OF BUILDINGS

ASSOCIATIONS

Apartment Owners and Managers Association
of America
65 Cherry Plaza
Watertown, CT 06795
203-274-2589
203-274-2580 Fax
Robert McGough, President
Members are builders who manage the multi-unit buildings they constructed and own.

International Facility Management Association
1 E. Greenway Plaza, 11th Fl.
Houston, TX 77046
713-623-IFMA
713-623-6124 Fax
Dennis Longworth, Executive Director
Offers information to facilities managers who design and manage the workspaces of hospitals, banks, and other public and private institutions.

Institute of Real Estate Management
430 N. Michigan Ave.
Chicago, IL 60611
312-329-6000
Ronald Vukas, Executive Vice President
Offers educational programs to professional real estate managers.

National Property Management Association
220 Patricia Ave.
Dunedin, FL 34698
813-736-6707
813-736-6707 Fax
James Lerch, Executive Director
A clearinghouse for managers of facilities and equipment.

National Society of Professional Resident
Managers
1518 K St. N.W., Ste. 503
Washington, DC 20005
202-737-0204
202-638-4833 Fax
Elizabeth Greene, Exec.Dir.
An information exchange for managers of residential apartment complexes.

Property Management Association of America
8811 Colesville Rd., Ste. G106
Silver Spring, MD 20910
301-587-6543
301-589-2017 Fax
John Bachner, Executive Vice President
Members include managers of commercial and residential property.

PERIODICALS

Buildings
Stamats Communications, Inc.
c/o Wayne Bayliss
427 Sixth Ave., S.E.
Cedar Rapids, IA 52406
319-364-6167
Linda Monroe, Editor
Information about the planning, construction, and management of facilities and buildings.

Facilities Design and Management
Gralla Publications
1515 Broadway
New York, NY 10036
212-869-1300
Anne Falluchi, Editor
Written for managers of offices and other types of facilities.

Journal of Property Management
Institute of Real Estate Management
430 N. Michigan Ave.
Box 109025
Chicago, IL 60610-9025
312-661-1930
Mariwyn Evans, Editor
Advice and news for managers of office buildings, apartment buildings, shopping centers, and other types of investment real estate.

Property Management Monthly
Adler Group
8601 Georgia Ave., Ste. 400
Silver Spring, MD 20910
301-588-0681
Laura Zaner, Editor
Follows trends for those who manage income-producing properties.

LIBRARIES

American Public Works Association
Information Services
1313 E. 60th St.
Chicago, IL 60637
312-667-2200
Grounds management, buildings management, equipment services, and public works.

COMPANIES

ECL Industries, Inc.
(Subsidiary of Service Resources Corp.)
75 Varick St.
New York, NY 10013
212-941-2577
Facilities management services.

Innovative Tech Systems Inc.
589 Bethlehem Pike
Montgomeryville, PA 60604
215-997-2711
Facilities management software and consulting.

Lomas Mortgage USA
(Subsidiary of Lomas Financial Corp.)
2001 Bryan Tower, Box 655644
Dallas, TX 75265
214-746-7111
Mortgages, insurance, and property management.

Micros Systems Inc.
(Subsidiary of Westinghouse Electric Corp.)
12000 Baltimore Ave.
Beltsville, MD 20705
301-490-2000
Software for property management and other purposes.

Sverdrup Corp.
13723 Riverport Dr.
Maryland Heights, MO 63043
314-436-7600
Real estate development, construction, and facilities management.

PROSTHETICS INDUSTRY

ASSOCIATIONS

American Orthotic and Prosthetic Association
717 Pendleton St.
Alexandria, VA 22314
703-836-7116
703-836-0838 Fax
Ian Horen, Executive Director
Members manufacture and custom fit artificial limbs, other replacement parts for the human body, and braces. Affiliated with the American Board for Certification in Orthotics and Prosthetics, a physicians' organization located at the same address.

PERIODICALS

Journal of Arthroplasty
Churchill Livingstone Medical Journals
650 Ave. of the America
New York, NY 10011
212-206-4050
David Hungerford, Editor
Covers all aspects of joint replacement surgery.

Journal of Prosthetics and Orthotics
American Academy of Orthotists and Prosthetists
717 Pendleton St.
Alexandria, VA 22314
703-836-7116
Charles Pritham, Editor
A professional journal covering orthotics and prosthetics procedures and equipment.

LIBRARIES

Intermedics, Inc.
Library Information Services Department
240 W. 2nd St.
Box 617
Freeport, TX 77541
409-233-8611
409-233-6474 Fax
Biomedical engineering, bioprosthetics, and cardiology.

Orthotics and Prosthetics National Office Library
1650 King St., 5th Fl.
Alexandria, VA 22314
703-836-7116
Orthotics and prosthetics.

U.S. Department of Veterans Affairs
Office of Technology Transfer
Resource Center
VA Prosthetics Research & Development
    Center
103 S. Gay St.
Baltimore, MD 21202
301-962-1800
301-962-9670 Fax
*Prosthetics, orthotics, rehabilitation, and bio-
engineering.*

COMPANIES

Acor Orthopaedic, Inc.
18530 S. Miles Pkwy.
Cleveland, OH 44128
216-662-4500
Artificial limbs and orthotic devices.

Bell-Horn, Inc.
451 N. Third St.
Philadelphia, PA 19123
215-627-2773
Prosthetic appliances.

Hanger Orthopedic Group, Inc.
8200 Wisconsin Ave.
Bethesda, MD 20814
301-986-0701
Orthotic and prosthetic devices.

William H. Horn & Brother, Inc.
451 N. Third St.
Philadelphia, PA 19123
215-627-2773
Orthotic and prosthetic products.

Knit-Rite, Inc.
P. O. Box 208
Kansas City, MO 64141
816-221-5200
Orthotic and prosthetic devices.

Ohio Willow Wood Co.
15441 Scioto-Darby Rd.
Mount Sterling, OH 43143
614-869-3377
Orthotic and prosthetic products.

Orthopedic Services Inc.
2570 Blvd. of the Generals, Box 931
Valley Forge, PA 19482
215-631-9900
Orthotic and prosthetic services.

Rhode Island Limb Co.
1559 Elmwood Ave.
Cranston, RI 02910
401-941-6230
Prosthetic appliances.

Union Orthotics & Prosthetics Co.
3401 Liberty Ave.
Pittsburgh, PA 15201
412-621-2698
Artificial limbs and orthotic products.

FEDERAL GOVERNMENT

U.S. Department of Veterans Affairs
810 Vermont Ave., N.W.
Washington, DC 20420
202-233-4000
*Ask for the Rehabilitation and Prosthetics
division in the Clinical Affairs department.*

U.S. Patent and Trademark Office
Crystal Plaza 2
2011 Jefferson Davis Highway
Arlington, VA 22202
703-305-8000
*Ask for the Examining Group Director who is
a specialist in prosthetic products.*

PUBLIC ADMINISTRATION

See also: CIVIL SERVICE and MUNICIPAL GOVERNMENT

ASSOCIATIONS

American Society for Public Administration
1120 G St. N.W., Ste. 500
Washington, DC 20005
202-393-7878
202-638-4952 Fax
Shirley Wester, Executive Director
*Members include public officials, managers,
and others associated with the public administrative area.*

Institute of Public Administration
55 W. 44th St.
New York, NY 10036
212-730-5486
212-398-9305 Fax
Dwight Ink, President
*Conducts research and educational programs
in the fields of public administration, finance,
and related topics.*

National Forum for Black Public Administrators
777 N. Capitol St. N.E., Ste. 801
Washington, DC 20002
202-408-9300
202-408-8558 Fax
Quentin Lawson, Executive Director
*Members are Afro-American administrators,
city managers, and others.*

PERIODICALS

American City & County
Communication Channels, Inc.
6255 Barfield Rd.
Atlanta, GA 30328-4369
404-256-9800
Janet Ward, Editor
*Covers many issues of interest to administra-
tors of city, town, and county governments.*

County News
National Association of Counties
440 First St., N.W.
Washington, DC 20001
202-393-6226
Beverly Schlotterbeck, Editor
*Written for county administrators and offi-
cers.*

Governing
Congressional Quarterly Inc.
1414 22nd St., N.W.
Washington, DC 20037
800-432-2250
Peter Harkness, Editor
*Reports on issues and trends for local and
state officials and administrators.*

Government Executive
National Journal, Inc.
1730 M St., N.W., Ste. 1100
Washington, DC 20036
202-875-1400
Timothy Clark, Editor
*Business news for federal officials and man-
agers.*

Nation's Cities Weekly
National League of Cities
1301 Pennsylvania Ave., N.W.
Washington, DC 20004
202-626-3040
Alan Beals, Editor
*Offers examples of cities that have overcome
problems.*

Public Management
International City Management Association
777 North Capitol, N.E., Ste. 500
Washington, DC 20002-4201
202-289-4262
Beth Payne, Editor
*Practical information for managers of local
governments.*

LIBRARIES

U.S. Executive Office of the President
Library
725 17th St., N.W., Rm. G-102
Washington, DC 20503
202-395-3654
*Public administration, economics, political sci-
ence, policymaking, and related topics.*

University of Mississippi
Public Policy Research Center
University, MS 38677
601-232-5407
*Public administration, government, and
related topics.*

University of Texas, Austin
Wasserman Public Affairs Library
General Libraries
Sid Richardson Hall, 3.243
Austin, TX 78713-7330
512-471-4486
512-471-8901 Fax
*Public administration, public finance, and
public welfare.*

PUBLIC OPINION AND POLLS

See also: MARKET RESEARCH AND STATISTICS

ASSOCIATIONS

American Association for Public Opinion
   Research
PO Box 17
Princeton, NJ 08542
609-924-8670
Diana Druker, Administrator
*Members exchange information on the tech-
niques and uses of public opinion polls.*

Council of American Survey Research Organizations
3 Upper Devon Belle Terre
Port Jefferson, NY 11777
516-928-6954
Diane Bowers, Executive Director
*Members are survey research companies that
share data and techniques with each other.*

National Council on Public Polls
205 E. 42nd St., Rm. 1708
New York, NY 10017
212-986-8262
212-687-2102 Fax
Harry O'Neill, President
*Members take and analyze polls, and help
explain results to the public.*

Roper Organization
205 E. 42nd St.
New York, NY 10017
212-599-0700
212-687-2102 Fax
Burns Roper, Chairman
*Conducts and collects public opinion polls and
disseminates results.*

PERIODICALS

Index to International Public Opinion
Hastings Survey Research Consultants Inter-
   national, Inc.
Greenwood Press, Inc.
88 Post Rd. W.
Westport, CT 06881-9990
203-226-3511
Elizabeth Hastings, Editor
*Surveys public opinion polls around the
world.*

Polling Report
Polling Report, Inc.
509 Capitol Ct., N.E., No.100
Washington, DC 20002
202-544-5455
Thomas Silver, Editor
*Poll results and analyses by experts on numer-
ous topics.*

LIBRARIES

Louis Harris & Associates, Inc.
Information Services
630 Fifth Ave.
New York, NY 10111
212-698-9697
Public opinion.

University of California, Berkeley
Data Archive & Technical Assistnace
Survey Research Center
2538 Channing Way
Berkeley, CA 94720
510-642-6571
510-643-8292 Fax
Opinion polls, U.S. Census data, survey research methods, sociology, and vital statistics.

University of Chicago
National Opinion Research Center
Paul B. Sheatsley Library
1155 E. 60th St.
Chicago, IL 60637
312-702-1213
312-702-0857 Fax
Public opinion research, demography, statistics, and sociology.

University of Connecticut
Institute for Social Inquiry
341 Mansfield Rd., Rm. 421
Box U-164
Storrs, CT 06269-1164
203-486-4440
203-486-2123 Fax
Public opinion surveys, census data, and election data.

COMPANIES

Center for Public Interest Polling
Rutgers University
Eagleton Institute of Politics
New Brunswick, NJ 08901
201-828-2210
Conducts survey research.

The Daniel Yankelovich Group, Inc.
1350 6th Ave.
New York, NY 10150
212-247-1313
Conducts public opinion polls.

The Gallup Organization, Inc.
53 Bank St.
Princeton, NJ 08540
609-924-9600
Conducts public opinion polls.

Institute for Social Research
University of Michigan
426 Thompson St.
Ann Arbor, MI 48106
313-764-8363
Studies survey methodology.

Institute for Survey Research
Temple University
1601 N. Broad St.
Philadelphia, PA 19122
215-787-8355
Studies survey methodology.

Louis Harris & Associates, Inc.
630 Fifth Ave.
New York, NY 10020
212-698-9600
Conducts public opinion polls.

A. C. Nielsen Co.
Nielsen Plaza
Northbrook, IL 60062
312-498-6300
Conducts public opinion polls.

Roper Organization, Inc.
205 E. 42nd St., 17th Fl.
New York, NY 10017
212-599-0700
Conducts public opinion polls.

Starch/Inra/Hooper, Inc.
E. Boston Post Rd.
Mamaroneck, NY 10543
914-698-0800
Conducts public opinion polls.

PUBLIC RELATIONS AND PUBLICITY

ASSOCIATIONS

Institute for Public Relations Research and
Education
310 Madison Ave.
New York, NY 10017
212-370-9353
Don Bates, Adminisrator
*Conducts and reports public relations
research.*

Public Relations Society of America
33 Irving Pl., 3rd Fl.
New York, NY 10003-2376
212-995-2230
212-995-0757 Fax
Elizabeth Kovacs, Executive Vice President
*A large professional society that offers
research and educational programs to public
relations personnel in the public and private
sectors.*

Society of Consumer Affairs Professionals in
Business
4900 Leesburg Pike, Ste. 400
Alexandria, VA 22302
703-998-7371
Louis Garcia, Executive Director
*An information clearinghouse for managers of
consumer affairs departments in companies.*

PERIODICALS

Media News Keys
Television Index, Inc.
40-29 27th St.
Long Island City, NY 11101
718-937-3990
Timothy Hunter, Editor
Lists contacts in the media.

Public Relations News
127 E. 80th St.
New York, NY 10021
212-879-7090
Denny Griswold, Editor
*Offers industry news and trends, and detailed
reports about successful public relations campaigns.*

Public Relations Quarterly
44 W. Market St.
Box 311
Rhinebeck, NY 12572
914-876-2081
Howard Penn Hudson, Editor
*Covers practical and theoretical information
about public relations and communications.*

Public Relations Review
J A I Press Inc.
55 Old Post Rd., No.2
Box 1678
Greenwich, CT 06836-1678
203-661-7602
Ray Hiebert, Editor
*Details public relations research, issues, and
trends.*

LIBRARIES

Burson-Marsteller
Information Service
One E. Wacker Dr.
Chicago, IL 60601
312-329-9292
312-329-7583 Fax
Public relations.

Hill and Knowlton, Inc.
Information Center
111 E. Wacker Dr., Ste. 1700
Chicago, IL 60601
312-565-1200
312-565-4360 Fax
Public relations.

University of Illinois
Communications Library
122 Gregory Hall
Urbana, IL 61801
217-333-2216
Public relations, communication theory,
broadcasting, and related topics.

University of Missouri, Columbia
Journalism Library
117 Walter Williams Hall
Columbia, MO 65202
314-882-7502
Journalism, public relations, news writing,
and broadcasting.

COMPANIES

Ackerman, Hood & McQueen, Inc.
1100 Citizens Plaza
Oklahoma City, OK 73118
405-843-7777
Advertising and public relations services.

Creswell, Munsell, Fultz & Zirbel
(Division of Young & Rubicam L.P.)
P.O. Box 2879
Cedar Rapids, IA 52406
319-395-6500
Advertising and public relations services.

Daniel J. Edelman, Inc.
211 E. Ontario St.
Chicago, IL 60611
312-280-7000
Public relations services.

Hill & Knowlton, Inc.
(Subsidiary of WPP Group plc)
420 Lexington Ave.
New York, NY 10017
212-697-5600
Public relations services.

Lewis, Gilman & Kynett, Inc.
(Subsidiary of Foote, Cone & Belding Com-
    munications, Inc.)
200 S. Broad St.
Philadelphia, PA 19102
215-790-4100
Advertising and public relations services.

Mallory Factor Inc.
275 Seventh Ave.
New York, NY 10001
212-242-6000
Public relations and investor relations ser-
vices.

Robert Marston and Assoc., Inc.
485 Madison Ave.
New York, NY 10022
212-371-2200
Public relations services.

Poppe Tyson Inc
(Subsidiary of Bozell, Jacobs, Kenyon & Eck-
    hardt Inc.)
475 Park Ave. South
New York, NY 10016
212-725-2900
Advertising and public relations services.

Ruder-Finn, Inc.
301 E. 57th St.
New York, NY 10022
212-593-6440
Public relations and investor relations ser-
vices.

PUBLIC TRANSPORTATION

See also: MOTOR BUSES; RAILROAD INDUSTRY; and each
of the 50 states under transportation

ASSOCIATIONS

American Public Transit Association
1201 New York Ave. N.W., Ste. 400
Washington, DC 20005
202-898-4000
202-898-4070 Fax
Jack Gilstrap, Executive Vice President
*Members include bus and rail transit systems,
manufacturers, and others.*

International Mass Transit Association
PO Box 40247
Washington, DC 20016-0247
202-362-7960
202-842-0621 Fax
C. Carroll Carter, Executive Director
*Offers research and promotional programs for
manufacturers and consultants in the mass
transit field.*

Transportation Research Board
2101 Constitution Ave. N.W.
Washington, DC 20418
202-334-2934
Thomas Deen, Executive Director
*Conducts research on all planning, technologi-
cal, and operating subjects in the transportation field.*

PERIODICALS

Journal of Urban Planning and Development
Urban Planning and Development Division
American Society of Civil Engineers
345 E. 47th St.
New York, NY 10017-2398
212-705-7288
David Pearson, Editor
*Reports on the civil engineering aspects of
urban planning, including public transporta-
tion.*

National Cooperative Transit Research and
    Development Program Synthesis of Tran-
    sit Practice
Transportation Research Board
National Research Council
2101 Constitution Ave., N.W.
Washington, DC 20418
202-334-3214
Analyzes practices in public transit.

Passenger Transport
American Public Transit Association
1201 New York Ave., N.W., Ste. 400
Washington, DC 20005
202-898-4119
Dennis Kouba, Editor
Surveys the public transit field.

Urban Transport News
Business Publishers, Inc.
951 Pershing Dr.
Silver Spring, MD 20910-4464
301-587-6300
Dede Ryan, Editor
Reports on such topics as urban transportation management, funding, ridership, technology, and federal government news that has an impact on public transportation.

LIBRARIES

American Public Transit Association
1201 New York Ave. N.W., Ste. 400
Washington, DC 20005
202-898-4000
Urban transportation systems.

U.S. Department of Transportation
Library and Distribution Services Division
400 7th St., S.W.
M-493.3, Rm. 2200
Washington, DC 20590
202-366-0746
Urban mass transit, highways, and railroads.

U.S. Urban Mass Transportation Administration
Transportation Research Information Center
400 7th St., S.W., Rm. 6100
Washington, DC 20590
202-366-9157
Urban transportation, rail technology, new systems and technology, service, and planning.

University of California, Irvine
Institute of Transportation Studies
Information Center
Room 419, GSM Bldg.
Irvine, CA 92717
714-856-5989
213-206-3421 Fax
Urban transportation.

FEDERAL GOVERNMENT

U.S. Department of Transportation
400 Seventh St., S.W.
Washington, DC 20590
202-366-4000
Ask for the public information office to find an appropriate expert.

PUBLIC UTILITIES

See also: ELECTRIC POWER; NATURAL GAS INDUSTRY;
and each of the 50 states under public utilities

ASSOCIATIONS

American Public Gas Association
PO Box 1426
Vienna, VA 22183
703-281-2910
Robert Cave, Executive Director
*Members are publicly owned gas utilities and
the firms that service them.*

American Public Power Association
2301 M St. N.W.
Washington, DC 20037
202-467-2900
202-467-2910 Fax
Larry Hobart, Executive Director
*Publicly owned electric utilities and other elec-
tric systems.*

Association of Edison Illuminating Companies
600 N. 18th St.
PO Box 2641
Birmingham, AL 35291-0992
205-250-2530
W. O. Whitt, Executive Director
Public utilities owned by investors.

Automatic Meter Reading Association
PO Box 500
Westwood, NJ 07675
202-666-0902
Donald Schlenger, Executive Officer
*Manufacturers of telemetry-based equipment
to read meters and to control energy use.*

Edison Electric Institute
701 Pennsylvania Ave. N.W.
Washington, DC 20004-2696
202-508-5000
Thomas Kuhn, President
Electric utilitites owned by investors.

Institute of Public Utilities
Michigan State Univ.
113 Olds Hall
East Lansing, MI 48824
517-355-1876
517-355-1854 Fax
Harry Trebing, Director
*Offers educational programs to privately-
owned utility companies.*

National Association of Regulatory Utility
    Commissioners
PO Box 684
1102 ICC Bldg.
Constitution Ave. and 12th St. N.W.
Washington, DC 20044-0864
202-898-2200
202-898-2213 Fax
Paul Rodgers, Administrative Director
*Represents the commissioners who protect the
public's interest by regulating public utilities
and transportations firms.*

Water and Sewer Distributors of America
PO Box 34595
Bethesda, MD 20817
301-897-3191
Glenn Northup, Executive Director
Members distribute equipment and supplies to water and sewer systems.

Water and Wastewater Equipment Manufac-
   turers Association
PO Box 17402
Dulles Intl. Airport
Washington, DC 20041
703-444-1777
Dawn Kristof, President
Firms that make equipment used in water works and waste water facilities.

PERIODICALS

Accounting for Public Utilities
Matthew Bender & Co., Inc.
11 Penn Plaza
New York, NY 10001
212-967-7707
Detailed information about accounting and rate-determination for utilities.

Analysis of Public Utility Financing
Ebasco Services Inc.
145 Technology Park—Atlanta
Norcross, GA 30092
404-662-2098
J. Nichols, Editor
Covers various financial topics relating to new issues of utility securities.

Moody's Public Utility Manual
Moody's Investors Service
99 Church St.
New York, NY 10007
212-553-0300
Robert Hanson, Editor
Provides statistics about finances and other information of all utilities in the U.S. A sister publication, Moody's Public Utility News Reports, covers news of all these utilities.

Public Utilities Fortnightly
Public Utilities Reports, Inc.
2111 Wilson Blvd., Ste. 200
Arlington, VA 22201
703-243-7000
Cheryl Romo, Editor
Surveys trends and news of public utilities.

Public Utilities Newsletter
National Safety Council
444 N. Michigan Ave.
Chicago, IL 60611
800-621-7619
Advises on safety matters for utilities.

Utility Construction and Maintenance
Practical Communications, Inc.
Box 183
Cary, IL 60013-0183
708-639-2200
Alan Richter, Editor
Offers advice to managers of utilities about utility construction and maintenance.

LIBRARIES

Portland General Electric
Corporate Library
121 S.W. Salmon St. 3WTC-5
Portland, OR 97204
503-464-8700
503-464-8706 Fax
Environmental sciences, alternative energy sources, and electrical engineering.

Public Utility Commission of Texas
Library
7800 Shoal Creek Blvd.
Austin, TX 78757
512-458-0254
512-458-0254 Fax
*Public utilities, electric utilities, energy, and
economics.*

Virginia Power
Research/Records Services
Box 26666
Richmond, VA 23261
804-771-3657
804-771-3168 Fax
*Nuclear power, electric power, and environ-
ment.*

COMPANIES

American Electric Power Co., Inc.
One Riverside Plaza
Columbus, OH 43215
614-223-1000
Electric light and power utility.

Illinois Power Co.
500 S. 27th St.
Decatur, IL 62525
217-424-6600
Electric and gas utility.

Jamaica Water Supply Co.
(Subsidiary of JWP Inc.)
410 Lakeville Rd.
Lake Success, NY 11042
516-488-4600
Water public utility.

Memphis Light Gas and Water Division
220 S. Main St.
Memphis, TN 38101
901-528-4011
Electric, gas, and water utility.

Michigan Power Co.
(Subsidiary of American Electric Power Co.,
    Inc.)
123 Portage Ave., Box 367
Three Rivers, MI 49093
616-279-5261
Electric and gas public utility.

San Diego Gas & Electric Co.
P.O. Box 1831
San Diego, CA 92112
619-696-2000
Electric and gas utility.

Southern California Water Co.
3625 W. Sixth St.
Los Angeles, CA 90020
213-251-3600
Water and electric public utility.

Wisconsin Power & Light Co.
(Subsidiary of WPL Holdings, Inc.)
222 W. Washington Ave.
Madison, WI 53703
608-252-3311
Gas, water, and electric public utility.

PUMP AND COMPRESSOR INDUSTRY

ASSOCIATIONS

Compressed Air and Gas Institute
c/o John H. Addington
Thomas Assocs., Inc.
1230 Keith Bldg.
Cleveland, OH 44115
216-241-7333
216-241-0105 Fax
John Addington, Executive Officer
Firms that make air and gas compressors and related equipment.

Contractors Pump Bureau
PO Box 5858
Rockville, MD 20855
301-340-2094
Walter Anderson, Executive Director
Manufacturers of pumping engines and equipment used primarily in the construction industry.

Hydraulic Institute
30200 Detroit Rd.
Cleveland, OH 44145-1967
216-899-0010
216-892-1404 Fax
Allen Wherry, Secretary
Firms that make and service hydraulic pumps used in industry.

National Fluid Power Association
3333 N. Mayfair Rd.
Milwaukee, WI 53222
414-778-3344
414-778-3361 Fax
William Wilberg, Executive Director
Manufacturers of pumps, hoses, valves, and other items used in the transmission of pressurized fluid.

Submersible Wastewater Pump Association
600 S. Federal St., Ste. 400
Chicago, IL 60605
312-922-6222
312-922-2734 Fax
Charles Stolberg, Managing Director
Members make submersible wastewater pumps.

Sump and Sewage Pump Manufacturers Association
PO Box 298
Winnetka, IL 60093
708-835-8911
708-835-8913 Fax
Pamela Franzen, Managing Director
Manufacturers of sewage pumps and sump pumps, which are used to drain residential cellars of water.

PERIODICALS

Compressed Air
Compressed Air Magazine Co.
253 E. Washington Ave.
Washington, NJ 07882
908-850-7818
S.M. Parkhill, Editor
Technological and industrial management information about compressed air products.

COMPANIES

Copeland Corp.
(Subsidiary of Emerson Electric Co.)
1675 Campbell Rd.
Sidney, OH 45365
513-498-3011
Pumps, compressors, and other equipment used in air conditioners, refrigerators, and heating systems.

Eagle Industries, Inc.
(Subsidiary of Great American Management
    & Investment, Inc.)
Two N. Riverside Plaza
Chicago, IL 60606
312-906-8700
Air compressors and many other types of products.

Goulds Pumps, Inc.
240 Fall St.
Seneca Falls, NY 13148
315-568-2811
Pumps and water systems.

Ingersoll-Rand Co.
200 Chestnut Ridge Rd.
Woodcliff Lake, NJ 07675
201-573-0123
Pumps, compressors, and other products.

Ladish Co. Inc.
5481 S. Packard Ave.
Cudahy, WI 53110
414-747-2611
Valves, pumps, and other products.

Pentair Inc.
1700 W. Hwy. 36
St. Paul, MN 55113
612-636-7920
Water pumps and many other types of products.

Tecumseh Products Co.
100 E. Patterson St.
Tecumseh, MI 49286
517-423-8411
Compressors for refrigerators, pumps, and other equipment.

Thomas Industries Inc.
4360 Brownsboro Rd.
Louisville, KY 40207
502-893-4600
Vacuum pumps, air compressors, and other types of products.

Trinova Corp.
3000 Strayer
Maumee, OH 43537
419-867-2200
Fluid pumps, hydraulic systems, and other products.

FEDERAL GOVERNMENT

U.S. International Trade Administration
Department of Commerce
14th St. and Constitution Ave., N.W.
Washington, DC 20230
202-377-2000
Ask for the Commodity Analyst who is an expert in pumps and compressors.

U.S. International Trade Commission
500 E St., S.W.
Washington, DC 20436
202-205-2000 Office of the Secretary
202-205-3296 Industries locator
Ask for the Trade Analyst who is an expert in pumps and compressors.

PURCHASING

See also: Each of the 50 states under purchasing

ASSOCIATIONS

American Purchasing Society
11910 Oak Trail Way
Port Richey, FL 34668
813-862-7998
Harry Hough, President
Provides seminars, research and consulting to personnel responsible for purchasing.

National Association of Purchasing Management
2055 E. Centennial Circle
PO Box 22160
Tempe, AZ 85285
602-752-6276
800-888-6276
602-752-7890 Fax
R. Jerry Baker, Executive Vice President
A large organization offering information on procurement techniques, market trends and related subjects.

National Association of State Purchasing Officials
c/o Council of State Governments
Iron Works Pike
PO Box 11910
Lexington, KY 40578
606-231-1877
606-231-1928 Fax
Linda Carroll, Staff Director
A professional group of state purchasing officials.

National Institute of Governmental Purchasing
115 Hillwood Ave.
Falls Church, VA 22046
703-533-7300
703-532-0915 Fax
Robin Zee, Executive Vice President
Sets specifications and standards for local, state, county, and federal purchasing officials.

PERIODICALS

Industrial Purchasing Agent
Publications for Industry
21 Russell Woods Rd.
Great Neck, NY 11021
516-487-0990
Pearl Panes, Editor
Describes new products of interest to purchasing agents.

Purchasing
Cahners Publishing Co.
275 Washington St.
Newton, MA 02158-1630
617-946-3030
James Morgan, Editor
Offers news about products, prices, economic conditions, and advice about purchasing methods and strategies.

Purchasing Management
Purchasing Management Association, Twin
    City
14 N. Seventh Ave.
St. Cloud, MN 56303
612-259-4000
Marie Castle, Editor
How-to information for purchasing agents.

Southern Purchasor
Purchasing Management Association of
    Carolinas-Virginia, Inc.
405 Battleground Ave., Ste. 203
Greensboro, NC 27402
919-272-6186
V. Gilbert Snyder, Editor
*Advises on how to be a more effective
purchasor.*

Purchasing Executive's Bulletin
Bureau of Business Practice
24 Rope Ferry Rd.
Waterford, CT 06386
203-442-4365
Wayne Muller, Editor
*Reports news that affects purchasing deci-
sions.*

LIBRARIES

National Association of Purchasing Manage-
    ment
Information Center
Box 22160
Tempe, AZ 85285-2160
602-752-6276
602-752-7890 Fax
*Purchasing, inventory management, and value
analysis.*

QUALITY CONTROL

See also: PRODUCTIVITY

ASSOCIATIONS

American Society for Quality Control
310 W. Wisconsin Ave.
Milwaukee, WI 53203
414-272-8575
800-248-1946
414-272-1734 Fax
Paul Borawski, Executive Director
*A large professional society of quality control
managers, engineers, and others. Offers
courses in quality control management,
inspection, cost-control, and related topics.*

Association for Quality and Participation
801-B W. 8th St., Ste. 501
Cincinnati, OH 45203
513-381-1959
Cathy Kramer, Executive Vice President
*Educates executives about Quality Circles: a
team approach to solving problems, increasing
productivity, and improving the quality of
manufactured goods.*

ASTM
1916 Race St.
Philadelphia, PA 19103
215-299-5400
J.G. O'Grady, President
A very large group of engineers, executives, scientists, and others concerned with the testing of products, materials, and systems.

PERIODICALS

Journal of Quality Technology
American Society for Quality Control
310 W. Wisconsin Ave.
Milwaukee, WI 53203
414-272-8575
John Cornell, Editor
Focuses on quality control from an engineering and statistical point of view.

Quality Assurance
Academic Press, Inc., Journal Division
1250 Sixth Ave.
San Diego, CA 92101
619-230-1840
Frederick Coulston, Editor
Detailed information about the technological, engineering, regulatory, and legal issues involved in quality control and quality assurance.

Quality Assurance Bulletin
Bureau of Business Practice
24 Rope Ferry Rd.
Waterford, CT 06386
203-442-4365
Anna Trusky, Editor
Follows news and trends in quality assurance.

Quality Control and Applied Statistics
Executive Sciences Institute
1005 Mississippi Ave.
Davenport, IA 52803
319-324-4463
Bruce Brocka, Editor
Digests the worldwide technical literature in quality control.

Quality Progress
American Society for Quality Control
310 W. Wisconsin Ave.
Milwaukee, WI 53203
414-272-8575
Brad Stratton, Editor
Advises industrial managers about quality control.

LIBRARIES

American Productivity & Quality Center
Information Services
123 N. Post Oak Ln.
Houston, TX 77024
713-681-4020
713-681-8578 Fax
Productivity, industrial economics, and quality control.

California Institute of Technology
Industrial Relations Center
Management Library
383 S. Hill
Pasadena, CA 91125
818-356-4048
818-795-7174 Fax
Productivity management, new product development, quality control, advanced manufacturing systems, and related topics.

University of Maryland, College Park
Maryland Center for Quality and Productivity
Library
College of Business and Management
College Park, MD 20742
301-405-2189
301-454-0179 Fax
Productivity, quality control, labor-management cooperation, and related topics.

Work in America Institute, Inc.
700 White Plains Rd.
Scarsdale, NY 10583
914-472-9600
914-472-9606 Fax
Productivity, work innovations, quality control, industrial relations, and related topics.

COMPANIES

Aerodyne Products Corp.
76 Treble Cove Rd.
North Billerica, MA 01862
508-663-7411
Quality control products.

Bio-Tek Instruments, Inc.
Highland Park
Winooski, VT 05404
802-655-4040
Medical and quality assurance testing equipment.

Brand Companies, Inc.
1420 Renaissance Dr.
Park Ridge, IL 60068
708-298-1200
A wide variety of technical services including quality assurance.

ESA, Inc.
45 Wiggins Ave.
Bedford, MA 01730
617-275-0100
Analytical instruments used for quality control, testing, and other purposes.

Federal Products Co.
(Division of Esterline Technologies Corp.)
1144 Eddy St.
Providence, RI 02940
401-781-9300
Quality control instruments used for inspection and measurement.

Lawson-Hemphill Inc.
96 Hadwin St.
Central Falls, RI 02863
401-724-7130
Instuments used for quality control in the textile industry.

Standard Gage Co. Inc.
(Subsidiary of Brown & Sharpe Mfg. Co.)
P.O. Box 271
Poughkeepsie, NY 12602
914-471-3100
Instuments used for quality control.

United States Testing Co., Inc.
(Subsidiary of S.G.S. North America Inc.)
1415 Park Ave.
Hoboken, NJ 07030
201-792-2400
A variety of testing, inspection, and engineering services, including quality control testing.

X-Rite, Incorporated
3100 44th St. S. W.
Grandville, MI 49418
616-534-7663
Instruments used for quality control in the x-ray and photographic industry.

QUARRY AND STONE INDUSTRY

See also: MINES AND MINING INDUSTRY

ASSOCIATIONS

Allied Stone Industries
PO Box 288145
Chicago, IL 60628
312-928-4800
Jack Van Etten, Secretary
Members are stone quarriers and fabricators.

Barre Granite Association
PO Box 481
Barre, VT 05641
802-476-4131
Norman James, Exeouive Vice President
Firms that quarry granite for building construction and cemetery use.

Building Stone Institute
420 Lexington Ave.
New York, NY 10170
212-490-2530
914-997-1106 Fax
Dorothy Kender, Executive Vice President
A group of quarriers and stone dealers who answer questions for builders, architects, masons, and others.

Cultured Marble Institute
435 N. Michigan Ave., Ste. 1717
Chicago, IL 60611
312-644-0828
312-644-8557 Fax
Edward Kawala, Executive Director
Members make cultured marble products and supply the industry. Provides research, training, and promotional services.

Marble Institute of America
33505 State St.
Farmington, MI 48335
313-476-5558
Robert Hund, Managing Director
Represents all parts of the dimension stone industry, including those who quarry, distribute, install, and finish marble.

National Stone Association
1415 Elliot Pl. N.W.
Washington, DC 20007
202-342-1100
202-342-0702 Fax
Robert Bartlett, President
Quarriers and processors of crushed stone and manufacturers of equipment.

PERIODICALS

Cement, Quarry and Mineral Aggregates
    Newsletter
National Safety Council
444 N. Michigan Ave.
Chicago, IL 60611
800-621-7619
Safety information for the quarry industry.

Mine & Quarry Trader
Allied Publications
7355 N. Woodland
Box 603
Indianapolis, IN 46206-0603
317-297-5500
For buyers and sellers of equipment for the mining and quarry industries.

Pit & Quarry
Edgell Communications
7500 Old Oak Blvd.
Cleveland, OH 44130
216-243-8100
Robert Drake, Editor
*Surveys the market for cement, gravel,
crushed stone, and other products.*

COMPANIES

Continental Materials Corp.
325 N. Wells St.
Chicago, IL 60610
312-661-7200
*Sand, concrete, quarry products, and other
types of products.*

Georgia Marble Co.
1201 Roberts Blvd., Building 100
Kennesaw, GA 30144
404-421-6500
Marble and other quarry products.

Harmony Blue Granite Co.
Harmony Dr.
Elberton, GA 30635
912-283-3111
Granite and other quarry products.

Heritage Marble of Ohio, Inc.
7086 Huntley Rd.
Columbus, OH 43229
614-736-1464
Marble and other quarry products.

Hinkle Corp.
N. Middletown Rd.
Paris, KY 40361
606-987-3670
*Stone quarries and concrete and asphalt
plants.*

Kline's Quarry Inc.
Front St.
Wrightsville, PA 17368
717-252-1584
Limestone quarry.

New England Stone Industries, Inc.
Providence Pike
Smithfield, RI 02917
401-232-2040
Granite quarry.

North Carolina Granite Corp.
P.O. Drawer 151
Mount Airy, NC 27030
919-786-5141
Granite quarry.

Telsmith, Inc.
(Division of Astec Industries, Inc.)
P. O. Box 723
Milwaukee, WI 53201
414-242-6600
Mining and quarrying machinery.

Wichert Tile, Ltd.
2003 Kalia Rd.
Honolulu, HI 96815
808-955-6631
Ceramic tile, marble, and granite.

FEDERAL GOVERNMENT

Bureau of Mines
810 7th St., N.W.
Washington, DC 20747
202-501-9770
*Ask for the Mining & Quarrying Trends
department.*

RADIO BROADCASTING INDUSTRY

See also: TELEVISION BROADCASTING INDUSTRY

ASSOCIATIONS

American College of Radio Marketing
710 Arendell, Ste. 103
PO Box 1801
Morehead City, NC 28557
919-247-7131
919-726-8800 Fax
Charles Campbell, President
Offers training to radio salespeople and managers of sales forces.

Country Radio Broadcasters
50 Music Sq., W., #604
Nashville, TN 37203
615-327-4487
Frank Mull, Executive Director
Represents owners, programmers, and managers of country radio stations.

Manufacturers Radio Frequency Advisory
   Committee
1041 Sterling Rd., Ste. 106
Herdon, VA 22070
703-532-7459
J.B. Parker, President
Studies radio frequencies and makes suggestions about frequencies to equipment manufacturers.

National Association of State Radio Networks
400 Sibley Blvd.
Harvey, IL 60426
708-210-3463
Tom Dobrez, Marketing Director
Members broadcast live programs on multiple radio stations within certain states.

PERIODICALS

Radio Advertising Bureau. Radio Facts
Radio Advertising Bureau
304 Park Ave., S.
New York, NY 10010
212-254-4800
Statistics about the radio industry.

Radio Business Report
Box 782
Springfield, VA 22150
703-866-9300
Reports news and trends for executives of radio stations.

Radio Week
National Association of Broadcasters
1771 N St., N.W.
Washington, DC 20036
202-429-5416
Leslie Stimson, Editor
Covers all aspects of the radio industry.

Radio World
Industrial Marketing Advisory Services, Inc.
5827 Columbia Pike, Ste. 310
Falls Church, VA 22041
703-998-7600
Judith Gross, Editor
Focuses on radio technology.

LIBRARIES

Library of Congress
Motion Picture, Broadcasting & Recorded
    Sound Division
James Madison Memorial Bldg., LM-338
Washington, DC 20540
202-707-5840
202-707-2371 Fax
*Huge collection of radio programs on disc,
tape, wire, and cylinder from 1920s to present.*

National Association of Broadcasters
Library and Information Center
1771 N St., N.W.
Washington, DC 20036
202-429-5490
202-775-3520
Radio broadcasting and allied subjects.

National Public Radio
Broadcast Library
2025 M St., N.W.
Washington, DC 20036
202-822-2064
202-822-4329 Fax
Music, drama, and current events.

Radio Advertising Bureau
Marketing Information Center
304 Park Ave., S., 7th Fl.
New York, NY 10010-4302
212-254-4800
212-254-8713 Fax
*Radio, consumer markets, marketing, competi-
tive media, and advertising.*

COMPANIES

American Broadcasting Companies, Inc.
(Subsidiary of Capital Cities/ABC Inc.)
77 W. 66th St.
New York, NY 10023
212-456-7777
Radio and television broadcasting.

CBS Inc.
51 W. 52 St.
New York, NY 10019
212-975-4321
Radio and television broadcasting.

Gaylord Broadcasting Co.
(Subsidiary of Oklahoma Publishing Co.)
P.O. Box 25125
Oklahoma City, OK 73125
405-232-3311
Radio and television broadcasting.

Great American Broadcasting
(Subsidiary of Great American Communica-
    tions Co.)
One E. Fourth St.
Cincinnati, OH 45202
513-721-1414
Radio and television broadcasting.

Infinity Broadcasting Corp.
600 Madison Ave.
New York, NY 10022
212-750-6400
Radio broadcasting.

Jefferson-Pilot Communications Co.
(Subsidiary of Jefferson-Pilot Corp.)
One Julian Price Pl.
Charlotte, NC 28208
704-374-3500
Radio and television broadcasting.

King Broadcasting Co.
333 Dexter Ave. N.
Seattle, WA 98109
206-448-5555
Radio and television broadcasting.

National Broadcasting Co.
30 Rockefeller Plaza
New York, NY 10112
212-644-4444
Radio and television broadcasting.

Westinghouse Broadcasting Co.
(Subsidiary of Westinghouse Electric Corp.)
888 Seventh Ave.
New York, NY 10106
212-307-3000
Radio and television broadcasting.

FEDERAL GOVERNMENT

Federal Communications Commission
1919 M St., N.W.
Washington, DC 20554
202-632-7106
*Ask for the Consumer Assistance & Small
Business Division; the AM Branch or the FM
Branch in the Mass Media Bureau; or the
Satellite Radio Branch in the Common Car-
rier Bureau.*

RAILROAD INDUSTRY

ASSOCIATIONS

American Railway Car Institute
Bldg. 5
19900 Governor's Dr., Ste. 10
Olympia Fields, IL 60461
708-747-0511
708-747-0783 Fax
Elwyn Ahnquist, President
Manufacturers of railroad and freight cars.

American Short Line Railroad Association
2000 Massachusetts Ave. N.W.
Washington, DC 20036
202-785-2250
202-887-0275 Fax
W. E. Loftus, President
*Members are short line railroads, generally
under 100 miles in length.*

Association of American Railroads
American Railroads Bldg.
50 F St. N.W.
Washington, DC 20001
202-639-2100
William Dempsey, President
*The primary research organization for the
railway industry. Studies such topics as railroad maintenance, safety, costs, security, and
much more.*

High Speed Rail Association
206 Valley Ct., Ste. 800
Pittsburgh, PA 15237
412-366-6887
412-364-6113 Fax
Robert Casey, Executive Director
*A clearinghouse for information on high speed
rail systems.*

Railway Supply Association
478 Pennsylvania Ave., Rm. 202
Glen Ellyn, IL 60137
708-469-5676
708-469-5732 Fax
John Bergen, Executive Director
Manufacturers of rolling stock equipment and firms that service rolling stock.

Railway Systems Suppliers
561 Middlesex Ave., Ste. 5
Metuchen, NJ 08840
201-494-2910
W. E. Rowland, Executive Director
Firms that manufacture, distribute, and service railroad communications, control devices, and signaling equipment.

PERIODICALS

Passenger Train Journal
Interurban Press
Box 6128
Glendale, CA 91225
Carl Swanson, Editor
Surveys the city-to-city passenger rail industry nationwide.

Railway Age
Simmons-Boardman Publishing Corp.
345 Hudson St.
New York, NY 10014
212-620-7200
Luther Miller, Editor
Surveys all aspects of the railroad, rapid transit, and railroad equipment industries.

Railway Track & Structures
Simmons-Boardman Publishing Corp.
345 Hudson St.
New York, NY 10014
212-620-7200
Robert Tuzik, Editor
Covers the technologies and equipment used to construct and maintain rail track, bridges, and other rail structures.

U S Rail News
Business Publishers, Inc.
951 Pershing Dr.
Silver Spring, MD 20910-4464
301-587-6300
Andrew Stephens, Editor
Follows technical, industry, and regulatory developments for railroad executives.

LIBRARIES

Association of American Railroads
Library
50 F St., N.W., Rm. 5800
Washington, DC 20001
202-639-2334
202-639-2312 Fax
Covers American railroad topics such as law, history, engineering, and research.

Consolidated Rail Corp.
Saw Library
1138 Six Penn Center Plaza
Philadelphia, PA 19103
215-977-5044
215-977-4817 Fax
Railroads and interstate commerce.

Transportation-Communications Union
Library
3 Research Place
Rockville, MD 20850
301-948-4910
301-948-1369 Fax
Rail industry.

U.S. Department of Transportation
Library and Distribution Services Division
400 7th St., S.W.
M-493.3, Rm. 2200
Washington, DC 20590
202-366-0746
Railroads and mass transit.

COMPANIES

Amtrak
60 Mass. Ave., N.E.
Washington, DC 20002
202-906-3000

Burlington Northern Inc.
777 Main St.
Ft. Worth, TX 76102
817-878-2000
Railroad company.

Chicago and Northwestern Holdings Corp.
Two Manhattanville Rd.
Purchase, NY 10577
914-694-3764
Railroad company.

Consolidated Rail Corp.
6 Penn Center Plaza
Philadelphia, PA 19103
215-977-4699
Railroad freight transportation.

General Electric Railcar Service Corp.
(Subsidiary of General Electric Co.)
33 W. Monroe St.
Chicago, IL 60603
312-853-5000
Lease, service, and sell railroad cars.

Illinois Central Corp.
233 N. Michigan Ave.
Chicago, IL 60601
312-819-7500
Railroad company.

Itel Corp.
Two N. Riverside Plaza
Chicago, IL 60606
312-902-1515
Lease railroad cars and other types of capital equipment.

New York Air Brake Co.
Starbuck Ave.
Watertown, NY 13601
315-782-7000
Brakes for railroads and other types of equipment.

TTX Co.
101 N. Wacker Dr.
Chicago, IL 60606
312-853-3223
Manufacture and lease various types of railroad cars.

Thrall Car Mfg. Co.
(Subsidiary of Duchossois Industries, Inc.)
26th & State, Box 218
Chicago Heights, IL 60411
708-757-5900
Manufacture and lease railroad cars.

FEDERAL GOVERNMENT

Consolidated Rail Corp.
6 Penn Center Plaza
Philadelphia, PA 19103
215-596-2000
Ask for the public relations office.

Interstate Commerce Commission
12th St. and Constitution Ave., N.W.
Washington, DC 20423
202-275-0885
Ask for the Railroad Service Board.

U.S. Customs Service
Department of the Treasury
U.S. Customshouse
6 World Trade Center
New York, NY 10048
212-466-5550
Ask for the Commodity Specialist in charge of railroad equipment.

U.S. Department of Transportation
400 Seventh St., S.W.
Washington, DC 20590
202-366-4000
Ask for the Federal Railroad Administration.

U.S. International Trade Administration
Department of Commerce
14th St. and Constitution Ave., N.W.
Washington, DC 20230
202-377-2000
Ask for the Commodity Analyst who is an expert in railroad services or equipment.

U.S. International Trade Commission
500 E St., S.W.
Washington, DC 20436
202-205-2000 Office of the Secretary
202-205-3296 Industries locator
Ask for the Trade Analyst who is an expert in railroad services.

REAL ESTATE BUSINESS

See also: REAL ESTATE INVESTMENTS and each of the 50 states under real estate

ASSOCIATIONS

American Land Title Association
1828 L St. N.W., Ste. 705
Washington, DC 20036
202-296-3671
202-223-5843 Fax
James Maher, Executive Vice President
Members include title insurance firms and real estate attorneys.

American Society of Professional Appraisers
100 Galleria Pkwy., Tower 1, Ste. 400
Atlanta, GA 30339
404-951-1994
Lee McCutchan, Director
Appraisers of commercial and residential real estate.

American Society of Real Estate Counselors
430 N. Michigan Ave.
Chicago, IL 60611
312-329-8427
312-329-8881 Fax
Lois Hofstetter, Executive Vice President
Members are consultants on real estate matters who are paid a fee or salary rather than a commission for their services.

International Foundation for Timesharing
1220 L St. N.W., Ste. 510
Washington, DC 20005
202-371-6700
202-289-8544 Fax
Stephany Madsen, Executive Secretary
Offers a variety of courses on real estate timesharing.

National Association of Master Appraisers
303 W. Cypress St.
PO Box 12617
San Antonio, TX 78212-0617
512-271-0781
800-227-5907
George Harrison, Executive Director
Offers seminars to real estate appraisers and others with an interest in appraising.

National Association of Real Estate Brokers
1629 K St. N.W.
Washington, DC 20006
202-785-4477
Evelyn Reeves, President
A relatively small group of real estate professionals who designate themselves "Realtists." Offers educational programs.

National Association of Realtors
430 N. Michigan Ave.
Chicago, IL 60611-4087
312-329-8200
312-329-8576 Fax
William North, Executive Vice President
A huge association of real estate professionals who designate themselves "Realtors." Offers a large range of education and research programs.

PERIODICALS

Appraiser News
Appraisal Institute
875 N. Michigan Ave., Ste. 2400
Chicago, IL 60611-1980
312-335-4100
Grace Hayek, Editor
Reports on the business and regulatory trends that affect working real estate appraisers.

Assessment Digest
International Association of Assessing Officers
1313 E. 60th St.
Chicago, IL 60637-9990
312-947-2053
Annie Aubrey, Editor
How-to information for assessors.

Commercial Property News
Gralla Publications
1515 Broadway
New York, NY 10036
212-869-1300
Kenneth Lelen, Editor
Surveys the commercial real estate business.

Practical Real Estate Lawyer
American Law Institute
4025 Chestnut St.
Philadelphia, PA 19104
215-243-1604
Mark Carroll, Editor
How-to information and standard forms for real estate attorneys.

Real Estate Forum
Real Estate Forum, Inc.
12 W. 37th St.
New York, NY 10018
212-563-6460
Harold Kelman, Editor
Follows news of real estate development, financing, investments, and management nationwide.

Real Estate News
Real Estate News Corp.
2600 W. Peterson Ave.
Chicago, IL 60659
Steven Polydoris, Editor
Written for executives involved in real estate building and investment.

Real Estate Review
Warren, Gorham and Lamont Inc.
One Penn Plaza
New York, NY 10119
800-950-1217
Alvin Arnold, Editor
A forum for successful real estate executives and investors to share advice and opinions about the industry.

LIBRARIES

National Association of Realtors
Library
430 N. Michigan Ave.
Chicago, IL 60611-4987
312-329-8292
312-329-5960 Fax
Real estate, selling, and city planning.

Real Estate Research Corp.
Library
2 N. LaSalle St., Ste. 400
Chicago, IL 6062
312-346-5885
Real estate management, land use, urban planning, and appraisal.

Urban Land Institute
Library
1090 Vermont Ave., N.W.
Washington, DC 20005
202-624-7116
202-624-7141 Fax
Real estate, environmental issues, land use, and urban planning.

Williams-Kuebelbeck & Associates, Inc.
Library
1301 Shoreway Rd., Ste. 317
Belmont, CA 94002
415-593-7600
415-593-4147 Fax
Real estate market.

COMPANIES

Century 21
Century Centre
2601 S.E. Main St.
P.O. Box 19564
Irvine, CA 92713
714-553-2100
Chain of real estate agencies.

Coldwell Banker
Xerox Center Bldg.
55 W. Monroe, Ste. 3100
Chicago, IL 60603
312-875-5200
Chain of real estate agencies.

ERA
4900 College Blvd.
Shawnee Mission, KS 66211
913-491-1000
Chain of real estate agencies.

Fine Homes International, Inc.
10 Stamford Forum
Stamford, CT 06901
203-356-1400
Real estate brokerage firm.

Merrill Lynch Hubbard Inc.
(Subsidiary of Merrill Lynch & Co., Inc.)
2 Broadway
New York, NY 10004
212-635-2027
Syndication of real estate developments.

Ranger Development Corp.
(Subsidiary of American Ranger, Inc.)
One Commercial Plaza
Hartford, CT 06103
203-549-1674
Developers of residential real estate.

Remax International
P.O. Box 3907
Englewood, CO 80155-3907
1-800-525-7452
Chain of real estate agencies.

Rouse Co.
10275 Little Patuxent Pkwy.
Columbia, MD 21044
301-992-6000
Developer and manager of office buildings and retailing centers.

Sverdrup Corp.
13723 Riverport Dr.
Maryland Heights, MO 63043
314-436-7600
Planning, design, construction, and management of real estate projects.

Taubman Co., Inc.
200 E. Long Lake Rd., Box 200
Bloomfield Hills, MI 48303
313-258-6800
Developer of various real estate projects.

FEDERAL GOVERNMENT

General Services Administration
18th and F St., N.W.
Washington, DC 20405
202-708-5082
Ask for the Real Estate Policy & Sales division in the Federal Property Resources Service.

REAL ESTATE INVESTMENTS

See also: INVESTMENTS; REAL ESTATE BUSINESS; and each of the 50 states under real estate

ASSOCIATIONS

American Conference of Real Estate Investment Trusts
7201 Wisconsin Ave., Ste. 703
Bethesda, MD 20814
301-654-6400
Joseph Baldinger, Secretary
A clearinghouse for information about real estate investment trusts.

Association of Foreign Investors in U.S. Real Estate
2300 M St. N.W.
Washington, DC 20037
202-887-0937
James Low, Executive Vice President
Members include foreign firms that invest in U.S. real estate and the American firms that provide consulting, legal, and other services to these investors.

National Council of Real Estate Investment
  Fiduciaries
PO Box 970
Tacoma, WA 92401-0970
206-596-5400
Joseph Diehl, Executive Officer
*Offers educational programs and promotes
real estate as an investment for pension funds.*

Commercial-Investment Real Estate Council
430 N. Michigan Ave.
Chicago, IL 60611
312-321-4460
312-329-8882 Fax
Steven Pope, Executive Vice President
*Offers research and seminars designed to
enhance the professionalism of commercial
investment real estate brokers, property developers, and others in the field.*

National Association of Real Estate Investment Trusts
1129 20th St. N.W., Ste. 705
Washington, DC 20036
202-785-8717
Mark Decker, President
*Members include real estate investors, real
estate investment trusts, companies, and other
entities that manage or own group-owned real
estate properties.*

Pension Real Estate Association
95 Glastonbury Blvd.
Glastonbury, CT 06033
203-657-2612
Robert Stavey, President
*Members include pension funds, developers
and sponsors of real estate investment funds,
and individuals in the field.*

PERIODICALS

Commercial Investment Real Estate Journal
Commercial Investment Real Estate Institute
430 N. Michigan Ave., Ste. 500
Chicago, IL 60611-4092
312-670-3780
Lorene Norton, Editor
*A wide range of news and advice for profes-
sionals in the commercial real estate business.*

Distressed Property Investor's Monthly
Real Estate Publications, Inc.
Box 20027
Tampa, FL 33622-0027
800-356-2317
Thomas Lucier, Editor
*Advises on opportunities to buy foreclosed,
probated, and other distressed real estate.*

John T. Reed's Real Estate Investor's Monthly
Reed Publishing
342 Bryan Dr.
Danville, CA 94526
415-820-6292
John Reed, Editor
*Surveys trends in management, finance, laws,
and other aspects of real estate investment.*

Mortgage and Real Estate Executives Report
Warren, Gorham and Lamont Inc.
One Penn Plaza
New York, NY 10119
800-950-1217
Alvin Arnold, Editor
*Advice, forecasts, and news for real estate
executives and investors.*

National Real Estate Investor
Communication Channels, Inc.
6255 Barfield Rd.
Atlanta, GA 30328-4369
404-256-9800
Paula Stephens, Editor
*Focuses on commercial real estate manage-
ment, development, financing, and investment.*

Real Estate Investment Situations
High Tech Publishing Co.
Box 1923
Brattleboro, VT 05301
802-254-3539
*Suggests real estate investment opportunities
in the U.S. and abroad.*

Real Estate Syndication Alert
Warren, Gorham and Lamont Inc.
One Penn Plaza
New York, NY 10119
800-950-1217
Offers case studies of real estate syndications.

LIBRARIES

Real Estate Research Corp.
Library
2 N. LaSalle St., Ste. 400
Chicago, IL 6062
312-346-5885
*Real estate management, land use, urban plan-
ning, and appraisal.*

Williams-Kuebelbeck & Associates, Inc.
Library
1301 Shoreway Rd., Ste. 317
Belmont, CA 94002
415-593-7600
415-593-4147 Fax
Real estate market.

COMPANIES

Ameribanc Investors Group
7630 Little River Trpk.
Annandale, VA 22003
703-658-2720
Real estate and other types of investments.

Countrywide Mortgage Investments Inc.
155 N. Lake Ave.
Pasadena, CA 91109
818-304-8400
Real estate investment trust.

Marcus & Millichap Incorporated
2626 Hanover St.
Palo Alto, CA 94304
415-494-8900
Brokers of investment real estate.

RPS Realty Trust
733 3rd Ave.
New York, NY 10017
212-370-8585
Real estate investment trust.

Rockefeller Center Properties Inc.
1166 Ave. of the Americas
New York, NY 10036
212-841-7760
Real estate investment trust.

Sierra Real Estate Equity Trust/82
(Subsidiary of Meridian Point Properties Inc.)
100 California St.
San Francisco, CA 94105
415-956-3031
Real estate investment trust.

Southmark Corp.
1601 LBJ Freeway
Dallas, TX 75234
214-241-8787
Invests in real estate.

RECORDING INDUSTRY

See also: AUDIOVISUAL INDUSTRY and MUSIC INDUSTRY

ASSOCIATIONS

Audio Engineering Society
60 E. 42nd St., Rm 2520
New York, NY 10165
212-661-8528
Donald Plunkett, Executive Director
Conducts research and offers educational programs to audio engineers, recording technicians, and others in the field.

National Academy of Recording Arts and Sciences
303 N. Glenoaks Blvd., Ste. 140
Burbank, CA 91502-1178
213-849-1313
Christine Farnon, Executive Vice President
Represents musicians, composers, recording engineers, and others involved with the professional recording industry. Presents the Grammy Awards.

National Association of Independent Record Distributors and Manufacturers
PO Box 568
Maple Shade, NJ 08052
609-547-3331
609-547-4762 Fax
Holly Cass, Executive Director
Promotes sales for independent manufacturers and distributors of recordings.

Recording Industry Association of America
1020 19th St. N.W., Ste. 200
Washington, DC 20036
202-775-0101
202-775-7253 Fax
Jason Berman, President
Provides a range of information services to manufacturers of recordings, including compact disks, cassettes and music videos.

Society of Professional Audio Recording Services
4300 Tenth Ave., N.
Lake Worth, FL 33461
407-641-6648
407-642-8263 Fax
Shirley Kaye, Executive Director
Offers technical, management, and industry information for the owners of recording and video studios and others who supply the industry.

PERIODICALS

Audiocraft
National Federation of Community Broadcasters
666 11th St. N.W., Ste. 805
Washington, DC 20001
202-393-2355
Randy Thom, Editor
How-to information for audio producers and broadcasters.

Billboard's International Recording Equipment & Studio Directory
Billboard Publications, Inc.
1515 Broadway, 39th Fl.
New York, NY 10036
212-764-7300
Information about professional recording equipment and studios.

Mix Annual Directory of Recording Industry Facilities and Services
Act III Publishing
6400 Hollis, Ste. 12
Emeryville, CA 94608
415-653-3307
Blair Jackson, Editor
A list of recording studios and services nationwide.

Mix Magazine
Act III Publishing
6400 Hollis, Ste. 12
Emeryville, CA 94608
415-653-3307
David Schwartz, Editor
Technical and creative advice for recording engineers and producers.

Pro Sound News
P S N Publications
2 Park Ave., 4th Fl.
New York, NY 10016
212-213-3446
Debra Pagan, Editor
Covers news and trends for the professional recording and sound production industry.

Recording Engineering Production
Intertec Publishing Corp.
9221 Quivira Rd.
Overland Park, KS 66212-9981
913-888-4664
Mike Joseph, Editor
Practical information for audio engineers and producers.

Soundtrack
Soundtrack Publishing
317 Skyline Lake Dr.
Box 609
Ringwood, NJ 07456
201-831-1317
Don Kulak, Editor
A wide range of business information for independent record labels.

LIBRARIES

Ampex Corp.
Technical Information Services
401 Broadway
Redwood City, CA 94063
415-367-3368
Management, business, magnetic recording, electronics, physics, and television.

Bowling Green State University
Music Library
Jerome Library
Bowling Green, OH 43403-0179
429-372-2307
419-372-7996 Fax
Recording industry, classical music, and popular music.

University of California, San Diego
Center for Magnetic Recording Research
Information Center
La Jolla, CA 92093-0175
619-534-6213
619-534-2720 Fax
Recording technology, optical recording technology, magnetic media.

COMPANIES

Atlantic Recording Corp.
75 Rockefeller Plaza
New York, NY 10019
212-484-6000
Recording and sales of cassettes and compact discs.

CBS Records
51 W. 52nd St.
New York, NY 10019
212-975-4321
Recording and sales of cassettes and compact discs.

Capitol Industries-EMI, Inc.
(Subsidiary of THORN EMI plc)
1750 N. Vine St.
Hollywood, CA 90028
213-462-6252
Recording and sales of cassettes and compact discs.

MCA Records
70 Universal City Plaza
N. Hollywood, CA 91608
818-777-1000
Recording and sales of cassettes and compact discs.

Nightingale-Conant Corp.
7300 N. Lehigh Ave.
Chicago, IL 60648
708-647-0300
Educational and self-help recordings.

Nimbus Records, Inc.
P.O. Box 7305
Ruckersville, VA 22968
804-985-1100
Recording and sales of cassettes and compact discs.

Sam Ash Music Corp.
278 Duffy Ave.
Hicksville, NY 11801
516-932-6400
Retailer of professional recording equipment, musical instruments, and other products.

Warner Brothers Records Co.
3300 Warner Blvd.
Burbank, CA 91505
818-846-9090
Recording and sales of cassettes and compact discs.

FEDERAL GOVERNMENT

Copyright Royalty Tribunal
1825 Connecticutt Ave., N.W.
Ste. 918
Washington, DC 20009
202-606-4400
Ask for the public affairs office for help finding an expert in royalties.

U.S. International Trade Administration
Department of Commerce
14th St. and Constitution Ave., N.W.
Washington, DC 20230
202-377-2000
Ask for the Commodity Analyst who is an expert in the recording industry.

U.S. International Trade Commission
500 E St., S.W.
Washington, DC 20436
202-205-2000 Office of the Secretary
202-205-3296 Industries locator
Ask for the Trade Analyst who is an expert in the recording industry.

U.S. Patent and Trademark Office
Crystal Plaza 2
2011 Jefferson Davis Highway
Arlington, VA 22202
703-305-8000
Ask for the Examining Group Director who is a specialist in recording equipment.

RECORDS MANAGEMENT

See also: LIBRARIES; MANAGEMENT INFORMATION SYSTEMS (MIS); MICROFORMS; and OFFICE AUTOMATION

ASSOCIATIONS

Association of Records Managers and Administrators
4200 Somerset, Ste. 215
Prairie Village, KS 66208
913-341-3808
James Souders, Executive Director
Offers research and seminars in creating and keeping records of all kinds.

National Association of Government Archives and Records Administrators
c/o Executive Secretariat
New York State Archives, Rm. 10A46
Cultural Education Center
Albany, NY 12230
518-473-8037
Bruce Dearstyne, Executive Director
A forum for government records managers and others at the federal, state, and local levels to discuss how to better administer governmental records.

National Records Management Council
60 E. 42nd St.
New York, NY 10165
212-697-0290
Alan Andolsen, President
Provides educational, research, and consulting services to help organizations improve their records handling systems.

PERIODICALS

I M C Journal
International Information Management Congress
345 Woodcliff Dr.
Fairport, NY 14450-4201
716-383-8330
William McArthur, Editor
Covers a wide range of information management trends and technologies, including those used for records management.

Infocus
Business Forms Management Association, Inc.
519 S.W. Third Ave., Ste. 712
Portland, OR 97204
503-227-3393
William Urban, Editor
Reports on new products, form designs, hardware, software, and other topics regarding records and information management.

Information Management
Center for Management Systems
Box 208
Sioux City, IA 51102
712-568-3370
John Siefer, Editor
Surveys news and provides advice in the field of records management, micrographics, and office automation.

LIBRARIES

National Archive & Records Administration
Library
8th & Pennsylvania Ave., N.W.
Washington, DC 20408
202-501-5400
Records management, history, archives, U.S. biography, and manuscripts.

University of California, Berkeley
Library School Library
2 South Hall
Berkeley, CA 94720
510-642-2253
Library science, records management, information storage and retrieval, history, and related topics.

University of Texas, Austin
Library and Information Science Collection
General Libraries, PCL 6.102
Austin, TX 78713-7330
512-471-7668
512-471-1790 Fax
Library science, records management, and related topics.

RECREATIONAL VEHICLES INDUSTRY

See also: AUTOMOTIVE INDUSTRY and MOBILE HOME INDUSTRY

ASSOCIATIONS

Family Motor Coach Association
8291 Clough Pike
Cincinnati, OH 45244
513-474-3622
513-474-2332 Fax
Delmer Davis, President
A consumer group of motor home owners who use their vehicles for travel and camping.

International Snowmobile Industry Association
3975 University Dr., Ste. 310
Fairfax, VA 22030
703-273-9606
703-273-9271 Fax
Roy Muth, President
Represents manufacturers of snowmobiles and snowmobile accessories.

Recreation Vehicle Dealers Association of
North America
3251 Old Lee Hwy., Ste. 500
Fairfax, VA 22030
703-591-7130
Robert Strawn, Executive Vice President
*Members are retailers of such recreational
vehicles as motor homes, camping trailers, and
travel trailers.*

Recreation Vehicle Industry Association
1896 Preston White Dr.
PO Box 2999
Reston, VA 22090
703-620-6003
David Humphreys, President
*An information center for firms that manufac-
ture and supply equipment and accessories for
recreational vehicles of all kinds.*

PERIODICALS

M H—R V Builders News
Dan Kamrow & Associates, Inc.
Box 72367
Roselle, IL 60172
708-893-8872
Pat Finn, Editor
*Written for manufacturers of mobile homes
and recreational vehicles.*

R V Business
T L Enterprises, Inc.
29901 Agoura Rd.
Agoura, CA 91301
818-991-4980
Mike Schneider, Editor
*Surveys business and financial news of the R V
industry.*

R V Trade Digest
Continental Publishing Co. of Indiana, Inc.
Box 1805
Elkhart, IN 46517
219-295-1962
Thomas Russell, Editor
*Covers sales and marketing topics for manu-
facturers, wholesalers, and retailers of recre-
ational vehicles.*

Snowmobile Business
Ehlert Publishing Group, Inc.
319 Barry Ave., S.
Wayzata, MN 55391-1603
612-476-2200
Dick Hendricks, Editor
*Industry news and merchandising advice pri-
marily for snowmobile dealers.*

COMPANIES

Airstream, Inc.
419 W. Pike
Jackson Ctr., OH 45334
513-596-6111
Motor homes.

Atlantic Mobilehome & RV Supply
4828 High Point Rd.
Greensboro, NC 27407
919-299-4691
*Distributes supplies for recreational vehicles
and mobile homes.*

Fleetwood Enterprises, Inc.
3125 Myers St.
Riverside, CA 92503
714-351-3500
Motor homes.

Harley-Davidson Motor Co., Inc.
3700 W. Juneau Ave.
Milwaukee, WI 53201
414-935-4680
Motorcycles.

Hi-Lo Trailer Co.
100 Elm St.
Butler, OH 44822
419-883-3000
Recreational vehicles.

Myers Electric Products Inc.
(Subsidiary of Shirmar Corp.)
1130 S. Vail
Montebello, CA 90640
213-724-0450
*Equipment for servicing recreational vehicles
and other types of products.*

National R.V., Inc.
3411 N. Perris Blvd.
Perris, CA 92370
714-943-6007
Equipment for recreational vehicles.

RECREATION INDUSTRY

See also: SPORTING GOODS INDUSTRY and SWIMMING POOL INDUSTRY

ASSOCIATIONS

American Spa and Health Resort Association
PO Box 585
Lake Forest, IL 60045
312-234-8851
Melanie Ruehle, Director
*Owners and operators of health spas and
resorts.*

Association of Physical Fitness Centers
600 Jefferson St., Ste. 202
Rockville, MD 20852
301-424-7744
301-762-1758 Fax
Jimmy Johnson, President
*A clearinghouse for information on physical
fitness centers and the manufacturers that
supply the industry.*

Barbecue Industry Association
710 E. Ogden Ave., Ste. 113
Naperville, IL 60563
708-369-2404
Sandy Burton, Executive Director
*Manufacturers of grills, charcoal, and other
items used to barbecue food.*

International Tanning Manufacturers Association
5100 Poplar Ave., Ste. 2116
Memphis, TN 38137
901-761-3084
Bill Richey, President
Firms that make suntanning equipment.

Kampground Owners Association
E. Arizona Biltmore Circle, Ste. 144
Phoenix, AZ 85016
602-381-8742
Marj Cole, Executive Director
Offers educational programs to KOA franchisees.

National Campground Owners Association
11307 Sunset Hills Rd., Ste. B7
Reston, VA 22090
703-471-0143
703-481-9661 Fax
David Gorin, Executive Vice President
Members include owners and operators of campgrounds and suppliers to the industry.

National Forest Recreation Association
Rt. 3, Box 210
Hwy. 89, N.
Flagstaff, AZ 86004
602-526-4330
Gaylord Staveley, President
Represents the interests of owners and operators of resorts, restaurants, camps, and other types of businesses in or near national forests.

Resort and Commercial Recreation Association
PO Box 1208
New Port Richey, FL 34656
813-845-7373
Frank Oliveto, Executive Director
Serves as an information exchange for all kinds of individuals who work in the commercial recreation and resort industry.

Society of Recreation Executives
PO Drawer 17148
Pensacola, FL 32522
904-477-2123
K. W. Stephens, President
Professional group of corporate executives who work for firms in the leisure and recreation industry.

PERIODICALS

Campground Management
Woodall Publishing Co.
28167 N. Keith Dr.
Lake Forest, IL 60045
708-362-6700
Mike Byrnes, Editor
Advice on how to manage, maintain, and improve campgrounds and other outdoor recreation facilities.

Federal Parks & Recreation
Resources Publishing Co.
1010 Vermont Ave., N.W., Ste. 708
Washington, DC 20005
202-638-7529
James Coffin, Editor
News about federal legislation and regulations affecting parks and other recreational areas.

Journal of Hospitality & Leisure Marketing
Haworth Press, Inc.
10 Alice St.
Binghamton, NY 13904-1580
800-342-9678
Francis Buttle, Editor
Detailed advice on how to improve the marketing of hospitality, leisure, and recreational services.

Journal of Park and Recreation Administration
Sagamore Publishing Inc.
302 W. Hill St.
Box 673
Champaign, IL 61824-0673
217-359-5940
Helps planners and managers of leisure and recreation organizations to improve their marketing, profitability, and organizational structures.

Leisure Industry Report
Leisure Industry—Recreation News
Box 43563
Washington, DC 20010
202-232-7107
Marj Jensen, Editor
*Summarizes news and trends in the leisure
and recreation industries.*

Leisure Sciences
Taylor & Francis
1900 Frost Rd., Ste. 101
Bristol, PA 19007
215-785-5800
Robert Ditton, Editor
*Scholarly articles about recreation, leisure,
and travel.*

Recreation and Parks Law Reporter
National Recreation and Park Association
3101 Park Center Dr.
Alexandria, VA 22302
703-820-4940
James Kozlowski, Editor
*Reports on legislation, litigation, and other
legal topics of concern to parks and recreation
managers.*

Recreation Resources
Lakewood Publications, Inc.
50 S. Ninth
Minneapolis, MN 55402
612-333-0471
Galynn Nordstrom, Editor
*Covers products and services purchased by
managers of recreation, fitness, and leisure
activities.*

LIBRARIES

Indiana University
Health, Physical Education & Recreation
    Library
HPER Bldg. 031
Bloomington, IN 47401
812-855-4420
812-855-6615 Fax
*Recreation and park administration, coaching,
therapeutic recreation, health, safety, psychology, and other topics.*

Laventhol and Horwath
National Information Center
1845 Walnut St.
Philadelphia, PA 19103
215-299-1995
215-299-8645 Fax
Leisure time industries and health care.

North Carolina State University
D.H. Hill Library
Natural Resources
P.O. Box 7114
Raleigh, NC 27695-7114
919-737-2306
Recreation administration and other topics.

COMPANIES

Busch Entertainment Corp.
1 Busch Pl.
St. Louis, MO 63118
314-577-4736
Theme parks and other leisure properties.

Club Mediterranee
40 W. 57th St.
New York, NY 10019
212-977-2100
Michael Kubin, President
Vacation villages in 26 countries.

Bally's Health & Tennis Corp.
(Subsidiary of Bally Manufacturing Corp.)
2029 Century Park E.
Los Angeles, CA 90067
213-552-6941
Recreation and sports clubs, recreational services and equipment.

Caesars World, Inc.
1801 Century Park East
Los Angeles, CA 90067
213-552-2711
Resorts, casinos, and wide variety of leisure services.

Florida Cypress Gardens, Inc.
2641 S. Lake Summitt Rd.
Winter Haven, FL 33880
813-324-2111
Theme parks and other leisure properties.

Killington Ltd.
Killington Rd.
Killington, VT 05751
802-422-3333
Skiing facilities.

KOA Kampgrounds of America
3938 W. Northview
Phoenix, AZ 85051
602-939-0012
Camping and recreational areas.

National Recreation Products, Inc.
(Subsidiary of Fuqua Industries Inc.)
14760 Santa Fe Trail Dr.
Lenexa, KS 66215
913-492-3206
Camping, sporting, and other leisure products.

Pratt Hotel Corp.
13455 Noel Rd.
Dallas, TX 75240
214-386-9777
Hotels and recreation services.

FEDERAL GOVERNMENT

U.S. Department of Agriculture
14th St. and Independence Ave., S.W.
Washington, DC 20250
202-720-8732
Ask for the Recreation Management division in the Forest Service.

U.S. Department of the Interior
1800 C St., N.W.
Washington, DC 20240
202-208-7220
Ask for the Recreation Resources Assistance division in the National Park Service; or for the Recreation & Cultural Resources division in the Bureau of Land Management.

RECYCLING

See also: ENVIRONMENTAL CONSERVATION AND POLLUTION
CONTROL and WASTE MANAGEMENT

ASSOCIATIONS

Aluminum Recycling Association
1000 16th St. N.W., Ste. 603
Washington, DC 20036
202-785-0951
Richard Cooperman, Executive Director
Firms that use scrap aluminum.

Asphalt Recycling and Reclaiming Association
3 Church Circle, Ste. 250
Annapolis, MD 21401
301-267-0023
Michael Krissoff, Executive Director
*Companies and engineers that recycle and
reuse asphalt.*

Council on Plastics and Packaging in the Environment
1275 K St. N.W., Ste. 900
Washington, DC 20005
202-789-1310
202-289-1389 Fax
Edward Stana, Executive Director
*Provides information about the environmental
problems caused by plastic packaging and
solutions offered by recycling.*

Glass Packaging Institute
1801 K St. N.W., Ste. 1105
Washington, DC 20006
202-887-4850
202-785-5377 Fax
Lewis Andrews, President
*Promotes the use of glass containers and recy-
cled glass products.*

Institute of Scrap Recycling Industries
1627 K St. N.W., Ste. 700
Washington, DC 20006
202-466-4050
Herschel Cutler, Executive Director
*Conducts research and offers educational pro-
grams concerning the recycling of scrap metals
and other types of recyclable materials.*

National Recycling Coalition
1101 30th St. N.W.
Washington, DC 20007
202-625-6406
202-625-6409 Fax
David Loveland, Executive Director
*A clearinghouse for information on all kinds of
recycling.*

Plastics Recycling Foundation
1275 K St. N.W., Ste. 500
Washington, DC 20005
202-371-5200
Wayne Pearson, Executive Director
*Conducts research into the recycling of plas-
tics.*

Steel Can Recycling Institute
Foster Plaza X
680 Anderson Dr.
Pittsburgh, PA 15220
412-922-2772
800-876-7274
412-922-3213 Fax
Kurt Smalberg, President
Offers information on a wide range of issues and technologies involving the recycling of cans.

PERIODICALS

Bottle—Can Recycling Update
Resource Recycling, Inc.
Box 10540
Portland, OR 97210
800-227-1424
Jerry Powell, Editor
Focuses on technological, business, and regulatory aspects of recycling glass, metals, plastics, and other refuse.

Paper Recycler
Miller Freeman Publications, Inc.
600 Harrison St.
San Francisco, CA 94107
415-905-2200
Debra Garcia, Editor
Technical and business information for paper recycling firms.

Plastic Bottle Reporter
Plastic Bottle Information Bureau
Society of the Plastics Industry, Inc
1275 K St., N.W., Ste. 400
Washington, DC 20005
202-371-5244
Advises how to collect and recycle plastic bottles.

Plastics Recycling Update
Resource Recycling, Inc.
Box 10540
Portland, OR 97210
800-227-1424
Jerry Powell, Editor
Surveys all aspects of plastics recycling.

Recycling Times
Richard H. Freeman
1730 Rhode Island Ave., N.W., Ste. 1000
Washington, DC 20036
202-861-0708
Kathleen Meade, Editor
Information for municipal and corporate officials who control the buying, selling, and recycling of solid wastes.

Recycling Today
G.I.E. Inc. Publishers
4012 Bridge Ave.
Cleveland, OH 44113
216-961-4130
Jeff Solomon-Hess, Editor
Focuses on the markets for solid waste recycling.

Scrap Processing and Recycling
Institute of Scrap Recycling Industries
1627 K St., N.W., Ste. 700
Washington, DC 20006
202-466-4050
Elise Brown, Editor
Keeps scrap recyclers abreast of industry news and technological developments.

LIBRARIES

Earthworm, Inc.
Recycling Information Center
186 South St.
Boston, MA 02111
617-426-7344
Recycling, pollution, enviornmental education, and solid waste management.

Rogers, Golden and Halpern, Inc.
Information Resource Center
1216 Arch St.
Philadelphia, PA 19107
215-563-4220
Recycling and environmental planning.

Rutgers University, the State University of
    New Jersey
Center for Plastics Recycling Researh
Busch Campus, Bldg. 3529
Piscataway, NJ 08855
908-932-4402
908-932-5636 Fax
Plastics recycling.

FEDERAL GOVERNMENT

U.S. Environmental Protection Agency
401 M St., S.W.
Washington, DC 20460
202-260-2090
Ask for the public relations office to locate an appropriate expert in recycling.

U.S. International Trade Administration
Department of Commerce
14th St. and Constitution Ave., N.W.
Washington, DC 20230
202-377-2000
Ask for the Commodity Analyst who is an expert in recycling.

REGULATION OF INDUSTRY

ASSOCIATIONS

Federation of Associations of Regulatory
    Boards
555 S. Perry St, No. 112
Montgomery, AL 36104
205-834-2415
205-269-6379 Fax
Randolph Reaves, President
Members are state regulatory board associations that share information.

National Association of Regulatory Utility
    Commissioners
1102 ICC Bldg.
Constitution Ave. and 12th St. N.W.
Washington, DC 20044
202-898-2200
202-898-2213 Fax
Paul Rodgers, Administrative Director
Members are federal and state commissioners who regulate public utilities and transportation firms.

National Clearinghouse on Licensure,
    Enforcement and Regulation
c/o Council of State Governments
Iron Works Pike
PO Box 11910
Lexington, KY 40578
606-231-1901
606-231-1928 Fax
Eugene Ketchum, Executive Director
*Acts as a center for information on state
licensing and regulation in all 50 states. Offers
educational programs to regulatory officials.*

Regulatory Affairs Professionals Society
1101 Connecticut Ave. N.W., Ste. 700
Washington, DC 20036
202-857-1148
202-775-2675 Fax
Carter Keithley, Executive Director
*Members are individuals responsible for regu-
lation of health care products such as pharmaceuticals, cosmetics, medical equipment, and
biotechnology products.*

PERIODICALS

Regulatory Watchdog Service
Washington Business Information, Inc.
1117 N. 19th St., Ste. 200
Arlington, VA 22209
703-247-3434
Alice Rogers, Editor
*Advises which regulatory documents are avail-
able from Congress and federal agencies.*

Federal Regulation of Energy
Shepard's—McGraw-Hill, Inc.
Box 35300
Colorado Springs, CO 80935-3530
800-525-2474
*Reports on government regulations affecting
energy industries, especially those that pro-
duce hazardous waste.*

Federal Regulation of the Chemical Industry
Shepard's—McGraw-Hill, Inc.
Box 35300
Colorado Springs, CO 80935-3530
800-525-2474
*Reports on government regulations affecting
chemical industries.*

Federal Regulatory Directory
Congressional Quarterly Inc.
1414 22nd St. N.W.
Washington, DC 20037
202-887-8500
*A detailed listing of all federal agencies that
write and enforce regulations.*

Government Relations Watch
American Academy of Actuaries
1720 I St., N.W., 7th Fl.
Washington, DC 20006
202-223-8196
Gary Hendricks, Editor
*Covers state and federal regulations and laws
that affect employee benefits and the insurance industry.*

Legislative and Regulatory Update
Compliance Division
American Bankers Association
1120 Connecticut Ave., N.W.
Washington, DC 20036
202-663-5497
*Follows new legislation and regulations in the
banking industry.*

FEDERAL GOVERNMENT

U.S. Department of Commerce
14th St. & Constitution Ave., N.W.
Washington, DC 20230
202-377-2000
*Ask for the Regulatory-Legislative Analysis
department.*

RELOCATION OF EMPLOYEES

See also: MOVING AND STORAGE INDUSTRY

ASSOCIATIONS

Employee Relocation Council
1720 N St. N.W.
Washington, DC 20036
202-857-0857
H. Cris Collie, Executive Vice President
Offers information to executives at large cor-
porations responsible for the transfer and relo-
cation of employees, and to members of the
relocation industry.

PERIODICALS

E-R-C Directory
Employee Relocation Council
1720 N St., N.W.
Washington, DC 20036
202-857-0857
Tina Lung, Editor
A listing of firms that serve the relocation
industry, including relocation consultants, real
estate professionals, and others.

Expansion Management
New Hope Communications, Inc.
1301 Spruce St.
Boulder, CO 80302-4832
303-939-8440
James Sample, Editor
Covers employee relocation and other issues of
concern to executives who plan and manage
corporate expansions and relocations.

National Relocation and Real Estate Direc-
tory
Relocation Information Service, Inc.
113 Post Rd., E.
Westport, CT 06880
203-227-3800
Peter Featherston, Editor
A listing of relocation services and consultants.

Relocation Report
Runzheimer International
Runzheimer Park
Rochester, WI 53167
800-942-9949
Kenneth Groh, Editor
Surveys news of the relocation industry for
consultants, appraisers, and real estate bro-
kers.

COMPANIES

Coldwell Banker Relocation Management
Services, Inc.
(Subsidiary of Coldwell Banker Real Estate
Group, Inc.)
27271 Las Ramblas
Mission Viejo, CA 92691
714-367-2121
Employee relocation services.

Fine Homes International, Inc.
10 Stamford Forum
Stamford, CT 06901
203-356-1400
Real estate brokers and relocation manage-
ment services.

Genesis Relocation Co.
501 Merritt, #7
Norwalk, CT 06852
203-845-8400
Employee relocation consulting services for Fortune 1000 firms.

Metropolitan Relocation Consultants, Inc.
93 S. Finley Ave.
Basking Ridge, NJ 07920
908-766-0703
Employee relocation and homefinding consultants.

PHH Homequity
(Subsidiary of PHH Corp.)
249 Danbury Rd.
Wilton, CT 06897
203-834-8500
Employee relocation services.

Prudential Relocation Management
(Division of Prudential Residential Services, L.P.)
200 Summit Lake Dr.
Valhalla, NY 10595
914-741-6111
Employee relocation services.

Relocation Experts, Inc.
2210 Midwest Rd., Ste. 201
Oak Brook, IL 60521
708-571-9779
Employee relocation and homefinding consultants.

Runzheimer International
Runzheimer Park
Rochester, WI 53167
414-534-3121
Cost-of-living data used in determining fair compensation for relocated employees.

Travelers Relocation Corp.
(Subsidiary of General Electric Capital Mortgage Insurance Companies)
5850 T.G. Lee Blvd.
Orlando, FL 32812
407-826-9000
Buys the homes of corporate employees who have been relocated.

RENTAL AND LEASING SERVICES

See also: AUTOMOBILE LEASE/RENTAL SERVICES

ASSOCIATIONS

American Association of Equipment Lessors
1300 N. 17th St., Ste. 1010
Arlington, VA 22209
703-527-8655
703-527-2649 Fax
Michael Fleming, President
Offers information to and about firms whose main business is leasing equipment of all kinds.

American Rental Association
1900 19th St.
Moline, IL 61265
309-764-2475
800-334-2177
James Irish, Executive Vice President
Firms that rent tools, equipment of all kinds, home health care machinery, party items, and other types of goods.

Association of Progressive Rental Organizations
6300 Bridgepoint Pkwy.
Austin, TX 78730-5016
512-794-0095
Bill Keese, Executive Director
Serves companies that offer a rental service with an option to buy for such products as furniture, appliances, and home electronics.

PERIODICALS

Equipment Leasing Newsletter
New York Law Publishing Co.
Marketing Dept.
111 Eighth Ave.
New York, NY 10011
212-741-8300
Covers industry, regulatory, and tax news that affects equipment leasing firms.

Equipment World
Randall Publishing Co.
Box 2029
Tuscaloosa, AL 35401
800-633-5953
Offers financial advice to those who rent, lease, and use all types of equipment.

Leasing Sourcebook
Bibliotechnology Systems & Publishing Co.
Box 657
Lincoln, MA 01773
617-259-0524
A directory of the U.S. capital equipment leasing industry.

Rental
Johnson Hill Press, Inc.
1233 Janesville Ave.
Ft. Atkinson, WI 53538
414-563-6388
Newton Berry, Editor
Marketing advice for retail rental firms.

Rental Dealer News
Rental Dealer News, Inc.
2900 Bristol, Ste. G-204
Costa Mesa, CA 92626
714-755-1440
Carl Calvert, Editor
*Management and merchandising information
for rent-to-own dealers.*

COMPANIES

Aratex Services, Inc.
(Subsidiary of ARA Services, Inc.)
115 N. First St.
Burbank, CA 91502
818-973-3700
Rental of uniforms.

AT & T Capital Corp.
(Subsidiary of AT&T)
44 Whippany Rd.
Morristown, NJ 07960
201-397-3000
Equipment leasing and financing.

Circle Business Credit, Inc.
(Subsidiary of Xerox Credit Corp.)
8720 Castle Creek Pkwy.
Indianapolis, IN 46250
317-845-0771
Leasing and finance services.

Ellco Leasing Corp.
(Subsidiary of General Electric Capital Corp.)
10251 Vista Sorrento Pkwy.
San Diego, CA 92121
619-458-4400
Financing and leasing of equipment.

Inspiration Resources Corp.
600 Fourth St., Terra Centre
Sioux City, IA 51101
712-277-1340
*Leasing of industrial equipment and other
businesses.*

Itel Corp.
Two N. Riverside Plaza
Chicago, IL 60606
312-902-1515
*Leasing of capital equipment, particularly
railroad cars.*

LDI Corp.
One Cleveland Ctr., 1375 E. 9th St.
Cleveland, OH 44114
216-687-0100
*Leasing of computers and other types of
equipment.*

Norwest Financial, Inc.
(Subsidiary of Norwest Financial Services,
    Inc.)
206 8th St.
Des Moines, IA 50309
515-243-2131
Equipment leasing and other businesses.

Transport International Pool, Inc.
(Subsidiary of General Electric Capital Corp.)
Two Bala Cynwyd Plaza
Bala-Cynwyd, PA 19004
215-667-7100
Equipment leasing and other businesses.

U. S. Leasing International, Inc.
(Subsidiary of Ford Motor Co.)
733 Front St.
San Francisco, CA 94111
415-627-9000
Equipment leasing and rental.

FEDERAL GOVERNMENT

Federal Trade Commission
Pennsylvania Ave. at 6th St., N.W.
Washington, DC 20580
202-326-2000
Ask for the Credit Practices department in the Bureau of Consumer Protection.

U.S. International Trade Administration
Department of Commerce
14th St. and Constitution Ave., N.W.
Washington, DC 20230
202-377-2000
Ask for the Commodity Analyst who is an expert in rental and leasing services.

RESEARCH AND DEVELOPMENT

ASSOCIATIONS

American Association of Small Research Companies
c/o Lawrence Levy
222 3rd St., Ste. 3150
Cambridge, MA 02142
617-491-7906
Lawrence Levy, President
Represents small R & D firms, particularly those working on new high technology products.

Association of Research Directors
c/o Mr. Lynn Lander
Unilever Research U.S. Inc.
45 River Rd.
Edgewater, NJ 07020
201-943-7100
Lynn Lander, Secretary
A professional group of scientists, executives, engineers, and others who direct R & D programs in industry.

Association of University Related Research Parks
4500 S. Lakeshore Dr., Ste. 475
Tempe, AZ 85282
602-752-2002
Chris Boettcher, Executive Director
University parks are collections of R & D firms located on the same property and associated with the same univerity. This association provides information about all aspects of building, joining, and managing university parks.

Council on Research and Technology
1735 New York Ave. N.W., Ste. 500
Washington, DC 20006
202-662-8407
202-331-1024 Fax
Kenneth Kay, Executive Director
A group of companies, universities, research centers, and other organizations that lobby to increase appropriations and tax benefits to R & D programs.

Industrial Research Institute
1550 M St. N.W.
Washington, DC 20005
202-872-6350
202-872-6356 Fax
Charles Larson, Executive Director
Serves as a clearinghouse to help firms manage and operate their R & D laboratories more effectively and economically.

PERIODICALS

Research & Development
Cahners Publishing Co.
1350 E. Touhy Ave.
Box 5080
Des Plaines, IL 60017-5080
708-635-8800
Rob Cassidy, Editor
Technical information about R & D programs and results.

R & D Contracts Monthly
Government Data Publications
1661 MacDonald Ave.
Brooklyn, NY 11230
718-627-0819
Siegfried Lobel, Editor
News of government contracts that were just awarded and other news for research organizations and manufacturers.

R & D Management Digest
Lomond Publications, Inc.
Box 88
Mt. Airy, MD 21771
301-829-1633
Lowell Hattery, Editor
Topics covered include science policy, technology assessment, technology transfer, federal programs, international development, and project management.

R & D Strategist
Auerbach Publishers
One Penn Plaza
New York, NY 10119
212-971-5000
Advice for R & D managers.

LIBRARIES

Erico Products, Inc.
Information Resources Center
34600 Solon Rd.
Solon, OH 44139
216-248-0100
Research and development, materials, science, and technology.

Arthur D. Little, Inc.
Research Library
25 Acorn Park
Cambridge, MA 02140-2390
617-864-5770
617-661-8024 Fax
Research administration, science, food, mechanical engineering, chemistry, and physics.

National Research Council
Library
2101 Constitution Ave., N.W.
Washington, DC 20418
202-334-2125
202-334-1651 Fax
Science policy.

Research Triangle Insitute
Technical Information Center
Box 12194
Research Triangle Park, NC 27709
919-541-6455
919-541-5985 Fax
Industrial processes, health research, computer science, and related topics.

Teledyne Brown Engineering
Technical Library
Cummings Research Park
300 Sparkman Dr., N.W.
P.O. Box 070007
205-726-1809
Research and development.

COMPANIES

Analysis & Technology, Inc.
Route 2, Technology Park, Box 220
North Stonington, CT 06359
203-599-3910
Electronics R & D and engineering services.

Battell Memorial Institute
505 King Ave.
Columbus, OH 43201
614-424-6424
R & D in various industries.

Genentech, Inc.
(Subsidiary of Roche Holdings Inc.)
460 Point San Bruno Blvd.
San Francisco, CA 94080
415-266-1000
Pharmaceutical R & D.

General Magnaplate Corp.
1331 U. S. Hwy. 1
Linden, NJ 07036
908-862-6200
Contract R & D in metals and materials.

Mechanical Technology Inc.
968 Albany-Shaker Rd.
Latham, NY 12110
518-785-2211
Contract R & D in machinery and other areas.

Montana Energy Research & Development
    Institute, Inc.
220 N. Alaska
Butte, MT 59701
406-782-0463
Energy R & D.

Nova Pharmaceutical Corp.
6200 Freeport Ctr.
Baltimore, MD 21224
301-558-7000
Pharmaceutical R & D.

Reliant Testing Laboratories
16312 S. Main St.
Gardena, CA 90248
213-327-6352
R & D testing.

Research Triangle Institute
3040 Cornwallis Rd.
Research Triangle Park, NC 27709
919-541-6000
R & D in various areas.

Southwest Research Institute
6220 Culebra Rd.
San Antonio, TX 78284
512-684-5111
Contract R & D in various areas.

Spire Corp.
Patriots Park
Bedford, MA 01730
617-275-6000
Electronics R & D.

SRI International
333 Ravenswood Ave.
Menlo Park, CA 94025
415-326-6200
R & D in various areas.

FEDERAL GOVERNMENT

U.S. International Trade Administration
Department of Commerce
14th St. and Constitution Ave., N.W.
Washington, DC 20230
202-377-2000
*Ask for the Commodity Analyst who is an
expert in research and development.*

U.S. International Trade Commission
500 E St., S.W.
Washington, DC 20436
202-205-2000 Office of the Secretary
202-205-3296 Industries locator
*Ask for the Trade Analyst who is an expert in
research and development.*

RESTAURANT INDUSTRY

See also: FOOD SERVICE INDUSTRY

ASSOCIATIONS

Hotel Employees and Restaurant Employees
    International Union
1219 28th St., N.W.
Washington, DC 20007
202-393-4373
Herman Leavitt, Secretary
*A very large union of hotel and restaurant
employees.*

National Association of Restaurant Managers
5322 N. 78th Way
Scottsdale, AZ 85250
602-941-3059
800-777-NARM
Kenneth Paulson, President
*Offers educational programs to owners and
managers of restaurants and to industry suppliers.*

National Soft Serve and Fast Food Association
516 S. Front St.
Chesaning, MI 48616
517-845-3336
Ward Anderson, Executive Director
*A small group of independent owners of soft
serve ice cream restaurants.*

National Restaurant Association
1200 17th St. N.W.
Washington, DC 20036
202-331-5900
800-424-5156
202-331-2429 Fax
William Fisher, Executive Vice President
*Members include restaurants, foodservice
firms, cafeterias, and other entities that serve
food. Offers educational programs in management, table service, and other topics.*

PERIODICALS

Cameron's Foodservice Promotions Reporter
5325 Sheridan Dr.
Box 1160
Williamsville, NY 14231-1160
716-833-4369
Nina Cameron, Editor
Advises restaurants, hotels, and other organizations that provide food service about promotions to increase their business.

Chef Institutional
Talcott Publishing Co.
206 W. Huron St.
Chicago, IL 60610
312-664-4040
Alfreda Vaughn, Editor
News and trends for chefs, managers of restaurants, and institutional food servicers.

Nation's Restaurant News
Lebhar-Friedman, Inc.
425 Park Ave.
New York, NY 10022
212-371-9400
Charles Bernstein, Editor
Surveys the restaurant business.

Restaurant Business
Bill Communications, Inc.
633 Third Ave.
New York, NY 10017
212-986-4800
Peter Berlinski, Editor
Reports on equipment, personnel, supplies, and services for restaurant owners, managers, and others in the food service business.

Restaurants and Institutions
Cahners Publishing Co.
1350 E. Touhy Ave.
Box 5080
Des Plaines, IL 60017-5080
708-635-8800
Michael Bartlett, Editor
Describes new products, recipes, marketing trends, and other subjects for managers of restaurants and institutions.

LIBRARIES

City of College of San Francisco
Hotel and Restaurant Department
Alice Statler Library
50 Phelan Ave.
San Francisco, CA 94112
415-239-3460
Restaurants, catering services, hotels, cooking, tourism, and beverages.

Cornell University
School of Hotel Administration Library
Statler Hall
Ithaca, NY 14853-6901
607-255-3673
607-255-0742 Fax
Restaurant administration, food and beverages, sales promotion, marketing, public relations, and the tourist industry.

Culinary Institute of America
Katharine Angell Library
651 S. Albany Post Rd.
Hyde Park, NY 12538-1499
914-452-9700
Restaurant management and food service.

New York City Technical College of the City
    University of New York
Library
300 Jay St.
Brooklyn, NY 11201
718-260-5470
718-260-5467 Fax
Restaurant management and business fields.

COMPANIES

A & W Restaurants, Inc.
(Subsidiary of Taubman Investment Co.)
17197 N. Laure Park Dr.
Livonia, MI 48152
313-462-0029
Fast food restaurants.

Burger King Corp.
(Subsidiary of Grand Metropolitan PLC)
17777 Old Cutler Rd.
Miami, FL 33157
305-378-7011
Fast food restaurant chain.

McDonald's Restaurants
1 McDonald's Plaza
Oak Brook, IL 60521
708-575-3000
Fast food restaurant chain.

Pizza Hut, Inc.
(Subsidiary of PepsiCo, Inc.)
9111 E. Douglas
Wichita, KS 67207
316-681-9000
Fast food restaurant chain.

Restaurant Enterprise Group Inc.
One Park Plaza
Irvine, CA 92714
714-852-5700
Owns and operates restaurants.

Sizzler International, Inc.
12655 W. Jefferson Blvd.
Los Angeles, CA 90066
213-827-2300
Restaurant chain.

Sky Chefs, Inc.
(Subsidiary of Onex Food Services, Inc.)
601 Ryan Plaza
Arlington, TX 76012
817-792-2123
Airport restaurants and food service in institutions.

Sonic Industries Inc.
120 Robert S. Kerr
Oklahoma City, OK 73102
405-478-0731
Fast food, restaurant equipment, and franchise fees.

Spartan Food Systems Inc.
(Subsidiary of TW Services Inc.)
Frontage Rd., Box 3168
Spartanburg, SC 29304
803-596-8000
Owns and operates restaurants.

Wendy's International Inc.
4288 W. Dublin Granville Rd.
Dublin, OH 43017
614-764-3100
Fast food restaurant chain.

White Castle System Inc.
555 W. Goodale St.
Columbus, OH 43215
614-228-5781
Fast food restaurant chain.

FEDERAL GOVERNMENT

U.S. International Trade Administration
Department of Commerce
14th St. and Constitution Ave., N.W.
Washington, DC 20230
202-377-2000
*Ask for the Commodity Analyst who is an
expert in the restaurant industry.*

U.S. International Trade Commission
500 E St., S.W.
Washington, DC 20436
202-205-2000 Office of the Secretary
202-205-3296 Industries locator
*Ask for the Trade Analyst who is an expert in
the restaurant industry.*

RETAIL TRADE

See also: CHAIN STORES; POINT-OF-SALE INDUSTRY;
SHOPPING CENTERS AND MALLS; STORE DISPLAYS; and
SUPERMARKETS AND CONVENIENCE STORES

ASSOCIATIONS

Institute of Store Planners
25 N. Broadway
Tarrytown, NY 10591
914-332-1806
Newton Fassler, President
*Planners, designers, and suppliers to the retail
industry.*

International Mass Retail Association
1901 Pennsylvania Ave. N.W., 10th Fl.
Washington, DC 20006
202-861-0774
202-785-4588 Fax
Richard Hersh, President
*Discount retailing chains and firms that ser-
vice them. Offers research and education in
the field of self-service retailing.*

National Association of Catalog Showroom
   Merchandisers
PO Box 725
Hauppauge, NY 11788
516-979-0166
800-334-4177
516-979-9585 Fax
Jean Coticchio, President
*Firms that operate catalog showrooms and
supply the industry.*

National Association of College Stores
528 E. Lorain St.
Oberlin, OH 44074
216-775-7777
800-622-7498
216-774-1335 Fax
Garis Distelhorst, Executive Director
*Offers research and educational programs to
college stores and their suppliers.*

National Association of Retail Dealers of
America
10 E. 22nd St.
Lombard, IL 60148
312-953-8950
708-953-8957 Fax
John Shields, Executive Director
*Members include retailers of furniture, home
appliances, computers, electronics goods, and
other products. The association offers consulting services, and training in retail advertising,
management, and sales.*

National Retail Federation
100 W. 31st St.
New York, NY 10001
212-244-8780
212-594-0487 Fax
John Schultz, President
*A large group of chain, department, and other
types of retailers. Offers a wide range of information services and workshops on such topics
as retail management, finance, credit, theft
control, window display, and many other
areas.*

PERIODICALS

Retail Info Systems News Directory
Edgell Enterprises, Inc.
One West Hanover Ave., Ste. 107
Randolph, NJ 07869
201-895-3300
Georgia Colicchio, Editor
*Follows developments and new products in
software for retail executives.*

Retail Observer
1442 Sierra Creek Way
San Jose, CA 95132
408-272-8974
*Advises retailers on the merchandizing of elec-
tronics and kitchen goods, including appliances.*

Retail Store Image
Communication Channels, Inc.
6255 Barfield Rd.
Atlanta, GA 30328-4369
404-256-9800
Katherine Fields, Editor
*Advises interior decorators, visual merchan-
disers, architectural consultants, store planners, and others responsible for the image and
appearance of stores.*

Retailing Today
Robert Kahn and Associates
Box 249
Lafayette, CA 94549
415-254-4434
Robert Kahn, Editor
Informs CEO's about retailing trends.

Stores
National Retail Federation
100 W. 31st St.
New York, NY 10001
212-244-8780
Joan Bergmann, Editor
Reports on retailing and merchandising issues.

Value Retail News
Off-Price Specialists, Inc.
13773 Icot Blvd., No. 507
Clearwater, FL 34620-3711
813-536-4047
Tom Kirwan, Editor
*Covers marketing, real estate, and other topics
of concern to off-price and discount retailers.*

LIBRARIES

Dayton Hudson Corp.
Research/Information Center
777 Nicollet Mall
Minneapolis, MN 55402
612-370-6769
Retailing and business.

Montgomery Ward and Co.
Information Services
One Montgomery Ward Plaza
Chicago, IL 60671
312-467-7351
Retailing.

National Association of Convenience Stores
NACS Information Center
1605 King St.
Alexandria, VA 22314-2792
703-684-3600
703-836-4564 Fax
Retail trade and convenience stores.

National Retail Federation
100 W. 31st St.
New York, NY 10001
212-244-8780
212-594-0487 Fax
All retailing topics.

Purdue University
Consumer and Family Sciences Library
Stone Hall
West Lafayette, IN 47907
317-494-2914
317-494-9007 Fax
Retail management, consumer affairs, hotel management, tourism, and other topics.

COMPANIES

Dayton Hudson Corp.
777 Nicollet Mall
Minneapolis, MN 55402
612-375-2200
Retail chain.

Kenzer Corp.
777 3rd Ave.
New York, NY 10017
212-563-4400
Management consulting and executive search services for retailers and other industries.

R.H. Macy and Co.
151 W. 34th St.
New York, NY 10001
212-560-4249
Retail chain.

Meret, Inc.
645 S. Grant Ave.
Columbus, OH 43206
614-469-0444
Consulting and design services to retailers.

Montgomery Ward Holding Corp.
1 Montgomery Ward Plaza
Chicago, IL 60671
312-467-2000
Retail chain.

Rouse Co.
10275 Little Patuxent Pkwy.
Columbia, MD 21044
301-992-6000
Developers and managers of retail centers.

Sears Roebuck and Co.
Sears Tower
Chicago, IL 60684
312-875-2500
Retail chain.

Wal-Mart Stores, Inc.
702 S.W. 8th St.
Bentonville, AR 72712
501-273-4000
Retail chain.

FEDERAL GOVERNMENT

U.S. Bureau of the Census
Washington, DC 20233
301-763-4040
*Ask for the Economic Programs Office to get
information about the Census of Retail Trade.*

U.S. International Trade Administration
Department of Commerce
14th St. and Constitution Ave., N.W.
Washington, DC 20230
202-377-2000
*Ask for the Commodity Analyst who is an
expert in retail trade.*

RETIREMENT

See also: EMPLOYEE BENEFITS; NURSING HOMES; and PENSIONS AND PROFIT-SHARING PLANS

ASSOCIATIONS

American Association of Retired Persons
1909 K St. N.W.
Washington, DC 20049
202-872-4700
Horace Deets, Executive Director
*Usually known as AARP, this huge organiza-
tion of people 50 years of age and older offers
a wide range of services including a program
for planning retirement.*

International Society for Retirement Planning
c/o L. Malcolm Rodman
11312 Old Club Rd.
Rockville, MD 20852
301-881-4113
800-327-ISRP
301-816-2379 Fax
L. Malcolm Rodman, Executive
    Vice President
*This group of financial planners, personnel
executives, and businesses offers information
on all aspects of preretirement planning.*

National Conference on Public Employee
    Retirement Systems
311 Roosevelt Ave.
San Antonio, TX 78210
512-534-3262
512-534-5877 Fax
Carlos Resendez, Secretary
*Organizations at all levels of government that
safeguard the retirement systems of public
employees.*

National Institute on Age, Work and Retire-
    ment
c/o National Council on the Aging
600 Maryland Ave. S.W., W. Wing 100
Washington, DC 20024
202-479-1200
Daniel Thursz, President
*Offers information to companies on employ-
ment and retirement subjects.*

Service Corps of Retired Executives Association
1825 Connecticut Ave. N.W., Ste. 503
Washington, DC 20009
202-653-6279
John Daniels, Executive Director
Organizes volunteer programs of retired and active business people who offer free consultations to new and ongoing businesses.

PERIODICALS

Retirement and Benefit Planning
Butterworth Legal Publishers
90 Stiles Rd.
Salem, NH 03079
800-548-4001
Randolph Goodman, Editor
Reports on the legal aspects of retirement planning and employee benefits.

Retirement Letter
Phillips Publishing, Inc.
7811 Montrose Rd.
Potomac, MD 20854
301-340-2100
Peter Dickinson, Editor
Advises consumers on the financial aspects of planning for retirement.

LIBRARIES

International Personnel Management Association
Center for Personnel Research
Alexandria, VA 22314
703-549-7100
703-684-9048 Fax
Covers human resource management topics, including retirement planning.

The National Council on the Aging, Inc.
Ollie A. Randall Library
600 Maryland Ave., S.W., West Wing 100
Washington, DC 20024
202-479-1665
202-470-0735 Fax
Retirement, senior centers, aging, economics, and nursing homes.

Program Planners, Inc.
Library/Information Center
230 W. 41st St., 19th Fl.
New York, NY 10036
212-840-2600
Retirement systems, public employee pensions, insurance, and health care.

COMPANIES

Beverly Enterprises, Inc.
1200 S. Waldron Rd.
Fort Smith, AR 72903
501-452-6712
Builds and manages retirement centers and long-term health facilities.

Forum Group, Inc.
8900 Keystone Crossing, Box 40498
Indianapolis, IN 46240
317-846-0700
Builds and operates retirement centers and long-term health facilities.

Geriatric & Medical Centers, Inc.
5601 Chestnut St.
Philadelphia, PA 19139
215-476-2250
Operates retirement centers and nursing homes.

Mutual Life Insurance Co. of New York
1740 Broadway
New York, NY 10019
212-708-2000
Insurance and retirement plans for employees, families, and individuals.

Paul Revere Life Insurance Co.
(Subsidiary of Textron Inc.)
18 Chestnut St.
Worcester, MA 01608
508-799-4441
Insurance and retirement plans.

Retirement Care Associates Inc.
212 N. Kirkwood Rd.
St. Louis, MO 63122
314-822-8383
Operates retirement centers.

Standard Insurance Co.
1100 S. W. Sixth Ave.
Portland, OR 97204
503-248-2700
Insurance and retirement plans.

FEDERAL GOVERNMENT

U.S. Department of Labor
200 Constitution Ave., N.W.
Washington, DC 20210
202-523-6666
Ask for the Pension Welfare Benefits Administration.

U.S. Department of the Treasury
1500 Pennsylvania Ave., N.W.
Washington, DC 20220
202-566-2111
Ask for the Employee Plans, Technical & Actuarial Division or the Employee Plans & Exempt Organizations Operations department.

Office of Personnel Management
1900 E St., N.W.
Washington, DC 20415
202-606-2424
Ask for the Retirement and Insurance Group.

RHODE ISLAND

STATE OFFICE LOCATOR (*for referrals to all state government offices*)

401-277-2000

ARCHIVES AND RECORDS

Archives Division
State House
Room 217
Providence, RI 02903
401-277-2535

ATTORNEY GENERAL

Attorney General Department
72 Pine Street
Providence, RI 02903
401-274-4400

BANKING

Business Regulations Department
233 Richmond Street
Providence, RI 02903
401-277-2405

COMMERCE

Economic Development
7 Jackson Walkway
Providence, RI 02903
401-277-2601

CONSUMER AFFAIRS

Consumer Affairs
100 Orange Street
Providence, RI 02903
401-277-2443

EDUCATION

Education Department
22 Hayes Street
Providence, RI 02908
401-277-2031

ENERGY

Housing, Energy & Intergovernmental Rela-
tions Office
State House
Room 143
Providence, RI 02903-5872
401-277-2850

ENVIRONMENTAL AFFAIRS

Environmental Coordination Office
83 Park Street
Providence, RI 02903
401-277-3434

HEALTH

Health Department
3 Capitol Hill
Providence, RI 02908
401-277-2231

HOUSING

Housing, Energy & Intergovernmental Rela-
tions Office
State House
Room 143
Providence, RI 02903
401-277-2080

HUMAN RIGHTS

Human Rights Commission
10 Abbott Park Place
Providence, RI 02920
401-277-2661

INSURANCE

Business Regulations Department
233 Richmond Street
Providence, RI 02903
401-277-2246

LABOR

Labor Department
220 Elmwood Avenue
Providence, RI 02907
401-457-1800

LEGISLATION

Legislative Council
State House
Room 101
Providence, RI 02903
401-277-3757

LIBRARY SERVICES

State Library Services Department
300 Richmond Street
Providence, RI 02903
401-277-2726

LICENSING—CORPORATE

Corporations Division
State House
Room 217
Providence, RI 02903
401-277-3040

LICENSING—PROFESSIONAL AND OCCUPATIONAL

Professional Regulations Division
3 Capitol Hill
Providence, RI 02908
401-277-2827

MOTOR VEHICLES

Motor Vehicles Division
210 State Office Building
Providence, RI 02903
401-277-6900

OCCUPATIONAL HEALTH AND SAFETY

Occupational Safety Division
220 Elmwood Avenue
Providence, RI 02907
401-457-1800

PUBLIC UTILITIES

Public Utilities Commission
100 Orange Street
Providence, RI 02903
401-277-3500

PURCHASING

Purchases Office
1 Capitol Hill
Providence, RI 02908
401-277-2321

REAL ESTATE

Licensing & Consumer Protection Division
233 Richmond Street
Providence, RI 02903
401-277-2416

SECURITIES

Banking Division
233 Richmond Street
Providence, RI 02903
401-277-3048

TAXATION AND REVENUE

Taxation Office
1 Capitol Hill
Providence, RI 02908
401-277-3050

TOURISM

Tourism & Promotion Division
7 Jackson Walkway
Providence, RI 02903
401-277-2601
800-556-2484 (in New England and Mid-
   Atlantic Region)

TRANSPORTATION

Transportation Department
210 State Office Building
Providence, RI 02903
401-277-2481

UNEMPLOYMENT

Unemployment Insurance & Tax Operations
24 Mason Street
Providence, RI 02903
401-277-3649

WORKER'S COMPENSATION

Workers Compensation Department
610 Mantun Avenue
Providence, RI 02909
401-272-0700

RICE INDUSTRY

ASSOCIATIONS

Rice Council for Market Development
PO Box 740123
Houston, TX 77274
713-270-6699
713-270-9021 Fax
Bill Goldsmith, Executive Vice President
Offers promotional, advertising, and public relations services to growers, millers, and other rice industry companies.

Rice Millers' Association
Crystal Gateway 1, Ste. 302
1235 Jefferson Davis Hwy.
Arlington, VA 22202
703-920-1281
703-521-5814 Fax
David Graves, President
Offers information on rice processing, packaging, and related topics to rice milling operators.

PERIODICALS

Rice Farming and Rice Industry News
Little Publications, Inc.
6263 Poplar Ave., Ste. 540
Memphis, TN 38119
901-767-4020
Patrick Shepard, Editor
Technical and business information for rice farmers and processors.

Rice Journal
Specialized Agricultural Publications, Inc.
3000 Highwoods Blvd., Ste. 300
Box 95075
Raleigh, NC 27625
919-872-5040
Follows technical and industry trends for rice producers.

Rice World & Soybean News
Box 219
Folsom, LA 70437-0219
504-796-3012
J.P. Gaines, Editor
Surveys the rice and soybean business.

LIBRARIES

U.S.D.A.
National Agricultural Library
10301 Baltimore Blvd.
Beltsville, MD 20705
301-344-3755
301-344-5472 Fax
Plant science, soils, fertilizers, alternative farming, and other agricultural topics.

University of Florida
Everglades Research & Education Center
Belle Glade Library
Inst. of Food & Agricultural Sciences
Box 8003
Belle Glade, FL 33430
407-996-3062
Rice, soils science, and agriculture.

COMPANIES

Arrow Industries, Inc.
2625 Belt Line Rd.
Carrollton, TX 75006
214-416-6900
Packages and distributes rice, dried beans, peas and other items.

Comet Rice, Inc.
(Subsidiary of Erly Industries Inc.)
10960 Wilshire Blvd.
Los Angeles, CA 90024
213-478-0069
Rice and products made from rice.

Connell Co.
45 Cardinal Dr.
Westfield, NJ 07092
908-233-0700
Wholesaler of rice and other foods.

Erly Industries Inc.
10990 Wilshire Blvd.
Los Angeles, CA 90024
213-879-1480
Rice, products made from rice, and other foods.

Producers Rice Mill Inc.
N. Anna St., Box 461
Stuttgart, AR 72160
501-673-4444
Processor and marketer of rice.

Riceland Foods, Inc.
2120 Park Ave.
Stuttgart, AR 72160
501-673-5500
Rice and other food products.

Riviana Foods Inc.
2777 Allen Pkwy.
Houston, TX 77019
713-529-3251
Rice and products made from rice.

FEDERAL GOVERNMENT

U.S. Department of Agriculture
14th St. and Independence Ave., S.W.
Washington, DC 20250
202-720-8732
Ask for the Economic Research Service.

U.S. International Trade Administration
Department of Commerce
14th St. and Constitution Ave., N.W.
Washington, DC 20230
202-377-2000
Ask for the Commodity Analyst who is an expert in the rice industry.

U.S. International Trade Commission
500 E St., S.W.
Washington, DC 20436
202-205-2000 Office of the Secretary
202-205-3296 Industries locator
Ask for the Trade Analyst who is an expert in the rice industry.

RISK MANAGEMENT

Risk management refers to a profession and a group of techniques used to study, prevent, or minimize loss to business and other organizations due to theft, accidents, and litigation. Risk managers employ insurance, safety measures, and education to control loss. A related term—political risk—refers to the potential dangers of traveling in or doing business in certain countries.

See also: INSURANCE

ASSOCIATIONS

Associated Risk Managers International
200 Colorado Bldg.
702 Colorado St.
Austin, TX 78701
512-479-6886
512-479-0577 Fax
John Atkinson, President
Insurance agencies that have a specialty in providing risk management services.

Council for International Business Risk Management
PO Box 811765
Dallas, TX 75381
214-352-5801
214-350-7609 Fax
George Barnes, Executive Director
Members study government policies, political risk, and other issues that can affect international businesses.

Public Agency Risk Managers Association
5750 Almaden Expy.
San Jose, CA 95118
408-265-2600
Ben Francis, Secretary
Serves as a forum for discussing risk management in the public sector.

Public Risk Management Association
1117 N. 19th St., Ste. 900
Arlington, VA 22209
703-528-7701
703-528-7966 Fax
Brad Johnson, Executive Director
A clearinghouse to share ideas on risk management, insurance, and safety for officials from cities, counties, villages, school boards, and other public entities.

Society of Risk Management Consultants
c/o John J. Crout
Blades & Macaulay
2444 Morris Ave.
Union, NJ 07083
201-687-3735
John Crout, Secretary
Members are insurance and risk management consultants involved with selling insurance.

PERIODICALS

Corporate Risk Management
Oster Communications, Inc.
219 Main St.
Cedar Falls, IA 50613
319-277-1271
Advises corporate risk managers on how to solve common problems.

Governmental Risk Management Manual
Management Publishing Co.
2030 E. Broadway, Ste. 106
Tucson, AZ 85719
602-622-5174
Sabina Dunton, Editor
Focuses on the problems faced by government risk managers.

Insurance and Risk Management
Buraff Publications
1350 Connecticut Ave. N.W., Ste. 1000
Washington, DC 20036
202-862-0990
Corby Anderson, Editor
Covers a variety of topics in the field of loss control and risk management.

Merritt Risk Management Review
Merritt Co.
1661 Ninth St.
Box 955
Santa Monica, CA 90406
213-450-7234
Mary Ann Giorgio, Editor
Follows news and trends in insurance and risk management.

Political Risk Yearbook
Political Risk Services
Box 6482
Syracuse, NY 13217-6482
315-472-1224
William Coplin, Editor
Reports on political risks in nearly 100 countries for international business managers and investors.

Risk & Insurance
Axon Group
747 Dresher Rd., Ste. 500
Box 980
Horsham, PA 19044
215-784-0860
Richard Jaccoma, Editor
Analyzes such insurance and risk management issues as environmental liability, and compensation and benefits for employees.

Risk and Benefits Journal
Curant Communications, Inc.
1849 Sawtelle Blvd., Ste. 770
Los Angeles, CA 90025
213-479-1769
*Detailed examination of corporate experiences
with risk and benefits matters.*

LIBRARIES

American Institute for Property & Liability
    Underwriters
Insurance Institute of America
Library
720 Providence Rd.
Malvern, PA 19355
215-644-2100
215-251-9995 Fax
Risk management, insurance, and economics.

FEDERAL GOVERNMENT

Export-Import Bank
811 Vermont Ave., N.W.
Washington, DC 20571
202-566-2117
Ask for the Export Finance Group.

ROADS AND HIGHWAYS

See also: PUBLIC TRANSPORTATION; TRAFFIC ENGINEERING
AND MANAGEMENT; TRAFFIC SAFETY; and each of the
50 states under transportation

ASSOCIATIONS

American Association of State Highway and
    Transportation Officials
444 N. Capitol St., N.W., Ste. 225
Washington, DC 20001
202-624-5800
Francis Francois, Executive Director
*An information exchange for officials nation-
wide who work for state highway and other
public transportation systems.*

American Road and Transportation Builders
    Association
501 School St. S.W.
Washington, DC 20024
202-488-2722
202-488-3631 Fax
T. Peter Ruane, President
*Members include construction firms, highway
contractors, government officials, engineers,
suppliers of construction equipment and materials, and others interested in promoting the
the building of roads.*

Better Roads and Transportation Council
501 School St. S.W.
Washington, DC 20024
202-488-2722
A lobbying group that promotes funding to improve state highways.

Highway Loss Data Institute
1005 N. Glebe Rd., Ste. 800
Arlington, VA 22201
703-247-1600
Brian O'Neill, President
Provides statistical information on highway accidents and the loss of life and property that results.

The Road Information Program
1200 18th St. N.W., Ste. 314
Washington, DC 20036
202-466-6706
202-785-4722 Fax
William Wilkins, Executive Director
Provides information to the public about highways.

PERIODICALS

From the State Capitals: Transportation Policies
Wakeman-Walworth, Inc.
300 N. Washington St.
Alexandria, VA 22314
703-549-8606
Reports news of building, funding, and other topics that involve roads and mass transit.

I T E Journal
Institute of Transportation Engineers
525 School St., S.W., Ste. 410
Washington, DC 20024
202-554-8050
Kathy Harrington-Hughes, Editor
Technical information for transportation engineers, including those involved with road and highway planning, building, and maintenance.

Pavement Maintenance
Aberdeen Group
426 S. Westgate
Addison, IL 60101
708-543-0870
Follows trends in road and highway maintenance.

LIBRARIES

Michigan (State) Department of Transportation
Resource Center
425 W. Ottawa
Box 30050
Lansing, MI 48909
517-373-1545
517-373-0168 Fax
Transportation planning, and highway engineering, design, and safety.

National Research Council
Transportation Research Information Service
Transportation Research Board
2101 Constitution Ave., N.W.
Washington,DC 20418
202-334-2995
202-334-2003 Fax
Highway transport, design, operations, planning, and construction.

U.S. Department of Transportation
Library and Distribution Services Division
400 7th St., S.W.
M-493.3, Rm. 2200
Washington, DC 20590
202-366-0746
Highways and urban mass transit.

COMPANIES

Apac Inc.
(Subsidiary of Ashland Oil Holdings, Inc.)
3340 Peachtree Rd., N.E.
Atlanta, GA 30326
404-261-2610
Highway construction.

Beazer East, Inc.
(Subsidiary of Beazer PLC)
436 7th Ave.
Pittsburgh, PA 15219
412-227-2000
Street and highway construction.

Caterpillar Inc.
100 N.E. Adams St.
Peoria, IL 61629
309-675-1000
Road construction equipment and vehicles.

Greiner Engineering, Inc.
909 E. Las Colinas Blvd.
Irving, TX 75039
214-869-1001
Design and engineering services for highway construction and other transporation systems.

Haulpak Division
(Division of Komatsu Dresser Co.)
2300 N.E. Adams St., Box 240
Peoria, IL 61650
309-672-7000
Highway construction equipment.

IA Holdings Corp.
Rte. 202
Concordville, PA 19331
215-459-3136
Street and highway construction.

Medusa Corp.
Lee & Monticello Blvd.
Cleveland Heights, OH 44118
216-371-4000
Construction of guard rails, signs, median barriers, and other products for highways.

Quixote Corp.
One E. Wacker Dr.
Chicago, IL 60601
312-467-6755
Highway safety devices and other computerized products.

Rogers Group, Inc.
P.O. Box 25250
Nashville, TN 37202
615-242-0585
Highway and other types of construction.

Western-Mobile, Inc.
(Subsidiary of Redland PLC)
1400 W. 64th Ave., Box 21588
Denver, CO 80221
303-534-3165
Highway paving.

FEDERAL GOVERNMENT

U.S. Department of Transportation
400 Seventh St., S.W.
Washington, DC 20590
202-366-4000
Ask for the National Highway Institute in the Federal Highway Administration; or for the Construction & Maintenance division in the Engineering & Program Development department.

U.S. International Trade Administration
Department of Commerce
14th St. and Constitution Ave., N.W.
Washington, DC 20230
202-377-2000
Ask for the Commodity Analyst who is an
expert in roads and highways.

U.S. International Trade Commission
500 E St., S.W.
Washington, DC 20436
202-205-2000 Office of the Secretary
202-205-3296 Industries locator
Ask for the Trade Analyst who is an expert in
roads and highways.

ROBOT INDUSTRY

See also: COMPUTER-AIDED DESIGN/MANUFACTURING/ ENGINEERING (CAD/CAM/CAE) and PRODUCTION AND PROCESS CONTROL

ASSOCIATIONS

Automated Imaging Association
900 Victors Way
Ann Arbor, MI 48106
313-994-6088
313-994-3338 Fax
Jeffrey Burnstein, Managing Director
Offers research and educational programs to
manufacturers and users of machine vision
products.

IEEE Robotics and Automation Council
c/o Institute of Electrical and Electronics
    Engineers
345 E. 47th St.
New York, NY 10017
212-705-7867
An information clearinghouse for engineers
interested in all aspects of robotics.

Machine Vision Association
PO Box 930
Dearborn, MI 48121
313-271-1500
313-271-2861 Fax
Kristi Hansen, Manager
Offers educational programs on machine
vision to engineers. Associated with the
Robotics International of SME at the same
addresses.

National Service Robot Association
900 Victors Way
Ann Arbor, MI 48106
313-994-6088
313-994-3338 Fax
Jeffrey Burnstein, Managing Director
Provides information on service robots, which
are used for education, household work, and
other purposes.

Robotic Industries Association
900 Victors Way
Ann Arbor, MI 48106
313-994-6088
313-994-3338 Fax
Donald Vincent, Executive Vice President
Offers seminars to researchers, manufacturers, educators, and others interested in robotics.

PERIODICALS

Advances in Automation and Robotics
J A I Press Inc.
55 Old Post Rd., No. 2
Box 1678
Greenwich, CT 06836-1678
203-661-7602
George Saridis, Editor
Technical information about robotics and automated manufacturing.

IEEE Transactions on Robotics and Automation
Institute of Electrical and Electronics Engineers, Inc.
345 E. 47th St.
New York, NY 10017-2394
212-705-7366
Russell Taylor, Editor
Reports new theories and applications of robotics.

I E N: Industrial Equipment News
Thomas Publishing Co.
Five Penn Plaza
250 W. 34th St.
New York, NY 10001
212-695-0500
Mark Devlin, Editor
Covers new industrial parts, materials, and equipment, including robotics.

International Journal of Robotics Research
M I T Press
55 Hayward St.
Cambridge, MA 02142
617-253-2889
Michael Brady, Editor
Technical information for robotics scientists and researchers.

Journal of Robotic Systems
John Wiley & Sons, Inc.
605 Third Ave.
New York, NY 10158-0012
212-692-6000
Gerardo Beni, Editor
Reports on the new designs, implementations, and uses for robots. Written for engineers and scientists.

Robotics and Computer-Integrated Manufacturing
Pergamon Press, Inc.
Maxwell House
Fairview Park
Elmsford, NY 10523
914-592-7700
Toshio Sata, Editor
Technical articles on the use of robots and flexible manufacturing systems.

Robotics Today
Society of Manufacturing Engineers
One SME Dr.
Box 930
Dearborn, MI 48121-0930
313-271-1500
Robert Stauffer, Editor
Technical information on how robots are used to automate manufacturing.

Robotics World
Communication Channels, Inc.
6255 Barfield Rd.
Atlanta, GA 30328-4369
404-256-9800
Larry Anderson, Editor
Covers all aspects of the robotics and computer-integrated manufacturing industries.

LIBRARIES

Cincinnati Milacron Inc.
Information Resource Center
4701 Marburg Ave.
Cincinnati, OH 45209-1025
513-841-8589
513-841-8059 Fax
Robotics, electronic controls, processing machinery, and related topics.

Rensselaer Polytechnic Institute
Center for Manufacturing Productivity and
    Technology Transfer
Library
110 Eighth St.
Troy, NY 12180
518-266-6724
518-276-2990 Fax
Robotics, computer-aided design, artificial intelligence, and sensor technologies.

Society of Manufacturing Engineers
SME Library
One SME Dr.
Box 930
Dearborn, MI 48121
313-271-1500
313-271-2861 Fax
Robotics, computerized automation in manufacturing, and related topics.

COMPANIES

Automated Assemblies Corp.
25 School St.
Clinton, MA 01510
508-368-8914
Robotics equipment used in the plastics industry.

Bra-Con/X-Mation, Inc.
(Subsidiary of CDI Transportation Group,
    Inc.)
43850 W. 10 Mile Rd.
Novi, MI 48376
313-348-0200
Industrial robotics systems.

ESAB Automation, Inc.
(Subsidiary of ESAB Group, Inc.)
P.O. Box 2286
Fort Collins, CO 80522
303-225-7600
Robotics equipment for metal cutting and welding.

I. S. I. Manufacturing, Inc.
31915 Groesbeck Hwy.
Fraser, MI 48026
313-294-9500
Industrial robotics systems.

IDAB, Incorporated
3200 W. 84th St.
Hialeah, FL 33016
305-823-4000
Robotics and materials handling machinery.

Odetics Inc.
1515 S. Manchester Ave.
Anaheim, CA 92802
714-774-5000
Robotics systems.

Prab Robots, Inc.
5944 E. Kilgore Rd., Box 2121
Kalamazoo, MI 49003
616-329-0835
Robots and other types of industrial equipment.

Process Equipment Co.
6555 S. State Rte. 202
Tipp City, OH 45371
513-667-4451
Robotics systems.

Quad Systems Corp.
2 Electronic Dr.
Horsham, PA 19044
215-657-6202
Robotics used for circuit board assembly.

Robotic Vision Systems, Inc.
425 Rabro Dr. E.
Hauppauge, NY 11788
516-273-9700
Robotics systems.

FEDERAL GOVERNMENT

National Science Foundation
1800 G St., N.W.
Washington, DC 20550
202-357-9859
Ask for the Robotics & Machine Intelligence department.

U.S. International Trade Administration
Department of Commerce
14th St. and Constitution Ave., N.W.
Washington, DC 20230
202-377-2000
Ask for the Commodity Analyst who is an expert in the robot industry.

U.S. International Trade Commission
500 E St., S.W.
Washington, DC 20436
202-205-2000 Office of the Secretary
202-205-3296 Industries locator
Ask for the Trade Analyst who is an expert in the robot industry.

ROOFING INDUSTRY

See also: ASPHALT INDUSTRY

ASSOCIATIONS

Asphalt Roofing Manufacturers Association
6288 Montrose Rd.
Rockville, MD 20852
301-231-9050
301-881-6572 Fax
Richard Snyder, Executive Vice President
Firms that make roofing shingles, rolls, and related materials from asphalt.

National Roofing Contractors Association
O'Hare International Center
10255 W. Higgins Rd., Ste. 600
Rosemont, IL 60018-5607
708-299-9070
708-299-1183 Fax
William Good, Executive Vice President
Offers educational programs to contractors who work with all types of roofing materials.

National Tile Roofing Manufacturers Association
3127 Los Feliz Blvd.
Los Angeles, CA 90039
213-660-4411
800-248-TILE
213-660-6259 Fax
Walter Pruter, Executive Vice President
Members manufacture "firesafe" roofing tiles made from concrete and clay.

Roof Coatings Manufacturers Association
60 Revere Dr., Ste. 500
Northbrook, IL 60062
708-480-9080
708-480-9282 Fax
Kevin Hacke, Executive Director
Manufacturers of roof coatings that use the cold process.

Roof Consultants Institute
7424 Chapel Hill Rd.
Raleigh, NC 27607
919-859-0742
Robert Phillips, Executive Manager
A group of consultants who advise builders, building owners, architects, and engineers about roofing subjects.

Single Ply Roofing Institute
104 Wilmot Rd., Ste. 201
Deerfield, IL 60015
708-940-8800
708-940-7218 Fax
Ruth Warshaw, Managing Director
Represents manufacturers and distributors of the rubber, plastic, and other materials used in single ply roofing systems.

PERIODICALS

Contractor's Guide
Century Communications, Inc.
6201 W. Howard St.
Niles, IL 60648
708-647-1200
Greg Ettling, Editor
Covers products used by the roofing, window, insulation, and siding industries.

Handbook of Commercial Roofing Systems
Edgell Communications
7500 Old Oak Blvd.
Cleveland, OH 44130
216-826-2839
Teresa O'Dea, Editor
Technical advice for roofing contractors.

International Journal of Roofing Technology
National Roofing Contractors Association
10255 W. Higgins Rd., Ste. 600
Rosemont, IL 60018
708-299-9070
Reports on roofing research and technical data.

R S I
Edgell Communications
7500 Old Oak Blvd.
Cleveland, OH 44130
216-243-8100
Michael Russo, Editor
Covers industry news, marketing ideas, and roofing products.

Roofer Magazine
D & H Publications
12120 Amedicus Ln.
Ft. Myers, FL 33907
813-275-7663
Kaerrie Simons, Editor
Surveys the roofing industry for contractors and others.

LIBRARIES

Certainteed Corp.
Corporate Library/Information Center
1400 Union Meeting Rd.
Blue Bell, PA 19422
215-341-6283
215-341-6429 Fax
Roofing and insulation.

Construction Consultants, Inc.
Library
900 Pallister
Detroit, MI 48202
313-874-2770
313-874-1693 Fax
Roofing, construction, and waterproofing.

COMPANIES

Allied Building Products Corp.
15 E. Union Ave.
East Rutherford, NJ 07073
201-935-0800
Roofing, insulation, siding, and waterproofing products.

Carlisle Syntec Systems
(Division of Carlisle Corp.)
P.O. Box 7000
Carlisle, PA 17013
717-245-7000
Waterproofing and roofing systems.

Centimark Corp.
3000 Industrial Blvd.
Bethel Park, PA 15102
800-558-4100
Roofing and flooring products.

Elcor Corp.
14643 Dallas Pkwy.
Dallas, TX 75240
214-851-0500
Roofing and other types of products.

Georgia-Pacific Corp.
133 Peachtree St., N. E.
Atlanta, GA 30303
404-521-4000
A wide variety of building products, including those used for roofing.

Gibson-Homans Co.
1755 Enterprise Pkwy.
Twinsburg, OH 44087
216-425-3255
Roof and other types of coatings and adhesives.

Gifford-Hill & Co., Inc.
(Subsidiary of Beazer PLC)
2515 McKinney Ave.
Dallas, TX 75201
214-754-5500
Roofing gravel and other types of products.

Goodyear Tire & Rubber Co.
1144 E. Market St.
Akron, OH 44316
216-796-2121
Tires, roofing, and other types of products.

Manville Sales Corp.
(Subsidiary of Manville Corp.)
P.O. Box 5108
Denver, CO 80217
303-978-2000
Insulation and roofing systems, and other products.

Owens-Corning Fiberglas Corp.
Fiberglas Tower
Toledo, OH 43659
419-248-8000
Insulation, shingles, roofing systems, and other types of products.

FEDERAL GOVERNMENT

U.S. International Trade Administration
Department of Commerce
14th St. and Constitution Ave., N.W.
Washington, DC 20230
202-377-2000
*Ask for the Commodity Analyst who is an
expert in the roofing industry.*

U.S. International Trade Commission
500 E St., S.W.
Washington, DC 20436
202-205-2000 Office of the Secretary
202-205-3296 Industries locator
*Ask for the Trade Analyst who is an expert in
the roofing industry.*

RUBBER AND RUBBER GOODS INDUSTRY

ASSOCIATIONS

International Institute of Synthetic Rubber
    Producers
2077 S. Gessner Rd., Ste. 133
Houston, TX 77063-1123
713-783-7511
713-783-7253 Fax
W. E. Tessmer, Managing Director
*Manufacturers of synthetic rubber who share
technical and market information.*

Malaysian Rubber Bureau
1925 K St. N.W., Ste. 204
Washington, DC 20006
202-452-0544
202-659-5150 Fax
Paul Hurley, President
*Represents producers of natural rubber from
Malaysia.*

Rubber Manufacturers Association
1400 K St. N.W.
Washington, DC 20005
202-682-4800
Thomas Cole, President
*Members manufacture all kinds of rubber
products, including tires, roofing, industrial
goods, and other items.*

Rubber Trade Association of New York
17 Battery Pl.
New York, NY 10004
212-344-7776
Gail Coury, Secretary
*This group local to New York represents firms
that import natural rubber into the U.S.*

United Rubber, Cork, Linoleum and Plastic
    Workers of America
87 S. High St.
Akron, OH 44308
216-376-6181
Kenneth Coss, Secretary
*The largest union of workers in the rubber and
allied industries.*

PERIODICALS

Elastomerics
Communication Channels, Inc.
6255 Barfield Rd.
Atlanta, GA 30328-4369
404-256-9800
Ann Barker, Editor
Technical information for manufacturers of rubber and synthetic rubber products of all kind.

Rubber & Plastics News
Crain Communications Inc.
1725 Merriman Rd., Ste. 300
Akron, OH 44313-3185
216-836-9180
Edward Noga, Editor
Covers the worldwide rubber industry offering news of technological, legislative, and business developments.

Rubber and Plastics Newsletter
National Safety Council. Industrial Section
444 N. Michigan Ave.
Chicago, IL 60611
800-621-7619
Provides safety recommendations for the rubber and plastics industry.

Rubber Chemistry and Technology
University of Akron
Akron, OH 44325-3801
216-375-7814
G.R. Hamed, Editor
Reports original research in the fields of rubber chemistry and engineering.

Rubber World
Lippincott & Peto, Inc.
1867 W. Market St.
Akron, OH 44313
216-864-2122
Don Smith, Editor
Technical advice for manufacturers of rubber goods.

Vanderbilt Rubber Handbook
R.T. Vanderbilt Co., Inc.
30 Winfield St.
Norwalk, CT 06855
203-853-1400
Robert Ohm, Editor
Technical data for chemists, engineers, and technicians who make rubber compounds and other elastomers of all kinds.

LIBRARIES

American Chemical Society
Rubber Division
John Gifford Memorial Library & Information
  Center
1155 16th St., N.W.
Washington, DC 20036
202-872-4600
Rubber and rubber history.

Bridgestone/Firestone Inc.
Central Research Library
1200 Firestone Pkway.
Akron, OH 44317-0001
216-379-7430
216-379-6144 Fax
Rubber, chemical engineering, polymer chemistry, and plastics.

Gates Rubber Co.
Information Center
900 S. Broadway
Box 5887
Denver, CO 80217
303-744-4150
303-744-4000 Fax
Rubber, plastics, and chemistry.

Uniroyal Goodrich Tire Co.
Akron Information Center
600 S. Main St.
Akron, OH 44397-0001
216-374-3884
Rubber, polymers, and tires.

COMPANIES

Bandag, Inc.
Bandag Center
Muscatine, IA 52761
319-262-1400
Rubber tread supplies and equipment, and other rubber products.

Carlisle Companies Incorporated
101 S. Salina St.
Syracuse, NY 13202
315-474-2500
A variety of rubber and plastic products.

Cooper Tire & Rubber Co.
Lima & Western Aves.
Findlay, OH 45840
419-423-1321
Rubber tires and other rubber products.

Crompton & Knowles Corp.
One Station Pl., Metro Center
Stamford, CT 06902
203-353-5400
Machinery used to extrude rubber and other types of products.

Gates Rubber Co.
(Subsidiary of Gates Corp.)
990 S. Broadway, Box 5887
Denver, CO 80217
303-744-1911
Rubber products used in mechanical systems, including rubber belts and hose.

Gencorp Inc.
175 Ghent Rd.
Fairlawn, OH 44333
216-869-4200
Rubber products used in industry and other types of products.

Mohawk Rubber Co.
(Division of Yokohama Rubber Co.)
3560 W. Market St.
Akron, OH 44313
216-666-8177
Extruded and molded rubber products including tires and tubes.

Orcomatic Inc.
(Division of Eagle-Picher Industries, Inc.)
Ohio Ave.
Norwich, CT 06360
203-886-2451
Molded rubber products.

Rubbermaid Incorporated
1147 Akron Rd.
Wooster, OH 44691
216-264-6464
A wide variety of rubber products for consumer and industrial use.

A. Schulman, Inc.
3550 W. Market St.
Akron, OH 44313
216-666-3751
Synthetic rubber and plastic compounds.

FEDERAL GOVERNMENT

U.S. Customs Service
Department of the Treasury
U.S. Customshouse
6 World Trade Center
New York, NY 10048
212-466-5550
Ask for the Commodity Specialist in charge of rubber and rubber goods.

U.S. International Trade Administration
Department of Commerce
14th St. and Constitution Ave., N.W.
Washington, DC 20230
202-377-2000
*Ask for the Commodity Analyst who is an
expert in rubber and rubber goods.*

U.S. International Trade Commission
500 E St., S.W.
Washington, DC 20436
202-205-2000 Office of the Secretary
202-205-3296 Industries locator
*Ask for the Trade Analyst who is an expert in
rubber and rubber goods.*

U.S. Patent and Trademark Office
Crystal Plaza 2
2011 Jefferson Davis Highway
Arlington, VA 22202
703-305-8000
*Ask for the Examining Group Director who is
a specialist in synthetic rubber and rubber
goods.*

SAFETY

See also: INDUSTRIAL HYGIENE; PRODUCT SAFETY; TRAFFIC SAFETY; and each of the 50 states under occupational health and safety

ASSOCIATIONS

Academy of Hazard Control Management
8009 Carita Ct.
Bethesda, MD 20817
301-984-8969
Harold Gordon, Executive Director
*Hazard control managers who share informa-
tion about environmental and occupational
safety.*

American Society of Safety Engineers
1800 E. Oakton St.
Des Plaines, IL 60016
708-692-4121
Judy Neel, Executive Director
*Offers training to safety engineers and others
in the accident-prevention field.*

Industrial Safety Equipment Association
1901 N. Moore St., Ste. 501
Arlington, VA 22209
703-525-1695
703-528-2148 Fax
Frank Wilcher, President
*Members make all types of industrial safety
equipment and clothing.*

National Safe Workplace Institute
122 S. Michigan Ave., Ste. 1450
Chicago, IL 60603
312-939-0690
312-939-8105 Fax
Joseph Kinney, Executive Director
Studies safety issues and offers information on litigation and legal matters.

National Safety Council
444 N. Michigan Ave.
Chicago, IL 60611
312-527-4800
312-527-9381 Fax
T. C. Gilchrest, President
A huge organization that offers safety training and research in many fields.

National Safety Management Society
3871 Piedmont Ave.
Oakland, CA 94611
415-653-4148
Robert LeClerg, Secretary
Advises managers on safety issues and the risks and benefits of accident prevention and loss control.

Safety Equipment Distributors Association
111 E. Wacker Dr., Ste. 600
Chicago, IL 60601
312-644-6610
312-565-4658 Fax
James Elsener, Executive Director
Distributors of industrial safety equipment.

System Safety Society
Technology Trading Park
5 Export Dr., Ste. A
Sterling, VA 22170
703-450-0310
Harris Yeager, President
Offers educational programs to persons involved with promoting safety in industrial and other settings.

PERIODICALS

Chilton's Industrial Safety & Hygiene News
Chilton Co.
One Chilton Way
Radnor, PA 19089
215-964-4028
Dave Johnson, Editor
Covers news and new equipment in the fields of safety, hygiene, fire, security and emergency protection.

Job Safety Consultant
Business Research Publications, Inc.
817 Broadway
New York, NY 10003
212-673-4700
Gail Hayden, Editor
Teaches corporate safety managers how to comply with OSHA and other safety regulations, how to reduce accidents, and how to train workers in safety techniques.

OSHA Training Bulletin for Supervisors
Business & Legal Reports, Inc.
39 Academy St.
Madison, CT 06443-1513
203-245-7448
John Brady, Editor
Advises how to comply with OSHA regulations.

Occupational Hazards
Penton Publishing
1100 Superior Ave.
Cleveland, OH 44114-2543
216-696-7000
Stephen Minter, Editor
Covers the control of industrial and environmental dangers, insurance matters, medical treatment after accidents, and related topics.

Occupational Safety & Health Reporter
The Bureau of National Affairs, Inc.
1231 25th St., N.W.
Washington, DC 20037
202-452-4200
Mary Worobec, Editor
Follows new regulations, research, legislation, and other legal matters in the occupational safety field.

Safety Compliance Letter
Bureau of Business Practice
24 Rope Ferry Rd.
Waterford, CT 06386
203-442-4365
Shelley Wolf, Editor
Advises on complying with safety regulations.

LIBRARIES

ITT Hartford
Technical Research Services Unit and Loss
    Control Library
Hartford Plaza
Hartford, CT 06115
203-547-3099
203-547-6004 Fax
Safety engineering, occupational safety, toxicology, fire protection, and other topics.

National Safety Council
444 N. Michigan Ave.
Chicago, IL 60611
312-527-4800
All safety subjects.

U.S. Department of Labor
OSHA
Technical Data Center
200 Constitution Ave., N.W.
Rm. N-2625
Washington, DC 20210
202-523-9700
202-523-5046 Fax
Fire safety, material safety, occupational safety, toxicology, hazardous materials, electrical safety, and farm safety.

Wausau Insurance Companies
Media and Reference Services
2000 Westwood Dr.
Box 8017
Wausau, WI 54402-8017
715-847-8504
715-847-8740 Fax
Industrial safety and insurance.

COMPANIES

Briggs-Weaver, Inc.
(Subsidiary of Sammons Enterprises, Inc.)
5000 Harry Hines Blvd.
Dallas, TX 75235
214-631-3600
Industrial safety equipment and supplies, and other products for industry.

Dames & Moore
911 Wilshire Blvd.
Los Angeles, CA 90017
213-683-1560
Consultants offering environmental studies, site selection studies, safety studies, and related services.

Lion Apparel
2735 Kearns Ave.
Dayton, OH 45414
513-278-6531
Uniforms and safety apparel.

Lukens Inc.
50 S. First Ave.
Coatesville, PA 19320
215-383-2000
Industrial safety products and other businesses.

Mine Safety Appliances Co.
P.O. Box 426
Pittsburgh, PA 15230
412-967-3000
Safety equipment for mines.

Mr. Gasket Co.
8700 Brookpark Rd.
Cleveland, OH 44129
216-398-8300
Equipment and supplies for automobiles, including safety products.

Quixote Corp.
One E. Wacker Dr.
Chicago, IL 60601
312-467-6755
Highway safety devices and other products.

Vallen Corp.
13333 Northwest Freeway
Houston, TX 77040
713-462-8700
Safety equipment for industry.

FEDERAL GOVERNMENT

U.S. Department of Labor
200 Constitution Ave., N.W.
Washington, DC 20210
202-523-6666
Ask for the Occupational Safety and Health Administration.

U.S. International Trade Administration
Department of Commerce
14th St. and Constitution Ave., N.W.
Washington, DC 20230
202-377-2000
Ask for the Commodity Analyst who is an expert in safety equipment.

U.S. International Trade Commission
500 E St., S.W.
Washington, DC 20436
202-205-2000 Office of the Secretary
202-205-3296 Industries locator
Ask for the Trade Analyst who is an expert in safety equipment.

SALES MANAGEMENT

See also: MANAGEMENT; MARKETING; and SALESPEOPLE AND
SALES TECHNIQUES

ASSOCIATIONS

Association of Sales Administration Managers
PO Box 737
Harrison, NJ 07029
201-481-4800
Bill Martin, Secretary
*A forum for sales managers of consumer goods
firms to share information about efficiency,
distributors, and other topics.*

Sales and Marketing Executives International
Statler Office Tower, No. 458
Cleveland, OH 44115
216-771-6650
Jack Criswell, Executive Director
*Offers research and educational programs to
sales and marketing executives who wish to
improve selling techniques and management
skills.*

PERIODICALS

Competitive Advantage
Competitive Advantage, Inc.
1901 N.W. 23rd Ave.
Box 10091
Portland, OR 97210
503-274-2953
James Moran, Editor
*Practical advice for sales and marketing man-
agers to increase profits.*

Conference Board's Marketing Briefing
Conference Board, Inc.
845 Third Ave.
New York, NY 10022
212-759-0900
*Covers a variety of issues that concern man-
agers of sales and marketing.*

Income in Sales—Marketing Management
Sales & Marketing Executives International
Abbott, Langer & Associates
548 First St.
Crete, IL 60417
708-672-4200
Steven Langer, Editor
*Information to help sales and marketing man-
agers excel in their careers.*

Personal Selling Power
Personal Selling Power, Inc.
1127 International Parkway
Fredericksburg, VA 22405
703-752-7000
L.B. Geschwandtner, Editor
Advice for sales and marketing executives.

Sales & Marketing Management
Bill Communications, Inc.
633 Third Ave.
New York, NY 10017
212-986-4800
Richard Kern, Editor
*Covers information useful to managers of mar-
keting and sales within their own companies.*

Sales Manager's Bulletin
Bureau of Business Practice
24 Rope Ferry Rd.
Waterford, CT 06386
203-442-4365
*News of hiring, training, motivational, and
management techniques that increase sales.*

LIBRARIES

Amway Corp.
Corporate Library
7575 E. Fulton St.
Ada, MI 49355
616-676-6308
616-676-7142 Fax
Direct selling and business.

Dartnell Corp.
Publishing-Research Library
4660 N. Ravenswood Ave.
Chicago, IL 60640
312-561-4000
*Salesmanship, sales management, direct mail,
and customer service.*

SALESPEOPLE AND SALES TECHNIQUES

See also: SALES MANAGEMENT

ASSOCIATIONS

National Association for Professional
Saleswomen
PO Box 2606
Novato, CA 94948
415-898-2606
415-897-5347 Fax
Gaye Garcia, President
*Offers research and educational programs to
women working in sales and marketing.*

National Council of Salesmen's Organizations
303 5th Ave., Rm. 1303
New York, NY 10016
718-835-4591
Michael Gale, Representative
*Represents commissioned salespeople who sell
all types of products.*

National Network of Women in Sales
710 E. Ogden, Ste. 113
Naperville, IL 60563
800-321-6697
Eloise Haverland, Director
*Offers information , counseling, and training
to saleswomen and others interested in a sales
career.*

National Society of Sales Training Executives
203 E. 3rd St., Ste. 201
Sanford, FL 32771
407-322-3364
800-752-7613
James Egbert, Manager
Provides clinics to executives in charge of corporate sales training.

LIBRARIES

National Association for Professional
　　Saleswomen
Library
Box 2606
Novato, CA 94948
415-898-2606
514-897-5347 Fax
Sales and business.

PERIODICALS

Peak Performance Selling
Bureau of Business Practice
24 Rope Ferry Rd.
Waterford, CT 06386
203-442-4365
Michele Rubin, Editor
Suggests techniques for increasing sales.

Personal Selling Power
Personal Selling Power, Inc.
1127 International Parkway
Fredericksburg, VA 22405
703-752-7000
L.B. Geschwandtner, Editor
Helps motivate and train salespeople.

Professional Selling
Bureau of Business Practice
24 Rope Ferry Rd.
Waterford, CT 06386
203-442-4365
Paulette Kitchens, Editor
Advice for salespeople of high tech goods and services.

Sales and Marketing Strategies & News
Hughes Communications, Inc.
211 W. State St.
Box 197
Rockford, IL 61105
800-435-2937
Bill Hughes, Editor
Gives example of successful sales and marketing campaigns.

Sales Upbeat
Economics Press, Inc.
12 Daniel Rd.
Fairfield, NJ 07004
201-227-1224
Techniques and methods for increasing sales.

SALES PROMOTION

See also: MARKETING and PREMIUMS AND INCENTIVES

ASSOCIATIONS

ARMS—The Association of Retail Marketing Services
3 Caro Ct.
Red Bank, NJ 07701
201-842-5070
George Meredith, Executive Director
A clearinghouse for retailers and others interested in promotions, incentives, and premiums at retail stores.

Council of Sales Promotion Agencies
750 Summer St.
Stamford, CT 06901
203-325-3911
203-969-1499 Fax
Jeffrey McElnea, President
Members are sales promotion agencies that share information about marketing and communications.

Promotion Industry Club
PO Box 5243
Palatine, IL 60078-5243
708-991-3285
Karen Eiff, President
Provides seminars and information to the manufacturers, buyers, salespeople, and others interested in sales promotions, incentives, premiums, and related topics.

Promotion Marketing Association of America
322 8th Ave., Ste. 1201
New York, NY 10001
212-206-1100
212-929-1408 Fax
Christopher Sutherland, Executive Director
Provides research and educational programs to firms that offer and use sales incentives as well as promotional services and products.

PERIODICALS

Creative
Magazines Creative, Inc.
37 W. 39th St.
New York, NY 10018
212-840-0160
David Flaserstein, Editor
Suggests ideas for promotion and marketing.

Journal of Promotion Management
Haworth Press, Inc.
10 Alice St.
Binghamton, NY 13904-1580
800-342-9678
Fred Crane, Editor
Reports on innovations in sales promotions, advertising, personal selling, and public relations.

Promo
Smith Communications, Inc.
261 Main St.
Danbury, CT 06812
203-778-4007
Kerry Smith, Editor
Covers promotional marketing and sales.

Promotion Power
Donnelley Directory
287 Bowman Ave.
Purchase, NY 10577
914-933-6718
Tibor Taraba, Editor
A newsletter for those in charge of sales promotions.

LIBRARIES

Adams Advertising Agency, Inc.
Library
111 N. Canal St.
Chicago, IL 60606
312-930-9446
Sales promotion and psychology.

COMPANIES

D.L. Blair Corp.
1051 Franklin Ave.
Garden City, NY 11530
516-746-3700
Sweepstakes, games, and sales promotion programs.

Burke Communication Industries, Inc.
1165 N. Clark St.
Chicago, IL 60610
312-951-0500
Sales promotion products.

Comart Associates, Inc.
(Subsidiary of RSC & G)
360 W. 31st St.
New York, NY 10001
212-714-2550
Marketing and sales promotion services.

Communications Diversified, Inc.
440 Park Ave., S.
New York, NY 10016
212-213-3400
Marketing and sales promotion services.

Frankel & Co.
111 E. Wacker
Chicago, IL 60601
312-938-1900
Marketing and sales promotion services.

Don Jagoda Associates, Inc.
100 Marcus Dr.
Melville, NY 11743
516-454-1800
Sweepstakes, games, and sales promotion programs.

Marden-Kane, Inc.
410 Lakeville Rd.
Lake Success, NY 11042
516-326-3666
Sales promotions, sweepstakes, incentive programs, and related services.

Videocart Inc.
564 W. Randolph St.
Chicago, IL 60606
312-466-5000
Advertising and sales promotion.

SALT INDUSTRY

ASSOCIATIONS

Salt Institute
Fairfax Plaza, Ste. 600
700 N. Fairfax
Alexandria, VA 22314-2040
703-549-4648
Richard Hanneman, President
Salt producers and users.

PERIODICALS

Mineral Industry Surveys: Salt Production and
    Distribution
U.S. Bureau of Mines
Cochrans Mill Rd.
Box 18070
Pittsburgh, PA 15236
412-892-4411
Offers statistics on salt import, export, production and usage.

Salt and Trace Minerals Report
Salt Institute
700 N. Fairfax St., Ste. 600
Alexandria, VA 22314-2040
703-549-4648
Lou Priebe, Editor
Surveys the salt industry.

COMPANIES

Akzo America Inc.
(Subsidiary of Akzo N.V.)
111 W. 40th St.
New York, NY 10018
212-382-5500
Chemicals, salt, salt products, and other items.

American Salt Co.
6950 W. 56th St.
Shawnee Missions, KS 66202
913-362-6150
Salt and other products.

International Salt Co.
Abington Executive Park
Clark Summit, PA 18411
717-587-5131
Salt and other products.

Leslie Salt Co.
7220 Central Ave.
Newark, CA 94560
415-797-1820
Salt and other products.

Morton Salt Division
(Division of Morton International Inc.)
100 N. Riverside Plaza
Chicago, IL 60606
312-807-2000
Salt for eating, animal feed, and industrial uses.

Portion Pac, Inc.
(Division of H. J. Heinz Co.)
7325 Snider Rd.
Mason, OH 45040
513-691-6380
Salt, ketchup, and other foods in individual servings.

Savannah Food Service
30600 Oregon Rd.
Perrysburg, OH 43551
419-666-1190
Packaging of sugar, salt, cream substitute, and other foods.

Western Salt Co.
7220 Trade St.
San Diego, CA 92121
619-566-6600
Salt and other products.

Westin, Inc.
4727 Center
Omaha, NE 68106
402-553-3363
Salt and other foods.

FEDERAL GOVERNMENT

Bureau of Mines
810 7th St., N.W.
Washington, DC 20747
202-501-9770
Ask for the analyst in charge of salt.

U.S. Customs Service
Department of the Treasury
U.S. Customshouse
6 World Trade Center
New York, NY 10048
212-466-5550
Ask for the Commodity Specialist in charge of salt.

U.S. International Trade Administration
Department of Commerce
14th St. and Constitution Ave., N.W.
Washington, DC 20230
202-377-2000
Ask for the Commodity Analyst who is an expert in the salt industry.

U.S. International Trade Commission
500 E St., S.W.
Washington, DC 20436
202-205-2000 Office of the Secretary
202-205-3296 Industries locator
Ask for the Trade Analyst who is an expert in the salt industry.

SANITATION INDUSTRY

See also: CLEANING PRODUCTS AND SERVICES and INDUSTRIAL HYGIENE

ASSOCIATIONS

American Society of Sanitary Engineering
PO Box 40362
Bay Village, OH 44140
216-835-3040
Gael Dunn, Executive Secretary
Sanitary engineers, plumbers, engineers, inspectors, physicians, and others concerned with water-borne diseases.

Environmental Management Association
255 Detroit St., Ste. 200
Denver, CO 80206
303-320-7855
303-393-0770 Fax
Dianna Rampy, Representative
An information resource for those in charge of environment sanitation programs, primarily for industry.

International Sanitary Supply Association
7373 N. Lincoln Ave.
Lincolnwood, IL 60646
708-982-0800
800-CAL-ISSA
800-BEP-ISSA
708-982-1012 Fax
E. Allen James, President
Manufacturers of janitorial, maintenance, and cleaning supplies.

National Sanitation Foundation
3475 Plymouth Rd.
Ann Arbor, MI 48106
313-769-8010
313-769-0109 Fax
Nina McClelland, President
Conducts extensive research and offers seminars to a wide range of those involved in sanitation, public health, business, and environmental conservation.

Portable Sanitation Association International
7800 Metro Pkwy., Ste. 104
Bloomington, MN 55425
612-854-8300
612-854-7560 Fax
Dorothy Sansom, Representative
Firms that rent portable toilets and other sanitation facilities for use at construction sites and elsewhere.

Sanitary Supply Wholesalers Association
PO Box 8008
Sylvania, OH 43560
419-885-2134
James Ferris, President
Represents wholesalers of janitorial supplies.

PERIODICALS

American City & County
Communication Channels, Inc.
6255 Barfield Rd.
Atlanta, GA 30328-4369
404-256-9800
Janet Ward, Editor
Written for local government officials in charge of administration, engineering, sanitation, and operations.

Environmental Management
Environmental Management Association
255 Detroit, Ste. 200
Denver, CO 80206-4821
303-320-7855
Dianna Rampy, Editor
Focuses on building and facilities management and industrial sanitation.

Sanitary Maintenance
Trade Press Publishing Corp.
2100 W. Florist Ave.
Milwaukee, WI 53209
414-228-7701
Austin Weber, Editor
Reports news, trends, and product information for the sanitary supply industry.

LIBRARIES

U.S. Environmental Protectiion Agency
Environmental Research Laboratory, Athens
Library
College Station Rd.
Athens, GA 30613-7799
404-546-3154
Sanitary engineering, biology, and environmental subjects.

Zimpro Passavant Environmental Systems, Inc.
Reference and Resource Center
301 W. Military Rd.
Rothschild, WI 54474
713-359-7211
715-355-3221 Fax
Sewage treatment and environmental control systems.

FEDERAL GOVERNMENT

U.S. Department of the Interior
1800 C St., N.W.
Washington, DC 20240
202-208-7220
Ask for the Environmental Sanitation division in the National Park Service.

SAVINGS AND LOAN ASSOCIATIONS

See also: BANKS AND BANKING

ASSOCIATIONS

United States League of Savings Institutions
1709 New York Ave. N.W., Ste. 801
Washington, DC 20006
202-637-8900
Frederick Webber, President
Offers a variety of advertising, promotional, financial, and education services for savings and loan associations and banks.

PERIODICALS

Failed Bank and Thrift Litigation Reporter
Andrews Publications
1646 West Chester Pike
Box 1000
Westtown, PA 19395
215-399-6600
Barbara Murphy, Editor
Reports on litigation and other legal matters involving banks and S & L's.

S & L—Savings Bank Financial Quarterly
I D C Financial Publishing, Inc.
Box 140
Hartland, WI 53029
800-544-5457
Financial data on S & L's.

S & L Quarterly
United Communications Group
11300 Rockville Pike, Ste. 1100
Rockville, MD 20852-3030
301-816-8950
Martin Zook, Editor
Offers detailed financial data including ratios for all S & L's and federal savings banks in the U.S.

Savings & Loan Reporter
Mortgage Commentary Publications
Box 30240
Bethesda, MD 20814
301-654-5580
Andrew Mandala, Editor
Surveys the S & L industry.

Savings and Loan Investor
Box 7163
Long Beach, CA 90807-0163
213-427-1905
Mary Marks, Editor
Reports news and trends of the thrift industry, particularly publicly traded S & L associations and banks.

LIBRARIES

U.S. League of Savings Institutions
Library
1709 New York Ave., N.W.
Washington, DC 20006
202-637-8920
Savings, loans, and economics.

U.S. League of Savings Institutions
Library
111 E. Wacker Dr.
Chicago, IL 60601
312-644-3100
312-938-2541 Fax
Savings and loans, savings banks, electronic funds transfer, and mortages.

U.S. Office of Thrift Supervision
Law Library
1700 G St., N.W.
Washington, DC 20552
202-906-6470
202-906-7495 Fax
Savings and loan associations.

COMPANIES

Capitol Federal Savings & Loan Assn. of
    Denver
(Subsidiary of First Capitol Financial Corp.)
3300 S. Parker Rd.
Aurora, CO 80014
303-671-1000
Savings and loan association.

DFSoutheastern, Inc.
250 E. Ponce de Leon Ave.
Decatur, GA 30030
404-371-4000
Savings and loan association.

Farm & Home Savings Assn.
(Subsidiary of Farm & Home Financial Corp.)
221 W. Cherry
Nevada, MO 64772
816-891-7778
Savings and loan association.

First Federal of Michigan
(Subsidiary of FirstFed Michigan Corp.)
1001 Woodward
Detroit, MI 48226
313-965-1400
Savings and loan association.

First Federal Savings & Loan Assn. of
    Rochester
One First Federal Plaza
Rochester, NY 14614
716-454-4010
Savings and loan association.

First Nationwide Bank, a Federal Savings Bank
(Subsidiary of First Nationwide Financial
    Corp.)
135 Main St.
San Francisco, CA 94105
415-904-1100
Savings and loan association.

Fortune Savings Bank
(Subsidiary of Fortune Financial Group, Inc.)
16120 U.S. 19 N.
Clearwater, FL 34624
813-538-1000
Savings and loan association.

Great Western Bank
(Subsidiary of Great Western Holding Co.)
251 W. Garden St.
Pensacola, FL 32501
904-435-3036
Savings and loan association.

Western Savings & Loan Assn.
6001 N. 24th St.
Phoenix, AZ 85016
602-468-4600
Savings and loan association.

FEDERAL GOVERNMENT

U.S. Department of the Treasury
1500 Pennsylvania Ave., N.W.
Washington, DC 20220
202-566-2111
Ask for the Financial Institutions Policy Office; or the Research Division in the Thrift Supervision Office.

SCHOOLS

See also: EDUCATION

ASSOCIATIONS

Educational Dealers and Suppliers Association International
711 W. 17th St., Ste. J-5
Costa Mesa, CA 92627
714-642-3986
800-654-7099
714-642-7960 Fax
Allen Warren, Director
Represents manufacturers, distributors, publishers, and other suppliers of educational materials and equipment used by schools.

National Association of Independent Schools
75 Federal
Boston, MA 02110
617-451-2444
617-482-3913 Fax
John Esty, President
Provides research and other services to independent elementary and secondary schools.

National PTA—National Congress of Parents and Teachers
700 N. Rush St.
Chicago, IL 60611
312-787-0977
312-787-8342 Fax
Ann Lynch, President
A huge organization of parents, teacher, and school officials. Offers information on a wide range of educational and school issues.

National School Boards Association
1680 Duke St.
Alexandria, VA 22314
703-838-6722
703-683-7590 Fax
Thomas Shannon, Executive Director
Provides information on legislation, educational matters, and other subjects.

National School Supply and Equipment Association
2020 N. 14th St., Ste. 400
Arlington, VA 22201
703-524-8819
800-395-5550
703-525-4199 Fax
Tim Holt, Executive Vice President
Members make, wholesale, and retail school supplies and equipment of all kinds.

PERIODICALS

American School & University
North American Publishing Co.
401 N. Broad St.
Philadelphia, PA 19108
215-238-5300
Joe Agron, Editor
Advice for public school and university administrators in charge of facilities, purchasing, and business matters.

Handbook of Private Schools
Porter Sargent Publishers, Inc.
11 Beacon St.
Boston, MA 02108
617-523-1670
Surveys independent (private) schools.

Independent School
National Association of Independent Schools
75 Federal St.
Boston, MA 02110-1904
617-451-2444
Blair McElroy, Editor
Covers news and trends that affect private schools.

School and College
Penton Publishing
1100 Superior Ave.
Cleveland, OH 44114-2543
216-696-7000
Roger Morton, Editor
Covers issues involving educational facilities, business topics, new technologies, and management.

School Business Affairs
Association of School Business Officials
11401 N. Shore Dr.
Reston, VA 22090-4232
P.D. Kirkpatrick, Editor
Business management advice for school administrators.

LIBRARIES

ERIC Clearinghouse on Elementary and Early Childhood Education
University of Illinois
805 W. Pennsylvania Ave.
Urbana, IL 61801
217-333-1386
217-333-5847 Fax
Elementary education, day care, child development through early adolescence, and early childhood education.

ERIC Clearinghouse on Information Resources
030 Huntington Hall
Syracuse University
Syracuse, NY 13244-2340
315-443-3640
315-443-5732 Fax
Programmed instruction, educational media, educational technology, library science, and related topics.

Santa Clara County Office of Education
EMC/Professional Library
100 Skyport Dr.
Mail Code 232
San Jose, CA 95115
408-453-6800
Education and administration.

School Management Study Group
Library
860 18th Ave.
Salt Lake City, UT 84103
801-532-5340
Educational management and administration.

FEDERAL GOVERNMENT

Office of Management and Budget
725 17th St., N.W.
Washington, DC 20503
202-395-3000
Ask for the specialist in elementary and secondary education.

U.S. Department of Education
400 Maryland Ave., S.W.
Washington, DC 20202
202-708-5366
Ask for the public information office to find an appropriate expert.

SCIENTIFIC INSTRUMENTS AND SUPPLY INDUSTRY

See also: MEDICAL AND HOSPITAL EQUIPMENT INDUSTRY

ASSOCIATIONS

Association for the Advancement of Medical
    Instrumentation
3330 Washington Blvd., Ste. 400
Arlington, VA 22201-4598
703-525-4890
800-332-2264
703-276-0793 Fax
Michael Miller, Executive Director
A forum for engineers, physicians, technicians, and manufacturers to share information about medical instruments.

IEEE Instrumentation and Measurement
    Society
c/o Institute of Electrical and Electronics
    Engineers
345 E. 47th St.
New York, NY 10017
212-705-7867
Members research the use of electrical and electronic technologies in the manufacture and use of instruments.

Instrument Society of America
67 Alexander Dr.
Research Triangle Park, NC 27709
919-549-8411
919-549-8288 Fax
Glenn Harvey, Executive Director
Offers research and training to those who design, make, and use scientific and industrial instruments.

PERIODICALS

Analytical Instrumentation
Marcel Dekker Journals
270 Madison Ave.
New York, NY 10016
212-696-9000
John Wampler, Editor
Covers the design and use of instruments in the chemical, biomedical, and environmental sciences.

C L R
Medical Laboratory Observer
Medical Economics Co. Inc.
680 Kinderkamack Rd.
Oradell, NJ 07649
201-262-3030
Robert Fitzgibbon, Editor
News and trends involving instruments, equipment, and other products used in medical laboratories.

Chilton's I A N
Chilton Co.
Chilton Way
Radnor, PA 19089
215-964-4419
Pat Pool, Editor
Covers the technology and business of scientific instruments and equipment.

Guide to Biotechnology Products and Instruments
American Association for the Advancement of Science
1333 H St., N.W.
Washington, DC 20005
202-326-6500
Daniel Koshland, Editor
A directory of laboratory equipment and scientific instrument manufacturers.

Intelligent Instruments & Computers
Elsevier Science Publishing Co., Inc.
655 Ave. of the Americas
New York, NY 10010
212-989-5800
Richard Graham, Editor
Reports on the use of computers in science and engineering laboratories.

Personal Engineering & Instrumentation News
Personal Engineering Communications, Inc.
Box 300
Brookline, MA 02146-0015
617-232-3625
Paul Schreier, Editor
Discusses the use of personal computers and software in scientific laboratories.

Review of Scientific Instruments
American Institute of Physics
335 E. 45th St.
New York, NY 10017
212-661-9404
Thomas Braid, Editor
Technical data about scientific instruments.

LIBRARIES

Rural Enterprises, Inc.
Central Industrial Applications Center
422 Cessna
P.O. Box 1335
Durant, OK 74702
405-924-5094
Instrumentation, mathematics, computer science, and physics.

Tektronix, Inc.
Corporate Library
Box 500, MS 50-210
Beaverton, OR 97077
503-627-5388
503-627-5502 Fax
Instrumentation, electron optics, solid state physics, and electronics.

Varian Associates
Technical Library
3075 Hansen Way, K-100
Palo Alto, CA 94304
415-424-5071
415-424-6988 Fax
Instrumentation, electronics, and engineering.

COMPANIES

Applied Biosystems, Inc.
777 Lincoln Centre Dr.
Foster City, CA 94404
415-570-6667
Scientific instruments and biochemicals.

Autoclave Engineers, Inc.
2901 W. 22nd St.
Erie, PA 16506
814-838-5700
Scientific and engineering laboratory equipment.

Fischer & Porter Co.
125 E. County Line Rd.
Warminster, PA 18974
215-674-6000
Scientific and other types of instruments.

GE Reuter-Stokes, Inc.
(Subsidiary of General Electric Co.)
8499 Barrow Rd.
Twinsburg, OH 44087
216-425-3755
Scientific instruments.

Harvard Apparatus, Inc.
22 Pleasant St.
South Natick, MA 01760
508-655-7000
Scientific instruments for education.

Micromeritics Instrument Corp.
One Micromeritics Dr.
Norcross, GA 30093
404-662-3620
Scientific instruments.

Spectra-Physics, Inc.
(Subsidiary of Ciba-Geigy Corp.)
3333 N. First St.
San Jose, CA 95134
408-432-3333
Laser-based scientific instruments and other laser products.

Varian Associates
611 Hansen Way
Palo Alto, CA 94303
415-493-4000
Scientific instruments and other products.

Weksler Instruments Corp.
80 Mill Rd.
Freeport, NY 11520
516-623-0100
Scientific measurement instruments.

FEDERAL GOVERNMENT

U.S. Customs Service
Department of the Treasury
U.S. Customshouse
6 World Trade Center
New York, NY 10048
212-466-5550
*Ask for the Commodity Specialist in charge of
scientific instruments and supplies.*

U.S. International Trade Administration
Department of Commerce
14th St. and Constitution Ave., N.W.
Washington, DC 20230
202-377-2000
*Ask for the Commodity Analyst who is an
expert in scientific instruments and supplies.*

U.S. International Trade Commission
500 E St., S.W.
Washington, DC 20436
202-205-2000 Office of the Secretary
202-205-3296 Industries locator
*Ask for the Trade Analyst who is an expert in
scientific instruments and supplies.*

U.S. Patent and Trademark Office
Crystal Plaza 2
2011 Jefferson Davis Highway
Arlington, VA 22202
703-305-8000
*Ask for the Examining Group Director who is a
specialist in scientific instruments and supplies.*

SECRETARIES AND OFFICE WORKERS

See also: OFFICE MANAGEMENT and WORD PROCESSING

ASSOCIATIONS

Data Entry Management Association
101 Merritt 7, 5th Fl.
Norwalk, CT 06851
203-846-3777
203-846-6883 Fax
Marilyn Bodek, Executive Director
Offers training to data entry managers.

National Association of Executive Secretaries
900 S. Washington St.
Falls Church, VA 22046
703-237-8616
Susan Young, Executive Officer
Represents executive secretaries.

National Association of Legal Secretaries
2250 E. 73rd St., Ste. 550
Tulsa, OK 74136
918-493-3540
918-493-5784 Fax
Stan Orr, Executive Director
*Offers training to secretaries in law offices and
other secretaries who work on legal matters.*

National Association of Secretarial Services
3637 4th St. N, Ste. 330
St. Petersburg, FL 33704-1336
813-823-3646
800-237-1462
813-894-1277 Fax
Frank Fox, Executive Director
A clearinghouse for information on independent secretarial services.

Professional Secretaries International
10502 N.W. Ambassador Dr.
PO Box 20404
816-891-6600
816-891-9118 Fax
Jerome Heitman, Executive Director
A large professional association of working secretaries.

PERIODICALS

Office Skills Workshop
Bureau of Business Practice
24 Rope Ferry Rd.
Waterford, CT 06386
800-243-0876
Joyce Grabel, Editor
How-to information to help clerical workers improve their productivity.

Personal Report for the Professional Secretary
National Institute of Business Management
1328 Broadway
New York, NY 10001-0208
212-971-3300
Barry Lenson, Editor
Advice on career advancement and productivity for secretaries.

Secretary
Professional Secretaries International
10502 N.W. Ambassador Dr.
Box 20404
Kansas City, MO 64195-0404
816-891-6600
Debra Stratton, Editor
Helps secretaries improve their skills and advance their careers.

SECURITIES

See also: FINANCIAL ANALYSTS; INVESTMENT BANKING; INVEST-
MENTS; and each of the 50 states under securities

ASSOCIATIONS

American Stock Exchange
86 Trinity Pl.
New York, NY 10006
212-306-1000
James Jones, Chairman
*The well-known market for U.S. and interna-
tional securities and options.*

Association of Publicly Traded Companies
1707 L St., N.W., Ste. 950
Washington, DC 20036
202-785-9200
202-785-8869 Fax
John Guion, President
*Represents the interests of corporations whose
stock is publicly traded.*

Corporate Transfer Agents Association
c/o Martin McDermott
Merck & Co., Inc.
PO Box 2000
Rahway, NJ 07065
201-594-5603
201-594-6736 Fax
Martin McDermott, President
*Transfer agents and other employees of corpo-
rations who handle stock transfers.*

National Association of Securities Dealers
1735 K St. N.W.
Washington, DC 20006
202-728-8000
202-429-9503 Fax
Joseph Hardiman, President
*A large group of stock brokerage firms that
regulates itself and sponsors the NASDAQ
(National Association of Securities Dealers
Automated Quotations) computer system of
over-the-counter stock market quotations.*

National Association of Securities Professionals
10 E. 87th St.
New York, NY 10128
212-427-8100
212-876-6278 Fax
*A small group of minority securities firm
employees.*

North American Securities Administrators
    Association
555 New Jersey Ave. N.W., Ste. 750
Washington, DC 20001
202-737-0900
202-783-3571 Fax
Lee Polson, Executive Director
*Government officials who monitor and enforce
laws regarding securities sales.*

New York Stock Exchange
11 Wall St.
New York, NY 10005
212-656-3000
Judith Poole, Executive Officer
One of the world's best-known markets for securities.

Public Securities Association
40 Broad St., 12th Fl.
New York, NY 10004-2373
212-809-7000
212-797-3895 Fax
Heather Ruth, President
Conducts research and offers information regarding public securities offered by the U.S. government and municipalities, and other securities.

Securities Industry Association
120 Broadway
New York, NY 10271
212-608-1500
212-608-1604 Fax
Edward O'Brien, President
Offers information to securities and bond dealers, underwriters, investment bankers, and others.

Security Traders Association
1 World Trade Center, Ste. 4511
New York, NY 10048
212-524-0484
John Watson, President
Provides educational programs to brokers and dealers of all kinds of securities, stocks, and bonds.

PERIODICALS

Equities
O T C Review Inc.
37 E. 28th St., Rm. 706
New York, NY 10016
215-685-6244
Robert Flaherty, Editor
Covers news about over-the-counter equities.

Individual Investor
Financial Data Systems, Inc.
38 E. 29th St., 4th Fl.
New York, NY 10016
212-689-2777
Advises investors about the stocks of small companies.

Institutional Investor
Institutional Investor, Inc.
Circulation Department
488 Madison Ave.
New York, NY 10022
212-303-3570
Gilbert Kaplan, Editor
Reports news and trends for fund managers, corporate investment executives, and others responsible for investing for institutions.

Investment Reporter
Olympia Capital Corp.
325 N. Newport Blvd., No. 100
Newport Beach, CA 92663
714-548-8035
Peggy Powel, Editor
Follows investments in securities and other instruments for stockbrokers, stock analysts, and others.

M P T Review
Navellier and Associates, Inc.
Box 5695
Incline Village, NV 89450
702-831-7800
Louis Navellier, Editor
*Technical information about over-the-counter
stocks and funds.*

Market Guide Over-the-Counter Stock Edition
Market Guide Inc.
49 Glen Head Rd.
Box 106
Glen Head, NY 11545
516-759-1253
*Offers very detailed information about 800
OTC stock firms.*

O T C Growth Stock Watch
O T C Research Corp.
Box 305
Brookline, MA 02146
617-327-8420
Geoffrey Eiten, Editor
Advice for investors who watch OTC stocks.

O T C Stock Reports
Standard & Poor's Corp.
25 Broadway
New York, NY 10004
212-208-8000
Stephen Vallance, Editor
Reports on the performance of OTC stocks.

Personal Finance
K C I Communications, Inc.
1101 King St., Ste. 400
Alexandria, VA 22314
703-548-2400
Richard Band, Editor
Advice to consumers on investing in stocks.

Professional Investor
Lynatrace, Inc.
Box 2144
Pompano Beach, FL 33061-2144
800-826-2122
Robert Gross, Editor
*Reports news and trends of interest to profes-
sional investors and traders.*

Registered Representative
Plaza Communications, Inc.
18818 Teller Ave., No. 280
Irvine, CA 92715
Tolman Geffs, Editor
*Management, selling, and other information
for stockbrokers who are registered represen-
tatives.*

Securities Product News
Investment Dealers' Digest
Two World Trade Center, 18th Fl.
New York, NY 10048
212-227-1200
*Describes new securities products for stock-
brokers.*

Today's Investor
P S N Communications, Inc.
Box 86
Columbia, MD 21045-0086
301-498-8544
Jerome Wenger, Editor
News about emerging growth stocks.

LIBRARIES

Lehman Brothers
Corporate Library
American Express Tower, 15th Fl.
200 Vesey St.
New York, NY 10285-1500
212-298-2783
212-619-9457 Fax
*Securities and Exchange Commission (SEC)
investments, filings, and pricings.*

Merrill Lynch Capital Markets
Library
250 Vesey St., 24 Fl.
New York, NY 10281-1324
212-449-3814
212-449-3875 Fax
Securities, investments, acquisitions, and economics.

National Association of Securities Dealers
Library
1735 K St., N.W.
Washington, DC 20006
202-728-8000
Securities, commercial standards and related topics.

New York Stock Exchange
Research Library
11 Wall St.
New York, NY 10005
212-656-5049
Finance, banking, securities, and economics.

U.S. Securities and Exchange Commission
Library
450 5th St., N.W.
Washington, DC 20549
202-272-2618
Securities, finance, stock exchanges, statistics, and corporations.

COMPANIES

Bear, Stearns & Co. Inc.
(Subsidiary of Bear Stearns Companies Inc.)
245 Park Ave.
New York, NY 10167
212-272-2000
Securities brokerage and other financial services.

Charles Schwab Corp.
101 Montgomery St.
San Francisco, CA 94104
415-627-7000
Discount securities brokerage.

Depository Trust Co.
55 Water St.
New York, NY 10041
212-898-1200
Depository for securities.

A. G. Edwards, Inc.
One N. Jefferson Ave.
St. Louis, MO 63103
314-289-3000
Securities brokerage and other financial services.

Merrill Lynch and Co.
North Tower
World Financial Center
New York, NY 10281-1332
212-449-1000
Securities brokerage and other financial services.

Morgan Stanley Group Inc.
1251 Ave. of the Americas
New York, NY 10020
212-703-4000
Securities brokerage and other financial services.

Oppenheimer & Co., Inc.
(Subsidiary of Oppenheimer & Co., L.P.)
Oppenheimer Tower, World Fin. Ctr.
New York, NY 10281
212-667-7000
Securities brokerage and other financial services.

Salomon Brothers Inc
(Subsidiary of Salomon Inc)
One New York Plaza
New York, NY 10004
212-747-7000
Securities brokerage and other financial services.

Shearson Lehman Brothers Inc.
(Subsidiary of American Express Co.)
World Financial Center
New York, NY 10285
212-298-2000
Securities brokerage and other financial services.

S.G. Warburg & Co. Inc.
(Subsidiary of S.G. Warburg Group)
787 Seventh Ave., Equitable Tower
New York, NY 10019
212-459-7000
Securities brokerage and other financial services.

FEDERAL GOVERNMENT

U.S. International Trade Administration
Department of Commerce
14th St. and Constitution Ave., N.W.
Washington, DC 20230
202-377-2000
Ask for the Commodity Analyst who is an expert in stock brokerage firms.

U.S. Securities and Exchange Commission
450 5th St., N.W.
Washington, DC 20549
202-272-3100
The following departments may be able to help you: the Broker-Dealer Examination Branch; the Securities Industry Analysis Branch in the Economic Analysis Office; the Transfer Agent Regulations Branch; the Government Securities Regulator in the Bureau of Public Debt; or the Exchange & Options Regulations department.

SECURITY AND DETECTIVE SERVICES AND EQUIPMENT

See also: HARDWARE AND LOCKSMITH INDUSTRY

ASSOCIATIONS

American Society for Industrial Security
1655 N. Ft. Myer Dr., Ste. 1200
Arlington, VA 22209
703-522-5800
703-243-4954 Fax
E. J. Criscuoli, Executive Vice President
Provides educational programs for corporate security professionals who work to reduce theft and loss of property.

Computer Security Institute
500 Howard St.
San Francisco, CA 94105
415-267-7666
415-945-2487 Fax
Philip Chapnick, Director
Offers seminars to those concerned about the security of their computer systems.

Retail Loss Prevention Association
222 Middle Country Rd.
Smithtown, NY 11787
516-366-4290
Robert Barry, Vice President
Helps retailers reduce theft and pilfering.

Committee of National Security Companies
2714 Union Ave., Extended, Ste. 310
Memphis, TN 38112
901-323-0173
Gail Simonton, Executive Director
Represent large security guard firms.

International Association of Security Service
PO Box 8202
Northfield, IL 60093
312-973-7712
Howard Ross, President
Offers training to security and guard services.

International Security Management Association
PO Box 11161
Moline, IL 61265-8661
309-787-0085
Gerald O'Neill, President
A small group of senior security managers in large companies and chiefs of large security services firms who share management information.

National Council of Investigation and Security
  Services
PO Box 449
Severna Park, MD 21146
301-647-3227
800-445-8408
301-544-6181 Fax
Frank Rogers, President
Reports on legislation, regulations, and other information that affects the security and guard business.

Security Industry Association
2800 28th St., Ste. 101
Santa Monica, CA 90405
213-450-4141
213-452-7524 Fax
Donna Gentry, Executive Director
Provides technical and industry information to manufacturers and distributors of security equipment.

PERIODICALS

Corporate Security Digest
Washington Crime News Services
3918 Prosperity Ave., Ste. 318
Fairfax, VA 22031-3334
703-573-1600
Betty Bosarge, Editor
Follows news, trends, and products for security managers of companies.

Fraud & Theft Newsletter
Fraud & Theft Information Bureau
217 N. Seacrest Blvd.
Box 400
Boynton Beach, FL 33425
407-737-7500
Larry Schwartz, Editor
Updating service on all types of theft, crime, and fraud against individuals and corporations.

International Counterterrorism & Security
Counterterrorism & Security, Inc.
Box 10265
Arlington, VA 22210
703-243-0993
Dale Andrade, Editor
Covers techniques to prevent terrorism.

Police and Security News
Days Communications Inc.
1690 Quarry Rd.
Kulpsville, PA 19443
215-538-1240
James Devery, Editor
Advises administrators in police and security forces on new products, training methods, and related topics.

Private Security Case Law Reporter
Strafford Publications, Inc.
1201 Peachtree St., N.E., Ste. 1150
Atlanta, GA 30361
404-881-1141
R. Keegan Federal, Editor
Reports on state and federal court decisions that may affect managers of security services and personnel.

Safety & Security for Supervisors
Business Research Publications, Inc.
817 Broadway
New York, NY 10003
212-673-4700
Gail Hayden, Editor
Advice for managers in charge of safety and security.

Security and Special Police Legal Update
Americans for Effective Law Enforcement, Inc.
5519 N. Cumberland Ave., No. 1008
Chicago, IL 60656-1471
312-763-2800
Reports on legislation and regulations that affect security personnel.

Security Distributing & Marketing
Cahners Publishing Co.
1350 E. Touhy Ave.
Box 5080
Des Plaines, IL 60017-5080
708-372-6880
Gary Parr, Editor
Covers technology, management techniques, and merchandising methods for the security products industry.

Security Journal
ASIS Foundation
Butterworth—Heinemann Ltd.
80 Montvale Ave.
Stoneham, MA 02180
617-438-8464
Robert McCrie, Editor
Advice on crime prevention, security management, and related topics.

LIBRARIES

Eastern Kentucky University
Law Enforcement Library
Stratton Bldg.
Richmond, KY 40475
606-622-1798
606-622-1174 Fax
Security, criminal law, law enforcement, loss prevention, and fire science.

International Association of Security Service
Library
Box 8202
Northfield, IL 60093
708-973-7712
Guard services and security.

National Crime Prevention Institute
Information Center
University of Louisville, Shelby Campus
Louisville, KY 40292
502-588-6987
502-588-6990 Fax
Security systems and environmental design for crime prevention.

COMPANIES

Allied Security, Inc.
2840 Library Rd.
Pittsburgh, PA 15234
412-884-2636
Security guard services.

Borg-Warner Corp.
200 S. Michigan Ave.
Chicago, IL 60604
312-322-8500
Security services and manufacturing businesses.

Globe Security Systems, Inc.
(Division of Baker Industries, Inc.)
520 N. Delaware Ave.
Philadelphia, PA 19123
215-592-9205
Security guard and investigative services.

ISS International Service System Inc.
(Subsidiary of ISS International Service System A/S)
1430 Broadway
New York, NY 10018
212-382-9800
Building maintenance, security, and other services.

Network Security Corp.
9901 E. Valley Ranch
Irving, TX 75063
214-402-8440
Burglar alarms and other security products.

Pinkertons's Security & Investigation Services
6727 Odessa Ave.
Van Nuys, CA 91406
818-373-8800
Security guard and investigative services.

Protection One Alarm Services
15951 S.W. 72nd St.
Portland, OR 97224
503-624-0244
Burglar alarms and other security products.

Wackenhut Corp.
1500 San Remo Ave.
Coral Gables, FL 33146
305-666-5656
Security guard and investigative services.

FEDERAL GOVERNMENT

U.S. International Trade Administration
Department of Commerce
14th St. and Constitution Ave., N.W.
Washington, DC 20230
202-377-2000
Ask for the Commodity Analyst who is an expert in security services or products.

U.S. International Trade Commission
500 E St., S.W.
Washington, DC 20436
202-205-2000 Office of the Secretary
202-205-3296 Industries locator
Ask for the Trade Analyst who is an expert in security services of products.

SEED INDUSTRY

See also: AGRICULTURE

ASSOCIATIONS

American Seed Research Foundation
Executive Bldg., Ste. 964
1030 15th St. N.W.
Washington, DC 20005
202-223-4080
202-293-2617 Fax
Robert Falasca, Secretary
Offers technical information to breeders, growers, and marketers of seeds. Associated with the American Seed Trade Association, at the same address, which studies the seed business.

Association of Official Seed Analysts
c/o Jim Lair
Illinois Dept. of Agriculture Seed Lab.
Box 19281
Springfield, IL 62794
217-782-7655
Jim Lair, Secretary
Members are researchers and testers at government seed testing laboratories.

PERIODICALS

Crop Science
Crop Science Society of America
677 S. Segoe Rd.
Madison, WI 53711
608-273-8080
William Luellen, Editor
Technical information about various aspects of crops including seed production.

Seed Industry Journal
Freiberg Publishing Co.
2302 W. First St.
Cedar Falls, IA 50613
319-277-3599
Bill Freiberg, Editor
Business and technological news for the seed industry.

Seed Savers Exchange
R.R.3, Box 239
Decorah, IA 52101
319-382-5990
Kent Whealy, Editor
Seed information for amateur gardeners and others.

Seed Trade Buyer's Guide
Scranton Gillette Communications, Inc.
380 E. Northwest Hwy.
Des Plaines, IL 60016-2282
708-298-6622
Lynn Whitmore, Editor
A directory of seed laws and of seed suppliers in each state.

Seed Trade News
Dean Enterprises Inc.
7535 Office Ridge Circle
Eden Prairie, MN 55344
612-941-5820
Steve Fox, Editor
Covers news of interest to the seed industry.

Seed World
Scranton Gillette Communications, Inc.
380 E. Northwest Highway
Des Plaines, IL 60016
708-298-6622
Lynn Whitmore, Editor
Reports technological, production, and marketing news to the seed industry.

LIBRARIES

American Seed Trade Association
Library
Executive Bldg., Ste. 964
1030 15th St., N.W.
Washington, DC 20005
202-223-4080
202-293-2617 Fax
Seed production and marketing.

The California Seed Laboratory
Library
121 E. Grant St., Ste. 1
P.O. Box 668
Winters, CA 95694
916-795-4546
Covers topics about seeds such as identification, viability, and germination.

Cornell University
New York State Agricultural Experiment
    Station
Library
Geneva, NY 14456
315-787-2214
315-787-2397 Fax
Seeds, plant pathology, fruit breeding, and vegetable breeding.

U.S. National Arboretum
Library
3501 New York Ave., N.E.
Washington, DC 20002
202-475-4828
202-475-5252 Fax
Horticulture, plant genetics, and plant breeding.

COMPANIES

Agrigenetics Co.
(Division of Lubrizol Corp.)
35575 Curtis Blvd.
Eastlake, OH 44094
216-942-2210
Seeds and other products.

Andersons
P.O. Box 119
Maumee, OH 43537
419-893-5050
A wide variety of agricultural products, including seeds.

Asgrow Seed Co.
(Subsidiary of Upjohn Co.)
P.O. Box 7570
Des Moines, IA 50322
319-347-6633
Seed corn and other products.

Ciba-Geigy Seed Division
(Division of Ciba-Geigy Corp.)
P.O. Box 18300
Greensboro, NC 27419
919-547-1800
Various seed products.

Growmark, Inc.
1701 Towanda Ave., Box 2500
Bloomington, IL 61702
309-557-6000
A wide variety of agricultural products, including seeds.

Northrup King Co.
(Subsidiary of Sandoz Corp.)
7500 Olsen Memorial Hwy.
Golden Valley, MN 55427
612-593-7333
Wholesaler of seeds.

Pioneer Hi-Bred International, Inc.
700 Capital Sq., 400 Locust
Des Moines, IA 50309
515-245-3500
Various seed products.

O. M. Scott & Sons Co.
(Subsidiary of Scotts Co.)
14111 Scottslawn Rd.
Marysville, OH 43041
513-644-0011
Seeds for lawn grass and other lawn products.

Southern States Cooperative, Inc.
6606 West Broad St.
Richmond, VA 23230
804-281-1000
*A wide variety of agricultural products,
including seeds.*

FEDERAL GOVERNMENT

U.S. Department of Agriculture
14th St. and Independence Ave., S.W.
Washington, DC 20250
202-720-8732
*Ask for the Livestock & Seed division in the
Agricultural Marketing Service department.*

U.S. International Trade Administration
Department of Commerce
14th St. and Constitution Ave., N.W.
Washington, DC 20230
202-377-2000
*Ask for the Commodity Analyst who is an
expert in the seed industry.*

U.S. International Trade Commission
500 E St., S.W.
Washington, DC 20436
202-205-2000 Office of the Secretary
202-205-3296 Industries locator
*Ask for the Trade Analyst who is an expert in
the seed industry.*

SEMICONDUCTOR INDUSTRY

ASSOCIATIONS

American Electronics Association
5201 Great America Pkwy.
Santa Clara, CA 95054
408-987-4200
408-970-8565 Fax
J. Richard Iverson, President
*Represents U.S. electronics firms, including
those that manufacture or use semiconductors.*

Semiconductor Equipment and Materials
    International
805 E. Middlefield Rd.
Mountain View, CA 94043
415-964-5111
415-967-5375 Fax
William Reed, Executive Director
*Offers technical and industry information to
firms that provide materials and equipment to
the semiconductor industry.*

Semiconductor Industry Association
4300 Stevens Creek Blvd., No. 271
San Jose, CA 95129
408-246-2711
408-246-2830 Fax
Andrew Procassini, President
*Manufacturers of microprocessors, integrated
circuits, and other semiconductors.*

PERIODICALS

Digital I Cs D.A.T.A. Digest
D.A.T.A. Business Publishing
15 Inverness Way E.
Box 6510
Englewood, CO 80155-6510
800-447-4666
*Industry news for executives in the electronics
and semiconductor field.*

E D N Magazine
Cahners Publishing Co.
275 Washington St.
Newton, MA 02158-1630
617-964-3030
Jonathan Titus, Editor
*Design and technical information about elec-
tronics for engineers involved with computers,
semiconductors, and other electronic devices.*

Microcontamination
Canon Communications, Inc.
3340 Ocean Park Blvd., Ste. 1000
Santa Monica, CA 90405-3207
213-392-5509
Bob Keeley, Editor
*Practical information on controlling contami-
nation during the manufacture of computer
disk drives, semiconductors, and other high
technology products.*

Microelectronic Manufacturing and Testing
Lake Publishing Corp.
17730 W. Peterson Rd.
Box 159
Libertyville, IL 60048-0159
708-362-8711
Terrence Thompson, Editor
*Covers the techniques, materials, and machin-
ery used to manufacture and test integrated
circuits and semiconductors.*

Semiconductor Industry & Business Survey
    Newsletter
H T E Research, Inc.
400 Oyster Point Blvd., Ste. 220
S. San Francisco, CA 94080
415-871-4377
Steve Szirom, Editor
*Detailed profiles of semiconductor firms, tech-
nologies, and markets.*

Semiconductor International
Cahners Publishing Co.
1350 E. Touhy Ave.
Box 5080
Des Plaines, IL 60017-5080
708-635-8800
Peter Singer, Editor
*Reports on all aspects of semiconductor
design, manufacture, marketing, and use.*

Solid State Technology
PennWell Publishing Co.
14 Vanderventer Ave.
Port Washington, NY 11050
516-883-6200
Sidney Marshall, Editor
*Covers news of the semiconductor and inte-
grated circuit industry.*

LIBRARIES

Burr-Brown Corp.
Library
Box 11400
Tuscon, AZ 85734
602-746-7186
602-746-7211 Fax
Semiconductors and microelectronics.

Raytheon Co.
Research Division
Library
131 Spring St.
Lexington, MA 02173
617-860-3190
617-860-3196 Fax
*Semiconductor physics, advanced materials,
and applied physics.*

Rockwell International Corp.
Science Center Library
1049 Camino Dos Rios
Thousand Oaks, CA 91360-2362
805-373-4721
805-373-4775 Fax
*Semiconductor devices, fluid mechanics, elec-
tronics, and related topics.*

Texas Instruments, Inc.
Semiconductor Group Library
Box 655303, MS 8240
Dallas, TX 75265
214-997-2135
*Semiconductor technology, electronics, and
computer science.*

COMPANIES

Applied Materials Inc.
3050 Bowers St.
Santa Clara, CA 95054
408-727-5555
*Equipment and materials for semiconductor
fabrication.*

Cypress Semiconductor Corp.
3901 N. First St.
San Jose, CA 95134
408-943-2600
Semiconductors.

Harris Semiconductors
(Division of Harris Corp.)
2450 Walsh Ave.
Santa Clara, CA 95051
408-996-5000
Semiconductor and other electronic devices.

Kulicke & Soffa Industries, Inc.
2101 Blair Mill Rd.
Willow Grove, PA 19090
215-784-6000
Equipment used to produce semiconductors.

LSI Logic Corp.
1551 McCarthy Blvd.
Milpitas, CA 95035
408-433-8000
Semiconductors.

Motorola, Inc.
1303 E. Algonquin Rd.
Schaumburg, IL 60196
708-397-5000
Semiconductors and other products.

National Semiconductor Corp.
P.O. Box 58090
Santa Clara, CA 95052
408-721-5000
Semiconductors and other products.

Silicon Valley Group Inc.
2240 Ringwood Ave.
San Jose, CA 95131
408-434-0500
Equipment for semiconductor fabrication.

Texas Instruments Incorporated
P.O. Box 655474
Dallas, TX 75265
214-995-2011
Semiconductors, computers, and many other products.

Varian Associates
611 Hansen Way
Palo Alto, CA 94303
415-493-4000
Equipment for semiconductor fabrication and other types of products.

FEDERAL GOVERNMENT

U.S. International Trade Administration
Department of Commerce
14th St. and Constitution Ave., N.W.
Washington, DC 20230
202-377-2000
Ask for the Commodity Analyst who is an expert in semiconductors.

U.S. International Trade Commission
500 E St., S.W.
Washington, DC 20436
202-205-2000 Office of the Secretary
202-205-3296 Industries locator
Ask for the Trade Analyst who is an expert in semiconductors.

U.S. Patent and Trademark Office
Crystal Plaza 2
2011 Jefferson Davis Highway
Arlington, VA 22202
703-305-8000
Ask for the Examining Group Director who is a specialist in semiconductors.

SHEEP INDUSTRY

See also: LIVESTOCK INDUSTRY

ASSOCIATIONS

American Sheep Industry Association
6911 S. Yosemite St.
Englewood, CO 80112-1414
303-771-3500
303-771-8200 Fax
John Obson, Executive Director
Represents farmers and producers of sheep and wool.

National Lamb Feeders Association
PO Box 238
Bristol, IL 60512-0238
708-553-5512
Howard Wyman, Secretary
Represents firms that manufacture feed and drugs for lambs.

PERIODICALS

National Wool Grower
American Sheep Industry Association
6911 S. Yosemite St.
Englewood, CO 80112-1414
303-771-3500
Janice Grauberger, Editor
Discusses sheep industry issues and management practices.

Sheep Breeder and Sheepman
Mead Livestock Services
Box 796
Columbia, MO 65205
314-442-8257
Larry Mead, Editor
Business and technical information for sheep farmers.

Sheep! Magazine
Sheep! Magazine Inc.
W. 2997 Markert Rd.
Helenville, WI 53137
414-674-3020
Dave Thompson, Editor
Practical information for sheep farmers and ranchers.

Shepherd
Sheep and Farm Life, Inc.
5696 Johnston Rd.
New Washington, OH 44854
419-492-2364
Guy Flora, Editor
Advice for sheep farmers.

LIBRARIES

Delaware Valley College of Science and Agriculture
Joseph Krauskopf Memorial Library
Doylestown, PA 18901
215-345-1500
215-345-1711 Fax
Animal science, dairy science, agribusiness, and related topics.

Michigan State University
Animal Industries Reference Room
208 Anthony Hall
East Lansing, MI 48824
517-355-8483
517-353-9806 Fax
Animal breeding and animal production.

University of Illinois
Agriculture Library
226 Mumford Hall
1301 W. Gregory Dr.
Urbana, IL 61801
217-333-2416
217-244-0398 Fax
Animal science and agricultural economics.

FEDERAL GOVERNMENT

U.S. Department of Agriculture
14th St. and Independence Ave., S.W.
Washington, DC 20250
202-720-8732
Ask for the Economic Research Service.

U.S. International Trade Administration
Department of Commerce
14th St. and Constitution Ave., N.W.
Washington, DC 20230
202-377-2000
Ask for the Commodity Analyst who is an expert in the sheep industry.

U.S. International Trade Commission
500 E St., S.W.
Washington, DC 20436
202-205-2000 Office of the Secretary
202-205-3296 Industries locator
Ask for the Trade Analyst who is an expert in the sheep industry.

SHIPS AND SHIPPING INDUSTRY

See also: CONTAINER INDUSTRY; FREIGHT TRANSPORTATION;
and WATERWAYS AND PORTS

ASSOCIATIONS

Intermodal Marketing Association
2111 Wilson Blvd., Ste. 700
Arlington, VA 22201
703-875-8665
703-528-7510 Fax
John McQuaid, Executive Director
*Provides research to agents who consolidate
shipments of freight to earn lower transport
rates.*

Maritime Association of the Port of New
    York/New Jersey
17 Battery Pl., Ste. 1006
New York, NY 10004
212-425-5704
212-635-9498 Fax
N. Nick Cretan, Executive Director
*Offer statistical and other types of information
to steamship firms, shipbuilders, marine supply firms, and others in the shipping industry.*

New York Shipping Association
Two World Trade Center, 20th Fl.
New York, NY 10048
212-323-6600
Anthony Tozzoli, President
*Represents steamship lines, stevedoring firms,
and other employers along the New York/New
Jersey waterfront.*

Professional Mariners Alliance
370 W. Park Ave.
Long Beach, NY 11561-3292
516-431-4441
516-889-5111 Fax
Thomas O'Hara, Executive Vice President
*A professional group of people working in the
maritime industry.*

Shippers for Competitive Ocean Transportation
1090 Vermont Ave. N.W., Ste. 410
Washington, DC 20005
301-253-1910
H. George Miller, Executive Director
*Represents U.S. importers and exporters by
monitoring international shipping regulations
that may reduce competition among ocean
shippers.*

Society of Marine Port Engineers
PO Box 466
Avenel, NJ 07001
908-381-7673
James Dickey, Secretary
*A professional group of port engineers and
others holding management positions in ship-
ping firms.*

United Shipowners of America
1627 K St., N.W., Ste. 1200
Washington, DC 20006
202-466-5388
202-466-5392 Fax
William Verdon, President
A trade group of U.S. merchant lines.

PERIODICALS

American Shipper
Howard Publications, Inc.
33 S. Hogan St., Ste. 230
Box 4728
Jacksonville, FL 32201
904-355-2601
David Howard, Editor
Covers issues and news about ports, ships, and related topics.

Journal of Maritime Law and Commerce
Anderson Publishing Co.
2035 Reading Rd.
Cincinnati, OH 45202
513-421-4142
Nicholas Healy, Editor
Analyses of legal and business issues affecting the shipping industry.

Journal of Ship Production
Society of Naval Architects and Marine Engineers
601 Pavonia Ave.
Jersey City, NJ 07306-2907
201-798-4800
Covers the world of ship building.

Maritime Reporter and Engineering News
Maritime Activity Reports
118 E. 25th St.
New York, NY 10010
212-477-6700
Charles O'Malley, Editor
Business and technical news for the shipping industry.

Shipping Digest
Geyer-McAllister Publications, Inc.
51 Madison Ave.
New York, NY 10010
212-689-4411
Covers news about shipping for export and transportation executives.

LIBRARIES

Clyde Leavitt Inc.
Library
13901 Puerto Dr.
Ocean Springs, MS 39564-2019
601-875-5711
Ship construction, marine safety, naval architecture, and maritime history.

Manalytics, Inc.
Library
625 3rd St., 3rd Fl.
San Francisco, CA 94107
415-788-4143
415-777-0540 Fax
Maritime consulting.

U.S. Department of Transportation
Library and Distribution Services Division
400 7th St., S.W.
M-493.3, Rm. 2200
Washington, DC 20590
202-366-0746
Marine transportation and other topics.

U.S. Federal Maritime Commission
Library
1100 L St., N.W.
Washington, DC 20573
202-523-5762
202-523-3782 Fax
Marine transportation and shipping law.

COMPANIES

American Commercial Lines, Inc.
(Subsidiary of CSX Corp.)
1701 E. Market St.
Jeffersonville, IN 47130
812-288-0100
Inland waterway shipping and shipbuilding.

American President Lines Ltd.
1800 Harrison St.
Oakland, CA 94612
415-272-8000
Shipping line.

Avondale Industries, Inc.
P. O. Box 50280
New Orleans, LA 70150
504-436-2121
Shipbuilding and other businesses.

Carnival Cruise Lines, Inc.
3655 N. W. 87th Ave.
Miami, FL 33178
305-599-2600
Cruise ship operator.

CSX Corp.
1 James Ctr.
Richmond, VA 23219
804-782-1400
Shipping and other businesses.

General Steamship International, Ltd.
One California St.
San Francisco, CA 94111
415-772-9200
Ship agents, shipping terminal operators, and other businesses.

Matson Navigation Co., Inc.
(Subsidiary of Alexander & Baldwin, Inc.)
333 Market St., Box 7452
San Francisco, CA 94120
415-957-4000
Shipping operator.

Newport News Shipbuilding and Dry Dock Co.
(Subsidiary of Tenneco Inc.)
4101 Washington Ave.
Newport News, VA 23607
804-380-2000
Shipbuilding and repair.

Norfolk Shipbuilding & Drydock Corp.
P. O. Box 2100
Norfolk, VA 23501
804-494-4000
Shipbuilding and repair.

Sea-Land Services, Inc.
379 Thornall St.
Edison, NJ 08837
201-558-6000
Shipping line.

Seatrain Lines, Inc.
270 Sylvan Ave.
Englewood Cliffs, NJ 07632
201-871-8900
Shipping line.

Todd Shipyards Corp.
1801 16th Ave. S. W.
Seattle, WA 98134
206-623-1635
Shipbuilding and repair.

FEDERAL GOVERNMENT

Federal Maritime Commission
1100 L St., N.W.
Washington, DC 20573
202-523-5773
Ask for the Freight Forwarders & Passenger Vessel Operations department.

U.S. Department of Transportation
400 Seventh St., S.W.
Washington, DC 20590
202-366-4000
Ask for the Production Division in the Ship Construction Office; or, in the Maritime Administration, ask for the Commercial Cargo Market Development division or the Industry Analysis Division.

U.S. Patent and Trademark Office
Crystal Plaza 2
2011 Jefferson Davis Highway
Arlington, VA 22202
703-305-8000
*Ask for the Examining Group Director who is
a specialist in ships.*

SHOE INDUSTRY

ASSOCIATIONS

National Shoe Retailers Association
9861 Broken Land Pkwy.
Columbia, MD 21046
301-381-8282
301-381-1167 Fax
William Boettge, President
*Offers training and research services to shoe re-
tailers, including chain stores and independents.*

National Shoe Traveler's Association
11701 Borman Dr., Ste. 324
St. Louis, MO 63146
314-993-3141
314-862-8361 Fax
Norman Weaver, President
*Offers educational programs to traveling sales-
people who sell shoes and related products.*

Shoe Service Institute of America
5024-R Campbell Blvd.
Baltimore, MD 21236
301-931-8100
301-529-4612 Fax
Ronald Sohn, Executive Vice President
*Members include wholesalers of equipment
and supplies used for shoe repair, and also
manufacturers of these products.*

PERIODICALS

American Shoemaking
Shoe Trades Publishing Co.
Box 198
Cambridge, MA 02140
617-648-8160
James Sutton, Editor
Covers the shoe industry for manufacturers.

Footwear News
Fairchild Publications, Inc.
7 E. 12th St.
New York, NY 10003
212-741-4310
Dick Silverman, Editor
*Reports on the shoe industry for manufactur-
ers, distributors, and retailers.*

Footwear Plus
Earnshaw Publications, Inc.
225 W. 34th St., Ste. 1212
New York, NY 10001
212-563-2742
Christina Gruber, Editor
*Surveys the footwear and hosiery market for
retailers.*

World Footwear
Shoe Traders Publishing Co., Inc.
Box 198
Cambridge, MA 02140
617-684-6810
*International news for shoe manufacturers in
the U.S. and abroad.*

LIBRARIES

Footwear Industries of America, Inc.
Library
1420 K St., N.W., Ste. 600
Washinton, DC 20005
202-789-1420
202-789-4058 Fax
Footwear industry and shoe technology.

COMPANIES

Etonic Inc.
(Subsidiary of Tretorn Sweden)
147 Center St.
Brockton, MA 02403
508-583-9100
Athletic footwear.

Kinney Shoe Corp.
(Subsidiary of Woolworth Corp.)
233 Broadway
New York, NY 10279
212-720-3700
Shoe retail chain.

Nike, Inc.
1 Bowerman Dr.
Beaverton, OR 97005
503-641-6453
Athletic shoes and clothing.

Nunn-Bush Shoe Co.
(Subsidiary of Weyco Group, Inc.)
P. O. Box 2047
Milwaukee, WI 53201
414-263-8800
Shoes for men.

Payless Shoesource
(Division of May Department Stores Co.)
3231 E. Sixth St.
Topeka, KS 66607
913-233-5171
Shoe retailer.

Shoe-Town, Inc.
994 Riverview Dr.
Totowa, NJ 07512
201-785-1900
Shoe retail chain.

Stride Rite Corp.
5 Cambridge Center
Cambridge, MA 02142
617-491-8800
Shoes for children and adults.

Timberland Co.
11 Merrill Industrial Dr., Box 5050
Hampton, NH 03842
603-926-1600
Shoes and boots.

U. S. Shoe Corp.
One Eastwood Dr.
Cincinnati, OH 45227
513-527-7000
Shoe retailer.

Wolverine World Wide Inc.
9341 Courtland Drive
Rockford, MI 49351
616-866-5500
Shoes for children and adults.

FEDERAL GOVERNMENT

U.S. Customs Service
Department of the Treasury
U.S. Customshouse
6 World Trade Center
New York, NY 10048
212-466-5550
*Ask for the Commodity Specialist in charge of
shoes.*

U.S. International Trade Administration
Department of Commerce
14th St. and Constitution Ave., N.W.
Washington, DC 20230
202-377-2000
Ask for the Commodity Analyst who is an expert in shoes or shoemaking machinery.

U.S. International Trade Commission
500 E St., S.W.
Washington, DC 20436
202-205-2000 Office of the Secretary
202-205-3296 Industries locator
Ask for the Trade Analyst who is an expert in shoes or shoemaking machinery.

U.S. Patent and Trademark Office
Crystal Plaza 2
2011 Jefferson Davis Highway
Arlington, VA 22202
703-305-8000
Ask for the Examining Group Director who is a specialist in shoemaking machinery.

SHOPPING CENTERS AND MALLS

See also: RETAIL TRADE

ASSOCIATIONS

International Council of Shopping Centers
665 5th Ave.
New York, NY 10022
212-421-8181
212-486-0849 Fax
John Riordan, Executive Vice President
Offers research and educational programs to everyone connected to the shopping center industry, including developers, owners, managers, retailers, real estate brokers, and others.

PERIODICALS

Carlsonreport for Shopping Center Management
Jonesreport, Inc.
Report Communications
9595 Whitley Dr., Ste., 100
Indianapolis, IN 46240
317-844-9024
William Wilburn, Editor
News for senior executives in the shopping center industry.

Monitor
Four Stamford Forum
Stamford, CT 06901-3202
203-977-2900
Robert O'Neill, Editor
Surveys the shopping center and chain store industry.

Shopping Center Digest
Jomurpa Publishing Inc.
Box 1708
7 S. Myrtle Ave.
Spring Valley, NY 10977
914-426-0040
Murray Shor, Editor
Reports on space availability of planned, new, and expanding shopping centers.

Shopping Center Newsletter
National Research Bureau, Inc.
424 N. Third St.
Burlington, IA 52601
319-752-5415
R. Wilson, Editor
Focuses on special promotions and events at shopping centers nationwide.

Shopping Center World
Communication Channels, Inc.
6255 Barfield Rd.
Atlanta, GA 30328-4369
404-256-9800
Teresa DeFranks, Editor
Covers such topics as developing, building, managing, leasing, and promoting shopping centers.

LIBRARIES

Dayton Hudson Corp.
Research/Information Center
777 Nicollet Mall
Minneapolis, MN 55402
612-370-6769
Retailing and business.

International Council of Shopping Centers
Library/Information Center
665 Fifth Ave.
New York, NY 10022
212-421-8181
Covers shopping center topics such as development, law, marketing, and design.

Montgomery Ward and Co.
Information Services
One Montgomery Ward Plaza
Chicago, IL 60671
312-467-7351
Retailing.

The Vineyard
Real Estate, Shopping Center & Urban
    Development
Information Center
50 W. Shaw Ave.
Fresno, CA 93704
209-222-0182
Shopping centers, urban planning, and market research.

COMPANIES

Crown American Corp.
Pasquerilla Plaza
Johnstown, PA 15907
814-536-4441
Builder, owner, and operator of shopping centers and malls.

Edward J. DeBartolo Corp.
7620 Market St.
Youngstown, OH 44512
216-758-7292
Operates shopping malls.

Ingles Markets Inc.
P.O. Box 6676, Hwy. 70
Asheville, NC 28816
704-669-2941
Owns and operates shopping centers and grocery stores.

Lennar Corp.
700 N. W. 107th Ave.
Miami, FL 33172
305-559-4000
Builder of homes, office buildings, condominiums, and shopping centers.

Lloyd's Shopping Centers, Inc.
330 Rte. 211 E.
Middletown, NY 10940
914-342-3905
Operates supermarkets and shopping centers.

Sizeler Property Investors Inc.
2542 Williams Blvd.
Kenner, LA 70062
504-466-5363
Invests in shopping malls.

SHORTHAND AND SHORTHAND REPORTING

ASSOCIATIONS

National Shorthand Reporters Association
118 Park St. S.E.
Vienna, VA 22180
703-281-4677
Charles Hagee, Executive Director
Represents shorthand reporters who work for courts, business, and government.

COMPANIES

Ace-Federal Reporters, Inc.
444 N. Capitol St., N.W.
Washington, DC 20001
202-347-3700
Shorthand reporting services.

Adler Reporting Service, Inc.
15 Park Row
New York, NY 10038
212-267-3343
Court reporting services.

Commerce Reporting Co.
139 East 59th St.
New York, NY 10022
212-750-9696
Shorthand reporting services.

Pengad Co's., Inc.
55 Oak St.
Bayonne, NJ 07002
201-436-5625
Supplies for court reporters and attorneys.

Quixote Corp.
One E. Wacker Dr.
Chicago, IL 60601
312-467-6755
Equipment for stenography and other purposes.

Stenograph Corp.
(Subsidiary of Quixote Corp.)
1500 Bishop Ct.
Mount Prospect, IL 60056
708-803-1400
Equipment and supplies for shorthand and stenography.

Vertical Software Systems, Inc.
2801 Youngfield
Golden, CO 80401
303-233-4213
Computer systems for stenographers and court reporters.

SIGN INDUSTRY

ASSOCIATIONS

National Electric Sign Association
801 N. Fairfax St., Ste. 205
Alexandria, VA 22314
703-836-4012
George Kopecky, President
*Offers seminars to manufacturers of electric
and nonelectric signs, and suppliers to the
industry.*

World Sign Associates
8774 Yates Dr.
Westminster, CO 80030
303-427-7252
303-427-7090 Fax
Jerry Righthouse, Executive Vice President
*Offers training to manufacturers who special-
ize in custom electrical signs.*

PERIODICALS

Marking Industry
Marking Devices Publishing, Inc.
113 Adell Pl.
Elmhurst, IL 60126-3301
708-832-5200
Terri Andrews, Editor
*Covers the market of marking products and
signs.*

Signcraft
Signcraft Publishing Co., Inc.
Box 06031
Ft. Myers, FL 33906
813-939-4644
Tom McIltrot, Editor
*Advises owners and operators of sign shops
about business practices, creative sign design,
and related topics.*

Signs of the Times
S T Publications Inc.
407 Gilbert Ave.
Cincinnati, OH 45202
513-421-2050
Tod Swormstedt, Editor
*News and how-to information for manufactur-
ers and others in the sign and advertising display business.*

COMPANIES

Acme-Wiley Corp.
2480 Greenleaf
Elk Grove Village, IL 60007
708-364-2250
Plastic and neon signs.

Ad Art Signs, Inc.
3133 N. Ad Art Rd.
Stockton, CA 95215
209-931-0860
Electric signs.

BG Holding Co., Inc.
P.O. Box 280366
Columbia, SC 29228
803-794-2290
Signs.

Benco Industries Inc.
One Benco Industrial Dr.
Fort Deposit, AL 36032
205-227-4333
Illuminated and non-illuminated signs.

Dualite, Inc.
One Dualite Lane
Williamsburg, OH 45176
513-724-7100
Illuminated signs and clocks.

Emed Co., Inc.
P.O. Box 369
Buffalo, NY 14240
716-626-1616
Advertising displays and signs.

Everbrite Electric Signs, Inc.
4949 S. 110th St.
Greenfield, WI 53220
414-529-3500
Indoor and outdoor signs.

Plasti-Line, Inc.
623 E. Emory Rd., Box 59043
Knoxville, TN 37950
615-938-1511
Illuminated signs.

Tencon Inc.
(Subsidiary of Plasti-Line, Inc.)
400 Rivers Rd.
Centerville, TN 37033
615-729-5103
Electric signs.

Zimmerman Sign Co.
(Subsidiary of Stamford Capital Group, Inc.)
8140 Walnut Hill Lane
Dallas, TX 75231
214-691-8797
Illuminated and non-illuminated signs.

FEDERAL GOVERNMENT

U.S. International Trade Administration
Department of Commerce
14th St. and Constitution Ave., N.W.
Washington, DC 20230
202-377-2000
*Ask for the Commodity Analyst who is an
expert in signs and the sign board industry.*

U.S. International Trade Commission
500 E St., S.W.
Washington, DC 20436
202-205-2000 Office of the Secretary
202-205-3296 Industries locator
*Ask for the Trade Analyst who is an expert in
signs and the sign board industry.*

SMALL BUSINESS AND SELF-EMPLOYMENT

See also: ENTREPRENEURS

ASSOCIATIONS

American Federation of Small Business
407 S. Dearborn St.
Chicago, IL 60605-1115
312-427-0207
Thomas Latimer, Executive Vice President
Primarily a lobbying group that represents the interests of small businesses and self-employed people against what it sees as the "big business" monopolies.

American Small Businesses Association
PO Box 612663
Dallas, TX 75261
800-880-2722
Ronald Frano, Executive Director
Lobbies for the interests of small business owners and offers seminars on business topics.

American Society of Independent Business
c/o Keith Wood
777 Main St., Ste. 1600
Ft. Worth, TX 76102
817-870-1880
Keith Wood, President
Helps self-employed people and small businesses obtain employee benefits and be competitive as employers.

Independent Small Business Employers of
    America
520 S. Pierce
Mason City, IA 50401
515-424-3187
Jim Collison, President
800-728-3187
Helps small businesses with their employee management skills.

International Association of Business
701 Highlander Blvd., Ste. 220
Arlington, TX 76015
817-465-2922
817-468-0098 Fax
Paula Rowe, Vice President
Offers seminars and advises small businesses how to obtain the same benefits as large corporations.

National Association of Investment Companies
1111 14th St. N.W., Ste. 700
Washington, DC 20005
202-289-4336
JoAnn Price, President
Offers services to Small Business Investment Companies (SBICs) that invest in minority-owned businesses.

National Association of Private Enterprise
PO Box 470397
Ft. Worth, TX 76147
817-870-1971
800-223-NAPE
817-332-4525 Fax
D'Ann Dagen, Executive Director
Offers educational and benefits programs to small businesses and the self-employed.

National Association for the Self-Employed
2328 Gravel Rd.
Ft. Worth, TX 76118
800-232-6273
817-595-5456 Fax
William Witcher, President
A very large group of self-employed people. Offers variety of educational and benefit programs.

National Association of Small Business Investment Companies
323 W. 8th St.
5501 Lucas Place
Kansas City, MO 64105
816-374-6708
202-775-9158 Fax
Harold Ewossaman, Executive Officer
Represents SBIC's that are licensed to invest in small businesses.

National Business Association
14875 Landmark Blvd., Ste. 100
Dallas, TX 75240
214-991-5381
800-456-0440
Robert Allen, President
Helps self-employed people and small businesses obtain loans, insurance, and other services. Offers educational programs.

Small Business Service Bureau
554 Main St.
PO Box 1441
Worcester, MA 01601-1441
508-756-3513
Francis Carroll, President
Offers group insurance, health plans, management advice, and other services to firms with under 100 employees.

PERIODICALS

Family Business
Family Business Publishing Co., Inc.
229 S. 18th St.
Philadelphia, PA 19103
215-790-7000
Steven Solomon, Editor
Advises owners and managers of family businesses on a wide range of issues.

Family Business Review
Family Firm Institute
Jossey-Bass Inc., Publishers
350 Sansome St., 5th Fl.
San Francisco, CA 94104
415-433-1767
Ivan Lansberg, Editor
Technical and scholarly information for small businesses run by families.

Inc.
Goldhirsh Group, Inc.
38 Commercial Wharf
Boston, MA 02110
617-248-8000
George Gendron, Editor
News, trends, profiles of successful companies, and management advice for small and mid-sized businesses.

Journal of Small Business Finance
J A I Press Inc.
55 Old Post Rd., No. 2
Box 1678
Greenwich, CT 06836-1678
203-661-7602
Rassoul Yazdipour, Editor
Reports on financial issues of concern to small companies.

Journal of Small Business Management
Bureau of Business Research
West Virginia University
Box 6025
Morgantown, WV 26506-6025
304-293-7534
Stanley Kloc, Editor
Detailed advice for managers of small businesses.

Small Business Opportunities
Harris Publications, Inc.
1115 Broadway, 8th fl.
New York, NY 10010
212-807-7100
Susan Rakowski, Editor
Advises on how to start and operate a small business.

Small Business Reports
Business Research and Communications
203 Calle del Oaks
Monterey, CA 93940
408-899-7221
Bryon Radaker, Editor
Surveys news and trends that concern executives at small businesses.

Small Business Tax Control
Business Tax Publishers, Inc.
1101 King St., Ste. 400
Box 1463
Alexandria, VA 22314
703-548-2400
Larry Witner, Editor
Tax advice for small businesses.

Small Business Tax Review
Hooksett Publishing, Inc.
Box 895
Melville, NY 11747-0895
516-549-4090
Steven Hopfenmuller, Editor
Tax news and advice for small businesses.

LIBRARIES

American Federation of Small Business
Information Center
407 S. Dearborn St., Ste. 500
Chicago, IL 60605
312-427-0207
Small business, legislation, and business education.

Georgia State University
Small Business Development Center
1 Park Place, S., Ste. 1056
Atlanta, GA 30303
404-651-3550
404-651-2804 Fax
Small business, marketing, and finance.

Small Business Administration
Reference Library
409 Third St., S.W., 5th Fl.
Washington, DC 20416
202-205-7033
Small business, management, and venture capital.

FEDERAL GOVERNMENT

Small Business Administration
2100 K St., N.W.
Washington, DC 20416
202-653-6600
Ask for Information Services or the Answer Desk.

SOCIAL SECURITY

ASSOCIATIONS

National Academy of Social Insurance
505 Capitol Ct. N.E., Ste. 300
Washington, DC 20002
202-547-9592
202-547-9595 Fax
Pamela Larson, Executive Director
Acts as a clearinghouse for information on Social Security, unemployment, worker's compensation, and other forms of social insurance.

National Committee to Preserve Social Security and Medicare
2000 K St. N.W., Ste. 800
Washington, DC 20006
202-822-9459
202-822-9612 Fax
Martha McSteen, President
Conducts research and represents the interests of those who recieve Social Security and Medicare.

PERIODICALS

Senior Law Report
Community Development Services, Inc.
C D Publications
5204 Fenton St.
Silver Spring, MD 20910-2889
301-588-6380
Herb Weiss, Editor
Reports on many legal matters of concern to senior citizens, including Social Security.

Social Security Manual
National Underwriter Co.
505 Gest St.
Cincinnati, OH 45203
513-721-2140
Describes Social Security rights and rules.

Social Security Practice Guide
Matthew Bender & Co., Inc.
11 Penn Plaza
New York, NY 10001
212-967-7707
Information for attorneys about disability claims under the Social Security laws.

LIBRARIES

Cornell University
New York State School of Industrial and Labor Relations
Martin P. Catherwood Library
Ives Hall
Ithaca, NY 14851-0952
607-255-2184
607-255-9641 Fax
Social security, labor economics, labor-management relations, and related topics.

U.S. Social Security Administration
Branch Library
Van Ness Centre, Rm. 206
4301 Connecticut Ave., N.W.
Washington, DC 20008
202-282-7000
202-282-7219 Fax
Social Security programs, pension benefits, retirement, and income maintenance.

U.S. Social Security Administration
Information Resources Branch
Library Services Section
Altmeyer Bldg., Rm. 570
P.O. Box 17330
Baltimore, MD 21235
301-965-6107
Social insurance, law, and operations research.

FEDERAL GOVERNMENT

Social Security Administration
Department of Health and Human Services
6401 Security Blvd.
Baltimore, MD 21235
301-594-7700
Ask for the Public Inquiries office to find an appropriate expert.

SOLAR ENERGY

See also: ENERGY

ASSOCIATIONS

American Solar Energy Association
c/o John Lillard
1667 K St. N.W., Ste. 395
Washington, DC 20006
202-347-2000
John Lillard, General Counsel
Represents manufacturers, architects, engineers, and others in the solar energy field.

American Solar Energy Society
2400 Central Ave., B-1
Boulder, CO 80301
303-443-3130
303-443-3212 Fax
Larry Sherwood, Director
A professional society whose members share technical information about solar energy.

Passive Solar Industries Council
1090 Vermont Ave. N.W., Ste. 1200
Washington, DC 20005-4905
202-371-0357
202-682-0168 Fax
Helen English, Executive Director
Members include designers, manufacturers, engineers, and builders who use or sell passive solar products. These products are usually built into structures—for example windows that face south or water reservoirs that catch sunlight.

Solar Energy Industries Association
777 N. Capitol St. N.E., Ste. 805
Washington, DC 22202
202-408-0660
202-408-8536 Fax
Scott Sklar, Executive Director
This group of manufacturers, distributors, and engineers of solar energy products runs a research foundation and promotes the use of solar energy systems.

PERIODICALS

C A Selects. Solar Energy
Chemical Abstracts Service
2540 Olentangy River Rd.
Box 3012
Columbus, OH 43210
614-447-3600
Technical information regarding the conversion of solar energy.

Journal of Solar Energy Engineering
American Society of Mechanical Engineers
345 E. 47th St.
New York, NY 10017
212-705-7722
Frank Kreith, Editor
How-to information for solar engineers.

Solar Energy
Pergamon Press, Inc., Journals Division
Maxwell House
Fairview Park
Elmsford, NY 10523
914-592-7700
John Duffie, Editor
Technological information for scientists and engineers.

Solar Today
American Solar Energy Society
2400 Central Ave., B-1
Boulder, CO 80301
303-443-3130
Maureen McIntyre, Editor
Articles include case histories and technological reviews.

LIBRARIES

Burt Hill Kosar Rittelmann Associates
Library
400 Morgan Center
Butler, PA 16001
412-285-4761
Solar energy, engineering, architecture, and related topics.

Solar Energy Research Institute
SERI Technical Library
1617 Cole Blvd.
Golden, CO 80401
303-231-1415
303-231-1422 Fax
Solar, wind, biomass, and other renewable energy sources.

Sunsearch, Inc.
Library
P.O. Box 590
Guilford, CT 06437
203-453-6591
Solar energy and energy-conversion technology.

Companies
Alpha Solarco, Inc.
11534 Gondola
Cincinnati, OH 45241
513-771-1690
Solar energy consultants.

Berkeley Solar Group
3140 Martin Luther King, Jr.
Berkeley, CA 94703
415-843-7600
Solar energy consultants.

Ford Products Corp.
Ford Products Rd.
Valley Cottage, NY 10989
914-358-8282
Solar, oil, and electric water heaters, and other products.

Mor-Flo Industries, Inc.
18450 S. Miles Rd.
Cleveland, OH 44128
216-663-7300
Water, gas, electric, and solar heaters.

Sealed Air Corp.
Park 80 Plaza E.
Saddle Brook, NJ 07662
201-791-7600
Solar pool blankets, solar collectors, and other products.

Spectrolab, Inc.
(Subsidiary of Hughes Aircraft Co.)
12500 Gladstone Ave.
Sylmar, CA 91342
818-365-4611
Silicon solar cells for use in space, solar cell power testing systems, and other equipment.

Taco, Inc.
1160 Cranston St.
Cranston, RI 02920
401-942-8000
Control equipment for solar and other energy systems.

FEDERAL GOVERNMENT

U.S. International Trade Administration
Department of Commerce
14th St. and Constitution Ave., N.W.
Washington, DC 20230
202-377-2000
Ask for the Commodity Analyst who is an expert in solar energy.

U.S. Department of Energy
1000 Independence Ave., S.W.
Washington, DC 20585
202-586-5000
Ask for the Solar Energy Research Institute.

SOUTH CAROLINA

STATE OFFICE LOCATOR (*for referrals to all state government offices*)

803-734-1000

ARCHIVES AND RECORDS

Archives & History Department
Box 11669
Columbia, SC 29211
803-734-8577

ATTORNEY GENERAL

Attorney General's Office
P.O. Box 11549
Columbia, SC 29211
803-734-3970

BANKING

Treasurer
P.O. Box 11778
Columbia, SC 29211
803-734-2101

COMMERCE

State Development Board
P.O. Box 927
Columbia, SC 29202
803-737-0400

CONSUMER AFFAIRS

Consumer Affairs Department
P.O. Box 5757
Columbia, SC 29250
803-734-9458

EDUCATION

Education Department
1429 Senate Street
Columbia, SC 29201
803-734-8492

ENERGY

Energy Research & Development Center
Clemson University
386-2 College Avenue
Clemson, SC 29634-0929
803-656-2267

ENVIRONMENTAL AFFAIRS

Environmental Qualtiy Control Division
2600 Bull Street
Columbia, SC 29201
803-734-5360

HEALTH

Health & Environmental Control Department
2600 Bull Street
Columbia, SC 29201
803-734-4880

HOUSING

Housing Authority
P.O. Box 7008
Columbia, SC 29211
803-734-8831

HUMAN RIGHTS

Human Affairs Commission
P.O. Box 11009
Columbia, SC 29211
803-253-6336

INSURANCE

Insurance Department
P.O. Box 100105
Columbia, SC 29202-3105
803-737-6117

LABOR

Labor Department
P.O. Box 11329
Columbia, SC 29211-1329
803-734-9594

LEGISLATION

Legislative Council
P.O. Box 11489
Columbia, SC 29211
803-734-2145

LIBRARY SERVICES

State Library
P.O. Box 11469
Columbia, SC 29211
803-734-8666

MOTOR VEHICLES

Motor Vehicle Division
P.O. Box 1498
Columbia, SC 29216
803-737-1135

OCCUPATIONAL HEALTH AND SAFETY

Occupational Safety & Health Division
P.O. Box 11329
Columbia, SC 29211-1329
803-734-9644

OMBUDSMAN

Ombudsman & Citizen Services Division
Edgar A. Brown Building
1205 Pendleton Street
Room 308
Columbia, SC 29201
803-734-0457

PUBLIC UTILITIES

Utility Division
P.O. Box 11649
Columbia, SC 29211
803-737-5120

PURCHASING

Material Management Office
1201 Main Street
Ste. 420
Columbia, SC 29201
803-737-3880

REAL ESTATE

Real Estate Commission
1201 Main Street
Ste. 1500
Columbia, SC 29201
803-737-0700

SECURITIES

Securities Division
P.O. Box 11350
Columbia, SC 29211
802-734-1087

TAXATION AND REVENUE

Tax Commission
P.O. Box 125
Columbia, SC 29214
803-737-9820

TOURISM

Division of Tourism
1205 Pendleton Street
Columbia, SC 29201
803-734-0122 or 0135

TRANSPORTATION

Highways & Public Transportation Department
P.O. Box 191
Columbia, SC 29202
803-737-1302

UNEMPLOYMENT

Unemployment Compensation Division
P.O. Box 995
Columbia, SC 29202
803-737-2787

WORKER'S COMPENSATION

Workers Compensation Fund
P.O. Box 102100
Columbia, SC 29221-5000
803-737-9450

SOUTH DAKOTA

STATE OFFICE LOCATOR (*for referrals to all state government offices*)

605-773-3011

ARCHIVES AND RECORDS

State Historical Society
State Library Building
800 Governors Drive
Pierre, SD 57501
605-773-3804

ATTORNEY GENERAL

Attorney General's Office
State Capitol
910 E. Sioux
Pierre, SD 57501
605-773-3215

BANKING

Banking Division
State Capitol
910 E. Sioux
Pierre, SD 57501
605-773-3177

COMMERCE

Commerce & Regulations Department
State Capitol
910 E. Sioux
Pierre, SD 57501
605-773-3177

CONSUMER AFFAIRS

Consumer Protection Division
State Capitol
910 E. Sioux
Pierre, SD 57501
605-773-4400

EDUCATION

Education Division
700 Governors Drive
Pierre, SD 57501-2293
605-773-3243

ENERGY

Energy Office
217 1/2 W. Missouri
Pierre, SD 57501
605-773-3603

ENVIRONMENTAL AFFAIRS

Water & Natural Resources Department
Joe Foss Building
523 E. Capitol Avenue
Pierre, SD 57501
605-773-3151

HEALTH

Health Department
523 E. Capitol
Pierre, SD 57501
605-773-3361

HOUSING

Housing Development Authority
P.O. Box 1237
Pierre, SD 57501-1237
605-773-3181

HUMAN RIGHTS

Human Rights Division
State Capitol
910 E. Sioux
Pierre, SD 57501
605-773-4493

INSURANCE

Insurance Division
State Capitol
910 E. Sioux
Pierre, SD 57501
605-773-4104

LABOR

Labor Department
700 Governors Drive
Pierre, SD 57501
605-773-3101

LEGISLATION

Legislative Research Council
State Capitol Annex
500 E. Capitol Avenue
Pierre, SD 57501-5088
605-773-3251

LIBRARY SERVICES

Education & Cultural Affairs Department
700 Governors Drive
Pierre, SD 57501
605-773-3131

LICENSING—CORPORATE

Corporations Divison
State Capitol Annex
500 E. Capitol Avenue
Ste. 204
Pierre, SD 57501-5077
605-773-4845

LICENSING—PROFESSIONAL AND OCCUPATIONAL

Professional & Occupational License Division
State Capitol
910 E. Sioux
Pierre, SD 57501
605-773-3177

MOTOR VEHICLES

Motor Vehicle Division
700 Governors Drive
Pierre, SD 57501-2276
605-773-3541

OMBUDSMAN

Social Services Department
700 Governors Drive
Pierre, SD 57501
605-773-3165

PUBLIC UTILITIES

Public Utilities Commission
State Capitol
910 E. Sioux
Pierre, SD 57501
605-773-3201

PURCHASING

Purchasing & Printing Division
500 E. Capitol
Pierre, SD 57501
605-773-3405

REAL ESTATE

Real Estate Commission
P.O. Box 490
Pierre, SD 57501
605-773-3600

SECURITIES

Securities Division
State Capitol
910 E. Sioux
Pierre, SD 57501
605-773-4823

TAXATION AND REVENUE

Revenue Department
700 Governors Drive
Pierre, SD 57501-2276
605-773-3311

TOURISM

Division of Tourism
Capital Lake Plaza
711 Wells Avenue
Pierre, SD 57501
605-773-3301
800-952-2217
800-843-1930 (in South Dakota)

TRANSPORTATION

Transportation Department
700 Broadway Avenue, E.
Pierre, SD 57501-2586
605-773-3265

UNEMPLOYMENT

Unemployment Insurance Division
P.O. Box 4730
Aberdeen, SD 57402-4730
605-622-2452

WORKER'S COMPENSATION

Division of Labor & Management
700 Governors Drive
Pierre, SD 57501-2277
605-737-3681

SOYBEAN INDUSTRY

ASSOCIATIONS

American Soybean Association
540 Maryville Centre Dr.
St. Louis, MO 63141
314-576-1770
Kenneth Bader, Chief Executive
Provides technical and industry informtion to soybean farmers and producers.

Soyfoods Association of North America
PO Box 234
Lafayette, CA 94549
415-283-2991
William Shurtleff, Director
Promotes the use of soybeans in food.

PERIODICALS

Rice World & Soybean News
J.P. Gaines, Ed. & Pub.
Box 219
Folsom, LA 70437-0219
504-796-3012
Surveys the rice and soybean industry.

Soybean Digest
American Soybean Association
777 Craig Rd.
Box 41309
St. Louis, MO 63141-1309
314-432-1600
Gregg Hillyer, Editor
Covers the soybean industry.

LIBRARIES

Central Soya Co., Inc.
Food Research Library
Fort Wayne National Bank Bldg.
P.O. Box 1400
Fort Wayne, IN 46801-1400
219-425-5906
219-425-5838 Fax
Soybeans, proteins, nutrition, and food science.

Soyfoods Center Library and Information
    Center
P.O. Box 234
Lafayette, CA 94549
415-283-2991
415-283-9091 Fax
Soybean nutrition, marketing, history, and commercial soy products.

COMPANIES

AG Processing Inc
11717 Burt St.
Omaha, NE 68154
402-496-7809
Soybeans, soy flour, soybean meal and oil, and other products.

Agrex Inc.
7007 College Blvd.
Overland Park, KS 66211
913-345-5400
Storage and marketing of wheat, corn, soybeans, and other grains.

Central Soya Co., Inc.
(Subsidiary of SMRK Equity Holdings, Inc.)
1300 Ft. Wayne National Bank Bldg.
Ft. Wayne, IN 46802
219-425-5100
Soybeans, soybean meal and oil, and other products.

Dekalb Genetics Corp.
3100 Sycamore Rd.
De Kalb, IL 60115
815-758-3461
Seed corn, sunflowers, soybeans, and other products.

Ferruzzi Trading USA Inc.
1114 Ave. of the Americas
New York, NY 10036
212-997-7100
Trader of corn, wheat, soybeans, and other products.

Perdue Farms Inc.
P. O. Box 1537
Salisbury, MD 21801
301-543-3000
Poultry and soybean products.

FEDERAL GOVERNMENT

U.S. Department of Agriculture
14th St. and Independence Ave., S.W.
Washington, DC 20250
202-720-8732
Ask for the Economic Research Service.

U.S. International Trade Administration
Department of Commerce
14th St. and Constitution Ave., N.W.
Washington, DC 20230
202-377-2000
Ask for the Commodity Analyst who is an expert in the soybean industry.

U.S. International Trade Commission
500 E St., S.W.
Washington, DC 20436
202-205-2000 Office of the Secretary
202-205-3296 Industries locator
Ask for the Trade Analyst who is an expert in the soybean industry.

SPICE INDUSTRY

ASSOCIATIONS

American Spice Trade Association
Box 1267
Englewood Cliffs, NJ 07632
201-568-2163
201-568-7318 Fax
Thomas Burns, Executive Vice President
Members manufacture and distribute spices.

PERIODICALS

Journal of Herbs, Spices & Medicinal Plants
Haworth Press, Inc.
10 Alice St.
Binghamton, NY 13904
800-342-9678
Lyle Craker, Editor
Surveys the breeding, growing, and marketing of herbs, spices, and medicinal plants.

COMPANIES

Baltimore Spice Inc.
Reisterstown Rd.
Garrison, MD 21055
301-363-1700
Seasonings and spices.

Crescent Foods Inc.
25 S. Hanford
Seattle, WA 98134
206-461-1400
Spices, seasonings, extracts, and salad dressings.

Farmer Bros. Co.
20333 S. Normandie Ave.
Torrance, CA 90502
213-775-2451
Spices, coffee, and supplies for restaurants.

Fitzpatrick Co.
832 Industrial Dr.
Elmhurst, IL 60126
708-530-3333
Equipment for processing foods, chemicals, spices, and other purposes.

Gel Spice Co., Inc.
48 Hook Rd.
Bayonne, NJ 07002
201-339-0700
Spices.

McCormick & Co. Inc.
18 Loveton Circle, Box 6000
Sparks, MD 21152
301-771-7301
Seasonings, herbs, spices, flavorings, and essential oils.

Reckitt & Colman Inc.
(Subsidiary of Reckitt & Colman plc)
1655 Valley Rd., Box 943
Wayne, NJ 07474
201-633-3600
Spices, mustards, sauces, and food extracts.

Smart & Final, Inc.
524 Chapala St.
Santa Barbara, CA 93101
805-564-6700
Wholesaler of coffee, spices, and food.

Tone Bros. Inc
(Subsidiary of Rykoff-Sexton Inc.)
Box AA
Des Moines, IA 50301
515-262-9721
Teas, spice extracts, and processed foods.

FEDERAL GOVERNMENT

U.S. Customs Service
Department of the Treasury
U.S. Customshouse
6 World Trade Center
New York, NY 10048
212-466-5550
Ask for the Commodity Specialist in charge of spices and spice products.

U.S. International Trade Administration
Department of Commerce
14th St. and Constitution Ave., N.W.
Washington, DC 20230
202-377-2000
Ask for the Commodity Analyst who is an expert in the spice industry.

U.S. International Trade Commission
500 E St., S.W.
Washington, DC 20436
202-205-2000 Office of the Secretary
202-205-3296 Industries locator
Ask for the Trade Analyst who is an expert in the spice industry.

SPORTING GOODS INDUSTRY

ASSOCIATIONS

Athletic Footwear Association
200 Castlewood Dr.
North Palm Beach, FL 33408
407-840-1161
407-863-8984 Fax
Gregg Hartley, Executive Director
Conducts research and education programs on behalf of manufacturers of athletic footwear.

American Canoe Manufacturers Union
439 E. 51st St.
New York, NY 10022
212-421-5220
212-421-5999 Fax
Dwight Rockwell, President
Promotes the sport of canoeing on behalf of canoe manufacturers.

American Fishing Tackle Manufacturers Association
1250 Grove Ave., Ste. 300
Barrington, IL 60010
312-381-9490
Robert Kavanagh, President
Members import and manufacture fishing tackle and related items.

American Tennis Industry Federation
200 Castlewood Dr.
North Palm Beach, FL 33408
407-848-1026
407-863-8984 Fax
Brad Patterson, Executive Director
Offers informtion to tennis equipment manufacturers, builders of courts, and other suppliers to the industry.

Archery Manufacturers Organization
200 Castlewood Dr.
North Palm Beach, FL 33408
407-840-1139
407-863-8984 Fax
Nancy Ainger, Executive Director
Manufacturers of archery supplies and equipment.

Billiard and Bowling Institute of America
200 Castlewood Dr.
North Palm Beach, FL 33408
407-840-1120
Sebastian DiCasoli, Administrator
Firms that make and distribute billiard and bowling equipment.

Diving Equipment Manufacturers Association
PO Box 217
Tustin, CA 92681
714-744-5287
Robert Gray, Executive Director
Promotes scuba diving.

National Association of Sporting Goods
    Wholesalers
PO Box 11344
Chicago, IL 60611
312-565-0233
Rebecca Maddy, Executive Director
Firms that wholesale camping, sporting, and athletic equipment.

National Ski Retailers Association
1699 Wall St.
Mt. Prospect, IL 60056-5780
708-439-4000
708-439-0111 Fax
Thomas Doyle, Managing Director
Provides services to retailers of skiing equipment.

National Sporting Goods Association
Lake Center Plaza Bldg.
1699 Wall St.
Mt. Prospect, IL 60056-5780
708-439-4000
James Faltinek, President
Provides a wide range of research services to manufacturers, distributors, and retailers of all kinds of sporting goods.

Soccer Industry Council of America
200 Castlewood Dr.
North Palm Beach, FL 33408
407-840-1171
407-863-8984 Fax
Keith Heyes, Chairman
Represents all segments of the soccer equipment industry.

Sporting Goods Manufacturers Association
200 Castlewood Dr.
North Palm Beach, FL 33408
407-842-4100
407-863-8984 Fax
John Riddle, President
Provide information to manufacturers of sporting goods, including clothing and footwear used for sports.

Water Ski Industry Association
200 Castlewood Dr.
North Palm Beach, FL 33408
407-842-3600
James Hotchkiss, Executive Director
Represents the water ski equipment industry.

PERIODICALS

Army—Navy Store & Outdoor Merchandiser
Howmark Publishing Corp.
567 Morris Ave.
Elizabeth, NJ 07208
201-353-7373
Paul Bubney, Editor
Management and merchandising information for retailers of camping, sporting goods, and military surplus goods.

NSGA Retail Focus
National Sporting Goods Association
1699 Wall St.
Mt. Prospect, IL 60056-5780
708-439-4000
Larry Weindruch, Editor
Follows industry news for executives of sporting goods firms.

Sporting Goods Business
Gralla Publications
1515 Broadway
New York, NY 10036
212-869-1300
Robert Carr, Editor
Covers news and trends for the sporting goods industry.

Sporting Goods Dealer
Sporting News Publishing Co.
1212 N. Lindbergh Blvd.
St. Louis, MO 63132
314-997-7111
Steve Fechter, Editor
Management, merchandizing, and new product information for sporting goods retailers.

Sports Trend
Shore Communications, Inc.
180 Allen Rd., N.E., Ste. 300 N
Atlanta, GA 30328
404-252-8831
Jeff Atkinson, Editor
Focuses on merchandising techniques for sporting goods retailers.

COMPANIES

AMF Bowling Companies, Inc.
P.O. Box 31640
Richmond, VA 23294
804-747-6300
Bowling and other types of sporting goods.

Brunswick Bowl/Billiard
525 W. Laketon
Muskegon, MI 49443
616-725-3300
Bowling and billiard products.

BSN Corp.
1901 Diplomat Dr.
Dallas, TX 75234
214-484-9484
Football equipment and other sporting goods.

Dunlop Slazenger Corp.
P.O. Box 3070
Greenville, SC 29602
803-271-9767
Tennis and other types of sporting goods.

Herman's Sporting Goods, Inc.
(Subsidiary of Isoceles PLC)
2 Germak Dr.
Carteret, NJ 07008
908-541-1550
Chain of sporting goods stores.

K 2 Corp.
19215 99th S.W.
Vashon, WA 98070
206-463-3631
Ski equipment.

MacGregor Sporting Good
25 E. Union Ave.
E. Rutherford, NJ 07073
201-935-6300
Baseball and other types of sporting goods.

Marcy Fitness Products
1900 S. Burgundy
Ontario, CA 91761
714-986-2729
Rowing machines and other types of fitness equipment.

Oshman's Sporting Goods, Inc.
2302 Maxwell Lane
Houston, TX 77023
713-928-3171
Chain of sporting goods stores.

Prince Manufacturing
P.O. Box 2031
Princeton, NJ 08543
609-896-2500
Tennis and other types of equipment.

Rawlings Sporting Goods Co.
(Division of Figgie International Inc.)
1859 Intertech Dr.
Fenton, MO 63026
314-349-3500
Athletic equipment and sporting goods.

Wilson Sporting Goods
2233 West St.
River Grove, IL 60171
312-456-6100
Various types of sports equipment.

FEDERAL GOVERNMENT

U.S. Customs Service
Department of the Treasury
U.S. Customshouse
6 World Trade Center
New York, NY 10048
212-466-5550
Ask for the Commodity Specialist in charge of sporting goods.

U.S. International Trade Administration
Department of Commerce
14th St. and Constitution Ave., N.W.
Washington, DC 20230
202-377-2000
Ask for the Commodity Analyst who is an expert in the sporting goods industry.

U.S. International Trade Commission
500 E St., S.W.
Washington, DC 20436
202-205-2000 Office of the Secretary
202-205-3296 Industries locator
Ask for the Trade Analyst who is an expert in the sporting goods industry.

STANDARDS, WEIGHTS, AND MEASUREMENTS

ASSOCIATIONS

American National Standards Institute
1430 Broadway
New York, NY 10018
212-354-3300
212-302-1286 Fax
Manuel Peralter, President
Acts as a clearinghouse for a wide range of industries that seek to create, maintain, and follow standards relating to weight, size, terminology, materials, and more.

International Society of Weighing and Measurement
2299 Brockett Rd.
Tucker, GA 30084
404-939-2200
404-939-7924 Fax
Mimi Strozier, Executive Director
Individuals who make, sell, or service scales, and also government officials in charge of weights and measures.

National Conference of Standards Laboratories
1800 30th St., Ste. 305B
Boulder, CO 80301
303-440-3339
Wilbur Anson, Manager
Members work for laboratories involved with the measurement of standards and with calibration.

National Conference on Weights and Measures
PO Box 4025
Gaithersburg, MD 20878
301-975-4009
301-926-0647 Fax
A. D. Tholen, Executive Secretary
*Local and state officials in charge of weights
and measures, and firms that manufacture
equipment for weighing and measuring.*

Precision Measurements Association
3685 Motor Ave., Ste. 240
Los Angeles, CA 90034
213-287-0941
213-287-1851 Fax
Robert Myers, Executive Director
*Offers training in the use of all types of mea-
surement instruments to technicians, scientists, and engineers.*

PERIODICALS

Index and Directory of Industry Standards
Information Handling Services
15 Inverness Way. E.
Englewood, CO 80150
303-790-0600
Liz Prigge, Editor
*A guide to finding domestic and international
standards.*

Standards and Specifications Information
Bulletin
National Standards Association, Inc.
1200 Quince Orchard Blvd.
Gaithersburg, MD 20878
301-590-2300
*Reports news concerning standards and speci-
fications.*

LIBRARIES

American Standards Testing Bureau, Inc.
Sam Tour Library
40 Water St.
New York, NY 10004
212-943-3160
212-825-2250 Fax
*Covers standards and specifications for chem-
istry, engineering, physics, mathematics, and
other fields.*

U.S. National Institute of Standards and Technology
National Center for Standards and Certification Information
Administration Bldg., Rm. A629
Gaithersburg, MD 20899
301-975-4040
301-963-2871 Fax
*Product standards, specifications, codes, certi-
fication rules, engineering standards, and
related subjects.*

U.S. National Institute of Standards and Tech-
nology
Research Information Center
E106 Administration Bldg.
Gaithersburg, MD 20899
301-975-3052
301-869-8071 Fax
Statistics, mathematics, technology, standards.

STATISTICS

ASSOCIATIONS

American Statistical Association
1429 Duke St.
Alexandria, VA 22314
703-684-1221
703-684-2037 Fax
Barbara Bailar, Executive Director
A professional society for those who study and use statistics and statistical methods for all purposes and in all fields.

Econometric Society
Department of Economics
Northwestern University
Evanston, IL 60208-2400
708-491-3615
Julie Gordon, Executive Director
Statisticians and economists who study the apllication of statistics and mathematics to economic subjects.

Institute for Econometric Research
3471 N. Federal Hwy.
Ft. Lauderdale, FL 33306
305-563-9000
Norman Fosback, President
Offers educational programs to economists and others who study financial events and trends, including the stock markets, by using econometric methods.

Council of Professional Associations on Federal Statistics
1429 Duke St., Ste. 402
Alexandria, VA 22314
703-836-0404
703-684-2037 Fax
Katherine Wallman, Executive Director
Studies statistical issues of concern to the federal government and to statisticians employed by the government.

International Society of Statistical Science in Economics
536 Oasis Dr.
Santa Rosa, CA 95407
707-575-3529
Vladislav Shvyrkov, Chairperson
An international association of statisticians.

PERIODICALS

Journal of the American Statistical Association
American Statistical Association
1429 Duke St.
Alexandria, VA 22314-3402
703-684-1221
Technical articles for statisticians.

Statistical Science
Institute of Mathematical Statistics
3401 Investment Blvd., Ste. 7
Hayward, CA 94545
510-783-8141
Robert Kass, Editor
Technical information for statisticians.

LIBRARIES

U.S. Department of Commerce
Library
14th & Constitution Ave., N.W., Rm. 8060
Washington, DC 20230
202-377-3611
*Business and economic statistics, economic
conditions, economic theory, and industry
information.*

University of California, Berkeley
Astronomy-Mathematics-Statistics
Library
100 Evans Hall
Berkeley, CA 94720
510-642-3381
*Statistical methods, applied mathematics, and
mathematics of computer science.*

University of Illinois
Mathematics Library
216 Altgeld Hall
1409 W. Green St.
Urbana, IL 61801
217-333-0258
217-244-0398 Fax
*Statistical methods, pure mathematics, applied
mathematics, and computer sciences.*

STEEL AND IRON INDUSTRY

See also: FOUNDRY INDUSTRY and METALS INDUSTRY

ASSOCIATIONS

American Institute for International Steel
555 13th St. N.W., Ste. 500
Washington, DC 20004-1109
202-628-3878
202-737-3134 Fax
Bess Feig, Executive Director
Members import and export steel.

American Institute of Steel Construction
1 E. Wacker Dr., Ste. 3100
Chicago, IL 60601-2001
312-670-2400
Neil Zundel, President
*Firms that erect structural steel, primarily for
bridges, buildings, and industrial plants.*

American Iron and Steel Institute
1133 15th St. N.W.
Washington, DC 20005
202-452-7100
202-463-6573 Fax
Milton Deaner, President
*Conducts technological research for iron and
steel manufacturers, iron ore mining firms,
and other segments of the industry.*

Association of Iron and Steel Engineers
3 Gateway Center, Ste. 2350
Pittsburgh, PA 15222
412-281-6323
412-281-4657 Fax
Herschel Poole, Managing Director
A forum for engineers to share production and technical information about iron and steel processing.

Association of Steel Distributors
401 N. Michigan Ave.
Chicago, IL 60611-4390
312-644-6610
312-321-6869 Fax
Edward Craft, Executive Director
Members distribute steel products of all kinds.

Iron and Steel Society
410 Commonwealth Dr.
Warrendale, PA 15086
412-776-1535
412-776-0430 Fax
Lawrence Kuhn, Executive Director
Offers seminars and information about iron and steel metallurgy and engineering.

Steel Manufacturers Association
815 Connecticut Ave. N.W., Ste. 304
Washington, DC 20006
202-342-1160
202-331-7675 Fax
James Collins, President
Facilitates the exchange of technical, production, and industry information between steel manufacturers.

Steel Plate Fabricators Association
2400 S. Downing Ave.
Westchester, IL 60154
708-562-8750
708-562-8436 Fax
Ward Gill, Executive Director
Firms that make heavy steel plates for use by a variety of industries.

Steel Service Center Institute
1600 Terminal Tower
Cleveland, OH 44113
216-694-3630
Andrew Sharkey, President
Conducts research and offers advice on how to make steel distribution more efficient.

PERIODICALS

Iron & Steelmaker
Iron and Steel Society
410 Commonwealth Dr.
Warrendale, PA 15086
412-776-1535
Thomas McAloon, Editor
Technical information for iron and steel engineers and executives.

Iron Age
Hitchcock Publishing
191 S. Gary Ave.
Carol Stream, IL 60188
708-462-2286
Anne Armel, Editor
Information for iron and steel company executives.

Iron and Steel Engineer
Association of Iron and Steel Engineers
Three Gateway Center, Ste. 2350
Pittsburgh, PA 15222
412-281-6323
Charles Labee, Editor
Technical data for steel engineers.

Iron and Steel Works of the World
Metal Bulletin Inc.
220 Fifth Ave.
New York, NY 10001
212-213-6202
Information about mid-sized and large iron and steel producers worldwide.

Steel Digest
Intersteel Technology, Inc.
3041 Shallowood Lane
Charlotte, NC 28277
704-542-8210
John Vallomy, Editor
Technical information about the continuous steelmaking process and related technologies.

Steels Alert
A S M International, Materials Information
Materials Park, OH 44073
216-338-5151
Business information about the steel industry.

LIBRARIES

Bethlehem Steel Corp.
Corporate Information Center
701 E. Third St., Rm. 320A
Bethlehem, PA 18016
215-694-3325
215-694-3290 Fax
Steelmaking economics, metallurgy, engineering, and steelmaking technology.

LTV Steel Co.
Technology Center Library
6801 Brecksville Rd.
Independence, OH 44131
216-642-7100
Steel, engineering, and metallurgy.

USX Corp.
USS Division
Information Resource Center
4000 Tech Center Dr.
MS 88
Monroeville, PA 15146
412-825-2344
412-825-2050 Fax
Steel manufacture, metallurgy, materials science, physical chemistry, and related topics.

COMPANIES

Allegheny Ludlum Corp.
1000 Six PPG Pl.
Pittsburgh, PA 15222
412-394-2800
Steel and steel alloys.

Bethlehem Steel Corp.
1170 Eighth Ave.
Bethlehem, PA 18016
215-694-2424
Steel products.

Cyclops Industries, Inc.
650 Washington Rd.
Pittsburgh, PA 15228
412-343-4000
Steel sheets, plates, and related products.

Inland Steel Industries, Inc.
30 W. Monroe St.
Chicago, IL 60603
312-346-0300
Steel products.

LTV Steel Co., Inc.
(Subsidiary of LTV Corp.)
25 W. Prospect Ave.
Cleveland, OH 44115
216-622-5000
Steel products.

National Steel Corp.
(Subsidiary of NII Capital Corp. & NKK
       U.S.A. Corp.)
National Steel Ctr., 20 Stanwix St.
Pittsburgh, PA 15222
412-394-4100
Steel sheets, plates, and other steel products.

Nucor Corp.
4425 Randolph Rd.
Charlotte, NC 28211
704-366-7000
Steel products.

Joseph T. Ryerson & Son, Inc.
(Subsidiary of Inland Materials Distribution
    Group, Inc.)
2621 W. 15th Place
Chicago, IL 60608
312-762-2121
Steel bars, sheets, tubes, and other steel products.

Timken Co.
1835 Dueber Ave, S. W.
Canton, OH 44706
216-438-3000
Steel and steel alloys.

Wheeling-Pittsburgh Steel Corp.
(Subsidiary of Wheeling Pittsburgh Corp.)
1134 Market St.
Wheeling, WV 26003
304-234-2400
Steel and coke products.

FEDERAL GOVERNMENT

Bureau of Mines
810 7th St., N.W.
Washington, DC 20747
202-501-9770
Ask for the analyst who is an expert in the steel industry.

U.S. Customs Service
Department of the Treasury
U.S. Customshouse
6 World Trade Center
New York, NY 10048
212-466-5550
Ask for the Commodity Specialist in charge of steel products.

U.S. International Trade Administration
Department of Commerce
14th St. and Constitution Ave., N.W.
Washington, DC 20230
202-377-2000
Ask for the Commodity Analyst who is an expert in the steel industry.

U.S. International Trade Commission
500 E St., S.W.
Washington, DC 20436
202-205-2000 Office of the Secretary
202-205-3296 Industries locator
Ask for the Trade Analyst who is an expert in the steel industry.

STORE DISPLAYS

See also: POINT-OF-SALE INDUSTRY and RETAIL TRADE

ASSOCIATIONS

Institute of Store Planners
25 N. Broadway
Tarrytown, NY 10591
914-332-1806
Newton Fassler, President
*Members include store planners, designers,
and the visual merchandisers responsible for
displays.*

National Association of Display Industries
470 Park Ave. S., 17th Fl.
New York, NY 10016
212-213-2662
212-889-0727 Fax
Marvin Dorfmann, Executive Director
*Manufacturers and distributors of the dis-
plays, mannequins, equipment, and other merchandising supplies used by stores to display
their goods.*

PERIODICALS

Display & Design Ideas
Shore Communications, Inc.
180 Allen Rd., N.E., Ste. 300 N.
Atlanta, GA 30328
404-252-8831
Karen Benning, Editor
*Focuses on display techniques and products
for retailing designers and those responsible
for visual merchandising in stores.*

Produce Merchandising
Vance Publishing Corp.
7950 College Blvd.
Shawnee Mission, KS 66210
913-451-2200
Bill O'Neill, Editor
*Surveys new ideas in merchandising and retail
display for produce stores.*

V M & S D
International Authority on Visual Merchandising and Store Design
S T Publications Inc.
407 Gilbert Ave.
Cincinnati, OH 45202
513-421-2050
P.K. Anderson, Editor
*Covers the products and methods used by suc-
cessful visual merchandisers, store designers,
and window decorators.*

COMPANIES

Bon-Art International, Inc.
99 Evergreen Ave.
Newark, NJ 07114
201-623-6615
*Mannequins, store display products and fix-
tures.*

Hamilton Fixture Co.
4805 Hamilton-Middletown Rd.
Hamilton, OH 45012
513-868-2144
Displays and fixtures for stores.

Lozier Corp.
6336 Pershing Dr.
Omaha, NE 68110
402-457-8000
Displays and fixtures for stores.

Madix, Inc.
P. O. Box 729
Terrell, TX 75160
214-563-5744
Displays, fixtures, and checkout counters for stores.

Meg Mfg. Corp.
502 S. Green St.
Cambridge City, IN 47327
317-478-3141
Displays and fixtures for stores.

Miller/Zell Inc.
4750 Frederick Dr., S.W.
Atlanta, GA 30336
404-691-7400
Displays and fixtures for stores.

F. M. Thorpe Manufacturing Co.
(Subsidiary of L. A. Darling Inc.)
1801 Gulf
Lamar, MO 64759
417-682-3375
Point-of-purchase displays.

SUGAR INDUSTRY

ASSOCIATIONS

American Sugar Alliance
1225 Eye St. N.W., Ste. 400
Washington, DC 20005
202-457-1437
202-408-0763 Fax
Vickie Myers, Executive Director
A lobbying and public relations group for U.S. producers of sugarcane, corn, and sugar beets, the raw materials for most sweeteners.

American Sugar Cane League of the U.S.A.
PO Drawer 938
Thibodaux, LA 70302
504-448-3707
504-448-3722 Fax
P. J. deGravelles, General Manager
Members grow and process sugar cane.

The Sugar Association, Inc.
1101 15th St., N.W., No. 600
Washington, DC 20005
Charles Shamel, President
202-785-1122
202-785-5019 Fax
Offers scientific information to processors and marketers of cane and beet sugar.

PERIODICALS

Sugar Bulletin
American Sugar Cane League of the U.S.A.
201 N. Canal Blvd.
Thibodauy, LA 70301
504-448-3707
J. Kelly Nix, Editor
Surveys the U.S. sugar industry.

Sugar Journal
Kriedt Enterprises, Ltd.
4640 S. Carrollton Ave., Ste. 1D
New Orleans, LA 70119
504-482-3914
Lowell McCormick, Editor
Reports news of the U.S. and foreign sugar industry.

Sugar Producer
Harris Publishing, Inc.
520 Park Ave.
Idaho Falls, ID 83402
208-524-7000
News for the U.S. sugar beet industry.

Sugarbeet Grower
Sugar Publications
503 Broadway
Fargo, ND 58102
701-237-5747
Don Lilleboe, Editor
Technical and business information for sugar beet growers.

Weekly Review of the Market
Coffee, Sugar & Cocoa Exchange, Inc.
Four World Trade Center
New York, NY 10048
212-938-2800
Covers coffee, sugar, and cocoa market activity.

LIBRARIES

Amstar Corp.
Research and Development Library
266 Kent Ave.
Brooklyn, NY 11211
718-387-6800
718-599-0354 Fax
Sugar technology and food technology.

Hawaiian Sugar Planters' Association Experiment Station
Library
99-193 Aiea Heights Dr.
Box 1057
Aiea, HI 96701
808-487-5561
808-486-5020 Fax
Sugar technology, plant pathology, plant breeding, and agriculture.

The Sugar Association, Inc.
Library
1101 15th St., N.W., No. 600
Washington, DC 20005
202-785-1122
202-785-5019 Fax
Sugar, food technology, and nutrition.

COMPANIES

Amalgamated Sugar Co.
(Subsidiary of Valhi, Inc.)
P. O. Box 1520
Ogden, UT 84402
801-399-3431
Beet sugar products and molasses.

American Crystal Sugar Co.
101 N. Third St.
Moorhead, MN 56560
218-236-4400
Beet sugar products and molasses.

California and Hawaiian Sugar Co.
1390 Willow Pass Rd., Box 4126
Concord, CA 94520
415-356-6000
Sugar and molasses.

Colonial Sugars, Inc.
(Subsidiary of Savannah Foods & Industries, Inc.)
P.O. Box 339
Savannah, GA 31406
912-234-1261
Sugar.

Hamakua Sugar Co. Inc.
P.O. Box 250
Paauilo, HI 96776
808-776-1511
Cane sugar and molasses.

Holly Sugar Corp.
(Subsidiary of Imperial Holly Corp.)
P.O. Box 1052
Colorado Springs, CO 80901
719-471-0123
Beet sugar products.

Refined Sugars Inc.
(Subsidiary of Lantic Sugar Ltd.)
One Federal St.
Yonkers, NY 10702
914-963-2400
Cane sugar products.

Southern Minnesota Beet Sugar Cooperative
P.O. Box 500
Renville, MN 56284
612-329-8305
Beet sugar products and molasses.

Spreckels Industries
4234 Hacienda Dr.
Pleasantoli, CA 94566
415-460-0840
Sugar and other businesses.

FEDERAL GOVERNMENT

U.S. Customs Service
Department of the Treasury
U.S. Customshouse
6 World Trade Center
New York, NY 10048
212-466-5550
Ask for the Commodity Specialist in charge of sugar.

U.S. Department of Agriculture
14th St. and Independence Ave., S.W.
Washington, DC 20250
202-720-8732
Ask for the Economic Research Service.

U.S. International Trade Administration
Department of Commerce
14th St. and Constitution Ave., N.W.
Washington, DC 20230
202-377-2000
Ask for the Commodity Analyst who is an expert in the sugar industry.

U.S. International Trade Commission
500 E St., S.W.
Washington, DC 20436
202-205-2000 Office of the Secretary
202-205-3296 Industries locator
Ask for the Trade Analyst who is an expert in the sugar industry.

SUPERCONDUCTORS

Superconductors, an emerging technology, involves the efficient production and transmission of electrical energy by use of highly conductive (resistance-free) materials.

ASSOCIATIONS

Superconductor Applications Association
27692 Deputy Cir.
Laguna Hills, CA 92653
714-362-9701
714-362-9803 Fax
Tim Runner, Executive Director
A clearinghouse for information about the commercial use of superconductors.

PERIODICALS

IEEE Transactions on Applied Superconductivity
Institute of Electrical and Electronics Engineers, Inc.
345 E. 47th St.
New York, NY 10017-2394
212-705-7366
Theodore Van Duzer, Editor
Technical information on applied superconductivity and related technologies.

Journal of Superconductivity
Plenum Press
233 Spring St.
New York, NY 10013
212-620-8000
D.U. Gubser, Editor
Technical information about the full range of superconductivity topics.

Superconductor Industry
Rodman Publications, Inc.
17 S. Franklin Tpk.
Box 555
Ramsey, NJ 07446
201-825-2552
Lee Carlson, Editor
Covers companies, products, and markets for the superconductor industry.

Superconductor Week
Atlantic Information Services, Inc.
1050 17th St., N.W., Ste. 480
Washington, DC 20036
David Chaffee, Editor
Reports on new research and products involving superconductivity.

COMPANIES

Eriez Magnetics
Asbury Rd. at Airport
Erie, PA 16514
814-833-9881
Separating equipment employing superconductivity technology.

Hypres, Inc.
175 Clearbrook
Elmsford, NY 10523
914-592-1190
Electronics test equipment employing superconductivity technology.

Intermagnetics General Corp.
P.O. Box 566
Guilderland, NY 12084
518-456-5456
Superconducting magnets and related products.

Satcon Technology Corp.
12 Emily St.
Cambridge, MA 02139
617-661-0540
Superconducting magnet products.

Supercon, Inc.
830 Boston Tpke.
Shrewsbury, MA 01545
508-842-0174
Insulated wire employing superconductivity technology.

Xsirius Superconductivity Inc.
1110 N. Glebe Rd.
Arlington, VA 22201
703-522-8601
Research on superconductivity.

FEDERAL GOVERNMENT

U.S. Department of Energy
1000 Independence Ave., S.W.
Washington, DC 20585
202-586-5000
Ask for the Superconducting Supercollider division in the Energy Research Administration.

U.S. International Trade Administration
Department of Commerce
14th St. and Constitution Ave., N.W.
Washington, DC 20230
202-377-2000
Ask for the Commodity Analyst who is an expert in superconductors.

SUPERMARKETS AND CONVENIENCE STORES

See also: GROCERY BUSINESS and RETAIL TRADE

ASSOCIATIONS

Food Marketing Institute
1750 K St. N.W., Ste. 700
Washington, DC 20006
202-452-8444
202-429-4519
Robert Aders, President
Offers seminars and services to convenience store owners and grocers.

National Association of Convenience Stores
1605 King St.
Alexandria, VA 22314-2792
703-684-3600
703-836-4564 Fax
Kerley LeBoeuf, President
Members own convenience stores that sell groceries, cigarettes, gasoline, fast food, and other items.

PERIODICALS

Convenience Store News
B M T Publications, Inc.
7 Penn Plaza
New York, NY 10001-3900
212-594-4120
Barbara Grondin, Editor
News and feature articles about the convenience store industry.

Food Industry Newsletter
Newsletters, Inc.
Box 2730
Bethesda, MD 20827
301-469-8507
Max Busetti, Editor
Written for managers of firms that sell food products through supermarkets.

General Merchandise News
712 Fair Oaks Ave., Ste. 211
South Pasadena, CA 91030
818-799-0231
Marian Bond, Editor
Covers developments for firms that sell beauty, health, and general merchandise through supermarkets and chain stores.

Supermarket News
Fairchild Publications, Inc.
7 W. 34th St.
New York, NY 10001
212-630-3770
Tim Simmons, Editor
Surveys news, trends, and opinions for supermarket executives and others.

Supermarket Strategic Alert
Pollack Associates
140 E. 81st St., Ste. 5E
New York, NY 10028
212-734-0563
Mary Pollack, Editor
Reports on the supermarket industry as covered by other business and trade periodicals.

COMPANIES

Albertson's Inc.
250 Parkcenter Blvd.
Boise, ID 83726
208-385-6200
Owns and operates supermarkets.

Dillon Companies, Inc.
(Subsidiary of Kroger Co.)
700 E. 30th Ave.
Hutchinson, KS 67501
316-663-6801
Owns and operates supermarkets and convenience stores.

Food Lion Inc.
P.O. Box 1330
Salisbury, NC 28144
704-633-8250
Owns and operates supermarkets.

Giant Food, Inc.
6300 Sheriff Rd.
Landover, MD 20785
301-341-4100
Owns and operates supermarkets.

Hy-Vee Food Stores, Inc.
1801 Osceola Ave.
Chariton, IA 50049
515-774-2121
Owns and operates supermarkets and drug stores.

Price Chopper Operating Co.
(Subsidiary of Golub Corp.)
501 Duanesburg Rd.
Schenectady, NY 12306
518-355-5000
Owns and operates supermarkets.

Purity Supreme Supermarkets
(Division of Supermarkets General Corp.)
101 Billerica Ave.
North Billerica, MA 01862
508-663-0750
Owns and operates supermarkets and conve-
nience stores.

Southland Corp.
2711 N. Haskell Ave.
Dallas, TX 75221
214-828-7011
Owns and operates convenience stores.

Stop & Shop Holdings Inc.
(Subsidiary of SSC Holdings Corp.)
P.O. Box 369
Boston, MA 02101
617-380-8000
Owns and operates supermarkets.

Tom Thumb Stores, Inc.
(Subsidiary of Cullum Companies, Inc.)
14303 Inwood Rd.
Dallas, TX 75244
214-661-9700
Owns and operates supermarkets.

Vons Companies, Inc.
618 Michillinoa
Arcadia, CA 91007
818-821-7019
Owns and operates supermarkets.

FEDERAL GOVERNMENT

U.S. International Trade Administration
Department of Commerce
14th St. and Constitution Ave., N.W.
Washington, DC 20230
202-377-2000
Ask for the analyst who is an expert in super-
markets and convenience stores.

SURPLUS PRODUCTS

ASSOCIATIONS

Associated Surplus Dealers
PO Box 250046
Los Angeles, CA 90025
213-477-2556
800-421-4511
W. J. Fletcher, Executive Director
Represents close-out dealers, surplus dealers,
manufacturers, and others.

Investment Recovery Association
30200 Detroit Rd.
Cleveland, OH 44145-1967
216-899-0010
216-892-1404 Fax
Allen Wherry, Executive Director
Provides seminars and advice to all industries
which wish to sell their surplus assets, yet are
not sales firms and wish to minimize their lia-
bility risks.

National Association State Agencies for Surplus Property
522 South 700 West
Salt Lake City, UT 84104
801-533-5885
Marvin Titzman, Executive Officer
State agencies that distribute surplus goods on behalf of the federal government to local nonprofit organizations.

Resources Exchange Association Foundation
PO Box 2876
Petersburg, VA 23804
804-733-0287
804-733-0441 Fax
James Jones, Executive Officer
Helps nonprofits, colleges, and schools collect surplus goods and gifts-in-kind from the corporations that donate these goods.

PERIODICALS

Army—Navy Store & Outdoor Merchandiser
Howmark Publishing Corp.
567 Morris Ave.
Elizabeth, NJ 07208
201-353-7373
Merchandising and management information for retailers selling military surplus, closeout products, and related items.

Auction and Surplus
News Circle Publishing House
1250 W. Glenoaks Blvd., Unit E.
Box 3684
Glendale, CA 91201-0684
818-545-0333
Joseph Haiek, Editor
Offers information about liquidations, closeouts, surplus sales, and auctions to corporate buyers of surplus goods.

Surplus Record
Surplus Record, Inc.
20 N. Wacker Dr.
Chicago, IL 60606
312-372-9077
Thomas Scanlan, Editor
A listing of surplus and used capital equipment such as machinery, equipment, and electrical good available throughout the U.S.

COMPANIES

Commodities Recovery Corp.
217 Brook Ave.
Passaic, NJ 07055
201-778-8777
Buys and sells all kinds of surplus goods.

Elgin Salvage & Supply Co.
464 McBride St.
Elgin, IL 60120
708-742-9500
Surplus machinery and scrap metals.

Pic 'n' Save Corp.
2430 E. Del Amo Blvd
Dominguez, CA 90220
213-537-9220
Retailer of close-out products.

Surplus International
409 Almonesson Rd.
Blenheim, NJ
609-227-1796
Buys and sells surplus industrial and consumer goods of all kinds.

Value Merchants, Inc.
710 N. Plankinton Ave.
Milwaukee, WI 53209
414-274-2575
Distributor and retailer of close-out items.

Wisconsin Toy Co., Inc.
710 N. Plankinton Ave.
Milwaukee, WI 53203
414-274-2575
Distributor and retailer of close-out toys.

SWIMMING POOL INDUSTRY

ASSOCIATIONS

National Spa and Pool Institute
2111 Eisenhower Ave.
Alexandria, VA 22314
703-838-0083
703-549-0493 Fax
William Sadd, Executive Director
Offers information to pool and spa designers, manufacturers, builders, dealers, suppliers, and others.

National Swimming Pool Foundation
10803 Gulfdale, Ste. 300
San Antonio, TX 78216
512-525-1227
512-344-3713 Fax
Evelyn Robinson, Executive Director
A small group that promotes research into pool construction, maintenance, safety, and related issues.

PERIODICALS

Aquatics
Communication Channels, Inc.
6255 Barfield Rd.
Atlanta, GA 30328-4369
404-256-9800
Terri Simmons, Editor
Reports on the design, management, maintenance, and programming of public and semi-public swimming facilities, including pools and beaches.

Pool & Spa News
Leisure Publications, Inc.
3923 W. 6th St.
Los Angeles, CA 90020
213-385-3926
Covers news, trends, and equipment for swimming pool and spa executives and owners.

Swimming Pool—Spa Age
Communication Channels, Inc.
6255 Barfield Rd.
Atlanta, GA 30328-4369
404-256-9800
Terri Simmons, Editor
Offers swimming pool, hot tub, and spa dealers and contractors information about building, installing, and maintaining their products.

Swimming Pool and Spa Dealer News
Creative Media, Inc.
10244 Best Dr.
Dallas, TX 75229
Alice Pies, Editor
Product and merchandising information for pool dealers.

Swimming Pools Today
National Swimming Pool Owner's Association
1213 Ridgecrest Circle
Denton, TX 76205
Tom Doron, Editor
Advice for swimming pool owners about pool cleaning, safety, repair, and related topics.

LIBRARIES

International Swimming Hall of Fame
Museum & Library
One Hall of Fame Dr.
Fort Lauderdale, FL 33316
305-462-6536
305-525-4031 Fax
Pool care and management, swim officiating, swimming history, and other subjects.

COMPANIES

Bio-Lab, Inc.
(Subsidiary of Great Lakes Chemical Corp.)
627 E. College Ave.
Decatur, GA 30030
404-378-1753
Swimming pool chemicals.

Delair Group Inc.
8600 River Rd.
Delair, NJ 08110
609-663-2900
Swimming pools and spa builders.

Hayward Industries, Inc.
900 Fairmount Ave.
Elizabeth, NJ 07207
908-351-5400
Swimming pool equipment and supplies.

Heldor Industries, Inc.
One Cory Rd.
Morristown, NJ 07960
201-898-9445
Swimming pools, chemicals, ladders, and other pool accessories.

Jacuzzi Inc.
(Subsidiary of Hanson Industries North
    America)
12401 I-30
Little Rock, AR 72209
501-455-1234
Whirlpool, spa, and swimming pool equipment.

KD Holdings, Corp.
5721 Dragon Way
Cincinnati, OH 45227
513-272-1421
Swimming pools and equipment.

KDI Sylvan Pools, Inc.
(Subsidiary of KDI Corp.)
Rte. 611
Doylestown, PA 18901
215-348-9011
Swimming pools and equipment.

Muskin, Inc.
(Subsidiary of U.S. Leisure, Inc.)
401 E. Thomas St.
Wilkes-Barre, PA 18705
717-825-4501
Swimming pools and equipment.

Poseidon Pools of America, Inc.
50th St. & First Ave.
Brooklyn, NY 11232
718-788-8060
Swimming pools and equipment.

Sta-Rite Industries, Inc.
(Subsidiary of WICOR, Inc.)
777 E. Wisconsin Ave.
Milwaukee, WI 53202
414-276-6888
*Pumps and filters for swimming pools and
other uses.*

SWINE INDUSTRY

See also: LIVESTOCK INDUSTRY

ASSOCIATIONS

National Feeder Pig Marketing Association
c/o Keith E. Myers
Rt. 1
Grundy Center, IA 50638
319-824-6996
Keith Myers, Secretary
*A small group that offers marketing informa-
tion to those in the feeder pig industry.*

National Pork Producers Council
PO Box 10383
Des Moines, IA 50306
515-223-2600
515-223-2646 Fax
Russ Sanders, Executive Vice President
*A very large group representing swine breed-
ers and pork producers.*

PERIODICALS

Iowa Pork Producer
Iowa Pork Producers Association
Box 71009
Clive, IA 50325-0009
515-225-7675
Andrew Baumert, Editor
*Covers a wide range of issues concerning the
swine industry in Iowa and around the nation.*

Swine Practitioner
Vance Publishing Corp.
7950 College Blvd.
Shawnee Mission, KS 66210
913-451-2200
Thomas Quaife, Editor
*Technical and industry information for swine
growers.*

COMPANIES

W. H. Conyngham & Co., Inc.
1234 United Penn Bank Bldg.
Wilkes-Barre, PA 18701
717-822-7188
Beef and pig farming.

Dekalb Genetics Corp.
3100 Sycamore Rd.
De Kalb, IL 60115
815-758-3461
Swine breeding stock and other products.

K.G. Johnson Livestock Equip., Inc.
Rte. 3, Hwy. 33 W.
Baraboo, WI 53913
608-356-4547
Equipment for swine production.

Snowflake Pig Farms, Inc.
P.O. Box AF
Snowflake, AZ 85937
602-536-7183
Pig farming.

United Supplies, Inc.
Airport Rd.
Eldora, IA 50627
515-858-2341
Swine semen and other products.

Waldo Farms
RR1
DeWitt, NE 68341
402-683-5225
Swine breeding stock.

FEDERAL GOVERNMENT

U.S. Department of Agriculture
14th St. and Independence Ave., S.W.
Washington, DC 20250
202-720-8732
Ask for the Economic Research Service.

U.S. Food and Drug Administration
7500 Standish Place
Rockville, MD 20855
301-443-4500
Ask for the Swine & Poultry Drugs division.

U.S. International Trade Administration
Department of Commerce
14th St. and Constitution Ave., N.W.
Washington, DC 20230
202-377-2000
*Ask for the Commodity Analyst who is an
expert in the swine industry.*

U.S. International Trade Commission
500 E St., S.W.
Washington, DC 20436
202-205-2000 Office of the Secretary
202-205-3296 Industries locator
*Ask for the Trade Analyst who is an expert in
the swine industry.*

TABLEWARE INDUSTRY

See also: GIFT INDUSTRY and GLASS AND GLASS PRODUCTS

ASSOCIATION

American Cutlery Manufacturers Association
1101 14th St. N.W., Ste. 1100
Washington, DC 20005
202-371-1262
202-371-1090 Fax
David Barrack, Executive Director
Provides research and educational seminars to manufacturers of cutlery, knives, and scissors.

American Pewter Guild
c/o Fischer Pewter Hdqtrs.
440 Southlake Blvd.
Richmond, VA 23236
804-379-3282
Nellie Fischer, Secretary
Represents manufacturers and distributors of pewter.

American Restaurant China Council
PO Box 1417
Alexandria, VA 22313
707-938-5909
Irving Mills, Executive Director
Represents firms that make china used in hotels and restaurants.

Associated Glass and Pottery Manufacturers
c/o Harold L. Hayes
2800 E. Military Rd.
Zanesville, OH 43701
614-452-8329
Harold Hayes, Secretary
Serves the ceramic dinnerware industry.

China, Glass and Giftware Association
1115 Clifton Ave.
Clifton, NJ 07013
201-779-1600
201-779-3242 Fax
Donald Doctorow, Executive Secretary
Provides information on the china, glass, and giftware industry.

National Tabletop Association
355 Lexington Ave., 17th Fl.
New York, NY 10017
212-661-4261
212-370-9047 Fax
Mark Holland, Executive Director
Offers statistical data and seminars to manufacturers of flatware, crystal, linens, and other forms of tableware.

Sterling Silversmiths Guild of America
312-A Wyndhurst Ave.
Baltimore, MD 21210
301-532-7062
Robert Johnston, Executive Vice President
Helps promote sales of sterling silver tableware through sales training and public relations programs.

PERIODICALS

China Glass & Tableware
Doctorow Communications, Inc.
1115 Clifton Ave.
Clifton, NJ 07013
201-779-1600
Amy Stavis, Editor
Reports on new trends and products in the tableware business.

Gift & Stationery Business
Gralla Publications
1515 Broadway
New York, NY 10036
212-869-1300
Joyce Washnick, Editor
Offers management and merchandising information, as well as industry news, to retailers of paper and gift items including tableware.

Gifts & Decorative Accessories
Geyer-McAllister Publications, Inc.
51 Madison Ave.
New York, NY 10010
212-689-4411
Phyllis Sweed, Editor
Surveys trends and new products in the gift, tableware, gourmet, home accessory, greeting card, and social stationery industries.

Giftware News
Talcott Communications Corp.
1414 Merchandise Mart
Chicago, IL 60654
312-670-0800
Anthony Demasi, Editor
Covers products and news for corporate buyers of gifts, china and glass, stationery and home accessories.

COMPANIES

Bartlett-Collins Co., Inc.
(Subsidiary of Lancaster Colony Corp.)
P.O. Box 1288
Sapulpa, OK 74067
918-224-1860
Glass tableware.

Blenko Glass Co., Inc.
P.O. Box 67
Milton, WV 25541
304-743-9081
Glass tableware made by hand.

Ebeling & Reuss Co.
477 N. Lewis
Royers Ford, PA 19468
215-687-8930
Wholesale importers of glass and china tableware.

Lifetime Hoan Corp.
820 3rd Ave.
Brooklyn, NY 11232
718-499-9500
Stainless steel tableware and flatware.

Lunt Silversmiths
(Subsidiary of Rogers, Lunt & Bowlen Co.)
298 Federal St.
Greenfield, MA 01301
413-774-2774
Tableware and cutlery made from sterling silver.

Oneida Ltd.
Kenwood Station
Oneida, NY 13421
315-361-3000
Sterling silver and stainless steel tableware and related products.

Utica Cutlery Co.
820 Noyes St.
Utica, NY 13502
315-733-4663
Stainless steel cutlery and tableware, and related products.

Wheaton Industries
Wheaton Ave.
Millville, NJ 08332
609-825-1400
Crystal and glass tableware, and related products.

Towle Manufacturing Co.
260 Merrimac St.
Newburyport, MA 01950
617-229-1919
Sterling silver and stainless steel flatware, crystal tableware, and related products.

FEDERAL GOVERNMENT

U.S. Customs Service
Department of the Treasury
U.S. Customshouse
6 World Trade Center
New York, NY 10048
212-466-5550
Ask for the Commodity Specialist in charge of tableware products.

U.S. International Trade Administration
Department of Commerce
14th St. and Constitution Ave., N.W.
Washington, DC 20230
202-377-2000
Ask for the Commodity Analyst who is an expert in the tableware industry.

U.S. International Trade Commission
500 E St., S.W.
Washington, DC 20436
202-205-2000 Office of the Secretary
202-205-3296 Industries locator
Ask for the Trade Analyst who is an expert in the tableware industry.

TAXATION

See also: ACCOUNTING and each of the 50 states under taxation and revenue

ASSOCIATIONS

American Taxation Association
c/o American Accounting Association
5717 Bessie Dr.
Sarasota, FL 34233
813-921-7747
Kenneth Heller, President
A group of university professors and researchers who study the effect of taxation on the U.S.

Business and Tax Planning Board
10 Paragon Dr.
Montvale, NJ 07645
201-573-6219
201-573-8185 Fax
J. B. Schiff, Consulting Director
Provides educational programs to chief executives and other senior executives responsible for their company's tax planning.

Center for Local Tax Research
121 E. 30th St.
New York, NY 10016
212-889-8020
Steven Cord, Executive Director
Members share information on local taxation.

International Tax Institute
787 7th Ave.
New York, NY 10019
212-407-3398
Jim Tobin, President
Members are CPA's, tax lawyers, and executives concerned with U.S. taxation of foreign income.

National Association of Tax Practitioners
720 Association Dr.
Appleton, WI 54914
414-749-1040
Gene Honn, Executive Director
Offers promotional and educational programs for CPA's and other tax preparers.

National Tax Association—Tax Institute of America
5310 E. Main St., Ste. 104
Columbus, OH 43213
614-864-1221
Frederick Stocker, Executive Director
Supports a wide range of taxation research for governments, businesses, and the accounting profession.

Research Institute of America
90 5th Ave.
New York, NY 10011
212-337-4100
Allan Morse, President
Produces and sells a wide range of technical publications for accountants, executives, and others.

Tax Executives Institute
1001 Pennsylvania Ave. N.W., Ste. 320
Washington, DC 20004
202-638-5601
Thomas Kerester, Executive Director
An information resource for corporate executives responsible for their employers' tax decisions.

Tax Foundation
470 L'Enfant Plaza East S.W., Ste. 7112
Washington, DC 20024
202-863-5454
202-638-5607 Fax
Wayne Gable, President
Conducts research on federal, state, and local tax and fiscal issues.

PERIODICALS

Journal of Taxation
Warren, Gorham and Lamont Inc.
One Penn Plaza
New York, NY 10119
800-950-1217
Ronald Klinger, Editor
Follows rulings and news about taxes and offers advice to tax accountants.

Monthly Digest of Tax Articles
Newkirk Products, Inc.
15 Corporate Circle
Albany, NY 12203
518-452-1000
James Blake, Editor
Surveys tax writings in other publications.

National Tax Journal
National Tax Association—Tax Institute of
    America
5310 E. Main St., Ste. 104
Columbus, OH 43213
614-864-1221
Daniel Holland, Editor
Covers tax issues in the U.S. and abroad.

Practical Tax Lawyer
American Law Institute
4025 Chestnut St.
Philadelphia, PA 19104
215-243-1604
Mark Carroll, Editor
How-to advice, checklists, and forms for tax attorneys.

Tax Adviser
American Institute of Certified Public
    Accountants
1211 Ave. of the Americas
New York, NY 10036-8775
212-575-6200
N. Fiore, Editor
Advice for accountants about tax planning, trends, techniques.

LIBRARIES

American Institute of Certified Public
    Accountants
1211 Ave. of the Americas
New York, NY 10036
212-575-6200
212-575-3846 Fax
800-223-4155 Library services
800-522-5434 Library services in NY state
800-223-4158 Technical information
800-522-5430 Technical information in NY
    state
Philip Chenok, President
Covers the full range of accounting and taxation subjects.

National Association of Accountants
10 Paragon Dr.
Montvale, NJ 07645
201-573-9000
800-638-4427
201-573-8185 Fax
Gary Scopes, Executive Director
Accounting, taxation, accounting practice management, and related topics.

Tax Foundation
470 L'Enfant Plaza East S.W., Ste. 7112
Washington, DC 20024
202-863-5454
202-638-5607 Fax
Tax and fiscal issues.

COMPANIES

Arthur Andersen & Co.
69 West Washington St.
Chicago, IL 60602
312-346-6262
Accounting firm.

Matthew Bender & Co. Inc.
(Subsidiary of Times Mirror Co.)
1275 Broadway
Albany, NY 12201
518-487-3000
Publisher of technical books on taxation and legal subjects.

CCH Computax Inc.
(Subsidiary of Commerce Clearing House, Inc.)
21250 Hawthorne Blvd.
Torrance, CA 90503
213-543-6200
Computerized tax-processing services for professional tax preparers.

General Business Services, Inc.
20271 Goldenrod Lane
Germantown, MD 20874
301-428-1040
Record-keeping, data processing, and tax services for small businesses.

H & R Block, Inc.
4410 Main St.
Kansas City, MO 64111
816-753-6900
Preparation of income tax returns.

Computer Language Research, Inc.
2395 Midway Rd.
Carrollton, TX 75006
214-250-7000
Automated income tax services.

Coopers & Lybrand
1251 Avenue of the Americas
New York, NY 10020
212-536-2000
Accounting firm.

Price Waterhouse & Co.
1251 Avenue of the Americas
New York, NY 10020
212-489-8900
Accounting firm.

SCS/Compute Inc.
12444 Powerscourt Dr.
St. Louis, MO 63131
314-966-1040
Software for tax return preparers.

FEDERAL GOVERNMENT

Internal Revenue Service
Department of the Treasury
1111 Constitution Ave., N.W.
Washington, DC 20224
202-566-5000
Ask for the public relations office to find an appropriate expert.

TAXICAB AND LIMOUSINE INDUSTRY

ASSOCIATIONS

International Taxicab Association
3849 Farragut Ave.
Kensington, MD 20895
301-946-5701
Alfred LaGasse, Executive Vice President
Represents owners of taxi, limousine, and van fleets.

National Limousine Association
1300 L St. N.W., Ste. 1050
Washington, DC 20005
202-682-1426
800-NLA-7007
202-898-0484 Fax
Wayne Smith, Executive Director
Provides management training to owners and operators of limousines.

COMPANIES

Carey Limousine, Inc.
62-07 Woodside Ave.
Queens, NY
212-599-1122
Limousine service.

Metro Transportation Co.
3111 Grays Ferry Ave.
Philadelphia, PA 19146
215-551-6650
Taxicab service.

Rudy's Limousine Service, Inc.
P.O. Box 295
Riverside, CT 06878
203-869-0014
Limousine service.

Specialty Hearse & Ambulance Sales Corp.
180 Dupont St.
Plainview, NY 11803
516-349-7700
Builder of ambulances, hearses, and customized limousines.

Yellow Cab Co.
(Subsidiary of Yellow Transportation, Inc.)
2100 Huntington Ave.
Baltimore, MD 21211
301-727-7300
Taxicab and limousine service.

TECHNOLOGY TRANSFER

Technology transfer is the study of how to efficiently and profitably sell or license patents to businesses that will commercialize the new technology. Universities, government laboratories, and small companies are usually the sources of technology that is transferred.

ASSOCIATIONS

Industry Coalition on Technology Transfer
1400 L St. N.W., 8th Fl.
Washington, DC 20005-3502
202-371-5994
202-371-5950 Fax
Eric Hirschhorn, Executive Secretary
Consists of ten associations, primarily in the electronics industry, that study legislation and regulations that affect technology transfer.

Licensing Executives Society
71 East Ave.
Norwalk, CT 06851
203-852-7168
203-838-5714 Fax
James Menge, Executive Director
Teaches about technology transfer techniques and issues to business people, scientists, attorneys and others. Affiliated with the Association of University Technology Managers at the same telephone number and address, which helps patent managers at universities.

Technology Transfer Society
611 N. Capitol Ave.
Indianapolis, IN 46204
317-262-5022
317-262-5044 Fax
F. Timothy Janis, President
A clearinghouse for information about technology transfer techniques and issues.

PERIODICALS

Federal Technology Transfer
National Technology Transfer Institute
1200 Pennsylvania Ave.
Box 7206
Washington, DC 20044
703-931-0511
Kurt Willinger, Editor
Surveys laboratories sponsored by the federal government and the technologies they transfer to businesses in the U.S.

Healthcare Technology & Business Opportunities
Biomedical Business International
1524 Brookhollow Dr.
Santa Ana, CA 92705-5426
714-755-5757
Lists patents and technologies available for sale and license in the healthcare field.

Journal of Technology Transfer
Technology Transfer Society
611 N. Capitol Ave.
Indianapolis, IN 46204
317-262-5022
Ralph Segman, Editor
Advises how to successfully transfer technology for commercial application.

Technology Management Action
Technology News Center
Box 335
Morgan Hill, CA 95037
408-778-0889
Norman Lynn, Editor
Reports on how technology is distributed and used.

LIBRARIES

Association of University Related Research
　　Parks
Reference Library
4500 S. Lakeshore Dr., Ste. 475
Tempe, AZ 85282
602-752-2002
602-752-2003 Fax
High technology, research parks, technology transfer, and planning issues.

Chapman Research Group, Inc.
Library
5601 S. Broadway, Ste. 306
Littleton, CO 80121
303-730-2226
Technology transfer and new venture development.

Technology Transfer Society
Library
611 N. Capitol Ave.
Indianapolis, IN 46204
317-262-5022
317-262-5044 Fax
Technology transfer.

University of Oklahoma
Science and Public Policy Program
Library
601 Elm Ave., Rm 431
Norman, OK 73019
405-325-2554
Technology assessment, energy policy, information transfer, and science policy.

TELECOMMUNICATIONS INDUSTRY

See also: MOBILE TELEPHONE INDUSTRY

ASSOCIATIONS

Computer and Communications Industry
  Association
666 11th St. N.W., Ste. 600
Washington, DC 20001
202-783-0070
202-783-0534 Fax
A. Biddle, President
*Provides market, technological, and other
types of information to manufacturers of computers and computer telecommunications
products.*

IEEE Communications Society
c/o Inst. of Electrical and Electronics Engineers
345 E. 47th St.
New York, NY 10017
212-705-7867
*A professional society for engineers, computer
scientists, and others interested in telecommunications and computer telecommunications.*

International Association of Telecomputer
  Networks
660 E. Hwy. 434, Ste. A
Winter Springs, FL 32708
407-327-3270
Michael Sprouse, Executive Vice President
*A clearinghouse for information about tele-
computer networks (in which computer users
can send and receive messages and data trans-
mitted by modems).*

National Association of Telecommunications
  Dealers
1255 23rd St. N.W.
Washington, DC 20037
202-872-8420
202-833-3636 Fax
Mark Engle, Executive Director
*Members recondition and sell used telecom-
munications equipment.*

North American Telecommunications Association
2000 M St. N.W., Ste. 550
Washington, DC 20036
202-296-9800
202-296-4993 Fax
Edwin Spievack, President
*Offers a variety of educational, research, and
public relations services to manufacturers and
suppliers of computers, communications and
office equipment, and to others in the telecommunications industry.*

Society of Telecommunications Consultants
PO Box 810776
Boca Raton, FL 33481-0776
800-782-7670
212-262-8341 Fax
Effie Cooper, Executive Director
*A professional society that promotes the
employment of telecommunications consultants.*

Telecommunications Cooperative Network
505 Eighth Ave., Ste. 1805
New York, NY 10018
212-714-9780
Robert Loeb, President
This group of hospitals, universities, and other nonprofit institutions offers information about and discounts on telecommunication equipment.

Telecommunications Industry Association
2001 Pennsylvania Ave. N.W., Ste. 800
Washington, DC 20006-1813
202-457-4912
202-457-4939 Fax
Allen Frischkorn, President
Manufacturers of telecommunications products and firms that offer services to manufacturers.

PERIODICALS

Business Communications Review
B C R Enterprises, Inc.
950 York Rd.
Hinsdale, IL 60521-2939
312-986-1432
Fred Knight, Editor
Provides telecommunications managers with information about new products, industry trends, and issues.

Communications in Finance
Investment Dealers' Digest
2 World Trade Ctr., 18th Fl.
New York, NY 10048
212-227-1200
Covers the technologies and management of data and voice telecommunications in the finance and banking industries.

Datapro Management of Telecommunications
Datapro Research Corp.
1805 Underwood Blvd.
Delran, NJ 08075
609-764-0100
Lance Lindstrom, Editor
Advice and how-to information for telecommunications managers.

F C C Week
Capitol Publications Inc.
1101 King St., Ste. 444
Box 1455
Alexandria, VA 22313-2055
800-327-7205
Anne LaLena, Editor
Focusses on Federal Communications Commission telecommunications policies and regulations.

Independent Telco News
Capitol Publications, Inc.
1101 King St., Ste. 444
Box 1455
Alexandria, VA 22313-2055
800-327-7205
Beth Melville, Editor
News of technologies, markets, regulations, and issues of concern to managers of independent telephone companies.

Link-UpLearned Information, Inc.
143 Old Marlton Pike
Medford, NJ 08055
609-654-6266
Joseph Webb, Editor
Information for computer owners who use their modems to search online databases.

Long-Distance Letter
Phillips Publishing, Inc.
7811 Montrose Rd.
Potomac, MD 20854
301-340-2100
Ray Py, Editor
Surveys the long distance telecommunications industry.

Telecom Gear
Link House Publications, Inc.
15400 Knoll Trail., Ste. 500
Dallas, TX 75248
214-233-5131
Information about telecommunications equipment.

Telecom Insider
International Data Corp.
5 Speen St.
Box 9015
Framingham, MA 01701
508-872-8200
Alan Pearce, Editor
Covers telecommunications markets, technology, policy, and regulations.

Telecommunications Alert
United Communications Group
11300 Rockville Pike, Ste. 1100
Rockville, MD 20852-3030
301-816-8950
Doug O'Boyle, Editor
Surveys news about the telecommunications industry that appears in major business and telecommunications publications.

Telecommunications Product Review and
    CPE Strategies
Aries Group—MPSG
1350 Piccard Dr., Ste. 300
Rockville, MD 20850
301-840-0800
Sue Rubinstein, Editor
Reviews telecommununications products and services.

Telecommunications Week
Business Research Publications, Inc.
817 Broadway
New York, NY 10003
212-673-4700
Karen Kinard, Editor
Helps telecommunications executives keep abreast of industry news and trends.

LIBRARIES

AT & T Consumer Products
Teletype Library
7600 Interstate 30
P.O. Box 8912
Little Rock, AR 72219
501-569-4260
Telecommunications and systems engineering.

GTE Telephone Operations Headquarter
Market Research Library
4500 Fuller Dr.
MCF04P01
Irving, TX 75038
214-718-5549
214-718-5276 Fax
Telecommunications and technology.

Michigan Bell Telephone Co.
Corporate Reference and Development
    Center
1365 Cass Ave., Rm. 1200
Detroit, MI 48226
313-223-8045
313-223-8095 Fax
Telecommunications, marketing, and management.

U.S. Federal Communications Commission
Library
1919 M St., N.W.
Washington, DC 20554
202-632-7100
Telecommunications, law, public utility regulation and management.

COMPANIES

Contel Corp.
(Subsidiary of GTE Corp.)
One Stamford Forum
Stamford, CT 06904
203-965-2000
Telecommunications services.

DSC Communications Corp.
1000 Coit Rd.
Plano, TX 75075
214-519-3000
Telecommunications equipment and other products.

GTE Communication Systems Corp.
(Subsidiary of GTE Products of Connecticut
    Corp.)
One Stamford Forum
Stamford, CT 06904
203-965-2000
Telecommunications products and services.

NEC America, Inc.
(Subsidiary of NEC Corp.)
8 Old Sod Farm Rd.
Melville, NY 11747
516-753-7000
Telecommunications equipment and other products.

Nynex Corp.
335 Madison Ave.
New York, NY 10017
212-370-7400
Telecommunications services.

Southwestern Bell Co.
(Subsidiary of Southwestern Bell Corp.)
1010 Pine St.
St. Louis, MO 63101
314-235-9800
Telecommunication services.

Toshiba America, Inc.
(Subsidiary of Toshiba Corp.)
375 Park Ave.
New York, NY 10152
212-308-2040
Telecommunications and many other types of products.

United Telecommunications, Inc.
P.O. Box 11315
Kansas City, MO 64112
913-676-3000
Telecommunications equipment.

Wisconsin Bell, Inc.
(Subsidiary of Ameritech Corp.)
722 N. Broadway
Milwaukee, WI 53202
414-549-7102
Telecommunications services.

FEDERAL GOVERNMENT

General Services Administration
18th & F St., N.W.
Washington, DC 20405
202-708-5082
Ask for the Office of Telecommunications Customer Requirements or the Office of Telecommunications Services.

U.S. Customs Service
Department of the Treasury
U.S. Customshouse
6 World Trade Center
New York, NY 10048
212-466-5550
Ask for the Commodity Specialist in charge of telecommunications equipment.

U.S. International Trade Commission
500 E St., S.W.
Washington, DC 20436
202-205-2000 Office of the Secretary
202-205-3296 Industries locator
*Ask for the Trade Analyst who is an expert in
telecommunications.*

U.S. Patent and Trademark Office
Crystal Plaza 2
2011 Jefferson Davis Highway
Arlington, VA 22202
703-305-8000
*Ask for the Examining Group Director who is
a specialist in telecommunications equipment.*

TELEMARKETING

See also: MARKETING

ASSOCIATIONS

American Telemarketing Association
5000 Van Nuys Blvd., No. 400
Sherman Oaks, CA 91403
818-995-7338
800-441-3335
Cheryl Green, Executive Director
*Helps telemarketers run their businesses more
effectively. Tries to increase public acceptance
of telephone sales.*

Alliance Against Fraud in Telemarketing
c/o National Consumers League
815 15th St. N.W., Ste. 516
Washington, DC 20005
202-639-8140
Sara Cooper, Coordinator
*Trade associations, government agencies, and
consumer groups who work to reduce telemarketing fraud.*

PERIODICALS

T S R Hotline
F.G.I. and Affiliated Publishing Companies,
    Inc.
80 Scenic Dr., Ste. 7
Freehold, NJ 07728
908-780-7020
Lee Van Vechten, Editor
Teaches sales and telephone techniques.

Telemarketer
Actel Marketing
200 Park Ave., Ste. 303
New York, NY 10166
212-674-2540
Aldyn McKean, Editor
*Surveys such telemarketing topics as generat-
ing leads, selling techniques, and fund raising.*

Telemarketing
Technology Marketing Corp.
One Technology Plaza
Norwalk, CT 06854
203-852-6800
Linda Driscoll, Editor
*Advice for managers of telemarketing opera-
tions.*

Telemarketing Update
Update Publicare Co.
c/o Prosperity & Profits Unlimited
Box 570213
Houston, TX 77257-0213
Art Sobczak, Editor
Suggests telemarketing scripts and techniques.

Telephone Selling Report
Telemarketing Design, Inc.
5301 S. 144th St.
Omaha, NE 68137
402-895-9399
A. Doyle, Editor
How-to information for everyone who sells over the phone.

COMPANIES

American Transtech
(Subsidiary of AT&T)
8000 Baymeadows Way
Jacksonville, FL 32256
904-636-1000
Inbound and outbound telemarketing.

C & C Information Systems
54 Willow Park Center
Farmingdale, NY 11735
800-424-7669
Inbound and outbound telemarketing.

FCB/Direct
(Subsidiary of Foote, Cone & Belding Communications, Inc.)
11601 Wilshire Blvd.
Los Angeles, CA 90025
818-571-6600
Direct mailing and telemarketing services.

Marketing Missions, Ltd.
19 W. 44th St.
New York, NY
212-575-2525
Inbound and outbound telemarketing.

The Telemarketing Co.
5306 W. Lawrence
Chicago, IL
312-545-0407
Inbound and outbound telemarketing.

Telephone Marketing Services
(Subsidiary of Cincinnati Bell Co.)
2727 Madison Rd.
Cincinnati, OH
513-321-1888
Inbound and outbound telemarketing.

TMI Fulfillment
(Division of TMI Corp.)
155 Allen Blvd.
Farmingdale, NY 11735
516-249-0860
Inbound telemarketing and other services.

TELEPHONE ANSWERING SERVICE INDUSTRY

ASSOCIATIONS

Association of Telemessaging Services, International
1150 S. Washington St., Ste. 150
Alexandria, VA 22314
703-684-0016
Joseph Laseau, Executive Vice President
Offers technical and industry information to telephone answering services.

Association of Telephone Answering Services
c/o Monte Engler
Phillips, Nizer, Benjamin, Krim & Ballon
40 W. 57th St.
New York, NY 10019
212-977-9700
Monte Engler, Counsel
Members are telephone answering services, primarily in New York City.

PERIODICALS

Answer
Association of Telemessaging Services
International, Inc.
1150 S. Washington, Ste. 150
Alexandria, VA 22314
703-684-0016
Surveys news of the telephone answering industry.

Enhanced Services Outlook
Capitol Publications Inc.
1101 King St., Ste. 444
Alexandria, VA 22313-2055
800-327-7205
Dick Stirba, Editor
Covers a wide variety of communications services, including voice mail, value added networks, and automated answering machines.

FEDERAL GOVERNMENT

U.S. Patent and Trademark Office
Crystal Plaza 2
2011 Jefferson Davis Highway
Arlington, VA 22202
703-305-8000
Ask for the Examining Group Director who is a specialist in telephone answering equipment.

TELEVISION BROADCASTING INDUSTRY

See also: CABLE TELEVISION INDUSTRY

ASSOCIATIONS

Academy of Television Arts and Sciences
3500 W. Olive Ave., Ste. 700
Burbank, CA 91505
818-953-7575
James Loper, Executive Director
*Members work in the film and television
industry. Maintains one of the largest archives
of television programs in the world.*

Advanced T.V. Systems Committee
1776 K St. N.W., Ste. 300
Washington, DC 20006
202-828-3130
202-828-3131 Fax
Robert Hopkins, Executive Director
*Sets standards and promotes research into
high definition and other advanced forms of
television.*

American Sportscasters Association
5 Beekman St., Ste. 814
New York, NY 10038
212-227-8080
Louis Schwartz, President
*Offers training and other programs to sport-
casters and aspiring sportscasters.*

Association of Independent Television Stations
1200 18th St. N.W., Ste. 502
Washington, DC 20036
202-887-1970
Preston Padden, President
*Provides marketing and promotional services
to independent, commercial television stations.*

Association for Public Broadcasting
1350 Connecticut Ave., N.W., Ste. 200
Washington, DC 20036
202-887-1700
202-293-2422 Fax
David Brugger, President
*Provides a wide range of information about
public broadcasting to public television
licensees and the public.*

Broadcast Promotion and Marketing Executives
6255 Sunset Blvd., Ste. 624
Los Angeles, CA 90028
213-465-3777
213-469-9559 Fax
Linda Nix, President
*An information clearinghouse for radio and
television executives in charge of promotions,
public relations, marketing, and advertising.*

National Association of Broadcasters
1771 N St. N.W.
Washington, DC 20036
202-429-5300
202-429-5343 Fax
Edward Fritts, President
*A lobbying and research group comprised of
numerous radio and television stations.*

National Association of Farm Broadcasters
26 E. Exchange St.
St. Paul, MN 55101
612-224-0508
612-224-1956 Fax
Roger Olson, Executive Director
*Members are radio and television directors
and broadcasters who do farm programming.*

Radio-Television News Directors Association
1717 K St. N.W., Ste. 615
Washington, DC 20006
202-659-6510
202-223-4007 Fax
David Bartlett, President
Promotes journalistic freedom for the heads of radio and television news departments and broadcast journalists.

National Black Programming Consortium
929 Harrison Ave., Ste. 104
Columbus, OH 43215
614-299-5355
Mabel Haddock, Executive Director
Promotes the creation and distribution of television programming of special interest to black Americans.

Public Broadcasting Service
1320 Braddock Pl.
Alexandria, VA 22314
703-739-5000
Bruce Christensen, President
Members are public television stations.

American Federation of Television and Radio
    Artists
260 Madison Ave.
New York, NY 10016
212-532-0800
John Hall, Executive Secretary
A large union of radio and television performers and artists.

PERIODICALS

Broadcast Engineering
Intertec Publishing Corp.
9221 Quivira Rd.
Box 12901
Overland Park, KS 66212-9981
913-888-4664
Covers broadcast technology.

Broadcasting
Cahners Publishing Co.
475 Park Ave. S.
New York, NY 10016-6901
212-779-1999
Donald West, Editor
Surveys the broadcasting industry.

Broadcasting and the Law
Broadcasting and the Law, Inc.
1 S.E. 3rd Ave., Ste. 1450
Miami, FL 33131-1715
800-933-IFCC
John Spencer, Editor
Reports on regulatory and legal matters for station operations.

Nielsen Newscast
Nielsen Media Research
Nielsen Plaza
Northbrook, IL 60062
708-498-6300
L. Frerk, Editor
Reports on television audiences, products, industry trends, and the media.

Satellite T V Week
Fortuna Communications Corp.
Box 308
Fortuna, CA 95540
707-725-6951
James Scott, Editor
A listing of television programs available on satellite channels and articles surveying the satellite industry.

T V Technology
Industrial Marketing Advisory Services, Inc.
5827 Columbia Pike, Ste. 310
Falls Church, VA 22041
703-998-7600
Marlene Lane, Editor
Covers television trends, products, and technologies.

LIBRARIES

Library of Congress
John F. Kennedy Center for the Performing
    Arts
The Performing Arts Library
John F. Kennedy Ctr.
Washington, DC 20566
202-707-5507
*Broadcasting, theater, film, music, and related
topics.*

U.S. Federal Communications Commission
Library
1919 M St., N.W.
Washington, DC 20554
202-632-7100
*Telecommunications, broadcasting, and other
topics.*

COMPANIES

American Broadcasting Companies, Inc
(Subsidiary of Capital Cities/ABC Inc.)
77 W. 66th St.
New York, NY 10023
212-456-7777
Radio and television broadcasting.

CBS Inc
51 W. 52 St.
New York, NY 10019
212-975-4321
Radio and television broadcasting.

Gaylord Broadcasting Co.
(Subsidiary of Oklahoma Publishing Co.)
P.O. Box 25125
Oklahoma City, OK 73125
405-232-3311
Radio and television broadcasting.

Great American Broadcasting
(Subsidiary of Great American Communica-
    tions Co.)
One E. Fourth St.
Cincinnati, OH 45202
513-721-1414
Radio and television broadcasting.

Lin Broadcasting Corp.
(Subsidiary of McCaw Cellular Communica-
    tions Inc.)
5295 Carillon Pt.
Kirkland, WA 98033
206-828-1902
Television broadcasting and other businesses.

National Broadcasting Co.
30 Rockefeller Plaza
New York, NY 10112
212-644-4444
Radio and television broadcasting.

News America Publishing Inc.
(Subsidiary of News Corp. Ltd.)
1211 Ave. of the Americas
New York, NY 10036
212-852-7000
*Newspapers, television broadcasting, and
other businesses.*

Pulitzer Publishing Co.
900 N. Tucker Blvd.
St. Louis, MO 63101
314-622-7000
Newspapers, radio and television broadcasting.

Turner Broadcasting System, Inc.
One CNN Ctr., Box 105366
Atlanta, GA 30348
404-827-1700
Television broadcasting.

Westinghouse Broadcasting Co.
(Subsidiary of Westinghouse Electric Corp.)
888 Seventh Ave.
New York, NY 10106
212-307-3000
Radio and television broadcasting.

FEDERAL GOVERNMENT

U.S. Federal Communications Commission
1919 M St. N.W.
Washington, DC 2554
202-632-7106
*Ask for the TV Branch in the Mass Media
Bureau; or for the Consumer Assistance &
Small Business Division.*

U.S. International Trade Administration
Department of Commerce
14th St. and Constitution Ave., N.W.
Washington, DC 20230
202-377-2000
*Ask for the Commodity Analyst who is an
expert in television broadcasting.*

TEMPORARY EMPLOYEES

See also: EMPLOYMENT SERVICES AND EXECUTIVE SEARCH FIRMS

ASSOCIATIONS

Association of Manpower Franchise Owners
611 E. Wells St.
Milwaukee, WI 53202
414-276-2651
414-276-3349 Fax
Rick Iber, Executive Director
*Members are Manpower International fran-
chisees who share information.*

Association of Part-Time Professionals
Crescent Plaza
7700 Leesburg Pike, No. 216
Falls Church, VA 22043
703-734-7975
Maria Laqueur, Executive Director
*Provides research and educational programs
to part-time professional workers, free-lancers,
job-sharers, and others.*

National Association of Temporary Services
119 S. St. Asaph St.
Alexandria, VA 22314
703-549-6287
Samuel Sacco, Executive Vice President
*Offers information and seminars to companies
that supply temporary workers of all kinds.*

PERIODICALS

Contemporary Times
National Association of Temporary Services,
    Inc.
119 S. Saint Asaph St.
Alexandria, VA 22314
703-549-6287
Louise Seghers, Editor
*Surveys the temporary help industry and
offers management advice.*

Part-Time Professional
Association of Part-Time Professionals
Crescent Plaza, Ste. 216
7700 Leesburg Pike
Falls Church, VA 22043
703-734-7975
*Follows news, trends, and job search advice
for part-time professional workers.*

COMPANIES

Adia Services Inc.
64 Willow Pl.
Menlo Park, CA 94025
415-324-0696
Temporary personnel agencies.

Diversified Human Resources Group Inc.
5001 Spring Valley
Dallas, TX 75244
214-458-8500
*Permanent and temporary employment agen-
cies.*

Interim Systems Corp.
(Subsidiary of H & R Block, Inc.)
Four Brighton Rd.
Clifton, NJ 07015
201-778-3899
Temporary personnel agencies.

Kelly Services, Inc.
999 W. Big Beaver Rd.
Troy, MI 48084
313-362-4444
Temporary office help.

Mainstream Engineering Co., Inc.
(Subsidiary of Raycomm Transworld Indus-
    tries, Inc.)
17277 Ventura Blvd.
Encino, CA 91316
818-783-4405
Temporary technical personnel.

Olsten Corp.
Merrick Ave.
Westbury, NY 11590
516-832-8200
Temporary personnel agencies.

Raycomm Transworld Industries, Inc.
P.O. Box 971 Rt. 33
Freehold, NJ 07728
908-431-2500
Temporary technical personnel.

Snelling and Snelling, Inc.
4000 S. Tamiami Trail
Sarasota, FL 33581
813-922-9616
Franchise of temporary personnel agencies.

Staff Builders, Inc.
1981 Marcus Ave.
Lake Success, NY 11042
516-358-1000
Temporary health care personnel.

Uniforce Temporary Personnel, Inc.
1335 Jericho Turnpike
New Hyde Park, NY 11040
516-437-3300
Temporary personnel agencies.

FEDERAL GOVERNMENT

U.S. International Trade Administration
Department of Commerce
14th St. and Constitution Ave., N.W.
Washington, DC 20230
202-377-2000
*Ask for the Commodity Analyst who is an
expert in temporary personnel agencies.*

TENNESSEE

**STATE OFFICE LOCATOR (*for referrals
to all state government offices*)**

615-741-3011

ARCHIVES AND RECORDS

State Library & Archives Division
403 7th Avenue, N.
Nashville, TN 37243
615-741-7996

ATTORNEY GENERAL

Attorney General's Office
450 James Robertson Parkway
Nashville, TN 37243
615-741-6474

BANKING

Bank Examinations Division
500 Charlotte Avenue
Room 408
Nashville, TN 37219
615-741-2236

COMMERCE

Economic & Community Development
    Department
320 6th Avenue, N.
Nashville, TN 37243-0405
615-731-1888

CONSUMER AFFAIRS

Division of Consumer Affairs
500 James Robertson Parkway
5th Floor
Nashville, TN 37243-0600
615-741-4737

EDUCATION

Education Department
Cordell Hull Building
Room 100
Nashville, TN 37243-0375
615-741-2731

ENERGY

Community Development
320 6th Avenue, N.
Nashville, TN 37243-0405
615-741-2373

ENVIRONMENTAL AFFAIRS

Health & Environment Department
Cordell Hull Building
Room 313
Nashville, TN 37219
615-741-3111

HEALTH

Health & Environment Department
Cordell Hull Building
Room 313
Nashville, TN 37219
615-741-3111

HOUSING

Housing Development Agency
700 Landmark Center
401 Church Street
Nashville, TN 37243-0900
615-741-2473

HUMAN RIGHTS

Human Rights Commission
226 Capitol Boulevard
Ste. 602
Nashville, TN 37219-5095
615-741-5825

INSURANCE

Commerce & Insurance Department
500 James Robertson Parkway
Nashville, TN 37243-0566
615-741-2241

LABOR

Labor Department
501 Union Building
Nashville, TN 37243-0655
615-741-2582

LEGISLATION

Legislative Services Office
War Memorial Building
Room G-20
Nashville, TN 37219
615-741-3511

LIBRARY SERVICES

State Library & Archives Division
403 7th Avenue, N.
Nashville, TN 37243-0312
615-741-7996

LICENSING—CORPORATE

Uniform Commercial Code Section
State Capitol
1st Floor
Nashville, TN 37243-0305
615-741-3276

LICENSING—PROFESSIONAL AND OCCUPATIONAL

Regulatory Boards
500 James Robertson Parkway
Nashville, TN 37243-0566
615-741-3449

MOTOR VEHICLES

Motor Vehicle Division
705 Andrew Jackson State Office Building
500 Deaderick Street
Nashville, TN 37242
615-741-3381

OCCUPATIONAL HEALTH AND SAFETY

Occupational Safety Division
501 Union Building
Nashville, TN 37243-0655
615-741-2793

OMBUDSMAN

Office of the Governor
State Capitol Building
Nashville, TN 37243-0001
615-741-1208

PUBLIC UTILITIES

Utility Service Division
460 James Robertson Parkway
Nashville, TN 37243-0505
615-741-3939

PURCHASING

Procurement & Purchasing Service
Central Services Building
C-2 200
Nashville, TN 37243-0530
615-741-5922

REAL ESTATE

Real Estate Commission
500 James Robertson Parkway
Nashville, TN 37243-0566
615-741-2273

SECURITIES

Securities Division
500 James Robertson Parkway
Nashville, TN 37243-0566
615-741-2947

TAXATION AND REVENUE

Revenue Department
1200 Andrew Jackson Building
Nashville, TN 37242
615-741-2461

TOURISM

Tourist Department
P.O. Box 23170
Nashville, TN 37202
615-741-7994

TRANSPORTATION

Transportation Department
700 James K. Polk Department
Nashville, TN 37243-0349
615-741-2848

UNEMPLOYMENT

Unemployment Insurance Division
Volunteer Plaza Building
12th Floor
Nashville, TN 37245-0001
615-741-3178

WORKER'S COMPENSATION

Workers Compensation Division
501 Union Building
Nashville, TN 37243-0655
615-741-2793

TESTING

See also: EDUCATION and SCHOOLS

ASSOCIATIONS

International Test and Evaluation Association
4400 Fair Lakes Ct.
Fairfax, VA 22033-3899
703-631-6220
703-631-4693 Fax
Sherry Sieg, Administrator
An information clearinghouse for test and evaluation professionals.

American College Testing
Box 168
Iowa City, IA 52243
319-337-1000
319-337-1551 Fax
Richard Ferguson, President
Offers a wide range of tests and questionnaires taken by high school and college students each year.

Association for Measurement and Evaluation
   in Counseling and Development
c/o American Association for Counseling and
   Development
5999 Stevenson Ave.
Alexandria, VA 22304
703-823-9800
800-545-AACD
703-823-0252 Fax
Theodore Remley, Executive Director
A forum for those who design, administer, score, and interpret tests of all kinds.

The College Board
45 Columbus Ave.
New York, NY 10023
212-713-8000
Donald Stewart, President
Also known as College Entrance Examination Board, this group provides the Scholastic Aptitude Test (SAT) and other tests for high school students applying for college.

Educational Testing Service
Rosedale Rd.
Princeton, NJ 08541
609-921-9000
609-734-5410 Fax
Eleanor Horne, Secretary
Supplies a wide range of tests to schools, various professions, and governmental agencies. Conducts research on testing and measurement.

National Council on Measurement in Education
1230 17th St. N.W.
Washington, DC 20036
202-223-9318
202-775-1824 Fax
William Russell, Executive Officer
Publishers of tests for students and test specialists who study measurement techniques.

National Society for Performance and Instruction
1300 L St. N.W., Ste. 1250
Washington, DC 20005
202-408-7969
202-408-7972 Fax
Paul Tremper, Executive Director
Members study ways to increase worker productivity by measuring performance and offering appropriate instruction and training.

PERIODICALS

Educational and Psychological Measurement
Educational and Psychological Measurement, Inc.
Box 6856
College Station
Durham, NC 27708
919-688-3227
William Michael, Editor
Covers issues in the development and application of tests for educational and psychological measurements.

Employee Testing & the Law
Vanguard Information Publications
Box 667
Chapel Hill, NC 27514
919-967-2420
Ted Shults, Editor
Reports on legal, technical, and business developments in employee testing.

Tests in Print
Buros Institute of Mental Measurements
135 Bancroft
University of Nebraska-Lincoln
Lincoln, NE 68588-0348
402-472-6203
A listing of tests that are available for purchase or use.

LIBRARIES

ERIC Clearinghouse on Tests, Measurement and Evaluation
American Institutes for Research
333 K St., N.W., Ste. 200
Washington, DC 20007
202-342-5060
202-342-5033 Fax
Tests, evaluation, measurement, learning theory, human development, and research methodology.

International Test and Evaluation Association
Library
4400 Fair Lakes Ct.
Fairfax, VA 22033-3899
703-631-6220
703-631-4693 Fax
Test and evaluation processes.

U.S. Equal Employment Opportunity Commission
Library
1801 L St., N.W., Rm. 6502
Washington, DC 20507
202-663-4630
202-663-4629 Fax
Testing, employment descrimination, labor law, civil rights, and related topics.

TEXAS

STATE OFFICE LOCATOR (*for referrals to all state government offices*)

512-463-4630

ARCHIVES AND RECORDS

Archives Division
P.O. Box 12927
Austin, TX 78711
512-463-5480

ATTORNEY GENERAL

Attorney General's Office
P.O. Box 12548
Austin, TX 78711
512-463-2191

BANKING

Banking Department
2601 N. Lamar
Austin, TX 78705
512-479-1200

COMMERCE

Commerce Department
P.O. Box 12728
Austin, TX 78711
512-472-5059

CONSUMER AFFAIRS

Consumer Protection Division
P.O. Box 12548
Austin, TX 78711-2548
512-463-2070

EDUCATION

Education Agency
1701 N. Congress Avenue
Austin, TX 78701
512-463-8985

ENERGY

Energy Management Center
P.O. Box 12428
Austin, TX 78711
512-463-1931

ENVIRONMENTAL AFFAIRS

Environmental Protection Division
P.O. Box 12548
Austin, TX 78711-2548
512-463-2012

HEALTH

Health Department
1100 W. 49th Street
Austin, TX 78756
512-458-7375

HOUSING

Community Development Program
410 E. 5th Street
Room 400
Austin, TX 78701
512-320-0110

HUMAN RIGHTS

Human Services Departmbet
P.O. Box 2960
Austin, TX 78769
512-450-3030

INSURANCE

Insurance Board
1110 San Jacinto
Austin, TX 78701-1998
512-463-6464

LABOR

Licensing & Regulation Department
P.O. Box 12157
Austin, TX 78711
512-463-3172

LEGISLATION

Legislative Council
P.O. Box 12128
Austin, TX 78711
512-463-1151

LIBRARY SERVICES

Library & Archives Commission
P.O. Box 12927
Austin, TX 78711
512-463-5460

LICENSING—CORPORATE

Corporation Division
P.O. Box 12887
Austin, TX 78711-2887
512-463-5586

LICENSING—PROFESSIONAL AND OCCUPATIONAL

Licensing & Certification Bureau
1100 W. 49th Street
Austin, TX 78756
512-458-7538

MOTOR VEHICLES

Motor Vehicle Division
11th and Brazos
Austin, TX 78701-2483
512-465-7365

OCCUPATIONAL HEALTH AND SAFETY

Occupational Health
4200 N. Lamar Street
Austin, TX 78756
512-459-1611

OMBUDSMAN

Governor's Citizen Assistance Office
P.O. Box 12428
Austin, TX 78711
512-463-1780

PUBLIC UTILITIES

Public Utility Commission
7800 Shoal Creek Boulevard
Room 400 N.
Austin, TX 78757
512-458-0291

PURCHASING

Purchasing Division
P.O. Box 13047
Austin, TX 78711-3047
512-463-3443

REAL ESTATE

Real Estate Commission
P.O. Box 12188
Austin, TX 78711-2188
512-465-3900

SECURITIES

Securities Commission
P.O. Box 13167
Austin, TX 78711
512-474-2233

TAXATION AND REVENUE

Comptroller of Public Accounts
111 E. 17th Street
Austin, TX 78774
512-463-4000

TOURISM

Tourist Development
P.O. Box 12008
Austin, TX 78711
512-426-9191
512-320-9422
800-888-8839

TRANSPORTATION

Highways & Public Transportation Department
11th and Brazos
Austin, TX 78701-2483
512-463-8616

UNEMPLOYMENT

Unemployment Insurance
15th Street and Congress Avenue
Austin, TX 78778
512-463-2661

WORKER'S COMPENSATION

Workers Compensation Division
1110 San Jacinto
Austin, TX 78701-1998
512-322-3490

TILE INDUSTRY

See also: FLOOR COVERINGS AND FLOORING INDUSTRY

ASSOCIATIONS

Ceramic Tile Distributors Association
15 Salt Creek Ln., Ste. 422
Hinsdale, IL 60521
708-655-3270
708-655-3282 Fax
Eleanor Schulte, Executive Director
Manufacturers and wholsalers of ceramic tile.

Ceramic Tile Institute of America
700 N. Virgil
Los Angeles, CA 90029
213-660-1911
213-660-4102 Fax
Timothy Hengst, Coordinator
Offers educational programs to tile manufacturers and contractors about various topics, especially tile installation.

Italian Tile Center
Division of Italian Trade Commission
499 Park Ave.
New York, NY 10022
212-980-1500
212-758-1050 Fax
Pier Celeste, Executive Officer
Helps promote Italian tiles through research and public relations compaigns.

National Tile Contractors Association
PO Box 13629
Jackson, MS 39236
601-939-2071
601-932-6117 Fax
Joe Tarver, Executive Director
Offers training in tile installation and related topics.

Tile Council of America
PO Box 326
Princeton, NJ 08542
609-921-7050
609-452-7255 Fax
Robert Kleinhans, Executive Director
Members make ceramic tile for floors and walls.

PERIODICALS

Eastern Floors
Specialist Publications, Inc.
17835 Ventura Blvd., Ste. 312
Encino, CA 91316
818-345-3550
Howard Olansky, Editor
Covers industry news for floor covering and tile manufacturers, wholesalers, and retailers east of the Mississippi.

Tile and Decorative Surfaces
20335 Ventura Blvd., Ste. 400
Woodland Hills, CA 91364
John Maynard, Editor
818-704-5555
Describes new tile products.

COMPANIES

American Biltrite Inc.
57 River St.
Wellesley Hills, MA 02181
617-237-6655
Rubber floor tiles and other products.

American Olean Tile Co.
(Subsidiary of Armstrong World Industries
   Inc.)
1000 Cannon Ave
Lansdale, PA 19446
215-855-1111
Ceramic floor and wall tiles.

Azrock Industries Inc.
(Subsidiary of Domco U.S. Inc.)
P.O. Box 696060
San Antonio, TX 78269
512-558-6400
Vinyl floor tile.

Biltrite Corp.
P. O. Box 9045
Waltham, MA 02254
617-647-1700
Rubber floor tiles and other products.

Ceramicus, Inc.
10233 Sandyville Rd.
East Sparta, OH 44703
216-866-5531
Ceramic tiles.

Color Tile, Inc.
(Subsidiary of Color Tile Holding, Inc.)
515 Houston St.
Fort Worth, TX 76102
817-870-9630
Tiles, wallpaper, paint, and related products.

Mannington Ceramic Tile
(Subsidiary of Mannington Mills, Inc.)
P. O. Box 1777
Lexington, NC 27292
704-249-3931
Ceramic tiles.

Monarch Tile Inc.
(Subsidiary of Monarch Industries, Inc.)
834 Rickwood Rd.
Florence, AL 35630
205-764-6181
Ceramic tiles.

Sikes Corp.
(Subsidiary of Premark International Inc.)
One Sikes Blvd.
Lakeland, FL 33801
813-687-7171
Ceramic tiles.

Vinyl Plastics, Inc.
3123 S. Ninth St.
Sheboygan, WI 53081
414-458-4664
Vinyl tile and other products.

FEDERAL GOVERNMENT

U.S. International Trade Administration
Department of Commerce
14th St. and Constitution Ave., N.W.
Washington, DC 20230
202-377-2000
*Ask for the Commodity Analyst who is an
expert in the tile industry.*

U.S. International Trade Commission
500 E St., S.W.
Washington, DC 20436
202-205-2000 Office of the Secretary
202-205-3296 Industries locator
*Ask for the Trade Analyst who is an expert in
the tile industry.*

TIRE INDUSTRY

See also: AUTOMOBILE EQUIPMENT INDUSTRY

ASSOCIATIONS

American Retreaders' Association
PO Box 17203
Louisville, KY 40217
502-367-9133
502-367-9570 Fax
John Wagner, Managing Director
Provides market research and technical information to tire dealers and retreaders.

National Tire Dealers and Retreaders Association
1250 I St. N.W., Ste. 400
Washington, DC 20005
202-789-2300
800-87-NTDRA
202-682-3999 Fax
Philip Friedlander, Executive Vice President
Members are tire dealers and retreaders.

Tire Retread Information Bureau
26555 Carmel Rancho Blvd., Ste. 3
Carmel, CA 93923
408-625-3247
408-625-1660 Fax
Harvey Brodsky, Managing Director
Provides public relations services to the tire retread industry.

Tire and Rim Association
175 Montrose Ave. W.
Copley, OH 44321
216-666-8121
J. F. Pacuit, Executive Vice President
Provides standards for interchangeable tires, rims, and other parts of motor vehicles.

PERIODICALS

Elastomerics
Communication Channels, Inc.
6255 Barfield Rd.
Atlanta, GA 30328-4369
404-256-9800
Ann Barker, Editor
Reports technical advances about elastomers that interest manufacturers of rubber goods, including tires.

Modern Tire Dealer
Bill Communications, Inc.
341 White Pond Dr.
Box 3599
Akron, OH 44309-3599
216-867-4401
Lloyd Stoyer, Editor
News and advice for dealers who sell tires and service cars.

Retreading—Repair Journal
Tire Technical Services, Inc.
Box 17203
Louisville, KY 40217
502-361-9219
E.J. Wagner, Editor
Technical information for tire retreaders.

Tire and Tube Import and Export Report
Rubber Manufacturers Association
1400 K St., 9th Fl.
Washington, DC 20005
202-682-4860
Statistics of tire imports and exports.

Super Automotive Service
Irving-Cloud Publishing Co.
7300 N. Cicero Ave.
Lincolnwood, IL 60646
708-647-7300
Bob Weber, Editor
Industry news and merchandising advice for service stations, tire retailers, and repair garages.

Tire Business
Crain Communications Inc.
1725 Merriman Rd., Ste. 300
Akron, OH 44313-5251
216-836-9180
David Zielasko, Editor
Covers new products, trends, and selling techniques for independent tire dealers.

Tire Review
Babcox Publications
11 S. Forge St.
Box 1810
Akron, OH 44309-1810
216-535-6117
Jim Davis, Editor
Covers the tire industry for dealers.

LIBRARIES

Uniroyal Goodrich Tire Co.
Akron Information Center
600 S. Main St.
Akron, OH 44397-0001
216-374-3884
Rubber, polymers, and tires.

COMPANIES

Dunlop Tire Corp.
(Subsidiary of SRI International Inc.)
2761 Long Rd.
Grand Island, NY 14072
716-773-8200
Tires.

General Automotive Inc.
(Subsidiary of Paccar Inc)
1400 N. 4th St.
Renton, WA 98055
206-939-3363
Retailer of automobile equipment, accessories, and tires.

Goodyear Tire & Rubber Co.
1144 E. Market St.
Akron, OH 44316
216-796-2121
Tires, tubes, and many other products.

Hennessy Industries, Inc.
(Subsidiary of Danaher Corp.)
1601 J.P. Hennessy Rd., Box 3002
La Vergne, TN 37086
615-793-7533
Tire changing and balancing equipment.

Hercules Tire & Rubber Co.
1300 Morrical Blvd.
Findlay, OH 45840
419-423-7204
Tires, tubes, and other automobile products.

Mohawk Rubber Co.
(Division of Yokohama Rubber Co.)
3560 W. Market St.
Akron, OH 44313
216-666-8177
Tires, tubes, repair materials, and other products.

Myers Industries, Inc.
1293 S. Main St.
Akron, OH 44301
216-253-5592
Tire repairing and recapping supplies and equipment.

Teknor Apex Co.
505 Central Ave.
Pawtucket, RI 02861
401-725-8000
Tire repair materials and other products.

Uniroyal Goodrich Tire Co.
600 S. Main St.
Akron, OH 44397
216-374-3000
Tires.

Western Auto Supply Co.
(Subsidiary of Sears, Roebuck and Co.)
2107 Grand Ave.
Kansas City, MO 64108
816-346-4000
Chain of automobile accessory and tire stores.

FEDERAL GOVERNMENT

U.S. Customs Service
Department of the Treasury
U.S. Customshouse
6 World Trade Center
New York, NY 10048
212-466-5550
Ask for the Commodity Specialist in charge of tires.

U.S. International Trade Administration
Department of Commerce
14th St. and Constitution Ave., N.W.
Washington, DC 20230
202-377-2000
Ask for the Commodity Analyst who is an expert in the tire industry.

U.S. International Trade Commission
500 E St., S.W.
Washington, DC 20436
202-205-2000 Office of the Secretary
202-205-3296 Industries locator
Ask for the Trade Analyst who is an expert in the tire industry.

TOBACCO INDUSTRY

ASSOCIATIONS

Cigar Association of America
1100 17th St. N.W., Ste. 504
Washington, DC 20036
202-223-8204
Norman Sharp, President
Offers information to cigar manufacturers, importers, distributors, and others.

Leaf Tobacco Exporters Association
3716 National Dr., Ste. 114
Raleigh, NC 27612
919-782-5151
J. T. Bunn, Executive Vice President
Members buy, pack, and export tobacco that has not been manufactured. Associated with the Tobacco Association of U.S., which promotes tobacco sales in the U.S.

Pipe Tobacco Council
1100 17th St. N.W., Ste. 504
Washington, DC 20036
202-223-8207
Norman Sharp, President
*Firms that deal in pipe and other forms for
loose tobacco.*

Tobacco Associates
1725 K St. N.W., Ste. 512
Washington, DC 20006
202-828-9144
Kirk Wayne, President
Promotes tobacco exports.

Tobacco Growers' Information Committee
PO Box 12300
Raleigh, NC 27605
919-821-0390
919-821-4564 Fax
Lisa Eddington, Managing Director
An information resource for tobacco growers.

Tobacco Institute
1875 I St. N.W., Ste. 800
Washington, DC 20006
202-457-4800
800-424-9876
202-457-9350 Fax
Samuel Chilcote, President
*Provides research and public relations services
to the tobacco industry.*

Tobacco Merchants Association of United
States
PO Box 8019
231 Clarksville Rd.
Princeton, NJ 08543
609-275-4900
609-275-8379 Fax
Farrell Delman, President
*Provides market information to the tobacco
industry and others.*

Tobacconists' Association of America
c/o Milan Brothers
106 S. Jefferson St.
Roanoke, VA 24011
703-344-5191
Ellis Milan, Treasurer
Members are retail tobacconists.

PERIODICALS

Flue Cured Tobacco Farmer
Specialized Agricultural Publications, Inc.
Box 95075
Raleigh, NC 27625
919-872-5040
Dayton Matlick, Editor
*Agricultural and business information for
tobacco farmers.*

Recent Advances in Tobacco Science
Tobacco Chemists' Research Conference
　　Board
Tobacco Literature Service
2314 D.H. Hill Library
Raleigh, NC 27695-7111
919-737-2836
Technical information about tobacco growing.

Retail Tobacconist
Leo Douglas, Inc.
9607 Gayton Rd.
Richmond, VA 23233
804-741-6704
Merchandising advice for tobacco retailers.

Smokeshop
B M T Publications, Inc.
7 Penn Plaza
New York, NY 10001-3900
212-594-4120
Paul Dworin, Editor
*Product and merchandising information for
tobacco retailers.*

T M A Tobacco Weekly
Tobacco Merchants Association of the United
 States, Inc.
231 Clarksville Rd., Ste. 6
Box 8019
Princeton, NJ 08543-8019
609-275-4900
Surveys news of the tobacco industry.

Tobacco Industry Litigation Reporter
Andrews Publications
1646 West Chester Pike
Box 1000
Westtown, PA 19395
215-399-6600
Jay Steinberg, Editor
*Follows law suits involving the tobacco
industry.*

Tobacco Reporter
Specialized Agricultural Publications, Inc.
Box 95075
Raleigh, NC 27625
919-872-5040
Dayton Matlick, Editor
*Covers the processing, trading, and manufac-
turing of tobacco.*

LIBRARIES

North Carolina State University
Tobacco Literature Service
2314 D.H. Hill Library
P.O. Box 7111
Raleigh, NC 27695
919-737-2837
Tobacco.

R.J. Reynolds Tobacco Co.
R & D Scientific Information Services
Library
Bowman Gray Technical Ctr., 611-12, 205C
Winston-Salem, NC 27102
919-741-4360
Tobacco, chemistry, and agriculture.

Tobacco Institute
Information Center
1875 I St., N.W., Ste. 800
Washington, DC 20006
202-457-9325
202-457-9350 Fax
Tobacco, health, and smoking.

Tobacco Merchants Association of the U.S.
Howard S. Cullman Library
Box 8019
Princeton, NJ 08543-8019
609-275-4900
609-275-8379 Fax
Tobacco industry and products.

COMPANIES

American Maize-Products Co.
250 Harbor Dr.
Stamford, CT 06904
203-356-9000
*Cigars, smokeless tobacco, and many food
products.*

Brooke Group Ltd.
65 E. 55th St.
New York, NY 10022
212-486-6100
Cigarettes.

Core-Mark International, Inc.
395 Oyster Point Blvd.
South San Francisco, CA 94080
415-589-9445
*Wholesaler of cigarettes, tobacco products,
and other products.*

Dalfort Corp.
(Subsidiary of Hyatt Air, Inc.)
P.O. Box 7556
Dallas, TX 75209
214-358-6282
Tobacco products and other businesses.

Dibrell Brothers, Inc.
512 Bridge St.
Danville, VA 24543
804-792-7511
Import and export of tobacco.

Hanson Industries North America
(Division of Hanson PLC)
99 Wood Ave., S.
Iselin, NJ 08830
908-603-6600
Tobacco products and many other types of products.

Lorillard, Inc.
(Subsidiary of Loews Corp.)
One Park Ave.
New York, NY 10016
212-545-3000
Cigarettes.

Philip Morris Incorporated
(Subsidiary of Philip Morris Companies Inc.)
120 Park Ave.
New York, NY 10017
212-880-5000
Cigarettes.

R. J. Reynolds Tobacco Co.
(Subsidiary of RJR Nabisco, Inc.)
401 N. Main St.
Winston-Salem, NC 27102
919-741-5000
Cigarettes.

Standard Commercial Corp.
P.O. Box 450
Wilson, NC 27893
919-291-5507
Wholesaler of leaf tobacco and other commodities.

FEDERAL GOVERNMENT

U.S. Department of Agriculture
14th St. and Independence Ave., S.W.
Washington, DC 20250
202-720-8732
Ask for the Tobacco Information Division in the Agricultural Marketing Service; or for the Economic Research Service.

U.S. Department of the Treasury
1500 Pennsylvania Ave., N.W.
Washington, DC 20220
202-566-2111
Ask for the Public Affairs office in the Bureau of Alcohol, Tobacco and Firearms.

U.S. International Trade Administration
Department of Commerce
14th St. and Constitution Ave., N.W.
Washington, DC 20230
202-377-2000
Ask for the Commodity Analyst who is an expert in tobacco.

U.S. International Trade Commission
500 E St., S.W.
Washington, DC 20436
202-205-2000 Office of the Secretary
202-205-3296 Industries locator
Ask for the Trade Analyst who is an expert in tobacco.

U.S. Patent and Trademark Office
Crystal Plaza 2
2011 Jefferson Davis Highway
Arlington, VA 22202
703-305-8000
Ask for the Examining Group Director who is a specialist in tobacco-related machinery.

TOY INDUSTRY

See also: HOBBY INDUSTRY

ASSOCIATIONS

American Toy Export Association
c/o Kraemer Mercantile Corp.
200 5th Ave., Rm. 1303
New York, NY 10010
212-255-1772
212-807-8324 Fax
Robert Urquiola, Executive Officer
Helps toy manufacturers increase exports through a variety of programs.

Greater Toy Center
200 5th Ave., Rm. 303
New York, NY 10010
212-675-4633
212-691-1179 Fax
Thomas Atkinson, Executive Secretary
Toy companies that have showrooms and sales offices at two group locations in New York City.

National Association of Doll and Stuffed Toy
    Manufacturers, Inc.
200 E. Post Rd.
White Plains, NY 10601
914-682-8900
914-761-0747 Fax
Ralph Katz, Administrator
Represents the interests of firms that make dolls and stuffed toys.

Toy and Hobby Wholesalers Association of
    America
PO Box 955
Marlton, NJ 08053
609-985-2878
William MacMillan, Executive Director
Distributors of toys and games.

Toy Manufacturers of America
200 Fifth Ave., Rm. 740
New York, NY 10010
212-675-1141
212-633-1429 Fax
Charles Riotto, Executive Director
Offers educational and other programs to U.S. toy manufacturers.

PERIODICALS

Playthings
Geyer-McAllister Publications, Inc.
51 Madison Ave.
New York, NY 10010
212-689-4411
Frank Reys, Editor
Surveys toys, hobbies, and industry news for toy merchandisers.

Small World
Earnshaw Publications, Inc.
225 W. 34th St., Ste. 1212
New York, NY 10001
212-563-2742
Thomas Hudson, Editor
Covers products, news, and trends for the toy, nursery furniture, and children's accessories industry.

Toy & Hobby World
Toy & Hobby World
463 Seventh Ave., Ste. 202
New York, NY 10018
212-594-4237
Larry Carlat, Editor
Surveys news and new products for toy and hobby retailers and buyers.

Toy Shop
Krause Publications, Inc.
700 E. State St.
Iola, WI 54990
715-445-2214
Specializes in collectible toys, dolls, and models.

Toy Trade News
Edgell Communications
270 Madison Ave.
New York, NY 10016
212-951-6600
Holly McMunn, Editor
Covers all aspects of the toy industry.

COMPANIES

Child World, Inc.
(Subsidiary of Trefoil Capital Investors, L.P.)
25 Littlefield St.
Avon, MA 02322
508-588-7300
Retail chain of toy stores

Fisher—Price
636 Girard Ave.
East Aurora, NY 14052
716-687-3000
Toys, children's clothing, and other juvenile products.

Lewis Galoob Toys, Inc.
500 Forbes Blvd.
South San Francisco, CA 94080
415-952-1678
Toys.

Hasbro, Inc.
1027 Newport Ave.
Pawtucket, RI 02861
401-431-8697
Toys and games.

Lionel Corp.
220 Mill Rd.
Edison, NJ 08817
201-287-3488
Toys and games.

Mattel Inc.
333 N. Continental Blvd.
El Segundo, CA 90246
213-978-5150
Toys and games.

Playskool Inc.
(Subsidiary of Milton Bradley Co.)
1027 Newport Ave., Box 1059
Pawtucket, RI 02862
401-431-8697
Toys and other juvenile products.

Tonka Corp.
(Subsidiary of Hasbro, Inc.)
6000 Clearwater Dr.
Minnetonka, MN 55343
612-936-3300
Toys.

Toys R Us Inc.
395 W. Passaic St.
Rochelle Park, NJ 07662
201-262-7800
Toy retail chain.

Tyco Toys, Inc.
6000 Midlantic Dr.
Mt. Laurel, NJ 08054
609-234-7400
Toys.

FEDERAL GOVERNMENT

U.S. Customs Service
Department of the Treasury
U.S. Customshouse
6 World Trade Center
New York, NY 10048
212-466-5550
Ask for the Commodity Specialist in charge of toys.

U.S. International Trade Administration
Department of Commerce
14th St. and Constitution Ave., N.W.
Washington, DC 20230
202-377-2000
Ask for the Commodity Analyst who is an expert in the toy industry.

U.S. International Trade Commission
500 E St., S.W.
Washington, DC 20436
202-205-2000 Office of the Secretary
202-205-3296 Industries locator
Ask for the Trade Analyst who is an expert in the toy industry.

U.S. Patent and Trademark Office
Crystal Plaza 2
2011 Jefferson Davis Highway
Arlington, VA 22202
703-305-8000
Ask for the Examining Group Director who is a specialist in toys.

TRADE SHOWS, CONVENTIONS, AND FAIRS

ASSOCIATIONS

Association for Convention Operations Management
William H. Just & Assoc., Inc.
1819 Peachtree St. N.E., Ste. 560
Atlanta, GA 30309
404-355-2400
404-351-3348 Fax
William Just, Executive Vice President
Members include directors of conventions, convention centers, convention bureaus, hotel managers, and others who supply the convention industry.

Exhibit Designers and Producers Association
611 E. Wells St.
Milwaukee, WI 53202
414-276-3372
414-276-3349 Fax
Georgia Halvorsen, Executive Officer
Companies that design and manufacture displays used in trade shows and exhibit halls.

Healthcare Convention and Exhibitors Association
5775 Peachtree-Dunwoody Rd., Ste. 500
Atlanta, GA 30342
404-252-3663
404-252-0774 Fax
Robert Gelardi, Executive Director
A forum for health care companies that exhibit their products and services at conventions, and for the firms that supply conventions with products and services.

International Association of Convention and
     Visitor Bureaus
PO Box 758
Champaign, IL 61824-0758
217-359-8881
217-359-0965 Fax
Richard Newman, President
Agencies in cities that promote and organize conventions.

International Association for Modular
     Exhibitry
Corporate Pl. 128, Bldg. 3, Ste. 29
Wakefield, MA 01880
617-245-8410
Irving Sacks, Executive Director
Firms that manufacture modular exhibits used at trade shows and conventions.

International Exhibitors Association
5501 Backlick Rd., Ste. 200
Springfield, VA 22003
703-941-3725
703-941-8275 Fax
Peter Manguelli, President
A clearinghouse for information about how to improve sales and marketing at trade shows.

Professional Convention Management Association
100 Vestavia Office Park, Ste. 220
Birmingham, AL 35216
205-823-7262
205-822-3891 Fax
Roy Evans, Executive Vice President
Convention managers and executives who share information on how to make conventions successful.

Trade Show Bureau
1660 Lincoln St., Ste. 2080
Denver, CO 80264
303-860-7626
303-860-7429 Fax
E. Jane Lorimer, President
Conducts research on such topics as trade show audiences, exhibitors, and marketing tactics.

PERIODICALS

Conventions and Expositions
American Society of Association Executives
Conventions and Exhibitions Managers Section
1575 I St., N.W.
Washington, DC 20005
202-626-2723
Advice for planners of association meetings.

Conventionsouth
Covey Communications Corp.
Box 2267
Gulf Shores, AL 36547
205-968-5300
J. Talty O'Connor, Editor
How-to information and profiles of sites for conventions in 11 southeastern states.

Directory of Conventions
Successful Meetings Data Bank
633 Third Ave.
New York, NY 10017
212-986-4800
Jean Jaworek, Editor
A listing of conventions, their dates and locations.

Directory of North American Fairs, Festivals
    and Expositions
B P I Communications, Inc.
Box 24970
Nashville, TN 37202
615-321-4250
Tom Powell, Editor
A listing of state and county fairs nationwide.

Meetings and Conventions
Reed Travel Group
500 Plaza Dr.
Secaucus, NJ 07096
201-902-2000
Kate Roudns, Editor
Advice for convention planners.

Trade Shows & Exhibits Schedule
Bill Communications, Inc.
633 Third Ave.
New York, NY 10017
212-986-4800
Stan Itzkowitz, Editor
A listing of trade shows and exhibits.

TradeShow Convention Guide
B P I Communications, Inc.
Box 24970
Nashville, TN 37202
615-321-4250
Tom Powell, Editor
A listing of trade shows, conventions, available sites, and much more information for the convention planner.

COMPANIES

Conference Management Co.
200 Connecticut Ave.
Norwalk, CT 06854
202-852-0500
Trade show, conference, and exhibit organization and management.

Conferon, Inc.
2285 Enterprise Pkwy., E.
Twinsburg, OH 44087
216-425-8333
Meeting consultants.

Corporate Promotions Group, Inc.
305 Madison Ave.
New York, NY 10165
212-972-0230
Organizes trade shows and sales meetings.

Giltspur, Inc.
(Subsidiary of Giltspur North America, Inc.)
500 Park Blvd.
Itasca, IL 60143
708-250-3930
Displays and exhibits for conventions and trade shows.

Security Van Lines, Inc.
100 W. Airline Hwy.
Kenner, LA 70062
504-468-7711
Convention and trade show storage and moving.

Slack Inc.
6900 Grove Rd.
Thorofare, NJ 08086
609-848-1000
Management of conventions and exhibits.

TRAFFIC ENGINEERING AND MANAGEMENT

See also: ROADS AND HIGHWAYS and each of the 50 states
under transportation

ASSOCIATIONS

American Association of State Highway and
    Transportation Officials
444 N. Capitol St., N.W., Ste. 225
Washington, DC 20001
202-624-5800
Francis Francois, Executvie Director
*Studies the construction, management, and
integration of highway systems nationwide.*

American Road and Transportation Builders
    Association
501 School St. S.W.
Washington, DC 20024
202-488-2722
202-488-3631 Fax
T. Peter Ruane, President
*Contractors that build highways and airports,
firms that make highway equipment, and individual engineers.*

Institute of Transportation Engineers
525 School St. S.W., Ste. 410
Washington, DC 20024-2729
202-554-8050
202-863-5486 Fax
Thomas Brahms, Executive Director
Professional society of traffic engineers.

National Industrial Transportation League
1090 Vermont Ave. N.W., Ste. 410
Washington, DC 20005
202-842-3870
202-842-3520 Fax
James Bartley, Executive Vice President
Studies transportation issues and legislation.

PERIODICALS

Better Roads
William O. Dannhausen, Publisher
Box 558
Park Ridge, IL 60068
708-693-7710
Ruth Stidger, Editor
*Reports on road construction, bridge manage-
ment, traffic zone safety, and related subjects.*

I T E Journal
Institute of Transportation Engineers
525 School St., S.W., Ste. 410
Washington, DC 20024
202-554-8050
Kathy Harrington-Hughes, Editor
*Helps engineers keep abreast of the latest in
traffic flow improvements, highway safety,
and transportation planning.*

National Cooperative Highway Research Pro-
    gram
Synthesis of Highway Practice
National Research Council Transportation
    Research Board
2101 Constitution Ave., N.W.
Washington, DC 20418
202-334-3214
Surveys highway industry practices.

Traffic Management
Cahners Publishing Co.
275 Washington St.
Newton, MA 02158-1630
617-964-3030
Francis Quinn, Editor
Reports on new products, regulations, other topics for buyers of transportation services, and equipment.

Urban Transportation Monitor
Lawley Publications
2701 C West 15th St., Ste. 501
Plano, TX 75075
214-596-6680
Daniel Rathbone, Editor
Covers urban transportation, traffic engineering, survey data, and related subjects.

LIBRARIES

Institute of Transportation Engineers
Library
525 School St., S.W., Ste. 410
Washington, DC 20024
202-554-8050
202-863-5486 Fax
Traffic engineering and transportation planning.

JHK & Associates
Technical Library
East
4660 Kenmore Ave.
Alexandria, VA 22304
703-370-2411
703-823-8347 Fax
Transportation, traffic engineering, and environmental studies.

New York (State) Department of Motor Vehicles
Research Library
Swan St. Bldg., Rm 418
Empire State Plaza
Albany, NY 12228
518-473-5467
Traffic accident research, driver education, traffic safety, traffic laws, and other subjects.

U.S. Federal Highway Administration
Office of the Chief Counsel
Law Library
400 Seventh St., S.W., Rm. 4232
Washington, DC 20590
202-366-1388
202-366-7499 Fax
Road and highway law.

COMPANIES

Eagle Signal Controls
(Division of Mark IV Industries, Inc.)
8004 Cameron Rd.
Austin, TX 78753
512-837-8300
Traffic control systems and other products.

Econolite Control Products, Inc.
(Subsidiary of Arroyo Holdings, Inc.)
3360 E. La Palma Ave.
Anaheim, CA 92806
714-630-3700
Traffic control systems.

Interstate Highway Sign Co.
(Division of Mark IV Industries, Inc.)
P. O. Box 8911
Little Rock, AR 72219
501-565-8484
Highway signs.

L & C Flashing Barricades, Inc.
60 Walpole St.
Canton, MA 02021
617-828-3481
Traffic control systems and signs.

Parking Control Systems Corp.
(Subsidiary of Dover Resources Inc.)
P.O. Box 849
Harrison, AR 72601
501-741-5481
Parking meters and traffic control equipment.

Signal Inc.
(Subsidiary of Flex-O-Lite Inc.)
16330 Phoebe Ave.
La Mirada, CA 90638
714-994-3880
Traffic control systems.

Welsbach Electric Corp.
(Subsidiary of Welsbach Corp.)
19-49 42 St.
Astoria, NY 11105
718-274-4200
Lighting and traffic signal systems.

FEDERAL GOVERNMENT

U.S. Department of Transportation
400 Seventh St., S.W.
Washington, DC 20590
202-366-4000
Ask for the public affairs office to find an appropriate expert in traffic engineering or traffic management.

TRAFFIC SAFETY

See also: SAFETY

ASSOCIATIONS

Alliance for Traffic Safety
c/o Glenn Carriker
Safety Center
Humphreys Bldg., Ste. 213
Central Missouri State Univ.
Warrensburg, MO 64093
816-429-4830
Glenn Carriker, Executive Officer
A clearinghouse for a variety of organizations that share information on traffic safety issues.

American Automobile Association
1000 AAA Dr.
Heathrow, FL 32746-5063
407-444-7000
407-444-7380 Fax
J. B. Creal, President
A huge organization that provides information on travel and traffic safety, among other subjects.

American Driver and Traffic Safety Education
    Association
239 Florida Ave.
Salisbury, MD 21801-5814
301-860-0075
301-742-2601 Fax
Jefferson Keith, Executive Director
Driver education and traffic safety experts.

American Insurers Highway Safety Alliance
1501 Woodfield Rd., Ste. 400 W.
Schaumburg, IL 60173
708-330-8500
708-330-8602 Fax
Franklin Nutter, President
*Provides traffic safety programs on behalf of
automobile insurance companies.*

American Traffic Safety Services Association
ATSSA Bldg.
5440 Jefferson Davis Hwy.
Fredericksburg, VA 22401
703-898-5400
703-898-5510 Fax
Robert Garrett, Executive Director
*Members sell highway safety signs, traffic con-
trol equipment, and related goods.*

Center for Auto Safety
2001 S St. N.W., Ste. 410
Washington, DC 20009
202-328-7700
Clarence Ditlow, Director
*A consumers' rights and research organization
devoted to reducing traffic deaths. Ralph
Nader is the founder.*

Motorcycle Safety Foundation
2 Jenner St., Ste. 150
Irvine, CA 92718
714-727-3227
800-447-4700
714-727-4217 Fax
Alan Isley, Executive Officer
*Provides motorcycle safety programs on behalf
of motorcycle manufacturers.*

National Safety Council
444 N. Michigan Ave.
Chicago, IL 60611
312-527-4800
312-527-9381 Fax
T. C. Gilchrest, President
*A large safety training and research organiza-
tion that provides information on traffic safety
and many other subjects.*

PERIODICALS

Fatal Accident Reporting System
National Center for Statistics and Analysis
National Highway and Traffic Safety Adminis-
    tration
U.S. Department of Transportation
400 Seventh St., S.W.
Washington, DC 20590
202-366-5820
*Statistics and descriptions of fatal accidents in
the U.S.*

Highway Safety Directions
Highway Safety Research Center
University of North Carolina at Chapel Hill
134 1-2 E. Franklin St.
CB 3430
Chapel Hill, NC 27599-3430
919-962-2202
Jeffrey Lowrance, Editor
*Covers highway traffic laws, passenger safety,
accident analysis, and other safety topics.*

Traffic Safety
National Safety Council
444 N. Michigan Ave.
Chicago, IL 60611
800-621-7619
Dawn DeLong, Editor
*News and advice for people working in traffic
safety.*

Traffic Safety Series
Transaction Publishers
Transaction Periodicals Consortium
Department 3091
Rutgers University
New Brunswick, NJ 08903
908-932-2280
Peter Cooper, Editor
*Follows traffic safety topics including driver
behavior, passenger safety, and driving while
intoxicated.*

LIBRARIES

U.S. National Highway Traffic Safety Admin-
    istration
Technical Reference Division
400 7th St., S.W., Rm. 5110
Washington, DC 20590
202-366-2768
*Motor vehicle safety, automobile occupant
protection, emergency medical services, and
highway safety.*

University of Michigan
Transportation Research Institute
Research Information & Publications Center
2901 Baxter Rd.
Ann Arbor, MI 48109-2150
313-764-2171
313-936-1081 Fax
*Driver behavior, highway safety, and other
transportation subjects.*

University of North Carolina, Chapel Hill
Highway Safety Research Center
Library
CB 3430 234 1/2 E. Franklin St.
Chapel Hill, NC 27599
919-962-8701
919-962-8710 Fax
*Highway safety, driver education, restraint
systems usage, traffic records, and other
topics.*

FEDERAL GOVERNMENT

U.S. Department of Transportation
400 Seventh St., S.W.
Washington, DC 20590
202-366-4000
*Ask for the National Highway Traffic Safety
Administration; or for the Safety & Operations Division in the Federal Highway Administration.*

TRAINING OF PERSONNEL

See also: EDUCATION; MOTIVATION (PSYCHOLOGY);
and PERSONNEL MANAGEMENT

ASSOCIATIONS

American Society for Training and Development
Box 1443
1640 King St.
Alexandria, VA 22313
703-683-8100
703-683-8103 Fax
Curtis Plott, Executive Vice President
A large professional society of trainers, and others involved with training and development of personnel in business, government, education, and other fields.

International Association for Continuing Education and Training
1101 Connecticut Ave., N.W., Ste. 300
Washington, DC 20036
202-857-1122
202-223-4579 Fax
Donna Cantor, Executive Director
Serves as a forum for universities, business training groups, associations, and other groups to share information about training and continuing education.

National Training Systems Association
2425 Wilson Blvd., Ste. 457
Arlington, VA 22201
703-243-1655
703-243-1659 Fax
Robert Reed, Executive Director
Manufacturers of computer systems used for military training and simulation, and providers of training programs under contract to the military.

Training Directors' Forum
c/o Lakewood Publications
50 S. 9th St.
Minneapolis, MN 55402
612-333-0471
800-328-4329
612-333-6526 Fax
Brian McDermott, Executive Director
Offers information to training managers on how to improve results.

PERIODICALS

TechTrends
Association for Educational Communications and Technology
1025 Vermont Ave, N.W., Ste. 820
Washington, DC 20005-3516
202-347-7834
Nancy Klinck, Editor
Advises professionals in education and training on how to employ new technologies.

Training
Lakewood Publications, Inc.
50 S. Ninth
Minneapolis, MN 55402
612-333-0471
Jack Gordon, Editor
Helps executives in charge of human resources development to improve their problem-solving strategies, employee training, and use of new technology.

Training & Development
American Society for Training and Development
1640 King St.
Box 1443
Alexandria, VA 22313
703-683-8129
Patricia Galagan, Editor
Follows training and development trends and theories.

Training Trends
T P C Training Systems
750 Lake Crook Rd.
Buffalo Grove, IL 60089-5080
708-537-6610
Patricia Horn, Editor
Describes training programs in industrial plants.

LIBRARIES

American Society for Training and Development
1640 King St.
Alexandria, VA 22313
703-683-8100
703-683-8103 Fax
Training methods and products.

Michigan State University
Labor and Industrial Relations Library
Library E109
East Lansing, MI 48824
517-355-4647
517-353-9806 Fax
Employment and training, labor unions, and labor law.

Sandy Corp.
Library
1500 W. Big Beaver Rd.
Troy, MI 48084
313-649-0800
313-649-3619 Fax
Training and communications.

COMPANIES

Bureau of National Affairs, Inc.
1231 25th St., N.W.
Washington, DC 20037
202-452-4200
Publisher of books, magazines, and training films.

Carlson Marketing Group Inc.
(Subsidiary of Carlson Companies, Inc.)
Carlson Parkway, Box 59159
Minneapolis, MN 55459
612-449-1000
Motivation and training programs, and other types of services.

Drake Beam Morin, Inc.
(Subsidiary of Harcourt Brace Jovanovich, Inc.)
100 Park Ave.
New York, NY 10017
212-692-7700
Management consulting services that include training and development services.

Maritz Inc.
1375 N. Highway Dr.
Fenton, MO 63026
314-827-4000
Training, motivation, and incentive travel programs.

National Education Corp.
18400 Von Karman Ave.
Irvine, CA 92715
714-474-9400
Educational publishing, and industrial and vocational training programs.

National Education Training Group, Inc.
(Subsidiary of National Education Corp.)
1751 W.Diehl Rd.
Naperville, IL 60563
708-369-3000
Multi-media training courses.

Science Management Corp.
P.O. Box 0600
Basking Ridge, NJ 07920
201-647-7000
Management consulting services that includes training and development programs.

Wilfred American Educational Corp.
1657 Broadway
New York, NY 10019
212-582-6690
Career training schools.

FEDERAL GOVERNMENT

U.S. Department of Labor
200 Constitution Ave., N.W.
Washington, DC 20210
202-523-6666
Ask for the Employment & Training Administration.

TRANSLATION AND TRANSLATORS

ASSOCIATIONS

American Society of Interpreters
PO Box 9603
Washington, DC 20016
703-998-8636
Eva Desrosiers, President
An information clearinghouse for professional interpreters and those who hire them.

The American Association of Language Specialists
1000 Connecticut Ave. N.W., Ste. 9
Washington, DC 20036
301-986-1542
Remco Krafft, President
Members are translators and interpreters who have worked at international organizations or conferences.

American Translators Association
109 Croton Ave.
Ossining, NY 10562
914-941-1500
914-941-1330 Fax
Deanna Hammond, President
Represents translators and interpreters.

Translators' and Interpreters' Educational Society
1259 El Camino Rd., Ste. 160
Menlo Park, CA 94025
415-369-0952
Etilvia Arjona, Executive Director
A professional society that conducts research about translation and interpretation.

PERIODICALS

Translation
Translation Center
412 Dodge Hall
Columbia University
New York, NY 10027
212-854-2305
Frank MacShane, Editor
Publishes well-regarded translations of literature.

Translation Services Directory
American Translators Association
109 Croton Ave.
Ossining, NY 10562
914-941-1500
Offers a listing of working translators and interpreters.

LIBRARIES

Frank C. Farnham Co., Inc.
Library
Box 8187
Philadelphia, PA 19101
215-567-1500
Scientific translations, medicine, mining, chemistry, and related topics.

University of Iowa
Translation Laboratory
W 615 Seashore Hall
Iowa City, IA 52242
319-335-2002
319-335-2951 Fax
Translation, subtitling, and interpreting.

University of Texas, Dallas
Center for Translation Studies
Translation Library
McDermott Library
P.O. Box 830688
Richardson, TX 75083-0688
214-690-2092
Literary translations.

TRAVEL AGENCIES

See also: TRAVEL INDUSTRY and each of the 50 states
under tourism

ASSOCIATIONS

American Society of Travel Agents
1101 King St.
Alexandria, VA 22314
703-739-2782
*A large professional society of travel agents,
travel and tourism services, and tourist organizations. Acts as an information clearinghouse for the travel industry.*

Association of Community Travel Clubs
2330 S. Brentwood Blvd.
St. Louis, MO 63144
314-961-2300
314-961-9828 Fax
George White, Vice President
*Members are community travel clubs that
organize trips for group travel.*

Greater Independent Association of National
    Travel Services
915 Broadway
New York, NY 10010
212-505-5665
800-442-6871
212-260-1227 Fax
Susan Shapiro, President
*A relatively small group of travel agencies that
cooperate in their marketing efforts.*

Institute of Certified Travel Agents
148 Linden St.
Wellesley, MA 02181
617-237-0280
617-237-3860 Fax
Judith Zacek, President
*Accredits travel agents as Certified Travel
Counselors and offers training programs.*

PERIODICALS

Travel Agent Magazine
825 Seventh Ave.
New York, NY 10019
215-887-1900
Mikki Dorsey, Editor
Follows all aspects of travel for travel agents.

Travel Marketing and Agency Management
    Guidelines
19235 Village 19
Camarillo, CA 93012
805-987-0563
Evelyn Reichman, Editor
Advice about travel agency management.

TravelAge West
49 Stevenson, No. 460
San Francisco, CA 94105-2909
415-905-1155
Robert Carlsen, Editor
*Reports on national and regional news, and
offers travel agents suggestions to increase
sales.*

LIBRARIES

Institute of Certified Travel Agents
Travel Reference Library
148 Linden St.
Box 82-56
Wellesley, MA 02181
617-237-0280
617-237-3860 Fax
Travel agency management, travel, tourism, and related topics.

Reed Travel Group
Travel Weekly Library
500 Plaza Dr.
Secaucus, NJ 07094
201-902-1636
201-319-1755 Fax
Tourism and travel.

U.S. Travel Data Center
Library
2 Lafayette Centre
1133 21st St., N.W.
Washington, DC 20036
202-293-1040
202-293-3155 Fax
Tourism and travel.

COMPANIES

Acquisition Capability, Inc.
Seven Penn Plaza
New York, NY 10001
212-869-8905
Travel agency and airline ticket wholesaler.

American Express Travel Related Service
American Express Plz.
New York, NY 10285
212-640-2000
Travel agency.

Carlson Travel Group Inc.
(Subsidiary of Carlson Companies, Inc.)
Carlson Parkway, Box 59159
Minneapolis, MN 55459
612-449-1000
Chain of travel agencies.

Thomas Cook Travel, Inc.
2 Penn Plaza
New York, NY 10121
212-967-4390
Travel agencies.

Cruise Ventures, Inc.
501 Front St.
Norfolk, VA 23510
804-627-8000
Travel agency and cruise ticket wholesaler.

Hapag Lloyd Travel, Inc.
1640 Hempstead Tpk.
East Meadow, NY 11554
516-228-4970
Travel agency.

Holland America Line Westours, Inc.
(Subsidiary of Holland America Line, Inc.)
300 Elliott Ave. W.
Seattle, WA 98119
206-281-3535
Travel agency and cruise operator.

Liberty Travel Co.
69 Spring St.
Ramsey, NY 07446
201-934-3500
Travel agencies.

Passport Travel, Inc.
6340 Glenwood
Overland Park, KS 66202
913-677-7777
Travel agencies.

Space & Leisure Time Ltd.
119 N. Park Ave.
Rockville Center, NY 11570
516-764-6767
Travel wholesaler and marketing services for agencies.

FEDERAL GOVERNMENT

U.S. International Trade Administration
Department of Commerce
14th St. and Constitution Ave., N.W.
Washington, DC 20230
202-377-2000
Ask for the Commodity Analyst who is an expert in travel agencies.

U.S. International Trade Commission
500 E St., S.W.
Washington, DC 20436
202-205-2000 Office of the Secretary
202-205-3296 Industries locator
Ask for the Trade Analyst who is an expert in travel agencies.

TRAVEL INDUSTRY

See also: TRAVEL AGENCIES and each of the 50 states under tourism

ASSOCIATIONS

American Automobile Touring Alliance
888 Worcester St.
Wellesley, MA 02181
617-237-5200
617-237-2763 Fax
David Thibodeau, Vice President
Offers information on international automobile touring.

American Sightseeing International
211 E. 43rd St.
New York, NY 10017
212-687-6611
212-686-0818 Fax
Richard Valerio, President
Offers public relations and sales programs to sightseeing companies.

Association of Corporate Travel Executives
PO Box 5394
Parsippany, NJ 07054
201-537-7630
800-228-3669
Robert Graze, Executive Director
Managers of corporate travel, purchasing directors, meeting planners, travel agents, and others.

Cruise Lines International Association
500 5th Ave., Ste. 1407
New York, NY 10110
212-921-0066
212-921-0549 Fax
James Godsman, President
Offers promotional and training services for the cruise industry.

National Bed-and-Breakfast Association
PO Box 332
Norwalk, CT 06852
203-847-6196
Phyllis Featherston, President
Owners and operators of small inns and bed-and-breakfasts.

National Business Travel Association
516 Fifth Ave., Ste. 406
New York, NY 10036
212-221-6782
212-944-5513 Fax
Margie Crace, President
Corporate travel managers who represent the interests of business travelers.

National Tour Association
546 E. Main St.
Lexington, KY 40596
606-253-1036
W. James Host, Executive Vice President
Members operate tour groups or are hotels, restaurants, and other service firms that work with tour operators.

Society of Incentive Travel Executives
21 W. 38th St., 10th Fl.
New York, NY 10018
212-575-0910
212-575-1838 Fax
Nancy Lian, Executive Vice President
Serves as a forum for corporate users of incentive travel services to exchange information with airlines, hotels, resorts, incentive travel agencies, and others.

Travel Industry Association of America
2 Lafayette Center
1133 21st St. N.W.
Washington, DC 20036
202-293-1433
Edward Book, President
A collection of travel executives, government officials and others who promote the growth of the U.S. travel industry.

Travel and Tourism Research Association
PO Box 58066
Salt Lake City, UT 84158
801-581-3351
801-581-3354 Fax
Mari Lou Wood, Executive Director
Offers research services to travel directors and others in the travel industry.

Share-A-Ride International
c/o Richard Bartell
PO Box 703
Burtonsville, MD 20866-0703
301-330-6750
Richard Bartell, President
Provides a service that matches travelers with the owners of cars, planes, and boats who will be traveling to the same destination.

International Airline Passengers Association
4341 Lindburg Dr.
Dallas, TX 75244
214-404-9980
James Dunne, Chairman
An association of frequent fliers of all airlines.

PERIODICALS

Business Travel Management
Coastal Communications Corp.
488 Madison Ave.
New York, NY 10022
212-888-1500
Stephen Arrendell, Editor
Advice for executives in charge of business travel.

Business Travel News
C M P Publications, Inc.
600 Community Dr.
Manhasset, NY 11030
516-562-5000
Follows the business travel industry and advises on organizing trips.

Business Traveler Magazine
National Association of Business Travel Agents
3255 Wilshire Blvd., Ste. 1514
Los Angeles, CA 90010
213-382-3335
Stuart Faber, Editor
Publishes information on airlines, cities, hotels, and other topics of interest to the business traveler.

Outlook for Travel and Tourism
U S Travel Data Center
Two Lafayette Ctr.
1133 21st St., N.W.
Washington, DC 20036
202-293-1040
Forecasts of economic trends, and demographic and market changes that affect the tourism and travel industry.

Travel Expense Management
American Business Publishing
3100 Hwy. 138
Box 1442
Wall Township, NJ 07719-1442
908-681-1133
Robert Jenkins, Editor
Advises how to reduce travel expenses for executives at large coporations.

Travel & Tourism Executive Report
Association of Travel Marketing Executives
Leisure Industry—Recreation News
Box 43563
Washington, DC 20010
202-232-7107
Marj Jensen, Editor
Reports on demographics and news to help executives better promote and sell travel products.

LIBRARIES

Maritz Travel Co.
Travel Library
1385 N. Highway Dr.
Fenton, MO 63026
314-827-1402
314-827-3271 Fax
Covers travel topics such as restaurants, sightseeing, foreign countries, and hotels.

Reed Travel Group
Travel Weekly Library
500 Plaza Dr.
Secaucus, NJ 07094
201-902-1636
201-319-1755 Fax
Tourism and travel.

U.S. Travel Data Center
Library
2 Lafayette Centre
1133 21st St., N.W.
Washington, DC 20036
202-293-1040
202-293-3155 Fax
Tourism and travel.

FEDERAL GOVERNMENT

U.S. International Trade Administration
Department of Commerce
14th St. and Constitution Ave., N.W.
Washington, DC 20230
202-377-2000
*Ask for the Commodity Analyst who is an
expert in the travel industry.*

U.S. International Trade Commission
500 E St., S.W.
Washington, DC 20436
202-205-2000 Office of the Secretary
202-205-3296 Industries locator
*Ask for the Trade Analyst who is an expert in
the travel industry.*

TRUCK AND TRAILER
MANUFACTURING

See also: AUTOMOBILE EQUIPMENT INDUSTRY; ENGINES; and
TRUCKING INDUSTRY

ASSOCIATIONS

International Truck Parts Association
7127 Braeburn Pl.
Bethesda, MD 20817
202-544-3090
202-457-9121 Fax
Venlo Wolfsohn, Executive Director
*Members buy and sell used and rebuilt parts
used in heavy-duty trucks.*

Motor Vehicle Manufacturers Association of
the United States
7430 2nd Ave., Ste. 300
Detroit, MI 48202
313-872-4311
313-872-5400 Fax
Thomas Hanna, Executive Officer
*Offers information on automotive and truck
safety, energy efficiency, pollution control, legislation, and other topics.*

National Truck Equipment Association
38705 7 Mile Rd., Ste. 345
Livonia, MI 48152
313-462-2190
800-866-NTEA
313-462-2108 Fax
James Carney, Executive Director
Members include manufacturers, distributors, and installers of truck bodies and equipment. Studies legislative and management issues of concern to the industry.

Truck Cap Industry Association
10417 Englishman Dr.
North Bethesda, MD 20852
800-283-TCIA
301-897-9265 Fax
Frank Brown, Executive Director
Represents firms that manufacture truck caps, which are used in pickup trucks to enclose the bed.

Truck Trailer Manufacturers Association
1020 Princess St.
Alexandria, VA 22314
703-549-3010
703-549-3014 Fax
Richard Bowling, President
Members make commercial truck trailers and provide services to the industry.

Used Truck Sales Network
29 N. Wacker Dr.
Chicago, IL 60606
312-726-2802
800-621-9907
312-726-2574 Fax
Marvin Gordon, General Manager
Promotes the used truck industry.

PERIODICALS

Auto Age
M H West, Inc.
6633 Odessa Ave.
Van Nuys, CA 91406
818-997-0644
C.D. Bohon, Editor
Reports news for truck dealers, car dealers, leasing companies, body shops, and other automotive related industries.

Trailer-Body Builders
Tunnell Publications, Inc.
Box 66010
Houston, TX 77266
713-523-8124
Paul Schenck , Editor
Covers the manufacturing of school buses, truck bodies and equipment, van containers, and related products.

Truckers—U S A
B P S Inc.
1416 Greensboro Ave.
Tuscaloosa, AL 35401
205-758-3070
Dave Adams , Editor
Focuses on industry news, manufacturing trends, and the latest products.

LIBRARIES

American Trucking Associations, Inc.
Information Center
2200 Mill Rd.
Alexandria, VA 22314
703-838-1880
703-634-4324 Fax
Trucking regulation, engineering, equipment, and related topics.

Navistar International Transportation Corp.
Corporate Library
455 N. Cityfront Plaza, 9th Fl.
Chicago, IL 60611
312-836-2061
312-836-2192 Fax
Trucks and engines.

COMPANIES

Budd Co.
(Subsidiary of Thyssen Aktiengesellschaft)
3155 W. Big Beaver Rd., Box 2601
Troy, MI 48084
313-643-3500
Car and truck body components and related products.

Caterpillar Inc.
100 N.E. Adams St.
Peoria, IL 61629
309-675-1000
Off-highway trucks and other vehicles.

Ford Motor Co.
The American Road
Dearborn, MI 48121
313-322-3000
Automobiles and trucks.

Freightliner Corp.
(Subsidiary of Daimler-Benz AG)
P. O. Box 3849
Portland, OR 97208
503-283-8000
Trucks.

Fruehauf Trailer Corp.
(Subsidiary of Terex Corp.)
26999 Central Park Blvd.
Southfield, MI 48076
313-267-1000
Trucks and trailers.

General Motors Corp.
3044 W. Grand Blvd.
Detroit, MI 48202
313-556-5000
Automobiles, trucks, and many other products.

Great Dane Trailers, Inc.
(Subsidiary of International Controls Corp.)
P. O. Box 67
Savannah, GA 31402
912-232-4471
Truck trailers.

Hyster-Yale Materials Handling
2701 N.W. Vaughn
Portland, OR 97210
503-721-6000
Forklift trucks.

Navistar International Transportation Corp.
(Subsidiary of Navistar International Corp.)
455 N. Cityfront Plaza Dr.
Chicago, IL 60611
312-836-2149
Heavy-duty trucks and truck engines.

Oshkosh Truck Corp.
2307 Oregon St.
Oshkosh, WI 54901
414-235-9150
Heavy-duty trucks and chassis.

Paccar Inc
777 106th Ave., N. E.
Bellevue, WA 98004
206-455-7400
Heavy-duty trucks and other products.

FEDERAL GOVERNMENT

U.S. International Trade Commission
500 E St., S.W.
Washington, DC 20436
202-205-2000 Office of the Secretary
202-205-3296 Industries locator
Ask for the Trade Analyst who is an expert in truck and truck trailer manufacturing.

U.S. International Trade Administration
Department of Commerce
14th St. and Constitution Ave., N.W.
Washington, DC 20230
202-377-2000
Ask for the Commodity Analyst who is an expert in truck and truck trailer manufacturing.

TRUCKING INDUSTRY

See also: FREIGHT TRANSPORATION and each of the 50 states under transportation

ASSOCIATIONS

American Truck Dealers
8400 Westpark Dr.
McLean, VA 22102
703-821-7116
James Westlake, Director
Offers research and lobbying services on behalf of medium-duty and heavy-duty truck retailers.

American Trucking Associations
2200 Mill Rd.
Alexandria, VA 22314
703-838-1700
Thomas Donohue, President
Offers a wide range of research services on truck regulations, safety, statistics, and other topics.

Commission of Accredited Truck Driving Schools
1899 L St., N.W., Ste. 500
Washington, DC 20036
202-331-8866
202-872-0896 Fax
James McAlpin, Executive Director
Offers information to and about accredited truck driving schools.

Independent Truck Owner/Operator Association
PO Box 621
Stoughton, MA 02072
617-828-7200
Marshall Siegel, President
Offers educational programs and research designed to benefit the small and independent truck owner/operator.

National Private Truck Council
1320 Braddock Pl., Ste. 720
Alexandria, VA 22314
703-683-1300
703-683-1217 Fax
Gene Bergoffen, Executive Vice President
Helps shippers, manufacturers, and other firms that operate their own trucking fleets to increase efficiency and safety.

National Truck Leasing System
2625 Butterfield Rd.
Oak Brook, IL 60521
800-SAY-NTLS
William Ford, President
Helps independent truck leasing firms to operate their businesses more effectively.

Owner-Operator Independent Drivers Association
PO Box 88
Oak Grove, MO 64075
816-229-5791
800-821-6190
816-229-0518 Fax
James Johnston, President
Offers a wide range of insurance, advertising, research, and lobbying services to owners and operators of trucks.

Professional Truck Driver Institute of America
8788 Elk Grove Blvd., Ste. 20
Elk Grove, CA 95624
916-686-5146
916-686-4878 Fax
E. Kynaston, President
Sets standards and certifies courses that train truck drivers.

Regional and Distribution Carriers Conference
2200 Mill Rd., Ste. 640
Alexandria, VA 22314
703-838-1990
Sheridan Brinley, Executive Director
Provides management training and other services to short haul carriers and local trucking firms.

Truck Renting and Leasing Association
2011 I St., N.W., 5th Fl.
Washington, DC 20006
202-775-4859
202-457-9121 Fax
J. Michael Payne, Executive Vice President
Offers marketing and management information to firms that rent and lease trucks, trailers, and tractors.

PERIODICALS

Chilton's Commercial Carrier Journal
Chilton Co.
1 Chilton Way
Radnor, PA 19089
215-964-4000
Gerald Standley, Editor
News about bus and truck fleets.

Modern Bulk Transporter
Tunnell Publications, Inc.
Box 66010
Houston, TX 77266
713-523-8124
Charles Wilson, Editor
Covers tank trucking of food products, chemicals, and other commodities.

Refrigerated Transporter
Tunnell Publications, Inc.
Box 66010
Houston, TX 77266
713-523-8124
Gary Macklin, Editor
Information about shipping and handling of products requiring temperature-control.

Tow-Age
Kruza Kaleidoscopix, Inc.
Box 389
Franklin, MA 02038
308-528-6211
J.A. Kruza, Editor
Publishes how-to articles for the road service and towing profession.

Transport Fleet News
Transport Publishing Co.
1300 W. Exchange Ave.
Chicago, IL 60609
312-523-6669
Phillip Scopelite, Editor
Helps fleet supervisors keep abreast of industry trends and new products.

Trucks
Trucks Magazine Inc.
765 Churchville Rd.
Southampton, PA 18966
215-355-1034
John Stevens, Editor
Covers numerous topics of interest to truck drivers and fleet owners.

LIBRARIES

American Trucking Associations, Inc.
Information Center
2200 Mill Rd.
Alexandria, VA 22314
703-838-1880
703-634-4324 Fax
Trucking regulation, engineering, transportation, financial analysis, and related topics.

Atlas Traffic Consultatnts
Tariff Department Library
13-42 College Point Blvd.
Flushing, NY 11356
718-461-0556
718-461-0657 Fax
Interstate Commerce Commissions reports.

Western Highway Institute
Research Library
1200 Bayhill Dr., Ste. 112
San Bruno, CA 94066
415-952-4900
415-588-0424 Fax
Trucking, transportation engineering, and highway engineering.

COMPANIES

Carolina Freight Corp.
P.O. Box 545
Cherryville, NC 28021
704-435-6811
Trucking services.

Frozen Food Express Industries, Inc.
318 Cadiz St., Box 655888
Dallas, TX 75265
214-428-7661
Temperature-controlled trucking.

KLLM Transport Services Inc.
3475 Lakeland Dr., Box 6098
Jackson, MS 39208
601-939-2545
Temperature-controlled trucking.

Landstar System Inc.
Four High Ridge Park, Box 120052
Stamford, CT 06904
203-329-9735
Common carrier trucking services.

M S Carriers Inc.
3150 Starnes Cove
Memphis, TN 38116
901-332-2500
Long-distance trucking services.

Munson Transportation, Inc.
N. 6th St. Rd.
Monmouth, IL 61462
309-734-9393
Long-distance trucking services.

Roadway Services, Inc.
1077 Gorge Blvd.
Akron, OH 44309
216-384-8184
Trucking services.

Ryder System, Inc.
3600 N.W. 82nd Ave.
Miami, FL 33166
305-593-3726
Rentals and leasing of trucks.

TNT Red Star Express, Inc.
(Subsidiary of TNT Transport Group, Inc.)
24 Wright Ave.
Auburn, NY 13021
315-253-2721
Long-distance trucking services.

Werner Enterprises, Inc.
Interstate 80 & Hwy. 50, Box 37308
Omaha, NE 68137
402-895-6640
Long-distance trucking services.

FEDERAL GOVERNMENT

U.S. Department of Transportation
400 Seventh St., S.W.
Washington, DC 20590
202-366-4000
Ask for the Motor Carrier Standards Review department in the Federal Highway Administration.

U.S. International Trade Administration
Department of Commerce
14th St. and Constitution Ave., N.W.
Washington, DC 20230
202-377-2000
Ask for the Commodity Analyst who is an expert in trucking services.

TRUSTS AND ESTATES

See also: LAWYERS and RETIREMENT

ASSOCIATIONS

American College of Trust and Estate Counsel
2716 Ocean Park Blvd., Ste. 1080
Santa Monica, CA 90405
213-450-2033
213-450-5565 Fax
Gerry Vogt, Executive Director
A professional society of attorneys who work in the field of probate law.

National Association of Estate Planning Councils
98 Dennis Dr.
Lexington, KY 40503
606-276-4659
606-276-3294 Fax
Members include attorneys, insurance firms, bank trust officers, CPA's, and others involved in estate planning.

PERIODICALS

Journal of Taxation of Estates and Trusts
Faulkner & Gray, Inc.
106 Fulton St.
New York, NY 10038
212-766-7800
Leslie Laffie, Editor
Reports trusts and estates news from the courts and the IRS.

Tax Management Estates, Gifts and Trusts
   Journal
Tax Management, Inc.
1231 25th St., N.W.
Washington, DC 20037
202-452-4200
Glenn Davis, Editor
Advice about gifts, trusts, and estates.

Trusts and Estates
Communication Channels, Inc.
6255 Barfield Rd.
Atlanta, GA 30328-4369
404-256-9800
Michael Klim, Editor
Helps professionals in trust administration, estate planning, and related areas keep abreast of taxes, laws, property appraisal, accounting rules, and other subjects.

ULTRASONICS

ASSOCIATIONS

Acoustical Society of America
500 Sunnyside Blvd.
Woodbury, NY 11797
516-349-7800
516-349-7669 Fax
Murray Strasberg, Secretary
Scientists and engineers who study all facets of accoustics, including ultrasonics.

IEEE Ultrasonics, Ferroelectrics and Frequency Control Society
c/o Bruce McAvoy
Westinghouse R & D Center
1310 Beulah Rd.
Pittsburgh, PA 15235
412-256-1470
Bruce McAvoy, President
Members of this society conduct research into accoustics, ultrasonics, and their practical applications.

Ultrasonic Industry Association
PO Box 5126
Old Bridge, NJ 08857
201-679-9666
Bette Katz, Executive Director
Offers research and other services to manufacturers of ultrasonic equipment.

PERIODICALS

IEEE Transactions on Ultrasonics, Ferroelectrics and Frequency Control
IEEE. Ultrasonics, Ferroelectrics and Frequency Control Society
Institute of Electrical and Electronics Engineers, Inc.
345 E. 47th St.
New York, NY 10017-2394
212-705-7366
William O'Brien, Editor
Technical and theoretical information about ultrasonics.

Ultrasonic Imaging
Academic Press, Inc.
1250 Sixth Ave.
San Diego, CA 92101
619-230-1840
Melvin Linzer, Editor
Surveys the theories and applications of ultrasonic imaging in medicine and other fields.

Ultrasonics Symposium
Proceedings IEEE Ultrasonics, Ferroelectrics, and Frequency Control Society
Institute of Electrical and Electronics Engineers, Inc.
345 E. 47th St.
New York, NY 10017-2394
212-705-7900
Follows new technologies, equipment, and applications for ultrasonics.

LIBRARIES

Texas Research Institute, Inc.
Nondestructive Testing Information Analysis
　Center
415A Crystal Creek Dr.
Austin, TX 78756
512-283-2106
512-263-3530 Fax
Covers ultrasonic topics such as optical-visual and audible-sonic devices.

COMPANIES

Badger Meter, Inc.
4545 W. Brown Deer Rd.
Milwaukee, WI 53223
414-355-0400
Ultrasonic flow measurement equipment and other types of products.

Branson Ultrasonics Corp.
(Subsidiary of Emerson Electric Co.)
41 Eagle Rd.
Danbury, CT 06810
203-796-0400
Ultrasonic welding and cleaning equipment.

Crestek Inc.
Scotch Rd., Mercer County Airport
Trenton, NJ 08628
609-883-4000
Ultrasonic equipment.

Dapco Industries, Inc.
241 Ethan Allen Hwy.
Ridgefield, CT 06877
203-438-9696
Ultrasonic testing equipment.

Imex Medical Systems Inc.
6355 Joyce Dr.
Golden, CO 80403
303-431-9400
Ultrasonic medical equipment.

Krautkramer Branson, Inc.
(Subsidiary of Emerson Electric Co.)
Mifflin County Ind. Pk., Box 350
Lewistown, PA 17044
717-242-0327
Ultrasonic equipment used for measurement,
inspection, and testing.

Magnetic Analysis Corp.
535 S. 4th Ave.
Mount Vernon, NY 10550
914-699-9450
Ultrasonic testing equipment.

Philips Medical Systems North America Co.
(Subsidiary of North American Philips Corp.)
710 Bridgeport Ave.
Shelton, CT 06484
203-926-7674
Ultrasonic diagnostic equipment and other
medical instrumentation.

Sonicor Instrument Corp.
100 Wartburg Ave.
Copiague, NY 11726
516-842-3344
Ultrasonic cleaning equipment.

Sonics & Materials, Inc.
Kenosia Ave.
Danbury, CT 06810
203-744-4400
Ultrasonic welding equipment.

FEDERAL GOVERNMENT

U.S. Patent and Trademark Office
Crystal Plaza 2
2011 Jefferson Davis Highway
Arlington, VA 22202
703-305-8000
Ask for the Examining Group Director who is
a specialist in ultrasonic equipment.

UNDERWEAR, HOSIERY, AND INTIMATE APPAREL INDUSTRY

See also: CLOTHING INDUSTRY

ASSOCIATIONS

Allied Underwear Association
100 E. 42nd St.
New York, NY 10017
212-867-5720
Sidney Orenstein, Executive Director
Firms that make underwear and sleepwear for
women and children.

Greater Blouse, Skirt and Undergarment
  Association
225 W. 34th St.
New York, NY 10122
212-563-5052
Howard Morris, Executive Director
Manufacturers of women's blouses, underwear,
and negligees.

Intimate Apparel Manufacturers Association
475 Fifth Ave., Ste. 1908
New York, NY 10017
212-725-5599
Manufacturers of lingerie, nightwear, and leisure wear.

National Association of Hosiery Manufacturers
447 S. Sharon Amity Rd.
Charlotte, NC 28211
704-365-0913
Manufacturers of all kinds of hosiery.

PERIODICALS

Body Fashions—Intimate Apparel
Edgell Communications
7500 Old Oak Blvd.
Cleveland, OH 44130
216-826-2839
Jill Gerson, Editor
Helps retail executives in the intimate apparel business keep abreast of fashion trends, advertising, and management techniques.

Contours
Communications, Conferences and Exhibitions, Ltd.
112 E. 42nd St., Ste. 1104
New York, NY 10168
212-867-5159
Reports on swimwear, hosiery, leisure wear, lingerie, and bodywear.

Hosiery and Underwear
Edgell Communications
7500 Old Oak Blvd.
Cleveland, OH 44130
216-826-2839
Jill Gerson, Editor
Covers the merchandising and retailing of underwear and hosiery.

Hosiery News
National Association of Hosiery Manufacturers
447 S. Sharon Amity Rd.
Charlotte, NC 28211
704-365-0913
Gina Carroll Howard, Editor
Reports on all aspects of the hosiery market.

LIBRARIES

National Association of Hosiery
    Manufacturers
Library
447 S. Sharon Amity Rd.
Charlotte, NC 28211
704-365-0913
704-362-2056 Fax
Covers hosiery statistics, regulatory matters, and industry standards.

North Carolina State University
Burlington Textiles Library
P.O. Box 8301
Raleigh, NC 27695-8301
919-737-6602
919-737-3926 Fax
Textiles and clothing.

COMPANIES

I. Appel Corp.
136 Madison Ave.
New York, NY 10016
212-685-3900
Intimate apparel and other clothing products.

Danskin Division
(Division of Esmark Apparel, Inc.)
305 State St.
York, PA 17403
717-852-6100
Hosiery and dancewear.

Fruit of the Loom, Inc.
(Subsidiary of Farley, Inc.)
6300 Sears Tower
Chicago, IL 60606
312-876-7000
Underwear.

J.E. Morgan Knitting Mills, Inc.
(Subsidiary of Dawson International)
P.O. Box 390
Tamaqua, PA 18252
717-668-3330
Thermal underwear.

NCC Industries, Inc.
163 Main St.
Cortland, NY 13045
607-756-2841
Intimate apparel.

Neuville Industries, Inc.
96-50 Neuville Ave.
Hildebran, NC 28637
704-397-5566
Hosiery.

Pennaco Hosiery
(Division of Esmark Apparel, Inc.)
111 W. 40th St., 18th Fl
New York, NY 10018
212-764-4630
Hosiery.

Playtex Apparel Inc.
(Subsidiary of Apparel Partners, L.P.)
700 Fairfield Ave.
Stamford, CT 06904
203-356-8000
Intimate apparel.

VF Corp.
1047 N. Park Rd.
Wyomissing, PA 19610
215-378-1151
Intimate apparel and other clothing products.

FEDERAL GOVERNMENT

U.S. Customs Service
Department of the Treasury
U.S. Customshouse
6 World Trade Center
New York, NY 10048
212-466-5550
Ask for the Commodity Specialist in charge of underwear, hosiery, or intimate apparel.

U.S. International Trade Administration
Department of Commerce
14th St. and Constitution Ave., N.W.
Washington, DC 20230
202-377-2000
Ask for the Commodity Analyst who is an expert in underwear, hosiery, or intimate apparel.

U.S. International Trade Commission
500 E St., S.W.
Washington, DC 20436
202-205-2000 Office of the Secretary
202-205-3296 Industries locator
Ask for the Trade Analyst who is an expert in in underwear, hosiery, or intimate apparel.

UNEMPLOYMENT AND UNEMPLOYMENT INSURANCE

See also: Each of the 50 states under unemployment

ASSOCIATIONS

International Association of Personnel in
Employment Security
1801 Louisville Rd.
Frankfort, KY 40601
502-223-4459
502-223-4127 Fax
Michael Stone, Executive Director
*A professional group of officials and adminis-
trators in local, state, and federal government
agencies who work with unemployment compensation and job placement issues.*

Interstate Conference of Employment Security Agencies
444 N. Capitol St. N.W. Ste. 126
Washington, DC 20001
202-628-5588
202-783-5023 Fax
Emily DeRocco, Executive Vice President
*Members are state agencies that share infor-
mation on improving the administration of
unemployment insurance and related topics.*

National Foundation for Unemployment Compensation and Workers Compensation
600 Maryland Ave. S.W., Ste. 603
Washington, DC 20024
202-484-3346
J. Eldred Hill, President
*Conducts research into a wide range of unem-
ployment and work compensation issues,
including benefits, injury, and loss of wages.
Helps public officials and others improve compensation systems.*

PERIODICALS

Employment and Training Reporter
MII Publications Inc.
1211 Connecticut Ave., N.W.
Washington, DC 20036
202-293-1740
Cecilio Morales, Editor
*Reports on government-funded programs for
the unemployed and disadvantaged.*

NABE Outlook
National Association of Business Economists
28790 Chagrin Blvd., Ste. 300
Cleveland, OH 44122
216-464-7986
*Provides statistics on the Gross National Prod-
uct, housing starts, and unemployment.*

Unemployment Insurance Reports with Social
  Security
Commerce Clearing House, Inc.
4025 W. Peterson Ave.
Chicago, IL 60646
312-583-8500
A.E. Schecter, Editor
*Information on disability benefits, unemploy-
ment insurance, social security taxes, and
related topics.*

LIBRARIES

College of Insurance
·Insurance Society of New York
Kathryn and Shelby Cullom Davis Library
101 Murray St.
New York, NY 10007
212-962-4111
212-964-3381 Fax
*Unemployment insurance, worker's compensa-
tion, and other topics.*

U.S. Social Security Administration
Information Resources Branch
Library Services Section
Altmeyer Bldg., Rm 570
P.O. Box 17330
Baltimore, MD 21235
301-965-6107
*Social insurance, personnel administration,
law, and other topics.*

W.E. Upjohn Institute for Employment
  Research
Library
300 S. Westnedge Ave.
Kalamazoo, MI 49007
616-343-5541
*Causes and effects of unemployment, labor
economics, and urban affairs.*

FEDERAL GOVERNMENT

U.S. Department of Labor
200 Constitution Ave., N.W.
Washington, DC 20210
202-523-6666
*Ask for the Monthly Industry Employment
Statistics division, the Current Employment
Analysis division, or the Unemployment Insur-
ance Service.*

UPHOLSTERY INDUSTRY

See also: FABRICS AND TEXTILES

ASSOCIATIONS

Association of Specialists in Cleaning and
    Restoration
10830 Annapolis Junction Rd., Ste. 312
Annapolis Junction, MD 20701
301-604-4411
Martin Berry, Executive Vice President
Provides technical and business information to
companies that clean, repair, and restore car-
pets, draperies, upholstery, and other fabrics.

International Institute of Carpet and Uphol-
    stery Certification
2715 E. Mill Plain Blvd.
Vancouver, WA 98661
206-693-5675
206-693-4858 Fax
Kenway Mead, Administrator
Firms and individuals who restore and repair
carpets, upholstery, and other fabrics.

National Association of Decorative Fabric
    Distributors
3008 Milwood Ave.
Columbia, SC 29205
803-252-5646
800-445-8629
803-765-0860 Fax
Mary Ann Eubanks, Executive Director
Members are wholesalers of upholstery fab-
rics.

PERIODICALS

F D M—Furniture Design & Manufacturing
Delta Communications, Inc.
400 N. Michigan Ave., 13th Fl.
Chicago, IL 60611
312-222-2000
Michael Chazin, Editor
Reports on bedding, furniture, and the uphol-
stering industry.

UFAC 1992
Upholstered Furniture Action Council
Box 2436
High Point, NC 27261
919-885-5065
E.L. Briggs, Editor
Advice about cigarette-resistant upholstering
methods.

Upholstery Design & Manufacturing
Delta Communications, Inc.
400 N. Michigan Ave., 13th Fl.
Chicago, IL 60611
312-222-2000
Michael Chazin, Editor
Surveys the upholstery industry.

COMPANIES

Burlington Industries, Inc.
(Subsidiary of Burlington Holdings, Inc.)
3330 W. Friendly Ave.
Greensboro, NC 27410
919-379-2000
Textiles, including those used for upholstery.

Collins & Aikman Corp.
(Subsidiary of Wickes Companies, Inc.)
210 Madison Ave.
New York, NY 10016
212-578-1200
Textiles, including those used for automobile and airline upholstery.

Culp, Inc.
2020 Logan St., Box 2686
High Point, NC 27263
919-889-5161
Upholstery fabrics.

La-z-Boy Chair Co.
1284 N. Telegraph Rd.
Monroe, MI 48161
313-242-1444
Upholstered furniture.

Malden Mills Industries Inc.
46 Stafford St.
Lawrence, MA 01841
508-685-6341
Textiles, including those used for upholstery.

Minnesota Fabrics, Inc.
(Subsidiary of Hancock Fabrics, Inc.)
P.O. Box 2400
Tupelo, MS 38803
601-842-2834
Upholstery and drapery fabrics.

Mohasco Upholstered Furniture Corp.
(Subsidiary of Mohasco Corp.)
666 Lake Shore Dr.
Chicago, IL 60611
312-642-5604
Upholstered furniture.

F. Schumacher & Co.
79 Madison Ave.
New York, NY 10016
212-213-7900
Upholstery and drapery fabrics.

Albert Trostel & Sons Co.
(Subsidiary of Everett Smith Investment Co.
 of Delaware)
10201 W. Lincoln Ave.
West Allis, WI 53227
414-327-4870
Furniture and automotive upholstery.

FEDERAL GOVERNMENT

U.S. International Trade Administration
Department of Commerce
14th St. and Constitution Ave., N.W.
Washington, DC 20230
202-377-2000
Ask for the Commodity Analyst who is an expert in upholstery and fabrics.

U.S. International Trade Commission
500 E St., S.W.
Washington, DC 20436
202-205-2000 Office of the Secretary
202-205-3296 Industries locator
Ask for the Trade Analyst who is an expert in upholstery and fabrics.

UTAH

STATE OFFICE LOCATOR (*for referrals to all state government offices*)

801-538-3000

ARCHIVES AND RECORDS

Archives Division
3120 State Office Building
Salt Lake City, UT 84114
801-538-3012

ATTORNEY GENERAL

Attorney General's Office
236 State Capitol
Salt Lake City, UT 84114
801-538-1015

BANKING

Financial Institutions Department
324 S. State
Ste. 201
Salt Lake City, UT 84110
801-538-8830

COMMERCE

Commerce Department
P.O. Box 45802
Salt Lake City, UT 84145-0801
801-530-6701

CONSUMER AFFAIRS

Consumer Protection Division
P.O. Box 45802
Salt Lake City, UT 84145-0801
801-530-6619

EDUCATION

Board of Education
250 E. 500 South
Salt Lake City, UT 84111
801-538-7510

ENERGY

Energy Office
355 W. N. Temple
Ste. 450
Salt Lake City, UT 84180-1203
801-538-5428

ENVIRONMENTAL AFFAIRS

Environmental Health Division
P.O. Box 16700
Salt Lake City, UT 84116-0700
801-538-6121

HEALTH

Health Department
P.O. Box 16700
Salt Lake City, UT 84116-0700
801-538-6111

HOUSING

Community Development Division
324 S. State
Ste. 300
Salt Lake City, UT 84111
801-538-8723

HUMAN RIGHTS

Labor Division & Anti-Discrimination Division
P.O. Box 510910
Salt Lake City, UT 84151-0910
801-530-6921

INSURANCE

Insurance Department
P.O. Box 45803
Salt Lake City, UT 84145
801-530-6406

LABOR

Labor Division & Anti-Discrimination Division
P.O. Box 510910
Salt Lake City, UT 84151-0910
801-530-6921

LEGISLATION

Legislative Research & General Counsel
Office
State Capitol
Room 436
Salt Lake City, UT 84114
801-538-1032

LIBRARY SERVICES

State Library
2150 S. 300 West
Salt Lake City, UT 84115
801-466-5888

LICENSING—CORPORATE

Corporations & Uniform Commercial Code
Division
P.O. Box 45802
Salt Lake City, UT 84145-0801
801-530-6027

LICENSING—PROFESSIONAL AND OCCUPATIONAL

Occupational & Professional Licensing Division
P.O. Box 45802
Salt Lake City, UT 84145-0801
801-530-6620

MOTOR VEHICLES

Motor Vehicle Division
160 E. 300 South
Salt Lake City, UT 84134
801-538-8320

OCCUPATIONAL HEALTH AND SAFETY

OSHA Division
P.O. Box 51910
Salt Lake City, UT 84151-0910
801-530-6901

PUBLIC UTILITIES

Public Service Commission
P.O. Box 45585
Salt Lake City, UT 84145
801-530-6716

PURCHASING

Purchasing Division
3210 State Office Building
Salt Lake City, UT 84114
801-538-3026

REAL ESTATE

Real Estate Division
P.O. Box 45802
Salt Lake City, UT 84145-0801
801-530-6747

SECURITIES

Securities Division
P.O. Box 45802
Salt Lake City, 84145-0801
802-530-6600

TAXATION AND REVENUE

Tax Commission
160 E. 300 South
Salt Lake City, UT 84134
801-530-6077

TOURISM

Travel Council
Council Hall
Capitol Hill
Salt Lake City, UT 84114
801-538-1030

TRANSPORTATION

Transportation Department
4501 S. 2700 West
Salt Lake City, UT 84119
801-965-4113

UNEMPLOYMENT

Unemployment Insurance Division
P.O. Box 11249
Salt Lake City, UT 84147
801-533-2201

WORKER'S COMPENSATION

Workers Compensation
P.O. Box 45580
Salt Lake City, UT 84145-0580
801-530-6880

VALUATION AND APPRAISAL

ASSOCIATIONS

American Association of Certified Appraisers
800 Compton Rd., Ste. 10
Cincinnati, OH 45231
513-729-1400
800-543-2222
Anthony Brueneman, Executive Director
Provides educational programs to appraisers who work for banks, real estate firms, and state and local governments.

American Society of Appraisers
PO Box 17265
Washington, DC 20041
703-478-2228
A. W. Carson, Executive Director
A professional society for appraisers of all kinds of property.

American Society of Professional Appraisers
100 Galleria Pkwy., Tower 1, Ste. 400
Atlanta, GA 30339
404-951-1994
Lee McCutchan, Director
Appraisers of real estate.

Appraisal Institute
225 N. Michigan Ave., Ste. 724
Chicago, IL 60601-7601
312-819-2400
800-331-7732
312-819-2360 Fax
Offers educational programs to real estate appraisers.

Appraisers Association of America
60 E. 42nd St.
New York, NY 10165
212-867-9775
Victor Wiener, Executive Director
Members appraise a wide range of personal property, including art, books, furniture and furnishings, and related items.

Association of Machinery and Equipment
   Appraisers
1110 Spring St.
Silver Spring, MD 20910
301-587-9335
301-588-7830 Fax
Fred Mervis, President
Members appraise all kinds of machinery and equipment used primarily for industry.

Independent Automotive Damage Appraisers
   Association
707 N. York Rd., 2nd Fl.
Elmhurst, IL 60126
708-834-0010
708-834-0052 Fax
Richard Devermann, Executive Vice President
A group of companies that are hired by insurance firms and car rental agencies to appraise damaged cars.

Institute of Business Appraisers
PO Box 1447
Boynton Beach, FL 33435
407-732-3202
Raymond Miles, Executive Director
Offers a variety of educational programs to professional appraisers and valuators of businesses.

International Association of Assessing Officers
1313 E. 60th St.
Chicago, IL 60637
312-947-2069
312-363-2246 Fax
John Eckenroad, Executive Director
Tax assessing officials who work for state and local governments.

International Society of Appraisers
PO Box 726
Hoffman Estates, IL 60195
708-882-0706
708-885-2116 Fax
Maurice Fry, Executive Director
Offers educational programs and other services to appraisers of personal property.

International Society of Fine Arts Appraisers
PO Box 280
River Forest, IL 60305
708-848-3340
Elizabeth Carr, President
Provides research and training to fine arts appraisers and others who work for museums, appraisal firms, and other organizations.

National Association of Real Estate Appraisers
8383 E. Evans Rd.
Scottsdale, AZ 85260
602-948-8000
800-537-2069
602-998-8022 Fax
E. Kenneth Twichell, Managing Director
A large association of real estate appraisers.

PERIODICALS

Appraisal Journal
Appraisal Institute
875 N. Michigan Ave., Ste. 2400
Chicago, IL 60611-1980
312-335-4100
Jennifer Roberts, Editor
Covers real estate appraisal issues.

Appraiser News
Appraisal Institute
875 N. Michigan Ave., Ste. 2400
Chicago, IL 60611-1980
312-335-4100
Grace Hayek, Editor
*Reports on the real estate appraisal business
and related financial and legislative news.*

Appraisers Standard
New England Appraisers Association
5 Gill Terrace
Ludlow, VT 05149
802-228-7444
Linda Tucker, Editor
*Helps auctioneers and appraisers keep abreast
of their business.*

Jewelry Appraiser
National Association of Jewelry Appraisers
4210 N. Brown Ave., No. A
Scottsdale, AZ 85251
602-941-8088
Richard Baron, Editor
*How-to information for appraising gems and
jewels.*

LIBRARIES

Appraisal Institute
Library
225 N. Michigan Ave., Ste. 724
Chicago, IL 60601
312-819-2400
312-819-2360 Fax
Investment analysis and real estate appraisal.

International Association of Assessing Officers
Research and Technical Services Department
Paul V. Corusy Memorial Library
1313 E. 60th St.
Chicago, IL 60637-9990
312-947-2050
*Appraisal, property taxation, and assessment
administration.*

Valuation Research Corp.
Corporate Research and Reference Library
411 E. Wisconsin Ave.
Milwaukee, WI 53202
414-271-8662
414-271-3240 Fax
*Appraisal, valuation, taxation, and property
assessment.*

COMPANIES

CCC Information Services Inc.
(Subsidiary of Financial Protection Services,
Inc.)
640 N. LaSalle St.
Chicago, IL 60610
312-787-2640
Insurance valuation services.

Cole-Layer-Trumble Co.
(Subsidiary of Day & Zimmermann, Inc.)
3199 Klepinger Rd.
Dayton, OH 45406
513-276-5261
*Computer systems for appraisals by local and
state governments.*

Farmers National Co.
(Subsidiary of Metropolitan Life Insurance
Co.)
11516 Nicholas St.
Omaha, NE 68154
402-496-3276
Farm appraisals and other services.

International Realty Group, Inc.
111 N.W. 183rd St.
Miami, FL 33169
305-944-8811
Real estate appraisal and other services.

Lloyd-Thomas/Coats & Burchard Co.
6676 Howard St.
Niles, IL 60648
708-470-1800
Valuation consultants.

Marshall & Stevens Incorporated
(Subsidiary of SGS North America Inc.)
600 S. Commonwealth Ave.
Los Angeles, CA 90005
213-385-1515
Valuation consultants.

Sabre Systems & Service, Inc.
(Division of Moore Data Management Services)
9111 Springboro Pike, Box 327
Dayton, OH 45459
513-866-6000
Real estate appraisal systems.

Simat/Hellies/Eich
(Subsidiary of Reed International PLC)
90 Park Ave.
New York, NY 10018
212-682-8455
Aircraft appraisal and other services.

Sotheby's Inc.
(Subsidiary of Sotheby's Holdings, Inc.)
1334 York Ave.
New York, NY 10021
212-606-7000
Art, antiques, and jewelry auctions and appraisals.

Valuation Research Corp.
411 E. Wisconsin Ave.
Milwaukee, WI 53202
414-271-8662
Industrial appraisals.

VALVE INDUSTRY

See also: PIPE AND PIPE FITTINGS INDUSTRY and PUMP AND
COMPRESSOR INDUSTRY

ASSOCIATIONS

Manufacturers Standardization Society of the
  Valve and Fittings Industry
127 Park St. N.E.
Vienna, VA 22180
703-281-6613
Olen Thornton, Executive Director
Offers information about engineering, standards, and specifications to manufacturers of valves, pipe fittings and related products.

Offshore Valve Association
1620 I St. N.W., Ste. 202
Washington, DC 20006
202-452-8811
202-659-5427 Fax
George Pagonis, Executive Director
Represents the interests of foreign manufacturers and distributors of valves.

Valve Manufacturers Association of America
1050 17th St. N.W., Ste. 701
Washington, DC 20036
202-331-8105
202-296-0378 Fax
J. Stephen Larkin, President
Members make valves of every imaginable type.

PERIODICALS

Valve Magazine
Valve Manufacturers Association of America
1050 17th St., N.W., Ste. 701
Washington, DC 20036
202-331-8105
Margaret Newton, Editor
*Reports on industry news, major issues, and
new technologies for valve manufacturers.*

LIBRARIES

Valve Manufacturers Association of America
Library
1050 17th St., N.W., Ste. 701
Washington, DC 20036
202-331-8105
*Distribution valves, industrial valves, and
actuators.*

COMPANIES

BTR Inc.
(Subsidiary of BTR p.l.c.)
750 Main St.
Stamford, CT 06902
203-352-0000
Valves and many other products.

Babcock & Wilcox Co.
(Subsidiary of Babcock & Wilcox Investment
   Co.)
1010 Common St., Box 61038
New Orleans, LA 70161
504-587-5700
Control valves and many other products.

Commercial Intertech Corp.
1775 Logan Ave., Box 239
Youngstown, OH 44505
216-746-8011
*Oil and water valves, pumps, and other prod-
ucts.*

Fisher Controls International, Inc.
(Subsidiary of Monsanto Co.)
8000 Maryland Ave.
St. Louis, MO 63105
515-754-2452
*Valves, controllers, regulators, and other prod-
ucts.*

Keystone International Inc.
9600 W. Gulf Bank Dr.
Houston, TX 77240
713-466-1176
Butterfly valves.

Ladish Co. Inc.
5481 S. Packard Ave.
Cudahy, WI 53110
414-747-2611
Valves, pumps, and other products.

Pittway Corp.
333 Skokie Blvd.
Northbrook, IL 60065
708-498-1260
Aerosol valves and other products.

Vinson Supply Co.
(Subsidiary of Sammons Enterprises, Inc.)
P.O. Box 1860
Tulsa, OK 74101
918-587-6681
Oil field valves, pipes, and related products.

Watts Industries Inc.
Rte. 114 & Chestnut St.
North Andover, MA 01845
508-688-1811
Valves and related products.

FEDERAL GOVERNMENT

U.S. Customs Service
Department of the Treasury
U.S. Customshouse
6 World Trade Center
New York, NY 10048
212-466-5550
Ask for the Commodity Specialist in charge of valves.

U.S. International Trade Administration
Department of Commerce
14th St. and Constitution Ave., N.W.
Washington, DC 20230
202-377-2000
Ask for the Commodity Analyst who is an expert in the valve industry.

U.S. International Trade Commission
500 E St., S.W.
Washington, DC 20436
202-205-2000 Office of the Secretary
202-205-3296 Industries locator
Ask for the Trade Analyst who is an expert in the valve industry.

U.S. Patent and Trademark Office
Crystal Plaza 2
2011 Jefferson Davis Highway
Arlington, VA 22202
703-305-8000
Ask for the Examining Group Director who is a specialist in valves.

VENDING MACHINE INDUSTRY

ASSOCIATIONS

National Automatic Merchandising Association
20 N. Wacker Dr.
Chicago, IL 60606
312-346-0370
312-704-4140 Fax
James Rost, President
Firms that make and operate automatic vending machines, coffee machines, and the suppliers of food, cigarettes and other items sold through vending machines.

National Bulk Vendors Association
200 N. LaSalle St., Rm. 2100
Chicago, IL 60601
312-346-3100
312-621-1750 Fax
Morrie Much, Counsel
Firms that manufacture, distributute, and service bulk vending equipment.

National Coffee Service Association
4000 Williamsburg Sq.
Fairfax, VA 22032
703-273-9008
703-273-9011 Fax
Provides research and educational programs to firms that manufacture and operate vending machines and coffee machines.

PERIODICALS

American Automatic Merchandiser
Edgell Communications
7500 Old Oak Blvd.
Cleveland, OH 44130
216-826-2839
Mark Dlugoss, Editor
Covers equipment, products, and management issues for coffee service operators and vending machine operators.

Sunbelt Vending and O C S
B G Group
4016 Flowers Rd., Ste. 440A
Atlanta, GA 30360
404-451-2345
Ben Ginsberg, Editor
Merchandising advice for the coffee service and vending machine business.

Vending Times
Vending Times, Inc.
545 Eighth Ave.
New York, NY 10018
212-714-0101
Arthur Yohalem, Editor
Surveys the vending machine industry.

COMPANIES

Amadeus Holdings Inc.
3822 Charthouse Circle
Westlake Village, CA 91361
818-707-2133
Machines that vend video cassettes.

Canteen Corp.
(Subsidiary of TW Services, Inc.)
222 N. LaSalle St.
Chicago, IL 60601
312-701-2000
Operates food, cigarette, and beverage vending machines.

Federal Machine Corp.
8044 University Ave., Box 1779
Des Moines, IA 50306
515-274-1555
Vending machines of all types.

Gross-Given Mfg. Co.
75 W. Plato Blvd.
St. Paul, MN 55107
612-224-4391
Candy and cigarette vending machines.

Dixie-Narco, Inc.
(Subsidiary of Maytag Corp.)
Lawrence St.
Ranson, WV 25438
304-725-3481
Vending machines.

Refreshment Machinery Industries
(Subsidiary of Automatic Products Co.)
300 Jacksonville Rd.
Warminster, PA 18974
215-675-4200
Beverage vending machines.

Rowe International, Inc.
75 Troy Hills Rd.
Whippany, NJ 07981
201-887-0400
Vending machines and jukeboxes.

Seeburg Phonograph Corp.
1105 Westwood Ave.
Addison, IL 60601
708-543-1270
Vending machines and jukeboxes.

Vendors Exchange
4020 Payne Ave.
Cleveland, OH 44103
216-432-1800
Vending machines.

FEDERAL GOVERNMENT

U.S. Customs Service
Department of the Treasury
U.S. Customshouse
6 World Trade Center
New York, NY 10048
212-466-5550
Ask for the Commodity Specialist in charge of vending machines.

U.S. International Trade Administration
Department of Commerce
14th St. and Constitution Ave., N.W.
Washington, DC 20230
202-377-2000
Ask for the Commodity Analyst who is an expert in the vending machine industry.

U.S. International Trade Commission
500 E St., S.W.
Washington, DC 20436
202-205-2000 Office of the Secretary
202-205-3296 Industries locator
Ask for the Trade Analyst who is an expert in the vending machine industry.

U.S. Patent and Trademark Office
Crystal Plaza 2
2011 Jefferson Davis Highway
Arlington, VA 22202
703-305-8000
Ask for the Examining Group Director who is a specialist in vending machines.

VENTURE CAPITAL

See also: INVESTMENTS and SMALL BUSINESS AND SELF-EMPLOYMENT

ASSOCIATIONS

International Venture Capital Institute
PO Box 1333
Stamford, CT 06904
203-323-3143
Carroll Greathouse, President
Offers a variety of services to venture capital funds that are starting up.

National Venture Capital Association
1655 N. Fort Myer Dr., Ste. 700
Arlington, VA 22209
202-528-4370
703-525-8841 Fax
Daniel Kingsley, Executive Director
Acts as a forum for venture capitalists and financiers to discuss the funding of young companies.

PERIODICALS

Corporate Finance Sourcebook
National Register Publishing Co.
3004 Glenview Rd.
Wilmette, IL 60091
708-256-6067
*Provides information on potential financing
sources, including venture capital firms and
banks.*

Corporate Financing Week
488 Madison Ave.
New York, NY 10022
212-303-3591
Tom Lamont, Editor
*Helps executives keep abreast of corporate
finance, investment banking, venture capital,
equity issues, and related topics.*

Coup
Venture Capital Consultants America
Box 1553
Owosso, MI 48867
*Advice about private placements, mergers,
corporate financing, and other subjects that
concern venture capital consultants.*

International Venture Capital Network
High Tech Publishing Co.
Box 1923
Brattleboro, VT 05301
802-254-3539
Ben Campbell, Editor
*Helps venture capitalists evaulate proposals
for investment.*

Venture Capital Journal Venture Economics,
    Inc.
75 Second Ave., Ste. 700
Needham, MA 02194
617-431-8100
John Bonnanzio, Editor
Analyzes the small business investment industry.

COMPANIES

Capital Southwest Corp.
12900 Preston Rd.
Dallas, TX 75230
214-233-8242
Venture capital investments.

Dominion Ventures, Inc.
44 Montgomery St., Ste. 4200
San Francisco, CA 94104
415-362-4890
Venture capital investments.

Enterprise Partner
5000 Birch St., Ste. 6200
Newport Beach, CA 92660
714-833-3650
Venture capital investments.

Hambrecht & Quist Incorporated
(Subsidiary of Hambrecht & Quist Group)
One Bush St.
San Francisco, CA 94104
415-576-3300
*Investment banking, underwriting, and ven-
ture capital.*

Jupiter Industries, Incorporated
5454 Wisconsin Ave.
Chevy Chase, MD 20815
301-656-0626
Venture capital investments.

New Enterprise Associates
235 Montgomery St., Ste. 1025
San Francisco, CA 94104
415-956-1579
Venture capital investments.

North American Co. Ltd.
P.O.Box 14758
Fort Lauderdale, FL 33302
305-463-0681
Venture capital investments.

Oxford Venture Corp.
Soundview Plaza
1266 Main St.
Stamford, CT 06902
203-964-0592
Venture capital investments.

Pinnacle West Capital Corp.
400 E. Van Buren
Phoenix, AZ 85004
602-379-2500
Venture capital and other businesses.

Rothschild Inc.
(Subsidiary of Rothschild North America Inc.)
One Rockefeller Plaza
New York, NY 10020
212-757-6000
Investment banking and venture capital.

VERMONT

STATE OFFICE LOCATOR (*for referrals to all state government offices*)

802-828-1110

ARCHIVES AND RECORDS

State Archives Division
26 Terrace Street
Montpelier, VT 05602
802-828-2369

ATTORNEY GENERAL

Attorney General's Office
109 State Street
Montpelier, VT 05602
802-828-3171

BANKING

Banking & Insurance Division
Administration Building
Montpelier, VT 05602
802-828-3301

COMMERCE

Development & Community Affairs Agency
Pavilion Office Building
Montpelier, VT 05602
802-828-3211

CONSUMER AFFAIRS

Public Protection Division
109 State Street
Montpelier, VT 05602
802-828-3171

EDUCATION

Education Department
State Office Building
Montpelier, VT 05602
802-828-3135

ENERGY

Public Service Department
120 State Street
Montpelier, VT 05602
802-828-2321

ENVIRONMENTAL AFFAIRS

Natural Resources Agency
103 S. Main Street
Waterbury, VT 05676
802-244-7347

HEALTH

Health Department
P.O. Box 70
Burlington, VT 05402
802-863-7280

HOUSING

Housing & Community Affairs Department
Pavilion Office Building
Montpelier, VT 05602
802-828-3217

HUMAN RIGHTS

Public Protection Division
109 State Street
Montepelier, VT 05602
802-828-3171

INSURANCE

Banking & Insurance Department
89 Main Street
2nd Floor
Montpelier, VT 05602
802-828-3301

LABOR

Labor & Industry Department
State Office Building
120 State Street
Montpelier, VT 05602
802-828-2286

LEGISLATION

Legislative Council
State House
115 State Street
Montpelier, VT 05602
802-828-2231

LIBRARY SERVICES

Libraries Department
State Office Building
120 State Street
Montpelier, VT 05602
802-828-3265

LICENSING—CORPORATE

Corporations Division
26 Terrace Street
Montpelier, VT 05602
802-828-2371

LICENSING—PROFESSIONAL AND OCCUPATIONAL

Secretary of State
26 Terrace Street
Montpelier, VT 05602
802-828-2363

MOTOR VEHICLES

Motor Vehicles Department
State Office Building
Montpelier, VT 05602
802-828-2011

OCCUPATIONAL HEALTH AND SAFETY

OSHA
7 Court Street
Montpelier, VT 05602
802-828-2286

PUBLIC UTILITIES

Public Service Board
89 Main Street
3rd Floor
Montpelier, VT 05602
802-828-2358

PURCHASING

General Services Department
133 State Street
Montpelier, VT 05602
802-828-3288

REAL ESTATE

Secretary of State
26 Terrace Street
Montpelier, VT 05602
802-828-2363

SECURITIES

Securities Division
89 Main Street
2nd Floor
Montpelier, VT 05602
802-828-3301

TAXATION AND REVENUE

Tax Department
109 State Street
Montpelier, VT 05602
802-828-2505

TOURISM

Travel Division
134 State Street
Montpelier, VT 05602
802-828-3236

TRANSPORTATION

Transportation Agency
133 State Street
Montpelier, VT 05602
802-828-2657

UNEMPLOYMENT

Employment & Training Programming
P.O. Box 488
Montpelier, VT 05602
802-229-0311

WORKER'S COMPENSATION

Labor & Industry Department
7 Court Street
Montpelier, VT 05602
802-223-7226

VETERINARY PRODUCTS INDUSTRY

See also: PET INDUSTRY

ASSOCIATIONS

American Veterinary Distributors Association
106 W. 11th St.
Kansas City, MO 64105
816-221-5909
816-842-2603 Fax
James Fries, Executive Director
Offers promotional and educational programs to distributors of veterinary products.

American Veterinary Exhibitors Association
PO Box 6842
Santa Barbara, CA 93160
805-683-0489
Fred Hamlin, Executive Director
Represents manufacturers and suppliers of veterinary products that exhibit their goods at conventions.

American Veterinary Medical Association
930 N. Meacham Rd.
Schaumburg, IL 60196
708-605-8070
800-248-2862
708-330-2862 Fax
Michael Walters, Director of Public Information
A large professional society of veterinarians that offers research and educational programs.

Animal Health Institute
119 Oronoco St.
Alexandria, VA 22313
703-684-0011
703-684-0125 Fax
Fred Holt, President
Members research and manufacture drugs and vaccines used in animal health.

PERIODICALS

Apis
CITA International
Box 70
Phoenix, AZ 85001
602-234-2642
E.M. Morsy, Editor
Reports on the development and manufacture of new veterinary products for livestock and pets.

D V M Newsmagazine
Edgell Communications
7500 Old Oak Blvd.
Cleveland, OH 44130
216-826-2839
Maureen Hrehocik, Editor
Reports on veterinary issues, practices, and technologies.

Large Animal Veterinarian
Watt Publishing Co.
Sandstone Bldg.
122 S. Wesley Ave.
Mt. Morris, IL 61054-1497
815-734-4171
Tim Phillips, Editor
Advises equine and large animal veterinarians on such topics as herd management, nutrition, new technology, and genetics.

Topics in Veterinary Medicine
SmithKline Beecham Animal Health
812 Springdale Dr.
Exton, PA 19341-2803
215-363-3100
Kathleen Etchison, Editor
Practical information for veterinarians about medical advances and other topics.

Veterinary Economics
Veterinary Medicine Publishing Co.
9073 Lenexa Dr.
Lenexa, KS 66215
913-492-4300
Rebecca Turner, Editor
Covers the management of veterinary practice, financial management, public relations, office procedures, and related subjects.

Veterinary Forum
Forum Publications, Inc.
1610-A Frederica Rd.
St. Simons Island, GA 31522-2509
912-638-4848
Michael Sollars, Editor
Advice about practical and medical management for vets.

Veterinary Medicine
Veterinary Medicine Publishing Co.
9073 Lenexa Dr.
Lenexa, KS 66215
913-492-4300
Dr. Tracy Revoir, Editor
Reports on technical advances and research results in the veterinary field.

LIBRARIES

U.S.D.A.
National Agricultural Library
10301 Baltimore Blvd.
Beltsville, MD 20705
301-344-3755
301-344-5472 Fax
Veterinary medicine, animal industry, agriculture, and other topics.

COMPANIES

Baxter International
1 Baxter Pkwy
Deerfield, IL 60015
312-948-2000
Surgical, medical, and veterinary instruments, and other products.

Becton Dickinson and Co.
1 Becton Dr.
Franklin Lakes, NJ 07417
201-848-6800
Medical and veterinary products.

Colorado Serum Co.
4950 York St.
Denver, CO 80216
303-295-7527
Veterinary drugs and supplies.

Fort Dodge Laboratories Inc.
(Division of American Home Products Corp.)
800 5th St. N.W.
Fort Dodge, IA 50501
515-955-4600
Veterinary drugs.

IGI, Inc.
2285 E. Landis Ave.
Vineland, NJ 08360
609-691-2411
Veterinary drugs.

Ideal Instruments Inc.
(Subsidiary of Neogen Corp.)
607 N.Western Ave.
Chicago, IL 60612
312-997-3370
Veterinary instruments.

Nelson Laboratories
1000 Benson Rd.
Sioux Falls, SD 57101
605-336-2451
Veterinary drugs.

Neogen Corp.
620 Lesher Pl.
Lansing, MI 48912
517-372-9200
Veterinary instruments and other products.

Syntex Animal Health, Inc.
(Subsidiary of Syntex Agribusiness, Inc.)
4800 Westown Pkwy.
West Des Moines, IA 50265
515-224-2400
Wholesaler of veterinary drugs.

Veterinary Reference Laboratories, Inc.
(Subsidiary of Animed Inc.)
25 Lumber Rd.
Roslyn, NY 11576
516-484-2700
Laboratory services for veterinarians.

FEDERAL GOVERNMENT

U.S. International Trade Administration
Department of Commerce
14th St. and Constitution Ave., N.W.
Washington, DC 20230
202-377-2000
Ask for the Commodity Analyst who is an expert in veterinary products.

U.S. International Trade Commission
500 E St., S.W.
Washington, DC 20436
202-205-2000 Office of the Secretary
202-205-3296 Industries locator
Ask for the Trade Analyst who is an expert in veterinary products.

U.S. Patent and Trademark Office
Crystal Plaza 2
2011 Jefferson Davis Highway
Arlington, VA 22202
703-305-8000
Ask for the Examining Group Director who is a specialist in veterinary equipment.

VIDEO RECORDING INDUSTRY

See also: AUDIOVISUAL INDUSTRY and MOTION PICTURE INDUSTRY

ASSOCIATIONS

International Society of Videographers
c/o American Society of T.V. Cameramen
Box 296
Washington St.
Sparkill, NY 10976
914-359-5569
Steve Jambeck, Secretary
A professional society for video, camera, and lighting personnel who exchange technical information.

International Teleproduction Society
990 Ave. of the Americas, Ste. 21E
New York, NY 10018
212-629-3266
Janet Luhrs, Executive Director
Firms that produce audio and video tapes of all kinds.

Professional Film and Video Equipment Association
PO Box 9436
Silver Spring, MD 20906
301-460-8084
Chuck Sorensen, Administrator
Members manufacture, wholesale, and retail professional equipment used in the video and film industry.

Society of Motion Picture and Television Engineers
595 W. Hartsdale Ave.
White Plains, NY 10607
914-761-1100
914-761-3115 Fax
Lynette Robinson, Executive Director
A professional society of engineers who work in film, television, and video.

VIDION/International Association of Video
1440 N St., N.W., Ste. 601
Washington, DC 20005
202-332-7166
202-347-5829 Fax
David Rice, Executive Director
A clearinghouse for information about the video industry.

PERIODICALS

A V Video
Montage Publishing, Inc.
701 Westchester Ave.
White Plains, NY 10604
914-329-9157
Phillip Kurz, Editor
How-to information for audio-video production and presentation.

Film & Video
Optic Music, Inc.
8455 Beverly Blvd., Ste. 508
Los Angeles, CA 90048
213-653-8053
David Swartz, Editor
Focuses on the production of commercials, motion pictures, and films.

Sound & Communications
Testa Communications, Inc.
25 Willowdale Ave.
Port Washington, NY 11050
516-767-2500
Judith Morrison, Editor
Reports on the design and construction of audio and video studios.

Sound & Image
Hachette Magazines, Inc.
1633 Broadway
New York, NY 10009
212-767-6000
Michael Riggs, Editor
Surveys the recording and video industry, and editing studios.

Video Business
Capital Cities
825 Seventh Ave., 6th Fl.
New York, NY 10019
212-887-8400
John Gaffney, Editor
Advice for retailers of video tapes, both pre-recorded and blank.

Video Specialist Newsletter
J. Lahm Consultants Inc.
2630 Coronado Dr.
Fullerton, CA 92635
714-738-8422
James Lahm, Editor
Covers the home video industry with news of products, marketing strategies, and other topics.

COMPANIES

Andersen Group
1280 Blue Hills Ave.
Bloomfield, CT 06002
203-242-0761
Video equipment and other electronics.

CMX Corp.
(Subsidiary of Chyron Corp.)
2230 Martin Ave.
Santa Clara, CA 95050
408-988-2000
Video and audio editing systems.

Comprehensive Video Supply Co.
148 Veteran's Dr.
Northvale, NJ 07647
201-767-7990
Video editing supplies.

EMC Corp.
300 York Ave.
St. Paul, MN 55101
612-771-1555
Tape duplicating services.

Plastic Reel Corp. of America
Brisdon Ave.
Lyndhurst, NJ 07071
201-933-5100
Post-production equipment and supplies.

Video Station Inc.
220 Santa Monica Blvd.
Santa Monica, CA 90401
213-393-0391
Wholesaler of video equipment.

FEDERAL GOVERNMENT

U.S. Customs Service
Department of the Treasury
U.S. Customshouse
6 World Trade Center
New York, NY 10048
212-466-5550
Ask for the Commodity Specialist in charge of video recording equipment.

U.S. International Trade Administration
Department of Commerce
14th St. and Constitution Ave., N.W.
Washington, DC 20230
202-377-2000
Ask for the Commodity Analyst who is an expert in the video recording industry.

U.S. International Trade Commission
500 E St., S.W.
Washington, DC 20436
202-205-2000 Office of the Secretary
202-205-3296 Industries locator
Ask for the Trade Analyst who is an expert in the video recording industry.

U.S. Patent and Trademark Office
Crystal Plaza 2
2011 Jefferson Davis Highway
Arlington, VA 22202
703-305-8000
Ask for the Examining Group Director who is a specialist in video recording equipment.

VIDEOTEX/TELETEXT

Videotex and teletext are electronic technologies that allow consumers to receive and transmit text and graphics, do electronic banking, and shop by using their television sets or home computers.

ASSOCIATIONS

Videotex Industry Association
8403 Colesville Rd., Ste. 865
Silver Spring, MD 20910-3366
301-495-4955
301-495-4959 Fax
Robert Smith, Execuive Director
Offers public relations and research services to companies involved with videotex and teletex equipment and publishing.

PERIODICALS

Enhanced Services Outlook
Capitol Publications Inc.
Telecom Publishing Group
1101 King St., Ste. 444
Alexandria, VA 22313-2055
800-327-7205
Dick Stirba, Editor
Reports on business, technology, and other information about videotex and other telecommunications industries.

Information & Interactive Services Report
Telecommunications Reports
1333 H St., N.W., Ste. 1100-W.
Washington, DC 20005
202-842-3006
Victoria Mason, Editor
Follows the information industry, including videotex and teletex.

ViewText
Phillips Publishing, Inc.
7811 Montrose Rd.
Potomac, MD 20854
301-340-2100
David Hold, Editor
Helps managers keep abreast of the teletext and videotex business with information on software, financing, and related subjects.

FEDERAL GOVERNMENT

U.S. International Trade Administration
Department of Commerce
14th St. and Constitution Ave., N.W.
Washington, DC 20230
202-377-2000
Ask for the Commodity Analyst who is an expert in videotex/teletex services.

U.S. International Trade Commission
500 E St., S.W.
Washington, DC 20436
202-205-2000 Office of the Secretary
202-205-3296 Industries locator
Ask for the Trade Analyst who is an expert in videotex/teletex services.

VIRGINIA

STATE OFFICE LOCATOR (*for referrals to all state government offices*)

804-786-0000

ARCHIVES AND RECORDS

State Library
Library Building
Richmond, VA 23219
804-786-5579

ATTORNEY GENERAL

Attorney General's Office
101 N. 8th Street
Richmond, VA 23219
804-786-2071

BANKING

Financial Institutions Bureau
701 E. Byrd Street
Room 16090
Richmond, VA 23219
804-786-3657

COMMERCE

Economic Development
9th Street Office Building
Room 723
Richmond, VA 23219
804-786-7831

CONSUMER AFFAIRS

Consumer Affairs Office
1100 Bank Street
Room 210
Richmond, VA 23219
804-786-2042

EDUCATION

Department of Public Instruction
101 N. 14th Street
Richmond, VA 23216
804-225-2023

ENERGY

Energy Division
2201 W. Broad Street
Richmond, VA 23220
804-367-1310

ENVIRONMENTAL AFFAIRS

Council on the Environment
202 N. 9th Street
Room 900
Richmond, VA 23219
804-786-4500

HEALTH

Health Department
109 Governor Street
Room 400
Richmond, VA 23219
804-786-3561

HOUSING

Community Development Division
205 N. 4th Street
Richmond, VA 23219
804-786-7891

HUMAN RIGHTS

Civil Rights Office
Nelson Building
1503 Santa Rosa Road
Richmond, VA 23288
804-662-9971

INSURANCE

Insurance Bureau
P.O. Box 1197
Richmond, VA 23219
804-786-3741

LABOR

Labor & Industry Department
P.O. Box 12064
Richmond, VA 23241
804-786-2377

LEGISLATION

Legislative Services Division
P.O. Box 3-AG
Richmond, VA 23208
804-786-3591

LIBRARY SERVICES

State Library
Library Building
Richmond, VA 23219
804-786-2332

LICENSING—CORPORATE

Personne & Central Administrative Division
P.O. Box 1197
Richmond, VA 23219
804-786-1200

LICENSING—PROFESSIONAL AND OCCUPATIONAL

Commerce Department
3600 W. Broad Street
Richmond, VA 23230
804-367-8519

MOTOR VEHICLES

Motor Vehicles Department
2300 W. Broad Street
Richmond, VA 23220
804-367-6600

OCCUPATIONAL HEALTH AND SAFETY

Occupational Safety & Enforcement Division
P.O. Box 12064
Richmond, VA 23241
804-786-2391

OMBUDSMAN

Office of the Governor
P.O. Box 1475
Richmond, VA 23212
804-786-2211

PUBLIC UTILITIES

State Corporation Commission
P.O. Box 1197
Richmond, VA 23219
804-786-3601

PURCHASING

Purchases & Supplies Division
General Services Department
P.O. Box 1199
Richmond, VA 23219
804-786-3846

REAL ESTATE

Real Estate Board
3600 W. Broad Street
Richmond, VA 23230
804-367-8552

SECURITIES

Securities & Retail Franchising Bureau
P.O. Box 1197
Richmond, VA 23219
804-786-7751

TAXATION AND REVENUE

Taxation Department
2220 W. Broad Street
Richmond, VA 23282
804-367-8005

TOURISM

Division of Tourism
202 N. 9th Street
Ste. 500
Richmond, VA 23239
804-786-4484
800-847-4882

TRANSPORTATION

Transportation Department
1401 E. Broad Street
Richmond, VA 23219
804-786-2701

UNEMPLOYMENT

Unemployment Insurance Division
703 E. Main Street
Richmond, VA 23219
804-786-3004

WORKER'S COMPENSATION

Industrial Commission
P.O. Box 1794
Richmond, VA 23214
804-367-8615

VITAMIN AND DIET INDUSTRY

See also: HEALTH FOOD INDUSTRY

ASSOCIATIONS

Association of Vitamin Chemists
c/o Deborah Becker
801 Waukegan Rd.
Glenview, IL 60025
708-998-7457
Deborah Becker, President
*Chemists, nutritionists, and others who study
and manufacture vitamins.*

American Dietetic Association
216 W. Jackson Blvd., Ste. 800
Chicago, IL 60606
312-899-0040
312-899-1979 Fax
Dawn Treadwell, Executive Officer
A very large group of professional dietitians.

Calorie Control Council
5775 Peachtree-Dunwoody Rd.
Atlanta, GA 30342
404-252-3663
404-252-0774 Fax
Robert Geraldi, Executive Director
*An information resource representing produc-
ers of diet and low-calorie foods and drinks.*

PERIODICALS

Advances in Nutritional Research
Plenum Publishing Corp.
233 Spring St.
New York, NY 10013
212-620-8000
Harold Draper, Editor
*A professional journal covering the latest
nutritional research.*

Diet & Health Magazine
Fell Publishers, Inc.
2131 Hollywood Blvd.
Hollywood, FL 33020
305-925-5242
Barbara Newman, Editor
*Advice about dieting and health written for
consumers.*

Executive Fitness Newsletter
Rodale Press, Inc.
33 E. Minor St.
Emmaus, PA 18098
215-967-5171
William Gottlieb, Editor
*How-to information for executives who want
to be fit and healthy.*

Health Shopper
Swanson Health Products
1318 39th St., N.W.
Box 2803
Fargo, ND 58102
800-437-4148
Advice about health, weight-reduction, and nutrition.

Nutrition & Dietary Consultant
American Association of Nutritional Consultants
1641 E. Sunset Rd., B 117
Las Vegas, NV 89119
702-361-1132
Myra Zelikovics, Editor
Offers news for nutritional consultants.

LIBRARIES

U.S. Food & Drug Administration
Center for Food Safety & Applied Nutrition
Library
200 C St., S.W., Rm. 3321, HFF-37
Washington, DC 20204
202-245-1235
202-245-6694 Fax
Food technology, nutrition, analytical chemistry, and toxicology.

COMPANIES

Amurol Products Co.
(Subsidiary of Wm. Wrigley Jr. Co.)
1100 E. Chicago Ave., Box 3026
Naperville, IL 60566
708-355-3000
Dietetic and sugarless candies and confections.

American Vitamin Products, Inc.
505 Halls Mill Rd.
Freehold, NJ 07728
908-308-3000
Vitamins.

Atlantic Group Inc.
10 W. Adams St.
Jacksonville, FL 32202
904-359-3075
Vitamins and health foods.

Estee Corp.
169 Lackawanna Ave.
Parsippany, NJ 07054
201-335-1000
Diet foods and confections.

Evergood Products Corp.
175 Lauman Lane
Hicksville, NY 11801
516-822-1230
Vitamins and related products.

General Nutrition Inc.
921 Penn Ave.
Pittsburgh, PA 15222
412-288-4600
Vitamins and food supplements.

Herbalife International of America, Inc.
9800 La Cienega Blvd.
Inglewood, CA 90301
213-410-9600
Dietary and vitamin products.

P. Leiner Nutritional Products Corp.
1845 W. 205th St.
Torrance, CA 90501
213-328-9610
Vitamins and other products.

Stur-Dee Health Products, Inc.
2 Austin Blvd.
Island Park, NY 11558
516-889-6400
Vitamins.

Vitamin Products Co.
1200 W. Royal Lee Dr., Box 904
Palmyra, WI 53156
414-495-2122
Vitamins and dietary foods.

FEDERAL GOVERNMENT

U.S. International Trade Administration
Department of Commerce
14th St. and Constitution Ave., N.W.
Washington, DC 20230
202-377-2000
Ask for the Commodity Analyst who is an expert in vitamins and diet supplements.

U.S. International Trade Commission
500 E St., S.W.
Washington, DC 20436
202-205-2000 Office of the Secretary
202-205-3296 Industries locator
Ask for the Trade Analyst who is an expert in vitamins and diet supplements.

WALLPAPER INDUSTRY

See also: PAINT AND PAINTING INDUSTRY

ASSOCIATIONS

National Decorating Products Association
1050 N. Lindbergh Blvd.
St. Louis, MO 63132-2994
314-991-3470
314-991-5039 Fax
Robert Petit, Chief Executive
Provides research and training programs to wholesalers and retailers of wallpaper, paint, and other products used for decorating.

Wallcovering Distributors Association
401 N. Michigan Ave.
Chicago, IL 60611-4390
312-644-6610
312-321-6869 Fax
Edward Craft, Executive Director
Wholesalers of wallpaper and other wallcoverings.

Wallcovering Manufacturers Association
355 Lexington Ave., 17th Fl.
New York, NY 10017
212-661-4261
212-370-9047 Fax
Mauro Checchio, Executive Director
Offers educational and technical programs to manufacturers of wallpapers and other wallcoverings.

PERIODICALS

Decorative Products World
Chilton Co.
Chilton Way
201 King of Prussia Rd.
Radnor, PA 19089
215-964-4275
Terrence Gallagher, Editor
*Surveys new products and industry trends for
paint and wallpaper retailers.*

Wallcoverings
Publishing Dynamics Inc.
15 Banks St., Ste. 101
Stamford, CT 06901
203-357-0028
Martin Johnson, Editor
*Reports news of interest to manufacturers and
distributors of wallcoverings.*

COMPANIES

Color Tile, Inc.
(Subsidiary of Color Tile Holding, Inc.)
515 Houston St.
Fort Worth, TX 76102
817-870-9630
Tile, paint, and wallpaper products.

Eisenhart Wallcoverings Co.
(Subsidiary of Eisenhart Corp.)
Pine St.
Hanover, PA 17331
717-632-5918
Wallpaper.

Excel Jerlee, Inc.
(Division of Excel Home Fashions)
420 Frelinghuysen Ave.
Newark, NJ 07114
201-824-7000
Wallpaper and tape products.

Gison Homas Cleveland
1755 Enterprise Pkwy.
Twinsburg, OH 44087
216-425-3255
Wallpaper paste and other adhesives.

Greeff Fabrics Inc.
(Division of Collins & Aikman Corp.)
150 Midland Ave.
Port Chester, NY 10573
914-939-6200
Upholstery fabrics and wallpaper coverings.

Katzenbach & Warren, Inc.
(Division of Collins & Aikman Corp.)
420 Hudson River Rd.
Waterford, NY 12188
518-235-6500
Wallpaper.

Kent-Bragaline, Inc.
27-35 Jackson Ave
Long Island City, NY 11101
718-784-2012
Wholesaler of fabrics and wallpaper.

Martin Paint Stores
182-20 Liberty Ave.
Jamaica, NY 11432
718-454-5100
Retailer of paint, wallpaper, and related products.

Quality Wall Covering, Inc.
8 Sutton Pl.
Edison, NJ 08817
908-985-3349
Wallpaper.

Red Devil Inc.
2400 Vauxhall Rd.
Union, NJ 07083
908-688-6900
*Painting and wallpapering tools, and other
types of products.*

FEDERAL GOVERNMENT

U.S. International Trade Administration
Department of Commerce
14th St. and Constitution Ave., N.W.
Washington, DC 20230
202-377-2000
Ask for the Commodity Analyst who is an
expert in the wallpaper industry.

U.S. International Trade Commission
500 E St., S.W.
Washington, DC 20436
202-205-2000 Office of the Secretary
202-205-3296 Industries locator
Ask for the Trade Analyst who is an expert in
the wallpaper industry.

WAREHOUSES

See also: DISTRIBUTORS AND WHOLESALERS and MOVING AND STORAGE INDUSTRY

ASSOCIATIONS

Affiliated Warehouse Companies
PO Box 295
Hazlet, NJ 07730
201-739-2323
201-739-4154 Fax
Jim McBride, President
Offers research, public relations, advertising,
and sales assistance to franchised public ware-
house companies.

Allied Distribution
2711 W. 183rd St., Ste. 219
Homewood, IL 60430
708-957-2113
708-957-7918 Fax
Ernest Brunswick, Executive Vice President
A network of associated distribution centers
and warehouses.

American Chain of Warehouses
PO Box 7216
Somerset, NJ 08875-7216
800-346-4113
Edward Deuchar, Executive Vice President
An association of commercial warehouses.

International Association of Refrigerated
    Warehouses
7315 Wisconsin Ave.
Bethesda, MD 20814
301-652-5674
301-652-7269 Fax
J. William Hudson, President
Owners of commercial refrigerated ware-
houses that store food and other perishable
goods of all kinds.

National Mini-Storage Institute
1331 P St. N.W.
Washington, DC 20005
202-943-9162
Frank Mason, President
Offers seminars to owners and operators of self-storage facilities.

Self Storage Association
60 Revere Dr., Ste. 500
Northbrook, IL 60062
708-480-9627
Provides marketing and public relations programs to owners and operators of self-storage facilities.

PERIODICALS

Direction
National Moving & Storage Association
1500 Beauregard St.
Alexandria, VA 22311-1715
703-671-8813
Joyce McDowell, Editor
Reports on labor relations, equipment, and news of interest to the moving and storage industry.

Distribution Center Management
Alexander Research & Communications, Inc.
1133 Broadway, Ste. 1407
New York, NY 10010
212-228-0246
Yvette Holland, Editor
Advice on how to streamline storage and distribution operations.

Material Handling Product News
Gordon Publications, Inc.
301 Gibraltar Dr.
Morris Plains, NJ 07950
201-292-5100
Dolly Grobstein, Editor
A directory of material handling systems and products used in warehouses and elsewhere.

COMPANIES

Americold Corp.
1515 S.W. Fifth
Portland, OR 97201
503-224-3480
Warehousing of frozen foods.

Crete Carrier Corp.
P. O. Box 81228
Lincoln, NE 68502
402-475-9521
Trucking and warehousing.

Exel Logistics Dedicated Distribution Inc..
(Subsidiary of NFC International Holdings
    (USA Inc.)
229 Huber Village Blvd.
Westerville, OH 43081
614-890-1730
Warehousing.

Kenwal Products Corp.
9301 Central Ave.
Detroit, MI 48204
313-933-4362
Warehousing of steel.

Leaseway Transportation Corp.
(Subsidiary of Leaseway Holdings, Inc.)
3700 Park East Dr.
Cleveland, OH 44122
216-765-5500
Trucking and warehousing.

Lennar Corp.
700 N. W. 107th Ave.
Miami, FL 33172
305-559-4000
Builder of homes, warehouses, and other real estate.

Smith Investment Co.
P.O. Box 23976
Milwaukee, WI 53223
414-359-4030
Public warehousing and other businesses.

WASHINGTON

STATE OFFICE LOCATOR (*for referrals to all state government offices*)

206-753-5000

ARCHIVES AND RECORDS

State Archives
Secretary of State
Mail Stop AS-22
Olympia, WA 98504
206-586-2660

ATTORNEY GENERAL

Attorney General's Office
Mail Stop PB-71
Olympia, WA 98504
206-753-2550

BANKING

Banking & Small Loans Division
218 General Administration Building
Olympia, WA 98504
206-753-6520

COMMERCE

Trade & Economic Development Department
Mail Stop AX-13
Olympia, WA 98504
206-753-7426

CONSUMER AFFAIRS

Department of Consumer Protection
Mail Stop PB-71
Olympia, WA 98504
206-586-2563

EDUCATION

Public Instruction Department
Mail Stop FG-11
Olympia, WA 98504
206-586-6904

ENERGY

Energy Office
Mail Stop FA-11
Olympia, WA 98504
206-956-2000

ENVIRONMENTAL AFFAIRS

Ecology Department
Mail Stop PV-11
Olympia, WA 98504
206-459-6188

HEALTH

Vital Records
Mail Stop ET-11
Olympia, WA 98504
206-753-5936

HOUSING

Housing Programs
Mail Stop GH-51
Olympia, WA 98504-4151
206-753-0515

HUMAN RIGHTS

Human Rights Commission
Mail Stop FJ-41
Olympia, WA 98504
206-753-6770

INSURANCE

Insurance Commissioner
Mail Stop AQ-21
Olympia, WA 98504-0321
206-753-7301

LABOR

Labor & Industries Department
Mail Stop HC-101
Olympia, WA 98504
206-753-6307

LEGISLATION

Program Research Office
Mail Stop AS-33
Olympia, WA 98504
206-786-7102

LIBRARY SERVICES

State Library
Mail Stop AJ-11
Olympia, WA 98504-0111
206-753-2915

LICENSING—CORPORATE

Municipal Corporations Division
Mail Stop AS-21
Olympia, WA 98504
206-753-2433

LICENSING—PROFESSIONAL AND OCCUPATIONAL

Professional Licensing Services Division
Mail Stop PB-01
Olympia, WA 98504
206-753-6681

MOTOR VEHICLES

Vehicle Services Division
Mail Stop PB-01
Olympia, WA 98504-0111
206-753-6914

OCCUPATIONAL HEALTH AND SAFETY

Industrial Safety & Health Division
P.O. Box 207
Olympia, WA 98504
206-753-6500

OMBUDSMAN

Lead Analyst & Constituent Contact
Mail Stop AS-13
Olympia, WA 98504
206-753-6780

PUBLIC UTILITIES

Utilities & Transportation Commission
1300 S. Evergreen Park Drive, S.W.
Olympia, WA 98504
206-753-6430

PURCHASING

Procurement Division
216 General Administration Building
Olympia, WA 98504
206-753-6461

REAL ESTATE

Real Estate Escrow Bureau
P.O. Box 9012
Olympia, WA 98504
206-753-6974

SECURITIES

Securities Division
Mail Stop PB-01
Olympia, WA 98504
206-753-6928

TAXATION AND REVENUE

Revenue Department
Mail Stop AX-02
Olympia, WA 98504
206-753-5574

TOURISM

Tourism Division
101 General Administration Building
Olympia, WA 98504
206-586-2088
800-544-1800

TRANSPORTATION

Transportation Department
Mail Stop KF-01
Olympia, WA 98504
206-753-6054

UNEMPLOYMENT

Unemployment Insurance Division
212 Maple Park
Olympia, WA 98504
206-753-5120

WORKER'S COMPENSATION

Workers Benefits Section
Mail Stop HC-101
Olympia, WA 98504
206-753-6376

WASTE MANAGEMENT

See also: ENVIRONMENTAL CONSERVATION AND POLLUTION CONTROL; RECYCLING; and each of the 50 states under environmental affairs

ASSOCIATIONS

Center for Hazardous Materials Research
320 William Pitt Way
University of Pittsburgh Applied Research
    Center
Pittsburgh, PA 15238
412-826-5320
800-334-CHMR
412-826-5552 Fax
Edgar Berkey, President
Conducts laboratory research, provides technical assistance, and studies policy issues concerning hazardous materials and waste management.

Coalition for Responsible Waste Incineration
1330 Connecticut Ave. N.W., Ste. 300
Washington, DC 20036
202-659-0060
William Murray, Executive Director
Offers information about the technical, safety, and health aspects of industrial waste incineration.

Hazardous Materials Control Research Institute
7237 Hanover Pkwy.
Greenbelt, MD 20770
301-587-9390
Harold Bernard, Executive Director
Provides educational programs and a wide range of information services on the prevention and cleanup of hazardous materials and wastes.

Hazardous Waste Treatment Council
1440 New York Ave. N.W., Ste. 310
Washington, DC 20005
202-783-0870
Richard Fortuna, Executive Director
Companies that use advanced and alternative technological methods to treat hazardous wastes.

National Solid Wastes Management Association
1730 Rhode Island Ave. N.W., Ste. 1000
Washington, DC 20036
202-659-4613
Eugene Wingerter, Executive Director
The Association provides research and information about all aspects of solid waste management equipment, services, technologies, and related topics.

PERIODICALS

BioCycle
J G Press, Inc.
419 State Ave.
Emmaus, PA 18049
215-967-4135
Jerome Goldstein, Editor
Covers collection, processing, recycling, and composting of waste.

Hazardous Materials Control
Hazardous Materials Control Resource
9300 Columbia Blvd.
Silver Spring, MD 20910-1702
301-587-9390
Christopher Hoelzel, Editor
Reports on regulations, technology, equipment, and other topics relevant to hazardous waste control.

Hazardous Substances & Public Health
U.S. Department of Health and Human Services
Agency for Toxic Substances and Disease Registry
1600 Clifton Rd., N.E.
Mailstop E-33
Atlanta, GA 30333
404-639-0736
Theresa Ramsey, Editor
Covers hazardous waste management and its medical aspects.

Hazardous Waste and Toxic Torts Law and
   Strategy
New York Law Publishing Co.
Marketing Dept.
111 Eighth Ave.
New York, NY 10011
212-741-8300
Follows regulatory and legislative matters regarding hazardous waste.

Hazardous Waste Consultant
McCoy and Associates, Inc.
13701 W. Jewell Ave., Ste. 202
Lakewood, CO 80228-4173
303-987-0333
Paul Gallagher, Editor
Offers information on hazardous waste technology, environmental policy, and regulatory rulings.

Hazardous Waste Management & Business
Opportunities Newsletter
C A E Consultants Inc.
41 Travers Ave.
Yonkers, NY 10705
914-963-3695
Lidia LoPinto, Editor
Reports on the latest hazardous waste technologies and systems for executives looking to invest in this field.

Management of World Wastes
Communication Channels, Inc.
6255 Barfield Rd.
Atlanta, GA 30328-4369
404-256-9800
William Wolpin, Editor
Surveys hazardous waste news and technology worldwide.

Waste Treatment Technology News
Business Communications Co., Inc.
25 Van Zant St.
Norwalk, CT 06855
203-853-4266
Donald Saxman, Editor
Covers new technologies for the treatment of hazardous waste.

LIBRARIES

Clayton Environmental Consultants, Inc.
Library and Information Center
22345 Roethel Dr.
Novi, MI 48050
313-344-1770
313-344-2654 Fax
Waste management, environmental pollution, industrial hygiene, and related topics.

Malcolm Pirnie, Inc.
Technical Library
2 Corporate Park Dr.
Box 751
White Plains, NY 10602
914-641-2954
914-694-9286 Fax
Hazardous waste management, environmental engineering, and air pollution.

Wehran Envirotech
Library
666 E. Main St.
Middletown, NY 10940
914-343-0660
914-692-7376
Wastewater, solid waste, industrial pollution abatement, and other subjects.

COMPANIES

Air & Water Technologies Corp.
U.S. Hwy. 22 W. & Station Rd.
Branchburg, NJ 08876
201-685-4600
A wide variety of waste management and environmental treatment services.

Canonie Environmental Services Corp.
800 Canonie Dr.
Porter, IN 46304
219-926-8651
Cleanup of hazardous wastes.

Chemical Waste Management, Inc.
(Subsidiary of Waste Management, Inc.)
3001 Butterfield Rd.
Oak Brook, IL 60521
708-218-1500
Cleanup of hazardous wastes.

Combustion Engineering Inc.
(Subsidiary of ABB Asea Brown Boveri Ltd.)
900 Long Ridge Rd., Box 9308
Stamford, CT 06904
203-329-8771
Engineering, design, and construction of pollution control systems.

Courter & Co., Inc.
(Subsidiary of NPS Technology Group Inc.)
300 Harmon Meadow Blvd.
Secaucus, NJ 07094
201-865-6550
Wastewater treatment plants and other engineering projects.

Nalco Chemical Co.
One Nalco Center
Naperville, IL 60566
708-305-1000
Chemicals used in waste treatment and other products.

Republic Waste Industries Inc.
314 N. Post Oak Lane
Houston, TX 77024
713-956-1110
Waste management services.

URS Corp.
100 California St.
San Francisco, CA 94111
415-774-2700
Pollution control and waste management services.

Waste Management, Inc.
3003 Butterfield Rd.
Oak Brook, IL 60521
708-572-8800
A wide range of waste management services.

FEDERAL GOVERNMENT

U.S. Environmental Protection Agency
401 M St., S.W.
Washington, DC 20460
202-260-2090
Ask for the public relations office to locate an appropriate expert in waste management.

U.S. International Trade Administration
Department of Commerce
14th St. and Constitution Ave., N.W.
Washington, DC 20230
202-377-2000
Ask for the Commodity Analyst who is an expert in waste management.

U.S. International Trade Commission
500 E St., S.W.
Washington, DC 20436
202-205-2000 Office of the Secretary
202-205-3296 Industries locator
Ask for the Trade Analyst who is an expert in waste management.

WATERWAYS AND PORTS

See also: SHIPS AND SHIPPING INDUSTRY

ASSOCIATIONS

American Waterways Operators
1600 Wilson Blvd., Ste. 1000
Arlington, VA 22209
703-841-9300
703-841-0389 Fax
Joseph Farrell, President
Firms that operate tugboats, barges, and related vessels in coastal and inland waterways.

Inland Rivers Ports and Terminals
c/o Kathy Pabst
204 E. High St.
Jefferson City, MO 65101
314-634-2028
Kathy Pabst, Executive Officer
Owners of ports and inland waterway terminals, facility operators, and others interested in promoting the use of inland waterways.

National Association of Dredging Contractors
1733 King St., Ste. 300
Alexandria, VA 22314
703-548-8300
703-548-0421 Fax
Mark Sickles, Executive Director
Contractors who dredge navigation channels and remove underwater rock.

National Waterways Conference
1130 17th St. N.W., Ste. 200
Washington, DC 20036
202-296-4415
202-835-3861 Fax
Harry Cook, President
Promotes the use of water transportation through educational and public relations programs.

Water Transport Association
c/o William Morelli
Ohio River Co.
PO Box 1460
Cincinnati, OH 45201
800-950-7707
William Morelli, Secretary
A small group of inland and coastal water carriers (transport firms) who are certified by the Interstate Commerce Commission.

PERIODICALS

Global Trade
North American Publishing Co.
401 N. Broad St.
Philadelphia, PA 19108
Karen Theurman, Editor
Covers numerous subjects for international trade executives, including ports.

Journal of Waterway, Port, Coastal, and Ocean Engineering
Waterway, Port, Coastal, and Ocean Division
American Society of Civil Engineers
345 E. 47th St.
New York, NY 10017-2398
212-705-7288
Philip Li-Fan Liu, Editor
Helps engineers keep abreast of how ice, floods, dredging, tidal wave action, and pollution affect waterways, ports, and seashores.

Seaway Review
Harbor House Publishers, Inc.
221 Water St.
Boyne City, MI 49712
616-582-2814
Michelle Cortright, Editor
Information about the St. Lawrence-Great Lakes waterway system.

U.S. Army. Corps of Engineers Information Exchange Bulletin Waterways Experiment Station
3909 Halls Ferry Rd.
Vicksburg, MS 39180-6199
601-634-2070
Surveys the latest in dredging research.

U.S. Custom House Guide
North American Publishing Co.
401 N. Broad St.
Philadelphia, PA 19108
215-238-5300
Tery Moran-Lever, Editor
Information on U.S. tariffs, customs regulations, customs ports.

Waterways Journal
Waterways Journal, Inc.
319 N. Fourth St.
666 Security Bldg.
St. Louis, MO 63102
314-241-7354
Jack Simpson, Editor
Follows the marine profession and commercial activity on inland waterways.

LIBRARIES

U.S. Army
Corps of Engineers
North Atlantic Divisiion
Technical Library
26 Federal Plaza
New York, NY 10278
212-264-0234
Water development, dams, locks, and civil engineering.

U.S. Army
Corps of Engineers
South Pacific Division
Library
630 Sansome St., Rm. 720
San Francisco, CA 94111-2206
415-705-1520
Water resources and civil engineering.

FEDERAL GOVERNMENT

U.S. Coast Guard
2100 2nd St., S.W.
Washington, DC 20593
202-267-2229
Ask for the community relations office to find an appropriate expert.

U.S. International Trade Administration
Department of Commerce
14th St. and Constitution Ave., N.W.
Washington, DC 20230
202-377-2000
Ask for the Commodity Analyst who is an expert in ports and waterways.

U.S. International Trade Commission
500 E St., S.W.
Washington, DC 20436
202-205-2000 Office of the Secretary
202-205-3296 Industries locator
Ask for the Trade Analyst who is an expert in ports and waterways.

U.S. Department of Transportation
400 Seventh St., S.W.
Washington, DC 20590
202-366-4000
Ask for the Port & Intermodal Marketing Operations department; or the Inland Waterways Shipping Marketing Division in the Maritime Administration.

WEATHER AND WEATHER FORECASTING

ASSOCIATIONS

Association of American Weather Observers
PO Box 455
Belvidere, IL 61008
815-544-9811
815-544-6334 Fax
Steven Steinke, Director
*Comprised of professional and amateur
weather observers and meteorologists.*

Commercial Weather Services Association
655 15th St., N.W., Ste. 310
Washington, DC 20005-5701
202-546-6993
Jeffrey Smith, Executive Director
*Firms that provide weather forecasting data
and reports.*

National Weather Association
4400 Stamp Rd., Rm. 404
Temple Hills, MD 20748
301-899-3784
Sol Hirsch, Executive Director
*A professional society of weather forecasters
and meteorologists.*

National Weather Service Employees Organi-
 zation
400 N. Capitol St., Ste. 326
Washington, DC 20001
202-783-3131
David Powell, President
*Members are employed by the National
Weather Service, the National Meteorological
Center, and other federal organizations that
deal with weather subjects.*

PERIODICALS

Journal of Applied Meteorology
American Meteorological Society
45 Beacon St.
Boston, MA 02108-3693
617-227-2425
Steven Hanna, Editor
*Offers technical information on weather modi-
fication, satellite meteorology, and clouds.*

Monthly Weather Review
American Meteorological Society
45 Beacon St.
Boston, MA 02108-3693
617-227-2425
Richard Rotunno, Editor
*Reports highly technical information about
weather and weather forecasting.*

LIBRARIES

U.S. National Weather Service
Central Region Headquarters
Library
601 E. 12th St., Rm 1836
Kansas City, MO 64106
813-426-5672
Climatology and hydrology.

Weather Research Center
Library
3227 Audley
Houston, TX 77098
713-529-3076
713-528-3538
Climatology, hydrology, and physics.

COMPANIES

Alden Electronics Inc.
40 Washington St.
Westboro, MA 01581
508-366-8851
Weather recording devices.

Belfort Instrument Co.
(Division of TransTechnology Corp.)
727 S. Wolfe St.
Baltimore, MD 21231
301-342-2626
Meteorological and other types of instruments.

Deepwater Inc.
P. O. Box 17599
Irvine, CA 92713
714-751-3522
*Chemicals used to modify the weather, and
other products.*

ISC Cardion Electronics Inc.
Long Island Expressway
Woodbury, NY 11797
516-921-7300
Meteorological and other types of equipment.

Leupold & Stevens, Inc.
P. O. Box 688
Beaverton, OR 97075
503-646-9171
Meteorological and other types of instruments.

Sunbeam Precision Measurements
(Subsidiary of Sunbeam Corp.)
76 Passaic St.
Wood-Ridge, NJ 07075
201-777-2900
Weather instruments and other products.

Swift Instruments, Inc.
952 Dorchester Ave.
Boston, MA 02125
617-436-2960
Weather instruments and other products.

Thermometer Corp. of America
(Division of Figgie International Inc.)
280 Cane Creek Rd., Box 1349
Fletcher, NC 28732
704-684-5178
Weather instruments and other products.

Transtechnology Corp.
15303 Ventura Blvd.
Sherman Oaks, CA 91403
818-990-5920
Meteorological and other types of instruments.

FEDERAL GOVERNMENT

U.S. Department of Agriculture
14th St. and Independence Ave., S.W.
Washington, DC 20250
202-720-8732
*Ask for the National Agricultural Statistics
Service.*

U.S. National Weather Service
1325 East-West Highway
Silver Springs, MD 20910
301-443-8910
*Ask for the public affairs office to find an
appropriate expert.*

WELDING

ASSOCIATIONS

American Council of the International Institute of Welding
550 N.W. LeJeune Rd.
Miami, FL 33135
305-443-9353
800-443-9353
H. Glenn Ziegenfuss, Secretary
Sponsors research and provides information on all aspects of welding. Affiliated with the American Welding Society at the same address.

American Welding Institute
10628 Dutchtown Rd.
Knoxville, TN 37932
615-675-2150
615-675-6081 Fax
H. Vanderveldt, President
An educational and research group of companies that offer and use specialized welding techniques employed in aerospace, robotics, and other industries.

Edison Welding Institute
1100 Kinnear Rd.
Columbus, OH 43212
614-486-9400
614-486-9528 Fax
Karl Graff, Executive Director
Offers training and information in welding and other material-joining technologies.

PERIODICALS

Welding—Brazing—Soldering Digest
A S M International, Materials Information
Materials Park, OH 44073
216-338-5151
H. David Chafe, Editor
Publishes articles about riveting, soldering, brazing, and other welding techniques.

Welding Design and Fabrication
Penton Publishing
1100 Superior Ave.
Cleveland, OH 44114-2543
216-696-7000
Rosalie Brosilow, Editor
Reports on welding technology, equipment, maintenance, and applications.

Welding Distributor
Penton Publishing
1100 Superior Ave.
Cleveland, OH 44114-2543
216-696-7000
Michael Vasilakes, Editor
Offers management and merchandising advice to distributors of welding equipment and supplies.

Welding Journal
American Welding Society
Box 351040
Miami, FL 33135
305-443-9353
Jeff Weber, Editor
Covers products, supplies, inspection, testing, construction, and related welding topics.

Welding Research News
Welding Research Council
345 E. 47th St.
New York, NY 10017
212-705-7956
Reports on the latest developments in the welding industry.

LIBRARIES

American Council of the International Institute of Welding
Library
550 N.W. LeJeune Rd.
Box 351040
Miami, FL 33135
405-443-9353
305-443-7559 Fax
Welding and international welding standards.

Babcock and Wilcox Co.
Corporate Information Center
Box 835
Alliance, OH 44601
2216-821-9110
216-823-0639 Fax
Welding, metallurgy, heat transfer, mechanics, and technology.

Hobart Institute of Technology
Hobart Brothers Co.
John H. Blankenbuehler Memorial Library
400 Trade Square East
Troy, OH 45373
513-332-5603
513-332-5200 Fax
Welding and metallurgy.

COMPANIES

Hobart Brothers Co.
Hobart Square
Troy, OH 45373
513-332-4000
Arc welding equipment and other products.

Inco United States, Inc.
(Subsidiary of INCO Limited)
One New York Plaza
New York, NY 10004
212-612-5690
Welding products and other businesses.

Lawson Products, Inc.
1666 E. Touhy Ave.
Des Plaines, IL 60018
708-827-9666
Welding equipment and supplies, and other types of products.

Miller Electric Mfg. Co.
(Subsidiary of Miller Group, Ltd.)
1635 W. Spencer, Box 1079
Appleton, WI 54912
414-734-9821
Welding equipment.

Miller Group, Ltd.
1635 W. Spencer St.
Appleton, WI 54914
414-734-9821
Welding equipment.

National-Standard Co.
1618 Terminal Rd.
Niles, MI 49120
616-683-8100
Welding wire and other kinds of wire.

Nibco Inc.
P. O. Box 1167
Elkhart, IN 46515
219-295-3000
Welding flanges and many other types of products.

Sandvik, Inc.
(Subsidiary of Sandvik AB)
1702 Nevins Rd.
Fair Lawn, NJ 07410
201-794-5000
Welding wire and many other types of products.

Thermadyne Industries
101 S. Hanley
St. Louis, MO 63105
314-721-5573
Welding and cutting equipment.

FEDERAL GOVERNMENT

U.S. Customs Service
Department of the Treasury
U.S. Customshouse
6 World Trade Center
New York, NY 10048
212-466-5550
Ask for the Commodity Specialist in charge of welding equipment.

U.S. International Trade Administration
Department of Commerce
14th St. and Constitution Ave., N.W.
Washington, DC 20230
202-377-2000
Ask for the Commodity Analyst who is an expert in welding equipment.

U.S. International Trade Commission
500 E St., S.W.
Washington, DC 20436
202-205-2000 Office of the Secretary
202-205-3296 Industries locator
Ask for the Trade Analyst who is an expert in welding equipment.

U.S. Patent and Trademark Office
Crystal Plaza 2
2011 Jefferson Davis Highway
Arlington, VA 22202
703-305-8000
Ask for the Examining Group Director who is a specialist in welding equipment.

WEST VIRGINIA

STATE OFFICE LOCATOR (*for referrals to all state government offices*)

304-348-3456

ARCHIVES AND RECORDS

Culture & History Division
Cultural Center
State Capitol Complex
Charleston, WV 25305
304-348-0230

ATTORNEY GENERAL

Attorney General's Office
State Capitol Complex
26 East
Charleston, WV 25305
304-348-2021

BANKING

Banking Division
State Capitol Complex
Building 3, Room 311A
Charleston, WV 25305
304-348-2294

COMMERCE

Community Development Division
State Capitol Complex
Building 6, Room 553
Charleston, WV 25305
304-348-4010

CONSUMER AFFAIRS

Consumer Protection
State Capitol Complex
26 East
Charleston, WV 25305
304-348-8986

EDUCATION

Education Division
State Capitol Complex
Building 6, Room B-358
Charleston, WV 23505
304-348-2681

ENERGY

Fuel & Energy Office
Building E
1204 Kanawha Boulevard
Charleston, WV 25301
304-348-4010

ENVIRONMENTAL AFFAIRS

Natural Resources Division
State Capitol Complex
Building 3
Charleston, WV 25305
304-348-2754

HEALTH

Health & Human Resources Department
State Capitol Complex
Building 3, Room 519
Charleston, WV 25305
304-348-2971

HOUSING

Housing Development Fund
814 Virginia Street, E.
Charleston, WV 25301
304-345-6475

HUMAN RIGHTS

Human Rights Commission
1321 Plaza East
Room 104-106
Charleston, WV 25301-1400
304-348-2616

INSURANCE

Insurance Commission
State Capitol Complex
Charleston, WV 25305
304-348-3394

LABOR

Labor Division
1800 Washington Street, E.
Charleston, WV 25305
304-348-7890

LEGISLATION

Legislative Services
State Capitol Complex
Room E-132
Charleston, WV 25305
304-348-2040

LIBRARY SERVICES

Library Commission
Cultural Center
State Capitol Complex
Charleston, WV 25305
304-348-2041

LICENSING—CORPORATE

Corporations Division
State Capitol Building
Charleston, WV 25305
304-345-4000

MOTOR VEHICLES

Motor Vehicles Division
State Capitol Complex
Building 3
Charleston, WV 25305
304-348-2723

OCCUPATIONAL HEALTH AND SAFETY

Radiological Health Program
State Capitol Complex
Building 3, Room 519
Charleston, WV 25305
304-348-3526

PUBLIC UTILITIES

Public Service Commission
P.O. Box 812
Charleston, WV 25323
304-340-0303

PURCHASING

Purchasing Division
State Capitol Complex
Building 1, Room E119
Charleston, WV 25305
304-348-2309

REAL ESTATE

Real Estate Management
State Capitol Complex
Building 3
Charleston, WV 25305
304-348-2224

SECURITIES

Securities Division
100 State Capitol Complex
1st Floor
Charleston, WV 25305
304-348-2257

TAXATION AND REVENUE

Tax & Revenue Department
Revenue Center
Room W300
Charleston, WV 25305
304-348-2500

TOURISM

Travel West Virginia
State Capitol Complex
Charleston, WV 25305
304-348-2286
800-CALL-WVA

TRANSPORTATION

Transportation Department
State Capitol Complex
Building 5, Room 109
Charleston, WV 25305
304-348-0444

UNEMPLOYMENT

Unemployment Compensation Section
112 California Avenue
Charleston, WV 25305
304-348-2624

WORKER'S COMPENSATION

Workmens Compensation Bureau
P.O. Box 3151
Charleston, WV 25332
304-348-0475

WHEAT INDUSTRY

ASSOCIATIONS

International Wheat Gluten Association
4510 W. 89th St.
Prairie Village, KS 66207-2282
913-341-1155
913-341-3625 Fax
J. Hesser, Executive Director
Offers technical and industry information to producers and users of wheat gluten and wheat starch.

National Association of Wheat Growers
415 2nd St. N.E., Ste. 300
Washington, DC 20002
202-547-7800
Carl Schwensen, Executive Vice President
Provides educational programs and conferences on wheat growing, shipping, and other topics.

U.S. Wheat Associates
1620 I St. N.W., Ste. 801
Washington, DC 20006
202-463-0999
202-785-1052 Fax
Winston Wilson, President
Members include state organizations of wheat growers and state wheat commissions that promote sales of U.S. wheat abroad.

Wheat Gluten Industry Council
4210 Shawnee Mission Pkwy., Ste. 312A
Shawnee Mission, KS 66205
913-362-0777
913-362-0872 Fax
J. Kirkpatrick, Executive Director
Comprised of wheat gluten and wheat starch producers.

Wheat Quality Council
404 Humboldt
Manhattan, KS 66502
913-776-6348
Thomas Roberts, Executive Vice President
Sponsored by bakeries and other users of wheat, the Council provides technical information designed to help growers maintain the quality of wheat supplies.

PERIODICALS

Wheat Grower
National Association of Wheat Growers Foundation
415 Second St., N.E., Ste. 300
Washington, DC 20002-4993
202-547-7800
Barry Jenkins, Editor
Agricultural and business advice for wheat growers.

Wheat Life
Washington Association of Wheat Growers
109 E. First Ave.
Ritzville, WA 99169-2394
509-659-0610
David Anderson, Editor
*Reports on research, legislation, and other
topics of concern to wheat growers.*

Wheat Situation and Outlook
U.S. Department of Agriculture
Economic Research Service
1301 New York Ave., N.W., Ste. 228
Washington, DC 20005-4789
202-786-1494
*Statistical information and forecasts about the
wheat industry.*

Wheat Technology
National Association of Wheat Growers Foun-
    dation
415 Second Street, N.E., Ste. 300
Washington, DC 20002-4993
202-547-7800
Richard Stuckey, Editor
Technical information for wheat growers.

COMPANIES

Adm-West
(Division of Archer-Daniels-Midland Co.)
309 W. Madison
Arkansas City, KS 67005
316-442-5500
Wheat flour and related products.

Agrex Inc.
7007 College Blvd.
Overland Park, KS 66211
913-345-5400
Storage and sales of wheat and other grains.

Bartlett Milling Co.
(Division of Bartlett and Co.)
4800 Main St.
Kansas City, MO 64112
816-531-6235
Wheat flour.

California Milling Corp.
(Subsidiary of Cereal Food Processors, Inc.)
1861 E. 55th St.
Los Angeles, CA 90058
213-585-0131
Wheat flour.

Keynes Brothers, Inc.
One W. Front St.
Logan, OH 43138
614-385-6824
Wheat flour.

Mennel Milling Co.
128 W. Crocker St.
Fostoria, OH 44830
419-435-8151
Wheat flour and related products.

Midwest Grain Products, Inc.
1300 Main St.
Atchison, KS 66002
913-367-1480
Wheat and other grain products.

Union Equity Co-operative Exchange
P.O. Box 3408
Enid, OK 73702
405-233-5100
Hard milling wheat and other products.

Tom W. Wade Co.
P.O. Box 265
Kenton, TN 38233
901-749-5305
Wheat and other products.

Wall-Rogalsky Milling Co.
416 N. Main St.
McPherson, KS 67460
316-241-2410
Hard wheat flour and related products.

FEDERAL GOVERNMENT

U.S. Department of Agriculture
14th St. and Independence Ave., S.W.
Washington, DC 20250
202-720-8732
Ask for the Economic Research Service.

WINE INDUSTRY

See also: LIQUOR AND SPIRITS INDUSTRY and LIQUOR STORES

ASSOCIATIONS

Academy of Master Wine Growers
703 Market St., Ste. 2101
San Francisco, CA 94103
415-957-5071
Louis Gomberg, Executive Secretary
A small group offering information about California wines.

American Society for Enology and Viticulture
PO Box 1855
Davis, CA 95617
916-753-3142
916-753-3318 Fax
Lyndie Boulton, Executive Director
A forum for the exchange of technical information about grape growing and wine production.

American Viticultural Area Association
Guenoc Winery
21000 Butts Canyon Rd.
Middletown, CA 95461
707-987-2385
707-987-9351 Fax
Orville Magoon, President
Promotes U.S. wines in the U.S.

American Wine Society
3006 Latta Rd.
Rochester, NY 14612
716-225-7613
Angel Nardone, Executive Director
Members include growers, winemakers, wine retailers, connoisseurs, and others. Offers educational programs, wine tastings, and other programs to increase the appreciation of wines.

Association of American Vintners
Box 307
East Rochester, NY 14445
716-383-8050
William Stockdale, Executive Officer
Reports to wine producers about legislation and regulation affecting the industry.

Wine Appreciation Guild
155 Connecticut St.
San Francisco, CA 94107
415-864-1202
415-864-0377 Fax
Donna Bottrell, President
Conducts research designed to increase wine consumption.

Wine Institute
425 Market St., Ste. 1000
San Francisco, CA 94105
415-512-0151
415-442-0742 Fax
John De Luca, President
Offers research and educational programs on technical, industry, and wine appreciation topics.

PERIODICALS

American Journal of Enology and Viticulture
American Society for Enology and Viticulture
Box 1855
Davis, CA 95617
916-753-3142
JoAnne Rantz, Editor
Covers grape farming and winemaking.

Beverage Alcohol Market Report
Peregrine Communications
160 E. 48th St.
New York, NY 10017
212-371-5237
Perry Luntz, Editor
Helps industry executives keep abreast of the wine, beer, and liquor market.

Jobson's Wine Marketing Handbook
Jobson Publishing Corp.
352 Park Ave. S.
New York, NY 10010
212-685-4848
Nicolas Furlotte, Editor
Information on sales, consumption, and other statistics about the wine business.

Practical Winery & Vineyard
Don Neel and Associates
15 Grande Paseo
San Rafael, CA 94903
415-479-5819
Don Neel, Editor
How-to information on grape growing, wine-making, and marketing.

Vineyard and Wine Management
Vineyard & Winery Services, Inc.
103 Third St.
Box 231
Watkins Glen, NY 14891
607-535-7133
J. William Moffett, Editor
Advice for grape growers and vintners to increase profitability.

Wine Investor: Buyers' Guide
Wine Investor
3284 Barham Blvd., Ste. 201
Los Angeles, CA 90068
213-876-8400
J.D. Kronman, Editor
Offers suggestions to consumers, retailers, and investors about which wines to buy.

Wines and Vines
Hiaring Co.
1800 Lincoln Ave.
San Rafael, CA 94901
415-453-9700
Philip Hiaring, Editor
Reports on the wine and grape industry.

LIBRARIES

E. & J. Gallo Winery
Library
Box 1130
Modesto, CA 95353
209-579-3230
209-579-4541 Fax
Wine technology, packaging, chemical research, and biological research.

Napa Valley Wine Library Association
Library
1492 Library Ln.
St. Helena, CA 94574
707-963-5244
707-963-5264 Fax
Wine, grapes, viticulture, and winemaking.

Wine Institute
Library
425 Market St., Ste. 1000
Ssan Francisco, CA 94105
415-512-0151
415-442-0742 Fax
Wine, viticulture, and winemaking.

COMPANIES

Canandaigua Wine Co. Inc
116 Buffalo St.
Canandaigua, NY 14424
716-394-3630
Winery.

Continental Distributing Co. Inc.
9800 W. Balmoral Ave.
Rosemont, IL 60018
708-671-7700
Wine and liquor wholesaler.

E & J Gallo Winery
600 Yosemite Blvd.
Modesto, CA 95354
209-579-3111
Winery.

Guild Wineries & Distilleries
P.O. Box 55
Woodbridge, CA 95258
415-798-7722
Winery.

Robert Mondavi Winery, Inc.
7801 St. Helena Hwy.
Oakville, CA 94562
707-963-9611
Winery.

National Winex Spirits
700 W. Morris St.
Indianapolis, IN 46206
317-636-4880
Wine and liquor wholesaler.

Schenley Industries, Inc.
(Subsidiary of Guinness plc)
12770 Merit Dr.
Dallas, TX 75251
214-450-6400
Liquor production and wine importing.

Joseph E. Seagram & Sons, Inc.
(Subsidiary of Seagram Co. Ltd.)
375 Park Ave.
New York, NY 10152
212-572-7000
Liquors and wines.

Sutter Home Winery, Inc.
277 St. Helena Hwy. S., Box 248
St. Helena, CA 94574
707-963-3104
Winery.

Taylor Wine Co.
(Subsidiary of Vintners International Co. Inc.)
County Rte. 88
Hammondsport, NY 14840
607-569-6111
Winery.

FEDERAL GOVERNMENT

U.S. Customs Service
Department of the Treasury
U.S. Customshouse
6 World Trade Center
New York, NY 10048
212-466-5550
Ask for the Commodity Specialist in charge of wine.

U.S. Department of the Treasury
1500 Pennsylvania Ave., N.W.
Washington, DC 20220
202-566-2111
Ask for the Wine & Beer Compliance Bureau in the Bureau of Alcohol, Tobacco and Firearms.

U.S. International Trade Administration
Department of Commerce
14th St. and Constitution Ave., N.W.
Washington, DC 20230
202-377-2000
Ask for the Commodity Analyst who is an
expert in the wine industry.

U.S. International Trade Commission
500 E St., S.W.
Washington, DC 20436
202-205-2000 Office of the Secretary
202-205-3296 Industries locator
Ask for the Trade Analyst who is an expert in
the wine industry.

WIRE INDUSTRY

ASSOCIATIONS

American Wire Producers Association
1101 Connecticut Ave. N.W., Ste. 700
Washington, DC 20036
202-857-1155
202-429-5154 Fax
Robert Chancler, Director
Comprised of firms that make steel, wire prod-
ucts, and machinery used to make wire prod-
ucts. Provides industry information on U.S.
and imported wire goods.

Wire Association International
1570 Boston Post Rd.
Guilford, CT 06437
203-453-2777
203-453-8384 Fax
Joseph Ring, Executive Director
Members include executives, operations man-
agers, metallurgists, engineers, and others who
work in wire mills and plants that make all
types of wire and wire products. Offers techni-
cal and production information.

Wire Fabricators Association
710 E. Ogden Ave., Ste. 113
Naperville, IL 60563
708-369-2406
Michael Hansen, Executive Director
Firms that use wire to produce shelving, bar-
beque grills, and similar products.

Wire Industry Suppliers Association
7297 Lee Hwy., Ste. N
Falls Church, VA 22042
703-533-9530
Harry Buzzerd, Executive Director
Manufacturers of the machinery used to pro-
duce, fabricate, shape, and cut wire and wire
products.

PERIODICALS

Wire Industry News
Business Information Services, Inc.
7 Hampden Rd.
Stafford Springs, CT 06076-9310
203-684-5877
Richard Callahan, Editor
Surveys market conditions, mergers, and
trends in the wire industry.

Wire Journal International
Wire Association International
Wire Journal, Inc.
1570 Boston Post Rd.
Guilford, CT 06437
203-453-2777
Cliff D'Addetta, Editor
Publishes manufacturing and technical information about wire and cable.

Wire Technology International
Initial Publications Inc.
3869 Darrow Rd., Ste. 101
Stow, OH 44224
216-686-9544
Thomas Drewer, Editor
Advice on how to manufacture wire and related products.

LIBRARIES

Siecor Corp.
Library/Information Services
489 Siecor Park
800 17th St., N.W.
Hickory, NC 28603-0489
704-327-5000
Cable industries, fiber optics, and telecommunications.

Southwire Co.
R & D Technical Library
One Southwire Dr.
Carrollton, GA 30119
404-832-5099
404-832-4949 Fax
Wire, cable, rods, copper, and aluminum.

Wire Association International
Technical Information Center
Box H
1570 Boston Post Rd.
Guildford, CT 06437
203-453-2777
203-453-8384 Fax
Wire technology, metallurgy, and fiber optics.

COMPANIES

Bekaert Corp.
(Subsidiary of NV Bekaert SA)
675 Third Ave.
New York, NY 10017
212-953-2255
Steel wire and products made from steel wire.

CF & I Steel Corp.
P.O. Box 316
Pueblo, CO 81002
719-561-6000
Wire and other steel products.

Central Steel & Wire Co.
3000 W. 51st St.
Chicago, IL 60632
312-471-3800
Wire and other products made from steel and other metals.

W. L. Gore & Associates
555 Paper Mill Rd.
Newark, DE 19711
302-738-4880
Insulated cable and wire, and other products.

Insteel Industries, Inc.
1373 Boggs Dr.
Mount Airy, NC 27030
919-786-2141
Wire mesh and other wire products.

Keystone Consolidated Industries, Inc.
5430 LBJ Freeway
Dallas, TX 75240
214-458-0028
Wire and wire products made from steel.

LPL Technologies Inc.
358 Hall Ave., Box 384
Wallingford, CT 06492
203-265-8600
Electrical cable and wire.

Northwestern Steel & Wire Co.
121 Wallace St.
Sterling, IL 61081
815-625-2500
Various types of steel wire and other products.

Okonite Co.
P. O. Box 340
Ramsey, NJ 07446
201-825-0300
Insulated cable and wire.

Southwire Co.
One Southwire Dr.
Carrollton, GA 30119
404-832-4242
Wire and cables made from copper and other metals.

FEDERAL GOVERNMENT

U.S. Customs Service
Department of the Treasury
U.S. Customshouse
6 World Trade Center
New York, NY 10048
212-466-5550
Ask for the Commodity Specialist in charge of wire.

U.S. International Trade Administration
Department of Commerce
14th St. and Constitution Ave., N.W.
Washington, DC 20230
202-377-2000
Ask for the Commodity Analyst who is an expert in the wire industry.

U.S. International Trade Commission
500 E St., S.W.
Washington, DC 20436
202-205-2000 Office of the Secretary
202-205-3296 Industries locator
Ask for the Trade Analyst who is an expert in the wire industry.

U.S. Patent and Trademark Office
Crystal Plaza 2
2011 Jefferson Davis Highway
Arlington, VA 22202
703-305-8000
Ask for the Examining Group Director who is a specialist in wire.

WISCONSIN

STATE OFFICE LOCATOR (*for referrals to all state government offices*)

608-266-2211

ARCHIVES AND RECORDS

Historical Society
816 State Street
Madison, WI 53707
608-262-7304

ATTORNEY GENERAL

Justice Department
P.O. Box 7857
Madison, WI 53707
608-266-1221

BANKING

Bank Commissioner
P.O. Box 7876
Madison, WI 53707-7876
608-266-1621

COMMERCE

Commerce Department
517 E. Wisconsin
Milwaukee, WI 53202
414-297-3473

CONSUMER AFFAIRS

Trade & Consumer Protection Division
P.O. Box 8911
Madison, WI 53708
608-266-7220

EDUCATION

Public Instruction Department
P.O. Box 7841
Madison, WI 53707-7841
608-266-1771

ENERGY

Energy & Intergovernmental Relations Division
P.O. Box 7868
Madison, WI 53707-7868
608-266-8234

ENVIRONMENTAL AFFAIRS

Natural Resources Department
P.O. Box 7921
Madison, WI 53707
608-266-2121

HEALTH

Health Division
P.O. Box 7850
Madison, WI 53707
608-266-1511

HOUSING

Housing & Economic Development Authority
P.O. Box 1728
Madison, WI 53701-1728
608-266-7884

HUMAN RIGHTS

Equal Rights Division
P.O. Box 8928
Madison, WI 53708
608-266-0946

INSURANCE

Insurance Commission
P.O. Box 7873
Madison, WI 53707-7873
608-266-3585

LABOR

Industry, Labor & Human Relations Department
P.O. Box 7946
Madison, WI 53707
608-266-7552

LEGISLATION

Legislative Reference Bureau
P.O. Box 2037
Madison, WI 53701-2037
608-266-0341

LIBRARY SERVICES

Library Services Division
P.O. Box 7841
Madison, WI 53707-7841
608-266-2205

LICENSING—CORPORATE

Corporations Division
P.O. Box 7848
Madison, WI 53707
608-266-3590

LICENSING—PROFESSIONAL AND OCCUPATIONAL

Regulation & Licensing Department
P.O. Box 8935
Madison, WI 53708-8935
608-266-8609

MOTOR VEHICLES

Motor Vehicles Division
P.O. Box 7910
Madison, WI 53707-7910
608-266-2233

OCCUPATIONAL HEALTH AND SAFETY

Safety & Buildings Division
P.O. Box 7903
Madison, WI 53707
608-266-1816

OMBUDSMAN

Constituent Relations
P.O. Box 7863
Madison, WI 53707
608-266-1212

PUBLIC UTILITIES

Public Service Commission
P.O. Box 7854
Madison, WI 53707
608-267-7897

PURCHASING

Procurement Division
P.O. Box 7864
Madison, WI 53707
608-266-2605

REAL ESTATE

Bureau of Direct Licensing & Real Estate
P.O. Box 8935
Madison, WI 53708-8935
608-266-3423

SECURITIES

Securities Commission
P.O. Box 1768
Madison, WI 53701
608-266-3431

TAXATION AND REVENUE

Revenue Department
P.O. Box 8933
Madison, WI 53708
608-266-1611

TOURISM

Division of Tourism
P.O. Box 7970
Madison, WI 53707
608-266-2161
800-432-8747
800-372-2737 (in Wisconsin and bordering
    states)

TRANSPORTATION

Transportation Department
P.O. Box 7910
Madison, WI 53707-7910
608-266-1113

UNEMPLOYMENT

Unemployment Compensation Division
P.O. Box 7905
Madison, WI 53707
608-266-7074

WORKER'S COMPENSATION

Workers Compensation Division
P.O. Box 7901
Madison, WI 53707
608-266-1340

WOMEN PROFESSIONALS AND EMPLOYEES

See also: ENTREPRENEURS

ASSOCIATIONS

Alliance of Minority Women for Business and
    Political Development
c/o Brenda Alford
Brasman Research
814 Thayer Ave., Ste. 202A
Silver Spring, MD 20910
301-565-0258
Brenda Alford, President
*A network of black women who own and oper-
ate businesses of all kinds.*

The International Alliance, An Association of
    Executive and Professional Women
8600 LaSalle Rd., Ste. 308
Baltimore, MD 21204
301-321-6699
301-823-2410 Fax
Marian Goetze, Executive Vice President
*Enables and promotes networking by women
executives and professionals. Offers educational programs that help women succeed in
business.*

Mothers' Home Business Network
PO Box 423
East Meadow, NY 11554
516-997-7394
Georganne Fiumara, Director
Offers information on how to start and run a small business for mothers who wish to take care of their children and work at home.

National Association of Minority Women in Business
906 Grand Ave., Ste. 200
Kansas City, MO 64106
816-421-3335
816-421-3336 Fax
Inez Kaiser, President
Offers a network for minority woman managers and business owners.

National Association of Women Business Owners
600 S. Federal St., Ste. 400
Chicago, IL 60605
312-922-0465
Natalie Holmes, Executive Director
Provides information services, education, and networking to women who own and operate businesses of all types.

Women in Management
2 N. Riverside Plaza, Ste. 2400
Chicago, IL 60606
312-263-3636
312-263-0923 Fax
Patricia Kelps, Administrator
Acts as a network for women executives and professionals who wish to share experiences and information.

PERIODICALS

Entrepreneurial Woman
Entrepreneur Inc.
2392 Morse Ave.
Irvine, CA 92714
714-261-2325
Rieva Lesonsky, Editor
How-to information for starting and operating a business.

Executive Female
National Association for Female Executives
127 W. 24th St.
New York, NY 10011
212-645-0770
Diane Burley, Editor
Covers career issues, money matters, and related topics for the professional woman.

National Business Woman
National Federation of Business and Professional Women's Clubs, Inc.
2012 Massachusetts Ave., N.W.
Washington, DC 20036
202-293-1100
Maryanne Costa, Editor
Offers articles about day care, equal opportunity, and other subjects of interest to the working woman.

Successful Woman in Business
American Society of Professional and Executive Women
1429 Walnut St.
Philadelphia, PA 19102
215-563-4415
Hennie Shore, Editor
Advice about business and career advancement for women.

Woman's Enterprise
Paisano Publications, Inc.
28210 Dorothy Dr.
Box 3075
Agoura Hills, CA 91301
818-889-8740
Caryne Brown, Editor
*Follows business ventures started by women
or in which women have an influential role.*

Working Woman
Lang Communications
230 Park Ave.
New York, NY 10169
212-309-9800
Lynn Povich, Editor
*Advice to working women on how to excel in
their careers.*

LIBRARIES

Business and Professional Women's Foundation
Marguerite Rawalt Resource Center
2012 Massachusetts Ave., N.W.
Washington, DC 20036
202-293-1200
*Women's employment and economic topics,
including occupational segregation, sexual
harassment, displaced homemakers, and comparable worth.*

Catalyst
Information Center
250 Park Ave., S., 5th Fl.
New York, NY 10003-1459
212-777-8900
212-477-4252 Fax
Women and work.

National Chamber of Commerce for
    Women, Inc.
Elizabeth Lewin Business Library & Information Center
10 Waterside Plaza, Ste. 6H
New York, NY 10010-2610
212-685-3454
*Women and the law, women and education,
and labor-management relations.*

FEDERAL GOVERNMENT

U.S. Department of Labor
200 Constitution Ave., N.W.
Washington, DC 20210
202-523-6666
Ask for the Women's Bureau.

WOODWORKING INDUSTRIES

ASSOCIATIONS

Architectural Woodwork Institute
2310 S. Walter Reed Dr.
Arlington, VA 22206
703-671-9100
703-820-7839 Fax
H. Keith Judkins, Executive Vice President
Provides training and technical information to firms that manufacture wood paneling, casework, and fixtures.

Machine Knife Association
30200 Detroit Rd.
Cleveland, OH 44145-1967
216-899-0010
Allen Wherry, Executive Secretary
Manufacturers of the knives used in woodworking and metal-cutting equipment.

National Wood Window and Door Association
1400 E. Touhy Ave., No. G54
Des Plaines, IL 60018
312-299-5200
312-299-1286 Fax
John Shoemaker, Executive Vice President
Conducts research and establishes quality standards for manufacturers of wooden windows, doors, and related products.

Southern Woodwork Association
PO Box 148
Macon, GA 31202
912-743-2642
John Willingham, Director
Firms that make such architectural woodwork products as doors, windows, and moldings.

Wood Machinery Manufacturers of America
1900 Arch St.
Philadelphia, PA 19103
215-564-3484
215-564-2175 Fax
Don White, Executive Vice President
Provides technical and industry information to firms that make heavy woodworking equipment used in woodworking plants, mills, and furniture factories.

Woodworking Machinery Distributors Association
Adams Bldg., Ste. 109
251 W. DeKalb Pike
King of Prussia, PA 19406
215-265-6658
215-265-3419 Fax
R. Franklin Brown, Executive Vice President
Members distribute equipment used in woodworking plants and sawmills.

Woodworking Machinery Importers Association of America
5024-R Campbell Blvd.
Baltimore, MD 21236
301-931-8100
301-931-8111 Fax
Calvin Clemons, Executive Vice President
Represents importers of woodworking machinery.

PERIODICALS

American Woodworker
Rodale Press, Inc.
33 E. Minor St.
Emmaus, PA 18098
215-967-5171
David Sloan, Editor
Advice for small-shop woodworkers.

Bits 'n Chips
Woodworking Machinery Distributors Association
251 W. DeKalb Pike, A-109
King of Prussia, PA 19406
215-265-6658
R. Franklin Brown, Editor
Helps machinery distributors keep abreast of government trends and management techniques.

Carpenter
United Brotherhood of Carpenters and Joiners of America
101 Constitution Ave., N.W.
Washington, DC 20001
202-546-6206
John Rogers, Editor
Focuses on issues of concern to carpenters.

Custom Woodworking Business
Vance Publishing Corp.
400 Knightsbridge Parkway
Lincolnshire, IL 60069
312-634-2600
Rich Christianson, Editor
Offers marketing and management information, technical knowledge, and design tips.

Fine Woodworking
Taunton Press, Inc.
63 S. Main St.
Box 5506
Newtown, CT 06470-5506
203-426-8171
Dick Burrows, Editor
Advice for woodworkers on creating useful and aesthetically pleasing pieces.

International Woodworking Magazine
Woodworking Association of North America
Glove Hollow Press
Rt. 3 and Cummings Hill Rd.
Box 706
Plymouth, NH 03264
603-536-3768
Doug Werbeck, Editor
Offers information of interest to small-shop woodworkers and serious amateur woodworkers.

Woodworker's Journal
Madrigal Publishing Co., Inc.
517 Litchfield Rd.
Box 1629
New Milford, CT 06776
203-355-2694
James McQuillan, Editor
How-to information about construction, tool use, and supply selection for the woodworker.

LIBRARIES

Fine Hardwood Veneer Asociation/American Walnut Manufacturers Association
Library
5603 E. Raymond, Ste. O
Indianapolis, IN 46241
317-244-3311
317-244-3386 Fax
Forestry production, wood technology, and furniture construction.

Forest Products Research Society
FOREST Information Retrieval System
2801 Marshall Ct.
Madison, WI 53705
608-231-1361
608-231-2152 Fax
Covers wood-related topics such as machining, energy, and timber resources.

COMPANIES

Creative Woodworking Co., Inc.
1370 Ralph Ave.
Brooklyn, NY 11236
718-451-0460
Architectural woodwork.

Ekstrom Carlson & Co.
1400 Railroad Ave.
Rockford, IL 61101
815-968-0961
Woodworking machinery and supplies.

John Langenbacher Co., Inc.
1345 Seneca Ave.
Bronx, NY 10474
212-328-7600
Architectural woodwork.

Leichtung Inc.
4944 Commerce Pkwy.
Cleveland, OH 44128
216-831-6191
Woodworking tools and do-it-yourself products.

Medalist Industries Inc.
10850 W. Park Pl.
Milwaukee, WI 53224
414-359-3000
Woodworking saws and machinery, and other products.

Mielach Co.
9 Kilmer Ct.
Edison, NJ 08817
908-287-1100
Architectural woodwork.

Newman Machine Co.
507 Jackson St.
Greensboro, NC 27403
919-273-8261
Woodworking machinery.

Pentair Inc.
1700 W. Hwy. 36
St. Paul, MN 55113
612-636-7920
Woodworking machinery and tools, and other types of products.

Wilton Corp.
300 S. Hicks Rd.
Palatine, IL 60067
708-934-6000
Woodworking machinery and other types of products.

Wisconsin Knife Works
(Division of Black & Decker Inc.)
2710 Prairie Ave.
Beloit, WI 53511
608-365-9581
Router bits and woodworking knives.

Woodwork Corp. of America
1432 W. 21st St.
Chicago, IL 60608
312-226-4800
Architectural woodwork and other products.

FEDERAL GOVERNMENT

U.S. Customs Service
Department of the Treasury
U.S. Customshouse
6 World Trade Center
New York, NY 10048
212-466-5550
Ask for the Commodity Specialist in charge of woodworking tools and equipment.

U.S. International Trade Administration
Department of Commerce
14th St. and Constitution Ave., N.W.
Washington, DC 20230
202-377-2000
Ask for the Commodity Analyst who is an expert in woodworking tools and equipment.

U.S. International Trade Commission
500 E St., S.W.
Washington, DC 20436
202-205-2000 Office of the Secretary
202-205-3296 Industries locator
Ask for the Trade Analyst who is an expert in woodworking tools and equipment.

U.S. Patent and Trademark Office
Crystal Plaza 2
2011 Jefferson Davis Highway
Arlington, VA 22202
703-305-8000
Ask for the Examining Group Director who is a specialist in woodworking tools and equipment.

WOOL AND WORSTED INDUSTRY

See also: SHEEP INDUSTRY

ASSOCIATIONS

American Wool Council
c/o American Sheep Industry Association
6911 S. Yosemite St.
Englewood, CO 80112
Rodger Wassen, Executive Director
Offers public relations and promotional services to the wool industry.

National Wool Marketing Corp.
3900 Groves Rd.
Columbus, OH 43232
614-863-3716
614-861-7531 Fax
V. Arnold MacDonald, General Manager
Represents state associations of sheep owners. Promotes wool usage.

Natural Colored Wool Growers Association
12628 Mid Ranch Ln.
Lakeside, CA 92040
619-443-8341
Sherry Carlson, Registrar
Members breed colored sheep and sell colored wool.

Wool Bureau
360 Lexington Ave.
New York, NY 10017
212-986-6222
212-949-5205 Fax
Paul Marois, Executive Officer
Funded by Southern Hemisphere wool growers. Provides technical information to manufacturers and others who use wool and woolen products.

Wool Manufacturers Council
c/o Northern Textile Association
230 Congress St.
Boston, MA 02110
617-542-8220
617-542-2199 Fax
Karl Spilhaus, President
Members are wool textile mills.

PERIODICALS

Montana Wool Grower
Montana Wool Growers Association
Box 1693
Helena, MT 59624
Robert Gilbert
Advice about sheep raising and care.

National Wool Grower
American Sheep Industry Association
6911 S. Yosemite St.
Englewood, CO 80112-1414
303-771-3500
Janice Grauberger, Editor
Surveys the sheep industry with information on business trends, management, and production.

Wool Sack
North Central Wool Marketing Corp.
Box 328
Brookings, SD 57006
605-692-2324
Dick Boniface, Editor
Covers sheep breeding and care.

Wyoming Wool Grower
Wyoming Wool Growers Association
Box 115
811 N. Glenn Rd.
Casper, WY 82602
307-265-5250
Carolyn Paseneaux, Editor
Follows marketing, technological, and legislative information for the wool industry.

LIBRARIES

University of Wyoming
Animal Science Division
Wool Library
Box 3354, University Sta.
Laramie, WY 82071
307-766-5212
Wool textiles and wool science.

COMPANIES

American Felt & Filter Co.
34 John St.
Newburgh, NY 12550
914-561-3560
Wool and synthetic felt and filters.

American Woolen Co.
4000 N.W. 30th Ave.
Miami, FL 33142
305-635-4000
Wool and other types of textiles.

Carleton Woolen Mills, Inc.
Box 317
Winthrop, ME 04364
207-377-2291
Wool and wool blend fabrics.

Faribault Woolen Mill Co.
1500 2nd Ave. N.
Faribault, MN 55021
507-334-6444
Wool robes and blankets.

Forstmann Textiles Inc.
1185 Ave. of the Americas
New York, NY 10036
212-642-6900
Wool and worsted textiles.

Forte, Dupee, Sawyer Co.
311 Summer St.
Boston, MA 02210
617-482-8434
Wool and other types of fibers.

Standard Commercial Corp.
P.O. Box 450
Wilson, NC 27893
919-291-5507
Tobacco and wool processing and sales.

Tennessee Woolen Mills
P. O. Box 728
Lebanon, TN 37088
615-444-6060
Wool and synthetic blankets and related products.

Worcester Co.
Greystone Ave.
North Providence, RI 02911
401-231-4500
Wool and wool-blend fabrics.

FEDERAL GOVERNMENT

U.S. Department of Agriculture
14th St. and Independence Ave., S.W.
Washington, DC 20250
202-720-8732
Ask for the National Agricultural Statistics Service for the Economic Research Service.

U.S. International Trade Administration
Department of Commerce
14th St. and Constitution Ave., N.W.
Washington, DC 20230
202-377-2000
Ask for the Commodity Analyst who is an expert in the wool and worsted industries.

U.S. International Trade Commission
500 E St., S.W.
Washington, DC 20436
202-205-2000 Office of the Secretary
202-205-3296 Industries locator
Ask for the Trade Analyst who is an expert in the wool and worsted industries.

WORD PROCESSING

See also: COMPUTERS and SECRETARIES AND OFFICE WORKERS

ASSOCIATIONS

National Association of Secretarial Services
3637 4th St. N, Ste. 330
St. Petersburg, FL 33704-1336
813-823-3646
800-237-1462
813-894-1277 Fax
Frank Fox, Executive Secretary
Members include secretarial services and word processing businesses.

National Association of Professional Word
    Processing Technicians
110 W. Byberry Rd., Ste. E2
Philadelphia, PA 19116
215-698-8525
Khalil Muhammad, Executive Director
An information resource for professional word processors and computer operators.

PERIODICALS

Office Products Dealer Buying Guide and
    Directory
Hitchcock Publishing
191 S. Gary Ave.
Carol Stream, IL 60188
708-462-2275
Wayne Siatt, Editor
Helps retailers and manufacturers keep abreast of new office machines, office supplies, computers, and word processing systems, software and related supplies.

P C Magazine
Ziff-Davis Publishing Co.
One Park Ave.
New York, NY 10016
212-503-5100
Bill Machrone, Editor
Reports on numerous software and hardware topics, including word processors.

Word Progress
American Bar Association
Law Practice Management Section
750 N. Lake Shore Dr.
Chicago, IL 60611
312-988-5000
Reports on word processing in the legal profession and offers articles about software and hardware use.

WordPerfect Magazine
WordPerfect Publishing Corp.
270 W. Center St.
Orem, UT 84057
801-226-5555
Clair Rees, Editor
How-to information about WordPerfect word processing software.

COMPANIES

Apple Computer, Inc.
20525 Mariani Ave.
Cupertino, CA 95014
408-996-1010
Word processing software and many other computer products.

International Business Machines Corp.
Old Orchard Rd.
Armonk, NY 10504
914-765-1900
Word processing software and many other computer products.

Lotus Development Corp.
55 Cambridge Pkwy.
Cambridge, MA 02142
617-577-8500
Word processing software and many other computer products.

Microsoft Corp.
1 Microsoft Way
Redmond, WA 98052
206-882-8080
Word processing software and many other computer products.

NBI Inc.
3375 Mitchell Lane, Box 9001
Boulder, CO 80301
303-444-5710
Word processing software.

Ruttle, Shaw & Wetherhill, Inc.
270 Commerce Dr.
Fort Washington, PA 19034
215-628-4620
Typesetting and word processing services.

Smith Corona Corp.
65 Locust Ave.
New Canaan, CT 06840
203-972-1471
Typewriters and word processors.

Wang Laboratories, Inc.
One Industrial Ave.
Lowell, MA 01851
508-459-5000
Word processing hardware and software.

WordPerfect Corp.
1555 N. Technology Way
Orem, UT 84057
801-222-7900
Word processing software and many other computer products.

Xerox Corp.
Long Ridge Rd., Box 1600
Stamford, CT 06904
203-968-3000
Word processing and other types of office equipment.

WORKERS' COMPENSATION

See also: Each of the 50 states under workers' compensation

ASSOCIATIONS

International Association of Industrial Accident Boards and Commissions
1575 Aviation Ctr. Pkwy, Ste. 519
Daytona Beach, FL 32114
904-255-2915
904-258-9965 Fax
Robert Collyer, Executive Officer
Offers educational programs to government officials, insurers, health care executives, attorneys, and others concerned with worker's compensation laws.

National Council on Compensation Insurance
One Penn Plaza
New York, NY 10119
212-560-1000
William Hager, President
Conducts research and other services for insurance companies that offer compensation insurance.

National Foundation for Unemployment Compensation and Workers Compensation
600 Maryland Ave. S.W., Ste. 603
Washington, DC 20024
202-484-3346
J. Eldred Hill, President
Conducts research on a wide range of worker's compensation issues.

PERIODICALS

Analysis of Workers' Compensation Laws
Chamber of Commerce of the U.S.
1615 H St., N.W.
Washington, DC 20062
202-659-6000
Publishes insurance, benefit, and compensation laws in each the 50 states and Canada.

B N A's Workers' Compensation Report
The Bureau of National Affairs, Inc.
1231 25th St., N.W.
Washington, DC 20037
202-452-4200
Jeffrey Nackley, Editor
Reports on legal issues and other topics that affect workers' compensation.

Worker's Compensation Law Review
William S. Hein & Co., Inc.
1285 Main St.
Buffalo, NY 14209
800-828-7571
William Moran, Editor
Publishes detailed legal information for attorneys about workers' compensation.

Workers' Compensation Law Reporter
Commerce Clearing House, Inc.
4025 W. Peterson Ave.
Chicago, IL 60646
312-583-8500
A.E. Schecter, Editor
Helps lawyers keep abreast of workers' compensation issues with information on laws, recent court decisions, and statutes.

LIBRARIES

College of Insurance
Insurance Society of New York
Kathryn and Shelby Cullom Davis Library
101 Murray St.
New York, NY 10007
212-962-4111
212-964-3381 Fax
Covers all insurance topics, including unemployment insurance.

University of California, Berkeley
School of Public Health
Labor Occupational Health Program Library
2521 Channing Way
Berkeley, CA 94720
510-642-5507
510-643-5698 Fax
Workers' compensation, insurance, education, and occupational hazards.

COMPANIES

Argonaut Insurance Co.
(Subsidiary of Argonaut Group, Inc.)
250 Middlefield Rd
Menlo Park, CA 94025
415-326-0900
Workers' compensation and other types of insurance.

Fireman's Fund Insurance Co.
(Subsidiary of Allianz AG Holdings)
777 San Marin Dr.
Novato, CA 94998
415-899-2000
Workers' compensation and other types of insurance.

R. E. Harrington, Inc.
(Subsidiary of Harrington Services Corp.)
811 Greencrest Dr.
Westerville, OH 43081
614-891-3480
Claims administration in the areas of unemployment, health, disability, and workers compensation.

Nationwide Corp.
(Subsidiary of Nationwide Mutual Insurance Co.)
One Nationwide Plaza
Columbus, OH 43216
614-249-7111
Workers' compensation and other types of insurance.

New Jersey Manufacturers Insurance Co.
Sullivan Way-CN 00128
West Trenton, NJ 08628
609-883-1300
Workers' compensation and other types of insurance.

Northwestern National Casualty Co.
(Subsidiary of Northwestern National Insurance Co.)
18650 W. Corporate Dr.
Brookfield, WI 53005
414-792-0414
Workers' compensation and other types of insurance.

Ohio Property & Casualty Insurance Co.
(Subsidiary of Ohio Casualty Corp.)
136 N. Third St.
Hamilton, OH 45025
513-867-3000
Workers' compensation and other types of insurance.

Preferred Mutual Insurance Co.
One Preferred Way
New Berlin, NY 13411
607-847-6161
Workers' compensation and other types of insurance.

Republic Indemnity Co. of America
(Subsidiary of Pennsylvania Co.)
15821 Ventura Blvd.
Encino, CA 91436
818-990-9860
Workers' compensation insurance.

FEDERAL GOVERNMENT

U.S. Department of Labor
200 Constitution Ave., N.W.
Washington, DC 20210
202-523-6666
Ask for the public relations office to locate an appropriate expert.

WRITING AND EDITING

See also: JOURNALISM; NEWSPAPERS; and PERIODICALS, MAGAZINES, AND TRADE JOURNALS

ASSOCIATIONS

American Society of Business Press Editors
4445 Gilmer Ln.
Cleveland, OH 44143
216-531-8306
Jeanne Ribinskas, Executive Vice President
A professional society for working editors whose employers are trade, business, and technical publications.

American Society of Magazine Editors
575 Lexington Ave.
New York, NY 10022
212-752-0055
212-888-4217 Fax
Marleen Kahna, Executive Director
A professional society of managing, executive, and other senior editors of magazines.

Association for Business Communication
Department of Management
College of Business
University of North Texas
Denton, TX 76203
817-565-4423
817-565-6540 Fax
John Pettit, Executive Director
A professional group of university teachers of business writing and communications, public relations writers, business communication consultants, advertising writers, and others.

Association of Editorial Businesses
116 Fourth St., S.E.
Washington, DC 20003
202-543-1800
Shirley Rosenberg, Representative
A professional society for owners of businesses that hire writers, editors, and those who provide other editorial services.

Association of Teachers of Technical Writing
c/o Dr. Dan Jones
Department of English
University of Central Florida
Box 2500
Orlando, FL 79409
407-275-2212
Dan Jones, Executive Secretary
Members include instructors of technical writing and technical communications, and working technical writers.

Authors Guild
234 W. 44th St.
New York, NY 10036
212-398-0838
Helen Stephenson, Executive Director
A professional society of professional writers of books and magazine articles.

Editorial Freelancers Association
PO Box 2050, Madison Square Sta.
New York, NY 10159
212-677-3357
Laurie Lewis, Executive Officer
Offers referrals and training to freelance editorial writers, editors, indexers, proofreaders, and other editorial professionals.

Investigative Reporters and Editors
100 Neff Hall
University of Missouri
Columbia, MO 65211
314-882-2042
314-882-5431 Fax
Steve Weinberg, Executive Director
Offers educational programs for investigative reporters and editors.

National Writers Club
1450 S. Havana, Ste. 620
Aurora, CO 80012
303-751-7844
James Young, Director
An association for published writers.

Society for Technical Communication
901 N. Stuart St., Ste. 304
Arlington, VA 22203
703-522-4114
703-522-2075 Fax
William Stolgitis, Executive Director
Members include technical writers and editors, documentation specialists, artists, engineers, publishers, and others interested in technical communications.

PERIODICALS

Communication Briefings
Encoders, Inc.
700 Black House Pike, Ste. 110
Blackwood, NJ 08012-1455
609-232-6380
Frank Grazian, Editor
Focuses on ways to improve writing, listening, speaking, problem-solving, and other decision-making skills for the executive.

Editorial Eye
Editorial Experts, Inc.
66 Canal Center Plaza, Ste. 200
Alexandria, VA 22314
703-683-0683
Ann Moldus, Editor
Keeps editors abreast of the standards and practices used in editing publications of all kinds.

Journal of Technical Writing and Communication
Baywood Publishing Co., Inc.
26 Austin Ave.
Box 337
Amityville, NY 11701
516-691-1270
David Carson, Editor
Focuses on technical writing and oral communication in business and industry.

Society for Technical Communication Anthology Series
Society for Technical Communication
901 N. Stuart St.
Arlington, VA 22203
703-522-4114
Covers technical writing, illustrating, desk-top publishing, editing, and related areas.

Writer
Writer, Inc.
120 Boylston St.
Boston, MA 02116
617-423-3157
Sylvia Burack, Editor
Advice about the craft of writing.

Writer's Digest
F & W Publications, Inc.
1507 Dana Ave.
Cincinnati, OH 45207
513-531-2222
Bruce Woods, Editor
Offers suggestions on writing and making a living as a writer.

LIBRARIES

Investigative Reporters and Editors
100 Neff Hall
University of Missouri
Columbia, MO 65211
314-882-2042
314-882-5431 Fax
Clippings, videotapes, and other examples of investigative reporting.

National Writers Club
Library
1450 S. Havana, Ste. 620
Aurora, CO 80012
303-751-7844
303-751-8593 Fax
Writing, writers' markets, and biographies of writers.

WRITING INSTRUMENT INDUSTRY

ASSOCIATIONS

National Association of Writing Instrument
    Distributors
5024-R Campbell Blvd.
Baltimore, MD 21236
301-931-8100
Calvin Clemons, Executive Director
Offers promotional services on behalf of writing instrument distributors.

Writing Instrument Manufacturers Association
2 Greentree Centre, Ste. 225
Marlton, NJ 08053
609-985-2878
609-985-3238 Fax
Lisa Hoover, Administrator
*Manufacturers of pens and many other types
of handwriting instruments.*

PERIODICALS

Pen World
World Publications
2240 North Park Dr.
Kingwood, TX 77339
713-359-4363
Nancy Olson, Editor
*Publishes articles about pens, antique pens,
writing tools, and pen collections.*

COMPANIES

Berol Corp.
(Subsidiary of Pen Holdings, Inc.)
44 Old Ridgebury Rd., Box 1302
Danbury, CT 06813
203-792-1900
Writing instruments of all kinds.

Bic Corp.
500 Bic Dr.
Milford, CT 06460
203-783-2000
Pens and other products.

A. T. Cross Co.
One Albion Rd.
Lincoln, RI 02865
401-333-1200
Writing instruments.

Faber-Castell Corp.
Four Century Dr.
Parsippany, NJ 07054
201-483-4646
Writing instruments.

Gillette Co.
Prudential Tower Bldg.
Boston, MA 02199
617-421-7000
Pens and other products.

Koh-i-Noor Rapidograph, Inc.
100 North St.
Bloomsbury, NJ 08804
908-479-4124
Technical fountain pens and art materials.

Sanford Corp.
2740 Washington Blvd.
Bellwood, IL 60104
708-547-6650
Felt-tip markers and other markers.

Sheaffer Eaton, Inc.
One Crown Mark Dr.
Lincoln, RI 02865
401-333-0303
Writing instruments.

Stationery Product Group
(Division of Gillette Co.)
Prudential Tower Bldg.
Boston, MA 02199
617-421-8018
Writing instruments and other products.

FEDERAL GOVERNMENT

U.S. International Trade Administration
Department of Commerce
14th St. and Constitution Ave., N.W.
Washington, DC 20230
202-377-2000
*Ask for the Commodity Analyst who is an
expert in the writing instrument industry.*

U.S. International Trade Commission
500 E St., S.W.
Washington, DC 20436
202-205-2000 Office of the Secretary
202-205-3296 Industries locator
*Ask for the Trade Analyst who is an expert in
the writing instrument industry.*

WYOMING

STATE OFFICE LOCATOR (*for referrals
to all state government offices*)

307-777-7220

ARCHIVES AND RECORDS

Archives & Records Management Division
Barrett Building
Cheyenne, WY 82002
307-777-7827

ATTORNEY GENERAL

Attorney General's Office
Capitol Building
200 W. 24th Street
Room 123
Cheyenne, WY 82002
307-777-7841

BANKING

State Auditor
Capitol Building
200 W. 24th Street
Room 114
Cheyenne, WY 82002
307-777-7831

COMMERCE

Economic Development & Stabilization
    Department
Herschier Building
122 W. 25th Street
Cheyenne, WY 82002
307-777-7284

CONSUMER AFFAIRS

Attorney General
Capitol Building
200 W. 24th Street
Room 123
Cheyenne, WY 82002
307-777-7841

EDUCATION

Education Department
Hathaway Building
2nd Floor
Cheyenne, WY 82002
307-777-7675

ENERGY

Energy Division
Herschier Building
122 W. 25th Street
Cheyenne, WY 82002
307-777-7284

ENVIRONMENTAL AFFAIRS

Environmental Quality Department
Herschier Building
122 W. 25th Street
4th Floor, W.
Cheyenne, WY 82002
307-777-7938

HEALTH

Health & Medical Services Division
117 Hathaway Building
Cheyenne, WY 82002-0710
307-777-7121

HOUSING

Economic Development & Stabilization
    Board
Herschier Building
122 W. 25th Street
3rd Floor
Cheyenne, WY 82002
307-777-7285

HUMAN RIGHTS

Labor Standards & Fair Employment Division
Herschier Building
122 W. 25th Street
2nd Floor, E.
Cheyenne, WY 82002
307-777-6381

INSURANCE

Insurance Department
Herschier Building
122 W. 25th Street
Cheyenne, WY 82002-0440
307-777-7401

LABOR

Labor & Statistics Department
Herschier Building
122 W. 25th Street
2nd Floor, E.
Cheyenne, WY 82002
307-777-7261

LEGISLATION

Legislative Service Office
State Capitol
200 W. 24th Street
Room 213
Cheyenne, WY 82002
307-777-7881

LIBRARY SERVICES

Library Department
Supreme Court Building
Cheyenne, WY 82002-0650
307-777-7281

LICENSING—CORPORATE

Corporations Division
State Capitol
Cheyenne, WY 82002-0020
307-777-7311

MOTOR VEHICLES

Driver Control Section
Herschier Building
122 W. 25th Street
Cheyenne, WY 82002
307-777-5262

OCCUPATIONAL HEALTH AND SAFETY

Occupational Health & Safety Department
Herschier Building
122 W. 25th Street
2nd Floor, E.
Cheyenne, WY 82002
307-777-7786

PUBLIC UTILITIES

Public Service Commission
700 W. 21st Street
Cheyenne, WY 82002
307-777-7427

PURCHASING

Purchasing & Property Control Division
2001 Capitol Avenue
Cheyenne, WY 82002
307-777-7253

REAL ESTATE

Real Estate Commission
Herschier Building
122 W. 25th Street
4th Floor
Cheyenne, WY 82002
307-777-7141

SECURITIES

Securities Division
State Capitol
Cheyenne, WY 82002-0020
307-777-7370

TAXATION AND REVENUE

Revenue & Taxation Department
Herschier Building
122 W. 25th Street
Cheyenne, WY 82002
307-777-5285

TOURISM

Travel Commission
I-25 and College Drive
Cheyenne, WY 82002
307-777-7777
800-225-5996

TRANSPORTATION

Highway Department
P.O. Box 1708
Cheyenne, WY 82002
307-777-7471

UNEMPLOYMENT

Unemployment Insurance Division
P.O. Box 2760
Casper, WY 82602
307-235-3200

WORKER'S COMPENSATION

Workers Compensation
Herschier Building
122 W. 25th Street
Cheyenne, WY 82002-0700
307-777-7441

YARN INDUSTRY

See also: COTTON INDUSTRY; FABRICS AND TEXTILES;
and WOOL AND WORSTED INDUSTRY

ASSOCIATIONS

American Yarn Spinners Association
2500 Lowell Rd.
Gastonia, NC 28053
704-824-3522
704-824-5358 Fax
Jim Conner, Executive Vice President
*Firms that make combed cotton yarn and
corded yarns spun from wool, cotton, and synthetic materials. Affiliated with the Craft Yarn
Council of America, which is comprised of
craft yarn manufacturers.*

Association of Yarn Distributors
c/o Henry M. Kamins Co.
1441 Broadway, Ste. 1904
New York, NY 10018
212-221-3315
Hermine Kamins, Secretary
*Represents wholesalers, brokers, and sales
agents of yarn.*

Hand Knitting Association
650 Danbury Rd.
Ridgefield, CT 06877
203-431-8226
203-431-0862 Fax
Kay Cook, Executive Director
Members include firms that spin and convert yarn, import yarn, and supply knitting accessories.

PERIODICALS

International Fiber Journal
McMickle Publications, Inc.
2919 Spalding Dr.
Atlanta, GA 30350-4628
404-394-6098
Wilbur Newcomb, Editor
Helps management keep abreast of yarn spinning, polymerizers, and other fiber-related developments.

Textile Pricing Outlook
Statistikon Corp.
Box 246
E. Norwich, NY 11732
516-922-0882
Jordan Yale, Editor
Offers insights on textile pricing, fibers, raw materials, and yarns.

COMPANIES

Avondale Mills Inc.
(Subsidiary of Walton Monroe Mills, Inc.)
P.O. Box 1109
Monroe, GA 30655
205-245-5221
Fabrics and knitting yarns.

Carisbrook Industries Inc.
(Subsidiary of Hanson PLC)
1114 Ave. of the Americas
New York, NY 10036
212-398-1180
Fabrics and yarns.

Carolina Mills, Inc.
618 Carolina Ave.
Maiden, NC 28650
704-428-9911
Fabrics and yarns.

Dixie Yarns, Inc.
P.O. Box 751
Chattanooga, TN 37401
615-698-2501
Cotton and synthetic yarns.

Dominion Yarn Corp.
(Subsidiary of Dominion Textile Inc.)
P.O. Box 8105
Landis, NC 28088
704-857-1121
Textile yarns.

Phillips Fibers Corp.
(Subsidiary of Phillips Co.)
P.O. Box 66
Greenville, SC 29602
803-242-6600
Synthetic yarn.

Regal Mfg. Co.
(Subsidiary of Willcox & Gibbs Inc.)
212 12th Ave. N.E.
Hickory, NC 28601
704-328-5381
Novelty and elastic yarns.

Spartan Mills
805 Spartan Blvd.
Spartanburg, SC 29303
803-574-0211
Fabrics and yarns.

Unifi Inc.
P. O. Box 19109
Greensboro, NC 27419
919-294-4410
Synthetic yarn.

FEDERAL GOVERNMENT

U.S. Customs Service
Department of the Treasury
U.S. Customshouse
6 World Trade Center
New York, NY 10048
212-466-5550
Ask for the Commodity Specialist in charge of yarn.

U.S. International Trade Administration
Department of Commerce
14th St. and Constitution Ave., N.W.
Washington, DC 20230
202-377-2000
Ask for the Commodity Analyst who is an expert in yarn.

U.S. International Trade Commission
500 E St., S.W.
Washington, DC 20436
202-205-2000 Office of the Secretary
202-205-3296 Industries locator
Ask for the Trade Analyst who is an expert in yarn.

APPENDIX

COMPUTER DATABASES

Of the many fields revolutionized by computers in the last decade, few have changed so dramatically as information retrieval. The days are over when your only options for finding information were telephoning experts and spending hours hunting down materials at a library.

Today, a computer, a modem (a communications device), communications software, and a subscription to one or more publicly available on-line database systems put a huge world of information at your fingertips. A database is a collection of related information. An "on-line" database can be accessed instantaneously with a properly equipped computer via telephone lines.

Today, a vast number of books, newspaper and magazine articles, reports, conference proceedings, statistical data, and many other types of information published in English can be located through a database search. These databases generally list information in bibliographic form and include the author, title, publication information, subject headings, and, in many cases, a summary of the contents. A large number of newspaper and magazine articles and other materials are also available in full-text form, which includes every word of the printed version.

ADVANTAGES OF COMPUTER DATABASES

A computer database search has significant advantages over library research:

1. Speed and convenience. The results of a computer search are in your hands immediately. If the information you need is available on a full-text database, a directory database, or certain other types, you need look no further. Even if the information you need can only be found on a bibliographic database—requiring you to obtain a photocopy of an article or other document from a library, the publisher, or another source—a computer search will still save a great deal of time by helping you to quickly identify which article you need.

2. Precision. Getting basic background information about a large company is easy using both traditional and newer methods: libraries, computer databases, or telephone. However, a computer search lets you find the proverbial needle in a haystack with just a few keystrokes. If you need to find statistics about women who use home-health-care devices to recover from exercise-related injuries, for example, the computer is by far the best choice. A computer database search can hone in on only those books, articles, and other sources in which all elements of your topic—women, home-health-care devices, and exercise-related injuries—appear together.

3. Up-to-date information. Many databases, both full-text and bibliographic, are updated on a monthly, weekly, or even daily basis. If you wish to follow a story covered in a major newspaper, the complete text of the newspaper can be searched on-line twenty-four hours after publication. In comparison, printed subject indexes to major newspapers lag several months behind.

DISADVANTAGES OF COMPUTER DATABASES

While powerful, databases may not provide the magic answer to all your information needs. Unless you do research on a regular basis and need data not easily found on the telephone, databases may not be worth the time and expense. Databases can be:

1. Time-consuming to learn. As with any new skill, it takes time to learn how to search databases effectively. First of all, you must decide which databases are most likely to contain the information you seek. I currently access over 1,500 databases because my clients ask for data on every subject imaginable. Most people will be satisfied with the several hundred business-oriented databases available on certain major on-line services. Those who frequently need specific types of data or who closely follow a single industry will need to find out which services carry the appropriate databases.

Once you subscribe to a suitable service, you need to learn the mechanics of on-line searching. If you are a savvy computer-user and need to search just a handful of databases, the basics can be learned in a few hours. But because each database is unique, searching requires intelligent planning so as not to waste time and money.

Many database systems now offer search menus as an option. Much like the menu in a restaurant, the on-line searcher selects from a number of choices when setting up a search strategy. On-line services offering menus claim that even first-time users can successfully perform searches. Unfortunately, while novices will get some of the answers they need, menu systems cause them to spend more time and money wading through extraneous information.

2. Potentially costly. Most of the databases containing business information cost $25-$125 per hour just for access to the information. Many databases charge additional amounts for telecommunications and for each record of information captured by the searcher. On-line database searches can be astonishingly inexpensive or expensive, depending, among other things, on the size of the search, which databases are searched, the skills of the searcher, and the on-line system used.

If your search is narrow and specific, a computer database search can be extremely cost-effective. It can literally find in a few minutes what might take hours (or days) to uncover manually at a library. But if your search is very broad or large, it may be more cost-effective to search at a major library, assuming you live near one.

HOW TO FIND SOMEONE TO DO COMPUTER SEARCHES FOR YOU

If you'd rather not do a computer search yourself, call a local library to see if they will do one for you. Some libraries offer free or low-cost searches for the public. Unfortunately, many libraries also make users wait days or even weeks before performing searches.

An alternative is to call one of the research services listed under Companies in the Information Industry section of this book.

HOW TO START DATABASE SEARCHING

If you would like to explore on-line searching further, you should contact some of the companies listed below. Collectively, these firms make available a large portion of English-language databases containing business-related information. In the unlikely event you need to search a database that surveys a specific industry or topic not covered by these firms, check the *Directory of On-line Databases* (Gale Research, Inc., 1-800-877-4253 or 1-313-961-2242). This directory lists nearly 5,000 databases around the world.

Aside from helping you determine if their databases contain the data you seek, the firms below can also advise you on the computer hardware and software you will need. A few firms sell their own customized search software.

MAJOR ON-LINE DATABASE SERVICES

BRS Information Technologies
Maxwell On-line, Inc.
8000 Westpark Dr.
McLean, VA 22102
800-955-0906
BRS is best known for its collection of medical and science databases. However, it also offers some of the most useful business, news, social science, education, and general interest databases as well. BRS has an inexpensive evening version called "After Dark," which contains many databases.

CompuServe, Inc.
5000 Arlington Center
Columbus, OH 43220
614-457-8600
Compuserve is a huge on-line system offering many services (such as games) of little use to serious business researchers. Compuserve does offer access to numerous business databases through an expensive menu system.

Data-star
D-S Marketing, Inc.
485 Devon Park Dr., Suite 110
Wayne, PA 19087
215-687-6777
Data-star is owned by a Swiss company. It is strongest in medical, pharmaceutical, and business databases that originate in Europe. If you need information on European business, Data-star is one of the best sources.

DataTimes
14000 Quail Springs Parkway, Ste. 450
Oklahoma City, OK 73134
405-751-6400
800-642-2525
405-755-8028 Fax
DataTimes offers what may be the world's largest collection of full-text newspaper databases. Aside from large newspapers, many smaller U.S. papers and some foreign papers are also available. In addition, DataTimes provides a select group of databases that cover business, companies, and news also available on many other systems listed in this appendix.

Dialog Information Service, Inc.
3460 Hillview Ave.
Palo Alto, CA 94304
415-858-3785
800-334-2564
415-858-7069 Fax
Dialog offers one of the largest collections of databases in the world. These databases cover news, business, companies, virtually every industry, governments, finance, science and technology, medicine, education, humanities, social sciences, and much more. Aside from bibliographic and directory databases, Dialog also features full-text newspaper and magazine databases.

For inexperienced business users, Dialog offers the Dialog Business Connection, a menu-based system for finding business information. Dialog also offers an evening version of 85 databases called Knowledge Index at substantially reduced rates. Some, but by no means all, business databases are available on Knowledge Index.

DRI/McGraw Hill
24 Hartwell Ave.
Lexington, MA 02173
617-863-5100
DRI offers highly specialized statistical databases for senior executives of major corporations. The databases are used for marketing and sales planning, sales forecasting, and other types of business forecasting.

Dow Jones News/Retrieval
Dow Jones & Co., Inc.
P.O. Box 300
Princeton, NJ 08543-0300
609-520-4649
609-452-1511
609-520-4660 Fax
Dow Jones, most famous for publishing the Wall Street Journal, *provides databases of interest to individual investors and corporations. Included are stock quotations, business and financial news services, major business publications, and a smattering of general interest databases.*

LEXIS/NEXIS
Mead Data Central
9393 Springboro Pike
Dayton, OH 45401
800-227-4908
513-865-1780 Fax
The LEXIS/NEXIS system comprises one of the world's largest collections of news, legal, regulatory, business, company, technological, medical, and general interest information. Approximately 750 sources include numerous full-text databases. The LEXIS/NEXIS databases are expensive but extremely useful if you require certain kinds of full-text information or legal information.

Newsnet
945 Haverford Rd.
Bryn Mawr, PA 19010
215-527-8030
800-952-0122

Newsnet provides the full text of nearly 600 business and industry newsletters, as well as 20 newswires and a handful of other business databases. These newsletters cover such topics as advertising and marketing, aerospace, biotechnology, electronics and computers, energy, finance, healthcare, investments, manufacturing, publishing, and telecommunications.

Orbit Search Service
Maxwell On-line, Inc.
8000 Westpark Dr.
McLean, VA 22102
703-442-0900
800-456-7248
703-893-4632 Fax

While Orbit focuses on science, technology, and patent databases, a few business databases are also available.

VU/TEXT
325 Chestnut St., Ste. 1300
Philadelphia, PA 19106
215-574-4400
800-323-2940
215-627-0194 Fax

VU/TEXT offers the full text of several dozen newspapers nationwide. Many of these newspapers are also available on the Dialog Information Services databases (see above).

W. H. Wilson Co.
950 University Ave.
Bronx, NY 10452
212-588-8400
800-367-6770
212-590-1617 Fax

For many years W. H. Wilson has published indexes of general interest, humanities, and social studies periodicals. Wilson is best known for its Readers' Guide to Periodical Literature. *Most of these indexes can be searched on-line. Their major business database is the* Business Periodicals Index, *a computerized version of the printed index with the same title.*

INDEX OF ASSOCIATIONS,
PERIODICALS, AND COMPANIES

A & W Restaurants, Inc., 891

ABA Banking Journal, 114

ABA Journal, 531

Abbey Newsletter, 136

Abbott Laboratories, 595

ABB Process Automation Inc., 824

ABC Liquors, Inc., 543

ABC-Treadco, Inc., 406

ABF Freight System, Inc., 387

Abracadabra, 136

Abrasive Engineering Society, 1

Abrasive Engineering Society Magazine, 1

Abrasive Industries Inc., 1

Abstract Newsletter: Government Inventions for Licensing, 499

Academe, 216

Academy for Health Services Marketing, 434

Academy of Accounting Historians, 156

Academy of Hazard Control Management, 916

Academy of Marketing Science, 575

Academy of Master Wine Growers, 1119

Academy of Motion Picture Arts and Sciences, 638

Academy of Television Arts and Sciences, 1015

ACCA Quality Contractor's Catalog, 38

Accounting for Public Utilities, 847

Accounting News, 6

Accounting Today, 6

Acco World Corp., 709

Accredited Gemologists Association, 412

Accu-Sort Systems, Inc., 94, 501

Ace-Federal Reporters, Inc., 959

Aceto Corp., 3

ACG, Inc., 685

Acheson Industries, Inc., 3

Ackerman, Hood & McQueen, Inc., 843

Acme-Cleveland Corp., 560

ACME—The Association of Management Consulting Firms, 569

Acme-Wiley Corp., 960

ACM Transactions on Graphics, 229

Acor Orthopaedic, Inc., 837

Acoustical Society of America, 1063

Acquisition Capability, Inc., 1052

Acquisition Mart, 597

Across the Board, 568

Acta Metallurgica et Materialia, 601

Activewear Business Magazine, 201

Actuarial Digest, 9

Actuarial Update, 9

Adage, Inc., 230

Ad Art Signs, Inc., 960

Addictions Alert, 60

Adhesive and Sealant Council, 12

Adhesives Age, 13

Adhesives Age Directory, 13

Adhesives D.A.T.A. Digest, 13

Adhesives Manufacturers Association, 12

Adhesive Trends, 13

Adia Services Inc., 1020

Adler Reporting Service, Inc., 959

Admar Research Co., 579

Administrative Management, 568, 703, 713

Administrative Management Society, 713, 759

ADM Milling Co., 364

Adm-West, 1118

Adobe Systems, Inc., 230, 279

Adult & Continuing Education Today, 15

Adult Education Quarterly, 15

Adult Learning, 16

Advanced Battery Technology, 122

Advanced Coatings & Surface Technology, 468

Advanced Materials & Processes, 587

Advanced Oil and Gas Recovery Technologies, 660

Advanced T.V. Systems Committee, 1015

Advanced Wireless Communication, 628

Advance Manufacturing Co., Inc., 558

Advances in Aerosol Physics, 22

Advances in Alcohol & Substance Abuse, 60

Advances in Automation and Robotics, 908

Advances in Consumer Research, 578

Advances in Econometrics, 290

Advances in Financial Planning and Forecasting, 346

Advances in Meat Research Series, 591

Advances in Motivation and Achievement, 642

Advances in Nutritional Research, 1095

Advances in Polymer Technology, 793

Advatex Associates, Inc., 85

Advertising Age, the International Newspaper of Marketing, 19, 576

Advertising & Graphic Arts Techniques, 423

Advertising Club of New York, 17

Advertising Photographers of America, 782

Advertising Research Foundation, 17

Advertising Typographers Association, 815

Advo-System Inc., 282

Adweek/East, 19

Adweek's Marketer's Guide to Media, 19

Adweek's Marketing Computers, 232

A-E-C Automation Newsletter, 226

Aerial Co., Inc., 119

Aerodyne Products Corp., 854

Aerojet, 25

Aerosol Age, the Magazine of Pressure Packaging, 22

Aerosol Science and Technology, 22

Aerospace America, 25

Aerospace Electronics Business, 106

Aerospace Industries Association of America, 47, 270

Aerospace Products, 25

Aetna Casualty and Surety Co., 482, 485

Aetna Life and Casualty Co., 491

Affiliated Advertising Agencies International, 17

Affiliated/Associated Drug Stores, 287

Affiliated Inventors Foundation, 499

Affiliated Warehouse Companies, 1099

Affirmative Action Register, 29

Affluent Markets Alert, 247

AFG Industries, Inc., 420

AFL-CIO News, 525

Aftermarket Business, 99

Agency Rent-a-Car, Inc., 102

Agency Sales, 575

AG Processing Inc., 718, 974

Agrex Inc., 974, 1118

Agrichemical Age, 35

Agricultural and Industrial Manufacturers' Representatives Association, 574

Agricultural Chemical Newsletter, 762

Agricultural Research, 35

Agricultural Research Institute, 35

Agriculture Council of America, 30

Agrigenetics Co., 946

Agway Inc., 268

Agweek, 31

Aicorp, Inc., 81

AIDS & Public Policy Journal, 27

AIDS Clinical Care, 27

AIDS Education and Prevention, 28

AIDS-HIV Treatment Directory, 27

AIDS Litigation Reporter, 28

AIDS Policy and Law, 28

AI Expert, 80

Air and Expedited Motor Carriers Conference, 386

Air & Water Technologies Corp., 322, 1106

Airborne Freight Corp., 42

Air Cargo News, 42

Air Cargo World, 42

Air Conditioning, Heating & Refrigeration News, 39

Air Conditioning & Heating Service & Repair—Domestic Cars, 39

Air-Conditioning and Refrigeration Institute, 38

Air-Conditioning and Refrigeration Wholesalers, 38

AirConditioning Contractors of America, 37

Aircraft Electronics Association, 106

Aircraft Owners and Pilots Association, 46

Aircraft Technician, 48

Air Freight Association of America, 41

Airline Executive International, 44

Airline Newsletter, 44

Airline Passengers of America, 52

Air Line Pilot, 47

Air Line Pilots Association, International, 46

Airport Consultants Council, 50

Airport Operators Council International, 50

Airport Pocket Guide, 51

Airports, 51

Airport Services Management, 51

Air Products And Chemicals, Inc., 187

Airstream, Inc., 873

Air Traffic Control Association, 50

Air Transport Association of America, 41, 44

Air Transport World, 44

AI Today, 80

Akzo America Inc., 925
Akzo Coatings Inc., 469
Alamo Iron Works, 382
Alamo Rent A Car, Inc., 102
Albertson's Inc., 993
Alcan Aluminium Corp., 62
Alcoa International Holdings Co., 62
Alcohol Health & Research World, 60
Alcoholics Anonymous World Services, 59
Alcon Laboratories, Inc., 726
Alden Electronics Inc., 1111
Aldus Corp., 230, 280
Alexander & Alexander Services Inc., 304, 493
Alexander & Baldwin, Inc., 634
Alexander-Seewald Co., Inc., 99
Alfa-Laval, Inc., 370
Algonquin Gas Transmission Co., 790
Allegheny International Inc., 66
Allegheny Ludlum Corp., 985
Allen-Bradley Co., 824
Allen County Motors, Inc., 97
Allen Group Inc., 99
Allen Organ Co., 652
Allergan, Inc., 726
Alliance Against Fraud in Telemarketing, 1013
Alliance for Traffic Safety, 1044
Alliance of American Insurers, 483
Alliance of Minority Women for Business and Political Development, 1127
Alliance of Motion Picture and Television Producers, 638
Alliance of State Car and Truck Renting and Leasing Association, 101
Alliance to Save Energy, 309
Allied Building Products Corp., 480, 912

Allied Construction Services, Inc., 791
Allied Distribution, 1099
Allied Industrial Worker, 526
Allied-Lyons North America Corp., 110
Allied Paper, Inc., 379
Allied Security, Inc., 944
Allied-Signal Inc., 25, 587
Allied Stone Industries, 855
Allied Underwear Association, 1065
Allied Van Lines, Inc., 634
All-Phase Electric Supply Co. Inc., 298
Allstate Insurance Co., 482, 485
Allwaste Inc., 322
Almond Board of California, 698
Aloha Airlines Inc., 45
Alpha Solarco, Inc., 967
Alpo Petfoods, Inc., 767
Alternative Energy Digests, 313
Alternative Energy Retailer, 65, 313
Alternative Energy Sourcebook, 313
Aluminum & Plastic Packaging Group, 736, 738
Aluminum Association, 61
Aluminum, Brick and Glass Workers International Union, 61
Aluminum Extruders Council, 61
Aluminum Foil Container Manufacturers Association, 61
Aluminum Recycling Association, 878
Amadeus Holdings Inc., 1080
Amalgamated Sugar Co., 989
Amana Refrigeration, Inc., 40
Amax Inc., 62, 205
Ambrit Inc., 454
Amcast Industrial Corp., 787
AMC Entertainment Inc., 641
Amdur Braude Riley, Inc., 535
Amerada Hess Corp., 410, 769

Ameribanc Investors Group, 867
American Academy of Actuaries, 8
American Academy of Matrimonial Lawyers, 531
American Agent and Broker, 493
American Agricultural Economics Association, 35
American Agricultural Law Association, 31
American Agriculturist, 31
American Airlines Employees Federal Credit Union, 266
American Airlines Inc., 45
American Angus Association, 171
American Apparel Contractors Association, 200
American Apparel Manufacturers Association, 200
American Arbitration Association, 70
American Architectural Manufacturers Association, 152
American Assembly of Collegiate Schools of Business, 292
American Association for Adult and Continuing Education, 15
American Association for Aerosol Research, 21
American Association for Affirmative Action, 29
American Association for Artificial Intelligence, 80
American Association for Budget and Program Analysis, 148
American Association for Higher Education, 216
American Association for Public Opinion Research, 840
American Association for Vocational Instructional Materials, 294
American Association of Advertising Agencies, 17
American Association of Airport Executives, 50

American Association of Certified Appraisers, 1074

American Association of Equipment Lessors, 884

American Association of Exporters and Importers, 461

American Association of Individual Investors, 504, 657

American Association of Insurance Services, 483

American Association of Inventors, 499

The American Association of Language Specialists, 1049

American Association of Meat Processors, 590

American Association of Nurserymen, 407

American Association of Nutritional Consultants, 1096

American Association of Preferred Provider Organizations, 437

American Association of Professional Consultants, 243

American Association of Retired Persons, 895

American Association of Small Cities, 648

American Association of Small Research Companies, 886

American Association of State Colleges and Universities, 216

American Association of State Highway and Transportation Officials, 904, 1042

American Astronautical Society, 24

American Automatic Merchandiser, 1080

American Automobile Association, 1044

American Automobile Touring Alliance, 1053

American Automotive Leasing Association, 101

American Bank Directory, 114

American Banker, Inc., 115, 116

American Bankers Association, 113, 116

American Bankruptcy Institute, 111

American Bar Association, 63, 156, 531

American Bar Association Standing Committee on Dispute Resolution, 70

American Beauty Association, 118

American Beekeeping Federation. Newsletter, 446

American Bicyclist & Motorcyclist, 129

American Biltrite Inc., 1029

American Biotechnology Laboratory, 131

American Boarding Kennels Association, 765

American Board of Industrial Hygiene, 473

American Boat and Yacht Council, 133

American Book Producers Association, 138

American Booksellers Association, 141

American Brewer Magazine, 145

American Broadcasting Companies, Inc., 858, 1018

American Building Maintenance Industries, 40, 566

American Bureau of Metal Statistics, 603, 811

American Bus Association, 644

American Business Computers Corp., 800

American Business Law Association, 157

American Butter Institute, 267

American Canoe Manufacturers Union, 977

American Car Rental Association, 101

American Cast Metals Association, 381

American Cement Alliance, 174

American Cement Directory, 174

American Cemetery Association, 396

American Chain of Warehouses, 1099

American Chamber of Commerce Executives, 181

American Chamber of Commerce Researchers Association, 181

American Cheese Society, 182

American Chemical Society, 187

American Cinema Editors, 638

American City & County, 649, 838, 927

American Coal Foundation, 204

American Coin-Op, 528

American Coin Portfolios Inc., 212

American Collectors Association, 214

American College of Bankruptcy, 111

American College of Health Care Administrators, 695

American College of Radio Marketing, 857

American College of Trust and Estate Counsel, 1062

American College Testing, 1024

American Commercial Collectors Association, 214

American Commercial Lines, Inc., 953

American Compensation Association, 224

American Concrete Pavement Association, 238

American Concrete Pipe Association, 786

American Conference of Real Estate Investment Trusts, 865

American Consultants League, 243

American Copper Council, 603

American Copyright Society, 494

American Corporate Counsel Association, 157, 531

American Council for an Energy Efficient Economy, 309

American Council for Drug Education, 59

American Council of Highway Advertisers, 17

American Council of Independent Laboratories, 523

American Council of Life Insurance, 489

American Council of Nanny Schools, 189

American Council of the International Institute of Welding, 1112

American Council on Alcoholism, 59

American Council on Education, 15

American Council on International Personnel, 460

American Craft Council, 442

American Crystal Sugar Co., 989

American Cultured Dairy Products Institute, 267

American Custom Gunmakers Guild, 347

American Cutlery Manufacturers Association, 1000

American Cyanamid Co., 32, 187

American Cycle Systems, Inc., 130

American Dairy Association, 267

American Dairy Products Institute, 267

American Dehydrated Onion and Garlic Association, 722

American Demographics, 247, 801

American Dental Trade Association, 275

American Dietetic Association, 1095

American Driver and Traffic Safety Education Association, 1045

American Drycleaner, 528

American Economic Association, 290

American Economic Review, 290

American Electric Power Co., Inc., 301, 848

American Electronics Association, 947

American Electroplaters and Surface Finishers Society, 467, 599

American Express Travel Related Service, 1052

American Facsimile Association, 327

American Family Corp., 488

American Farm Bureau Research Foundation, 31

American Federation of Small Business, 962

American Federation of State, County and Municipal Employees, 526

American Federation of Television and Radio Artists, 1017

American Federation of Violin and Bow Makers, 650

American Feed Industry Association, 333

American Felt & Filter Co., 1134

American Fiber Manufacturers Association, 338

American Fiber, Textile, Apparel Coalition, 338

American Film Marketing Association, 638

American Finance Association, 341, 343

American Firearms Industry, 347

American Fire Journal, 349

American Fishing Tackle Manufacturers Association, 977

American Floorcovering Association, 354

American Forestry Association, 320

American Foundrymen's Society, 381

American Franchise Association, 383

American Fruit Grower, 391

American Funeral Director, 396

American Fur Industry, 398

American Furniture Manufacturers Association, 400

American Galvanizers Association, 467

American Gas Association, 659

American Gem and Mineral Suppliers Association, 412

American Gem Society, 412, 511

American Gem Trade Association, 412

American Greenhouse Vegetable Growers Association, 389

American Greetings Corp., 418, 428

American Hardware Manufacturers Association, 429

American Helicopter Society, 47

American Hereford Association, 171

American Honey Producers Association, 446

American Horticultural Society, 407

American Hospital Association, 448

American Hotel & Motel Association, 451

American Immigration Lawyers Association, 460

American Independent Refiners Association, 774

American Industrial Hygiene Association, 473

American Inkmaker, 820

American Institute for Economic Research, 290

American Institute for Hollow Structural Sections, 604

American Institute for International Steel, 983

American Institute of Aeronautics and Astronautics, 24

American Institute of Architects, 71

American Institute of Baking, 108

American Institute of Building Design, 71

American Institute of Certified Public Accountants, 5

American Institute of Chemical Engineers, 184

American Institute of Floral Designers, 360

American Institute of Food Distribution, 365

American Institute of Graphic Arts, 220, 422

American Institute of Management, 567

American Institute of Steel Construction, 983

American Institute of Technical Illustrators Association, 220

American Insurance Association, 483

American Insurance Services Group, 483

American Insurers Highway Safety Alliance, 481, 1045

American Intellectual Property Law Association, 494

American Iron and Steel Institute, 983

American Journal of Enology and Viticulture, 1120

American Journal of Industrial Medicine, 473

American Journal of Occupational Therapy, 701

American Journal of Ophthalmology, 726

American Judges Association, 259

American Laboratory News, 523

American Ladder Institute, 429

American Land Title Association, 862

American Laundry Machinery Inc., 529

American Lawyer, 532

American Leather Manufacturing Co., 535

American Libraries, 536

American Library Association, 536

American Lighting Association, 538

American Luggage Dealers Cooperative, 554

American Machine Tool Distributors' Association, 559

American Machinist, 823

American Maize-Products Co., 1035

American Managed Care and Review Association, 437

American Management Association, 567, 759

American Marketing Association, 575, 578

American Marketplace, 247

American Meat Institute, 590

American Medical Association, 438

American Medical Directors Association, 695

American Medical International, Inc., 449

American Medical Publishers' Association, 138

American Medical Services, Inc., 697

American Metal Market, 605, 812

American Mining Congress, 616

American Mining Congress Journal, 616

American Mobilehome Association, 625

American Movers Conference, 634

American Mushroom Institute, 389

American Music Center, 654

American Music Conference, 654

American Music Teacher, 655

American National Cattle Women, 171

American National Standards Institute, 980

American Newspaper Markets Circulation, 679

American Nuclear Energy Council, 693

American Numismatic Association, 211

American Numismatic Society, 211

American Nurseryman, 408

American Occupational Therapy Association, 701

American Oil Change Corp., 406

American Olean Tile Co., 1029

American Optical Corp., 726

American Orthotic and Prosthetic Association, 593, 836

American Painting Contractor, 740

American Paper Institute, 745

American Pet Products Manufacturers Association, 765

American Petroleum Institute, 77, 410

American Pewter Guild, 1000

American Pharmaceutical Association, 287

American Philatelic Society, 213

American Pipe Fittings Association, 786

American Plywood Association, 375

American Polled Hereford Association, 171

American Postal Workers Union, 803

American Powdered Metals, 602

American President Lines Ltd., 954

American Printed Fabrics Council, 324

American Printer, 816

American Produce Association, 389

American Production and Inventory Control Society, 501, 823

American Productivity and Quality Center, 826

American Professional Pet Distributors, Inc., 765

American Public Gas Association, 846

American Public Power Association, 84, 300

American Public Transit Association, 644, 844

American Purchasing Society, 851

American Railway Car Institute, 859

American Rental Association, 436, 593, 884

American Republic Insurance Co., 488

American Restaurant China Council, 1000

American Retreaders' Association, 1029

American Road and Transportation Builders Association, 904, 1042

The American Safe Deposit Association, 113

American Salon, 118

American Salt Co., 925

American School & University, 931

American Seafood Retailers Association, 351

American Seed Research Foundation, 945

Americans for a Sound AIDS Policy, 27

American Sheep Industry Association, 950

American Shipper, 953

American Shoemaking, 955

American Short Line Railroad Association, 859

American Sightseeing International, 1053

American Small Businesses Association, 962

American Society for Concrete Construction, 238

American Society for Enology and Viticulture, 1119

American Society for Healthcare Human Resources Administration, 448

American Society for Hospital Materials Management, 448

American Society for Industrial Security, 941

American Society for Public Administration, 838

American Society for Quality Control, 852

American Society for Training and Development, 292, 1047

American Society of Access Professionals, 385

American Society of Agronomy, 31

American Society of Appraisers, 1074

American Society of Bakery Engineers, 109

American Society of Business Press Editors, 1140

American Society of Cinematographers, 638

American Society of Civil Engineers, 190

American Society of CLU and ChFC, 492

American Society of Composers, Authors and Publishers, 654

American Society of Furniture Designers, 400

American Society of Heating, Refrigeration and Air-Conditioning Engineering, 38

American Society of Independent Business, 962

American Society of Interior Designers, 496

American Society of Interpreters, 1049

American Society of Irrigation Consultants, 36

American Society of Landscape Architects, 71

American Society of Magazine Editors, 1140

American Society of Magazine Photographers, 782

American Society of Medical Technology, Inc., 523

American Society of Newspaper Editors, 678

American Society of Pension Actuaries, 8, 302

American Society of Perfumers, 254

American Society of Professional Appraisers, 862, 1074

American Society of Real Estate Counselors, 862

American Society of Safety Engineers, 916

American Society of Sanitary Engineering, 926

American Society of Travel Agents, 1051

American Society of Women Accountants, 5

American Solar Energy Association, 966

American Solar Energy Society, 966

American Southwest Mortgage Investments Corp., 634

American Soybean Association, 974

American Spa and Health Resort Association, 874

American Spice Trade Association, 975

American Sportscasters Association, 1015

American Stamp Dealers Association, 213

American Standard Inc., 154

American Statistical Association, 982

American Stock Exchange, 937

American Sugar Alliance, 988

American Sugar Cane League of the U.S.A., 988

American Supply and Machinery Manufacturers Association, 470

American Supply Association, 797

American Systems Corp., 548

American Taxation Association, 1003

American Tea & Coffee Co., Inc., 206

American Technical Education Association, 294

American Telemarketing Association, 1013

American Television & Communications Corp., 159

American Tennis Industry Federation, 977

American Textile Manufacturers Institute, 324

American Tin Trade Association, 604

American Tourister, Inc., 554

American Toy Export Association, 1037

American Traffic Safety Services Association, 1045

American Translators Association, 1049

American Transtech, 282, 1014

American Truck Dealers, 1059

American Trucking Associations, 1059

American Tunaboat Association, 351

American Vegetable Grower, 391

American Veterinary Distributors Association, 1086

American Veterinary Exhibitors Association, 1086

American Veterinary Medical Association, 1086

American Video Association, 90

American Vitamin Products, Inc., 1096

American Viticultural Area Association, 1119

American Vocational Association, 294

American Watch Association, 198

American Watchmakers Institute, 198

American Waterways Operators, 1107

American Welding Institute, 1112

American Wind Energy Association, 312

American Wine Society, 1119

American Wire Producers Association, 1122

American Wood-Preservers' Association, 375

American Woodworker, 1131

American Wool Council, 1133

American Woolen Co., 1134

American Yarn Spinners Association, 1147

America's Hobby Center, Inc., 442

America West Airlines Inc., 45

Americold Corp., 1100

Ameron, Inc., 787

Ames Co., 409

AMF Bowling Companies, Inc., 979

Amfac Foods Inc., 183

AM General Division, 271

Amherst Systems, Inc., 501

Amkor Electronics Inc., 246

Amlings Flowerland, 361

AMR Recovery Association Inc., 214

Amtrak, 861

Amurol Products Co., 1096

Analysis & Technology, Inc., 888

Analysis of Public Utility Financing, 847

Analysis of Workers' Compensation Laws, 1138

Analytical Instrumentation, 933

Analytics, 81

Anchor Glass Container Corp., 250, 420

Arthur Andersen & Co., 7, 1005

Andersen Group, 1090

Anderson Report on Computer Graphics, 229

Andersons, 32, 946

Angelica Corp., 529

Anheuser-Busch Companies, Inc., 146

Animal Health Institute, 1086

Annals of Nuclear Energy, 693

Annual Directory of Pipelines and Equipment, 771

Annual Editions: Business Ethics, 155

Annual Report on Privatization, 822

Answer, 1015

Michael Anthony Jewelers Inc., 199, 413

Anti-Friction Bearing Manufacturers Association, 124

Antique Appraisal Association of America, 78

Antique Market Report, 78

Antique Monthly, 78

Antiques and Auction News, 78, 89

Antiques Dealers' Association of America, 78

Antique Trader Price Guide to Antiques and Collectors' Items, 78

Antitrust, 64

Antitrust Bulletin, 64

Apac Inc., 906

Apartment Owners and Managers Association of America, 834

APG, Inc., 23

API Industries, 600

Apis, 1086

Apogee Enterprises, Inc., 421

Apollo Space Systems, Inc., 92

Apparel Industry Magazine, 201

Apparel Merchandising, 201

I. Appel Corp., 1066

Apple Computer, Inc., 234, 280, 1136

Appleton Papers Inc., 424

Appliance Manufacturer, 66

Appliance Parts Distributors Association, 65

Appliance Service News, 66

Applied Biochemistry and Biotechnology, 131

Applied Biosystems, Inc., 934

Applied Materials Inc., 949

Applied Networks Report, 547

Applied Occupational & Environmental Hygiene, 473

Appraisal Institute, 1075, 1076

Appraisal Journal, 1075

Appraiser News, 863, 1076

Appraisers Association of America, 1075

Appraisers Standard, 89, 1076

Apricot Producers of California, 389

APV Crepaco, Inc., 370

APWA Reporter, 190

AQP Report, 826

Aquatics, 996

Aquatic Systems, Inc., 69

ARA Environmental Services, Inc., 566

ARA Services, Inc., 373

Aratex Services, Inc., 884

Arbor Drugs, Inc., 289

Arcade Building Maintenance, Inc., 566

Arcata Corp., 818

Archer-Daniels-Midland Co., 110

Archery Manufacturers Organization, 977

Architectural Digest, 496

Architectural Lighting, 538

Architectural Record, 71

Architectural Woodwork Institute, 152, 1130

Arco Chemical Co., 187

Arco Pipe Line Co., 790

Arctic Alaska Fisheries, 352

Argonaut Insurance Co., 1139

Arlington Corp., 397

Armanetti, Inc., 543

Armed Forces Journal International, 270

ARMS—The Association of Retail Marketing Services, 923

Armstrong World Industries Inc., 356

Army-Navy Store & Outdoor Merchandiser, 955, 879

Arnold Constable Corp., 180

Aro Corp., 553

Arrowhead Mountain Spring Water Co., 127

Arrow Industries, Inc., 901

Art & Antiques, 79

Art at Auction: The Year at Sotheby's and Parke-Bernet, 89

Art Dealers Association of America, 78

Art Direction, 423

Artificial Intelligence Abstracts, 80

Artificial Intelligence Markets, 81

Artificial Intelligence Technologies, Inc., 81

Artistic Greetings Inc., 425

Arts Management, 83, 655

Artsoft Inc., 548

Asbestos Abatement Report, 85

Asbestos Case Law Quarterly, 85

Asbestos Control Report, 85

Asbestos Information Association/North America, 84

Asbestos Litigation Group, 84

Asbestos Victims of America, 84

Asgrow Seed Co., 946

Ash Grove Cement Co., 174

Ashland Oil, Inc., 410, 776

Sam Ash Music Corp., 653, 870

ASHRAE Journal, 39

ASM International, 601

Asphalt Emulsion Manufacturers Association, 86

Asphalt Institute, 86

Asphalt Recycling and Reclaiming Association, 87, 878

Asphalt Roofing Manufacturers Association, 87, 910

Asphalt Rubber Producers Group, 87

Assessment Digest, 863

Associated Accounting Firms International, 5

Associated Builders and Contractors, 149

Associated Building Material Distributors of America, 152

Associated Construction Distributors International, 153

Associated Credit Bureaus, 262

Associated Equipment Distributors, 470

Associated Funeral Directors Service International, 396

Associated Glass and Pottery Manufacturers, 1000

Associated Locksmiths of America, 429

Associated Pipe Organ Builders of America, 650

Associated Risk Managers International, 902

Associated Surplus Dealers, 994

Associated Wholesale Grocers, Inc., 428

Association for Business Communication, 1140

Association for Computing Machinery, 231

Association for Consumer Research, 247

Association for Convention Operations Management, 1039

Association for Finishing Processes of Society of Manufacturing Engineers, 467

Association for Information and Image Management, 613

Association for Innovative Marketing, 576

Association for Intelligent Systems Technology, 80

Association for Investment Management and Research, 344, 504

Association for Measurement and Evaluation in Counseling and Development, 1024

Association for Public Broadcasting, 1015

Association for Quality and Participation, 642, 852

Association for Systems Management, 572

Association for the Advancement of Medical Instrumentation, 594, 943

Association Management, 568

Association of American Colleges, 216

Association of American Pesticide Control Officials, 762

Association of American Publishers, 138

Association of American Railroads, 859

Association of American Vintners, 1119

Association of American Weather Observers, 1110

Association of Asphalt Paving Technologists Proceedings, 87

Association of Audio-Visual Technicians, 90

Association of Automotive Aftermarket Distributors, 98

Association of Bank Holding Companies, 113

Association of Battery Recyclers, 121

Association of Biotechnology Companies, 131

Association of Bituminous Contractors, 204

Association of Collegiate Entrepreneurs, 318

Association of Community Travel Clubs, 1051

Association of Computer Users, 231

Association of Consulting Chemists and Chemical Engineers, 184

Association of Corporate Travel Executives, 52, 1053

Association of Cosmetologists and Hairdressers, 118

Association of Crafts and Creative Industries, 442

Association of Credit Union League Executives, 265

Association of Diesel Specialists, 316

Association of Edison Illuminating Companies, 846

Association of Editorial Businesses, 1141

Association of Energy Engineers, 209

Association of Executive Search Consultants, 306

Association of Food Industries, 365

Association of Foreign Trade Representatives, 461

Association of Home Appliance Manufacturers, 65

Association of Immigration Attorneys, 460

Association of Independent Television Stations, 1015

Association of Industrial Metallizers, Coaters and Laminators, 467

Association of Internal Management Consultants, 570

Association of International Automobile Manufacturers, 103

Association of Iron and Steel Engineers, 984

Association of Jewish Book Publishers, 138

Association of Machinery and Equipment Appraisers, 1075

Association of Manpower Franchise Owners, 1019

Association of National Advertisers, 17

Association of North American Directory Publishers, 138

Association of Official Seed Analysts, 945

Association of Oil Pipe Lines, 774, 789

Association of Oilwell Servicing Contractors, 774

Association of Outplacement Consulting Firms, 306

Association of Part-Time Professionals, 1019

Association of Physical Fitness Centers, 874

Association of Physical Plant Administrators of Universities and Colleges, 565

Association of Private Pension and Welfare Plans, 756

Association of Productivity Specialists, 826

Association of Professional Color Laboratories, 782

Association of Professional Design Firms, 496

Association of Professional Energy Managers, 309

Association of Progressive Rental Organizations, 884

Association of Publicly Traded Companies, 937

Association of Records Managers and Administrators, 871

Association of Research Directors, 886

Association of Rotational Molders, 793

Association of Sales Administration Managers, 920

Association of Specialists in Cleaning and Restoration, 195, 1070

Association of Steel Distributors, 984

Association of Talent Agents, 82

Association of Teachers of Technical Writing, 1141

Association of Telemessaging Services, International, 1015

Association of Telephone Answering Services, 1015

Association of the Wall and Ceiling Industries, 84, 153, 791

Association of Travel Marketing Executives, 53

Association of Trial Lawyers of America, 531, 829

Association of University Related Research Parks, 886

Association of Vitamin Chemists, 1095

Association of Yarn Distributors, 1147

Astec Industries, Inc., 88

ASTM, 853

Atalanta Corp., 167

AT & T Capital Corp., 884

Atapco Office Products Group, 709

Athletic Footwear Association, 977

Atlantic Dairy Cooperative, 268

Atlantic Group Inc., 441, 1096

Atlantic Mobilehome & RV Supply, 873

Atlantic Recording Corp., 869

Atlantic Richfield Co., 205

Atlantic Seafarms, Inc., 69

Atlantis Group, Inc., 795

Atomic Energy Clearinghouse, 693

Attorneys and Agents Registered to Practice U.S. Patent Office, 495

Atwood Richards, Inc., 120

Auction and Surplus, 89, 995

Auction Prices of American Artists, 89

Auction Weekly, 89

Audiocraft, 868

Audio Engineering Society, 868

Audiovideo International, 245

Audio-Visual Communications, 91

Audio-Visual Management Association, 91

Auric Corp., 600

Aurora Casket Co., Inc., 397

Ausimont N.V., 4

Auster Co. Inc., 393

Authors Guild, 1141

Auto Age, 101, 1057

Auto and Flat Glass Journal, 420

Autoclave Engineers, Inc., 934

Autodesk Inc., 227

Auto Glass Specialists, Inc., 406

Autoland Chevrolet Inc., 97

Automated Assemblies Corp., 909

Automated Builder, 150, 626

Automated Imaging Association, 907

Automatic Identification Manufacturers, 93

Automatic Meter Reading Association, 846

Auto Merchandising News, 99

Automobile Insurance Losses, Collision Coverages, 482

Automobile Law Reports—Insurance Cases, 482

Automotive, Tooling, Metalworking Newsletter, 558

Automotive & Consumer Group, 445

Automotive Body Parts Association, 98

Automotive Engine Rebuilders Association, 557

Automotive Executive, 96

Automotive Industries, 104

Automotive Industry Action Group, 103

Automotive Information Council, 103

Automotive Market Research Council, 98

Automotive News, 104

Automotive Parts and Accessories Association, 98

Automotive Parts Rebuilders Association, 98

Automotive Refrigeration Products Institute, 37

Automotive Service Association, 405

Automotive Service Industry Association, 98

AutoWeek, 104

Avco Financial Services, Inc., 263

Avery Dennison Corp., 521

Aviation Distributors and Manufacturers Association, 48

Aviation Maintenance Foundation International, 48

Aviation Week & Space Technology, 25

Avionics, 106
Avionics Newsletter, 107
Avionics News Magazine, 106
Avionics Review, 107
Avis, Inc., 102
AV Market Place, 91
Avondale Industries, Inc., 608, 954
Avondale Mills Inc., 1148
Avon Products, Inc., 255
AV Video, 91, 1089
AVX Corp., 178
AW Computer Systems, Inc., 800
Axel Johnson Inc., 471
N. W. Ayer Inc., 20
Azrock Industries Inc., 1029
Aztar Corp., 404

Babcock & Wilcox Co., 1078
Babco Textron, Inc., 558
Bacardi Imports, Inc., 541
Bachman's Inc., 361, 409
Backer Spielvogel Bates World-
    wide Inc., 20
Backstage, 83
Henry Bacon Building Materials,
    154
Badger Meter, Inc., 1064
Baker Commodities Inc., 718
JE Baker Co., 178
Baker Industries, Inc., 350
Bakery Equipment Manufactur-
    ers Association, 109
Bakery Production and Market-
    ing, 109
Bakery Production and Marketing
    Red Book, 109
Baldwin Technology Co., Inc., 589
L. G. Balfour Co., Inc., 643, 814
Ball Manufacturers Engineers
    Committee, 124
Bally Manufacturing Corp., 404
Bally's Grand, Inc., 404
Bally's Health & Tennis Corp.,
    877

Baltimore Spice Inc., 976
Bandag, Inc., 406, 915
B & C Corp., 558
Bank Administration Institute,
    113
BankAmerica Corp., 117
Bank Capital Markets Associa-
    tion, 113
Bankcard Holders of America,
    262
Bank Director, 115
Bankers Magazine, 115
Bankers Monthly, 115
Banking Law Institute, 113
Bank Management, 115
Bank Marketing Association, 114
Bank New Product News, 115
Bankruptcy Strategist, 112
Banta Corp., 818
Bantam Doubleday Dell Publish-
    ing Group, Inc., 139
Banyan Corp., 398
Banyan Systems, Inc., 548
Barbecue Industry Association,
    874
E. Barber and Sons Livestock, 545
Barber-Greene Co., 88
Barnes and Noble, Inc., 142
Baroid Drilling, Fluids, Inc., 772
Barre Granite Association, 855
Barrister, 532
Barron's National Business and
    Financial Weekly, 506
Barry's Jewelers, Inc., 512
Barter Advantage, Inc., 120
Barter Communique, 120
Barter Exchange, Inc., 120
BarterNews, 120
Barter Update, 120
Bartlett and Co., 364
Bartlett Cattle Co., 171
Bartlett-Collins Co., Inc., 1001
Bartlett Milling Co., 1118
Barton-Malow Co., 150
Base Ten Systems Inc., 107

Basf Corp., 339
Baskin-Robbins USA Co., 454
Felix V. Bass & Co., Inc., 443
Batesville Casket Co., Inc., 397
Battelle Memorial Institute, 587,
    888
Battery Council International,
    121
Battery Man, 122
Baumann Paper Co. Inc., 743
Baxter International Inc., 436,
    524, 1087
Bayer USA Inc., 187
BBDO Worldwide Inc., 20
B C & T News, 109
BCI News, 122
Beals Royal Glass and Mirror, 421
Bear, Stearns & Co. Inc., 507, 940
Bearings, Inc., 125
Bearing Specialists Association,
    124
Beatrice/Hunt-Wesson   Foods,
    167, 367
Beauty Age, 118
Beauty and Barber Supply Insti-
    tute, 118
Beazer East, Inc., 906
Bechtel Group, Inc., 152, 191
Becton, Dickinson & Co., 524,
    595, 1087
Beech Aircraft Corp., 49
Beef Business Bulletin, 171
Beef Today, 171
Beefweek, 171
Beer Institute, 145
Beer Marketer's Insights, 145
Beer Statistics News, 145
Beer Wholesaler, 146
Bekaert Corp., 1123
Bekins Moving & Storage Co.,
    634
Belfort Instrument Co., 1111
W. Bell & Co., 199
Bell & Howell Publication Sys-
    tems Co., 614

Bell Atlantic Business Systems Services, Inc., 235
Bell Farms, Inc., 33
Bell-Horn, Inc., 837
Bell Industries, Inc., 40
Bell Packaging Corp., 736
Bemis Co., Inc., 736
Ben & Jerry's Homemade Inc., 454
Benco Industries Inc., 961
Beneficial Corp., 263
Benefits, 303
Benefits News Analysis, 303
Benefits Today, 305
Berbiglia, Inc., 543
Berke Co., 154
Berkeley Solar Group, 967
Berol Corp., 1143
Russ Berrie & Co., Inc., 419, 692
Charles Beseler Co., 738
Best's Agents Guide to Life Insurance Companies, 491
Best's Insurance Management Reports: Life-Health Edition, 490
Best's Insurance Report: Life—Health, 487
Best's Insurance Report: Property—Casualty, 484
Bethlehem Steel Corp., 606, 985
Better Homes and Gardens Home Products Guide, 153
Better Roads, 1042
Better Roads and Transportation Council, 905
Beverage Alcohol Business Scene, 146, 543
Beverage Alcohol Market Report, 1120
Beverage Beacon—Ledger, 127
Beverage Dynamics, 543
Beverage Industry, 127
Beverage Network, 126
Beverage World, 127
Beverage World's Databank, 127
Beverly Enterprises, Inc., 896
BG Holding Co., Inc., 960

BHP-Utah International Inc., 615
Bibb Co., 324
Bic Corp., 1143
Bicycle Dealer Showcase, 129
Bicycle Dealer Showcase Buyers Guide, 129
Bicycle Guide, 129
Bicycle Institute of America, 129
Bicycle Manufacturers Association of America, 129
Bicycling, 130
Biddle Sawyer Corp., 4
Big Gus Onion Rings, 723
Billboard, 655
Billboard's International Recording Equipment & Studio Directory, 869
Billboard's International Talent and Touring Directory, 83
Billiard and Bowling Institute of America, 977
Biltrite Corp., 1029
Binswanger Glass Co., 421
BioCycle, 1104
BioEngineering News, 131
Biogen Research Corp., 132
Bio-Lab, Inc., 997
Biological Farming News, 34
Biomass Energy Research Association, 312
Biopharm, 778
Bioresearch Today: Food Additives & Residues, 10
Biotech Business, 131
BioTechnica International, Inc., 132
Biotechnology and Bioengineering, 131
Biotechnology Directory, 131
Biotechnology Progress, 132
Bio-Tek Instruments, Inc., 854
Birdsong Corp., 700
Bird Talk, 766
Biscuit and Cracker Manufacturers Association, 109

Bits 'n Chips, 1131
Bitstream, Inc., 230
Bituminous Coal Operators' Association, 204
Blacks in Government, 192
D. L. Blair Corp., 924
Bland Cadillac Co., 97
Barry Blau & Partners Inc., 282
Blaw Knox Corp., 370, 589
Bleached Paperboard Group, 750
Blenko Glass Co., Inc., 1001
Block Distributing Co., Inc., 541
Blue Anchor, Inc., 389
Blue Bell, Inc., 201
Blue Cross and Blue Shield of Michigan, 488
Blue Cross and Blue Shield of the National Capital Area, 488
Blue Cross of Western Pennsylvania, 488
Blue Diamond Growers, 698
The Blue Sheet, 779
Blumberg Communications, Inc., 92
BMI Refractories, 382
BMW of North America, Inc., 105
BNA's Alternative Dispute Resolution Report, 70
BNA's Patent, Trademark & Copyright Journal, 495
BNA's Workers' Compensation Report, 1138
Board Converting News, 749
Board of Certified Product Safety Management, 831
Board of Governors of the Federal Reserve System, 116
Boat & Motor Dealer, 134
Boat & Motor Dealer's Market Manual, 134
Boating, 134
Boating Industry, 134
Body Fashions—Intimate Apparel, 1066
Boehringer Mannheim Corp., 595

Boeing Co., 49

Boeing Employees Credit Union, 266

Boise Cascade Corp., 376, 746

Wm. Bolthouse Farms, Inc., 723

Bon-Art International, Inc., 987

Bond Leather Co., Inc., 534

Bonneville Pacific Corp., 210

Book Binders, Inc., 136

Book Dealers World, 141

Book Industry Study Group, 138

Book Industry Trends, 139

Book Manufacturers Institute, 136

Boosey & Hawkes, Inc., 655

Borden, Inc., 183, 454, 556

Borden Packaging & Industrial Products Division, 14

Borg-Warner Corp., 944

Borland International, Inc., 234

Boston Co. Family of Funds, 658

Boston Computer Society, 232

Bottle-Can Recycling Update, 61, 879

Boxboard Containers, 143, 749

Boxoffice, 638

Bra-Con/X-Mation, Inc., 824, 909

Braden-Sutphin Ink Co., 820

Brand Companies, Inc., 854

Brand Names Education Foundation, 494

Branson Ultrasonics Corp., 1064

Brass and Bronze Ingot Manufacturers, 604

Breeders Journal, 545

Brenlin Corp., 382

Brewers' Association of America, 145

Brewers Digest, 146

Brick Institute of America, 153

Briggs & Stratton Corp., 317

Briggs Industries, Inc., 798

Briggs—Weaver, Inc., 589, 918

Bristol Corp., 798

Bristol—Myers Squibb Co., 780

Broadcast Engineering, 1017

Broadcasting, 1017

Broadcasting and the Law, 1017

Broadcast Promotion and Marketing Executives, 1015

Brodart Co., 537

Brodhead—Garrett Co., 295, 401

Broker World, 487, 490, 493

Brooke Group Ltd., 1035

Brookover Feed Yards, 171

Brooks Beverage Management, Inc., 128

Brother International Corp., 252, 327

Alex Brown & Sons, Inc., 503

Browning, 348

Brunswick Bowl/Billiard, 979

Brush Wellman Inc., 178

BSN Corp., 979

BTR Inc., 1078

Budd Co., 1958

Budget Rent a Car Corp., 102

Builder-Dealer, 150

Builders' Hardware Manufacturers Association, 429

Builders Specialties Co., 154

Building Design & Construction, 150

Building Owners and Managers Association International, 706

Building Products Digest, 153

Buildings, 835

Building Service Contractors Association International, 565

Building Stone Institute, 855

Building Supply Home Centers, 153, 444

Bullion Advisory, 812

Bunge Corp., 334

Bureau of Business Practice, 677

Bureau of National Affairs, Inc., 1048

Bureau of Salesmen's National Associations, 200

Burger King Corp., 891

Burgoyne, Inc., 425

Burke Communication Industries, Inc., 924

Burke Marketing Research, Inc., 579

Burlington Air Express Inc., 42, 387

Burlington Industries, Inc., 168, 339, 1070

Burlington Northern Inc., 861

Burmax Co., Inc., 119

Ed Burnett Consultants, Inc., 282

Busch Entertainment Corp., 876

Bushkin Associates, Inc., 598

Business and Health, 487

Business and Institutional Furniture Manufacturers Association, 400

Business & Professional Ethics Journal, 155

Business and Tax Planning Board, 1003

Business Communications Review, 1010

Business Computer Digest, 703

Business Economics, 290

Business Education Forum, 293

Business Education Index, 293

Business Education World, 293

Business Ethics Resource, 155

Business Forms, Labels and Systems, 378

Business Forms Management Association, 378

Business History Conference, 156

Business History Review, 156

Business Horizons, 293

Business Interiors, 72, 497

Business Law Monographs, 157

Business Lawyer, 157

Business of Fur, 398

Business Organizations: Franchising, 384

Business Traveler Magazine, 1055

Business Travel Management, 1055

Business Travel News, 1055
Bus Operator, 644
Bus World, 644
Busy Beaver Building Centers, Inc., 445
Butane-Propane News, 832
Butler International Inc., 51
Butler Manufacturing Co., 32
BWD Automotive Corp., 99
Byte, 233

Cable Television Administration and Marketing Society, 158
Cable TV Advertising, 158
Cable TV and New Media Law and Finance, 158
Cable TV Programming, 159
Cable TV Technology, 159
CableVision, 159
Cablevision Systems Corp., 159
Cable World, 159
CACI Marketing Systems, 579
Cactus Feeders, Inc., 171
Cadbury Beverages, Inc., 128
CAD-CAM Abstracts, 226
Cadillac Products, Inc., 743
Cadmium Council, Inc., 604
Cadnetix Corp., 227
Caesars World, Inc., 452, 877
Cagle's Inc., 808
Calavo Growers of California, 393
Calcot, Ltd., 258
CAL Electric Supply Inc., 298
Calgene, Inc., 132
California Almond Growers Exchange, 700
California and Hawaiian Sugar Co., 989
California Fig Institute, 389
California Iceberg Lettuce Commission, 389
California Melon Research Board, 389
California Milling Corp., 1118

California Mining Journal, 616
California Portland Cement Co., 175
California Raisin Advisory Board, 390
California Shellfish Co., Inc., 353
California Table Grape Commission, 390
California Tomato Grower, 391
Caliper Management, Inc., 761
Calorie Control Council, 1095
Calstar, Inc., 212, 214
Cambridge Holdings Ltd., 647
Cambridge Street Metal Co. Inc., 609
Cameron's Foodservice Promotions Reporter, 372, 890
Camp Dresser & McKee Inc., 322
Campground Management, 875
Canandaigua Wine Co. Inc., 1121
C & C Information Systems, 1014
C & D Power Systems, Inc., 122
Candy Buyers Directory, 163
Candy Wholesaler, 163
Canned Food Information Council, 165
Canon Business Machines, Inc., 252, 327
Canonie Environmental Services Corp., 1106
Canteen Corp., 1080
Capital Credit Corp., 215
Capital Southwest Corp., 1082
Capitol Federal Savings & Loan Association of Denver, 929
Capitol Industries-EMI, Inc., 870
Car and Driver, 104
Carbonated Beverage Institute, 126
Carborundum Co., 178
Car Dealer Insider Newsletter, 96
Cardinal Distribution Inc., 256
Card Player, 403
Careercom Corp., 293
Career Pilot, 47

Career Success, 294
Carey Limousine, Inc., 1006
Cargill, Inc., 364
Cargill Fertilizer, Inc., 337
Carisbrook Industries Inc., 1148
Jack Carl/312 Futures, Inc., 223
Carleton Woolen Mills, Inc., 1134
Carlisle Companies Inc., 914
Carlisle Syntec Systems, 912
Carlson Hospitality Group Inc., 452
Carlson Marketing Group Inc., 643, 1048
Carlson Report for Shopping Center Management, 957
Carlson Travel Group Inc., 1052
Carnival Cruise Lines, Inc., 954
Carolco Pictures Inc., 639
Carolina Freight Carriers Corp., 388, 1061
Carolina Mills, Inc., 1148
Carpenter, 1131
Carpet and Rug Industry Review, 168
Carpet Manufacturers Marketing Association, 168
Car Rental & Leasing Insider Newsletter, 102
Carson International Inc., 237
Carter-Wallace, Inc., 767
Cartier, Inc., 512
Carvel Corp., 454
Carver Boat Corp., 135
Car Wash Owners and Suppliers Association, 405
J. I. Case Co., 32
CA Selects. Adhesives, 13
CA Selects. Amino Acids, Peptides and Proteins, 3
CA Selects. Batteries & Fuel Cells, 122
CA Selects. Ceramic Materials, 177
CA Selects. Coatings, Inks, & Related Products, 820

CA Selects. Corrosion—Inhibiting Coatings, 468

CA Selects. Detergents, Soaps, & Surfactants, 196

CA Selects. Fats & Oils, 717

CA Selects. Flavors & Fragrances, 10

CA Selects. Food, Drugs, & Cosmetics, 254

CA Selects. Hot-Melt Adhesives, 13

CA Selects. Lubricants, Greases, & Lubrication, 552

CA Selects. Omega-3 Fatty Acids & Fish Oil, 3

CA Selects. Pesticide Analysis, 762

CA Selects. Solar Energy, 967

Cash Box, 655

Cash Flow Enhancement Report, 170

Cash Management Performance Report, 170

Casino World, 403

Casket Manufacturers Association of America, 396

Casting Industry Suppliers Association, 381

Casualty Actuarial Society, 9

Catering Today, 372

Caterpillar Inc., 906, 1058

Cat Fancy, 766

Catfish Farmers of America, 68

Catholic Book Publishers Association, 138

CBC Features, 139

CBS Inc., 858, 1018

CBS Records, 870

CCC Information Services Inc., 1076

CCH Computax Inc., 1005

CDI Corp., 308

Cellcom Corp., 629

Cell Technology, Inc., 132

Cellular Business, 628

Cellular Marketing, 628

Cellular Sales & Marketing, 629

Cement and Concrete Research, 174, 238

Cement, Quarry and Mineral Aggregates Newsletter, 855

Centel Corp., 629

Center for Auto Safety, 1045

Center for Dispute Settlement, 70

Center for Entrepreneurial Management, 318

Center for Hazardous Materials Research, 1104

Center for Local Tax Research, 1003

Center for Management Effectiveness, 568

Center for Migration Studies of New York, 801

Center for Office Technology, 707

Center for Packaging Education, 734

Center for Public Interest Polling, 841

Center Management, 189

Centimark Corp., 356, 912

Central Maine Power Co., 301

Central Point Software, Inc., 235

Central Soya Co., Inc., 334, 975

Central Sprinkler Corp., 350

Central States Diversified Inc., 144, 743

Central Steel & Wire Co., 62, 1123

Central Wholesalers Association, 797

Century 21, 864

Ceramic Engineering and Science Proceedings, 177

Ceramic Industry, 177

Ceramic Tile Distributors Association, 1029

Ceramic Tile Institute of America, 1029

Ceramicus, Inc., 1029

Cereal Foods World, 362

Certified Coin Dealer Newsletter, 212

Cessna Aircraft Co., 49

Cetus Corp., 132

CF & I Steel Corp., 1123

CF Industries, Inc., 337

CG Professional, 229

Chain Drug Review, 288

Chain Store Age General Merchandise Trends, 179

Chamber of Commerce of the United States, 181

Champion Co., 397

Channel Home Centers Inc., 409

Charter Arms Corp., 348

Charter Power Systems, Inc., 122

Chaselle, Inc., 401

Chase Manhattan Corp., 117

Checkpoint Systems, Inc., 537

CheckRobot Inc., 94

Cheese Importers Association of America, 182

Cheese Market News, 182

Cheese Reporter, 182

Chef Institutional, 890

Chelsea Industries, Inc., 795

Chemical and Engineering News, 184, 186

Chemical Engineering, 184, 186

Chemical Engineering Progress, 185, 587

Chemical Manufacturers Association, 186

Chemical Sources Association, 10

Chemical Specialties Manufacturers Association, 186, 762

Chemical Waste Management, Inc., 1106

Chemical Week, 185, 186

Chemical Worker, 187

Chemistry and Biochemistry of Amino Acids, Peptides, and Proteins, 3

Chemists' Club Library, 187

Chempower Inc., 85
Chesapeake Corp., 800
Chesapeake Utilities Corp., 833
Chesebrough-Pond's USA Co., 256
Chevron Chemical Co., 4, 553, 764
Chevron Corp., 88, 410
Cheyenne Software, Inc., 548
Chicago and Northwestern Holdings Corp., 861
Chicago Hair Goods Co., 119
Chicago Tribune Co., 679
Chief Executive Magazine, 569
ChildCare, 189
Child Care Action Campaign, 189
Children's Book Council, 138
Childrenswear Manufacturers Association, 200
Child World, Inc., 1038
Chilled Foods Association, 365
Chilton Co., 757
Chilton's Automotive Marketing, 96
Chilton's Commercial Carrier Journal, 645, 1060
Chilton's Distribution Magazine, 283, 401
Chilton's Food Engineering, 366
Chilton's Hardware Age, 153, 430
Chilton's IAN, 933
Chilton's Industrial Safety & Hygiene News, 473, 917
Chilton's Jewelers' Circular—Keystone, 198, 512
Chilton's Review of Optometry, 726
China, Glass and Giftware Association, 417, 1000
China Glass & Tableware, 1001
Chiquita Brands International, Inc., 367
Chock Full o'Nuts Corp., 206
Chocolate and Nut World, 699
Christian Booksellers Association, 141

Chronicle of Higher Education, 216
Chrysler Corp., 105
Chubb Corp., 482, 485
Ciba-Geigy Seed Division, 946
Cider Association of North America, 126
Cigar Association of America, 1033
Cincinnati Milacron Inc., 560
Circle Business Credit, Inc., 884
Circuit City Stores Inc., 66
Circulation Management, 757
Cissell Manufacturing Co., 529
Cit-Con Oil Corp., 553
Citicorp, 117
Citicorp/Citibank, 116
Citizens for Sensible Control of Acid Rain, 320
Citrus and Vegetable Magazine, 391
Citrus Industry Magazine, 392
City Hall Digest, 649
Civil Service Employees Association, 192
Clabir Corp, 454
Claire's Stores Inc., 418
Claritas/NPDC, 579
Classification and Compensation Society, 224
Clay Minerals Society, 193
Clayton Homes, Inc., 626
Clean Coal Technologies, 204
Clean Harbors Inc., 322
Cleaning Business, 196, 565
Cleaning Equipment Trade Association, 195
Cleaning-Finishing-Coating Digest, 599
Cleaning Management Institute, 195, 565
Cleveland Builders Supply Inc., 792
Clinical Homecare Ltd., 436
Clinical Laboratory Science, 523

Clinical Pharmacology & Therapeutics, 779
Clock Manufacturers and Marketing Association, 198
Clorox Co., 196
Clothing & Textiles Research Journal, 324
CLR, 594, 933
CLSI, Inc., 537
Club Mediterranee, 876
CMX Corp., 1090
CNF Constructors, Inc., 210
Coal, 205
Coal and Slurry Technology Association, 204
Coalition for Responsible Waste Incineration, 1104
Coalition of Adult Education Organizations, 15
Coalition of Labor Union Women, 525
Coalition of Publicly Traded Partnerships, 504
Coal Mine Directory, 205
Coal Mining Newsletter, 205
Coal Week, 205
Coastal Corp., 661
Coast Oyster Co., 353
Coated Abrasives Manufacturers Institute, 1
Cobe Laboratories, Inc., 596
Coca-Cola Enterprises Inc., 11, 128
Cocaine Anonymous World Services, 59
Cockshaw's Construction Labor News & Opinion, 150
Coffee Development Group, 126, 206
Coffee, Sugar & Cocoa Exchange, Inc., 223
Cogeneration, 209
Cogeneration and Independent Power Coalition of America, 209

Cogeneration Journal, 209
Cohen Furniture Co., 356
Coin Laundry Association, 528
Coin Prices, 212
Coins, 212
Coin World, 212
Coldwell Banker, 864
Coldwell Banker Relocation Management Services, Inc., 882
Cole-Layer-Trumble Co., 1076
Collector, 215
Collectors Club, 213
The College Board, 1024
Collins & Aikman Corp., 326, 1070
Collins Commercial Avionics, 107
Collins Industries, Inc., 645
Colonial Sugars, Inc., 990
Colorado Serum Co., 1087
Color Tile, Inc., 1029, 1098
Columbia Journalism Review, 514
Columbian Advertising, Inc., 282
Columbus McKinnon Corp., 589
Columbus Mills, Inc., 169
Comart Associates, Inc., 924
Combustion Engineering Inc., 1106
Comcast Corp., 159
Comdata Holdings Corp., 263
Comet Rice, Inc., 901
Comex Weekly Market Report, 222
Comments on Money and Credit, 262
Commerce Reporting Co., 959
Commercial Building Maintenance Co., Inc., 566
Commercial Food Equipment Service Association, 368
Commercial Intertech Corp., 1078
Commercial-Investment Real Estate Council, 866
Commercial Investment Real Estate Journal, 866
Commercial Lending Newsletter, 115

Commercial Products Division, 40
Commercial Programming Unlimited, Inc., 293
Commercial Property News, 863
Commercial Steel Treating Corp., 600
Commercial Weather Services Association, 1110
Commission of Accredited Truck Driving Schools, 1059
Committee for Small Business Exports, 461
Committee for Sustainable Agriculture, 34, 440
Committee of National Security Companies, 942
Committee to Support the Antitrust Laws, 63
Commodities Recovery Corp., 995
Commodity Closeup, 222
Commodity Perspective, 222
Commodore Environmental Services Inc., 85
Communicating for Agriculture, 30
Communication Arts, 19
Communication Briefings, 1141
Communications, 629
Communications Diversified, Inc., 924
Communications in Finance, 1010
Communications Industries Report, 91
Communications Workers of America, 526
Community Service Credit Union Council, 265
Commuter Air International, 44
Commuter-Regional Airline News, 44
Compaq Computer Corp., 234
Compensation & Benefits Management, 225

Compensation and Benefits Review, 225
Compensation Strategy and Management, 225, 303
Competitive Advantage, 920
Composite Catalog of Oil Field Equipment & Services, 772
Composites & Adhesives Newsletter, 13
Comprehensive Video Supply Co., 1090
Compressed Air, 849
Compressed Air and Gas Institute, 849
CompuServe, Inc., 477
Compute, 233
Computer Aided Design Report, 227
Computer-Aided Engineering, 227
Computer Aided Manufacturing International, 226
Computer and Business Equipment Manufacturers Association, 707
Computer and Communications Industry Association, 1009
Computer Associates International, Inc., 235
Computer Graphics World, 229
Computer Language Research, Inc., 1005
Computer Microfilm Corp., 614
Computers & Operations Research, 724
Computer Sciences Corp., 724
Computer Security Institute, 941
Computer Shopper, 233
Computers in Banking, 115
Computerworld, 233, 573, 703
Computing & Management, 573
Conagra, Inc., 32, 334
ConAgra Flour Milling Co., 364
Concessionaire, 237
Concord Career Colleges Inc., 295

Concord Custom Cleaners, 530

Concrete Construction, 239

Concrete Producers News, 787

Concrete Products, 239

Cone Mills Corp., 326

The Conference Board, 290

Conference Board's Human Resources Briefing, 759

Conference Board's Marketing Briefing, 920

Conference Management Co., 1041

Conference of Casualty Insurance Companies, 484

Conference of National Park Concessioners, 236

Conference of State Court Administrators, 259

Conferon, Inc., 1041

Congoleum Corp., 356

Congress of Independent Unions, 525

Connecticut General Life Insurance Co., 491

Connecticut Yankee Atomic Power, 694

Connell Co., 901

Conopco, Inc., 718

Conservation and Renewable Energy Inquiry and Referral Service, 312

Consolidated Rail Corp., 388, 861

Consolidation Coal Co., 205

Constar International Inc., 250

Consultants and Consulting Organizations Directory, 243

Consultants News, 570

Consultation, 243

Consulting Rates and Business Practices. Annual Survey, 243

Consumer Confidence Survey, 248

Consumer Federation of America, 247

Consumer Product Litigation Reporter, 829

Consumer Reports, 66

Consumer Selection Guide for Room Air Conditioners, 39

Consumers' Research, 247

Consumers Union of United States, 247

Consumer Trends, 248

Containerboard and Kraft Paper Group, 748

Containerization and Intermodal Institute, 249

Container Marketing Committee, 249

Container News, 249

Contel Corp., 1012

Contemporary Long-Term Care, 696

Contemporary Times, 1020

Continental Airlines Inc., 45

Continental Cablevision Inc., 160

Continental Distributing Co. Inc., 541, 1121

Continental Materials Corp., 856

Contours, 1066

Contracting Business, 39

Contractor: The Newsmagazine of Mechanical Contracting, 39, 797

Contractor's Guide, 480, 911

Contractors Pump Bureau, 849

Control Data Corp., 234

Control Engineering, 470

Controllers Council, 5

Control Transaction Corp., 800

Convenience Store News, 993

Convenient Automotive Services Institute, 405

Conventions and Expositions, 1040

Conventionsouth, 1040

Conversion Industries Inc., 314

Converting Magazine, 745, 749

W. H. Conyngham & Co., 447

Thomas Cook Travel, Inc., 1052

Coopers & Lybrand, 7, 1005

Cooper Tire & Rubber Co., 914

Adolph Coors Co., 146

Coors Porcelain Co., 178

Copeland Corp., 40, 850

Copier Dealers Association, 251

Copier Duplicator News, 251

Coplay Cement Co., 175

Copper and Brass Fabricators Council, 607

Copper and Brass Servicenter Association, 604

Copyright Clearance Center, 494

Copyright Law Reports, 495

Copyright Society of the U.S.A., 494

Core-Mark International, Inc., 1035

Cornell International Industrial and Labor Relations Reports, 475

Corning Glass Works/Corning Engineering, 421

Corporate Cashflow, 170

Corporate Finance, 341

Corporate Finance Sourcebook, 341, 1082

Corporate Financing Week, 502, 1082

Corporate Promotions Group, Inc., 1041

Corporate Risk Management, 903

Corporate Security Digest, 942

Corporate Transfer Agents Association, 937

Cosmetic, Toiletry and Fragrance Association, 254

Cosmetic Industry Buyers and Suppliers, 254

Cosmetic Insider's Report, 255

Cosmetic Science and Technology Series, 255

Cosmetic World, 255

Costume Jewelry Review, 512

Cotter & Co., 430

Cotton Council International, 257

Cotton Digest International, 258

Cotton Farming, 258

Cotton Foundation, 257

Cotton Gin and Oil Mill Press, 258

Cotton Grower, 258

Cotton Inc., 257

Coty Division, 256

Council for Export Trading Companies, 461

Council for International Business Risk Management, 902

Council for Periodical Distributors Associations, 756

Council of American Survey Research Organizations, 840

Council of Consulting Organizations, 570

Council of Defense and Space Industry Associations, 270

Council of Fashion Designers of America, 329

Council of Graduate Schools, 216

Council of Institutional Investors, 504

Council of Logistics Management, 283

Council of Professional Associations on Federal Statistics, 982

Council of Sales Promotion Agencies, 923

Council on Alternate Fuels, 312

Council on Family Health, 778

Council on Plastics and Packaging in the Environment, 878

Council on Research and Technology, 886

Countertrade Outlook, 120

Countrymark, Inc., 32

Country Music Association, 654

Country Radio Broadcasters, 857

Countrywide Mortgage Investments Inc., 867

County News, 838

Coup, 1082

Courter & Co., Inc., 1106

Cox Enterprises Inc., 90

CPA Client Bulletin, 6

CPC International Inc., 110, 167, 268

CPI Corp., 783

Cracker Barrel Old Country Store, Inc., 418

Crawford and Co., 493

CRB Futures Chart Service, 222

Creative, 923

Creative, the Magazine of Promotion and Marketing, 19

Creative Education Foundation, 261

Creative Industries Group, Inc., 609

Creative Management, 826

Creative Woodworking Co., Inc., 1132

Creativity in Action, 261

Creativity Research Journal, 261

Credit, 262

Credit & Finance, 262

Credit Bureau Reports, Inc., 215

Credit Professionals International, 262

Credit Research Foundation, 262

Credit Union Executives Society, 265

Credit Union National Association, 265

Credit Union News, 265

Credit Union Week, 266

Crescent Foods Inc., 976

Crestek Inc., 1064

Creswell, Munsell, Fultz & Zirbel, 843

Crete Carrier Corp., 1100

Critical Industries Inc., 86

H. S. Crocker Co., Inc., 424

Crompton & Knowles Corp., 11, 914

Crop Science, 945

Philip Crosby Associates, Inc., 571

A. T. Cross Co., 1143

Crowley Foods, Inc., 183

Crown American Corp., 958

Crown Books Corp., 142

Crown Cork & Seal Co., Inc., 739

CRS Sirrine Engineers, Inc., 191

Cruise Lines International Association, 1054

Cruise Ventures, Inc., 1052

Cruising World, 134

Crum and Forster, Inc., 482, 485

Cryovac Division, 739

CSX Corp., 634, 954

Culp, Inc., 1070

Cultured Marble Institute, 855

Cumberland Farms, Inc., 411

Cupples Co. Manufacturers, 743

Current, Inc., 425

Current Employment, 307

Current Industrial Reports: Fats and Oils, 717

Current Issues in the Financial Services Industries, 6

Curtice-Burns Foods Inc., 167, 393

Custom Applicator, 336

Custom Roll Forming Institute, 607

Custom Woodworking Business, 1131

CVI Inc., 694

Cycle Composites, Inc., 130

Cycle News, 646

Cycle Parts and Accessories Association, 129

Cycle World, 130

Cyclops Industries, Inc., 985

Cypress Semiconductor Corp., 949

Daicolor-Pope, Inc., 820

Dairy and Food Industries Supply Association, 267

Dairy Foods, 267

Dairy Herd Management, 267

Dairymen, Inc., 183, 268

Dairy Today, 268

Daisy/Cadnetix Inc., 227

Dalfort Corp., 1035

Dalgety, Inc., 373

B. Dalton Bookseller, Inc., 141

Dames & Moore, 918

Damon Corp., 524

D & B Reports, 569

D & C Stores, 180

Daniel Industries, Inc., 772

John Dannreuther Rare Coins, Inc., 212

Danskin Division, 1066

Dapco Industries, Inc., 1064

D'Arcy Masius Benton & Bowles, Inc., 20

Darkroom & Creative Camera Techniques, 783

Darr Equipment Co., Inc., 471

Dart Group Corp., 97

Data Entry Management Association, 935

Data General Corp., 234

Datapoint Equipment Corp., 704

Data Probe Inc., 580

Data Processing Management Association, 232

Datapro Management of Office Automation, 704

Datapro Management of Telecommunications, 1010

Datapro Reports on Copiers & Duplicators, 252

Davis Polk and Wardwell, 532

Davy McKee Corp., 602

A. J. Daw Printing Ink Co., 821

Dawn Food Products, Inc., 110

Day-brite Lighting Inc., 539

Dayton Hudson Corp., 894

DCA Food Industries Inc., 110

Dealer Communicator, 423

Dealer Progress, 336

Dealerscope Merchandising, 245

Dean Witter, 223

Edward J. DeBartolo Corp., 958

De Bruyn Produce Co., 393

DEC International, Inc., 370, 541

Decision Sciences Institute, 293

Decorative Laminate Products Association, 793

Decorative Products World, 1098

Deepwater Inc., 1111

Deere & Co., 317

Defense-Aerospace Business Digest, 270

Defense and Aerospace Markets, 270

Defense Organization Service— Industry, 270

De Francisci Machine Corp., 555

Degussa Corp., 187, 606, 813

John H. Dekker & Sons, Inc., 137

Dekalb Genetics Corp., 975, 999

Delair Group Inc., 997

De Laurentiis Entertainment Group Inc., 639

Dell Computer Corp., 234

Deloitte & Touche, 7

Delta Air Lines Inc., 45

Delta Beverage Group, 128

Delta Woodside Industries, 326

Demert & Dougherty, Inc., 23

Dennison Manufacturing Co., 14, 379, 709

Dental Dealers of America, 275

Dental Economics, 276

Dental Gold Institute, 811

Dental Laboratory Conference, 276

Dental Laboratory Review Buyer's Guide, 276

Dental Lab Products, 276

Dental Management, 276

Dental Manufacturers of America, 276

Dentsply International Inc., 277

Depository Trust Co., 940

Design for Manufacturability Alert, 226

Designers Illustrated, 497

Desktop Communications, 278

Desktop Publishing Applications Association, 278

Desktop Publishing: Office Automation Buyer's Guide, 278

Detroit Ball Bearing Co. of Michigan, 125

DFSoutheastern, Inc., 929

DHL Airways Inc., 42

Dial Corp., 196

Dialog Information Services, Inc., 477

Diamond Insight, 412

Diamond Petroleum Co., 395

Diamond Rug and Carpet Mills, Inc., 169

Diamond Shamrock Inc., 411

Diamond Walnut Growers, 698, 700

Dibrell Brothers, Inc., 1036

A. B. Dick Co., 252, 818

Diebold, Inc., 502

Diesel & Gas Turbine Worldwide, 316, 809

Diet & Health Magazine, 1095

Digital Equipment Corp., 234, 704

Digital I Cs D.A.T.A. Digest, 948

Digital Solutions, Inc., 761

Dillon Companies, Inc., 993

Diners Club International, 263

Direct, 281

Direction, 634, 1100

Direct Mail Corp. of America, 283

Direct Mail List Rates and Data, 281

Direct Marketing Association, 281

Direct Marketing Educational Foundation, 281

Direct Marketing Magazine, 281

Direct Marketing Market Place, 282

Direct Response Specialist, 282

Directions, 401

Directory of Consumer Electronics 1992, 245
Directory of Conventions, 1041
Directory of Executive Recruiters, 307
Directory of Leading Chain Stores, 179
Directory of Management Consultants, 570
Directory of Merger and Acquisition Firms and Professionals, 597
Directory of North American Fairs, Festivals and Expositions, 1041
Directory of Oil Well Supply Companies, 772
Directory of Selected U S Cogeneration . . . Power Plants, 209
Directory of Steel Foundries in the U.S., Canada and Mexico, 381
Directory of the Canning, Freezing, Preserving Industries, 166
Discipline and Grievances, 70, 475
Disclosure, Inc., 478
Discover Credit Corp., 263
Walt Disney Co., 639
Display & Design Ideas, 987
Distilled Spirits Council of the United States, 540
Distressed Property Investor's Monthly, 866
Distribution Center Management, 283, 1100
Distributors & Wholesalers' Advisory, 283
Distributors Association, 434
Diversco Inc., 566
Diversicare Corp. of America, 436
Diversified Energies, Inc., 311
Diversified Human Resources Group, Inc., 308, 1020
Diving Equipment Manufacturers Association, 977

Dixie-Narco, Inc., 1080
Dixie Yarns, Inc., 339, 1148
DM Camp and Sons, 33
DMS Market Intelligence Reports: Civil Aircraft, 48
Doall Co., 561
Dobbs Houses, Inc., 237
Dog Fancy, 766
Do-it-Yourself Retailing, 444
Dole Nut Co., 700
DollarSense, 506
Dominion Textile (USA) Inc., 326
Dominion Ventures, Inc., 1082
Dominion Yarn Corp., 1148
Domsea Farms, Inc., 69
Donaldson, Lufkin & Jenrette, Inc., 503
Donaldson Industrial Group, 322
Don Jagoda Associates, Inc., 924
Door and Hardware Institute, 429
Dorr-Oliver Inc., 370, 602
Double Envelope Corp., 521
Douglas & Lomason Co., 100
Douglas Battery Manufacturing Co., 647
Dow Chemical Co., 32, 795
Down Beat, 655
Dow Plastics & Hydro-Carbons, 187
Dow U.S.A., 606
Drake Beam Morin, Inc., 761, 1048
Dresser Industries, Inc., 311
Dreyer's Grand Ice Cream, Inc., 454
Dreyfus Corp., 658
DRI-McGraw-Hill Energy Review: Natural Gas Review, 660
Drug Emporium, Inc., 289
Drug Information Association, 288
Drugs Anonymous, 59
Drugs in the Workplace, 60
Drug Store Market Guide, 288

Drug Store News, 288
Drug Topics Red Book, 288
Drycleaners News, 528
Dryclean U.S.A., Inc., 530
DSC Communications Corp., 1012
Dualite, Inc., 961
Dubois Chemicals, Inc., 196
Dubrowsky & Perlbinder, Inc., 399
Ductile Iron Pipe Research Association, 786
Duffens Optical Inc., 726
Dukane Corp., 614
Dun & Bradstreet Information Services NA, 263
Dun & Bradstreet Receivable Management Services, 215
Dun & Bradstreet Software Services, Inc., 761
Duncan Enterprises, 792
Dundee Cement Co., 175
Dunlop Slazenger Corp., 979
Dunlop Tire Corp., 1032
Dun's Employment Opportunities Directory—The Career Guide, 307
Dun's Industrial Guide—The Metalworking Directory, 608
Duplex Products Inc., 379
E. I. Du Pont de Nemours & Co., 340, 764, 795
Duracell Inc., 123
Duriron Co. Inc., 787
Duron, Inc., 740
Durum Kernels, 362
Dutch Gold Honey, Inc., 447
Duty Free International Inc., 418
DVM Newsmagazine, 1086
Dynamic Supervision, 713
Dynix, Inc., 537

EAC USA, Inc., 472
Eagle Industries, Inc., 850
Eagle Signal Controls, 1043
E & J Gallo Winery, 1121

Earnshaw's Infants, Girls and Boys Wear Review, 201

Earnshaw's Plus Sizes, 201

Eastern Floors, 355, 1029

Eastman, Inc., 711

Eastman Kodak Co., 784

East Penn Manufacturing Co., 123

Ebeling & Reuss Co., 1001

Echlin Inc., 317

EC Industries, Inc., 600

Jack Eckerd Corp., 289

ECL Industries, Inc., 835

Econolite Control Products, Inc., 1043

Econometric Society, 982

Economy Electric Supply, Inc., 298

Daniel J. Edelman, Inc., 843

Edgcomb Metals Co., 62

Edgell Communications, Inc., 163, 757

Edison Brothers Stores, Inc., 201

Edison Electric Institute, 300, 846

Edison Welding Institute, 1112

Editor & Publisher—the Fourth Estate, 679

Editorial Eye, 757, 1142

Editorial Freelancers Association, 1141

Editors' Notes, 757

EDN Magazine, 948

Educational and Psychological Measurement, 1024

Educational Dealers and Suppliers Association International, 930

Educational Technology, 92

Educational Testing Service, 1024

A. G. Edwards, Inc., 503, 507, 940

EEO Report, 29

EE Product News, 66

EG & G Idaho, Inc., 694

Egg Industry, 807

Eisenhart Wallcoverings Co., 1098

Ekstrom Carlson & Co., 1132

Elastomerics, 914, 1031

Elcor Corp., 912

Eldon Industries, Inc., 709

Electrical Apparatus Service Association, 297

Electrical Generating Systems Association, 297

Electrical World, 300

Electric Light and Power, 300

Electric Power Research Institute, 300

Electric Specialty & Supply Corp., 298

Electronic and Electrical Equipment Newsletter, 298

Electronic Funds Transfer Association, 114

Electronic Industries Association, 244, 245

Electronic Market Trends, 245

Electronic Servicing & Technology, 245

Electronics Purchasing, 298

Elgin Salvage & Supply Co., 995

Elgin Watch Co., 199

Elixir Industries, 626

Eljer Industries Inc., 798

Ellco Leasing Corp., 884

Embalming Chemical Manufacturers Association, 396

EMC Corp., 1090

Emed Co., Inc., 961

Emerson Radio Corp., 246

Emery Worldwide, 42, 388

Empire Airlines Inc., 43

Empire Diamond Corp., 413

Employee Benefit Cases, 303

Employee Benefit News, 303

Employee Benefit Research Institute, 302

Employee Benefits Report, 225

Employee Communication, 759

Employee Relations in Action, 475

Employee Relations Report, 476

Employee Relocation Council, 882

Employee Testing & the Law, 1024

Employers Council on Flexible Compensation, 224

Employer's Guide Purchasing Managed Health Care Services, 437

Employment and Training Reporter, 1069

Employment Management Association, 29

Encomp Corp., 350

Endata, Inc., 614

Ener-G Foods Inc., 441

Energy, 310

Energy Conservation Coalition, 310

Energy Daily, 310

Energy Factors, Inc., 210

Energy Report, 310

Energy Review, 310

Energy Sources, 310

Energy Today, 310

Engelhard Corp., 587

Engineered Systems, 39

Engineering & Mining Journal, 605

Engineers and Engines Magazine, 316

Engine Manufacturers Association, 316

Engine Service Association, 316

Engraph, Inc., 736

Enhanced Services Outlook, 1015, 1091

ENR, 150, 190

ENR Directory of Contractors, 150

Enron Corp., 311

Enserch Corp., 311

Entenmann's, Inc., 110

Enterprise Leasing Co., 102

Enterprise Partner, 1082

Entertainment Law Reporter, 638

Enthone, Inc., 600

Entrepreneur, 319

Entrepreneurial Economy Review, 319

Entrepreneurial Woman, 319, 1128

Entrepreneur's Guide to Franchise & Business Opportunities, 384

The Entrepreneurship Institute, 319

Entrepreneurship: Theory and Practice, 319

Entwistle Co., 144

Environmental Business Journal, 321

Environmental Compliance Update, 321

Environmental Control Group Inc., 86

Environmental Management, 927

Environmental Management Association, 565, 926

Environmental Manager, 322

Environmental Protection, 321

Environment Today, 321

Environment Week, 321

Envirosource, Inc., 322

EPA Pesticide Label File, 763

Epic Healthcare Group Inc., 450

Lucas Epsco, Inc., 107

Equal Employment Advisory Council, 29

Equifax, Inc., 263

Equipment Leasing Newsletter, 884

Equipment Manufacturing Institute, 36

Equipment World, 884

Equitable Life Assurance Society of the United States, 491

Equities, 938

Equity Cooperative Livestock Sales Association, 545

ERA, 864

E-R-C Directory, 882

Eriez Magnetics, 991

ERISA Industry Committee, 303

Erly Industries Inc., 901

Ernst & Young, 7

ESA, Inc., 854

ESAB Automation, Inc., 909

ESOP Association, 305

Esselte Business Systems Inc, 424, 709

Estate and Financial Planners Alert, 346

Estee Corp., 1096

Estee Lauder, Inc., 256

Eta Kappa Nu, 296

Etonic Inc., 956

E-II Holdings, 180

Evans & Sutherland Computer Corp., 230

Everbrite Electric Signs, Inc., 961

Evergood Products Corp., 1096

Eveready Battery Co., 123

Excel Jerlee, Inc., 1098

Executive Compensation Reports, 225

Executive Female, 1128

Executive Fitness Newsletter, 1095

Executive Report on Managed Care, 437

Exel Logistics Dedicated Distribution Inc., 1100

Exhibit Designers and Producers Association, 1039

Exide Corp., 123

Exolon-ESK Co., 1

Expanded Shale Clay and Slate Institute, 193

Expansion Management, 882

Expert Systems, Inc.,81

Export, 462

Exporter, 463

Export Today, 462

Exterior Insulation Manufacturers Association, 479

Exxon Corp., 776

Exxon Pipeline Co., 790

Eyecare Business, 726

EZ Loader Boat Trailers, Inc., 135

Faber-Castell Corp., 1143

Fabric & Fiber Sourcebook, 339

Facilities Design and Management, 835

Facts and Advice for Airline Passengers, 53

Fadal Engineering Co., Inc., 561

Fadler Co., Inc., 393

Failed Bank and Thrift Litigation Reporter, 928

Fair Employment Practices Summary of Latest Developments, 30

Fairfax Opportunities Unlimited, Inc., 308

Familian Pipe & Supply Co., 798

Family Business, 963

Family Business Review, 963

Family Circle, Inc., 758

Family Handyman, 444

Family Motor Coach Association, 872

Famtec International, Inc., 561

Fancy Food, 163, 366

Faribault Woolen Mill Co., 1134

Farley Candy Co., 164

Farm & Home Savings Association, 929

Farm & Power Equipment Dealer, 36

Farm Chemicals, 35, 336

Farm Chemicals International, 763

Farm Credit Bank of Baltimore, 33

Farm Equipment Catalog, 37

Farm Equipment Wholesalers Association, 36

Farmer Bros. Co., 976

Farmers National Co., 1076

Farmers Union Central Exchange, Inc., 33, 335

Farm Fish, Inc., 69

Farm Labor Research Project, 36

Farmland Foods Inc., 592

Farmland Industries, Inc., 335, 337

Farr Co., 685

Fashion Newsletter, 329

Fatal Accident Reporting System, 1045

Fax Magazine, 327

Faxon Co., Inc., 537

FCB/Direct, 1014

FCC Week, 1010

FDM—Furniture Design & Manufacturing, 401, 1070

FEDAPT, 83

Federal Court Clerks Association, 259

Federal Express Corp., 43

Federal Information Disclosure, 2-E, 386

Federal Machine Corp., 1080

Federal-Mogul, 125

Federal National Mortgage Association, 634

Federal Paper Board Co., Inc., 750

Federal Parks & Recreation, 875

Federal Products Co., 854

Federal Regulation of Energy, 881

Federal Regulation of the Chemical Industry, 881

Federal Regulatory Directory, 881

Federal Reserve Bank Atlanta, 116

Federal Reserve Bank Boston, 116

Federal Reserve Bank Chicago, 116

Federal Reserve Bank Cleveland, 116

Federal Reserve Bank Dallas, 116

Federal Reserve Bank Kansas City, 116

Federal Reserve Bank Minneapolis, 116

Federal Reserve Bank New York, 117

Federal Reserve Bank Philadelphia, 117

Federal Reserve Bank Richmond, 117

Federal Reserve Bank St. Louis, 117

Federal Reserve Bank San Francisco, 117

Federal Technology Transfer, 1007

Federal Times, 192

Federated Pecan Growers' Associations of the United States, 698

Federation of American Health Systems, 448

Federation of Apparel Manufacturers, 200

Federation of Associations of Regulatory Boards, 880

Federation of Materials Societies, 586

Federation of Societies for Coatings Technology, 467

Feed and Grain Times, 333

Feed Control Comment, 333

Feed Industry Red Book, 333

Feed Management, 334

Alan Feinstein & Associates, 677

Fellowes Manufacturing Co., 709

Ferman Motor Car Co., 97

Fermont Co., 210

Ferro Corp., 178, 469

Ferruzzi Trading USA Inc., 975

Fertilizer and Agricultural Chemical Newsletter, 336

The Fertilizer Institute, 336

Fertilizer Science and Technology Series, 336

Feuer Leather Corp., 535

Fiberglass Petroleum Tank and Pipe Institute, 771

Fiber Society, 338

Fibreboard Corp., 480

Fibre Box Association, 143, 249

Fiduciary Standards in Pension and Trust Fund Management, 754

Figgie International Inc., 350

Film & Video, 1090

Financial Analysts Federation, 344

Financial Analysts Journal, 345

Financial Executives Research Foundation, 341

Financial Management, 345

Financial Manager, 342

Financial Managers Society, 341, 498

Financial Planners and Planning Organizations Directory, 346

Financial Planning, 346

Financial Product News, 506

Findex, 578

Find/SVP, 478

Fine Homebuilding, 153

Fine Homes International, Inc., 864, 882

Finevest Foods, Inc., 268

Fine Woodworking, 1131

Finger Lakes Livestock Exchange, Inc., 546

Finishers' Management, 599

Finlay Fine Jewelry Corp., 512

Fire, Casualty & Surety Bulletin, 484

Firearms Import & Export Corp., 348

Fireman's Fund Insurance Co., 1139

Fire News, 350

Fire Protection Contractor, 350

Fire Publications, Inc., 350

Fire Technology, 350

First Coinvestors, Inc., 212, 214

First Data Resources Inc., 263

First Federal of Michigan, 929

First Federal Savings & Loan Association of Rochester, 929

FirstFed Financial Corp., 634

First Nationwide Bank, a Federal Savings Bank, 929

First Options of Chicago, Inc., 223

Fischer & Porter Co., 934

George Fischer Corp., 382

Fish Culture Section, 68

Fisher Business Systems, Inc., 800

Fisher Controls International, Inc., 824, 1078

Fisher Foods, Inc., 180

Fisheries Product News, 352

Fisher-Price, 1038

Fisher Scientific, 524

Fishery Products International USA, 353

Fitzpatrick Co., 976

Flanigan's Enterprises, Inc., 543

Flat Glass Marketing Association, 419

Flavor and Extract Manufacturers Association of the U. S., 10

Fleetwood Enterprises, Inc., 626, 873

Fletcher Oil & Refining Co., 395

Flexible Corp., 645

Flexible Packaging Association, 734

Flight Safety Foundation, 24

Floor Covering Installation Contractors Association, 354

Floor Covering News, 355

Flooring, 355

Floral and Nursery Times, 361, 408

Florasynth, Inc., 11, 256

Florida Citrus Mutual, 390

Florida Citrus Packers, 390

Florida Cypress Gardens, Inc., 877

Florida Fruit and Vegetable Association, 390

Florida Grower and Rancher, 392

Florida Nurseryman, 408

Florida Rock Industries, Inc., 239

Florida Tomato Exchange, 390

Florists' Review, 361

Florists' Transworld Delivery Association, 360

Flower News, 361

Flowers Industries, Inc., 110

Flue Cured Tobacco Farmer, 1034

FMC Corp., 32, 472

FOIA Update, 386

Folding Carton, 734

Follet Corp. (Chicago, Ill.), 142

Food & Beverage Marketing, 366, 541

Food and Drug Packaging, 734, 779

Food Chemical News Guide, 10

Food Industries Suppliers Association, 368

Food Industry Newsletter, 993

Food Lion Inc., 993

Food Machinery Service Institute, 369

Food Marketing Institute, 992

Food People, 426

Food Processing, 366, 369

Food Processing Machinery and Supplies Association, 166, 369

Food Processors Institute, 166, 365

Food Production—Management, 366, 369

Foodservice Consultants Society International, 371

FoodService Director, 372

Foodservice Distributor, 372

Foodservice Equipment & Supplies Specialist, 369

Foodservice Equipment Distributors Association, 369, 371

Foodservice Product News, 369, 373

Food Technology, 366

Footwear News, 955

Footwear Plus, 955

Ford Motor Co., 105, 1058

Ford Products Corp., 967

Forest City Bookbindery, 137

Forest Products Research Society, 375

Forms & Label Purchasing, 521

Forms Tech Reference Series, 378

Michael Forrest Inc., 339

Forstmann Textiles Inc., 1135

Fort Dearborn Lithograph Co., 521

Fort Dodge Laboratories Inc., 1088

Forte, Dupee, Sawyer Co., 1135

Fortune Savings Bank, 929

Forum Corp. of North America, 827

Forum Group, Inc., 697, 869

Foster Natural Gas Report, 660

Foster Wheeler Corp., 191

Foster Wheeler International Corp., 191

Foundation Center, 380

Foundation Directory, 380

Foundation for Accounting Education, 5

Foundation Giving Watch, 380

Foundation Grants Index, 380

Foundation News, 380

Foundry Focus, 382

Foundry Management & Technology, 382

J. H. France Refractories Co., 193

Franchise Annual, 384

Franchise Consultants International Association, 383

Franchise Law Journal, 384

Franchising Adviser, 384

Franchising World, 384

Frankel & Co., 924

Frankford Candy & Chocolate Co., Inc., 692

Franklin Custodian Funds, Inc., 658

Frank's Nursery & Crafts Inc., 409

Fraud & Theft Newsletter, 942

Freedom of Information Center, 385

Freedom of Information Clearinghouse, 385

Freeman Products Inc., 814

Freeport Area Inc., 193

Freeport-McMoRan Resource Partners LP, 337, 616

Freightliner Corp., 1058

Freight Management Report, 387

Frequency Electronics, Inc., 199

Fresh Garlic Association, 722

Friden-Alcatel Corp., 803

Friendly Ice Cream Corp., 454

Fritz Chemical Co., 69

Fromm Industries, 119

From the State Capitals: Civil Rights, 30

From the State Capitals: Transportation Policies, 905

Frozen Food Express Industries, Inc., 1061

Frozen Potato Products Institute, 805

Frozen Vegetable Council, 390

Fruehauf Trailer Corp., 1058

Fruit Basket Gardens, Inc., 361

Fruit Country, 392

Fruit of the Loom, Inc., 1066

Fruit Varieties Journal, 392

Fry Foods, Inc., 723

Fuel Oil News, 394

Fujitsu Imaging Systems of America, Inc., 327

Fuller Brush Co., 23

Fuller Co., 175

George A. Fuller Co., 151

H. B. Fuller Co., 14, 469

Fuqua Industries, Inc., 409

Furniture Rental Association of America, 400

Furniture Retailer, 401

Furniture—Today, 401

Furniture Transporter, 401

Fur Rancher, 398

Fur Takers of America, 398

Fur Vault Inc., 399

Futures Industry Association, 222

Futures Magazine Reference Guide to Futures Markets, 223

Galaxy Carpet Mills, Inc., 169

A. F. Gallun & Sons Co., L.P., 535

The Gallup Organization, Inc., 841

G & M Oil Co., Inc., 395

Gane Bros. & Lane, Inc., 137

Gannett Co., Inc., 680

Gans Ink & Supply Co., Inc., 821

Garden Club of America, 408

Garden Supply Retailer, 408

Garlic Times, 723

Garrard County Stockyard, 546

Gas Appliance Manufacturers Association, 65

Gas Inc., 833

Gasoline and Automotive Service Dealers Association, 405

Gas Price Index, 660

Gas Processors Suppliers Association, 659

Gas Research Institute, 660

Gas Storage Report, 660

Gates Corp., 123

Gates Rubber Co., 914

Gaylord Broadcasting Co., 858, 1018

Gaylord Bros., 537

Gaylord Container Corp., 250, 743

Gay Men's Health Crisis, 27

GCA Bar Code Reporter, 94

GC Services Corp., 215

Geer Drug Co., 436

Gel Spice Co., Inc., 976

Gem East Corp., 413

Gemological Institute of America, 412

Gems & Gemology, 412

Gencorp Inc., 914

Genentech, Inc., 888

General Automotive Inc., 1032

General Aviation Manufacturers Association, 106

General Business Services, Inc., 1005

General Chemical Corp., 784

General Cinema Corp., 641

General Dentistry, 276

General Educational Development Institute, 15

General Electric Canada Inc., 49

General Electric Co., 2, 298, 317

General Electric Railcar Service Corp., 861

General Employment Enterprises, Inc., 308

General Foods Manufacturing Corp., 744

General Host Corp., 409

General Magnaplate Corp., 888

General Merchandise Distributors Council, 283

General Merchandise News, 993

General Motors Corp., 105, 317, 1058

General Motors Truck and Bus Division, 645

General Nutrition Inc., 1096

General Refractories Co., 480

General Ship Corp., 558

General Signal Corp., 472

General Steamship International, Ltd., 954

General Technologies Group Ltd., 804

Generic Pharmaceutical Industry Association, 778

Genesee Brewing Co., Inc., 146
Genesis Relocation Co., 883
Genesys Software Systems, Inc., 761
Genetic Engineering News, 132
Geneva Steel, 788
Genlyte Group, Inc., 539
Genmar Industries, Inc., 135
Genovese Drug Stores, Inc., 289
Georgia Marble Co., 856
Georgia-Pacific Corp., 480, 912
Georgia Peanut Commission, 699
Gerber Scientific Products, Inc., 729
GE Reuter-Stokes, Inc., 934
Geriatric & Medical Centers, Inc., 697, 896
Gerson's International, 214
Gestetner Corp., 253
Getty Petroleum Corp., 411
Geyer's Office Dealer, 708
Giant Food Inc., 428, 993
C. R. Gibson Co., 784
Gibson Dunn and Crutcher, 532
Gibson Greetings Inc., 426
Gibson Guitar Corp., 652
Gibson-Homans Co., 912
Giddings & Lewis, Inc., 561
Gifford-Hill & Co., Inc., 912
Gifford-Hill Cement Co., 175, 239
Gift & Stationery Business, 417, 1001
Gift Association of America, 417
Gift Basket Review, 417
Gift Box Corp. of America, 744
Gift Digest, 417
Gifts & Decorative Accessories, 418, 425, 1001
Giftware News, 418, 1001
Giles & Ransome, Inc., 88
Gilkey Farms, Inc., 33
Gillette Co., 67, 1143
Gilroy Foods, Inc., 723
Giltspur, Inc., 1041
Gioia Pasta Co., Inc., 555

Gison Homas Cleveland, 1098
Givaudan Corp., 11
Glass Digest, 420
Glass Packaging Institute, 878
Glazier Park, Inc., 237
Glemby Co., 256
Glen-Gery Corp., 175
Glitsch, Inc., 772
Global Appliance Report, 66
Global Trade, 463, 1108
Globe Security Systems, Inc., 944
GNB, Inc., 123
Gold Bond Ice Cream Inc., 454
Golden Grain Co., 555
Golden 1 Credit Union, 266
Golden Peanuts Co., 700
Golden Poultry Co., Inc., 808
Goldin-Karabeles International, Inc., 399
Gold Institute, 811
Gold Kist Inc., 335, 337
Gold Mining Stock Report, 812
Gold Standard Enterprises, Inc., 543
Gold Standard News, 812
Gold Star Electronics Co. Inc., 67
Good Packaging Magazine, 734, 738
B. F. Goodrich Co., 25, 795
Goodyear Tire & Rubber Co., 912, 1032
W. L. Gore & Associates, 1123
Gosiger Inc., 561
Goulds Pumps, Inc., 850
Governing, 649, 838
Government Accountants Journal, 6
Governmental Risk Management Manual, 903
Government Auctions Update, 90
Government Executive, 838
Government Finance Officers Association of U. S. and Canada, 343
Government Finance Review, 344

Government Relations Watch, 881
W. R. Grace & Co., 187, 311
Grace Energy Corp., 772
Gradco Systems, Inc., 253
Grain Age, 334
Grain & Feed Marketing, 334
W. W. Grainger, Inc., 299
Granada Foods Corp., 171
Graphic Artists Guild, 220, 422
Graphic Arts Blue Book, 817
Graphic Arts Marketing Information Service, 422
Graphic Arts Monthly, 423
Graphic Arts Product News, 423
Graphic Arts Suppliers Association, 422
Graphic Arts Technical Foundation, 422
Graphic Communications World, 817
Graphic Industries, Inc., 818
Graphic Technology, Inc., 94, 521
Graves-Humphreys Co., 295
Great American Broadcasting, 858, 1018
Great Atlantic & Pacific Tea Co., Inc., 428
Great Dane Trailers, Inc., 1058
Greater Blouse, Skirt and Undergarment Association, 1065
Greater Independent Association of National Travel Services, 1051
Greater Toy Center, 1037
Great Lakes Chemical Corp., 187
Great Northern Corp., 144
Great Northern Nekoosa Corp., 376
Great Western Bank, 930
Great Western Systems Inc., 90
Greeff Fabrics Inc., 1098
Greendale Bicycle Co., 130
Greenleaf Wholesale Florists, 361
Greeting Card Association, 425

Greiner Engineering, Inc., 906

Greyhound Lines Inc., 645

Grieger's Inc., 413

Griffith-Consumers Co., 395

Grinding Wheel Institute, 1

Grocery Manufacturers of America, 426

Grocery Marketing, 426

Grolier, Inc., 139

Groom & Board, 766

Gross-Given Manufacturing Co., 1080

Groundwater Technology Inc., 524

Group Health Association of America, 437

J. Groves & Sons Co., 51

Grow Group Inc., 14, 469

Growmark, Inc., 337, 946

Gruen Marketing Corp., 199

Grumman Allied Div., 645

Grumman Data Systems Institute, 293

Grumman Electronics Systems Division, 107

GTE Communication Systems Corp., 1012

GTE Products Corp., 539

Guide to Biotechnology Products and Instruments, 933

Guild CPO, 740

Guild of Book Workers, 136

Guild Wineries & Distilleries, 1121

Guilford Mills, Inc., 326

Guitar and Accessories Music Marketing Association, 651

Gulfstream Aerospace Corp., 49

Gummed Industries Association, 12

Gustafson Inc., 764

Häagen-Dazs Co., Inc., 454

Frank B. Hall and Co., Inc., 493

Halliburton Co., 772

Hallmark Cards Inc., 426

Hamakua Sugar Co. Inc., 990

Hambrecht & Quist Inc., 1082

Hamburg Brothers Co., 356

Hamilton Fixture Co., 987

John H. Hampshire, Inc., 792

John Hancock Mutual Life Insurance Co., 491

Handbook for Internal Auditors, 498

Handbook of Commercial Roofing Systems, 911

Handbook of Private Schools, 931

Hand Knitting Association, 1148

Hand Papermaking, 745

H & R Block, Inc., 1005

Handy & Harman, 813

Hanger Orthopedic Group, Inc., 837

Hanson Industries North America, 1036

Hapag Lloyd Travel, Inc., 1052

HAPPI: Household & Personal Products Industry, 22

Harbert Corp., 210

Harbridge House, Inc., 571

Harcourt Brace Jovanovich, Inc., 140

Harcros Chemicals Inc., 4

Hardware Trade, 430

Hardware Wholesalers, Inc., 154, 430

Hardwood Manufacturers Association, 375

John H. Harland Co., 818

Harley-Davidson Motor Co., Inc., 647, 873

Harmony Blue Granite Co., 856

Harnischfeger Industries, Inc., 589

HarperCollins Publishers, 140

Harper Group Inc., 388

R. E. Harrington, Inc., 1139

Louis Harris & Associates, Inc., 841

Harris Semiconductors, 949

Harsco Corp., 788

Harte-Hanks Communications, Inc., 680

Hartford Accident and Indemnity Co., 488

Hartford Bindery, Inc., 137

Hartman Bindery, Inc., 137

Hartmann Luggage Co., 554

Hartmarx Corp., 201

Hartz Mountain Corp., 767

Harvard Apparatus, Inc., 934

Harvard Business Review, 569

Harvard Cooperative Society, 142

Harvard Industries, Inc., 402

Harvest States Cooperatives, 335

Hasbro, Inc., 1038

Hasco International, Inc., 784

Haulpak Division, 906

Haygood, Inc., 406

Hayward Industries, Inc., 997

Hazardous Materials Control, 1105

Hazardous Materials Control Research Institute, 1104

Hazardous Substances & Public Health, 1105

Hazardous Waste and Toxic Torts Law and Strategy, 1105

Hazardous Waste Consultant, 1105

Hazardous Waste Management & Business, 1105

Hazardous Waste Treatment Council, 1104

Hazard Prevention, 831

Hazelden Foundation, 59

HB Reese Candy Co., Inc., 164

Health Care & Retirement Corp., 697

Healthcare Community Relations & Marketing Letter, 435

Healthcare Convention and Exhibitors Association, 1040

Healthcare Information Management, 435

Health Care Marketer, 435

Healthcare Services Group, Inc., 530

Health Care Strategic Management, 435

Healthcare Technology & Business Opportunities, 1007

Healthco International Inc., 277

Health Devices Sourcebook, 594

Healthdyne Inc., 436

Health Foods Business, 440

Health Industry Distributors Association, 594

Health Industry Manufacturers Association, 434, 594

Health Insurance Association of America, 486

Health Insurance Medical Records Risk Management Report, 487

Health Marketing Quarterly, 435, 696

Health Shopper, 1096

HealthStaffers, Inc., 308

Healthtrust Inc., 450

Hearst Business Communications, Inc., 677

Heating-Piping-Air Conditioning, 40

Hechinger Co., 377

Heidelberg Harris, Inc., 818

Heidrick and Struggles International, Inc., 571

Heinold Hog Market, Inc., 546

H. J. Heinz Co., 167, 367

Heldor Industries, Inc., 997

Helicopter News, 48

Helmsley-Spear, Inc., 706

Henkel Corp., 4

Henkels and McCoy, Inc., 191, 790

Hennessy Industries, Inc., 1032

Herbalife International of America, Inc., 1096

Hercules Inc., 340

Hercules Tire & Rubber Co., 1032

Heritage Marble of Ohio, Inc., 856

Herman Miller, Inc., 711

Herman's Sporting Goods, Inc., 979

Hermes Abrasives Ltd., 2

Hershey Foods Corp., 164, 367

Hershey Pasta Group, 555

Hertz Corp., 102

Herzing Institutes, Inc., 295

Heucotech Ltd., 821

Hewitt Associates, 304

HFD—Retailing Home Furnishings, 401

HGH Associates, Inc., 827

Hickok Electrical Instrument Co., 100

Hickok Manufacturing Co., 137

Hide and Leather Bulletin, 534

J. E. Higgins Lumber Co., 356

Higher Education and National Affairs, 216

Highland Superstores, Inc., 246

Highsmith Co., Inc., 92

High Speed Rail Association, 859

High Volume Printing, 817

Highway and Heavy Construction, 190

Highway Common Carrier Newsletter, 387

Highway Loss Data Institute, 905

Highway Safety Directions, 1045

Hill & Knowlton, Inc., 843

Hi-Lo Trailer Co., 874

Hilton Hotels Corp., 452

Hinkle Corp., 856

HMK Enterprises, Inc., 169

HMO Practice, 438

Hobart Brothers Co., 1113

Hobby Industry Association of America, 442

Hobby Merchandiser, 442

Hoboken Wood Flooring Corp., 356

Hoechst Celanese Corp., 340, 795

Hoge-Warren-Zimmerman Co., 792

Holco Commodities Inc., 223

Holiday Corp., 452

Holland America Line Westours, Inc., 1052

Hollandia Dairy, 171

Holly Farms Corp., 335

Holly Farms Foods, Inc., 808

Holly Sugar Corp., 990

Hollywood Reporter, 639

Holmes Limestone Co., 193

Holmes Protection, Inc., 350

Holstein-Friesian Association of America, 171

Holston Builders Supply Co., Inc., 154

Home Baking Association, 362

Home Depot, Inc., 445

Home Furnishings Review, 401

Home Health Care Dealer, 436

Home Health Care Services Quarterly, 436

Home Improvement Center, 445

Home Improvement Research Institute, 444

Home Lighting & Accessories, 539

Home Office Computing, 233

Home Shopping Network, Inc., 160

Homestake Mining Co., 813

Home Textiles Today, 324

Honda Co., 173

Honda of America Manufacturing, Inc., 105, 647

Honey Market News, 446

Honeywell Inc., 825

H. P. Hood Inc., 183, 268

Hoover Co., 196

Horizon Healthcare Corp., 697

William H. Horn & Brother, Inc., 837

Horn & Hardart Co., 373

Hornsmatch, 171

Hosiery and Underwear, 1066
Hosiery News, 1066
Hospital, 448, 594
Hospital & Health Services Administration, 448
Hospital Corp. of America, 450
Hospitality Management, 451
Hospitality Manager, 451
Hospital News, 449
Hospital Practice, 449
Hospital Purchasing News, 449
Hospitals, 449
Host International, Inc., 52, 418, 452
Hotel and Motel Management, 451
Hotel Employees and Restaurant Employees International Union, 889
Hotel Sales and Marketing Association International, 451
Hot Line Farm Equipment Guide, 37
Houghton Mifflin Co., 140
House of Adjustments Inc., 215
Houze Glass Corp., 814
Howes Leather Co. Inc., 535
H-R International Inc., 769
H R Reporter, 759
Hubbard Hall Inc., 600
Hubbard Milling Co., 364
J. M. Huber Corp., 821
Hudson Foods, Inc., 592
Hudson General Corp., 52
Hudson's Bay New York Inc., 399
Huffy Corp., 130, 502
Hughes Aircraft Employees Federal Credit Union, 266
Hughes Supply, Inc., 154
Humana Inc., 450
Human Capital, 760
Human Performance, 642
Human Resource Management Review, 760
Human Resource Professional, 760

Human Resources Research Organization, 642, 759
Hunter-Melnor Inc., 409
Huntsinger Farms, Inc., 33
Huntway Partners, 88
Hurco Companies Inc., 561
Huttlinger's Pipeline Report, 789
HVAC Product News, 39
Hydraulic Institute, 849
Hydril Co., 772
Hydrocarbon Processing, 775
Hydro-Mill Co., 558
Hydroponic Society of America, 68
Hypres, Inc., 991
Hyster-Yale Materials Handling, 1058
Hy-Vee Food Stores, Inc., 993

IA Holdings Corp., 906
Iams Co., 767
I and N Reporter, 460
IBM Credit Corp., 263
IBP, Inc., 592
Iceland Seafood Corp., 353
ICF Kaiser Engineers, Inc., 191
ICM/Krebsoge, 602
ICMA—The Professional Local Government Management Association, 648
IDAB, Inc., 909
Idaho Potato Commission, 805
Idaho Supreme Potatoes, Inc., 805
Ideal Instruments Inc., 1088
Idex Corp., 609
ID Systems, 94
IEEE Communications Society, 1009
IEEE Computer Graphics and Applications, 229
IEEE Computer Society, 232
IEEE Consumer Electronics Society, 244
IEEE Engineering Management Review, 296

IEEE Industry Applications Society, 823
IEEE Instrumentation and Measurement Society, 932
IEEE Network, 547
IEEE Robotics and Automation Council, 907
IEEE Spectrum, 296
IEEE Transactions on Applied Superconductivity, 991
IEEE Transactions on Robotics and Automation, 908
IEEE Transactions on Ultrasonics, Ferroelectrics, 1064
IEEE Ultrasonics, Ferroelectrics and Frequency Control Society, 1063
IEN: Industrial Equipment News, 471, 908
IFMT Magazine, 118
IGI, Inc., 1088
Illinois Central Corp., 861
Illinois Power Co., 301, 848
Illinois Range Co., 370
Illuminating Engineering Society of North America, 538
Illustrator, 221
Image Bank Inc., 784
Image Carpets, Inc., 169
IMC Fertilizer Group, Inc., 337
IMC Journal, 613, 871
Imex Medical Systems Inc., 1064
Immigration and Nationality Law Review, 460
Immigration Briefings, 461
Immigration Policy & Law, 461
Immunex Research and Development Corp., 132
IMO Industries Inc., 729
Impact, 541
Imperial Commodities Corp., 206
Implement & Tractor, 37
I.M.S. International, Inc., 580
Inbound Logistics, 387

Inc., 963

Incentive, 814

Incentive Manufacturers Representatives Association, 814

InCider—A Plus, 233

INCODA, 708

Income-Expense Analysis: Office Buildings, Downtown, 706

Income in Sales—Marketing Management, 920

Inco United States, Inc., 1113

INDA, Association of the Nonwoven Fabrics Industry, 324

Independent Automotive Damage Appraisers Association, 481, 1075

Independent Bakers Association, 109

Independent Bankers Association of America, 114

Independent Battery Manufacturers Association, 121

Independent Cash Register Dealers Association, 799

Independent Computer Consultants Association, 232

Independent Cosmetic Manufacturers and Distributors, 254

Independent Energy, 209, 313

Independent Gasoline Marketing, 410

Independent Insurance Agents of America, 492

Independent Investor Protective League, 505

Independent Jewelers Organization, 511

Independent Manufacturers Representatives Forum, 574

Independent Medical Distributors Association, 594

Independent Motorcycle Retailers of America, 646

Independent Petroleum Association of America, 774

Independent Professional Representatives Organization, 91

Independent School, 931

Independent Sewing Machine Dealers Association, 65

Independent Small Business Employers of America, 962

Independent Telco News, 1010

Independent Truck Owner/Operator Association, 1059

Independent Zinc Alloyers Association, 604

Index and Directory of Industry Standards, 981

Index of Patents Issued from the United States, 495

Index Technology Corp., 227

Index to International Public Opinion, 840

Individual Investor, 506, 938

Industrial Acoustics Co., Inc., 685

Industrial and Labor Relations Review, 476

Industrial Biotechnology Association, 131

Industrial Chemical News, 187

Industrial Chemical Research Association, 186

Industrial Distribution Association, 470

Industrial Engineering Works, 694

Industrial Health Foundation, 473

Industrial Hygiene News, 473

Industrial Lubricants Co., 553

Industrial Machinery News, 471

Industrial Machine Trader, 560

Industrial Management, 826

Industrial Market Place, 471

Industrial Perforators Association, 607

Industrial Purchasing Agent, 851

Industrial Relations Counselors, 475

Industrial Relations Law Journal, 476

Industrial Relations Research Association, 475

Industrial Research Institute, 887

Industrial Safety Equipment Association, 916

Industrial Welding, Inc., 792

Industry Coalition on Technology Transfer, 1007

Industry Statistics, 122

Industry Week, 643

Infinity Broadcasting Corp., 858

Inflight Food Service Association, 372

Infocus, 871

INFORM: International News on Fats, Oils & Related Materials, 718

Information & Interactive Services Report, 1092

Information Broker, 477

Information Industry Alert, 477

Information Industry Association, 477

Information Industry Bulletin, 477

Information Management, 871

Information Management: Strategies, Systems, and Technologies, 573

Information on Demand, 478

Information Processing & Management, 573

Information Today, 477

Information Week, 477, 573

Informix Corp., 704

InfoWorld, 233

Ingersoll-Rand Co., 125, 616, 850

Ingles Markets Inc., 958

Ingram Library Services, Inc., 537

Inland Container Corp., 250

Inland Enterprises, Inc., 193

Inland Mortgage Co., 634

Inland Rivers Ports and Terminals, 1107

Inland Steel Industries, Inc., 985

Innovative Tech Systems Inc., 835

In-Plant Reproductions, 817

Inspiration Resources Corp., 884

Instant & Small Commercial Printer, 817

Insteel Industries, Inc., 1123

Institute for a Drug-Free Workplace, 59

Institute for Alternative Agriculture, 34

Institute for Econometric Research, 982

Institute for Public Relations Research and Education, 842

Institute for Scientific Information, 478, 758

Institute for Social Research, 841

Institute for Survey Research, 841

Institute of Business Appraisers, 1075

Institute of Business Designers, 496

Institute of Certified Financial Planners, 346

Institute of Certified Management Accountants, 5

Institute of Certified Travel Agents, 1051

Institute of Electrical and Electronics Engineers, 296

Institute of Financial Education, 114

Institute of Gas Technology, 660

Institute of Industrial Launderers, 528

Institute of Internal Auditors, 6, 498

Institute of Labor and Industrial Relations, 475

The Institute of Management Sciences, 568

Institute of Noise Control Engineering, 684

Institute of Nuclear Power Operations, 693

Institute of Outdoor Advertising, 17

Institute of Packaging Professionals, 734

Institute of Public Administration, 838

Institute of Public Utilities, 846

Institute of Real Estate Management, 834

Institute of Scrap Recycling Industries, 878

Institute of Shortening and Edible Oils, 717

Institute of Store Planners, 892, 987

Institute of Transportation Engineers, 1042

Institutional Investor, 938

Instrumentalist, 652

Instrumentation in the Pulp and Paper Industry, 746

Instrument Society of America, 933

Insulation Contractors Association of America, 479

Insulation Materials Corp. of America, 480

Insurance and Risk Management, 903

Insurance Crime Prevention Institute, 484

Insurance Law Reports: Fire & Casualty, 484

Insurance Law Reports: Life, Health & Accident, 487, 490

InsuranceWeek, 484

Integrated Barter International, Inc., 121

Intellectual Property Law, 495

Intellectual Property Law Review, 495

Intellectual Property Owners, 494

Intelligent Instruments & Computers, 933

Inter-City Products Corp., 40

Interco Inc., 402

Intergraph Corp., 230

Interim Systems Corp., 1020

Interior Design, 497

Interior Design Society, 496

Interlake Corp., 26, 587

Intermagnetics General Corp., 992

Intermec Corp., 94, 383, 522

Intermodal Marketing Association, 952

Internal Auditing, 498

International Airline Passengers Association, 53, 1055

The International Alliance, 1127

International Alliance for Sustainable Agriculture, 34

International Apple Institute, 390

International Association for Computer Systems Security, 232

International Association for Continuing Education and Training, 1047

International Association for Energy Economics, 309

International Association for Financial Planning, 341, 345

International Association for Modular Exhibitry, 1040

International Association of Agricultural Economists, 35

International Association of Airport Duty Free Stores, 51, 236

International Association of Assessing Officers, 1075

International Association of Business, 962

International Association of Business Forecasting, 290

International Association of Concrete Repair Specialists, 238

International Association of Convention and Visitor Bureaus, 1040

International Association of Drilling Contractors, 774

International Association of Electronic Keyboard Manufacturers, 651

International Association of Geophysical Contractors, 774

International Association of Industrial Accident Boards and Commissions, 1138

International Association of Lighting Management Companies, 538

International Association of Machinists and Aerospace Workers, 526

International Association of Merger and Acquisition Consultants, 597

International Association of Personnel in Employment Security, 1069

International Association of Printing House Craftsmen, 815

International Association of Refrigerated Warehouses, 38, 1099

International Association of Registered Financial Planners, 346

International Association of Security Service, 942

International Association of Telecomputer Networks, 1009

International Banana Association, 390

International Bottled Water Association, 126

International Brotherhood of Electrical Workers, 527

International Brotherhood of Teamsters, Chauffeurs, Warehousemen, 527

International Business Forms Industries, 378

International Business Machines Corp., 234, 280, 705, 1137

International Catering Corp., 374

International Center for Companies of the Food Trade and Industry, 179

International Coil Winding Association, 297

International Communications Industries Association, 91

International Cotton Advisory Committee, 257

International Council of Shopping Centers, 957

International Counterterrorism & Security, 942

International Credit Association, 262

International Data Group, Inc., 758

International Defense Equipment Exhibitors Association, 270

International Directory of Nuclear Utilities, 693

International Documentary Association, 638

International Drycleaners Congress, 528

International Exhibitors Association, 1040

International Fabricare Institute, 528

International Facility Management Association, 834

International Facsimile Association, 327

International Fiber Journal, 339, 1148

International Fiber Science and Technology Series, 339

International Financial Printers Association, 816

International Flavors & Fragrances Inc., 11

International Foodservice Distributors Association, 372

International Food Service Executive's Association, 372

International Formalwear Association, 200

International Foundation for Timesharing, 862

International Foundation of Employee Benefit Plans, 303

International Frozen Food Association, 365

International Ice Cream Association, 453

International Identification, Inc., 502

International Information Management Congress, 703

International Institute for Lath and Plaster, 791

International Institute of Carpet and Upholstery Certification, 1070

International Institute of Fisheries Economics and Trade, 352

International Institute of Site Planning, 71

International Institute of Synthetic Rubber Producers, 913

International Intellectual Property Association, 495

International Journal of Machine Tools & Manufacture, 560

International Journal of Micrographics & Optical Technology, 613

International Journal of Robotics Research, 908

International Journal of Roofing Technology, 911

International Leather Goods, Plastic and Novelty Workers' Union, 533, 691

International Magnesium Association, 604

International Management Council, 568

International Mass Retail Association, 892

International Mass Transit Association, 844

International Material Management Society, 588

International MIDI Association, 651

International Minilab Association, 782

International Multifoods Corp., 335, 364, 367, 374

International Newspaper Advertising and Marketing Executives, 18, 678

International Paper Co., 747

International Personnel Management Association, 759

International Planned Music Association, 654

International Precious Metals Institute, 811

International Realty Group, Inc., 1076

International Reciprocal Trade Association, 120

International Recovery Corp., 323

International Salt Co., 925

International Sanitary Supply Association, 927

International Security Management Association, 942

International Silo Association, 36

International Snowmobile Industry Association, 872

International Society for Retirement Planning, 895

International Society of Appraisers, 1075

International Society of Certified Employee Benefit Specialists, 303

International Society of Fine Arts Appraisers, 1075

International Society of Interior Designers, 496

International Society of Performing Arts Administrators, 82

International Society of Statistical Science in Economics, 982

International Society of Videographers, 1089

International Society of Weighing and Measurement, 980

International Stamp Collectors Society, 214

International Tanning Manufacturers Association, 874

International Taxicab Association, 1006

International Tax Institute, 1003

International Teamster, 526

International Technology Corp., 323

International Technology Education Association, 294

International Teleproduction Society, 1089

International Test and Evaluation Association, 1024

International Trade Council, 462

International Traders Association, 462

International Trading Group Ltd., 224

International Truck Parts Association, 1056

International Union, United Automobile, Aerospace Workers, 527

International Union, United Mine Workers of America, 615

International Venture Capital Institute, 1081

International Venture Capital Network, 1082

International Wheat Gluten Association, 1117

International Window Cleaning Association, 195

International Woodworking Magazine, 1131

Internet Communications Corp., 705

Interphase Corp., 548

Interpublic Group of Companies, Inc., 20

Intersearch Group, Inc., 761

Interstate Auto Auction, Inc., 90

Interstate Bakeries Corp., 111

Interstate Conference of Employment Security Agencies, 1069

Interstate Food Processing Corp., 806

Interstate Highway Sign Co., 1043

Interstate/Johnson Lane, Inc., 224

Interstate Mining Compact Commission, 615

Interstate Natural Gas Association of America, 660

Interstate Professional Applicators Association, 762

Interstate Towing Association, 405

Intimate Apparel Manufacturers Association, 1066

Inventing and Patenting Sourcebook, 499

Invention Marketing Institute, 499

Inventors Clubs of America, 499

Inventor's Gazette, 500

Inventors Workshop International Education Foundation, 499

Investigative Reporters and Editors, 1141, 1142

Investment Co. Institute, 505, 657

Investment Counsel Association of America, 505

Investment Management Consultants Association, 505

Investment Partnership Association, 505

Investment Recovery Association, 994

Investment Reporter, 506, 938

Investor Responsibility Research Center, 505

Iowa Pork Producer, 998
Ireland Coffee-Tea, Inc., 208
Irex Corp., 480
Iron Age, 984
Iron and Steel Engineer, 984
Iron & Steelmaker, 984
Iron and Steel Society, 984
Iron and Steel Works of the World, 984
Irrigation Association, 35
Irving Tanning Co., 535
ISC Cardion Electronics Inc., 1111
ISDA—The Office Systems Cooperative, 708
I.S.I. Manufacturing, Inc., 909
Isolatek Corp., 685
ISR: Intelligent Systems Report, 81
ISS International Service System Inc., 196, 566, 944
Issues Management Association, 568
Italian Tile Center, 1029
ITE Journal, 905, 1042
Itel Corp., 250, 861, 884
ITT Corp., 271
ITT Hartford Insurance Group, 482, 485
ITT Rayonier, Inc., 377
ITT Sheraton Corp., 452
IVCI Corp., 441

Jacobs Engineering Group Inc., 151, 191
Jacobsen's Fats & Oils Bulletin, 718
Jacuzzi Inc., 997
Jamaica Water Supply Co., 848
Jani-King International, Inc., 566
Japan Automobile Manufacturers Association, Washington Office, 103
Jardine Insurance Brokers, Inc., 493

Jazz World Society, 654
Jefferson-Pilot Communications Co., 858
Jefferson Smurfit Corp., 250, 750
Jensen Corp., 530
Jet Cargo News, 42
Jewelers of America, 511
Jewelry Appraiser, 412, 1076
Jewelry Industry Council, 511
Jewelry Manufacturers Association, 511
Jewelry Manufacturers Guild, 512
Jewelry Workers' Bulletin, 198
Jiffy Lube International, Inc., 407
JLG Industries, Inc., 590
JMB Properties Urban Co., 706
Jobber-Retailer, 99
Job Safety Consultant, 917
Jobson's Liquor Handbook, 541
Jobson's Wine Marketing Handbook, 1120
Johnson and Higgins, 304, 493
Johnson & Quin, Inc., 283
Johnson Matthey Investments, Inc., 813
K. G. Johnson Livestock Equipment, Inc., 999
Joint Council on Economic Education, 290
Jones Day Reavis and Pogue, 532
Earle M. Jorgensen Holdings Co., Inc., 383
Journal of Accountancy, 7
Journal of Aerosol Medicine, 22
Journal of Aerosol Science, 22
Journal of Aircraft, 48
Journal of Applied Aquaculture, 68
Journal of Applied Corporate Finance, 342
Journal of Applied Meteorology, 1110
Journal of Arthroplasty, 836
Journal of Business and Economic Perspectives, 290

Journal of Business Venturing, 319
Journal of Career Development, 307
Journal of Cash Management, 170
Journal of Commercial Bank Lending, 115
Journal of Continuing Higher Education, 16
Journal of Direct Marketing, 282
Journal of Economic Theory, 290
Journal of Elastomers and Plastics, 793
Journal of Electronic Defense, 271
Journal of Employment Counseling, 307
Journal of Financial and Quantitative Analysis, 345
Journal of Food Process Engineering, 367, 370
Journal of Foodservice Systems, 373
Journal of Futures Markets, 223
Journal of Gambling Studies, 403
Journal of Herbs, Spices & Medicinal Plants, 975
Journal of Hospitality & Leisure Marketing, 875
Journal of Information Systems Management, 573
Journal of Insurance Medicine, 487
Journal of Labor Research, 476
Journal of Long-Term Care Administration, 696
Journal of Management Information Systems, 573
Journal of Manufacturing and Operations Management, 823
Journal of Maritime Law and Commerce, 953
Journal of Marketing Research, 578

Journal of Packaging Technology, 143

Journal of Park and Recreation Administration, 875

Journal of Petroleum Marketing, 775

Journal of Pharmaceutical Marketing and Management, 779

Journal of Productivity Analysis, 826

Journal of Products Liability, 829

Journal of Promotion Management, 923

Journal of Property Management, 706, 835

Journal of Prosthetics and Orthotics, 836

Journal of Protective Coatings and Linings, 468

Journal of Quality Technology, 853

Journal of Reinforced Plastics & Composites, 794

Journal of Robotic Systems, 908

Journal of Ship Production, 953

Journal of Small Business Finance, 963

Journal of Small Business Management, 963

Journal of Solar Energy Engineering, 967

Journal of Studies in Technical Careers, 294

Journal of Superconductivity, 991

Journal of Taxation, 1004

Journal of Taxation of Estates and Trusts, 1063

Journal of Technical Writing and Communication, 1142

Journal of Technology Transfer, 1007

Journal of the American Society of Brewing Chemists, 145

Journal of the American Statistical Association, 982

Journal of Thermal Insulation, 480

Journal of Thermoplastic Composite Materials, 794

Journal of Tribology, 552

Journal of Urban Planning and Development, 844

Journal of Waterway, Port, Coastal, and Ocean Engineering, 1108

Joyce International, Inc., 402

JPT: Journal of Petroleum Technology, 775

JSJ Corp., 609

Julius Schepps Wholesale Liquors, Inc., 542

Jupiter Industries, Inc., 1082

Justin Industries, Inc., 193, 239

Kahler Corp., 530

Kaiser Aerospace & Electronics Corp., 107

Kaiser Aluminum & Chemical Corp., 63

Kal Kan Foods, Inc., 767

Kampground Owners Association, 875

Kapco Library Products, 537

Karlshamns USA Inc., 718

M. W. Kasch Co., 443

Kash-n-Karry Food Stores Inc., 543

Katzenbach & Warren, Inc., 1098

Kawasaki Motor Manufacturing Corp. USA, 647

Kay Jewelers Inc., 512

KD Holdings, Corp., 997

KDI Sylvan Pools, Inc., 997

Ben E. Keith Co., 146

Walter T. Kelley Co., 447

Kellogg Co., 367

Kelly-Moore Paint Co., Inc., 741

Kelly Services, Inc., 1020

Kendall-Futuro Co., 596

Kennametal Inc., 602

Kennecott Corp., 616, 813

Kent-Bragaline, Inc., 1098

Kentucky-Tennessee Clay Co., 194

Kenwal Products Corp., 1100

Kenzer Corp., 894

Kerr Glass Manufacturing Corp., 421

Ketchum Communications Inc., 20

Keynes Brothers, Inc., 1118

Keynotes, 430

Keystone Consolidated Industries, Inc., 1123

Keystone International Inc., 1078

Kidder, Peabody and Co., 503

Kiewit Construction Group Inc., 239

Kiewit Continental Inc., 736

Kiewit Mining Group Inc., 813

Killington Ltd., 877

Kimball Office Furniture Co., 711

Kimball Piano & Organ Co., 652

Kinetics Noise Control, Inc., 685

King Broadcasting Co., 858

King Ranch, Inc., 173

King's North American Gas, 661

Kinney Shoe Corp., 956

Kiplinger Washington Editors, Inc., 677

Kitchen & Bath Business, 66

KK Motorcycle Supply, 647

Kliklok Corp., 739

Kline's Quarry Inc., 856

KLLM Transport Services Inc., 1061

K Mart Apparel Corp., 201

Knight-Ridder, Inc., 680

Knit-Rite, Inc., 837

Knitted Textile Association, 324

Knoll International Inc., 711

KOA Kampgrounds of America, 877

George Koch Sons, Inc., 741

Koh-i-Noor Rapidograph, Inc., 1143

Koken Manufacturing Co., Inc., 119

Koldfax, 40

Kollmorgen Corp., 730

Koontz-Wagner Electric Co., Inc., 299

Koret, Inc., 555

Korn-Ferry International, 308

W. A. Kraft Corp., 299

Kraft General Foods, Inc., 367

Krautkramer Branson, Inc., 1064

Kroch's and Brentano's, Inc., 142

Kronheim Co., 542

K 2 Corp., 979

Kulicke & Soffa Industries, Inc., 949

Kurt Salmon Associates, Inc., 571

Kurzweil Music Systems, Inc., 652

Kutzen Co., Inc., 598

Kwasha Lipton, 304

Label Printing Industries of America, 521

Labmedica, 523

Laboratory Equipment, 523

Labor Relations Today, 476

Labor Today, 526

Lacks Industries, 795

LaCroix Water Co., 128

Ladies Apparel Contractors Association, 200

Ladish Co. Inc., 850, 1078

Lafarge Corp., 175, 239

Lakehead Pipe Line Co., Inc., 790

Lake Shore, Inc., 383

Laldish Co., Inc., 383

LAN, 547

Lancaster Colony Corp., 418, 421

Lance, Inc., 164

LAN Computing, 547

L & C Flashing Barricades, Inc., 1044

Landis Manufacturing Systems, Inc., 558

Land O'Lakes, Inc., 33, 269

Landscape & Irrigation, 36

Landstar System Inc., 1061

L and W Supply Corp., 154

Lane Co., Inc., 711

John Langenbacher Co., Inc., 1132

Langston Co. Inc., 744

LAN Reporter, 547

LAN Technology, 547

LAN Times, 547

Lapidary Journal, 512

Large Animal Veterinarian, 1087

Lasalle-Deitch Co., Inc., 356

Later Years, 696

Latham and Watkins, 532

Lauhoff Grain Co., 364

Laundry News, 528

Laventhol & Horwath, 8

Law & Business Directory of Bankruptcy Attorneys 1992, 112

Law of Products Liability, 829

Lawrence Agency Corp., 493

Lawrence Insurance Group, Inc., 493

Lawson-Hemphill Inc., 854

Lawson Products, Inc., 1113

Lazare Kaplan International Inc., 413

La-Z-Boy Chair Co., 402, 1070

L D & A, 728

LDI Corp., 884

Leach & Garner Co., 513

Lead Industries Association, 604

Leaf Tobacco Exporters Association, 1033

Leanin Tree Inc., 426

Learjet Corp., 49

Leaseway Transportation Corp., 1100

Leasing Sourcebook, 884

Leather Crafters Journal, 534

Leather Industries of America, 533

Leco Corp., 602

Legg Mason, Inc., 503

Legislative and Regulatory Update, 881

Leichtung Inc., 445, 1132

Leider Horticultural, 361

P. Leiner Nutritional Products Corp., 1096

Leisure Industry Report, 876

Leisure Sciences, 876

Lennar Corp., 706, 958, 1101

Lepercq de Neuflize & Co. Inc., 598

Lerner Stores Corp., 180

Leslie Salt Co., 925

Leupold & Stevens, Inc., 1111

Level Valley Dairy Co., 719

Kenneth Leventhal & Co., 7

Levi Strauss Associates, Inc., 201

Levitz Furniture Corp., 402

Edward C. Levy Co., 88

Lewis, Gilman & Kynett, Inc., 843

Lewis Bear Co., 146

Lewis Galoob Toys, Inc., 1038

Lewis Letter on Cable Marketing, 159

Liberty Mutual Insurance Co., 485

Liberty Travel Co., 1052

Library and Information Technology Association, 613

Library Bureau, Inc., 537

Library Journal, 536

Licensing Executives Society, 1007

Life Insurance Marketing and Research Association, 489

Life Insurance Selling, 490

Lifestyle Market Analyst, 801

Lifetime Corp., 437

Lifetime Hoan Corp., 1001

Lighting Dimensions, 539

Lights of America, Inc., 539

Lightweight Concrete Information Sheets, 87

Eli Lilly and Co., 33
Lin Broadcasting Corp., 1018
Lincoln, 553
Link-UpLearned Information, Inc., 1010
Linn's Stamp News, 213
Lino & Associates, 121
Lion Apparel, 918
Lionel Corp., 1038
Thomas J. Lipton, Inc., 208
Literary Market Place, 139
Lithonia Lighting, 539
Litigation, 532
Litigation Under the Federal Open Government Laws, 386
Arthur D. Little, Inc., 571, 827
Litton Industries, Inc., 825
Litwin Engineers & Constructors Inc., 769
Livestock, Meat and Wool Market News, 591
Livestock Conservation Institute, 544
Livestock Industry Institute, 544
Livestock Market Digest, 545
Livestock Marketing Association, 544
Livestock Weekly, 545
Liz Claiborne, Inc., 201
L. J. Technical Systems, Inc., 295
Lloyd's Shopping Centers, Inc., 959
Lloyd-Thomas/Coats & Burchard Co., 1076
LMSC Federal Credit Union, 266
Local Government Center, 649
Lockheed Air Terminal, Inc., 52
Locksmith Ledger International, 430
Loctite Corp., 469
Loews Corp., 452, 641
Logan Co., 94
Log House Builder's Association of North America, 149
Lomas Mortgage USA, 835

Lone Star Industries, Inc., 239
Long-Distance Letter, 1011
Long Lake Energy Corp., 210
Long Term Care Management, 696
Loral Corp., 271
Lord Corp., 685
Lori Corp., 513
Lorillard, Inc., 1036
Los Angeles Nut House, 700
Los Angeles Times, 680
Lotus Development Corp., 235, 1137
Louisiana-Pacific Corp., 377
Lowe's Companies, Inc., 430, 798
Lozier Corp., 987
LPL Technologies Inc., 1123
LSI Logic Corp., 949
LTV Aerospace and Defense Co., 26, 49, 272
LTV Steel Co., Inc., 985
Lubricating Specialties Co., 553
Lubrizol Corp., 132, 188, 553
Lugbill Brothers, Inc., 90
Luggage and Leather Goods Manufacturers of America, 534, 554
Lukens Inc., 919
Lunt Silversmiths, 1001
LVI Group Inc., 86
Lykes Bros. Steamship Co., Inc., 388
Lyman Products Corp., 348
Lyondell Petrochemical Co., 769

McCann-Erickson USA, Inc., 20
McClatchy Newspapers, Inc., 680
McCormick & Co. Inc., 976
McCormick Stange Flavor Division, 11
McCrory Corp., 180
MacDermid Inc., 4, 600
McDermott Inc., 790
MacDonald & Co., Inc., 598
McDonald's Restaurants, 891
McDonnell Douglas Corp., 49

McGraw-Hill, Inc., 758
MacGregor Sporting Good, 979
Machine Knife Association, 1130
Machinery Dealers National Association, 470
Machine Vision Association, 907
McJunkin Corp., 788
McKinsey and Co., Inc., 571, 581
McKnight's Long Term Care News, 696
McLane Co., Inc., 428
McSwain Manufacturing Corp., 559
McWane Inc., 788
MacWorld, 233
R. H. Macy and Co., 894
Made to Measure, 201
Madison Avenue Handbook, 19
Madison Dairy Produce Co., 719
Madix, Inc., 987
Magazine & Bookseller, 141
Magazine and Paperback Marketing Institute, 756
Magazine Antiques, 79
Magazine Printers Section, 816
Magazine Publishers of America, 756
Magma Copper Co., 617
Magnetic Analysis Corp., 1065
Mail Advertising Service Association International, 281
Mail Boxes Coast to Coast Inc., 804
Mail Boxes Etc., 804
Maine Lobstermen's Association, 352
Maine Potato Growers, Inc., 806
Maine Potato News, 805
Maine Yankee Atomic Power Co., 694
Mainstream Engineering Co., Inc., 1020
Malaysian Rubber Bureau, 913
Malden Mills Industries Inc., 1070

Mallinckrodt Inc., 11
Mallory Factor Inc., 843
Managed Care Outlook, 438
Managed Futures Trade Association, 222
Management, 192, 713
Management of World Wastes, 1105
Management Recruiters International, Inc., 308
Management Review, 569
Manco, Inc., 522
M & A Dealmaker, 503, 597
Mannington Ceramic Tile, 1029
Manor Healthcare Corp., 450
Manufactured Homes, Inc., 626
Manufactured Housing Institute, 625
Manufacturers' Agents National Association, 575
Manufacturers Alliance for Productivity and Innovation, 470, 826
Manufacturers Radio Frequency Advisory Committee, 857
Manufacturers Standardization Society of the Valve and Fittings Industry, 1077
Manufacturing Confectioner, 164
Manville Corp., 377, 617
Manville Forest Products Corp., 736, 750
Manville Sales Corp., 340, 481, 912
Mapco Inc., 205
Marble Institute of America, 855
Marcus & Millichap Inc., 867
Marcy Fitness Products, 979
Marden-Kane, Inc., 815, 924
Maremont Exhaust Products, Inc., 788
Marine Retailers Association of America, 133
Marion Merrell Dow Inc., 780
Maritime Association of the Port of New York/New Jersey, 952

Maritime Reporter and Engineering News, 953
Maritz Inc., 643, 1048
Maritz Travel Co., 1055
Mark Controls Corp., 825
Markem Corp., 821
Market Facts, Inc., 580
Market Guide Over-the-Counter Stock Edition, 939
Marketing Grocery Products, 426
Marketing Insights, 576
Marketing Missions, Ltd., 1014
Marketing Research Association, 578
Marketing Research Review, 579
Marketing Science Institute, 576
Marking Industry, 960
Marks-O'Donnell Industries, Inc., 35
Marriott Corp., 453
Mars, Inc., 164
Mars Graphic Services Inc., 283
Marshall & Stevens Inc., 1077
Marshalls Inc., 201
Marsh and McLennan Companies, Inc., 304, 493
Robert Marston and Association, Inc., 843
C. F. Martin & Co., 652
Martin Marietta Corp., 26, 272
Martin Paint Stores, 1098
Mary Kay Cosmetics, Inc., 256
Masco Corp., 67, 430, 445
Massachusetts Mutual Life Insurance Co., 491
Massillon-Cleveland-Akron Sign Co., 800
Material Handling Engineering, 588, 738
Material Handling Product News, 589, 1100
Materials Edge, 587, 602
Materials Engineering, 587
Materials Research, Inc., 588
Materials Research Society, 586

Mathematics of Operations Research, 724
Matson Navigation Co., Inc., 954
Matsushita Electric Corp. of America, 67
Matsushita Industrial, 246
Mattel Inc., 1038
Matthew Bender & Co. Inc., 1005
Max Factor & Co., 256
May, Stern & Co., L.P., 707
Mayflower Group, Inc., 637
Mayflower Warehouseman, 634
Maytag Corp., 67
Mazda Motor Manufacturing (USA) Corp., 105
MCA Records, 870
M.D.C. Holdings, Inc., 634
Mead Corp., 377, 709, 747
Mead Data Central, Inc., 478
Meat and Poultry, 591, 807
Meat Business Magazine, 591
Meat Importers' Council of America, 590
Meat Industry Suppliers Association, 590
Meat Price Report, 591
Meat Processing, 592
Meat Sheet, 592
Mechanical Technology Inc., 888
Medalist Industries Inc., 1132
Medgroup Inc., 702
Media News Keys, 842
Media Week, 19
Medical Advertising News, 779
Medical Economics, 438
Medical Electronics and Equipment News, 595
Medical Laboratory Products, 524
Medical Letter on Drugs and Therapeutics, 779
Medical Library Association, 536
Medical Product Manufacturing News, 595
Medical Products Sales, 435
Medical Services Association, 488

Medico-Legal Advisor, 830

Medusa Corp., 906

Meetings and Conventions, 1041

Meg Manufacturing Corp., 987

MEI Diversified Inc., 164, 441, 700

Melridge, Inc., 362

Memo to Mailers, 803

Memphis Light Gas and Water Division, 301, 848

Mennel Milling Co., 1118

Menswear Retailers of America, 200

Mentor Graphics Corp., 235

Mercedes-Benz of North America, Inc., 105

William M. Mercer, Inc., 571, 828

William M. Mercer—Meidinger—Hansen Inc., 305

Merck & Co., Inc., 780

Meret, Inc., 894

Merger Management Report, 597

Mergers & Acquisitions, 598

Mergers and Acquisitions Law Reporter, 598

Merger Yearbook: Domestic Edition, 598

Merico Inc., 111

Merrill Lynch and Co., 503, 507, 940

Merrill Lynch Hubbard Inc., 864

Merritt Risk Management Review, 903

Metalex Manufacturing, Inc., 559

Metal Fabricating Institute, 608

Metal Finishing, 599

Metal Finishing Suppliers' Association, 599

Metalink, Inc., 609

Metallurg Inc., 2, 63

Metal Powder Industries Federation, 601

Metals Week, 605

Metal Treating Institute, 607

Metpath Inc., 524

Metrologic Instruments, Inc., 94

Metro Mobile CTS, Inc., 629

Metropolitan Circuits Inc., 694

Metropolitan Life Insurance Co., 491

Metropolitan Relocation Consultants, Inc., 883

Metro Transportation Co., 1006

MGM/UA Communications Co., 639

MH-RV Builders News, 626, 873

Miami Margarine Co., 719

Michaels Stores, Inc., 443

Michigan Livestock Exchange, 546

Michigan Mutual Insurance Co., 488

Michigan Power Co., 848

MicroComputer Investors Association, 505

Microcontamination, 948

Microelectronic Manufacturing and Testing, 948

Microfilm Holding Co., Inc., 614

Micro General Corp., 804

Micrographics and Optical Storage Equipment Review, 613

Micrographics Newsletter, 613

Micrographic Technology Corp., 614

Micromeritics Instrument Corp., 934

Micron Instrument Corp., 825

MicroPublishing Report, 279

Microsoft Corp., 235, 280, 1137

Micros Systems Inc., 800, 836

Mid-America Dairymen, Inc., 183

Midcon Corp., 311

Mid-Continent Oil and Gas Association, 410

Middleby Corp., 370

Midial USA Fanny Farmer Candy Shops, Inc., 164

Mid-Ohio Chemical Co., Inc., 764

Midwest Grain Products, Inc., 1118

Midwest Mutual Insurance Co., 647

Midwest Waltham Abrasive Co., 2

Mielach Co., 1132

Miles Inc., 780

Military Market, 271

Miller Brewing Co., 147

Miller Chemical & Fertilizer Corp., 764

Miller Electric Manufacturing Co., 1113

Miller Freeman, Inc., 677

Miller Group, Ltd., 1113

Millers' National Federation, 362

Miller/Zell Inc., 987

Milling & Baking News, 109, 362

Million Dollar Round Table, 492

Millmaster Onyx Group, Inc., 821

Mine & Quarry Trader, 616, 855

Mineral Industry Surveys. Cement, 174

Mineral Industry Surveys. Gold and Silver, 812

Mineral Industry Surveys: Salt Production and Distribution, 925

Minerals, Metals, and Materials Society, 601

Mine Safety Appliances Co., 919

Mini Lab Focus, 783

Mining and Metallurgical Society of America, 615

Mining Engineering, 616

Mini-Storage Messenger, 634

Minnesota Fabrics, Inc., 1070

Minnesota Mining & Manufacturing Co., 14, 92

Minorities in Business Insider, 30

Minstar Inc., 135

Mirage Resorts Inc., 404

Mission Bay Investments, Inc., 653

Mr. Gasket Co., 100, 919

Mitsubishi International Corp., 606

Mitsubishi Motor Sales of America, Inc., 105

Mix Annual Directory of Recording Industry Facilities and Services, 869

Mixin', 541

Mix Magazine, 869

MLX Corp., 41

Mobile Air Conditioning Society, 38

Mobile Homes and Mobile Home Parks, 626

Mobile Modular Office Association, 711

Mobile Product News, 629

Mobil Oil Corp., 776

Model Rectifier Corp., 443

Modern Bulk Transporter, 1060

Modern Business Systems, Inc., 253

Modern Courts, 260

Modern Grocer, 426

Modern Jeweler National, 512

Modern Machine Shop, 558

Modern Materials Handling, 94, 589

Modern Metals, 605

Modern Office Technology, 704

Modern Paint and Coatings, 468, 740

Modern Paint and Coatings Paint Red Book, 740

Modern Plastics, 794

Modern Salon, 119

Modern Tire Dealer, 1031

Mohasco Upholstered Furniture Corp., 1070

Mohawk Carpet Corp., 169

Mohawk Rubber Co., 914, 1032

Monarch Luggage Co.,Inc., 555

Monarch Marking Systems, Inc., 522

Monarch Tile Inc., 1029

Robert Mondavi Winery, Inc., 1121

Money Market Trust, 658

Monfort, Inc., 592

Monitor, 957

Monogram Models Inc., 443

Monroe Auto Equipment Co., 100

Monroe Systems For Business, Inc., 253

Monro Muffler and Brake, Inc., 407

Monsanto Co., 33, 764

Montana Energy Research & Development Institute, Inc., 888

Montana Wool Grower, 1134

Montgomery Ward Holding Corp., 894

Monthly Digest of Tax Articles, 1004

Monthly Weather Review, 1110

Monument Builders of North America, 396

Moody's Public Utility Manual, 847

Moody's Transportation News Reports, 645

Moorco International Inc., 694

Mor-Flo Industries, Inc., 967

Dan T. Moore Co., 685

Morgan Adhesives Co., 14

J. P. Morgan and Co., Inc., 117

J. E. Morgan Knitting Mills, Inc., 1066

Morgan Stanley and Co., 503

Morgan Stanley Group Inc., 507, 598, 940

Morning Glory Farms Region, 183, 269

Morningstar Foods Inc., 269

John Morrell & Co., 592

Morse Shoe, Inc., 180

Mortgage and Real Estate Executives Report, 633, 866

Mortgage Bankers Association of America, 114, 633

Mortgage Banking, 115

Mortgage Commentary, 634

Mortgage Insurance Companies of America, 633

Mortgage Market Insight, 634

Morton International Inc., 188

Morton Salt Division, 925

Mortuary Management, 396

Moss, Adams & Co., 8

O. F. Mossberg & Sons, Inc., 348

Mothers' Home Business Network, 1128

Motor and Equipment Manufacturers Association, 98

Motor Boating & Sailing, 134

Motorcycle Dealernews Buyers Guide, 646

Motorcycle Industry Council, 646

Motorcycle Industry Magazine, 647

Motorcycle Product News, 647

Motorcycle Safety Foundation, 1045

Motorola, Inc., 100, 472, 949

Motor Vehicle Manufacturers Association of the United States, 104, 644, 1056

Moyer Products, Inc., 764

MPA Newsletter of Research, 19

MPB Corp., 125

MPT Review, 939

MRCA Information Services, 580

MS Carriers Inc., 1061

MTV Networks, 160

Mueller Brass Co., 798

Multi-Amp Institute, 694

Multi-Housing Laundry Association, 528

Multi Housing News, 150

Multi-Level Marketing International Association, 576

Munford, Inc., 418

Municipal Litigation Reporter, 649

Municipal Treasurers Association of the U.S. and Canada, 343

Munson Transportation, Inc., 1062

Mushroom, 393

Mushroom News, 392

Musical America, 655

Music and Sound Retailer, 652, 655

Music City News, 655

Music Distributors Association, 651

Music Industry Conference, 651

Musicland Group Inc., 653

Music Publishers' Association of the United States, 654

Music Retailing, 652

Music Sales Corp., 656

Muskin, Inc., 997

Mutual Fund Charts, 657

Mutual Fund Education Alliance, 657

Mutual Fund Fact Book, 658

Mutual Fund Forecaster, 658

Mutual Fund Performance Report, 658

Mutual Fund Trends, 658

Mutual Life Insurance Co. of New York, 897

Myers Electric Products Inc., 874

Myers Industries, Inc., 1032

NABE Outlook, 1069

Nacco Industries, Inc., 206

NADA Official Used Car Guide, 96

Nalco Chemical Co., 1106

Nanny Times, 189

Nash-Finch Co., 367

National Academy of Arbitrators, 70

National Academy of Recording Arts and Sciences, 868

National Academy of Social Insurance, 965

National Account Marketing Association, 576

National Advertising Division, 18

National Aerosol Association, 21

National Agricultural Chemicals Association, 34

National AIDS Information Clearinghouse, 27

National Air Transportation Association, 44

National-American Wholesale Grocers' Association, 426

National Antique and Art Dealers Association of America, 78

National Asbestos Council, 84

National Asphalt Pavement Association, 87

National Association for Court Management, 259

National Association for Creative Children and Adults, 261

National Association for Family Day Care, 189

National Association for Home Care, 436

National Association for Professional Saleswomen, 921

National Association for the Self-Employed, 962

National Association for the Specialty Food Trade, 365

National Association of Accountants, 6

National Association of Aluminum Distributors, 61

National Association of Animal Breeders, 544

National Association of Band Instrument Manufacturers, 651

National Association of Bankruptcy Trustees, 112

National Association of Bank Women, 114

National Association of Business Economists, 290

National Association of Casual Furniture Retailers, 400

National Association of Casualty and Surety Executives, 484

National Association of Catalog Showroom Merchandisers, 892

National Association of Cellular Agents, 628

National Association of Chain Drug Stores, 288

National Association of Chemical Distributors, 186

National Association of Child Care Resource & Referral Agencies, 189

National Association of Civil Service Employees, 192

National Association of College Stores, 141, 892

National Association of Computer Consultant Businesses, 232

National Association of Concessionaires, 236

National Association of Container Distributors, 249

National Association of Convenience Stores, 179, 992

National Association of Corporate and Professional Recruiters, 306

National Association of Corporate Treasurers, 170

National Association of Corrosion Engineers, 3

National Association of County Treasurers and Finance Officers, 343

National Association of Criminal Defense Lawyers, 531

National Association of Decorative Fabric Distributors, 324, 1070

National Association of Desktop Publishers, 278

National Association of Display Industries, 987

National Association of Doll and Stuffed Toy Manufacturers, 1037

National Association of Dredging Contractors, 1107

National Association of Electrical Distributors, 298

National Association of Estate Planning Councils, 1062

National Association of Executive Recruiters, 306

National Association of Executive Secretaries, 935

National Association of Export Companies, 462

National Association of Farm Broadcasters, 1015

National Association of Fashion and Accessory Designers, 329

National Association of Federally Licensed Firearms Dealers, 347

National Association of Fleet Administrators, 101

National Association of Fleet Resale Dealers, 95

National Association of Floor Covering Distributors, 355

National Association of Flour Distributors, 362

National Association of Food Equipment Manufacturers, 369

National Association of Forensic Economists, 64

National Association of Freight Transportation Consultants, 386

National Association of Futures Trading Advisors, 222

National Association of Gambling Regulatory Agencies, 403

National Association of Government Archives, 871

National Association of Health Underwriters, 486

National Association of Home Builders of the U.S., 149

National Association of Hosiery Manufacturers, 1066

National Association of Independent Lighting Distributors, 538

National Association of Independent Lubes, 405

National Association of Independent Publishers, 139

National Association of Independent Record Distributors and Manufacturers, 868

National Association of Independent Schools, 931

National Association of Investment Companies, 962

National Association of Investors Corp., 505

National Association of Jewelry Appraisers, 1076

National Association of Legal Secretaries, 935

National Association of Letter Carriers of the U.S.A., 803

National Association of Life Companies, 489

National Association of Life Underwriters, 490

National Association of Margarine Manufacturers, 717

National Association of Marine Products and Services, 134

National Association of Market Developers, 576

National Association of Master Appraisers, 863

National Association of Meat Purveyors, 591

National Association of Medical Equipment Suppliers, 434, 594

National Association of Metal Finishers, 599

National Association of Minority Women in Business, 1128

National Association of Mortgage Brokers, 633

National Association of Music Merchants, 651

National Association of Noise Control Officials, 684

National Association of Off-Track Betting, 403

National Association of Performing Arts Managers and Agents, 82

National Association of Personal Financial Advisors, 346

National Association of Personnel Consultants, 307

National Association of Pharmaceutical Manufacturers, 778

National Association of Photographic Manufacturers, 782

National Association of Plastics Distributors, 793

National Association of Postmasters of the United States, 803

National Association of Power Engineers, 809

National Association of Printers and Lithographers, 816

National Association of Printing Ink Manufacturers, 820

National Association of Private Enterprise, 962

National Association of Professional Print Buyers, 816

National Association of Professional Word Processing Technicians, 1136

National Association of Purchasing Management, 851

National Association of Quick Printers, 816

National Association of Real Estate Appraisers, 1075

National Association of Real Estate Brokers, 863

National Association of Real Estate Investment Trusts, 866

National Association of Realtors, 863

National Association of Regulatory Utility Commissioners, 846, 880

National Association of Restaurant Managers, 889

National Association of Retail Dealers of America, 893

National Association of Retail Druggists, 288

National Association of Secretarial Services, 936, 1136

National Association of Securities Dealers, 937

National Association of Securities Professionals, 937

National Association of Small Business Investment Companies, 962

National Association of Sporting Goods Wholesalers, 977

National Association of State Agencies for Surplus Property, 995

National Association of State Auditors, Comptrollers, and Treasurers, 343

National Association of State Budget Officers, 148

National Association of State Purchasing Officials, 851

National Association of State Radio Networks, 857

National Association of State Treasurers, 343

National Association of Steel Pipe Distributors, 786

National Association of Tax Practitioners, 1003

National Association of Telecommunications Dealers, 1009

National Association of Temporary Services, 1019

National Association of Theatre Owners, 641

National Association of the Remodeling Industry, 149

National Association of Towns and Townships, 649

National Association of Trade and Technical Schools, 294

National Association of VA Physicians, 438

National Association of Wheat Growers, 1117

National Association of Wholesaler-Distributors, 283

National Association of Women Business Owners, 1128

National Association of Writing Instrument Distributors, 1143

National Auctioneers Association, 89

National Audubon Society, 320

National Auto Auction Association, 89

National Automatic Merchandising Association, 1079

National Automobile Dealers Association, 95

National Automobile Theft Bureau, 482

National Avionics Society, 106

National Bankruptcy Reporter, 112

National Bar Association, 531

National Beauty Culturists' League, 118

National Bed-and-Breakfast Association, 1054

National Beer Wholesalers' Association, 145

National Beverage Corp., 128

National Beverage Dispensing Equipment Association, 126

National Bicycle Dealers Association, 129

National Black Programming Consortium, 1017

National Blacksmiths and Weldors Association, 557

National Broadcasting Co., 858, 1018

National Broiler Council, 807

National Building Material Distributors Association, 153

National Bulk Vendors Association, 1079

National Business Association, 963

National Business Education Association, 293

National Business Forms Association, 378

National Business Travel Association, 53, 1054

National Business Woman, 1128

National Bus Trader, 645

National Bus Traffic Association, 644

National By-Products, Inc., 719

National Cable Television Association, 158

National Cable Television Institute, 158

National Campground Owners Association, 875

National Candy Brokers Association, 163

National Candy Wholesalers Association, 163

National Car Rental Systems, Inc., 102

National Cattlemen's Association, 171

National Cellular Resellers Association, 628

National Center for Business and Economic Communication, 514

National Center for Freedom of Information Studies, 385

National Center for State Courts, 260

National Cheese Institute, 182

National Cherry Growers and Industries Foundation, 390

National Clay Pipe Institute, 786

National Clearinghouse on Licensure, Enforcement and Regulation, 881

National Coal Association, 204

National Coffee Association of U.S.A., 126, 206

National Coffee Service Association, 1079

National Commercial Refrigeration Sales Association, 38

National Committee to Preserve Social Security and Medicare, 965

National Computer Graphics Association, 229

National Computer Systems, Inc., 502

National Concrete Masonry Association, 238

National Confectioners Association of the U.S., 163

National Conference of Standards Laboratories, 523, 980

National Conference on Public Employee Retirement Systems, 895

National Conference on Weights and Measures, 981

National Congress of Floor Covering Associations, 355

National Convenience Stores Inc., 428

National Cooperative Highway Research Program, 1042

National Cooperative Transit Research and Development Program, 844

National Corporate Cash Management Association, 170

National Corporate Investigations Bureau, Inc., 215

National Corrugated Steel Pipe Association, 786

National Cotton Council of America, 258

National Cottonseed Products Association, 717

National Council of Administrators of Adult Education, 15

National Council of Agricultural Employers, 36

National Council of Farmer Cooperatives, 31

National Council of Investigation and Security Services, 942

National Council of Moving Associations, 634

National Council of Real Estate Investment Fiduciaries, 754, 865

National Council of Salesmen's Organizations, 921

National Council of the Housing Industry, 149

National Council on Compensation Insurance, 1138

National Council on Measurement in Education, 1024

National Council on Public Polls, 840

National Credit Union Management Association, 265

National Customs Brokers and Forwarders Association of America, 462

National Data Book of Foundations, 380

National Decorating Products Association, 1097

National Dipper, 453

National Dog Groomers Association of America, 765

National Education Association, 527

National Education Corp., 1048

National Education Training Group, Inc., 761, 1048

National Electrical Manufacturers Association, 298

National Electric Sign Association, 960

National Electronic Sales and Service Dealers Association, 245

National Employee Benefits Institute, 303

National Energy Specialist Association, 310

National Engine Parts Manufacturers Association, 316

National Enterprises Inc., 627

National Federation of Federal Employees, 192

National Federation of Independent Unions, 525

National Feeder Pig Marketing Association, 988

National Feed Ingredients Association, 333

National Fertilizer Solutions Association, 336

National Fire Protection Association, 349

National Fisheries Institute, 352

National Fluid Power Association, 849

National Food Processors Association, 166, 366

National Forest Products Association, 375

National Forest Recreation Association, 875

National Forge Co., 383

National Forum for Black Public Administrators, 838

National Foundation for Unemployment Compensation and Workers, 1069, 1138

National Foundation for Manufactured Home Owners, 626

National Frame Builders Association, 149

National Free Lance Photographers Association, 782

National Freight Transportation Association, 387

National Frozen Food Association, 366

National Funeral Directors Association, 396

National Futures Association, 222

National Glass Association, 419

National Grain and Feed Association, 333

National Graphic Arts Dealers Association, 423

National Grocers Association, 426

National Gypsum Co., 792

National Hardwood Lumber Association, 375

National Hay Association, 333

National Health Care Anti-Fraud Association, 487

National Healthcorp L.P., 437, 697

National Health Laboratories Inc., 524

National Heritage Inc., 697

National Home Furnishings Association, 400

National Honey Packers and Dealers Association, 446

National Housewares Manufacturers Association, 65

National Ice Cream and Yogurt Retailers Association, 453

National Ice Cream Mix Association, 453

National Immigration Law Center, 460

National Independent Automobile Dealers Association, 96

National Industrial Transportation League, 1042

National Institute for Dispute Resolution, 70

National Institute Of Careers Inc., 295

National Institute of Governmental Purchasing, 851

National Institute of Oilseed Products, 717

National Institute of Pension Administrators, 754

National Institute on Age, Work and Retirement, 895

National Institute on Community-Based Long-Term Care, 696

National Insulation and Abatement Contractors Association, 84, 479

National Inventors Foundation, 499

National Investor Relations Institute, 505

National Jeweler, 413

National Juice Products Association, 126

National Knitwear and Sportswear Association, 200

National Kosher Food Trade Association, 366

National Lamb Feeders Association, 950

National Leadership Coalition on AIDS, 27

National League of Cities, 649

National Licensed Beverage Association, 543

National Limousine Association, 1006

National Liquor Stores Association, 543

National Live Stock and Meat Board, 591

National Locksmith Suppliers Association, 429

National Lubricating Grease Institute, 552

National Luggage Dealers Association, 534, 554

National Machine Tool Builders' Association, 559

National Mail Order Association, 281

National Management Association, 568

National Manufactured Housing Federation, 626

National Marine Electronics Association, 134

National Marine Manufacturers Association, 134

National Medical Enterprises, Inc., 450

National Mental Health Association, 434

National Metal Spinners Association, 607

National Mini-Storage Institute, 634, 1100

National Music Publishers' Association, 654

National Music Services Inc., 656

National Network of Women in Sales, 921

National Newspaper Association, 678

National Oats Co., Inc., 364

National Office Machine Dealers Association, 251, 708

National Office Machine Service Association, 251, 708

National Office Products Association, 708

National Oilseed Processors Association, 717

National Onion Association, 722

National Ornamental and Miscellaneous Metals Association, 608

National Ornament and Electric Lights Christmas Association, 538

National Outerwear and Sportswear Association, 201

National Paint and Coatings Association, 467, 740

National Paint Distributors, 740

National Paperbox and Packaging Association, 143

National Paper Trade Association, 745

National Pasta Association, 555
National Peach Council, 391
National Peanut Council, 699
National Pecan Marketing Council, 699
National Pesticide Telecommunication Network, 762
National Petroleum Refiners Association, 768, 775
National Pork Producers Council, 998
National Potato Council, 805
National Potato Promotion Board, 805
National Potteries Corp., 362
National Precast Concrete Association, 238
National Premium Sales Executives, 814
National Press Photographers Association, 782
National Printing Equipment and Supply Association, 816
National Private Truck Council, 1060
National Productivity Review, 826
National Propane Gas Association, 832
National Property Management Association, 834
National PTA—National Congress of Parents and Teachers, 930
National Ready Mixed Concrete Association, 238
National Real Estate Investor, 866
National Recreation Products, Inc., 877
National Recycling Coalition, 878
National Red Cherry Institute, 391
National Reloading Manufacturers Association, 347
National Relocation and Real Estate Directory, 882

National Repair Center, Inc., 235
National Resource Network, 345
National Restaurant Association, 889
National Retail Federation, 179, 893
National Retail Hardware Association, 429, 444
National Rifle Association of America, 347
National Roofing Contractors Association, 910
National Rural Electric Cooperative Association, 300
National R.V., Inc., 874
National Safety Council, 917, 1045
National Safety Management Society, 917
National Safe Workplace Institute, 917
National Sanitation Foundation, 927
National School Boards Association, 930
National School Bus Report, 645
National School Supply and Equipment Association, 931
National School Transportation Association, 644
National Second Mortgage Association, 114, 633
National Security Industrial Association, 270
National Semiconductor Corp., 949
National Service Industries, Inc., 196
National Service Robot Association, 907
National Shoe Retailers Association, 955
National Shoe Traveler's Association, 955
National Shorthand Reporters Association, 959

National Ski Retailers Association, 977
National Society for Computer Applications in Engineering, 226
National Society for Performance and Instruction, 1024
National Society of Professional Engineers, 315
National Society of Professional Resident Managers, 834
National Society of Public Accountants, 6
National Society of Sales Training Executives, 922
National Soft Drink Association, 127
National Soft Serve and Fast Food Association, 889
National Solid Wastes Management Association, 1104
National Spa and Pool Institute, 996
National Space Society, 24
National Sporting Goods Association, 978
National Spray Equipment Manufacturers Association, 740
National-Standard Co., 1113
National Steel Corp., 985
National Stone Association, 855
National Supply Distributors Association, 444
National Swimming Pool Foundation, 996
National Tabletop Association, 1000
National Tax Association-Tax Institute of America, 1003
National Tax Journal, 1004
National Tile Contractors Association, 1029
National Tile Roofing Manufacturers Association, 911
National Tire Dealers and Retreaders Association, 1029

National Tour Association, 1054

National Training Systems Association, 1047

National Truck Equipment Association, 1057

National Truck Leasing System, 1060

National Turkey Federation, 807

National Underwriter. Property & Casualty Insurance Ed, 484

National Unfinished Furniture Institute, 400

National Union Electric Corp., 196

National United Affiliated Beverage Association, 540

National Utility Contractor, 190

National Vehicle Leasing Association, 101

National Venture Capital Association, 1081

National Waterbed Retailers Association, 400

National Waterways Conference, 1108

National Weather Association, 1110

National Weather Service Employees Organization, 1110

National Wholesale Hardware Association, 429

National Wildlife Federation, 320

National Winex Spirits, 542, 1121

National Wood Energy Association, 312

National Wooden Pallet and Container Association, 143

National Wood Flooring Association, 355

National Wood Window and Door Association, 1130

National Wool Grower, 951, 1134

National Wool Marketing Corp., 1133

National Writers Club, 1141, 1142

Nation's Cities Weekly, 839

Nation's Restaurant News, 890

Nationwide Cellular Service Inc., 629

Nationwide Corp., 1139

Nationwide Mutual Insurance Group, 485

Natural Colored Wool Growers Association, 1133

Natural Gas, 661

Natural Gas Supply Association, 660

Natural Product Broker Association, 440

Natural Resources Defense Council, 320

Naturipe Berry Growers, 393

Navistar International Transportation Corp., 1058

Navy Federal Credit Union, 266

NBI Inc., 1137

NCC Industries, Inc., 1066

NCH Corp., 196

NCITD—The International Trade Facilitation Council, 462

NCLC Reports: Bankruptcy & Foreclosures, 112

NCLC Reports: Debt Collection & Reposessions, 215

NCNB Corp., 117

NCR Corp, 234, 705

NEC America, Inc., 1012

Neiss Corp., 685

Nelson Laboratories, 1088

Nelson's Directory of Pension Fund Consultants, 754

Neogen Corp., 1088

Nestle Foods Corp., 165

NetFrame Systems Inc., 548

Network Equipment Technologies, Inc., 705

Network General Corp., 548

Network Security Corp., 944

Neumade Products Corp., 641

Neuville Industries, Inc., 1066

Nevada Association Race and Sports Book Operators, 403

New England Business Service, Inc., 379

New England Stone Industries, Inc., 856

New Enterprise Associates, 1082

New Equipment Digest, 471

New Equipment Reporter, 471

New Hampshire Ball Bearings, Inc., 125

New Jersey Manufacturers Insurance Co., 1139

New Jersey Transit Bus Operation Inc., 645

New Line Cinema Corp., 639

Newman Machine Co., 1132

Newmont Gold Co., 813

Newmont Mining Corp., 617

Newport News Shipbuilding and Dry Dock Co., 954

News America Publishing Inc., 1018

Newsletter Association, 677

Newsletter on Newsletters, 677

Newspaper Advertising Bureau, 18, 678

Newspaper Financial Executives Journal, 679

Newspaper Research Council, 678

Newspaper Research Journal, 679

New York Air Brake Co., 861

New York Law Publishing Co., 677

New York Life Insurance Co., 491

New York Shipping Association, 952

New York Society of Security Analysts, 345

New York Stock Exchange, 938

New York Testing Laboratories, Inc., 602

New York Times Co., 680

Nibco Inc., 799, 1113

NICEM Index to AV Producers and Distributors, 92
A. C. Nielsen Co., 841
Nielsen Marketing Research, 580
Nielsen Newscast, 19, 1017
Nightingale-Conant Corp., 870
Nike, Inc., 956
Nikko Securities Co. International, Inc., 503
Nikon Inc., 730, 784
Nimbus Records, Inc., 870
Nissan Motor Manufacturing Corp. USA, 105
Noise Control Association, 684
Noise Control Engineering Journal, 684
Noise-News, 684
Noise Regulation Reporter, 684
Noland Co., 41, 799
Nomura Securities Co., 503
Non-Ferrous Founders Society, 381
Non-Ferrous Metals Producers Committee, 604
Nonprescription Drug Manufacturers Association, 778
Nordstrom, Inc., 201
Norfolk Shipbuilding & Drydock Corp., 954
Norfolk Southern Corp., 637
North American Association of Inventory Services, 501
North American Blueberry Council, 391
North American Bookdealers Exchange, 141
North American Co. Ltd., 1082
North American Computer Service Association, 232
North American Electric Reliability Council, 300
North American Gold Mining Stocks, 812
North American Limousine Foundation, 171

North American Philips Corp., 277
North American Publishing Co., 677
North American Securities Administrators Association, 937
North American Telecommunications Association, 1009
North American Van Lines of Texas, 637
North American Ventures, Inc., 308
North American Watch Corp., 199
North Carolina Granite Corp., 856
Northern Lights Studies in Creativity, 261
Northern Logger and Timber Processer, 376
Northrop Corp., 49, 272
Northrup King Co., 946
Northwest Airlines Inc., 45
Northwestern Mutual Life Insurance Co., 491
Northwestern National Casualty Co., 1139
Northwestern Steel & Wire Co., 1123
Northwest Motor Welding, Inc., 407
Norton Co. Coated Abrasives, 2
Norwest Financial, Inc., 884
Novacare Inc., 702
Nova Pharmaceutical Corp., 133, 888
Novell Inc., 549
Noveltex Miami Inc., 692
Novo Corp., 23
NSC Corp., 86
NSGA Retail Focus, 978
Nuclear Information and Resource Service, 693
Nuclear Management and Resources Council, 693
Nuclear Plant Journal, 693
Nuclear Reactors and Technology, 694

Nucor Corp., 985
Numerical Control Society/AIM Tech, 560
Nunn-Bush Shoe Co., 956
Nursery Business, 408
Nursing Home Information Service, 696
Nursing Homes and Senior Citizen Care, 697
NUS Corp., 323
Nutech, Inc., 695
Nut Grower, 699
Nutritional Enterprises, Inc., 441
Nutrition & Dietary Consultant, 1096
Nu-West Industries, Inc., 337
Nynex Corp., 1012

OAG Air Cargo Guide, 42
OAG Business Travel Planner. North American Edition, 53
OAG Pocket Flight Guide North American Edition, 45
Oakwood Homes Corp., 627
O'Brien Environmental Energy Inc., 210, 314
Occidental Chemical Corp., 188, 795
Occidental Petroleum Corp., 776
Occupational Hazards, 917
Occupational Health & Safety Asbestos Control Buyer's Guide, 85
Occupational Safety & Health Reporter, 918
Occupational Therapy Forum, 701
Occupational Therapy in Mental Health, 701
Ocean Beauty Seafoods, Inc., 353
OCLC, 537
Odetics Inc., 909
OE Reports, 729
Oerlikon Motch Corp., 561
Office, 708

Office Automation Society International, 703
Office Club Inc., 709
Office Dealer, 252, 708
Office Depot Inc., 709
Officemation Product Reports, 709
Office Products Analyst, 252, 327, 709
Office Products Dealer Buying Guide and Directory, 252, 709, 711, 1136
Office Skills Workshop, 936
Office Technology Management, 704
Offshore Valve Association, 1077
Ogden Allied Services Corp., 197
Ogden Services Corp., 566
Ogilvy Group Inc., 20
Ohio Art Co., 653
Ohio Mattress Co., 402
Ohio Property & Casualty Insurance Co., 1139
Ohio Willow Wood Co., 837
Ohm Corp., 323
Oil, Gas & Petrochem Equipment, 768, 772
Oil and Gas Investor, 775
Oil & Gas Journal, 775, 789
Oil Daily Co., 677
Oil-Dri Corp. of America, 767
Oji Brothers Farms, Inc., 33
Okonite Co., 1123
Old Dominion Box Co., 144
Olin Corp., 188
Olive Oil Association, 717
Olsten Corp., 1020
OMI International Corp., 600
On!, 245
Oneida Ltd., 1001
Onion World, 723
Operations Research, 724
Operations Research Society of America, 724
Ophthalmology Times, 726

Oppenheimer and Co., 503, 507, 940
Oppenheimer Fund Management, Inc., 658
Opportunity Magazine, 384
Optical Coating Laboratory, Inc., 730
Optical Engineering, 729
Optical Laboratories Association, 725
Optical Manufacturers Association, 725
Optical Materials and Engineering News, 729
Optical Micro Systems, 727
Optical Physics and Engineering, 729
Optical Radiation Corp., 727, 730
Optical Society of America, 728
Optometric Economics, 726
Optometric Management, 726
Oracle Corp., 235
Orcomatic Inc., 914
Oregon Potato Co., 806
Ore-Ida Foods Co., Inc., 723, 806
Organic Crop Improvement Association, 34, 440
Organic Foods Production Association of North America, 440
Oriental Rug Importers Association, 168
Oriental Rug Review, 168
Orion Pictures Corp., 640
Orita Land and Cattle, 173
Orkin Exterminating Co., 764
Orthopedic Products News, 595
Orthopedic Services Inc., 837
Osco Drug, Inc., 289
OSHA Training Bulletin for Supervisors, 917
Oshkosh Truck Corp., 1058
Oshman's Sporting Goods, Inc., 979
Oster/Sunbeam Appliance Co., 119

OTC Growth Stock Watch, 939
OTC Stock Reports, 939
Outboard Marine Corp., 135, 317
Outdoor Amusement Business Association, 236
Outlook for Travel and Tourism, 1055
Overnite Transportation Co., 388
R. S. Owens & Co., 815
Owens-Corning Fiberglas Corp., 481, 912
Owens-Illinois, Inc., 250
Owner-Operator Independent Drivers Association, 1060
Oxford Chemicals Inc., 764
Oxford Venture Corp., 1082
Oxy Petrochemical Inc., 769

Pabst Brewing Co., 147
Paccar Inc, 272, 1058
Pacific Clay Products, Inc., 194
Pacific Coast Oyster Growers Association, 352
Pacific Fishing, 352
Pacific Hide & Fur Depot, 399
Pacific Resources Inc., 833
Package Design Council, 734
Package Printing & Converting, 743
Packaging, 143, 735
Packaging Concepts Ltd., 800
Packaging Corp. of America, 250
Packaging Digest, 144, 735, 738
Packaging Machinery Manufacturers Institute, 738
Packaging Marketplace, 735
Packaging Strategies, 249, 735
Packerland Packing Co., Inc., 592
Paint & Coatings Industry, 468, 740
Painting and Wallcovering Contractor, 740
Pan American Diamond Corp., 413
P & C Food Markets, Inc., 428

P & IM Review, 824
Panhandle Eastern Corp., 661
Pan Pacific Fisheries, 353
Paper Age, 746, 749
Paper Bag Institute, 743
Paperboard Packaging, 144, 749
Paperboard Packaging Council, 734, 749
Paper Corp. of America, 747
Papercraft Corp., 418
Paper Distribution Data Source, 746
Paper Industry Management Association, 745
Paper Manufacturers Co., 522
Paper Recycler, 746, 879
Paper Sales, 746
Paper Stock Report, 746
Paper Tree Letter, 376
Paracelsus Healthcare Corp., 450
Paragon Family Services, Inc., 397
Paramount Pictures Corp., 640
Parish Division, 609
Parker Hannifin Corp., 26
Parking Control Systems Corp., 1044
Parkway Ford, Inc., 97
Partnership for a Drug-Free America, 59
Parts, Inc., 100
Parts Industries Corp., 407
Part-Time Professional, 1020
Party and Paper Retailer, 425
Passenger Train Journal, 860
Passenger Transport, 844
Passive Solar Industries Council, 966
Passport Travel, Inc., 1052
Patterson Dental Co., 277
Pavement Maintenance, 905
Paxall Group, Inc., 739
Paxar Corp., 522
Payless Cashways, Inc., 430
Payless Shoesource, 956

PCA International, Inc., 784
PC Magazine, 233, 1136
PC Sources, 233
Peabody Coal Co., 206, 617
Peaches Entertainment Corp., 653
Peak Performance Selling, 922
Peanut Butter and Nut Processors Association, 699
Peanut Farmer, 699
Peanut Grower, 699
Peanut Research, 700
Pearle, Inc., 727
Peat, Marwick, Main & Co., 8
Penford Products Co., 806
Pengad Co's., Inc., 959
Pennaco Hosiery, 1066
Pennock Co., 361
Pennsylvania & Southern Gas Co., 833
Penobscot Frozen Foods, Inc., 806
Pension and Profit-Sharing Plans: Forms and Practice, 755
Pension and Profit-Sharing Plans Compliance Guide, 755
Pension Fund Litigation Reporter, 755
Pension Fund News, 755
Pension Real Estate Association, 754, 866
Pension Research Council, 754
Pension Rights Center, 754
Pensions & Investments, 506, 755
Pension World, 755
Pentagon Federal Credit Union, 266
Pentair Inc., 553, 747, 850, 1132
Pen World, 1143
Penzoil Products Co., 553
Peoples Drug Stores, Inc., 289
People With AIDS Coalition, 27
Pep Boys, 180
Pepsi-Cola Co., 128
Perdue Farms Inc., 808, 975

Perfumer & Flavorist, 10, 255
Perini Corp., 151
Periodicals Institute, 756
Perry Drug Stores Inc., 289
Personal Engineering & Instrumentation News, 933
Personal Finance, 939
Personal Financial Planning, 346
Personal Publishing, 279
Personal Report for the Professional Secretary, 713, 936
Personal Selling Power, 920, 922
Personnel, 760
Personnel Management, 760
Personnel News, 760
Personnel Psychology, 760
Pesticide & Toxic Chemical News, 763
Pet Dealer, 766
Peterson Builders, Inc., 135
Peterson Industries Inc., 808
Petfood Industry, 766
Pet Food Institute, 766
Pet Industry Distributors Association, 766
Pet Industry Joint Advisory Council, 766
Petrie Stores Corp., 203
Petrochemical Energy Group, 768
PetroChemical News, 768
Petroleum Equipment Suppliers Associatiom, 771
Petroleum Heat & Power Co., 395
Petroleum Management, 775
Petroleum Marketers Association of America, 394, 775
Petroleum Taxation & Legislation Report, 775
Pets, Supplies, Marketing, 766
Pettibone Corp., 383, 590
Pfizer Inc., 781
Pharmaceutical Engineering, 779
Pharmaceutical Executive, 779
Pharmaceutical Manufacturers Association, 778

Pharmaceutical Representative, 779

Pharmaceutical Technology, 779

Phelps Dodge Corp., 813

PHH Homequity, 883

Phibro Energy, Inc., 311, 776

Philadelphia Macaroni Co., Inc., 555

Philip Morris Inc., 1036

Philipp Brothers, Inc., 606

Philips Consumer Electronics Co., 246

Philips Lighting Co., 539

Philips Medical Systems North America Co., 1065

Phillips & Jacobs, Inc., 424

Phillips Fibers Corp., 1148

Phillips Petroleum Co., 411, 661, 776

PHM Corp., 634

Photo & Sound Co., 92

Photo Business, 783

Photographic Manufacturers and Distributors Association, 783

Photo Lab Management, 783

Photo Marketing Association International, 782

Physician's Management, 439

Piano Manufacturers Association International, 651

Pic 'n' Save Corp., 995

Piccadilly Cafeterias, Inc., 374

Pillsbury Co., 364

PIMA Magazine, 746

Pinkertons's Security & Investigation Services, 944

The Pink Sheet, 779

Pinnacle West Capital Corp., 1082

Pioneer Electronics (USA), Inc., 67

Pioneer Feed Yards, Inc., 173

Pioneer Financial Services, Inc., 488

Pioneer Hi-Bred International, Inc., 947

Pipe Fabrication Institute, 786

Pipeline & Gas Journal, 789

Pipe Line Contractors Association, 771, 789

Pipe Line Industry, 789

Pipe Tobacco Council, 1034

Pit & Quarry, 174, 855

Pitney Bowes Inc., 804

Pittston Co., 43, 206

Pittway Corp., 23, 1078

Pizza & Pasta, 555

Pizza Hut, Inc., 891

Plains Cotton Cooperative Association, 258

Planning Review, 148

Plastic Bag Association, 743

Plastic Bottle Reporter, 879

Plastic Pipe and Fittings Association, 786

Plastic Reel Corp. of America, 1090

Plastics Business News, 794

Plastics Compounding, 794

Plastics Design Forum, 794

Plastic Shipping Container Institute, 249

Plastics Institute of America, 793

Plastics Machinery and Equipment, 794

Plastics News, 794

Plastics Pipe Institute, 786

Plastics Recycling Foundation, 878

Plastics Recycling Update, 879

Plastics Technology, 794

Plastics World, 794

Plasti-Kote Co., Inc., 23

Plasti-Line, Inc., 961

Platt's Oilgram Marketscan. US Edition, 775

Platt's Petrochemicalscan, 769

Player, 403

Playskool Inc., 1038

Playtex Apparel Inc., 1066

Playthings, 442, 1037

Plumbing and Drainage Institute, 797

Plumbing & Mechanical, 797

Plumbing Business, 798

Plumbing Engineer, 798

Plumbing Manufacturers Institute, 797

Pneumatic Scale Corp., 739

Pneumo Abex Corp., 26

PNP Prime Corp., 445

Point-of-Purchase Advertising Institute, 18

M. Polaner, Inc., 723

Polaroid Corp., 784

Police and Security News, 943

Political Risk Yearbook, 903

R. L. Polk & Co., 283

Polk's Bank Directory. North American Edition, 116

Polling Report, 840

Pollution Engineering Locator, 321

Pollution Equipment News, 321

Polychrome Corp., 424, 819

Polystyrene Packaging Council, 734

Pontiac Livestock Sales, 546

Pool & Spa News, 996

Poppe Tyson Inc., 843

Popular Photography, 783

Population Association of America, 801

Population Reference Bureau, 801

Population Trends and Public Policy, 801

Portable Sanitation Association International, 927

Portion Pac, Inc., 925

Portland Cement Association, 174

Poseidon Pools of America, Inc., 997

POS News, 799

Postal Watch, 803

Postal World, 803

Potato Grower of Idaho, 805

Potlatch Corp., 356, 377, 747

Potomac Electric Power Co., 301

Potsmokers Anonymous, 60

Poultry and Egg Marketing, 807

Poultry and Egg News, 807

Poultry Digest, 807

Poultry Processing, 807

Poultry Science Association, 807

Powder Coating Institute, 467

Power, 810

Power Transmission Design, 124, 810

PPO Letter, 438

Prab Robots, Inc., 910

Practical Accountant, 7

Practical Financial Planning, 346

Practical Real Estate Lawyer, 863

Practical Tax Lawyer, 1004

Practical Winery & Vineyard, 1120

Practicing Architect, 72

Prairie Farms Dairy, Inc., 269

Prairie Livestock, Inc., 546

Pratt & Lambert, Inc., 741

Pratt Hotel Corp., 877

Pre-, 817

Precision Measurements Association, 981

Precision Metalforming Association, 608

Predicasts, Inc., 478

Preferred Hotels Association, 451

Preferred Mutual Insurance Co., 1140

Premium-Incentive Business, 814

Prepared Foods, 166

Prescolite Inc., 539

Presstime, 514, 679

Pressure Sensitive Tape Council, 12

Prestressed Concrete Institute, 238

Prevor Marketing International, Inc., 393

Price Chopper Operating Co., 993

Price Co., 430, 543

Price Waterhouse & Co., 8, 1005

Prime Computer, Inc., 228

Prime Tanning Co., Inc., 535

Prince Co., Inc., 555

Prince Manufacturing, 979

Print Buyers Review, 817

Printers' Bindery, Inc., 137

Printers Hot Line, 817

Printing Brokerage Association, 816

Printing Industries of America, 816

Printing News-East, 818

Private Pilot, 47

Private Security Case Law Reporter, 943

Privatization, 822

Privatization Council, Inc., 822

Privatization Watch, 822

Proceedings of the Annual Meeting American Society of Bakery Engineers, 109

Process Equipment Co., 910

Procter & Gamble Co., 197

Produce Merchandising, 987

Produce Packaging Handling Digest, 735

Producers Rice Mill Inc., 901

Production and Inventory Management, 501

Productivity Communication Center, 826

Productivity Measures for Selected Industries, 827 Product Liability: Design and Manufacturing Defects, 830

The Product Liability Alliance, 829

Product Liability Law and Strategy, 830

Product Liability Prevention and Defense, 829

Product Liability Trends, 830

Product Safety & Liability Reporter, 831

Product Safety Letter, 831

Product Safety News, 831

Product Safety Up To Date, 832

Pro-Fac Cooperative, Inc., 393

Professional and Technical Consultants Association, 243

Professional Arts Management Institute, 83

Professional Audiovideo Retailers Association, 91

Professional Builder & Remodeler, 150

Professional Cleaning Journal, 196

Professional Consultant Information, 570

Professional Convention Management Association, 1040

Professional Film and Video Equipment Association, 1089

Professional Investor, 506, 939

Professional Mariners Alliance, 952

Professional Numismatists Guild, 211

Professional Packaging Corp., 23

Professional Photographers of America, 783

Professional Plant Growers Association, 408

Professional Secretaries International, 936

Professional Selling, 922

Professional Surveyor, 190

Professional Truck Driver Institute of America, 1060

Profit Freight Systems, Inc., 43

Profit Sharing Council of America, 754

Progress in Materials Handling and Logistics, 589

Progressive Architecture, 72

Progressive Farmer, 31

Progressive Grocer, 426

Promo, 923
Promotion Industry Club, 923
Promotion Marketing Association of America, 923
Promotion Power, 924
Property Management Association of America, 834
Property Management Monthly, 835
Proprietary Holding, Inc., 33
Pro-Quip Corp., 769
Pro Sound News, 869
Protection One Alarm Services, 944
Provena Foods Inc., 555
Prudential Insurance Co. of America, 491
Prudential Relocation Management, 883
PSE Inc., 211
Psychology of Learning and Motivation, 643
Public Agency Risk Managers Association, 902
Public Broadcasting Service, 1017
Public Budgeting and Finance, 148
Public Budgeting and Financial Management, 148
Public Management, 839
Public Personnel Management, 760
Public Power, 300
Public Productivity and Management Review, 827
Public Relations News, 842
Public Relations Quarterly, 842
Public Relations Review, 842
Public Relations Society of America, 842
Public Risk Management Association, 903
Public Securities Association, 938
Public Service Enterprise Group Inc., 211

Public Utilities Fortnightly, 847
Public Utilities Newsletter, 847
Publish!, 279
Publishers Weekly, 139, 141
Publishing Trends and Trendsetters, 757
Pulaski Furniture Corp., 199
Pulitzer Publishing Co., 680, 1018
Pulp, Paper and Paperboard Export Association of the U.S., 745
Pulp & Paper International, 746
Purchasing, 851
Purchasing Executive's Bulletin, 852
Purchasing Management, 852
Puritan-Bennett Corp., 23
Purity Supreme Supermarkets, 994
Purpa Lines, 210
Putnam Berkeley Group, Inc., 140
PVA-EPVA, Inc., 426

Quad Systems Corp., 910
Quaker Oats Co., 368, 767
Quality and Productivity Management Association, 826
Quality Assurance, 853
Quality Assurance Bulletin, 853
Quality Control and Applied Statistics, 853
Quality Progress, 853
Quality Wall Covering, Inc., 1098
Quarterly Journal of Economics, 290
Quebecor Printing, 819
Quick Printing, 818
Quintessence Inc., 256
Quixote Corp., 906, 919, 959
Quotron Systems, Inc., 479

Racetrac Petroleum, Inc., 411
Radiac Abrasives, Inc., 2
Radio Advertising Bureau, 18, 857
Radio Advertising Bureau. Radio Facts, 857
Radio Business Report, 857

Radio-Electronics, 245
Radio-Television News Directors Association, 1017
Radio Week, 857
Radio World, 857
Railway Age, 860
Railway Supply Association, 859
Railway Systems Suppliers, 860
Railway Track & Structures, 860
Ralston Purina Co., 111, 123, 767
Rancho Flowers, Inc., 362
R & D Contracts Monthly, 887
R & D Management Digest, 887
R & D Strategist, 887
Rand International, Inc., 130
Random House, Inc., 140
Ranger Development Corp., 864
Ransburg Corp., 741
Rapistan Corp., 590
Rare Fruit Council International, 391
Raster Technologies, Inc., 230
Ravarino & Freschi, Inc., 555
Rawlings Sporting Goods Co., 979
Raycomm Transworld Industries, Inc., 1020
Raymond Corp., 590
Rayovac Corp., 123
Reactive Metal & Alloys Corp., 603
REA International Corp., 107
Real Estate Forum, 863
Real Estate Investment Situations, 867
Real Estate News, 863
Real Estate Review, 864
Real Estate Syndication Alert, 867
Recent Advances in Tobacco Science, 1034
Reckitt & Colman Inc., 764, 976
Recon/Optical, Inc., 730
Recording Engineering Production, 869
Recording Industry Association of America, 868

Recovery Now, 60

Recreation and Parks Law Reporter, 876

Recreation Resources, 876

Recreation Vehicle Dealers Association of North America, 873

Recreation Vehicle Industry Association, 873

Recruiting and Search Report, 307

Recruiting Trends, 307

Recycling Times, 879

Recycling Today, 879

Red Devil Inc., 1098

Red's Market, Inc., 393

Reed Publishing (USA), Inc., 140

John T. Reed's Real Estate Investor's Monthly, 866

Reed Travel Group, 1055

HB Reese Candy Co., Inc., 164

Reeves Communications Corp., 640

Refined Sugars Inc., 990

Refreshment Machinery Industries, 1080

Refrigerated Transporter, 1060

Refrigeration Service Engineers Society, 38

Regal Manufacturing Co., 1148

Regional Airline Association, 44

Regional and Distribution Carriers Conference, 1060

Registered Representative, 939

Regulatory Affairs Professionals Society, 881

Regulatory Watchdog Service, 881

Rehab Management, 701

Reichel & Drews Inc., 825

Reichhold Chemicals, Inc., 14

Wm. B. Reily & Co., 208

Reliable Automatic Sprinkler Co., Inc., 351

Reliance Electric Co., 299

Reliant Testing Laboratories, 888

Relocation Experts, Inc., 883

Relocation Report, 882

Remax International, 865

Renew America, 312

Rennoc Corp., 692

Renrob Coins Inc., 212

Rental, 884

Rental Dealer News, 884

Republic Health Corp., 450

Republic Indemnity Co. of America, 1140

Republic Waste Industries Inc., 1106

Resco Products, Inc., 178

Research Alert, 579

Research & Development, 887

Research and Engineering Council of the Graphic Arts Industry, 422

Research in Marketing, 579

Research Institute, 312

Research Institute of America, 1003

Research Network, 479

Research Organics, Inc., 133

Research Triangle Institute, 888

Resilient Floor Covering Institute, 355

Resort and Commercial Recreation Association, 875

Resorts International/Casino Hotel Inc., 404

Resources Exchange Association Foundation, 995

Restaurant Business, 890

Restaurant Enterprise Group Inc., 891

Restaurants and Institutions, 890

Retail Advertising Conference, 18

Retail Bakers of America, 109

Retail Bakers of America. Government Bulletin, 110

Retail Confectioners International, 163

Retail Information Systems News Directory, 893

Retailing Today, 893

Retail Loss Prevention Association, 942

Retail Observer, 893

Retail Office Furniture Forum, 711

Retail Store Image, 893

Retail Tobacconist, 1034

Retirement and Benefit Planning, 896

Retirement Care Associates Inc., 897

Retirement Letter, 896

Retreading-Repair Journal, 1031

Revco D.S., 289

Paul Revere Life Insurance Co., 897

Review of Scientific Instruments, 933

Rex, Inc., 213

Rexham Inc., 736

Reynolds and Reynolds Co., 379

Russell Reynolds Associates, Inc., 308

Reynolds Metals Co., 63, 813

R. J. Reynolds Tobacco Co., 1036

Rhode Island Limb Co., 837

Rice Council for Market Development, 900

Rice Farming and Rice Industry News, 900

Rice Journal, 900

Riceland Foods, Inc., 901

Rice Millers' Association, 900

Rice World & Soybean News, 900, 974

Richards Brick Co., 194

Richmond Motor Co., 97

Riggs Supply Co., 154

Right Management Consultants, Inc., 761

Riley's Inc., 348

Ringhaver Equipment Co., 472

Ringier America, Inc., 819

Rinker Materials Corp., 240

Rip Griffin Truck/Travel Center, Inc., 411

Risdon Corp., 23

Riser Foods Inc., 428

Risk and Benefits Journal, 904

Risk & Insurance, 487, 903

Rite Aid Corp., 289

River Garden Farms Co., 34

Riviana Foods Inc., 901

RJR Nabisco, Inc., 368, 719

The Road Information Program, 905

Roads & Bridges, 191

Roadway Motor Plazas, Inc., 411

Roadway Package System, Inc., 388

Roadway Services, Inc., 1062

Robertshaw Controls Co., 825

Robotic Industries Association, 908

Robotics and Computer-Integrated Manufacturing, 908

Robotics Today, 908, 909

Robotic Vision Systems, Inc., 910

Rocco Enterprises, Inc., 808

Rock & Gem, 413

Rockaway Corp., 804

Rockefeller Center Properties Inc., 867

Rock-Tenn Co., 144, 750

Rodale Press, Inc., 677

Rodico, Inc., 739

Rogers Group, Inc., 906

Rohm & Haas Co., 188, 795

Rolling Stone, 655

Ronzoni Macaroni Co., Inc., 555

Roof Coatings Manufacturers Association, 911

Roof Consultants Institute, 911

Roofer Magazine, 911

A. I. Root Co., 447

Roper Organization, Inc., 840, 841

Rose Hills Co., 397

Rosemount Varec Division, 770

Ross Roy, Inc., 20

Rothschild Inc., 1082

Rough Notes, 493

Rouse Co., 707, 865, 894

Rowe International, Inc., 656, 1080

Rowe Price New Income Fund, Inc., 659

Royal Crown Cola Co., 128

Royal Dutch/Shell Group, 606, 777

Royal Zenith Corp., 424

Royster Co., 337

RPM Inc., 469

RPS Realty Trust. 867

RSI, 911

RSVP: The Directory of Illustration and Design, 221

Rubber & Plastics News, 914

Rubber and Plastics Newsletter, 914

Rubber Chemistry and Technology, 914

Rubbermaid Inc., 914

Rubber Manufacturers Association, 913

Rubber Trade Association of New York, 913

Rubber World, 914

Ruder-Finn, Inc., 843

Rudy's Limousine Service, Inc., 1006

Runzheimer International, 883

Ruttle, Shaw & Wetherhill, Inc., 1137

RV Business, 873

RV Trade Digest, 873

Ryan Homes, Inc., 151

Ryder System, Inc., 1062

Joseph T. Ryerson & Son, Inc., 986

Saatchi & Saatchi Compton Inc., 21

Sabre Systems & Service, Inc., 1077

Safety & Security for Supervisors, 943

Safety Compliance Letter, 918

Safety Equipment Distributors Association, 917

Sailboat & Equipment Directory, 134

St. Ives Laboratories, Inc., 256

St. Louis Journalism Review, 514

St. Paul Fire and Marine Insurance Co., 486

Salem Carpet Mills, Inc., 169

Sales and Marketing Executives International, 920

Sales & Marketing Management, 576, 920

Sales and Marketing Strategies & News, 922

Sales Manager's Bulletin, 921

Sales Rep's Advisor, 575

Sales Upbeat, 922

Kurt Salmon Associates, Inc., 571

Salomon Brothers Inc., 507, 941

Salt and Trace Minerals Report, 925

Salt Institute, 925

Sammons Enterprises, Inc., 472

Samsonite Corp., 555

Sanders Associates, Inc., 230

Sanderson Farms, Inc., 808

San Diego Gas & Electric Co., 301, 848

S & L Quarterly, 928

S & L—Savings Bank Financial Quarterly, 928

Sandoz Corp., 33

Sands Hotel & Casino Corp., 404

Sandvik, Inc., 1114

Sanford Corp., 1143

Sanitary Maintenance, 927

Sanitary Supply Wholesalers Association, 927

Sanyo Business Systems Corp., 327

Sanyo Manufacturing, 246

Satcon Technology Corp., 992
Satellite TV Week, 1017
Sathers, Inc., 165
Savage Industries, Inc., 348
Savannah Food Service, 925
Savin Corp., 253, 328
Savings & Loan Investor, 929
Savings and Loan Reporter, 928
Scana Corp., 301
SCAN Newsletter, 94
Henry Schein, Inc., 277
Schenley Industries, Inc., 1121
Julius Schepps Wholesale Liquors, Inc., 542
Schering-Plough Corp., 781
Schlumberger Ltd., 772
School and College, 931
School Business Affairs, 931
School Food Service Journal, 373
School Library Journal, 536
School Specialty Supply, Inc., 92
Schottenstein Stores Corp., 402
Schott Glass Technologies Inc., 727
A. Schulman, Inc., 795, 915
Schult Homes Corp., 627
F. Schumacher & Co., 1071
Charles Schwab Corp., 507, 940
Schwinn Bicycle Co., 130
Science Management Corp., 571, 828, 1049
Sci-O-Tech, Co., 437
O. M. Scott & Sons Co., 947
Scott Paper Co., 377, 747
Scotts Co., 409
Scott Stamp Monthly, 213
Scotty's Inc., 155
Scrap Processing and Recycling, 879
E. W. Scripps Co., 680
Scripps Howard Broadcasting Co., 160
Scrivner, Inc., 368
SCS/Compute Inc., 1005
SDI Operating Partners L.P., 421

Seaberg Precision Corp., 559
Seaboard Corp., 364
Sea Farms West, Inc., 69
Seafood Business, 352
Seafood Leader, 352
Seafood Price—Current, 352
Joseph E. Seagram and Sons, Inc., 542, 1121
Sea-Land Services, Inc., 954
Sealant Waterproofing and Restoration Institute, 12
Sealed Air Corp., 736, 968
Sears Roebuck and Co., 894
Seatrain Lines, Inc., 954
Sea View Fillet Co., Inc., 353
Seaway Review, 1108
Secondary Marketing Executive, 634
Secretary, 936
Securities Industry Association, 502, 938
Securities Product News, 939
Security and Special Police Legal Update, 943
Security Distributing & Marketing, 943
Security Industry Association, 942
Security Journal, 943
Security Pacific Corp., 117
Security Traders Association, 938
Security Van Lines, Inc., 1041
Seeburg Phonograph Corp., 1080
Seed Industry Journal, 945
Seed Savers Exchange, 945
Seed Trade Buyer's Guide, 945
Seed Trade News, 945
Seed World, 946
See's Candy Shops, Inc., 165
Seidman & Seidman/BDO, 8
Self Storage Association, 634, 1100
Semiconductor Equipment and Materials International, 947
Semiconductor Industry & Business Survey Newsletter, 948

Semiconductor Industry Association, 948
Semiconductor International, 948
Seneca Foods Corp., 167
Senior Law Report, 697, 965
Sequa Corp., 317
Service Corp. International, 397
Service Corps of Retired Executives Association, 896
Service Employees International Union, 527
ServiceMaster Co. LP, 566
Service Station Dealers of America, 406
Service Station Management, 406
Servistar Corp., 377, 430
Sessions Co. Inc., 700
Seward Luggage Co., 555
Seybold Report on Desktop Publishing, 279
Patricia Seybold's Office Computing Report, 709
Shalom International Corp., 692
Share-A-Ride International, 1054
Shasta Beverages Inc., 128
Shaw Industries, Inc., 169
Sheaffer Eaton, Inc., 1144
Shearman and Sterling, 532
Shearson Lehman Brothers Inc., 507, 941
Sheep Breeder and Sheepman, 951
Sheep! Magazine, 951
Sheet Metal and Air Conditioning Contractors' National Association, 604
Shell Oil Co., 661, 777
Shemin Nurseries, Inc., 362
Shepherd, 951
Sherrill Farms, Inc., 34
Sherwin-Williams Co., 14, 742
Sherwood Medical Co., 277
Shippers for Competitive Ocean Transportation, 952
Shipping Digest, 953

Shoe Service Institute of America, 955

Shoe-Town, Inc., 956

Shopping Center Digest, 958

Shopping Center Newsletter, 958

Shopping Center World, 179, 958

Shoreline Products Inc., 648

Shorewood Packaging Corp., 750

Showboat Inc., 404

Showell Farms, Inc., 808

Shuron Inc., 727

Sidley and Austin, 533

Sierra Real Estate Equity Trust, 82, 867

Sigel Liquor Stores, Inc., 543

Signal Inc., 1044

Signcraft, 960

Signs of the Times, 960

Sikes Corp., 1029

Silberman Fur Corp., 399

Silgas, Inc., 833

Silicon Graphics Inc., 231

Silicon Valley Group Inc., 949

Silvar-Lisco, 228

Silvercrest Corp., 627

SilverPlatter Information, 479

Silver Institute, 811

Silver Users Association, 811

Simat/Hellies/Eich, 1077

Simplex Time Recorder Co., 199

Simplimatic Engineering Co., 739

Single Ply Roofing Institute, 911

Singleton Seafood Co., 353

SinterMet Corp., 2

Sioux Honey Association Co-op, 447

Sirco International Corp., 555

Sizeler Property Investors Inc., 959

Sizzler International, Inc., 891

Skadden Arps Slate Meagher and Flom, 533

SKF USA, Inc., 125

Sky Chefs, Inc., 52, 374, 891

Skyway Luggage Co., 555

Slack Inc., 1041

Sloan Management Review, 569

Small Business Opportunities, 964

Small Business Reports, 964

Small Business Service Bureau, 963

Small Business Tax Control, 964

Small Business Tax Review, 964

Small Luxury Hotels Association, 451

Small World, 1037

Smart & Final, Inc., 976

Smith & Wesson Corp., 348

Smith Corona Corp., 1137

Smithfield Foods, Inc., 592

Smith Industries, Inc., 351

Smith Investment Co., 119, 351, 1101

SmithKline Beecham Corp., 524, 781

Smokeshop, 1034

J. M. Smucker Co., 700

Smyth Manufacturing Co., 137

Snappy Car Rental, Inc., 102

Snelling and Snelling, Inc., 1020

Snokist Growers, 393

Snowflake Pig Farms, Inc., 999

Snowmobile Business, 873

SnyderGeneral Corp., 41

Soap and Detergent Association, 3

Soccer Industry Council of America, 978

Social Security Manual, 965

Social Security Practice Guide, 965

Society for Advancement of Management, 568

Society for Business Ethics, 155

Society for Computer-Aided Engineering, 226

Society for Foodservice Management, 372

Society for Glass Science and Practices, 420

Society for Information Management, 572

Society for Machine Intelligence, 80

Society for Scholarly Publishing, 139

Society for Technical Communication, 1141

Society for Technical Communication Anthology Series, 1142

Society for the Advancement of Material and Process Engineering, 586

Society of Actuaries, 9

Society of Actuaries. Transactions, 9

Society of American Florists, 360

Society of Certified Insurance Counselors, 492

Society of Cleaning Technicians, 195

Society of Collision Repair Specialists, 406

Society of Consumer Affairs Professionals in Business, 842

Society of Cosmetic Chemists, 254

Society of Experimental Test Pilots, 46

Society of Fire Protection Engineers, 349

Society of Fire Protection Technicians, 349

Society of Flavor Chemists, 10

Society of Illustrators, 220

Society of Incentive Travel Executives, 1054

Society of Independent Gasoline Marketers of America, 410

Society of Logistics Engineers, 823

Society of Marine Port Engineers, 952

Society of Motion Picture and Television Engineers, 1089

Society of Plastics Engineers, 793

Society of Professional Audio Recording Services, 868

Society of Professional Journalists, 514

Society of Recreation Executives, 875

Society of Risk Management Consultants, 903

Society of Telecommunications Consultants, 1009

Society of the Plastics Industry, 793

Society of Tribologists and Lubrication Engineers, 552

Society of Vacuum Coaters, 468

Society of Women Engineers, 315

Sohio Pipe Line Co., 790

Solar Energy, 967

Solar Energy Industries Association, 966

Solar Today, 967

Solid State Technology, 968

Solon Automated Services, Inc., 530

SonicAir Couriers, Inc., 43

Sonic Industries Inc., 891

Sonicor Instrument Corp., 1065

Sonics & Materials, Inc., 1065

Sotheby's Inc., 90, 513, 1007

Sound & Communications, 1090

Sound & Image, 1090

Sound and Vibration, 684

Soundtrack, 869

Source Book of Franchise Opportunities, 384

Southdown, Inc., 175, 240

Southern California Gas Co., 661

Southern California Rapid Transit District, 645

Southern California Water Co., 848

Southern Clay Products Inc., 194

Southern Microfilm Corp., 614

Southern Minnesota Beet Sugar Cooperative, 990

Southern Purchasor, 852

Southern States Cooperative, Inc., 33, 947

Southern Woodwork Association, 1130

Southland Corp., 994

Southmark Corp., 867

Southwest Airlines Co., 45

Southwest Research Institute, 888

Southwestern Bell Co., 1012

Southwire Co., 63, 1123

Souvenir, 691

Souvenir and Novelty Trade Association, 691

Souvenirs and Novelties, 418, 691

Soybean Digest, 974

Soyfoods Association of North America, 974

Space & Leisure Time Ltd., 1053

Spacelabs Inc., 596

Space Studies Institute, 24

Spartan Food Systems Inc., 891

Spartan Mills, 1148

Spaulding Co., Inc., 614

Special Interest Group on Artificial Intelligence, 80

Special Interest Group on Computer Graphics, 229

Special Interest Group on Data Communication, 547

Special Interest Group on Office Information Systems, 703

Special Libraries Association, 536

Specialty Advertising Association International, 18

Specialty Equipment Companies Inc., 370

Specialty Food Merchandising, 440

Specialty Hearse & Ambulance Sales Corp., 1006

Specialty Paperboard, Inc., 750

Spectra-Physics, Inc., 934

Spectrolab, Inc., 968

SpeeDee Oil Change and Tune-up, 407

Spencer Gifts, Inc., 419

Spic and Span, Inc., 530

SPIE—The International Society for Optical Engineering, 728

Spire Corp., 888

Sporting Goods Business, 978

Sporting Goods Dealer, 978

Sporting Goods Manufacturers Association, 978

Sports Trend, 979

Sportswear International, 201

Spreckels Industries, 990

Springhouse Corp., 758

Springs Industries, Inc., 326

Spudman, 805

SRI International, 888

Stack's, 213

Staff Builders, Inc., 1020

A. E. Staley Manufacturing Co., 718, 841

Stamp Collector, 213

Stamping Quarterly, 608

Standard Abrasives Co., 2

Standard Brands Paint Co., 356, 742

Standard Commercial Corp., 1036, 1135

Standard Directory of Advertisers, 20

Standard Gage Co. Inc., 854

Standard Insurance Co., 897

Standard Microsystems Corp., 549

Standard Register Co., 379

Standards and Specifications Information Bulletin, 981

Stanhome Inc., 197

Stanley Works, 430

Staplcotn, 258

Starch/Inra/Hooper, Inc., 580, 841

Sta-Rite Industries, Inc., 988
Star-Kist Foods, Inc., 167, 767
State and Local Government Review, 650
State Employees Credit Union, 266
State Farm Fire and Casualty Co., 486
State Farm Mutual Automobile Insurance Co., 482
Stationery Product Group, 1144
Statistical Process Control Society, 823
Statistical Science, 982
Stauffer Chemical Co., 33
Steel Can Recycling Institute, 879
Steelcase Inc., 402, 712
Steel Digest, 985
J. C. Steele & Sons, Inc., 194
Steel Founders' Society of America, 381
Steel Manufacturers Association, 984
Steel Plate Fabricators Association, 984
Steels Alert, 985
Steel Service Center Institute, 984
Steel Shipping Container Institute, 249
Stendig Industries Inc., 424
Stenograph Corp., 959
Sterling Drug Co., 781
Sterling Inc., 513
Sterling Optical Corp., 277
Sterling Silversmiths Guild of America, 1000
Sterling Supply Corp., 530
Jacob Stern & Sons, Inc., 4, 719
Stern Metals, Inc., 609
Steuart Petroleum Co., 395
J. P. Stevens & Co., Inc., 326
Stevens Graphics Corp., 739
Harry M. Stevens, Inc., 237, 374
Stewart & Stevenson Services, Inc., 317

Stewart's Ice Cream Co., Inc., 454
Stewart-Warner Corp., 553, 742
Stimson Lane Wine and Spirits Ltd., 542
Stone Construction Equipment, Inc., 792
Stone Container Corp., 250, 744
Stop & Shop Holdings Inc., 994
Storage Council, 634
Storer Communications, Inc., 160
Stores, 893
Stotler Group Inc., 224
Stouffer Hotel Co., 453
Strategic Planning Associates, Inc., 571, 828
Strategic Planning for Magazine Executives, 757
W. F. Straub & Co., 447
Stride Rite Corp., 956
Strings, 652
Stroh Brewery Co., 147
Structural Dynamics Research Corp., 228
Stryker Corp., 596
D. A. Stuart Ltd., 553
Stuart Petroleum Co., 395
Studies in Operations Research, 724
Studley Products Co., Inc., 744
Stur-Dee Health Products, Inc., 1096
Sturm Ruger & Co., Inc., 348
Subaru of America, Inc., 105
Submersible Wastewater Pump Association, 849
Suburban Newspapers of America, 678
Suburban Propane, 833
Successful Woman in Business, 1128
The Sugar Association, Inc., 988
Sugarbeet Grower, 989
Sugar Bulletin, 988
Sugar Journal, 989
Sugar Producer, 989

Sullivan and Cromwell, 533
Sullivan Graphics, Inc., 819
Summagraphics, 231
Sump and Sewage Pump Manufacturers Association, 849
Sunarhauserman, Inc., 712
Sunbeam Precision Measurements, 1111
Sunbelt Marketing Investment Corp., 351
Sunbelt Nursery Group Inc., 409
Sunbelt Vending and OCS, 1080
Sun Co., Inc., 311
Sun-Diamond Growers of California, 700
Sundstrand Data Control, Inc., 107
Sun Electric Corp., 100
Sunkist Growers, 391
Sun-Land Products of California, 394
Super Automotive Service, 406, 1032
Supercon, Inc., 992
Superconductor Applications Association, 991
Superconductor Industry, 991
Superconductor Week, 991
Super Food Services, Inc., 428
Superior Brands, Inc., 767
Supermarket News, 993
Supermarket Strategic Alert, 993
Suppliers of Advanced Composite Materials Association, 586
Supply House Times, 798
Surplus International, 995
Surplus Record, 560, 995
Surrette America, 314
Survey Sampling, Inc., 580
Sutter Home Winery, Inc., 1121
Sverdrup Corp., 835, 865
Swank, Inc., 419
Jake Sweeney Automotive, Inc., 97
Swift-Eckrich, Inc., 593

Swift Instruments, Inc., 1111

Swimming Pool and Spa Dealer News, 997

Swimming Pool—Spa Age, 996

Swimming Pools Today, 997

Swine Practitioner, 998

Sybron Acquisition Co., 277

Symbol Technologies, Inc., 95, 502, 522

Synerjy, 313

Syntex Animal Health, Inc., 1088

Synthesis of Highway Practice, 1042

Syntrex Inc., 705

Syracuse Supply Co., 437

Sysco Corp., 368

System Safety Society, 917

Systems Builders Association, 149

Systems Management American Corp., 705

Tab Products Co., 712

Taco, Inc., 968

Tag and Label Manufacturers Institute, 521

Takashimaya, Inc., 692

Talon Inc., 203

Tandy Corp., 246

Tapjac Home Centers, 445

TAPPI, 745

TAPPI Information Resources Center, 738, 743

Target Marketing, 282

Tatung Co. of America, Inc., 67

Taubman Co., Inc., 865

Tax Adviser, 1004

Tax Executives Institute, 1003

Tax Foundation, 1004

Tax Management Estates, Gifts and Trusts Journal, 1063

Taylor Wine Co., 1121

Tea and Coffee Trade Journal, 206

Tea Board of India, 206

Tea Council of the United States of America, 127, 206

J. J. Teaparty, 212

Tea Talk, 206

Technical Ceramics Manufacturers Association, 177

Technical Education News, 294

Technical Marketing Society of America, 578

Technology Management Action, 1008

Technology Transfer Society, 1007

TechTrends, 1047

Techtron, 424

Tecumseh Products Co., 317, 851

Tejon Ranch Co., 173

Teknor Apex Co., 1033

Telecom Corp., 692

Telecom Gear, 1011

Telecom Insider, 1011

Telecommunications Alert, 1011

Telecommunications Cooperative Network, 1010

Telecommunications Industry Association, 1010

Telecommunications Product Review and CPE Strategies, 1011

Telecommunications Reports, 1092

Telecommunications Week, 1011

Telecredit, Inc., 263

Teleflora, 360

Telemarketer, 1013

Telemarketing, 1013

The Telemarketing Co., 1014

Telemarketing Update, 1014

Telephone Marketing Services, 1014

Telephone Selling Report, 1014

Television, Audio & Appliance Dealer, 66

Television Bureau of Advertising, 18

Telocator, The Mobile Communications Industry Association, 628

Telsmith, Inc., 856

Temco Service Industries Inc., 52, 566

Tempglass, Inc., 421

Temple-Inland Forest Products Corp., 340

Tencon Inc., 961

Tenneco Oil Co., 411, 770, 770

Tennessee Gas Pipeline Co., 661

Tennessee Woolen Mills, 1135

Terex Corp., 617

Terra International, Inc., 33

Testor Corp., 443

Tests in Print, 1024

Texaco Chemical Co., 770

Texaco Inc., 777

Texas Gas Transmission Corp., 662, 790

Texas Instruments Inc., 950

Texas Utilities Electric Co., 301

Textile Business Outlook, 324

Textile Chemist and Colorist, 324

Textile Distributors Association, 324

Textile Fibers and By-Products Association, 338

Textile Laundry Council, 528

Textile Manufacturing, 324

Textile Pricing Outlook, 1148

Textile Research Journal, 324

Textron Inc., 26, 272

Theatre Equipment Association, 641

Theodore Presser Co., 656

Thermadyne Industries, 1114

Thermal Insulation Manufacturers Association, 479

Thermo Electron Corp., 211

Thermometer Corp. of America, 1111

Thiokol Corp., 272

Third Branch, 260

33 Metal Producing, 605

Roy Thomas, Inc., 283

Thomas Industries Inc., 540, 850

J. Walter Thompson Co., 21

K. W. Thompson Co., Inc., 348

F. M. Thorpe Manufacturing Co., 987

Thrall Car Manufacturing Co., 861

3Com Corp., 548

Thrift Drug Co., 289

Thrifty Rent-A-Car System, Inc., 102

Thunderbird Products Corp., 135

Tilcon Inc., 175, 240

Tile and Decorative Surfaces, 1029

Tile Council of America, 1029

Timber Harvesting, 376

Timberland Co., 956

Timber Processing, 376

Timber Producer, 376

Time, Inc., 758

Time-Life Books, Inc., 140

Timken Co., 125, 606, 986

Tin Research Institute, 605

Tiny Tots, 443

Tire and Rim Association, 1031

Tire and Tube Import and Export Report, 1031

Tire Business, 1032

Tire Retread Information Bureau, 1030

Tire Review, 1032

Tishman Construction Corp., 707

Titan Corp., 81

Titanium Development Association, 605

TJX Companies, Inc., 203

TMA Tobacco Weekly, 1035

TMI Fulfillment, 1014

TNT Ltd., 43

TNT Red Star Express, Inc., 1062

Tobacco Associates, 1034

Tobacco Growers' Information Committee, 1034

Tobacco Industry Litigation Reporter, 1035

Tobacco Institute, 1034

Tobacco Merchants Association of United States, 1034

Tobacconists' Association of America, 1034

Tobacco Reporter, 1035

Toccoa Casket Co., 397

Today's Farmer, 31

Today's Investor, 939

Todd Shipyards Corp., 954

Together, Inc., 29

R. Tolerton Co., 295

Tom Thumb Stores, Inc., 994

Tone Bros. Inc, 208, 976

Tonka Corp., 1038

Tootsie Roll Industries, Inc., 165

Topics in Veterinary Medicine, 1087

Toshiba America, Inc., 67, 246, 1012

Toshiba America Information Systems, Inc., 253, 328

Tow-Age, 1061

Towers, Perrin, Forster & Crosby, Inc., 572, 828

Towle Manufacturing Co., 1002

Toy and Hobby Wholesalers Association of America, 1037

Toy & Hobby World, 442, 1037

Toy Manufacturers of America, 1037

Toyota Motor Manufacturing USA, Inc., 105

Toy Shop, 1038

Toys R Us Inc., 1038

Toy Trade News, 1038

TPI Enterprises, Inc., 641

TPQ: The Tube & Pipe Quarterly, 787

Tracor, Inc., 272

Trade Show Bureau, 1040

TradeShow Convention Guide, 1041

Trade Shows & Exhibits Schedule, 1041

Traditional Industries, Inc., 784

Traffic Management, 1043

Traffic Safety, 1045

Traffic Safety Series, 1046

Training, 1047

Training & Development, 1048

Training Directors' Forum, 1047

Training Trends, 1048

Translation, 1050

Translation Services Directory, 1050

Translators' and Interpreters' Educational Society, 1049

Transmedia Network Inc., 121

Transportation in America, 387

Transportation Research Board, 844

Transport Fleet News, 1061

Transport International Pool, Inc., 884

Transtechnology Corp., 1111

Trans World Airlines Inc., 45

Travel Agent Magazine, 1051

TravelAge West, 1051

Travel & Tourism Executive Report, 1055

Travel and Tourism Research Association, 1054

Travelers Corp., 491

Travelers Insurance Co., 486

Travelers Relocation Corp., 883

Travel Expense Management, 1055

Travel Industry Association of America, 1054

Travel Marketing and Agency Management Guidelines, 1051

Travel News, 53

Travelware, 554

Treasury Manager, 170, 342

Tree of Life, Inc., 441

Trek Bicycle Corp., 130

Tremco Inc., 14, 469

Trial, 532

Triangle Pacific Corp., 356

Tribune Co., 680

Tri-Chem, Inc., 443

Trinity Industries, Inc., 250

Trinova Corp., 850

Tri-Pack Corp., 737

Triple H Fish Farms, 69

Tri/Valley Growers Inc., 167, 394

Albert Trostel and Sons Co., 535, 1071

Truck Cap Industry Association, 1057

Truckers-USA, 1057

Truck Renting and Leasing Association, 1060

Trucks, 1061

Truckstops of America, 411

Truck Trailer Manufacturers Association, 1057

Trump Organization, 707

Trusts and Estates, 1063

Trust Services of America, Inc., 305

TRW, Inc., 235, 264

TRW Space & Defense Sector, 272

TSR Hotline, 1013

TTX Co., 861

Tube and Pipe Fabricators Association, International, 787

Tube Council of North America, 734

Turkey World, 808

Turnaround Management Association, 112

Turner Broadcasting System, Inc., 1018

Tuscarora Plastics, Inc., 795

TV Technology, 1017

Twentieth Century-Fox Film Corp., 640, 656

Twentieth Century Investors, Inc., 659

21 International Holdings, 712

TW Services, Inc., 374

Tyco Laboratories, Inc., 351

Tyco Toys, Inc., 1038

U: The National College Newspaper, 216

Uarco Inc., 379

UFAC 1992, 1070

U-Haul International, Inc., 637

Ultrasonic Imaging, 1064

Ultrasonic Industry Association, 1064

Ultrasonics Symposium, 1064

Underwriters Laboratories, 523, 831

Underwriters Salvage Co., 100

Unemployment Insurance Reports with Social Security, 1069

Uniforce Temporary Personnel, Inc., 1021

Uniform Code Council, 93

Union Camp Corp., 747

Union Carbide Corp., 188, 795

Union Equity Co-operative Exchange, 1118

Union Orthotics & Prosthetics Co., 837

Union Pacific Corp., 606

Uniroyal Goodrich Tire Co., 1033

Uniservice Corp., 397

United Airlines Employees Credit Union, 266

United Airlines Inc., 46

United Artists Entertainment Co., 641

United Association of Journeymen and Apprentices. Plumbing Industry, 797

United Brotherhood of Carpenters and Joiners of America, 527

United Bus Owners of America, 644

United Cities Gas Co., 833

United Dominion Industries Ltd., 151

United Engineering Trustees, 315

United Engineers and Constructors International, Inc., 191

United Farm Workers of America, 36

United Food and Commercial Workers International Union, 527

United Fresh Fruit and Vegetable Association, 391

United Gas Pipe Line Co., 662

United Liquors Ltd., 542

United Mortgage Bankers of America, 633

United Mutual Fund Selector, 658

United Parcel Service of America, Inc., 388

United Process, Inc., 685

United Rubber, Cork, Linoleum and Plastic Workers of America, 913

United Shipowners of America, 952

United States Advanced Ceramics Association, 177

United States Banknote Corp., 804

United States Cheese Makers Association, 182

United States Conference of Mayors, 649

United States Distribution Journal, 164

United States League of Savings Institutions, 928

United States Leather Holdings, Inc., 535

United States Luggage Corp., 555

United States Meat Export Federation, 591

United States Space Foundation, 25

United States Testing Co., Inc., 854

United Stationers Inc., 709

United Supplies, Inc., 999

United Technologies Corp., 26, 49, 272

United Telecommunications, Inc., 1012
Unitrode Corp., 178
Universal Group Ltd., 11
Universal Health Services, Inc., 450
Universal Luggage Co., Inc., 555
Universal-Rundle Corp., 799
University Microfilms Inc., 614
University of California, Berkeley, 725
University of Pennsylvania, 725
UOP, 770
Upholstery Design & Manufacturing, 1070
Upjohn Co., 781
Urban Transportation Monitor, 1043
Urban Transport News, 844
URS Corp., 1106
USAir Inc., 46
U.S. Army Corps of Engineers Information Exchange Bulletin, 1108
U.S. Auto Glass Centers, Inc., 407
U.S. Cellular Corp., 629
US Custom House Guide, 1108
Used Car Dealer, 96
Used Equipment Directory, 471
Used Truck Sales Network, 1057
U.S. Feed Grains Council, 333
US Glass, Metal & Glazing, 420
U.S. Hide, Skin and Leather Association, 534
US Immigration, 461
US Industrial Export Directory, 463
US Leasing International, Inc., 884
US Lodging Industry, 452
US Medicine, 439
US Non-Alcoholic Beverage Market, 127
U.S. Pipe & Foundry Co., 788
US Rail News, 860

US West NewVector Group, Inc., 629
U.S. Wheat Associates, 1117
U.S. Shoe Corp., 956
USX Corp., 206
Utica Cutlery Co., 1001
Utility Construction and Maintenance, 847

Vacco Industries, 695
Vacuum Cleaner Manufacturers Association, 65
Vacuum Dealers Trade Association, 65
Valero Natural Gas Partners, L.P., 662
Valid Logic Systems Inc., 228
Vallen Corp., 920
Valleylab, Inc., 596
Valley Packing Service, 394
Valmont Industries, Inc., 540
Valspar Corp., 742
Valuation Research Corp., 1077
Value Merchants, Inc., 996
Value Retail News, 893
Valve Magazine, 1078
Valve Manufacturers Association of America, 1078
Vanderbilt Rubber Handbook, 914
Vanguard Cellular Systems, Inc., 629
Vanier Graphics Corp., 379
Varian Associates, 934, 950
Vari-Care Inc., 698
Variety, 639, 655
Varlen Corp., 773
Vawtpower Inc., 314
Vecellio & Grogan, Inc., 88
Vega Biotechnologies, Inc., 133
Vegetable and Specialty Crop Situation and Outlook, 392
Vehicle Leasing Today, 102
Vending Times, 1080
Vendors Exchange, 1080

Vengroff Williams & Association Inc./Western Division, 215
Ventura Software, Inc., 280
Venture Capital Journal Venture Economics, Inc., 1082
Venture Dyne Ltd., 323
Vernon Co., 815
Vertical Software Systems, Inc., 959
Vestro Foods Inc., 441
Veterinary Economics, 1087
Veterinary Forum, 1087
Veterinary Medicine, 1087
Veterinary Reference Laboratories, Inc., 1088
Vetter Products, Inc., 648
VF Corp., 203, 1066
Vibration Mountings & Controls Inc., 686
Video Business, 1090
Videocart Inc., 924
Video Software Dealers Association, 91
Video Specialist Newsletter, 1090
Video Station Inc., 1090
Videotex Industry Association, 1091
VIDION/International Association of Video, 1089
ViewText, 1092
Vigoro Industries, Inc., 337
Vineyard and Wine Management, 1120
Vinson and Elkins, 533
Vinson Supply Co., 773, 788, 1078
Vintage Sales Stables, Inc., 546
Vinyl Plastics, Inc., 1029
Virco Manufacturing Corp., 712
Vision Council of America, 726
Vitamin Products Co., 1097
Vivitar Corp., 785
VM & SD, 987
Vocational Training News, 294
Vogel and Fey Farms, Inc., 34
Volkswagen of America, Inc., 105

Volt Delta Resources, Inc., 235
Volvo North America Corp., 105
Vons Companies, Inc., 994
Vulcan-Hart Corp., 370
Vulcan Materials Co., 88
VWR Corp., 524

Wackenhut Corp., 52, 944
Tom W. Wade Co., 1118
Walbridge Aldinger Co., 151
Walden Book Co., Inc., 142
Waldo Farms, 999
Walgreen Co., 289
Wallace Computer Services Inc., 379
Wallcovering Distributors Association, 1097
Wallcovering Manufacturers Association, 1097
Wallcoverings, 1098
Wall-Rogalsky Milling Co., 1118
Walls & Ceilings, 791
Wall Street Journal, 506
Wal-Mart Stores, Inc., 894
Wang Laboratories, Inc., 1137
S. G. Warburg & Co., Inc., 504, 508, 941
Ward's Engine Update and Vehicle Technology, 316
Warner Bros. Inc., 640
Warner Brothers Records Co., 870
Warner-Lambert Co., 767, 781
Washington National Insurance Co., 489
Washington Post Co., 680
Washington State Apple Commission, 391
Waste Management, Inc., 1106
Waste Treatment Technology News, 1105
Watch and Clock Review, 198
Water and Sewer Distributors of America, 847
Water and Wastewater Equipment Manufacturers Association, 847

Water Farming Journal, 68
Water Pollution Control Federation, 321
Water Ski Industry Association, 978
Water Transport Association, 1108
Waterways Journal, 2208
Watkins Oil Co., Inc., 395
J. C. Watson Co., 806
Watts Industries Inc., 1078
Weber Marking Systems, Inc., 522
Webster Industries, Inc., 737
Wedding Photographer, 783
Weed Science Society of America, 35
Weekly Cotton Trade Report, 258
Weekly Livestock Reporter, 545
Weekly Propane Newsletter, 833
Weekly Review of the Market, 989
Weksler Instruments Corp., 934
Welbilt Corp., 41, 371
Welch Allyn, Inc., 726
Welding-Brazing-Soldering Digest, 1112
Welding Design and Fabrication, 1112
Welding Distributor, 1112
Welding Journal, 1112
Welding Research News, 1113
Well Gotshal and Manges, 533
Wellington Fund, Inc., 659
Wellman, Inc., 340
Welsbach Electric Corp., 1044
Wendy's International Inc., 891
Wenger Corp., 656
Werner Enterprises, Inc., 1062
West Coast Grocery Co., 428
Western Auto Supply Co., 123, 180, 1033
Western Floors, 355
Western Livestock Reporter, 545
Western Mobile News, 626, 906
Western Optical Corp., 727
Western Paper Co., 819

Western Publishing Group, Inc., 140
Western Salt Co., 926
Western Savings & Loan Association, 930
Western Wooden Box Association, 143
West Homestead Engineering & Machine Co., 559
Westin, Inc., 723, 926
Westinghouse Broadcasting Co., 858, 1019
Westinghouse Electric Corp., 235
Roy F. Weston, Inc., 323, 525
West Point-Pepperell, Inc., 326
Westvaco Corp., 144, 747
Weyerhaeuser Co., 377, 747
Wheat Gluten Industry Council, 1117
Wheat Grower, 1117
Wheat Life, 1118
Wheaton Industries, 1002
Wheat Quality Council, 1117
Wheat Situation and Outlook, 1118
Wheat Technology, 1118
Wheelabrator Technologies Inc., 311
Wheeling-Pittsburgh Steel Corp., 986
White Castle System Inc., 891
White Consolidated Industries, Inc., 472
Whiting-Turner Contracting Co., 151
Whole Foods, 441
Wholesale Florists and Florist Suppliers of America, 360
Who's Who in the Egg and Poultry Industries, 808
Whyco Chromium Co., 600
Wichert Tile, Ltd., 856
Wick Building Systems, Inc., 627
Wickes Companies, Inc., 100, 445
Wiland Services Inc., 283

Wilbur Curtis Co., Inc., 206
Wilfred American Educational Corp., 1049
Willamette Industries, Inc., 144, 377, 744
Willert Home Products, 764
Williams Companies, 662, 790
Willis Corroon Corp., 493
Wilson Industries, Inc., 472, 773
Wilson Jones Co., 379
Wilson Sporting Goods, 979
Wilton Corp., 1132
Win, 403
Wind Energy News, 313
Windsor Funds, Inc., 659
Wine and Spirits Shippers Association, 541
Wine and Spirits Wholesalers of America, 541
Wine Appreciation Guild, 1119
Wine Institute, 1120
Wine Investor: Buyers' Guide, 1120
Wines and Vines, 1120
Winn-Dixie Stores, Inc., 428
Wire Association International, 1122
Wire Fabricators Association, 1122
Wire Industry News, 1123
Wire Industry Suppliers Association, 1122
Wire Journal International, 1123
Wire Technology International, 1123
Wisconsin Bell, Inc., 1012
Wisconsin Dairies Co-Op, 183
Wisconsin Knife Works, 1132
Wisconsin Paperboard Corp., 750
Wisconsin Power & Light Co., 848
Wisconsin Toy Co., Inc., 995
Witco Corp., 588
Wolcott & Lincoln Inc., 224
A. R. Wolfson Associates, 598
Wolverine World Wide Inc., 956

Woman's Enterprise, 1129
Women in Cable, 158
Women in Management, 1128
Women's Wear Daily, 201, 329
Woodland Farms, Inc., 34
Wood Machinery Manufacturers of America, 1130
Woodwork Corp. of America, 1132
Woodworker's Journal, 1131
Woodworking Machinery Distributors Association, 1130
Woodworking Machinery Importers Association of America, 1130
Wool Bureau, 1134
Wool Manufacturers Council, 1134
Wool Sack, 1134
Worcester Co., 1135
WordPerfect Corp., 235, 280, 1137
WordPerfect Magazine, 1136
Word Progress, 1136
Workers' Compensation Law Reporter, 1138
Worker's Compensation Law Review, 1138
Working Press of the Nation, 679
Working Woman, 1129
World Aluminium Databook, 62
World Aluminum Abstracts, 62
World Aquaculture Society, 68
World Carpets, Inc., 169
World Coffee & Tea, 206
World Cogeneration, 210
World Color Press, Inc., 819
World Export Processing Zones Association, 462
World Footwear, 956
World International Nail and Beauty Association, 118
World Leather, 534
World Military Avionics Inventory & Forecast, 107
World Modeling Association, 329

World Oil, 776
World Sign Associates, 960
Writer, 1142
Writer's Digest, 1142
Writing Instrument Manufacturers Association, 1143
Wurzburg, Inc., 522
Wyoming Wool Grower, 1134

Xerox Corp., 253, 328, 1137
X-Rite, Inc., 854
Xsirius Superconductivity Inc., 992

Yachting, 135
Yamaha Music Manufacturing Inc. USA, 653
The Daniel Yankelovich Group, Inc., 841
Year Book Medical Publishers, Inc., 758
Yellow Book News, 397
Yellow Cab Co., 1006
Yellow Pages Publishers Association, 18
York Group, Inc., 398
Yosemite Park & Curry Co., 237
Young & Rubicam Inc., 21
Young Entrepreneurs Organization, 319
Young-Phillips Sales Co., 424
Yuasa Exide Battery Corp., 648

H. B. Zachry Co., 52, 791
Zale Corp., 413, 513
Zapata Haynie Corp., 353
Zebra Technologies Corp., 95
Zeigler Brothers, Inc., 69
Ziff-Davis Publishing Co., 758
Zimmerman Sign Co., 961
Zinetics Medical, Inc., 596

INDEX OF SUBJECTS

Abrasives, 1–2
Accident insurance, 486–89
Accounting, 5–8
  actuarial science and, 8–9
  internal auditing, 498
  taxation and, 1003–5
  see also specific states
Acids, 3–4
Acquisitions, 597–98
  see also Investment banking;
    Securities
Actuarial science, 8–9
Addiction, 59–61
Additives, 10–12
  perfumes, 254–57
Adhesives, 12–14, 469
Adult education, 15–16
Advertising, 17–21
  see also Marketing; Sales pro-
    motion
Aerosols, 21–24
Aerospace, 24–26
  airplane industry, 47–50
  airports, 50–52
  avionics and, 106–8
  helicopter industry, 47–50
Affirmative action, 29–30
Affluent consumers, 247
Agriculture, 30–37
  alternative and organic farming,
    34
  chemicals in, 32, 33, 34–35
  dairy industry, 267–69
  economics and research in, 35
  farms, 33–34
  feed industry and grain, 333–35

  fertilizers in, 336–38
  fruit and vegetable industry,
    389–94
  irrigation in, 35–36
  labor in, 36
  machinery for, 36–37
  nut industry, 698–701
  onion and garlic industry,
    722–24
  pesticides in, 762–65
  potato industry, 805–6
  poultry industry, 807–9
  seed industry and, 945–47
  soybean industry, 974–75
  wheat industry, 1117–19
  see also Foods and food indus-
    try; Livestock
AIDS, 27–28
Air conditioning, 37–41, 797–99
Air freight, 41–43
  see also Freight transportation
Airline industry, 44–46
Air pilots, 46–47
Airplane industry, 47–50
  see also Aerospace
Airports, 50–52
  concessions in, 51, 236–37
  see also Aerospace
Air travel, 52–53
Alabama, 54–56
Alaska, 56–58
Alcohol abuse, 59–61
Almonds, 698, 700
Alternative energy, 312–14
  cogeneration and, 209–11
Alternative farming, 34

Aluminum, 61–63
  see also Metals
Antiques, 78–79
  auctions and, 89–90
Antitrust, 63–64
Apparel, *see* Clothing
Apple cider, 126
Apple computers, 233
Apples, 390
Appliances, 65–67
  consumer electronics, 244–46
Appraisal and valuation, 1074–77
  of real estate, 862–65
Apricots, 389
Aquaculture, 68–69
  see also Fish and seafood indus-
    try
Arbitration, 70–71
Archery equipment, 977
Architecture, 71–72
Archives, 871–72
Arizona, 72–75
Arkansas, 75–77
Arms, *see* Weapons
Army–Navy stores, 995
Art:
  commercial, 220–21
  computer graphics, 229–31
Artificial intelligence, 80–82
  see also Computers
Artificial limbs, 836–37
Art market, 78–79
  auctions and, 89–90
Arts management, 82–83
Asbestos, 84–86
  see also Product liability

Asphalt, 86–88
Assessment (appraisal), 1074–77
    of real estate, 862–65
Astronautics, 24–26
Athletic equipment, 977–80
Auctions, 89–90
Audio engineering, 868–70
Audiovisual industry, 90–93
Auditing, internal, 498
Automatic identification, 93–95
    label industry and, 521–22
    point-of-sale   industry   and,
        799–800
Automobile dealers, 95–97
Automobile equipment, 98–101
    batteries, 121–24
    lubrication of, 552–54
    tires, 1031–33
    trucks and truck trailers, 1056–59
Automobile insurance, 481–83
Automobile lease/rental services,
    101–3
Automotive industry, 103–6
    buses, 644–46
    motorcycles, 646–48
    recreational vehicles, 872–74
    see also specific states under
        Motor Vehicles
Automotive repairs, 405–7
Avionics, 106–8

Bags, paper and plastic, 743–44
Baking industry, 108–11
    flour and, 363–64
Ball bearings, 124–25
Bananas, 390
Bankruptcy, 111–12
Banks and banking, 113–17
    credit unions, 265–66
    investment, 502–4
    mortgages and, 633–35
    savings and loan associations,
        928–30
    see also specific states under
        Banking

Barbecue equipment, 874
Barber shops, 118–19
Bar-codes, 93–95
    label industry and, 521–22
Barrels, 249
Barter, 120–21
Batteries, 121–24
    see also Automobile equipment
Bearings, 124–25
Beauty shops, 118–19
Beef:
    cattle industry and, 171–73
    meat industry and, 590–93
    see also Livestock
Beekeeping, 446–47
Beer, 145–47
Beet sugar, 988–90
Beverages, 126–28
    beer, 145–47
    coffee and tea, 206–8
    dairy products, 267–69
    liquor and spirits, 540–42
    wine, 1119–22
Bicycles, 129–30
Billiards, 977
Biomass, 312
Biotechnology, 131–33
Blueberries, 391
Boats, 133–35
    see also Ships and shipping
Bonds, 937–41
Bookbinding, 136–37
    printing and, 815–19
Book publishing, 138–40
Bookselling, 141–42
Bowling equipment, 977
Boxes, 143–44
    see also Containers
Brass, 604
Brewing, 145–47
    see also Beverages; Liquor and
        spirits
Bronze, 604
Budgeting, 148
Building industry, 149–52

    carpenters, 1130–33
    roofing and, 910–13
    see also Plumbing
Building maintenance, 565–67
    cleaning and cleaning products
        in, 195–97
Building materials, 152–55
    asphalt, 86–88
    cement, 174–76
    concrete, 238–40
    plaster, 791–92
Burglar alarms, 941–44
Buses, 644–46
    see also Automotive industry;
        Public transportation
Business education, 292–93
Business ethics, 155–56
Business forms, 378–79
Business history, 156–57
Business law, 157
    see also Law and lawyers; spe-
        cific states under Attorney
        General
Butane, 832–33
    see also Natural gas
Butter, 267–69

Cable television, 158–60
    see also Television broadcasting
Cadmium, 604
Cafeterias, 889
California, 160–62
Camping and campgrounds, 875,
    877
Candy, 163–65
Canned food, 165–67
    food machinery and equipment
        and, 368–71
    see also Foods and food industry
Canoes, 977
Carbonated beverages, 126–28
Carnivals, 236–37
Carpenters, 1130–33
Carpets, 168–69
Cartons, 143–44

Cash management, 170

Casinos, 403–4

Castings, 381–83

Casualty insurance, 483–86

Cattle, 171–73

 see also Livestock

CD-ROM, 478, 479

Cellular telephones, 628–30

Cement, 174–76

 see also Concrete

Census data, 176

Ceramics, 177–78

Certified Financial Planners, 345–46

Chain stores, 179–80

Chambers of Commerce, 181

Charcoal, 874

Cheese, 181–84

 see also Dairy products

Chemical engineering, 184–85

Chemical industry, 186–88

Chemicals, agricultural, 32, 33, 34–35

 pesticides, 762–65

Cherries, 390

Chickens, 807–9

Child care, 189–90

China, 417–18, 1000–1002

Cigarettes, 1033–36

Cigars, 1033–36

Cinema:

 motion picture industry, 638–40

 motion picture theaters, 641–42

Citrus fruit, 391

Civil engineering, 190–91

Civil service, 192

 see also Federal government; Municipal government; *specific states*

Clay, 193–94

Cleaning products and services, 195–97

 building maintenance and, 565–67

 laundry and dry cleaning, 528–30

sanitation industry, 926–28

Clerical workers, 935–36

Clocks, 198–99

Close-out dealers, 994–96

Clothing, 200–203

 fashion industry and, 329–30

 furs, 398–99

 shoes, 955–57

 underwear, hosiery, and intimate apparel, 1065–67

Coal, 204–6

 see also Energy

Coatings:

 industrial, 12–14, 467–69

 metal finishing, 599–601

 paint and painting, 740–42

Coffee, 206–8

 see also Beverages

Coffee machines, 1079

Cogeneration, 209–11

 see also Alternative energy

Coins, 211–13

Collectibles, 211–14

 art and antiques, 78–79

 auctions of, 89–90

Collection agencies, 214–16

Collective bargaining, 70–71

Colleges, 216–17

 see also Education

Colorado, 217–20

Comex, 222

Commercial art, 220–21

 graphic arts, 422–24

Commodity futures, 222–24

Compensation and pay, 224–25

Compressors, 849–50

Computer-aided design/manufacturing/engineering (CAD/CAM/CAE), 226–28

 robots in, 907–10

Computer graphics, 229–31

 see also Desktop publishing

Computers, 231–36

 artificial intelligence and, 80–82

hardware companies, 234

local area networks and, 547–49

management information systems and (MIS), 572–74

repair and maintenance of, 235

semiconductor industry and, 947–50

software companies, 234–35

telecommunications and, 1009–13

Computer system security, 232

Computer viruses, 232

Concessions, 51, 236–37

Concrete, 238–40

 see also Cement

Confectionery, 163–65

Connecticut, 240–43

Construction, *see* Building industry; Building materials

Consultants, 243–44

 management, 570–72

Consumer electronics, 244–46

 appliances, 65–67

Consumers, 247–48

 population and demographic data on, 801–2

 see also Market research and statistics; *specific states under Consumer Affairs*

Contact lenses, 725–28

Containers, 249–51

 boxes, 143–44

Continuing education, 15–16

Contractors, 149–52

Controllers, 343

Convenience stores, 180, 992–94

 grocery business and, 426–28

 see also Retail trade

Conventions, 1039–41

Copper, 603

Copying machines, 251–53

 see also Office equipment and supplies

Copyrights, 494–96, 654

Corporate finance, 341–42

Cosmetics, 254–57
Cotton, 257–59
Countertrade, 120–21
Court reporting services, 959
Courts, 259–60
   see also Law and lawyers
Craft supplies, 442–43
Creativity, 261
Credit, 262–64
Credit unions, 265–66
Crime, security and detective ser-
   vices and, 941–44
Cutlery, 1000–1002

Dairy industry, 267–69
   cheese, 181–84
   ice cream, 453–54
Data processing, 231–36
Debt collection, 214–16
Defense industries, 270–72
Delaware, 273–75
Demographics, 801–2
Dental industry, 275–78
Design, computer-aided (CAD),
   226–28
Desktop publishing, 278–80
   computer graphics and, 229–31
Detective services and equip-
   ment, 941–44
Detergents, 195–97
Diet industry, 1095–97
   see also Health food
Direct mail and marketing,
   281–83
   see also Marketing
Directory publishers, 138–40
Disability:
   employee benefits and, 302–5
   Social Security and, 965–66
Displays, store, 18, 987–88
Distributors, 283–84
   material handling and, 588–90
District of Columbia, 285–87
Do-it-yourself industry, 444–46
   see also Hardware

Dolls, 1037–39
Doors, 152
Drug abuse, 59–61
Drugs (pharmaceuticals), 778–81
Drug stores, 287–89
Dry cleaning, 528–30
Drywall, 791–92
Duplicating machines, 251–53
   see also Office equipment and
     supplies
Duty-free concessions, 51, 236–
   37

Econometrics, 291–92
Economics, 290–92
   agricultural, 35
Editing, see Writing and editing
Education, 292–96
   adult or continuing, 15–16
   business, 292–93
   at colleges and universities,
     216–17
   personnel training, 1047–49
   schools and, 930–32
   technical and vocational,
     294–95
   testing in, 1024–25
   see also specific states under
     Education
Efficiency, operations research
   and, 724–25
Electrical engineering, 296–97
Electric equipment, 297–99
Electric power, 300–302
   public utilities and, 846–48
   superconductors and, 991–92
   see also Energy
Electronics, consumer, 244–46
Electroplating, 467, 599–601
Emigration, 460–61
Employee benefits, 302–5
   actuarial science and, 8–9
   compensation and pay, 224–25
   pensions and profit sharing
     plans, 754–56

   stock ownership plans, 305–6
Employees:
   industrial hygiene and, 473–74
   relocation of, 882–83; see
   also Moving industry
   training of, 15–16, 1047–49
   see also Personnel management
Employment services, 306–9
   temporary employees and,
     1019–21
Energy, 309–14
   alternative, 312–14
   coal, 204–6
   cogeneration and, 209–11
   conventional, 309–11
   electric power, 300–302
   fuel oil, 394–95
   gasoline, 410–11
   natural gas, 659–62
   nuclear, 693–95
   petroleum, 774–77
   propane and butane, 832–33
   solar, 966–68
   utility companies and, 846–48
   see also specific states under
     Energy
Engineering, 315
   audio, 868–70
   chemical, 184–85
   civil, 190–91
   computer-aided (CAE), 226–
     28
   electrical, 296–97
   sanitary, 926–28
   traffic, 1042–44
Engines, 316–18
Entrepreneurs, 318–20
   see also Self employment; Small
     businesses
Environmental conservation,
   320–23
   recycling, 61, 878–80
   waste management, 1104–7
   see also specific states under
     Environmental Affairs

Equal employment opportunity, 29–30

ERISA (Employee Retirement Income Security Act), 303

ESOPs (employee stock ownership plans), 305–6

Essential oils, 10–12, 254–57

Estate planning, 1062–63

Ethics, business, 155–56

Evaluation and testing, 1024–25

Executive search firms, 306–9

Exhibit halls, 1039–41

Expert systems, 80–82

Eye care, 725–28

Fabrics and textiles, 324–26
  cotton, 257–59
  fiber industry and, 338–40
  upholstery, 1070–71
  wool and worsted, 1133–35

Facility management, 834–36
  building maintenance and, 565–67

Facsimile (fax) machines, 327–28
  see also Office equipment and supplies

Fairs, 1039–41

Farms, 33–34
  see also Agriculture

Fashion industry, 200–203, 329–30
  see also Clothing

Fast food restaurants, 891

Fats, 717–19

Fatty acids, 3–4

FAX (facsimile) machines, 327–28

Federal government:
  Agriculture Department, 37
  Bureau of Mines, 63
  civil service and, 192
  Commerce Department, 2
  Customs Service, 49
  Defense Department, 272
  Education Department, 16
  Energy Department, 211

Environmental Protection Agency, 323
  Federal Communications Commission, 859
  Federal Trade Commission, 21
  Health and Human Services Department, 439
  Housing and Urban Development Department, 152
  Interior Department, 237
  International Trade Administration, 2
  International Trade Commission, 2
  Justice Department, 64
  Labor Department, 225
  National Institutes of Health, 28
  National Science Foundation, 235
  Patent and Trademark Office, 2
  Securities and Exchange Commission, 941
  Small Business Administration, 964
  telephone referral numbers for, 330–32
  Transportation Department, 43
  Treasury Department, 117
  Veterans Affairs Department, 295

Feed, for livestock, 333–35

Fertilizers, 336–38
  see also Agriculture

Fibers, 338–40
  see also Fabrics and textiles

Film industry, 638–40

Finance:
  cash management and, 170
  corporate, 341–42
  mergers and acquisitions and, 597–98
  public, 343–44

Financial analysts, 344–45
  see also Investments; Securities

Financial planning, 345–46

Financiers, 1081–83

Finishes, industrial, 467–69

Firearms, 347–49

Fire prevention and protection, 349–51

Fiscal issues, taxation and, 1003–5

Fish and seafood industry, 351–54
  aquaculture, 68–69

Fishing equipment, 977

Fitness centers, 874, 876

Fittings, 786–88

Flatware, 1000–1002

Flavorings, 10–12
  perfumes, 254–57

Floor coverings and floorings, 357
  carpets and rugs, 168–69
  tiles, 1029–30

Florida, 357–60

Florists, 360–62
  garden supply and plant nurseries and, 407–9

Flour, 363–64
  see also Baking industry

Flower industry, 360–62
  garden supply and plant nurseries and, 407–9

Food machinery and equipment, 368–71

Food preserving, 166

Foods and food industry, 365–68
  baked, 108–11
  candy, 163–65
  canned, 165–67
  cheese, 181–84
  dairy products, 267–69
  diet, 1095–97
  fish and seafood, 351–54
  flour, 363–64
  fruits and vegetables, 389–94
  health, 440–41
  honey, 446–47
  ice cream, 453–54
  kosher, 366
  macaroni and pasta, 556–57

Foods and food industry (*cont'd*)
    meat, 590–93; *see also* Cattle;
        Livestock; Sheep; Swine
    nuts, 698–701
    oils, fats, and margarine, 717–19
    onions and garlic, 722–24
    pet, 765–68
    pork, 998–99
    potatoes, 805–6
    poultry, 807–9
    rice, 900–902
    salt, 925–26
    soybeans, 974–75
    spices, 975–76
    sugar, 988–90
    wheat, 1117–19
    see also Beverages
Food services, 371–74
    restaurants, 889–92
    vending machines, 1079–81
Football equipment, 979
Footwear, 955–57
Foreign trade, 461–64
Forensic economists, 64
Forest products, 375–77
    paper and pulp, 745–48
    paperboard, 748
Forgings, 381–83
Forms for business, 378–79
    see also Office equipment and
        supplies
Foundations, 380–81
Foundries, 381–83
    see also Iron; Metals; Steel
Fragrances, 10–12
Franchises, 383–85
    see also Self employment; Small
        businesses
Fraud, security and detective ser-
    vices and, 941–44
Freedom of Information Act,
    385–86
Free-lance workers, 1019–21
Freight transportation, 386–88
    air freight, 41–43

by ship, 952–55
    trucking, 1059–62
Fruit and vegetable industry,
    389–94
    onions and garlic, 722–24
    potatoes, 805–6
Fuel oil, 394–95
    see also Petroleum
Funeral industry, 396–98
Furniture, 400–402
    office, 711–12
    upholstery for, 1070–71
Furs, 398–99

Gambling, 403–4
Games, 1037–39
Garages and service stations, 405–7
    gasoline industry and, 410–11
    lubrication industry and, 552–
        54
    see also Automobile equipment
        industry
Garden supply, 407–9
    florists and flower industry,
        360–62
Garlic, 722–24
Gasoline, 410–11
    at garages and service stations,
        405–7
    see also Petroleum industry
Gas propellants, 21–24
Gems, 412–14
    see also Jewelry
Genetic engineering, 131–33
Georgia, 414–17
Geothermal energy, 313
Gifts, 417–18
    greeting cards, 425–26
    novelties and souvenirs, 418,
        691–92
    tableware, 1000–1002
Glass and glass products, 419–21
    see also Tableware
Glues, 12–14
Gold, 811–13

Government:
    municipal, 648–50
    see also Federal government;
        specific states
Grains, 333–35
Granite, 855–56
Grant sources, 380–81
Grapes, 389
Graphic arts, 422–24
    commercial art and illustration,
        220–21
Graphics, computer, 229–31
Greeting cards, 425–26
    see also Gifts
Grills, barbecue, 874
Grinding products, 1–2
Grocery business, 426–28
Grocery industry:
    supermarkets and convenience
        stores, 180, 992–94
    see also Foods and food indus-
        try
Grounds management, 834–36
Gums, adhesive, 12–14

Handicapped people, affirmative
    action and equal employ-
    ment opportunity for, 29–30
Hardware, 429–31
    do-it-yourself or home improve-
        ment industry and, 444–46
Hardwood, 375–77
Hawaii, 431–33
Hazardous materials, 1104–7
Health care, 434–39
    AIDS and, 27–28
    dental industry, 275–78
    home, 436–37
    hospitals, 448–50
    long-term, 695–98
    medical and hospital equip-
        ment for, 593–96, 932–35
    mental health and, 434
    nursing homes, 695–98
    occupational therapy, 701–2

ophthalmic industry, 725–28
physicians, 438–39
preferred provider organizations (PPOs), 437–38
prosthetics, 836–37
see also specific states under Health and Occupational Health and Safety
Health food, 440–41
vitamin and diet industry and, 1095–97
Health insurance, 486–89
Medicare, 965–66
Health maintenance organizations (HMOs), 437–38
Health spas, 874, 996–98
Heating, 37–41, 797–99
Heating oil, 394–95
Helicopters, 47–50
see also Aerospace
Herbicides, 762
Highways, 904–7
History, business, 156–57
HMOs (health maintenance organizations), 437–38
Hobbies, 442–43
see also Collectibles; Toys
Home health care, 436–37
machinery for, 884
Home improvement, 444–46
see also Hardware
Honey, 446–47
Hosiery, 1065–67
see also Clothing
Hospitals, 448–50
equipment for, 593–96, 932–35
see also Health care; Nursing homes
Hotels, 451–53
Housewares, 65
Housing, 72
manufactured, 625–27
see also Building industry; Building materials
Human performance, 642–43

Human resources, 759–61
Hydroponics, 68

IBM and compatible microcomputers, 233
Ice cream, 453–54
Ice cream restaurants, 889
Idaho, 455–57
Illinois, 457–60
Illustration, 220–21
see also Commercial art
Immigration, 460–61
Import-export, 461–64
Incentives and premiums, 814–15
Indiana, 464–66
Industrial coatings, 467–69
paint, 740–42
Industrial control, 823–25
Industrial equipment, 470–72
machine tools, 559–61
Industrial hygiene, 473–74
Industrial relations, 475–77
labor unions and, 525–27
see also specific states under Labor
Information access laws, 385–86
Information industry, 477–79
Information management, *see* Records management
Inks, 820–21
Insecticides, 762
Instruments, musical, 650–53
Insulation, 479–81
Insurance:
actuarial science and, 8–9
automobile, 481–83
casualty and property, 483–86
health and accident, 486–89
life, 489–92
Medicare, 965–66
unemployment, 1068–69
see also specific states under Insurance
Insurance agents, 492–93
Integrated circuits, 947–50

Intellectual property, 494–96
inventions, 499–500
music, 654–57
Interior decoration, 496–97
Intermodel shipping, 249
Internal auditing, 498
Intimate apparel, 1065–67
see also Clothing
Inventions, 499–500
see also Intellectual property
Inventory control, 501–2
automatic identification and, 93–95
materials handling and, 588–90
operations research and, 724–25
point-of-sale equipment in, 799–800
Investigative services, 941–44
Investment banking, 502–4
mergers and acquisitions and, 597–98
see also Banks and banking; Securities
Investments, 504–8
commodity futures, 222–24
employee stock ownership plans, 305–6
financial analysts and, 344–45
mutual funds, 657–59
real estate, 865–67
securities, 937–41
trusts and estates and, 1062–63
venture capital, 1081–83
Iowa, 508–11
Iron, 983–86
foundries, 381–83
see also Metals
Irrigation, 35–36

Janitorial services, 565–67
see also Cleaning products and services
Jewelry, 511–13
gems and, 412–14

Journalism, 514–15
  see also Media; Writing and
    editing
Judges, 259–60
Juices, 126
Jukeboxes, 1080

Kansas, 515–17
Kennels, 765
Kentucky, 518–20
Kosher food products, 366

Label industry, 521–22
  see also Packaging
Laboratories, 523–25
  see also Medical and hospital
    equipment; Research and
    development
Labor relations, 475–77
Labor unions, 525–27
Lamb:
  meat industry and, 590–93
  sheep industry and, 950–51
Laminators, industrial, 467
Landscape architecture, 71
Land use, 862–65
Laundry, 528–30
Law and lawyers, 531–33
  antitrust, 63–64
  bankruptcy, 111–12
  business, 157
  information access and, 385–86
  trusts and estates and, 1062–63
Lawn products, 945–47
Lead, 604
Leasing services, 884–86
  automobile, 101–3
Leather, 533–35
Legal system:
  courts in, 259–60
  see also Law and lawyers
Leisure industry, 874–77
  gambling and casinos, 403–4
Lenses, ophthalmic, 725–28
Lettuce, 389

Liability, 829–30
Libraries, 536–37
  see also specific states under
    Library Services
Licensing, 881
Life insurance, 489–92
  see also Insurance agents
Lighting, 538–40
Limousines, 1006
Lingerie, 1065–67
  see also Clothing
Liquor and spirits, 540–42
  beer, 145–47
  wine, 1119–22
Liquor stores, 544–45
Liscensing, of technology, 1007–8
Livestock, 544–46
  cattle, 171–73
  feed for, 333–35
  meat industry and, 590–93
  sheep, 950–51
  swine, 998–99
  veterinary   products   and,
    1086–88
Local area networks, 547–49
  see also Computers; Telecom-
    munications
Locksmiths, 429–31
Long-term health care, 695–98
Louisiana, 549–51
Low-calorie foods, 1095–97
Lubrication, 552–54
  see also Garages and service sta-
    tions
Luggage, 554–55
Lumber, 375–77

Macaroni, 556–57
Machinery:
  farm, 36–37
  industrial, 470–72
Machine shops, 557–59
  metal working and, 607–9
Machine tools, 559–61
  industrial equipment, 470–72

Machine vision, 907
Magazines, 756–58
  journalism and, 514–15
  writing and editing, 1140–42
  see also Newsletters
Magnesium, 604
Mail, 803–4
Mailing lists, 281–83
Maine, 562–64
Maintenance of buildings, 565–67
  cleaning and cleaning products
    in, 195–97
Malls, 957–59
  see also Retail trade
Management, 567–69
  arts, 82–83
  office, 713
  personnel, 759–61
  sales, 920–21
Management consultants, 570–72
  see also Consultants
Management information systems
    (MIS), 572–74
Manufactured housing, 625–27
Manufacturer's   representatives,
    574–75
  see also Salespeople and sales
    techniques
Manufacturing:
  computer–aided (CAM), 226–28
  production and process control
    in, 823–25
  robots in, 907–10
Marble, 855–56
Margarine, 717–19
Marine biology, 68–69
Marine products, 133–35
Maritime industry, see Ships and
    shipping
Marketing, 575–77
  advertising in, 17–21
  direct mail, 281–83
  premiums and incentives in,
    814–15
  sales promotion and, 923–24

store displays in, 987–88
telemarketing and, 1013–14
see also Consumers
Market research and statistics, 578–80
population and demographic data in, 801–2
public opinion and polls in, 840–41
Maryland, 580–83
Massachusets, 583–86
Mass transit, *see* Public transportation
Materials (engineered or advanced), 586–88
metallurgy and, 601–3
see also Metals
Materials handling, 588–90
distributors or wholesalers and, 283–84
inventory control and, 501–2
operations research and, 724–25
warehouses and, 1099–1101
Mattresses, 402
Measurements, 980–81
Meat industry, 590–93
see also Livestock
Media:
cable television, 158–60
journalism and, 514–15
radio broadcasting, 857–59
television broadcasting, 1016–19
see also Publishing
Mediation, 70–71
Medical and hospital equipment, 593–96, 932–35
laboratories and, 523–25
see also Health care
Medicare, 965–66
Meeting planners, 1054
Melons, 389
Mental health, 434
Mergers, 597–98
see also Investment banking; Securities

Metal finishing, 599–601
Metallizers, 467
Metallurgy, 601–3
advanced or engineered materials and, 586–88
foundries and, 381–83
Metals, 603–7
aluminum, 61–63
mining and, 615–17
precious, 811–13
steel and iron, 983–86
Metal working, 607–9
machine shops and, 557–59
Meteorology, 1110–11
Michigan, 610–12
Microfilms, 613
Microforms, 613–15
see also Records management
Micrographics, 613
Microprocessors, 947–50
Migration data, 801–2
Military goods, 270–72
Milk, 267–69
Mines and mining, 615–17
coal, 204–6
quarry and stone industry, 855–56
Minnesota, 617–20
Minorities, affirmative action and equal employment opportunity for, 29–30
MIS (management information systems), 572–74
Missiles, 270–72
Mississippi, 620–22
Missouri, 623–25
Mobile homes, 625–27
see also Building industry
Mobile telephones, 628–30
Molasses, 988–90
Montana, 630–32
Mortgages, 633–35
see also Banks and banking; Real estate investments
Mortuary industry, 396–98

Motels, 451–53
Motion picture industry, 638–40
Motion picture theaters, 641–42
Motivation (psychology), 642–43
Motor buses, 644–46
see also Automotive industry; Public transportation
Motorcycles, 646–48
see also Automotive industry
Motor homes, 872–74
Movie industry, 638–40
Movie theaters, 641–42
Moving industry, 636–37
see also Warehouses
Municipal government, 648–50
civil service and, 192
see also specific states
Mushrooms, 389
Musical instruments, 650–53
Music industry, 654–57
recording and, 868–70
Mutual funds, 657–59
see also Investments; Securities

Natural food, 440–41
Natural gas, 659–62
pipelines for, 789–91
propane and butane, 832–33
public utilities and, 846–48
see also Petrochemicals; Petroleum industry
Nebraska, 663–65
Nevada, 665–68
New Hampshire, 668–70
New Jersey, 671–73
New Mexico, 674–76
Newsletters, 677–78
journalism and, 514–15
writing and editing, 1140–42
Newspapers, 678–80
advertising in, 18
journalism and, 514–15
writing and editing, 1140–42
New York, 681–83
Noise control, 684–86

North Carolina, 686–88
North Dakota, 689–91
Novelties, 418, 691–92
Nuclear power, 693–95
    see also Energy
Numerical control, 823–25
Numismatics, 211–13
Nursing homes, 695–98
    see also Health care; Hospitals
Nuts, 698–701

Occupational health and safety
    industrial hygiene, 473–74
Occupational therapy, 701–2
Office buildings, 706–7
    see also Real estate investments
Office equipment and supplies,
    707–10
    business forms, 378–79
    copying and duplicating ma-
        chines, 251–53
    facsimile (fax) machines, 327–28
    furniture, 711–12
    see also Computers
Offices:
    automation of, 703–5; see also
        Computers; Local area
        networks; Management in-
        formation systems
    management of, 713; see also
        Management; Secretaries
Office workers, 935–36
    temporary employees and,
        1019–21
    word processing and, 1136–37
Ohio, 714–16
Oils (food), 717–19
Oklahoma, 720–22
Onions, 722–24
    see also Fruit and vegetable
        industry
Operations research, 724–25
Ophthalmic industry, 725–28
Optical character recognition,
    93–95

Optics, 728–30
Options, 222–24
Optoelectronics, 728–30
Optometry, 725–28
Oregon, 731–33
Organic farming, 34
Organic food, 440–41
Orthotics, 836–37
OSHA regulations, 917
Over-the-counter stocks, 937–41

Packaging, 734–37
    aerosols, 21–24
    boxes, 143–44
    labels and, 521–22
    machinery for, 738–40
    paper and plastic bags, 743–44
Paging systems, 628–30
Paint and painting, 740–42
    see also Wallpaper
Paper and pulp industry, 745–48
    see also Forest products
Paper bags, 743–44
Paperboard, 748
Paper boxes, 143–44
Part-time professional workers,
    1019–21
Passengers, airline, 52–53
Pasta, 556–57
Patents, 494–96
Pavement:
    asphalt, 86–88
    concrete, 238–40
Pay, 224–25
Peaches, 391
Peanuts, 699–700
Pecans, 698, 700
Pennsylvania, 751–53
Pens, 1143–44
Pensions, 754–56
    actuarial science and, 8–9
    see also Employee benefits
Perfumes, 254–57
Periodicals, 756–58
    journalism and, 514–15

writing and editing, 1140–42
    see also Newsletters
Personnel, see Employee benefits;
    Employees; Employment ser-
    vices
Personnel development, 1047–49
Personnel management, 759–61
    industrial relations and, 475–
        77
    see also Management
Pesticides, 762–65
    see also Agriculture
Pet industry, 765–68
    veterinary products, 1086–88
Petrochemicals, 768–70
    fuel oil, 394–95
    gasoline, 410–11
    see also Chemical engineering;
        Chemical industry; Natu-
        ral gas
Petroleum industry, 774–77
    equipment for, 771–73
    pipelines for, 789–91
Pharmaceuticals, 778–81
    drug stores and, 287–89
Philanthropy, 380–81
Philately, 213–14
Photocopiers, 251–53
Photography, 782–85
Physicians, 438–39
Pigs, 998–99
Pilots, 46–47
Pipelines, 789–91
    see also Natural gas; Petroleum
Pipes and pipe fittings, 786–88
    see also Plumbing; Valves
Plant nurseries, 407–9
    florists and flower industry,
        360–62
Plaster and plastering, 791–92
    see also Building materials
Plastic bags, 743–44
Plastics, 793–96
    advanced or engineered materi-
        als and, 586–88

Platinum, 811–13

Plumbing, 797–99

pipes and pipe fittings for, 786–88

valves for, 1077–79

see also Hardware

Plywood, 375–77

Point-of-purchase advertising, 18

Point-of-sale equipment, 799–800

automatic identification and, 93–95

see also Retail trade

Polishing products, 1–2

Political risk, 902–4

Polls and public opinion, 840–41

see also Market research and statistics

Pollution control, 320–23

see also Environmental conservation

Polyvinyl chloride, 795

Population and demographics, 801–2

see also Consumers; Market research and statistics

Pork:

meat industry and, 590–93

swine industry and, 998–99

Ports, 1107–9

see also Ships and shipping

Postal services and equipment, 803–4

Potatoes, 805–6

see also Fruit and vegetable industry

Poultry, 807–9

Power:

mechanical, 809–10

see also Energy; Engineering; Engines

Power plants:

cogeneration at, 209–11

electric, 300–302

nuclear, 693–95

Precious metals, 811–13

see also Metallurgy; Metals

Preferred provider organizations (PPOs), 437–38

Premiums and incentives, 814–15

see also Marketing; Sales promotion

Printing and printing equipment, 815–19

bookbinding and, 136–37

see also Graphic arts

Printing inks, 820–21

Privatization, 822

Probate, 1062–63

Process control, 823–25

Procurement, 851–52

Production and process control, 823–25

computer-aided design/manufacturing/engineering (CAD/CAM/CAE), 226–28

Productivity, 825–28

motivation and (psychology), 642–43

see also Quality control

Product liability, 829–30

asbestos industry and, 84–86

Product safety, 831–32

see also Safety

Profit sharing plans, 754–56

see also Employee benefits

Promotion, 923–24

Propane, 832–33

see also Natural gas

Property appraisals, 1074–77

Property insurance, 483–86

Property management, 834–36

building maintenance and, 565–67

Prosthetics, 836–37

Psychology, motivation and, 642–43

Public administration, 838–39

civil service and, 192

municipal government, 648–50

see also Federal government; *specific states*

Publicity, 842–43

Public opinion and polls, 840–41

see also Market research and statistics

Public relations, 842–43

Public transportation, 844–45

buses, 644–46

railroad, 859–62

roads and highways, 904–7

see also specific states under Transportation

Public utilities, 846–48

see also Electric power; Natural gas; *specific states under Public Utilities*

Publishing:

book, 138–40

bookbinding and, 136–37

desktop, 278–80

newsletters, 677–78

newspapers, 678–80

periodicals, magazines, and trade journals, 756–58

Pulp and paper industry, 745–48

paperboard, 748–50

see also Forest products

Pumps, 849–50

Purchasing, 851–52

see also specific states under Purchasing

Quality circles, 642, 852

Quality control, 852–54

see also Productivity

Quarries, 855–56

see also Mines and mining

Questionnaires, 1024–25

Radio broadcasting, 857–59

advertising in, 18

journalism and, 514–15

Railroads, 859–62

Raisins, 390

Real estate appraisals, 1074–77
Real estate business, 862–65
    see also specific states under
        Real Estate
Real estate investments, 865–67
    mortgages and, 633–35
    office buildings, 706–7
    see also Investments
Recording industry, 868–70
    see also Audiovisual industry;
        Music industry
Records management, 871–72
    libraries and, 536–37
    management information sys-
        tems (MIS), 572–74
    microforms, 612–14
    office automation and, 703–5;
        see also Computers; Local
        area networks
Recreational vehicles, 872–74
    see also Automotive industry;
        Mobile homes
Recreation industry, 874–77
    sporting goods, 977–80
    swimming pools, 996–98
Recycling, 61, 878–80
    see also Environmental conser-
        vation; Waste management
Refrigeration, 37–41
Regulation of industry, 880–81
Relocation of employees, 882–
    83
    moving and storage industry
        and, 636–37
Remodeling, 153
Rental services, 884–86
    automobile, 101–3
Repossession, 214
Research, market, see Market
    research and statistics
Research and development, 886–
    89
    laboratories in, 523–25
Resins, plastic, 793–96
Resorts, 874, 875

Restaurants, 889–92
    see also Food services
Retail advertising, 18
Retail trade, 892–95
    bookselling, 141–42
    chain stores, 179–80
    drug stores, 287–89
    liquor stores, 544–45
    point-of-sale equipment in,
        799–800
    shopping centers and malls,
        957–59
    store displays in, 18, 987–88
    supermarkets and convenience
        stores, 992–94
Retirement, 895–97
    employee benefits and, 302–5
    pensions and profit sharing
        plans for, 754–56
Retread industry, 1031–33
Rhode Island, 897–900
Rice, 900–902
Risk management, 902–4
    see also Insurance
Roads and highways, 904–7
    see also Public transportation;
        Traffic enginering and
        management; Traffic safety;
        specific states under Trans-
        portation
Robots, 907–10
    see also Computer-aided de-
        sign/ manufacturing/ engi-
        neering (CAD/CAM/CAE);
        Production and process
        control
Roofing, 910–13
    asphalt, 86–88
Rubber and rubber goods, 913–16
Rugs, 168–69

Safety, 916–19
    industrial hygiene and, 473–74
    product, 831–32
    traffic, 1044–46

    see also specific states under
        Occupational Health and
        Safety
Salaries, 224–25
Sales management, 920–21
    see also Management; Market-
        ing
Salespeople and sales techniques,
    921–22
    manufacturer's representatives,
        574–75
Sales promotion, 923–24
    premiums and incentives, 814–
        15
    see also Marketing
Salt, 925–26
Sanitation, 926–28
    cleaning products and services
        in, 195–97
Savings and loan associations,
    928–30
    see also Banks and banking
Sawmills, 1130–33
Scales, 980–81
Scanners, 93–95
Schools, 930–32
    colleges and universities, 216–17
    see also Education
Science, R&D and, 886–89
Scientific instruments and sup-
    plies, 932–35
    medical and hospital equip-
        ment, 593–96
Scuba diving, 977
Seafood industry, 351–54
    aquaculture, 68–69
Sealants, 12–14, 469
Secretaries, 935–36
    word processing and, 1136–37
    see also Offices
Securities, 937–41
    financial analysts and, 344–45
    investment banking and, 502–4
    mergers and acquisitions and,
        597–98

mutual funds, 657–59
see also Investments; specific
    states under Securities
Security services and equipment,
    941–44
    locksmith industry and, 429–31
    see also Hardware
Seed industry, 945–47
    see also Agriculture
Self-employment, 962–64
    entrepreneurs and, 318–20
    franchises and, 383–85
Self-storage facilities, 1100
Semiconductors, 947–50
Service stations, see Garages and
    service stations
Sewer systems, 847
Sewing machines, 65
Sharpening products, 1–2
Sheep, 950–51
    see also Livestock
Ships and shipping, 952–55
    containers for, 249–51
    waterways and ports for,
        1107–9
    see also Freight transportation
Shoes, 955–57
Shopping centers, 957–59
    see also Retail trade
Shorthand and shorthand report-
    ing, 959
Sightseeing, 1053–56
Signs, 960–61
Silver, 811–13
Skiing equipment, 977
Small businesses, 962–64
    entrepreneurs and, 318–20
    franchises, 383–85
    venture capital and, 1081–83
Small Business Investment Com-
    panies (SBICs), 962
Snowmobiles, 872–74
Soaps, 195–97
Soccer equipment, 978
Social Security, 965–66

Sofabeds, 402
Soft drinks, 126–28
Solar energy, 966–68
    see also Energy
South Carolina, 968–70
South Dakota, 971–73
Souvenirs, 418, 691–92
    see also Gifts
Soybeans, 974–75
Spaghetti, 556–57
Spas, 874, 996–98
Specialty advertising, 18
Spices, 975–76
Sporting goods, 977–80
    bicycles, 129–30
    boats, 133–35
Sports clubs, 877
Stamps, 213–14
Standards, weights, and measure-
    ments, 980–81
Statistics, 982–83
    actuarial science and, 8–9
    census data, 176
    marketing research and,
        578–80
    population and demographic
        data, 801–2
    public opinion and polls,
        840–41
Steel, 983–86
    foundries, 381–83
    see also Metals
Stenography, 959
Stocks, 937–41
Stones, 855–56
Storage industry, 636–37
    warehouses and, 1099–1101
Stores, see Retail trade
Substance abuse, 59–61
Sugar, 988–90
Suntanning equipment, 874
Superconductors, 991–92
Supermarkets, 992–94
    grocery business and, 426–28
    see also Retail trade

Surgical instruments, 593–96
Surplus products, 994–96
Surveys, 840–41
Sweepstakes, 924
Swimming pools, 996–98
Swine, 998–99
    see also Livestock
Synthetic fuels, 312

Tableware, 1000–1002
    see also Gifts; Glass and glass
        products
Tanning, of leather, 533–35
Tapes, adhesive, 12–14
Taxation, 1003–5
    accounting and, 5–8
    see also specific states under
        Taxation and Revenue
Taxicabs, 1006
Tea, 206–8
    see also Beverages
Technical education, 294–95
Technical writing, 1141
Technology:
    R&D and, 886–89
    transfer of, 1007–8
Telecommunications, 1009–13
    local area networks and, 547–49
    mobile telephones, 628–30
    videotex/teletext, 1091–92
Telemarketing, 1013–14
    see also Marketing
Telephone answering services,
    1015
Teletext, 1091–92
Television broadcasting, 1016–19
    advertising in, 18, 19
    cable, 158–60
    journalism and, 514–15
Temporary employees, 1019–21
Tennessee, 1021–23
Tennis equipment, 977
Testing, 1024–25
    see also Education; Schools
Texas, 1026–28

Textiles, *see* Fabrics and textiles

Theaters, motion picture, 641–42

Theft, security and detective services and, 941–44

Thrift industry, 928–30

Tiles, 1029–30
  see also Floor coverings and floorings

Timesharing, 862

Tin, 604, 605

Tires, 1031–33
  see also Automobile equipment

Titanium, 605

Tobacco, 1033–36

Toiletries, 254–57

Toilets, 927

Tomatoes, 390

Tourism, 1053–56

Toys, 1037–39
  see also Hobbies

Trade journals, 756–58
  journalism and, 514–15
  writing and editing, 1140–42
  see also Newsletters

Trademarks, 494–96

Trade shows, 1039–41

Traffic engineering and management, 1042–44
  roads and highways and, 904–7
  see also specific states under Transportation

Traffic safety, 1044–46
  see also Safety

Trailers, 872–74

Training of personnel, 1047–49
  motivation and (psychology), 642–43
  see also Education; Personnel management

Training programs, 15–16

Translation and translators, 1049–50

Transportation:
  air, 44–46, 52–53
  bus, 644–46

motorcycle, 646–48

public, 844–45

railroad, 859–62

taxicab and limousine, 1006

Travel agencies, 1051–53

Travel industry, 1053–56
  air, 44–46, 52–53
  see also specific states under Tourism

Treasurers, 343

Tribologists, 552–54

Trucking industry, 1059–62
  see also Freight transportation; *specific states under Transportation*

Trucks and truck trailer manufacturing, 1056–59
  see also Automobile equipment; Engines

Trusts, 1062–63
  see also Law and Lawyers; Retirement

Turkeys, 807–9

Typesetting, 815–19

Ultrasonics, 1063–65

Underwear, 1065–67
  see also Clothing

Unemployment and unemployment insurance, 1068–69
  see also specific states under Unemployment

Unions, labor, 525–27

Universities, 216–17
  see also Education

University parks, 886

Upholstery, 1070–71
  see also Fabrics and textiles

Urban planning, 72

Used car dealers, 95–97

Utah, 1072–74

Utilities, 846–48

Vacuum cleaners, 65

Valuation and appraisal, 1074–77

Valves, 1077–79
  aerosol, 21–24
  see also Pipes and pipe fittings; Pumps

Vegetable industry, *see* Foods and food industry; Fruit and vegetable industry

Vending machines, 1079–81

Ventilation, 37–41

Venture capital, 1081–83

Vermont, 1083–85

Veterinary products, 1086–88
  see also Pet industry

Vibration control, 686

Video recording industry, 1089–91
  see also Audiovisual industry; Motion picture industry

Videotex, 1091–92

Violins, 650

Virginia, 1092–95

Visual merchandising, 987–88

Vitamins, 1095–97
  see also Health food

Vocational education, 294–95

Wallpaper, 1097–99
  see also Paint and painting

Walnuts, 698, 700

Warehouses, 1099–1101
  moving and storage industry and, 636–67
  see also Distributors; Wholesalers

Washington (state), 1101–3

Waste management, 1104–7
  recycling, 61, 878–80
  see also Environmental conservation; *specific states under Environmental Affairs*

Watches, 198–99

Waterbeds, 400

Waterproofing, 12, 912

Water skiing equipment, 978

Waterways, 1107–9
  see also Ships and shipping

Water works, 847

Weapons:
  defense industries, 270–72
  firearms, 347–49

Weather forecasting, 1110–11

Weighing and measurement, 980–81

Welding, 1112–14

West Virginia, 1114–17

Wheat, 1117–19

Wholesalers, 283–84
  materials handling and, 588–90

Wind energy, 312, 313

Windows, 152

Wine, 1119–22
  see also Liquor and spirits; Liquor stores

Wire, 1122–24

Wisconsin, 1124–27

Women:
  affirmative action and equal employment opportunity for, 29–30
  as professionals and employees, 1127–29; see also Entrepreneurs

Wood, 375–77
  as energy source, 312

Woodworking, 1130–33

Wool, 1133–35
  sheep industry and, 950–51
  see also Sheep

Word processing, 1136–37

Workers' compensation, 1138–40
  see also specific states under Workers' Compensation

Worsteds, 1133–35
  see also Sheep

Writing and editing, 1140–42
  journalism, 514–15
  newsletters, 677–78
  for newspapers, 678–80
  for periodicals, magazines, and trade journals, 756–58

Writing instruments, 1143–44

Wyoming, 1144–47

Yarn, 1147–49
  see also Cotton; Fabrics and textiles; Wool

Yellow pages, advertising in, 18, 19

Yogurt, 267–69

Zinc, 604